The Oxford Companion to

Theatre and Performance

Dennis Kennedy is Beckett Professor of Drama Emeritus at Trinity College Dublin. His award-winning books include *The Spectator and the Spectacle: audiences in modernity and postmodernity*, *Looking at Shakespeare: a visual history of twentieth-century performance*, and *Granville Barker and the Dream of Theatre*. He edited *The Oxford Encyclopedia of Theatre and Performance*, *Foreign Shakespeare*, and *Shakespeare in Asia: contemporary performance* (with Yong Li Lan). He has held distinguished visiting professorships around the world and has worked as a playwright, dramaturg, and director in theatres from London to Beijing.

(((⊕)) SEE WEB LINKS)

This is a web-linked volume. There is a list of recommended web links at the end of the Companion on page 688. To access the websites, go to the Companion's web page at www.oup.com/uk/reference/resources/theatreandperformance, click on **Web links** in the Resources section and click straight through to the relevant websites.

The most authoritative and up-to-date reference books for both students and the general reader.

Oxford Paperback Reference

Many of these titles are also available online at www.Oxfordreference.com

The Oxford Companion to

Theatre and Performance

FIRST EDITION

Edited by DENNIS KENNEDY

OXFORD
UNIVERSITY PRESS

OXFORD

UNIVERSITY PRESS

Great Clarendon Street, Oxford OX2 6DP

Oxford University Press is a department of the University of Oxford.
It furthers the University's objective of excellence in research, scholarship,
and education by publishing worldwide in

Oxford New York

Auckland Cape Town Dar es Salaam Hong Kong Karachi
Kuala Lumpur Madrid Melbourne Mexico City Nairobi
New Delhi Shanghai Taipei Toronto

With offices in

Argentina Austria Brazil Chile Czech Republic France Greece
Guatemala Hungary Italy Japan Poland Portugal Singapore
South Korea Switzerland Thailand Turkey Ukraine Vietnam

Oxford is a registered trade mark of Oxford University Press
in the UK and in certain other countries

Published in the United States
by Oxford University Press Inc., New York

© Oxford University Press 2010, 2011

The moral rights of the author have been asserted
Database right Oxford University Press (maker)

First published 2010
First published in the Oxford Paperback Reference series 2011

British Library Cataloguing in Publication Data
Data available

Library of Congress Cataloging in Publication Data
Data available

Typeset by SPI Publisher Services, Pondicherry, India
Printed in Great Britain
on acid-free paper by
Clays Ltd, St. Ives plc

ISBN 978-0-19-957457-5

10 9 8 7 6 5 4 3 2 1

Contents ✒

Preface and principles

This Companion is a concise and updated version of *The Oxford Encyclopedia of Theatre and Performance* (2 volumes, 2003). The new book treats the most important aspects of theatre, performance in the theatre, and performance in a broader sense, over time and on a worldwide scale. The work attempts to see theatre and performance as human expressions with large cultural significance: what goes on and has gone on in playhouses is the centre of interest but the discussion has been expanded to incorporate key issues in censorship, dance and dance-drama, opera, ritual, some para-theatrical activities (e.g. animal fights, public executions), and other types of live entertainment (circus, sport, Wild West shows).

In a concise work the most precious resource is space, and it has been impossible to include all the material that might be desirable to cover. The longer and theoretical essays from the parent volumes have given way here to shorter entries of practical use. A few topical categories have been eliminated (entries on cities and regions, for example) and others reduced in scope (only the most important venues and theatre companies have been retained). Readers who wish further information or discursive treatment of performance concepts are referred to the original volumes, which are also available on-line by subscription through www.oxfordreference.com.

Three major principles have affected the selection of topics:

• Literary matters about drama are handled in many other reference books; here they are de-emphasized in favour of performance-related ones.

• In order to include a large number of biographies, some of them must be fairly short. In general, we have attempted to correlate the length of an entry with the significance of its topic, and have preferred professional issues over personal life stories.

• The perspective is international. Some entries address global matters (e.g. diaspora, interculturalism), others treat issues specific to the theatre of individual nations (kabuki, kathakali, expressionism), and those on general performance topics also attempt a wider viewpoint (acting, applause, playhouse).

The advisory editors listed on page ix had oversight of specific areas of the field for the parent volumes, and were augmented for this Companion by Mark Fearnow. The work of concision for the Companion was my responsibility, but I am most grateful to the many advisory editors and contributors who assisted me in revising, updating, and providing new entries for the current work.

DK

Editors and contributors

EDITOR

Dennis Kennedy is Beckett Professor of Drama Emeritus at Trinity College Dublin. His award-winning books include *The Spectator and the Spectacle: audiences in modernity and postmodernity, Looking at Shakespeare: a visual history of twentieth-century performance*, and *Granville Barker and the Dream of Theatre*. He edited *The Oxford Encyclopedia of Theatre and Performance, Foreign Shakespeare*, and *Shakespeare in Asia: contemporary performance* (with Yong Li Lan). He has lectured on performance subjects and has held distinguished visiting professorships around the world, and his own plays have been performed in many places. He regularly gives workshops on acting Shakespeare and he has worked as a dramaturg and director in professional theatres from London to Beijing.

ADVISORY EDITORS

Rustom Bharucha
Writer and director, Calcutta

Jacky Bratton
University of London

Edward Braun
University of Bristol

Marvin Carlson
City University of New York

John Conteh-Morgan (1948–2008)
Ohio State University

Mark Fearnow
Hanover College

David Kerr
University of Botswana

Kate McLuskie
Shakespeare Institute, University of Birmingham

Brooks McNamara (1937–2009)
New York University

Kirstin Pauka
University of Hawai'i

J. Thomas Rimer
University of Pittsburgh

Adam Versényi
University of North Carolina

Ronald W. Vince
McMaster University

KEY TO CONTRIBUTOR INITIALS

AA	Arnold Aronson	DaK	David Kerr
AB	Annemarie Bean	DC	David Carnegie
ACB	Albert Bermel	DG	Daniel Gerould
ACH	Arthur Holmberg	DGM	David G. Muller
ADW	David Williams	DJP	Derek Paget
AEM	Anna McMullan	DK	Dennis Kennedy
AF	Ann Featherstone	DLF	Debra Freeberg
AFJ	Alexandra F. Johnston	DM	David Mayer
AH	Alexander C. Y. Huang	DMcM	Donatella Fischer McMillan
AHK	Amelia Howe Kritzer	DR	Dan Rebellato
AJG	Andrew Gurr	DRP	David Pellegrini
AL	Ananda Lal	DT	David Thomas
AlR	Alain Ricard	DWJ	Denis Johnston
AMB	Ananda Mohan Bhagawati	DZS	David Z. Saltz
AMCS	Anamaria Crowe Serrano		
ANG	Arthur Gelb	EB	Eckhard Breitinger
ARJ	Anthony Jackson	EEC	Eileen Cottis
ARY	Alan Young	EEP	Eric Pourchot
AS	Adrienne Scullion	EGC	Eric Csapo
ATS	Antonio Scuderi	EJS	Elizabeth Schafer
AV	Adam Versényi	EJW	E. J. Westlake
AW	Alan Woods	EN	Edna Nahshon
AWF	Adrian Frazier	ER	Eli Rozik
		ES	Elaine Savory
BB	Birgit Beumers	EW	Eric Weitz
BBL	Barbara Lewis		
BGW	Brian Woolland	FAK	Fawzia Afzal-Khan
BJR	Beatriz J. Rizk	FD	Frances Dann
BMC	Bruce McConachie	FHL	Felicia Hardison Londré
BRK	Baz Kershaw	FJH	Franklin J. Hildy
BRS	Brian Singleton	FL	Frazer Lively
BSG	Barbara Gelb		
BWFP	Brian Powell	GAO	Gwen Orel
		GAR	Gary A. Richardson
CAG	C. Andrew Gerstle	GB	Günter Berghaus
CAL	Cathy A. Leeney	GBB	Gilli Bush-Bailey
CBB	Christopher Balme	GES	Gretchen Elizabeth Smith
CD	Charles Davis	GG	Gerald Groemer
CDC	David Cottis	GGE	Gabriele Erasmi
CEC	Claire Cochrane	GJG	Greg Giesekam
CFS	Christopher Fitz-Simon		
CHB	C. Henrik Borgstrom	HD	Hazel Dodge
ChM	Chris Morash	HJA	Judit Horgas
CJM	Christiane Makward	HMA	Hazem M. Azmy
CJW	Christa J. Williford		
CLB	Christopher Baugh	IDW	Ian Watson
CM	Cynthia Marsh		
CMC	Charlotte Canning	JAB	John Agee Ball
CP	M. Cody Poulton	JAH	Jorge Huerta
CR	Christopher Rawson	JB	John Barnes
CRG	Cobina Ruth Gillitt	JCa	Jose Camõens
CS	Catherine Swatek	JCC	Juanamaría Cordones-Cook
CT	Caldwell Titcomb	JCD	Julia Dietrich
		JCM	John Conteh-Morgan

JD	John Degen	LK	Loren Kruger
JDM	Jeffrey D. Mason	LQM	Lisa Merrill
JDV	Jozef De Vos	LRG	Luis A. Ramos-García
JE	John Emigh	LRK	Laurence Kominz
JEH	Jane E. House	LSR	L. S. Rajagopalan
JF	Joseph Farrell	LT	Lib Taylor
JG	John Golder	LTC	Lynne Conner
JGJ	Jean Graham-Jones	LW	Lisa Wolford
JGR	Janelle Reinelt		
JLRE	José Luis Ramos Escobar	MA	Mohd Anis Md Nor
JM	Jane Moody	MAF	Mark Fearnow
JMcC	John McCormick	MAK	Michal Kobialka
JMG	James Gibbs	MAR	Mario A. Rojas
JMM	Judith Mossman	MAS	Melissa Sihra
JMW	J. Michael Walton	MC	Marvin Carlson
JOB	Jose Oliveira Barata	MCH	Mary C. Henderson
JOC	Jae-Oh Choi	MD	Michael Dobson
JoG	Jose George	MDC	Matthew Causey
JR	John Rouse	MDG	Melissa Dana Gibson
JRB	John Russell Brown	MDS	Michael Slater
JRS	John Russell Stephens	MHS	Maria Helena Serôdio
JSB	Jacky Bratton	MJ	Margot Jones
JSM	James S. Moy	MJB	Maria João Brilhante
JTD	Jim Davis	MJD	Moira Day
JTR	J. Thomas Rimer	MJK	Matthew J. Kinservik
JuJ	Julie Greer Johnson	MJW	Martin Wiggins
JWH	John Wesley Harris	ML	Milan Lukeš
		MLa	Maximilien Laroche
KB	Kazimierz Braun	MM	Meg Mumford
KC	Katherine Carlitz	MMcG	Moray McGowan
KF	Karen Fricker	MMD	Maria M. Delgado
KFN	Kirsten Nigro	MMe	Mohamed Mediouni
KFo	Kathy Foley	MMu	Magaly Muguercia
KG	Keith Gregor	MNS	Modali Nagabhushana Sarma
KGo	Kiki Gounaridou	MOC	Marion O'Connor
KH	Kathryn Hansen	MPB	Mark Patrick Bates
KJ	Kirti Jain	MPH	Marion Peter Holt
KM	Kim Marra	MPYC	Martha P. Y. Cheung
KMC	Kathleen Coleman	MR	Milla Riggio
KMM	Katherine Mezur	MRB	Michael R. Booth
KMN	Katherine Newey	MRo	Martin Rohmer
KN	Katie Normington	MS	Michael Shapiro
KNP	Kavalam Narayana Panikkar	MSh	Michael Schuster
KP	Kirstin Pauka	MW	Martin White
KPK	Klaus Peter Köpping	MWP	Michael Patterson
KS	Karthigesu Sivathamby	MWS	Matthew Wilson Smith
KVA	K. V. Akshara		
KWB	Karen Brazell	NC	Noel Carroll
		NG	Nicholas Grene
		NGT	Nicanor Tiongson
LC	Linda Charnes	NGu	Nancy Guy
LCL	Luis Chesney-Lawrence	NHB	Nicholas Barker
LDP	Lois Potter	NMSC	Neelam Man Singh Chowdhry
LED	Leonard E. Doucette	NW	Nick Worrall
LEM	Lydie Moudileno		
LHD	Leslie Damasceno	OD	Ousmane Diakhaté

PAD	Peter Davis	SEW	S. E. Wilmer
PBON	Patrick B. O'Neill	SF	Simon Featherstone
PCR	Paola Catenaccio Roblin	SGG	Shanta Gokhale
PDH	Peter Holland	SJA	Syed Jamil Ahmed
PEC	Paulo Eduardo Carvalho	SJCW	Simon Williams
PH	Pamela Howard	SLL	Samuel L. Leiter
PNN	Pius Nkashama Ngandu	SN	Steve Nelson
PR	Prasanna Ramaswamy	SPC	S. P. Cerasano
PS	Patricia Sieber	SPJ	Susan Pertel Jain
PWM	Peter W. Marx	STC	Scott T. Cummings
PZ	Phillip B. Zarrilli	SV	Surapone Virulrak
		SWL	Stephen Lacey
RAA	Richard Andrews	SYL	Siyuan Liu
RAC	Richard Allen Cave	SYV	Sophie Volpp
RAH	Roger Hall		
RB	Rustom Bharucha	TEH	Thomas Hays
RCB	Richard Beacham	TFC	Thomas Connolly
RCN	Robert Nunn	TH	Ton Hoenselaars
RI	Riad Ismat	TK	Tonia Krueger
RJ	Russell Jackson	TL	Thomas Leabhart
RM	Rosemary Malague	TP	Thomas Postlewait
RN	Richard Niles		
RV	Rodolfo Vera	VDa	Vasudha Dalmia
RVL	R. Valerie Lucas	VEE	Victor Emeljanow
RWH	Roger W. Herzel	VFD	Victor Dixon
RWS	Richard W. Schoch	VLC	Valerie Cumming
RWV	Ronald W. Vince	VRS	Victoria Stec
		VS	Virginia Scott
SA	Simon Amegbleamé		
SB	Sally Banes	WDH	W. D. Howarth
SBB	Sarah Bryant-Bertail	WFC	William F. Condee
SBe	Susan Bennett	WJS	William Slater
SBM	Susan McCully		
SBS	Susan Bradley Smith	YH	Yvette Hutchison
SD	Sudhanva Deshpande	YLL	Yong Li Lan
		YS	Yvonne Shafer

Note to the reader 🌿

Alphabetic arrangement. Entries are arranged alphabetically letter by letter in the order of their headwords, except that 'Mc' and 'St' are treated as if spelled 'Mac' and 'Saint'. In order to avoid an unhelpful series of entries that begin with a form of the word 'theatre', most such entries are recorded under the next significant word (e.g. theatre of the oppressed is placed under 'oppressed', Théâtre du Soleil under 'Soleil'). Exceptions include institutions commonly known by their initials (Théâtre National Populaire) or that would be confusing to list otherwise (Theatre Guild, Theatre Workshop).

Names and romanization. Names of persons used as headwords are those the figure is best known by. They follow the form of the relevant country or language; thus Chinese, Japanese, and Korean names, whether in headwords or text, are normally given with the family name first followed by the given name without a separating comma (e.g. Gao Xingjian and Ninagawa Yukio). Accents are included for languages with Roman alphabets. In transliterating other alphabets, the standards of the Library of Congress on romanization have been followed and diacritical marks have normally been left out. The major exceptions are Japanese and Korean, where the macron or long mark has been used because of its significance in establishing meaning (e.g. *kyogen* and *nō* in Japanese, *kamyŏngŭk* in Korean). Chinese names and terms in headwords are given first in the *pinyin* system, followed by the Wade-Giles system in parenthesis: *canjun xi* (*ts'an chün hsi*), Gao Ming (Kao Ming).

Dates of plays and translation of titles. Dates of plays are of first production, unless otherwise noted. Foreign play titles follow the most commonly seen version when an English translation of the work is known to exist, but often there is no standard translated title, and more often no translation at all. In such circumstances the contributor has given a translation designed to convey the sense and quality of the original title.

Cross references. An asterisk (*) in front of a word signals a cross reference to a relevant entry. Any reasonable form of the referenced headword is marked in the text (*naturalist for 'naturalism', *neoclassic for 'neoclassicism'). When the mention in the text is not directed towards the content of the entry by that name, however, the word is usually not marked as a cross reference ('actor' and 'director', which appear very frequently, are tagged only when they refer to the substance of the entries on acting and directing). It has seemed unnecessary to mark the many occurrences of the name Shakespeare. Cross references are indicated the first time they appear in an entry only. '*See*' and '*see also*' followed by a headword in small capitals draw attention to relevant entries that have not been specifically mentioned in the text.

Contributor signatures are given as initials at the end of each entry. A key to these begins on page x.

Bibliography. A selective bibliography ('Further Reading') is at the end of the volume.

Web resources. General resources on theatre and performance available on the world wide web are listed by links on the Oxford University Press site. (A list of these recommended web links is printed at the end of the Companion on page 688.) To access the websites go to the Companion's web page at http://www.oup.com/uk/reference/resources/theatreandperformance, click on Web links in the Resources section, then click straight through to the relevant websites.

Abbey Theatre Home of the National Theatre of Ireland. The Irish National Theatre Society (INTS) was created by Frank and W. G. Fay's National Dramatic Company following its performances of *Cathleen ni Houlihan* (by *Yeats and Lady *Gregory) and *Deirdre* (by Æ) in 1902. Yeats, its first president, fostered a 'theatre of beauty', not of commerce or propaganda. English heiress Annie *Horniman, who detested all things Irish' but was fond of Yeats, bought the Hibernian Theatre of Varieties and Mechanics' Institute on Abbey Street, Dublin, and let it rent free and refurbished to the INTS. The Abbey Theatre opened on 27 December 1904. The acting area was tight and shallow, the pit and horseshoe-shaped balcony seated 562. Frequently, the executive—*Synge, Gregory, and Yeats, all authors and Protestants—quarrelled with the actors, Horniman (bought out in 1911), or the audience during a period of Catholic nationalist agitation for Irish independence, especially over the disruptions during the opening of Synge's *The Playboy of the Western World* (1907) (*see* RIOTS).

Periodically unpopular in Dublin, the INTS *toured England and the USA for money and fame. After the death of Synge in 1909, domestic dramas in a *realist style predominated, and 'kitchen comedies' set in a peasant's cottage. Dozens of playwrights appeared before *O'Casey arrived with urban *tragicomedies (*The Shadow of a Gunman*, 1923; *Juno and the Paycock*, 1924; *The Plough and the Stars*, 1926). The acting of Sara *Allgood and Barry *Fitzgerald in these plays was a culmination of the Abbey style. With a subsidy in 1925 from the new Irish Free State came state appointments: Ernest Blythe, *manager from 1941 to 1967, passionately wanted to make Ireland Irish speaking. In addition to nightly plays in Irish, popular *comedies of 'peasant quality' and O'Casey revivals were the staple, not the later O'Casey nor the new Irish writers *Johnston, *Beckett, and *Behan. The Abbey burned in 1951; fifteen years later a new theatre opened on the same site, a modernist block of a building, with seating for 628 and a much wider and deeper stage. The *box sets of the old repertoire are now remote from the audience, but by the later 1960s playwrights such as Tom *Murphy, *Friel,

and *Kilroy learned to exploit more open concepts of stage space. The Abbey still searches for playwrights, and some new works are produced in its studio space, the Peacock. The company of state-employed actors has been dissolved. 'Ireland' remains a problem that writers dramatize, but 'national theatre' is now defined as just theatre in Ireland. With the *artistic directors of the 1990s Garry *Hynes and Patrick *Mason—the performance styles of the past gave way to high production values and overtly theatrical staging, and under the directorship of Fiach Mac Conghail the *auditorium was remodelled in 2007 to seat 500 in a more open plan. A move to completely new premises is under discussion.   AWF

Abbott, George (1889–1995) American playwright, director, and producer, a prime inventor of Broadway as an artistic and commercial enterprise. Influenced by George Pierce *Baker's playwriting class, he directed 113 Broadway shows, many of which he co-authored, adapted, or produced, and became a major film director-writer-producer. As *director, he demanded complete control over actors, often dictating line-readings and specifying exact gestures and timing. After an early career as an actor (1913–25), Abbott turned to playwriting, co-authoring *The Fall Guy* (1925), and the hit *comedy-*melodrama *Broadway* (1926), which he also directed. He helped to create four hit *farces of the 1930s: producing, writing and/or directing *Twentieth Century* (1932), *Three Men on a Horse* (1935), *Boy Meets Girl* (1935), and *Room Service* (1937). *Jumbo* (1935) was the first *musical he directed, and he dominated that profession into the 1960s, working in various capacities for *On your Toes* (1936), *The Boys from Syracuse* (1938), *Pal Joey* (1940), *On the Town* (1944), *High Button Shoes* (1947), *Where's Charley?* (1948), *Call Me Madam* (1950), *The Pajama Game* (1954), *Damn Yankees* (1955), *Wonderful Town* (1954), and *A Funny Thing Happened on the Way to the Forum* (1962). Abbott was working on New York revivals and new projects until the time of his death.   MAF

Abdoh, Reza (1963–95) Iranian-born experimental director and video artist. Hailed by some as an *avant-garde visionary at the time of his death due to AIDS, he began directing at the age of 14 in London, where he grew up. After settling in Los Angeles in the early 1980s, his work was seen at various venues. In 1991 he organized the Dar a Luz ensemble and created a series of large-scale *multimedia spectacles with provocative and enigmatic iconography, aggressive and high-decibel intensity, and a concern for moral and social decay. These included *The Hip-Hop Waltz of Eurydice* (1990), *Bogeyman* (1991), *The Law of Remains* (1992), *Tight, Right, White* (1993), and *Quotations from a Ruined City* (1993), which were performed in derelict storefronts, lofts, and warehouses in Los Angeles and New York and in major European festivals.   STC

Abe Kōbō (1924–93) Japanese existentialist novelist, playwright, and director. The experience of being raised in Manchuria and repatriated to Japan after the war bred in Abe a sense of rootless individualism, an aversion to nationalist ideologies, and an abiding suspicion of authority. His influences ranged from Dostoevsky and Heidegger to Kafka and *Beckett. Beginning with *The Uniform* (1955), Abe wrote some twenty plays, including *Slave Hunt* (1955), *The Ghost Is Here* (1959; trans. 1993), *You, Too, Are Guilty* (1965; trans. 1979), *The Man Who Turned into a Stick* (1969; trans 1975), and *Involuntary Homicide* (1971; trans. 1993). Abe's most famous play, *Friends* (1967), became a cult classic in Czechoslovakia and Poland. A member of the Communist Party, he was expelled in 1957 after criticizing the Soviet invasion of Hungary. His plays feature men thrust into absurd situations in an unjust and hostile social environment; vaguely allegorical in nature, they defy easy analysis. With his Abe Kōbō Studio (1971–9) he explored forms of theatrical expression that were increasingly anti-literary. His last play, *The Little Elephant Is Dead* (1979), contained almost no *dialogue.   CP

abhinaya *Acting in the classical Indian tradition. The word signifies leading spectators towards theatrical pleasure as delineated in Bharata's *Natyasastra, the ancient Sanskrit text on Indian aesthetics and *dramaturgy. *Abhinaya* is made up of four interrelated components of acting: *angika* (the body), *vacika* (the voice), *sattvika* (mental states), and *aharya* (*costumes, make-up, scenery).   KNP

Abington, Fanny (Frances) (1737–1815) English actress, an influential performer on and off the stage. Born into a poor family in London, she became a rich woman, a wildly popular comic actress, and a leader of fashion in late Georgian Dublin and London. Her contracts at *Drury Lane and *Covent Garden included generous clothing allowances, and she is said to have earned another £1,500 a year as a fashion consultant. On stage, her forte was *comedy, especially young woman roles. She created Lady Teazle in *Sheridan's *The School for Scandal* (1777) and was also popular as Beatrice in *Much Ado* and Millamant in *Congreve's *The Way of the World*. While her range was not wide, her graceful gestures, expertly modulated voice, and skill at ironic pronouncements kept her acting from becoming monotonous. Her value to the Drury Lane company is evident from *Garrick's refusal to dismiss her, despite their perpetual clashes and combative correspondence. Joshua Reynolds immortalized her in his *Mrs Abington as the Comic Muse*, a companion piece to his better-known painting of Sarah *Siddons.   MJK

absurd, theatre of the Term coined by Martin Esslin (*The Theatre of the Absurd*, 1961) to describe the work of a number of (chiefly) European playwrights writing in the 1950s and early 1960s. Notably included were a group of exiles in Paris, among them *Beckett from Ireland, *Ionesco from Romania, the Russian-Armenian *Adamov, and *Genet, who, though French, had spent most of his early life as an itinerant criminal. The first three were not writing in their native languages and brought an outsider's view of language as constructed and arbitrary, and thus ultimately absurd. Other absurdist writers include *Pinter, *Albee, and later, such widely various figures as *Abe Kōbō, Václav *Havel, and *Gao Xingjian. None was connected in any way to the others and the theatre of the absurd was never more than a convenient critical amalgam of a shared view of the world and human existence. 'Absurdism' never became a theatre movement as such. Nonetheless the absurdist authors had stheir shared roots in modernist experiments like *Jarry's *Ubu roi* (1896), Guillaume Apollinaire's *The Breasts of Teiresias* (1917), and particularly *Maeterlinck's *symbolist drama *The Blind* (1890), which—like Beckett's *Waiting for Godot*—features a group of people waiting beside a tree for a saviour who never arrives. The *dadaists and *surrealists, with their spontaneous writing, are further predecessors.

The notion of the 'absurd' was first proposed by *Camus in his essay *The Myth of Sisyphus* (1942). Camus's existentialism derived from growing up French in colonized Algeria, and particularly from his research on the effects of pestilence and plague (similar to *Artaud). In times of extreme stress, Camus thought, human beings abandon social conventions and morals in an effort to survive; this leads to arbitrary and gratuitous actions which are separated from their consequences. The historical connective between existentialist philosophy and absurd theatre is the Second World War, which provided ample evidence of atrocity on a mass scale. Hitler's industrialization of murder, and the atomic devastation of Hiroshima and Nagasaki, revealed that during the war language was used as an instrument of death, like any other weapon of destruction. The existentialist theatre of Camus and *Sartre, despite its attention to parallel issues, was conventional in its drawing-room settings and articulation of a philosophy in *dialogue form. The theatre of the absurd, on the other hand, has been called the theatricalization of existentialism. No *character discusses the philosophy; characters exist within it and embody it. Absurd things happen and they know not why. They desire to escape but know they cannot. They sometimes talk of death but it is usually denied them. They exist in a perpetual state of meaninglessness.

The most celebrated of the absurdist plays is Beckett's *Waiting for Godot*, initially directed by Roger *Blin as *En attendant Godot* (Paris, 1953). It features two tramps on a roadside who wait, passing the time with comic theatrical routines, a self-referential or *metatheatrical tactic common to much absurdist drama. Nothing happens and Godot never comes, denying plot and *action. In Ionesco's *La Cantatrice chauve* (1950, translated as *The Bald Prima Donna* and *The Bald Soprano*), a knock is heard at the door but there is no one there, and a clock strikes thirteen—a staging of the detachment of signifier from signified. And in *The Balcony* (1960), Genet shows how existence is created only through its reflection by others.

The unsettling form used in absurdist drama is a reflection and symptom of a society which has lost value and meaning. Stories cannot be told within traditional or recognizable forms; a play's action is in the image or the word; character motivations are, at best, opaque; there is no dramatic conflict. The world of the absurd has lost the unifying factors of logic, reason, and rationality—those qualities so admired in the French tradition deriving from Descartes—which is why the stage cannot maintain the qualities of *realism. In the absurdist view, everything is possible, and the *dramaturgical mechanics of traditional theatre are exposed as false (Ionesco called *La Cantatrice chauve* an 'anti-play'). Though located historically in the wake of the Second World War, the absurdist tradition lived on into the new millennium and transcended

its European borders: postmodern theatre thrives on, and makes a virtue of, disruption and *bricolage*.   BRS

Achurch, Janet (1864–1916) English actress. From a Manchester theatrical family, Achurch appeared at the Olympic Theatre in London in 1883, then *toured with the recently formed *Benson company, taking leading Shakespearian roles. She was a tall, golden-haired, statuesque, open-featured actress, independent of mind and interested in the 'New Drama', much admired by *Shaw, for whom she played Candida and Lady Cicely Waynflete in *Captain Brassbound's Conversion*. She and her second husband Charles Charrington are best remembered for mounting the first professional production of *Ibsen in London, *A Doll's House* (1889), in which she played Nora. In *Archer's translation and partly under his direction, the play was highly successful and led to a series of Ibsen productions in the 1890s. *Little Eyolf* (1896) was less well received; in spite of a rapturous review for Achurch by Shaw, she was soon replaced as Rita by Mrs Patrick *Campbell, to Shaw's fury. She retired from the stage in 1911.   EEC

Ackermann family German theatre company active between 1753 and 1767 under the leadership of **Konrad Ernst Ackermann** (1712–71). The troupe performed in numerous towns, basing itself initially in Königsberg (1755) where Ackermann built the first private theatre in Germany. In the turmoil of the Seven Years War the troupe was itinerant, finally settling in Hamburg with its own house (Comödienhaus am Gänsemarkt) in 1765. In 1767 the building, *costumes, and scenery were leased to the newly formed Hamburg National Theatre enterprise with which the troupe effectively merged. After the failure of the national theatre Ackermann resumed *touring with a smaller troupe until his death. The troupe occupies an important place in the history of German theatre. Not only did it première many important works (for example, *Lessing's *Miss Sara Sampson* in 1755), but leading members were dedicated to theatre reform and establishing theatre as an artistically and socially respectable institution. Among its members were many of the leading actors of the day such as Sophie Charlotte *Schröder (Ackermann's wife), Friedrich Ludwig *Schröder (Ackermann's stepson), Konrad *Ekhof, and Sophie Hensel.   CBB

Acquart, André (1922–) French *scenographer and painter, who studied fine art in Algiers while designing for the university theatre. His first production in Paris (Montherlant's *Pasiphaé*, 1951)

led to work with Michel *Vinaver (*Coréens*, 1957), Roger *Blin (*Genet's *The Blacks*, 1959), and seven productions with Jean *Vilar. Always seeking new ways to enlarge the stage space, Acquart used raw materials—wood, metal, water—often combined with mirrors to abstract reality. To enhance his three-dimensional approach to scenic movement he designed various schemes of folding panels for Roger *Planchon's *Troilus and Cressida* (1964), sliding wooden platforms for his *Bleus, Blancs, Rouges* (*Blues, Whites, Reds*, 1971), and paper screens for Blin's production of Genet's *The Screens* (1966). An instinctive artisan, Acquart trusts his intuition rather than intellect, insists he is not a theoretician, and always visualizes actual materials when making sketches and models. A large retro-spective installation exhibition in *Avignon (1986) showed the breadth and sculptural quality of his work.   PH

Acquaye, Saka (1923-2007) Ghanaian artist, composer, and playwright. A trained art teacher, whose sculptures occupy important positions in Accra and whose canvases have been shown in major international exhibitions, Acquaye's extraordinary gifts, which include writing, chore-ography, and administration, were brought to-gether in a series of productions that included *Obadzeng Goes to Town* and *Lost Fisherman*, which used a *total theatre approach to cut through problems of language, became an almost permanent part of the Ghanaian national repertoire during the 1960s and early 1970s. Ac-quaye worked with various groups, such as the Dumas Choir and Wulomei, and produced a body of texts that included *Sasabonsam, Modzawe, TroTro*, and *Scholarship Woman*.   JMG

acrobatics Ancient popular entertainment. Petronius describes rope *dancers and acrobats in the *Satyricon*. In thirteenth-century Bourbon, acrobats 'somersaulted on the ground', and by the sixteenth century 'feats of activity' were dis-played at feasts and carnivals. At the great Euro-pean fairs, competitions for leaping and balancing were held, and rope dancers, who combined ac-robatic balancing with artistic dancing, amazed *audiences with speciality acts, such as Mlle Charini, who danced on the rope with her feet in chains while playing the mandolin. With the coming of the *circus in the late eighteenth cen-tury, acrobats found a more permanent home. Leaping—over horses, through balloons of fire—and multiple somersaults were popular, and the Bedouin Arabs were famed for their reverse-pyramid-building act. The Risley act—one acro-bat juggling another with his feet—combined

adult and child performers and was seen in the circus and in the street. Balancing on a rolling globe was made popular in the middle of the nineteenth century by the elegant Signor Ethardo, and the bottle equilibrist, who balanced on the necks of wine bottles, was a frequent sight in the circus. Later circus acrobats tended to utilize apparatus more extensively, though those in the Chinese State Circus, drawing on over 3,000 years of history, still feature stunning feats of foot juggling, ladder balancing, and pyramid building without the aid of technology or nets.   AF

acting/actor Acting is the art of performing an *action or of representing human experience on stage or in some other mode of performance, in which the actor's body and voice serve as the principal expressive tools.

Traditional Western acting *Mimesis—the art of imitation—is one of the basic traits of human beings, who replicate the world around them out of a desire to control their immediate envir-onment, or adapt to it, or laugh at it. Acting is the fundamental art of the theatre and from the earli-est days the actor has been its prime interpreta-tive artist. Few records of acting exist until the *Greek theatre of the fifth century BC and even then evidence is scant. Only men acted in ancient Athens. As they played to *audiences of over 15,000 in open-air arenas, their gestures were broad and the emotional states they con-veyed instantly recognizable. *Masks were worn to establish *character and, in later centuries, massive headpieces and raised boots (*cothor-nus) were assumed to enlarge the performer's stature. The most prized actors were those who spoke with strength and clarity. In a politicized society like Athens, rhetoric was a valued weapon and actors achieved eminence as purveyors of rhetorical skills to citizens.

For 2,000 years after the heyday of the *Diony-sia festivals, actors lived in uncertainty, obscurity, and indigence. Despite the centrality of perfor-mance as entertainment in the late *Roman Republic and Empire, actors in plays and other spectacles were slaves and few earned freedom. There is virtually no documentation of acting for several centuries following the fall of Rome, though the art stayed alive during the early *medieval period in Europe in the activities of minstrels, *acrobats, comic performers, and story-tellers who performed at fairs, taverns, and ban-quets in the halls of feudal lords. *Liturgical drama was performed solely by those in holy orders and later the *mystery and *biblical plays were staged mainly by amateur members of the local community, with some participation, perhaps in lead and comic roles, of professional entertainers.

In the sixteenth century we can identify the beginnings of the modern acting profession. There were two formations that actors employed to structure their professional work, which led to different modes of theatre. In Italy, where actors had little access to indoor theatres and few written scripts to perform, from mid-century they formed troupes which *toured the towns and, whenever possible, the courts of Italy. Their generic name, *commedia dell'arte*, highlighted the professional nature of these activities, but *commedia* is known best to history for *improvisation, a practice whose origins may go back to the *mimes of ancient Rome. Each troupe included between ten or twelve actors who specialized in *stock characters; their repertoire was composed of *scenarios in which these characters were involved in a variety of (usually) comic actions. *Commedia*, above all, catered to the pleasure humans take in playing with appearance; performances were not a literal representation of life but a game played with it.

By the seventeenth century *commedia* had spread far beyond Italy. But eventually improvisation fell prey to the desire among actors and authorities to make theatre predictable and respectable, by requiring actors to interpret a written script, and permanent companies of actors assembled in specially constructed *playhouses, initially in Madrid, London, and Paris, to perform a repertoire of scripted drama, interpreting the invention of another's mind. Fortunately, as the playwrights of Spain and England at this time included Lope de *Vega, Shakespeare, *Calderón, and *Jonson, to mention a few, actors had to develop techniques of in-depth characterization that the earlier, simpler roles in morality plays and *pasos had not required. In England especially, Edward *Alleyn and Richard *Burbage were noted for their charismatic stage presence.

Acting did not attract attention as a discrete art until the Enlightenment. In the eighteenth century, theatre in England and Europe was employed as one means of cultivating civility in a dangerously violent society. While plays aspired to be morally improving, actors served as models of civilized behaviour, both by the elegance of their demeanour and because the very process of acting required them to feel sympathy for a character other than themselves. The actor became an icon of enlightenment, strikingly with such players as *Baron and *Lekain in France, *Garrick in England, and *Ekhof in Germany, who represented their roles with fullness and elicited empathy from the audience. 'Emotionalist'

theorists considered effective acting to be a product of the emotional sensitivity of the actor, while *Diderot argued that the actor must not feel with the character, but subject the performance to a controlling, aesthetic consciousness.

In the course of the eighteenth century, the most prominent actors achieved public respect and social status to a degree previously unequalled. Nevertheless, acting remained one of the least respected of all professions, and actresses especially were considered to exercise a corrupting influence over audiences gathered to gaze at them. Women had performed with the wandering troupes of Italy, France, and Spain, but they were not seen on the English stage until the Restoration of 1660. For two centuries after this, actresses, being the object of male fantasy, were regularly pilloried from the pulpit as prostitutes (*see* ANTI-THEATRICAL POLEMIC).

Virtuoso star actors and *actor-managers dominated nineteenth-century theatre: Edmund *Kean, *Devrient, *Lemaître, *Forrest, *Siddons, *Macready, *Rachel, *Irving, *Bernhardt. But the Europe-wide *tours of the *Meiningen company (1874–90) and the advent of *naturalistic drama suggested that a deeper ensemble acting was desirable. Among ensemble companies, the most influential was the *Moscow Art Theatre under the direction of *Stanislavsky, whose great achievement was to develop exercises that allowed actors to explore the psychological depths of their characters. Stanislavsky's commentaries remain basic to the art of representation in the modern theatre. Almost all actors in the Western tradition encounter his work in their training and most incorporate it into performance in some fashion, though both *Brecht and *Artaud have also been significant as counter influences.

Until the end of the nineteenth century, most actors trained as apprentices in a *repertory company. In modern times actor training in conservatories or universities has become common. But theatre is expensive to produce and often requires subsidy, and the prospects of an actor sustaining a lifelong career in live theatre are not good. In the USA, and increasingly elsewhere, films and television offer more jobs and larger salaries than commercial, *regional, or local theatres, and many actors regard the stage as preparation for more lucrative cinema work. Nevertheless, the acting profession in theatre is far from dead. As always, public interest is centred around the stars of the profession, and the modern stage has produced a whole array of virtuoso actors as polished and charismatic as their forebears, from *Olivier and *Weigel and *Gielgud to *Brando and *Dench and *McKellen. The compulsion to imitate, play with appearance, penetrate and exemplify extreme states of mind is so embedded in human nature that the art of acting will always survive.   SJCW

Non-Western approaches Given the association of acting with mimesis and representation in the West, when applied to many non-Western genres of performance which are non-representational the term is best understood etymologically—from the Latin *actus*, meaning 'to do' or perform. In pre-colonial Africa, Asia, and the Americas, performance cultures fulfilled socio-cultural needs for *ritual, teaching, as well as entertainment, and ranged across dramas, *dance-dramas, ritual dramas, and a variety of orature from storytelling to recitation of epics and delivery of praise poems; performers were as likely to make use of dance, conventionalized movement, song, mime, or masking, as the spoken word.

Acting can be understood as a culture-specific mode of embodiment and awareness deployed to achieve an aesthetic ideal in performance. Each culture's understanding of acting as a form of embodiment is based on indigenous paradigms of the body in movement (including voicing), the body–mind relationship, and consciousness or awareness. To understand acting in India, for example, one would need to be informed about vibratory theories of sound, yoga physiology/philosophy, and *Ayurveda* ('science of life'), the indigenous system of medicine which provides a humoural understanding of the body, physiology, and health.

Non-Western acting cannot be limited to 'an' actor interpreting 'a' role. In Javanese *shadow-puppet theatre (*wayang kulit*), the solo puppeteer (*dalang*) performs all the roles in all-night performances of epic stories, transforming voice and register into easily recognizable characters, managing archaic languages and contemporary dialects, and serving as a conduit for dynamic performative energies, bringing alive on the shadow screen everything from refined females to dynamic, rough demons to the bawdy comic byplay of *clowns speaking in the vernacular. In the *kutiyattam Sanskrit dramas in Kerala, India, a single actor playing a primary character takes the stage alone for several days as he interprets, narrates, and enacts the stories and all the characters necessary as background to the action performed by the full company on the final day.

The source of knowledge and authority in most non-Western performance lies, not with the text, but with the actor and his lineage of performing a particular style transmitted across generations. What is most important is not what is performed, but how a story, play, or role is elaborated in

performance. This concern is evident not only in the lengthy process of training often required, but also in extant written texts about acting, particularly those from India and Japan. India's *Natyasastra* (perhaps *c.*200 BC to AD 200) is an encyclopedic work on all aspects of drama (*natya*). Its 36 chapters classify and describe in minute detail every aspect of production necessary for an acting company to achieve success when performing the then popular Sanskrit dramas at courts. The twenty or more early fifteeenth-century treatises of *Zeami, the founder with his father *Kan'ami of Japanese *nō theatre, provide the first sole-authored general theory of acting. Zeami's treatises on acting were secret texts, written for exclusive use within his own family lineage of performers, and were unavailable to the public until 1908. His writings give practical advice on teaching, convey an understanding of the subtleties of the psychophysical process of acting, analyse how to capture the audience's attention, and articulate the way of nō as a Buddhist path toward enlightenment. In contrast, the flamboyant *kabuki theatre produced *The Actors' Analects* (1776), a collection of tales, gossip, criticism, and instruction that actors wrote for fellow actors. The best-known item is 'The words of Ayame', a record of the sayings of *Yoshizawa Ayame, the first great performer of female roles (*onnagata). In contrast to the non-representational approach of the nō actor to playing female roles, Ayame asserts that the *onnagata* should play his role offstage as well as on.

The question of 'how' to perform continues to be a preoccupation of many master teachers of non-Western acting, since it is the 'how' that produces the next generation of virtuosic actors within each lineage of performance. But throughout the non-Western world the colonial era brought Western models of 'spoken drama', especially the plays of *Ibsen, *Chekhov, and Shakespeare, and the concomitant introduction of Stanislavskian character acting. Most early forms of spoken drama were mounted by educated amateurs who performed translations of Western classics, and whose acting often slavishly imitated Western models. The birth of a post-colonial consciousness, especially after the Second World War, brought a critique of this imitation of the West and a search for indigenous modes of embodiment that could inform contemporary actor training and performance.   PZ

Approaches since 1945 Although the cult-like status of star actors is a ubiquitous part of many theatre histories, in the post-war period the influence of the global film industries of Hollywood and Bollywood, the rise of television, and popular presses vying for access to the personal life of stars have helped to create the notion of the actor-as-personality in which the lines between private/public and self/character are blurred. Acting has always been considered problematic because it plays with such boundary crossing, and many actors intentionally transgress the boundaries in life and performance. By the end of the twentieth century, however, two developments seemed distinctive: a number of stars had entered political life (in India, the USA, and elsewhere), and the media established performativity as a part of public life. Politicians regularly engage coaches to help shape their public images and rehearse their public performances.

This sociological development runs counter to contemporary trends in acting and actor training. Stanislavsky revolutionized nineteenth-century acting in the West by ushering in a new sense of the actor's work on stage as the product of extensive systematic training and 'rehearsal. Following *Copeau's philosophy and approach, after the Second World War *Saint-Denis founded schools of theatre in London and Strasbourg intended to discover new ways of stimulating the creative imagination distinctively anti-commercial in nature. Western models have internationalized both training and paradigms of performance around the globe, just as yoga and Indian philosophy had earlier played an important role in some of Stanislavsky's key concepts and approaches to acting.

After 1959 *Grotowski developed a highly influential psychophysical pathway aimed at self-transcendence in which the actor strips the self down to become a living incarnation, inspired in part by the intensive training of actor-dancers in *kathakali. *Lecoq, another key figure, founded a school in Paris in 1956 where the methods and 'laws' of movement are constantly (re-)explored through the use of masks, clowning, and practical explorations of the styles of *melodrama, buffoonery, or *tragedy. Lecoq-based work is fundamental to Theatre de *Complicité in England, *Mnouchkine in France, and other companies.

The primacy of collaboration and the notion of the actor-as-creator were simultaneously developed by other practitioners and ensembles during the 1960s and 1970s in order to democratize the theatrical process, moving away from the top-down model of *director's theatre. *Collective ensembles such as *Bread and Puppet Theatre, the *Living Theatre, the *Open Theatre, and *Theatre Workshop developed a variety of collaborative working methods. Reflecting scientific

thinking about relativity and indeterminacy, the notions of spontaneity, improvisation, and 'being in the now' were developed through the playing of games by Clive Barker in Britain and Viola Spolin in America. In the UK *devising new work around a social issue, historical period, or incident became the preferred creative method for numerous companies and some university drama courses. In all such instances the actor is no longer considered an interpreter of a playwright's text, but the locus and beginning point of creation.

Ironically, changes in dramatic writing also forced the development of new approaches to accommodate the quite different tasks expected of the actor, as in many of *Beckett's later plays, such as *Not I* (1972) and *A Piece of Monologue* (1979), where no recognizable characters exist to act, and the physical demands on the performer are often extreme. The psychologically whole character was no longer central to many types of theatre after the 1960s, as can be seen in the deconstructive work of the *Wooster Group or Robert *Wilson or *Suzuki Tadashi. Such alternative approaches have often been inspired by Artaud, who called for a rebellion against 'the subjugation of the theatre to the text' and wanted the actor to be an 'athlete of the heart'. Artaud's vision of the actor has been actualized in much contemporary *physical theatre, which intentionally blurs the boundaries between dance, movement, and traditional theatre, as in *butoh, DV-8 in the UK, and *Bausch in Germany.

Many of these developments have led to an emphasis on theatre process rather than product, establishing the actor as social facilitator, seeking not the development of the virtuosic professional performer but rather the empowerment of the 'spect-actor', to use *Boal's term. This new actor dramatizes issues of concern in local settings such as schools, prisons, hospitals, youth clubs, village squares, or on the streets. Theatre games and improvisation techniques are often used in community-based workshops not as a means of training actors but of raising social awareness, developing alternative voices, and assisting in the making and expression of perspectives that are not normally heard in the regular theatres.

The modes of acting in the post-war period outlined here—the actor-as-personality, the actor-as-interpreter, the actor-as-creator, and the actor-as-facilitator—illustrate that the field of acting is now characterized by multiple perceptions, in work that might take place in community halls, the streets, or even in formal playhouses.   PZ

action The two most common meanings of action derive from *Aristotle's Poetics*, where *tragedy is defined as 'an imitation of an action...with persons performing the action rather than through narrative' (*see* MIMESIS). Action, then, is both (*a*) the core of meaning, motive, and purpose embodied in the drama, and (*b*) the actual physical movements and speeches of the actors (dramatic action as opposed to narrative action). Action in its deeper sense was for Aristotle a form whereby reality was made intelligible, and imitated in drama principally by the plot. The connection between plot and action is close, but the two are not identical, and their confusion lies behind the mistaken *neoclassical idea that Aristotle insisted on a single plot (*see* UNITIES): he certainly preferred a single *action*, but does not object to a single action imitated by several plots. Since dramatic action represents human behaviour, which is governed by *character and thought, it is possible to distinguish an intermediary level of action where the term refers to characters' internal psychological, moral, or intellectual progression. But whether identified with dramatic action, character progression, or deep form, action invariably involves a movement—psychic, moral, intellectual—that, often defined in terms of motive, progresses to a new perception.   RWV

actor *See* ACTING/ACTOR.

actor-manager A leading actor and *manager of his or her own theatre or company. *Garrick, at *Drury Lane in London from 1747 to 1776, was the prototypical actor-manager: a leading actor, administrator, investor in his own theatre, he cast, hired, and fired actors, determined their wages, chose the repertory, and oversaw the wardrobe, *costuming, scenery, scene painting, box office, *finances, public relations, and all the multifarious operations of a large business employing several hundred people, among them actors, musicians, *prompters, scene painters, property men, seamstresses, cleaners, candle-snuffers, box-office keepers, and doorkeepers. Several other candidates provide notable examples of the actor-manager, such as *Molière and *Bernhardt in France, *Duse in Italy, and Edwin *Booth in New York, but it was in England at the end of the nineteenth century that the actor-manager completely dominated the theatre of the metropolis as well as providing first-class *tours to the provinces and overseas. *Irving at the Lyceum, George *Alexander at the St James's, John *Hare at the Garrick, Charles *Wyndham at Wyndham's, Charles *Hawtrey at the Comedy, Cyril *Maude at the *Haymarket, Lillie *Langtry

at the Imperial, Mrs Patrick *Campbell at the Royalty, Beerbohm *Tree at Her Majesty's—and this is not a complete list. They were building on the previous managerial accomplishments of *Vestris, *Macready, Charles *Kean, *Phelps, and Marie *Wilton (the first actor-manager to depend on the long run), and all took middle-class West End theatres after they had established themselves as leading actors of ability and reputation. Each manager acted in the repertory appropriate to the theatre and to his or her strengths, carefully composed to mark the theatre's distinctive identity and style in a crowded commercial market and attract a substantial *audience of loyal repeaters. The golden period of English actor-managers ended abruptly with the 1914 war and the subsequent huge demand for light entertainment. After the war, with the old actor-managers retired or dead, and the expenses of production rapidly inflating, theatres and production passed out of the hands of the individual actor and into the hands of *producers, speculators, and business syndicates. The same thing happened at the end of the nineteenth century in America. There are few modern examples of the actor-manager; Brian *Rix with his *farce company at the Whitehall Theatre in London (1950–67) is one.   MRB

Actors Studio Workshop founded in New York in 1947 by *Group Theatre alumni Cheryl Crawford, Robert *Lewis, and Elia *Kazan, intended as a training institution for professional actors. The Studio has been in the same West 44th Street space since 1955. Because Lewis and Kazan were too busy to teach, Lee *Strasberg, another Group alumnus, joined in 1949. From the time he took over as artistic leader in 1951 to his death in 1982, Strasberg ran two weekly two-hour sessions, emphasizing his interpretation of the *Stanislavsky acting system, which came to be known as the *Method. This involved exercises aiming at getting actors to 'unblock' their emotional resources. As more and more of America's respected actors of the 1950s, such as Marlon *Brando, James Dean, Geraldine *Page, Kim Stanley, and Shelly Winters, came to be associated with the Studio, its reputation as the home of deeply felt, psychologically authentic *acting was established. However, its many detractors, perhaps confusing the neorealistic *characters played by Studio actors—often in Kazan's films and plays—with the Method itself, criticized its proponents for sloppy speech and selfish stage habits in which they put personal expression before the needs of the ensemble, the play, or the *audience. Eventually, the Studio created directors', playwrights', and production units.   SLL

Actors Theatre of Louisville American *regional theatre and state theatre of Kentucky. Established in 1964, ATL came to international renown for new American plays and playwrights under the leadership of Jon *Jory. In 1969 he became the producing director and in 1976 inaugurated the annual Humana Festival of New American plays, which continues. Important festival productions include D. L. Coburn's *The Gin Game* (1977), *Henley's *Crimes of the Heart* (1979), and Donald Margulies's *Dinner with Friends* (1998), each of which went on to win the Pulitzer Prize, as well as plays by Marsha *Norman, *Kushner, Naomi Wallace, and Charles L. *Mee. ATL has provided sustained support to pseudonymous playwright Jane Martin and experimental director *Bogart. For twelve years (1985–97), an annual Classics-in-Context Festival surrounded productions of classical and modern European plays with lectures, panel discussions, gallery exhibits, and film exhibitions. Jory left ATL in 2000 and was replaced by Marc Masterson.   STC

Adam de la Halle (Adam Le Bossu) (*c.*1240–*c.*1288) Professional entertainer (*trouvère*). A versatile poet, Adam composed two of the most remarkable vernacular plays of the thirteenth century. *The Play of the Feuillée* (1376), set and performed in his native Arras in France, is a blend of fantasy and reality in which local fools and sinners are pilloried. *Robin and Marion* (*c.*1283), probably written for Robert of Artois's expatriate court in southern Italy, where Adam spent his final years, is in the tradition of *pastoral dancing-games and features an equally traditional cast of maid, knight, and rustic.   RWV

Adamov, Arthur (1908–70) French playwright, born in Russia of an Armenian family who settled in Paris in 1924. Adamov was befriended by *Artaud and Roger *Blin and joined their *surrealist circle as a poet. Nearly twenty years of depression, drifting, and prison term followed. In 1946, influenced by Strindberg, Freud, and *expressionism, Adamov wrote his first play, *The Parody*, staged in 1952 by Blin. Other plays that also combine dream structure with socio-political critique include *Le Professeur Taranne* (1953) and *Le Ping-pong* (1957). As Adamov's work became more *realistic and historical, he drew on *Brechtian *epic theatre while retaining absurdist elements. *Paolo Paoli* (1956) examines the causes of the First World War, while *Le Printemps '71* (1961) reconstructs the Paris Commune, and *The Politics of Waste* (1962) attacks racism in the United States. Adamov's work, and his adaptations of *Büchner, *Chekhov, and *Gorky, have

been staged by Blin, *Vilar, *Planchon, and *Mnouchkine. Often compared to *Beckett and *Ionesco, Adamov's bleak plays with their harsh language never gained the same popularity.   SBB

Adams, Maude (1872–1953) American actress and educator. On stage from infancy, an actress's daughter, Maude Adams appeared in adult roles in 1888, becoming John *Drew's leading lady (1892–6). She starred in her own company from 1897, opening with J. M. *Barrie's dramatization of *The Little Minister*, earning a reputation as Barrie's foremost American interpreter. Adams's low, musical voice, delicate beauty, and slight physique made her especially effective playing young girls and androgynous roles. She was the first American to act in *Rostand's *L'Aiglon* (1900), and in Barrie's *Peter Pan* (1905). Her repertory included Barrie's *Quality Street* (1901), *What Every Woman Knows* (1908), *A Kiss for Cinderella* (1917), and Rostand's *Chanticleer* (1912). Her acting career effectively ended in 1918. In 1937 she founded the drama programme at Stephens College in Missouri, teaching and directing until 1950. Adams was reclusive, rarely appearing in public other than on the stage, and never married.   AW

Addison, Joseph (1672–1719) English writer and editor. Although Addison is now mostly remembered for his periodical partnership with Richard *Steele, he was also famous as the author of *Cato* (1713), a play that enjoyed tremendous popularity in both Britain and America for its portrayal of patriotism and stoical virtue. Throughout the eighteenth century, all parties were able to see *Cato* as an endorsement of themselves, ensuring its popularity. His moral *comedy *The Drummer* (1716), loosely based on the last books of the *Odyssey*, was much less successful, as was his effort to capitalize on the vogue for Italian *opera with *Rosamond* (1707)   MJK

Adler, Jacob P. (1855–1926) Latvian-American actor, considered the greatest dramatic actor of the Yiddish theatre. A powerful *actor manager with a flair for scenic effects, he began his career in Russia, moved to London, and in 1890 settled in New York. In 1891 he produced and starred in Jacob *Gordin's drama *Siberia*, a historic event that marked the beginning of the golden age of Yiddish theatre. Other milestone parts were in Gordin's *Yiddish King Lear* (1892) and *The Wild Man* (1905), and Lev *Tolstoy's *The Power of Darkness* (1903) and *The Living Corpse* (1911). Adler left his mark on the mainstream stage when in 1903 he played Shylock in Yiddish with an English speaking cast. *See* DIASPORA   FN

Adler, Stella (1901–92) American actress and teacher. The daughter of Jacob *Adler and Sara Levitsky, major figures in the Yiddish theatre of New York, Adler was acting from the age of 5. Seeking a systematic approach to *acting, in 1925 she enrolled at the American Laboratory Theatre, an outpost of the *Stanislavsky system. In 1930 she joined the newly formed *Group Theatre and studied with Lee *Strasberg. After meeting with Stanislavsky in Paris in 1934 she returned to challenge Strasberg's emphasis on 'affective memory'. The *Method, she argued, had been rejected by Stanislavsky as both artistically inefficient and psychologically damaging. She offered the Group her own classes, emphasizing 'given circumstances' and 'actions' derived from the play and its context rather than the actor's own memories. She left the Group in 1937 to accept a series of film roles, but returned to New York in 1942 to found her own studio in 1949. Adler quickly became a major force in theatre and film, attracting students such as Marlon *Brando, Warren Beatty, and Robert DeNiro, emerging as the major rival to Strasberg's *Actors Studio. MAF

Admiral's Men, Lord The Elizabethan Lord Admiral, Charles Howard, Lord Effingham, kept a company of players from 1576 until King James made his elder son Henry their patron in 1603, when it became the Prince's Men, running unchanged for 49 years. Its most famous player was Edward *Alleyn, who became Howard's servant in the 1580s. He played at the *Rose Theatre in London from 1592, as a member of Strange's Men, keeping his Admiral's livery, while the rest of the Admiral's Men *toured the country. In 1594 he formed a new Admiral's Men, one of the two new companies replacing the old *Queen's Men, licensed to play in London exclusively at the Rose. Alleyn had become the son-in-law of the Rose's owner, Philip *Henslowe, in 1592, and the two ran the company together, as part of the newly authorized 'duopoly' of companies along with the Lord *Chamberlain's Men. The Admiral's Men had almost all of *Marlowe's plays, and many more produced by a team of collaborative writers, including *Munday, *Dekker, *Chapman, *Jonson and others, all of whose dealings are listed in Henslowe's 'diary', the notebook of his playmaking business. These papers show that from 1594 the Admiral's staged roughly 30 plays each year, performing a different play each afternoon for six days every week except for Lent. They played at the Rose for six years until the other half of the duopoly built the *Globe just across the road. In 1600 they moved to the other side of the river, having the *Fortune built for them in

Clerkenwell. Under different names they played at the Fortune for the next 25 years. After Prince Henry died they became the servants of the Elector Palatine, husband of Henry's sister Elizabeth.   AJG

Aeschylus (*c.*525–456 BC) The first great writer of *tragedy and the foundation of our knowledge of *Greek theatre. Aeschylus fought against the Persians at the battle of Marathon (490 BC), a deed recorded in his epitaph to the exclusion of his dramatic achievements, and which probably suggested aspects of *Aristophanes' *parody of him in *Frogs* as austere and old-fashioned. Of his total of 70 to 90 plays, only seven survive (or six, if *Prometheus Bound* is not his). Aeschylus was extremely successful, gaining thirteen victories in the competitions held at the *Dionysia, the Athenian dramatic festivals, and his plays quickly became classics, reperformed after his death and winning more victories. Unlike *Sophocles and *Euripides, Aeschylus composed many (though not all) of his plays as connected tetralogies, with three tragedies forming a connected story and a *satyr-play on a loosely related theme. There is only one such group of tragedies extant, *Agamemnon, Libation-Bearers*, and *Eumenides*, collectively known as the *Oresteia*, which deals with the murder of Agamemnon by his wife and her lover, the revenge taken for it by his son Orestes, and Orestes' pursuit by the Furies and trial in Athens. This trilogy was accompanied by a (lost) satyr-play, *Proteus*, whose hero was Agamemnon's brother Menelaus.

This surviving trilogy, first performed in 458 BC, best exemplifies Aeschylus' dramatic genius. *Seven against Thebes* and *Suppliants* are the sole survivors of their tetralogies, and though they are powerful in themselves their part in Aeschylus' original grand design can only be guessed at; *Prometheus Bound* may have been the middle play of a trilogy begun with the theft of fire in *Prometheus Fire-Bearer* and ending with *Prometheus Unbound*, but this is not certain, and the stylistic arguments against Aeschylus being the play's author, or at any rate its sole author, are strong.

Persians (472) was not part of a connected trilogy. Remarkably, it is a historical drama which imagines Persian reactions to their defeat at Salamis (479), where Aeschylus probably also fought. It has some features which anticipate the later *Oresteia*, particularly the role of the *chorus of elders, left behind, too old to fight. The Persian Queen is very different in character from the terrifying Clytemnestra of *Agamemnon*, but her interaction with the chorus is used to set the scene in a similar, if less subtle, manner.

Her entry on a chariot illustrates the wealth and pride of Persia, so soon to be laid in the dust by Athens, and provides a striking visual contrast with the later entry of the wretched Xerxes, alone and in rags.

The *Oresteia* uses the myth of the accursed house of Atreus to explore issues of revenge and justice, human and divine. The trilogy shows Aeschylus' technique fully developed and makes full use of the stage resources available in 458 BC, some of which were probably not in use earlier. In particular, the *skene*, or background building, with a central door and a solid roof, before which the actors played, is constantly prominent in the *Oresteia* but not in *Persians*. In *Agamemnon* it represents the palace, which is accursed and where horrible things have happened; the play opens with the Watchman placed precariously on the roof, looking out for the signal which will herald the sack of Troy and Agamemnon's return; Clytemnestra controls and dominates its central door, and although others enter the palace, only she leaves it alive. Aeschylus also employed the *ekkyklema*, a low wooden platform on wheels which, rolled through the door of the *skene*, was used to show what has been happening inside. In *Agamemnon* the triumphant Clytemnestra stands over the corpses of Agamemnon and Cassandra displayed on the *ekkyklema*; in *Libation-Bearers* that tableau is mirrored, as the matricidal Orestes stands over Clytemnestra and Aegisthus.

Visual as well as poetic imagery is used to bind the trilogy together: red fabric flows out of the house like blood in *Agamemnon* when Clytemnestra lays out tapestries for Agamemnon to tread on as he goes into the house to death; in *Libation-Bearers* Orestes holds up the red bloody robe in which Agamemnon was killed; finally the bloodthirsty Furies are transformed into the awe-inspiring Eumenides when they are clothed with red robes at the end of *Eumenides*. This visual symbol expresses the move from the savage *lex talionis* of the first two plays, enacted without guilt or shame by Clytemnestra and more hesitatingly by Orestes, to the justice system of the Athenian courts laid down by Athena in *Eumenides*, and given further divine authority by the Eumenides' cultic presence. Nothing is perfect; divine vengeance can be as harsh and arbitrary as that of men; but the final scene of *Eumenides*, with its torchlight procession in honour of the newly named goddesses, seems to illuminate with modified hope the darkness in which *Agamemnon* begins.

In terms of modern adaptation and performance Aeschylus was slower to attain prominence than Sophocles and Euripides. There was no English translation until the eighteenth century, though in the twentieth the *Oresteia* prompted distinguished adaptations: *O'Neill's *Mourning Becomes Electra* (1931) and *Eliot's *The Family Reunion* (1939). There was an early production of *Agamemnon* in ancient Greek in 1880 at Balliol College, Oxford. In 1914 *Agamemnon*, in an Italian translation, was the first play produced at the dramatic festival at Syracuse. A viciously distorted Nazi version of the whole *Oresteia* was produced in Berlin in 1936; *Guthrie adapted it as *The House of Atreus* in 1966; and more recent landmark productions took place in Berlin in 1980, directed by *Stein, and at the *National Theatre in London in 1981, directed by Peter *Hall, using *masks and an all-male cast, in an adaptation by *Harrison.   JMM

African-American theatre After the war of 1812, William Henry *Brown offered alfresco amusements for blacks in a tea garden behind his house in New York. By 1821, whites formed much of the *audience at the African Grove, which presented Shakespeare and contemporary plays commenting on slavery. In 1822 Brown built a 300-seat theatre in Greenwich Village, where Ira *Aldridge played as part of the African Company. One of its last productions was Brown's *The Drama of King Shotaway*, reputed to be the first play by an American dramatist of African descent. It is symbolic that Brown's African Grove started outdoors, since black American performance has always had to push its way inside.

During the Reconstruction period, segregationist (or 'Jim Crow') legislation placed all black artists under the same *minstrel roof. Comics, dancers, lyricists, dramatists, and *opera singers all participated in this complex entertainment form. Prominent African-American performers at the turn of the century included Henrietta Vinton *Davis, who produced a play about Dessalines at the Haitian Pavilion in Chicago's Columbian Exposition (1893). *The Octoroons*, featuring a *chorus of African-American women in contrast to the minstrel show format, was also performed there. Its director's next show, *Oriental America*, was one of the first all-black *musical productions on Broadway (1896). Successful musical shows by Bert *Williams and George Walker, one of the most popular musical teams of the era, included *In Dahomey*, *The Sons of Ham*, *Abyssinia*, and *Bandana Land*. After Walker's death around 1912, Williams moved to the *Ziegfeld Follies*, where he continued to wear blackface.

In 1915 Anita Bush founded the Lafayette Players in Harlem, the most important stock company during the Harlem Renaissance. In 1916 the National Association for the Advancement of Colored People produced *Rachel* in Washington, partially in response to D. W. Griffith's film *The Birth of a Nation*. Written by Angelina Weld Grimke, *Rachel* is thought to be the first full-length drama to have a black director, black actors, a black producer, and a black playwright. *Shuffle Along*, the Sissle and *Blake musical, opened in 1921, and was responsible for promoting the careers of Josephine *Baker and Paul *Robeson. *Connelly's *Green Pastures* was a success on Broadway in 1930 with an all-black cast, and a few years later, *Stein's *Four Saints in Three Acts* featured black performers. Nonetheless, theatrical prospects for blacks declined during the Depression. Only the vogue of the stage mammy was in the ascendant, exemplified by Ethel *Waters and Rose *McClendon. The Negro Unit of the *Federal Theatre Project was the leading theatrical venue for African Americans before its closure in 1939, and several black playwrights were produced under its aegis. The Harlem Unit based at the Lafayette Theatre was one of 22 such units in major cities, presenting plays by *Shaw and Shakespeare under *Welles and *Houseman. Langston *Hughes, whose play *Mulatto* was produced in 1935, also founded several theatres in Harlem, Chicago, and Los Angeles.

In the summer of 1940 Frederick O'Neal and Abram Hill motivated a group to create a black company in Harlem: the American Negro Theatre (ANT). In 1945 their *Anna Lucasta* opened on Broadway and toured nationally for two years before being made into a film. Harry Belafonte, Alice *Childress, Ossie *Davis, Ruby *Dee, Sidney Poitier, and Clarice Taylor are some of the black actors associated with ANT, which lasted ten years. The actor Canada *Lee appeared on Broadway during the 1940s in several productions, including a significant lead role in the dramatized version of Richard Wright's *Native Son*, directed by Welles.

While a few plays by black writers were staged in the 1950s, the signal event was the 1959 opening of *A Raisin in the Sun*. *Hansberry's play had a black director, Lloyd *Richards, and a stellar black cast, including Dee, Poitier, and Claudia McNeil. In the aftermath of the Second World War, African Americans wanted change, and they were not in the mood to wait, as indicated by the play's title, taken from a line in a Langston Hughes poem on the repercussions of deferring a dream.

Finally the dam broke in the early 1960s. Black theatre was never the same after LeRoi Jones (later Amiri *Baraka) wrote *Dutchman* in 1964, followed by his *Slave Ship*, works with an unmistakable, new, and irrepressible voice. In the early 1960s, Douglas Turner *Ward bemoaned in print the dearth of black theatre companies. The foundations listened, and in 1967 he was given a chance to create one, the Negro Ensemble Company, where playwrights such as Philip Hayes Dean, Lonnie *Elder III, Charles *Fuller, and Joseph Walker found a home. *Genet's *The Blacks* had been performed a few years earlier in the same space with Cicely Tyson, Godfrey Cambridge, and Maya Angelou. Within walking distance, *Papp was giving black actors a greater presence in productions at the *New York Shakespeare Festival, and Adrienne *Kennedy was produced at *La Mama. Uptown in Harlem, Robert Macbeth received a grant establishing the New Lafayette Theatre; *Bullins would become resident playwright. Further downtown, Woodie King founded the New Federal Theatre, which became a central force in black theatre. The decade ended with Charles *Gordone becoming the first black playwright to receive a Pulitzer Prize, for *No Place to Be Somebody*.

The most significant breakthrough of the 1970s was Ntozake *Shange's *for colored girls*, produced jointly by King and Papp before moving to Broadway in 1976, where it stayed several years before an international tour. Other notable ventures were Carroll's *Your Arm's Too Short to Box with God* and Dean's *Robeson* (with James Earl *Jones). Within six years of the establishment of the Black Theatre Alliance, over 50 theatres had joined, but when arts funding was cut at the end of the decade few remained. Even NEC fell victim to *finance. One black *regional theatre, Crossroads in New Jersey, came to attention when it produced *The Colored Museum* by *Wolfe in 1986.

At the beginning of the 1980s, Charles Fuller's *A Soldier's Story* earned a Pulitzer and was made into a film, while a new energy emerged in August *Wilson, whose work was nurtured by Richards. Wilson, a playwright of epic vision, before his early death completed a cycle of ten historical dramas from the perspective of the black community in Pittsburgh, which won numerous awards.

In the 1990s three new women playwrights moved into the limelight: Kia Corthron, Suzan-Lori *Parks, and Anna Deavere *Smith. Smith acts in her own *documentary dramas about racial malaise. Her two most significant works are about contemporary race riots: *Fires in the Mirror* (1993) and *Twilight: Los Angeles, 1992* (1993). Parks is interested in revamping African-American history in works such as *The Death of the Last Black Man in the Whole Entire World* (1990), *The America Play* (1995), and *Topdog/Underdog* (2001). Corthron writes contemporary problem plays (*Breath, Boom*, 2000; *Safe Box*, 2001) focused on social maladjustment issues such as drugs, gangs, homelessness, abortion, and suicide.

The relative lack of financial support for African-American theatre was the key issue that emerged during a 1997 public debate, which Smith moderated, between Wilson and the critic and *producer *Brustein, in which Wilson called for the establishment of a network of black theatres separate from the dominant regional theatre movement. His proposal underscored the fact that the difficulties of black theatre are primarily institutional. In an environment of protracted struggle, African-American theatre can boast of admirable progress but it still stands outside, in the backyard of the nation, without an established centre where it can develop and sustain itself. *See also* DIASPORA.   BL

agitprop Political theatre which presents urgent social issues from a partisan viewpoint through bold rhetorical techniques, aiming to inform and mobilize its *audience. The term, from the Russian for the Department of Agitation and Propaganda established in 1920 by the Soviet Communist Party, has been applied retrospectively to earlier periods. While Soviet agitprop theatre troupes promoted state policy, their more Western counterparts addressed issues ranging from industrial action to the legalization of abortion and racial discrimination, often from a Marxist position. The troupes *toured widely, performing at political meetings or spontaneously in *streets and tenement courtyards. Agitprop presentations were structured as a series of punchy and fast-moving sketches containing references to topical and local news. Intelligibility was ensured by sloganistic banners, songs, mass chants, heroic tableaux, stereotyped or satirical characterizations, emblematic props and *costumes, direct address, and audience participation. Financial restraints and the demands of touring fostered an emphasis on the ensemble, and often groups tried to combine national popular traditions with *avant-garde experimentation. The rise of *fascism and economic stabilization after the Depression contributed to the demise of inter-war agitprop. Since then it has increasingly served political activists, from the anti-Vietnam War and civil rights demonstrators of the 1960s to *feminist and AIDS awareness campaigners. In both developing and affluent countries agitprop continues to provide an educational vehicle at moments of crisis and change. *See also* OPPRESSED, THEATRE OF THE.   MM

agon A Greek term originally meaning 'assembly', especially an assembly to watch athletic events, *agon* came to refer to the competition itself. In the case of dramatic competition, it also referred to the contest between *actors (*agonistes*) and eventually, by association, to the conflict between *characters in a drama. In *Aristophanic *comedy, the *agon* was a formal part of the play in which characters debated a topical issue. This *agon* at the centre of *Greek drama also pointed to its supposed origins in the myth of the dying-and-reviving god Dionysus, and in the *ritual combat between the forces of life and death. So seemingly integral was *agon* to the forms and origins of Greek drama that Western dramatic theory has deemed conflict an essential *dramaturgical principle. The structural analysis of traditional drama has been concerned largely with the development and resolution of dramatic conflict. Usual typologies find the central character (*protagonist) in a drama in conflict with some power or principle beyond human control, with a society that denies individual integrity, with another character over matters ranging from a mutual love interest to philosophical differences, or with opposing thoughts or feelings within him- or herself. Freudian psychology added to internal conflict psychopathological conflict, wherein the conflict is between conscious intention and subconscious impulse. It has been objected that the agonistic principle is not applicable to all drama, that it is irrelevant, for instance, to the so-called theatre of the *absurd, to *epic theatre, and to much Asian theatre. Nevertheless, so flexible is the notion, and so ingrained in Western theory, that it persists in both dramatic analysis and *audience expectation.   RWV

Aguirre, Isidora (1919–) Chilean playwright and novelist, who became known with *Carolina* (1955) and *Las Pascualas* (1957), based on a Chilean legend. Her *musical *The Flower Market* (Santiago, 1960) became an instant hit and was taken on European *tour. Subsequently Aguirre's plays have been closely modelled on *Brecht's *epic theatre. In *Los papeleros* (*The Paper Gatherers*, 1963) and *Los que van quedando en el camino* (*Those Left by the Wayside*, 1969: the title is a quotation from Che Guevara), she continued her socio-political concerns. In *Lautaro* (1982), she used an epic fictitious *character to refer to the situation of the Mapuche people, and in *Retablo de Yumbel* (*Yumbel's Altarpiece*, 1986) the victims of the dictatorship are likened to St Sebastian the martyr. Her latest plays are *Manuel* (1999), whose main character is a legendary hero of Chilean independence; and *Marrichiweu* (2000), in which she returned to the Mapuche theme. MAR

Ainley, Henry (1879–1945) English actor, noted for the beauty and musicality of his voice, who first won success playing Paolo in Stephen *Phillips's Paolo and Francesca* (1902). Though excelling in Shakespearian romantic roles, Ainley was frequently attracted to demanding experimental ventures: Hippolytus (1904), Orestes (1906), Malvolio and Leontes (1912), and the Reader in *The Dynasts* (1914) for Granville *Barker; Young Cuchulain for *Yeats (1916); and J. E. Flecker's Hassan (1923). The intensity of his performances led twice to breakdowns forcing him to retire, the first following his Macbeth of 1926. His late achievements included the husband in *Ervine's *The First Mrs Fraser* (1929) and the Archangel in *Bridie's *Tobias and the Angel* (1930). RAC

Ajoka Founded in 1980 by Madeeha Gauhar in Lahore, Ajoka is a leading alternative theatre in Pakistan. Meaning 'dawn of a new day' in Punjabi, Ajoka began with *street theatre against the cultural repression of General Zia-ul-Haque's military and Islamist regime. When the former trade unionist, political activist, and playwright Shahid Nadeem joined Ajoka, it developed into a professional company producing plays by Nadeem on social issues like family murders, rape, religious repression, the population explosion, and female education. It has expanded its repertoire to translations and adaptations, especially of the plays of *Brecht, whose themes have major relevance to South Asia. Some of Ajoka's most popular plays have been *Barri* (*Acquittal*), *Eik Thi Nani* (*There Was Once a Grandmother*), *Jum Jum Jeevay Jummanpura* (*Population Explosion in Jummanpura*), *Bala King* (an adaptation of Brecht's *The Resistible Rise of Arturo Ui*), and *Dukhini* (*The Abused Woman*), performed bilingually in Urdu and Bengali. *Acquittal* was performed in English at the Los Angeles Biennale (2001).   FAK

Akalaitis, JoAnne (1937–) American director and actor. Akalaitis travelled with her fiancé, composer Philip *Glass, to Paris in 1965, where she worked with other American actors on productions of *Beckett's plays, and studied with *Grotowski in 1969. In 1970 with those American colleagues, she formed the *collective *Mabou Mines. The group's early productions at *La Mama caught the eye of *Papp, who invited them to his *New York Shakespeare Festival in 1976. Akalaitis directed and co-created many productions with Mabou Mines, including *Dressed Like an Egg* (1977), based on the writings of Colette, and *Dead End Kids: A History of Nuclear Power* (1981). Beckett disowned Akalaitis's

1984 production of *Endgame* at the *American Repertory Theatre because she deviated from his strict stage directions. In 1991, Papp named Akalaitis his successor at the NYSF, despite her lack of administrative experience and specific artistic vision. The NYSF board cited these reasons when they fired her in 1993. She has since directed many plays and *operas around the USA, and is the recipient of numerous awards.   KF

Akimoto Matsuyo (1911–2001) One of the leading women playwrights of post-war Japan, Akimoto was a student of the leftist playwright Miyoshi Jūrō (1902–58), and her debut work, *A Sprinkling of Dust*, was published in 1947. She wrote for the major *shingeki* companies and from 1967 to 1970 ran her own company, the Theatre Troupe (Engekiza). Many of her plays, like *Muraoka Iheiji* (1960), *Kaison, Priest of Hitachi* (1967; trans. 1988), and *The Cape of Seven* (1975), are deft critiques of modern Japanese militarism and patriarchy. She also wrote a number of plays based loosely on classical puppet (*bunraku) and *kabuki dramas, the most successful of which, *Double Suicide after Chikamatsu* (1979), was directed by *Ninagawa Yukio and toured Europe in 1989.   CP

Albee, Edward (1928–) American playwright. Namesake of the American *vaudeville tycoon Edward F. Albee, into whose family he was adopted, Albee rejected school, the patrician pretensions of his wealthy family, and throughout his career subverted their manners and diction. Fleeing to Greenwich Village in the 1950s, he struggled as a poet, and turned to playwriting at Thornton *Wilder's urging. Albee's earliest works were identified as *absurdist, but his later, longer dramas defy categorization. His first play, *The Zoo Story* (Berlin, 1959), is an intense confrontation between two men, ostensibly over a park bench, that touches on emotional and philosophical concerns of modern life. Produced *Off-Broadway in 1960 with *The Sand Box*, Albee was critically anointed and his next plays, *The American Dream* and *The Death of Bessie Smith* (1961), seemed further evidence of the absurdist trend. He responded with a trenchant essay, 'Which Theatre Is the Absurd One?', in the *New York Times* shortly before his most successful play, *Who's Afraid of Virginia Woolf?*, opened on Broadway (1962). The play's psychic bloodletting has been declared everything from Cold War parable to neo-*Strindbergian *realism.

In 1964 Albee's career turned. Baffled by the complexity of *Tiny Alice*, actors, critics, and *audiences complained that he was deliberately opaque. Always impatient with his critics, Albee publicly called the reviewers too stupid and the actors too lazy to understand his play. For the next three decades, in spite of two Pulitzer Prizes (*A Delicate Balance*, 1967; *Seascape*, 1975), Albee seemed to alienate his audience by writing remonstrative and untheatrical dramas. Play after play was rejected by the commercial establishment, and after the debacle of *The Man Who Had Three Arms* (1983) Albee gave up on New York, though he continued working in Vienna, London, and in American *regional theatres. *Three Tall Women*'s ecstatic critical reception in 1994 re-established his Broadway reputation. A third Pulitzer for this play, a Kennedy Center lifetime achievement award in 1996, and the National Medal of Arts in 1997 enthroned him as a great American playwright. In 2001 *The Play about the Baby* won acclaim, even as it teased audiences with its seeming reference to the famous non-existent child in *Who's Afraid of Virginia Woolf?* Clearly audiences could now accept Albee's richly allusive *dialogue as well as his challenging symbolism. His latest play, *Me, Myself and I*, opened in 2008.   TFC

Albee, Edward Franklin *See* KEITH, B. F.

Albery, James (1838–89) English playwright. Influenced by the *comedies of Tom *Robertson, Albery wrote the sentimental *Two Roses* (1870), a success for Henry *Irving as Digby Grant, the comically proud and hypocritical father of two idealized young women. The greatest hit of Irving's career came as the tormented innkeeper Mathias in Albery's version of a French *melodrama, *The Bells* (1871). One of the first adaptations of risqué French *farce, *The Pink Dominos* (1877), for Charles *Wyndham was also successful. The rest of Albery's work was dismissed by his contemporaries as failing to live up to his early promise.   MRB

Alcalá de Henares, Corral de Spain's oldest surviving theatre, in Alcalá de Henares near Madrid, was discovered in 1981, when a disused cinema was found to contain substantial remains of a small *playhouse built in 1601 by a local carpenter, Francisco Sánchez, in a yard behind a house in the market square. Modelled on the Corral de la *Cruz, it had an open-air patio and a roofed stage, flanked by *gradas* (raked seating), with two tiers of galleries and *boxes and a tiring house with balcony and machine loft; the stage, the yard and well, numerous timbers, and two boxes beside the stage survive from this phase. In 1769 the yard was roofed and a *proscenium arch installed. In 1831 the venue was converted

into a *romantic theatre with elliptical tiers of boxes, called the Teatro Cervantes, and from 1927 to 1972 it was used as a cinema. It was restored in the 1990s, preserving its intriguing combination of structures from three centuries of Spanish theatre history. *See* CORRALES DE COMEDIAS.   CD

Aldridge, Ira (1807–67) *African-American actor. As a boy in New York he worked backstage at the Chatham Theatre and studied the performances of major actors at the Park. He launched his career at the African Company in *Sheridan's adaptation of *Kotzebue's *Pizarro*, but, convinced he could not have an acting career in America because of race laws and racial bias, he left in 1824 for England, working the minor and provincial theatres. He acted in a variety of plays about race, including *Othello*, and, taking the abolitionist cause abroad, often concluded his performances with anti-slavery songs. Shortly he was appearing in white roles as well as black in plays such as *Bickerstaffe's *The Padlock*, *A Slave's Revenge*, *Titus Andronicus*, *The Merchant of Venice*, *King Lear*, and *Richard III*. His reputation increased after he replaced the dying Edmund *Kean as Othello (*Covent Garden, 1833). In 1852 he began the first of several continental tours, performing in Berlin, Budapest, Munich, Prague, and Vienna. In 1858 he played Richard III, Othello, and Macbeth in Serbia and *toured Russia. The recipient of many foreign honours, Aldridge was the first African-American theatre artist to receive wide international recognition—though not in his own country.   BBL

Aleichem, Sholem (Sholem Rabinowitz) (1859–1916) Ukrainian Yiddish writer who settled in New York in 1907. Aleichem began to write playlets in 1887, shifting in 1894 to full-length plays, mostly based on his own stories and novels. His first important theatrical success came in 1905 with the Warsaw production of *Scattered and Dispersed*. His American theatrical career began poorly in 1907 with mediocre productions by Jacob P. *Adler and Boris *Tomashefsky, and he did not live to see his folksy *tragicomedies become the high points of the Jewish repertoire worldwide, with companies as diverse as the Yiddish Art Theatre, ARTEF, the Moscow State Yiddish Theatre, and the Habima. Aleichem's best-known plays include *People*, *Stempenyu*, *Hard to Be a Jew*, *The Big Win*, and *The Treasure*. *Tevye the Milkman*, one of Maurice Schwartz's great roles on stage (1919) and film (1939), served as the basis for Jerry *Bock's *musical *Fiddler on the Roof* (1964). *See* DIASPORA.   EN

Aleotti, Giovan Battista (1546–1636) Italian architect and engineer in the service of the Estense family who constructed many secular and religious buildings in Ferrara, in the manner of *Palladio. He showed more originality as a designer of theatre machines and stage sets (*see* SCENOGRAPHY), both for dramatic performances and public spectacles. In 1605–6 he constructed his first permanent *playhouse, in the old granary of Cesare d'Este, followed in 1610 by a temporary stage in the Castello Estense with a scaenae frons inspired by the *Teatro *Olimpico. In 1612 this structure, with an *auditorium for 4,000, was turned into a permanent theatre. Aleotti's masterpiece was the *proscenium-arch theatre of the Pilotta in Parma, known as Teatro *Farnese (constructed 1618–19).   GB

Alexander, George (1858–1918) English *actor-manager who joined *Irving at the Lyceum in 1881, distinguishing himself as Faust (1885) and Macduff (1888). Alexander managed the Avenue Theatre in 1890 and then embarked upon a long tenure of the St James's (1891–1918). Here he did his best work, both as an actor and a *manager, producing *Wilde's *Lady Windermere's Fan* (1892) and *The Importance of Being Earnest* (1895), in which he played Jack Worthing. He also staged important plays by *Pinero, such as *The Second Mrs Tanqueray* with Mrs Pat *Campbell (1893), *His House in Order* (1902), and *Mid-Channel* (1909). Other dramatists whose plays were seen at the St James's included Stephen *Phillips, Jerome K. Jerome, and Henry *James, whose *Guy Domville* was withdrawn after a rowdy first night in 1895. Alexander's management was socially conservative and solidly upper middle class; the St James's was an attractive, well-run theatre with a loyal *audience. As an actor Alexander was handsome, dignified, and well bred, as successful in romantic, dashing parts as he was in troubled husbands.   MRB

Alfieri, Vittorio (1749–1803) Italy's pre-eminent writer of *neoclassical *tragedy was born into the French-speaking nobility of Piedmont. After his first play, *Cleopatra* (1774), he moved to Florence to improve his knowledge of pure Tuscan, and there met the Countess d'Albany, wife of Bonnie Prince Charlie, and the 'worthy love' he had been seeking. Alfieri also wrote several treatises denouncing tyranny and advocating the freedom of the writer, as well as several *comedies, an autobiography, and volumes of verse. Although his hatred of despotism links Alfieri with the Enlightenment, his cult of individualism and portrayal of overwhelming feeling

make him a precursor of *romanticism. He accepted unquestioningly the *Aristotelian *unities, eliminated the Racinian *confidant to focus on the *protagonists alone, and stated that his ideal was tragedy 'as dark and fierce as nature permits and with all the fire that is in me'. The cliché 'titanic' is routinely employed to describe the great, despotic protagonists against whom the younger heroes struggle, even if Alfieri is ambiguous in his depiction of these supposed *villains. In *Filippo* (1780), which pits Don Carlos against his tyrannical father, Philip II of Spain, the struggle is external, but in his finest works, *Saul* (1782) and *Mirra* (1786), his protagonists are at war with themselves.   JF

Alfreds, Mike (1934–) English director. In 1975 Alfreds founded the actor-based storytelling company Shared Experience, having previously worked in the USA and Israel. His groundbreaking adaptation of *Dickens's *Bleak House* (1977), with seven actors swapping roles and sharing the narrative, was a precursor to the *Royal Shakespeare Company's production of David *Edgar's *Nicholas Nickleby*. Other notable productions included an adaptation of Evelyn Waugh's *A Handful of Dust* (1982). After leaving Shared Experience in 1987, Alfreds worked briefly as associate director for the *National Theatre (*Chekhov's *The Cherry Orchard* and an adaptation of Eugène Sue's *The Wandering Jew*). In 1991 he became the artistic director for the *touring Cambridge Theatre Company, renamed Method and Madness in 1995, which operated as a permanent touring company between 1997 and 2000. Since then he has worked freelance, achieving particular success with productions for the *Globe. He published a guide to rehearsal techniques, *Different Every Night* (2007).   KN

alienation effect *See* VERFREMDUNG.

Alkazi, Ebrahim (1925–) Indian director and teacher. Trained in London, Alkazi returned to India in 1950 and later formed the Theatre Unit in Bombay, whose productions of *Antigone, Medea*, and *Oedipus Rex*, all in English, were path-breaking for their energy, aesthetic power, and professionalism. In 1962 he became director of the National School of Drama, New Delhi, and remained at its helm until 1977, where his productions set new standards. Of the 50 or so plays he directed at NSD, *Andha Yug* (*The Blind Age*, 1963), staged in the Ferozshah Kotla ruins, and *Tughlaq* (1973) in the Old Fort achieved legendary status for their innovative use of space and stunning visual impact. Exemplifying Western standards of professionalism, Alkazi's theatre was sometimes criticized for its lack of connection to Indian realities. KJ

Allalou (Sellali Ali) (1902–?) Algerian actor, playwright, and director, one of the founders of modern Algerian theatre. A singer and popular storyteller, Allalou switched to the theatre by creating the Zahia Troupe in 1925. The next year he co-wrote and staged *Djaha*, the first Algerian *comedy. He drew his material and *characters from *The Thousand and One Nights* and popular narratives. Allalou's plays deal with the daily lives of ordinary people, achieving their comic effect through atmosphere and a series of puns that delighted *audiences in Algiers. His ironic approach encompassed the heroes of Arab mythology and the venerated caliphs and their symbols. MMe

Allen, Gracie *See* BURNS, GEORGE.

Alleyn, Edward (1566 1626) English actor, entrepreneur, and founder of Dulwich College. The son of a prominent inn holder and porter to the Queen, by 1586 Edward was a player with the Earl of Worcester's Men and two years later he and his actor-brother were owners of playbooks and theatrical properties. By 1592 Alleyn was lauded as one of the greatest actors of his time, his reputation being largely earned through his performances with the Lord *Admiral's Men in *Marlowe's plays. Alleyn definitely performed the roles of Tamburlaine and Dr Faustus, probably played Barabas in *The Jew of Malta*, along with a number of other roles. Primarily a tragedian, Alleyn's style was powerful and charismatic and his exceptional physical stature was an asset for the conquering *heroes he performed. He was described by one of his contemporaries as 'strutting and bellowing' and he became known through some of his eulogies as 'the *Roscius of his age'. By comparison with Richard *Burbage, the leading actor in Shakespeare's company, Alleyn is thought by some historians to have been bombastic and highly stylized. In addition to his talents as an actor, Alleyn held many financial investments, largely in the entertainment business. Together with his partner and father-in-law Philip *Henslowe, Alleyn came to own the *Rose Theatre, as well as the *Fortune and *Hope *playhouses and the Bear Garden. In 1604 Alleyn and Henslowe also acquired the patent for the Mastership of the Bears, Bulls, and Mastiff Dogs (*see* BAITING). By 1606 Alleyn had purchased Dulwich Manor on which he constructed a joint orphanage and pensioners' home now known as Dulwich College SPC

Allgood, Sara (1883–1950) The most celebrated of the first generation of *Abbey Theatre actresses, she joined the National Theatre Society in Dublin in 1903. Her musical voice was expertly handled, initially under Frank Fay's tutelage, over a remarkable range of tragic and comic roles: Cathleen Ni Houlihan, Emer, Deirdre for *Yeats; Maurya and the Widow Quin for *Synge; others for Lady *Gregory and Lennox *Robinson. Allgood had a richly warm stage persona, but she could encompass roles as driven as T. C. *Murray's Mrs Harte and as embittered as his Ellen Keegan. It was, however, *O'Casey who exploited her range to the full with his Juno and Bessie Burgess, the former impersonation being preserved on film by Hitchcock (*Juno and the Paycock*, 1930). Allgood often toured away from Dublin, notably with *Poel, Mrs Patrick *Campbell, and in J. Hartley Manners's *Peg o' my Heart* throughout Australia (1916–20). After 1940 she lived in Hollywood, performing in over 30 films. RAC

Allio, René (1924–95) French *scenographer, painter, filmmaker, greatly influenced by *Piscator and the *Berliner Ensemble. Following a period in France, Allio created ten designs for *Planchon from 1957 to 1967, including Shakespeare's *Henry IV*, *Molière's *Georges Dandin*, Planchon's own *La Remise*, and *Racine's *Bérénice*. He designed several productions for the *National Theatre in London with director *Gaskill: *Farquhar's *The Recruiting Officer* (1963) and *The Beaux' Stratagem* (1971), and *Arden's *Armstrong's Last Goodnight* (1965). He also designed Molière's *Tartuffe* for *Guthrie (1967). His work typically explored all the planes of the stage space, especially exploiting its full depth. His interest in film extended from the visual to writing and directing, and he made over twelve films between 1962 and 1993. He also continuously painted, exhibiting in Paris 1958 and 1961, and collaborated with architects in reshaping and restoring *playhouses in Paris, Tunisia, and Marseille. PH

Alloula, Abdalkder (1923–94) Algerian actor and director. At Théâtre National Algérien he staged an adaptation of *Gogol's *Diary of a Madman* (1971) and his own play *El-Khobza* (*The Bread*, 1972), which set a new direction for contemporary Algerian practice. His most important period was at Oran Regional Theatre from 1978, where he created work that intervened in social and political issues. Attending to popular aesthetics, he found in the tradition of the *gaoual* (reciting poet) the elements of a distinctive *epic theatre form. His *Lagoual* (*The Statements*, 1980), *Lajouad* (*The Generous*, 1983), and *Litham* (*Mask,

1988) formed a trilogy that defined Algerian theatre in that decade. He was assassinated by the Armed Islamic Group (GIA) as part of a campaign to eradicate Algerian artists, journalists, and intellectuals. MMe

Almagro, Corral de The surviving *playhouse in the main square of Almagro (south central Spain) dates from 1628 and was discovered in 1953. This fairly small, rectangular *corral de comedias* (14.3 m by 24 m; 47 by 79 feet) has an open-air yard and roofed stage surrounded on three sides by a stone colonnade with two upper galleries. Originally there were *gradas* (raked seating) and benches on the ground floor and the galleries were divided into *boxes, with a women's gallery at the back. The stage, 1.5 m (5 feet) high, occupies the width of the yard and is 4.5 m (15 feet) deep. At the back are wooden posts supporting the tiring house gallery, which has three balustraded openings; these posts delimit three similar openings at stage level, originally curtained, with the tiring house wall set nearly a metre further back. The *corral*, always privately owned, was opened by a prosperous local chaplain, Leonardo de Oviedo, in the patio of an inn, and remained in use until the nineteenth century. CD

Alonso, José Luis (1924–90) Spanish director, one of the most important of the Franco era. He played a significant role, even while director of the Teatro Nacional María Guerrero in the early 1960s, in introducing alternative international works to Spain. His role in promoting contemporary *dramaturgy, most visible in his staging of numerous of Antonio *Gala's plays, his productions of forgotten classics like *Valle-Inclán's *Ballad of Wolves* in 1970 and *Calderón's *The Goblin Lady* in 1966, as well as his championing of important trends in international drama—*Cocteau, *Claudel, *Ionesco, *Williams—accorded him a unique role in the modernization of the Spanish stage. A prolific translator and critic, Alonso continued to dominate in the post-Franco era, bringing *Casares for a landmark production of Rafael Alberti's *The Absurdity* in 1976. MMD

Alonso de Santos, José Luis (1942–) Spanish playwright, actor, and director. After experience with Madrid's independent collective groups Tabano and the Teatro Libre in the 1970s, he first achieved recognition with an original play in 1975. *Hostages in the Barrio* (1981) and *Going down to Marrakesh* (1985) brought him both critical respect and box-office success. These seriocomic plays, dealing with marginal *characters speaking contemporary slang, were appealing to younger *audiences in particular and both were adapted into films. Other major works are *The Last Pirouette* (1986), *Unhinged* (1987), and the *tragicomedy *The Generals' Dinner* (2000). In 1978 he joined the faculty of the Royal School of Dramatic Arts as professor of *acting and playwriting. He was named *artistic director of Spain's National Company for Classical Theatre in 2000, beginning his new duties with a revisionist staging of *Calderón's *The Phantom Lady*. MPH

Alsina, Arturo (1897-1984) Paraguayan playwright. Born in Argentina, Alsina came to Paraguay when he was 12 and remained for the rest of his life. He founded the Paraguayan Company of Drama and Comedy in 1926. Considered the greatest of Paraguayan national dramatists, much of his work was influenced by *Ibsen. His prolific output includes *The Firemark* (1926), *Evangelist* (1926), *Birthright* (1927), *Intruso* (1928), *La llama flota* (1940), *The Shadow of the Statue* (1947), and *The Dreamed City* (1968). EJW

Álvarez Quintero, Serafín (1871–1938) and **Joaquín Álvarez Quintero** (1873–1944) Spanish playwrights. The Álvarez Quintero brothers formed a popular literary duo composing for both the stage and the new medium of radio. The inheritors of nineteenth-century Spanish *naturalism, they were joint authors of many successful *entremeses, *comedias, new plays, and *sainetes, as well as the librettos for several *zarzuelas. The 'golden brothers' produced over 200 pieces that filled Spanish theatres for nearly half a century. Their stylized, somewhat episodic depictions of life and customs in Seville and lower Andalusia were especially popular with Madrid *audiences, though they were frequently accused of producing a false and dulcified picture of Spanish rural reality, which sacrificed a vision of social hardship for an ingenuous picture of local customs. KG

American Repertory Theatre (Cambridge, Massachusetts) *Regional theatre. Following his term of office at the Yale School of Drama, *Brustein founded the ART at Harvard in 1980, bringing many staff and students with him. He soon established the company in the vanguard of regional theatres by hiring visionary directors and designers to interpret an ambitious repertoire of Shakespeare, classical *comedies, new plays, and modernist dramas by *Ibsen, *Chekhov, *Shaw, *Pirandello, *Brecht, and *Beckett. *Şerban mounted numerous productions, including a popular version of *Gozzi's *King Stag*, with *scenography by *Taymor. Other landmark productions include Brustein's adaptation of Pirandello's

Six Characters in Search of an Author (1984); *Akalaitis's controversial treatment of *Endgame* (1984, disavowed by Beckett); and a major section of Robert *Wilson's *the CIVIL warS* (1985). In the 1990s, *Mamet premièred several of his plays at ART, including *Oleanna* (1992). Since 1987 ART has operated a training institute, which formalized a joint programme with the *Moscow Art Theatre School in 1998. In 2002 Brustein stepped down as *artistic director, replaced by Robert Woodruff, succeeded by Diane Paulus in 2008.   STC

Ames, Winthrop (1871–1937) American director and producer. Harvard educated and independently wealthy, Ames surprised his friends in 1904 by entering commercial theatre—then regarded as a grubby affair dominated by the *Theatrical Syndicate. After producing and directing three seasons in Boston, Ames toured European art theatres in 1907 and 1908. He returned to become director of the New Theatre in New York, and its failure convinced him of the need for smaller venues. He supervised designs for two intimate venues in the Broadway district: the Little Theatre (1912, 299 seats) and the Booth Theatre (1913, 712 seats). Ames offered carefully prepared and self-financed productions of plays by *Galsworthy, *Shaw, Granville *Barker, and *Gilbert and *Sullivan, as well as American works, such as *Kaufman and *Connelly's *Beggar on Horseback* (1924). Despite many long-running productions and critical praise, Ames's career slowly decimated his personal fortune.   MAF

amphitheatre Literally, 'theatre on two sides', first attested archaeologically in Pompeii about 70 BC. Its form was normally elliptical, with doors for animals and performers at each end. In the western Roman Empire it largely replaced the public forum as a space for the performance of spectacles (*munera*), especially *gladiatorial contests, *animal fights, and dramatized public executions (*damnatio*). In the east the classic amphitheatre form is less common, since stadiums, hippodromes, or theatres were adapted, or multi-purpose facilities were specially built, but it is found in many centres of Roman influence such as Corinth or Pergamum. Constant improvement led to underground chambers with gangways, trapdoors, and lifts operated by capstans, capable of swiftly elevating beasts, trees, or buildings into the arena. Canvas coverings (*vela*) against the sun could be provided. Aqueducts supplied water in quantity to flush underground rooms or sometimes flood parts of the arena (*see* NAUMACHIA). Front seats were always reserved for dignitaries and the tendency to class-based seating, as in the theatre, grew. Rome possessed the greatest amphitheatre in the Amphitheatrum Flavium (the Colosseum) built from the spoils from Jerusalem by Vespasian.

The term is also used to describe contemporary outdoor theatres and, referring to the Elizabethan age, to distinguish the open-air *public theatres (like Shakespeare's *Globe) from indoor *private theatres (like Shakespeare's *Blackfriars).   WJS

amusement arcades Commercial venues of light and often mechanical entertainment particularly popular in the late nineteenth and early twentieth centuries, especially in North America. Amusement arcades have many antecedents, but in the early 1890s entrepreneurs began to exploit automatic amusement machines, called in the USA 'nickel-in-the-slots', adapted from Edison's phonographs and kinescopes. Louis Glass of San Francisco installed two converted Edison phonographs in the Palais Royal Saloon in 1890, and within six months he owned over a dozen machines in various saloons and waiting rooms, netting an extraordinary $4,000. Nickel-in-the-slot machines were soon installed in hotel lobbies, resorts, and the midways of local and world's fairs. To attract a wider *audience and a higher class of clientele, entrepreneurs moved their machines into storefront facilities in commercial districts in most major American cities and added other automatic novelty machines, including candy and chewing-gum dispensers, and even early X-ray machines and fluoroscopes. The arcade changed in 1893 with the arrival of Edison's kinescope, the technological forerunner to film. Thomas Lombard opened the first kinescope arcade in 1894 in New York. By 1897 the fad was waning and many owners sold their equipment to 'tenderloin' arcades and shooting galleries. The lurid nature of the arcades' pictures and their attraction for young men drew increased opposition, but these new 'penny arcades' flourished. Adolph Zukor and Morris Kohn founded the Automatic Vaudeville Company in 1903 and built a number of 'peep-show' arcades in New York, Newark, Boston, and Philadelphia. By 1905 many arcades had converted to the new nickelodeon format, only to be replaced in 1907 by the one-reel 'screen shows'—the immediate predecessors to movie houses. But amusement arcades never entirely lost their appeal, and made a comeback in the latter part of the twentieth century with the development of games based on computer simulations. *See also* PENNY THEATRES.   PAD

anagnorisis In *Aristotle's *Poetics*, *anagnorisis* (recognition) refers to a change in the *protagonist from ignorance to knowledge, leading to happiness (*comedy) or misery (*tragedy). In tragedy, *anagnorisis* is often the mechanism whereby *peripeteia* (reversal) is brought about. Taken together, recognition and reversal are central to a complex plot, revealing the *hamartia* (error) underlying the protagonist's tragic act, and precipitating his suffering. In Aristotle's discussion of the techniques of recognition—made much of in *early modern criticism—he argues that those dependent on external signs or tokens, or on self-revelation, are inferior to those arising from a logical analysis of the incidents themselves, as in *Sophocles' *Oedipus the King.* Ironically, the inartistic token became the *sine qua non* of *New Comedy and its Renaissance descendants. Late twentieth-century theory has applied *anagnorisis* to the *audience, either as a sympathetic 'recognition-acceptance' of the situation as perceived by the *characters, or as a detached 'recognition-criticism' of the situation. RWV

Anderson, Judith (1898–1992) Australian actress who enjoyed a highly acclaimed career in the USA. She gained early experience in the Julius Knight company, which *toured Australia during the First World War. Her American work began in 1918, and included Broadway successes such as *O'Neill's *Strange Interlude* (1928) and *Mourning Becomes Electra* (1932), and classical roles. She played Lady Macbeth opposite *Olivier at the *Old Vic in London in 1937, and opposite Maurice *Evans in New York in 1941. Anderson was much praised for her Gertrude, against *Gielgud's Hamlet (1936), and her Medea, (1947), both on Broadway, the latter adapted by Robinson Jeffers from *Euripides. Her talent for heavy *villainesses and emotional acting is clearly on display in her performance as Mrs Danvers in the film of *Rebecca* (Hitchcock, 1940). In later life Anderson toured the USA in recitals, and was a regular on the television soap opera *Santa Barbara* (1984–7). She was created Dame of the British Empire in 1960, the first Australian actress so honoured. EJS

Anderson, Laurie (1947–) American pioneering *performance artist who created work during the 1970s that combined *happenings with her training as a classical violinist. She developed her mature performance style during the early 1980s by fusing elaborate technological effects with short, comically *surrealistic *monologues. Her first major work in this style, *The United States, Parts I–IV,* premièred at the Brooklyn Academy of Music in 1983 (much was reprised in her 1986 film *Home of the Brave*). Besides *avant-garde acclaim, songs from her performances attracted a popular music audience. Warner Brothers

released the first of her several albums and music videos, *Big Science,* in 1982, establishing her as one of the first 'crossover' performance artists in the United States. Anderson *toured extensively in the 1990s and assembled a retrospective, *Stories from the Nerve Bible,* in 1993. She branched out again in 1999 by collaborating with director Anne *Bogart on *Songs and Stories from Moby Dick.* A musical performance, *Homeland,* was on tour from 2007. JAB

Anderson, Mary (1859–1940) American actress who made her professional debut as Juliet in Louisville in 1875 at the age of 16. Immediately recognized as an actress of great beauty, dramatic passion, and power, her many successes included Perdita and Hermione in *The Winter's Tale* and Rosalind in *As You Like It.* Other roles included Parthenia in *Ingomar* by Maria Lovell, Galatea in *Gilbert's *Pygmalion and Galatea,* and Clarice in Gilbert's *Comedy and Tragedy,* a role written for her. In 1878 Anderson moved to London, attaining great success throughout the 1880s; she was the first to double Perdita and Hermione (1887). Her marriage to a wealthy American allowed her to retire from the stage in 1889, at the height of her fame. She wrote in her memoirs (*A Few Memories,* 1896) that like Frances *Kemble, 'the *practice* of my art... had grown as time went on more and more distasteful to me'. KMN

Anderson, Maxwell (1889–1959) American playwright who was regarded for his verse plays in the 1930s as one of America's foremost dramatists, rivalling *O'Neill, though his work has been little produced since 1960. His verse plays were seen by some critics as pretentious or bombastic. Others disparaged his poetry—a loose blank verse—as only so much prose set in fixed lines. When *Winterset* (1935) was given the first New York Drama Critics Circle award (1936) on the fifth ballot, Percy Hammond of the *Herald Tribune* made a speech representing the dissenters, calling the play 'spinach'. *Elizabeth the Queen* (1930) was the first of Anderson's successful verse plays, and *Mary of Scotland* (1933), about the rivalry between Elizabeth I and her cousin, was regarded by many critics as his outstanding work; the 'Tudor Trilogy' was completed with *Anne of the Thousand Days* (1948). Anderson's talents seemed well suited to *musical collaboration; he wrote book and lyrics for *Knickerbocker Holiday* (1938) and *Lost in the Stars* (1949) for composer *Weill. MAF

Anderson, Robert (1917–2009) American playwright. His first full-length play on Broadway, *Tea and Sympathy* (1953), was a study of a misunderstood and sensitive boy at an elite American prep school. It was helped by the direction of *Kazan and the appearance of the film star Deborah Kerr in the leading role. A succession of plays on Broadway followed, with varying success: *All Summer Long* (1954), *Silent Night, Lonely Night* (1959), *You Know I Can't Hear You When the Water's Running* (1967), *I Never Sang for my Father* (1968), and *Solitaire, Double Solitaire* (1971). *The Days Between*, premièred at the Dallas Theatre Center in 1965, was subsequently produced at 51 *regional, *community, and university theatres, to prove that dramatic works can survive away from Broadway. Anderson's plays are sometimes autobiographical but never plot-heavy, and provide telling glimpses into the psychology of the mostly well-bred, intelligent *characters through his graceful *dialogue. He also wrote for film, radio, and television, and taught playwriting at universities throughout the United States.   MCH

Andreev, Leonid (1871–1919) Russian writer who completed twenty full-length and eight shorter plays between 1905 and 1916. Closely associated with the *symbolist movement, his drama of man's journey from cradle to grave, *The Life of Man* (1906), is more akin to German *expressionism and was staged by *Meyerhold in St Petersburg and *Stanislavsky at the *Moscow Art Theatre, in 1907. His most famous play, *He Who Gets Slapped* (1915), is set in a *circus and, in a manner anticipatory of Chaplin's film *The Circus* (1928), dramatizes the problem of the alienated individual. Andreev's own conflicts were reflected in at least three suicide attempts and political vacillation which began with affiliation to Lenin's Social Democratic Party and concluded with outright opposition to the Russian Revolution. A painter, amateur photographer, and author of two strikingly original theatrical essays (*Letters on the Theatre*, 1912–13), Andreev finally settled in Finland.   NW

Andreini family Italian professional practitioners of *commedia dell'arte* and related genres. The Tuscan **Francesco** (1548–1624) embarked on a theatrical career in the late 1570s, and married the young Paduan **Isabella Canali** (1562–1604) in 1578. They quickly became celebrated, the core of the *Gelosi company, with Francesco playing the part of the braggart Capitano, and Isabella becoming the first professional actress in history to establish a respectable reputation, while playing the part of the Innamorata (*see* GENDER AND PERFORMANCE). She refuted accusations of immodesty, composed a *pastoral play and a large number of occasional rhymes, was fêted in society, and elected to a literary academy. Both of them left behind in print some important repertoire material from their *arte* improvisations. Their son **Giovan Battista** (1576–1654) followed them into the profession, defended its respectability vigorously in print, and had a long career as *actor-manager with his own troupe called the *Fedeli. His twenty published plays cover a remarkable range of tones and structures, though the majority are forms of *comedy: they include history's first attempt at a comic *opera libretto (*La Ferinda*, 1622, never actually set to music). His first wife **Virginia** was both actress and singer: she premièred the title role in Monteverdi's *Arianna* in 1608.   RAA

angura Japanese *avant-garde movement, also called 'little theatre' (*shōgekijō*) movement. *Angura* ('underground') rose from a dissatisfaction with the politics and aesthetics of orthodox modern theatre (*shingeki*); many of its proponents were involved in the nationwide protests over the ratification of the 1960 USA–Japan Security Treaty. The movement centred on *Kara Jūrō, *Satoh Makoto, *Shimizu Kunio, *Terayama Shūji, *Suzuki Tadashi, and *Hijikata Tatsumi. The styles of *angura* vary widely, from the carnivalesque to the austere, but in general it discarded the *realism and humanism of *shingeki* in favour of fantasy and myth, trying to make sense of a world rendered absurd by the war and its aftermath. *Angura* typically employed *metatheatrical devices, often in an attempt to recapture the energy and spirit of pre-modern Japanese theatre. It also radically questioned the roles of text, performance space, actors, and *audience. Where *shingeki* privileged the text, *angura* tended to stress the physicality of the actor, though excellent playwrights like Shimizu and Kara have emerged from it. Performances were typically held in small studio theatres, in tents, or on the *street. Initially marked by revolutionary roots, *angura* became increasingly apolitical. Some fix its demise around the mid-1970s, but many of its creators are still active, and its stylistic legacy continues in the work of younger artists like *Noda Hideki.   CP

animal fights (*venationes*) The Romans displayed *animals variously as curiosities, to perform tricks, and to engage in combat. Staged hunts developed at Rome during the third and second centuries BC, perhaps stimulated by contact with North African civilizations, and became an integral feature of Romanization throughout the known world. They combined the allure of exotic species with the excitement of the chaos.

In the late republic the *aediles* (urban magistrates) became responsible for providing regular *venationes*, and competed energetically to acquire animals. There is some evidence that tribesmen from the animals' native habitat were imported to hunt them. Under the empire professional organizations supplied animals and personnel, at least to venues in North Africa, and at Rome a training school for beast-fighters is first mentioned in the reign of Nero (AD 54–68). Republican installations under the Roman Forum indicate that its use as a temporary arena included provision for the display of animals. For massed hunts the largest venue at Rome was the Circus Maximus, while *amphitheatres or converted *Greek theatres and stadia were equipped for spectator protection. Under Augustus (27 BC–AD 14) *venationes* became regularly combined with *gladiatorial contests; sometimes the two halves of the programme would be punctuated by a *damnatio*. The number and type of animals were advertised in advance, and frequently recorded in sponsors' epitaphs. A local community could take pride in an event even if the total number of animals displayed remained in single figures. At Rome, however, the emperors competed in conspicuous consumption. Augustus dispatched 3,500 'African beasts' in 26 displays, Trajan (reputedly) 11,000 animals during his Dacian triumph. Animals were also pitted against one another individually, sometimes chained together to ensure an engagement. Encounters were contrived that balanced the odds: bull versus elephant, rhinoceros versus bison. An animal could also be matched with a beast-fighter who was trained and equipped to outwit it. A theatrical setting sometimes contributed verisimilitude: at the Ludi Saeculares in AD 204 Septimius Severus staged a 'shipwreck' in the Circus Maximus that disgorged a cargo of live animals onto the track. Despite logistical difficulties, *venationes* persisted into the sixth century. *See also* CIRCUS, ROMAN. KMC

animals Animals have featured in performance from ancient times. The *Romans had bears and dogs in dramas, elephants who performed rope walking, and built gruesome shows of *animal fights. Throughout Europe, trained animals accompanied itinerant performers to the great fairs—the dancing bear, the tame lion, and the intelligent goat. In *The Winter's Tale*, Shakespeare's famous stage direction 'Exit, pursued by a hear' is considered by some historians to indicate the availability of trained performing bears, rather than those from the nearby Bear-Pit at Southwark (*see* BAITING). By the seventeenth

century animals featured in performances in their own right. At Bartholomew Fair in London, *fairground booths exhibited animal as well as human performers: the tiger who, in 1701, 'pulled the feathers so nicely from live fowls', the *morris-dancing dogs (who danced before Queen Anne), and an Italian singing pig. It was in the fairs that performing horses established their popularity. Not only were they *animaux savants*, they also demonstrated tricks and feats which formed the basis of the modern *circus. An ape dressed in a soldier's uniform rode a horse, and human riders exhibited trick horsemanship on expertly trained animals in open fields and riding schools.

Astley's Circus opened in London in 1768, and *Astley's Amphitheatre in 1784, featuring mainly equestrian acts. The popularity of the horses encouraged the development of *hippodrama, plays constructed around feats of equestrianism by star performers. Popular themes were *Dick Turpin's Ride to York* (in which the death of Black Bess was the climax) and plays by Shakespeare such as *Richard III* and *Henry V*, where galloping and leaping horses could shine in the battle scenes. By the 1870s dog dramas such as *The Forest of Bondy* and *My Poor Dog Tray* were hugely popular, written to display the talents of well-trained dogs like Sam Wild's retriever Nelson, who would ascend a 12-m (40-foot) ladder, fire a cannon on a perch, and descend on the opposite side. Trainers used meat secreted in a pocket or a handkerchief to encourage a dog to 'take the seize', that is, attack or fasten its teeth on an actor's clothing. When such highly trained animals were sold, they took their acts with them.

The exhibition of performing animals continued throughout the nineteenth century. Menageries were extremely popular *touring shows. In booths, public houses, and exhibition rooms, animal anomalies—the six-legged horse, the two-headed calf, the monster pig—were often challenged by a human-animal, like Jo-Jo the Dog-faced boy, the Leopard or Zebra Child, or Zip (William Henry Johnson) Coon, billed as the 'Man-Monkey' or 'What Is It?' by P. T. *Barnum (*see also* FREAK SHOW). Lion taming was featured in both menageries and circuses.

Trainers proliferated in the nineteenth and early twentieth centuries as the demand for animal novelties moved from the circus to the *music halls and *variety theatres. The Hungarian M. Nivin was a famed monkey trainer, and his 'Blondin' monkey —who walked, somewhat reluctantly, across a horizontal bar with his head in a sack— was the rage of the London halls during 1894.

Animals frequently became stars in their own right. Jumbo, the elephant so coveted by Barnum, was the focus of British outrage when he was sold by the London Zoo to the showman in 1881. Having shipped him to America, Barnum realized his potential even after the unfortunate animal was killed in a locomotive collision. In Barnum's grand circus parade, Jumbo's skin and the skeleton were mounted on two great wagons, followed by Alice, another elephant from the London Zoo, and a long line of the circus's regular elephants, all carrying in their trunks black-bordered bed sheets and trained to wipe their eyes every few steps.

Convincing animal impersonators are a rare breed. Charles Lauri worked as a famously accurate *pantomime monkey who had trained by observing Sally, a real specimen at London Zoo. He played a *realistic Poodle in the 1888 *Drury Lane pantomime of *Sindbad the Sailor*. He specialized in monkeys, cats, and dogs, and famously walked around the edge of the circle among the audience in animal *character. George *Conquest played a similar range of pantomime animals, including an octopus and a gigantic ape in the *Grim Goblin* (1876) and a grotesque toad in *Harlequin Rokoko, the Rock Fiend* (1878). A reviewer wrote that 'the Octopus not only looks like the real thing, but in its movements we trace an exact resemblance'. Despite a growing cultural repulsion to performing animals and their human imitators, animal impersonations have not disappeared; in fact they have moved into the mainstream theatre in contemporary *musicals like *Lloyd Webber's *Cats* (1972) and the Disney Company's *The Lion King* (1997), which still realize the human-animal on stage.   AF

ankiya nat Traditional *dance-drama performed in the north-eastern state of Assam, India. Attributed to Sankaradeva (1459–1568), a saint-poet and social and religious reformer, the form dramatizes the avatars of the Hindu god Vishnu for the spiritual edification of ordinary people. Following Sanakaradeva's first venture, *Chihnyatra*, he wrote other *nats* (plays) on mythological themes: *Patni-prasada, Kali-damana, Keli-gopala, Rukmini-harana, Parijata-harana*, and *Rama-vijaya*. The saint-poet Madhavadeva (1489–1596), continuing Sanakaradeva's spiritual legacy, also composed devotional plays, although most of them are popularly known as *jhumura* rather than *ankiya nat*, because of their short duration. The performance of *ankiya nat* follows the procedures of Sanskrit drama outlines in the *Natyasastra*. Apart from verses in Sanskrit, the songs, *dialogue, and commentary are in a vernacular form of Assamese called Brajavali. The performance is highlighted by exquisite dances

and simple yet elegant *costumes and *masks. Performed more often than not in a prayer-hall within a monastery, the *ankiya nat* remains an integral part of Assamese culture today.   AMB

Anouilh, Jean (1910–87) French dramatist. Employed as *Jouvet's secretary (1931–2), he wrote his first play, *L'Hermine* (1932), a modest success. *Pitoëff's productions of *Le Voyageur sans bagage* (1937) and *La Sauvage* (*Restless Heart*, 1938) established Anouilh's reputation for slick *dramaturgy with a comic touch and mordant bite. His decade-long collaboration with director *Barsacq yielded some of his most enduring work: *Thieves Carnival* (1938), *Time Remembered* (1940), *Antigone* (1944), *L'Invitation au château* (*Ring round the Moon*, 1947).

Anouilh's plays include reinterpretations of classics by *Sophocles, Shakespeare, and *Wilde, and historical subjects like Joan of Arc in *The Lark* (1953) and *Becket* (1959). Social *comedies with risqué overtones include *Waltz of the Toreadors* (1952) and *L'Hurluberlu* (1959). A frequent *character type is the *gamine*, a self-aware young woman whose obsession with purity enables her to handle would-be seducers with aplomb, as in *The Rehearsal* (1950), *Colombe* (1951), and *Cécile* (1954). *Metatheatrical devices abound, for theatre itself is one of Anouilh's persistent themes, its artifice serving to expose falseness in social interactions. Besides his 60 or so plays, Anouilh wrote and directed screenplays. Perhaps more than any other French dramatist of the twentieth century, Anouilh found an international *audience.   FHL

antagonist *See* PROTAGONIST.

antiquarianism A method of historically accurate *mise-en-scène. Antiquarianism was a widespread cultural movement to preserve, collect, and study historical objects and documents. While novels, paintings, and museums could represent the past, the theatre alone could re-enact it, transforming historical records and monuments into a live, embodied experience.

From the late eighteenth to the early twentieth centuries theatrical antiquarianism meant using historically correct *scenography. The series of Gothic architectural designs which William Capon created for John Philip *Kemble at both *Drury Lane and *Covent Garden between 1794 and 1809 represent its first sustained use, while Charles *Kemble and J. R. *Planché's 1823 revival of *King John* at Covent Garden was the first to feature historically precise *costumes. Shakespeare's plays became the principal focus of antiquarian propriety, especially in productions by *Macready, Charles *Kean, *Irving, and *Tree, who all relied upon historically correct—and increasingly elaborate—stage and costume designs. Even plays with no fixed time or setting, such as *The Tempest*, were assigned a precise history and geography in order that they could be staged as historical spectacles. The value placed upon historical accuracy meant that researchers had to track down archival sources. The theatre ranged far in its quest for historical truth, sometimes interpolating re-enactments of documented events into plays which do not dramatize them, such as Henry's triumphal return to London after the victory at Agincourt which Kean added to *Henry V* in 1859.

Dismissed for most of the twentieth century, more recently scholarship has shown that theatrical antiquarianism helped create a popular audience for historical study. *See also* REALISM AND REALITY. RWS

anti-theatrical polemic In the Western tradition, moral or religious objections to the theatre have been raised during most of the periods in which it has enjoyed prosperity and influence and during many in which it has not. Towards the close of the great era of *Greek theatre, Plato (c.428–348 BC) included the theatre centrally in his attack on the mimetic arts in *The Republic*—all poets were to be banished from his ideal commonwealth, not least the playwrights—and while classical Roman writers rarely bothered to follow his example they barely needed to, since by law *Roman actors, even celebrities such as *Roscius, were denied citizenship and treated to the social opprobrium otherwise reserved for prostitutes. Plato was eagerly seconded by the early church fathers, who supplemented his view of the theatre as a place of base mimickry calculated to raise our animal passions against our reason by adducing biblical prohibitions against falsity in general and dressing up in particular. Tatian's 'Address to the Greeks' (c.AD 160) argued that actors were guilty of inciting the crimes they depicted, and Tertullian's *De Spectaculis* (c.210) claimed that drama was devised by devils to lure men into idolatry. St Augustine was more ambivalent: although his *Confessions* (c.400) repent of his youthful addiction to theatregoing, they acknowledge the power of live *tragedy. Organized Christianity has been divided ever since between the desire to repudiate the theatre and the desire to appropriate it. Anti-theatrical polemic enjoyed its European heyday during the Reformation and Counter-Reformation, when both the courtly and the commercial theatres of England, France, Spain, and Italy found themselves under attack from various ecclesiastical factions. In England, though some Puritans (such as Milton) loved

drama and some high churchmen (such as the lapsed playwright Stephen Gosson and, more influentially, the Restoration pamphleteer Jeremy *Collier) wrote against it, the theatre's most vociferous opponents, associating drama with courtly corruption and Popish ritual, were Puritans such as Phillip Stubbes (*The Anatomy of Abuses*, 1583) and William *Prynne, who lost his ears for criticizing Queen Henrietta Maria's participation in *masques (in *Histriomastix*, 1633). On the Continent, by contrast, the major campaign against drama was led by senior Jansenists, among them Cardinal Carlo Borromeo and Armand de Bourbon, Prince de Conti (*Traité de la comédie et des spectacles*, 1669). Anti-theatrical attitudes continued to flourish through the nineteenth century, sometimes less visibly in Europe than in the United States—perhaps unsurprisingly given its Puritan heritage and the influence of another man-of-the-theatre turned anti-theatricalist, *Rousseau. While the stage has occasionally drawn fire since, it has generally had to be quite strenuously obscene or provocative in order to do so, moralists' attentions having largely transferred to film, television, and the Internet. *See also* CENSORSHIP. MD

Antoine, André (1858–1943) French actor and director. His modest beginnings as an employee of the Paris Gas Company belied the reformative zeal and commitment with which he was to revolutionize stage practice. In 1887, after experimentation with his amateur drama group, the Cercle Gaulois, Antoine founded the Théâtre *Libre, funded primarily through subscriptions, which enabled him to avoid the *censor. From the first season he hit on a successful formula of combining unproduced works by known authors with the work of new dramatists, and he refused to rest on the laurels of one playwright's success. His theatre quickly became the refuge for many playwrights rejected by the larger stages; his turnover policy, however, also led to disagreements with authors, as did the emphasis on *realism, which shifted the balance of power away from author and *actor to *director. His insistence on continuous novelty, often in programmes of short one-act plays, expanded to include stage adaptations of well-known novels, new prose and verse drama, and translations of foreign plays. Few indigenous works were to enter the French canon, though significant premières of foreign works included *Ibsen's *Ghosts* (1890), *Strindberg's *Miss Julie* (1891), and *Hauptmann's *The Weavers* (1893). Antoine's passion for realism in production linked him falsely with *Zola's project of *naturalism in the theatre, and yet authenticity and exactitude in *costumes, scenery, and *lighting, and his quest for realistic *acting, did not harm the naturalist cause.

Bankruptcy forced him to close in 1894 but he reopened the same venue in 1897 as Théâtre Antoine. In 1906 recognition came with his appointment to the Théâtre de l'*Odéon, where he was able to put in place what would become standard procedures, such as the abolition of *footlights and darkening of the *auditorium. There he mounted notable productions of European classics by Shakespeare, *Goldoni, *Racine, *Corneille, and *Sheridan, which were characterized by historical realism and scenic exactitude. Ticket receipts during his tenure rose dramatically, but so did production costs. At the Odéon he produced over 360 plays between 1906 and 1914. One major hurdle was attracting audiences across the river—by the beginning of the twentieth century most theatres were situated on Paris's Right Bank. After the First World War, Antoine, faced with the anti-naturalism of *Copeau and *Jouvet, dabbled in film and continued to call for reforms in theatre through his dramatic criticism.　　RRS

Appia, Adolphe (1862-1924) Swiss designer and theorist, one of the creators of modernist theatre practice. In *Music and the Art of the Theatre* (1899), inspired by the staging requirements of *Wagner's *operas, Appia suggested that the musical score should dictate the quality of performance, actors' movement, and the nature of scenic space. He called for three-dimensional scenery, for creative and form-revealing *lighting, and for settings expressive of the inner reality of the work. The actor must perform within a supportive and responsive *scenography where light, symbolic colouring, and sculptured space would be used to evoke atmosphere and psychological nuance, harmoniously correlated by the new theatrical artist, the 'designer-director'. The *audience should no longer be thought of as passive spectators but as active mental participants.

The second phase of Appia's career began in 1906 and involved the system of eurhythmics devised by his compatriot Émile *Jaques-Dalcroze, designed to enhance performers' perception of music through the movement of their bodies in space. Appia prepared a series of designs, termed 'rhythmic spaces', which would revolutionize future scenic practice further. These were essentially abstract arrangements of solid stairs, platforms, podia, and the like, whose rigidity, sharp lines and angles, and immobility, when confronted by the softness, subtlety, and movement of the body, would by opposition take on a kind of borrowed life.

Together with Dalcroze, Appia helped plan and present demonstrations at Dalcroze's institute in Hellerau, Germany, highlighting the potential of eurhythmics for both performance and design. The *proscenium arch was abolished and the lighting, operated from a central 'organ', carefully coordinated with music and movement. The festivals at Hellerau in 1912 and 1913 caused astonishment and exercised a profound influence upon later scenic practice, as well as directly and indirectly upon the development of modern *dance.

In the last decade of his life Appia realized that what had begun as an analysis and critique of the state of the theatre must end in a fundamental attack on contemporary culture itself. People observed art passively because it had lost its power to activate them emotionally and spiritually. The solution was to return to the well-spring of all art, the living experience of the human body to express and share the reality of oneself and one's communal relationship with society. In *The Work of Living Art* (1921), Appia detailed the social implications of this new collaborative art. This speculative treatment is less concrete than his earlier writings but provided a programme for many developments of subsequent theatrical art. Appia was shy and reclusive, and, despite the eminently practical basis of most of his ideas, found collaborative work difficult and frustrating. His productions were very few, his radical ideas brought him into conflict with traditionalists, and his contributions have been insufficiently recognized. *See also* CRAIG, EDWARD GORDON.　　RCB

applause Spectators' appreciation for performances has often been demonstrated through the clapping of hands. Applause is part of a larger set of social behaviours intimately related to the reception of performance: approbative signals like cheering, or shouting bravo or encore; disapprobative signals like *booing, hissing, or catcalls; and instinctive emotive reactions like *laughter and weeping. These *audience gestures are not universal; they are culturally specific and have histories just as do the curtain call and the institution of the *claque. The *Romans had an organized series of approbative gestures, ranging from finger snapping to hand clapping (*applaudere* means to strike upon) to waving the flap of the toga or a special handkerchief. Roman comedians customarily ended a play with 'valete et plaudite' (farewell and applaud), a convention that easily worked its way into the *epilogues of early modern *comedy throughout Europe, as in Shakespeare's *A Midsummer Night's Dream* (*c.*1595), which ends with Puck's lines 'Give me your hands, if we be friends | And Robin shall restore amends.'

Clapping is considered out of place in some traditional Asian performance modes, especially when they evoke a religious or ceremonial disposition. In the *dance-drama of *krishnattam, for example, performed at the Guruvayur temple in the state of Kerala in the south of India, no applause will be heard. Habits of applause are also affected by spectators' class, race, gender, and nation, since all public gestures are ultimately subject to social order and control. They are affected by time and place as well: the rowdy cheering and jeering that was common in nineteenth-century popular theatre is now welcomed in sporting events but not in the *bourgeois *playhouse. Virtuoso displays—in *sport, *opera, or even *juggling—seem to generate spontaneous outbursts of applause more readily than the *realistic or spoken theatre, suggesting that spectators take particular delight in the exhibition of skills that are technically difficult and beyond the scope of ordinary people. In India the modern secular traditions of entertainment regularly evoke applause as in the West, though the approbation is usually expressed during or immediately after a particularly pleasing moment in a performance rather than at a final curtain call. In Indian classical dance and music, spectators may use onomatopoeic verbal expressions (clicking of the tongue, or other culture-specific signs) rather than clapping. Thus applause may be considered universal, but it is not universally the same.

In the final analysis, applause in the modern theatre signifies more than approval; it also is the clearest way that spectators, who are otherwise mostly passive witnesses, actively enter the event. When a curtain call is used the audience's formal applause brings closure to the performance more completely than the end of the drama itself, since it is what Erving Goffman calls an 'interaction ritual' that gives the audience some measure of reciprocity with the actors. By signalling that their part in the event is fulfilled, spectators at the curtain call officially recognize themselves as an audience in a group, and thereby acknowledge their ultimate power over the performance. *See also* RIOTS.   DK

Arbuzov, Aleksei (1908–86) Soviet/Russian playwright. Arbuzov trained as an actor before turning to dramatic writing in the 1930s. His play *Tanya* (1938) exemplifies the demands of socialist realism for 'conflictless' drama: Tanya is not allowed to find happiness by devoting herself to her husband and abandoning her career, but

only after her transformation into a committed doctor. During the war Arbuzov worked in a 'joint stock' method in his studio for young dramatists. His post-war plays are concerned with the young generation: *Years of Wandering* (1954) deals with the self-centredness of young people, a theme that also dominates *My Poor Marat* (also known as *The Promise*, 1964), where love is placed above duty when Lika marries an invalid although she loves Marat, with whom she is eventually reunited. Arbuzov's plays of the 1970s (*An Old-Fashioned Comedy, Tales of the Old Arbat, Cruel Games*) focus on the disintegration of family life and the difficulty of sustaining relationships, and quickly formed part of the repertoire of Moscow's leading theatres.   BB

Archer, William (1856–1924) Scottish critic, translator, and playwright who spent part of his childhood in Norway. For more than 40 years a London dramatic critic, including 21 years on the *World*, Archer travelled widely to theatres in Europe and elsewhere. He campaigned for *realistic, socially aware, and *naturalistically acted plays, and his fluent Norwegian enabled him to become the leading English-language authority on *Ibsen and to translate most of his plays; his faithful though somewhat stiff versions held the stage for many years. He also anonymously helped direct many of the first London performances, including *A Doll's House* (1889), *Ghosts* (1891), and *Little Eyolf* (1896). He was an austere, high-principled man, a free-thinker and supporter of women's suffrage, an opponent of *censorship, and a lifelong campaigner for a *national theatre, for which he wrote detailed plans with Granville *Barker in 1904. For 40 years he had an argumentative friendship with *Shaw, encouraging him in many ways while criticizing his plays for levity and prolixity. His many publications include collected criticism, *Masks or Faces?* (1888), and *Play-Making* (1912), and he had an unexpected late international success with a well-constructed *melodrama, *The Green Goddess* (1921).   EEC

architecture of theatres *See* PLAYHOUSE.

Arden, John (1930–) British dramatist, theatre-maker, and novelist, one of the most political and literate of the post-*Osborne generation. His best-known plays were written between 1958 (*The Waters of Babylon*) and 1963 (*Armstrong's Last Goodnight*), after which time he began collaborating with his wife, the Irish writer and political activist Margaretta D'Arcy. After an acrimonious row with the *Royal Shakespeare Company over its production of their Arthurian trilogy, *The*

Island of the Mighty (1973), Arden and D'Arcy stopped writing for mainstream British theatre. They moved to Ireland, where they have produced political and *community theatre and have written a number of plays for radio. He became increasingly committed to revolutionary socialist and Irish nationalist politics after 1968; while his early plays are also political, the politics they proceed from is libertarian and anarchist. Other important plays include *Live Like Pigs*, (1958) and *The Workhouse Donkey* (1963).   SWL

Arena Stage American *regional theatre in Washington, DC, founded in 1950 by Zelda *Fichandler, Thomas C. Fichandler, and Edward Mangum in an abandoned movie house renovated as an arena theatre. The configuration was maintained in 1956 when the company moved into an old brewery, and in 1961 in a purpose-built *playhouse. In the 1970s two further spaces were added, a *proscenium stage and a *cabaret. Under the dynamic leadership of Fichandler, and with substantial support from the Ford Foundation, Arena went from pioneer to paragon in the resident theatre movement. Its landmark 1967 production of Howard Sackler's *The Great White Hope*, starring James Earl *Jones, moved to Broadway and won the Pulitzer and Tony awards, thereby helping to establish regional theatres as breeding grounds for new American plays. Living Stage became a pioneer of outreach programming with its *improvisation workshops and free performances for non-traditional *audiences. Many famous actors, directors, and *scenographers have worked there. After 40 years as *artistic director, Zelda Fichandler stepped down in 1991. The facilies underwent major renovation in 2008-10.   STC

Aretino, Pietro (1492-1556) Italian man of letters and dramatist. Born relatively humbly in Arezzo, Aretino established a fearsome reputation as a pamphleteer, satirist, and a man not to be crossed. Non-dramatic writings range from religious treatises to outright *pornography—it was the latter which made his name internationally proverbial. His theatre production consists of one *tragedy, *Orazia*, and five highly original and scurrilous *comedies, written for court and academic circles, dense with linguistic innovation and with overtly judgemental references to contemporary luminaries. The titles are *The Courtier's Play*, *The Stablemaster*, *Talanta*, *The Hypocrite*, and *The Philosopher*. Despite Aretino's initial anti-literary pose, they are all carefully composed, with passages of structured rhetoric and polemic; but some individual scenes are influenced by the techniques of improvised *street theatre, and it is possible that collaboration was envisaged in performance between amateurs and professionals. After Aretino's works were all placed on the Catholic Church's Index of Forbidden Books, the comedies were reissued after 1600 with false titles and attributions, thus attesting their lasting attraction to readers seeking under-the-counter material.   RAA

Argüelles, Hugo (1932-2003) Mexican playwright, screenwriter, and educator. Considered one of Mexico's major living dramatists, he had his first stage success in 1960 with *The Crows Are in Mourning*, a dark *comedy about black magic, death, and dying in rural Mexico. Many of his other plays have similar settings, such as *The Prodigious Ones* (1961), *The Savage Cocks* (1986), and *Scarabs* (1991), which assume an ironic, often cruel look at the violence born of middle-class hypocrisy, sexual repression, and homophobia. Argüelles is also the author of numerous historical plays, such as *Royal Eagle* (1992) and *The Rounds of the Bewitched Ones*, which opened the cultural programme for the 1968 Olympics in Mexico City.   KFN

Ariosto, Ludovico (1474-1533) Ferrarese poet and dramatist. As well as the epic masterpiece *Orlando furioso*, Ariosto composed four stage *comedies, plus one more unfinished. *La cassaria* (*The Strongbox Play*) and *I suppositi* (*The Substitutes*) were staged in Ferrara in 1508 and 1509: they were the first original five-act plays in Italian vernacular in the classical mode of *Plautus and *Terence. They thus effectively inaugurated modern European theatre, in that they were scripts subsequently published and treated (like classical plays) as high cultural products, rather than ephemeral texts linked to single performances. They were also the first full-length Western dramas to be written in prose—though Ariosto may never have intended them to be published in this form, and his later plays (including rewrites of the first two) were in verse. Like comedies of Plautus, the first two plots deal with amorous intrigues and conflicts between youth and age in the context of a middle-class urban family. For *I suppositi*, Ariosto moved to a local contemporary setting, rather than the distant neutral locations of *Roman comedy; and his plot details are based more on medieval Italian novella than on Plautus. The later comedies of the 1520s, *Il negromante* (*The Magician*) and *Lena*, accompany similar stories with greater satirical bite.   RAA

Aristophanes (c.448-c.380 BC) *Greek comic playwright. The work of no other writer of *Old Comedy or *Middle Comedy has survived, a tribute to how far the reputation of Aristophanes out-stripped that of his rival comic dramatists. His relationship with the *tragic playwrights was ambivalent. *Euripides is satirized as a *character in three plays and is mentioned in fun at least once in all of the others. Though much younger than either *Sophocles or Euripides, Aristophanes over-lapped their careers from 427 BC, the date of the production of his first play, *The Banqueters*, until 406 BC when both the tragedians died. The follow-ing year Aristophanes presented *Frogs* at the *Le-naea; all three tragedians appear as characters. Aristophanes himself turns up as a character in Plato's *Symposium*, a dramatic dialogue on the nature of love, where he is a teller of fanciful tales, a fictional portrait that accords well with his extant work. Eleven of his plays survive: nine Old Come-dies produced between 425 and 405 BC, and two Middle Comedies (sometimes called *New Come-dies) written late in his life.

The Old Comedies are set in manufactured stage worlds. *Acharnians* (425), his third play but the first to survive, is set in and around Athens where Dicaeopolis is so upset by the war with Sparta (the Peloponnesian War, then in its sixth year) that he engineers a private peace confined to his own farm. The play won first prize. *Knights* (424) was a concerted attack on Cleon, the most belligerent of the city's demagogues. Three years later, after Cleon's death in battle, Aristo-phanes returned to the same theme with *Peace* (421), in which an Athenian farmer flies up to heaven on the back of a dung-beetle to rescue Peace who has been thrown down a well by the god of War. Perhaps the best known of his plays is *Lysistrata* (411), where the women of Greece im-pose a sex strike on their husbands in order to force them to make peace. All these were written and played at a time when the city was committed to the war his characters refuse to endorse. In other plays Aristophanes' targets were political in a broader sense, dealing with issues of the day: *Wasps* (422), which satirizes the law courts and the enthusiasm of the elderly for jury service; education in *Clouds* (uncertain date), in which Socrates appears as one of the characters swing-ing in a balloon and indulging in philosophical contemplation of the heavens; *Birds* (414), where two Athenian citizens create a new city in mid-air, undertaking, and winning, a holy war against the gods of Olympus; and *Thesmophoriazusae* (*Women at the Thesmophoria*, also 411) which concerns the attempted revenge of the women of Athens on Euripides for portraying them in such a poor light.

All these plays posit a stage world in which gods, heroes, contemporary celebrities, and in-vented characters intermingle. Usually Aristo-phanes creates some dominant concept which develops through the wildest fantasy into the ex-ploration of current ideas. Indeed, there is more to be learnt from the plays of Aristophanes about the processes of everyday life in Athens than from any other source. The sheer theatricality is infec-tious. The *choruses are often animals or unreal creatures, though they can be ordinary Athenians. They and the main characters were *masked and all were played by male actors. Most of them wore exaggerated *costumes, possibly including the *phallus, but the general scurrility and references to sexual and other bodily functions no longer seem outrageous. Amongst the productions that rescued Aristophanes for the stage those of *Koun in modern Greek were the most influential. His productions, seen all over the world, include *Birds*, which was banned in Athens in the late 1950s, *Frogs*, and *Lysistrata*. In all three the cho-rus was the focal point of the drama and of the *comedy, masked and ever mobile, blending fantasy and sexual *farce with a political hard edge. Spurred by Koun's example other directors have presented most of the surviving plays at one time or another at the Athens and *Epidaurus festivals, and at the Greek National Theatre.

Outside Greece Aristophanes has taken longer to establish himself in the repertoire. This has been partly as a result of his earthy humour, partly because of his seemingly parochial politics, though *Wealth* was a popular 'moral' play in the early modern period, and both *Goethe and *Planché presented versions of *Birds*. More recent attitudes towards translation and production have given licence to directors to stray widely from the text and update situations. Though this has on occasion resulted in strained parallels, the adap-tation of *Frogs* by Burt Shevelove and *Sondheim gives some indication of how Aristophanes might return to the repertoire. In this *musical version, set in a swimming pool, Aeschylus and Euripides are revived as Shakespeare and *Shaw.

In his last two plays, *Ecclesiazusae* (*Women in Assembly*, 392/1) and *Wealth* (388), Aristo-phanes marks the transition to a less robust and more parochial kind of comedy. *Ecclesiazusae* raises the prospect of the women of Athens (male actors, of course) taking over the state by disguising themselves as their husbands and then attempting, with conspicuous lack of success, to institute a kind of Platonic communism. *Wealth* follows the efforts of Chremylus to restore the blind god of wealth to sight, and the uncomfort-able consequences for a number of characters, including the god Hermes. The war, it appears, had been Aristophanes' source of inspiration. Its ending soon after *Frogs* altered the whole nature of Athenian comedy.   JMW

Aristotle (384–322 BC) Greek philosopher, whose *Poetics* (*c*.330 BC) is the seminal document of Western dramatic theory. Its cryptic style encouraged its interpretation as a collection of precepts, but it is now conceded that the treatise is highly organized. But the *Poetics* was separated from the *Greek theatre of fifth-century Athens by nearly a century, by which time drama had been stripped of the political and religious ideology of its performance at the Theatre of *Dionysus; it was increasingly separated in conception from the *music and spectacle of its presentation, acquiring a new literary status independent of performance. The *Poetics* reflects these changes. Text and performance, drama and *theatre are conceptualized as separate phenomena. Aristotle preferred the literary to the theatrical, and the *Poetics* reflects his analytical bent. Poetry is conceived as an art distinguished by its medium (language); drama as a species of poetry distinguished by its manner of presentation (dramatic *dialogue); and *tragedy and *comedy as variants of drama distinguished on the basis of the object imitated (men as better or worse than the average). Aristotle may have intended to include a discussion of comedy, but the *Poetics* as we have it is concerned mainly with tragedy, which is analysable in terms of its constituent parts: plot, *character, thought, diction, song, and spectacle, listed in decreasing importance, indicative of his preference for the literary over the theatrical. He argued for plot as the 'soul' of tragic art, and dismissed spectacle as belonging to the 'art of staging'. His schematized and problematic 'history' of dramatic genres, in which tragedy is held to have developed from the *dithyramb and comedy from phallic songs, is similarly devoid of reference to circumstances of performance.

Aristotle provides a lexicon of familiar terms and concepts, at least three of which continue to stimulate thought. While it has proved almost impossible to define unequivocally what Aristotle meant by *mimesis, *catharsis, and *hamartia, taken together they can be seen as providing an answer to Plato's attack on poetic imitation as twice removed from reality, arousing passions dangerous to intellectual health and moral action, and incapable of embodying or communicating knowledge. Aristotle saw poetry as a rational art devoted to the imitation, not of ordinary reality, but of the unrealized possibilities of human action. The learning and pleasure derived from poetic imitation may be linked to the emotional pleasure of tragedy, the arousal and catharsis ('cleansing' or 'purifying') of pity and fear. *Hamartia*, the error that precipitates tragic suffering, can thus be either intellectual or emotional, or both. As slippery as these concepts are, Aristotle's attempt to explain and justify the pleasure produced by poetic imitation, especially tragedy, has not been superseded.

When the *Poetics* was rediscovered by Italian critics at the end of the fifteenth century, it was interpreted in the context of medieval rhetoric and moral philosophy, and, together with the Roman critic Horace's *Ars Poetica*, provided the ancient authority for 250 years of *neoclassical theory and practice. More importantly, Aristotle and his interpreters have bequeathed two unfortunate constants to Western theory: that the essence of theatre lies in the script, which governs theatrical 'interpretation'; and that the forms of drama are to be defined on literary rather than theatrical grounds.   RWV

Arlecchino *See* HARLEQUIN; COMMEDIA DELL'-ARTE.

Arlen, Harold (1905–86) American composer. Born Hyman Arluck, he dropped out of school to pursue a career in music, working as a dance-band pianist and Tin Pan Alley songwriter during the 1920s. Teaming in 1929 with lyricist Ted Koehler, he wrote his first huge hit, 'Get Happy' (1930). The song's interpolation into a Broadway *revue brought him into the theatre, and he began writing scores for Broadway revues—and, significantly, revues at Harlem's Cotton Club. One of the first white composers to delve seriously into *African-American musical forms, he worked closely throughout his career with black performers. In Hollywood in the 1930s, he first collaborated with lyricist E. Y. Harburg, with whom he would write scores for several films, including the classic *The Wizard of Oz* (1939), as well as three major stage works dealing with political and racial issues: *Hooray for What?* (1937), *Bloomer Girl* (1944), and *Jamaica* (1957). He also wrote with lyricists Johnny Mercer (*St Louis Woman* for a black cast, 1946) and Ira *Gershwin (the Oscar-winning score for *A Star is Born*, 1954).   JD

Armfield, Neil (1955–) Australian director, known for his thoughtful, provocative productions of the classics as well as his challenging productions of supposedly difficult modern Australian playwrights such as Patrick *White. Armfield promotes an ensemble feel at the Belvoir Street Theatre, Sydney, where he became *artistic director in 1994, but his work is distinguished enough to attract stars such as Geoffrey *Rush and Cate Blanchett to work with him. His theatre has presented work focusing on Aboriginal issues, and Armfield's production of *Cloudstreet*, which addressed the loaded topic of reconciliation in Australia, *toured internationally in 1999 with great success. EJS

Armin, Robert (*c.*1568–1615) English comic actor and writer, the creator of Shakespeare's Jacobean *clowns, among them Feste and Lear's Fool. He was also a dramatist, and, according to his own *Quips upon Questions* (1600), a solo performer of improvised comedy. He replaced *Tarlton as comedian with Chandos's Men. His collection of merry tales, *Fool upon Fool*, appeared in 1600 under the pseudonym 'Clonnico de Curtanio Snuffe' (Snuff, the clown at the *Curtain); it was reissued in 1605 under that of 'Clonnico del Mondo Snuffe' (Snuff, the clown at the *Globe) and finally under Armin's own name (as *A Nest of Ninnies*) in 1608. By then he had made his name, largely because he had taken over as principal clown with the Lord *Chamberlain's (subsequently King's) Men after the departure of *Kempe in 1599. A less physical performer than his predecessor, Armin's expert singing and verbal wit may have prompted the cerebral and melodious style of Shakespeare's clown roles after 1599, though Armin's own *comedy *Two Maids of More-Clacke* is considerably less subtle. MD

Aronson, Boris (1898–1980) American scene designer. Born in Russia, he studied with *Ekster and was deeply influenced by *constructivism and cubism. Arriving in New York, he worked in Yiddish theatre and for Eva *Le Gallienne, then designed several early *Group Theatre plays, notably *Odets's *Awake and Sing* and *Paradise Lost* (both 1935). His first significant Broadway commissions were for the *revue *Walk a Little Faster* (1932) and J. C. Holm and *Abbott's *Three Men on a Horse* (1935). Although he was given his share of *realistic settings he always injected a metaphorical abstraction, which led to *opera and *ballet commissions. Aronson's reputation blossomed in the 1940s and 1950s when he designed for emerging playwrights, including *Williams's *The Rose Tattoo*, *Miller's *The Crucible* (1953), and *Inge's *Bus Stop* (1955). Late in his career, he became renowned as an innovative designer of *musicals, his sets combining his early constructivist leanings with a metaphorical, almost lyrical environment. *Fiddler on the Roof* (1964) was followed by a string of Harold *Prince musicals: *Cabaret* (1966), *Zorba* (1968), and *Sondheim's *Company* (1970), *Follies* (1971), *A Little Night Music* (1973), and *Pacific Overtures* (1976). MCH

Arrabal, Fernando (1932–) Spanish playwright, novelist, and filmmaker. After a traumatic childhood and law studies, he moved to Paris, where he became linked with the theatre of the *absurd through French versions of his early iconoclastic plays. *Lavelli's staging of *The Architect and the Emperor of Assyria* (1967) in Paris, and Tom O'Horgan's in New York (1976), presented his work at its best. Arrabal himself directed the New York production of *And They Put Handcuffs on the Flowers* (1972), the most political of his works. New York's INTAR theatre championed his later plays with stagings of *The Red Madonna; or, A Damsel for a Gorilla* (1986) and *The Body-Builder's Book of Love* (1990). Returning to Spain after Franco, he proved controversial with his frequent pronouncements and a turn to the right politically; but his numerous new plays were as scenically inventive and thematically provocative as his early works, such as *The King of Sodom* (1983). In 2000, a revival of *The Automobile Graveyard* (1958) focused new interest on this absurdist piece as it *toured throughout Spain. MPH

Art, Théâtre d' French company, formed in Paris in 1890 after the amalgamation of Paul *Fort's Théâtre Mixte, committed to young writers, and Louis Germain's Théâtre Idéaliste, whose aim was to resist *naturalism. Germain swiftly parted company, and much of the work presented in Fort's first year would have found a home at the Théâtre *Libre, but his company quickly became associated with the *symbolist movement. The 1891 version of Shelley's *The Cenci* featured a three-minute silent tableau at the end of each performance, the silent stage which Mallarmé had been advocating. Subsequently Fort declared his theatre symbolist, and premièred some notable plays, including *Maeterlinck's *The Intruder* (1891) and *The Blind* (1892), as well as work by Quillard and Van Leberghe, productions which gave rise to the term 'static theatre'. The curtain came down on the project in March 1892, the result of Fort's inexperience and a programme of limited appeal to an intellectual elite. BRS

Artaud, Antonin (1896–1948) French actor, director, playwright, and theorist, who shook up the intellectual French elite in his lifetime and whose writings and manifestos came to wield extraordinary influence on post-war theatre. A theatrical jack of all trades, Artaud's legacy came in the form of an immense quantity of epistolary communication with the *avant-garde advocating a revolution in theatre. Artaud was inspired first by the *surrealist movement in the 1920s and published a number of treatises in the surrealist vein, though it was as a film actor that he made his name. He acted in over twenty films, his most notable roles being Marat in Abel Gance's *Napoléon* (1927), and Brother Jean in Carl Dreyer's *The Passion of Joan of Arc* (1928).

After walk-on parts at the Théâtre de l'Œuvre he joined *Dullin's Théâtre de l'Atelier in 1921 and became obsessed with the potential of theatre for breaking with *realism. His treatise 'The Evolution of Set Design' (1924) was the first of many such writings, culminating in the collection of essays *The Theatre and its Double* (1938), which became the manifesto for theatre revolutionaries growing up in the political unrest of the 1960s.

Artaud's practical theatre career centred on two periods of intense activity around the formation of theatres. The first was entitled the Alfred *Jarry Theatre (in homage to the precursor of surrealism), which mounted four productions in various Parisian theatres between 1927 and 1929, including *Strindberg's *A Dream Play* and *Vitrac's *Victor; or, Children Take Over*. The second was the Theatre of *Cruelty, which survived for only one production in 1935, Artaud's own adaptation of *Shelley's *The Cenci*. Uneven in *acting style, it played to poor houses for seventeen performances. The demise of his cherished project of 'cruelty' (based on a Gnostic belief that the essence of life is cruel and beyond redemption) forced Artaud to reject theatre altogether. It was followed by world travels in search of authentic primitive cultures, and a nine-year period in psychiatric hospitals. Upon his release in 1946 he turned to radio as a medium for his ideas and recorded three programmes. The last, *To Put an End to the Judgement of God*, was banned in 1948 on the eve of transmission for blasphemy (*see* CENSORSHIP). Artaud's spirit was crushed.

But if his theatrical career let him down, his own life was his true performance. His lectures were legendary; fuelled by psychoses and drug addiction, he acted out his philosophies of affective theatre. His entire life was haunted by psychiatric illnesses which both tortured and inspired him. He had a personal relationship with two notable psychiatrists, through whom he encountered much of the inspiration for his revolutionary theatre: research he conducted for them on the psychophysical effects of plague provided for Artaud an allegory of what he thought of as 'true' theatre, and even the electro-shock therapy he underwent (although he abhorred its use personally) provided him with opportunity to explore the actor's split between self and other.

After his release he continued to upset the establishment. At a fundraising lecture called 'Tête-à-tête with Antonin Artaud' in 1947 he tore up his notes and, before a shocked *audience of celebrities, performed rather than narrated the notion of cruelty. This instance again demonstrated that he was far ahead of his time, obsessed with the codification of traditional Asian theatres, the structuring of the unconscious, and the deconstruction of signs and systems of signification. *The Theatre and its Double*, and a seemingly endless series of his *Complete Works*, testify to the myth of a living failure and a posthumous revolutionary.   BRS

artistic director A *manager who controls and oversees artistic policy. Though related in function to the German *Intendant* and to the directors of older European national theatres like the *Comédie-Française, the artistic director arose internationally after the Second World War with the rapid establishment of companies whose *finance was dependent on state or private subsidy. In many countries, but especially in England and North America, the earlier model of theatrical control implied a capitalist form of production in which sharers, a manager, or an *actor-manager owned or leased the *playhouse, chose the scripts, and hired the acting and production company, thus taking the financial risks and reaping the rewards. An extension of this model was the development in the early twentieth century of the *producer, a commercial coordinator who controls a production in the interests of profit—the regular pattern still in the West End and on Broadway—but has no long-term investment in a particular playhouse or company. The artistic director, on the other hand, is normally contracted by the board of directors of a stable company and is insulated from the legal and financial responsibility of the institution, which most often is designated as a charitable or non-profit enterprise and thinks of itself as a public service.

The duties of an artistic director can vary considerably, but in most cases involve setting and maintaining standards of production, selecting annual seasons, and supervising casting, choice of *directors and designers, and maintaining public and governmental relations. Sometimes the artistic director has fiscal, personnel, and material responsibilities as well, though for larger companies these functions fall to a specialist manager without artistic obligations. Artistic directors may be hired for a specified term, as at the *National Theatre in London, or may remain in post for almost 40 years, as Zelda *Fichandler did at *Arena Stage in Washington. It is a sign of the power structure of contemporary theatre that most artistic directors have been stage directors. Almost no designers or playwrights have been appointed to such posts, and relatively few *actors. *Olivier at the National in Britain was a highly visible exception to custom; in other cases actors elevated to power have rapidly converted to directing, as *Newton at the *Shaw Festival did. Notable artistic directors of the post-war period include *Vilar (another actor-director) and *Planchon of *Théâtre National Populaire, *Mnouchkine of Théâtre du *Soleil in Paris, Peter *Stein of the Berlin *Schaubühne, *Suzuki Tadashi of Suzuki Company of Toga in Japan, and Habib *Tanvir of Naya Theatre in India. DK

Artists of Dionysus An organization of free Greek festival performers, first attested *c.*300 BC, which continued until nearly AD 300. It was widespread in all Greek lands, being the most powerful, best-organized, and most enduring of all ancient groups of artisans. Indispensable for Greek religious festivals and for their promoters, the organization gained access to Roman emperors or Hellenistic kings. It swiftly learned how to exact ever greater privileges for members, such as freedom from arrest, freedom of travel, front seating, the right to wear purple, and tax concessions, all confirmed by surviving inscriptions. WJS

Asakura Setsu (1922-) Japanese designer. Born in Tokyo, Asakura began her career as a painter but after study in New York in 1970 took up a theatrical career. She soon became a favourite designer for such important figures in the *avant-garde movement as *Kara Jūrō and *Shimizu Kunio and worked on Japanese productions of Western works, among them a celebrated production of the *Brecht–*Weill *Threepenny Opera* in 1977. Asakura became the best-known Japanese stage designer in Europe and the United States. She designed the sets for a *Medea* seen in Greece and Italy in 1983, and the *costumes for Richard Strauss's *opera *Die Frau ohne Schatten* for the Bavarian State Opera in 1993. In 1985 she designed *Jōruri* by the leading Japanese composer Miki Minoru for the Opera Theatre of St Louis, and returned to do sets and costumes for the world première of Miki's *The Tale of Genji* in 2000. Asakura's goal, in her words, is to express 'the director's image in solid form', but her highly personal use of light, colour, and space invariably provides a sense of innovation and visual surprise. JTR

Asch, Solomon (Sholem Asch) (1880–1957) Polish-born Yiddish novelist and playwright,

whose one-act play *The Eldest Sister* inaugurated the Moscow Habima Studio in October 1918. Asch wrote over twenty plays, the earliest of which, *Returned* (1904) and *The Time of Messiah* (1905), deal with the conflict between old and new Jewish lifestyles, a theme also reflected in *God and Vengeance* (1907), staged by *Reinhardt at the *Deutsches Theater in Berlin, which has a lesbian theme combined with a brothel setting. Many of his plays fuse an idyllic romanticism with a sense of harsh realism and express a love of nature. *See* DIASPORA. NW

Asche, Oscar (1871–1936) Australian *actor-manager and playwright who made a career in London. Starting in *Benson's company (1893–1901) he married the actress Lily Brayton, and in 1904 they joined *Tree at His Majesty's Theatre to play a succession of Shakespearian lead couples, which quickly became their trademark. But it was in the realm of popular culture that Asche was to make a mark and a sizeable fortune. Three orientalist spectaculars—*Kismet* (1911), *Chu Chin Chow* (1916), and *Cairo* (1921)—accrued mass appeal in their lavish decors, Arabian Nights fantasies, *dancing orgies, and *costume parades. *Chu Chin Chow* was the most successful, running until 1921 at His Majesty's for 2,238 performances, at that time the longest continuous run in London. These productions featured the jingoistic claptraps of *melodrama, the oriental settings and *characters of *musical comedy, and the *stock figures and scene transformations of *pantomime, acting as theatrical respite for the fears and anxieties of a nation at war. BRS

Ashcroft, Peggy (1907–91) English actress who began her career at the *Birmingham Rep in 1926. In London Ashcroft appeared in work by many dramatists from Shakespeare, *Congreve, and *Goldsmith to *Shaw, *Hauptmann, and *Pirandello. She played Desdemona to *Robeson's Othello (1930) and Juliet to *Gielgud's and *Olivier's Romeos (1935). At the *Old Vic in the mid-1930s she took on further Shakespearian roles, including Portia and Rosalind, and during the next three decades would play most of the major female parts in Shakespeare (except for Lady Macbeth), the title roles in *Webster's *The Duchess of Malfi* (1945) and *Sophocles' *Electra* (1951), and triumphed in Gielgud's production of *The Importance of Being Earnest* (1942) and in *Hedda Gabler* (1954).

During the 1950s and early 1960s she appeared often in Stratford, including Margaret in *Hall's *Wars of the Roses* (1963), and elsewhere in *Ibsen, *Chekhov, *Pinter, *Albee, and Grass; her Winnie in *Beckett's *Happy Days* (1975) was particularly remarkable. In 1957 she became a member of the *English Stage Company; in 1960 she was a founding member of the *Royal Shakespeare Company. Performing on stage in great drama remained her paramount purpose for six decades, though on occasion she also appeared in film, and won an Academy award as Mrs Moore in *A Passage to India* (1984). TP

Ashwell, Lena (1869–1957) English actress, *manager, and writer, born Lena Pocock. Ashwell's most applauded performances were as strong, passionate women in ambiguous moral circumstances, such as Mrs Dane, the woman with a past in H. A. *Jones's *Mrs Dane's Defence* (1900), or the reluctant burglar heroine in *Leah Kleschna* (1905), a part written for her. She managed the Kingsway Theatre, London, from 1907 to 1909; notable successes included Cecily Hamilton's *Diana of Dobson's* (1908) with herself in the lead. During the First World War she ran a massive operation to entertain the troops abroad with concerts, extracts from plays, and recitals. From 1919 to 1929 she managed the Lena Ashwell Players, a company which *toured extensively, particularly around London, performing a different play each week and targeting non-traditional *audiences. EJS

Asian-American theatre *See* DIASPORA.

Astaire, Fred (1899–1987) and **Adele Astaire** (1898–1981) American brother–sister *dance team. Born Fred and Adele Austerlitz in Omaha, the Astaires' mother enrolled them in dance school when the family moved to New York in 1904. The children began appearing in *vaudeville the next year and made their Broadway debut in 1917 with *Over the Top*. They were featured in eleven Broadway *musicals between 1918 and 1932, including *Gershwin's *Lady, Be Good* (1924) and *Funny Face* (1927). The last show in which they performed together was *The Band Wagon* (1931). As a brother–sister team, the Astaires avoided the traditionally sexual basis of male–female dancing, and offered instead an asexual elegance and wit. Adele retired from performing in 1932 when she married Lord Cavendish, the 9th Duke of Devonshire, and moved with him to a castle in Ireland. Fred moved to Hollywood in the same year and began a long film career. MAF

Astley's Amphitheatre London *circus theatre. Built as an *amphitheatre in 1784 by Philip Astley, a retired cavalryman who invented the modern circus, it became, after remodelling and rebuilding in 1795 and 1804 (following two fires), a theatre for *hippodrama, a new form of equestrian *melodrama—and later *pantomime—employing both the circus ring and an attached stage and using large numbers of trained horses in military spectacles based upon historical and contemporary battles such as Agincourt, Jerusalem, Waterloo, and the Alma in the Crimea. This kind of spectacle continued through the nineteenth century. After Astley's death the theatre was managed by *Ducrow, a superb horseman, William Batty, and William Cooke, who equestrianized *Richard III*, *Macbeth*, and *I Henry IV* in 1856–7. Reconstructed and enlarged in 1873 by George *Sanger, it became Sanger's Amphitheatre, with the same kind of repertory. It closed in 1893 and was demolished in 1895. MRB

Atkins, Eileen (1934–) English actress. Atkins *danced in working men's clubs as a child, then trained at the Guildhall School. She played at Stratford in 1957–8, but was not conventionally attractive when young and did not come into her own until her thirties. An intelligent and energetic actress, who chose her parts carefully, Atkins did first-rate work for many years in Britain and the USA, usually outside the subsidized companies. She won awards for playing Childie in *The Killing of Sister George* (1965) and Elizabeth in *Vivat! Vivat Regina* (1970); other favourite roles include Celia Coplestone in *The Cocktail Party* (1968) and St Joan (1977). She has often appeared on television; with Jean Marsh she created the popular series *Upstairs, Downstairs*. She enjoyed playing Virginia Woolf, who was also tall and angular: she adapted *A Room of One's Own* (1989), and *devised *Vita and Virginia* (1994), which she performed in New York with Vanessa *Redgrave. EEC

Atkins, Robert (1886–1972) English actor, director, and *manager. Atkins began acting in 1906 at *Tree's His Majesty's Theatre, playing minor Shakespearian roles. Before the war he also acted with *Martin-Harvey, *Forbes-Robertson, and *Benson. In 1915 he joined the *Old Vic, playing Iago, Richard III, Macbeth, and Prospero. After serving in the First World War, he returned to the Old Vic as a director and actor (1920–5). In 1925 he began to manage his own company, performing in London and Stratford, and also *toured. During the 1930s and the early 1940s he produced plays at the Open Air Theatre in Regent's Park and at the *Shakespeare Memorial Theatre, and after 1945 he presented annual seasons in the Park, usually featuring Shakespeare. He excelled in comic roles such as Sir Toby Belch and Bottom. TP

Auden, W. H. (Wystan Hugh) (1907–73) English writer. Though best known as a poet, his first staged play, *The Dance of Death* (1934), broke open the conventional *dance-drama to introduce vibrant social *satire. Subsequent plays, conceived in collaboration with *Isherwood, were equally eclectic: into a basic *expressionist format were introduced elements of popular *revue and *pantomime in *The Dog beneath the Skin* (1936); social critique, Freudian psychology, and the redemptive metaphysics of miracle plays in *The Ascent of F6* (1937); *melodrama and Shakespearian tragic romance in *On the Frontier* (1938). Later Auden became fascinated by the complex demands of *operatic librettos, working notably on *Paul Bunyan* for Britten (1939–41), and with Chester Kallman on *The Rake's Progress* for Stravinsky (1947–8), *Elegy for Young Lovers* (1959–60), and *The Bassarids* (1963) for Henze. He wrote incisive criticism of theatre in performance, included in *The Dyer's Hand* (1962) and *Secondary Worlds* (1968). RAC

Audiberti, Jacques (1899–1965) French dramatist. Born in Antibes, he came to Paris in 1924, worked as a journalist, and made his reputation as a poet and novelist, but theatre took precedence with *Quoat-Quoat* (1946) and *Le Mal court* (*Evil Rampant*, 1947). The latter remains best known of his 30 or so plays. The force of evil thematically pervades Audiberti's work, arising from his nihilist philosophy of 'abhumanism'. Yet his prolix style has been called 'a feast', incorporating baroque, *surrealist, erotic, fantastic, humorous, and nightmarish elements in loosely structured plots. Among his darker plays are *The Black Festival* (1948) and *La Hobereaute* (1956). Some, like *Pucelle* (1950) and *An Unscratchable Itch* (1962), have been classed as historical *'operettas'. Women dominate the action in *The Glapion Effect* (1959), *The Landlady* (1960), and others; a ferocious purity is often the source of their mystery and power. FHL

audience One or more persons assembled to see a performance. The constituency of audiences varies widely according to the social, political, and cultural circumstances of the performance: for the City *Dionysia of the first *Greek theatre, audiences were as large as 14,000; intimate alternative spaces of *Off-Off-Broadway may seat only a dozen people. Since performance assumes the presence of an audience, the attraction of spectators to the live event as well as engagement with them during the event are crucial.

Knowledge of who went to theatres at different historical moments and the relative successes of performances they saw tells us much about the values and beliefs of a particular society. A day at the three-day City Dionysia opened with a ceremony of purification, followed by proclamations, three *tragedies, a *satyr-play, a break for dinner, and then a *comedy. This suggests the degree of commitment required as well as the integration of the audience's religious and civic life into the festival performance. At the other extreme, *censorship has endeavoured to prohibit audiences from viewing productions that might encourage or incite beliefs or behaviours considered dangerous. More typically, the audience for a performance comes together as a result of its collective and individual expectations as well as more general cultural conditions. While much theatregoing is a leisure or entertainment activity, it can also be an expression of faith (such as for audiences in India for the *ritual *ras lila).

Many different components of pre-performance inform an audience's attitudes. Foremost among these is the cultural capital afforded to theatre. Is theatre considered a high culture activity? Or a popular form? Are there many opportunities to see theatre? Or is it a rare event? Is theatre considered primarily an 'art' activity or is it tied to other cultural experiences such as religion, politics, tourism, or education? The audience's relation to the generally held concept of theatre, to specific theatre products within their home culture, and to the specifics that inform attendance at an actual performance combine to produce a spectator's attraction to and expectations for the theatrical event itself. A production of *Hamlet* would be outside the traditions of a Korean audience, but might draw audiences in Seoul because of Shakespeare's global cultural capital or because of the involvement of a leading Korean theatre practitioner or because of its use of local theatre methods. Further, expectations are likely to be quite different for a theatregoer who has bought a ticket months in advance for a blockbuster Broadway show than for the *dantai* (groups of workers and their families sent to the theatre by Japanese companies as an employment perk) or for the tourist audiences of the Mandalay *marionettes (*yokthe pwe*) in Myanmar.

The conditions that underlie performance are also relevant. How a play is funded and advertised will shape the spectator's willingness to buy a ticket or devote time. Reviews, discussions, prizes, popularity of an author or actor, price of a ticket, scholarship, teachers, word-of-mouth encouragement, and critics all serve to market a performance.

The spectator's arrival at the performance space triggers another level of expectation and preparation. How did the spectator travel to the theatre? Was the journey difficult or easy? Is this part of the spectator's leisure time or is it connected to the workplace or an educational setting? What kind of environment surrounds the performance space? Is it part of an arts district or is it in an isolated or unwelcoming neighbourhood? What is the performance space like? Are there foyers, bars, eating places for socializing before the event? Is the spectator alone or with others? How is the audience positioned in relation to the *action? Once the performance begins, spectators respond to a combination and succession of visual and aural signs. Some will be fixed (a set that does not change), but the majority will be in flux; all enable an audience to posit the existence of a fictional world with its own dynamic and governing rules.

Visual and aural signs created by an *actor emanate from language, voice, movement, and physical appearance (including *costume, make-up, and facial expression). Individual performers are linked in their interrelationships within the world of the play and in the context of external signs that derive from the set, props, lighting, sound, and *music. In the first few minutes of a performance, spectators are likely to focus on all signs so as to establish a context for the fictional world; as the performance continues, some elements will draw less attention unless they are in some way respecified (a set change) and more spectatorial energy can be devoted to local details (facial expressions, gestures, costume changes).

The spectator's experience is one of constant revision, confirmation, and negation within a fixed time period. The only times available for reflection are likely to be determined by performers (use of intervals, set changes). Moreover, responses result not only from the interaction between the audience and the represented world but also from the interaction with the performers as actors. In Western theatre, the presence of a star actor is particularly laden; in some West African theatres, audience members go onto the stage to stick coins on the foreheads of popular actors or musicians. Responses are also generated from spectator–spectator interaction. A shared collective reaction can be expected (*laughter at the same event), but this can never be guaranteed. Within even the most seeming homogeneity of response, some may be experiencing the performance very differently or may not be paying attention at all. Individual reactions in areas of identification, desire, and fantasy also impact response whether or not an individual expresses these reactions as part of the collective.

Post-performance expressions of *applause or *booing or other signals are an explicit recognition of spectator presence. Devices such as curtain calls, receptions, and other social events all further contribute to the degree of pleasure experienced. Since theatre audiences tend to comprise varying sizes of groups, their experience often extends to specific social interactions after the performance. Also, reading an available text, reading reviews or other descriptions, seeing another or the same production or a film version, or discussions with others all have the potential to reconstitute a spectator's understanding and response after the event. In short, the audience is always an interactive and productive part of performance.   SBe

auditorium From the Latin 'a place for hearing', since the 1720s 'auditorium' has been used in English to refer to the space in a *playhouse or similar building where the spectators sit or stand while watching the play, often called 'the house'. The form and shape of the auditorium have varied a great deal in history for both performance reasons and social reasons, as the desirable *audience size and degree of class segregation has changed. The contemporary auditorium is generally steeply raked (by the standards of past generations), with considerable attention paid to sight lines and acoustics, thus allowing the spectators to experience the play as individually as possible. It is also highly democratic, with social distinctions reflected by the *box, pit, and gallery, the stalls and dress circle of past centuries mostly replaced by the single standard of a higher price for the seats with the best visibility and audibility.   JB

Augier, Émile (1820–89) French playwright, champion of early *realism, along with *Dumas *fils*. Augier came to prominence in 1844 with *La Ciguë* (*The Love of Hippolyta*). Its professed morality was in direct opposition to *romantic drama and heralded a new era in the theatre, beyond the *well-made play, of *bourgeois morals, taste, and social concerns in Second Empire France. In his large dramatic output, the themes of money and class shine out. But although he exposed hypocrisy, he often wrote from within the dominant ideology and failed to see the narrowness of his petty morality, which did not reflect the inequity of society as a whole. His most notable creation was the 'personnage sympathique', the *character who could right wrong, the best example being the *hero of *The Son of Giboyer* (1862), a play with similarities to his most successful work, *M. Poirier's Son-in-Law* (1854), written in collaboration with Jules Sandeau, and revived periodically from 1864 by the *Comédie-Française. *Gabrielle* (1849) won the Prix Montyon, and in 1857 Augier was elected to the Académie Française and stopped writing.   BRS

auto sacramental One-act devotional plays produced in Spain at *Corpus Christi from the sixteenth until late eighteenth century. Two floats were drawn up beside a platform at successive points on the route of a procession, which incorporated *street theatre of other kinds, most notably *tarascas* (mechanized dragons). As they came to be financed by rival townships and written and played by professionals, *costumes, scenery, and mechanical effects grew ever more spectacular. In Madrid, though the number of plays was reduced from four to two in 1647, each required four elaborate, two-storeyed floats. After performances over three days, they were played for another fortnight at the *corrales* and especially in nearby villages. Since the companies were well paid, and given exclusive use of the *corrales* for the lucrative post-Lenten season, contracts to perform them were eagerly sought. Sixteenth-century *autos* were often based on stories from the *Bible or the lives of saints, and included profaner episodes, but under Counter-Reformation pressure they became celebrations of the message that mankind is redeemed by Christ's body and blood. All the leading playwrights contrived, through allegory especially, to illustrate that doctrine, but the most accomplished were a specialist, José de Valdivielso, and above all *Calderón. The *auto sacramental* became the supreme example of the fusion of religious and secular life in Golden Age Spain.   VFD

avant-garde A French military term, 'advance guard', became synonymous with progressivism in both art and politics in the later nineteenth century in Europe, and has since been applied to distinguish socially engaged art movements from other strands of modernism. 'Avant-garde' still denotes non-commercial and experimentally minded artists, though not necessarily overtly political ones. If the 'historical' avant-garde movements that arose in the inter-war era may be characterized as the 'modernism of modernism', that was mainly the result of their collision with volatile social contexts. The avant-garde manifesto, frequently incorporated in performance, often exalted the potential of industrialism at the expense of Western cultural traditions. Like the

political tracts from which they borrowed their rhetoric, the avant-gardists' chief target was bourgeois society, particularly the conventions that privileged an art devoid of social consequences. In *constructivism and the *agitprop groups born in the ebullient spirit of the Soviet Revolution, the anti-bourgeois critique appears most organic. *Expressionism and *dada, both of which gained momentum in the aftermath of the First World War, were overtly reactionary; disorientation and shock were their favoured performance techniques. The Italian *futurists made political agitation a staple of their activities.

The avant-garde was too diffuse geographically and politically to have a cohesive social programme, though many of its artists were affiliated with anarchism or communism; for theorists of the historical movements their broadside against aesthetic autonomy has become paramount. Rooted in the Enlightenment, the doctrine of aesthetic autonomy rationalized the separation of art from the social sphere, reaching its apotheosis in the art-for-art's-sake movements of the late nineteenth century. By contrast, the eradication of the boundaries between art and life became the avant-garde credo, and as early as 1909 *Marinetti and the futurists were satirizing traditional representational modes. With its brevity, mechanical allusions, and *music-hall conventions, the futurist 'synthetic theatre' was an amalgam of performance forms that heralded the fusion of art and common social experience. For both futurists and dadaists, shock tactics became a performance staple to rupture the passivity of their *audiences by encouraging *rioting, *booing, police raids, and the much welcomed negative publicity.

Meanwhile the Soviet-sanctioned agitprop troupes, whose chief interest in theatre was its potential for educating the masses, created a host of forms through *collective means that were indictments of the bourgeois individualism traditionally associated with artistic genius. Operating in factories, groups such as the Blue Blouse collectives, a network of performers that grew to around 100,000 members by 1923, abstracted the new technologies of labour into the physical properties of the performers. *Foregger's 'mechanical ballets', which owed more to the *circus than to the *dance establishment, and *Meyerhold's *biomechanics were two examples of new forms that could be mastered by workers as well as dancers, exemplifying the fusion of labour and art.

What further distinguished the Russian avant-garde was early support by the revolutionary cultural bureaucracy; under the tutelage of the Commissariat of Enlightenment, Soviet avant-gardists enjoyed ideological kinship with the state as well as *financial sustenance. Elsewhere such intersections between the avant-garde and the public sector were never as congenial. *Wedekind, for example, excoriated bourgeois sensibilities with his political and scatological *cabaret *revues as early as 1901, resulting in *censorship and obscenity charges. The expressionists, whose apocalyptic exaltation of personal suffering in the face of social desolation appeared prophetic in the aftermath of the First World War, consciously placed themselves on the fringe of society and the art market.

The historical avant-garde has also been important in illuminating how totalitarian arts policies developed in the inter-war years and ultimately were used to legitimize the politics that lay behind them (*see* FASCISM AND THEATRE). The political spectacles organized by Mussolini's cultural ministers and perfected by the National Socialists in Germany aestheticized the military rally, which submerged the individual into the collective and achieved a symbiosis between spectacle and audience that the avant-gardists could only dream of.

Historians have often categorized the avant-garde as a subset of modernism, and the avant-gardists recognized their influence over what have become the canonical figures of high theatrical modernism, citing parallels between futurist tactics of audience disruption and *Pirandello's *metatheatre, between dadaist montage and the *epic theatre of *Piscator and *Brecht, as well as the general suffusion of expressionism into early film. Of such figures, Brecht is perhaps the most contested since he is alternately granted avant-garde status for practices such as collective *dramaturgy and *Verfremdung, or excluded on the grounds that he laboured within rather than against the institutions of theatre.

Interest in the historical avant-garde was reinvigorated in the 1960s and 1970s through a series of museum retrospectives and by the professed indebtedness of a new generation of socially minded artists, including *collectives such as the *Living Theatre and *Théâtre du *Soleil, playwrights such as *Weiss, and directors such as *Stein. The cumulative effect was to galvanize the historical avant-garde as the institutional standard for advanced art production.

Exactly how the term relates to theatre and performance in the present—and whether it should be applied at all—is not settled. In general usage 'avant-garde' often merely signifies work that appears formally innovative or is somehow in opposition to mainstream theatre practice. At other times the term is used more critically to designate art and artists attempting to undermine the political and social status quo by inventing or

drawing upon subversive content and form. But in an age when the novelty sought by the historical avant-garde has become a matter for immediate commodification and routine absorption into a throwaway global culture, it is difficult to sustain for long the idea that an 'advance guard' is leading the public or other artists into a new or revolutionary aesthetic condition, much less a social one. In the late 1980s and 1990s the Next Wave Festival at the Brooklyn Academy of Music perhaps best exemplified the contradictions of oppositional art in postmodernity, by seeking pioneering work and then marketing it to bourgeois audiences according to the procedures of contemporary capitalism.

The major festivals anxiously seek the newest and most innovative work of directors like Robert *Wilson, *Lepage, or *Ninagawa, practitioners already established as avant-gardists. Operating on a large and transnational scale, annual events such as the *Avignon Festival and the *Edinburgh Festival can support the extremely expensive productions of such artists, which are rarely exhibited in regular theatre runs, while an international audience of progressive cultural tourists avidly follow. There are numerous examples of companies and artists who create theatre that is both innovative and politically or socially oppositional, troupes like *Societas Raffaello Sanzio and the *Wooster Group, performance artists like Karen *Finley and *Gómez-Peña, playwrights like *Kara Jūrō and Suzan-Lori *Parks. But designating such work as avant-garde, despite the handy properties of the term, in the end only highlights the enormous contradictions that have accompanied its use from the start.   DRP/DK

Avignon Festival Theatre festival created by *Vilar in 1947 in the ancient city of Avignon in Provence. Vilar intended to liberate theatre from the urban elite. The initial festival lasted one week and consisted of three productions, including the first staging in France of Shakespeare's *Richard II*, performed outside in the courtyard of the fourteenth-century papal palace. For many years the festival was closely associated with the *Théâtre National Populaire (TNP), which Vilar directed from 1951 until 1963. Some of the most notable productions of this early period were *Corneille's *Le Cid* and *Kleist's *The Prince of Homburg* in 1951, both featuring the charismatic young actor Gérard *Philipe. Vilar staged *Brecht's *The Resistible Rise of Arturo Ui* in 1960, just as de Gaulle was negotiating with the right-wing factions in the military, and two years later, he presented *Giraudoux's *Tiger at the Gates* in the wake of France's war with Algeria. After he left the TNP, Vilar dedicated himself to enlarging the festival, which was attracting upwards of 50,000 spectators. He invited younger directors, like *Planchon and *Lavelli, and added new performance spaces, which allowed greater diversity in the offerings. In 1968 the *Living Theatre staged a massive protest against the festival, demanding that all performances be free of charge. One year later saw the birth of an independent fringe festival, which, known as 'Avignon Off', rapidly grew to hundreds of productions, from *mimes and *street performances to European classics. Today, the festival takes place each July and attracts an average of 130,000 spectators to over 500 productions running virtually around the clock. With supplementary *finance provided by the French government and corporate sponsors, the official festival includes *dance, music, film, lectures, and discussions. The fringe still dominates, with companies from all over Europe and an increasing presence of francophone African and Caribbean troupes. CHB

Ayckbourn, Alan (1939–) English director and playwright, director of the Stephen Joseph Theatre, Scarborough, since 1971, for which he has written the majority of his plays. His manipulation of narrative was visible in his first major success, the intricately *farcical *Relatively Speaking* (1967). In the trilogy *The Norman Conquests* (1973), the same events are retold from three different vantage points, a device partially reused in the linked plays *House* and *Garden* (1999). In *Sisterly Feelings* (1978) and *Intimate Exchanges* (1982) decisions made by *characters on stage lead to alternative routes for the *action, creating a great variety of possible versions of the plays.

In the mid-1970s Ayckbourn's work took on a wintry tone, as in *Absurd Person Singular*

(1972) and *Absent Friends* (1974). Though rarely political, he explored the ethics of political extremism in the allegorical *Way Upstream* (1981), and the relationship between entrepreneurial capitalism and family values in *A Small Family Business* (1987). In *A Chorus of Disapproval* (1984) and *Man of the Moment* (1988), he examined the difficulty of being good in a corrupt world, and he has explored the position of women within marriage, most thoroughly in *Woman in Mind* (1985).

Ayckbourn has also written *musicals, *revues, and several very successful plays for *youth. He directs most of his own work, and completed a successful season as a director at the *National Theatre in 1987, where his production of *Miller's *A View from the Bridge* was widely acclaimed. The design of the new in-the-round Stephen Joseph Theatre (1996) reflects his collaborative view of theatre, with a *playhouse architecture that ensures the intermingling of *audiences, backstage crew, and actors. DR

Aylmer, Felix (1889–1979) English actor. Aylmer maintained a long career in West End theatres, from the 1910s to the 1960s. His early roles were in productions by *Hicks, Fred *Terry, *Tree, and Granville *Barker. In London from the 1920s to 1940s he regularly appeared in plays by *Shaw, *Galsworthy, and Barker. He also acted in a steady run of popular *melodramas and *comedies, and occasionally appeared in New York. He appeared in many films from the 1930s forward, including *Henry V, St Joan, The Doctor's Dilemma, Ivanhoe, Exodus*, and *The Chalk Garden*, and by the 1960s he was performing often in television roles. From 1949 to 1969 he served as president of British Actors' Equity Association. TP

Babel, Isaak (1894–1941) Russian/Soviet writer from the Jewish quarter of Odessa. A protégé of *Gorky, who encouraged him to acquire experience of real life, Babel joined Budenny's Cossack cavalry as a Civil War correspondent. Babel's diary notes became a group of stories, *Red Cavalry*, based on his experiences as a bespectacled Jew, full of violent and disturbing incident. A group of them was staged in adaptation at the Vakhtangov Theatre in the late 1960s. Babel wrote film scripts and a play based on life in Odessa, *Sunset* (*Moscow Art Theatre, 1928). *Marya* (1935) concerns city life during the worst days of the Civil War. Condemned by Budenny for a 'false' picture of cavalry life, Babel fell silent and was obliged to account for his inactivity at the First Soviet Writers' Congress in 1934. He was arrested in 1939 and 'disappeared', the full circumstances of his death remaining unclear until the 1990s.　　　NW

Bacheterzi, Mahieddine (1896–1985) Algerian playwright, director, and *manager who, with *Allalou and *Ksentini, established modern Algerian theatre. He wrote and directed 70 plays, starting with *comedy (*Yes, Yes, Beni*, 1935; *Perfidious*, 1937; *Liars*, 1939), then dealt with social and political drama, directing, for example, Tawfiq al- Madani's *Hannibal* (1947). Bacheterzi's talents as a singer and actor added to his flair for management: he was among the first Algerian artists to succeed in provincial and overseas *tours, and in 1947 headed the *opera of Algiers. By force of personality and example he encouraged a number of artists in his long and diverse career. His memoirs, published in three volumes (1968, 1984, 1986), are a mine of information on Algerian theatre.　　　MMe

Bahr, Hermann (1863–1934) Austrian dramatist, critic, and director. Bahr's multifaceted career covered the major trends of the *fin de siècle*. While his first full-length drama *The New Men* (1887) was heavily influenced by *Ibsen, the programmatic essays of the early 1890s proclaimed the passing of *naturalism and promulgated impressionism and neo-*romanticism. Bahr's work in the theatre included stints as a *dramaturg and director with *Reinhardt, as well as a short term as

director of the *Burgtheater in Vienna in 1918–19. Of his many plays only the social *comedy *The Concert* (1909) became an accepted part of the repertory. Bahr's sensitivity to artistic trends made him an important broker between aesthetic developments and the wider public. His essay *Expressionismus* (1913) contributed to the popularization of the term *expressionism.　　　CBB

baiting The goading, torturing, and usually killing of *animals as a form of public or private entertainment. A variety of animals have been baited in a variety of circumstances, from elephants in *Roman arenas to bulls in Spanish *plazas de toros*, from gamecocks in pits to foxes in the English countryside. Often animals are set on other animals (bear-baiting, dogfights), but humans are sometimes directly involved as participants (bullfighting, Roman staged *animal fights).

In terms of numbers and varieties of animals baited and slaughtered the Romans exceeded all others. Rhinoceros, elephants, lions, tigers, bulls, and bears were set upon one another in many combinations, often with one or the other restrained by a chain. Other animals, such as deer, were cast as victims (as were criminals or war prisoners; *see* DAMNATIO). The setting of hounds or lions after deer is a precedent for modern fox-hunting. The pitting of armed men against savage beasts developed into a form of *corrida*, in which a single man dispatched an animal that had been goaded into attacking.

Bulls and bears were the animals of choice in traditional English baiting, which flourished from the twelfth to the nineteenth century. An annual bull running, in which the animal was chased to exhaustion and killed, was a feature of several English towns. A royal official in charge of 'bears and apes' was appointed in 1484, and the warrant extended to bulls and dogs in 1573. The position was held after 1604 by Philip *Henslowe and Edward *Alleyn. At least two baiting-rings stood in London in the mid-sixteenth century, although by 1574 there appears to have been one only, the Bear Garden, rebuilt by Henslowe in 1583 as a three-storey *amphitheatre. This structure, torn down in 1613, was replaced the following year by the *Hope, a dual-purpose *playhouse and baiting arena. Baiting traditionally took place on Sundays. Typically, dogs were set on a chained bear or bull, although there were also lion baitings in the early years of the seventeenth century. The baiting was often accompanied by other diversions: monkeys on horseback, cockfights, dogfights, the whipping of a blinded bear. Parliament banned animal baiting in 1642, but it was revived after the Restoration and persisted in some areas until the late eighteenth century. Baiting was officially forbidden in 1835 but continued in England and on the Continent well into the nineteenth century. Currently four main forms of baiting remain. Cockfighting is prohibited in most jurisdictions, although it continues unofficially. Dog fighting is practised surreptitiously in rural areas of North America, among other locations. Bullfighting, enveloped in ceremony and legitimized by 'grace', continues in Spain and Latin America. Fox-hunting, practised in many places, remains a controversial pastime; chasing foxes with hounds was banned in the United Kingdom from 2005.   RWV

Baker, George Pierce (1866–1935) American teacher and theorist, creator of the first US playwriting course, at Harvard (1905–24). The list of Baker alumni comprises a Who's Who of American theatre between 1906 and 1950: playwrights *O'Neill, Philip *Barry, *Behrman, and Sidney *Howard; directors *Abbott and *Kazan; designers Robert Edmond *Jones, *Oenslager, and *Simonson; and critic *Macgowan. His first playwriting course (English 47) in 1905–6 produced a hit play—Edward Sheldon's *Salvation Nell*—and in 1914 Baker began to stage student work. Regarded with suspicion by Harvard, Baker resigned in 1924 and moved to Yale, where he established the first graduate programme in theatre.   MAF

Baker, Josephine (1906–75) *African-American performer. She appeared at the end of the *chorus line of *Shuffle Along*, the 1921 hit *musical, and then in *Chocolate Dandies* in 1924. The next year she went to Paris with *La Revue nègre* and in the finale danced the Charleston wearing only a feathered belt. Remaining in France as a celebrated personality, she seemed the jungle transposed, elegant, tame, and pettable. 'La Baker', as she became known, kept her American passport until her disappointing 1936 trip to the USA to appear in the *Ziegfeld Follies. During the war she joined the French Resistance. In 1951 she returned to the USA but refused to perform for segregated *audiences, and returned again for the March on Washington in 1963. Ten

years later, she toured America for the last time. Her one-woman show, *Josephine*, premièred in Monaco in 1974 and was restaged in Paris in 1975. Her name was synonymous, the world over, with exoticism and libidinal freedom.   BBL

Bakst, Leon (1866–1924) Russian designer who made his debut in St Petersburg in 1902 with *Euripides' *Hippolytus*. A collaboration with *Diaghilev began in Paris with designs for *Cléopâtre* (1909) and *Scheherazade* (1910). His interest in the art forms of ancient Greece, stimulated by a visit to that country in 1907, was apparent in his designs for Debussy's *Prélude à l'après-midi d'un faune* and Ravel's *Daphnis and Chloe*, in 1912. He was also influenced by the styles of ancient Egypt and Asia, seen to best effect in *ballets such as *Scheherazade* and Stravinsky's *The Firebird* (1910) and in *Le Dieu bleu*, a Hindu legend in one act by *Cocteau (Paris, 1912). His work was seen in London for *The Sleeping Beauty*, also staged by Diaghilev (1921). His designs amazed *audiences by their extravagance of colour, fluidity of line, and transparency of *costume, revealing the dynamic force of the human body and lending it a sensuously erotic power, though some critics objected to his exotic (and over-ripe) lushness of style.   NW

Balanchine, George (1904–83) Russian-American choreographer. Georgi Melintonovitch Balanchivadze was born in St Petersburg, spent a number of years in Europe with his own company and with *Diaghilev's *Ballets Russes, and emigrated to New York in 1933 to start (with the critic Lincoln Kirstein) the School of American Ballet, the first step towards the founding of the New York City Ballet in 1948. Balanchine's achievement as a choreographer spanned five decades and more than 400 *dance works, including *ballets, *opera ballets, dance sequences for *musicals, *revues, plays, films, *cabarets, television shows, and a *circus parade. His career links the old-world concept of a ballet master with the modern concept of a choreographer. Beginning in the mid-1930s, Balanchine moved between the concert stage and Broadway, choreographing dance pieces for the *Ziegfeld Follies*, *Babes in Arms*, *The Boys from Syracuse*, *Song of Norway*, and the groundbreaking 'Slaughter on 10th Avenue' dream ballet for *On your Toes* (1936). In the late 1930s and early 1940s he worked on several films, including *On your Toes* and *Star-Spangled Rhythm*.   LTC

Baldwin, James (1924–87) American writer, considered the most insightful and powerful black literary voice during the civil rights era.

Best known for his fiction, he also wrote two important plays, *Blues for Mister Charlie* (1964) and *Amen Corner* (1967). Both concern the black Church and its leadership role in the *African-American community. In *Blues*, the son of a southern pastor goes north, but returns home and is murdered, which precipitates an intense moral confrontation between blacks and whites. In *Amen*, a female minister in a northern church is troubled when her son follows in his father's footsteps and becomes a jazz musician.   BBL

Bale, John (1495–1563) English playwright, priest, and Protestant polemicist. At various times stripped of clerical office, imprisoned, or forced to flee the country, Bale began playwriting in the early 1530s for the Earl of Oxford, but undertook his most intensive dramatic activity 1530–9 under the patronage of Thomas Cromwell. During Bale's brief tenure in Ireland, several of his anti-papal plays were acted on the occasion of Mary Tudor's coronation, to local outrage. The best known of Bale's five plays, *King John*, was probably performed at Archbishop Cranmer's house in 1539 and was revised in 1558, possibly for a performance before Queen Elizabeth.   RWV

Balgandharva (1888–1967) Indian legendary actor of *sangeet natak* (music drama) who specialized in female roles. Born Narayan Shripad Rajhans in Pune, he dominated the Marathi stage from 1911 to 1934. Endowed with a naturally sweet voice, Balgandharva's first female role was Shakuntala in Kirloskar's *Shakuntala*, and he achieved stardom as Bhamini in Khadilkar's *Manapaman* (1911). He set up his own company, Gandharva Natak Mandali, in Pune in 1913, playing in Bombay with a repertoire of several popular plays. Balgandharva's most admired role was Sindhu, an alcoholic lawyer's long-suffering wife in Gadkari's *Ekach Pyàla* (*Just One More Glass*). With his elaborate hairstyles and specially designed saris, he became a model of fashion for women, who emulated his mannerisms. The opulence of his productions drove the company into debt; when it had recovered in 1927, Balgandharva had lost his charisma and stopped performing in 1934. Modern audiences considered *female impersonation crude, and cinema had begun to marginalize the theatre.   SGG

Ball, William (1931–91) American director. In 1965 Ball abandoned a successful *Off-Broadway directing career in order to create the American Conservatory Theatre at the Pittsburgh Playhouse, relocated in 1967 to San Francisco. There he produced a season of 27 plays in *repertory, using a resident ensemble of actors, a model

of the *regional theatre movement. As a director Ball was widely acknowledged for his energetic interpretations of the classics, highlighted in his crisp version of *Tartuffe* (1965–7). Other acclaimed productions from Ball's first San Francisco season included *Pirandello's *Six Characters in Search of an Author* and *Albee's *Tiny Alice*. Ball achieved his goal of combining training with performance by instituting workshops that evolved into a two-year certificate programme for young actors. Though his management style and policies had detractors, he retained a loyal following until his resignation from ACT in 1986.   LTC

ballad opera A play with songs. Ballad opera flourished after the production in London in 1728 of *Gay's *Beggar's Opera*, a wildly popular *satire on Walpole's corrupt government, set among the city's lowlife. The music, based in part on *opera seria*, lampooned that genre's high seriousness. Although Gay's work spawned scores of imitations, only *Fielding exploited the satirical potential of ballad opera with *burlesques produced at the Little Theatre *Haymarket and *Drury Lane during the late 1720s and 1730s. Its satirical purpose meant the appeal of ballad opera was purely temporary. Only *The Beggar's Opera* is revived today.   SJCW

ballet A theatrical *dance genre and a dance technique. The technique, also known as classic dancing or *danse d'école*, developed out of *early modern and *neoclassic performances in Europe and crystallized in the late eighteenth century. Related to other bodily disciplines (such as fencing), ballet treats the body as a machine for beautiful artifice. The diverse national schools of ballet technique are based primarily on the principles of verticality, five standard positions of the feet, and turn-out (the rotation of the legs and hips so that the feet form an angle approaching 180 degrees). Secondarily, there is a codified use of space (facings of the body that assume the use of a *proscenium stage), of the arms and shoulders, and of various movements, such as turns, jumps, and transitions. At first, male virtuosity reigned in ballet performance, but during the nineteenth century, female performers took centre stage, especially with the development of pointework, or toe-dancing, which began as a tentative, graceful, feathery action but gradually took on a steely strength, vigour, and sense of female agency. Although various national academies contributed to ballet's technical development, it is the Russian style that came to dominate. A strongly athletic Soviet style, using the back expressively, emerged in the mid-twentieth century. And, as Russian émigrés settled in Western Europe and America in the 1930s, two new styles emerged in the West: the British school, characterized by gentle precision, and the American school, stressing speed, expansiveness, and strength.

As a performance genre, ballet has roots in the court entertainments of Renaissance Europe. The earliest ballets, blending music, dancing, and poetry, involved amateur performers and social dance movements. But as a professional class of dancers emerged, especially in France in the seventeenth century, a more specialized, refined technique arose. Allegorical political performances in the Renaissance gave way to grandiose baroque narratives of gods and kings. Until the late nineteenth century, ballets were generally subsumed within *opera and *variety programmes. In the early nineteenth century, the *romantic ballet focused on themes of folklore and the supernatural, and the late nineteenth-century grand Russian imperial ballet often took fairy-tale themes as a pretext for elaborating evening-length movement spectacles, as in *Swan Lake* (1895), choreographed by Marius Petipa and Lev Ivanov to music by Tchaikovsky. During the twentieth century, myriad experiments repeatedly tested the resiliency of ballet, ranging from technical distortions to abstract structures to eschewing music to a synthesis with other genres, such as jazz and postmodern dance. *Balanchine, the most important ballet choreographer of the twentieth century, was part of a generation who experimented radically with the Russian tradition in exile. Despite its origins in an outmoded Western hierarchical culture, ballet has spread to every corner of the contemporary world and remains one of the most popular forms of dance theatre internationally, both East and West. SB

Ballets Russes, Les (de Serge Diaghilev) *Ballet company that began as a *tour to Paris in 1909 by dancers and opera singers from the Mariinsky Theatre in St Petersburg. The company lasted for twenty years, producing some of the twentieth century's most *avant-garde experiments in *dance, music, and visual art. *Diaghilev had organized Russian exhibitions, concerts, and *opera in Paris; after 1909 he became the visionary impresario of a world-renowned dance company. At first he exported the collaborative work of Russian dancers, composers, and visual artists to Europe and the Americas. *The Rite of Spring* (1913), choreographed by Vaslav Nijinsky to music by Igor Stravinsky, was sensational for its anti-balletic dancing, polyrhythmic music, and folkloric images of pagan Russia. After 1917 the company settled in Paris and then Monte Carlo, and became more international; its participants included *Picasso, *Cocteau, *Bakst, Matisse, Ravel, and Satie, and its choreographers included Bronislava Nijinska and *Balanchine. After Diaghilev's death in 1929, his dancers settled in various countries, founding companies and schools in Europe and the USA. Several subsequent companies known as Ballet Russe (singular) operated with parts of the original repertory until the early 1950s. SB

Bancroft, Squire (1841–1926) English *actor-manager, one of the leading figures of the mid-Victorian stage. Joining Marie *Wilton at the Prince of Wales Theatre in London in 1865, he assumed leading parts in the extraordinarily successful *comedies of Tom *Robertson: *Society* (1865), *Ours* (1866), *Caste* (1867), and *School* (1869). A tall, handsome man, Bancroft acted against *stock company stereotyping and with a polished restraint that matched Robertson's writing. This restraint also marked his period of management, which he shared with Marie Wilton, whom he married in 1867. In collaboration with Robertson at the Prince of Wales's and the larger *Haymarket (1880–5), they presented a quiet middle-class domestic *realism, in both *acting and production style, which influenced later playwrights and *managers. At the Haymarket Bancroft introduced the full picture-frame stage and controversially abolished the pit, replacing it with stalls (*see* BOX, PIT, AND GALLERY). The Bancrofts retired in 1885 with £180,000, mostly derived from Robertson's plays. He was knighted in 1897, the first actor after *Irving to be so honoured. MRB

Bandō Tamasaburō V (1950–) Japanese *onnagata* (female-gender role specialist) in *kabuki and *shimpa*, and choreographer. He was adopted into the kabuki family of Morita Kanya in 1956, and *Nakamura Utaemon VI, the foremost *onnagata* of the post-war period, recognized his unusual talent and beauty in his early roles such as Hototogisu in *Gosho no Gorozo* (1967) and tutored him. That same year Tamasaburō and the young Kataoka Takao made a sensation in their couple roles in *Sakurahime Azuma Bunshō* (1967). Performing both the young acolyte and the princess in *Sakurahime*, Tamasaburō established his quintessential feature of gender ambiguity. Known for his aloof beauty and cool sensuality, he excels in the *akuba* (evil woman) parts such as Kirare Otomi and Unzari Omatsu in the plays of those titles. Tamasaburō has worked extensively outside kabuki, choreographing and performing in collaboration with artists such as Maurice Béjart, Andrzej *Wajda, Nuria *Espert and Yo Yo Ma. Among his Western female roles are Medea, Lady Macbeth, and Queen Elizabeth in Francisco Orrs's *Contradance*. He also directs and performs in films.   KMM

bangsawan Popular Malaysian and Indonesian commercial urban theatre. *Parsi theatre troupes touring from Bombay in the 1880s are believed to have provided the model. *Bangsawan* was Malaysia's (and later Indonesia's) first purely secular and commercial theatre, characterized by shameless self-promotion, star appeal, and troupe rivalries. It also introduced indigenous *audiences to the *proscenium stage, scenery, and *lighting. Flashy and theatrical, *bangsawan* performances appealed across ethnic and class lines. Stories were drawn from popular Middle Eastern, Indian, and Malay sources as well as from adaptations of Western literary classics and films. *Dialogue, performed in Malay, was improvised around loose *scenarios—a single play could take several nights to complete if a good rapport with the audience was established. In the 1890s Malay troupes toured to Sumatra and Java where local companies subsequently formed, becoming generally known in Indonesia as *opera melayu* (Malay opera) or *stambul*. Its popularity peaked during the 1920s and 1930s and began to decline in the 1940s, as intellectuals from the nationalist movements in both Malaysia and Indonesia criticized it as coarse and unrealistic.   CRG

Baraka, Imamu Amiri (LeRoi Jones) (1934-) *African-American poet and playwright. As LeRoi Jones, he emerged out of the beatnik era to express the anger and force of black cultural determination. In the 1950s and 1960s in New York he joined *Albee's playwrights' workshop and founded the American Theatre for Poets with Diane di Prima in 1961. That same year his provocative race play *The Toilet* caught critical fire, and was followed three years later by *The Baptism*, but it was *Dutchman* (1964) that brought him and race issues powerfully to the public eye. Set in a subway car, *Dutchman* pits a cocky black male against a seductive white female in a violent tug of war which ends in the young man's death, and suggests an endless cycle of the same *action. Jones changed his name and affiliated with the Black Arts Repertory Theatre and School in Harlem, which took performance to the *streets. *The Slave* (1964), *A Black Mass* (1966), and *Slave Ship: An Historical Pageant* (1967) confirmed his artistic and political reorientation. He returned to Newark, where he was born, and

created the Spirit House Theatre. *The Motion of History* (1975) shows his rejection of black separatism for a more broadly based international socialism. *See* DIASPORA.   BBL

Barba, Eugenio (1936-) Italian director, theorist, and teacher. Barba founded the Odin Teatret in 1964 in Oslo after working with *Grotowski for three years in Poland. Moving to Holstebro in Denmark in 1966, he established the Nordisk Teaterlaboratorium, a research organization modelled loosely on Grotowski's Polish Lab Theatre. Barba published the first English version of Grotowski's *Towards a Poor Theatre* (1968) and arranged his first workshops and performances outside of Poland. Barba is one of the leading figures of the independent group theatre movement and was among the first to realize its relevance through his concept of the 'third theatre'. He was also an early practitioner of what he terms 'barter', that is, using performance as a means of generating contact between different cultures. He established the International School of Theatre Anthropology in 1979, a research organization predicated upon what he terms theatre anthropology, investigating performance universals that function across cultures. He has directed more than twenty productions with the Odin and has conducted workshops in many parts of the world. A prolific author, he has written or collaborated on twelve books and more than 80 articles, which have been widely translated. *See also* INTERCULTURALISM.   IDW

Barbeau, Jean (1945-) Québécois playwright. Barbeau's use of colourful Canadian French, following that of *Tremblay, proved immensely popular, in plays such as *Manon Lastcall* and *Joualez-moi d'amour* (*Speak to Me of Love*, both 1970), the latter a reference to *joual*, a hitherto pejorative term for the language of working-class francophones. Politically committed and savagely parodic of Québec society, Barbeau's black humour entertained *audiences until the election of the separatist Parti Québécois (which he supported) in 1976. His output and influence have declined noticeably since then.   LED

Barberio Corsetti, Giorgio (1951-) Italian director, actor, and author. A leading figure of the 'post *avant-garde', Barberio Corsetti founded La Gaia Scienza in 1976 and the Barberio Corsetti Company in 1984 to perform his original, experimental works. Many of these reflected his desire to seek nourishment in myth and sacred texts and to express ideas through video-theatre (*see* MULTIMEDIA PERFORMANCE). Among the best of them have been *The Abstract Room* (1987),

Mefistofele... (1995, based on *Goethe's Faust*), *America* (1990) and *The Trial* (1998), both adapted from Kafka, and *Notte* (1998), a mythic meditation on city nightlife.   JEH

baris Several types of ceremonial Balinese warrior *dances classified into different categories based on the types of weapons used. *Baris* has been in existence since at least the sixteenth century and was first mentioned in the context of funeral processions. It is customarily performed during temple anniversary festivals (*odalan*) and the dancers are considered the bodyguard of the visiting deities. *Baris* literally means 'line' or 'row', and it is presented by rows of men who perform stylized fighting moves and military drills in pairs. Often two lines face each other and execute complex stylized mock battles in unison. The dancers wear characteristic triangular pointed helmets and use various heirloom weapons (spears, lances, bows and arrows, clubs, shields) depending on the type of dance. *Baris gedé* (grand *baris*) is the most elaborate kind, involving large groups of up to 60 dancers and accompanied by the gamelan *gong gedé*. Several secular types of *baris* exist as well, such as the *baris melampahan*, which includes dramatic elements. A solo *baris* developed in the late twentieth century as part of the repertoire of tourist performances.   KP

Barker, Harley Granville (1877–1946) English actor, playwright, director, *manager, critic, and theorist. Self-educated, he began acting in 1891, writing plays in 1895, and directing in 1899. As an actor Barker excelled in roles that combined intelligence with romantic dreaminess, and *Shaw thought his subtle but natural playing particularly suited for lover-poets like Marchbanks in *Candida*, Tanner in *Man and Superman*, Cusins in *Major Barbara*, and Dubedat in *The Doctor's Dilemma*, the last two written with Barker in mind. But *acting did not appeal to him and he gave it up in 1911. At a time when *directing was barely acknowledged in England, Barker built on the models of *Antoine and *Reinhardt, and almost single-handedly transformed the quality of production in London. His first assignments were under the limited auspices of the *Stage Society, but at the *Royal Court Theatre from 1904 to 1907 he became the major reformer of the Edwardian stage. With his business manager J. E. Vedrenne, he mounted almost 1,000 performances, mostly of new works (or new translations of *Euripides by *Murray); 701 of the performances were of eleven plays by Shaw. Barker collaborated with Shaw in staging his plays, and directed all the others himself. He also acted a number of important roles.

In 1906 he married the actress Lillah *McCarthy, soon after they played opposite each other in *Man and Superman*.

Barker's own play *The Voysey Inheritance* (1905) remains one of the masterworks of the Edwardian stage. But his other plays, which are highly nuanced in thought, did not much appeal to Edwardian *audiences, who sometimes found them incomprehensible. Unlike his friend and mentor Shaw, Barker was closer in method to *Chekhov, putting *action under the surface. Despite his subtle method, Barker did not avoid important and controversial issues: *Waste* was banned in 1907 because of its twinned subjects of abortion and politics (*see* CENSORSHIP), and *The Madras House* (1910) treated the economic domination of women using the embryonic fashion business to analyse contemporary sexual relationships.

The Vedrenne–Barker seasons established Shaw as a major playwright but did not mean financial stability. A second repertory experiment at the Duke of York's in 1910, briefly funded by the American impresario *Frohman, reinforced for Barker the need for an endowed *repertory company. In 1904 he had written a book with *Archer arguing for a national theatre, and he continued to champion the cause; his failure to achieve it was the greatest disappointment of his life. His persistent advocacy nonetheless encouraged the growth of the *regional repertory movement in Britain and ultimately influenced the founding of the subsidized English theatres in the 1960s.

Barker's directing reached its height in three famous productions of Shakespeare at the Savoy: *The Winter's Tale* and *Twelfth Night* (1912) and *A Midsummer Night's Dream* (1914). Partly influenced by *Poel, for whom he played Richard II in 1899, Barker used nearly complete texts, revoked Victorian pictorial traditions for the sake of modernist design, and emphasized ensemble acting. But the war changed everything and in the 1920s he devoted himself to the study, where he said he always wanted to be. He divorced Lillah McCarthy and in 1918 married a minor American writer, Helen Huntington, who disliked the stage, most actors, and especially Shaw. Her wealth allowed them the freedom to write. Hyphenating his name to Granville-Barker, he appeared remote and lost the support of his theatrical allies, who believed he had abandoned the battle for a life of luxury. He attended to the stage from a distance, in books like *The Exemplary Theatre* (1922), *The National Theatre* (1930), and *The Use of Drama* (1944). He wrote two more plays—*The Secret Life* (1923) and *His Majesty* (1928)—and with his wife he translated the *comedies of *Martínez Sierra and the *Álvarez Quintero brothers. His most enduring critical work is *Prefaces to Shakespeare* (1927–46), the first major Shakespeare study to attend to practical matters of staging.

In recent years Barker's plays, which now seem prescient in style and theme, have attracted serious attention. The *Royal Shakespeare Company produced *The Marrying of Ann Leete* in 1975 and *Waste* in 1985. The *National Theatre presented *The Madras House* in 1977, *The Voysey Inheritance* was seen there and in many venues in Britain and North America in the late 1980s and 1990s (most recently in an adaptation by *Mamet, 2005), and even Barker's difficult late plays were at last given productions, at the Orange Tree Theatre in London, directed by Sam *Walters. Between 1988 and 2002 the *Shaw Festival in Canada undertook to establish Barker as a major playwright by producing most of his plays under the direction of Neil Munro, and the *Edinburgh Festival mounted a major retrospective in 1992. At the same time Barker's general contributions have been re-evaluated and his importance for modern theatre securely acknowledged, so that he is now seen as one of the twentieth century's leading innovators.   DK

Barker, Howard (1946–) English dramatist and director. Barker's early work seemed to place him in the political movement of the late 1960s, but soon he evaded neat classification, and his historical subjects became acts of imaginative speculation in which *comedy and desire could mingle and clash. *The Castle* (1985), set after the crusades, pits the hierarchical values of the returning male warriors against the spiritual socialism created by the wives they left behind. Barker is unusually prolific: he has written an astounding number of plays, six books of poetry, and dramatic manifestos, many of them collected in *Arguments for a Theatre* (1989, 1997). Through these he articulated a 'theatre of catastrophe' that renounces moral and narrative clarity, and the consequent solidarity of the *audience, in favour of complexity and excess. These goals are realized in *The Possibilities* (1988), based around perverse moral acts, and the hugely ambitious *The Bite of the Night* (1988). Having lost his early champions like the *Royal Shakespeare Company and *Royal Court, Barker founded the Wrestling School in 1988, which became his main British conduit in pieces such as *Seven Lears* (1989), *Judith* (1995), *Wounds to the Face* (1997), *A House of Correction* (2001), and *The Dying of Today* (2008)   DR

Barker, James Nelson (1784–1859) American playwright, politician, and poet. Son of a prominent Philadelphia family, notable among his early efforts were *Tears and Smiles* (1806), a *comedy contrasting French and American social mores; a pro-Jeffersonian piece, *The Embargo* (1808), that occasioned *riots at the Chestnut Street Theatre; and *The Indian Princess* (1808), a retelling of the Pocahontas legend with a happy ending. This piece with *music was the first 'Indian play' written by an American to be produced in the United States. He continued in a distinctly nationalistic vein in his 1812 anti-British adaptation of Scott's novel *Marmion*, and in *The Armourer's Escape* (1817). Also in 1817 Barker wrote *How to Try a Lover*, a light comedy unproduced until 1836. After a term as Philadelphia's mayor, Barker penned his masterpiece, *Superstition* (1824), a moving indictment of Puritan fanaticism. Thereafter he became absorbed in politics and confined his literary production to poetry.   GAR

Barnes, Peter (1931–) English playwright and director. His first plays, *Time of the Barracudas* (1963) and *Sclerosis* (1965), received little attention, but *The Ruling Class* (1968) was groundbreaking, an uncompromising mixture of grotesque spectacle, dark humour, and acerbic *satire on the relationships between the vested interests of Church, state, money, and power. Barnes's distinctive voice and savage comic satires about serious subjects often resulted in controversy, most evident in the mixed reception of *Laughter!* (1978), a two-part play which measures Ivan the Terrible's personalized reign of terror against the depersonalized bureaucracy of the Nazi extermination machine. Barnes adapted numerous *early modern plays for stage and radio, directing many of them himself. The influence of *Jonson, *Marston, and *Middleton can be seen in his major plays, juxtaposing dense neo-Jacobean language with wittily anachronistic allusions to popular culture. Barnes's dislike of *naturalism and love of spectacle is evident throughout, perhaps most notably in *The Bewitched* (1974). He has won several major awards, including the Olivier for *Red Noses* (1985). His screenplay for *Enchanted April* (1991) was nominated for an Academy Award.   BGW

Barnum, P. T. (Phineas Taylor) (1810–91) American impresario of *freak shows, museums, *variety, theatre, and *circus. Initially styling himself as a confidence man sympathetic to working-class and slaveholding interests, Barnum presented several exhibits which undermined the values of the emerging middle class, most famously Joice Heth, an elderly slave who Barnum claimed had been the nurse of George Washington. Soon after opening Barnum's American Museum in New York in 1841, he changed tactics to represent himself and his exhibits as icons of middle-class respectability and a classless America. One of his most successful publicity ventures was the European *tour of the midget Tom Thumb (Charles Stratton). In 1850–1 Barnum organized the successful American tour of Swedish singer Jenny Lind, packaged as a sentimental nightingale conforming to middle-class ideals of womanhood. Barnum's second autobiography, *Struggles and Triumphs* (1869; five others would follow), announced his rebirth as a post-Civil War Republican. After he entered the circus business in 1871, Barnum's new conceptions of race and class emerged, especially in the racial exhibitions that dominated his Great Roman Hippodrome of 1874–5. In 1881 Barnum combined his circus interests with those of James A. Bailey to create 'The Greatest Show on Earth', but took little interest in managing it. Barnum virtually invented popular commercial entertainment in the USA; his enormous legacy continues.   BMC

Baron (Michel Boyron) (1653–1729) French actor and playwright. While acting in a children's company, the 13-year-old Baron was discovered by *Molière and became his pupil and protégé. On Molière's death he moved, first, to the *Hôtel de Bourgogne, where he created some of *Racine's young leading men, and then in 1680 to the newly established *Comédie-Française, where he played *tragedy and high *comedy. Inexplicably, in 1691 Baron retired from the stage, giving occasional private and court performances, until 29 years later, aged 67, he returned and not only resumed his former repertoire of *heroes and lovers, including Rodrigue in *Corneille's *Le Cid*, but also created a dozen new roles. Baron had all the attributes of a leading actor—good looks, graceful attitudes, striking presence, and versatility. He also had an equal measure of vanity, and *L'Homme à bonnes fortunes* (*The Philanderer*, 1686), the best of the ten comedies he wrote, was a role he played onstage and off.   JG

barong Large mythical supernatural beasts that appear in Balinese ritual performances. Different types of large *barong* *masks, considered spiritually powerful objects when consecrated, are used in *rituals and performances; they show iconographic features of lions, elephants, dogs, boars, or dragons. Typically a pair of male dancers play the creature, one in front animating the large mask and front legs, one at the rear. *Barong kekek*, the most spiritually powerful and well known, features prominently in ritual processions and performances. The mask has large bulging eyes, a movable jaw with large fangs, a protruding tongue, and a wing-shaped leather collar. It is associated with the animistic spirit Banaspati Raja (Lord of the Forest) as well as with the Hindu deity Shiva. The *barong* is considered a guarding spirit and the opponent of the witch-widow Rangda, who is associated with the legendary figure of Calonarang, witches, and the Hindu deity Durga. Barong and Rangda appear in exorcistic ritual performances that often include dramatic elements from the Calonarang story. Such a performance is intended to re-establish harmony in the community by balancing the supernatural powers of Barong and Rangda, therefore the conflict or battle-dance between them is the central element of the drama. Other dramatic elements often include *clown scenes, *dance scenes performed by the young apprentices of Rangda, and the dramatic *dialogue between Calonarang in her human form and her human opponent, a minister or king. The most spectacular element is the *ngurek*, often referred to as '*kris* dance'. In this section, human followers of Barong go into trance while defending him against Rangda. During this trance, it is believed, Rangda's powerful influence drives them to attack themselves with *kris* daggers; however, the power of the Barong protects them from injuries.

Performers of Barong and Rangda also go into trance under the influence of the spiritually powerful masks. The dance of Barong and Rangda, together with the *ngurek* trance-dance, have become famous in tourist performances where they are advertised as 'Barong and *kris* dance' and shortened to an hour-long show in which non-consecrated masks are used. The dancers generally do not go into trance.   KP

Barraca, La Spanish theatre company. A product of the Second Republic's ambitious cultural programme, La Barraca was formed in 1932 by students of the University of Madrid with the aim of taking serious Spanish theatre to the provinces and, in the words of the company's manifesto, 'aesthetically renovating the Spanish stage'. Under the artistic direction of Federico *García Lorca and Eduardo Ugarte, La Barraca drew on innovative Spanish artists for scenery and *costume design, in a quest for 'plasticity' of dress, *lighting, and movement, with which they revolutionized the performance of plays by authors such as *Cervantes, Lope de *Vega, and *Calderón. KG

Barrault, Jean-Louis (1910–94) French actor and director. Eclectic in his choice of repertory, Barrault shifted his *directing and *acting style accordingly, whether *epic, *expressionist, *ritualist, or pantomimic. Opposing 'psychologism', he was a proponent of *total theatre, with *mime, gesture, movement, vocal intonation, and rhythm being primary. In 1931 Barrault joined *Dullin's acting school. Influenced by *Artaud, *Copeau, and *Decroux, Barrault's first independent production, *Autour d'une mère* (1935) was adapted with *Camus from Faulkner's novel *As I Lay Dying*. Surrounded by a swaying, chanting *chorus that evoked the sea and wind was Barrault himself as the 'centaur-horse', creating through movement and vocalization a horse and rider simultaneously, as well as birds of prey overhead. His acting is memorialized in the 1935 film *Les Enfants du paradis*, in the role of *Deburau.

After army service, Barrault joined the *Comédie-Française as actor and director, where he met Madeleine *Renaud, whom he married in 1940. His major productions there included *Racine's *Phèdre* (1942), *Claudel's *The Satin Slipper* (1943), and *Antony and Cleopatra* (1945). Barrault shared Claudel's vision of a *tragicomic, epic-lyrical 'holy' theatre and continued to produce his works over the next four decades. In 1946 Barrault and Renaud left to found the private Compagnie Renaud–Barrault. Invited by Copeau, Barrault became *artistic director of the *Odéon Theatre from 1958 to 1968. For his own company and the Odéon, Barrault directed, acted in, or hosted works ranging from *Feydeau, *Marivaux, and Shakespeare to Claudel, *Anouilh, *Genet, *Ionesco, *Fry, *Duras, Kafka, *Brecht, and *Beckett. In May 1968, Barrault, in sympathy with student protesters, allowed them to occupy the Odéon, which led to his resignation. At 58 he started anew, and in a year opened triumphantly in a former *sports arena with *Rabelais*, a carnivalesque creation featuring actors, *clowns, and *bunraku *puppeteers. In 1980 Barrault and Renaud settled into the Théâtre du Rond-Point, where they continued to produce classical and modern works, and they died in the same year.   SBB

Barrett, Lawrence (1838–91) American *actor-manager. Barrett ran away from home at the age of 10, teaching himself to read by memorizing a dictionary. Working in *stock companies, he eventually appeared in New York in 1857. In 1869 he managed the company at the California Theatre in San Francisco with John McCullough, and was among the first actor-managers to *tour an entire company (1872). He regularly toured

in Shakespearian roles thereafter and in other classic works. Barrett managed the enormously successful final tours of Edwin *Booth (1886–90), playing second leads to the great tragedian. Regarded as an intellectual actor, Barrett's performances were studied and somewhat artificial, and were increasingly regarded as old-fashioned in the last two decades of the nineteenth century, although his performances as Cassius, Macbeth, and Othello were recognized as the leading ones of the 1880s.   AW

Barrett, Wilson (1846–1904) English *actor-manager. Of powerful voice and physique, Barrett established a reputation playing melodramatic *heroes such as Harold Armytage in George Sims's *The Lights o' London* (1881) and Wilfrid Denver in *The Silver King* (1882) by Henry Arthur *Jones and Henry Herman, characters wrongfully accused of murder. These plays first appeared under his own management (1881–6) of the Princess's Theatre in London; Barrett also undertook provincial management. He enjoyed further success with *Wills's religious spectacle drama, *Claudian* (1883), in which he played a profligate and murderous pagan aristocrat cursed for his sins and unable to die, left untouched even by an earthquake. *Hamlet*, in 1884, was not so well received, although it ran for 116 performances. Other Shakespeare parts included Romeo, Mercutio, and Benedick. In his own enormously popular religious *melodrama *The Sign of the Cross* (1895), Barrett played a dissolute Roman prefect converted to Christianity by the love of a Christian girl, with whom he goes to his death and 'the light beyond' in the jaws of the Colosseum's lions.   MRB

Barrie, J. M. (James Matthew) (1860–1937) Scottish novelist and playwright, who began his career as a journalist, moving to London in 1885. In the late 1880s he began to write novels, including *The Little Minister* (1891), which he later turned into a successful play (1897). In the 1890s he wrote *farces, but soon found his dramatic voice with a series of popular and long-running social *comedies, including *Walker, London* (1892), *The Professor's Love Story* (1894), *The Admirable Crichton* (1902), and *What Every Woman Knows* (1908). He also wrote romantic *costume plays, such as *Quality Street* (1901), and social fantasies, such as *Dear Brutus* (1917) and *Mary Rose* (1920). His greatest success was *Peter Pan* (1904), which starred Nina Boucicault as Peter and Gerald *du Maurier as Hook. It became an annual event, revived each Christmas until 1914. Since the mid twentieth century most of his plays have been dismissed as sentimental and superficial, except for *Peter Pan*, which remains popular as a children's drama.   TP

Barry, Elizabeth (*c.*1658–1713) English actress and *manager. Adopted into the *Davenant household, Barry made her first appearance in *Otway's *Alcibiades* (1675). She rose swiftly to become the leading actress in the *patent company and *Dryden, *Lee, Otway, and other prominent playwrights soon wrote parts for her. Renowned for her passionate yet sympathetic tragic heroines, Barry also established herself in *comedy. Her early successes included Hellena in Aphra *Behn's *The Rover* (1677), and later *Congreve wrote *Love for Love* (1695) and *The Way of the World* (1700) to capitalize on her eighteen-year acting partnership with Anne *Bracegirdle. Barry was the first actress to negotiate a personal bonus payment in the form of a *benefit performance and, with Bracegirdle and *Betterton, was instrumental in forming and managing a breakaway company which occupied the theatre at Lincoln's Inn Fields between 1695 and 1705. For the first time actresses as well as actors shared in the company's profits and their management premièred at least seventeen plays by female playwrights such as Mary *Pix, Catherine *Trotter, and Susannah *Centlivre.   GBB

Barry, Philip (1896–1949) American playwright. *Holiday* (1928) and *The Philadelphia Story* (1939), the most successful and highly regarded of his plays, are animated by conflicting American dreams—the accumulation and enjoyment of wealth versus egalitarian and communitarian ideals. Both plays revolve upon the decision of an intelligent and witty young woman to reject an easy life and socially acceptable marriage to pursue a more adventurous path through marriage with a poor but industrious young man. A 1919 graduate of Yale, Barry attended George Pierce *Baker's 47 Workshop at Harvard (1919–21) and saw his first Broadway success with *You and I* in 1923. Other major plays are the *comedies *Paris Bound* (1927) and *The Animal Kingdom* (1932), and the less successful philosophical dramas *Hotel Universe* (1930) and *Here Come the Clowns* (1938).   MAF

Barry, Sebastian (1955–) Irish writer whose novel *The Secret Scripture* (2008) won the Costa Prize. Barry (his mother was the Abbey actor Joan O'Hara) was established as a dramatist by *Boss Grady's Boys* (1988) in which he found his own style of poetic impressionism. Since then, he has produced a series of 'family' plays, *Prayers of Sherkin* (1990), *White Woman Street* (1992), *The*

Only True History of Lizzie Finn (1995), taking their origins from sketchy facts about his own ancestors. Barry's greatest international success has been *The Steward of Christendom* (1995), produced by London's *Royal Court. The central *character, a senile retired policeman (outstandingly performed by Donal *McCann), meditates on his past as a loyalist Catholic in the period of the Irish revolution. The effect of Barry's work has been to give theatrical expression to forgotten voices from Ireland's history, though the two-hander *The Pride of Parnell Street* (2007) represented a move into the contemporary period and proletarian Dublin.   NG

Barry, Spranger (1719–77) Irish actor and *manager. Known as the 'Irish *Roscius', Barry was the most serious rival to *Garrick, the 'English Roscius'. Barry was so effective as Othello that Garrick, who acknowledged him as the best lover on the stage, gave up the role rather than force comparisons. The two did compete, however, as rival Romeos in 1750. Barry was strikingly handsome, tall, and graceful. His voice was not strong and expressions of violent rage were beyond his range; he excelled as a dignified, tragic lover. Perhaps his most successful role was Castalio in *Otway's *The Orphan*. When he created the majestic title role in John Home's *Douglas* in 1757, he was at the height of his powers, performing at *Covent Garden and planning the construction of the Crow Street Theatre in Dublin. But he lost great sums of money and property, selling out in Dublin in 1767 and returning to London. In his final years frequent bouts of illness and a temperamental nature led him to cancel many performances. His final role was the elderly Evadner in Arthur *Murphy's *The Grecian Daughter*.   MJK

Barrymore family American acting family. In 1876 expatriate English leading man **Maurice Barrymore** (1847–1905) married Georgiana *Drew, herself of a famous stage dynasty. Maurice made his American debut in *Under the Gaslight* in Boston (1875). His most notable co-star was *Modjeska, for whom he wrote *Nadjezda* (1886), one of his several successful plays. A noted Orlando and Romeo, his greatest success was as Rawdon Crawley in *Becky Sharp* (1899). Refusing to settle into star vehicles, he insisted on independence, sued *Sardou for plagiarism (*Tosca* is a paraphrase of *Nadjezda*), quarrelled endlessly with *managers, and was reduced to appearing in *vaudeville when paresis ended his career in 1901. His irresponsibility and Georgiana's premature death caused their three children to be raised by their maternal grandmother, Mrs John Drew.

Lionel Barrymore (1874–1954) was hustled on the stage by his grandmother as Thomas to her Mrs Malaprop in 1893. Successful from the first, his contempt for *acting almost kept him from stardom. He won great acclaim in *The Copperhead* (1918) and when he played *villains opposite the sensitive *heroes of his brother in *Peter Ibbetson* (1917) and *The Jest* (1919). His failure as Macbeth (1921) probably caused him to forsake the stage for the screen. He made over 200 films, won an Oscar (for *A Free Soul*, 1931), and, though rheumatic illness left him in a wheelchair, became 'America's most beloved actor' and Hollywood's definitive Grand Old Man.

Ethel Barrymore (1879–1959) first appeared in *The Rivals* with Mrs Drew and in *The Bauble Shop* with her uncle John Drew (both 1894). She then went to London with *Gillette's *Secret Service*. Joining *Irving's company prepared her for American stardom, which came in 1901 with her Madame Trentoni in *Captain Jinks of the Horse Marines*. For the next 44 years her deep voice, peerless poise, and majestic beauty reigned over the theatre. Most successful in contemporary plays as sympathetic and romantic heroines, her greatest success was the inspiring teacher Miss Moffat in Emlyn *Williams's *The Corn Is Green* (1940). Her final years were spent in Hollywood.

John Barrymore (1882–1942) hated acting even more than Lionel but gained the greater fame. Reaching New York in 1903, he was content to show off his matchless profile in light *comedies until Edward *Sheldon convinced him to try serious parts. Barrymore electrified Broadway in *Justice* (1916). There followed a series of wrenching portrayals culminating in a magnificent Richard III (1920) and Hamlet (1922). Though he was the hope of the American theatre, he proved unable to sustain a part beyond its initial creation. After a triumphant London *Hamlet* he fled to films in 1925. Fourteen years of alcoholism and Hollywood excesses dissipated his talents, and his final stage appearance was in a travesty of his own life, *My Dear Children* (1939).

The next generation found notoriety if little fame. John's daughter **Diana** (1921–60) had a fitful stage life but failed to overcome the family curse of alcoholism, which also doomed the career of his son **John Barrymore, Jr.** (1932–2004). Sundry cousins and collateral relations fought to keep the tradition alive, but only John, Jr.'s daughter **Drew Barrymore** (1975–) has succeeded. She began as a child star like her great-great-grandmother, appearing in the film *ET* (1982), and, after her own bouts of dissipated living, twenty years later achieved Hollywood stardom.   TFC

Barsacq, André (1909–73) French designer and director. Trained as a visual artist and architect, Barsacq began painting scenery for *Dullin, for whom he would later design many productions. His designs for *opera and *ballet, including the first production of Stravinsky's *Perséphone* (1934) at the Paris Opéra, were also celebrated. Having been an occasional assistant to *Copeau, in 1936 he co-founded the Théâtre des Quatre Saisons with *Dasté. He succeeded Dullin as director of the Théâtre de l'Atelier in 1940, where he enjoyed a significant collaboration with *Anouilh, directing his *Antigone* (1943) with celebrated modern-dress *costumes at the height of the German Occupation. Barsacq directed for 30 more years after the war, continuing the tradition of textual fidelity and scenic experimentation championed by the *Cartel des Quatre.   DGM

Bart, Lionel (1930–99) English lyricist, playwright, and composer. Bart wrote lyrics for *Lock up your Daughters* (1959), and in the same year collaborated with Frank Norman on the *musical *Fings Ain't Wot They Used t' Be* (1959) for *Littlewood's *Theatre Workshop. A story of small-time criminals in London's Soho, it established a distinctively English version of the American musical genre, and ran for two years in the West End. Bart pursued the London underworld theme in his most popular work, *Oliver!* (1960), an adaptation of *Dickens's *Oliver Twist*, which had 2,618 performances in London and successfully transferred to New York and film. *Blitz!* (1962), a wartime spectacular, and *Maggie May* (1964), the story of a Liverpool prostitute, were also successful, but *Twang!!* (1965), a parody of the Robin Hood story, was critically and commercially disastrous. His later work never recovered the popularity of *Fings* and *Oliver*. It included the short-lived *La Strada* (1969) and the retrospective *Lionel* (1977).   SF

Barton, John (1928–) English director, one of the most influential interpreters of the classic repertory since he joined Peter *Hall's *Royal Shakespeare Company in 1960. He initially edited playable texts for the company and began a revolution in verse speaking. His principles are best demonstrated in *Playing Shakespeare*, televised and published in 1982. Since *The Wars of the Roses* (1963–4) his many Shakespeare productions have shown a deep engagement with the politics of the plays, exploring the relationship between power and passion. But his work is notable too for its narrative clarity while allowing for psychological nuances of considerable complexity, especially evident in his staging of *Twelfth Night* (1969) and *Richard II* (1971), where the device of actors alternating the roles of Richard and Bolingbroke enhanced patterns of psychological discrimination. After 1980 he made two attempts to stage cycles depicting the Trojan War and its aftermath: *The Greeks* (1979), largely used adapted texts from the *Greek tragedians; *Tantalus* (2001), comprised ten plays of his own devising. Since *Pillars of the Community* (1977), Barton directed *Chekhov, *Ibsen, and *Strindberg in productions notable for their moral precision and the actor-centred simplicity, qualities evident too in his chamber production of Granville *Barker's *Waste* (1985).   RAC

Bassermann, Albert (1867–1952) German actor. Bassermann first attracted attention as a character actor at the *Meiningen Court Theatre in the early 1890s. In 1895 he settled in Berlin where for *Brahm's *realistic repertoire he played leading roles in *Tolstoy, *Ibsen, and *Hauptmann. After joining *Reinhardt he concentrated on the classical repertoire, giving outstanding performances as Shylock, Othello, and as Mephisto in *Goethe's *Faust*. The latter he played as a mixture of cavalier, fallen angel, and *clown. Between 1915 and 1919 he went on extended *tours, including the USA. After 1919 he joined *Jessner at the Prussian Staatstheater, performing the title role in *William Tell*. An actor of exceptional range, Bassermann was considered the finest realistic performer of his generation for classical as well as contemporary roles. In 1933 he emigrated to the United States with his Jewish wife. He returned to Germany in 1946 but continued to divide his time between that country and America. He died in a plane crash over the Atlantic.   CBB

Bateman family Hezekiah Bateman (1812–75), an American theatrical entrepreneur known in England as Colonel Bateman, took London's Lyceum Theatre in 1871; it was under his management that *Irving first played in *The Bells* (1871). Bateman had four daughters who went on stage in their childhood. **Kate** (1842–1917) *toured America as a child with her younger sister **Ellen** (1844–1936), performing duets from Shakespeare. Ellen retired from the theatre after her marriage in 1860. Kate played several roles at the Lyceum, including Emilia and Lady Macbeth with Irving, and also acted with her sister **Isabel** (1854–1934), whom Colonel Bateman intended as

Irving's leading lady. She did Ophelia to his 1874 Hamlet and Desdemona to his Othello. However, when Irving took over the Lyceum from **Mrs Sidney Bateman** (1823–81), he quickly hired Ellen *Terry as his leading lady. Isabel went to *Sadler's Wells under her mother's brief management. **Virginia Bateman** (1855–1940) also appeared at the Lyceum and then, after marrying Edward Compton, with the Compton Comedy Company.   MRB

Bates, Alan (1934–2003) English actor, who made his London mark in 1956 as Cliff in the première of *Osborne's *Look Back in Anger*. Four years later he was Mick in *Pinter's *The Caretaker* (1960). Other stage work mixed modern with classical: Simon *Gray's *Butley* (1971), *Otherwise Engaged* (1975), and *Melon* (1987), Pinter's *One for the Road* (1984), *Chekhov's *Ivanov* (1989), and, for the *Royal Shakespeare Company, *The Taming of the Shrew* (1973) and *Antony and Cleopatra* (1999). His stage persona shifted away from youthful certainty and sexual assurance to angry physicality and, in his later career, to a raft of *characters weighted by suffering, anguish, and mourning, such as Fenchurch in *Storey's *Stages* (1992) and Solness in *Ibsen's *The Master Builder* (1995). Bates has also had a distinguished film career, appearing in *The Entertainer* (1960), *Georgy Girl* (1966), *Far from the Madding Crowd* (1967), *Women in Love* (1968), and *The Go-Between* (1971). His television work included *The Mayor of Casterbridge* (BBC, 1978) and Alan *Bennett's *An Englishman Abroad* (BBC, 1982).   AS

Baty, Gaston (1885–1952) French director whose career began in 1919 in Paris, alongside *Gémier at the Cirque d'Hiver, *lighting the monumental production of *Oedipus, King of Thebes*. At the same time he began to direct, study theatre history, and developed a passion for *puppets. *The Mask and the Censer* (1926) presented his early ideas, including a polemic against the hegemony of literature and the spoken text. His theoretical and historical writings established him as the theoretician of the *Cartel des Quatre. From 1924 to 1928 he took the helm of the Studio des Champs-Élysées, where he directed many contemporary plays, developed lighting as a key element of his *mise-en-scène, and began to champion a French *expressionism. From 1930 to 1947, Baty headed the Théâtre Montparnasse, where he nurtured the work of young playwrights, created groundbreaking adaptations of novels (*Crime and Punishment*, 1933; *Madame Bovary*, 1936), and produced a wide range of classics, including a celebrated historicist production of *Racine's *Phèdre* (1940).   DGM

Bauer, Wolfgang (1941–2005) Austrian dramatist. After early experiments in the mid-1960s with *absurdist pieces Bauer first came to attention in 1968 with his short play *Magic Afternoon*, which was hailed as an early dramatization of pop culture and remains his most frequently performed work. To combat boredom two young couples indulge in alcohol, drugs, and finally violence. The *realism of the play manifests itself in the use of dialect (a feature of most of Bauer's work) but transcends mere slice of life mimeticism to thematicize wider issues of social values and subjectivity. The role of the impotent artist or writer is also a central theme in many works, reflecting Bauer's preoccupation with issues of creativity and self-determination. The author of over twenty plays and film or television scripts, Bauer's reputation still rests mainly on the 'pop' plays of the late 1960s, such as *Change* (1969) and *Party for Six* (1967).   CBB

Bauhaus German art school, founded by Walter Gropius, originally situated in Weimar (1919–25), then active in Dessau (1925–32), where most of the theatre works were created. Due to right-wing pressure the school was forced to relocate to Berlin (1932–3) and then to Chicago. The first phase of the Bauhaus was strongly influenced by *expressionism; during the Dessau years a new *constructivist and technological orientation gave rise to the classic Bauhaus style. The principal aim of the institution was to overcome the division between arts and crafts and to bring different artistic disciplines under the umbrella of architecture. The theatre workshop offered a practical exploration of this philosophy and allowed artists from different backgrounds to collaborate in the exploration and composition of a 'total artwork of the stage', much of it under the direction of *Schlemmer.   GB

Bausch, Pina (1940–2009) German dancer, choreographer, and *manager. Bausch studied with two masters of expressive ballet: Kurt Jooss in Germany and Antony Tudor in New York. She also studied modern *dance. Bausch succeeded Jooss as director of the Folkwang Ballet in 1969 and in 1973 founded the Wuppertal Tanztheater. Heir to the German *Ausdruckstanz* (expressive dance) movement of the 1920s and 1930s, she developed a neo-*expressionism form of dance-theatre that often centred on issues of *gender, violence, and, more generally, human angst. Episodic and plotless, her dance-theatre pieces were emotionally intense. Her *mise-en-

scène included extravagant sets (a stage covered with water, a dirt mountain), props (10,000 artificial carnations), practicables (a construction that turns two dancers into a hippopotamus), and *costumes (at times, *cross-dressing); *animal performers (sheep, fish, dogs); spoken text; both popular and classical recorded music; film projections; and dancing that is extremely high energy and virtuosic, though not following the specialized technique of any dance genre. *Café Müller* (1978) still impressed London audiences in 2009, when it won an Olivier Award.   SB

Baylis, Lilian (1874–1937) English *manager and entrepreneur. In 1897 she agreed to assist her aunt Emma Cons, a social reformer who had renovated the Royal Victoria Theatre (the *Old Vic) as a temperance hall which provided *musical and *variety entertainment. When Cons died in 1912, Baylis took over management, expanding the *opera programme and adding plays and films. Determined to make the arts accessible to working men and women, between 1914 and 1923 she presented all of the Shakespeare plays in the First Folio, and also *Pericles*. In the 1920s she added *ballet to her ambitious programme. In 1925 she purchased *Sadler's Wells Theatre, which reopened in 1931 after major renovation. For a few years ballet, opera, and drama were performed in both *playhouses, but soon Sadler's Wells became the home of ballet, featuring the choreography of Ninette de Valois and Frederick Ashton. An ambitious opera programme was also established there, with 50 productions between 1931 and 1937. The Old Vic also became the home of drama, under the directorship of Harcourt *Williams and *Guthrie. Baylis struggled with *finance, yet bolstered by religious faith, love of the arts, and fierce willpower, she created the model and rationale for what became the English National Opera (1956), Royal Ballet (1956), and *National Theatre (1963).   TP

Bayreuth Festival An annual festival, founded by *Wagner for the model performance of his own works and other German *operas. It is held in the Festspielhaus, in the suburbs of Bayreuth in northern Bavaria, which opened in 1876 with the first performance of *The Rhinegold*. The theatre is noted for its near-perfect sight lines and acoustics. The *auditorium is wedge-shaped so that most *audience members have a clear view of the stage. Because of the size of the Wagnerian orchestra, the orchestra pit is sunken, which has the effect of homogenizing the sound. The double *proscenium is repeated in the architectural abutments that frame the auditorium which creates the *illusion, unique in *playhouse design, that the audience occupies the same space as the singer-actors. Wagner intended to equip the stage with the latest technology in *lighting and *scenography and today the Festival Theatre is still one of the best-equipped opera houses in Germany.

The annual festival was held regularly only after Wagner's death, under the direction of his widow Cosima (1838-1930), who limited the repertoire solely to her husband's ten mature music dramas, a restriction that still applies. Bayreuth has acquired a reputation for conservatism, but while it preserves Wagner's work, it does so in the most current theatre styles. *Expressionism was introduced under the direction of the composer's son Siegfried (1869-1930). From 1951 on, under the direction of Wagner's grandsons Wolfgang (1919-2010) and Wieland *Wagner, Bayreuth led the way in innovative design and staging. The Wagner brothers were the first to apply the principles of *Appia to all the music dramas. Since then, many leading directors of European theatre have directed there, including *Chéreau, *Dorn, Peter *Hall, Werner Herzog, and *Müller.

From the start Bayreuth attracted an international audience and so served as a model for other festivals, such as the *Shakespeare Memorial Theatre in Stratford, *Salzburg, and Glyndebourne, though Bayreuth's reputation suffered immense damage when it became associated with Hitler. Since then, due primarily to the efforts of Wieland and Wolfgang, the Festival has been restored to its position as one of the prime events in the European opera calendar. Wolfgang retired in 2008 and was controversially replaced by his daughters Eva Wagner-Pasquier and Katharina Wagner.   SJCW

Beale, Simon Russell (1961-) Penang-born English actor. For the *Royal Shakespeare Company his roles include Oliver in *Dear's *The Art of Success* (1986), *Marlowe's *Edward II* (1991), Konstantin in *Chekhov's *The Seagull*, Richard III (1992), Ariel (1993), and Edgar in *King Lear* (1994). He was hugely successful as the narrator Voltaire and Dr Pangloss in *Caird's revival of *Candide* for the *National Theatre (1999). In 2000 he played Hamlet in Caird's production and in 2001 the stuttering astrophysicist Felix Humble in Charlotte Jones's *Humble Boy*. He has had relatively few film roles but was an effective Second Gravedigger in *Branagh's *Hamlet* (1996), while for television he was a gentle Charles Musgrove in *Persuasion* (1995) and a monstrous Widmerpool in *A Dance to the Music of Time* (1997). Recent parts include Uncle Vanya

(Oliver Award, 2003) and at the National, Face in *Jonson's *The Alchemist* (2006), Benedick (2007), and Undershaft in *Shaw's *Major Barbara* (2008).   AS

bear-baiting *See* BAITING.

Beaton, Cecil (1904-80) English designer, photographer, and painter, equally famous for his high-society photographs and the grandeur of his scenery and *costumes for theatre and *ballet. From the 1930s to 1960s he created stylish designs, mainly in London but also New York. Best known for the costumes for *My Fair Lady* (New York, 1956; London, 1958), he also provided set and costume designs for a wide range of productions, from *Gielgud's revival of *Lady Windermere's Fan* (1946) to the *musical *Coco* (1969). He won two Academy awards for production design for the films *Gigi* (1958) and *My Fair Lady* (1964).   TP

Beatty, John Lee (1948-) American designer. Beginning *Off-Broadway in the 1970s, Beatty moved to Broadway as his productions transferred, and has since designed over 53 Broadway productions. His scenery, usually *realistic and highly detailed, like that for David Auburn's *Proof* (2000), has a subtle lyricism, though his designs for *musicals are more fanciful. He has done a number of what he calls 'American porch plays', including those of Lanford *Wilson (Tony award for *Talley's Folley*, 1979) and Beth *Henley (*Crimes of the Heart*, 1980). Other memorable work includes the musical *Ain't Misbehavin'* (1978), a revival of Robert *Anderson's *Abe Lincoln in Illinois* (1993), and *Fugard's *The Road to Mecca* (Washington, 1990).   GAO

Beaumarchais, Pierre-Augustin Caron de (1732-99) French playwright. One of the most conspicuous and controversial public figures of his generation, Beaumarchais is best known for his first two Figaro plays, which were soon to reach an even wider public through the *operas of *Mozart and Rossini. However, his career as dramatist began with a series of *parades*—short, spicy sketches written for private performance— and in the very different genre of sentimental domestic drama in which he followed *Diderot's example with *Eugénie* (1767) and *Les Deux amis* (1770). The first Figaro play, *The Barber of Seville*, was a great success at the *Comédie-Française in 1775 with some rewriting after the first night; but *The Marriage of Figaro* was performed in 1784 only after battles with a series of censors extending over several years, and in the face of royal opposition. Advance publicity in the form of readings and private performance led to a wildly successful opening night at the Comédie-Française, the most notorious première of the century, which was followed by a record run of over 70 performances.

Though a lifelong critic of social abuses, Beaumarchais was no revolutionary: he was a self-made nobleman, and was to suffer exile and loss of civil rights during the revolution. The third play of the Figaro trilogy, *La Mère coupable* (*Marais Theatre, 1792), shows an older and more disillusioned Beaumarchais. It reverts to the manner of his early *drames *bourgeois*, but it bears the imprint of *melodrama in the *villain Bégearss who must be driven out of decent society. Figaro, now middle-aged and sententious, does some smart detective work, and achieves this result. A revival at the Comédie-Française in 1797 brought Beaumarchais the final triumph of an onstage reception in front of an enthusiastic *audience.   WDH

Beaumont, Francis (*c.*1584–1616) English dramatist, best known for his collaboration with *Fletcher: a Folio collection of their work in 1647 made 'Beaumont-and-Fletcher' a cultural fixture, though Beaumont had a hand in no more than ten plays (compared with more than 50 by Fletcher). Already an established poet, Beaumont began as the sole playwright of two sharp, satirical *comedies for the London *boy companies: *The Woman Hater* (1606) contains a *parody of Shakespeare's *Hamlet*, and *The Knight of the Burning Pestle* (1607) comprehensively spoofs plebeian preferences when members of the *audience take over the performance and replace the billed play with their own choice.

The partnership with Fletcher began in 1609, and produced a run of plays, mainly for the King's Men (*see* CHAMBERLAIN'S MEN, LORD), of which *The Maid's Tragedy* (1611) and the *tragicomedies *Philaster* (1609) and *A King and No King* (1611) are the most significant. The plays are noted for their romantic tone, remote settings, and strong emotional scenes, but also for an interest in the limits on the power of absolute monarchy. Beaumont was the senior collaborator and responsible for the plays' final form. Their last work together was *The Scornful Lady* (1613), a comedy popular into the eighteenth century. Earlier in 1613 he scripted a *masque for Princess Elizabeth's wedding, but thereafter gave up writing for the theatre, possibly as a result of his marriage to the heiress Ursula Isley.

The Maid's Tragedy proved Beaumont's most durable stage work: it was frequently revived until the 1740s, latterly with music by Henry Purcell,

it also saw through the Victorian era in an adaptation, *The Bridal*, a vehicle for *Macready. In the twentieth century both it and *The Knight of the Burning Pestle* received intermittent professional productions.   MJW

Beaumont, Hugh (1908–73) Welsh *producer, who worked for H. M. Tennent management company from 1936 and became managing director in 1941. 'Binkie' Beaumont dominated London theatre for twenty years, famous for lavish productions, star casts, and glamorous settings. But he also produced serious work, including *Priestley's *They Came to a City* (1943), *Rattigan's *The Deep Blue Sea* (1952), and *Whiting's *Marching Song* (1954), knowing precisely how far to test the limits of middle-class taste. One of his shrewdest moves was to exploit a loophole that exempted 'partly educational' productions from the entertainment tax, by setting up a non-profit subsidiary for classics and new work, including the British première of *Williams's *A Streetcar Named Desire* in 1949. Unfounded allegations of a 'gay mafia' dogged Beaumont's reputation. His empire went into decline in the late 1950s, though he remained on the board of the *National Theatre throughout the 1960s.   DR

Beck, Julian (1925–85) American designer, director, actor, and activist. He began his artistic life as a painter in the abstract expressionist school and exhibited at the Peggy Guggenheim gallery. In 1947 he founded the *Living Theatre with his wife Judith *Malina. Under their artistic direction the company was instrumental in the development of *Off-Broadway in the 1950s, promoting new American and European drama. In the 1960s and 1970s Beck's work combined a radical politics of anarchism and pacifism with processes of *collective creation. He performed in and designed the scenery for the Living Theatre productions of *Mysteries and Smaller Pieces* (1964), *Frankenstein* (1965), *Antigone* (1967), and *Paradise Now* (1968), which were presented throughout Europe and the USA. His theoretical and biographical text *The Life of the Theatre* (1972) sets forth his political and aesthetic concerns, which he viewed as symbiotic. In the later years of his life, while suffering from cancer, Beck played in several Hollywood feature films such as *Poltergeist II: The Other Side* (1986) and *The Cotton Club* (1984), and television series such as *Miami Vice* (1984).   MDC

Beckett, Samuel (1906–89) Irish writer, one of the major innovators of modernist drama and fiction. Born on Good Friday 13 April into a middle-class Protestant family on the outskirts of

Dublin, Beckett attended Trinity College, Dublin, and taught English at the École Normale Supérieure in Paris (1928–30), where he first met James Joyce. Returning to Dublin, he taught briefly at Trinity, lived in London, and eventually settled in Paris in 1937. During the Second World War he was involved in the French Resistance; when their cell was infiltrated, he and his future wife fled Paris for Roussillon in southern France, where they stayed until the Liberation. His return to Paris initiated a particularly creative period during which he wrote in French a trilogy of novels, *Molloy*, *Malone Dies*, *The Unnamable*, and two plays, *Eleuthéria*, begun in 1947, and *En attendant Godot* (*Waiting for Godot*), begun in 1948. Both plays were submitted to the actor and director Roger *Blin, who chose to produce *Godot*, partly because it had a smaller cast and simpler set. It opened at the Théâtre de Babylone in Montparnasse in January 1953. With these early works Beckett began the practice of translating his own work from French to English (and in reverse when he wrote originally in English).

For *Godot* Beckett developed a radical *dramaturgy, linked thematically to the theatre of the *absurd, focusing on a formally conceived visual image and a tight, non-linear rhythmic structure. *Godot* re-creates on stage the experience of waiting, using *comedy, *metatheatrical commentary, and popular entertainment references to present theatre and life as passing time, diversionary tactics to keep the void at bay. The bare stage, apart from tree and mound, foregrounds the shifting relationships of power and dependency between the tramps Vladimir and Estragon, the landowner Pozzo and his servant Lucky, the mysterious Boy, and the eponymous Godot who fails to appear. The work initially baffled and scandalized *audiences and critics but became one of the most critically acclaimed plays of the twentieth century and undoubtedly Beckett's best-known work. After *Waiting for Godot* opened in London (directed by Peter *Hall, 1955), *Tynan remarked: 'It forced me to re-examine the rules which have hitherto governed the drama; and, having done so, to pronounce them not elastic enough.'

Fin de partie (*Endgame*) was performed in French at the *Royal Court in 1957, directed by Blin. Alan *Schneider directed the English-language première in New York in 1958. Like the terminal chess moves its title refers to, *Endgame* presents the last stages of the relationship between the *protagonist and storyteller Hamm, his factotum and son substitute Clov, and Hamm's parents Nagg and Nell who, having lost their shanks, are kept in ash cans. Conceived, like *Godot*, within a decade of the Second World War,

and set in a shelter after some devastation has apparently destroyed all life beyond its walls, *Endgame* embodies the anxieties of its era: it presents a history and a language in ruins, and yet the performance of daily life and the consciousness of the performance called life continue until the last moment.

The next two plays were written first in English. *Krapp's Last Tape* (1958) shows an old man on his 69th birthday listening to the voice of his past selves in a series of tape recordings made on previous birthdays; *Happy Days* (1962) features Beckett's first leading female *character, Winnie, buried up to her waist in a mound of earth. Since the visual image and rhythmic structure of his work are as important as the spoken text, from 1966 to 1984 Beckett directed productions of his plays in London, Paris, and Berlin in order to supervise the *mise-en-scène and the actors.

Beckett also relied on a handful of directors who worked with or consulted him, including Blin, Schneider, Donald McWhinnie and George *Devine in England, Pierre Chabert in France, and Antoni Libera in Poland. Beckett also worked regularly with particular actors, including Jack *MacGowran, Patrick Magee, Billie *Whitelaw, and David Warrilow. Although flexible with directors he admired, Beckett objected to certain productions of his plays which departed from his stage directions, including the 1984 production of *Endgame* for the *American Repertory Theatre which the director JoAnne *Akalaitis set in an abandoned subway station (see *also* COPYRIGHT; DIRECTING). In 1991 Dublin's Gate Theatre produced all nineteen of Beckett's stage plays in a festival which *toured to New York (1996) and London (1999).

Beckett's stage works from *Play* (1963) onwards are shorter and meticulously structured. Most of them open in darkness, against which an image emerges, defined by light. The visual focus is almost entirely on the body or body fragments, such as the three heads above urns in *Play* or the suspended Mouth spewing words uncontrollably while observed by a silent, cloaked Auditor in *Not I* (1972). There is little *action, as the drama is interiorized, becoming the scene of a fragmented consciousness struggling with the detritus of body, language, memory, and history. These late plays, including *Come and Go* (1966), *Footfalls* (1976), *Rockaby* (1981), *Ohio Impromptu* (1981), and *Catastrophe* (1982), focus intently on modes of perception, on the efforts to see, hear, and comprehend on the part of character and audience.

Beckett's experiments with the possibilities of sound and camera came at an influential time in the development of his own aesthetic. Between 1957 and 1972 he wrote six radio plays: *All That Fall*, *Embers*, *Cascando*, *Words and Music*, *Rough for Radio I* and *II*. Following his one generically titled *Film* (directed by Schneider, 1964)—which uses the camera's eye as agent of self-perception pursuing the fleeing figure of Buster Keaton—Beckett turned to television, investigating the possibilities of space, structure, and the role of the camera in the BBC productions *Eh Joe* (1966), *Ghost Trio*, and *…but the clouds…* (1977); and the German productions of *Quad I* and *II* (1981) and *Nacht und Traüme* (1983). He adapted his last stage play, *What Where* (1983), for German TV in 1985.

Beckett won the Nobel Prize for Literature in 1969. Sometimes described as spanning the aesthetics of European modernism and postmodernism, he rigorously revised the materials and structures of both traditional and new media in the Sisyphean task of telling, as he put it in a title, 'how it is'.   AEM

Becque, Henri (1837–99) French dramatist. Championed by *Zola, Becque fell between two *dramaturgical movements, the *realism of the *well-made play and slice-of-life *naturalism. His life was characterized by money worries, a theme which runs through his brief output, which presents a rapacious and amoral picture of middle-class French society. His early play *Michel Pauper* (1870) revealed him as a committed socialist, while *La Navette* (1878) depicted a woman with three lovers. The first of his 'rough' or bitter plays (*comédies rosses*), *Les Corbeaux* (*Comédie-Française, 1882), is a harsh and cynical drama of money and class in which greed conquers all. *La Parisienne* (1885), which starred *Réjane, shows a Parisian woman's web of relationships with her husband and two lovers: a woman's sexual life is an economic instrument based on ownership and return on investment. It entered the repertoire of the Comédie-Française in 1890, but was followed only by a series of sketches, an unfinished work (*Les Polichinelles*), and Becque's memoirs (1895).   BRS

Beeston, Christopher (*c*.1580–1639) English actor and *manager. Beeston began his career as an actor, appearing with the Lord *Chamberlain's Men in *Jonson's *Every Man in his Humour* (1598). Between 1603 and 1619 he was an actor and sometime business manager of Queen Anne's Men at the *Rose. In 1617 he built the Phoenix Playhouse, where he housed a series of companies: Queen Anne's (1617–19), Prince Charles's (1619–22), Lady Elizabeth's (1622–5), Queen

Henrietta's (1625–37), and the King and Queen's Young Company or Beeston's Boys (1637–42). He was succeeded at his death by his son William Beeston.   RWV

Behan, Brendan (1923–64) Irish playwright. From a strongly Irish Republican background, he was imprisoned for political offences as a teenager in Britain, an experience recorded in his memoir *Borstal Boy* (1958), and later in Ireland, where he began to write both in English and in Irish. His first play, *The Quare Fellow*, produced by the tiny Pike Theatre in Dublin in 1954, after it had been rejected by the *Abbey, shows a day in the life of a prison on the eve of an execution. The freshness of the writing, the unfamiliarity of the subject, and the fierceness of the play's attack on capital punishment attracted the attention of *Littlewood, who staged it with her *Theatre Workshop (London, 1956). Littlewood's 1958 production of his other major play, *The Hostage*, a translated adaptation of the Irish-language version *An Giall*, brought Behan an international reputation, much influenced by the Workshop's *Brechtian style of ensemble *improvisation. Behan's later years were given over to drunken self-publicizing, and he never completed his last play, *Richard's Cork Leg*.   NG

Behn, Aphra (1640–89) English playwright and novelist. Reputed to be the first woman to earn a living by her pen, details about Behn's life are notoriously unreliable. She was a prolific playwright with at least nineteen plays produced during her lifetime and two more produced posthumously. The first, *The Forc'd Marriage* (1670), was performed by *Davenant's Duke's Company, which then produced sixteen more. Behn's most popular *comedy, *The Rover* (1677), was frequently revived, with Elizabeth *Barry playing the spirited Hellena, a young woman determined to fulfil her own social and sexual destiny. Behn wrote at least seven parts for Barry which challenge patriarchal authority, particularly in the realm of love and marriage. Behn was frequently accused of immorality, a charge she defended in her preface to *The Lucky Chance* (1686), vehemently insisting on her rights as a writing woman. The topicality of her plays and her royalist politics attracted fierce criticism but she continued to be commercially successful. Feminist criticism has done much to restore Behn's work to the contemporary stage. *Barton's production of *The Rover* for the *Royal Shakespeare Company (*Swan Theatre, 1986) was the first of many revivals.   GBB

Behrman, S. N. (Samuel Nathaniel) (1893–1973) American playwright. From the *Theatre

Guild's production of *The Second Man* in 1927 until his last play, *But for Whom Charlie* in 1964, Behrman held a place with serious, humane, and sophisticated New York *comedies. The author of twenty-six plays or adaptations and one *musical (*Fanny*, with Harold Rome, 1954), Behrman was highly esteemed by critics of his era, though quickly forgotten in the upheavals of the 1960s. His greatest productivity was in the 1930s, when he faced a special challenge writing social comedy in an era of world economic depression and preparations for war. Major plays of the period revolve around a charming and witty woman contested for by pompous businessmen, fascist sympathizers, idealistic Marxists, and cynical aesthetes. Behrman's plays include *Biography* (1932), *Rain from Heaven* (1934), *End of Summer* (1936), and *No Time for Comedy* (1939).   MAF

Beier, Karin (1965–) German director. Beier began directing while still a student at the University of Cologne, where she founded the group Countercheck Quarrelsome in 1986, producing radically modernized versions of nine Shakespeare plays in English. In 1990 she was appointed assistant director at the Düsseldorf Schauspielhaus. Her breakthrough came in 1993 with a production of *Romeo and Juliet* which was invited to the Berlin *Theatertreffen. Beier's most renowned production is *A Midsummer Night's Dream* (Düsseldorf, 1995), with actors from nine European countries, all speaking their own languages. Designed to demonstrate both Shakespeare as a 'European' author and the possibility of multilingual theatre, it was followed in 1997 by a multilingual version of *The Tempest* in Cologne. In 2007 she became director of the Frankfurt Schauspielhaus. Although best known for Shakespeare, Beier has directed a wide range in both the classical and modern repertoire, including Bizet's *Carmen*.   CBB

Beijing opera *See* JINGJU.

Béjart family Seventeenth-century French actors inextricably linked with *Molière. **Madeleine** (1618–72) was the guiding spirit of the ragtag Parisian troupe that willed itself into existence in 1643 under the name L'Illustre Théâtre; Jean-Baptiste Poquelin, not yet known as Molière, four years her junior and her presumed lover, was one of three actors who rotated the assignment of the *hero, while Madeleine had the contractual right to play any role she chose. She was by all accounts a powerful actress, a talented writer, a free spirit, and a shrewd businesswoman, and after the troupe failed in Paris she held it together through a thirteen-year exile in the

provinces. By the time they returned to the capital her age was beginning to limit the range of roles the *audience would accept; still, Molière wrote for her such formidable *characters as Dorine in *Tartuffe* and Uranie in *The Critique of the School for Wives*, and he may well have intended Philaminte in *The Learned Ladies* for her. She died before it opened, one year to the day before Molière's death.

Madeleine's brother **Joseph** (1616–59) and sister **Geneviève** (1624–75) were also founding members of the troupe, while **Louis** (1630–78) joined during the provincial years. Joseph played romantic leads, despite his stammer; he died a few months after the troupe returned to Paris, and *La Grange took over his roles. Louis's best feature was his pronounced limp, which was copied by actors playing roles he created and which made him a memorable Mme Pernelle in *Tartuffe*. He retired in 1670 to pursue a military career. **Geneviève**, acting under her mother's name of Hervé, is a mystery: she did almost nothing in the plays of Molière, but continued quietly to collect her pay for 32 years; perhaps she played *confidantes in *tragedy.

The youngest member of the clan was **Armande** (1642/3–1700), officially registered as their sister but believed at the time to be Madeleine's daughter. In any case, she married Molière and entered the troupe in 1662, and went on to create a number of youthful roles of considerable liveliness and charm. Her greatest part was Célimène opposite Molière's Alceste. She, along with La Grange, held the troupe together after Molière's death. She remarried four years later, to the actor Guérin d'Estriché (1636–1728).   RWH

Belasco, David (1853–1931) American *manager and director. The son of English immigrants who arrived during the gold rush, Belasco was born in San Francisco, playing occasional roles as a child. By 1871 he was *touring mining camps and towns. He served briefly as secretary and personal assistant to *Boucicault while in Nevada and was thereafter *stage manager in San Francisco where he began an association with *Herne and eventually caught the eye of the *Frohman brothers, who invited Belasco to New York as stage manager and dramatist (1882–4). His first solo play was the romantic melodrama *May Blossom* (1884). Two years later he wrote such hits as *The Charity Ball* and *Lord Chumley* with Henry C. DeMille.

Belasco's 1890 production of *The Heart of Maryland* started his career as an independent playwright-*director-*producer. Between 1895 and 1902 he produced a string of hits as well as a collection of new stars for the *Theatrical Syndicate. Among his biggest successes were his own *Zaza* (1899) and *Madame Butterfly* (1900). Belasco leased a *playhouse on 42nd Street in 1902, and for fourteen years successfully challenged the Syndicate by writing, directing, and producing spectacular shows. In 1907 he built a remarkable venue on 44th Street, writing and producing more than three dozen hits, including his own *The Girl of the Golden West* (1905) and Eugene Walter's *The Easiest Way* (1909). For his 1912 production of Bradley's *The Governor's Lady*, Belasco built an exact replica of the dining room in Child's Restaurant in New York. Belasco became the premier director in America, writing or adapting in excess of 100 plays and producing hundreds more. As a director he was renowned for his adherence to scenic *realism and attention to the smallest details. Innovations in *lighting and *scenography were his hallmarks. His plays were among the most spectacular ever staged—and two quickly became the basis for *operas by *Puccini, *Madama Butterfly* (1904) and *La fanciulla del West* (1910). Belasco created a stable of stars, presaging the film industry, carefully crafting their professional personae through manipulation of publicity.   PAD

Belbel, Sergi (1963-) Spanish-Catalan playwright, director, and film scenarist. A major contributor to the resurgence of theatre in Barcelona in the post-Franco democracy, he quickly gained attention with his irreverent plays that challenged conventional structure and *dialogue. *Caresses* (1991) has been widely staged in Europe and Latin America and was filmed by Ventura Pons in 1999. *After the Rain* (1993), his most popular play, was staged at London's Gate Theatre in 1996 and a production in Paris received the Mollère Prize for the best comic play of 1999. *Blood* (1999) was a startling depiction of mindless terrorist brutality. Belbel has directed plays by *Beckett, *Mamet, *Benet i Jornet, *Müller, and *Koltès. He was appointed artistic director of Catalonia's National Theatre in 2006.   MPH

Bel Geddes, Norman (1893–1958) American designer of stage sets, trains, and automobiles. A leader in the 1920s streamlining movement, his modernist theatre work was typified by steps, ramps, and platforms arranged to create the *illusion of solid material as a sculpted mass. His most ambitious work—such as a monumental 1921 design for Dante's *The Divine Comedy*—was unrealized. An exception was his 1924 design for *Reinhardt's New York production of *The Miracle*. Bel Geddes built over the seating area and expanded the stage to the building's rear wall to convert a Broadway *playhouse into a Gothic cathedral. His *scenography was reminiscent of *Appia but imagined on a far larger scale, though much of his realized work was *realist scenery for Broadway productions. His set for *Kingsley's *Dead End* (1935), with its detailed building exteriors and the illusion of the East River into which actors dived and swam, came to epitomize American *naturalism.   MAF

Bell, John (1940-) Australian actor and director, leader of the Bell Shakespeare Company, which from 1991 toured the country with energetic and distinctively Australian productions of Shakespeare. In the 1970s Bell was part of the nationalist theatre revival. He co-founded the Nimrod Theatre in Sydney, promoted the work of David *Williamson, and helped make popular a larrikin, irreverent, Australian theatre, epitomized in the anti-*realistic, *revue-based *Legend of King O'Malley* (1970) which he directed. As an actor Bell is compelling and intelligent with a powerful ability to convince.   EJS

Bellamy, George Ann (c.1727–88) Irish actress, famous onstage and infamous off. Praised by *Quin after a triumphant *Covent Garden debut as Monimia in *Otway's *The Orphan*, by the middle of the next decade she received as much attention for her gaming, love affairs, and *playhouse squabbles as for her *acting. Very beautiful, with a plaintive voice and expressive face, and blessed with an ability to cry easily, she was best suited for pathetic roles such as Indiana in *Steele's *The Conscious Lovers*, Cordelia (in *Tate's version of *Lear*), Lady Randolph in John Home's *Douglas*, and Imoinda in *Oroonoko*. She was criticized for Lady Macbeth opposite *Barry; neither had the necessary vocal or emotional range. Hard living took its toll: by 31 she looked old, and despite a number of rich lovers, died poor.   MJK

Belleroche See POISSON, RAYMOND.

Bellotti-Bon, Luigi (1820–83) Italian *actor-manager and playwright. Trained in *commedia dell'arte* by his stepfather, the actor and playwright F. A. Bon, he became known as a courtly performer with a quick wit in *improvisation. Through his experience in the 1840s and 1850s with various companies—*Modena, the Reale Sarda, and *Ristori (who was his cousin)—he became concerned about the lack of a modern Italian repertory. As actor-manager of the Bellotti-Bon company (1859–73), he commissioned over 70 new plays from prominent authors such as

*Ferrari, *Giacometti, and *Giacosa. These Italian works were produced lavishly with fine actors under his meticulous direction. Due in great part to his efforts, Italian theatre from 1860 to 1870 enjoyed a period of prosperity despite the upheavals of the Risorgimento. In expanding to three companies in 1873, he met with artistic difficulties, and a financial shortfall drove him to suicide. JEH

Bemba, Sylvain (1934–95) Francophone Congolese novelist and dramatist who became head of the Division of Culture of the Ministry of Information of Zaire in 1973. His writing for the stage began with radio competition plays such as *Hell Is Orpheus* (1970) and stage plays like *The Man Who Killed the Crocodile* (1973). His work is full of irony created through the distancing technique of the figure of the public entertainer, the buffoon who comments on political events. *Black Tarantula and White Devil* (1976) explores psychological dislocation connected with the slave trade, while *A Bloody Awful World for a Too Honest Laundryman* (1979) shows the plight of urban communities. One of his last plays, *The Posthumous Nuptials of Santigone*, is a variation on the Antigone theme. Visual elements are strong in Bemba's work, sometimes relegating his parodic intentions to second place. PNN/trans. JCM

Ben-Ami, Jacob (1890–1977) Yiddish playwright, born in Minsk, Belarus. He joined the Hirshbein Troupe in Odessa, worked with the Vilna Troupe, and in 1912 settled in New York. In 1917 he joined Maurice Schwartz's theatre but left to found the Jewish Art Theatre (1919–20), a Yiddish company that opposed the star system and was committed to sophisticated scripts and ensemble *acting. In 1920 Ben-Ami began a successful English-language career associated with *Le Gallienne's Civic Repertory Theatre and the *Theatre Guild. On Broadway he starred in *Samson and Delilah* (1920), *Welded* (1924), *Evening Song* (1934), and *The Tenth Man* (1959); in Yiddish, he performed in numerous plays by *Asch, David Pinski, *Gordin, and *Aleichem. *See* DIASPORA. EN

Benavente, Jacinto (1866–1954) Spanish playwright, recipient of the Nobel Prize (1922). For more than four decades his plays were prominently staged in Spain and Latin America, and several reached Broadway and the West End. His complex female *characters were performed by *Guerrero, *Xirgu, and other renowned Spanish actresses. Although his popularity is often attributed to plays with characters of privilege speaking elegant *dialogue, he wrote effectively in a variety

of styles from *symbolism and fantasy to *naturalism and *melodrama. One of his most enduring plays, *Witches' Sabbath* (1903), was written early in his career; his international fame derived from *The Bonds of Interest* (1907), with characters based on *commedia dell'arte prototypes, and *The Passion Flower* (1913), a stark rural *tragedy. In *The Night Aglow* (1927) filmmaking is integral to the plot, and actors impersonate well-known personalities of the silent era. His professional standing enabled him to resume his career under the Franco dictatorship but his later plays were staged only in Spain and dismissed abroad. MPH

Ben Ayed, Ali (1930–72) Tunisian actor, director, and *manager who was central to the establishment of modern theatre in the country. In 1962 he was named manager of the Tunisian National Theatre, the only institutional professional theatre. A disciple of *Vilar, Ben Ayed used the post to reform practice in Tunisia by selecting the best texts, establishing an aesthetic approach, and creating a compatible team of fellow workers. He expanded the company's work beyond Tunis by national *tours, and transformed production in the mode of European modernism through functional use of *lighting, suggestive *scenography, and stylized *acting. He varied classic and contemporary European plays (*Sophocles, Shakespeare, *Molière, *Goldoni, *García Lorca, *Camus) with those by Arab and Tunisian playwrights (including Izzedine *Madani's *Revolt of the Man on the Ass*, 1970). MMe

Bene, Carmelo (1937–2002) Italian actor, director, and playwright. After his debut in 1959 in *Camus's *Caligula*, he directed his own work *The Mayakovsky Show* (1960), and thereafter made a reputation for subversive, provocative, and often outrageous adaptations of Shakespeare (*Hamlet*, 1975; *Romeo and Juliet*, 1976; *Richard III*, 1977), *Wilde, *Marlowe, and others. His purpose was to create an anti-establishment theatre that questioned traditional repertories, theatrical rules, and the idea of authorship. In *Romeo and Juliet*, for example, Mercutio refused to die. Bene moved towards a negative, almost nihilistic concept of the theatre, going so far as to picture a theatre without spectators, where the actor was a lonely and destructive presence, a mere acting machine. His *Manfred* (1989, from *Byron), *Egmont* (1990, from *Goethe), and *Hamlet Suite* (1994, from Laforgue) were examples of Bene's unorthodox and deconstructive view. *See also* CRUELTY, THEATRE OF. DMCM

benefit performance A special performance intended to benefit financially a playwright, actor, theatrical employee, or philanthropic cause. In English theatre it appears to have been used first in 1681, and Elizabeth *Barry the first performer to have been given the right to an annual benefit in 1686, on the grounds of her immense popularity. Originally such occasions arose in response to special needs. Theatre managements allowed actors in their companies or their families who found themselves in straitened circumstances to solicit public support. By the end of the eighteenth century, however, the system of annual benefits for all members of the theatre, including its minor functionaries, became part of the regular season. It was much vilified on the grounds that *managers were able to depress performers' salaries by the promise of a benefit, and that it forced performers and others who hoped to augment their meagre incomes to become virtual beggars in soliciting *audiences. Nevertheless the system whereby performers and managers negotiated a share of the gross proceeds persisted throughout the nineteenth century, and benefit performances to assist charities have endured into the twenty-first century.   VEE

Benelli, Sem (1877–1949) Italian poet, playwright, and screenwriter. After *La Trignola* (1908), a *naturalistic play with existential overtones, Benelli attempted to break with the *realistic tradition and experimented with verse, writing a series of historical *tragedies that inspired many imitators: *La cena delle beffe* (1909) and *The Love of Three Kings* (1910). The first of these, translated as *The Jest*, a drama of *character and intrigue set in fifteenth-century Florence, served as a vehicle for *Bernhardt in Paris and John *Barrymore in New York. Benelli returned to prose in later plays: *The Spider* (1935), *L'Elefante* (1937), and *L'Orchidea* (1938).   JEH

Benet i Jornet, Josep M. (1940–) Spanish-Catalan playwright and screenwriter. A leading figure in the post-Franco resurgence of theatre in Barcelona, he writes exclusively in Catalan; but Spanish translations have been staged regularly and several plays have been performed abroad. *The Disappearance of Wendy* (1977), *Description of a Landscape* (1979), and *Witches' Revolt* (1980) focused critical attention on his work. *Legacy*, first staged in 1996 at the Teatro Nacional María Guerrero, and then directed by *Belbel for the 1997 Festival Grec in Barcelona, was one of his major successes and was filmed as *Friend/Lover* by Ventura Pons. *Smells* (2000) completed

a trilogy about a decrepit neighbourhood in Barcelona that he had begun in 1964.   MPH

Bennett, Alan (1934–) English playwright, actor, and director. He co-wrote and performed in *Beyond the Fringe* (1960), a *revue that also featured Peter Cook, Dudley Moore, and Jonathan *Miller. Its innovative *satire on English life, institutions, and rhetoric established the concerns and style of Bennett's subsequent work. *Forty Years On* (1968) maintains a revue format, while *Getting On* (1971) and *Habeas Corpus* (1973) are elegiac *comedies that pitch the decline of their male *protagonists against the decline of England. *The Old Country* (1977) addresses similar concerns through the nostalgia of an English defector to the Soviet Union, returned to in his television play about the spy Guy Burgess, *An Englishman Abroad* (1983). Bennett's later work maintains a distinctive comic relish of everyday cliché and an interest in versions of Englishness. *Talking Heads* (1987) is a series of bitter-sweet *monologues for television, the screenplays *A Private Function* (1984), and *Prick up your Ears* (1987) are studies in provincial repression and rebellion. Wider cultural and historical concerns are exhibited in *Kafka's Dick* (1986), *The Insurance Man* (1986), and *The Madness of George III* (1991; film, 1994). *The History Boys* (2004; film, 2006) returned to the themes of education and Englishness.   SF

Bennett, Arnold (1867–1931) English writer. Best known as a social novelist, Bennett also had some success in London with romantic *comedies (*Cupid and Common Sense*, 1908), and social dramas (*The Great Adventure*, 1911, adapted from his novel *Buried Alive*). In collaboration with Edward Knoblock he wrote *Milestones* (1912), which starred the popular *Ainley and ran for 607 performances. After the war he wrote two plays on metaphysical questions, *Sacred and Profane Love* (1919, adapted from his novel) and *Body and Soul* (1922). He had more success with *Mr Prohack* (1927), a social drama co-written with Knoblock that starred *Laughton.   TP

Bennett, Michael (1943–87) American choreographer and director. A self-described Broadway 'gypsy', Bennett began his career as a show *dancer in the 1960s. His early choreography earned him a series of Tony nominations culminating in *Follies* (1971), the ambitious *Sondheim *musical that also marked Bennett's debut as a director. In 1974 Bennett began supervising a workshop to create a new musical based on the professional experiences of a group of New York-based gypsies. Though attribution for the book of

A Chorus Line remains in dispute, Bennett is credited with guiding its development and contributing a cinematic look to the staging and the choreography. *A Chorus Line* (1975) was among the most successful musicals of the American stage, running on Broadway for fifteen years and earning nine Tony awards, including Bennett's for best direction and best choreography. His career continued to flourish with *Dreamgirls* (1981). LTC

Benois, Alexandre (1870–1960) Russian artist, designer, and director. Benois made his design debut in 1902 with *Wagner's Twilight of the Gods*. His first major success was *Le Pavillon d'Armide* (St Petersburg, 1907) for which he also wrote the *scenario, staged by *Diaghilev in Paris in 1909, becoming a key work in the *Ballets Russes repertoire. Benois's trademark was historical detail; in this last case, precise evocation of the age of Versailles. In 1909 Benois became *artistic director of the *Moscow Art Theatre where, working closely with *Stanislavsky, he directed and designed productions of plays by *Molière, *Goldoni, and *Pushkin (1913–15). Closely associated with the 'World of Art' movement and Diaghilev, Benois's career peaked in 1911, which saw the Paris production of Stravinsky's *Petrushka* with designs by Benois derived from Russian folk art. He emigrated to France in 1926 and worked in Paris, Monte Carlo, and at La Scala in Milan. NW

Benson, Frank (1858–1939) English actor and *manager. Most of Benson's career was spent outside London, either performing Shakespeare in Stratford-upon-Avon during the summers from 1886 to 1919 (except for two years during the First World War) or *touring the country during the other months. He also took companies to the United States, Canada, and South Africa. Over the years he performed all of Shakespeare's plays except *Titus Andronicus* and *Troilus and Cressida*. Although Benson brought his productions to London on several occasions for short runs, he never established himself there, though many of the actors he trained became featured performers in the capital. He was an athletic actor, blessed with noble features that served him well in roles such as Henry V and Richard II, but his sometimes awkward gestures and sing-song voice hindered his style. His wife Constance acted in his companies and helped with management. TP

Benthall, Michael (1919–74) English director. His *expressionist *King John* (1948) at the *Shakespeare Memorial Theatre was influenced by his partner *Helpmann's *ballet *Adam Zero* (1946), for which he wrote the *scenario; Benthall's other vivid Stratford productions included *Hamlet* (1948), *Cymbeline* (1949), and *The Tempest* (1951–2). As director of the *Old Vic between 1953 and 1962, he reclaimed the company from financial and artistic decline during his project (1953–8) to present all the plays of Shakespeare's First Folio. His policies provided significant opportunities in *repertory theatre for young performers such as *Neville and *Dench, while star players such as *Gielgud and Katharine Hepburn were also accommodated within the company's work in London and on a series of high-profile overseas *tours. His non-Shakespearian work included *The White Devil* (1947), *The Millionairess* (1952), *The Importance of Being Earnest* (1959), and *Man and Boy* (1963). He also directed a number of *operas, including *Turandot* (1947) and *Queen of Spades* (1950) at *Covent Garden. VRS

Bentley, Eric (1916–) Anglo-American critic, translator, and playwright who introduced *Brecht to America. Bentley worked with Brecht in Los Angeles in the 1940s, and directed his translation of *The Good Person of Setzuan* in New York (1956). He preferred the theatre of commitment (in a book of that title, 1967) that engaged politics with theatre. Viewed alternatively as elitist and pioneering, Bentley's highly influential criticism includes *In Search of Theatre* (1957), *The Life of the Drama* (1965), and translations of *Pirandello and *Büchner, as well as extensive translations of Brecht. Drama critic of the *New Republic* from 1952 to 1956, Bentley 'retired' to playwriting. His plays portray historical subjects battling oppressive institutions, and include *Are You Now or Have You Ever Been…?* (1972), *The Recantation of Galileo Galilei* (1973), and *Lord Alfred's Lover* (1979). GAO

Berain, Jean (1637–1711) French designer. Berain was appointed *scenographer to Louis XIV in 1674, responsible for *costumes and scenery for court entertainments, weddings, and state funerals. Working with Carlo *Vigarani, he was in charge of costumes for *Thésée* (1675), *Atys* (1676), and *Isis* (1677) by *Lully and *Quinault, all first performed at Saint-Germain-en-Laye. In 1680 Berain succeeded Vigarani as designer for the Opéra in Paris, being followed in turn by his son Jean Berain II (1678–1726). WDH

Bérard, Christian (1902–49) French *scenographer. An accomplished painter, Bérard became celebrated during the 1930s and 1940s for designs for *ballet, *opera, and theatre, as well as for Parisian fashion. After his first ballet work for *Fokine and *Diaghilev he became resident designer at the Théâtre de l'Athénée, embarking on a significant and long-standing collaboration with *Jouvet, for whom he designed several groundbreaking productions including *Cocteau's *La Machine infernale* (1934) and *Giraudoux's *The Madwoman of Chaillot* (1945). Their celebrated version of *The School for Wives* (1936), with a three-dimensional scenic transformation that moved from a Louis XIV interior to a garden exterior amid the overarching theatricality of overhead chandeliers—like those found in a seventeenth-century French *playhouse—was said to have revolutionized the staging of *Molière. DGM

Berghaus, Ruth (1927–96) German director. Initially trained as a *dancer and choreographer at the Palucca-Schule in Dresden, Berghaus began working as a director in the 1950s. In 1954 she married the composer Paul Dessau, whose works she also directed. She was appointed director-in-residence at the *Berliner Ensemble in 1964 and brought out a number of highly acclaimed productions, including *Weiss's *Vietnam Discourse* (1968), *Brecht's *In the Jungle of Cities* (1971), and *Müller's *Cement* (1973). From 1971 to 1977 she was *artistic director of the Berliner Ensemble. After 1977 she attained an international reputation as a director of *opera with acclaimed productions in Frankfurt (*Wagner's *Ring*, 1985–7), Hamburg (*Tristan and Isolde*, 1988), and Brussels (Alban Berg's *Lulu*, 1988). Berghaus's productions were renowned for their visual quality and choreographic staging of both singers and actors. CBB

Berghof, Herbert (1909–90) Austrian-American actor, director, and teacher. Trained in Vienna, he also studied with *Reinhardt and eventually moved to New York, working with *Strasberg and becoming a charter member of the *Actors Studio. From the early 1940s Berghof appeared in various plays and revivals in his adopted country, including *Ibsen's *The Lady from the Sea* (1950); he played the accused Confederate prison-camp officer in Saul Levitt's *The Andersonville Trial* (1959). His film appearances include *Five Fingers* (1952) and *Cleopatra* (1963). Among his directorial credits, Berghof staged the first Broadway production of *Beckett's *Waiting for Godot* (1956). He is perhaps best remembered as an *acting teacher, founding the Herbert Berghof Studio in 1945, which he directed with his wife Uta *Hagen. EW

Bergman, Ingmar (1918–2007) Swedish director. In his films Bergman probed complex patterns of human interaction, often reaching into the darkest recesses of human experience, as in *Cries and Whispers* (1972). He has also explored man's sense of alienation from God, as in *Winter Light* (1962), and the emptiness of a life without overall meaning, as in *Through a Glass Darkly* (1961). In his final film, *Fanny and Alexander* (1982), however, the action concludes with a joyful celebration of art triumphing over darkness and despair. Bergman tended to rely on the same group of trusted actors and his theatre work was distinguished by the passion for clarity and simplicity of technique that characterize his films. He repeatedly returned to *Molière, *Ibsen, and *Strindberg, and was long associated with *Dramaten. His seminal productions of *The Misanthrope* (1973), *Hedda Gabler* (1964), *The Wild Duck* (1972), *A Dream Play* (1970), and *The Ghost Sonata* (1973) were all marked by stripping away unnecessary visual detail to highlight the complex human issues addressed in the plays. During the 1980s Bergman directed disturbing minimalist productions of *King Lear* (1984) and *Hamlet* (1986), both of which showed a world in which all moral values had imploded in the face of anarchy and violence. DT

Bergner, Elisabeth (1897–1986) Austrian actress and director who settled in Berlin in 1922. She worked mainly for *Reinhardt at the *Deutsches Theater but also at the Staatstheater under *Fehling. Famous roles included Miss Julie, Portia, Queen Christina in *Strindberg's play, and Juliet. She quickly established herself as one of the leading actresses of her generation, distinguished by psychological subtlety and vocal finesse, in a wide range of roles in theatre and film. In 1933 she went into exile in London where she successfully continued her acting career; in 1942 she moved to New York, where she began to direct. She resumed her acting and directing career in Germany in 1954. Her final performance was in 1973 in London. CBB

Berkoff, Steven (1937–) English director, playwright, and actor who trained with *Lecoq. In 1968, after six years in *repertory theatre, he formed the London Theatre Group. Influenced by *Brecht, *Artaud, and the *Living Theatre, Berkoff celebrated the physical inventiveness and primal energy of the actor in productions such as *Agamemnon* (1973). Berkoff's plays chart the extremes of the human condition, revealing a sensuous love for the spoken word, juxtaposing London slang with Shakespearian-style verse. His adaptations from Kafka, Poe, and *Strindberg were followed by the quasi-autobiographical *East* (1975) and *West* (1980), savage critiques of the class system in *Decadence* (1981) and of the Falklands War in the *Sink the Belgrano* (1987), and the lyrical *The Secret Love Life of Ophelia* (2001). A theatrical iconoclast, Berkoff nonetheless directed *Salome* (1988) and *The Trial* (1991) at the *National Theatre. His solo performance, *Shakespeare's Villains* (1999) was still *touring in 2010, and he directed *Richard II* in 1994 and 2005. Stints as Hollywood *villains and (ironically) as Hitler in the television epic *War and Remembrance* (1986) bankrolled his own productions, enabling him to retain artistic independence. RVL

Berlin, Irving (1888–1989) American composer, lyricist, and performer. Berlin personified American popular song for more than 50 years. Born the son of a cantor in Russia, Berlin and family emigrated to New York where he wrote his first published song, 'Marie from Sunny Italy', in 1907. His career took off in 1911 with 'Alexander's Ragtime Band' and the First World War standard 'Oh! How I Hate to Get up in the Morning', which he performed on stage (and reprised during the Second World War). During the 1920s Berlin produced his own *revues and contributed songs for the *Marx Brothers' show *The Cocoanuts* (1925) and the *Ziegfeld Follies of 1927. As Thousands Cheer* (1933) was one of the last successful revues of the era, and *Top Hat* (1935) was one of the more popular Fred *Astaire films, with such hits as 'Cheek to Cheek' and 'Let's Face the Music and Dance'. Berlin's stage *musical *Louisiana Purchase* (1940) was a *satire of southern politics, which he followed with the patriotic revue *This Is the Army* (1942). In 1946 Berlin wrote one of the most successful Broadway musicals of all time, *Annie Get your Gun*, and had another hit with *Call Me Madam* (1950), both of which were movie successes. His last Broadway show was *Mr President* in 1962. SN

Berliner Ensemble Company founded in 1949 by *Brecht and *Weigel, originally as a group within the *Deutsches Theater, since 1954 at the Theater am Schiffbauerdamm. Under Brecht's guidance, the company developed a version of *epic theatre suited to the post-war situation. Triumphant *tours to Paris (1954–5) and London (1956) helped establish a style for performing Brecht's plays and practising such theoretical concepts as *Verfremdung; the production of *Mother Courage* attracted particular attention. Brecht also trained a cadre of young directors, including *Besson, *Palitzsch, and *Wekwerth.

After Brecht's death in 1956, the Ensemble became guided more by his model than his spirit of experimentation. The transition resulted in several famous productions, including Palitzsch and Wekwerth's *Arturo Ui* (1959), and *Coriolan*

directed by Wekwerth and Joachim Tenschert (1964). The Ensemble toured these and other productions around the world in the 1960s and 1970s, although it reached North America only in 1986 with a visit to Toronto. By the late 1960s, however, the company was in danger of becoming a stylistic showcase. *Berghaus, its director after Weigel's death in 1971, resisted this tendency, but several of her projects angered the East German authorities and Brecht's stylistically conservative daughter, who controlled German-language production rights. Berghaus was replaced by Wekwerth in 1976.

The collapse of East Germany in 1990 prompted re-evaluation. Wekwerth was replaced in 1992 by a band of five directors, though by 1995 only *Müller remained. Müller's sudden death caused disarray; the old company was replaced and *Peymann took over the Ensemble in 1999. Under Peymann, the Ensemble became Berlin's most visited theatre, and Brecht's plays remain a significant part of the repertory. JR

Berman, Sabina (1953–) Mexican playwright, director, poet, novelist, and screenwriter. Berman belongs to a generation of writers who grew up during 'the crisis', a protracted period of political and economic instability and corruption which bred a deeply cynical view of the country's leadership and moral values. Its imprint is everywhere evident in Berman's work: in the trio of estranged youths who inhabit an abandoned apartment building in *Sudden Death* (1989); in *Krisis* (1996), a dark, twisted *satire of Mexican politics in the 1990s; and in the Kafkaesque world of *The Crack* (1997). Berman stands out for her continuous record of successes, including *Between Pancho Villa and a Naked Woman* (1993), a *comedy about machismo; *Molière* (1998); and *Happy New Century, Doktor Freud* (2000), a *tragicomedy about the repercussions of psychotherapy on its originator and his patients. KFN

Bernhard, Thomas (1931–89) Austria's most eminent post-war playwright. His collaboration with the director *Peymann led to a string of successful works, but his criticism of Austrian conservatism and culture made him an extremely controversial figure. Regarding his countrymen as incorrigible, he stipulated in his will that none of his works be performed or published in Austria as long as they remain in copyright. His 21 plays are existentialist studies of the search for purpose in a meaningless universe. Bernhard shows a typically Austrian distrust of language as a means of communication. Endless repetition of stock phrases *parodies the banality of life and points towards the senseless patterns of existence. He has often been compared to *Beckett and the *absurd, but his bleak world-view is more relentless and rarely offers playful respite. His work shows little concern for plot and *character development and disregards traditional *audience expectations. Dialogues are often interrupted by long, aria-like *monolgues of musical quality, delivered by misanthropic, belligerent shrews. They were rendered unforgettable by *Minetti, who became a congenial interpreter of these roles in *Hunting Society* (*Burgtheater, 1974), *The Force of Habit* (1974), *Minetti* (1976), *The World Reformer* (1980), *Appearances Are Deceptive* (1984), and *Simply Complicated* (1986).   GB

Bernhardt, Sarah (1844–1923) French actress. Bernhardt made her mark at the *Comédie-Française in 1872 with a triumphant performance as the Queen in *Hugo's *Ruy Blas*. Her Phèdre in *Racine's *tragedy was equally outstanding in 1874. While she played virtually the whole of Racine's tragic repertoire, her exceptionally wide range also included *Molière, *Marivaux, *Beaumarchais, Shakespeare (Cordelia and Desdemona), *Dumas *père*, *Dumas *fils*, *Sardou, and *Rostand. Impatient with the Comédie-Française, she resigned in 1880, forming her own company, and later *managing her own theatres. Her enormous international reputation was built up by repeated foreign *tours, especially in England and the USA. A particular feature of the latter part of her career was her fondness for male roles (see MALE IMPERSONATION): Hamlet in 1899, Napoleon's son in Rostand's *L'Aiglon* (1900), Lorenzo in *Musset's *Lorenzaccio* (1897). Her Hamlet won admiring reports, even in London, though *Punch* suggested that her performance should be followed by *Irving playing Ophelia.

Performing the heroine in Sardou's *La Tosca* in South America in 1905, Bernhardt threw herself off the stage battlements and fell heavily onto an unprotected floor. The injury remained untreated too long, and although she concluded her American tour of over 60 cities, she was never afterwards free of pain. In 1915, at the age of 70, she had her right leg amputated; so that for the many stage appearances she continued to make, she was either completely static or had to be carried in a chair. The graceful movements might have gone, but the modulations of the voice were as rich as ever; and by all accounts, it was the distinctive character of her voice that was the basis of Bernhardt's star quality. She was the archetypal 'monstre sacré' of the French theatre of the *belle époque*, with an extravagant

lifestyle and an insatiable need for a vast personal income to support herself and her spendthrift son Maurice. But she was adored by an enormous public, on both sides of the Atlantic: a growing public, once she had begun to experiment with the new medium of film. Offstage, she fed the appetite of the gossips and scandalmongers with her numerous affairs, but there was no doubt about her devotion to the national cause during the 1914–18 war, when, even after her amputation, she insisted on visiting the front to entertain the French troops.   WDH

Bernini, Gian Lorenzo (1598–1680) As well as being the greatest Italian sculptor and architect of his day, Bernini was a dramatist, amateur actor, and *scenographer in the heyday of spectacular stage machinery. He designed apparatuses for the popes from 1630, mounted his own plays from 1634; and during a visit to Paris in 1665 his adverse comments on the *Petit-Bourbon Theatre disturbed the projects and status of the *Vigarani family. As an actor and dramatist, Bernini offered plays in *commedia dell'arte* style (now lost), producing caricatures of current personalities which were sometimes cutting enough to get him into trouble. In 1637, for his play *Of Two Theatres*, he constructed a mirror-image set: the *audience was faced from the back of the stage with a representation of itself, with individual portrait *masks, first listening to the *prologue (delivered by two actors simultaneously), then leaving to go home.   RAA

Bernstein, Leonard (1918–90) American composer, conductor, pianist, and lyricist, one of the most prominent musicians of the twentieth century. As a Broadway composer Bernstein brought a classical wit, elegance, and unity to the musical-theatre score. His reputation was established in 1944 with the spirited *ballet *Fancy Free*, choreographed by *Robbins. It was quickly expanded to Broadway *musical comedy proportions as *On the Town* (1944), with book and lyrics by *Comden and Green, and direction by *Abbott. Following his score for an adaptation of *My Sister Eileen*, called *Wonderful Town* (1953), Bernstein invested his musical sophistication into an adaptation of *Voltaire's satiric romp *Candide* (1956, revised 1974 for Harold *Prince). Bernstein and Robbins had long discussed the project which would become *West Side Story* (1957), with lyrics by *Sondheim. The show's innovations in music and *dance blended with an up-to-the-minute transposition of *Romeo and Juliet*, and it remains a pinnacle of the Broadway musical's golden age. Bernstein's diverse compositional output also included song cycles, symphonies, *opera, a film soundtrack, and *Mass: a theater piece for singers, players and dancers* (1971). EW

Besson, Benno (1922–2006) Swiss actor and director. Besson moved to Paris in 1945 to work with *Blin, and joined *Brecht in Berlin in 1949. He directed a number of productions at the *Berliner Ensemble in the 1950s, including *Molière's *Don Juan* (1954), Brecht's *Trumpets and Drums* (1955) and *The Good Person of Setzuan* (1957). Between 1961 and 1969 he directed mainly at the *Deutsches Theater, producing important interpretations of Greek plays (*Aristophanes, *Sophocles) and contemporary dramatists such as *Hacks. From 1969 to 1978 he was *artistic director of the *Volksbühne, where he continued a repertoire mixing contemporary drama and adaptations of the classics. Besson's directorial style combined a keen analytical, Brechtian approach with radical, often burlesque exaggeration and witty modernizations. In 1982 Besson moved to the Comédie in Geneva, where his productions achieved European prominence. CBB

Betsuyaku Minoru (1937–) Manchurian-born Japanese *absurdist playwright. In 1961 Betsuyaku established the Free Stage (Jiyū Butai) with *Suzuki, the precursor to the Waseda Little Theatre. His *Elephant* (1962, trans. 1986), a play in the style of *Beckett and *Ionesco, was instrumental in breaking Japanese drama free from the gridlock of *realism. Both the Free Stage and the WLT produced many of his best plays, like *The Little Match-Girl* (1966). Betsuyaku left the WLT in 1969 and has since written freelance for various major *shingeki* troupes like Bungakuza (the Literary Theatre) and Gekidan En (Theatre Circle). His style is austere, with spare sets and understated, wry, and enigmatic *dialogue. His plays, which often feature couples—husbands and wives, parents and children, colleagues, masters and servants—focus on the hidden violence of apparently normal human relationships. Representative works include *The Move* (1973), *The Legend of Noon* (1973), and *The Cherry in Bloom* (1980). Betsuyaku is also a writer of children's stories and television and film scripts. CP

Betterton, Mary (c.1637–1712) English actress, one of the first women to appear on the English stage, as Ianthe in *Davenant's *Siege of Rhodes* (1661), making such an impression on the diarist *Pepys that he always referred to her by that name. She married Thomas *Betterton in 1662, forging a popular acting partnership. Colley *Cibber considered her without equal in Shakespeare. Mary was a gifted teacher, coaching the Princesses Mary and Anne in court *masques and imparting her greatest skills to the next generation of actresses, notably to Anne *Bracegirdle, who was adopted into her household as a young child. GBB

Betterton, Thomas (c.1635–1710) English actor, *manager, and playwright, the most prominent performer of the Restoration. He was recruited into *Davenant's Duke's Company where he was the leading player and, following Davenant's death in 1668, manager under Lady Davenant's direction. The highest-paid actor of the time, his contemporaries heaped praises upon his emotional range in *tragedy (his fame as Hamlet was such that he continued to play the part successfully into his seventies), and equally popular in *comedy. Betterton managed the Duke's Company for Davenant's son Charles, and continued as manager when the two *patent companies united in 1682. He employed his first-hand knowledge of French theatrical effects in successful adaptations of Shakespeare and *Fletcher, and during the 1690s directed his energies toward producing a number of spectacular *operas. When the theatrical patent passed to Christopher *Rich, Betterton's rule of the company was challenged. The leading players eventually rebelled against Rich, and by 1695 Betterton, Elizabeth *Barry, and Anne *Bracegirdle had received a royal licence to form their own company at *Lincoln's Inn Fields. In 1705 Betterton joined forces with *Vanbrugh and the company moved to the Queen's Theatre in the *Haymarket. He married the actress Mary *Betterton in 1662. GBB

Betti, Ugo (1892–1953) Italian writer, author of 25 plays. A magistrate by profession, he proclaimed his disbelief in all earthly justice and set his *characters on a quest for some transcendental, divine standard. His representative character is intent on his career and worldly affairs until some inner crisis causes him to question the values by which he has lived. This was the case of the judge Parsc presiding over the investigation into the disaster which was the subject of *Accident at the North Station* (1932). Parsc, when required to pronounce on individual responsibility, calls instead for universal compassion. Holders of power invariably turn out to be weak and ineffectual, like the fugitive monarch in *The Queen and the Rebels* (1949) or the statesman in *The Burnt Flowerbed* (1952). These seemingly political plays advocate no recognizable ideology, but dissolve into the notion that the pursuit of earthly objectives represents surrender to a code of beliefs which is intrinsically mistaken and inappropriate for human beings.   JF

Bhaduri, Sisir (1889–1959) Bengali *actor-manager, often considered the first modernist director in India. His breakthrough came when he produced two plays titled *Sita* (1923–4) on the heroine of the epic *Ramayana*. His own company, Natyamandir, was the start of a new phase of respectability for Bengali theatre. Bhaduri directed meticulously, with taste and sensitivity; he acted *heroes *naturalistically and with refinement. The intelligentsia, who had shunned the commercial stage, flocked to his shows and wrote effusively about him, while younger actors emulated his style. He introduced writers like *Tagore (*Tapati*, 1929) to *audiences, though they rejected such unconventional drama. He formed the first Bengali troupe to travel abroad, staging *Sita* in New York (1931) to critical acclaim and financial disaster. He recovered at the Srirangam Theatre in Calcutta (1941–56), recapturing much of his artistry.   AL

bhagavata mela South Indian traditional theatre performed in the villages around Thanjavur, Tamil Nadu, involving popular plays (*yakshaganas*) by a troupe (*melam*) of Brahman actors trained in *dance, *music, and speech. Originally performed as a part of a *ritualistic offering to Lord Narasimha, an incarnation of Vishnu, the tradition of *bhagavata mela* goes back to the eighteenth century. Later the performance tradition was consolidated by Venkatarama Sastry, who was responsible for bringing the *dance-drama from the court to the street, directly for the entertainment and religious edification of the people. The plays were performed annually during the Narasimha Jayanthi celebrations in front of the temple of Sri Varadaraja Perumal, Melattur. By far the most popular of Sastry's plays is *Prahlada Charitam*, which has a deep religious content and emotional intensity.   MNS

bhand North Indian storyteller, joker, and buffoon. The name derives from the Hindi word *bhanda* (buffooning). *Bhands* were employed by rich landlords or wealthy men, somewhat like the jesters of aristocratic Europe, acting as entertainers and as 'fixers' for their patrons. Now *bhands* are travelling minstrels, roaming the countryside and performing for *street *audiences. Though their position in the social hierarchy is very low, they entertain at weddings and other auspicious occasions. Apart from singing and dancing, they also recite genealogies through gags and double entendres, always working in pairs. They perform stories about avaricious moneylenders, the evils of dowry traditions, and other social issues. Satiric, irreverent, and subversive, they beg forgiveness from their patron before the show, hoping for licence from retaliation. NMSC

Bharata Muni *See* NATYASASTRA.

Bhasa (*c.* fourth century AD) *Sanskrit playwright, a precursor of *Kalidasa, whose works were unknown until rediscovered in 1910. The thirteen plays attributed to Bhasa contain a variety of themes depicting human character in its varied dimensions. Bhasa drew from the Hindu epics, the *Mahabharata* and the *Ramayana*, and folk tales. Among his plays based on the *Mahabharata*, *The Middle One*, *Karna's Task*, and *The Broken Thighs* demonstrate flexibility of structure and *acting potential. Bhasa's most popular play, *The Vision of Vasavadatta*, is a love story with a political undercurrent as well as a dream-play. Individual acts from many of Bhasa's plays are performed in the temple theatres of Kerala known as *kuttampalam* where the traditional *cakyar* community keeps alive the tradition of Sanskrit plays in *kutiyattam* performances. Since 1956 there have been attempts to produce Bhasa in contemporary versions in Hindi and other Indian languages.   KNP

Bhattacharya, Bijon (1915–78) Bengali dramatist and actor. Born in the countryside of what is now Bangladesh, he saw rural life at first hand, using this knowledge as primary material. Moving to Calcutta in 1930, he became a Communist Party member and co-founded the Bengal unit of the Indian People's Theatre Association, which staged his first full-length drama, *Nabanna* (*New Harvest*, 1944). The prototype of contemporary Bengali theatre, it showed with stark *realism the disastrous effects of the recent Bengal famine in which millions perished. Bhattacharya started his own group, Calcutta Theatre, in 1951 with his play *Dead Moon*. He wrote fifteen major plays; the others include *Change of Caste* (1959), on east Bengali migration to Calcutta after Partition, *The Goddess Roars* (1966), and *Pregnant Mother* (1969), which questions traditional dogmas.   AL

Bhavabhuti (*c.* seventh century AD) Sanskrit poet and dramatist. From a Brahman family of Vedic scholars, Bhavabhuti was a poet and scholar in the court of Raja Yesovarman of Kanyakubja, and is famous for three dramas: *Malati Madhava*, *Mahavira Charita*, and *Uttararamacharita*. The first has an invented plot, while the second is the dramatization of the epic *Ramayana* in seven acts, culminating in Rama's return to Ayodhya, and Sita's 'test through fire' to prove her chastity. *Uttararamacharita* deals in a highly distilled poetic language with the abandoning of Sita in the forest by Rama's brother Lakshmana, her subsequent experiences as she casts herself in the River Bhageerathi, and her recovery by the goddesses of the Earth and the River Ganga. In contrast to the sensuous love that assumes poetic dimensions in *Kalidasa's plays, Bhavabhuti presents a love which is rooted firmly in spiritual sacrifice.   KNP

Biancolelli family Italian *commedia dell'arte* actors settled in France in the seventeenth and eighteenth centuries. The founders of the dynasty were **Francesco** (d. after 1640) and his wife Isabella Franchini, daughter of a Pantalone. **Giuseppe Domenico** ('Dominique', c.1637–88) was born in Bologna and transferred to Paris in 1661 after creating a reputation in Italy and Vienna. He took possession of the role of *Harlequin, and initiated the process by which that mask was transformed from a rough, aggressive, demonic figure into something more refined, balletic, and also protean in its ability to assume disguises and *parody social or theatrical stereotypes. He was on familiar jester's terms with Louis XIV; and he began to introduce passages of French language into the plays of the *Comédie Italienne. He also left a collection of his *scenarios in manuscript. His son **Pierre-François** ('Dominique fils', 1680–1734) then became a pivotal figure in the transition between the first and the second Comédie Italienne, as both actor and dramatist. He performed in the French provinces after the expulsion of the Italian troupe from Paris in 1697, returned to the Paris Foire in 1710, and joined the revived Italian company under *Riccoboni in 1717. He performed as Harlequin, or in the similar servant role of Trivelin, by now entirely in French. His daughter **Marie-Thérèse de la Lalande** (1723–88) also had a distinguished career as an actress.   RAA

Bibiena family Italian painters, architects, and *scenographers. Students of the baroque, an age that loved *illusion, they adopted an exuberant style that made use of new architectural forms, ornate columns, *trompe l'œil*, overstatement, and exaggerated modelling. Their patrons were the great throughout Europe and Russia, who kept them busy designing gardens, palaces, villas, churches; organizing spectacular royal coronations, weddings, and funerals; constructing *playhouses; and engineering scenery and stage machinery for *operas and *ballets.

Ferdinando (1657–1743), as leading painter and architect for almost 28 years at the Duke of Parma's court, was chief scenographer for the Teatro *Farnese and Piacenza's Teatro Ducale and Teatro Nuovo. In 1711 the German Emperor Charles VI appointed him court architect in Vienna, the imperial seat of the Habsburgs, and gave him command over set designs and decorations for court festivals, opera, and ballet. Ferdinando wrote important theoretical tracts in which he discusses the *scena per angolo*, or sets at an angle, a *perspective technique that became a family trademark.

Ferdinando's brother **Francesco** (1659–1739) travelled to Naples in 1702 to organize magnificent festivities welcoming the new ruler, Philip V of Spain, and his Habsburg Queen Maria Theresa. Shortly thereafter Francesco was summoned to Vienna by Emperor Leopold I to build Teatro Nuovo (completed in 1704). He built four or five other theatres, including the great theatre at Nancy (1707), Rome's Teatro Alibert (1720, constructed with his nephew Antonio), and Verona's Teatro Filarmonico (1720), none of which has survived.

Giuseppe (1696–1757), having followed his father Ferdinando to Vienna in 1712, designed over 30 catafalques for the funerals of nobility. Among the splendid court festivities he planned was the 1723 celebration in Prague of the crowning of Charles VI and his Empress as king and queen of Bohemia. For this he created an open-air theatre holding 8,000 spectators, a stage 60 m (200 feet) deep, and stage machinery that facilitated startling tricks of transformation during the performance of the opera *Costanza e fortezza*. Giuseppe is best known for his interior of the Opera House in Bayreuth, a prime example of Bibiena court-theatre design which has been faithfully restored. **Antonio** (1700–74), another of Ferdinando's sons, was unrivalled in his time for the number of public theatres he constructed, among which is Bologna's Teatro Communale (1756–63). Ferdinando had two other sons, **Giovanni Maria** (n.d.) and **Alessandro** (1687–1769), who were active in Prague and Mannheim, respectively. Francesco's son **Giovanni Carlo** (d.1760) spent his career in Portugal. The last artist in the family, Giuseppe's son **Carlo** (1725–87), was in demand throughout Europe and in St Petersburg.   JEH

biblical plays Plays that dramatize portions of the scriptures, sometimes embellished with material from the Apocrypha, sacred legend, or historical writings such as those of Josephus, were the dominant form of *medieval theatre in Europe. They were part of a wider movement that included artistic representations in stained glass, wall paintings, and alabaster carvings, and non-dramatic literary works such as poems retelling Bible stories or offering emotive reflections on Jesus' life. Called variously *Corpus Christi plays, *mystery plays, miracle plays, *laude*, *Passion plays, Easter plays, Creed plays, or even Pater Noster plays, they have in common subject matter rooted in scripture and performance largely by and for the laity. As a dramatic form they first appear in the mid- to late fourteenth century and seem to have taken their inspiration not from the existing *liturgical drama or the extra-liturgical Latin drama but from didacticism and personal or 'affective' piety that characterized the religious life of the late fourteenth and fifteenth centuries. Similar types of drama appear all over Western Europe, varying only in their mix of didacticism with 'emotive response to the events of the Christian story. The proponents of affective piety emphasized the humanity and suffering of Christ to stimulate a closer relationship with him and so enhance faith.

Perhaps the most popular of the biblical dramas were the Passion plays—longer episodic biblical sequences normally performed in 'place and scaffold' configurations that added to the Resurrection story the trials, the beating, and humiliation, and the Crucifixion itself. This was the most common form of community drama in France. The base text for many of the French productions was composed about 1440 by Arnoul Gréban, a canon of Notre Dame Cathedral in Paris. Redactions of this text with omissions and additions were performed in many French cities over the next 100 years. French biblical drama tended to be mounted sporadically on a very large scale, sponsored by *confréries* (*see* CONFRÉRIE DE LA PASSION) or simply groups of individuals brought together to mount a single, often multi-day production, rather than undertaken regularly by cities as they were in northern England and the Germanic towns such as Frankfurt, Heidelberg, Marburg, and Zurich. England had at least two free-standing Passion plays unattached to major cities. Passion plays were rare in Italy and only one has been discovered in the Low Countries in Maastricht, but there are surviving examples in Provençal and Spanish. Some of the plays performed in the competitions of the *Chambers of Rhetoric had biblical subjects.

Biblical plays that dramatize the whole of salvation history beginning with the Creation and ending with the Last Judgement are confined to England and the Germanic areas, including the play from Bozen in the southern Tyrol performed by the craft guilds and the play at Künzelsau, the most complete of the German sequences. Two

surviving English examples are the cycles of plays from York and Chester, both performed in procession by the craft guilds and produced by the city councils. The play in York was performed in one day on the feast of Corpus Christi while the play in Chester was spread over three days at Pentecost. Two other English cycle plays, traditionally called 'N-Town' and 'Towneley', appear to be collections from different sources rather than written and revised for performance in one location.

Less well-known types include Creed plays, which follow the twelve clauses of the Apostles' Creed and might include scenes based on the Creation, the Nativity, the trials of Jesus (particularly the trial before Pilate), the Crucifixion, the Burial, the Resurrection, the Ascension, and Judgement; and, in England, the Pater Noster plays, based on the petitions of the Lord's Prayer, which apparently combined biblical narrative with an allegorical treatment of the deadly sins (no texts survive).

Plays on biblical subjects survived into the Reformation and, indeed, the early reformers adapted the form for their own purposes. New dramatizations of the stories were written from a Protestant perspective by such writers as Théodore de Bèze and John *Bale (c.1539). In Lutheran towns biblical plays continued while those associated with liturgical practice did not. In 1561 Hans Sachs wrote a new Passion play and humanists like Nicholas Grimaud wrote Latin plays on biblical subjects. Although in some parts of Eastern Europe the old traditions lasted into the seventeenth century, the medieval form of biblical drama did not survive the religious upheavals of the sixteenth century in the West.   AFJ

Bickerstaffe, Isaac (1735–1812) Irish playwright, perhaps the only person in Britain to make a living in the second half of the eighteenth century solely by writing plays. He specialized in short *musical plays and *farces, including *Love in a Village* (1762) and *The Maid of the Mill* (1765). His career was cut short in 1772 when he was accused of attempted sodomy and fled England, never to return. Despite his abrupt and scandalous departure from the London stage, his plays remained favourites and Elizabeth *Inchbald considered him one of the best farceurs of the eighteenth century.   MJK

Bieito, Calixto (1963–) Catalan director. A radical innovator who has embraced a versatile repertoire, from *Sondheim to *Shaw and *García Lorca to *Bernhard, Bieito built a formidable reputation in the early 1990s in Barcelona and more recently in Madrid. His reinvention of classics included contentious productions of *Calderón's *Life Is a Dream*, produced in both English (1998) and Spanish (2000), *Valle-Inclán's cruel *Barbaric Comedies* (2000), and *Ibsen's *Peer Gynt* (2006). His regular *mise-en-scène makes the audience appear as much on display as the performers. A series of radical, aggressive Shakespeares further consolidated his reputation as a political moralist, dissecting the commercial mores and social excesses of a postmodern world. Since 2000 he has been artistic director of Barcelona's Theatre Romea securing a young *audience.   MMD

Binodini Dasi (*c.*1863–1941) Bengali actress. Foremost among the first women to act on the Bengali stage, she was born in the community of prostitutes in Calcutta. Her meteoric career was short (1874–87), but encompassed nearly 100 roles in around 80 productions; an example of her versatility was the six *characters she played in *The Killing of Meghnad*. Trained by her mentor, the *actor-manager Girish *Ghosh, she played every kind of character—mythical, realistic, tragic, comic. Her cross-dressed performance as the Hindu religious reformer Chaitanya so overwhelmed the mystic Ramakrishna that he went backstage to bless her, at a time when the educated public considered theatre immoral. Binodini's memoirs, *My Story*, have significance as theatre history, for women's studies, and as a record of her artistic insight.   AL

biomechanics A term associated with the *acting theories of *Meyerhold. A former member of the *Moscow Art Theatre, and familiar with the acting theories of *Stanislavsky, Meyerhold parted company with his mentor in developing a theory based on external mastery of physical movement, rather than on inner emotional states of empathetic feeling. His ideas derived from more physically oriented and popular forms such as the *circus, *pantomime, and *commedia dell'arte, but also owed a debt to *acrobatics, *Jaques-Dalcroze's eurhythmics, and gymnastics, to the 'time and motion' theories of Frederick Taylor, to Japanese acting traditions, to oriental martial arts, and to Pavlovian theories of reflexology. The training courses which Meyerhold instituted immediately after the Russian Revolution eschewed individual expressiveness in favour of collectivist action where actors, dressed often in identical overalls, performed stage tasks in the hyper-efficient manner of workers on a production line. Meyerhold devised specific exercises, such as

'Shooting the Bow', 'Throwing the Stone', and 'The Leap onto the Chest', in which each movement was prefaced by a dialectical counter-movement, concluding with a synthesizing resolution of oppositions, signalled by a verbal exclamation. Following practical stage experiments in 1922, the method became largely confined to actor training and, though discredited during the Stalinist period, was revived during the 1960s and now features prominently in acting schools alongside the methods of Stanislavsky, *Brecht, and others. *See also* PHYSICAL THEATRE.   NW

Birmingham Repertory Theatre One of the earliest of the *regional repertory theatres in the UK, the Birmingham Rep was founded and funded by Barry *Jackson, and had its origins in an amateur group, the Pilgrim Players. Its purpose-built *playhouse opened in 1913 with *Twelfth Night*; Jackson was *artistic director and the playwright John Drinkwater the general *manager. In the early decades the repertoire was bold, including premières of works by *Shaw (notably *Back to Methuselah*, 1923) and Drinkwater (*Abraham Lincoln*, 1918), and actors included Edith *Evans, *Olivier, and *Richardson. Jackson's many Shakespeare productions (credit as director actually goes to H. K. Ayliff) were dominated by a pioneering series in modern dress, of which '*Hamlet* in plus-fours' (1925) attracted particular attention. European plays included *Kaiser's *Gas* (1923), with *expressionist sets by the house designer *Shelving. Jackson's post-war protégés included the young *Brook and *Scofield. A new 900-seat theatre opened in 1971, with a studio theatre for experimental work.   RJ

Bjørnson, Bjørn (1859–1942) Norwegian actor and director. The eldest son of playwright Bjørnstjerne *Bjørnson, he first made his mark as an actor. Trained in Germany, Bjørnson was the only non-German member of the *Meiningen Players in the early 1880s. In Norway he launched his career as an actor and director at the Christian Theatre in Bergen in 1884, playing the title role in *Richard III*. His Meiningen training was evident in his meticulous direction and rapid dynamic pacing: *audiences were astounded to see crowds turn their backs to them, and hear live sound effects. Bjørnson's 'authentic' *realism in productions of *The Wild Duck, Peer Gynt, John Gabriel Borkman*, and *Enemy of the People*, among other works, set the national standard for *Ibsen interpretation into the 1930s. The first director of the Nationaltheatret, Bjørnson directed over 120 productions during his tenure there, a repertoire that included his father, Shakespeare, *Holberg, and *Molnár.   DLF

Bjørnson, Bjørnstjerne (1832–1910) Norwegian playwright who wrote plays in styles that *Ibsen later adopted. Bjørnson wrote his national *romantic trilogy *Sigurd Slembe* (1862) the year before Ibsen wrote *The Pretenders*. A decade later Bjørnson wrote plays debating contemporary issues, *The Bankrupt* and *The Editor* (1875), two years before Ibsen turned his attention to contemporary issues with *Pillars of Society*. But in contrast to Ibsen, Bjørnson was an extrovert campaigner and journalist who fought for women's emancipation, Norwegian independence, and human rights, issues reflected in plays such as *The King* (1877), *Leonarda* (1879), *A Gauntlet* (1883), and *Beyond Our Powers* (1883). His most complex drama, *Paul Lange and Tora Parsberg* (1898), dealt frankly with political issues involved in the suicide of a contemporary politician. At times the artistic quality of Bjørnson's work suffered because of the depth of his social and political conviction, but its idealistic temper brought him the Nobel Prize for Literature in 1903.   DT

Björnson, Maria (1949–2002) British designer. Born in Paris of Romanian and Norwegian parents, apprenticeship at Glasgow *Citizens' Theatre led to collaboration with director David Pountney, and she designed his Welsh National Opera/Scottish Opera Janáček cycle. Awarded the 1983 Prague Bienniale Prize and Prague Quadrenniale Silver Medal, those expressive, bold designs demonstrate Björnson's view that designing 'is about finding out what the problems are by asking the right questions' and offering visual information *audiences 'can't get from the play, but which helps them to understand it'. In addition to spectacular West End productions of *Follies* (1987) and *Aspects of Love*, she is renowned for designing *The Phantom of the Opera* (1987), an opulent Parisian fantasy that captured numerous awards. Later work included *Verdi's Macbeth* (La Scala, 1997), *Cherry Orchard* (*National Theatre, 2000), *Plenty*, and *Britannicus* (1998).   RVL

Black, Stephen (1880–1931) South African playwright, actor, and *mime. He wrote two novels (*The Dorp* and *The Golden Calf*) and was a journalist, but is best known as the first South African to write drama in the local context. His first play, *Love and the Hyphen* (1908), commented on Cape society. Others include *Helena's Hope Ltd.*, based on his experiences of a Rhodesian gold mine, *Van Kalabas Does his Bit* (1916), based on his war experiences, *The Uitlanders*,

and *Outspan*. He also translated French texts into English (for instance, *The Flapper*, 1911). He travelled to London (1913–15) and France (1918–27), marketing his work, writing, and negotiating foreign rights. Black's satirical plays offer a useful early record of the social mores of early twentieth-century Cape society with its complicated racial interactions.   YH

blackface *See* MINSTREL SHOW.

Blackfriars Theatre The pre-eminent indoor *playhouse of Shakespeare's time. A hall theatre built in 1596 by James *Burbage, who planned it to replace the open-air *Theatre, which he built in 1576, Blackfriars was located in a 'liberty', free from the Lord Mayor of London's control because it had belonged to the Dominican friars. An earlier theatre was established in the same precinct in 1576 by Richard Farrant, the choirmaster of the *Chapel Royal, for commercial performances by his *boy company. Burbage hoped to use his for the same purpose but was stopped by the residents. Shakespeare's company began to use it as their winter playhouse in 1608. Set in a large stone hall 18 by 12 m (60 by 40 feet), its stage had *boxes on each flank, a pit with benches, and galleries curving round the pit. Gallants could hire stools to sit on the stage itself.   AJG

Blake, Eubie (1883–1983) *African-American performer-playwright, who broke into show business in the 1890s playing ragtime piano in a Baltimore bordello. He danced in *minstrelsy and worked in medicine shows before moving to New York in 1905. Later he teamed with Noble Sissle (1889–1975) in a *vaudeville act called the Dixie Duo. The two sold their first song, 'It's All your Fault', to Sophie *Tucker, who made it a big hit. With another vaudeville team, Miller & Lyles, they produced and starred in *Shuffle Along* (Broadway, 1921), the first all-black *musical to become a box-office smash. The *dancing was infectious and the songs unforgettable, including 'Love Will Find a Way' and 'I'm Just Wild about Harry' (later the campaign song for President Truman). Blake also wrote *The Chocolate Dandies* (with Sissle, 1924) and *Blackbirds of 1930*. In 1933 and 1952, he and Sissle revived *Shuffle Along*, though without the success of the first version. Retired for some years, Blake was back in the public mind in 1978 with *Eubie*, a Broadway musical celebrating his life and music.   BBL

Blakely, Colin (1930–87) Irish actor, whose rich stage career was paralleled by a prolific career as a character actor in film and television.

His first professional engagement was with the Group Theatre, Belfast. He progressed to the *Royal Court, *Royal Shakespeare Company, and *National Theatre, where he was a member of the acting company from its earliest days, playing the Norwegian Captain in the company's first production, *Hamlet*, directed by *Olivier (1963). Other early roles there include Kite in *Gaskill's mounting of *Farquhar's *The Recruiting Officer* (1963), as well as appearances in Lindsay Anderson's production of *Frisch's *Andorra*, *Shaffer's *The Royal Hunt of the Sun* (both 1964), and *Seneca's *Oedipus* (1968). In 1971 he was in Peter *Hall's première of *Pinter's *Old Times* for the RSC at the Aldwych, and in 1975 in John Schlesinger's National Theatre revival of *Shaw's *Heartbreak House*. In 1985 he appeared in Pinter's *Other Places* in the West End.   AS

Blakemore, Michael (1928–) Australian director and actor, resident in England. Blakemore's direction is distinguished by attempted self-effacement, attention to detail, and concern for actors. He is particularly known for his work with *Nichols, *Frayn, *Miller, and fellow Australian David *Williamson. Blakemore worked as an actor for fifteen years in Britain before directing at the Glasgow *Citizens' Theatre, where he premièred Nichols's *A Day in the Death of Joe Egg* (1966). He became an associate director at the *National Theatre, and directed several acclaimed productions including *Long Day's Journey into Night* (1971), starring *Olivier. Unhappy with the new regime under *Hall, Blakemore pursued a career in commercial theatre. During the 1990s he had great success with *musicals in the USA, and in 2000 won two Tony awards, one for *Kiss Me, Kate* and the other for Frayn's *Copenhagen*. He was back on Broadway in 2009 with *Coward's *Blithe Spirit*.   EJS

Blau, Herbert (1926–) American director, *producer, playwright, and scholar. In 1952 he and Jules Irving started the Actors Workshop of San Francisco, where he directed more than 25 productions, including the American premières of *Brecht's *Mother Courage* (1956) and *Arden's *Serjeant Musgrave's Dance* (1962). Blau also directed the legendary production of *Beckett's *Waiting for Godot* that played in San Quentin prison. In 1965, Blau and Irving took over the Repertory Theatre of *Lincoln Center in New York. Within two years, Blau resigned amid much controversy, ending his career in large institutional theatre. In 1971, after three years as dean and provost at the newly formed California Institute of the Arts, Blau formed KRAKEN,

an experimental acting ensemble which developed *physical theatre pieces as a *collective, including *Seeds of Atreus* (1973), *The Donner Party*, *its Crossing* (1974), and *Elsinore* (1976). After its dissolution, he concentrated on teaching and scholarship. His prolific writings on performance theory, Beckett, fashion, and other subjects demonstrate the same qualities that marked his work as a director: intellectual rigour and passion, commitment to experiment, fierce and uncompromising idealism.   STC

Blauwe Maandag Compagnie Belgian troupe founded in 1984 when actor-director Luk Perceval abandoned the conservative Koninklijke Nederlandse Schouwburg at Antwerp. With Guy Joosten, he launched a new fringe company with Ghent as its home base, performing mainly at Flemish arts centres and on modest festival stages. With unorthodox productions of *Othello*, *Chekhov's *Seagull*, and *Strindberg's *The Father*, Blauwe Maandag (Blue Monday) soon became the best known of Belgium's nearly 35 experimental companies. Using a *collective approach, Perceval produced classical plays in a multidisciplinary, deconstructionist, and non-*illusionist, *Brechtian manner, and also commissioned new writing. With the versatile writer and performer Tom Lanoye, Perceval directed *Ten Oorlog* (*To War*, 1997–8), a three-part adaptation of Shakespeare's English history plays twelve hours in length, later mounted in German as *Schlachten!* in Hamburg and at the *Salzburg Festival. To counter the fractured Flemish theatre scene and increase the opportunities for large-scale productions, Blauwe Maandag merged in 1998 with Perceval's former theatre to form a new company, Het Toneelhuis (the Playhouse).   TH

Blin, Roger (1907–84) French director, actor, and designer who played a crucial role in discovering the works of the *absurdist playwrights. A friend of *Artaud and member of the Paris *surrealist group in the 1920s, Blin welcomed the brilliant, troubled *Adamov and produced his first play, *La Parodie* (1952). In the 1930s he studied *mime and acted with *Barrault and in Artaud's *The Cenci* (1935). Blin believed that the text should not be overwhelmed with design, which endeared him to *Beckett. Blin directed the French premières of *Beckett's major plays, and acted in the first two: *Waiting for Godot* (1953) and *Endgame* (1957). These were followed by *Krapp's Last Tape* (1960) and *Happy Days* (1963). Blin also directed premières of *Genet's *The Blacks* (1959), and *The Screens* (1966), defending Genet from right-wing attacks. Blin's stagings of Genet were his most visually stunning and theatrical, not to display his own virtuosity but because the plays demanded it.   SBB

Blitzstein, Marc (1905–64) American composer, lyricist, and cultural critic. At the age of 21 Blitzstein made a concert hall debut as a pianist with the Philadelphia Orchestra, but later became committed—partly through his exposure to the manifestos of *Brecht and Hans Eisler—to the belief that 'music must have a social as well as artistic base; it should broaden its scope and reach not only the select few but the masses'. During the 1930s he wrote provocative articles on the form and function of socially conscious art while composing his own proletarian pieces, most notably *The Cradle Will Rock* (1937). Though this *agitprop 'play in *music' was ordered closed during *rehearsals by the *Federal Theatre Project, director *Welles managed to open it under now legendary performance conditions. *Regina*, Blitzstein's operatic version of *Hellman's *The Little Foxes*, appeared briefly on Broadway in 1949 and has since entered the *opera repertoire. His adaptation of *Weill and Brecht's *The Threepenny Opera* was mounted *Off-Broadway in the 1950s, offering Blitzstein some commercial success in his later career. LTC

Blok, Aleksandr (1880–1921) Russian poet, dramatist, and essayist. Blok's *Balaganchik* (*The Puppet Show/The Fairground Booth*) and *Neznakomka* (*The Female Stranger*) were both poems before they were plays; the first premièred at *Komissarzhevskaya's theatre (St Petersburg, 1906), directed by *Meyerhold, who also played the leading role of Pierrot. The play's conception of life as theatre, which exposes the world as immaterial illusion, is both playful and sophisticated: *symbolist mysticism and the *mystery play are parodied, as is death itself in the shape of a mortally wounded *clown who declares that he is bleeding cranberry juice. The play was one of a trilogy including *The King on the Town Square* and *The Female Stranger*. It was also staged by Meyerhold, alongside a revised version of *The Puppet Show* (1914). *The Rose and the Cross* (1913), set in thirteenth-century Provence, was rehearsed by *Stanislavsky but never staged. NW

Bloom, Claire (1931–) English actress. At the *Shakespeare Memorial Theatre (1948) she was Ophelia to the alternating Hamlets of *Scofield and *Helpmann; at the *Old Vic (1953) she played opposite *Burton. Her Romeos, both at the Old Vic, were Alan Badel (1952) and *Neville (1956). Her work with *Gielgud included the roles of Alizon Eliot in *Fry's *The Lady's Not for Burning* (1949), Cordelia in *King Lear* (1955), and Sasha in *Chekhov's *Ivanov* (1965). She countered accusations of emotional reserve with strong performances as Nora in *Ibsen's *A Doll's House* (1971), and Blanche in *Williams's *A Streetcar Named Desire* (1974). Bloom had a substantial screen career, including *Limelight* (1952) and *The Spy Who Came in from the Cold* (1966) and the television series *Brideshead Revisited*.   VRS

Boal, Augusto (1931–2009) Brazilian theoretician, director, and playwright. After studying with John Gassner in New York in the early 1950s, Boal became a core member of São Paulo's Arena Theatre in 1956, where he adapted *Actors Studio techniques to the development of a national *dramaturgy. As a playwright he was best known as co-author, with Gianfrancesco Guarnieri, of a series of *musicals about history that contested the Brazilian dictatorship, including *Arena Narratos Zumbi* (1965). Given the real dangers of artistic protest during the dictatorship, Boal chose exile in 1971. His book *Theatre of the Oppressed* (1974) laid the theoretical ground for the theatre of the *oppressed, largely developed in periods of exile, a political theatre movement that remains hugely important worldwide. Boal returned to Brazil in 1986, actively entered politics, and served as a city councillor (1992–6), while continuing his work as a cultural activist and teaching and directing internationally. Always interested in *opera and the *Brechtian possibilities of *music, after 2000 he turned his talents to developing a genre he called *sambópera*, producing Brazilianized versions of *Carmen* and *La traviata* with the melodies of Bizet and *Verdi transposed to the Brazilian rhythms of samba, maracatu, baião, and carnival marches. His other books include *Legislative Theatre*, *The Rainbow of Desire*, and *The Aesthetics of the Oppressed*.   LHD

Boar's Head Located on the eastern edge of London in Whitechapel, the Boar's Head was originally a tavern, a square of buildings surrounding an open yard. It was converted into a *playhouse in 1597, once the use of London's inns for staging plays was prohibited. It was further rebuilt in the succeeding years, as new companies arrived in London, challenging the duopoly of the *Admiral's and *Chamberlain's Men. The Worcester's Men had the Boar's Head designated as their regular playhouse in 1601. That made it the third licensed place for London playing after the *Globe and *Fortune. As an open air playhouse it did not have a long life, and Worcester's, now Queen Anne's Men, left it for the Red Bull in 1604. With only one level of galleries, its capacity was markedly smaller than the other *amphitheatres of the time. AJG

Bocage (Pierre-Martinien Tousez) (1797–1863) French actor. Bocage failed to gain acceptance at the *Comédie-Française, but began a successful career at the Porte-Saint-Martin. Lacking the robust stage presence of *Lemaître, he was ideally suited, in physique and delivery, to the more sombre and melancholy roles in the romantic repertory. The title role in *Dumas père's Antony (1831) was his most memorable success. It received a more enthusiastic reception than any other play of the period, due more to the playing of Marie *Dorval and Bocage than the author's craftsmanship. *Hugo's Marion de Lorme (also 1831) was only moderately successful. In 1832 Bocage played in Dumas's Teresa, for once choosing a middle-aged *character with greater psychological nuance; but later in 1832 the same author's La Tour de Nesle, a sensational historical *melodrama, offered him in the role of Buridan little more than a caricature of the fatalistic romantic hero. WDH

Bock, Jerry (1928–2010) American composer. Teaming with lyricist Larry Holofcener, Bock's first Broadway score, Mr Wonderful, was a successful vehicle for Sammy Davis, Jr. Bock then began a fruitful collaboration with lyricist Sheldon Harnick and had a huge success with Fiorello (1959). The *musical Tenderloin (1960) was followed by the charming pocket *operetta She Loves Me (1963), in which Bock managed to insert a tango, a beguine, and even a bolero. The next year brought the team its greatest hit, Fiddler on the Roof. Based on stories by *Aleichem, directed and choreographed by *Robbins, and designed in the style of Chagall by *Aronson, it played around the world and became a popular film (1971). An experimental work, The Apple Tree (1966), followed, as did The Rothschilds (1970), another period, Jewish-flavoured work, this time with a continental sweep. It marked the end of the partnership, and Bock remained relatively inactive thereafter, though starting in 1997 he produced some new music-theatre works at the University of Houston. JD

Bogart, Anne (1953–) American director. Bogart's early work was influenced by postmodern *dance and by several stays in Germany, from which she returned intent on exploring American forms, themes, and writers. She created theatrical collages and dance-theatre pieces for experimental venues until 1989, when she became *artistic

director of Trinity Repertory Company in Providence, a troubled appointment that lasted only one year. In 1992 she directed the world première of *Vogel's The Baltimore Waltz, for which she won her second Obie award. That same year, with *Suzuki Tadashi she co-founded the Saratoga International Theatre Institute (SITI) as a training ground and laboratory for developing new work rooted in Suzuki's rigorous physical and vocal techniques and Bogart's elaboration of the 'Viewpoints', a stage-movement vocabulary first outlined by choreographer Mary Overlie. With the SITI company she created a number of dense, abstract pieces inspired by twentieth-century culture heroes, including one-person portraits of Robert *Wilson, Virginia Woolf, and *Bernstein, and ensemble pieces inspired by Marshall McLuhan, Andy Warhol, and *Welles. Several SITI projects, including a *metatheatrical reflection on theatrical convention and the role of the *audience called Cabin Pressure (1999), started at *Actors Theatre of Louisville, where Bogart also mounted revisionist versions of *Inge and *Coward plays. A version of Antigone opened in New York in 2009. STC

Bogdanov, Michael (1938–) Welsh director. Bogdanov worked to make Shakespeare accessible by forming the *English Shakespeare Company with actor *Pennington in 1986. His *touring productions, such as the seven-play history cycle The War of the Roses (1987), have been popular successes. His direct, modern-dress, socio-political readings are considered 'un-English', and ignore trends for cerebral, text-based interpretations. Bogdanov has a curious relationship with institutions. The son of a Ukrainian father and Welsh mother, for two years he combined running a Welsh pub with assistant directing at the *Royal Shakespeare Company (including *Brook's A Midsummer Night's Dream, 1970). His early reputation for *youth theatre included an award-winning Taming of the Shrew (RSC, 1979). In 1980 *Hall appointed him an associate at the *National Theatre, where he notoriously faced prosecution under the Sexual Offences Act by Mary Whitehouse for staging gross indecency in *Brenton's Romans in Britain (1981). From 1989 to 1992 Bogdanov was director of the Deutsches Schauspielhaus, Hamburg; his populist productions increased attendance but received mixed critical reception. During the 1990s he produced Shakespeare for film and television, including the series Shakespeare on the Estate, and directed world tours for the sporadically funded ESC, and classic and epic texts for the RSC, RNT, and international theatres. Since 2003 he has been artistic director of Wales Theatre Company, based in Swansea. Two volumes of *Shakespeare: The Director's Cut* were published in 2003 and 2005.   KN

Bogosian, Eric (1953–) American playwright and actor. Bogosian began creating *characters and performing *monologues while working at New York's experimental venue the Kitchen (1976–9). His characters evolved into his first *Off-Off-Broadway *revue, *Careful Moment* (1977). He performed his one-person shows *Men Inside* and *Voices of America* at the *New York Shakespeare Festival's Public Theatre (1981–2) and achieved wide acclaim for his monologue *Drinking in America* (1986). Bogosian's gritty, serio-comic urban characters evolved into his first multi-character play, *Talk Radio* (1987). His one-man performance *Pounding Nails in the Floor with my Forehead* premièred in 1993 and the plays *subUrbia* (1994) and *Griller* (1998) were presented by major *regional theatres. Bogosian has also appeared in a number of film and television productions.   MAF

Boleslavsky,   Richard   Valentinovich (1889–1937) Actor, teacher, and director. Born Boleslaw Ryszard Srzednicki in Poland, Boleslavsky was the vital link between *Stanislavsky and the United States. He moved with his family to Odessa, joined a professional Russian-language troupe in 1904, and was accepted by the *Moscow Art Theatre in 1908. Strikingly handsome, he quickly became a leading actor. Appointed head of the MAT's First Studio, Boleslavsky quarrelled with Stanislavsky over artistic matters and left for New York in 1922; in 1923 he founded the American Laboratory Theatre, the first American school presenting the Stanislavsky approach. Future luminaries of American *acting studied with Boleslavsky and his colleague Maria Ouspenskaya, most notably *Strasberg and Stella *Adler, important in the *Group Theatre (1931–41) and as rival acting teachers thereafter. Many others were introduced to Stanislavskian techniques through Boleslavsky's *Acting: the first six lessons* (1933). He had a minor Broadway directing career, but moved to Hollywood in 1929 and was an 'A-list' film director at the time of his death.   MAF

Bolger, Ray (1904–87) American comic actor and eccentric *dancer, known for his loose-jointed style. He played *vaudeville in an act called 'Stanford and Bolger: a pair of nifties'. Bolger made his Broadway debut in *The Merry Whirl* (1926). Following two years in vaudeville on the Orpheum circuit, he returned to Broadway

in *Heads Up!* (1929), *George White's Scandals* (1931), *Life Begins at 8:40* (1934), and *On your Toes* (1936), in which he gained renown for the 'Slaughter on 10th Avenue' *ballet, choreographed by *Balanchine. In the 1940s Broadway saw him in *Keep off the Grass* (1940), *By Jupiter* (1942), *Three to Make Ready* (1946), and *Where's Charley?* (1948), in which he introduced his signature song, 'Once in Love with Amy'. His last two Broadway shows, *All American* (1962) and *Come Summer* (1969), were flops. Bolger also appeared in film (notably as the Scarecrow in *The Wizard of Oz*, 1939), on television, and in a series of one-person shows.   SLL

Bolt, Robert (1924–95) English dramatist and screenwriter. Bolt's first plays were staged in 1957: *The Critic and the Heart* and the successful *Flowering Cherry*, starring Ralph *Richardson. His work investigates the individual's moral responsibility in the face of social pressure. *Scofield starred as Thomas More in both the stage (1960) and film (1966) versions of his best-known work, *A Man for All Seasons*. The use of a *character called the Common Man as narrator, often called *Brechtian, actually reflects the play's origins in radio (1954). The academic crisis in *The Tiger and the Horse* (with Michael and Vanessa *Redgrave, 1960) mirrors Bolt's involvement with the Campaign for Nuclear Disarmament. Subsequent plays, including *Gentle Jack* (1963), *Vivat! Vivat Regina* (1970), and *State of Revolution* (*National Theatre, 1977), about Lenin and Trotsky, increasingly experimented with form. Bolt's screenplays include *Lawrence of Arabia* (1962), and *Dr Zhivago* (1965).   GAO

Bolton, Guy (1883–1979) American librettist, an early architect of the American *musical form. He and *Kern wrote a string of musicals for the Princess Theatre, including the hit *Very Good Eddie* (1915), which was the first of its kind to mine comedy from *character and situation rather than *vaudevillian *clowning. *Wodehouse joined the team, collaborating with Bolton on a number of librettos to Kern-scored shows like *Leave it to Jane* (1917) and *Porter's *Anything Goes* (1930). Bolton also worked on several shows with George and Ira *Gershwin, joining forces with Fred Thompson for *Lady, Be Good!* (1924) and John McGowan for *Girl Crazy* (1930). Among his non-musical works, Bolton wrote an adaptation for Broadway of *Anastasia* (1954). His contributions for film include *Easter Parade* (1948).   EW

Bond, Edward (1934–) English playwright. His first plays emerged from the Writers' Group at the *Royal Court, run by *Gaskill, who directed all his major work until *The Fool* (1975). *The Pope's Wedding* (1962), *Saved* (1965), *Early Morning* (1968), *Narrow Road to the Deep North* (1969), and *Lear* (1971) established Bond's reputation— and through the controversies surrounding *Saved* and *Early Morning*, forced key battles against *censorship. Bond has discussed his methods and *dramaturgy in extended prefaces and letters which amount to a theory not unlike *Brecht's, whose work Bond's often resembles. He creates what he called 'aggro-effects' of violence, such as the stoning of the baby in *Saved*, to break the limits of rationality and *naturalistic characterization. Similarly he often draws on events long past or projected into the future for his subject matter, sometimes reworking previous sources (*The Trojan Women* became *The Woman* and *King Lear* became *Lear*). His plays offer parables for our times, interpreting the present in light of the past or future in order to intervene, a move that identifies his work as *epic and politically committed.

Bond has proved to be difficult for English *audiences, and became alienated from his national theatres. His resistance to what he perceived as commercial conventions of *acting, *directing, and writing resulted in a desire to control the production of his work. He directed *The Woman* (1979), *Restoration* (1981), and *Summer* (1982) himself. He walked out of *rehearsals of *The War Plays* (1985) at the *Royal Shakespeare Company because of frustrations with the actors' stylistic habits and technique. During the late 1980s, as he became increasingly difficult to produce at home, his popularity grew in Europe. Beginning with *In the Company of Men* (1992), Bond has enjoyed increased critical appreciation in France, especially in *Françon's *mises-en-scène. The production of *The War Plays* at the *Avignon Festival in 1994 achieved what, for Bond, the RSC production lacked. French, not British, productions of *Jackets* (1993), *Coffee* (2000), and *The Crime of the Twenty-First Century* (2001) have been particularly striking. *Summer* and *The Sea*, which originated in England decades earlier, received important new stagings by French directors in 1993 and 1998.   JGR

Bondy, Luc (1948–) Swiss-German director. Bondy received a bilingual education in Switzerland and Paris before training at the *Lecoq school. His breakthrough in Germany came in 1974 with a much acclaimed production of *Bond's *The Sea* (Munich), and thereafter Bondy established himself as a European director, dividing his time between Berlin, Hamburg, Paris, and Vienna. From the mid-1980s he worked increasingly at the *Schaubühne where his most acclaimed production was *Marivaux's *Triumph of Love* (1987) in a dazzling set by *Herrmann. Bondy has a clear preference for authors of the *fin de siècle* (*Ibsen, *Schnitzler) as well as for contemporary dramatists such as Botho *Strauss, whose plays he has frequently premièred, most recently *Viol* in Paris. His directorial style is distinguished by wit, psychological sophistication, and keen attention to textual nuances in comparison to the confrontational approach frequently prevailing in German theatre. In recent years he has directed *opera with productions ranging from Monteverdi to *Mozart to Alban Berg.   CBB

booing Typically an expression of disapproval (literally, to imitate the sound of oxen), along with other behaviours such as jeering, hissing, and catcalls. Booing might be used by an *audience at any time to indicate dislike of a play or of a performance. Customs and practices of disapproval vary according to historical period, cultural location, and types of performance. In *Greek theatre fruit throwing and foot stamping would be expected when plays ran too long or did not engage the audience. Booing can also be explicitly directed at a particular *character, such as the *villain of a *melodrama. Popular theatre forms (and perhaps especially theatre for *youth) often expect significant audience participation, and booing might be encouraged as a response to the *action. Disapproval can be explicitly sought: in the *anansesem* of Ghana, actors often go into the audience to incite responses including boos and jeers. In *pantomimes, placards and other visual or verbal directions from actors are used to build the volume of boos for the show's villain. In such instances, booing is a sign of pleasure rather than disapproval and can contribute to the overall success of the performance. *See also* APPLAUSE.   SBe

Booth, Barton (1681–1733) English actor and *manager. Along with *Wilks and Colley *Cibber, Booth was part of the triumvirate of *actor-managers who ruled *Drury Lane during the 1710s and 1720s. He achieved his managerial status on the strength of his success as the original Cato in *Addison's play (1713), which established him as a leading tragedian. Booth eschewed comic parts, choosing the more stately and impressive parts of the Ghost in *Hamlet*, Oroonoko, Jaffeir in *Otway's *Venice Preserv'd*, Timon, and Brutus. He was exemplary of the 'declamatory school of acting that *Garrick and *Macklin displaced, though the young Macklin was nonetheless mesmerized by seeing him act. Cibber praised Booth for the musical harmony of his voice. Booth was considered one of the most learned actors of his day, having been educated at the Westminster School in London.   MJK

Booth, Edwin (1833–93) American actor, second son of Junius Brutus *Booth. Accompanying his erratic and frequently inebriated father on *tour, and occasionally appearing for him, Edwin made his official debut in Boston in 1849. In 1852 he and his father worked in theatres in California operated by his older brother, Junius Brutus Booth, Jr., and until 1856 Edwin toured California, Hawaii, and Australia, acting in companies with Laura *Keene. He achieved acclaim in New York in 1857 and became one of America's most highly regarded tragedians, particularly in the role of Hamlet; in 1865 he gave 100 consecutive performances, an unprecedented achievement. He was noted for emotional intensity, grace, and careful study of *characters. Booth's personal life was itself marked by tragedy. His wife, the actress Mary Devlin, died in 1863 at the age of 23 while he was on tour. He plunged into a melancholy that worsened after the assassination in 1865 of Abraham Lincoln by his brother John Wilkes *Booth. Edwin became *actor-manager of New York's Winter Garden Theatre, where he mounted distinguished productions of serious plays. The three Booth brothers appeared there together in 1864 in *Julius Caesar*, with Edwin as Brutus, John Wilkes as Mark Antony, and Junius Brutus, Jr., as Cassius, in a *benefit to fund a statue of Shakespeare in Central Park. After fire destroyed the Winter Garden, Edwin built Booth Theatre (1869), but poor management led to bankruptcy in 1874, though he continued to perform throughout the United States. Noteworthy foreign visits included the Princess's Theatre in London (1880–2); the Lyceum (1881), including Othello against *Irving's Iago; and an extremely successful German tour in 1883.   LQM

Booth, John Wilkes (1839–65) American actor. Son of Junius Brutus *Booth, his family was deeply divided over the Civil War. Wilkes, who began acting in 1857, travelled freely between the northern and southern states on *tour. His brother Edwin *Booth championed the Union cause, but Wilkes was an ardent supporter of the segregationist south. His last appearance as an actor was in March 1865 at Ford's Theatre in Washington. Almost a month later, on 14 April 1865, while Abraham Lincoln was attending a production of Tom *Taylor's *Our American Cousin* at the same venue, Wilkes stole into the presidential box, shot Lincoln, and jumped onto the

stage shouting, 'Sic semper tyrannis'. He escaped after the assassination but was captured and killed twelve days later.   LQM

Booth, Junius Brutus (1796–1852) Anglo-American actor. He came to attention in London as Richard III at *Covent Garden (1817). Reputed to be of Jewish descent, he incorporated Hebrew into his Shylock (1818). In 1821 he left his English wife and family and emigrated to America with Mary Ann Holmes. Three of their six children became noteworthy performers: Edwin *Booth, Junius Brutus Booth, Jr., and John Wilkes *Booth, the assassin of Abraham Lincoln. Often described as 'the mad tragedian' and compared to Edmund *Kean, the senior Booth was known for tumultuous *characters such as Richard III and Othello; his knowledge of languages; and his eccentric behaviour and alcoholic binges offstage and on. In later life Booth continued to *tour, often accompanied by his son Edwin.   LQM

Booth, Shirley (1898–1992) American actress, whose career spanned most of the twentieth century. She began in *stock companies in 1910, making her Broadway debut in 1926 (*Hell's Bells*, opposite Humphrey Bogart), her Oscar-winning film debut in 1952 (*Come Back, Little Sheba*, repeating her 1950 stage role), and starred in a hit television series (*Hazel*, 1961–6). She excelled in *comedy (*Three Men on a Horse*, 1935; *The Philadelphia Story*, 1939; *The Desk Set*, 1955), *musical comedy (*A Tree Grows in Brooklyn*, 1950; *Juno*, 1959), and drama (*The Time of the Cuckoo*, 1952). She played over 600 stage roles, acting into the 1970s on both stage and television. Throughout her somewhat rumpled, casual appearance and distinctive nasal voice, along with her virtuosity in suggesting concealed heartbreak, endeared her to *audiences.   AW

booth stage A temporary stage, outdoors, sized for the space allocated to a vendor in a market-place or fair. Generally it is a simple trestle stage with a rear curtain to mask a dressing space; the most elaborate might have traps in the stage floor, a canopy, or sometimes tent seating for the *audience. Booth stages have been used by *touring companies all over Europe from at least late *medieval times, and are possibly much older. In Britain and Ireland, professional shows touring the provinces as late as 1910 played on booth stages in a village green, known as 'fit-ups'.   JB

Borovsky, David (1934–2006) Soviet/Russian set designer. In 1969 Borovsky became chief designer for *Lyubimov at the Taganka Theatre.

Moscow, and began with *Alive: from the life of Fedor Kuzkin* (banned, 1968), *The Mother* (1969), and the famous set for *Hamlet* (1971), consisting of a heavy woven curtain that swept *characters off the stage into an open grave. For the war drama *But the Dawns Here Are so Calm* (1971) he created a variety of settings from the wooden panels of a truck. His sets for Trifonov's *The Exchange* (1979) and *The House on the Embankment* (1980) designated different times to distinct spaces. Borovsky worked with *Efros and *Efremov, as well as on *opera and theatre productions abroad. He temporarily joined the Sovremennik Theatre (1984–9) during Lyubimov's exile, and finally left the Taganka in 1999, becoming chief designer at the *Moscow Art Theatre in 2002.   BB

Boublil, Alain (1938–) and **Claude-Michel Schönberg** (1944–) French lyricist and composer team. They first collaborated in 1973 on a 'rock opera', *La Révolution française*; its Paris success led Boublil to suggest they attempt a similar musicalization of *Hugo's *Les Misérables*. Produced in Paris in 1980, it was an even greater success. In 1983 Boublil collaborated with producer *Mackintosh on *Abbacadabra*, a *musical based on songs by the Swedish pop group ABBA. Mackintosh then produced the English version of *Les Misérables* (1985), which became an international hit. Boublil and Schönberg's next collaboration, an adaptation of the *Madame Butterfly* story in the context of Vietnam titled *Miss Saigon* (1989), began in England and was similarly successful. *Martin Guerre* (1996) did not equal this success; subsequent work includes *The Pirate Queen* (2006). Their work is characterized by sweeping melodies used like *operatic leitmotifs, but infused with a rock beat. Schönberg has also had success as a pop composer in France, writing both music and lyrics.   JD

Bouchard, Michel Marc (1958–) Québec playwright and actor. His major play is *Les Feluettes* (*Lilies*, 1987), translated into several languages, staged on three continents, with a film version in English and French. As in most of his work male *protagonists, usually homosexual, challenge the homophobic intolerance of traditional Québec society. A complex drama operating on several linguistic levels while transcending usual concepts of space, time, and plot, it has been followed by some twenty others, notably *The Orphan Muses* (1988), *Coronation Voyage* (1995), and *Watched by Flies* (1998), the latter a dark drama on the topic of death.   LED

Bouchardy, Joseph (1810–70) French playwright. The enormous popularity of his *melodramas in Paris earned him the nickname 'King of the *Boulevard'. Resolutely populist, usually concluding with the destruction of a powerful *villain, his work was intended for an illiterate public. Often compared to *Pixérécourt, Bouchardy's plots are infinitely more complex than his predecessor's. Among his most celebrated works were *Gaspardo the Fisherman* (1837), *The Bellringer of St Paul*'s (1838), and *Lazarus the Shepherd* (1840). His last work, *The Armourer of Santiago*, was performed in 1868. Although Bouchardy's popularity with Parisians waned in the 1850s, many of his plays were translated into Catalan and continued to enjoy great success in Spain.   CHB

Boucicault, Dion (1822–1890) Irish actor, playwright, and *manager with a long career over three continents. Continual financial problems kept him writing or adapting plays to meet his needs, and he is credited with creating nearly 200 texts. His English provincial debut in 1838 was under the pseudonym of Lee Morton. Early success came with his *comedy *London Assurance* (staged by *Vestris at *Covent Garden, 1841), followed by over twenty works for Benjamin *Webster at the *Haymarket. During a sojourn in Paris Boucicault studied French sensational *melodrama, translating numerous works for the London stage. By 1852 he had returned to notice in London when Charles *Kean staged *The Corsican Brothers* and *The Vampire*. Boucicault joined Kean's company as actor but became estranged over Kean's ward and protégée Agnes Robertson.

The couple eloped to America in 1853. Her acting in the plays he wrote to exploit her talents won them fame and Boucicault created for himself a series of lovable, comic, down-at-heel, sentimental rogues, most notably Myles-na-Coppaleen in *The Colleen Bawn* (1860). On occasion a more exotically situated melodrama offered him the chance to play a resplendent *villain (Nana Sahib in his *Jessie Brown*, 1858) or a faithful servant (the American Indian Wahnotee in *The Octoroon*, 1859). In London from 1860 to 1872 the ever prodigal Boucicault veered between financial disaster or great success, especially with *Arrah-na-Pogue* (1864), *Rip Van Winkle* (1865), *Hunted Down* (1866) with *Irving as the villain Scudamore, *After Dark* (1868), and *Formosa* (1869). New York was to see the launch of his finest play, *The Shaughraun* (1874). In the 1880s the couple became estranged, while Dion lost money in management again. During a tour of New Zealand and Australia in 1885 he married the youthful Louise Thorndyke, without apparently divorcing Agnes. His final years were spent teaching *acting in New York.

As playwright and practitioner Boucicault effected notable innovations. He created the concept of the independent provincial *tour; he campaigned for better financial deals for dramatists, which resulted in the practice of *royalties. As dramatist, he popularized locating romantic or sensation scenes in 'authentic', especially Irish, landscapes. Though he deployed conventional sensational effects (the burning of boats, the onrush of an express train), Boucicault also used current scientific inventions unexpectedly to resolve his melodramatic plots (a camera as witness to a murder in *The Octoroon*; the telegraph in *The O'Dowd* of 1873).

Equally inventive was Boucicault's use of melodrama to engage with contemporary political events: slavery and miscegenation in *The Octoroon* (two years before the American Civil War); the motivation behind current political unrest in Ireland and the formation of the Fenian Brotherhood in *The Shaughraun*. At his best he brilliantly used the devices of melodrama to highlight differences between English and Irish modes of perception of colonial power. Boucicault was never afraid to combat the likely political sympathies of his spectators, and in this considerably influenced *Shaw and *O'Casey.   RAC

boulevard theatre At its simplest, 'le théâtre de boulevard' translates as 'commercial theatre': it refers, particularly in the period 1890–1914, to those Parisian establishments which were independent of state control, and developed their own types of play to appeal to a certain class of spectator. Limited licence to open new establishments gave way to complete freedom under Napoleon III, and many new theatres catered for the leisured affluence of the rising middle class in post-Haussmann Paris. An evening at one of the theatres built during the Second Empire—the Châtelet, the Gaîté, the Lyrique, and the Vaudeville, or the Porte-Saint-Martin—was a match for a visit to Charles Garnier's new Opéra: evening dress was obligatory, performances started after dinner, and spectators were there to be seen as well as to watch what was more often than not an exposé, either serious or light-hearted, of their own mores by playwrights like *Sardou or *Feydeau.   WDH

bourgeois theatre A cultural phenomenon which emerged during the rise of the European bourgeoisie in the eighteenth century. In Marxist parlance 'bourgeois' refers to the legal owners, or the managerial and state controllers, of merchant, industrial, and money capital who replaced the aristocracy as the class in control of the means of production. However, bourgeois theatre continues to be created by and appeal to a broader range of social groups, especially members of the diverse middle class, from professionals to clerical, technical, and service workers. Through its assertion of democratic liberalism, bourgeois theatre subversively challenged aristocratic absolutist order. In contrast to the French *neoclassical focus on plot, the *unities, and the tragic state affairs of royal figures, bourgeois drama emphasized characterization, especially of non-aristocratic *protagonists; displays of virtuous civil behaviour, especially by beneficent middle-class patriarchs; treatment of private issues in a manner which invited empathy and appealed to sentiment; and a move towards *realist *illusionism through, for example, the use of mundane prose instead of verse. In 1757 *Diderot, a prominent spokesperson for the new drama, called for a genre which embraced both 'serious *comedy', involving the virtue and duties of man, and 'bourgeois *tragedy', which dealt with domestic misfortunes. One of his sources of inspiration was *Lillo's *The London Merchant* (1731), with its story about a young businessman who steals for a prostitute and is ultimately executed.

Bourgeois theatre's association with pathos asserts self-expression and sensibility as sources of truth, while its promotion of empathy highlights what is shared by all mankind, regardless of rank. Methods of enhancing the beholder's emotional absorption in *character which gradually unfolded were: the removal of (upper-class) spectators from the stage; the fostering of fourth-wall illusionism; darkening of the *auditorium; and the focusing of concealed stage *lighting upon the actors. These methods, along with a shift from heightened theatricality to realist performance—as fostered early by *Garrick—have been interpreted as a retreat from the public to the private sphere and as an inscription of bourgeois codes of civility. A further display of these codes is to be found in nineteenth-century *playhouse auditoriums, where the introduction of seats in the stalls as well as increasingly plush decor helped to ensure quiet and disciplined spectatorship. During the nineteenth century bourgeois theatre became an increasingly conservative force. While *melodrama attracted a considerable number of spectators from the proletariat, their theatregoing was controlled by bourgeois entrepreneurs.

Many *avant-garde and politically engaged practitioners of the twentieth century have defined their work in opposition to bourgeois theatre. *Symbolism and *expressionism rejected the positivist overtones of *realism in favour of subjective abstractionism; theatres of *cruelty revolted against the disciplined body of civilized actor and spectator; and left-wing formations such as *agitprop challenged the hierarchical and commodity-oriented structures of commercial institutions. However, very few of these projects can be said to have extricated themselves from the influence of bourgeois capitalist forces, the staging of *Brecht and *Piscator's anti-bourgeois *epic theatre within mainstream institutions being a case in point. As Western theatre has become increasingly characterized by eclecticism in terms of form and content, the label 'bourgeois theatre' has tended to refer more to theatre events dominated by capitalist modes and relations of production than to specific types of drama and performance. As a descriptor which denotes cultural institutions owned, controlled, and frequented by the bourgeoisie and those who have assimilated its codes and values, 'bourgeois theatre' could be applied to the majority of theatre events in capitalist societies today.   MM

box, pit, and gallery *Audience areas in the *auditorium first established in English indoor *playhouses of the seventeenth century, such as the first *Drury Lane. The highest prices were charged for seats in a box, which might hold up to twenty people. Boxes were at stage level and ran continuously round three sides of the auditorium with at least two situated on the forestage. The pit occupied the floor of the theatre at a lower level than the stage and, unlike the standing pit of earlier *public theatres, contained rows of backless benches set on a raked floor. Seats in the pit were half the price of a seat in the box and attracted a mixed audience of men and women. The activity of the audience in the pit and the behaviour of the occupants of the boxes, especially with the King present, were part of the theatre-going spectacle. During the eighteenth century onstage boxes were gradually removed as the forestage was brought back to the *proscenium arch to accommodate larger audiences. References to the addition of middle and upper galleries in the *patent theatres appear in the 1690s with the highest gallery level, the 'gods', being first referred to in the 1750s. In the eighteenth century pit benches eventually gave way to rows of seats, with a standing pit at the back of the auditorium, while the last vestige of the early pit, immediately in front of the stage, was replaced by

the orchestra pit. In 1849 Drury Lane introduced three rows of orchestra stalls in front of the orchestra pit and by 1886 all West End London theatres had introduced stalls and enforced a dress code for stalls, boxes, and dress circle (the first gallery). Social divisions in the auditorium, apparent in the price difference between boxes and galleries in the seventeenth century, became deliberate moves toward social segregation, reflected by the dress codes that lasted until 1940. The price difference between the seating areas in traditional theatre buildings is still in force, with a stall in London costing about three times an upper gallery seat.   GBB

box set A stage set consisting of an interior room open to the *audience side, entirely framed by the *proscenium arch, within which all or most scenery will be practical. Developed in Paris for *melodrama and *boulevard *farce between 1800 and 1820, Madame *Vestris brought the box set to the Olympic Theatre in London in 1832. At first the English 'box scene' might have furniture, pictures, and windows painted on, but within two decades the box set would, as much as possible, resemble a real room sectioned by the proscenium. As *realism and *naturalism took hold of the theatre, the box set became the most 'natural' of settings, and by 1900 it had largely displaced horizontally sliding scenery. *Belasco and other Broadway *producers, during the boom years before the First World War, could afford both the materials and the technicians to create spaces in exacting detail; by 1930 most *audiences expected to experience the scenery as apparently 'real', a kind of vivid hallucination. With the subsequent development of the open stage, the box set began to seem quaint, static, distant, and contrived, requiring actors to speak, move, and turn as if they were conversing with an unmarked windowless wall. *See* SCENOGRAPHY.   JB

boy actor In all European theatrical traditions, female roles were regularly played by boys or young men until Italian popular companies introduced actresses in the mid-sixteenth century. Even these companies were not allowed to use actresses throughout Italy, and where actresses were permitted they used male performers to play bawdy female servants (*see* COMMEDIA DELL'-ARTE). Gradually, the use of actresses spread across Western Europe, but the English commercial theatre remained an all-male preserve until the enforced cessation of playing in 1642, and only introduced actresses after the Restoration in 1660. Before the 1590s, small itinerant English troupes, accustomed to doubling roles, often comprised 'four men and a boy', the latter taking all female roles. When larger troupes established permanent London *playhouses after the 1590s, three or four 'play-boys' in female roles could be on stage at the same time. As virtual if not actual apprentices, these young *female impersonators took female roles until their voices changed, as late as age 18 or 19, and thereafter played young men. Cross-gender casting was attacked by Puritans and other *anti-theatrical writers. *See also* GENDER AND PERFORMANCE.   MS

Bracegirdle, Anne (*c.*1673–1748) English actress and *manager. Adopted into the *Betterton household, Bracegirdle is named as a member of the United Company in 1688, though she probably performed earlier. Her reputation was as innocent and virtuous as the *characters she played in *tragedy, and she was a regular *prologue speaker and a popular comedienne, particularly in *breeches roles. With Elizabeth *Barry and Thomas Betterton, Bracegirdle co-managed the Players' Company at *Lincoln's Inn Fields (1695–1705) during which time *Congreve wrote *Love for Love* (1695) and Millament in *The Way of the World* (1700) for her. She retired from the stage in 1707, still at the height of her career.   GBB

Brahm, Otto (1856–1912) German critic and *manager. Brahm studied German literature in Berlin before becoming a theatre critic in 1881. In 1889 he co-founded the *Freie Bühne based on *Antoine's Théâtre *Libre. He also established and edited the periodical *Freie Bühne für modernes Leben* (1890–1), which became the most important organ for propagating the principles of *naturalism in Germany. The Freie Bühne, organized as a private society to avoid *censorship, was instrumental in introducing dramatists such as *Hauptmann and *Schnitzler and performing the more controversial plays by *Ibsen. In 1894 Brahm leased the *Deutsches Theater and built up one of the best *acting ensembles in Germany. Although he never appeared as *director on playbills, he closely supervised all aspects of production and the 'Brahm style' became a synonym for *dramaturgical exactitude and psychological *realism. In 1904 he leased the Lessing Theater, by which time his style was losing popularity against the flamboyant theatricality of his pupil *Reinhardt. He stayed with his repertoire but was in dire financial straits at his death. CBB

Braithwaite, Lilian (1873–1948) English actress. Braithwaite began her career in South Africa, performing Shakespeare with her husband Gerald Lawrence. She returned to England in 1900 and acted with the companies of *Benson and *Alexander, quickly establishing herself in the West End in revivals of Shakespeare and *Wilde. For the most part, her career over the next four decades consisted of roles in popular *melodramas and sentimental *comedies. In the 1920s she had great success in *Coward's *The Vortex* (1924), and she played in a series of Ivor *Novello comedies in the 1920s. For three years in London during the Second World War she appeared in *Arsenic and Old Lace*.   TP

Branagh, Kenneth (1960–) Irish actor, director, and *producer. Born in Belfast, Branagh made his London debut in 1982 in Julian *Mitchell's *Another Country*, and joined the *Royal Shakespeare Company in 1984 to play Henry V, Laertes, and the King of Navarre. Critics immediately drew comparisons with the young *Olivier. In 1987 he co-founded the Renaissance Theatre Company, and, extending the Olivier parallel, made his film directorial debut with *Henry V* (1989). For Renaissance he directed *Twelfth Night* (1987), *King Lear*, *A Midsummer Night's Dream* (both 1990), and *Uncle Vanya* (1991); and appeared as Hamlet, Benedick, and Touchstone in 1988, Quince and Edgar in 1990, and Coriolanus in 1992, when he also played Hamlet again, in a full text for the RSC. His film career focuses on Shakespeare: he has directed and starred in *Much Ado About Nothing* (1993), *Hamlet* (1996, running more than four hours), *Love's Labour's Lost* (2000), and *As You Like It* (2006). He played Iago opposite Laurence Fishburne in Oliver Parker's *Othello* (1995), and has appeared in a number of other Hollywood movies. Television includes *Shackleton* (2001) and *Wallander* (2008, based on Henning Mankell's detective novels). In the West End Branagh directed *The Play What I Wrote* (2001) and starred in *Stoppard's version of *Chekhov's *Ivanov* (2008).   AS

Brando, Marlon (1924–2004) American actor. Brando became famous for his *Method *acting style, learned from both *Adler and *Strasberg, in his stage and screen performances as Stanley Kowalski in *Williams's *A Streetcar Named Desire* (1947, 1951, directed by *Kazan). Though he never returned to the stage he continued to create moody, self-absorbed, and often aggressive *characters in films such as *The Wild One* (1954) and Kazan's controversial *On the Waterfront* (1954). Other notable films of the 1950s include *Julius Caesar* (1953), *Guys and Dolls* (1955), and *The Fugitive Kind* (1959). Brando received an Oscar for his performance as Don Corleone in

Coppola's *The Godfather* (1971). He remained uncomfortable with Hollywood stardom and continued to work in commercially risky ventures such as Bernardo Bertolucci's *Last Tango in Paris* (1972) and Coppola's *surreal epic about the Vietnam War, *Apocalypse Now* (1979). While he became increasingly reclusive as a person, Brando appeared in mainstream Hollywood movies during the 1980s and 1990s, most notably in a comic parody of Don Corleone in *The Freshman* (1990). JAB

Braun, Volker (1939-) German dramatist, essayist, and poet. Braun grew up in the German Democratic Republic, working as a printer and on construction sites before studying philosophy in Leipzig. From the mid-1960s he worked as a *dramaturg at the *Berliner Ensemble and then at the *Deutsches Theater. During this time he established himself as a dramatist, closely aligned to the ideals of the East German state, while at the same time able to criticize it within acceptable limits. The *characters in his plays are frequently rebels who channel their rebelliousness in a productive way. His best-known work is *Transitional Society* (1987), which was premièred in West Germany. Braun received major literary awards in both East and West Germany. CBB

Braunshweig, Stéphane (1964-) French director. After studying philosophy and theatre, Braunshweig became one of the most sought-after of younger directors, producing numerous plays and *operas throughout Europe, most notably *Brecht's *In the Jungle of the Cities* (Paris, 1997), *Measure for Measure* (*Edinburgh Festival, 1997), *The Merchant of Venice* (Paris, 1999), and a revelatory *Fidelio* (Berlin, 1995). From 1993 to 1998 he ran the Centre Dramatique National for Orléans-Loiret, and from 2008 was the director of Théâtre National de Strasbourg, directing (and often designing) a series of acclaimed productions of *Ibsen. DGM

Bread and Puppet Theatre German sculptor-puppeteer Peter Schumann (1934-) moved to New York in 1961, playing in poor neighbourhoods, baking and distributing bread at performances: his working assumption was that theatre, like bread, is a staple of life. In the 1960s Bread and Puppet began *street protests against capitalism and the Vietnam War, using giant figures—on a scale with the urban environment—*masks, and placards, reminiscent of Soviet *agitprop of the 1920s and the giant festive figures of Iberia. To be more in contact with nature, Schumann moved to a farm in Vermont, establishing an annual 'Resurrection Circus', involving hundreds of participants and huge *audiences. Rich in Christian references, and in a broad range of references to cultural myth, Schumann's work is profoundly humanitarian, and concerned with the false and exploitative values of a post-Cold War consumerism. Discovered at the Nancy Festival in 1968, Bread and Puppet paved the way for the introduction of the *puppet into modern theatre performance, notably with the Théâtre du *Soleil's *1789*. JMcC

Brecht, Bertolt (1898–1956) German playwright, director, theoretician, and poet, one of the most influential theatre practitioners of the twentieth century. Born in Augsburg in Bavaria, Brecht began publishing poetry while still in school. He studied medicine in Munich in 1917, but broke off the next year while working on his first play, *Baal*, to devote himself full time to writing. In 1922 he won the prestigious Kleist Prize for most promising young writer with his second play, *Drums in the Night*. The next year, both *Baal* and a new play, *In the Jungle of Cities*, received productions. All three plays provoked divided, often boisterous spectator response. Brecht rode this wave of notoriety from Munich to Berlin in 1924, where he took up a nominal position as one of *Reinhardt's *dramaturgs at the *Deutsches Theater while writing *A Man's a Man* (1926); he also worked with *Piscator in 1927-8. Brecht then collaborated with his childhood friend, the designer Caspar *Neher, and the composer Kurt *Weill on *The Threepenny Opera* (1928), which overnight became Weimar Germany's most successful theatre event.

Brecht's three early plays demonstrate his assimilation of *expressionist technique and a command of dramatic language that helped him develop one of the most significant styles in German. They also contain a violent rejection of the *bourgeois values with which he had been raised and a developing attack on the Weimar Republic's cold commercialism, which achieved its most exotic expression in the *opera *Rise and Fall of the City of Mahagonny* (music by Weill, 1930). By then, however, Brecht was more interested in creating a new kind of politically committed theatre, a proletarian theatre performed by workers' groups for worker *audiences. He had begun to study and practise Marxism in the mid-1920s; his initial interests are visible in the somewhat confused exploration of collective identity in *A Man's a Man*. Between 1929 and 1931 he wrote five *Lehrstücke*, or 'learning plays', the best known of which is *The Measures Taken* (1930), in which four agitators played by *actors report the story of their mission to China to a 'Control Chorus', played by several large workers' *choruses (and, by extension, by the spectators), to whom the agitators direct their physical demonstrations. *The Mother* (1932), one of the finest plays of this period, uses the *Lehrstück* style, but is written for professional rather than amateur actors and does not attempt to break the performer-spectator relationship.

Brecht directed his first production—the première of his own adaptation of *Marlowe's Edward II*—in 1924, and continued to work on productions of his plays, often as *director of record, often less openly. Until he fled Germany to avoid execution after the Nazis seized power in 1933, his various notes and statements about the theatre involved not abstract theorizing but direct response to a practice, leading to the *epic theatre he had been experimenting with throughout the decade.

After fleeing Germany, Brecht, his wife and collaborator, the actress Helene *Weigel, and their two children kept just ahead of expanding Nazi hegemony, moving first to Denmark (1933), then Sweden (1939), Finland (1940), and finally California (1941). During this period, he wrote several plays as direct contributions to the fight against Hitler, including the epic *Fear and Misery of the Third Reich* (1938), and the intentionally *melodramatic and hugely successful *Señora Carrar's Rifles* (1937). In exile Brecht wrote most of the theoretical essays and plays that secured his international reputation after his death, including *Life of Galileo* (1937), *Mother Courage and her Children* (1941), *The Good Person of Setzuan* (1943), and *The Caucasian Chalk Circle* (1948). Two political *comedies, *Mr Puntila and his Man, Matti* (1948) and *The Resistible Rise of Arturo Ui* (1958), have met with mixed receptions.

Brecht was unsuccessful in establishing himself as a Hollywood screenwriter and in getting his plays widely produced in the USA. In 1947 he was called to testify before the House Un-American Activities Committee. He defended himself well against charges of being a Communist Party member and writing communist propaganda, but left the next month for Switzerland, where in 1948 he directed productions of his adaptation of *Antigone* and *Puntila*, while working with Weigel towards setting up a new company, the *Berliner Ensemble, at the invitation of the East German authorities. In 1949 he moved to East Berlin. He left unfinished a new play, *Days of the Commune*, and did not complete another. Instead he concentrated on directing and on training a new generation of directors and actors. He developed new variations of his epic theatre, noting once that the

post-war, post-Nazi audience simply was not ready for the older, stronger epic theatre of the *Lehrstücke*. He did, however, stage *The Mother* (1951), along with *Mother Courage* (1949), and *Caucasian Chalk Circle* (1954). And he wrote several adaptations for the Ensemble that became influential, including *Lenz's *The Private Tutor* (1950), *Farquhar's *Trumpets and Drums* (1955), and Shakespeare's *Coriolanus*, unfinished at Brecht's early death and staged in 1964.

Brecht's work remained highly controversial in the German Democratic Republic until well after his death. The Berliner Ensemble survived its first few years in part thanks to the European-wide interest the company sparked on *tour, an interest that gradually extended to Brecht's plays. The initial reception took place, however, in the darkest moments of the Cold War, and gave more value to Brecht's exile plays, making comforting comparisons with the German classics and with Shakespeare, and focusing analysis on their seemingly sympathetic central *characters and their confrontation with large-scale but rather generalized moral dilemmas. Later readings and productions have achieved considerable success in wresting the plays away from this post-war liberalism.

By the end of the twentieth century, most of Brecht's plays could count on periodically finding new champions, even if the champions of one kind of Brecht play frequently despised the others. Adding to the controversy was a highly public flap over the true authorship of some of the plays, prompted by John Fuegi's claims in *The Life and Lies of Bertolt Brecht* (1994) that Brecht had exploited his female collaborators—claims which Fuegi exaggerated far beyond their sometimes legitimate basis in fact. More tellingly, new appreciations frequently refused close reference to Brecht's theory or to the practices of epic theatre, most of which had been absorbed into establishment theatre practice in Europe and America by the 1980s. But Brecht's enormous influence has continued into the new millennium, as his texts and theories still proved useful to populist practitioners and spectators in both the developed and developing worlds.   JR

Bredero, Gerbrant Adriaenszoon (1585–1618) Dutch poet and playwright. Like his contemporary *Hooft, Bredero was influenced by *early modern developments but his works also retain a popular, spontaneous stamp. He saw the *English Comedians in the Netherlands and may well owe something of his keen theatrical sense to them. He was a member of the Amsterdam *Chamber of Rhetoric, and wrote a number of

romances based on Spanish models, as well as *farces such as *The Farce of the Cow* (1612) which continued the *medieval tradition. More theatrically successful were his *comedies *Moortje* (1615), based on a French translation of Terence's *Eunuchus*, and *The Spanish Brabanter* (1617), the subject matter of which was borrowed from the Spanish picaresque novel *Lazarillo de Tormes*. In this play Bredero created a delightful *satiric picture of a destitute but blusterous Antwerp immigrant in Amsterdam. JDV

breeches role A part in which an actress appears in male attire. In English the term has been traditionally applied to parts written for men and performed by women. A commercially successful device in the seventeenth and eighteenth centuries, the breeches role began with the arrival of women on stage in the Restoration. New plays frequently included a female character who adopts male disguise in plots that ultimately turn on the discovery of her true sexual identity. All-female revivals of stock plays also proved to be financially successful, with Nell *Gwynn and Anne *Bracegirdle receiving popular acclaim in early breeches roles, and Peg *Woffington and Dorothy *Jordan demonstrating the continuing appeal in revivals of *Farquhar's *The Constant Couple*. As a device which revealed more of the female body than conventional dress, the extent to which the cross-dressed actress is an exploited object of the male gaze or active participant in the disruption of female constructs is the subject of ongoing debates (*see* MALE IMPERSONATION). *Behn's *The Rover* (1677) is an early example of playwriting by women in which the breeches role is used to disrupt conventional representations of female behaviour and challenge attitudes to female sexual desire. GBB

Brenton, Howard (1942–) English playwright. Many of Brenton's early plays were written for alternative theatre companies, including *Christie in Love* (1969), *Fruit* (1970), and *Scott of the Antarctic* (1971). He used a collage of styles to capture the 'society of the spectacle', Guy Debord's term for the superficial and mediatized world of images of Western society. Brenton was soon taken up by major theatres: he wrote a pungent intervention on political terrorism, *Magnificence* (1973), for the *Royal Court; *The Churchill Play* (1974, revised 1979), a dystopian vision of Britain under military rule, for the *Royal Shakespeare Company; and *Weapons of Happiness* (1976) for the *National Theatre. He worked with other writers and with collaborative *devising companies like Joint Stock (*Epsom Downs*,

1977). *The Romans in Britain* (NT, 1980) was the subject of a famous obsenity case for a scene which uses homosexual rape as an image of colonialism; the play compares the Roman invasion of Britain with Britain's treatment of Ireland. *Pravda* (written with *Hare, 1985) was an unsettling treatment of the relations between politics, industry, and the press.

Brenton wrote in the expectation of a final clash between the far left and far right, and his plays debate the ethics of revolutionary activity as well as offering scabrous portraits of the society to be overthrown. The election of Margaret Thatcher in 1979 was an opportunity for rethinking. *A Short Sharp Shock!* (1980) is a gleefully offensive portrait of the new government, but plays like *Sore Throats* (1979), *Bloody Poetry* (1984), and *Greenland* (1988) show an awareness of the increasing remoteness of the socialist utopia. Brenton returned to the immediacy of his early work with short *satirical pieces often co-written with another veteran of May 1968, Tariq Ali. *Iranian Nights* (1989) addressed the Salman Rushdie affair, *Ugly Rumours* (1998) lampooned the ideological drift of New Labour, and *Snogging Ken* (2000) satirized the Labour government's intrigues over the election of the first mayor of London. Brenton returned to main stages with *Paul* (2005), *In Extremis* (2006), and a surprisingly fond portrait of British Conservative prime minister, Harold Macmillan, in *Never So Good* (2008). DR

Breth, Andrea (1952–) German director. Breth's breakthrough came in 1983 with a production of *García Lorca's *The House of Bernarda Alba* in Freiburg. From 1986 to 1990 she was director-in-residence in Bochum, mounting a number of noted productions, and from 1992 to 1998 *artistic director of the *Schaubühne in Berlin, where she brought out highly acclaimed versions of *Ibsen and *Chekhov. In 2000 she was appointed director-in-residence at the *Burgtheater in Vienna. Her directorial style is characterized by psychological subtlety, highly charged atmosphere, and a preference for a slow pace with tension. She has been the recipient of many awards and invitations to the Berlin *Theatertreffen. CBB

Breuer, Lee (1937–) American playwright and director who co-founded *Mabou Mines in 1970. He adapted and directed three works by *Beckett, *Play*, *Come and Go*, and *The Lost Ones*, all of which received Obie awards. Breuer also wrote and directed a triology of what he has called 'performance poetry', inspired by Kafka's animal parables, called the 'Animations'. In 1980 *A Prelude to a Death in Venice* received acclaim for its innovative use of actors and *puppets. In the 1980s Breuer collaborated with composer Bob Telson on a series of *music theatre projects; in 1983 they presented *The Gospel at Colonus*, an oratorio set in an African-American Pentecostal church in which *Sophocles' *tragedy is the sermon text. Other collaborations include *Sister Suzie Camera* (1980) and *The Warrior Ant* (1986). His work has often been associated with minimalism and the 'theatre of images'.   JAD

Brewster, Yvonne (1938-) Jamaican actor and director, *artistic director of Talawa Theatre Company in London, which she co-founded. Its inaugural production was C. L. R. James's *The Black Jacobins* (1986). After training Brewster worked as an actor in London and as a radio announcer and television producer in Jamaica. With playwright Trevor *Rhone, she co founded Jamaica's first professional theatre company, the Barn Theatre in Kingston (1971). The early 1970s also saw her direct in London: Sally Durie's *Lippo, the New Noah* with an African Caribbean cast at the ICA in 1971; *Walcott's *Pantomime* in a pub; and a *musical version of Barry Reckord's *Skyvers*. In 1991 she directed *García Lorca's *Blood Wedding* for the *National Theatre. Innovative and challenging productions for Talawa include the first all-black production of *The Importance of Being Earnest* (1989), *Soyinka's *The Road* (1992), Shakespeare's *King Lear* (1994), *Ford's *'Tis Pity She's a Whore* (1995), Walcott's *farce *Beef, No Chicken* (1996), *Flyin' West* (1997) by *African-American Pearl Cleage, and *Medea in the Mirror* (1999) by *Triana.   AS

Brice, Fanny (1891-1951) Comic and singer. Brice was already a star in the Ziegfeld *revues when her 'Baby Snooks' *character was introduced in the *Ziegfeld Follies of 1934. Brice was adept at sketch- and song-based comedy (performed in a squawky Yiddish dialect) and at torch songs delivered in a powerful and unwavering alto. She began in amateur contests in 1906 before advancing through the ranks of *burlesque from 1907 to 1910. First hired by Ziegfeld for the *Follies* of 1910, she continued for 1911 but defected to the rival *Shubert brothers in 1912. She appeared on Broadway in *The Honeymoon Express* in 1913, played London, and returned to New York to appear in two of the *Kern/*Bolton 'Princess *musicals' in 1915—*Hands Up* and *Nobody Home*. She alternated among *Follies* appearances, Shubert musicals, the Orpheum vaudeville circuit, and Billy *Rose musicals—as well as forays

in film and radio—until her death from a brain haemorrhage. She was married to confidence-man Nick Arnstein (1919-27) and to composer/*producer Rose (1929-38).   MAF

Bridges-Adams, William (1889-1965) English director, director of the *Shakespeare Memorial Theatre (1919-34). Dubbed 'Unabridges-Adams' for using largely uncut texts, he nevertheless directed in a fluid manner, unhampered by scenic clutter. After the fire at the SMT in 1926, he maintained the continuity of the Stratford-upon-Avon Festival by transferring the repertoire to the local cinema. He intended the new theatre, opened in 1932, to be a flexible space for innovative work; guest director *Komisarjevsky's *The Merchant of Venice* (1932) and *Macbeth* (1933) fulfilled this aim. Insufficient administrative support for Bridges Adams's outward-looking policies led to his resignation in 1934. He later became dramatic adviser to the British Council (1937-44). His writings include *The Lost Leader* (1954), an essay on Granville *Barker, and *The Irresistible Theatre* (1957), a history of drama to the mid-seventeenth century.   VRS

Bridie, James (Osborne Henry Mavor) (1884-1951) Scottish playwright. Mavor wrote under a number of pseudonyms, including Mary Henderson and Archibald Kellock, before he finally settled on James Bridie after his fiftieth birthday. He also found his calling late; after qualifying as a doctor and serving in the Medical Corps during the First World War, *The Switchback* (1922) premièred at the *Birmingham Repertory Theatre. Bridie is most closely associated with Scottish theatre, which he worked hard to promote, founding the Glasgow *Citizens' Theatre and supporting the Royal Scottish Academy of Music and Drama. His major plays include *The Anatomist* (1931); *Tobias and the Angel* (1932), featuring *Guthrie who was later to direct several of his plays; *Storm in a Teacup* (1936), a *satire on Scottish provincialism and local politics; and *Daphne Laureola* (1949), a poetic look at postwar England, directed by *Olivier and starring Edith *Evans.   MDG

Brie, Mlle de (1630-1706) French actress. She joined *Molière's itinerant company in 1650, remained with it after his death, and retired from the *Comédie-Française in 1685. Mlle de Brie was the most consistently valuable interpreter of Molière's plays. In the early years she regularly played the *ingénue; the greatest of these roles, which transcends the type, was Agnès in *The School for Wives*, a popular favourite until her retirement. Molière gradually extended the psychological depth and complexity of her roles, especially after the younger and less experienced Mlle Molière (Armande *Béjart) became available to play conventional ingénues.   RWH

Brieux, Eugène (1858–1932) French dramatist who exposed the corruption, malaise, and illnesses of society. The sins of the flesh loom large in his work but he focuses his criticism on the social conditions which give rise to them. Two of his early plays were produced by *Antoine at the Théâtre *Libre, one a huge success (*Blanchette*, 1897). Three plays are of particular note: *The Three Daughters of M. Dupont* (1897) portrays the follies and the dangers of marriages of convenience; *Les Avariés* (*Damaged Goods*, 1902) is a teaching play about syphilis; *Maternity* (1903) treats the question of the legalization of contraception. These three 'thesis' plays were translated into English in 1909 and championed by *Shaw. *Damaged Goods* had the most effect and Shaw highlighted Brieux as the champion of social reform on the stage. Brieux is linked with *Zola's scientific principles of *naturalism, as the play presents three case studies in three acts that demonstrate that ignorance and fear of exposure are the causes of the spread of syphilis. Such was the vehemence of Brieux's attack on society that his plays often suffer *dramaturgically, as *characters give way to sermonizing.   BRS

Brighouse, Harold (1882–1958) English novelist and dramatist. Associated with the 'Manchester school' of playwrights, he wrote over 50 one-act and 16 full-length plays, often about contemporary Lancashire life and with a strong bias towards social themes, including *Dealing in Futures* (1910), the one-act *Lonesome Like* (1911), and *Garside's Career* (1916), all premièred at Manchester's Gaiety Theatre. Other notable plays include *The Northerners* (1914) and *Zack* (1916). His most famous work, and the archetypal Lancashire play, *Hobson's Choice*, was ironically given its first performance in New York before transferring to London in 1915. A *comedy set in Salford in 1880, challenging conventional expectations of how daughters should behave, it has remained a perennial favourite with repertory *audiences ever since its first performance, and was filmed in 1954, starring *Laughton and *Mills.   ARJ

Brome, Richard (*c.*1590–*c.*1653) English playwright. Nothing is known of Brome's origins and early years. He became a professional playwright after spending several years in the service of *Jonson, whose influence is often recognizable in his works. He was resident dramatist for the Salisbury

Court *playhouse from 1635 to 1638, afterwards moving to *Drury Lane. A prolific writer of *comedies and *tragicomedies, his work frequently indulges in *satire and radical political commentary. Among his best-known plays are the comedies *The Northern Lass* (1629), probably his greatest stage success, *The Antipodes* (1636), which contains a play-within-the-play full of remarks on contemporary theatre, *The Court Beggar* (1640), and *A Jovial Crew* (1641), which enjoyed numerous revivals in the late seventeenth century. The little-known *The Queen and Concubine* (1636), a tragicomedy on the dangers of absolutism, is outspoken in its commentary on contemporary topical issues.   PCR

Brook, Peter (1925–) English director, filmmaker, and theorist. Peter Brook's extraordinarily productive career spans more than 60 years since the end of the Second World War, and includes over 80 theatre and *opera productions and a dozen films. It will be useful to divide this extensive body of work into three periods.

Born in London, Brook was educated at Westminster and Gresham's schools, then Magdalen College, Oxford. The first phase of Brook's work as a *director (1945–63) comprises his hyperactive directorial apprenticeship in a wide range of performance contexts and styles. At the age of 22 he was already a director at the Royal Opera House, *Covent Garden; and by 1963, when Brook was 38, he had directed over 40 productions, including nine Shakespeare plays and seven major operas. Landmark productions included a luminous *Love's Labour's Lost*, inspired visually by Watteau, for the *Shakespeare Memorial Theatre (1946), a capriciously erotic reworking of *Strauss's *Salomé* (1949) with designs by Salvador Dalí, a shockingly austere *Titus Andronicus* (1955) with *Olivier and Vivien *Leigh, and an elemental, absurdist *King Lear* (1962) with *Scofield for the new *Royal Shakespeare Company. Although best known as a director of classical theatre, Brook also juggled productions of major twentieth-century European playwrights (*Cocteau, *Sartre, *Anouilh, *Genet, *Dürrenmatt) and works by seminal modernists (including *Eliot and *Miller), as well as overtly commercial projects—*boulevard and *musical comedies and television drama. Brook's immersion in a contradictory array of forms reflected his desire to fashion a complex, composite reality through the exploration of opposites. He referred to this period as a 'theatre of images', informed by an escapist aesthetic of illusionist decoration and artifice where the director's 'vision' was omnipotent. At the same time, he collaborated with many of the finest performers of his generation, including *Guinness, *Welles, and *Gielgud.

The second phase (1964–70) constituted a period of research, reappraisal, and maturation. Brook became increasingly disaffected with the dominant theatre forms and processes, which he stigmatized as convention bound and 'deadly'. In his search for theatre languages that could reflect the complexity of contemporary realities, he questioned the theatrical status quo at every level. This period of work reached fruition in a remarkable series of productions Brook characterized as a 'theatre of disturbance'. An explicit shift in his concerns and processes became evident in an experimental project conducted under the aegis of the RSC, with a group co-directed with *Marowitz. Public 'work-in-progress' showings of this early, tentative research in 1964 were entitled the 'Theatre of *Cruelty' in homage to *Artaud, culminating with the celebrated production of *Weiss's *Marat/Sade* (1964), a *collectively devised response to the Vietnam War ambiguously entitled *US* (1966), and a choral, *ritualized *Oedipus* (1968) in an abrasive new version (from *Seneca) by Ted Hughes.

This transitional phase was also characterized by a growing awareness of the performer's importance within an ensemble. Brook recognized that the creativity of *actors would be instrumental in challenging the complacency of prevalent practices and creative hierarchies, and in finding theatrical forms as multifaceted as Shakespeare's. Brook took Elizabethan *dramaturgy as his model. He particularly admired its shifts of gear in the mix of *comedy and *tragedy, its vivid language, its spatio-temporal fluidity, and the directness of its forms. Shakespeare became his prototype for a conflation of the 'rough' and the 'holy' into a textured totality he called the 'immediate'. This area of research reached its apogee with his joyously airborne production of *A Midsummer Night's Dream* (RSC, 1970), a *circus-inflected celebration which radically dismantled received ideas of the play and provided a buoyant counter-image to the harrowing, confrontational tenor of the earlier work of this period. Since that time, Brook's ideals and goals have remained constant: the amplification of actors' capacities as creatively responsive instruments within an ensemble conceived as 'a storyteller with many heads'; the practice of research as ongoing 'self-research', a process of individual development in which theatre serves as potent site and means, but rarely as the exclusive end; and the act of theatre as affirmative 're-membering', in which a mythical narrative or fable is actualized in the present to create tem-

porary communities of shared experience. Eventually the desire for conditions enabling the pursuit and refinement of such ideals took him from the restrictions of commercial theatre in England to a new base in France.

The third phase comprised Brook's work with his international group in Paris, the International Centre for Theatre Research (CIRT), from 1970 until 2008, when Brook finally announced plans for retirement at the age of 83. From the outset in Paris, Brook and his multicultural collaborators were cushioned by subsidy from the crippling demands and impositions of the commercial sector. The Centre's focus ranged from private research behind closed doors, to explorations of theatrical communication between cultures in the field (on journeys to Iran, Africa, and the USA), to forays into the fantastic inner landscapes of neurological disorders and abilities in *The Man Who* (1993). Core projects have included *Orghast* (1971), a site-specific music-theatre piece performed at Persepolis in a mixture of dead and invented languages; an adaptation of Colin Turnbull's anthropological study of the demise of a Ugandan tribe, *The Ik* (1975–6); a presentation of a twelfth-century Sufi poem, Attar's *Conference of the Birds* (1979), about the journey of a group of birds in search of their god; a nine hour version of the sacred Sanskrit epic *The Mahabharata* (1985–8); a spartan staging of Shakespeare's *The Tempest* with the African actor Sotigui Kouyaté as Prospero; and an abridged and physically dynamic version of *Hamlet* (2000–1) with Adrian Lester in the title role.

As a filmmaker Brook further developed in cinematic terms his concerns as a theatre director. Major films include *Moderato Cantabile* (1960), *Lord of the Flies* (1963), *Marat/Sade* (1966), *Tell Me Lies* (1968), *King Lear* (1971), *Meetings with Remarkable Men* (1979), and *The Mahabharata* (1989).

While at times Brook was suspected of cultural appropriation by some critics, his *intercultural practice with the Centre remained rigorously syncretic rather than synthetic. Cultural difference was consistently cherished as a source of creative friction, never erased in a quest for some imaginary theatrical 'esperanto'. Indeed, the make-up of the company itself implicitly offered a paradigm in microcosm of social and cultural coexistence, and of the act of theatre as meeting point. Similarly, throughout this period Brook's dramaturgical model remained one of narrative and psychological multiplicity in which the poetic, spiritual, political, and carnal can coexist. His characteristically unadorned *scenography at the company's base at the Théâtre des Bouffes du Nord in Paris was founded on proximity, openness, and fluidity. Like all popular theatre, it employed eclectic forms of a distilled and mutable simplicity which offered spectators active invitations to imaginative complicity. Brook's work with the Centre proposed a humanist social critique, suggesting that humankind's greatest threat remains the misanthropic ignorance of our fellow human beings. Nonetheless, these fables were ultimately restorative, outlining an itinerary in which fragmentation necessarily precedes reintegration and healing.

Finally, through his own writing Brook has made significant interventions to twentieth-century theory and practice, especially with *The Empty Space* (1968), *The Shifting Point* (1987), and a memoir, *Threads of Time* (1998).   ADW

Brown, John Russell (1923–) English scholar, director, and *dramaturg. Brown followed an international academic career, but from 1973 to 1988 was also an associate of the *National Theatre under *Hall, replacing *Tynan as script adviser. A leader of the performance-oriented approach to the study of Shakespeare and early modern playwrights, his many books have had wide influence; they include *Free Shakespeare* (1974), *Discovering Shakespeare* (1981), *The Oxford Illustrated History of the Theatre* (edited 1995), and *New Sites for Shakespeare: theatre, audience and Asia* (1999). He worked around the world as a director of Shakespeare and other plays, often experimenting in print and in practice with methods alternative to the modernist practice of *director's theatre, chiefly by recalling the *actor-led traditions of the Elizabethan stage.   DK

Brown, William Henry (fl. 1820s) *African-American playwright and *manager. Brown was a retired ship's steward from the West Indies who founded a pleasure garden for free blacks in New York in 1816. Called the African Grove, the facility featured occasional outdoor entertainments until officials closed it down in 1821. Undaunted, Brown re-formed his troupe into the African Company and continued performances indoors. Fearing competition, the nearby Park Theatre, in cooperation with the city sheriff, had the theatre closed and Brown was forced to perform illegally at various locations until 1823. He also wrote and produced *The Drama of King Shotaway* (1823), the first play by an African-American.   PAD

Browne, E. Martin (1900–80) English director. His enthusiasm for poetic and religious drama led Browne to make two remarkable contributions: the promotion of *Eliot's drama, and staging the York *mystery plays for the Festival of Britain in 1951. Browne toured the USA as an actor, then became director of religious drama for Chichester (1930). He commissioned Eliot's *Murder in the Cathedral*, and performed as the fourth Tempter in Canterbury Cathedral (1935); he later directed all Eliot's plays, and was instrumental in editing his *The Confidential Clerk* (1953). During the war he founded the Pilgrim Players and in 1945, as director of the Mercury Theatre, continued to support poetic drama.   KN

Browne, Maurice (1881–1955) English actor, *manager, writer, and champion of the *Little Theatre movement in the USA. Along with Ellen Van Volkenberg, he was founder and director of the Chicago Little Theatre (1912), which established the parameters of the little theatres in America: mixing professional and amateur performers, playing in a small venue (theirs seated 99 people), subscription-based seasons, and a repertoire heavily influenced by European drama. Browne was director of a repertory company (1918–26), and then a *producer and manager in London and New York (1928–37). He presented *Sherriff's *Journey's End* at the Savoy in London in 1929 and produced it internationally.   AS

Brustein, Robert (1927–) American critic, director, and playwright. As pre-eminent critic and influential *artistic director for 35 years, Brustein's career is unique. While at Columbia University, he became drama critic for *New Republic*. In 1966 he became dean of Yale School of Drama, where he founded Yale Repertory Theatre and pioneered the partnering of a university-based conservatory with a *regional theatre. In 1979 he shifted his operation to Harvard and started the *American Repertory Theatre, which he led until 2002. At both he hired inventive directors for classics, modernist works, and new American plays. He acted in eight productions, directed a dozen others, and produced his own plays as well as his adaptations of *Pirandello, *Ibsen, and others. He published a dozen books of essays, reviews, and memoirs, including *The Theatre of Revolt* (1962) and *Reimagining American Theatre* (1991). Brustein campaigned against commercialism, political correctness, and the incursion of popular culture on theatre as a high art, often courting controversy in the process.   STC

Bryceland, Yvonne (1925–92) South African actress known for playing *Fugard and co-founding South Africa's first internationally known non-racial theatre, the Space, in Cape Town. Bryceland found her voice reinterpreting Milly in Fugard's *People Are Living There* and especially creating Lena in *Boesman and Lena* in 1969. Bryceland, Fugard, and Bryceland's husband

Brian Astbury opened the Space with Fugard's *Statements after an Arrest...*, with Bryceland as Frieda and Fugard as Errol, her coloured lover (1972). Other roles included *Euripides' Medea and the definitive Hester in Fugard's *Hello and Goodbye* (1974) at the Space and *Brecht's *Mother Courage* at the Market Theatre (1976). Moving to London and the *National Theatre, Bryceland played Hecuba in *Bond's *The Woman* (1978) and Emilia in *Othello* (1979), as well as Miss Helen in Fugard's *Road to Mecca* (1985).   LK

Bryden, Bill (1942–) Scottish director and writer. Bryden assisted Tony *Richardson and *Gaskill before becoming director of the Royal Lyceum, Edinburgh. His tenancy of a resident Cottesloe (*National Theatre) ensemble in 1975 enabled him to produce populist, promenade productions such as *Lark Rise to Candleford* and *The Mysteries*. Bryden's desire to be '*the* director of *Mamet in this country' led to premières of *American Buffalo* and *Glengarry Glen Ross*. Bryden's screenplay *Long Riders*, and stage and television dramas *Benny Lynch* and *Willie Rough* have earned him considerable acclaim. His interest in TV was developed by his position as head of drama for Scottish TV (1978) and later for BBC Scotland (1984). In the 1990s Bryden moved to epic productions, directing *The Ship* and *The Big Picnic* in a disused Glasgow engine shed, and *opera such as *Parsifal* (*Covent Garden) and *The Silver Tassie* (English National Opera).   KN

Bsissou, Mouyin (1927–84) Palestinian writer. Born in Gaza, Bsissou's first collection of poetry (*The Battle*, 1952) already demonstrated a theatrical flair. He realized this promise in Cairo two decades later with plays such as *The Revolution of the Zenjs* (1970), *Samson and Delilah* (1971), *The Birds Build their Nests between Fingers* (1973), and *The Tragedy of Guevara*, which were staged by the best Egyptian directors. Bsissou was one of the first Arabic poets to use free-verse in drama. In his work the Palestinian cause is indissoluble from questions of social justice, freedom, and truth.   MMe

Büchner, Georg (1813–37) German dramatist. Born in Darmstadt into a liberal family, Büchner studied medicine and philosophy, became acquainted with radical thought and involved in political agitation, culminating in the pamphlet *The Hessian Country Messenger*. Threatened with prosecution, he fled to Zurich in 1836 where he died of typhus a year later. Büchner wrote only three plays. *Danton's Death* (1835) treats a central figure of the French Revolution caught

between hedonism and idealism, using techniques prefiguring *documentary drama. The *comedy *Leonce and Lena* (1836) mixes German and French *romanticism, Shakespeare, and *Gozzi. The unfinished *Woyzeck* (1836/7) is Büchner's best-known and most performed work. It combines the open, fragmentary style of *Sturm und Drang *dramaturgy with elliptical, regionally inflected language presaging *naturalism. *Woyzeck* was adapted into an *opera by Alban Berg and filmed a number of times. Büchner's works were not performed until the turn of the twentieth century when their formal innovation and radical social-critical stance was at last admired. *Reinhardt directed both *Danton's Death* (1916) and *Woyzeck* (1921). Though *Leonce and Lena* has been less popular, all three have become an integral part of German theatre, and Büchner is one of the few German playwrights to enter the world repertory.   CBB

Buckingham, 2nd Duke of (George Villiers) (1628–87) English playwright and politician. Reared in the family of Charles I, Buckingham shared exile with Charles II and after the Restoration became a member of the King's inner circle of ministers known as the Cabal. *Dryden caricatured him in *Absalom and Achitophel* (1681), probably payback for Buckingham's portrayal of him ten years earlier as the dramatist Bayes in *The Rehearsal*. Originally a satire on *Davenant and Robert Howard, Dryden's appointment as Poet Laureate in 1668, and his heroic drama *The Conquest of Granada* (1670), made him a more tempting target. *The Rehearsal* presents a *burlesque of a *heroic play in the context of its *rehearsal, with the pompous Bayes explaining his ideas to two critical companions. *The Rehearsal* became a model for the later burlesque drama of *Fielding and *Sheridan. RWV

Buckstone, John Baldwin (1802–79) English playwright, actor, and *manager. Buckstone began a London acting career in 1823, and for some years wrote and acted for a variety of minor theatres. His dramatic output was eclectic, embracing *burlettas, *melodramas, *farces, and *pantomime librettos, over 100 plays altogether. The thematically interesting three-act farces *Married Life* (1834) and *Single Life* (1839), and the melodramas *The Wreck Ashore* (1830), *The Dream at Sea* (1835), *The Green Bushes* (1845), and *The Flowers of the Forest* (1847), represent his best work. In 1853 he assumed the management of the *Haymarket Theatre, retiring in 1876. For years his was the best *comedy company in London. As an actor Buckstone was a distinguished low comedian, often performing in his own plays.   MRB

Buenaventura, Enrique (1925–2003) Colombian playwright, director, and poet. Buenaventura painstakingly developed a method of *collective creation for most of his plays, which he also directed. His more than 70 dramas are dominated by *At the Right Hand of God the Father* (1958), which was rewritten five times in 25 years. Influenced by *Brecht, *Weiss, *documentary, and historical drama, Buenaventura also produced, wrote, and directed successful work such as *Documents from Hell* (1973), a series of short episodes depicting the 'violent decade' of the 1950s; *The Story of a Silver Bullet* (1979), a free adaptation of *O'Neill's *The Emperor Jones*, a comment on the arrival of neo-liberalism in the Caribbean economies; and *Opera Bufa* (1983), based on the Somoza dynasty in Central America.   BJR

Buero-Vallejo, Antonio (1916–2000) Spain's leading playwright after 1950, whose plays often challenged the official culture of the Franco dictatorship. Imprisoned for six years at the end of the Spanish Civil War, upon release he began to write for the stage, and the production of his *Story of a Stairway* in 1949 began a revitalization of post-*García-Lorcan theatre. During *rehearsals of his second play, *In the Burning Darkness* (1950), he introduced a device that became fundamental to much of his subsequent work. In one scene in a school for the blind, the theatre was plunged into darkness to diminish aesthetic distance and allow the *audience to experience the physical condition of the *characters. The 'immersion effect' was used far more extensively in *The Sleep of Reason* (1970) to convey the isolation of deaf painter Goya, and in *The Foundation* (1974) to depict the mental delusion of a young political prisoner. His plays usually opened in Madrid, but the première of *The Double Case-History of Dr Valmy* (1968) was in Chester after *censorship prevented performance in Spain. *Wajda's Warsaw production of *The Sleep of Reason* in 1976 was instrumental in bringing wider international attention to his work.   MPH

bugaku Japanese court music that featured *dance. A sub-genre of *gagaku* (elegant music), the term *bugaku* is often used in contradistinction to purely instrumental pieces (*kangen*, winds and strings) of the larger *gagaku* court music tradition. *Bugaku* is roughly classified into two types, both consolidated and systematized during the Heian period (794–1185): 'dances of the left', accompanied by *tōgaku* ('music-dance of the Tang dynasty', from China); and 'dances of the right',

accompanied by *komagaku* music imported from the Korean peninsula. *Bugaku* makes use of elaborate *costumes, differing for the *tōgaku* and *komagaku* repertory and for the specific piece to be danced. Simple hand-held props are sometimes used; *masks, smaller and thinner than those used for *gigaku*, are now and then employed as well. Performances of *bugaku* today contain mostly highly restrained, stylized movements. Music is provided by the *gagaku* ensemble, including flutes and double-reed winds, mouth organs, percussion, and, in the case of *tōgaku* pieces, zithers and lutes. Some 50 *bugaku* pieces are still in the repertory of the imperial court today.   GG

buildings *See* PLAYHOUSE.

Bulgakov, Mikhail (1891–1940) Russian writer, born in Kiev. After the Civil War (he served as a doctor on the White side) Bulgakov was drawn to the *Moscow Art Theatre under *Stanislavsky, adapting his novel *The White Guard* as the play *The Days of the Turbins* (1926), about the life of a White officer's family in Kiev during the Civil War. Despite its focus on the Whites, the production was among Stalin's favourites. In 1925 the Vakhtangov Theatre commissioned a *comedy, *Zoya's Apartment*, a *satire which turns Moscow into a surreal, phantasmagoric place. His comedy *The Crimson Island* was banned in 1929; so was *The Flight* (1928), consisting of eight dreams about White émigrés.

The *Cabal of Hypocrites* (1929), Bulgakov's adaptation of his novel *Molière*, focuses on the conflict between the artist and authority. By the end of the 1920s all Bulgakov's plays had been removed from the repertoire after a press campaign against him. Only Stalin's intervention restored some of them and Bulgakov was offered the post of *dramaturg at the MAT. Staying safe in his choice of material, he completed a number of adaptations in the 1930s, such as *The Last Days* (1935) about *Pushkin's fatal duel, an adaptation of *Gogol's *Dead Souls* (1932), and *Don Quixote* (1938). Bulgakov's great novel *The Master and Margarita* was written in the last years of his life, but not published until 1966–7, and staged by *Lyubimov in 1976.   BB

bull-baiting *See* BAITING.

Bullins, Ed (1935–) *African-American playwright, a seminal figure in the Black Arts Movement. He co-founded Black Arts West and became director of Black House Theatre in Oakland, California, where the revolutionaries Bobby Seale, Eldridge Cleaver, and Huey Newton were affiliated as actors; through them he became minister of culture for the Black Panther Party. In 1967 Robert Macbeth of the New Lafayette Theatre invited Bullins to New York after reading *Goin' a Buffalo*, part of a cycle chronicling the lives of ordinary African Americans. Macbeth produced *In the Wine Time* (1968), *The Electronic Nigger* (1968), later done at *Lincoln Center, and *We Righteous Bombers* (1969), written under a pseudonym. Resident playwright at New Lafayette, Bullins also edited the house magazine, *Black Theatre*. When the company disbanded in 1973, Bullins became resident playwright at the American Place Theatre, and *The Taking of Miss Janie* (1975) won the Drama Critics Circle award. Bullins's career continued in the 1980s and 1990s, though without the force that marked his early work.   BBL

Bulwer-Lytton, Edward (1803–73) English playwright, politician, and novelist. In Parliament Bulwer chaired the 1832 Select Committee which was responsible for a bill to allow any *licenced theatre to play any kind of drama. Defeated in the Lords, it nonetheless prepared the ground for the Theatres Regulation Bill of 1843 which achieved the same ends. Already a successful novelist by the 1830s, Bulwer then took up the drama. After the failure of *The Duchesse de la Vallière* (1837), he had a great success with *The Lady of Lyons* (1838) and *Richelieu* (1839), the second adapted for the stage in collaboration with *Macready. Its themes of social pretence and ambition, wealth, class hostility, and the conflict between love and pride also distinguish *Money* (1840), the most significant *comedy of the century, which influenced much later writing. Eminently playable today, it has been performed by both the *Royal Shakespeare Company and the *National Theatre.   MRB

bunraku Sophisticated Japanese *puppet theatre, which developed out of the medieval storytelling tradition of blind minstrels and was the major dramatic form through Japan throughout the Tokugawa era (1600–1868). Today the only surviving professional troupe is based in Osaka and performs regularly at the Tokyo and Osaka National Theatres. The three elements of bunraku are chanter (*tayū*), *shamisen* (a stringed instrument), and puppets. Traditionally the chanter, who voices all the roles and the narration, has been the most prominent figure. The *shamisen* player accompanies him, both of them sitting on a dais stage left near the *audience. The puppets are about two-thirds life size and from 1734 each has been manipulated by three men. The senior

puppeteer works the puppet's head with his left hand and its right hand with his own right hand; the second works the left hand with his right hand; the third manipulates the feet. Chanters became sighted performers early in the seventeenth century, but *shamisen* players were usually blind until the mid-eighteenth century.

The story is of paramount importance. At the time of first performance playbooks were published in full, authorized editions, a situation different from *kabuki, bunraku's rival, which published no full texts until the modern era. As a result bunraku attracted outstanding playwrights, such as *Chūshingura: a treasury of loyal retainers* (1748) by *Namiki, *Takeda, and Miyoshi Shoraku. The greatest era of playwriting was from 1683 to 1800, when more than 1,000 day-long plays were written. *Chikamatsu Monzaemon, Namiki, Takeda, and *Chikamatsu Hanji all wrote primarily for bunraku. Successful bunraku plays were invariably adapted into kabuki and today form the core of its repertoire.

Bunraku chanting is based on musical principles, the chanter's art being to vary constantly the style between realistic declamation and various kinds of singing. From the late seventeenth century chanting became an important amateur activity among men and women, and plays were published with the chanter's code of musical notation. Amateur chanting was popular throughout Japan until the 1940s, and fostered a highly sophisticated audience for bunraku and kabuki. Bunraku theatres were found in all major cities, but Osaka was the creative centre where nearly all of the plays were composed. *Takemoto Gidayū founded the Takemoto-za theatre in 1684, and in the early 1700s his disciple founded the Toyotake-za; this rivalry produced the golden age of bunraku, and the modern art developed from the tradition then established. Indeed Gidayū (or *gidayū-bushi*) became the term for bunraku chanting and music. In the eighteenth century bunraku changed from a narrative art to a full dramatic one with the increasing sophistication of the puppetry and *shamisen* music. The nineteenth century saw further development of theatricality as the repertoire coalesced; a *shamisen* notation system led to increasingly complex musical accompaniment.

In performance, the chanter's voice and *shamisen* music infuse the puppets with life. The two junior puppeteers always wear black robes with faces covered by hoods, but the senior manipulator's face is visible in important scenes. Initially the puppets seem to be directed by the three men but as the intensity of *action, voice, and music increases, the puppets appear to lead the puppeteers, as they rush to the fateful climax. A remarkable aspect of bunraku is that the core of virtually every programme, past and present, is *tragedy, perhaps due to its Buddhist and folk-religious heritage. Takemoto Gidayū described a day of theatre as a cyclical experience, beginning in an auspicious setting, travelling through intrigue, insurrection, and battles, to an individual crisis which can only be resolved by death. A tragic action, usually in the middle of a play or programme, ultimately leads to a resolution of the original crisis, which had cast the world into chaos. After the tragic scene, the audience is led through a lyrical dance to a world restored to order, with hope for the future. This cyclical structure, originally inspired by *nō drama, is evident today in the orchestration of all bunraku programmes, and has influenced the *dramaturgy of kabuki as well. CAG

Buontalenti, Bernardo (1531–1608) Italian architect and *scenographer. He entered the service of the Medici in 1547 as a civil engineer and military architect. His inventions of entertaining gadgets, *fireworks, and decorations prepared him for a theatrical career at the side of *Vasari and Lanci. In 1574 he became principal designer at the Medici court in Florence, for whom he built the Teatro degli Uffizi (1585) with a capacity of 3,000. Its complex stage machinery allowed rapid changes of *perspective scenery, developed to unprecedented height in the 1589 theatre festival, for which Buontalenti also designed the *costumes. GB

Burbage, James (c.1530–1597) English actor, theatre owner, and *manager. A joiner by trade, by 1572 he was a prominent member of the Earl of Leicester's Men. In 1576 he leased property in Shoreditch and proceeded, with the financial backing of his brother-in-law Brayne, to erect the *Theatre, the second purpose-built public *playhouse in England. In 1583 several of Leicester's Men joined the newly organized *Queen's Men, who became the tenants of the Theatre. Burbage likely abandoned acting for full-time management and took up permanent residence in Shoreditch. Between 1583 and 1597, when it was abandoned and subsequently disassembled to provide timbers for the *Globe, the Theatre was home to several *acting companies, including the *Chamberlain's Men (1594–7). In early 1597 Burbage purchased one of the houses of Blackfriars and initiated an enterprise that would result in the second *Blackfriars Theatre. At his death, Burbage's interest in Blackfriars passed to his

younger son Richard *Burbage, and his interest in the Globe to his elder son Cuthbert. RWV

Burbage, Richard (c.1568–1619) English actor, the younger son of James *Burbage. Around 1590 Richard was playing major roles and at Christmas 1594 performed *interludes before the Queen. From 1595 he assumed a prominent place in the *Chamberlain's Men, remaining with the company when the players obtained a royal patent (1603) to the end of his professional life. He is best remembered for the leading roles in Shakespeare's plays. Burbage's contemporaries stated that he performed Hamlet, King Lear, and Othello; some historians suggest that Richard III, Romeo, Hieronimo (*Kyd's *The Spanish Tragedy*), and Ferdinand (*Webster's *The Duchess of Malfi*) were also his. Doubtless there were many others, largely unknown. Burbage's *acting style has been thought to have been more naturalistic and subtle than that of his contemporary *Alleyn, who played large, bombastic characters such as Faustus and Tamburlaine. *Middleton wrote an elegy claiming Burbage's Hamlet seemed so real that 'I would have sworn, he meant to die'. Burbage participated in many performances at court and in public pageants. In 1605 he negotiated with Robert Cecil a performance of *Love's Labour's Lost* (intended for Queen Anne); and in May 1610 he was employed by the city of London to deliver a speech to Prince Henry in a water pageant on the Thames. Moreover, Burbage was a shareholder in the *Globe and the *Blackfriars *playhouses, and he inherited part of the original *Theatre from his father. Surprisingly he excelled as a painter as well; a painting of Burbage (Dulwich Picture Gallery) is thought by some to have been a self-portrait. Of the many epitaphs which memorialized his acting talents, the shortest was 'Exit Burbage'. SPC

Burgos, Jerónima de (c.1580–1641) Spanish actress, married by 1594 to Pedro de Valdés (c.1568–1640), who led his own company with her assistance from 1613 at least until 1637. From 1607 she was closely involved with Lope de *Vega, who provided many plays for her, including *The Dumb Belle* in 1613. But by 1615 intimacy turned to enmity, and Lope wrote for others. That year she created the title role in *Tirso de Molina's *Don Gil of the Green Breeches*, but was apparently too old and fat for such parts. VFD

Burgtheater Founded in 1741 as the Habsburg court theatre in Vienna, in 1776 Emperor Josef II designated it as a 'German National Theatre'. The Burgtheater's first flowering came under Joseph

Schreyvogel (director 1814–32), who favoured classical German drama (*Goethe, *Schiller, *Kleist) and fostered new dramatists (*Grillparzer). Another important reformer was *Laube (director 1849–67), who continued the emphasis on highbrow literary theatre but also established a reputation for outstanding *acting. The present *playhouse was built by Gottfried Semper in 1888 in a monumental *neoclassical style. The famous ensemble was severely disrupted between 1939 and 1945 when many actors were forced into exile. A succession of directors rebuilt the ensemble in the post-war years, although none managed a distinctive stamp until the appointment of *Peymann (1986–99). Under his direction the 'Burg' became an innovative and highly controversial theatre, due chiefly to his preference for contemporary Austrian authors like *Bernhard, *Handke, and *Turrini, whose work was often critical of Austrian society. Under the director Klaus Bachler, the Burg was turned into an independent company, *financed but not administered by the state.   CBB

Burian, Emil František (1904–59) Czech director, playwright, and performer. In 1933 he opened D34, conceived as a cultural centre (the D stood for *divadlo* (theatre), and the number was changed annually to represent the next year). The opening production qualified Burian as a leftist, but his theatre was essentially poetic, as his adaptations of *romantic poets (*Pushkin, *Goethe) indicate. In a similar vein Burian directed *Wedekind's *Spring's Awakening* (1936) with a new principle of stage design, 'theatregraph', which used non-illustrative film and slide projection, achieving a dreamy and unrealistic effect. Burian's was a synthetic or *total theatre, where all the elements were of equal importance; the script, frequently non-dramatic or heavily adapted, was treated as a mere libretto for a richly orchestrated production. In March 1941, during the Nazi occupation, D41 was closed, and Burian was later sent to a concentration camp. During the post-war years he made (not completely successful) attempts to catch up with the present and to renovate his programme.   ML

burlesque In the Restoration and eighteenth-century English theatre the word 'burlesque' was applied to plays like *Fielding's *Tragedy of Tragedies* and *Sheridan's *The Critic*, which were *parodies of contemporary theatrical conventions of writing and staging. This tradition continued into the nineteenth century, with *melodrama and its *villain particular targets of comic *satire. *Jerrold's *Black-Ey'd Susan* and Pocock's *The Miller and his Men*, two popular melodramas, were frequently burlesqued for middle-class *audiences. *Opera and Shakespeare received the same irreverent treatment in dozens of plays. *Hamlet* was burlesqued at least five times and Shakespeare's plots and verse were reduced to the lowest level possible of eccentricity and the grotesque. Burlesque reduced its subject matter to the level of comic and urban domesticity. In stage performance burlesque, which also had roots in the relatively tasteful extravaganzas of *Planché, the *minstrel show, and the *music hall, was a frothy brew of topical songs, legs, limelight, puns good and bad, eccentric *dancing, and enormous energy. Increasing middle-class refinement and the growth of *musical comedy killed off the older burlesque at the end of the century. In America burlesque was a non-literary mixture of skimpily dressed women (and eventually strippers) and male low comedians, with dancing, songs, comic patter, and an increasing raunchiness frowned upon by the civic authorities, which began closing burlesque houses by edict, as in New York in 1942. As a living form, it had virtually expired by the 1950s.   MRB

burletta A form of light *comedy on the London stage in the 1820s and 1830s. The *licensing laws did not permit London's minor theatres to play *legitimate drama: traditional *comedy, *tragedy, and *farce. However, they were allowed to perform *melodrama and burletta. The word 'burletta' was applied to comic pieces containing a number of songs. Its heyday was the 1830s at the Olympic Theatre under *Vestris; *Planché was a chief contributor. At the Olympic a burletta was generally a two-act comedy with songs, written with restraint, refinement, and French polish, sometimes known as a *petite comédie*.   MRB

Burns, George (Nathan Birnbaum) (1896–1996) and **Gracie Allen** (1895–1964) American comedy team. Burns found *vaudeville success when in 1923 he teamed with Allen, a singer-dancer. They made their debut in Newark with an act called 'Sixty Forty' in which Allen played straight man to Burns's jokester. *Audiences found Allen funnier, and Burns rewrote their material to feature Gracie's surreal logic delivered cheerily in a childlike voice while Burns asked questions and patiently accepted her twisted statements. This basic act propelled them to stardom on the Orpheum circuit by 1925 and carried them through the next 35 years. Married in 1926, they soon signed a six-year contract for the Keith (later Keith-Orpheum) circuit at $750 per week. Their act translated successfully to radio (their show lasted 1933–50), to film (1934–44), and to television (1950–8). After Allen's retirement in 1958 Burns continued solo as comic and film actor. MAF

Burrows, Abe (1910–85) American playwright, lyricist, and director, who broke into show business in the 1930s on the Catskill Mountain 'Borscht Belt'. In 1939 he began a successful career as a Hollywood radio writer and performer, and was partly responsible for the popular show *Duffy's Tavern*. His Broadway career commenced with his collaboration on the book of the *musical *Guys and Dolls* (with *Loesser, 1950), which earned him a Tony award. Burrows wrote either the book or lyrics for such later musicals as *Can-Can* (1953), *Silk Stockings* (1955), *Say, Darling* (1958), *How to Succeed in Business without Really Trying* (1961)—a hit for which he shared the Pulitzer Prize and won two Tonys—and *What Makes Sammy Run?* (1964). Also respected as a 'script doctor', Burrows directed some of these shows as well as a number of *comedies. Plays he wrote, or co-wrote, included his hit adaptation of a French comedy, *Forty Carats* (1968). SLL

Burton, Richard (1925–84) Welsh actor whose talent on stage and film was all but squandered through alcoholism. His reputation as a young actor was won in *Fry's *The Lady's Not for Burning* (1949) and in a series of Shakespearian roles at the *Old Vic, including Hamlet (1953). All but abandoning the stage for an explosive film career, he appeared memorably opposite Elizabeth Taylor in the epic *Cleopatra* (1963) and in Mike *Nichols's film of *Albee's *Who's Afraid of Virginia Woolf?* (1966), the two stars conducting a hugely destructive relationship in public. Other significant film roles included *Becket* (1964), *The Spy Who Came in from the Cold* (1965), and *Shaffer's *Equus* (stage and film, 1977). He also narrated a famous radio adaptation of Dylan Thomas's *Under Milk Wood* (BBC, 1954). AS

Burton, William E. (1804–60) Anglo-American actor and *manager. By 1831 Burton was a major comic actor in London, performing with Edmund *Kean and at the *Haymarket. He arrived in the USA in 1834 and joined the Arch Street Theatre in Philadelphia where he quickly became renowned as America's top comic actor. Three years later he moved to the National Theatre in New York and by 1841 was its manager. After fire destroyed the *playhouse, he returned to Philadelphia and within a short time was managing four houses there and in Baltimore. In 1848 he assumed control of Palmo's Opera House in New York, renaming it Burton's Theatre, and for the next eight years ran

one of the best *stock companies in the USA. He produced and performed in a string of highly successful shows, including revivals of Shakespeare and adaptations of *Dickens. PAD

Bury, John (1925–2000) English *scenographer. After the war he joined *Littlewood's *Theatre Workshop, designing and constructing scenery and driving the van. His groundbreaking designs there included *Delaney's *A Taste of Honey*, *Behan's *The Quare Fellow*, and the ensemble *musicals *Fings Ain't Wot They Used t'Be* and *Oh! What a Lovely War*, which introduced solid materials and real objects into the stage. In 1963 he joined the *Royal Shakespeare Company and created sets and *costumes for *Barton and *Hall's *The Wars of the Roses* (1963–4), using heavy sheet-metal fixtures which allowed transformations on an epic scale, establishing the 'brutalist' style. In 1965 he was appointed head of design at the RSC. Increasing sophistication and developments in *light technology came together for *Pinter's *Landscape* and *Silence* (1969). Over ten *operas at Glyndebourne, including the *Mozart–da Ponte trilogy and Britten's *A Midsummer Night's Dream*, reflected on stage his lifelong love of nature. Following Hall to the *National Theatre, Bury was head of design from 1973 to 1985, where his productions included *Shaffer's *Amadeus* (1979). He was also consultant for new theatres at the Barbican and Glyndebourne. PH

Busch, Ernst (1900–80) German actor. Busch joined *Piscator at the *Volksbühne in Berlin in 1927. Thoroughly committed to left-wing politics, he performed in important productions such as *Toller's *Hoppla, wir leben!* (*Hoppla, We're Alive!*, 1928), *Brecht's film *Kuhle Wampe* (also known as *Whither Germany?*, 1932), and participated in political *cabaret. In 1933 he went into exile, served in the Spanish Civil War, and between 1939 and 1940 worked in Belgium, fleeing to France after the German invasion. He was interned in France, and then imprisoned in Germany for treason. After the war he joined the *Berliner Ensemble and played major roles in Brecht's own productions, and came to be recognized as a prototypical Brechtian actor. The most important theatre conservatory in Berlin, the Ernst-Busch-Schule, is named after him. CBB

busker Form of street entertainer dating back to Roman times and subsequently to the goliards, troubadours, minstrels, mountebanks, *acrobats, *puppeteers, and *commedia dell'arte* performers of the middle ages. Street performers were prevalent in nineteenth-century London; for some the work was a last resort before begging or the workhouse. In the early twentieth century buskers entertained queues waiting for admission to the pit and galleries of West End theatres and cinemas, and also performed at markets. They included barrel organists, street boxers, clog dancers, vocalists, boys singing popular *music-hall songs, 'out of work' actors reciting Shakespeare, *Dickens, or popular verses, paper-tearers, and chapeaugraphists. In the late 1930s, kerbside entertainment became more elaborate, with whole companies of buskers presenting regular programmes. Since the 1960s guitarists have been a familiar aspect of busking, while *jugglers, fireeaters, acrobats, *mimes, and *performance artists busk for crowds throughout the world.   JTD

butoh At first all modern *dance in Japan was called butoh, but the term has come to refer almost exclusively to an *avant-garde form created by dancers like *Hijikata and *Ono, who were both students of German expressionist *Neue Tanz*. Around 1960, Hijikata coined the term *ankoku butoh* (the dance of utter darkness) to describe his style. An underground *performance art during the 1960s, butoh's heyday in Japan was in the 1970s. It broke onto the international scene in the 1980s, and in recent years butoh groups have sprung up in Europe and the Americas. Based on the desire to discover a dance form congenial to the Japanese body, butoh's movements often echo *kabuki gestures or traditional agricultural practices. The body is regarded as a repository of repressed cultural memory; the grimaces and tortured gestures reflect the dancer's attempts to overcome physical and social inhibitions and to reconnect with primal energy. Spontaneous expression of the spirit has been considered more important than physical or technical virtuosity, especially in solo or small ensemble performances, but larger groups (like Maro Akaji's Dai Rakudakan, Ohsuka Isamu's Byakkosha, and Amagatsu Ushio's Paris-based Sankaijuku) are highly choreographed.   CP

Byron, George Gordon, Lord (1788–1824) English poet who had ambitions as a playwright. Of Byron's nine plays in verse only one, *Marino Faliero*, was staged in his lifetime (*Drury Lane, 1821), but it was not the success he hoped for. The plays are based on historical, biblical, or metaphysical subjects (only one, *The Blues*, is a *comedy); all focus on profound moral choices that have tragic social consequences; the verse owes more to *Alfieri than Shakespeare. The Venetian *tragedies, *Marino* and *The Two Foscari*, arguably his finest, communicate a deepening sense of place to heighten tragic event and deploy stage space to symbolic ends. *Macready produced four of the plays (*Werner* continued in his repertoire from 1830); Alfred Bunn staged a notoriously spectacular version of *Manfred* (1834), and Charles *Kean a pictorial *Sardanapalus* (1853).   RAC

Byron, Henry James (1834–84) English playwright, actor, and *manager. A very busy author, Byron became popular with *burlesques in the 1850s and 1860s. He was the chief punster of the Victorian stage, in both burlesque and *pantomime. Byron also wrote a strong *melodrama in *The Lancashire Lass* (1868), in which *Irving played the *villain, and several thematically interesting *comedies about marital difficulties rather than romantic courtship: *Cyril's Success* (1868), *Partners for Life* (1871), and *Married in Haste* (1876). His most successful comedy, in which he acted, was *Our Boys* (1875); it ran for over four years and was marked by Bryon's love of eccentric comedy. Byron was initially Marie *Wilton's partner in the management at the Prince of Wales's Theatre in 1865 and was instrumental in the acceptance of *Robertson's *Society* in that year. The partnership ended in 1867, Wilton being uninterested in producing Byron's speciality, burlesque; Byron then transferred his managerial energies to Liverpool.   MRB

cabaret One of the major performance forms of modernism, European in origin but with American variations, cabaret has been mythologized as excessive and decadent, dangerous and illicit, sophisticated and sexual. It has been imagined and re-created: in the art of Toulouse Lautrec, Otto Dix, and George Grosz; in *Isherwood's Berlin novels; on stage with *Van Druten's *I Am a Camera* and *Kander and Ebb's *musical *Cabaret*; in cinema in Josef von Sternberg's *Der Blaue Engel* and *Fosse's film of *Cabaret*.

The French word *cabaret* (tavern) came to mean a small entertainment in an intimate setting that might be *improvised and mix music, song, sketches, often commenting on social, economic, political, or artistic matters; the word applies to places of entertainment such as nightclubs as well as entertainments they provide. Modern cabaret began in Paris with Le Chat Noir in bohemian Montmartre in 1881 as an *avant-garde entertainment for an elite *audience. Its popularity soon grew and by the turn of the century similar venues were established in several French and German cities. Le Chat Noir, seating only 60, was designed in the style of Louis XIII and programmes included poetry readings and *shadow plays staged by leading artists. The venue's intimacy led to a new playing style that emphasized subtlety and preferred everyday *naturalistic subjects. French *diseuse* Yvette *Guilbert was at the forefront of this style.

French artists slipped between the intimacy of the cabaret stage and the glamorous *revues of the Parisian nightclubs and *music halls such as the *Folies-Bergère, and *Moulin-Rouge. From Guilbert to *Mistinguett, from Josephine *Baker to Édith *Piaf, from Maurice *Chevalier to Jacques Brel, the French tradition of cabaret has been eclectic and distinctively national, and has survived the onslaught of tourist buses as a unique contribution to popular theatre.

In Germany cabaret began at the Bunte Bühne, the so-called Überbrettl, in Berlin in 1901, followed immediately by Schall und Rauch, founded by *Reinhardt and actors from the *Deutsches Theater, and by the Elf Scharfrichter in Munich, where *Wedekind performed. These

cabarets shared the aesthetic of Le Chat Noir in testing what was new and experimental in the arts.

Elsewhere in Europe cabaret maintained this mixed economy of popular excess and aesthetic and political experimentation, the latter strong at the Zielony Balonik in Cracow and the Els Quatre Gats in Barcelona. In Russia cabarets functioned as a fringe for the theatre community: *Evreinov founded Crooked Mirror in St Petersburg in 1908; the Brodyachaya Sobaka (1913–15) was associated with the *futurists; and the Prival Komediantov (1916–19) with *Meyerhold. In Zurich the infamous Cabaret Voltaire (1916–17) provided an appropriate space for Hans Arp and Tristan Tzara to develop *dada.

Despite the impact of the First World War, cabaret flourished in the German capital, where it maintained associations with a counter-culture and anti-establishment sentiments. Though some were subject to heavy *censorship, performers used the cabaret stage, with its mixed bill of sketches, jazz, torch songs, and transvestism, to make a real social statement. *Kabarett* of the period include Trude Hesterberg's Wilde Bühne (1921), the Katakombe (1929), and the Tingel-Tangel (1930). Political *satire was a principal feature of the cabaret of the 1920s and 1930s in Germany, where *Weill and Hanns Eisler were protagonists. Under the liberal Weimar Republic cabaret achieved mythical status. By 1935, however, all the Berlin cabarets were closed in the aftermath of Hitler's declaration of martial law, reinstating censorship and strict social controls.

In the USA cabaret evolved several interconnected forms, almost all satellites of the nightclub: the shows of the supper rooms of New York in the 1950s with swing bands, big bands, and lounge singers; the entertainers, composers, and lyricists drawn from Broadway shows; the modern extravaganzas of Las Vegas; and the forms and traditions of *gay culture—none are cabaret proper but all owe something to the history and mythology of the form.

In England cabaret was a rather more genteel form, more like an intimate revue than its French or German counterparts. Nevertheless, something of the *Kabarett* spirit was aspired to by

*Auden in *The Ascent of F6* (1936), which included songs set to music by Benjamin Britten. Later *Coward and Marlene Dietrich entertained at elite venues like the Café de Paris, while Peter Cook's the Establishment (1961) attempted to extend the success of the satirical *Beyond the Fringe* revue to a fashionable after-hours club in London. The sleazier cabaret circuit of Soho evolved in the late 1970s and 1980s into an alternative cabaret scene that re-established stand-up comedy as a popular form of entertainment, while more recently the Pizza on the Park and Langans have re-established sophisticated jazz-based cabaret for the metropolitan market. *See also* CAFÉ-CONCERT.   AS

Cabrujas, José Ignacio (1937–95) Venezuelan director, actor, and scriptwriter, one of the most important Latin American playwrights. He made his debut as an actor with the Teatro de la Universidad Central, and while there wrote *Juan Francisco de León* (1959) and *Stone Soup* (1960). In 1961 he studied at the Piccolo Teatro in Milan. On his return he staged his plays *The Strange Journey of Simon the Evil* (1961), *The Insurgents* (1962), and wrote or co-wrote a number of works such as *Triángulo* (1962), *In the King's Name* (1963), *Testimonio* (1967), *Profundo* (1971), and *Cultural Act* (1976). In 1967 he formed El Nuevo Grupo together with Román Chalbaud and Isaac Chocrón. After 1976 he turned his attention to writing soaps for television. Other plays include *The Day You Love Me* (1979), *An Eastern Night* (1983), *Self-Portrait of the Artist with a Beard and Top Hat* (1990), and *Sonny* (1995), a version of *Othello* about the life of a boxer. LCL trans. AMCS

café-concert Also known as *cafés-chantants*, Paris cafés that employed a few singers and musicians and that flourished from the Second Empire to the *belle époque*. At a *caf'-conc'*, a labourer, often accompanied by his family, could relax with a drink while listening to a selection of songs geared to the local clientele: melodic musings on daily life, risqué numbers, comic ditties, rousing patriotic songs, *satirical lyrics. Some establishments encouraged patrons to join in the refrain, and because customers were expected to continue ordering drinks, the atmosphere could become rowdy, yet the singers and their pianists were required to wear evening clothes. Around 1900, Paris boasted about 265 *cafés-concerts*, the best known being the Alcazar, the Eden-Concert, the Eldorado, and the Ba-Ta-Clan. These names proliferated in provincial towns as the phenomenon spread. The popularity of this 'democratized theatre' and its offspring—the more intimate and intellectual *cabaret, the *variety entertain

ment of the *music halls—was seen as a threat by legitimate theatre owners. Though critics deplored their lowering of taste and drunkenness, it was only with the rise of film that the 'temples of song' declined.   FHL

Caffe Cino New York coffee house that became one of the first performance spaces of the *Off-Off-Broadway movement. Joseph Cino opened the café in 1958, and simultaneously opened his doors to a variety of poets, musicians, actors, and playwrights who would become the nucleus of New York's *avant-garde in the 1960s. Some of the important playwrights who made use of Caffe Cino's tiny 2.4-m (8-foot) square stage were Lanford *Wilson, *Fornés, *Shepard, *Terry, *Guare, and *Van Itallie. Ellen Stewart's *La Mama Experimental Theatre Club eclipsed Caffe Cino in importance after the space was destroyed by fire in 1965.   JAB

Caird, John (1948–) Canadian director who has worked extensively in England for the *Royal Shakespeare Company and the *National Theatre. His collaborations with *Nunn at the RSC led to the epic productions of *Edgar's *Nicholas Nickleby* (1980) and the *musical *Les Misérables* (1985). Caird has directed other large-scale productions including *Lloyd Webber's *Song and Dance* (1982), and a spectacular *Peter Pan* (NT, 1997) with designer *Napier. At the RSC Caird has staged *Jonson's *Every Man in his Humour* (1986) and *The New Inn* (1987) at the *Swan, and innovative interpretations of *A Midsummer Night's Dream* and *As You Like It* (both 1989). In the late 1990s during Nunn's tenure at the National Caird demonstrated versatility with new drama: *Gems's *Stanley* (1996) and Charlotte Jones's *The Humble Boy* (2001). Recently he has worked in Japan and Sweden.   KN

Calderón de la Barca, Pedro (1600–81) Spanish dramatist. Born in Madrid, and destined for the Church by his authoritarian father, he studied with the Jesuits in Alcalá and Salamanca, but refused in 1621 to become a priest. He saw his first plays performed in the next few years, and by the mid-1630s he was the dramatist most favoured by the court (and the leading writer of *autos sacramentales*), and in 1637 was made a Knight of Santiago. Having served and been wounded in Catalonia, he wrote far less in the 1640s (when the theatres were often closed), and in 1651 finally entered the priesthood. He ceased to work directly for the *corrales, but produced until his death a stream of spectacular plays and *operas for the court, and monopolized the composition of *auto for Madrid. Thus he dominated theatre in Spain for almost half a century, as had Lope de *Vega before him. Altogether he wrote nearly 80 *autos* and more than 100 *comedias*, plus a dozen in collaboration and a number of shorter works.

Calderón's plays are distinguished by intellectual depth and immaculate craftsmanship. His plots are tautly constructed, with relatively few shifts of scene and a limited range of metrics. His characteristic themes are the individual and society, freedom and constraint, illusion and reality, and above all passion and reason. Such conflicts both between and within his *characters are very clearly set out, often by the use of patterned exchanges and asides or in extended *monologues. His language is highly wrought, replete with rhetorical devices. His systematized exploitation of images of elemental discord reflects an essentially sombre view of our existence *vis-à-vis* the eternal. Though an orthodox Christian, he offers no complacent solutions to his characters' dilemmas, which are all the more intense for being of their own and others' making.

Life Is a Dream, his most performed play, charts the development of a prince whose father, to avert the acts of violence his horoscope predicted, has imprisoned him in secret from birth, but now has him brought to court for a test of his fitness to rule. He fails it and is persuaded it was a dream, but learns thereby that all human life is dreamlike. Though also concerned with the proper use of power, the play embodies fundamentally a philosophy of life.

Many famous works are more specifically religious, like *The Prodigious Magician* (1637), a *Faust*-like *saint-play, *The Constant Prince* (1629), a celebration of Christian fortitude, and *La cisma de Inglaterra* (1627), an account of the English schism often contrasted with Shakespeare's *Henry VIII*. Other plays are much more open to diverse interpretation. Three especially in which—as in *The Painter of Dishonour* (*c*.1645-50)—a husband murders his wife on suspicion of adultery seem shockingly unchristian. Less disturbing, but hardly less controversial, is *The Mayor of Zalamea* (1636). Its protagonist exceeds his civic authority by garrotting the nobly born captain by whom his own daughter has been raped.

Calderón's best works in lighter vein are his cloak-and-sword *comedies, like *The Phantom Lady* or *A House with Two Doors* (both 1629); in both of these a resourceful girl, confounding attempts to confine her, gets to marry the man she loves. By contrast, his palace plays and operas on mythological subjects exploited music and elaborate scenic effects, but within their obligatory celebration of royal power embody careful comments on fundamental matters of state. Perhaps his most remarkable works, however, are his *autos sacramentales*, for many of which his own detailed staging instructions have been preserved. *The Great Theatre of the World* (*c*.1633-4) is the one most often produced, but many others are more inventive. Fully versed in theology, he used all manner of allegories to bring its complexities to life on stage, and thereby gave the *mystery play a range, depth, and dynamism unparalleled elsewhere.

The Golden Age dramatist most widely known and performed in and since his day, he was hugely influential in nineteenth-century Germany, and is still popular there and in France. *Grotowski's version of *The Constant Prince* won universal acclaim, and other works are played worldwide, especially of course in Spain. Memorable performances in Britain include the *National Theatre's *The Mayor of Zalamea* (1981) and *The Painter of Dishonour* at Stratford (1994). A collaborative production of *Life Is a Dream* was mounted in Edinburgh, New York, London, and Madrid (1998-2000). But much of Calderón's diverse output remains to be revealed.   VFD

Caldwell, Zoë (1934–) American actress and director. Born in Australia, Caldwell made her reputation at the *Shakespeare Memorial Theatre in England and the *Stratford Festival in Canada in the late 1950s, then in the United States, where she understudied Anne Bancroft in *The Devils* (1965). Her career was centred in New York after her marriage to *manager-director Robert Whitehead. Her deep, rich voice and her vivid movements were suited for larger-than-life roles in such plays as *Slapstick Tragedy* (1966) and *The Prime of Miss Jean Brodie* (1968), as well as in *Medea* (1982) and as diva Maria Callas in *McNally's *Master Class* (1996). She also acted in McNally's *A Perfect Ganesh* (1995), and directed *Vita and Virginia* (1996), both *Off-Broadway. Caldwell is known for the thoroughness of her preparation and the details in her performances; she used *Hellman's own brand of perfume for *Lillian* (1985). Despite her reputation as a major actress, she appeared in only one major film, *The Purple Rose of Cairo* (1985).   AW

Callow, Simon (1949–) English actor, director, and writer. Callow joined Joint Stock in 1977 and appeared in *Hare's *Fanshen* and *Brenton's *Epsom Downs*. For the *National Theatre Callow has appeared as Orlando in *As You Like It* (1978), *Mozart in *Shaffer's *Amadeus* (1979), the Little Monk in *Brecht's *Galileo* (1980), and Face in *Jonson's *The Alchemist* (1996). His numerous films have included *Amadeus* (1983), *A Room with a View* (1986), *Four Weddings and a Funeral* (1994), and *Jefferson in Paris* (1995). In *musical theatre he has directed Strauss's *Die Fledermaus* for Scottish Opera (1989) and *Rodgers and *Hammerstein's *Carmen Jones* for the *Old Vic (1991), while his debut as a film director was with *The Ballad of the Sad Café* (1991). Recent performances include a one-man show on Shakespeare, *Three Reigns Love* (2008), and as Pozzo in *Beckett's *Waiting for Godot* (London, 2009) with *McKellen and *Stewart. Unusually articulate and literate, his books include *Being an Actor* (1984), biographies of *Laughton (1987) and *Welles (1995), and a short history of the NT, *The National* (1997).   AS

Calmo, Andrea (1509–71) Venetian comic dramatist and performer. He wrote six *comedies in a popular vein for a wide range of performing resources. In each one there is a part for a comic Venetian merchant speaking in dialect, a role which he performed himself: he thus imitated *Ruzante, with whom he may have worked, as a semi-professional practitioner who developed his own 'mask'. This makes him a figure of transition between scripted *commedia erudita* and improvised *commedia dell'arte*.   RAA

Cambridge Festival Theatre See GRAY, TERENCE.

Campbell, Ken (1941–2008) English actor, playwright, and director. He founded the Ken Campbell Roadshow in the late 1960s, *touring its anarchic *comedy and clowning around theatres, pubs, and working men's clubs. He wrote the book for the *musical *Bendigo* (1974), and his Science Fiction Theatre of Liverpool produced *The Great Caper* (1974) and *Illuminatus!* (1976). In 1979 he directed the 22-hour play *The Warp* at the ICA in London. Campbell became *artistic director of Liverpool's Everyman Theatre in 1980. His idiosyncratic one-person shows, part stand-up comedy, part eccentric lecture, include *The Bald Trilogy* (1993), *Ken Campbell's History of Comedy* (2000), and *I'm Not Mad: I've Just Read Different Books!* (2005).   SF

Campbell, Mrs Patrick (Beatrice Stella Tanner) (1865–1940) English actress who worked variously until she made a sensation in *Pinero's *The Second Mrs Tanqueray* (1893) and *The Notorious Mrs Ebbsmith* (1895). She had leading roles throughout the 1890s for *Alexander and *Forbes-Robertson, and still convinced as the

original Eliza Doolittle at the age of 49, opposite Beerbohm *Tree, in *Shaw's *Pygmalion* (1914). In her heyday she was a tall, willowy, Pre-Raphaelite beauty, with large dark eyes, a rich voice, and obvious star quality, but she rapidly became known as capricious and unprofessional. She wished to be taken seriously and to produce uncommon modern plays, but was constantly driven to pot-boilers to pay her frequent debts; however, she did play in *Ibsen and *Maeterlinck. Her correspondence with Shaw reveals a fascinating love–hate relationship; he wrote *Caesar and Cleopatra* for her, though she declined it. In later life she became fat and still more capricious, and refused to take supporting roles on stage; but she continued with radio work, and appeared in several films.   EEC

Campesino, El Teatro A Chicano theatre troupe founded by Luís *Valdez and a group of striking farmworkers in Delano, California, in 1965. Under Valdez's guidance, the Teatro members, who had never acted before, *collectively created *actos* or sketches intended to educate and entertain. This troupe of farmworkers gave instant visibility to the incipient farmworker's struggle, satirizing the growers and informing workers about the advantages of a labour union. The troupe left the union in 1968 in order to gain autonomy and to address other issues vital to the Chicanos such as the war in Vietnam, police brutality, and poor educational systems. The company moved into their permanent home in San Juan Bautista, California, in 1971, where they have offices and studios and produce a season of plays. An annual highlight is the centuries-old Christmas pageant performed in the eighteenth-century Mission San Juan Bautista. *See also* DIASPORA.   JAH

Camus, Albert (1913–60) French novelist, essayist, and playwright, born in Algeria. Expelled from the Algerian Communist Party in 1937 for rejecting Marx, he founded the Théâtre de l'Équipe and maintained his political and social focus until the outbreak of war. His war years were spent between Algeria and France and he was a member of the 'Combat' resistance. The first of four plays, *Le Malentendu* (*Cross Purpose*), was produced unsuccessfully during the Occupation, but *Caligula* (1945), with Gérard *Philipe in the title role, was well received. *Barrault directed *State of Siege* in 1948, and the following year *Les Justes* began a run of over 400 performances. Although he wrote no further plays, Camus was responsible for six successful theatrical adaptations of novels, including Dostoevsky's *The Possessed* (1959). Camus's focus on the existentialist notions of the 'absurd' and 'gratuitous action' in tragic situations link him back to *Artaud's notion of *cruelty and plague and forward to the theatre of the *absurd.   BRS

canjun xi (ts'an-chün hsi) An early form of Chinese drama popular during the eighth and ninth centuries (Tang Dynasty), which consisted of a variety of comic skits. The details of performance are long lost, and the origin of the term *canjun xi* (adjutant play) has received various explanations, but the humorous content of the plays is apparent. The plays involved both singing and *dialogue, and actresses as well as actors appeared. There is some indication that the plays were performed by groups of strolling players at temple sites for festivals and similar occasions. Actors wore make-up and were accompanied by a musical ensemble with, at minimum, string and percussion instruments. There are no direct influences of the adjutant plays discoverable in Yuan Dynasty and later forms of drama, but the nature of these entertainments indicates the basic parameters of subsequent Chinese theatre.   JTR

Cantor, Eddie (1892-1964) American singer and actor. With his warbling tenor, his timid persona, and his huge eyes which earned him the nickname 'Banjo Eyes', he began in *vaudeville, typically performing in blackface, before his discovery in the 1916 *Ziegfeld Midnight Frolic*. Promoted to the *Ziegfeld Follies* in 1917, he became a *Follies* headliner, appearing in every edition to 1920. He then embarked on a series of *musical comedies crafted to his talents, including *Kid Boots* (1923), *Whoopee* (1928), and *Banjo Eyes* (1941). He made more than fifteen films between 1926 and 1952, including *Whoopee* in 1930, as well as making regular appearances on radio and television. He also recorded hundreds of songs, including such signature tunes as 'If You Knew Susie' and 'Makin' Whoopee'.   JD

Cao Yu (Ts'ao Yü) (1910-96) Chinese playwright, pen-name of Wan Jiabao. Cao's theatrical education began in Nankai Middle School in Tianjin, which had one of the earliest Western-style theatre programmes in northern China. He attended Qinghua University in Beijing where he wrote his first play, *Thunderstorm*, in 1933; initially performed in Japan in 1935, it is now recognized as one of the greatest of *huajü* (spoken drama) plays. In 1936 Cao became a professor at the National School of Drama in Nanjing and wrote two more plays before the Sino-Japanese War: *Sunrise* and *Wilderness* (both 1937). During the war he moved with his school to the Chinese stronghold of south-western China where he

wrote *Beijing Man* (1941) and *Family* (1943). After 1949 Cao held several important theatrical positions, including artistic director of the Beijing People's Art Theatre, the best *huajü* theatre in China. He continued writing plays, *Bright Sky* (1954), *Gall and Sword* (1960), and *Wang Zhaojun* (1978) among them, but none reached the excellence of his earlier work.   SYL

Čapek, Karel (1890-1938) Czech playwright, novelist, and journalist. As a playwright he started in lyrical vein, but it was his post-war *expressionist plays, concerned about the technological future (*RUR*, 1921) and the self-indulgent, greedy, and militant character of man (*The Insect Comedy*, 1922), which drew international attention to him and to Czech theatre. Between 1921 and 1923 he was a *dramaturg in Prague's Vinohrady Theatre, occasionally directing plays, most notably his own *The Macropulos Secret* (1922), dealing with the problem of longevity, made into an *opera by Leoš Janáček. After *Adam the Creator* (1927) he dropped drama, returning to it as a social weapon in the late 1930s, deeply disturbed by the rise of dictatorship and totalitarianism (*The White Plague*, 1937; *Mother*, 1938), which, after the Munich appeasement, finally broke his spirit. Co-author of most of his earlier plays was his brother Josef (1887-1945), an outstanding painter and scene designer, who died in a German concentration camp.   ML

Capuana, Luigi (1839-1915) Italian playwright, novelist, and critic. Of Sicilian origin, Capuana studied the works of Hegel and the French *naturalists: Flaubert, the Goncourts, and *Zola. As a commentator on contemporary theatre, he promoted Italian *realism or *verismo, and with his and Giovanni Verga's encouragement, regional literature enjoyed a period of growth that produced the dialect theatre of *Pirandello. Capuana's plays in standard Italian and in Sicilian dialect served as vehicles for *actor-managers such as Giovanni Grasso and Angelo Musco. They include *Giacinta* (1888), an adaptation of his major novel; *Malia* (*Enchantment*, 1895); *Il cavaliere Pidagna* (1911).   JEH

Carballido, Emilio (1925-2008) Mexican playwright and novelist. A master of the quotidian, Carballido captures the bittersweet realities of simple but significant lives and the oppressive rhythms of provincial life. A prolific playwright, Carballido's method ranges from the *comedy of manners of his first successful play, *Rosalba and the Llavero Family* (1950)—repeated in many subsequent pieces, but with special artfulness in *Photograph on the Beach*

(1984)—to works with more political content, many of them under the influence of *Brecht, such as *A Short Day's Anger* (1966), which tells of a small town's brief uprising against a local injustice. Other Carballido plays explore the poetic, the inexplicable, and the twilight zones between the real and the perceived, as in *I Too Speak of the Rose* (1966). Carballido garnered many awards and was the author of two of Mexico's longest-running hits: *Orinoco* (1982) and *The Rose of Two Aromas* (1992), both of which are sensitive to the dilemma of women in a man's world.   KFN

Cariou, Len (1939–) Canadian actor. Between 1962 and 1964 Cariou played in *Rostand, *Molière, and Shakespeare at the *Stratford Festival. His New York debut as Orestes in *The House of Atreus* (1968) led to an expanding classical career at the *Chichester Festival (*Love's Labour's Lost*, 1964), the Goodman Theatre, Chicago (*Othello*, 1969), the *Guthrie Theatre (*As You Like It*, 1966; *Twelfth Night*, 1968), and the American Shakespeare Theatre (*Henry V*, 1969). Cariou's forceful stage presence and powerful voice have also allowed him to interpret effectively such contemporary strong men as Musgrave in *Arden's *Serjeant Musgrave's Dance* (1968), Stalin (David Pownall's *Master Class*, 1986), and Hemingway (John de Groot's *Papa*, 1996). An equally gifted interpreter of *musical theatre, and of *Sondheim in particular, he was nominated for a Tony in *A Little Night Music* (1963) and awarded both the Tony and Drama Desk awards for *Sweeney Todd* (1979). He has an active career in film and television.   MJD

Carnovsky, Morris (1897–1992) American actor. Born in St Louis, from 1923 to 1931 he acted regularly with the *Theatre Guild in New York and was a founding member of the *Group Theatre. Carnovsky created key roles for the Group, often playing characters far beyond his age, including the grandfather in *Odets's *Awake and Sing!* (1937) and the father in *Golden Boy* (1937). After the dissolution of the Group in 1941, Carnovsky worked on stage and film, but was blacklisted by Hollywood in the 1950s after his unfriendly appearance before the House Un-American Activities Committee. Carnovsky focused on Shakespeare and other classics for the rest of his life and succeeded in adapting the *Method to classical work. He began a long association with the American Shakespeare Theatre (Connecticut) in 1956 and later the *New York Shakespeare Festival. His performances of Lear, Shylock, and Claudius

established him as a leading Shakespearian during the 1960s and 1970s.   MAF

Carr, Marina (1964–) Irish playwright. *Ullaloo* (*Abbey Theatre, 1991) and other early works are largely experiments with *absurdist forms, but the memory play *The Mai* (1994) moved to the combination of lyrical language and idiomatic speech that has become Carr's hallmark. Her work centres around the fate of the outsider, aspects of motherhood, female abjection, and family behaviour patterns that lead to tragic outcomes. *Portia Coughlan* (1996), *By the Bog of Cats...* (1998), a variation on the Medea theme, and *On Raftery's Hill* (2000) moved away from strict regional speech. Recent plays such as *Woman and Scarecrow* (*Royal Court, 2006) explore the life of the unconscious using aspects of *surrealism and fantasy. *The Cordelia Dream* (*Royal Shakespeare Company, 2008) and *Marble* (Abbey, 2009) centre on the dream world and the unconscious.   MAS

Carraro, Tino (1910–95) Italian actor who forged the *acting style of the Piccolo Teatro in Milan, where between 1952 and 1962 he was the leading actor under the direction of *Strehler, playing many memorable roles, both classical and contemporary, in a characteristically understated style. His professional relationship with Strehler reached one of its high points in his 1956 interpretation of Mac the Knife in *Brecht's *Threepenny Opera*. After a falling out with Strehler, Carraro worked with *Visconti before returning to the Piccolo, first under the direction of *Chéreau and finally again under Strehler, appearing in the great Shakespeare productions as Lear (1972) and Prospero (1978). He retired from the stage in 1980 with *Pirandello's *The Mountain Giants*; in failing health, he was able to act only in the last part of the play.   DMcM

Carrière, Jean-Claude (1931–) French writer. He wrote the screenplays for six Luis Buñuel films, including *Belle de jour* and *The Discreet Charm of the Bourgeoisie*, as well as for *The Tin Drum*, *The Unbearable Lightness of Being*, and *Cyrano de Bergerac*. For *Brook in Paris Carrière successfully adapted *Timon of Athens* (1974); thereafter he became house translator, adapting other Shakespeare plays (*Measure for Measure*, 1978; *The Tempest*, 1990), *The Conference of the Birds* (1979), and other works. He used a very precise and direct French diction, avoiding conscious archaisms and also over-modern vocabulary; he applied the same approach for his and Brook's nine-hour *intercultural adaptation of the *Mahabharata

(1985), developed over a period of ten years. He later worked on both the screenplay and the English version of the text.   EEC

Carroll, Vinnette (1922–2002) *African-American actress and producer. Carroll was a clinical psychologist when she won a scholarship to the *Piscator Dramatic Workshop to study with *Strasberg and *Adler, making her debut in *Shaw's *Androcles and the Lion*. She created work for herself by writing and producing a one-person show that *toured, and in 1956 appeared on Broadway in a revival of *A Streetcar Named Desire*. Eleven years later she founded the Urban Arts Corps in New York, which promoted the work of black performers, writers, choreographers, and composers. She wrote the book for *Don't Bother Me I Can't Cope* (1972), which she also directed, making her the first African-American woman to direct a Broadway *musical. A collaboration with songwriter Micki Grant led to *Your Arm's Too Short to Box with God* (1977). In the 1980s Carroll left New York to found a 250-seat theatre in a renovated church in Fort Lauderdale, Florida.   BBL

Cartel des Quatre, Le Association of four Parisian directors and their theatres which led the French inter-war *avant-garde. Created in 1927 by two of *Copeau's former pupils, *Jouvet and *Dullin, together with *Pitoëff and *Baty, the Cartel embraced Copeau's aim of respecting the text. One aim of the association was to increase their *audience base by announcing their programmes in each other's publicity materials. The four directors had independent successes: Jouvet discovered a new playwright (*Giraudoux), Dullin trained a new generation of notable actors in memorable productions, the Pitoëffs brought a host of foreign plays to French audiences, and Baty experimented with pictorial elements. Their work was characterized by high production standards and it rejuvenated the theatre in a period of economic uncertainty.   BRS

Cartwright, Jim (1958–) English playwright. Though he draws on the language and attitudes of his industrial Lancashire origins, Cartwright eschews *naturalism in favour of a heightened, poetic style. *Road* (1986) follows the travellers on a road in northern Britain through a night out, elliptically drawing out a landscape of loss and longing in a town devastated by poverty and industrial collapse. His compelling language worked well in a promenade production which took the *audience into and around its characters' lives. His next major success was *The Rise and Fall of Little Voice* (1992), a romantic fantasy about a young girl's obsession with her absent father and

his record collection, which enjoyed a long West End run and was later filmed (as *Little Voice*, 1998). *I Licked a Slag's Deodorant* (1996) is comprised of intercut *monologues about a brutal encounter between a loveless man and a prostitute. *Hard Fruit* (2000) continued the investigation of masculinity in its portrait of a closeted gay man and his obsession with wrestling.   DR

Casares, María (1922–96) Franco-Spanish actress. Daughter of a prominent republican politician who fled Civil War Spain, Casares and her mother settled in Paris where, adding a grave accent to her surname to preserve the Spanish pronunciation, she went on to become one of the definitive tragediennes of the post-war era, premièring the dramas of *Camus and *Sartre before joining *Vilar's *Théâtre National Populaire (1954–9). Her deep, raspish voice, tinged with a Galician musical lilt, and her expressive almond-shaped eyes and controlled gestural language, were to make her a regular *Avignon performer. With *Lavelli, a fellow émigré, she was to realize a visceral *Medea in 1967, an influence on *Koltès. Among *Genet's preferred performers, she undertook the role of the mother in *The Screens* in 1966 under *Blin's direction, and in 1983 with *Chéreau. Casares was to work only sporadically in Spain, but her performance of the despotic Gorgo in Alberti's *The Absurdity* (1976) was a key moment in the cultural transition from dictatorship to democracy.   MMD

Casona, Alejandro (Alejandro Rodríguez Alvarez) (1903–65) Spanish playwright who chose exile in Argentina during the Spanish Civil War. His plays were characterized by fantasy, poetic undercurrents, and explorations of the role of illusion as an antidote to reality. Although his greatest successes were *The Lady of the Dawn* (1934) and *Trees Die Standing* (1949), his earlier prizewinning *The Stranded Mermaid* (Madrid, 1933) and *Suicide Prohibited in Springtime* (Mexico City, 1936), display more theatrical innovation. Several revivals of his plays accompanied his return to Spain in 1963, and a commercial production of *Trees Die Standing* in 1999 proved popular in Madrid.   MPH

Casson, Lewis (1875–1969) Actor and director of Welsh descent. He *toured with *Greet, acted at the *Royal Court Theatre under Granville *Barker, and at the Gaiety Theatre, Manchester, where he began directing. There he married Sybil *Thorndike in 1908, and they embarked on their 60-year theatrical partnership. Casson had several periods of *management of London theatres from 1922, and appeared with and directed his wife in

London and on many tours. He was a lifelong socialist, drama director of the Arts Council, and was president of Actors' Equity (1940 5). As an actor he was reliable and intelligent but not first rate, and played a wide variety of main and supporting parts, including Shakespeare's Glendower and Polonius, as well as *Shaw's Tanner in *Man and Superman*. He was a meticulous director, and supported his wife in serious and experimental productions, ranging from *Greek *tragedy through Shakespeare and *expressionist plays to contemporary drama and *Grand Guignol.   EEC

Castorf, Frank (1951-) German director. One of the most controversial figures in contemporary theatre, Castorf was born in East Berlin and throughout the 1980s worked at provincial East German theatres before returning to Berlin in 1988. He came to national attention after 1989 with productions of *Hamlet*, *Lessing's *Miss Sara Sampson*, and *Goethe's *Tasso*, which radically dismantled the texts. In 1992 he became *artistic director of the *Volksbühne and established it as an energetic forum for social debate. He confronts classical scripts with elements of pop culture, textual collage, the aesthetics of *performance art, and the ideology of *dada. His choice of texts is extremely catholic, ranging from the *Greeks to adaptations of *A Clockwork Orange* and *Trainspotting*. Recent productions include *Great and Small* by Botho *Strauss (2005) and a version of *Berlin Alexanderplatz* (2007).   CBB

Castro y Bellvis, Guillén de (1569–1631) Spanish dramatist. Influenced originally by the tragedians of his native Valencia, his plays show an increasingly symbiotic relationship with those of Lope de *Vega. The most famous is his many-faceted *The Young Cid*, recast by *Corneille as *Le Cid*, but he also wrote many *comedies (including three based on tales by *Cervantes), and dramatized both classical stories and the theme of resistance to tyranny.   VFD

catastrophe Literally 'downturn', the term in classical Greek implies a sudden and serious conclusion to an *action. In modern critical usage catastrophe usually refers to the disastrous unravelling of a *tragedy or to the climactic end of the process. The term has sometimes been used in a more neutral sense. In late antiquity catastrophe was the last of the four rhetorical parts of *comedy. (The others were the *prologue, the *protasis* or *exposition, and the *epitasis* or complication.) In the nineteenth century there were unsuccessful efforts to treat catastrophe as simply the closing action of any drama.   RWV

catharsis In the *Poetics* *Aristotle defines *tragedy in terms of its object of imitation (a serious action; *see* MIMESIS), its medium (language), and its manner of presentation (by *actors); but he then unexpectedly adds, 'through pity and fear bringing about the catharsis [purgation, purification] of emotions such as these'. Virtually every word in the clause is doubtfully translated, and there is no consensus on the meaning. Among the recurring questions over the centuries are: (1) Is catharsis a homoeopathic, therapeutic process? If so, are we to assume that spectators come to tragedy in need of a cure? (2) Are pity and fear the only passions involved in tragic catharsis, or are they representative? (3) Are the emotions that are purged in the spectator, or are they located in the play's structure? (4) Is catharsis the end of tragedy, or the means by which tragedy achieves its end? (5) Is catharsis brought about by the direct witnessing of pitiful and fearful events, or by the artistic representation of such events? Although the literature on catharsis is vast, interpretations can be roughly categorized as:

Moral. The view generally held in the *early modern period was that of *Giraldi Cinthio (1543): 'tragedy... by means of the pitiable and the terrible, purges the minds of the hearers from their vices and influences them to adopt good morals.'

Psychological. Since the late nineteenth century the most common interpretation of catharsis is that it is a process of emotional, even therapeutic, relief. In psychological and socio-psychological writing, drama, especially tragedy, is often cited with *ritual as a means whereby debilitating and repressed emotion, the result either of a specific trauma or of collectively held distresses, can be safely confronted and controlled.

Intellectual. In the twentieth century there were several efforts to explain catharsis as an intellectual clarification of the represented incidents, which results in a new perception on the part of the *audience. Once the tragic *protagonist's guilt is properly understood, the spectator is freed from pity and fear.

Structural. The most controversial interpretation of catharsis treats it as a constituent element of the tragedy, as an emotional element carried forward by the plot. Gerald Else (1967) argues that catharsis consists of the purification of the initially unclean tragic act through the demonstration of the protagonist's ignorance of its true nature. The spectator is consequently free to pity rather than execrate him.   RWV

cavittu natakam Indian performance, literally 'kicking' or 'stamping dramas', traditionally performed in the Malayalam language by large, all-male companies of Latin-rite Christians on feast days, at weddings, or other major celebrations during the dry season, primarily in the central region of Kerala. The tradition dates from the later half of the sixteenth century, when Jesuit missionaries travelled to the south-west coast of India with Portuguese traders and recruited Catholic converts (in contrast to the early Syrian Christians) to perform anonymous plays based on *biblical stories or lives of the great Christian saints. Performed by all-male companies in front of colourful backdrops, these all-night *dance-dramas derive their reputation for stamping and kicking from the large, wide, forceful leaping and arcing steps, kicks, jumps, and stamps used by the actor-dancers. For several centuries *cavittu natakam* performances were as popular at Catholic celebrations and festival days as were *kathakali* at Hindu temple festivals. Women began to appear onstage in women's roles around 1960. As late as the 1970s, a few new plays were written, but in spite of attempts to revive interest and patronage, performances were rare by the end of the century.   PZ

Cecchi, Carlo (1939–) Italian actor and director. Cecchi became a prominent figure with performances in alternative venues of his cooperative group Granteatro (1971-6). Synthesizing the Italian popular tradition with *avant-garde ideas—particularly those of the *Living Theatre—he presented works by the Neapolitan A. Petito, *Mayakovsky, *Brecht, *Büchner, *Molière, and *Pirandello. Cecchi went on to explore, as director and performer, the whole spectrum of European drama, including Shakespeare, *Goldoni, *Chekhov, *Beckett, *Pinter, and *Bernhard. A fine film actor, he appeared in *Le Mans* (1971), *Death of a Neapolitan Mathematician* (1992), *Stealing Beauty* (1996, directed by Bertolucci), *Hammam* (1997), and *Red Violin* (1998).   JEH

Cecchini, Pier Maria (1563-1645) *Commedia dell'arte* *actor-manager from Ferrara, who created the *Zanni-type mask Fritellino and directed the Accesi company. Frustrated in his career by quarrels with colleagues and patrons, he expressed his perfectionist vision of improvised theatre in a series of treatises and observations composed between 1610 and 1630.   RAA

Celeste, Madame (1814-82) French *dancer, actress, and *mime. Working in England and America, her passionate depictions of feeling began in thrilling physicality and only slowly moved to spoken English. Her most noted role was the Native American Miami in the *melodrama *Green Bushes* (1845). In London she *managed the melodrama house the Adelphi (1844-53), financially supporting her partner Benjamin *Webster's dramas at the *Haymarket. They appeared at the Adelphi together for six years more before they split and she moved on to manage the Lyceum, making a sensation there in her first season as Mme Defarge.   JSB

censorship In the theatre, the act of interference, usually by or on behalf of government or religious authority, in the content or representation of a dramatic work or other performance in order to ensure its conformity with what the authority considers to be political, moral, aesthetic, or religious norms. Plato banned poets from his ideal republic on the grounds that they were subversives, and something of that attitude infuses the censorship of drama and performance. Producing a text is as fraught with opportunities for *satire or subversion as the text itself, and in most cases censors have reserved the right to both pre- and post-performance control. Moreover, the presence of an *audience, disposed to make its opinions evident, has made governments sensitive to the dangers to public order implicit in theatre (*see* RIOTS).

Awareness of the power of the stage for the promulgation of vice rather than virtue was expressed on behalf of the early Christian Church by Tertullian in *De Spectaculis* (*c*.200), on to *Collier's *A Short View of the Immorality of the Stage* (1696), and well into the nineteenth century by evangelicals, mainly in the form of *anti-theatrical sermons. But political concerns have been at the forefront of censorship, and emerged with virulent effect in the twentieth century against dissidence in dictatorships in Spain, much of South America, South Africa, the Soviet Union, in certain rigidly controlled Islamic regimes, and elsewhere. Since it is impossible to detail all cases, the examples of Western Europe and East Asia treated here should be taken merely as representative of a complex series of censoring practices. For examples from other parts of the globe readers are referred to the long entry in the parent volume, *The Oxford Encyclopedia of Theatre and Performance*.

Western Europe to 1791 Strictly speaking the first 'censors' were the two elected magistrates in ancient Rome, who organized the census and as a secondary function had responsibility for public morals. During the *medieval period, as drama emerged from the Church to a secular theatre, censorships began to be established to control the stage. During the fifteenth century the authorities in France and Spain attempted to control religious drama (as in Charles VI's licensing of the *Confrérie de la Passion in 1402) and to curtail the troublesome activities of satiric troupes such as the Basochiens. *Mystery plays, often adulterated by secular accretions, were prohibited in France from 1538 and censorship was introduced also in England for religious reasons. The 1543 Act for the Advancement of True Religion was used to underline the changes wrought by the Protestant revolution, but references to the power of the Pope were suppressed in the Chester cycle plays as early as 1531. Inevitably Catholic doctrine was replaced by Protestant. The suppression of the Catholic feast of *Corpus Christi and its attendant dramatic activity took place in 1548, but a final ban on medieval *biblical plays and miracle plays was not fully realized until 1581, under Elizabeth I. Early in her reign an Act Prohibiting Unlicensed Interludes and Plays, Especially on Religion or Policy emphasized how concerned the authorities had become over the propaganda power of theatre, and a new system of censorship was instituted which handed the scrutiny of dramatic texts to local authorities (mayors and justices of the peace) throughout the realm.

Medieval and *early modern censorship throughout Europe was conducted in virtual secrecy. But in England from the appointment of Edmund Tilney as Master of the Revels in 1579, censorship acquired a human face and became more firmly established. Tilney's patent of 1581 introduced centralized control, empowering him 'to order and reform, authorise and put down, as shall be thought meet unto himself, or his... deputy', anything which he considered injurious to the interests of the state. On the face of it this gave him powers to interfere with the flowering of Elizabethan drama. Most famously, *Richard II* was supposedly given in performance by the *Chamberlain's Men on the night before the Earl of Essex's failed rebellion, which may have occasioned the removal of Richard's abdication scene from the first published version in 1600; it was not restored until 1608. The complete absence of oaths from the Folio text of *Othello* is undoubtedly the effect of the 1606 Act to Restrain Abuses of Players, a Puritan-inspired measure specifically directed at public performances.

At this period censorship usually emphasized the promptbook supplied to the censor and playwrights undoubtedly learned codes or strategies to avoid his attention by seeming to echo politically correct sentiments. While powers of post-production censorship did exist, little account seems to have been taken of the nature of representation, though there were exceptions. Thomas Nashe and *Jonson's *The Isle of Dogs* was staged at the *Swan in 1597 and may well never have existed in a fully written form, which is probably why the censor took some time to register its extreme subversiveness. It may also be that the actors pushed the political satire to more dangerous levels than sanctioned by the authors. In the ensuing controversy Nashe fled and Jonson was imprisoned for a short time for sedition. Jonson's *Every Man out of his Humour* also suffered when the original ending called for the representation of the Queen on stage. This was quickly stopped, initiating a ban lasting several centuries on any representation of the royal family. After Cromwell's victory in the Civil War, theatrical representations in England were prohibited from 1642, though the ban was not always obeyed. At the Restoration in 1660, for the companies which formed the *patent monopoly, the Lord Chamberlain reserved powers of censorship.

In France censorship was relatively weak during the seventeenth century; it was formally abolished in 1641 by Louis XIII and thereafter serious breaches of decorum by actors or political excess by playwrights were dealt with ad hoc. One victim who fell foul of the religious establishment was *Molière, whose portrayal of religious hypocrisy in *Tartuffe* (1664) proved too much for the archbishop of Paris, who demanded its prohibition following its première at Versailles. The play remained interdicted until 1669, when it acquired respectability by being performed before Louis XIV.

That King was responsible for formal reintroduction of censorship in 1701-6, in a structure that existed until the revolution, but the system was limited to the three royal theatres in Paris, especially the *Comédie-Française, which was expected to uphold the best standards of decency and establishment values (*see* NEOCLASSICISM). Authors were at liberty to stage prohibited plays—or those likely to be prohibited, as in the case of *Voltaire—in the provinces, where the powers of local magistrates had very limited effect. On the whole the censorship prohibited anything which might excite discontent or political disruption, interpreted to include personal allusion. Of banned plays the most prominent were those of *Beaumarchais, who enraged the authorities for his political stance on the abuses of the *ancien régime* and for his views on class in *The Barber of Seville* and *The Marriage of Figaro*. Both were prohibited for some years prior to production at the Comédie-Française in 1775 and 1784.

Britain's formal system of censorship, which lasted 231 years, was inaugurated with the Stage *Licensing Act of 1737, replaced by the wider authority of the Theatre Regulation Act of 1843. The original act was a blatant move by Robert Walpole's government to muzzle the political power of the theatre. The satire of *Gay's *Beggar's Opera* (1728) and its sequel *Polly* (1729) troubled authorities, and *Fielding acquired an increasing reputation for perfectly aimed political satire at *Drury Lane (1732–3) and particularly at the Little Theatre in the *Haymarket (1736–7) with *Pasquin, The Historical Register*, and *Eurydice Hiss'd*. Smarting at these attacks on corruption and incompetence, the government's case for censorship was strengthened in Parliament by the last-minute appearance of an obscene *farce, *The Golden Rump*, which may well have been written to order from Walpole. It is clear that Fielding was not the only target of the Licensing Act, a broad measure meant to curb the troublesome nature of the stage once and for all. It not only imposed strict censorship but also reasserted the Lord Chamberlain's right to restrict the performance of drama in the cities of London and Westminster to the patent *playhouses, and to exercise pre-censorship by requiring that *managers submit all plays for licensing prior to production.

An effect of pre-censorship was that audiences became attuned to seek out political allusion, whether or not it was present. James Thomson's veiled references to Walpole under the cloak of *Aeschylus in his *Agamemnon* (1738) were not picked up by the censor, who interfered only with the *prologue, but spectators saw the parallels immediately. Similarly in a production of *Richard III* in 1738, using a version of the original text rather than *Cibber's adaptation, the audience clapped and cheered at the line 'The King is not himself, but basely led | By flatterers'.

Throughout the century political considerations continued to influence the decisions of the censors, especially at times of political tension. Obvious political satire determined the fate of *Macklin's *The Man of the World* (1770), with its outrageously corrupt *character of Sir Pertinax MacSycophant. Submitted for licensing three times, it was finally allowed in 1781 for performance at Covent Garden by the new Examiner of Plays, John Larpent, who became the longest serving of all examiners (1778 to his death in 1824). Entrusted with full censoring powers by the Lord Chamberlain, Larpent was responsible for several notable suppressions, including Joseph Holman's translation (c.1799) of *Schiller's *The Robbers*—which in its original form had been censored in the German lands and many other parts of Europe.

Western Europe 1791–present Dramatic censorship in France was effectively abolished in January 1791 as inimical to revolutionary freedom. The new authorities, increasingly aware of its propaganda power, made the theatre serve the interests of the republic by providing lessons in good citizenship. By 1793 censorship was reintroduced discreetly through the agency of the Paris police, who deputed two officers to oversee new plays and revivals. Much of their interference was relatively minor, but Molière's *The Misanthrope*, purged of all references to the royal family, was like many other classic dramas ruthlessly republicanized. The formal 'vous' form of address was universally altered to 'tu' (hitherto mainly reserved for addressing children and inferiors), and 'monsieur' and 'madame' were abolished in favour of 'citoyen' and 'citoyenne'. All anti-revolutionary plays were forbidden. After the Reign of Terror and the fall of Robespierre, censorship was reconfirmed and the theatre's function as promoter of morals and republican principles reinforced. This decree remained in force until the reintroduction of conventional pre-production censorship by Napoleon in the wake of his coup in 1799.

Fear of the theatre as a forum for inculcating revolutionary ideas was common in most of Europe. Under the Habsburgs censorship was directed against anything considered harmful to the state and was strengthened under Metternich, who by 1819 had imposed a well-disciplined system of spies and censorship police throughout the empire. In divided Italy the Austrian censor had control in several areas to the north, while the Pope appointed a board of six *cavalieri* and a prelate to oversee the theatre in Rome and the Papal States.

The political situation in France affected Britain during the 1790s, when Larpent deleted all references to revolution (Irish or French), republicanism, anti-aristocratic or anti-monarchist ideas, whether or not intended, with the result that drama from about 1789 until after Waterloo became detached from the social and political tensions of the period. Successive censors in Britain continued to be wary. George Dibdin Pitt was tempting fate with his suppressed *Terry Tyrone (the Irish Tam O'Shanter)* (1847), which referred to the Irish patriot Robert Emmet and the 1798 rebellion. *Boucicault was circumspect enough for his Irish settings to pass muster with the censor, but in general any allusions to patriotism or the unruly state of affairs in Ireland were regularly prohibited, as was the singing of patriotic Irish songs like 'The Wearin' o' the Green'. The British censor was also wary of all plays dealing with violent crime, especially burglary and highway robbery, on the grounds of their bad example to the young.

This move marks a gradual shift in the censor's principal interest from the political to the moral, a change that began in the 1850s and was fully implemented by the 1870s. Protection of marriage and family life was considered paramount, but the censor's judgement was often poor. *Dumas's *La Dame aux camélias* and *Sardou's *Séraphine*, which treated sexual themes with some seriousness, tended to suffer more damage than inconsequential farces. In 1874 the Lord Chamberlain ordered the lengthening of the skirts of *ballet girls in the notorious 'ripercelle' *dance in *Offenbach's *Vert Vert*. With the explicit support of Queen Victoria, the cancan was resisted in London as long as possible into the 1880s.

Opposition to censorship, infrequent and unfocused before 1880, gathered momentum in parts of Western Europe as the nineteenth century drew to a close. It consolidated in the free theatre movement, begun in Paris with *Antoine's Théâtre *Libre in 1887, spread to Berlin (*Freie Bühne, 1889), and eventually to London (*Independent Theatre Society, 1891), where it was supported by keen anti-censorship campaigners such as *Archer and *Shaw. Censorship inhibited the 'advanced drama' of the period, represented by *Ibsen and others, through its inability to handle serious discussion of moral themes, particularly sexual. One of the most influential dramas of the period, Ibsen's *Ghosts* (written 1881), was banned almost everywhere in Europe for its (quite recessive) treatment of syphilis and marital infidelity, and was seen only in private performances for some years; it remained officially prohibited in Britain until 1914. Shaw's prefaces to his prohibited plays, including *Mrs Warren's Profession* (concerning prostitution as a business, 1893) and the *The Shewing up of Blanco Posnet* (a political satire, 1909), contain virulent attacks on censorship as an institution as well as on the individuals in charge of it. Other works of special merit were banned on grounds of sexual explicitness, including *Wedekind's *Spring's Awakening*, *Maeterlinck's *Monna Vanna*, *Brieux's *Damaged Goods*, and Granville *Barker's *Waste*. As a result of pressure from British playwrights, a parliamentary inquiry in 1909 effected some minor modifications to the system, but censorship remained as cautious and conservative as ever.

The drama of the *avant-garde suffered more than most, even those pieces which had attained

some international standing. *Pirandello's *Six Characters in Search of an Author* (1921) was suppressed in 1924 for its treatment of incest and dysfunctional family life; the ban was reluctantly lifted only in 1928. *Strindberg's *Miss Julie* (1888) was refused a licence as late as 1927. In the 1930s the British censor busily deleted references to foreign personalities in case they should give offence. *Rattigan suffered protracted negotiations over his burlesques of Hitler, Gœring, and Gœbbels in *Follow my Leader* (1938) and the play was only allowed after the outbreak of war. Over the same period the *fascist regimes of Germany and Italy operated rigorous controls on the drama. *Brecht and many of his colleagues left for exile on the appointment of Hitler as Chancellor in 1933, and all plays by Jews were banned completely, including those of *Schnitzler. In Italy performances of *Julius Caesar* were suppressed in case they offended Mussolini.

After the Second World War censorship came to an end in West Germany, but in several other countries, including Portugal, it became even more repressive. Under Franco there was a mass exodus of intellectuals from Spain, including a number of influential playwrights, such as *Arrabal. The climate was inhibiting for those who stayed. *Buero-Vallejo was imprisoned more than once and his long career punctuated by several conflicts. Franco's censorship, which lasted until 1975, was manifestly political in nature but Spain was somewhat unusual in that the influence of the Catholic Church was almost as strong. Eastern European countries under Soviet influence, such as Poland and the former Czechoslovakia, also suffered badly: *Havel was a notable victim of the Czech censors. Matters changed quickly in the later twentieth century, however. France was the first nation to abandon censorship officially, as far back as 1905, though controls remained possible at local level into the 1960s. Censorship collapsed entirely in the European socialist states with the fall of their communist governments in 1989–90, and by 2000 no Western democracy operated any formal control over drama.

But in Britain its abolition was a protracted business. The club device was used on various occasions to avoid the censor by the Arts Theatre, the *Cambridge Festival Theatre, *Littlewood's *Theatre Workshop, and the *Royal Court, which in the 1960s became a haven for several prohibited plays. Although *Osborne's landmark *Look Back in Anger* (1956) was passed, by the late 1950s censorship was regarded as seriously behind public opinion, particularly after the verdict in 1961 that permitted the paperback version of

*Lawrence's novel *Lady Chatterley's Lover*. There were many wrangles over 'bad language' which often seemed silly, and a ban on homosexuality as a subject remained until 1958, so that *Miller's *A View from the Bridge* and *Williams's *Cat on a Hot Tin Roof* had only club performances in 1955.

Several elements led to the abolition of censorship in 1968: club performances, the opposition of powerful institutions like the new *National Theatre, a long campaign in Parliament, and the activities of playwrights in conflict with the Lord Chamberlain's office. In *Pinter's *The Caretaker* the phrase 'piss off' was removed in 1960, but allowed for a revival in 1965 when it was discovered that the British Board of Film Censors had permitted the same phrase in a film. *Orton escaped a ban on *Loot* (1964), which the authorities found tasteless and unpleasant, only after considerable rewriting, mainly to do with the corpse. In the final years of British censorship the Lord Chamberlain refused Osborne's *A Patriot for Me* (1964) and *Bond's *Saved* (1965); Bond's *Early Morning* (1967) was also banned and his *Narrow Road to the Deep North* (1968) subjected to heavy cuts. That two major English playwrights, one established, one emergent, could be so thoroughly rejected by an arbitrary authority finally tipped the balance, and a new Theatres Act ended formal censorship a few months later. Prosecution under common law is still possible for offences to public standards. But since the failure of a private prosecution in 1982 against *Brenton's *The Romans in Britain* (directed by *Bogdanov at the National, 1980) no major case has been brought before the courts.

East Asia In China, the government attempted in varying degrees to censor the activities of troupes beginning in the Yuan Dynasty (1279–1368), when mature forms of theatre had become established. The authorities, recognizing the power of the theatre to communicate with a vast population, the majority of them illiterate, banned certain genres, themes, and titles; punishments were meted out to authors who overstepped established boundaries. The government of the Manchu Dynasty, the last of the pre-modern era, was especially suspicious over social and religious matters, expressing concern that because 'men and women were mixed together', the theatre had the potential to destroy proper family life. On the other hand, the Ming and Qing governments in the preceding dynasties encouraged plays that enshrined Confucian virtues and condemned those who ventured on the opposite path.

There was little organized censorship in the early twentieth century, but under the communist government of Mao and his successors in the post-war years the same mixture of positive and negative censorship was adopted. During the Cultural Revolution (1966–76) almost all forms of theatre were banned, both foreign and traditional. Mao's wife Jiang Qing led an effort to create 'revolutionary modern drama' (*geming xiandai xi*); 'model plays' were adopted by troupes everywhere as the only productions permitted. After Mao's death in 1976 virtually all forms of theatre were restored, although even at the start of the twenty-first century certain plays openly critical of contemporary social injustice have been banned, such as those of the Nobel laureate *Gao Xingjian which have not been on stage since the 1980s.

In Korea, little censorship was employed until the colonization of the country by Japan in 1910. In a limited sense, the court's Master of Revels during the first half of the Chosün Dynasty (1392–1912) might be looked on as a form of benevolent censorship, since he determined the performing arts appropriate for court celebrations. During the 36 years of the colonial period (1910–45), the Japanese government closely regulated the arts, both traditional and contemporary. When Western-style spoken drama by Ibsen and other progressive playwrights was introduced early in the twentieth century (ironically, via Japan), the Korean intelligentsia believed that this new form could provide a means to enlighten the larger population and help create a measure of spiritual independence from Japan. Such efforts, however, were increasingly suppressed by Japanese authorities. Three years after the country's liberation in 1945, the Korean peninsula was divided into two parts, with separate regimes established north and south with competing ideologies.

In the case of North Korea, the developments in post-war theatre are largely unknown to the outside world, although it seems clear that the government remains convinced that the theatrical arts are important in promoting the superiority of the socialist spirit. Plays are written under the guidance and control of government organizers; writers and directors are not permitted to change the wording of approved scripts without permission. In South Korea, many playwrights began to treat such issues as the division of the country, the Korean War, and political suppression. In the middle of the 1960s, however, the government organized the Committee for the Ethics of the Performing Arts as an official censoring agency. The committee was highly interventionist in theatre for two decades or more, but since about 1990 its major work has been to rate films and videos.

In Japan, there was no organized theatrical censorship before the Tokugawa Period (1600–1868), although the sponsorship of *nō performances by the aristocracy and Buddhist temples may be responsible, at least to some extent, for the fact that the nō seldom addressed political or social issues directly. With the coming of *kabuki in the seventeenth century, its existence as an urban theatre, dedicated to entertaining a large popular audience, brought its activities under the gaze of the government, which was concerned about questions of public order, morality, and political correctness. The controls imposed by the government were many, ranging from the lavishness of theatrical costume and the salaries of actors to the contents of the plays and a ban on women performers.

In the modern period, beginning in 1868, the theatre enjoyed increased freedom, although it was customary for kabuki scripts to be checked by government censors before production. Because of its progressive nature, *shingeki, the modern spoken theatre, caused the same difficulties it caused in colonial Korea. Censorship by the Home Ministry became particularly rigorous after 1937 with the increasing power of the militaristic regime. By 1940 the government had closed down all progressive modern companies, and a number of prominent directors, writers, and performers were jailed. Only those troupes professing purely artistic goals were permitted to continue.

After the war the American occupation forces, under the direction of General Douglas MacArthur, took over the censorship. Many left-wing theatre directors and writers, newly released from prison, became active again, though politically progressive productions did not begin in earnest until censorship was officially lifted in 1950. Kabuki, on the other hand, was examined closely by the occupation authorities because of the supposed danger of its 'feudalistic' elements. Some classic works were forbidden performance. These activities, and all theatrical censorship in Japan, came to an end a few years later. JRS/SYL/ JOC/JTR

Centlivre, Susannah (c.1667–1723) English playwright and actress. Centlivre had at least nineteen plays performed in London between 1700 and 1724; second to Shakespeare, she was the most performed playwright of the eighteenth and nineteenth centuries. *The Wonder! A Woman Keeps a Secret* (1715) was performed at least 250 times by 1800 with at least 65 of those revivals starring *Garrick, who chose the play for his fare-

well performance. Centlivre's popularity lay in her ability to capture and reproduce *realistic *characters and *dialogue. Her first play, *The Perjur'd Husband* (1700), was performed at *Drury Lane in a season containing plays by Catherine *Trotter and Mary *Pix, with whom Centlivre was closely associated. Writing in the heat of the *anti-theatrical polemic headed by *Collier, Centlivre did not attach her name to the publication of her next four *comedies, *The Beau's Duel* (1702), *The Stolen Heiress* (1702), *Love's Contrivance* (1703), and her first commercial hit, *The Gamester* (1705). These early plays challenge conventional constructs of virtuous female behaviour. The players were initially reluctant to perform *The Busie Body* (1709), although it proved to be her greatest success. *The Wonder!* and *A Bold Stroke for a Wife* (1718) had repeated success largely because Centlivre wrote plots and characters that attracted successive generations of players in Britain, Australia, and colonial America.   GBB

Cervantes Saavedra, Miguel de (1547– 1616) Spanish writer. The author of *Don Quixote* and the *Exemplary Novels* had gained a reputation as a popular dramatist before turning to prose fiction. The semi-autobiographical *Trade of Algiers*, based on Cervantes' captivity in North Africa, and *The Siege of Numantia*, a *tragedy mingling historical fact with popular legend and moral abstractions, were early proof of his theatrical talent. The reputation, however, was based primarily on the *comedies performed in Madrid during the 1580s, a small selection of which were published in the *Comedias y entremeses* of 1615. In a much quoted *prologue to the collection, Cervantes defends his decision to reduce the traditional five act structure of the Spanish *comedia to three and, after acknowledging his debt to writers like Lope de *Rueda, also defends the use of 'moral figures' as in *The Siege*. Though his *entremeses, with their blend of *realism, subtle characterization, and lively *dialogue, are generally considered to represent the high point of the genre (*see* ENTREMETS/ENTREMÉS), Cervantes quickly abandoned the stage in deference to the superior comic genius of Lope de *Vega. The continuing stageworthiness of *Pedro, The Great Pretender* was proved in a season of Golden Age plays by the *Royal Shakespeare Company (*Swan, 2004).   KG

Césaire, Aimé (1913–2008) Martinican writer and politician, considered one of the founders of African and Caribbean francophone literature.

Césaire read classics in Paris at the École Normale Supérieure, and achieved prominence in 1939 with *Cahier d'un retour natal*, a long autobiographical poem that was to launch the movement of *négritude*. He published six other acclaimed collections of poetry and two essays, but it was through drama that he sought to bridge the gap between his densely poetic vision and non-literate *audiences, especially in the developing world. His *tragic masterpiece, *La Tragédie du roi Christophe* (1963), reflects on the problems of African decolonization, a question pursued in *Une saison au Congo* (1966) through the tragic career of the leader of Congolese independence, Patrice Lumumba. Césaire's third play, *Une tempête* (1968), rewrites Shakespeare's *The Tempest* to speak to conditions of New World plantation slavery, colonial rule, and the master–slave dialectic.

Césaire's central *characters—Christophe, Lumumba, and Caliban—are all possessed of a sense of justice that impels them to rise up against historical conditions that wear the face of an implacable destiny. They invariably fail, but their failure exhilarates rather than depresses. Cesaire's work is especially notable for its combination of *Brechtian and indigenous Afro-Caribbean performance techniques.   JCM

Chaikin, Joseph (1935–2003) American actor, director, and playwright. Chaikin joined the *Living Theatre in 1959 and performed such roles as Galy Gay in *Brecht's *A Man's a Man* (1962), for which he won the first of six Obie awards, and appeared in *The Connection* (1959) and *In the Jungle of the Cities* (1961). Chaikin founded the *Open Theatre in 1963 in order to explore new methods of *acting practice and *collective creation. He directed productions of *Viet Rock* (1966), *The Serpent* (1968), *Terminal* (1969), *Mutation Show* (1971), and *Nightwalk* (1973). Chaikin's *directing strategies proved to be highly influential and included a *physical, *improvisatorial approach developed through the actor's voice and body. His book *The Presence of the Actor* (1972) sets forth his theories of performance as an organic process based in the body. The Open Theatre disbanded in 1973 and Chaikin went on to found the Other Theatre, where he directed productions of *Van Itallie's *Chekhov translations. Chaikin suffered a stroke in 1984 during heart surgery and was rendered aphasic, though he continued to direct, write, and teach, producing collaborations with *Shepard, Van Itallie, and Susan Yankowitz.   MDC

Chamberlain's Men, Lord Theatre company in London, formed in 1594 as half of a 'duopoly' along with the *Admiral's Men, and created to replace the *Queen's Men as providers of royal entertainment at Christmas. Its membership was drawn from several groups whose patrons had recently died. The new company's leading player was Richard *Burbage, son of the owner of the *Theatre, their allocated *playhouse. Shakespeare was a sharer and the company's contracted playwright. They began their long career with a rich repertory of Shakespeare's plays, and at the same time acquired several old Queen's Men plays, subsequently rewritten as *King John*, the *Henry IV* and *Henry V* series, *Hamlet*, and *King Lear*.

The two companies of the duopoly became the longest lived of all the playing companies in the Shakespearian era. The Chamberlain's Men, with James as their patron from 1603, ran on as the King's Men until the closure of the theatres in 1642, a total of 48 years. Their staple repertory included all of Shakespeare's plays that have survived, the work of *Jonson, *Middleton, *Massinger, *Davenant, and *Shirley, together with the 50 or more plays by several collaborative authors known as the *Beaumont and *Fletcher canon.

During the duopoly, between 1594 and 1603, they staged more than half the plays given at court for the winter entertainments. That ratio was sustained under the first Stuart kings, especially once the company had the *Blackfriars Theatre for winter playing indoors. Although Shakespeare wrote only one of his plays (*The Tempest*) for the Blackfriars instead of the *Globe, the indoor theatre had been built for them as early as 1596 to replace the old Theatre, though not until 1608 were they permitted to use it. From then on, using the Globe in summer and the Blackfriars in winter, they were unchallenged as the foremost playing company in England. AJG

Chambers of Rhetoric *Rederijkerskamers* were amateur literary guilds, possibly the descendants of earlier religious confraternities, but similar in their organization to contemporary archers' guilds. Varying in size from about fifteen to 150, the Chambers of Rhetoric dominated dramatic production in the Low Countries in the fifteenth and sixteenth centuries, regularly contributing *tableaux vivants* and dramas, both religious and secular, to public festivities. The stages used by the Rhetoricians could be very elaborate, featuring several levels and 'inner stages' behind decorated façades. The Chambers also competed with one another in drama, particularly in the *esbattement* (a short *farce), the *factie* (a comic street scene), and the more serious *spel van sinne* (*morality play). The best known among the latter are *The Blessed Apple Tree* (1500), *Man's Desire and Fleeting Beauty* (1546), and *Elekerlijc*, better known in its English translation as *Everyman* (c.1495).   RWV

Champion, Gower (1921–80) American choreographer and director. He began his career in the 1930s, *dancing in supper clubs with his partner June Taylor. By the late 1930s, their dancing was featured in Broadway *revues. After the Second World War, he teamed with his first wife Marge, and they danced together on stage and in films. In 1948 he began directing and choreographing for Broadway, but his reputation as a master director/choreographer was really established in the 1960s with *Bye Bye Birdie*, *Carnival*, and *Hello, Dolly!* While the first two were remarkably clever, the third introduced the Champion hallmark—a polished spectacle verging on over-production which rarely gave *audiences a chance to catch their breaths. Cleverness was also the mark of *I Do, I Do* (1966), which elevated an intimate two-character *musical to Broadway scale. But Champion's cleverness could sometimes harm a show, as in the case of *The Happy Time* (1968) or *Mack and Mabel* (1974). His last success was one of his most opulent: *42nd Street*, produced by *Merrick, which opened on the day he died.   JD

Champmeslé, Mlle (Marie Desmares) (1642–98) French actress. Moving with her husband in 1670 from the company at the *Marais Theatre in Paris to the more prestigious *Hôtel de Bourgogne, Mlle Champmeslé performed with great success in the *tragedies of *Racine (Bérénice, Roxane in *Bajazet*, Monime in *Mithridate*, Phèdre). Racine (whose mistress she became) is known to have coached her in the speaking of his verse. In 1679 a royal decree transferred the Champmeslés to the Guénégaud Théâtre, where the enlarged company was to form the Théâtre Français, with Mlle Champmeslé continuing to star in Racine's tragedies. Renouncing her profession on her deathbed, she was given a Christian burial.   WDH

Channing, Carol (1921–) American actress and singer. A long-legged blonde with peerless comic timing and a remarkably flexible voice that could shift from a shrill squeal to a deep rasp, she began her stage career in the early 1940s. She first attracted major notice in *Lend an Ear*, a 1948 *revue, and became a star as the quintessential gold-digger Lorelei Lee in *Gentlemen Prefer Blondes* (1949), in which she introduced 'Diamonds Are a Girl's Best Friend'. While attempts were made to find a suitable vehi-

cle for her unique talent, none appeared until 1964, when she created the title role in *Hello, Dolly!*, which she would continue to play for twenty years. She worked regularly in nightclubs, on television, and in film. Later film work was confined to voiceovers in animated features. In 1995 she was awarded a Tony for lifetime achievement.   JD

Channing, Stockard (1944–) American actress. After briefly appearing on Broadway in 1971, Channing divided her career between artistically challenging roles on stage and a host of mostly forgettable appearances in television and film—with the major exceptions of Betty Rizzo in the film of *Grease* (1978) and as the First Lady in the series *The West Wing* (1999-2006). Her theatre career experienced a rebirth with her award-winning performance as Sheila in a Broadway revival of Peter *Nichols's *A Day in the Death of Joe Egg* (1985). More critically acclaimed stage work followed, including a revival of *The House of the Blue Leaves* (1986), *Woman in Mind* (1988), and *Love Letters* (1989). She entered the 1990s playing the conscience-stricken New York socialite Ouisa in *Guare's *Six Degrees of Separation* (1990), which secured her reputation as one of the best actors of her generation, particularly of intelligent, offbeat *characters. Other notable credits include *Hapgood* (1995) and revivals of *The Little Foxes* (1997) and *The Lion in Winter* (1999).   JAB

Chapel Royal, Children of the A company of boy choristers who staged plays at court, and later for the public in the first *Blackfriars *playhouse in London. In 1576 Richard Farrant copied St Paul's, where in the previous year a playhouse was built adjoining the cathedral, by opening one in the nearby Blackfriars. The Children had played regularly at court since 1566, and now, in the year the *Theatre was built for adult players, they extended their offerings to the public. When Farrant died in 1580 the Chapel companies merged and *Lyly became their playwright and *manager. Some years later they joined with Paul's Boys, but were banned from playing in 1590. A boy company at a different Blackfriars playhouse from 1600 till 1608 used the same name.   AJG

Chapman, George (c.1560–1634) English dramatist who emerged only in his thirties but quickly became London's most brilliant comic writer. His first known play, *The Blind Beggar of Alexandria*, was a huge commercial success for the *Admiral's Men in 1596, and *The Comedy of Humours* (1597; printed as *A Humorous Day's*

Mirth) developed a new technique of comic *characterization based on individual idiosyncrasies. This strikingly original treatment of *comedy was soon imitated by Shakespeare (*Much Ado About Nothing*) and *Jonson.

Chapman continued to write for the Admiral's Men until 1599, but no other plays survive from this period. When the boys' companies reopened he transferred his services to them, writing his best-known *tragedy, *Bussy D'Ambois* (1604), for Paul's and a series of polished, sardonic comedies for *Blackfriars. One of these, *Eastward Hoe* (1605, with Jonson and *Marston), led to his imprisonment when its topical *satire offended the King. Chapman's interest in recent French history as tragic subject matter, first seen in *Bussy D'Ambois*, had similarly awkward consequences: in 1608, his two-part *Conspiracy and Tragedy of Charles, Duke of Biron* dramatized events of only six years earlier, and its undignified portrayal of living members of the French royal family caused the Blackfriars Boys to lose their theatre and royal patronage. Chapman stayed with the company in its new form; in 1610 he rewrote *Bussy D'Ambois* for their revival, along with a sequel, *The Revenge of Bussy D'Ambois*.

Chapman had links with the court, and wrote one of the *masques for Princess Elizabeth's wedding in 1613, but he was unlucky in his patrons. He returned home to Hitchin in debt, and concentrated on non-dramatic writing, including his famous translation of Homer. In 1631 he published *Caesar and Pompey*, but never again wrote for London. His long-term success rested on *Bussy D'Ambois*, which entered the repertory of the King's Men (see CHAMBERLAIN'S MEN, LORD) about 1616, with Nathan *Field in the title role.   MJW

character In narrative generally, a character is a person depicted within a story, either through description or direct speech; in drama the term usually refers only to persons portrayed by *actors. In either case, characters need not be human beings, but can be any kind of sentient agent: gods, animals, aliens, or even animated plants or household objects. *Aristotle ranks character second only to plot among the six elements of *tragedy, and in many modern plays, such as *Chekhov's, character is more important than plot. Though character is a ubiquitous term, its meaning has shifted over time and the concept remains highly ambiguous.

One way to conceive of dramatic character is as the representation of an individual person, either real or fictional. Each character has a biography and an array of personal characteristics—physical attributes, mannerisms, desires, objectives, beliefs—that the text defines incompletely and that the actor will elaborate in performance. It follows that when *Aeschylus, *Sophocles, and *Euripides each wrote plays about Electra, they created three distinct characters. It also follows that each actor who plays a role creates a distinct character, so that, for example, *Olivier's Hamlet was a different character from Mel Gibson's. This concept of character became prevalent toward the end of the nineteenth century as modernist playwrights such as *Ibsen and *Strindberg created increasingly individuated characters with complex and contradictory motivations and richly developed psychological histories. *Stanislavsky's system was predicated on a similar concept, enjoining actors to flesh out the 'given circumstances' of their characters. This view of character came under attack throughout the twentieth century by the New Critics (characters have no existence beyond the text), by Marxist critics (characters are defined by their socioeconomic circumstance rather than individual psychology), by post-structuralist theorists (the conception of the autonomous subject had not fully emerged during previous periods of theatre history).

Another way to conceive of character is as a type rather than an individual: not as something people *are* but something they *have*. For example, a person may have a brave or dishonest character. *Medieval *morality plays explicitly adopt a type concept, providing almost no individuating information, providing abstract names such as Everyman and Vice. Similarly, characters in the Stuart court *masques were almost pure types: aristocrats played idealized fairies, shepherds, and gods that represented the qualities they wished to connect to themselves.

Many theatrical traditions define a limited number of recurring character types. Greek *New Comedy introduced a set of conventional characters, such as the wily servant, the foolish pedant, and the braggart soldier, which carried into *Roman *comedy, resurfaced in the *commedia dell'arte* of the Italian *early modern period, and persisted throughout the twentieth century in popular films and television shows (*see* STOCK CHARACTER). Many non-Western traditions similarly rely on sharply delineated conventional types. For example, Sanskrit dramas draw on a set of character types defined in the *Natyasastra*, and the texts of the plays indicate the speaker by type name, such as *vidushaka* (*clown). In most theatrical traditions that rely on highly conventional character types, such as the *commedia dell'arte* or *Kutiyattam*, actors specialize in the portrayal of a particular type throughout their career (*see* LINES OF BUSINESS). In the first half of the twentieth century, performers in the British *music hall and American *vaudeville traditions, such as the *Marx Brothers, developed highly identifiable character types that they used for a wide variety of individual characters—Laurel and Hardy in the Old West or Abbott and Costello on Mars—highlighting the distinction between these two notions of character.

In the 1960s creators of *happenings, *performance artists, experimental theatre groups such as *Living Theatre, and playwrights such as *Handke tried to remove character from performance altogether. The goal was to produce an unmediated encounter between the *audience and the 'authentic' reality of the performers. *Grotowski replaced character with the performance 'score': a series of rigorously defined and *rehearsed actions constituting a kind of *ritual. Many theorists, however, came to regard attempts to eliminate character from theatre as quixotic, and Grotowski himself despaired that he stripped away his actors' *masks only to reveal new masks underneath.

A key feature of much postmodern theatre is a rejection of traditional notions of dramatic character, denying the possibility of a stable, coherent self onstage or off. In Robert *Wilson and *Glass's *Einstein on the Beach* (1976), for example, an actor *costumed like Einstein functions as an iconic image in an animated collage, making no attempt to embody the character he signifies, and in plays such as *Müller's *Hamletmachine* (1979), each speech evokes a dense network of fragmented characters and allusions to previous texts.   DZS

chariot races *See* CIRCUS, ROMAN.

Chaurette, Normand (1954–) Québec playwright. His early promise was confirmed in a series of seminal plays with innovative *dramaturgy and original thematic content, notably *Provincetown Playhouse, juillet 1919, j'avais 19 ans* (1982), now a classic of Québécois theatre. Focusing on the onstage murder of a child, it melds real and solipsistic theatrical time/space. *The Queens* (1982), set in London in 1483, explores the offstage world of the female *characters in Shakespeare's *Richard III*, while *Stabat Mater II* (1999) portrays a complexity of attitudes towards death.   LED

Cheek by Jowl British *touring company, founded in 1981 by Declan *Donellan and designer Nick Ormerod. They *toured widely at home and abroad with a changing small company of young players, mounting one or two classic plays every year, and usually appearing in London for several weeks, often at the Donmar Warehouse.

The company's first production, *The Country Wife*, was a great success, which continued with an adaptation of *Vanity Fair*, a good deal of Shakespeare, including a famous all-male *As You Like It* (1991), and foreign plays such as *Racine's *Andromaque* (1984), *Corneille's *Le Cid* (1986), and *Musset's *Don't Fool with Love* (1993). The company's hallmarks were clear and inventive treatment of the text, fast continuous action, ensemble *acting, and minimal but inventive sets. In 1989 Donnellan and Ormerod produced *Fuente Ovejuna* at the *National Theatre to general acclaim, and since then they have been increasingly in demand elsewhere. The company was in abeyance from 1998 to 2002.   EEC

Chekhov, Anton (1860–1904) Russian writer. Best known for his four major plays, *The Seagull* (1896), *Uncle Vanya* (1897), *Three Sisters* (1901), and *The Cherry Orchard* (1904), Chekhov also produced other dramatic works and more than 500 short stories. He began his literary career in the 1880s while qualifying as a doctor. The vast apprentice work that is now known as *Platonov* was completed in 1881 but not published until 1923 and first performed (in German) five years later. This was followed by the one-act plays and *vaudevilles *On the High Road* (1885), *Swansong* (*Kalkhas*, 1887), *The Bear* (1888), *The Proposal* (1888), *The Unwilling Tragedian* (1889), *Tatyana Repina* (1889), *The Wedding* (1890), *The Anniversary* (1892), and a dramatic *monologue *On the Harmfulness of Tobacco* (1886). Apart from *Platonov*, his first attempts at full-length plays were *Ivanov* (Moscow, 1887; revised for St Petersburg, 1889) and *The Wood Demon* (1889), subsequently reworked as *Uncle Vanya*.

The unsuccessful première of *The Seagull* in St Petersburg (1896) almost deflected Chekhov from playwriting, though the already composed *Uncle Vanya* was performed in the provinces in 1897. Chekhov was persuaded by *Nemirovich-Danchenko to allow the *Moscow Art Theatre to restage *The Seagull* in its opening season (1898, directed by him and *Stanislavsky), and the production epitomized the contemporaneity, *naturalistic sets, and *acting style for which the company became famous. *Uncle Vanya* followed in 1899. His reputation firmly established, Chekhov wrote his two final plays for MAT, *Three Sisters* (1901) and *The Cherry Orchard* (1904). He married Olga *Knipper, a leading actress at MAT, and introduced *Gorky to the company. There is little doubt that the partnership of Chekhov, Stanislavsky, Nemirovich-Danchenko, and the designer *Simov was responsible for the success of MAT in the peak period of 1898 to

1904, the year of the playwright's early death from tuberculosis. Chekhov and Stanislavsky frequently disagreed over interpretation, the playwright insisting his works were social *comedies, the director emphasizing their wistful fragility in order to create mood pieces about a dying way of life. Stanislavsky won this struggle, and the naturalistic productions by MAT set a programmatic style. The collaboration ensured a classic status for Chekhov, both in Russia and when MAT travelled abroad, but led to a constraint on production method which was only questioned in the latter half of the twentieth century. Stanislavsky had an acute ear for Chekhov's innovations in *dialogue, where the uttered text belied another drama hidden within (the *subtext), contributing greatly to Stanislavsky's understanding of concepts such as 'interior monologue' and 'the inner life of the role' central to his 'system' of acting.

The MAT monopolized first-rate productions of Chekhov until the revolution. Notable post-revolutionary productions of Chekhov, often seen as out of step with the new times, included *Vakhtangov's The Wedding (1921), the MAT restagings, notably by Nemirovich-Danchenko (Three Sisters, 1940), and *Meyerhold's 33 Swoons (a composite of The Bear, The Proposal, and The Anniversary, 1935). This latter production was an attempt to adapt Chekhov to a *socialist realist Russia. *Tairov's The Seagull (1944) and *Tovstonogov's Three Sisters (1965) were landmarks in the liberation of Chekhov from the MAT naturalistic house style and in the reassertion of his classic, as opposed to socialist realist, status. Abstract set design and *lighting effects came into their own. *Efros (Three Sisters, 1967) offered a highly physical carnival-like interpretation, followed by an equally controversial The Cherry Orchard (1975) acted out on a single, cemetery-like bleak set. *Efremov (The Seagull, 1970, and The Cherry Orchard, 1975) combined minimalist sets with the Stanislavskian tradition of emotional impact. *Lyubimov's Three Sisters (1981), visually and vocally defiant of convention, made a statement about the brutality of contemporary Russia, and contributed to Lyubimov's swift exodus to Europe. Perestroika was heralded by Efremov's moving, mellow Uncle Vanya (1985), capturing the uncertainty of the political moment. Subsequently the performance history is mixed: postmodern or deconstructive productions have appeared, while others returned to Stanislavskian tradition.

Exported during the MAT *tours, Chekhov's plays have outstripped their Russian beginnings and transcended cultural barriers to reach every corner of the globe. Britain has followed a naturalistic production tradition, regarding Chekhov almost as an untouchable classic. Great actors (*Olivier, *Gielgud, *Ashcroft, *Richardson, *Dench, Michael *Redgrave, *McKellan) have cut their teeth on Chekhov and then returned in later career with mature performances. Family productions such as those starring the *Cusacks (1990) and the *Redgraves (1990) enhanced the ensemble acting style and *realism still seen as quintessential Chekhov. Another thread of production transposed the Russian setting to more familiar territory, for nostalgia and isolation to Ireland (The Seagull, adapted by *Kilroy, 1981), or for politics to South Africa (The Cherry Orchard, directed by *Suzman, 1997). Gradually, productions have dropped period and introduced minimalist sets, such as Mike *Alfreds's The Seagull (1981). Alfreds's Cherry Orchard (1982) went for the carnival and clownish in an attempt to reach Chekhov's frequently elusive humour. In the British repertoire Chekhov is probably the most performed foreign dramatist; production of his plays is an international industry with landmark productions in the countries of East and West Europe, USA, Japan, and China. Like their British counterparts, these productions are as much engagements with cultural transference as they are interpretations of the plays. CM

Chekhov, Michael (Mikhail) (1891–1955) Russian actor, director, and theorist. The nephew of Anton *Chekhov, Mikhail came to prominence as an actor at the *Moscow Art Theatre Studios after 1912. Here he showed an intense psychological inwardness combined with improvisational brilliance, physical vitality, and plasticity of form in productions directed by *Vakhtangov and *Stanislavsky. Increasingly drawn to the anthroposophical works of Rudolf Steiner, Chekhov found theatrical life in the Soviet Union difficult and emigrated in 1928 and settled in England in 1936, opening a theatre studio at Dartington Hall in Devon.

The basis of Chekhov's theory is the 'psychological gesture' which can be roughly defined as a physical attitude which forms the outline of a role and aids the actor's capacity to think in creative images and radiate feeling in a closed circuit with other performers. Improvisation and inspiration are essential, and must be given full rein in *rehearsal through work conducted at maximum physical and emotional pitch. With the onset of the war Chekhov moved to the United States, opening another studio in Connecticut in 1939 before moving to Hollywood, where he supported his actor training with film work, notably as the psychiatrist in Hitchcock's *Spellbound* (1945). His major legacy consists of essays on *acting technique and approaches to production: *To the Actor* (1953) and *To the Director and Playwright* (1963).   NW

Cheng Changgeng (Ch'eng Ch'ang-keng) (1811–80) Chinese Beijing opera (*jingju*) performer. A native of Anhui province, for decades Cheng led the Sanqing (Three Celebrations) troupe, one of the four Anhui troupes that had migrated to the capital in the early nineteenth century. The Anhui companies fused their local music with a number of other regional styles, from the earthy *yiyang qiang* to the literary *kunqu*. In Beijing these regional styles were further melded with northern performance traditions to produce what would, by the twentieth century, be called *jingju* ('capital opera'). Chang's musical acumen and high, clear, and melodious voice made him instrumental in the development of the Beijing style, and his probity and refinement served to elevate the profession. Chang specialized in the mature male role (*laosheng*). He was famed for his performances as Wu Zixu, the knight errant of the Confucian age; as Yue Fei, the Song Dynasty general martyred for his loyalty; and as Guan Yu, the third-century military hero later revered as a god.   KC

Cheng Yanqiu (Ch'eng Yen-ch'iu) (1904–58) Chinese actor of the *dan* (female) category in *jingju* (Beijing opera). Born into a poor Manchu family, Cheng became an apprentice at the age of 6 and started stage performance at 11. Soon the scholar and theatre patron Luo Yinggong discovered him, secured his emancipation, and arranged for him to study with *Mei Lanfang and the respected *dan* teacher Wang Yaoqing. Like many young *dan* actors, Cheng had difficulty regaining an appropriate vocal style after his voice changed, and Wang helped him develop a method of singing with a soft, undulating, and haunting quality. This in part explains the large number of tragic *heroines in his repertoire, many written exclusively for him. In 1927 he was voted by fans the best *dan* actor. After a year studying in Europe, Cheng became head of the Chinese Theatre Training Academy in 1933. During the Sino-Japanese War he sold his *costumes in protest and became a farmer. He resumed performing after the war.   SYL

Chéreau, Patrice (1944–) French actor and director. Chéreau gained recognition as a director in 1967 with *Lenz's *The Soldiers*, and in 1972 was invited by *Planchon to be co-director of the

*Théâtre National Populaire at Villeurbanne, where his hallmark became archetypal *acting and brilliant *scenography created by Richard Peduzzi (1943–) in productions including *Marivaux's *The Dispute* (1973) and *Ibsen's *Peer Gynt* (1981). Most famously, Chéreau-Peduzzi gave a Marxist interpretation to the centenary staging of *Wagner's *Ring* at *Bayreuth (1976–80), set with massive forms and luminous colour in the Industrial Revolution. From 1982 to 1990, as *artistic director of the Théâtre des Amandiers in Nanterre, Chéreau produced works by *Genet, *Müller, *Chekhov, Shakespeare, and new playwrights, including *Koltès's *In the Solitude of the Cotton Fields* (1987), wherein Chéreau played the Dealer. Since 1990 Chéreau has worked independently. He has directed ten films, including *La Reine Margot* (1994) and *Persecution* (2009) and acted, among others, the role of General Montcalm in *The Last of the Mohicans* (1992). Recently on stage he directed *Racine's *Phèdre* (Paris and Vienna, 2003) and Wagner's *Tristan and Isolde* (Milan, 2007). Chéreau's aim is to reveal how we construct, through words and images, the reality that we inhabit.   SBB

Chevalier, Maurice (1888–1972) Debonair French actor, singer, and *dancer whose 50-year career began in the Paris *cabarets and *music halls, including the *Folies-Bergère, where his partner was the beautiful comedienne, dancer, and singer *Mistinguett. Already internationally known in the 1920s, Chevalier's fame increased enormously with two Hollywood film careers: as a romantic lead in *The Love Parade* (1930), *Love Me Tonight* (1932), and *Folies Bergère* (1935); and again as the avuncular elderly romantic in *Gigi* (1958), *Fanny* (1961), and *In Search of the Castaways* (1962). He became an international icon of Frenchness with his Parisian accent, romantic charm, grace, benign rakishness, and appreciation for women, food, wine, and music. His signature *costume included a tilted straw hat, cane, white spats, and tailcoat. His figure and voice survive as the most popular stereotype of the Frenchman in films, television, cartoons, and advertising.   SBB

Chicano theatre *See* DIASPORA.

Chichester Festival Theatre English *playhouse in Sussex. The building and stage were heavily influenced by *Guthrie's *Stratford Festival Theatre in Ontario and opened in 1962 with a ten-week summer season under the direction of *Olivier. The large *auditorium seats the *audience on three sides of an open stage with numerous entrances including two staircases in the auditorium. The stage is designed for large-scale productions like *Shaffer's *Royal Hunt of the Sun* (1964) and *Bolt's *Vivat! Vivat Regina* (1970), which premièred in the early years, alongside productions of Shakespeare and *Brecht. The original summer season was extended for up to five months. As part of the millennium celebrations a *community project was performed in the main house: *Barchester Chronicles* involved over 250 local inhabitants of all ages. In 1989 the Festival built a studio theatre, a more intimate and flexible space that offers a wide range of work from one-person shows to new *musicals. British and world premières of plays produced in the 1990s included *Harwood's *Taking Sides* (1995), directed by *Pinter, and William Nicholson's *Retreat from Moscow* (1999), starring *Suzman. GBB

Chikamatsu Hanji (1725–83) Japanese playwright. The son of the philosopher Hozumi Ikan, a friend of *Chikamatsu Monzaemon, Chikamatsu Hanji followed tradition in taking the name of his famous predecessor. Hanji began to write for the Osaka *bunraku *puppet theatre about 1751, and his name appears on 55 works. During his time playwrights worked as a team under a senior author who was responsible for the overall plot and for writing the climactic acts. Hanji became senior playwright about 1760 and many of his works are regularly performed today in both bunraku and *kabuki, including *Courtesans and the Straits of Naruto* (1768), *The Omi Genji Vanguard* (1769), *Mount Imo and Mount Se* (1771), *A New Edition of the Osome-Hisamatsu Ballad* (1780), and *A Travel Game while Crossing Iga* (1783). Hanji is known for his complex plots, music, theatricality, and for exploiting all three elements of bunraku (chanter, puppets, *shamisen*). CAG

Chikamatsu Monzaemon (1653–1725) Japanese playwright. Born Sugimori Nobumori in Fukui, the son of relatively high-ranking samurai, he was educated in Chinese and Japanese classics. The family moved to Kyoto where Chikamatsu served in courtier households; later he worked backstage at *kabuki theatres, performed as a street storyteller, and began writing plays in his late twenties. Experience of samurai, courtier, actor, and merchant life gave him a broad view of the highly stratified society of Japan. He wrote over 100 plays under contract with *bunraku and kabuki theatres in Kyoto and Osaka, and was considered the 'god of writers' soon after his death. Today he is sometimes compared with Shakespeare. Chikamatsu learned his craft as an apprentice to the performers

*Takemoto Gidayū and *Sakata Tōjūrō. As staff playwright at the Takemoto-za Theatre in Osaka, he produced his most famous plays during the last twenty years of his life, including *The Battles of Coxinga* (1715) and *Love Suicides at Amijima* (1721). His kabuki plays have survived only in summary form, but his nearly 100 bunraku *puppet theatre works survive in complete, authorized editions from the date of first performance.

Three-quarters of his bunraku plays were set in a historical period before 1600, epic five-act dramas that filled a whole day in performance from dawn to dusk. These works (*jidaimono*) have a structure of multiple plots and contrasts between picaresque, fantastical adventure and intense *tragedy. In 1703, however, after a decade of writing mostly for kabuki, he wrote his first domestic tragedy, *Love Suicides at Sonezaki*, a three-scene piece, comparable to the third act of a period play, based on an actual incident in Osaka. After its considerable success, Chikamatsu wrote 23 dramas based on contemporary incidents of love suicide, theft, smuggling, adultery, and murder, works that have been praised in modern times for their powerful *realism and *character portrayal. During these twenty years, he also produced his most famous period plays. In the last ten years of his life Chikamatsu focused on the nature and consequences of passion, crime, and responsibility. For example, over eighteen months he explored the theme of murder in three works, two period and one domestic: *Twins at the Sumida River* (1720), *Lovers Pond in Settsu Province* (1721), and *Woman-Killer and the Hell of Oil* (1721). His mature period plays show two trends: increasingly complex and realistic character portrayal in the context of tragedy in Act III, together with a fantastic theatricality representing the supernatural, particularly in Acts II and IV, achieved by sophisticated stage tricks.

Many of Chikamatsu's plays were revived and revised in the eighteenth and nineteenth centuries. After 1945 a strong movement developed to perform the original texts. The kabuki actor Nakamura Ganjirō III has led a Chikamatsu-za troupe since 1981 with the express intention of reviving the plays, and today Chikamatsu's work is regularly performed in bunraku and kabuki. CAG

children's theatre *See* YOUTH, THEATRE FOR.

Childress, Alice (1920–94) American playwright and novelist who began her career as an actress with the American Negro Theatre, a pioneering *African-American group in the 1940s and 1950s. She began writing in order to counter the tradition of demeaning roles for African-American women. Her plays include *Gold through the Trees* (1952), *Trouble in Mind* (1955), *Wine in the Wilderness* (1969), and *The Wedding Band: a love/hate story* (1966), acted by Ruby *Dee at the *New York Shakespeare Festival in the 1970s. BBL

Chin, Frank (1940–) American playwright and *manager. After university Chin was a writer for King Broadcasting in Seattle and a lecturer in Asian-American studies. In 1972 he established a workshop in San Francisco to encourage playwriting by *Asian-Americans; two years later it became the Asian American Theatre Company, America's first company dedicated exclusively to plays about Asian America. Both his *Chickencoop Chinaman* (1972) and *Year of the Dragon* (1974), which were the first plays by a Chinese American to be produced in New York, focus on the complexities of Asian identity in America. *See also* DIASPORA. JSM

Chitty, Alison (1948–) English *scenographer. As resident designer at the *National Theatre she designed over a dozen productions in eight years, ranging from *Shepard's *Fool for Love* (directed by *Gill, 1984) to *Euripides' *The Bacchae* (for *Hall) which *toured to *Epidaurus. She has also designed several Mike *Leigh films. Her designs for *opera have been seen around the world and include contemporary work by Harrison Birtwistle and a long collaboration with Francesca Zambello, for whom she designed a monumental, tiered ship for *Billy Budd* (*Covent Garden, 1994, Olivier Award). Her many other awards include Oliviers for best opera production (*Khovanshchina*, 1994) and best *costumes (*Remembrance of Things Past*, 2000). Recent London productions include Leigh's *Two Thousands Years*, Granville *Barker's *The Voysey Inheritance*, and J. P. Miller's *Days of Wine and Roses*, all in 2005-6. RVL

Ch'oe In-hun (1936–) Korean playwright. Born in Hoeryŏng in North Korea, he escaped to the south in 1950 during the Korean War and devoted himself to writing, at first as a novelist. During the 1970s he wrote exceptional plays that are characterized by a fine balance between poetry and prose, by multiple changes of sound and light, and by the adaptation of myths. His theatre work is frequently considered the first to succeed as both literature and drama in Korea, and is chiefly interested in the place of *tragedy and fate in Korean history. *Away, Away, Long Time Ago* (1976), about the birth of a hero who will create a new era, was published in English in *Modern Korean Literature* (Honolulu,

1990). Other work includes *Where We Will Meet as What We Are* (1970), *At Mountain and Field When Spring Comes* (1977), and *Tung Tung Nakrang Tung* (1978). JOC

Chong, Ping (1946–) American director, choreographer, and video and installation artist. Ping Chong was trained as a painter but began his *avant-garde performance work after studying with Meredith *Monk. He has frequently referred to his early pieces as 'bricolages', assembling 'luminous new worlds' out of bits and pieces of existing, older societies. Chong's *intercultural, interdisciplinary approach is evident in the well-regarded collaborations with Monk (*Paris, Chacon, Venice/Milan, The Games*), culminating in the mid-1980s, to his experimentation in the 1990s with community-specific pieces, notably in *Deshima, Chinoiserie, After Sorrow*, and *Pojag*, a quartet exploring East-West relations from a variety of national perspectives. Recently he has created large-scale *puppet works, including *Cathay: Three Tales of China* (2005). LTC

chorus A group of singers and/or *dancers who perform in concert; the performance of such a group. A chorus was central to the forms of *Greek performance from which Athenian drama evolved. Choral lyric featured several performance patterns: the chorus often sang and danced in unison, but it could also divide into semi-choruses and, together with the chorus leader, engage in statement and refrain, *exposition and response, or even *dialogue. One form, the *dithyramb, like *tragedy and *comedy a subject for competition at the *Dionysia, had a chorus of 50 that sang and danced in a circular formation about the leader. More obviously dramatic were the tragic chorus, originally numbering twelve but raised to fifteen by *Sophocles (the *satyr-play chorus remained at twelve], and the comic chorus, numbering 24. In both cases, the performance included *actors as well. The comic chorus, sometimes fantastically *costumed as birds or animals, was central to *Old Comedy, where, in a section of the play called the *parabasis*, it addressed the *audience directly both in character and as the poet's mouthpiece. The tragic chorus also had both a dramatic identity and an extra-dramatic role as commentator.

Dramatic choruses were in decline by the end of the fifth century BC. *Euripides' chorus retained its dramatic identity but its function was reduced to that of interlude between the episodes. Later, *Seneca's choral interludes were even more loosely connected to the dramatic action and *Roman comedy dropped the chorus altogether.

In sixteenth-century Italy and France, humanist authors made half-hearted attempts to include the chorus in their imitations of ancient drama, but had difficulty reconciling it with the *neoclassical demands of verisimilitude. In the twentieth century, the chorus was for the most part limited to adaptations or imitations of ancient Greek plays. An exception is *Eliot's *Murder in the Cathedral*, which, performed in the communal and ceremonial context of a church festival, endued its Chorus of Women of Canterbury with something of the quality of its ancient counterpart.

The character called 'Chorus' in some Elizabethan plays is derived, not from classical practice, but from figures developed in *medieval theatre, typically providing *prologues and *epilogues, summary sermons, or bridging narrative. In Shakespeare's *Henry V* and *Pericles* the Chorus functions as an epic-narrator, dividing the acts and connecting the dramatic action.

In the modern theatre, the chorus is largely restricted to oratorio, *opera, *musical comedy or *revue, and *ballet. But choric performance has continued as part of Western heritage, its rhythmic and coordinated sounds and movements expressed in forms as diverse as a massed choir, a military tattoo, or Las Vegas showgirls.   RWV

Christie, Agatha (1890–1976) English crime novelist whose commercial success as a playwright has been phenomenal. *The Mousetrap*, which began life as a radio play called *Three Blind Mice*, opened in London in 1952 and was still going strong in 2010, its over 23,000 performances probably holding the record for the longest-running play ever. Christie also had major theatrical hits on both sides of the Atlantic with *Ten Little Niggers* (1944, or *Ten Little Indians* and *And Then There Were None*) and *Witness for the Prosecution* (1954). She began writing plays seriously because she felt the stage adaptations of her novels had been too respectful of the original texts, and as a consequence too complex. With *Ten Little Indians*, Christie simplified and radically changed the outcome, although the strength of her playwriting in general is the audacious twisting and turning of the plot. Though one of the most successful women playwrights in British history, she is rarely considered in depth in dramatic studies.   EJS

Chronegk, Ludwig (1837–91) German actor and director. Chronegk's name is indissolubly linked with the *Meiningen Players. Trained in Berlin, he had a succession of engagements between Zurich and Königsberg before joining the court theatre in Meiningen in 1866. Initially an actor, the Duke of Meiningen soon recognized Chronegk's artistic and organizational abilities, appointing him director in 1871 and *artistic director (Intendant) in 1884. Chronegk was the key coordinator in the process of *mise-en-scène, putting into stage practice the Duke's conception and designs. He accompanied the troupe on their extended *tours, where he coordinated the involvement of locally hired supernumeraries.   CBB

chuanju (Sichuan opera) *See* DIFANGXI.

chuanqui (*ch'uan-ch'i*) Chinese operas written in the 'southern style' between the southern Sung and the Qing dynasties, often translated as 'romance' or 'southern drama'. *Chuanqi* flourished from the middle of the sixteenth to the end of the seventeenth centuries, roughly coinciding with the golden age of the *kunqu musical style. *Chuanqi* prevailed on the stage during this period along with northern drama (*zaju), though typically *zaju* have four acts and only one actor in a singing role, whereas *chuanqi* have between 20 and 50 acts and many actors singing.

During the *chuanqi* era it was common for gentlemen to be aficionados of the theatre; a number composed *chuanqi* and others owned and trained private troupes. The playwright *Li Yu (1611–80) included a chapter on writing drama in his guide to sophisticated living, *Essays Written in Idleness*, which appears next to chapters on interior decoration and the proper enjoyment of food and drink, suggesting that composing plays was a sign of social distinction. Among the *chuanqi* authors, most notable are Li Kaixian, *Tang Xianzu (especially *The Peony Pavilion*), Ruan Dacheng, Li Yu, *Kong Shangren (*The Peach Blossom Fan*), and Hong Sheng (*The Palace of Eternal Life*). Although *chuanqi* were primarily written by and for the gentry, some were designed for palace performances or for professional troupes. There were two musical styles: *kunqu*, which was popular in the banquet halls of the elite literati, and *yiyang*, a style popular in the outdoor theatres of the common people. When *jingju (Beijing opera) became enormously popular in the late eighteenth century, it ended the dominance of *chuanqi*, although many individual scenes from the form continue to be performed today.   SYV

Chunliu She (Ch'un liu she) The Spring Willow Society, the first Chinese Western-style theatre group. In 1907 a group of Chinese students in Tokyo performed an act from *The Lady of the*

Camellias by *Dumas *fils*. Some of the actors had studied the Japanese *shimpa* (new school) theatre and borrowed its techniques. Later that year the group staged *The Cry of the Black Slaves to Heaven*, a five-act play adapted from a Chinese translation of Harriet Beecher Stowe's *Uncle Tom's Cabin*. Written purely in *dialogue, it is generally considered the first *huaju* (spoken drama) play in Chinese. Chunliu She was active in Japan for a few more years, performing one-act plays and the four-act *Hot Blood* (1909), adapted from a Japanese translation of *Tosca* by *Sardou. Some of the participants, most noticeably *Ouyang Yuqian and Lu Jingruo, went on to become important forces in the Chinese new theatre movement. After 1910 a number of the group returned to Shanghai where they started the New Drama Society, which used the name Chunliu Jüchang (Spring Willow Theatre) during performance. Between 1912 and 1915, they were considered the most dedicated and best-trained Western-style *wenming xi* (civilized drama) group in China. Among the 81 plays they performed about one-third were translations or adaptations of foreign plays or novels, another third came from traditional Chinese themes, and the rest were original creations based on contemporary stories. Following the fashion of *wenming xi* few of these plays had finished scripts; most were *scenarios that relied heavily on *improvisation. But the insistence on European styles, and the high percentage of foreign and tragic plays in their repertoire, distanced Chunliu She from the average *audience. Lu Jingruo, who had become the leader of the group, died of overwork at the age of 30 in 1915, marking the end of Chunliu She and starting the decline of *wenming xi*.   SYL

church drama *See* BIBLICAL PLAYS; LITURGICAL DRAMA.

Churchill, Caryl (1938–) English playwright. Churchill wrote a number of student plays at Oxford, but during the mid-1960s she stayed at home with three young children and wrote for radio. *Owners* (1972) was produced at the *Royal Court in London, where she became the first woman writer in residence (1974). *Objections to Sex and Violence* and *Moving Clocks Go Slow* were both produced in 1975. In 1976 she began working with two theatre companies, Joint Stock and Monstrous Regiment, the latter a feminist socialist troupe. She wrote *Vinegar Tom* for the first and *Light Shining in Buckinghamshire* for the second; both plays, set in the seventeenth century, explore the complex relations between women and other outsiders and structures of law, morali-

ty, and religion. *Light Shining* was also her first collaboration with director *Stafford-Clark.

The 1980s consolidated Churchill's prestige as one of the most successful playwrights of her generation. *Cloud 9* (1981), *Top Girls* (1982), *Fen* (1983), and *Serious Money* (1986), all but *Fen* directed by Stafford-Clark, continued the analysis of women and politics, ranging from juxtapositions of colonial and post-colonial culture in *Cloud 9* to dramatic ethnography in *Fen*, to portraits of living in Thatcher's England in *Top Girls* and *Serious Money*. While Churchill was developing a sharp *epic style, she also began to experiment with form and movement, collaborating with choreographer Ian Spink and co-author David Lan on *A Mouthful of Birds* (1986). She became particularly important to *feminist performance theory. Her connections to *Brecht and her materialist analysis of economic, racial, and *gender experiences created graphic representations of women outside the dominant male gaze, and beyond a *realistic *dramaturgy.

Mad Forest (1990) continued her work in the epic mode while several experimental collaborations emphasized movement and music. *Lives of the Great Poisoners* (1991) featured *dance and *music (with Ian Spink and Orlando Gough). She continued with Spink and his dance company Second Stride on *The Striker* (1994), followed by *Hotel* (1997). Churchill also pushed the frontiers of language in *Blue Heart* (1997). Her work in this decade took on qualities of the fantastical fable, often nightmarish. In 2000, *Far Away* returned to a more traditional staging, but created an eerie world of threat. Recent work includes a translation of *Strindberg's *A Dream Play* (2005) and *Seven Jewish Children—a play for Gaza* (Royal Court, 2009).   JGR

ch'ŏyongmu, kŏmmu, muaemu Native *dance forms from Korea containing theatrical elements, originally developed during the long reign of the Silla kingdom (57 BC–AD 935). *Kŏmmu* is a *masked sword dance, inspired by the story of the death of a young warrior who killed an enemy king, while *muaemu* is a dance performed without masks to promulgate Buddhism. *Ch'ŏyongmu*, the most famous of the three, has dramatic elements that follow the legend of Ch'ŏyong, a son of the Dragon of the East Sea, who used a mask and incantatory song and dance to ward off the spirit of smallpox. *Ch'ŏyongmu* became a two-man dance in the Koryŏ Dynasty (936–1392) and a five-man dance in the early Chosŭn Dynasty (1392–1910). With each revision, the original *ritual purpose was modified for the sake of entertainment, and the dance is still performed today on special occasions. *See* KIAK. JOC

Cibber, Colley (1671–1757) English actor, *manager, and playwright. Cibber's *An Apology for the Life of Mr Colley Cibber* (1740), written in response to savage criticism from Pope and *Fielding, offers an invaluable account of seventeenth-century theatre. Cibber joined the *Drury Lane company as an actor in 1690. In his *Love's Last Shift* (1696) he played Sir Novelty Fashion, the first of many 'fop' *characters he successfully created, and in *Vanbrugh's satirical sequel, *The Relapse* (1696), Cibber played Lord Foppington to great public acclaim. *She Would and She Would Not* (1702) and *The Careless Husband* (1704) reflect the growing trend toward the sentimental comedies which dominated the eighteenth-century. As a performer he was less successful in *tragedy but his adaptation of *Richard III* (1700) was the standard acting edition well into the nineteenth century. In 1710 Cibber and fellow actors *Wilks and Thomas Doggett co-managed Drury Lane in a triumvirate that was successful until the arrival of Barton *Booth, which triggered a number of internal squabbles. One of Cibber's most successful plays, *The Double Gallant* (1707), was performed over 200 times by the end of the century, though the central plot was lifted directly from *Centlivre's *Love at a Venture* (1705), which Cibber had turned down the previous season. His less contentious version of Vanbrugh's unfinished work *Journey to London*, produced as *The Provok'd Husband* (1728), was also well received, but his appointment as Poet Laureate in 1730 was surrounded by further controversy. GBB

Cibber, Susannah (1714–66) English actress. Beginning her career as a singer, Susannah joined Theophilus *Cibber's breakaway company at the *Haymarket in 1733 and they married in 1734. Her dramatic debut in the title role of Aaron Hill's *Zara* (1736) brought her public acclaim and she quickly built her reputation as a great tragic actress; her use of a pocket handkerchief to convey emotion was greatly admired, though considered affected and overdone by her critics. Plagued by a scandalous court case, several difficult pregnancies, and repeated illness, Cibber was often absent from the stage. She made several appearances in Ireland and moved between the London houses. She finally settled in *Garrick's company at *Drury Lane (1753) where she became the highest-paid member of the troupe. GBB

Cibber, Theophilus (1703–58) English actor, *manager, and playwright. The first son of Colley *Cibber, Theophilus joined his father's company

at *Drury Lane aged 16. Before he was 20 he was playing leading parts and managing the summer company. His father appears to have blocked his son's succession to the managerial crown, possibly because of his dissolute reputation offstage. His performance as Pistol in *Henry IV* (1727) and his success as the manager of the *Haymarket company (1733–4) brought him popularity with *audiences but he lost their sympathy as details of his financial and sexual exploitation of his second wife, the actress Susannah *Cibber, were hauled through the courts. He continued to play minor parts and had some success as a hack writer. GBB

Ciceri, Pierre (1782–1862) French designer. After study under F. J. Belanger, Ciceri joined the staff of the Opéra and rose to the post of scenic director (1822–47). He also worked for the *Comédie-Française from 1826, and at other Paris theatres. His most notable designs for the Opéra included Liszt's *Don Sanche* (1825), Auber's *La Muette de Portici* (1828), and Rossini's *Le Comte Ory* (1828) and *Guillaume Tell* (1829); and at the Comédie-Française, *Henri III et sa cour* by *Dumas *père* (1829), and two major plays by *Hugo, *Hernani* (1830) and *Le Roi s'amuse* (1832). Characterized by elaborate spectacle, Ciceri's *romantic *scenography earned him Dumas's tribute as 'the father of modern stage design'. WDH

Cieślak, Ryszard (1937–90) Polish actor, best known for his work with the Polish Laboratory Theatre, of which he was a member from 1961 to its dissolution in 1984. Trained as a *puppeteer, Cieślak seemed an unlikely figure to become one of the most celebrated experimental performers of the twentieth century, the ultimate realization of *Grotowski's vision of the 'holy actor'. Cieślak's work in productions such as *The Constant Prince* (1965), in which he performed the role of a political martyr who achieved apotheosis through suffering, was taken as confirmation that Grotowski's vision of the performer's craft as a 'total act', an unveiling of the *actor's deepest truth as a confession in the presence of the spectator, could be realized. In the Laboratory Theatre's final production, *Apocalypsis cum Figuris* (1969), Cieślak performed the role of the Simpleton, an ironic figure for the Second Coming of Christ. His performance was lauded for its extraordinary intimacy, sincerity, and clarity of detail. Thereafter he participated in various para-theatrical projects and directed in Poland and abroad. His last notable role was as the blind King Dhritarastra in *Brook's *Mahabharata* (1985). LW

Cintra, Luís Miguel (1949–) Portuguese actor and director, known for acting in Manoel de Oliveira's films. Cintra is associated with the Teatro da Cornucópia, which he co-founded in Lisbon in 1973 with *Melo. As a director Cintra selects Portuguese classics (*Vicente, *Silva, and *Garrett), Shakespeare (*Cymbeline*, 2000), and contemporary writers like *Bond (*War Trilogy*, 1987) and *Müller (*Der Auftrag*, 1984 and 1992). His aesthetic choices rely on Marcuse's idea that great literature can be the spiritual rock against greed, relativism, and the decadence of modernity. MHS

circus, modern A quintessentially popular performance genre, in which highly skilled performers offer demonstrations of extreme physical virtuosity, precision, and daring. In its traditional form, circus refers to a travelling show, generally comprising a variety of acts, taking place in or above one or more circular stage areas called 'rings', with the *audience surrounding. The label has been used in a broader sense to evoke a circus-like style which features the performing body at its most astounding. The modern Western notion of circus arose in late eighteenth-century London as a collective programme for performative displays, emphasizing entertainment, sensation, and spectacle. Historically, circus acts fall into several general categories: aerial acts (e.g. tightrope and trapeze), ground acts (*acrobatics, balancing, *juggling); *clowning; *animal acts (equestrian, domestic, wild); and daredevils (knife-throwing, human cannonball). The circus act offers a triumph of the human body itself, not a representation—and the spectator's emotional reaction amounts to a 'real-life' response, rather than the empathized feeling of mimetic theatre. A predilection for the non-verbal makes it readily available to children, and affords travel across cultures.

Philip Astley, a former British cavalry officer, entertained a crowd of paying customers in 1768 by displaying his skills at handling horses while standing astride them as they galloped around a ring. Astley and his competitors quickly supplemented equestrian demonstrations with the other types of performative skills which have become synonymous with circus (*see* ASTLEY'S AMPHITHEATRE). Although these 'acts' would have been seen previously on streets and fairgrounds in some form, Astley gathered them within a containable staging area for a single admission price, the spectators encircling the action.

The circus spread quickly throughout Europe at the end of the eighteenth century, trading primarily on its equestrian roots and theatrical affinities, supplementing horse-riding with other human and animal displays, as well as clowning, *pantomimes, *melodramas, *burlettas, and *dances. The *hippodrama featured equine stars alongside human ones, playing out events with military, mythic, literary, and historic themes. One of the great names in British circus was the Belgian Andrew *Ducrow, an outstanding horseman, who ran Astley's Amphitheatre from 1825 to 1841. He introduced enduring entertainments like 'The Courier of St Petersburg', which presented a fictional messenger standing astride two horses and circling the ring, while other horses, each bearing the flag of a different country, galloped between his legs to join the charge. The emphasis on equestrian displays meant that *clowns, too, would explore the comic possibilities of horse and ring, and a common clowning strategy was to *burlesque whatever 'serious' act had preceded. The English actor-clown Joseph *Grimaldi is considered the progenitor of the Western circus clown.

In the nineteenth century prospective audiences in the USA were far apart and still moving westward. In 1825 J. Purdy Brown became the first proprietor to take his show on the road with a tent—a portable, constant performance space, distinguishing the American circus from its European counterparts. The European circus remained rooted to family or company tradition, while the American circus was driven by entrepreneurial spirit, epitomized by P. T. *Barnum, who, in 1871, combined his existing 'museum' of animal and human oddities with William Cameron Coup's travelling circus. Barnum and his partners began to invest in customized railway cars, moving to complete train transport in 1890.

Proprietors were trying to stretch their capacities in the 1850s. Barnum added two rings, ballooning the performance space and audience capacity, which could eventually accommodate well over 14,000 customers. The additional rings redefined the way circus was performed and received. Displays might be going on simultaneously in all the rings, so there developed a hierarchy among the acts, with the most highly touted taking place in the centre ring. This made it impossible for a spectator to focus on everything at once, though the overall sensation might be one of unfathomable excitement. Adjacent to the main tent one might find *freak shows, exotic animals, carnival performers, and animal menageries.

In Europe, some 200 indigenous companies were in operation by the end of the nineteenth century. George *Sanger operated Astley's from 1871 to 1893. By the turn of the twentieth century the American influence could be felt across the

Atlantic in an important way: the classic equestrian circus had given way to more extravagant feats of daring and wild-animal acts, both of which became the new stars of the show. Although Europeans would, for the most part, retain their one-ring tradition, tenting allowed them to spread the seeds of circus as far as Australia in the 1840s, India, China, and Japan in the 1860s, and South Africa in the 1870s. By the twentieth century, Latin American countries were already building strong circus traditions, generating their own top performers and companies.

Western circus proprietors have always collected striking acts from abroad: Indian and East Asian acrobats, Chinese plate-spinners, and Egyptian contortionists, among others, showed to the West the human body performing new feats while feeding a fascination for the 'exotic' which circus has always mined (see INTERCULTURALISM). The circus has traditionally played to the audience's orientalist tendencies to enhance a sense of wonder or unique opportunity, and perhaps capitalize on its culture's conceits of superiority.

Pressures exerted by the First World War, *music hall, and theatre, the increasing cost of travel, the Great Depression, and, of course, the eventual rise of film and television led to an overall reduction and consolidation of companies through the middle of the twentieth century, especially in the USA and Britain. Tenting circuses remained, but many switched to large, standing venues. In the later twentieth century, however, some moved away from animal acts, as cultural attitudes changed toward the training, caging, and 'performance' of beasts, and animal-rights groups became particularly aggressive in their protests. Although traditional circuses have continued to operate, a movement called New Circus emerged in the 1970s, applying a born-again interest in circus skills to contemporary aesthetics. New Circus generally takes a more environmentalist attitude toward animal acts, either avoiding animals entirely or attempting to foster a sense of respect for them on- and offstage. In form, New Circus steers closer to theatre: it features acts based on time-honoured skills but tends to channel them toward theme, narrative, or an *avant-garde aesthetic. Notable New Circus companies have included Circus Oz (Australia), Cirque de Soleil (Canada), Archaos (France), and the Pickle Family and Big Apple circuses (United States).

Circus has held a particular attraction for other art forms. As popular entertainment *par excellence*, it appealed to the *dada and *futurist movements, and *Artaud admired its visceral,

pre-verbal engagement between mass audience and the highly trained performing body. Elsewhere, circus or the circus-like have informed work by playwrights like *Wedekind and *Ionesco, and directors like *Meyerhold, *Brook, and *Mnouchkine. The romanticized images of circus life's daily swings from gaudy glamour to sawdust reality, its itinerant, communal lifestyle, its clowns with painted faces, the perceived innocence of a form which serves for many a child as an introduction to live performance: these and other circus themes have served as potent metaphors for theatre, film, dance, music, and *opera.   EW

circus, Roman Large entertainment building used first and foremost for chariot racing. The most famous of all circuses was the Circus Maximus in ancient Rome. Chariot racing was held as early as the sixth century BC in the area of what became the Circus Maximus in the valley between the Palatine and the Aventine Hills. During the later republic and the early empire the Circus Maximus, to a greater extent than any other circus, also served as the venue for other events. The first structure on the site is said to date back to the sixth century BC; it was not until Trajan (AD 98–117) that the structure reached its final form. Including the arena and seating the structure was 600 m (656 yards) long with an average width of 180 m (197 yards). Estimates of seating capacity vary from 150,000 to 350,000.

Games were held throughout the year as part of the religious and political life of the city, and the most popular and exciting events were the *ludi circenses*. On the day of a race, a procession was held that led into the circus. The crowd would cheer and place bets, a trumpet would blow, and the presiding magistrate would signal the start of the race by dropping a napkin. A maximum of twelve charioteers could compete in any one race and they entered the arena simultaneously from the twelve *carceres* or starting boxes at the open end of the circus. The racers travelled anticlockwise, normally circling seven times, for a total of about 5 km (3 miles), lasting just over eight minutes with speeds on the straight reaching 75 k.p.h. (47 m.p.h.).

Crashes were common, especially at the start of a race and at the turns. To overtake on the inside as one approached the turn was a tactic particularly admired, as well as extremely dangerous. Each chariot team had a *hortator*, an individual horseman in protective clothing whose job was to ride ahead of the team and act as guide through the dust and confusion of the race.

By the time of the empire (late first century BC) chariot racing had become highly professional, with large stables owned by prominent individuals supplying the horses, chariots, and drivers. All jockeys belonged to teams (*factiones*), and each team had its own colours. From Augustus' reign there were usually four, virtual companies under imperial patronage; they supplied teams to the magistrates giving the games and received money prizes in return. The charioteers by this time were mainly drawn from the lower social classes of freedmen and slaves. As with gladiators, those who succeeded were idolized by the public and could earn enough in prize money to retire as wealthy men.

By the imperial period a full day's programme included 24 races. As well as horse and chariot racing the circus could also be used for other types of spectacle, often put on as part of the entertainment between races: novelty races, exhibitions of trick riding, athletic displays including boxing, wrestling, and foot races. *Gladiatorial combat and *animal fights might also be staged. By the late Roman period the circus and chariot racing became increasingly associated with the emperor; the circus was one of the few places where he could be seen by ordinary people. *See* ROMAN THEATRE.   HD

Citizens Theatre Founded in Glasgow in 1943 by *Bridie, the 'Citz' took over the Royal Princess's, a Victorian theatre in the Gorbals, a notorious district south of the River Clyde. Although Bridie attempted to develop a national drama, encouraging Scottish writers and actors, under a succession of directors in the 1960s the theatre became indistinguishable from many other British *repertory theatres. Giles *Havergal's arrival in 1969 with Philip *Prowse heralded considerable change. With translator and writer Robert David MacDonald, they adopted a highly visual and visceral approach to production, presenting neglected plays on Prowse's extraordinary sets, where *Webster, *Tourneur, and *Wycherley rubbed shoulders with *Goldoni, *Lermontov, and *Genet, and MacDonald's adaptations of Proust and *Tolstoy. Although nudity and neglect of Scottish authors caused controversy, young *audiences flocked, attracted by cheap seats and a style which seemed to cross punk with *Meyerhold, *Wilde with deconstruction, and the Citz was regarded as one of Britain's most radical theatres. The addition of two studio theatres in 1993 allowed more attention to new writers and directors. From 2004, following the triumvirate's retirement, the theatre has relied increasingly on visiting productions to supple-

ment a more limited and conventional mixed repertory.   GJG

Ciulei, Liviu (1923–) Romanian director, designer, and actor. Trained in architecture and theatre, Ciulei began working in Bucharest in 1945, specializing in American plays banned during the war years. Under Soviet *censorship, Romanian theatre was dominated by *naturalism, and Ciulei turned to film. In 1956 his 'On the Theatricality of Scenery' sparked a turn away from *socialist realism to a rediscovery of theatricality and during the 1960s and 1970s his *scenography was marked by huge photos within architectural units, which moved in various configurations to suggest locale and mood, as in his *As You Like It* (1961). He served as *artistic director of the Bulandra Theatre in Bucharest (1963–72), but was dismissed for permitting *Pintilie's production of *Gogol's *The Government Inspector*. *Tours by the Bulandra during the 1970s to Western Europe, Australia, and the United States cemented Ciulei's reputation, especially with productions of *Büchner and *Gorky. He worked as designer/director for *opera and theatre at *Covent Garden, the Lyric Opera of Chicago, *Arena Stage, and the *New York Shakespeare Festival. He served as artistic director of the *Guthrie Theatre in Minneapolis (1980–5), where he redesigned the *auditorium and mounted a remarkable series of Shakespeare plays.   EEP

Cixous, Hélène (1937–) French writer. Cixous became known in the 1970s as one of four French feminists who developed the theory of *écriture féminine* (feminine writing), which proposes that representation is dominated by the male perspective, and that the female perspective must be liberated. Her first successful play, *Portrait of Dora* (1976), is a *feminist view of Freud's famous case study. Cixous's major theatre work was in collaboration with *Mnouchkine at the Théâtre du *Soleil. First hired to consult on *intercultural Shakespeare performances in Asian styles, Cixous was then urged to write original plays with contemporary themes. The first two deal with post-colonialism: *The Terrible but Unfinished History of Norodom Sihanouk, King of Cambodia* (1985) and *The Indiade; or, India of their Dreams* (1987). In *The Perjury City; or, The Furies' Awakening* (1994), the Furies return as mothers whose children have died from AIDS-contaminated blood. *Drums on the Dyke* (1999) concerns a disastrous, preventable flood, with *bunraku-style *puppets manipulated by actors.   SBB

Clairon, Mlle (Claire-Josèphe-Hippolyte Léris de La Tude) (1723–1803) French actress. Following a triumphant debut at the *Comédie-Française in 1743 as *Racine's *Phèdre*, she established a formidable reputation in *tragedy, playing the classical repertoire and new work. Unlike her rival, Mlle *Dumesnil, whose playing was intuitive and inspirational, Clairon was an intellectual actress grounded in research and study. To *Diderot's delight, her *acting underwent a revolutionary mid-career change: she abandoned tendencies towards the vehement and declamatory in favour of a more nuanced delivery and natural manner. Believing that '*realism in stage speech demand[ed] a similar realism in *costume', with the support of her colleague *Lekain she urged that the fashionable look be replaced by the appropriate and historically accurate look. As Idamé in *Voltaire's *The Orphan of China* (1755) she adopted 'foreign gestures' and wore 'Chinese' dress, without hoops or cuffs, with bare arms. She retired at age 42 in 1766 and opened an acting school, where she trained Larive and Mlle *Raucourt.   JG

claque A group of people who have been organized or hired, generally to applaud, as part of a theatre *audience. Common in Europe in the nineteenth century, especially in France, claque members received free admission from *managers. Some of the *chefs de claque* are reputed to have had a sliding scale of charges according to the length and intensity of *applause required.

Claques were so prevalent in Paris during the nineteenth century that several categories of *claqueur* were codified: *bisseurs* (who demanded 'bis', or encore), *chatouilleurs* (who kept the audience in good humour), *commissaires* (who memorized the text and loudly pointed out its merits), the *pleureuses* (women who cried in a *melodrama), and *rieurs* (who *laughed uproariously at *comedy). The *chef de claque* was an important force in the theatre and often attended *rehearsals to discover the optimum moments for applause. He would direct the response of the *claqueurs* through a variety of hand gestures. By the end of the nineteenth century, however, the claque had all but disappeared in the theatre, although it took longer to disappear from *opera.

The claque was not uncommon throughout history and in many settings. The first *Greek theatre was a competition and groups were organized to applaud enthusiastically to influence judges. In the Edo period (1603–1868) of *kabuki, it was customary for a predetermined spectator to stand when there was a slight pause in the acting and to shout out some encouragement to a particular actor. In some of the political theatre of the early twentieth century, actors were used as *claqueurs* to encourage the rest of the audience towards the desired message. The techniques of the claque take on an explicit form in television recorded before a live audience where stagehands hold placards directing audience responses, or when sitcoms rely on electronic 'laugh tracks' to simulate an audience response.   SBe

Clark-Bekederemo, John Pepper (1935–) Nigerian playwright and poet. Critical attention has focused on the early work of John Pepper Clark rather than the more recent plays published under the name Clark-Bekederemo. His responses to European *tragedy and concern with Delta conventions led to *Song of a Goat* (directed by *Soyinka, 1963) and its sequel *Masquerade* (1965). Political tensions in newly independent Nigeria prompted *The Raft* (directed by Soyinka, 1964). The large-scale *Ozidi* and *The Ozidi Saga* (1981) moved towards a *dance-like style. Starting in 1982 Clark-Bekederemo threw his energy into establishing a regular theatregoing habit among the Lagos elite by fostering the PEC Repertory Theatre. He also wrote a trilogy, *The Bikoroa Plays*, which follows the fortunes of a Delta family during the first half of the twentieth century. His plays of the 1990s, *The Wives' Revolt* and *All for Oil*, are meditations on the relevance of the past for contemporary society. The second, 'a history play about the present times in Nigeria', was presented in 2000.   JMG

Clarke, Martha (1944–) American choreographer and director. Trained as a modern *dancer, Clarke began developing an idiosyncratic, highly expressionistic theatre of movement and aural imagery that is sometimes given the label music theatre. In 1979 she founded Crowsnest, a chamber movement ensemble dedicated to producing her *auteur*-informed work. During the 1980s her pieces tended to re-envision well-known historical moments with a dreamlike, highly physical and sensual narrative voice. *The Garden of Earthly Delights* (1985), Clarke's version of the painting by Hieronymus Bosch, is among her most famous works of this genre. In the 1990s Clarke directed *opera in Beijing and for the Glimmerglass Company (Cooperstown, New York), collaborated with *Hampton on *Alice's Adventures Under Ground* for the *National Theatre, and created *Vers la flamme*, based in part on several short stories by *Chekhov and filled with her signature convolution of longing, grief, and sexuality. *Kaos* (2006) was based on stories by *Pirandello   ITC

classicism *See* NEOCLASSICISM.

Claudel, Paul (1868–1955) French playwright, poet, and essayist. A diplomat from 1890 to 1935, many of Claudel's plays were written decades before they were staged. Turn-of-the-century *audiences were not prepared for their complex structure and length, nor for the proselytizing nature of their Catholic world-view. Claudel sought to synthesize history in order to bring out its meaning, which always included *farce as well as epic versions of *tragedy and *comedy. He telescoped time, made every setting both real and symbolic, and used allegorical *characters and parable plots. Although his *Tidings Brought to Mary* was staged by *Lugné-Poe in 1912 and *The Exchange* by *Copeau in 1914, it was not until *Barrault's 1943 production of *The Satin Slipper* at the *Comédie-Française that Claudel gained wide recognition. Because the dramas accorded with Barrault's vision of a *total theatre synthesizing drama, *music, *dance, and film, he produced many of them over the years, including *Break of Noon* (1948), *The Exchange* (1951), *Christopher Columbus* (1953), *Golden Head* (1959), and *Under the Wind of the Balearic Isles* (1972).   SBB

Claus, Hugo (1929–2008) Flemish writer and painter. As a young artist he met *Artaud in Paris, whose influence is particularly apparent in *Moratorium* (1953) and in adaptations of *Seneca. Claus also wrote a number of *realistic plays, such as *A Bride in the Morning* (1955), which deals sensitively with brother-sister incest and appears to be influenced by Tennessee *Williams. In *Sugar* (1958) and *Friday* (1969), he wrote in a skilful mixture of standard Dutch and the Flemish dialect. Claus also wrote in an *epic or *documentary style, most notably *The Life and Works of Leopold II* (1970), a *burlesque of the Belgian king who colonized the Congo. Claus's wide-ranging personality is typified by his adaptations into Dutch of works from different languages. He was especially attracted to the freedom and verbal exuberance of Elizabethan drama and created fascinating renditions of Shakespeare, *Middleton, and others. His themes of human desire and family distress often touched on the basic Oedipal situation, and he wrote several pieces derived from Seneca and *Sophocles, such as *Blindeman* (1985).   JDV

Clive, Kitty (1711–85) English actress and playwright. Renowned for her singing voice and wry comic ability, Kitty Clive's personal triumph as Nell in Charles Coffey's *The Devil to Pay*, performed at *Drury Lane in the 1730–1 season, doubled her salary and she revived the role throughout her long career. She was a forthright woman who defended her rights

against *management moves to reallocate her parts and lower players' salaries. Clive wrote at least six comedies between 1750 and 1765. In her *The Rehearsal; or, Bays in Petticoats* (1750) she played the leading role of a vain female playwright who takes over from the absent leading lady, Kitty Clive.   GBB

Close, Glenn (1947–) American actress who made her Broadway debut in *Love for Love* (1974). Subsequent stage roles included Mary Tudor in *Rex* (1976), Leilah in *Uncommon Women and Others* (1977), Irene St Claire in *The Crucifer of Blood* (1978), Chairy in *Barnum* (1980), and Yeliena in *Uncle Vanya* with the Yale Repertory Theatre (1981). She won Tony awards for *The Real Thing* (1984), *Death and the Maiden* (1992), and *Sunset Boulevard* (1995). Her more prominent film roles demonstrate her unusual versatility: Jenny Fields in *The World According to Garp* (1982), Sarah in *The Big Chill* (1983), Alex in *Fatal Attraction* (1987), the Marquise de Merteuil in *Dangerous Liaisons* (1988), and Claire in *The Stepford Wives* (2004). She also produced and played the title role in the television movie *Sarah, Plain and Tall* (1991).   JDM

closet drama A play to be read instead of staged. Although the term sometimes carries a negative connotation, closet dramas have had a variety of dramatic features and purposes not tied to successful stage performance. They can be Platonic *dialogues, declamatory works (*Seneca's plays), *medieval dramas written for a narrator (*Hrotsvitha's plays), dramatic dialogues (*Diderot's *Le Neveu de Rameau*), verse dramas (Shelley's *Prometheus Unbound*), short *jeux d'esprit* (Wallace Stevens's plays), and grand epical works (*Ibsen's *Emperor and Galilean*). Following the invention of the printing press, the closet drama emerged as a viable dramatic text without need of performance. Such was the case with Milton's *Samson Agonistes* (1671), written for the reader alone. Women writers, often refused access to the theatre, wrote closet dramas, and many poets have shared a Platonic ambivalence about the theatre, even an *anti-theatrical prejudice. Unconfined by *actors and staging, the writer is free to create a complex, often philosophical dialogue and conflict in the lyrical mode (*Byron's *Manfred*). In the *romantic and modern ages closet dramas often investigate consciousness and self-identity. This virtual or mental drama locates the *action in a *theatrum mundi* of the imagination of both the poet and the reader. Perhaps the greatest closet drama of this type is *Goethe's two-part *Faust* (1808, 1832). Though its author considered the work unstageable, its vast range over time and space, untrammelled by considerations of nineteenth-century theatre practice, ironically made it an attractive challenge to *directors in the modernist tradition and numerous successful productions have resulted. TP

clown A dramatic *character serving stock comic functions, generally defined by the performer for whom the role was intended. The theatrical clown was literally a dim-witted rustic, found on the Elizabethan stage in characters like Costard in *Love's Labour's Lost.* The role was written by Shakespeare for William *Kempe of the *Chamberlain's Men, and the sense of a broadly recognizable comic character has become central to the clown identity. As a result, the clown label has sometimes embraced other comic types like *fools and jesters. Above all, the clown signals a predictable source of entertainment. A character for the common spectator, he usually occupies low or marginalized status, commenting upon human imperfection and the individual's place in society, often undermining the dominant discourse through naivety or wit. The clown usually enjoys a privileged relationship with the *audience, and has licence to take comic detours for scripted or *improvised turns.

Clown traditions have arisen in cultures worldwide, adapting indigenous, *ritual features to theatrical forms. During the *early modern period, the *Narr* became a stock figure on the German stage, the *gracioso* in Spanish companies. Loosely comparable traits appear in *stock characters of Italian *commedia dell'arte,* Chinese Sichuan, and West African theatres. The clown historically has been male, owing to long-standing codes of social propriety. The character's emblematic resonance has been mined by twentieth-century playwrights like *Brecht and *Beckett, while *Fo has explored the subversive possibilities of his own clowning persona.   EW

Clunes, Alec (Alexander Sheriff de Maro) (1912–70) British actor, director, and *manager. Best known for running the Arts Theatre in London from 1942 to 1952 and for performing alongside stars such as *Olivier, *Gielgud, and *Scofield, he began his professional acting career with *Greet's company in 1934. Subsequently he acted with major companies of his time, including *Guthrie's *Old Vic season in 1936–7, the *Shakespeare Memorial Theatre in 1954 (as Claudius to Scofield's Hamlet), and finally at the *National Theatre in *Hochhuth's controversial *Soldiers* in 1968. His influential Arts Theatre

seasons introduced new playwrights and staged forgotten classics.   BRK

Clurman, Harold (1901–80) American director and critic. Clurman worked as play reader for the *Theatre Guild from 1925. In 1930 he began weekly meetings, attracting young people with his passionate talk of moving beyond the 'art theatres' like the Guild to create a 'real theatre': an artistic expression of its members' ideas on 'the life of our times'. Along with *Strasberg and Cheryl Crawford, Clurman was made a director of the *Group Theatre when it emerged from the Guild in 1931. He first directed a production with *Awake and Sing!* (1935) by *Odets, followed by four other Odets plays and two by Irwin Shaw before the Group's collapse in 1941. Clurman worked as a producer in Hollywood during the war, but returned to prominence in theatre in 1945 with the publication of his book *The Fervent Years: the Group Theatre and the 1930s.* His direction of a prizewinning 1950 production of Carson McCullers's *Member of the Wedding* led to eighteen Broadway productions during the 1950s, including *Williams's *Orpheus Descending* (1956). In 1953 he became drama critic for the *Nation.* MAF

Cochran, C. B. (Charles Blake) (1872–1951) English *manager and impresario. Beginning in the USA as an actor, press agent, and manager, Cochran served as personal secretary to Richard *Mansfield, then as a *producer when he put *Ibsen's *John Gabriel Borkman* on Broadway (1897). He returned to London in 1902 to become an impresario of everything from *Reinhardt's *The Miracle* (1911) to *circus shows. He produced *ballet as well as popular *revues in the 1910s, the plays of *O'Neill, *O'Casey, and *Coward in the 1920s and 1930s, and *musicals in the 1940s. He was also manager of Royal Albert Hall (1926–38) and a promoter of rodeo and boxing. Everyone called him 'Cockie'.   TP

Cockpit-in-Court Built in 1629 as a replacement for a succession of temporary theatres used at Whitehall Palace to stage plays and *masques for the royal entertainments of the Christmas season, the Cockpit was designed by Inigo *Jones and reflected the distinctive qualities of *Palladio's Teatro *Olimpico at Vicenza (1583), which Jones had studied. An intimate theatre, it had a curved *scaenae frons* with five entry doors, and a complicated balcony area. Queen Henrietta Maria had introduced *perspective staging for a play at Somerset House in 1626, and Jones subsequently designed scenery for several other plays. This experience influenced his design for the new Whitehall Cockpit, although none of the professional company plays staged there in subsequent years made any use of scenery. It lost its function as a *playhouse in 1665, when the Hall Theatre was opened in Whitehall's great hall. *See also* SCENOGRAPHY. AJG

Cocteau, Jean (1889–1963) French writer, designer, and filmmaker. In a career that embraced virtually all the arts, ranging from classical influences to the *avant-garde, Cocteau called himself 'poet' and chose Orpheus to represent his multi-faceted artistry. After seeing *Diaghilev's *Ballets Russes in 1909, Cocteau devoted himself to writing *scenarios and designing for *ballet, notably *Parade* (1917) and *The Wedding at the Eiffel Tower* (1921). His wry dramatizations of classical mythology include *Orphée* (1926), *Oedipus Rex* (1927, with Stravinsky), and *La Machine infernale* (1934, about Jocasta). Other important plays are *La Voix humaine* (1930, a one-woman *tragedy), *Les Chevaliers de la Table Ronde* (1937), *Les Parents terribles* (1938), and *L'Aigle a deux têtes* (1946). Chief among his seventeen films are *Blood of a Poet* (1930), *Beauty and the Beast* (1946, incorporating his *surrealist design elements), *Orphée* (1950), and a virtual artistic farewell, *Le Testament d'Orphée* (1960). FHL

Cody, William Frederick ('Buffalo Bill') (1846–1917) American frontier scout, actor, and showman. Cody fought in the Civil War, and afterwards took a job killing buffalo to supply meat for railway workers, which established his nickname. When the railway work ended, he rejoined the army as a civilian scout and his exploits made him the subject of a serialized story in 1869 and a play in 1872. Cody took the stage as himself in 1872 in Chicago in *The Scouts of the Prairie*, and continued to act in a series of action-filled *melodramas over the next decade. In May 1883 Cody inaugurated his Wild West Exhibition, a stage show that became a phenomenal success both in America and Europe. Constantly in debt because of bad investments, he continued to perform in *Wild West shows up to the year of his death. RAH

cofradías Spanish religious associations dedicated to a holy patron. Though created for military or chivalric ends, these brotherhoods worked, from the twelfth century on, with Spain's municipal corporations and extended their membership to craftsmen belonging to different trades. Among the duties of the *cofradías* was the organization of religious ceremonies, especially the Holy Week processions (a role they still perform today), and of festivities connected with different patron saints. Particularly crucial was their involvement in the performance of *mystery plays. The numerous *cofrades* who made up the brotherhoods were charged with building and preparing the mansions used in the *parade, as well as playing all of the parts involved. Though the Spanish clergy placed severe constraints on the nature of those parts and banned the participation of women, the *cofradías* were decisive in popularizing and disseminating the *misterios* throughout the Iberian peninsula. KG

Cohan, George M. (1878–1942) American man of the theatre. Born to a family of *vaudeville performers, Cohan was on stage before the age of 10. A theatrical jack of all trades, Cohan gave Broadway its first distinctively American identity. A natural showman with a sure sense of the public, his breakthrough came in 1904 with *Little Johnny Jones*, where his cocksure portrayal of an American jockey stopped the show with 'Give my Regards to Broadway' and 'The Yankee Doodle Boy'. His 1906 *musicals *Forty-Five Minutes from Broadway* and *George Washington, Jr.* were also hits, the latter featuring 'You're a Grand Old Flag'. From 1906 to 1920 Cohan formed a highly successful *producing partnership with Sam Harris, which also saw the construction of the George M. Cohan Theatre in New York. While Cohan's stand against trade unions during the actors' strike of 1919 alienated him from his profession, his plays continued to find *audiences during the 1920s. Late in his career he had two notable successes as a performer in *O'Neill's *Ah, Wilderness!* (1933) and as President Roosevelt in *Rodgers and *Hart's *I'd Rather Be Right* (1937). SN

Coleman, Cy (1929–2004) American composer. Classically trained as a concert pianist, Coleman became interested in jazz, forming a successful trio in the 1950s. He also wrote pop songs with various lyricists, some of which found their way into stage *revues. His first Broadway score, with lyricist Carolyn Leigh, was *Wildcat* (1960), a vehicle crafted for Lucille Ball. His next two *musicals— *Little Me* (1962), *Sweet Charity* (1966)—were also star vehicles. He was notable for his ability to adapt his style to each project, rather than having a characteristic style. Thus the potpourri pop score for *I Love my Wife* (1977) sounded nothing like the sweeping *operetta-flavoured score of *On the Twentieth Century* (1978), nor the jazzy *City of Angels* (1989) like the rock-based *The Life* (1997). He also wrote two scores which place a historical figure's life in the musical context of their medium, the *circus-oriented *Barnum* (1980) and the *vaudevillian *Will Rogers Follies* (1991). JD

Coliseo The Coliseo del Buen Retiro in Madrid was the principal court theatre of later seventeenth- and eighteenth-century Spain. Built 1638–40 in the new royal palace of the Buen Retiro, it was designed by the Florentine engineer Cosimo (or Cosme) Lotti, *scenographer to Philip IV. It opened in 1640 but soon closed again for a decade because of war and theatrical prohibition. From the 1650s spectacular machine-plays by *Calderón and others were regularly staged in the Coliseo, as well as many ordinary *comedias. Among the first such productions were Calderón's *The Beast, the Thunderbolt, and the Stone* (1652) and *Fortunes of Andromeda and Perseus* the following year; a manuscript of the latter with elaborate scenographic drawings by Baccio himself has survived. Though gala performances were for the royal family and court, the public was admitted at other times. The *auditorium was modelled on Madrid's *playhouses, the *corrales de comedias* (though more luxurious and entirely roofed), but there was a *proscenium arch and a deep stage with changeable *perspective scenery, elaborate machinery, and *lighting. CD

collectives and collective creation Organizational structure for theatre companies and creative process for *devising, both emphasizing group dynamics and a non-hierarchical structure. Theatre is at its roots a community and collective effort, and examples of groups of artists and technicians pooling resources and talents can be found throughout history, but the social and political changes in the West during the 1960s sparked a particular desire for collectivity. Major collectives have included a number of American and European groups. The *Living Theatre (founded 1947) was led by *Beck and *Malina, whose anarchist and pacifist politics led to experimental productions which attempted to engender social revolution and new forms of theatrical experience. The *Open Theatre (1963–73), directed by *Chaikin, a former member of the Living Theatre, explored a new aesthetics of the actor devising performance through sound and movement. Théâtre du *Soleil (from 1964), directed by *Mnouchkine and formed as a social and artistic collective, has created a series of productions which developed radical and *intercultural forms of theatre through a borrowing of international performance forms. The Polish Theatre Laboratory (1957–69) directed by *Grotowski and the *Performance Group (1967) led by *Schechner looked to create theatre based in mythological narratives told through physicalized performance. Contemporary collectives such as the *Wooster Group, La *Fura dels Baus, *Socìetas Rafaello Sanzio, Theatre de *Complicité, and dumbtype (Japan) are loosely organized as collectives whose aesthetic concerns continue to explore new configurations of performance, but through a postmodern politics of incorporation as opposed to the earlier modes of confrontation and action.

Although each collective has different objectives and processes, politics and aesthetics, the collectives of the 1960s held a common concern for social activism and personal and group evolution filtered through leftist politics. This led to politically informed work that was not only representative of radical thought but strove to embody the principles of cultural revolution within the theatre. The dominance of the *director and the text gave way to actors engaged in *improvisation and *physically *devised *rehearsal, often creating their own texts or radically adapting them from classic sources. Contemporary collectives work in a comparable manner. MDC

Collier, Jeremy (1650–1726) English cleric and writer of *anti-theatrical polemic. Collier was not a Puritan but a high-church monarchist, yet achieved his greatest prominence with *Short View of the Immorality and Profaneness of the English Stage* (1698). This long, learned, and intemperate attack on contemporary dramatists, notably *Dryden, *D'Urfey, *Congreve, and *Vanbrugh, singles out in particular their alleged disrespect for marriage and their abuse of the clergy. It provoked an immediate pamphlet war, including replies from Vanbrugh. Ironically, it was the banishment of King James II, which Collier deplored, which left the *playhouses vulnerable to his assault: neither William and Mary nor Anne took protective interest in the Theatres Royal, nor any defence of actors and playwrights from the private prosecutions for blasphemy mounted by some of Collier's supporters. In the wake of the 'Collier controversy', Societies for the Reformation of Manners were established to uphold public virtue within the playhouses and beyond, which encouraged a trend away from the graphic *satire of the Restoration towards the more sentimental, *bourgeois morality exemplified by *Lillo. MD

Colman, George, the Elder (1732–94) English author and *manager. His first dramatic work, *Polly Honeycombe* (1760), was a popular *farce about a girl whose head is turned by novels like *Fielding's *Tom Jones*; ironically, his next and greatest success was *The Jealous Wife* (1761), a full-length *comedy derived from that work. By this time he had become the friend and protégé of *Garrick, with whom he wrote the best comedy of the mid-eighteenth century, *The Clandestine Marriage* (1766). The next year Colman made the mistake of buying a share of the *Covent Garden Theatre *patent. The partnership quickly foundered, leading to lengthy and costly litigation, and Colman left the management in 1774. His luck improved in 1776 when he leased Samuel *Foote's patent on the *Haymarket Theatre. After Foote died in 1777, Colman was permitted to continue the summer season under annual licences. He expanded the repertory and made many material improvements to the operation, which his son, George *Colman the Younger, took over in 1789.   MJK

Colman, George, the Younger (1762–1836) English author and *manager, ultimately a zealous Examiner of Plays in 1824 (*see* CENSORSHIP). He wrote several short pieces for the *Haymarket as a young man, the most popular being his *musical comedy *Inkle and Yarico* (1787). That work, like his full-length *comedy *The Heir at Law* (1797), became a repertory favourite. He took over management of the Haymarket in 1789 and ruined the profitable operation left to him by his father, *Coleman the Elder. Although he wrote several successful and lucrative plays, most famously *John Bull; or, The Englishman's Fireside* (1803), the financial problems led him to sell the Haymarket enterprise in 1820.   MJK

Comden, Betty (1915–2006) and **Adolph Green** (1915–2002) American lyricists, librettists, screenwriters, and performers. One of the most productive and enduring creative partnerships of all time, Comden and Green acquired a reputation for their sly wit, irrepressible spirit, and particular affection for New York. Working together since the 1930s, they had been writing material for their own comic troupe when in 1944 they were asked by *Bernstein to contribute lyrics and libretto for *On the Town*. They cleverly included roles for themselves, and have since performed individually and together, on stage and screen. Their canon is dominated by a number of collaborations with composer *Styne, beginning with the 1951 *revue *Two on the Aisle*, and going on to *Peter Pan* (1954), *Bells Are Ringing* (1956), *Do Re Mi* (1960), and *Hallelujah, Baby!* (1967), among others. They worked with Cy *Coleman for *On the Twentieth Century* (1978), and wrote the screenplays for *Singin' in the Rain* (1952), *The Band Wagon* (1953), and other films. Their best-known songs include 'The Party's Over' and 'Make Someone Happy'.   EW

comedia In Spain, *comedia* was used from the mid-sixteenth to the eighteenth centuries to refer to a full-length secular play, as opposed to *auto sacramental*, which designated a religious play. Modelled on the Italian *commedia erudita*, the Spanish *comedia* was introduced in the early sixteenth century by Bartolomé de Torres Naharro. Initially structured in five acts, the *comedia* was recast in its more typical three-act form by Lope de *Vega in the early seventeenth century.   RWV

Comediants Spanish company, formed in 1971 (as Els Comediants) as part of the movement for an independent Catalan theatre which rejected the official drama of the late Francoist period. Relying on *collective creation, Comediants avoids texts and *directors, instead employing actors, musicians, and artists of different styles to create an interdisciplinary performance event that echoes the travelling minstrels of the past. They tend to perform in unusual locales—streets, squares, rivers, meadows, or *sports stadiums—making a provocative 'theatre of the senses' that assaults the rigid conditions of everyday life. Their work, which ranges from the 'sacred drama' *Non Plus Plis* (1972) to *Maravillas de Cervantes* (*Marvels of Cervantes*, 2000) for the Compañía Nacional de Teatro Clásico, has also adapted and incorporated popular Spanish forms like the *auto sacramental*, the *farsa*, and the *entremés*.   KG

comédie-ballet A form of baroque court performance in France between 1661 and 1674. Among the artists who created the *comédies-ballets* were *Molière, *Lully, *Torelli, *Vigarani, and *Berain. While Louis XIV commissioned fourteen of the fifteen *comédies-ballets* for royal festivals, Molière alone participated in the creation of every one. The form drew some of its language and basic structure from *early modern festival and court *masque, combining a full-length play with vocal and instrumental music, *dancing, and spectacle between the acts, with an elaborate prologue and final *ballet. A unique feature was the staging of *comédies-ballets* within the formal gardens of Versailles, as well as at other royal chateaux. The genre began with *The Bores*, created by Molière and Beauchamp, which premièred at Vaux-le-Vicomte under the patronage of Nicolas Fouquet in August 1661; the final entry was *The Hypochondriac*, a Molière–Charpentier collaboration performed at Versailles in 1674, seventeen months after Molière's death.   GES

Comédie-Française France's oldest and most celebrated national theatre was created by order of Louis XIV in 1680 from the remnants of *Molière's troupe, the 'better' actors of the Théâtre du *Marais, and the company of the Théâtre de Guénégaud. There were to be three enterprises in Paris: the Comédie-Française for French *tragedy and *comedy, the *Comédie Italienne for Italian comedy and *farce, and the Académie de Musique for *opera. Each was subsidized by the state, though not generously; in return, each would provide entertainments for Louis's court.

When the Comédie-Française was established, the King took a hand in deciding the company, which consisted of ten men and seven women with full shares and five men and five women with partial shares. The state subvention was to be 12,000 livres. The new company was large enough that one group could perform daily in Paris while another answered calls to court. It opened at the Théâtre Guénégaud on 25 August with *Racine's *Phèdre* and *The Coaches of Orléans* by Jean de La Chapelle.

The most valuable property the actors brought was the repertory; the union of the troupes meant the union of the works of *Corneille, *Molière, and *Racine.

The 'Français' fought long and pugnaciously, but finally unsuccessfully, to defend its monopoly of spoken drama in French. First the Comédie Italienne, which had begun to add scenes in French in the late 1660s, and then theatres at the Paris fairs challenged the French troupe's entitlement. Important comic playwrights—*Regnard, Dufresny, *Lesage, *Marivaux—often turned to the competition. Tragedy remained the private property of the Comédie-Française, however, and after a long fallow period was revived by *Voltaire, who wrote for the troupe for 60 years beginning in 1718. The ambiguous status of the Comédie-Française, part private enterprise, part creature of the state bureaucracy, was first emphasized in 1687 when the actors learned that they were to be dispossessed of the theatre they owned on the rue Guénégaud because of objections by the Sorbonne, recently awarded tenancy of the nearby Collège de Quatre-Nations. Given only three months to move house, the actors were blocked at every turn in their efforts to find a suitable plot upon which to build. It was almost two years later that the troupe finally opened its new theatre, designed by François d'Orbay, on the rue Neuve des Fossés, where it was to remain until 1770.

In the eighteenth century the Comédie-Française was an actors' theatre, celebrated for the brilliant *Lecouvreur, the tragedy queens *Dumesnil and *Clairon, Voltaire's protégé *Lekain, the dazzling *Molé, Paris's first Hamlet, and many others. These actors, however, found themselves ever more at the mercy of the bureaucracy, which

now included an *intendant* who oversaw the day-to-day management of the royal theatres.

In 1770 the Comédie-Française left Orbay's decaying theatre and occupied a royal venue, the *Salle des Machines in the Tuileries palace, a most unsuitable space, while waiting for a new theatre to be built. They waited for twelve years. Their new Théâtre-Français, on the site of the present Théâtre de l'*Odéon, was finally completed after years of bureaucratic infighting in 1782, but in 1793 the Committee of Public Safety, led by Robespierre, ordered the theatre closed and the actors arrested. The troupe had already experienced a violent schism between the actors who supported the revolution and those who remained loyal to the monarchy. The actor-revolutionaries broke away and moved to a theatre on the rue de Richelieu, originally built for the Opéra, which they named the Théâtre de la République. The royalists remained at what they called the Théâtre de la Nation until their arrest. Thanks to the intervention of an amateur actor who was an employee of the Committee of Public Safety, the actors survived their eleven months of captivity, but found no way to re-establish themselves after their release. Finally, in 1799 the Comédie-Française troupe was reunited at the theatre on the rue de Richelieu where it has remained for more than 200 years.

Paris had enjoyed a 'freedom of the theatres' from 1790; by decree of the National Assembly 'any citizen could open a public theatre and produce there plays of any genre'. The actors of the 'Français' no longer enjoyed special status. In 1807, however, Napoléon re-established theatrical privilege, suppressing most of the new theatres, and granting monopolies to the surviving eight including the Comédie-Française.

Through most of the nineteenth century the actors retained some control over repertory, although successive commissioners and administrators encouraged certain playwrights to give their new plays to the Théâtre-Français. Baron Tayler, who was appointed commissioner in 1825, scheduled the new plays of *romanticism by *Dumas père, *Vigny, and *Hugo, including Hugo's infamous *Hernani* (1830). The romantics did not please, however, and the Comédie-Française entered a chaotic period of low popularity and lower receipts. Its salvation was a young actress named *Rachel who first appeared at the age of 17 in 1838 and filled the *auditorium. In the 1850s a cadre of new playwrights, including *Scribe, George Sand, and *Musset, helped the company recover from another loss of popularity.

A series of administrators have proposed and imposed a variety of ambitious plans over the last

150 years. What has not changed, at least from the point of view of the tenured actors (*sociétaires*), is the security of their appointments and their right to a share in the profits.

Few of the leading figures of the twentieth-century French theatre have been members of the Comédie-Française, perhaps because there has never been a provision made for a non-actor to become a *sociétaire*. In 1936 *Jouvet was invited to become the administrator, but rejected the offer. The man who accepted it, Édouard Bourdet, named four 'exterior' artists, Jouvet, *Copeau, *Dullin, and *Baty, as stage *directors, the first official notice of the theatre artist who became pre-eminent in the twentieth century. Although some members of the troupe have continued to direct, the trend has been to use outside directors or to appoint French directors as administrators. Among those who have been selected are the Italians *Zeffirelli, *Strehler, and *Fo, the English *Hands, and, as administrators, the French *Vincent, *Vitez, and Jacques Lassalle. Several *sociétaires* have also led the troupe since the end of the Second World War, directing and continuing to act. Actors, once elected *sociétaire*, are expected to remain with the troupe, and many do. Others, including such celebrated stars as Jeanne Moreau and Isabelle Adjani, have resigned while they were still *pensionnaires*, probationary actors or actors employed on short-term contracts. *Sociétaires* are restricted professionally, though now permitted to perform in television and film.

In 1930-1 the Comédie-Française produced 130 different plays; in 2001-2, it produced 16. Many factors have led to this decline, primary among them being a shift to longer runs. Although the company maintains a modified *repertory schedule at the Salle Richelieu, with at most three plays sharing the calendar at any given time, at its two smaller theatres each play has a discrete run. Still very much an institutional theatre, the Comédie-Française takes seriously its mission as an 'imaginary museum' of French dramatic art.

The Théâtre-Français on the rue Richelieu has been restored, remodelled, and rebuilt over the years, most fully after a fire in 1900, again in 1994 to accommodate modern stage technology. The status of the troupe has also been modified to suit modern bureaucratic structures. No longer a 'small republic', the Comédie-Française was declared in 1995 a 'public establishment of the industrial and commercial type' under the authority of the Ministry of Culture. In 2006 Muriel Mayette (born 1964), an accomplished actress and *sociétaire*, became the first woman appointed to lead the troupe.   VS

Comédie Italienne Name given by the French to the institutionalized presence of an Italian theatre company in Paris in the seventeenth and eighteenth centuries. At first the title meant performing in Italian, and improvising rather than learning a script, along with associations of liveliness, physicality, and populist subversive mockery. By the end of its history, however, the Comédie Italienne had merged, in most respects, with native French theatre. Italian actors began visiting France as early as the 1570s, Paris being a more metropolitan venue than their own divided peninsula could provide. The most prestigious were the object of royal invitations, stemming partly from successive Florentine queens of France, Marie and Catherine de Médicis. Two generations of the *Andreini family visited between 1603 and 1647. In 1680 theatre was organized into three monopolies: the new Opéra, the *Comédie-Française, and the Comédie Italienne. By this time performers from the *Biancolelli, *Gabrielli, Gherardi, and Romagnesi families were established stars; while imported *scenographers such as *Torelli and *Vigarani were contributing to large-scale royal spectacle. Texts for the Comédie Italienne began to be partly precomposed rather than improvised, and partly in French—thus beginning a process of naturalization which attempted nevertheless to retain the perceived exotic character.

Disaster came when the Italians were expelled from Paris in 1697 for an alleged scurrilous attack on Mme de Maintenon, Louis XIV's mistress. In 1716, under the Regent for the young Louis XV, a 'new' Comédie Italienne was re-established. Direction was entrusted to Luigi *Riccoboni, a second-generation immigrant. It lasted to 1762, when it lost its identity in a merger with the Opéra-Comique. In its second phase its material had been entirely in French: the company still offered lively and identifiably Italian star performers, but one of its chief playwrights was *Marivaux, the quintessence of purely French *sensibilité*. *See also* COMMEDIA DELL'ARTE.   RAA

comédie larmoyante In 'tearful comedy' the noun should be taken in the sense of 'play', for in the purest examples of the genre the sources of *laughter—extravagant characterization, the antics of comic servants—are absent, and the only feature belonging to traditional comedy is the happy ending. *Steele's *The Conscious Lovers* (1722) had aimed at 'a joy too exquisite for laughter'; and *La Chaussée followed suit in France, achieving considerable success with a formula which subjected a long-suffering *heroine to misunderstandings and other forms of adversity, as in

Le Préjugé à la mode (1735) or *Mélanide* (1741). Although *Voltaire poured scorn on La Chaussée's sentimental moralizing, his own *comedies owe more to sentiment than he would have admitted. The domestic drama of *Diderot and his contemporaries, as well as the *fin de siècle* *melodrama of *Pixérécourt, can both be seen to invest tearful comedy with a measure of prose *realism.   WDH

comedy A generic label usually taken in contemporary usage as an indication that a text, performance, or event features humorous intent. It may also imply that a story ends 'happily', and, to a lesser extent, that it orients itself toward the everyday world of the intended audience through vernacular language. None of these three elements, however, can be considered definitive, nor have they been consistently applied throughout Western dramatic history—and all can appear in texts which would not be considered comedies. It might be ventured that comedy renders the world with a distinctive sense of playfulness, even when its subject matter and themes are quite serious. It has been invoked with regard to a sprawling range of texts across media, as well as a model of improvised performance and a type of solo performance called 'stand-up comedy'.

As a dramatic form, comedy emerged in ancient *Greece as a complementary mode to *tragedy, offering playful relief from the senior genre's life-and-death themes. Comedy entered the formal competitions at the *Dionysia in Athens around 486 BC. The first historic wave is referred to as *Old Comedy, and our direct access to plays of this period remains limited to works by *Aristophanes. It is possible to see in these texts at least two of the broad elements we take to characterize comedy today, the first being a prevalence of humorous intent. The second is a *ritual festivity in the closing passages, from which it is not a huge step further to the romantic coupling or 'happy ending' we come to expect from comedy. Toward the end of the fourth century BC, comedy began to travel beyond Athens, and so it had to adopt a more broadly appealing approach for its content and humour. Plays began to focus upon the common travails of citizen life and developed a stable of social stereotypes. This more down-to-earth, observational inclination of *New Comedy, found in extant material by *Menander, establishes the third of the characteristic elements mentioned above. It was substantially revived in the *Roman era by *Plautus and *Terence.

A dramatic form by birth, the genetic heritage of today's comic performance can be traced to the patterns and practices of the *commedia dell'arte*, which arose in *early modern Italy. The *scenarios for *commedia* performance sought to contrive situations rife with comic irony, at the same time allowing for the lampooning of socio-cultural stereotypes like the bombastic doctor and aging skinflint (*see* STOCK CHARACTER). Two types of comic servant also emerged, one a wily schemer, the other a dull or naive rustic. *Commedia dell'arte* spread across Europe, and its influences can be seen in the dramatic literatures of France, Spain, Germany and Sweden, as well as Russia and England. Comic characterization will often attempt to epitomize the latest excesses of recognizable social types and behaviours. It remains occupied by the never-ending task of showing us more about our social selves than we can see from the midst of our lives.

Virtuosity in physical and vocal performance became a feature of *commedia* performance and its legacy extended to later English-speaking practices in British *music hall and American *vaudeville. Its performative patterns then transferred to screen and television with Charlie Chaplin, Buster Keaton, and the *Marx Brothers in the early twentieth century, and Lucille Ball, John Cleese, and Jim Carrey in the latter part. *Commedia*'s implications for characterization and the performing body can be seen in animated cartoons from Mickey Mouse and Bugs Bunny to *The Simpsons* and *Wallace & Gromit*.

Comedy thrives upon exploitation of its immediate production context and so Western dramatic history has thrown up an array of subgenres. The comedy of manners, for example, describes a kind of play situated in the upper strata of a class-conscious society, serving as critique of codes and postures. At the same time, it celebrates wit and verbal agility, a feature with particular implications for physical and vocal performance style. Typified by the plays of *Sheridan and *Goldsmith in the eighteenth century, the label has been applied to later works by *Wilde and *Coward. A number of plays written by Lope de *Vega during Spain's 'golden' seventeenth century are called *comedias de costumbres*, and similarly look at social manners in the city, country, and court. A tension between city and country can be found throughout the history of Western comedy, with pretence and intellectualism ridiculed on the side of city living, small-mindedness and naivety on the part of country life. The *character of the *clown, in fact, originally derives from the comic simplicity of the country bumpkin.

*Farce is another subgenre of comedy, exemplified by the works of *Feydeau in France. The plot is usually initiated by a male character's quest for extramarital sex, with subsequent machinations and misfortunes snowballing to the point of anarchy, before everything falls more or less back into place in the end. This form bred later variations, like the Aldwych farces of Ben *Travers and plays by *Kaufmann and Moss *Hart in the first half of the twentieth century, to more recent works by *Ayckbourn and *Frayn. Humour strategies and comic performance palettes have also been pressed into use by full-blown tragedy, as well as the theatre of the *absurd, and the cruel and violent worlds of Sarah *Kane, *McDonagh, and *Ravenhill.

Comedy is a curious specimen when placed under a political microscope. As a genre, which, by soliciting humour relationships with its audience, seeks the widest possible approval of its prejudices, comedy tends to mine a conservative vein of thought and feeling in society. Every joke has a target, and it is when a joke appears most 'innocent' that it should be inspected for the stereotypical features of social behaviour, *gender, race, class, or religion being held up for ridicule.

Comedy's 'happy ending' is also problematic in this regard. No matter how viably a text may challenge the dominant social order, a happy ending will most often seek to gather all parties under its normative embrace, ultimately diffusing any subversive points scored along the way. One should furthermore ask who defines the terms for 'happiness'—in most cases it is a Western white, male, middle-class, and heterosexual ethos that suits the status quo quite nicely. There is, on the other hand, an argument to be made on behalf of the political potency of comic strategies when wielded shrewdly. Dario *Fo's *Accidental Death of an Anarchist* (1970) and *Churchill's *Cloud Nine* (1979), for example, infiltrated conservative form to debase dominant discourses; more recently, *Albee's *The Goat* (2002) has employed comic means to interrogate the notion of sexual deviance.

The provisional nature of a dramatic text means its humour potential is always up for negotiation in actual production. Identifiable joking patterns in its words harbour a wide range of potential tone and feeling—it can be broadened or diminished, even imposed between the lines, all of which relates directly to the vectors and tones of bias seeking validation. Shakespeare's *As You Like It* (1599), which has been called the first romantic comedy, is almost presciently engaged with the cultural construction of gendered behaviour, and its production since the mid-twentieth century has swung among political positions from reactionary to feminist and queer readings.

*Satire may be considered a sly associate of comedy, which, while not necessarily adopting comic form, places an emphasis on caustic ridi-

cule. A dramatic text always harbours the possibility of addressing an audience in time, place, and culture through an expressive blueprint from another era. Plays like *Jonson's *Volpone* (1605) and *Molière's *Tartuffe* (1664, revised 1669) provided scathingly comic views of their societies, and have continued to support up-to-the-minute exposés of human venality and gullibility in subsequent performances.

Comedy as Westerners know it remains undeniably a cultural construct, deriving from European form and practice. Non-Western textual traditions, of course, also have time-honoured places for humour and comic irony, even though one would be mistaken in presuming a universal application of the Western template for comedy. Classical Sanskrit drama, rooted in the sacred texts and lore of India, includes forms that adopt comic themes, and otherwise avail of a jester figure; classical Chinese drama includes the *chou* (clown) as one of its four main role types. Classical Japanese drama has *kyōgen, a short comic form based on simple humorous situations meant to contrast with the seriousness of *nō drama. More recently, playwrights like *Soyinka and *Walcott treat the daily concerns and socio-cultural types of their respective African and Caribbean audiences with humour, despite differences from Western practice in their dramatic heritages. It might also be said that a vital aspect of comedy's spirit resides in the figure of the Trickster, a mischievous, nihilistic, shape-shifting, boldly playful persona found in folk traditions and mythologies around the world.   EW

commedia dell'arte The term we use for this form of theatre (which means simply 'professional *comedy') occurs late in its history. It is first found in a play by *Goldoni 1750, refering to the 'masked comedy', 'improvised comedy' or even simply 'Italian comedy' which had been in existence since the mid-sixteenth century. The precise origins of *commedia dell'arte* in Italy are not well documented: the earliest surviving company contract dates from 1545, and the earliest record of actresses appearing in public from 1548. By the 1560s there were already Italian *touring companies with female stars; by the 1570s troupes were visiting England, France, and Spain; and in 1589, during the landmark festivities for a Florentine granducal wedding, the improvisations of the *Gelosi company were given equal status with a scripted humanist *commedia erudita* ('learned' or 'erudite comedy'). For a couple of generations, the most celebrated performers and troupes won patronage in Florence, Mantua, and Turin, and commercial *audiences in Venice and throughout the peninsula. A military and economic crisis of 1630 ended the most glorious period of the genre in Italy; after that the best performers tended to go to France, to the *Comédie Italienne.

Although there may have been some input into *commedia dell'arte* from folk narrative and drama, its most important inspiration was the plot material of recent upper-class *commedia erudita*, together with its narrative stereotypes. The categorized distribution of roles in a standard company is enough to make this clear. The 'old men' (Vecchi)—usually Pantalone and the Dottore—were the miserly, lustful or pedantic fathers whose intentions were frustrated by the Lovers (Innamorati), and by the latter-day scheming *Plautine slaves (Servi), whose myriad names included Zani, Arlecchino, Brighella, Truffaldino, Pedrolino, and the female Franceschina and Colombina. A blustering but ultimately cowardly Capitano might be a free mover in the plot, usually a 'blocking' character like the old fathers, but sometimes allowed to be a lover. The solution to the intrigue was provided by a mixture of successful trickery and the discovery of lost family relationships. Every one of these elements—taken from *Roman comedy and from medieval novellas—was first dramatized and made familiar in *neoclassical comedy for courts and academies. The professionals simply stole them, fragmented them, turned them into a repertoire of permutable building blocks, and performed them in their own way. This involved three characteristics in particular: *masks, multilingualism, and *improvisation.

The use of facial half-masks by certain of the stereotypes (Vecchi and Servi, but not Innamorati and not always Capitani) may have helped to dictate an energetic and more visual performing style among the comic roles; and physical comedy, with mime and gesture, clearly helped the genre to be exportable. Even more important, however, is the very concept of a 'mask'—whether actually masked or not—as a permanent theatrical or fictional figure which the genre could constantly reuse, and which acquired a life of its own. In Italy the masks were identified not only by their *costume, but by their language—underlining the fact that this was verbal, as well as visual, comedy. Pantalone had to speak Venetian, the Dottore Bolognese, and the servants a Lombard dialect indicating up-country Bergamo, the homeland of the original *Zanni. (The initially French mask of *Harlequin became linguistically assimilated to the other male servants.) A Capitano was usually Spanish; whereas the Innamorati always spoke high-flown literary Tuscan. Later masks such as Tartaglia and Pulcinella brought in southern Ital-

ian dialects. Multilingualism was a feature which inevitably faded when performers went abroad; but within Italy it persisted through to Goldoni's time. Rather than supplying social *realism it rapidly became self-referential, providing an instantly recognizable comic badge for each relevant mask. Initially, the confrontation between Pantalone and Zani had alluded to a north Italian social reality. Later, Pantalone, Arlecchino, Pierrot, and Columbine (in all languages) had become the people's foolish but indestructible *heroes, taking on the fixed imaginative role since usurped by characters from animated cartoons. The stories in which they participated often had a cartoon-like implausibility.

The most obvious feature of all, however, was the practice of improvising on an outline *scenario instead of memorizing a written script. This may have been passed down from a first generation of illiterate *actors; though its permanent adoption is likely to have been commercially motivated, since it vastly increased the number of apparently different items which a company could offer. At all events, the technique won amazement and admiration, and became the defining characteristic of Comédie Italienne. The technique had little to do with the *improvisation practised by modern actors and drama students. Rather than a free use of the performer's imagination, aiming at innovation and stretching the creative faculties, it involved the memorization and redeployment of a huge amount of repertoire material. Actors specialized in a single mask, for which they 'learned their part' over a whole career, constantly accumulating in their commonplace books collections of jokes, speeches, and verbal routines in whatever language or dialect was appropriate. Much of this material was taken from written sources, just as the plots were cannibalized from written plays. Thus the majority of the material delivered in oral performance—details of which, by definition, scholars can never entirely recover—is likely to have been memorized in advance, in snippets and fragments, like the routine of a modern stand-up comedian. Naturally each single entertainment was leavened every time by genuine ad libs, by acknowledgements of the particular place and occasion, and (in the *audience's eyes) by an increase in the element of danger which always underlies live performance. But if this was theatrical acrobatics, it was performed with a safety-net: actors always knew where they were going, within a brief gag or within the plot as a whole. They were guided and constrained by constant mental and physical rehearsal, and by the directions of the scenario which told them what had to happen, and what had to be mentioned, in each scene. Preconceived *lazzi*, on a large scale or small, might figure as self-contained digressions, but also as components which actually advanced the plot.

The introduction of female performers was something else and their acceptance by society remains a mystery when one considers the formidable prejudices involved. Women who displayed themselves were assumed to be sexually immoral. It is probable, though not provable, that the earliest actresses were in fact high-class courtesans, who in any case learned a range of verbal accomplishments to entertain clients in their salons, including improvisation both of verse and of music. The rise of the actress may be inseparable from that of the *operatic prima donna. The virtuously married Isabella *Andreini worked hard to dispel the prejudice that she, at least, was a 'public woman'; and the emergence of theatrical family dynasties, similar to those in other artisan trades or *arti*, did modify the image. However, assumptions about sexual freedom continued in perception and in practice, and in the Papal States female performers of any kind were banned well into the eighteenth century. Nevertheless, their use spread from Italy to the rest of Europe, with England holding out until after the Restoration.

Since the 'texts' of *commedia dell'arte* were oral rather than written, their detailed content and tone remains very much a matter for speculation. Some seventeenth-century playscripts from both France and Italy, including those of *Molière, offer some clues as to how the 'modular' structures of improvised *dialogue, and the stock material of *monologues by individual masks, influenced subsequent comic dramatists who wanted to produce an analogous effect. Scenarios which have survived show that the emphasis of improvised theatre was indeed on comedy, leaving *tragedy and *pastoral more often to fully composed scripts. However, the plots of many comedies tend also to draw on the emotionally charged and picaresque formats of *tragicomedy: this leaves us in some permanent doubt as to how far, and how often, some roles—in particular those of the Innamorati—were played for pathos rather than for laughs. In the end the form existed in a state of permanent overlap, not only between genres, but also between itself and any written theatrical format which had a proven audience appeal. Goldoni's term *commedia dell'arte*, with its reference to a trade guild, implies a 'professional' theatre which therefore also had always to remain 'commercial'.   RAA

commedia erudita See COMMEDIA DELL'ARTE.

community theatre A term with various meanings depending on nation and period. It has many functions—it can enable communities collectively to share experiences and retell their own histories; it can encourage participation in political debate; and it can be a tool for social inclusion, embracing sections of society that feel themselves to be marginalized. Community theatre is found in forms as diverse as the functions it serves, but they can be grouped into the following four broad types. (1) Professional theatre devised for its local community, drawing on and retelling its stories, performed in conventional theatre spaces, sometimes by *regional repertory theatres but more usually on *tour to community centres in the area. Other variations include theatre companies who take their productions to a wider geographical area, playing to 'communities of interest'. (2) Community plays. Stories about the history of a locality are researched, *devised, and enacted, drawing on professional but mainly amateur resources for the *acting, *directing, *stage management, and backstage work. (3) Community arts centres. Theatres or other venues with performance spaces become a focus for community activity of various kinds, not only drama. (4) In America the term more usually refers to nonprofessional groups, influenced by the *Little Theatre Movement, based in local communities whose productions are a focus of heightened community activity at certain times of the year and are frequently a source of local pride.   ARJ

company theatre See PARSI THEATRE.

Complicité, Theatre de *Touring English company founded in 1983 by Simon *McBurney, Annabel Arden, and Marcello Magni, based on the notion of complicity with the *audience. More a loose association of like-minded collaborators with McBurney at its centre than a *collective ensemble, Complicité has been extremely influential since the 1990s, embodying an approach to theatre that owes much to *mime and *physically oriented European performance traditions. Work ranges from theatrical adaptations of literary texts (*The Three Lives of Lucie Chabrol*, 1994, based on a story by John Berger), to reinterpretations of classic texts (*Brecht's *The Caucasian Chalk Circle*, 1996), and *devised pieces (*Mnemonic*, 1999). Whatever the source, Complicité's process is constant, and involves a collaborative approach to *rehearsal, the juxtaposition of different media, and the integration of image, *music, and text within an overall production concept. The company tours internationally, and has pioneered collaborations with building-based theatres (*Street of Crocodiles*, 1992, with the *National Theatre in London, and *Shu-kin*, 2008–09, with the Setagaya Public Theatre, Tokyo). Increasingly, Complicité sees itself as a changing group of practitioners, with a research and education as well as production focus.   SWL

concert party African popular theatre based on *improvisation.

In Ghana: the easiest way now for many in Accra to watch performances by Ghanaian concert parties is to attend regular weekend matinées at the National Theatre, very different from the cocoa storage sheds and run-down open-air cinemas which were the usual venues. In such places shows often started at 9 p.m. and might, by popular demand, continue until near dawn. The concert party tradition began to coalesce in the 1930s from a variety of ingredients (*see* JOHNSON, BOB). Operated as 'Trios', the popular entertainers were, in effect, small-scale businesses whose fortunes rose and fell with the local economy. Performers criss-crossed the country in unreliable vehicles in pursuit of paying *audiences which expected little in the way of *mise-en-scène and were highly demonstrative in their responses. The pattern that evolved was for an extended 'warm-up' in which contemporary, inherited, and religious music played, to be followed, once the audience had assembled, by a moralistic drama in which *slapstick, pathos, caricature, *female impersonators, and a wide variety of musical numbers all found a place.

In Togo: Widely practised in bars during weekends, the concert party is composed of three parts: a street parade, a *prologue of humorous stories and songs, and the main performance which lasts several hours. Comedy, buffoonery, and pathos are the essence of the show. The setting of the concert party is usually simple, and the main *characters are *clowns dressed in rags; and their performance is built on interaction with the spectators and a subtle play of identification and alienation with the characters and plot. The performance is enhanced by song and *dance, creating a generally festive atmosphere conducive to collective enjoyment and depending on audience participation. The characters are defined by their social status, representing social types among the common folk—the houseboy, the idler, the drunk, the unemployed, the prostitute—or embodying high functions such as chief, company director, rich merchant, or bank executive. Female characters are played by cross-dressed men, and each actor plays several roles.   JMG/SA trans. JCM

Condell, Henry (fl. 1598–1627) English actor, a long-standing member the *Chamberlain's Men and its successor. A shareholder in the *Globe and *Blackfriars *playhouses, Condell edited the First Folio of Shakespeare's plays with John *Heminges (1623). During Condell's long career he performed in many plays, including *Jonson's *Every Man in his Humour*, *Webster's *The Duchess of Malfi*, and *Marston's *The Malcontent*. Like Shakespeare he was financially successful, and left a sizeable number of properties in London and environs.   SPC

confidant As the formal style of French *neoclassical *tragedy developed in the early seventeenth century, the retinues attached to royal or princely *characters tended to be reduced to a single confidant. Such characters were usually passive recipients of the *protagonist's hopes, fears, and projects in affairs of state or matters of the heart; when they offer advice, and particularly when that advice is harmful (for instance the case of Narcisse, Néron's adviser in *Racine's *Britannicus*), the label confidant ceases to be appropriate.   WDH

Confrérie de la Passion A religious and philanthropic fraternity of Parisian merchants and artisans which in 1402 was granted a monopoly on the production of religious drama. In 1548, its licence to perform *mystères sacrés* was revoked, but it continued to perform secular plays. At the same time it built the *Hôtel de Bourgogne where it staged plays until 1597, when it relinquished the responsibility in favour of acting simply as landlord. Between 1442 and 1597 the Confrérie had a cooperative arrangement with the Basochiens, who were responsible for comic performances.   RWV

Congreve, William (1670–1729) English playwright. Raised in Ireland, a graduate of Trinity College, Dublin, his first play appeared in London in 1693. Congreve's reputation as the foremost writer of Restoration comedy of manners rests on five plays, an unusually small output for the period. His first *comedy, *The Old Bachelor* (1693), underwent revisions by *Dryden and *Southerne before performance at *Drury Lane. Anne *Bracegirdle and Elizabeth *Barry contributed to its huge success and Congreve's subsequent plays were written specifically for them. *The Double Dealer* (1694) was not received with the same enthusiasm but Congreve threw his lot in with Barry, Bracegirdle, and *Betterton when they broke away from Drury Lane in 1695. The new company at *Lincoln's Inn Fields opened with *Love for Love* (1695), which ran for thirteen consecutive days, a highly successful run at the time. This was followed by Congreve's only *tragedy, *The Mourning Bride* (1697). Success attracted fierce criticism from the *anti-theatrical lobby, which accused Congreve of promoting immorality, charges which the playwright vociferously rebutted in counter-publications. This public war of words may have contributed to the comparative failure of his last comedy *The Way of the World* (1700)—a play that has attracted more revivals in the twentieth century than almost any other Restoration comedy. In 1707 Congreve was briefly involved in the *management of the *Haymarket Theatre with fellow playwright *Vanbrugh, but wrote no new plays.   GBB

conjuring *See* MAGIC SHOWS.

Conklin, John (1937–) American designer. Conklin began designing at Yale in the 1950s, where he studied with *Oenslager. Ten summers at Williamstown Theatre Festival and an early affiliation with Hartford Stage Company led to a career as one of the USA's most influential postmodern designers for theatre and *opera. Seen at most leading *regional theatres and at major opera houses in the USA and Europe, his abstract sets feature stunning imagery, a dynamic imbalance, quotations from art history, and the incorporation of the random or accidental. He collaborated with such major directors as Jonathan *Miller, *Akalaitis, and Robert *Wilson. In the 1990s, while still busy as a designer, he took up artistic staff positions at Glimmerglass Opera and City Opera in New York, promoting the migration of leading theatre directors, designers, and even playwrights into opera.   STC

Connelly, Marc (1890–1980) American playwright and director. Connelly amassed a sizeable body of work before writing *The Green Pastures*, for which he was awarded the Pulitzer Prize in 1930. He co-wrote ten plays and *musicals with *Kaufman between 1921 and 1924. Most notable were *Dulcy* (1921) and *To the Ladies!* (1922), both *satires of jingoistic business culture; a film industry *satire, *Merton of the Movies* (1922); and *Beggar on Horseback* (1924), a dream play which adapted *expressionism as a technique for satire of American business. Connelly's whimsical imagination seemed a suitable foil for Kaufman's biting irony. *The Green Pastures* was adapted from Roark Bradford's *Ol' Man Adam an' his Chillun*, a loose retelling of biblical stories in the supposed idiom of rural *African Americans. Connelly's play, which he directed, interweaves comic scenes with hymn-singing and a serious religious purpose. Despite criticism from African-American

intellectuals such as Langston *Hughes, the play was extraordinarily popular, running on Broadway for 640 performances, *touring for three years, then returning to New York for an additional 71 performances in 1935.   MAF

Conquest family English actors, *managers, and dramatists whose family name was originally Oliver. **Benjamin Oliver** (1804–72), a low comedian, managed the ill-fated Garrick Theatre from 1830 until it was destroyed by fire in 1846. He took over the Grecian Theatre in 1851, establishing a reputation for extravagant *pantomimes. His son **George Augustus Conquest** (1837–1901) was the *acrobatic draw, as the Spider Crab or the Grim Goblin, taking over management from his father in 1872, and in 1881 gaining the Surrey Theatre. There he collaborated with dramatists Paul Merritt and Henry Pettitt in writing highly successful spectacular *melodramas such as *Mankind* (1881). His son **George Benjamin Conquest** (1858–1926) specialized in giant roles, and took over the Surrey until 1904. Sons **Fred** (1871–1941) and **Arthur** (1875–1945) were famous animal impersonators.   AF

constructivism Artistic movement that flourished in Soviet Russia during the 1920s, which sought to bring art into public spaces, linking its materials and processes with those of industrial production and construction. First attempts to apply constructivist *scenography in the theatre were made at *Tairov's Kamerny Theatre by the designer *Ekster, with sets of varying levels for Annensky's *Thamira Kitharides* (1916), *Wilde's *Salome* (1917), and Shakespeare's *Romeo and Juliet* (1921). Aleksandr Vesnin produced an abstract setting of cubist-style levels for *Racine's *Phèdre* in 1922, and a gantry-style construction with working elevators for *The Man Who Was Thursday* (1926), both at the Kamerny, where the Stenberg brothers also produced constructivist settings for *Ostrovsky's *The Thunderstorm* (1924) and *O'Neill's *Desire under the Elms* (1926).

Meanwhile Vladimir Dmitriev designed a setting of geometrical components for *Meyerhold's production of Verhaeren's *Dawns*, in 1920, and *Popova built an 'acting machine' for Meyerhold's famous 1922 production of *The Magnanimous Cuckold*, whose moving parts also exploited the kinetic properties of constructivist work. Viktor Shestakov created a spiral staircase and walkway for Meyerhold's version of Ostrovsky's *A Lucrative Post* (1922) as well as an 'urbanist' construction of moving walkways and working lifts for a production of Faiko's *Lake*

Lyul. Meyerhold designed a constructivist setting for his production of Ostrovsky's *The Forest*, the principles of which were also applied to the text, which was taken apart and reassembled in 33 segments like machine components. Aleksander Rodchenko produced a constructivist setting for *Mayakovsky's *satire *The Bedbug*, staged by Meyerhold in 1929, while his *The Bathhouse* the following year had a design by Sergei Vakhtangov for the final scene that was somewhat reminiscent of Tatlin's unrealized Monument to the Third International. By that time constructivist practice was under official attack and was soon supplanted by more orthodox forms of staging.   NW

Contat, Louise-Françoise (1760–1813) and **Marie-Émilie** (1771–1846) French actresses. Louise made her debut at the *Comédie-Française in 1776 and quickly made her mark in high *comedy: her nickname was 'Thalie' (the Muse of Comedy). Although notable in *Molière, as Célimène (*The Misanthrope*) and Elmire (*Tartuffe*), she achieved celebrity status as the original Suzanne in *Beaumarchais's *The Marriage of Figaro* in 1784. Later that year, at *Figaro's* 51st performance, 13-year-old Émilie ('Mimi') joined the cast, as Fanchette. Mimi was formally admitted to the Comédie in 1785. Self-effacingly content to see her elder sister graduate from Beaumarchais to *Marivaux, Mimi remained for 32 years playing soubrettes. For their royalist sympathies the sisters were imprisoned in 1793. Narrowly escaping the guillotine, they rejoined the reconstituted Comédie-Française in 1799, Louise retiring in 1813 and Mimi two years later.   JG

Cooke, George Frederick (1756–1812) English actor, one of the most exciting performers of the *romantic era. Unlike his famous colleague John Philip *Kemble, Cooke eschewed stateliness and dignity in favour of energy and the powerful expression of malice and duplicity. He was most famous for his *villains, including Richard III, Shylock, and Pierre in *Otway's *Venice Preserv'd*, a role he altered into calculating hypocrite. Even in *comedy he excelled as Sir Pertinax MacSycophant in *The Man of the World* and Sir Archy MacSarcasm in *Love à la Mode*, both by *Macklin. Cooke favoured a natural style that emphasized the psychological life of the *character. He spent the first half of his career mostly on the provincial stage and began regular London engagements at *Covent Garden only in 1800. A lifelong battle with alcoholism affected his work and began to alienate *audiences. He became the first major British actor to perform in the United States, opening in New York in 1810, where he died two years later.   MJK

Cooke, T. P. (Thomas Potter) (1786–1864) English actor. The *hero of nautical *melodramas, and the archetypal British tar, Cooke's most famous roles were those of Long Tom Coffin in *Fitzball's *The Pilot* (1825) and William in *Jerrold's *Black-Ey'd Susan* (1829). As Harry Hallyard in J. T. Haines's *My Poll and my Partner Joe* (1835) he played a Thames waterman in the first act and, after being press-ganged into the navy, a heroic sailor on HMS *Polyphemus*, where he danced a double hornpipe, fought the captain of a slave ship, was heartbroken when he came home, and then made happy again. He took his nautical type casting very seriously, and frequently went into society in *costume, or at least wearing a naval medal. In a conversation with the Prime Minister, Lord Aberdeen, he was energetic in his opinions about reforms in the navy and suggested, 'If your Lordship likes to see what a real tar was, and what a real tar ought to be, come across the water some night... and see me as William in *Black-eyed Susan'.   AF

Copeau, Jacques (1879–1949) French director and *manager, considered the father of modern French theatre. He began as author and critic and was co-founder in 1908 of the influential *Nouvelle Revue française*. In 1913 he set up his own company, the Théâtre du Vieux-Colombier on the Left Bank in Paris. His aim was the renovation of theatre through a rejection of both the spectacular and the *naturalistic, through a focus on 'the beautiful, the good, and the true'. His reformation required a new actor-centred method with the long-term goal of creating a body of dramatic literature, since the reforms of the end of the nineteenth century carried out by *Antoine, among others, had left few plays of lasting merit. But first the company focused on Shakespeare and the French classics. Copeau also set up a model for training which broadened *acting to include the study of *masking, gymnastics, and general culture.

During the First World War the company decamped to New York, bringing its most notable success, *Twelfth Night*. Upon return in 1920 they played in the Vieux-Colombier, now remodelled to resemble an Elizabethan *playhouse, and designed to purify the theatre in a 'bare boards' approach in which *costume and *lighting were the principal signifiers. In 1924 a personal crisis— both an illness and a sense of isolation—led Copeau to decamp once again, this time to the Burgundian village of Pernand-Vergelesses, where he and his actors farmed for their sustenance while recouping their artistic and intellectual strength. Between 1925 and 1929, Les Copiaux *toured to great acclaim. Copeau's subsequent career included lectures, a spell at the helm of the *Comédie-Française (1940–1), and an influential essay *Le Théâtre populaire* (1941), which provided the template for the decentralization movement after the Second World War.   BRS

Copi (Raúl Damonte) (1939–87) Argentinian playwright, performer, and director. After staging his first play in Buenos Aires, Copi moved to Paris in 1962. Known for his irreverent *Le Nouvel Observateur* cartoon strips, 'Montmartre's transvestite' wrote and performed in France, Italy, and Spain. Copi's dozen plays (including his solos, *Loretta Strong* and *The Refrigerator*) take place in a hyperreal space. Their exuberant value inversions were especially amplified by fellow Argentinian expatriate Jorge *Lavelli, who directed five works, including *The Homosexual; or, The Difficulty of (S)expressing Oneself* (1971), *The Four Twins* (1973), and *An Inopportune Visit* (1987). The première of *Eva Perón* (1970) encountered violent response when right-wing Peronist sympathizers attacked cast members, including the male actor playing Evita, outside L'Épée-de-Bois theatre. Although several of Copi's plays have recently been produced in Buenos Aires, *Eva Perón* remains unstaged in its author's native country.   JGJ

copyright The exclusive legal right to prevent others from reproducing the creations of visual artists, writers, composers, choreographers, playwrights, film makers, broadcasters, and recording studios.

What copyright protects A copyright gives its owner a monopoly over the copying and performing of protected works. These works may include original creations from a statutory list of forms, regardless of artistic merit. Originality is the fundamental requirement for copyright protection. Thus, different artists, using the same or different mediums of expression, may recast the basic story of Ulysses or of the Nutcracker, since copyright protects the original expression of ideas, not the ideas themselves.

The history of dramatic copyright can be traced to ancient *Greece and the *Roman Empire, where writers were outspoken in their concern for receiving credit as the creators of their works. Over the centuries the emphasis for protection gradually shifted from the artistic or moral interests of creators to the economic interests of those who had invested in the commercialization of a work, aided to a great degree by the invention of the printing press. The commercial interests of publishers first received protection under the laws of England in 1534, which later adopted the first relevant statute, the Copyright Act of 1710. Early copyright statutes only protected literary works, but legal protection for the commercial interests in artistic works was firmly established as a general legal principle by the time of the founding of the United States, which expressly acknowledged in its Constitution protection for 'writings', a term that has been expanded to include 'any physical rendering of the fruits of creative, intellectual or aesthetic labour'. The first international treaty seeking to guarantee the rights of authors, the Berne Convention, came into effect after 1886.

In order to be protected, a work must be fixed in some permanent form. Like literary works, dramatic works must be original in their expression in order for copyright to apply, and must also be capable of being physically performed. Until the later half of the twentieth century, choreographed works of pure dance were not protected by copyright. Amendments to most national copyright statutes and to international treaties now provide choreography with the same protection as literary and dramatic works.

Any original graphic work, photograph, sculpture, collage, architectural work, or work of 'artistic craftsmanship' may be protected by copyright if the creation exhibits a minimum of skill, judgement, and labour, irrespective of the work's artistic quality. Thus a child's finger painting is as potentially protectable as a painting by Jackson Pollock. In the context of theatrical productions, copyrights might apply to backdrops painted by *Picasso or to playbill covers painted by Marc Chagall. It should be noted that a photograph of a performance has separate copyright protection. So long as others could not copy the performance from the photograph alone, the photograph does not infringe any performance-based copyright. This would not be the case where a film is made of a performance. Because the film would be a reproduction of the performance, itself making further reproductions possible, it is capable of infringing the rights embodied in a performance and different rules apply.

Cinema represents the first of the technology-driven variations on copyright protection. Until the 1990s the original copyright owner in a film, its 'author' in the context of a dramatic work, was considered to be the film's producer, as representative of the financial and administrative interests involved in film production, rather than the director of the film, the person with artistic control.

Now that copyright ownership is shared equally by its producers and directors, a compromise between commercial and artistic considerations. Broadcasts, cable-casts, and sound recordings are also capable of distinct copyright protection, though that protection is reduced in scope and term in comparison with a comparable live performance.

Scope and duration Copyright gives a limited amount of protection for a limited period of time against those who would exploit creative works without the permission of the creator. That protection comes in the form of the legal right to control the reproduction, distribution, first sale, and public performance of a work. For example, copyright ownership allows playwrights to control the copying of their scripts. It also gives film producers or directors the right to control the sales of videotaped copies of their films, and it allows composers to control the public performance of their musical compositions.

In most cases, the creator of the underlying work and the owner of the copyright are the same person, at least initially. An exception occurs when an artist creates something that is to be included in a larger work, in which case, if the commissioning contract specifies, the creation will be considered 'a work for hire' and the commissioner the copyright owner. This is the usual case, for example, with film scriptwriters, who have been employed by producers and thus do not own the copyright to their work.

The unauthorized use of another's protected creation is an infringement of the copyright in that creation. Infringement may be of a primary or of a secondary nature. Primary infringement is the unauthorized reproduction, in whole or in part, of the work of another. Dealing in unauthorized copies of a protected work is a secondary infringement of the copyright.

The copyright also allows its owner to control the public performance of the work. The performance rights, inherent in copyright protection, include the broadcasting, cable-casting, live performance, and the playing of a recorded performance of a protected work. Like infringement through copying, the infringement of performance rights may be divided into primary and secondary infringements.

There are exceptional uses of copyright-protected material that are not infringements when done without permission. A limited number of copies may be made of copyrighted works if those copies are to be used for private study, for instruction, examination, or performance in schools, or for inclusion in the collections of some libraries and archives. Other exceptions exist for news reporting, use in a criticism or review of the protected work, copies made under licence from a collective-licensing authority, retransmission by cable-cast of a broadcast, and in similar limited uses.

The copyright protection for new films, literary, artistic, dramatic, and musical works lasts for all of the creator's life and for an additional 70 years in most countries. This is an increase from a term of protection that existed throughout most of the twentieth century of 50 years after the life of the creator. Sound recordings, broadcasts, and cable-casts are protected for 50 years from the making of the recording or its first release or from the date of first transmission. Once the period of copyright protection ends, a work becomes part of the public domain, the cultural resource of society, and may be copied or performed by anyone, as is the case with the novels of *Dickens, the paintings of Caravaggio, and the plays of Shakespeare.

Formalities of protection and publication Under the laws of many countries, particularly those that are signatories of the Berne Convention, copyright protection arises automatically. A creator does not have to complete any formal registration or application requirements before the protection applies to the work. In all countries that have some form of copyright protection, especially those that subscribe to the Universal Copyright Convention, the marking of a published work with the symbol ©, the name of the creator, and the year the work was first published is sufficient to claim copyright protection. Many nations also provide a statutory scheme whereby creators can register their works through depositing a copy in a copyright depository, such as the British Library or the Library of Congress.

In a commercial sense, the copyright in a work is a collection of divisible rights, including the right to publish the work as a whole, in serialization, and in translation; the film rights, the performance rights in a dramatic work, and the right to dramatize a non-dramatic work; and the right to exploit electronic versions. The copyright owner may exploit each of these rights or all of them together, or, more commonly, the owner may confer them on others, either permanently or for a limited time. A licence of copyright is an agreement in which the copyright owner gives the licensee permission to exploit some or all of the rights of the owner for a limited time, usually in return for a fee, either in a single payment or as a portion of the income resulting from exploitation, called *royalties. An assignment of copyright is a permanent sale of some or all of the rights of the copyright owner.   TEH

Coquelin, Constant-Benoît (1841–1909) French actor. Coquelin made his debut at the *Comédie-Française in 1860, and became a *sociétaire* in 1864, having given an impressive performance as *Beaumarchais's Figaro in 1861. He soon became a leading member of the company, performing a wide range of *jeune premier* roles in the classical *comedy repertoire, and creating a number in contemporary plays by *Dumas *fils*, *Augier, and others. The desire to break out of the traditional repertoire at the Comédie, and also to have the freedom to undertake foreign *tours, led him to resign in 1886; in 1892 he moved to the Porte-Saint-Martin. The peak of his career was the creation of the title role written for him in *Rostand's *Cyrano de Bergerac* (1897), the most successful French play of the century. He played it over 400 times. He was to have performed in Rostand's *Chantecler* (1910) but died of a heart attack during *rehearsal. Coquelin was the author of two important books on *acting: *The Art of the Actor* (1880) and *Actors by an Actor* (1882).   WDH

Corneille, Pierre (1606–84) French playwright. Born in Normandy and trained as a lawyer, the elder Corneille was the most prolific and versatile of France's major seventeenth-century dramatists. Introduced to the theatre by *Montdory's itinerant company at Rouen, he saw his first play *Mélite*, a *comedy, played with success in Paris by Montdory in 1629. His *tragicomedy *Clitandre* (1631), a relative failure, was followed by four comedies, including *La Galerie du palais* (1632) and *La Place royale* (1633). Performed by Montdory at the *Marais, these illustrated the comedy of manners inaugurated by *Mélite*, which Corneille himself later defined as 'the portrayal of social intercourse among persons of good breeding'. This series was followed by his first *tragedy, *Médée* (1635), in which Corneille succeeded in making a sympathetic *heroine of the legendary sorceress Medea. Another sorcerer, Alcandre, presides as surrogate playwright over the comedy *L'Illusion comique* (*The Theatrical Illusion*, 1636), helping the hero Clindor, played by Montdory, to demonstrate that an acting career is not a source of shame to his bourgeois family, but of fame and glory. This imaginative work, which illustrates the range of current theatrical styles, regained favour in the twentieth century after lengthy neglect, and now ranks as one of Corneille's most stageworthy plays. It was followed by the tragicomedy *Le Cid* (1637), the author's most celebrated. Outstanding among the works of the talented playwrights of the 1630s, it presents the young Spanish hero Rodrigue, who triumphs over the Moors, but is forced to fight a duel in which he kills his beloved Chimène's father, who has insulted his own father. *Le Cid* stands at the very centre of the mid-century debate about genre (*see* NEOCLASSICISM; UNITIES). The 'quarrel of *Le Cid*' of 1637–40, while it did raise points of critical and theoretical interest, was largely an attack by vain and envious rivals, fuelled in part by Corneille's own oversensitive pride; Corneille himself had been recruited into the group of five playwrights who were commissioned to further the literary ambitions of *Richelieu but soon left, and the Cardinal's animosity may well have inspired some of the hostile criticism of *Le Cid*. By 1660, however, Corneille's position was much more assured: he had established his reputation as the author of a series of Roman tragedies, notably *Horace* (1640), *Cinna* (1641), *Polyeucte* (1642), *La Mort de Pompée* (1643), and *Nicomède* (1651), and he had been elected to the Académie Française in 1647. A break from the theatre between 1652 and 1659 was largely devoted to writing commentaries on his earlier plays, accompanied by three treatises on the theatre: the *Discours du poème dramatique*, *De la tragédie*, and *Des trois unités*. After *Le Menteur* (1643) and its inferior sequel, Corneille wrote no more comedies; however, in 1671 he turned to the spectacle-play, collaborating with *Molière in the 'tragédie-ballet' *Psyché* at the redesigned *Palais Royal. In his last years he was increasingly in competition with *Racine, their rivalry coming to a head in 1670 with simultaneous productions of Corneille's *Tite et Bérénice* at the Palais-Royal and Racine's *Bérénice* at the *Hôtel de Bourgogne. While fashionable opinion favoured Racine, Corneille maintained a following among an older generation of spectators. In his last play, the tragedy *Suréna* (1674) a neglected masterpiece—the hero's achievements are overshadowed by his resigned acceptance of death.

Throughout the eighteenth century, Corneille maintained his position alongside Racine as representing the outstanding achievement of seventeenth-century tragic theatre, with the acting profession, the theatregoing public, and playwrights like *Voltaire who continued to imitate Corneille's manner. In the nineteenth century, Corneille was championed as a 'reluctant' neoclassical dramatist, temperamentally closer to *Hugo and the other romantics than his rival Racine. More recently, while the *Comédie-Française continues to honour him by mounting an occasional production of *Horace*, *Polyeucte*, or *Nicomède*, much of his work has been mothballed, and enthusiasm tends to be reserved for the 'pre-classical' Corneille. Gérard *Philipe's revival of *Le Cid* at the *Avignon Festival (1951) and Georges Wilson's *Illusion comique* at the *Théâtre National Populaire (1965) provided two of the outstanding theatrical events of the early post-war period. WDH

Corneille, Thomas (1625–1709) French playwright. The younger brother of Pierre *Corneille, Thomas studied law but turned to the stage in his early twenties. Between 1647 and 1681 he wrote, alone or in collaboration, 46 plays, including four machine-plays (*see* SALLE DES MACHINES) and four *operas. Appointed co-editor of the periodical *Le Mercure galant* in 1681, and elected in place of Pierre to the Académie Française in 1684, Thomas devoted the remainder of his long life to work as a journalist, translator, and encyclopedist. As a dramatist, he was a follower rather than a setter of fashion, and although he achieved considerable contemporary success, few of his plays escape their historical moment. His most successful play, *Timocrate* (1656), reflected a current vogue for 'romanesque *tragedy', characterized by complex plots involving disguise and mistaken identity, and featuring gallant lovers in exotic settings. Later plays of note include *Ariane* (1672), *Le Comte d'Essex* (1678), and *Laodice* (1668). RWV

Cornell, Katharine (1898–1974) American actress and producer. Known for the dignity, intelligence, and articulation that she brought to her roles, Cornell shared with Helen *Hayes the title 'First Lady of the American Theatre'. Making her debut with the *Washington Square Players in 1916, she played a series of roles in *stock, and emerged as a leading player with a 1919 London production of *Little Women*. In 1921 she married *McClintic, who directed her productions after 1925. She starred in *Shaw's *Candida* in New York in 1924, a role so well suited that she revived it three times. Her breakthrough to Broadway commercial success was in *The Green Hat*, a 1925 *melodrama directed by McClintic. Elizabeth Barrett in *The Barretts of Wimpole Street* (1931) proved a defining role, revived four times. Critics saw her finest performances in serious work with McClintic: Juliet (1934), Shaw's St Joan (1936), Masha in *Chekhov's *Three Sisters* (1942), Antigone (1946), and Cleopatra (1947). Cornell last appeared as Mrs Patrick *Campbell in *Dear Liar* (1959–60). MAF

Cornish rounds *Medieval theatre in Cornwall was performed in 'the round'—the *action took place in an open round space surrounded by several *sedes* (scaffolds or mansions) representing the location of specific scenes. For example, the stage diagram for the first day of the *Ordinalia* specifies the *sedes* (clockwise from the east) as *Heaven, Bishop, Abraham, Solomon, David, Pharaoh, *Hell (in the north), and Torturers. For the episodes performed on the next two days all but the *sedes* for Heaven and Hell changed according to the requirements of the script. Unlike wagon staging, this convention had the effect of keeping the cosmic struggle between Heaven and Hell constantly before the *audience who sat around the periphery of the *platea* or 'place', a formation similar to the stage design for the fifteenth-century *morality play, *The Castle of Perseverance*. The round structure with a castle in the centre seems to have been created for *Castle* whenever it was performed, but the Cornish practitioners used earthworks, sometimes pre-existing, sometimes custom-built, to create open-air amphitheatres. AFJ

Corpus Christi plays The feast of Corpus Christi (body of Christ), which falls on the Thursday of the octave of Pentecost (between 21 May and 24 June), was established as part of late *medieval eucharistic devotion. Though Pope Urban IV authorized the feast in 1264, it did not achieve universal acceptance in the Western Church until it was established by Pope Clement V in 1311. The oldest surviving text of a Corpus Christi play, dated some time after 1360, comes from Orvieto in Italy and dramatizes a miracle of the host. The words 'The plaie called Corpus Christi' are written in a sixteenth-century hand at the beginning of the manuscript of the *N-Town Plays* from East Anglia. The manuscript contains plays covering all of salvation history from Creation to Doomsday. The most complete records for any English civic drama come from York, where an episodic play dramatizing salvation history was performed in procession. Until the third quarter of the fifteenth century the play and the procession honouring the Real Presence of Christ both took place on the feast of Corpus Christi, which led some scholars to assume that all *biblical plays depicted salvation history and were performed on that day in procession.

We now know that the nature of the presentations varied widely. Plays performed were frequently episodic biblical plays but more commonly modelled on the twelve clauses of the Apostles' Creed. The York salvation history play is the only text to survive in England that dramatizes the complete Creation, Redemption, and Judgement pattern that was performed on Corpus Christi day. Such complete sequences were commonly performed on Corpus Christi in the German-speaking countries, however, especially in the southern areas near the Swiss border. But smaller plays on other subjects were also performed on the feast day.

A more universal practice on Corpus Christi was the presentation of intricate *tableaux vivants as part of the procession honouring the eucharistic host. Elaborate processions with small dramas embedded in them took place in Bologna, Turin, and Toledo. In Britain several towns had processions with pageants. Among the most elaborate was one at Hereford that had 23 separate scenes depicting biblical events followed by three apparently unrelated tableaux of Pilate, Annas, and Caiphas with Mahound; knights in harness; and St Catherine and her torturers. In Bristol the craft guilds carried 'pageants' in the Corpus Christi procession, in Dublin the procession included Arthur and his knights and the Nine Worthies, and the one in Lanark in Scotland included St George and the dragon.

Corpus Christi Day was one of the two favourite summer feast days occasioning various processions and playmaking. Pentecost or Whitsun (which is also a movable feast and falls eleven days before Corpus Christi) was the time for many parish and village festivals and of the processional play in Chester. In Florence, the feast day of St John the Baptist (24 June), the city's patron, was celebrated by a procession and a sequence of plays from the Old and New Testaments, which after 1428 did not include the *Passion. Two more secular feast days filled out the summer festive calendar, particularly in England: May Day and Midsummer. In northern Europe in the period between mid-May and the end of June—after planting and before harvest—the weather would allow outdoor playmaking and revelry. But it is misleading to single out the feast of Corpus Christi for special significance. Different towns and parishes chose different festivals to present their traditional plays and entertainments, and each must be considered a unique event. *See also* MYSTERY PLAYS.   AFJ

corrales de comedias Public 'play yards' or *playhouses of *early modern Spain, also called *patios* or *casas de *comedias*. Some 50 at least were opened all over the country between about 1560 and 1680. Some were short-lived, others were rebuilt, but a number survived into the eighteenth century. The largest cities, Madrid and Seville, had two or three. Valladolid possibly had a playhouse by 1560, Seville and Madrid probably before 1570 and certainly in 1574, Toledo from 1576, and at least twenty other cities by 1610.

Most were founded by charitable brotherhoods (*cofradías*) or municipalities and the proceeds were generally used to subsidize hospitals. Relatively few were privately owned, though a number were leased and run by entrepreneurs. The largest held up to 2,000 people, possibly more. Typically the actors and the *management each collected a standard entrance charge, with further payments to the management for seating. The plays of Lope de *Vega, Tirso de *Molina, and *Calderón were normally first performed in one of the Madrid *corrales*, and later in cities and towns.

Unlike the English *public theatres, Spanish *corrales* were virtually never free-standing. They were usually installed in yards within blocks of houses, or occasionally in a hospital or an inn (*Almagro), often near the town centre, with entry through buildings adjoining the yard, which sometimes provided viewing spaces on upper floors. Most were rectangular, and all had a roofed thrust stage projecting from a tiring house (*vestuario*). At the sides of the yard there was usually raked seating (*gradas*); above them, along the sides and back of the yard and beside the stage, were two or three tiers of *boxes or galleries. All these were roofed but the yard itself was usually open air. It was normally occupied by standing groundlings (*mosqueteros*), but there was often some seating and occasionally the yard was largely filled with chairs or benches. Women had a separate entrance and were normally confined to the *cazuela* ('stewpot'), a large gallery usually at the back of the yard. Two *corrales* still survive, in *Alcalá de Henares and Almagro. *See also* CRUZ, CORRAL DE LA; PRÍNCIPE, CORRAL DEL.   CD

Corrêa, José Celso Martinez (1937–) Brazilian director. Also known as Zé Celso, Corrêa was one of the most creative forces in Brazilian theatre and a founder of Oficina Theatre in São Paulo (1958, reorganized as Uzina Uzona in 1971). In the 1960s his productions were important cultural responses to the dictatorship. His irreverent, transgressive *The Candle King* (1967) was a catalyst for cultural protest, as were his fine adaptations of *Brecht (for example, *Galileo*, 1968), allegories that attacked authoritarian repression. His theatre of aggression reached an apex with *Fast Track* (1968), in which the cast ate the 'live' liver of a dismembered rock star, tossing bits at the public. Although he has been attracted to a wide range of texts (*Genet, *Artaud, *Euripides, *Chekhov, Shakespeare), his approach has tended to the carnivalesque, including overtly homosexual pairings, scatology (such as freshly produced faeces), and general sexual euphoria. LHD

Cossa, Roberto Mario ('Tito') (1934-) One of Argentina's most important dramatists and screenwriters, Cossa has delved deeply into the failure of the country's middle class. Unlike his early plays, such as *Our Weekend* (1964) and *The Days of Julián Bisbal* (1966), which approached an almost *documentary *realism, the collaboratively written *The Black Airplane* (1970) was a biting socio-political *satire about Perón's anticipated comeback. Cossa returned to the theatre seven years later with *The Granny*, a long-running grotesque whose *protagonist symbolized the blind, destructive forces seizing the nation. In later plays such as *The Old Man-Servant* (1980) and *The Grey of Absence* (1981), Cossa mixed formal experimentation with such concrete cultural elements as the tango. By the mid-1980s his focus shifted to the historical and cultural circumstances conditioning middle-class failure, as in *Hand and Foot* (1984), *Gepetto* (1987), *Angelito* (1991), and *The Quack* (1999). Cossa's plays, purposefully local in dialect, cultural referent, and *character type, defy easy translation; with the notable exception of *The Granny*, few have been produced outside the Spanish-speaking world.JGJ

Costantini family Italian actors who built their reputations abroad in the seventeenth and eighteenth centuries. The most famous was **Angelo** (*c*.1654–1729), son of the Veronese cloth merchant Costantino who married an actress and then entered the profession, coming to Paris in the 1680s. Angelo made all his own the liveried servant mask of Mezzettino: on the death of Dominique *Biancolelli in 1688 he eventually preferred to stay with his own role, rather than stepping into Biancolelli's shoes. After the dismissal of the Italian troupe in 1697, he moved to Germany and Poland: his son Gabriele and others of the family performed all over Europe. *See* COMÉDIE ITALIENNE. RAA

costume Distinctive clothing for individuals or groups of performers, a visual presentation of *character or idea through clothed physical appearance. Disguising the human form in natural materials—feathers, furs, and vegetation—was used by early humans when preparing for ceremonies and *rituals. An individual became extraordinary, or was subsumed into an undifferentiated group, by using costumes, make-up, *masks, and wigs. Portable and adaptable, in performance the colours, fabrics, textures, and scale of costume signified roles, skills, or other identities which conveyed direct or symbolic messages.

Early European Evidence of costume practice between 500 BC and AD 1500 is patchy. We know the competitive nature of *Greek theatre and the large, open-air *theatron placed demands upon physical visibility. Much visual characterization was provided by masks, but costumes had to differentiate between *actors and the *chorus. In *tragedy the latter wore garments which reflected their nationality and/or role; in *comedy costumes and masks identified birds, clouds, wasps, as in *Aristophanes. Actors in tragedy wore variants of everyday garments, a full-length *chiton* but with the addition of sleeves, not a usual feature of Greek dress, and a long or short cloak. The garments were coloured and patterned so that the overall effect was of reality rendered larger than life. Comic characters were distinguished by broad exaggeration. Grotesques wore short, loose *chitons* with body padding and a long, protuberant *phallus.

Roman actors wore costume and masks appropriate to character in the Greek style, though with more exaggeration for tragedy. The dominant imperial architecture demanded massive, if less mobile performers. Comedy, *mime, and *pantomime acquired specific costumes: Apuleius' second-century account of a pantomime about the Judgement of Paris recorded that Paris was dressed 'after the likeness of a Phrygian herdsman, with barbaric mantle streaming from his shoulders, a fair tunic about his body, and a turban of gold on his head', Mercury was naked apart from 'the stripling's cloak that covered his left shoulder', and Venus' costume was 'a robe of thinnest silk which...clung to her and outlined...the charms of her fair limbs'.

The Christian Church denounced this type of decadence, but in the middle ages realized that performances on great feast days could provide instructive entertainment. The clothing of the clergy became, at its highest levels, as sumptuous as that of the imperial court in Byzantium. Towering headdresses and layers of richly ornamental robes impressed congregations with their ritualistic theatricality. *Liturgical dramas used garments distinguished by emblematic devices and symbolic colours, as in *Hildegard of Bingen's late 1140s allegory *Order of Virtues*. In the twelfth-century *Jeu d'Adam*, Christ was clothed in a dalmatic, Adam in a red tunic (red symbolized the blood of Christ and implicitly truth and justice), and Eve in a 'woman's garment' of white with a white silk headdress.

For the later *biblical plays, illuminated manuscripts, paintings, sculptures, stained glass, and tapestries provide some evidence of dress. The Three Kings and Herod offered opportunities for exotic costumes and headdresses, an orientalism informed by the mementoes of crusaders, merchants, and sailors. Devils and imps developed from frightening into comic figures covered in black hair or feathers, their faces disguised by grotesque masks. The records for the Smiths' guild in Coventry show that between 1449 and 1585 they regularly bought fabric for costumes, had them repaired, and hired a dress for Pilate's wife in 1490. Emblematic devices of nails, dice, and hammers crowned with thorns identified Christ's tormentors; Caiaphas and Annas wore bishops' mitres to signify their exalted religious roles, and both Christ and Peter had gilt wigs.

Early modern The rediscovery of classical art and literature in the fifteenth century, and an interest in humanism, found manifestation in the themes, designs, and costumes for triumphal *entries, pageants, and courtly entertainments throughout Europe. The first great age of *scenography was nurtured in the Italian states in the sixteenth century and disseminated by the printing presses. Italian theatre paralleled Italian art in Europe-wide influence and prestige. Leone de' Sommi, who worked at the Mantuan court, explained in the mid-1560s that he used rich costume in entertainments as propaganda in state displays. These styles superimposed elements of the classical past upon contemporary fashions, thereby creating a wholly artificial form of costume which influenced designers and theorists until the early eighteenth century.

Disguise and transformation in courtly entertainments was not so easily matched in popular plays. *Commedia dell'arte with its *stock characters and distinctive regional styles of Italian and Spanish dress infiltrated many European countries, but as the French moved towards *neoclassicism other sources for costumes became necessary. Professional actors usually provided their own, often acquired second hand. It was an expensive business acquiring costumes impressive enough to win an audience's approbation. The proximity of actors to audiences created its own demands. Courtly entertainments and municipal or religious presentations were impressive in scale, settings, and finance. They relied on a combination of costume and special effects to create a sense of awe and excitement. Professional actors had no such luxuries, but even the humblest artisan knew that a king must look the part and actors were, generally, exempted from sumptuary legislation, which otherwise reserved the wearing of certain colours, fabrics, and furs to high social groups.

What is known about the appearance of the actors in a Shakespeare play must, in the main,

be based on internal and contextual literary evidence. The only extant illustration is a rough sketch of a scene in *Titus Andronicus*, drawn in 1595; it is too slight to be compelling evidence. The six characters wear a haphazard mixture of contemporary, quasi-exotic, quasi-Roman garments, with odds and ends of armour. Although much has been read into *Henslowe's methods of buying, loaning, and pawning costumes, usually at the expense of gullible actors, the look of *Titus*, as with other productions, relied to great extent on the ingenuity of the theatre's wardrobe master and its actors. The inordinately high cost of clothing meant that the costumes for a new play depended upon ingenuity. The loan or gift of discarded court fashions, or their purchase from second-hand dealers, was part of performers' lives.

Surviving illustrations of seventeenth-century English court entertainments—*ballets, *masques, *operas—demonstrate the powerful influence of Italian designers and performers, especially in the work of Inigo *Jones. Court patronage allowed him to experiment with costumes, special effects, and staging techniques intended to glorify the new Stuart monarchy. In *Hymenaei* (1606) the male dancers wore costumes supposedly copied from antique Greek statues with breastplates of 'carnation cloth of silver, richly wrought, and cut to expresse the naked, in manner of the Greek Thorax', voluminous silk mantles of various colours, and white plumes as headdresses. Their female partners, cast as celestial beings, wore floating costumes of white and silver. The expenditure on visual display, and the emphasis on scenic and costume effects at the expense of the writing, led to a falling-out between Jones and *Jonson, author of the early masques.

Eighteenth century By the end of the seventeenth century opulent extravagance in costumes was questioned by books, engravings, and paintings which fed a growing appetite for historical accuracy. But the circumstances of performers had not improved much; many were required to provide their own costumes and properties out of piteously small incomes. Principal performers wore new or specially made costumes, but how they looked was rarely subjected to rigorous scrutiny. *Quin, whose long career overlapped with *Garrick, was declamatory in acting and determined to retain the traditional tragedian's costume of short, wide stiffened skirt, full wig, plumed headdress, and marshal's baton. Garrick, on the other hand, was a small man; the traditional *hero's costume would look foolish on him, so he introduced the Vandyke costume, much used for masquerades throughout the eighteenth century. It hinted at the historic past, and was elegant and easy to wear. His contemporary *Macklin dressed Shylock in a long gabardine coat and red hat, and Macbeth in a quasi-Scottish costume.

The Actor, written in 1750 by a former student of Macklin's, John Hill, asked for a greater realism in costume. He singled out actresses for dressing too finely when playing servants, and both sexes for not seeming to mirror the torments and turmoil of their roles in their appearance. Actresses found this type of advice unpalatable because their splendid appearance often attracted admirers and protectors. By 1790 Tate *Wilkinson's *Memoirs* expressed admiration for current costumes, and recalled that productions in his youth were not as splendidly dressed throughout. The key word is *throughout*, for a few decades earlier only two or three principals were well dressed. John Philip *Kemble's management of Drury Lane from 1794 was criticized for preferring dramas of ostentatious spectacle, But given the enlarged stage and huge audiences he had to attract, this was inevitable. He was alert to the changes in French theatre and introduced togas and sandals for *Coriolanus* and *Julius Caesar*, and his static acting style was enhanced by substantial draperies.

In France, well before 1789 there was a move away from the formal heroic styles of costume. Adrienne *Lecouvreur's adoption of English court dress and a Garter sash to play Elizabeth I in 1721 indicated a novel if inaccurate attempt at characterization, but the main changes originated with Mlle *Clairon, in the 1750s, who abandoned hoops under her skirt and bared her arms to play Roxane in 'the habit of a sultana', and followed it with an Electra in which she wore 'the simple habit of a slave'. Clairon's example was matched by her contemporary Mme *Favart, who wore simple costumes for peasant women and Turkish, Indian, and Chinese styles for roles which required them.

The actor who instituted major reform was *Talma. Influenced by his friend the painter Jacques-Louis David, Talma introduced the toga for classical roles and adopted a short, unpowdered hairstyle for Voltaire's *Brutus* (1791). *Macready, who met him in 1822, was impressed that Talma dressed for his role well in advance to familiarize himself with the costume's requirements and to use it as an interpretative tool.

Nineteenth century Many companies in Europe and America limped along with a curious mixture of styles which had existed for centuries,

but the seeds of artistry, archaeology, and heraldry now blossomed. The over-designed, over-furnished, and overdressed look of society at large was matched by opulent theatrical spectacles which gratified audiences by expanding their knowledge of the past while excluding its less pleasant aspects. 'Correct archaeology' extended to *Planché's designs for Charles *Kemble's 1823 production of *King John* at Covent Garden, which clothed all of the cast in accurate costumes and armour of the thirteenth century. The belief that there was a correct era, place, and style of costume for Shakespeare's plays became dominant. In Britain adherents to the pioneering work of Planché stretched from Macready in the 1820s to *Tree in the 1900s. Gradually, in well-established and financially secure companies, the plays of Shakespeare, works with historic settings, and *melodramas succumbed to the idea of pictorial splendour. Macready espoused historical accuracy erratically; in the late 1820s a German visitor to London was startled to see his Macbeth wearing 'a fashionable flowered chintz dressing-gown, perhaps the one he usually wears, thrown loosely over his steel armour'. By 1838 his *Coriolanus* was praised for its accurate costumes 'of antique Rome', and by the middle of the century public and critics alike expected historical accuracy and pageantry on the stage (*see* ANTIQUARIANISM).

Some critics deplored the meretricious glitter, others praised productions in which the performers 'appear to have stepped out of a Greek vase'. The *actor-manager who attracted the greatest criticism in the 1850s was Charles *Kean. His Shakespeare productions at the Princess's Theatre came with copious programme notes about sources used for costumes and sets, rationalized the choice of location and era in which he had placed the play, and justified his interpolation of hundreds of splendidly clad extras in processions and battle scenes.

Kean's work was admired by Georg II, Duke of Saxe-*Meiningen, whose court theatre company travelled to Berlin in 1874, to London in 1881, and to 38 other European cities; the young *Antoine saw it in Brussels and *Stanislavsky saw it in Moscow. Georg undertook detailed research, consulted historians, chose and cast the plays, designed the sets and costumes, and, through Ludwig *Chronegk, rehearsed the actors. He required them to work as a coherent unit, and to be familiar with costumes, properties, and sets well in advance of a performance, an anticipation of a modern *director.

At the Lyceum Theatre in London, where *Irving ruled with autocratic rigour, the ideal was to make each scene 'a very noble picture'. The *proscenium was the frame, and the gas and limelight, the scenery, costumes, properties, the actors and extras conjured up history paintings for an enthusiastic audience. But then as now, actors' hair, posture, mannerisms, and hesitations about strict period requirements, such as the use of the correct type of corsetry, mitigated against complete authenticity.

Actors continued to provide their own clothes, especially for contemporary plays. The expense involved meant that late in the century young actresses, such as Mrs Patrick *Campbell, made their own dresses for the stage but once well established patronized major couture houses in London and Paris. This might offer glamour and individuality but was little different from the competitive bid for attention of eighteenth-century actresses. Naturally this extravagance could only be borne if a play had a long run. In towns where theatres operated constantly changing programmes, there was a stronger dependence on company wardrobes and performers' personal costumes to dress everything from Shakespeare to modern comedies.

French standards were as variable as anywhere else. Antoine's *naturalist reforms at the Théâtre *Libre in 1894–5 placed actors in rough, ill-fitting clothes of the working classes and a young actress in underclothes. Such an approach was possible in a private theatre club but was not yet permissible in the mainstream. Other experiments in Paris included a highly stylized production of Pelléas et Mélisande (1893) for which the playwright *Maeterlinck had suggested designs and colours for the medieval costumes; and *Jarry's Ubu roi (1896) with costumes, designed by the author, caricaturing a childlike world of grotesque *puppets. Experiments with *symbolism drew upon interest in oriental theatre while rejecting gratuitous spectacle.

Twentieth century and beyond Although traditional approaches survived, costume in the twentieth century was the servant of philosophical, literary, and artistic interpretations of new works and revived classics. The emergence of the *director and the influence of designers sometimes threatened to bury the performer within a predetermined environment. Modernism seemed in general to impose physical and visual restraints upon the performer.

The stylized simplicity of *Craig and *Appia appeared at much the same time that the designers of the *Ballets Russes offered vibrant, sensual interpretations of stock and exotic figures from myth, folklore, and newly discovered foreign cultures. In the 1920s *Schlemmer in Germany and *Meyerhold in Russia used geometrical abstractions or didactic uniforms which made performers into illustrative symbols. Dramatists became more closely involved, describing and sometimes drawing what they required a character to wear. In a 1921 production of Six Characters in Search of an Author, *Pirandello dressed his principals in dark fabrics, rigidly pleated to suggest statues, a look reinforced by their black make-up which resembled 'antique masks of tragedy'. *Brecht experimented with the visual expression of his ideas, and understood that costume could illustrate intellectual and moral transformation.

Competing forms of visual entertainment, notably film and television, drawing on the spectacular costume effects of nineteenth-century theatre, went far beyond the theatre's ability to portray spectacle or historical accuracy. The theatre's response was often to use the clothes of ordinary life to reinforce the message of the text. Historic costumes were simplified or stylized; and productions in modern dress, or set within periods which added a new resonance to classic texts, became commonplace. Eclectic mixtures of period allusion, timelessness, contemporary and exotic styles taken from Eastern and African traditions created a different visual language. Audiences had more visual sophistication than at any previous time; to capture their attention required imagination and experimentation which drew upon complex sources of visual information. *Financial restraints had considerable impact on cast size, costumes, and scenery. Costume hire was standard practice even within large companies from the late nineteenth century, and by the 1930s few theatres had wardrobe departments. Costume designers, specialist costumiers, and wardrobes in large theatres drew upon a wide literature aimed at both professional and amateur companies. Collaboration among director, designer, and author reduced the input of the performer further; costume was no longer an actor's form of interpretative dress but an element in a process of visual construction.

Non-Western A notable feature of traditional Indian, Chinese, and Japanese styles of theatrical appearance is the complete integration of costume, make up or mask, and wig or other headdress. Any attempt to divide this physical transformation into categories is to misunderstand its purpose, for each element has a specific, often symbolic meaning. Colours, styles of costume, and its decoration assist in identifying distinct characters, their age, gender, status, state of mind, and role within a performance. Exaggeration, whether in the length of garments, ornamentation of fabrics, choice of colours, in make-up or masks, wigs, or headdress—all define the role but disguise the performer. Interpretation of the meaning of such physical disguise is aided by the stereotypical range of characters. Generally, naturalism exists only in modern forms of theatre.

Indian Sanskrit drama drew upon the encyclopedic treatise *Natyasastra for ideas on performance, including the costumes. The style and colour of costumes and the colour of make-up or mask delineated the caste, profession, and regional origins of a character. In *kathakali colours of make-up and costumes are taken from the *Mahabharata* and *Ramayana*. A not dissimilar approach can be detected in the best-known form of Chinese drama, Beijing opera (*jingju), which has depended upon vibrant costumes, make-up, and properties for its impact.

Japanese *kabuki offers sophisticated examples of the interrelationship between differing types of theatre and the physical manifestation suitable to them. Kabuki costume practice, which owes much to the traditions of *nō and *bunraku puppet theatre, can be summarized in the example of the stage kimono. This loose, full-sleeved garment worn by both sexes, is supplied in many different colours, distinguished by embroideries, styles of sash (*obi*), and length of hemline. In the historical *jidaimono* plays the kabuki heroine invariably wears a scarlet silk kimono with ornate embroidery whilst the discreet samurai wives are identified by their plain silk kimonos decorated with family crests. Courtesans are distinguished by excessively ornamental costumes; trailing layers of kimono skirts are turned back to reveal further skirts of differently coloured silks. Manipulating these flamboyant but heavy costumes requires great skill. Actors in male roles, especially those dressed in *suō*, the most formal of samurai styles, wear voluminous sleeved undergarments and loosely trailing divided skirts which require skilful movement. Further skill is required in the use of fans, long silk scarves, the lowering of sleeves, all symbolic expressions of recognizable emotions.

These complex styles of theatre costume have occasionally inspired Western imitation, as in *Puccini's *Madama Butterfly* (1904). More recently *Brook's *Mahabharata* (1985), and *Mnouchkine's *Les Atrides* of the early 1990s incorporated certain Eastern styles of costume and make-up in an *intercultural mode. However, the major impact of the bold colours, rich natural fabrics, and intricate designs found on Indian, Chinese, and Japanese costume has not been on Western the-

atre costume but on fashionable dress and interior design.   VLC

cothornus A calf-length, loose-fitting boot, often with upturned toes, which by 460 BC had become a standard feature of *tragic *costume in *Greek theatre. Flat soled until about 330 BC, cothorni in Roman times raised the actor 20-25 cm (8-10 inches) above the stage and came to symbolize tragedy's 'elevated' style.   EGC

Cottesloe Theatre *See* NATIONAL THEATRE OF GREAT BRITAIN.

coup de théâtre An unanticipated action in a drama that effects an abrupt change in a dramatic situation. As a technique for bringing about a *peripeteia or reversal, a *coup de théâtre* is distinguished by its theatricality, its detachment from the rest of the play. In *realism there is an attempt to disguise the artificiality of the *coup de théâtre*, whereas in non-realistic theatre the effect is prominently displayed. The unexpected appearance in a *melodrama of a *character thought dead may subsequently be accounted for in the plot, but the *deus ex machina* of *Euripidean *tragedy remains a completely external device.   RWV

court dance *See* MASQUE.

Courtney, Tom (1937–) English actor whose northern accent and unconventional good looks helped to undermine the gentility of English *acting in the early 1960s. Regional roots inflected his debut performance in *Chekhov's *The Seagull* in Edinburgh (1960) and his brilliance as a deadpan comic showed to great effect in *Billy Liar* (1961) when he took over the lead role from *Finney. By 1964 he was with the *National Theatre, as Andrei in *Frisch's *Andorra*. His range widened still further in the 1970s: notable roles included Lord Fancourt Babberly in *Charley's Aunt* (1970), Norman in *Ayckbourn's *The Norman Conquests* (1974), the poet-peasant John Clare in *Bond's *The Fool* (1975), plus Hamlet, Peer Gynt, the title role in *Harwood's *The Dresser* during several seasons with the 69 Company in Manchester. More classic parts followed with *Molière's *The Imaginary Invalid* (1987) and *The Miser* (1991). He *toured the one-person shows *Moscow Stations* (1993-4) and *Pretending to be Me* (2002). He starred in *Reza's *Art* (1996) and as a 2008 Christmas-guest in the television series *The Royle Family*.   BRK

Covent Garden Theatre After the success of *Beggar's Opera*, John *Rich had the original Covent Garden Theatre built in Bow Street in London, near *Drury Lane Theatre, by architect Edward Shephard. It opened in 1732 with a pit surrounded by three levels of side *boxes, with one level of boxes and two galleries at the rear, and a capacity of 1,397. Rich owned the *Davenant *patent, which remained with this theatre until such monopolies were abolished in 1843. Handel rented the theatre regularly from 1734 to 1737. When Rich died in 1761 Covent Garden became an *opera house until it was sold to playwright George *Colman and his associates in 1767. Thomas Harris had the theatre rebuilt by Henry Holland in 1792, with four levels of horseshoe-shaped tiers supported by cast-iron posts and a capacity of 3,000. John Philip *Kemble became *actor-manager in 1803. In 1808 the theatre was destroyed by fire.

The second *playhouse, built by John Smirke, Jr., in 1809, was the first major Greek revival building in London and the first public building with central heating. When it opened with a capacity of 2,800, higher ticket prices motivated the Old Price *riots, which ran for 61 nights. The lobby was illuminated with gas in 1815, the *auditorium in 1817. Charles *Kemble managed the theatre from 1817–32, *Macready was its actor-manager 1837–9, followed by *Mathews and *Vestris until 1842. In 1847 the theatre was redesigned by Benedetto Albano as the Royal Italian Opera House (capacity 4,000), but was destroyed by fire in 1856.

The current theatre was built by Edward W. Barry and opened in 1858 as the Royal English Opera, becoming the Royal Opera House in 1892. The theatre was remodelled in 1964 and closed from 1997 to 1999 for extensive renovations at a cost in excess of £250 million.   FJH

Coward, Noël (1899–1973) English playwright, performer, director, and songwriter, as famous for being himself as for any of his creative activities. Coward achieved success simultaneously as an actor and playwright in *I'll Leave It to You* (1920), *The Young Idea* (1923), and *The Vortex* (1924). *Hay Fever* (1925) is typical of the early plays, showing a highly theatrical family running rings around a group of staid outsiders. In *Private Lives* (1930), the pinnacle of the early work, a divorced couple meet on their respective honeymoons with new spouses and elope together; the evasion of moral judgement, and the blur of paradox and witticism, made it a perfect vehicle for Coward and his co-star Gertrude *Lawrence. Through the 1930s and 1940s, alongside classic *comedies like *Design for Living* (1939), *Blithe Spirit* (1941), and *Present Laughter* (1943), Coward wrote *revues, *musical comedies, straight

dramas, and a historical epic, *Cavalcade* (1931). His work can look flat on the page, the writing defiantly unliterary, yet as a performer he knew how to create dialogue that would release comic momentum. Although he appeared rakishly heterosexual on stage, other meanings could be derived from coded references to homosexuality in his work.

Coward cemented his reputation during the war with three successful plays, morale-boosting appearances for the troops, a stirring performance in his own propaganda film *In Which We Serve* (1942), and several songs of a patriotic or lightly satirical nature. He emerged a very establishment figure—*Relative Values* (1951) and *South Sea Bubble* (1956) had little of their author's earlier edge—but had already forged a new career as a *cabaret performer, with celebrated appearances in Las Vegas in 1955. His work continues to be performed worldwide.   DR

Cowley, Hannah (1743–1809) English dramatist. She wrote her first play, *The Runaway* (1776), out of a dissatisfaction with the new dramas of the time; it was a great success at *Garrick's *Drury Lane, an auspicious beginning to her career. The older Restoration repertory inspired much of her work, including *The Belle's Stratagem* (1780), *A Bold Stroke for a Husband* (1783), and *A School for Greybeards* (1786, from *Behn's *The Lucky Chance*). While Cowley claimed to be indifferent to popular success, her unhappiness with the bad taste of *audiences led her to stop writing plays in 1794.   MJK

Crabtree, Lotta (1846–1924) American actress. One of the best-loved performers of the nineteenth century, Crabtree parlayed her banjo picking, clog-dancing winsomeness into a $4 million fortune. A California gold prospector's daughter, she was spotted by Lola *Montez and taught to sing and *dance. From performing in mining camps and small time *variety shows she stormed San Francisco in 1858 with *The Loan of a Lover*. By 1864 she was starring in New York, three years later having her greatest success in the dual title roles of *Little Nell and the Marchioness*, an adaptation of *Dickens's *The Old Curiosity Shop*. Crabtree's popularity never dimmed, and after *touring extensively she retired in 1891.   TFC

Craig, Edith (1869–1947) English actress, designer, director, and political activist, daughter of Ellen *Terry. Craig directed pageants for the Actresses' Franchise League and devised *A Pageant of Great Women*, a suffrage piece remounted by Craig all over the UK with largely amateur casts, 1909–12. While her brother Edward Gordon

*Craig theorized about production, Edy attended to practicalities of *directing, usually away from the commercial mainstream. Her Pioneer Players (1911–25) presented plays largely on Sunday matinées in London, when friendly commercial theatres were available. The company's repertoire was eclectic and often woman centred: she staged work by *Hrostvitha, translated by Craig's long-term partner Christopher St John (Christabel Marshall), and later revived *Glaspell's *The Verge*, starring Sybil *Thorndike (1925). Edy Craig was known for her uncompromising approach and her ability to create spectacular effects on the smallest of budgets.   EJS

Craig, Edward Gordon (1872–1966) English actor, designer, director, one of the creators of modernist theatre. The son of Ellen *Terry and E. W. Godwin, architect and scene designer, Craig acted with *Irving's company (he was to write memoirs of both Irving and Terry); he left in 1893, partly because, realizing the excellence of Irving's artistry, he could not foresee ways in which *acting might be developed. And Craig wished fiercely to be an innovator. Also in 1893 he learned wood engraving, and relished the refinement and simplicity of expression imposed by the medium. In time he saw through it the means of revolutionizing the use of painted scenery, which he found artificial. His ideas were first put to the test when with Martin Shaw he staged Purcell's *Dido and Aeneas* (1900), *The Masque of Love* (1901), and Handel's *Acis and Galatea* (1902) in London. It was, however, his designs for his productions of *Housman's *Bethlehem* (1902), and of *Ibsen's *The Vikings* and Shakespeare's *Much Ado About Nothing* for his mother in 1903, which won him wide acclaim. Craig's first theoretical treatise, *The Art of the Theatre* (1905), defined the importance of the designer-*director in achieving the non-*naturalistic staging he envisaged as the theatre of the future. Count Harry Kessler's and *Brahm's enthusiasm for his work, and offers of commissions in Germany, now enticed Craig to leave England; he was to live and work chiefly on the Continent thereafter.

Craig did not prove an easy partner in collaboration. Only one of three projects for *Duse was realized (*Rosmersholm*, Florence, 1906). *Reinhardt, *Diaghilev, and *Tree rejected design schemes. Craig, like *Appia, sought to create credible architectural structures on stage, which would be given volume, mass, colour, and mood by angled (electric) *lighting not by painted effects of chiaroscuro (*see* SCENOGRAPHY). After settling in Florence in 1908 he began experimenting with series of movable screens of varying

heights and widths to achieve this effect in practicable terms. Later he envisaged a stage where pillar formations might rise or descend by electronic hoists, singly or in groups, to create stylized scenes. The fruits of this work were published in *Towards a New Theatre* (1913) and *Scene* (1923) with illustrative plates; and throughout the issues of the *Mask*, a magazine which Craig edited (1908–29).

The chance to test his concepts in practice came first from *Yeats to design at the *Abbey Theatre in Dublin, to whom Craig gave plans for a set of screens (first used in 1911). Next, *Stanislavsky commissioned a production of *Hamlet* (1912) for the *Moscow Art Theatre, although Craig lost the absolute control over the staging that he requested. Disillusioned with both the codification of classical *ballet (when compared with the freedom of his one-time lover Isadora *Duncan's *dance technique) and the mannerism of contemporary acting styles, Craig evolved over the decade the idea of a new mechanically operated 'performer', which he termed an *Über-marionette*. A crucial aspect of his agenda was that a director should keep absolute control over all aspects of a production in *rehearsal and performance, including the acting style.

This theme was restated vigorously in his revised *On the Art of the Theatre* (1911). Perhaps aware of Appia's parallel investigations, Craig had become highly defensive of his schemes. This attitude increasingly militated against his receiving that constructive criticism from sympathetic contemporaries which might have tempered his inspiration within the realms of the possible, enabling Craig to achieve in practical stagecraft the revolution he desired. However, Craig's output in books, illustrations, and stage designs after 1918 was prodigious and show his theories evolving from his experiences. Designs for two productions were commissioned in this decade: Ibsen's *The Pretenders* for Copenhagen in 1926, and George Tyler's New York staging of *Macbeth* (1928).   RAC

Craven, Hawes (1837–1910) English scene painter and designer. Craven learned the craft of scene painting at the Britannia Theatre, London. By his early twenties he was working at the major *playhouses, including *Drury Lane and *Covent Garden, and between 1862 and 1864 he served as resident designer at the Theatre Royal, Dublin. He later joined *Irving at the Lyceum, and became a leading designer in the 1880s and 1890s, preparing the sets for most of Irving's productions. Toward the end of his career he also designed for *Tree. Throughout his career he was committed to the principles of *illusionism and historical *antiquarianism. TP

Crimp, Martin (1956–) English playwright. Crimp's transformation of enigmatic, hyper-realistic *dialogue into minimalist stage poetry recalls *Pinter, but the *satire is harsher and the moral ambiguities deeper. First championed by the Orange Tree Theatre in Richmond, who produced *Dealing with Clair* (1988) and *Play with Repeats* (1989), in the 1990s his work was usually premièred at the *Royal Court. The central figure of *The Treatment* (1993) is a *character named Ann, maltreated first by her partner and then by film producers who want to buy her story. *Attempts on her Life* (1997) splinters her further in seventeen scenes. *Fewer Emergencies* (2005) further explored this territory in three concentric playlets revolving around 'Bobby'. *The Country* (2000) offers a more conventional narrative, but the riddling complexity of motivations shows the same harsh investigation into human identity, and has its own companion-piece in *The City* (2008). Other plays include *No One Sees the Video* (1990), *Getting Attention* (1991), and *Face to the Wall* (2002). Crimp has also been acclaimed for translations of plays from French. DR

crisis A decisive moment, or turning point, in a dramatic *action. In the late nineteenth century Gustav Freytag identified a traditional five-part pyramidal dramatic structure with a climax at the apex, and three crises: an initiating action that precipitates the complication, an action that ends the climax and initiates the *denouement, and an action that brings about the *catastrophe. It has become more common to recognize Freytag's climax as the central crisis, and to use 'climax' to refer to the highest point of *audience interest, which may or may not coincide with the central crisis. *Archer went further and identified crisis as the essence of drama. *See also* PERIPETEIA. RWV

Cronyn, Hume (1911–2003) Canadian actor, writer, and director. While attending McGill University, he appeared with the Montréal Repertory Company and the McGill Players' Club, and made his American debut in Washington in *Up Pops the Devil* (1931). After his Broadway debut in *Hipper's Holiday* (1934), Cronyn's roles there ranged from Polonius opposite *Burton's Hamlet to Tobias in *Albee's *A Delicate Balance* (1966). Beginning with Hitchcock's *Shadow of a Doubt* (1942), he performed in nearly 50 films, including *Lifeboat* (1944), *Cleopatra* (1963), and *Cocoon* (1988). His marriage to Jessica *Tandy in 1942 provided one of the great actor rapports on stage, screen, and

television. 'The first couple of American theatre' performed together at the *Guthrie Theatre, at the *Stratford Festival, and in *The Four Poster* (1952), *The Physicists* (1964), *The Gin Game* (1977), and *Foxfire* (1980, which Cronyn wrote with Susan Cooper). Cronyn directed Tandy in *Portrait of a Madonna* (1946) at the Actors' Laboratory Theatre, and later directed and *toured with his wife in *Triple Play* (1959). PBON

cross dressing *See* FEMALE IMPERSONATION; MALE IMPERSONATION.

Crothers, Rachel (1878–1958) A prolific playwright and skilled director, Crothers was arguably the most prominent woman in the American commercial theatre from her debut with *Elizabeth* in 1899 to her last play, *Susan and God*, in 1938. Thirty-two works were produced on Broadway during this period, with Crothers directing most of them and occasionally acting major roles. Committed to the ideal of a fully professional theatre, earning one's own living, and the value of entertaining while educating a large *audience, Crothers distrusted the art theatres of her time. Her plays—typically *realistic, serious *comedies—often focused on the double standard by which men and women were judged morally and the seeming incompatibility between modern woman's desire for a career and the demands of husband and children. Most successful were *The Three of Us* (1906), *A Man's World* (1910), *He and She* (1912), *When Ladies Meet* (1932), and *Susan and God*. MAF

Crouse, Russel (1893–1966) American librettist, playwright, and producer. Crouse was a journalist who began his theatre career with the libretto for *The Gang's All Here* (1931) and served as press agent for the *Theatre Guild. He had his first hit when he helped Howard Lindsay write the book for the Cole *Porter *musical *Anything Goes* (1934), and thereafter the pair had a highly successful 32-year collaboration in over seventeen *comedies. Their first non-musical, *Life with Father* (1939), ran for eight years, and *State of the Union* (1945), a political *satire, won the Pulitzer Prize. Crouse and Lindsay produced and substantially revised Joseph Kesselring's *Arsenic and Old Lace* (1941), and they wrote the book for *Rodgers and *Hammerstein's *The Sound of Music* (1959). FL

Crowley, Bob (1952–) Irish designer, associate artist of the *Royal Shakespeare Company and the *National Theatre, one of the busiest and most respected of contemporary *scenographers. For the RSC's *As You Like It* (1985), a forest was created without trees; ladders, rope, and muslin established multiple locations in *The Plantagenets* (1988). Rejecting period correctness, Crowley combined differing periods and conventions within the same design to resonate key themes. His RNT work ranges from giant hanging cloths for *Les Liaisons dangereuses* (1987) to a bridge to infinity in *Hedda Gabler* (1990) to the New England-inspired *Carousel* (1994), updated from the 1850s to 1900. With Stephen Rea, he designed and co-directed *The Cure at Troy* (1990). He designed the films *Suddenly Last Summer* and *Tales of Hollywood*, and *opera in Britain and abroad. He created a giant pyramid and postmodern fashionable *costumes for Elton John's *Aida* (1998). Among his many honours are the Olivier award for designer of the year (1990) and five Tony awards for *Aida*, *Carousel*, *Bennett's *The History Boys* (2006), *Mary Poppins* (2007), and *Stoppard's *The Coast of Utopia* (2007).   RVL

Cruelty, Theatre of Enterprise launched in Paris in 1935 by *Artaud, with his adaptation of Shelley's *The Cenci*. The production was the practical culmination of Artaud's long-held plan to revolutionize European theatre by challenging the dominant form of psychological *realism. Adverse critical response and financial difficulties curtailed the run of *The Cenci* to seventeen performances and marked Artaud's last practical experiment with theatre. The title derives from a heretical Gnostic belief that the very essence of life (creation and the struggle to survive) is 'cruel' and beyond redemption. This philosophy acted as an analogy for theatrical creation which, Artaud believed, should not be used to narrate or present cruelty but actually to transmit it. The psycho-physiological effects of such traumas, rather than the blood, gore, and violence associated with them, were the goals of Artaud's short-lived theatre. 'Cruelty' thus translated into theatrical production centred on the dramatization of moral and social crimes (such as murder, rape, and incest), which were the overriding themes of the first production. The notion was expounded in Artaud's celebrated manifesto, *The Theatre and its Double* (1938). Although he never succeeded in successfully realizing the theatre of cruelty himself, the idea acted as a touchstone for a post-war generation of practitioners seeking to revolutionize theatre in a post-totalitarian Europe, in an even more cruel world after the Holocaust. A Theatre of Cruelty season was held in London in 1504 under the aegis of the *Royal Shakespeare Company, directed by *Brook and *Marowitz. It featured sketches, scenes, *improvisations, a performance of Artaud's playlet *The Spurt of Blood*,

and, most importantly, Brook's mounting of *Weiss's *Marat/Sade*. That production and its film version (1966), coupled with the growing influence of Artaud's theories in the next decades, greatly affected *avant-garde performance worldwide and made the term 'theatre of cruelty' widely current.   BRS

Cruz, Corral de la The first of Madrid's two permanent *playhouses or *corrales de comedias, the other being the Corral del *Príncipe. Founded by the Brotherhoods (*cofradías) of the Pasión and the Soledad, the Cruz opened in rudimentary form on 29 November 1579, and survived, with modifications, until 1736, when it was replaced by a *coliseo* (*proscenium theatre). It was built in a rectangular walled yard (16.7 m by 24.2 m; 55 by 79 feet) within a block, behind a converted house which provided entrances and contained a women's gallery, some *boxes above, and a further gallery in the attic. At the far (south) end was a roofed stage (8 m by 4.5 m; 26 by 15 feet) projecting from a tiring house with a lower and upper gallery and a machine loft. Along the sides of the yard, adjoining the stage, were roofed platforms with benches and *gradas* (raked seating); above these were galleries (a distinctive feature of the Cruz). Lateral boxes gradually appeared after 1600 in privately owned buildings on adjoining sites. The yard was roofed in 1703.   CD

Cueva, Juan de la (1550–1610) Spanish poet and playwright. A prolific writer for the stage, he is distinguished by his blatant disregard for the *neoclassical *unities, his reduction of the traditional number of acts or *jornadas* from five to four, and his introduction of new metrical forms. With a keen eye for theatrical effect, Cueva often sacrificed theatrical decorum for the sensationalism of violent death and the supernatural, while in *The Slanderer*, he created the figure of the libertine who is generally regarded as a model for the Don Juan of Tirso de *Molina.   KG

Cumberland, Richard (1732–1811) English author. Cumberland is usually remembered as a sentimental playwright, attaching to his name all the opprobrium that is directed at that genre. His best plays, *The Brothers* (1669), *The West Indian* (1771), and *The Jew* (1794), were at once innovative and very popular. Not without humour, they aspire to serious social purpose, particularly the eradication of social prejudice against groups like the Irish, the British living in the West Indies, and Jews. Known at the time as the modern *Terence, Cumberland sought to write morally edifying *comedy that did not stoop to mimicry or topical attacks.   MJK

Cunillé, Lluïsa (1961–) Catalan playwright whose early enigmatic plays, such as *Roundabout* (1992), *Libration* (1994), and *The Meeting* (1998), polarized both critics and audiences. She demonstrated increasing versatility with *Barcelona, Map of Shadows* (2004), and *The Bald Soprano at McDonald's* (2006), a sequel to *Ionesco's *absurdist comedy. She was a co-founder of the Hongaresa Theatre Company in 1995 and has collaborated closely with director Xavier Albertí in the staging of her own plays and in other projects. In 2007 she received Catalonia's National Theatre Prize for *Après moi le deluge* and became playwright-in-residence at Barcelona's Teatre Lliure. MPH

Cunningham, Merce (1919–2009) American dancer and choreographer. Cunningham studied *dance at the Cornish School in Seattle, where he met John Cage. He danced in Martha *Graham's company from 1939 to 1945 and in 1942 began presenting his own work. He developed a distinctive dance technique, synthesizing the verticality, speed, and rapid rhythmic footwork of *ballet with modern dance's flexible use of the trunk and limbs. His characteristic choreographic method since the early 1950s, when he formed the Merce Cunningham Dance Company, used chance techniques that decentred space and generated new movements. He collaborated with numerous contemporary composers and visual artists, including Cage, Robert Rauschenberg, and Jasper Johns. Cunningham's collaborations freed dance from its previous dependence on music, although the two elements may share a time structure. A modernist choreographer, he made non-representational dances focusing on movement itself. He co-created several dances for film and video and after 1990 worked with computer software to create choreography. OD

Curtain Theatre Built in 1577, a year after the *Theatre, and located close by it on the main road north out of London through Shoreditch, the Curtain was probably of similar size and design. An open-air polygon of as many as twenty bays, with its stage built like the Theatre's, it was used by Shakespeare's company, the *Chamberlain's Men, from April 1597 when the Theatre was closed to mid-1599, when the *Globe opened. *Marston wrote in 1598 of law students praising and quoting *Romeo and Juliet* and giving it 'Curtain plaudities'. In the early seventeenth century it was one of the *playhouses with the most lower-class clientele, and no company used it for very long. But it did continue to stage plays until at least 1622, making it the longest-serving *amphitheatre of the period in London. AJG

Cusack, Cyril (1910–93) Irish actor and *manager. He first appeared onstage at the age of 7 with his mother and stepfather's *touring company. He joined the *Abbey Theatre Company in 1932, and over thirteen years played in 65 plays there. He ran his own company from 1946 to 1961, and played throughout Ireland, in London, and Europe. His best-known roles were in *Boucicault, *Synge, *O'Casey, and *Shaw. His idiosyncratic style of performance could erupt suddenly with intensely powerful passion and vigour. His playing of Christy Mahon in Synge's *Playboy* and Fluther Good in O'Casey's *The Plough and the Stars* was widely acclaimed. He believed his appearance in *Odd Man Out* (1947) established his international reputation as a cinema actor, and his work as a player of screen vignettes spanned 40 years. In 1990 he appeared at the Gate Theatre (Dublin) as Chebutykin in *Chekhov's *The Three Sisters* with three of his actress daughters, Sinéad *Cusack, Sorcha, and Niamh. CAL

Cusack, Sinéad (1948–) Irish actress, the daughter of Cyril *Cusack. She made her stage debut at the *Abbey Theatre before moving to London in the late 1960s. At the *Royal Shakespeare Company (1979–84) she played leading roles such as Lady Macbeth, Celia in *As You Like It*, Kate in *The Taming of the Shrew*, and Beatrice in *Much Ado About Nothing*. Her provocative and vivid characterizations contributed to the *feminist debate surrounding Shakespeare and representations of women. She said that Kate's 'submission' speech 'isn't a submission speech at all: it's a speech about how her spirit has been allowed to soar free...she has made her own rules'. Her work in television and cinema includes films with Bernardo Bertolucci and *Zeffirelli. For the *Royal Court Theatre she appeared in *Friel's *Faith Healer*, and for the *National Theatre played Mai in Sebastian *Barry's *Our Lady of Sligo* (1998). CAL

Cushman, Charlotte (1816–76) American actress of international fame. Known for her *breeches roles and female grotesques, Cushman often used her muscular body and unusual voice to create a masculine persona on stage (*see* MALE IMPERSONATION). Her lesbianism may have contributed to the erotic power of her male *characters, and her commanding presence and extravagant expressiveness attracted many female spectators. Cushman first appeared on stage as Lady Macbeth in 1836 and achieved her first notable success with Nancy in *Oliver Twist* in 1839.

She worked with *Macready during his American *tour and followed him to England in 1844 to seek stardom. A sensation in London, Cushman capitalized on her fame, living in London and Rome and touring internationally; except for her final years, she rarely returned to the United States. Following her London success, Cushman performed about 35 roles, repeating ten of them with some regularity. Among her most applauded characters were Meg Merrilies in *Guy Mannering*, Queen Katharine and Cardinal Wolsey in *Henry VIII*, Lady Macbeth, and Romeo, which she occasionally played opposite her sister Susan. Cushman retired from the stage in 1869.   BMC

cyclorama A smooth drape or wall used to produce the effect of a sky or of a neutral backdrop at indefinite distance. Though the principle of the 'cyc' was known as early as 1820, it was not until the early years of the twentieth century that European *lighting technicians and scene designers, notably Mariano Fortuny and Adolph Linnebach, demonstrated the advantages of a backdrop which was perfectly smooth under an even wash of coloured light. The human eye, when it is unable to find any irregularity on which to focus, cannot judge distance, and interprets the surface as infinity; thus the cyc works by mimicking the effect of daylight on the natural sky.

Fortuny had originally hoped that all lighting could be accomplished by reflection from the cyc, and several plaster 'sky domes' were constructed in Germany in the 1920s and 1930s. They worked badly in practice: the dome blocked flown scenery and cut off much of the wings, and since it was the brightest object in the space it pulled the eye up and away from the stage. Although 'Fortuny lighting' never became important, the cyclorama was immediately adopted by nearly all *scenographers for a wide range of problems. Besides the *realistic effect of sky, it can be used to create a backdrop that is more neutral than black, to suggest mood in impressionistic or *symbolist plays, or to create a feeling that the *action is somehow taking place in eternity, or in a universal space. In its cloth form, the cyc appears almost universal in Western theatres, and has been widely adopted in many non-Western nations as well.   JB

dada An international *avant-garde art movement created by Hugo Ball and Tristan Tzara in Zurich during the First World War. Their meeting place was the Cabaret Voltaire, where between February and June 1916 they created numerous performances of an experimental nature. In 1917 the group ran a gallery where they organized six dada soirées. The spaces were small and the *audience limited, to convey the ideas and aesthetic principles of dada to the general public they organized three soirées in Zurich guildhalls, which attracted up to 1,000 spectators each. After the war the centre of activities shifted to Paris and Berlin, where the dadaists continued the tradition of performing 'sound' poetry, simultaneous poems, movement pieces, and noise music. Audience reactions were often so violent that the actors watched the main action unfold in the *auditorium. In Berlin the dadaists became caught up in the November Revolution of 1918 and the tumultuous events of the early Weimar Republic. The Paris group produced literary soirées, public exhibits, and seven dada plays.   GB

Dadié, Bernard (1916–) Ivorian writer and politician, author of three volumes of poetry, three novels, and over a dozen full-length plays and dramatic sketches. Dadié worked in Senegal as a librarian-archivist until 1947 when he returned to Côte d'Ivoire, where he eventually became Minister of Education and Culture. His historical play, *Assémien Déhylé, roi du Sanwi* was performed in Dakar in 1936 and in Paris in 1937 at the International Exhibition. He co-founded in 1953 the Centre Culturel et Folklorique de la Côte d'Ivoire, for whose troupe he wrote five dramatic sketches between 1955 and 1960 on social themes. His first major play, *Béatrice du Congo* (1970), was inspired by *Césaire's *La Tragédie du roi Christophe* (1963), and written at the suggestion of Jean-Marie Serreau, who directed it at the *Avignon Festival (1971). Dadié's other major plays include *Islands of Tempest* (1973) on Toussaint L'Ouverture and the Haitian Revolution, *Voices in the Wind* (1970), a *tragedy of ambition, and the *satirical *comedy *Monsieur Thôgô-Gnini* (1970). In *Papassidi, maître escroc* (1975) and

Mhoi-ceul (1979) he returned to the vein of *farce that he wrote in the 1950s.   JCM

Dalcroze, Émile-Jaques *See* JAQUES-DALCROZE, ÉMILE.

Daldry, Stephen (1960–) English director. Daldry's deconstructed production of *Priestley's *An Inspector Calls* (*National Theatre, 1992; New York, 1994), with its 1940s air-raid sirens and collapsing Edwardian house, brought him Olivier and Tony awards. Daldry leans to spectacle and a form of *expressionism with classic, often leftist works (*Treadwell's *Machinal*, 1994, with Fiona *Shaw), and often collaborates with designer and companion Ian MacNeill. Daldry succeeded *Stafford-Clark as *artistic director of the *Royal Court (1992–7). His charismatic and generous leadership fostered an explosion of new playwrights, including Sarah *Kane, as well as successful fundraising and building renovation campaigns. *Billy Elliott* (2000), about a miner's son who wants to dance, was his debut as a film director, followed by *The Hours* (2002, screenplay by *Hare), and *The Reader* (2008, also by Hare). Daldry's production of *Billy Elliot: The Musical*, music by Elton John) was highly successful in London (2005) and New York (2008, nine Tony awards including best director).   GAO

dalit theatre Theatre of the oppressed castes (*dalit*) in India. In the state of Maharashtra the oppressed castes were once considered polluting and therefore untouchable, condemned to live outside villages and to perform menial jobs. Babasaheb Ambedkar, from the *dalit* Mahar caste, exhorted them to revolt against such work, educate themselves, and fight for human dignity. The earliest *dalit* theatre was designed to spread Ambedkar's ideas. Milind College in Aurangabad, established by Ambedkar's People's Education Society, was the centre of *dalit* theatre after independence. The first principal of the college, M. B. Chitnis, wrote *Yugyatra* (*The Journey of an Age*) in 1955 and staged it in Ambedkar's presence; the next year it was performed in Nagpur before 600,000 *dalits* who had gathered to convert to Buddhism. The play is composed of a series of episodes depicting the injustices inflicted on *dalits* through the centuries. Prakash Tribhuvan's (*Wait, Rama's Regime Is on the Way* and Datta Bhagat's *Routes and Escape Routes* are two of the many other plays staged in Auragabad. More recently *dalit* theatre has entered the *proscenium stage in an effort to expand its *audience to the middle class, though the different performance mode has occasionally compromised its political agenda.   SGG

Daly, Augustin (1836–99) American critic, playwright, and *manager. Unsuccessful in securing production of his early work, Daly turned to theatre criticism, writing for five different newspapers (1859–67). His first dramatic success came in 1862 with an adaptation of the German play *Deborah*, as *Leah the Forsaken*. Although he may have used collaborators, Daly is credited with numerous plays, both original compositions and adaptations, primarily from German and French sources. His more noteworthy original contributions include his great *melodrama *Under the Gaslight* (1867), *A Flash of Lightning* (1868), *Horizon* (1871), and *The Undercurrent* (1888). Daly carefully reworked his adaptations to suit American tastes, a strategy that produced substantial economic successes in *Frou-Frou* (1870), *Divorce* (1871), and *The Lottery of Love* (1888). He also owned a succession of *playhouses that were widely recognized for the quality of their productions. In 1879 he reopened New York's Wood's Museum as Daly's Theatre, quickly establishing it as a venue for elite society and for fine ensemble *acting. He used a *stock company of 44 actors—headed by Ada *Rehan and John *Drew—that excelled at melodrama, light *comedy, and Shakespeare, and provided a training ground for a host of rising American talent. Through its English and European *tours of the 1880s, Daly's troupe secured international recognition of maturing American practice.   GAR

Damiani, Luciano (1923–2007) Italian *scenographer who began a long career at the Piccolo Teatro in Milan in the 1950s. Under the direction of *Strehler he designed a large number of productions, including Bertolazzi's *El Nost Milan* (dialect for *Our Milan*, 1954), *Brecht's *Galileo* (1961), *Goldoni's *The Chioggian Squabbles* (1964), *Chekhov's *Cherry Orchard* (1973), and a magnificent *The Tempest* (1978). He also worked as designer for several *operas in Austria and Milan. Damiani considered the visual integral to the dramatic text. He frequently extended the stage into the stalls, rejecting the division between playing space and *audience. He has worked with numerous international directors, and in 1996 formed his own company, Teatro Documenti (Theatre of Documents), where the development of the scenography and theatrical space were recorded through his own preparatory drawings and sketches.   DMcM

damnatio Public *execution at Rome for non-citizens, prisoners of war, and slaves involved 'aggravated' death penalties, singly or in combination: crucifixion, *crematio* (burning alive), and *damnatio ad bestias* (exposure to wild beasts). These penalties were intended to cause the victim prolonged agony and humiliation. Occasionally their potential for spectator appeal was maximized by dramatization. The staging might exploit the miscreant's background or the nature of his crime: a Sicilian brigand in the age of Augustus who was known as 'son of Etna' was brought to Rome to be displayed in the forum on a contraption that 'erupted' and deposited him in a cage of wild animals. A Greek myth or Roman legend might be played out, sometimes with an unusual *denouement: at the opening of the Colosseum in AD 80 a popular *mime that ended in the crucifixion of the *protagonist was combined with *damnatio ad bestias* so that a criminal 'playing' the leading role was actually crucified and simultaneously exposed to a bear. Other myths performed on the same occasion included a version of the story of Orpheus in which, instead of being torn apart by Maenads, he was savaged by a bear; this scenario exploited the standard portrayal of Orpheus as the consummate musician who was able to charm the natural world into submission. A large-scale variant of these displays comprised massed combat involving thousands of participants. In 46 BC in the Circus Maximus, Julius Caesar constructed a 'camp' at either end of the track and staged a battle involving 1,000 infantry, 60 cavalry, and 40 elephants. On the Campus Martius in AD 52, on his return from the annexation of Britain, Claudius re-enacted the storming of a British town and the surrender of the kings, thereby turning the urban populace of Rome into a vicarious witness of his victory. The most extended form of dramatized *damnationes* was the *naumachia, a staged naval battle based upon a real or imaginary episode from Greek history. *See also* ROMAN THEATRE.   KMC

dance and dance-drama Dance may be defined as designed movement, or movement framed to be perceived as designed. Dance-drama implies a spoken text, and often a story, combined with movement. Both dance and drama seem to be part of every human culture. They occur in myriad folk, social, *ritual, therapeutic, and theatrical settings; dances may function as games, *sports, combat, psychological and physiological therapy, or social, cultural, and political events. This entry is concerned with dance and dance-drama as part of theatre and performance in the broadest sense, rather than as part of everyday life unframed as performance.

Because dance is so widespread it is impossible to write a comprehensive overview of its history and implications. However, one way of surveying this vast field briefly is to examine the binary 'dance and dance-drama' as a continuum. At one end of the spectrum is pure dance: abstract dance that consists only of movement sequences, without other expressive or communicative means, even music. For instance, in *Calico Min gling* (1973), by the American Lucinda Childs, four dancers walk, in six-step phrases, in similar but not identical paths that consist of circles, semicircles, and straight lines. Despite the simplicity of their basic movements, the slight variations in their paths and patterns result in a highly complex visual and rhythmic pattern of unison, divergence, interweaving, and intersection. Performed in silence, the dance itself seems to become a form of visual music, much as a solo or group tap dance without musical accompaniment creates a percussion piece that seems to occupy a position in the fields of both music and dance.

At the other end of the spectrum is the fully hybrid dance-drama, or *total theatre piece: a theatrical spectacle that consists of movement, speech, and song in the service of a narrative plot with *characters and *action. It may also employ other elements of *mise-en-scène, including scenery, *costumes, props, *lighting and other visual effects, *music and other sound effects, *masks, *puppets, performing *animals, machines, and aroma design. In both East and West, the great classical theatres have employed this rich, multi-sensory, multivalent genre. For instance, in *kathakali* masked and elaborately costumed actors perform tales from the Hindu epics and Puranas, or traditional stories. They use *mime and dance, a highly codified lexicon of hand gestures, colour coding in costume, mask, and make-up, symbolic uses of stage space, and music and poetic song to embody tales of heroism and military prowess. Similarly, Japanese *nō, Chinese *jingju* or Beijing opera, Balinese *topeng*, and ancient *Greek theatre, as well as *early modern and *neoclassical European *operas based on ancient Greek models, merged music, song, poetry, dance, mime, and other elements in order to achieve an integrated theatrical effect. In the con-

temporary world, some of these forms continue, and new forms have arisen, such as *musical theatre and film musicals that mix song, dance, and story.

In between these two poles are various admixtures of choreography, music, verbal texts, and narrative elements. Much world dance is performed to music, and thus, very close to the end of the pure dance spectrum is a category that contains dances that may be abstract, non-narrative, and non-dramatic, but that have some musical accompaniment, whether spare or full-bodied. These abstract dances, whose performers do not take on the role of characters beyond themselves dancing the dance, may nevertheless have expressive qualities derived from the music or the choreography. Into this category would fall a genre like *bugaku*, the ancient Japanese court dances, which are performed to instrumental music. Most are non-narrative, non-dramatic dances, slow and symmetrical, prized for their formal beauty and spiritual content.

A modern *ballet like *Balanchine's *Concerto barocco* (1941), to Bach's Double Violin Concerto in D Minor, is a dance about the aesthetic, formal tensions of architectural, polyphonic form, not about human drama. The dances created at the *Bauhaus in Germany during the 1920s by artists such as *Schlemmer often experimented, to percussive accompaniment or jazz music, with the geometry of the body and space, as well as with expressive properties of colours in the costumes and lights. On the border between pure dance without music and abstract dance with music, is the work of *Cunningham, whose storyless choreography occupies the same space-time continuum as the music in performance but is neither created nor danced *to* the music.

Moving from the pure dance end of the spectrum toward dance drama, the next category might be called imagistic dance. It has more meaning and often more elements of mise-enscène than pure or abstract dance, and it may even project the life of characters or a situation, but it does not have a fully fleshed-out narrative or dramatic conflict. Isadora *Duncan created lyric dances, set to symphonic music, that embodied emotional qualities such as joy or grief. In many traditional West African dances, what may look to Western eyes like abstract or formal patterns of rhythmic dancing carry symbolic meaning and serve a moral and spiritual purpose. A dance may celebrate fertility or coming of age; it may promote healing, counter death, or be an act of grieving; it may embody the attributes of gods and ancestors. In *butoh, choreographers such as *Hijikata and *Ōno and the group Dai Rakudakan create striking visual images and spiritual or psychological themes through techniques of bodily distortion, fantastic costumes, whitened faces and bodies, and extreme exertion, without overtly telling stories or creating characters.

A late eighteenth-century European debate about theatrical dancing casts some light on this discussion of dance and dance-drama. Right at the centre of the continuum is *ballet d'action*, or story ballets, created by critics of danced divertissements in operas that reduced dance to ornament. They argued that dancers could act dramas with strong narratives (especially *tragedies), without words, and recommended using well-known myths and stories. The ballets created by these choreographers were dance-dramas in the sense that they used choreography as the instrument for dramatic structure, combining mime and expressive dance to convey events and characters. This strand of ballet continued in romantic nineteenth-century ballets, the modernist ballets of *Fokine, and the narrative ballets of Frederick Ashton and the psychological dramas of Antony Tudor. However, even the imperial Russian ballets in the late nineteenth century, criticized by reformers like Fokine for devoting too much time to ornamental divertissements, were built on the story ballet model. In modern dance, Martha *Graham also created psychologically focused narrative dramas, especially in her dances of the 1940s and 1950s based on Greek myths. While narrative dance-dramas seem to exist in many cultures worldwide, in most non-Western cultures they include verbal storytelling, often in song. This category of mute choreographic storytelling—one result of the artistic specialization and fragmentation that has characterized the arts in Europe and its colonies since the eighteenth century—seems to be a largely Western invention, like absolute music.

Edging even closer to dance-drama is dance-theatre. Here the performances are still on the dance side of the dance/theatre divide, rather than existing as *physical theatre or a true marriage of dance and theatre. Movement predominates, but in addition to choreography these events include verbal components as well as dramatic structures. Contemporary forms of dance-theatre include the late twentieth-century German Tanztheater of *Bausch; many instances of postmodern dance in the West; and some modern dance.

Although dance and drama are sister arts, the emphasis in the former on the visual and kinaesthetic senses and in the latter on the aural sense, especially in verbal form, at times makes them seem worlds apart. While their different emphases have sometimes led to rivalry and aesthetic competition, especially in the history of dance theory in the West, in many world traditions pure music and pure dance occur rarely. Rather, the distinctive features of dance and drama complement one another, appearing together in varying proportions in a broad gamut of hybrid forms. SB

Dancourt, Florent-Carton (1665–1725) French actor and dramatist. Born into a good family and destined for the law, Dancourt met and married an actress, daughter of the celebrated actor La Thorillière, and followed her into the *Comédie-Française. He performed with distinction in *Molière's plays, earning the favour of Louis XIV and the Dauphin. He retired from the company in 1718. As a playwright Dancourt became a master of the *comedy of manners, exploiting topical foibles or abuses: gambling, social climbing, the lottery mania. In *Le Chevalier à la mode* (1687) the central *character is an impudent young adventurer trying to make his way by a rich marriage; *Les Bourgeoises à la mode* (1692) and *Les Bourgeoises de qualité* (1700) both show rich bourgeois wives imitating their 'betters'. Written in prose, Dancourt's plays make their *satirical point with considerable *realism. WDH

Dane, Clemence (Winifred Ashton) (1888–1965) English playwright. Clemence Dane was one of a handful of women playwrights to achieve West End success between the wars. A multi-faceted talent, Dane was a teacher, portrait artist, novelist, and actress as well as a dramatist. Similarly, her plays range widely in genre, encompassing social problems (*A Bill of Divorcement*, 1921; *The Way Things Happen*, 1924), poetic historical drama (*Will Shakespeare*, 1921), *musicals (*Adam's Opera*, 1928), religious drama (*The Saviors*, 1942), children's plays (*Shivering Shocks*, 1923), and adaptations (*The Happy Hypocrite*, 1936). Dane also wrote the screenplays for Greta Garbo's *Anna Karenina* (with Salka Viertel, 1935) and *Fire over England* (with Sergei Nolbandov, 1936). Her most successful work was *A Bill of Divorcement*, a *melodrama about mental illness and unfair divorce laws, which ran for over 400 performances in London and was filmed in 1932, starring Katharine Hepburn. MDG

Daniels, Ron (1942–) Brazilian-born British director. Having founded the Workshop theatre of São Paulo in 1960, Daniels came to England to train as an actor but soon Peter Cheeseman at Stoke-on-Trent invited him to direct. In 1974 he mounted *Rudkin's *Afore Night Comes* at the *Royal Shakespeare Company's the Other Place in Stratford, and was put in charge of that small theatre in 1979. At the RSC his interest in social and historical conditions led him to *Edgar's *Destiny* (1976) and to controversial productions such as Anthony Burgess's *A Clockwork Orange 2000* (1990). His versions of Shakespeare in the 1980s— *Romeo and Juliet* (repeated at the *Guthrie Theatre), *Pericles*, *Timon of Athens*, and *Hamlet*— were directed with simplicity and clarity. In the late 1980s Daniels ran the Mermaid Theatre in London. He directed Shakespeare extensively abroad, including productions of *Hamlet* (*American Repertory Theatre, 1991), *Titus Andronicus* (Tokyo, 1992), *Henry IV* (ART, 1993), and continues to work freelance in England (*Poliakoff's *Remember This* for the *National Theatre, 1999).   KN

Daniels, Sarah (1956–) One of the 'radical *feminist' playwrights in England of the 1980s, along with *Gems and *Churchill, Daniels was nurtured at the *Royal Court. Her provocative plays, like *Masterpieces* (1983), which presents *pornography as part of a gynocidal culture, feature women struggling with corrupt patriarchy. *Neaptide* (1986), the first play about *lesbian rights produced at the *National Theatre, was attacked for 'man-hating', loose structure, and didacticism. Daniels's other plays include *Ripen our Darkness* (1981), *Byrthrite* (1987), *The Gut Girls* (1988), *Beside Herself* (1990), *Morning Glory* (2000), and *Flying under Bridges* (2005).   GAO

Danjūrō family The Ichikawa family, whose senior actor usually took the stage name Danjūrō, was the dominant *kabuki acting family in Edo (Tokyo) from the 1690s until the twentieth century. **Danjūrō I** (1660–1704) is credited with inventing the bravura *acting style known as *aragoto* in which heroic men or deities engage in wild acts of superhuman strength. He wrote many of the plays he starred in. A dedicated artist and devoted family man, Danjuro was nonetheless partial to alcohol and bisexual love affairs; a devout believer in his gods, he also emulated his samurai ancestors in his ambition to master all competitors. He was murdered on stage by a rival actor.

Danjūrō II (1688–1758) dominated Edo kabuki for half a century. His innovations included striped make-up for *aragoto* *heroes, and a new, romantic *aragoto* *character with elements of commoner identity. He made *aragoto kabuki* essential to the calendar of kabuki events. **Danjūrō IV** (1711–82) added elements of *villain acting to *aragoto* and his son **Danjūrō V** (1741–1806) played a wider range of roles than any of his predecessors, relying less on the inherited body of family classics.

In 1832 **Danjūrō VII** (1791–1859) consolidated the authority of the line by establishing the 'Eighteen Great Plays' of the Danjūrō tradition, mostly by the first two Danjūrōs. In 1840 he created the *matsubamme* genre (a kabuki dance-drama based on *nō staging) but in 1842 was banished from Edo for ten years for breaking sumptuary laws in his productions. He spent most of his exile as a star actor in Osaka. **Danjūrō VIII** (1823–1854) blossomed during his father's exile. A beloved actor of romantic male leads, he committed suicide in Osaka for reasons that remain obscure. His younger brother, *Ichikawa Danjūrō IX (1838–1903), was kabuki's great figure in the late nineteenth century; he had no sons and his son-in-law was named Danjūrō X posthumously. From 1903 to 1952 there was no active Danjūrō in kabuki, but **Danjuro XII** (1946–) became a leading actor.   LRK

D'Annunzio, Gabriele (1863–1938) Italian writer and director. With his lover Eleonore *Duse, D'Annunzio dreamed of creating an open-air theatre where they would produce *Greek *tragedies and D'Annunzio's modern tragedies. Though the project never materialized, Duse inspired his major plays, though he promised his first, *The Dead City* (1898), to *Bernhardt in a French translation. In 1897 Duse premièred the dramatic poem *A Spring Morning's Dream* in Paris; and with the *realist actor *Zacconi, she played in *La Gioconda* (1899), *La Gloria* (1899), and the first Italian production of *The Dead City* (1901). That same year, under D'Annunzio's direction, she opened *Francesca da Rimini* (1901), his spectacular medieval tragedy, complete with *chorus. But the plays were considered too literary, formal, and badly structured. *Daughter of Jorio* (1904), a *pastoral tragedy in verse, was his only resounding success. His decision to allow Irma *Gramatica to première as the earthy prostitute Mila di Codra, a part he had promised to Duse, caused the break-up of their relationship. Facing bankruptcy and *censorship in Italy, D'Annunzio lived in Paris from 1911 to 1915 and wrote in French and Italian for theatre and film. Several works starred the Russian dancer Ida Rubinstein, including *Le Martyre de saint Sébastien* (1911, music by Debussy, *scenography by *Bakst, choreography by *Fokine), a *total theatre piece in the *symbolist style. D'Annunzio became a hero in the First World War.   JEH

Dasté, Jean (1904–94) French actor and director. Son-in-law of *Copeau, Dasté was instrumental in the development of decentralized theatre in post-war France, founding the Comédie de

Saint-Étienne as one of the first provincial Centres Dramatiques in 1947. His eclectic programming there ranged from an adaptation of a *medieval play, *Un miracle de Notre-Dame*, to the first French production of *Brecht's *The Caucasian Chalk Circle* (1957). An accomplished actor, Dasté appeared in such monumental films as Renoir's *La Grande Illusion* (1937), Vigo's *L'Atalante* (1934), Truffaut's *L'Enfant sauvage* (*The Wild Child*, 1970), and *Mnouchkine's *Molière*.   DGM

Davenant, William (1606–68) English playwright and *manager. Born to the wife of an Oxford innkeeper who later became mayor, Davenant was reputed to have been the godson of Shakespeare and did nothing to scotch the suggestion that the relationship may have been closer. By the early 1630s Davenant had done military service and thus gained royal favour; contracted syphilis, which left him disfigured; married the first of three wives; been convicted of murder (pardoned in 1638); and tried his hand at playwriting. The success in 1634 of a *comedy, *The Wits*, and especially of his heroic *tragicomedy *Love and Honour*, settled him on a theatrical career, and over the next five years he wrote at least seven more plays for the King's Men (*see* CHAMBERLAIN'S MEN). Davenant became the principal writer of court *masques after the success of *The Temple of Love* in 1635, and he was appointed Poet Laureate in 1638. In March 1639 he secured a *patent for a large new theatre for the presentation of 'music, musical presentments, scenes, dancing or other the like' by a company that he would assemble. The project was blocked but he retained the patent. The following year he was appointed governor of *Beeston's Boys, but was soon in the King's service in the Bishops' Wars, for which he was knighted in 1643.

Davenant remained a royalist through the Civil War and the Interregnum. By 1655 he was in London, planning representations and shows, and in May 1656 began a series of *operatic performances at Rutland House, his London residence, and continued later at the old Cockpit. The best known, *The Siege of Rhodes* (1656, revised 1661), was later cited by *Dryden as the first *heroic play. With the Restoration, Davenant resurrected his patent, and he and *Killigrew obtained exclusive rights to the performance of plays in London. Killigrew's King's Company eventually settled the Theatre Royal, *Drury Lane; Davenant's less experienced company at the Duke's Theatre, *Lincoln's Inn Fields, remodelled to accommodate changeable scenery. While Killigrew inherited rights to the large repertory of the King's Men, Davenant was granted

rights only for his own plays and nine by Shakespeare, with the proviso that they be 'improved' and modernized for production. The result was a series of Shakespearian adaptations (including *Macbeth* and *The Tempest*); other than these, a translation of a French play, and a dramatic medley (*A Playhouse Let*), Davenant contributed no original plays to the Restoration stage. He had found his true calling as an impresario.   RWV

Davidson, Gordon (1933–) American *producer and director. As *artistic director of the Mark Taper Forum in Los Angeles, Davidson held one of the longest tenures in *regional theatre (1967–2005), one that made him an influential national figure. As a producer he pioneered new plays at the Taper with a programme called New Theatre for Now. As a director he attracted early attention on two coasts with his productions of *In the Matter of J. Robert Oppenheimer* (1968) and *The Trial of the Catonsville Nine* (1970). In 1976 he won a Tony award for his direction of *The Shadow Box*, which started at the Taper before moving to Broadway. In 1989, while remaining head of the Taper, he became producing director for the Ahmanson Theatre, its larger commercial affiliate.   STC

Davies, Howard (1945–) Welsh director. Davies was an associate of the *National Theatre, the Almeida, and the *Royal Shakespeare Company, for which he ran the Donmar Warehouse in London. His work emphasizes social context, especially in acclaimed versions of Shakespeare and American drama. At the RSC he directed *Bond's *Bingo* (1976), *Gems's *Piaf* (1978), *Macbeth* (1982), *Hampton's *Les Liaisons Dangereuses*, and *Troilus and Cressida* (both 1985). At the National successful productions include *Williams's *Cat on a Hot Tin Roof* (1988), *Boucicault's *The Shaughraun* (1988), Nick Stafford's *Battle Royal* (1999), *Miller's *All my Sons* (2000), and O'Neill's *Mourning Becomes Electra* (2003). His work at the Almeida includes West End transfers such as *Albee's *Who's Afraid of Virginia Woolf?* (1996) with Diana *Rigg, and *O'Neill's *The Iceman Cometh* (1998) with Kevin Spacey. His Broadway productions of *My Fair Lady* (1993) and *Private Lives* (2002) were well received. *Operas in Britain include Rossini's *The Italian Girl* (1997), *Mozart's *Idomeneo* (1991), and *Verdi's *I due Foscari* (1993). His film of *Hare's *Secret Rapture* (1994) is also notable.   KN

Davies, Robertson (1913–95) Canadian writer. Internationally known as a novelist, Davies was first of all a man of the theatre. A leading actor at Queen's University, Ontario, and then at

Oxford, after graduation he worked at the *Old Vic (1938–40) as an actor and *dramaturg under *Guthrie. After returning to Canada, in 1942 he became editor of a daily newspaper in Peterborough, where he helped found the Peterborough Little Theatre and directed award-winning productions. He also wrote some widely produced Canadian *comedies such as *Overlaid* (1946), *Fortune my Foe* (1948), and *At my Heart's Core* (1950), which examined the place of art and imagination in a conservative post-war Canada that seemed indifferent to such ideas; another play, *Love and Libel*, directed by Guthrie, *toured widely in 1960. Davies helped in the founding of the *Stratford Festival, and wrote three books chronicling its first years (1953–5).   DWJ

Davis, Hallie Flanagan *See* FLANAGAN, HALLIE.

Davis, Henrietta Vinton (1860–1941) *African-American actress and *manager, an elocutionist and orator who specialized in Shakespearian *monologues. Encouraged by Frederick Douglass, Davis made her theatrical debut in 1883. A decade later she founded a theatre in Chicago where she produced and acted in work by black dramatists. At the turn of the century she *toured as an actress throughout the USA, the Caribbean, and Latin America, and for a time managed the Covent Garden Theatre in Kingston, Jamaica. She was dedicated to creating an *audience for black performance at a time when African Americans were excluded from the mainstream. Eventually Davis despaired of a full-fledged theatrical career to devote her energies to politics, being especially dedicated to the Marcus Garvey movement from 1919 to 1931.   BBL

Davis, Ossie (1917–2005) *African-American actor of multiple talents. In 1941 Davis landed a role with Harlem's Rose *McClendon Players. Five years later he starred in *Jeb* to great acclaim, and he met his future wife, the actress Ruby *Dee. In 1947 they *toured in *Anna Lucasta*, and Davis was on Broadway again in 1951 in a revival of *Connelly's *The Green Pastures*. During the McCarthy era, when Davis was blacklisted in Hollywood, the pair staged Davis's play about the politics of McCarthyism, *Alice in Wonder* (1953), appeared that same year in *The World of Sholem Aleichem*, and Davis replaced Sidney Poitier in *Hansberry's *A Raisin in the Sun*. Davis wrote and starred in *Purlie Victorious* (1961), a *satire of racial stereotypes, which became the Broadway *musical *Purlie* in 1970. Appearing in many roles in film and television, Davis was on Broadway again in 1986 in *Gardner's *I'm Not Rappaport*. His play for

young people about *Robeson was produced in New York in 1998.   BBL

Dawison, Bogumił (1818–72) Polish actor. Dawison gradually gained respect and star status in Lvov. Bilingual, he began to perform with the German company as well. At first this hampered his career, since the Polish-speaking public viewed the German theatre as a threat to native culture in Lvov, then under Austrian rule. Frustrated, Dawison moved to Hamburg (1847) and guest-starred in other German cities. He became the leading actor at the *Burgtheater, Vienna (1849–53), and the Royal Theatre, Dresden (1854–64). He *toured Western Europe, the United States (1866–7), and his native Poland to great critical acclaim. His penetrating gaze, internal energy, and the ability to imitate were put to excellent use in roles such as Othello, Richard III, Macbeth, Shylock, Mephistopheles, and Franz Moor (in *Schiller's *The Robbers*).   KB

Dear, Nick (1955–) English playwright. Dear gained early success with *Royal Shakespeare Company productions of *Temptation* (1984), followed by his portrait of William Hogarth, *The Art of Success* (1986, also New York), which was winner of the Whiting award and was nominated for the Olivier Award, as was *A Family Affair* (after *Ostrovsky; *Cheek by Jowl, 1988). Playwright in residence at the Royal Exchange, Manchester (1987–8), his later plays include *Food of Love* (1988), *The Last Days of Don Juan* (after Tirso de *Molina, 1990), and *In the Ruins* (1990). In 1993 *A Family Affair* premièred at the Almeida *Opera Festival as a libretto, as did *Siren Sony* in 1994. The RSC staged *Zenobia* (2001), and the *National Theatre *Summerfolk* (1999) and *Power* (2003). Screenplays include Dostoevsky's *The Gambler* for Channel 4 television, plus *The Last Days of Don Juan* and an adaptation of Jane Austen's *Persuasion* for Hollywood.   BRK

de Berardinis, Leo (1940–2008) Italian actor, director, and author. During the socio-political ferment of the mid-1960s and 1970s, under the influence of *Brecht and the *Living Theatre, de Berardinis and amateur actors created memorable dialect pieces that incorporated Neapolitan popular culture and music. After this counterculture movement failed, he moved to Bologna's cooperative company Nuova Scena to direct *Gelber's *The Connection* (1983), a series of productions based on Shakespeare, and poetic solo works—*Dante* and *Song of Songs*. In 1987 he formed his own company, Teatro di Leo, producing *Macbeth* (1988), *Acts IV and V of Othello* (1992), *King Lear* (1997), and *Strindberg's

To Damascus (1989). His *multimedia reinterpretations of the classics manipulated projections, *dance, *music, and non-traditional casting. Another solo work, *Like a Variety Star* (2000), revealed his reverence for the *variety star as a total man of the theatre, a description that applied to him. From 1994 to 1997 he headed Santarcangelo's summer festival of experimental theatre. JEH

Deburau, Jean-Gaspard (1796–1846) French *mime. Memorably brought to life by *Barrault in Marcel Carné's film *Les Enfants du paradis* (1945), Deburau was one of the outstanding figures of the French popular theatre during the 1830s and 1840s. Born as Jan Kaspar Dvorak in Bohemia, he came from a family of *acrobats and *circus performers, making his debut at the Théâtre des Funambules in 1816. Here he developed the mime *character *Pierrot in a long series of sketches which endeared him to the popular *audiences of the 'Boulevard du Crime'. A sad misanthrope, this alter ego was to take on a darker, even a threatening, character after April 1836; out walking with his wife, Deburau was insulted by a young apprentice, who called his wife a whore: he felled the youth with his stick, and the blow proved fatal. Acquitted of unlawful killing, he returned to an enthusiastic welcome from the Funambules audience, but his future performances were marked by the event. He was also the subject of a play by *Guitry in 1918. WDH

decorum *See* NEOCLASSICSM.

Decroux, Étienne (1889–1991) French *mime, actor, and theorist. Inspired by *Copeau, Decroux invented modern 'corporeal mime' as a reaction against the white-faced *pantomime of *Deburau and his followers. Corporeal mime emphasizes articulation of the torso and de-emphasizes expressive face and hands, which were of primary importance in Deburau's pantomime. Yet corporeal mime was almost eclipsed during Decroux's lifetime by the performances of his celebrated student *Marceau, who created his own pantomime form which owed more to Deburau than to Decroux's modernism. Decroux was also the teacher of *Barrault and thousands of other students during his 60-year teaching career. A stage, radio, and film actor (best known for his role as Deburau *père* in *Les Enfants du paradis*, 1945), Decroux had a passion for language, politics, and poetry, some of which is apparent in his *Words on Mime* (1962), which encapsulates his main lines of thought. *Barba wrote that Decroux is 'perhaps the only European master to have elaborated a system of rules comparable to that of an Oriental tradition'. TL

Dee, Ruby (1924–) *African-American actress and playwright, who first appeared on Broadway in 1943 and in the 1946–7 season starred in *Anna Lucasta*, which she *toured with her husband Ossie *Davis. Her career advanced greatly with her performance as Ruth in *Hansberry's *A Raisin in the Sun* (1959). She was back on Broadway in *Purlie Victorious* in 1961. At the American Shakespeare Theatre in Connecticut she was the first African-American actress to appear in leading roles, as Kate in *Taming of the Shrew* and Cordelia in *King Lear* (1965). *Off-Broadway she was featured with James Earl *Jones in *Fugard's *Boesman and Lena* (1970). Her own scripts include *Twin Bit Gardens* (1976), *Take It from the Top* (a *musical, 1979), and *Zora Is my Name*, on Zora Neale *Hurston. Dee's one-person show *My One Good Nerve* (1998) was based on her life. BBL

de Filippo, Eduardo (1900–84) Italian playwright, actor, and director, known throughout Italy simply as Eduardo. The illegitimate son of the playwright *Scarpetta and Luisa de Filippo, he made his debut at the age of 4 in his father's play *The Geisha*. After the success of his own one-act *Sik-Sik, the Masterful Magician* (1930), he formed a company with his brother Peppino and sister Titina, opening in 1931 in Naples, the next year collaborating with *Pirandello in adapting stories for the stage. The company dissolved after the war, largely due to tension between the brothers. In his long career, de Filippo wrote 39 plays, several collections of poetry, and many adaptations of works by Neapolitan writers. He directed all his plays and acted in most. His mature works, translated and produced widely, include *Christmas at the Cupiellos* (1937), *Filumena Marturano* (1946), *These Ghosts!* (1946), *Voices from Within* (1948), *Saturday, Sunday, Monday* (1959), and *The Art of Comedy* (1964). In London, *Zeffirelli's productions of *Saturday, Sunday, Monday* (*Old Vic, 1973) with *Olivier and *Plowright, and of *Filumena* with Plowright (1977), were particularly notable.

Most of de Filippo's works were written in a Neapolitan dialect designed to represent the character of ordinary people. Fascism and the war affected his work, which after 1945 became sombre and complex, as in *Napoli milionaria!*, about the moral damage of the war on ordinary people. In the 1950s and the 1960s his plays reflected major social changes in Italy: traditional corruption in Neapolitan politics was attacked in *The Local Authority* (1960) and *The Contract*

(1967), and his last play, *Exams Never End* (1973), written a few years after the legalization of divorce, treats disintegration of the family. De Filippo also wrote extensively for film, television, and *opera.   DMcM

de Graft, Joe (1924–78) Ghanaian dramatist, director, and teacher. His early domestic drama *Sons and Daughters* should be set beside a much more ambitious transposition of *Hamlet* to northern Ghana (*Hamile*) and *Through a Glass Darkly* (originally *Visitor from the Past*, 1962). Clashes within the University of Ghana led to his move to Kenya where he wrote *Muntu*, a pageant-drama about the experience of Africa. He also acted with distinction. Back in Ghana during the 1970s, de Graft found inspiration in Shakespeare and radically reworked *Macbeth* to incorporate the experience of politics in post-independence Africa. He also created more roles for female students. *Mambo* was premièred in 1978, by which time he was seriously ill.   JMG

De Groen, Alma (1941–) Australian *feminist playwright. De Groen's first performed work, *The Joss Adams Show* (1970), enjoyed an international reception. Her plays often represent marginalized women who respond to their entrapment with bizarre behaviour. In *The Rivers of China* (1987) De Groen interweaves the last days of Katherine Mansfield's life with a science fiction narrative. In *Vocations* (1981), women struggle to maintain integrity in the face of patriarchal demands, and *The Girl Who Saw Everything* (1991) is a study of generational responses to feminism. De Groen has also written for television, film, and radio.   SBS

Dekker, Thomas (*c.*1572–1632) English dramatist. As a playwright for the *Admiral's Men he contributed to more than 40 plays in the five years from 1598, and throughout his career often worked in collaboration: in 1604 with *Middleton, in 1604–5 with *Webster, in 1621–4 with *Ford. The frantic pace of his work reflects the dominant fact of his professional life, his driving poverty; he was imprisoned for debt at least three times. The longest spell was for seven years from 1612, probably as a result of expenses he incurred in devising that year's Lord Mayor's pageant. When he emerged, white-haired, it was into a different theatrical world: the figures who had dominated it—*Henslowe, *Burbage, Shakespeare—all dead, fashion now favouring courtlier modes of drama, to which he duly turned his hand. The Dekker plays which have lasted in the repertory, *The Shoemaker's Holiday* (1599) and *The Roaring Girl* (with Middleton, 1611), are notable for their bourgeois London settings and their racy, demot-

ic vitality more than complex narrative; but in his own time Dekker was a professional who could master any genre from intrigue *tragedy to rollicking *farce.   MJW

Delaney, Shelagh (1939–) English playwright, best known for *A Taste of Honey* (1958, filmed 1962), which concerns a pregnant young girl who is thrown out by her slatternly mother, directed by Joan *Littlewood at the *Theatre Workshop. When it transferred to the West End Delaney was recognized as one of the few 'angry young women' of the British new wave, and the play was instrumental in making regional accents and working-class lives serious dramatic subjects. *The Lion in Love* (1960), a bleak account of a dysfunctional and alcoholic family, was less well received. *The House That Jack Built* (television 1977, stage 1979) followed a marriage from the drunken aftermath of the wedding through crises to partial reconciliation. All of her plays are remarkable for the affection and resilience of the female *characters, and the tender concern displayed for the broken lives of the *protagonists. Delaney has also written successful screenplays, including *Charlie Bubbles* (1968) and *Dance with a Stranger* (1985).   DR

Delsarte, François (1811–71) French singing teacher and theorist. Delsarte studied voice at the Paris Conservatoire (1826–9) and performed as a tenor at the *Opéra-Comique. He took exception to the methods used, which he thought impaired his voice, and evolved his own method for teaching voice, expression, and *acting to actors (*Rachel, *Macready), singers (Jenny Lind), composers (Bizet), as well as the clergy, orators, painters, and sculptors. Delsarte's complex system is based on an infinite number of intersecting trinities such as: mind, soul, and body; head, heart, and lower trunk; Father, Son, and Holy Ghost; eccentric, concentric, and neutral. Delsarte's system taught precepts such as 'movement first, then speech', and 'to each spiritual function responds a function of the body. To each grand function of the body, corresponds a spiritual act.' Americans Steele *MacKay, Genevieve Stebbins, and Ted Shawn (*see* ST DENIS, RUTH) were most responsible for the continuation of Delsarte's teachings into the twentieth century. Practitioners as diverse as Mathias Alexander (founder of the Alexander Technique), *Grotowski, and Isadora *Duncan attributed primary importance to Delsarte. Much of contemporary performance practice, especially in modern *dance, would be unimaginable without his work.   TL

de Mille, Agnes (1905–93) American chore-ographer. The niece of Hollywood director Cecil B. DeMille, Agnes de Mille (family members chose different spellings) defied the discourage-ment of an early *ballet teacher and pursued training in London, where she studied with Marie Rambert, gave solo recitals, and began creating her own work. During the 1930s she travelled be-tween London, New York, and Hollywood, chor-eographing for film, Broadway, and the concert stage. Her association with Ballet Theatre began in the company's initial season (1939) and eventu-ally produced, among others, *Black Ritual* (1940), the first ballet to use black dancers, *Rodeo* (1942), first commissioned by the *Ballets Russes de Monte Carlo, and *Fall River Legend* (1948). In 1943, de Mille's eighteen-minute dream ballet for *Rodgers and *Hammerstein's *Oklahoma!* considerably ad-vanced the use of movement as an integral element in plotting and characterization in *musical come-dy; de Mille wrote the *scenario herself and directed the ballet. In the 1950s she launched a distin-guished literary career, writing memoirs, dance and cultural histories, and several lively and tart biographies.   LTC

Dench, Judi (1934–) English actress, the most distinctively voiced of her generation, who has consistently won acclaim for the psychological veracity, remarkable emotional range, warmth, and fearlessness of her portrayals. In her first *Old Vic seasons (1957–61) she was directed by *Zeffirelli as Juliet. Over 24 roles with the *Royal Shakespeare Company since 1961 include Tita-nia, Isabella, Viola, Beatrice, Lady Macbeth with *McKellen, Major Barbara, *O'Casey's Juno, and Mother Courage. At the *National Theatre since 1982 she notably played Lady Bracknell, Cleopatra, Arkadina, Mrs Rafi in *Bond's *The Sea*, and *Pinter's Deborah in *A Kind of Alaska*. In the commercial theatre unexpected successes showing her versatility were Lika in *The Promise* (1967) and Sally Bowles in *Cabaret* (1968). Since 1957, when she appeared in *Talking to a Stranger*, her numerous (often award-winning) television appearances include the series *A Fine Romance*, *Behaving Badly*, *Absolute Hell*, and *Last of the Blond Bombshells*. Memorable film roles include *Saigon: Year of the Cat*, *Chocolat*, *Iris*, and two queens in 1997–8, Victoria in *Mrs Brown* and Elizabeth in *Shakespeare in Love*.   RAC

Dennis, John (1657–1734) English critic and playwright who began his career in the early 1690s. *The Impartial Critic* (1693) demonstrated the tolerant *neoclassicism that characterized his best criticism. *A Plot and No Plot* (1697), his first play, was followed by *On the Usefulness of the Stage* (1698), his contribution to the *Collier con-troversy. Over the next twelve years Dennis wrote seven more plays and produced the bulk of the criticism that was to earn him the title 'The Critic'. After the failure of *Appius and Virginia* (1709), he forsook the stage for ten years, and his career was increasingly characterized by literary quarrels, his criticism fuelled by personal animosity. Dennis abandoned playwriting for good after the failure in 1719 of *The Invader of his Country* and died in poverty.   RWV

denouement Literally 'unravelling' or 'untying' in French, in traditional *dramaturgy that part of a dramatic *action which immediately follows the turning point or *crisis, during which the knot of complications created in the rising action is resolved. The nature of the play dictates whether the denouement is a logical outcome of the dramatic action or an artificially imposed solution (*deus ex machina). There are instances of false denouements which ironically introduce fresh complications, and of *absurd denoue-ments which merely bring the action back to its beginnings, resolutions in which nothing is resolved.   RWV

Deshpande, P. L. (1919–2000) Marathi writer who wrote and directed 24 films between 1947 and 1954, often acting in them. He also worked in radio, and when television arrived in 1972 he was invited to create the inaugural programme. Of his fourteen dramatic works, only *To Each His Own* (1957) was original, a *satire on the teachings of hypocritical ascetics. The rest were adaptations of plays like *Priestley's *An Inspector Calls*, *Brecht's *Threepenny Opera*, and *Shaw's *Pygmalion*. His one-person performance of his book *Batatyachi Chaal* (*The Potato Tenement*, 1958) was a land-mark in Marathi theatre, proving that drama could be created without spectacle and traditional trappings; Deshpande played all the eccentrics of his fictional tenement, changing voice and bear-ing for each *character. He described himself as above all a performer, asserting that his writing too was a form of performance.   SGG

design *See* SCENOGRAPHY.

deus ex machina Literally, 'god from the ma-chine' in Latin, the term derives from the ancient *Greek practice of having gods arrive on stage via a *mechane* (crane) to resolve an otherwise insoluble situation. It now means any unexpected resolution by any arbitrary means. *Aristotle re-stricted use of the device to matters outside the play, noting that it was otherwise inartistic. Its use in *tragedy as an instrument of superior will, or as an ironic commentary on that will (as in *Euripides' *Orestes*), is nevertheless appropriate; and its use in *comedy—usually a sign effecting the recognition (*anagnorisis*)—properly underscores the role of chance in the comic world.   RWV

Deutsch, Ernst (1890–1969) German actor. Born in Prague of Jewish descent, Deutsch achieved prominence as the 'prototypical' *expressionist actor in 1916 in the Dresden première of *Hasenclever's *The Son*. He joined *Reinhardt as a leading actor at the *Deutsches Theater until 1933. He was particularly noted for playing young rebellious *characters. Between 1939 and 1945 he worked in the USA in both English and German productions. On his return to Germany in 1947, Deutsch worked at leading theatres in West Germany and Austria. His most notable performances were of Jewish characters such as *Schnitzler's Professor Bernhardi, Shylock, and *Lessing's *Nathan the Wise*, whom he invested with a new dignity in the context of post-war German philo-Semitism.   CBB

Deutsches Theater Berlin *playhouse. Opened in 1883 by a group of literary-minded theatre professionals, the 'DT' was designed to provide high-quality theatre under the leadership of *L'Arronge. Although his repertoire was not strikingly progressive, the theatre became important for a new generation of actors such as *Kainz and *Sorma. A major shift came in 1894 when *Brahm assumed the lease. For the next decade the DT became synonymous with the 'Brahm style', contemporary drama performed in a *naturalistic mode. In 1905 *Reinhardt took charge and added the smaller and more intimate Kammerspiele, making the complex one of the premier theatres in the German-speaking world. In 1933 the DT was confiscated by the Nazis and placed under the control of the Ministry of Propaganda. The appointed director, Hilpert, managed nevertheless to create an ambitious programme remarkably free of direct political interference until the closure of the theatre in 1945. After the war the DT came under Soviet administration. In 1946 Wolfgang Langhoff was appointed artistic director, a position he held until 1963 when he fell foul of the East German authorities. None of his successors was able to make a major contribution, though they included a number of important directors such as Alexander Lang, until the appointment of Thomas Langhoff in 1991. The theatre then regained national prominence, based on a fine ensemble and a commitment to Germany's dramatic tradition.   CBB

development, theatre for Widely used term from Africa to describe instrumental organizations and performances which mobilize *audiences into community development in such fields as health, agriculture, literacy, and conflict resolution. An influential post-independence movement called Laedza Batanani (which means 'the sun is up—it is time to work together'), emerging in Botswana in the mid-1970s, gave theatre for development wide currency. A series of regional and international workshops in the late 1970s and early 1980s spread the Laedza Batanani model, whereby theatre activists researched the problems of a targeted community, created a *scenario through debate, built this into a play through *improvisation, and took the play back to the community for performance, discussion, and follow-up planning. The first and last stages of this process were in close collaboration with social activists such as extension workers or primary healthcare nurses. This model, fuelled by funding from non-government organizations, spread through most of anglophone Africa during the 1980s, though several theatre activists critiqued its parochialism, crudely modernizing ideology, reinforcement of passive attitudes, and tendency to isolate development goals from broader issues of political economy. Enthusiasts implemented more participatory and critical methodologies, partly under the influence of *Boal's theories and partly by way of a return to indigenous traditions of participatory performance. Theatre for development is now a widely used technique in informal communication in Africa, and has built links with similar movements on other continents, and with radio and television. *See also* OPPRESSED, THEATRE OF THE.   DaK

Devine, George (1910–65) English actor, director, and *manager. After Oxford he acted professionally, and from 1936 to 1939 taught at the London Theatre Studio, founded by Michel *Saint-Denis, with whom he continued to work at the *Old Vic School after the war. In 1955 he became the artistic director of the new *English Stage Company, based at the *Royal Court Theatre, where he remained until shortly before his death. Although the ESC became associated with social *realism in the wake of the phenomenal success of *Osborne's *Look Back in Anger* (1956), Devine's own theatrical values were broader, embracing the *physical performance style of *Copeau, theatre of the *absurd, and the work of *Brecht's *Berliner Ensemble (which performed at the Court in 1956). Perhaps Devine's principal achievement was that he supported new dramatists (even when *audiences were slow to arrive), and provided a means by which they could develop their craft. He encouraged playwrights to become involved in *rehearsal, allowing them to forge close working relationships with directors, and established a writer's workshop. *Bond, *Arden, *Wesker, as well as Osborne, owed much of their early success to his energy and clarity of vision.   SWL

devising An approach to making performance and theatre that depends on the participation of all the producing group in all or most stages of the creative process, from conception to presentation. Devising often utilizes *collective creation, in which every member of the production team works on an equal footing to the rest. It is often contrasted with the 'traditional' sequence of playwright/play—director/production—actors/ performance, but this is partly misleading since devising frequently involves all these elements, though not necessarily in that order. It often features unpredictable working methods, such as *improvisation or co-authorship and the exchange or blurring of creative roles, but there are probably as many ways to devise a show as there are groups devising.

Devising was crucial to the *dada, *futurist, and *Bauhaus movements in twentieth-century Europe, as well as the *dance traditions founded by *Duncan and *Graham. But it was in the second half of that century that devising came into its own in the upsurge of counter-cultural activity created by the underground, alternative, and independent theatre movements with their roots in the 1960s. The great pioneer company was the *Living Theatre, for whom devising was the root of revolution against the commercialism and bureaucracy of the affluent society. A similarly radical agenda shaped the practice of subsequent devising groups on both sides of the Atlantic. Important early devisers in the USA included Teatro *Campesino (1965), the *Open Theatre (1963), and the *Performance Group (1967). In England devising was pioneered by the first theatre-in-education company at the Coventry Belgrade Theatre (1965), by the People Show (1965), and the Pip Simmons Theatre Company (1968), and in mainland Europe by Théâtre du *Soleil (France, 1964), Teater Terzijde (the Netherlands, 1965), and others.

Many independent groups followed their example, as devising was variously used to involve *communities, to explore and strengthen different identities (in *feminist, *gay, disability, and black theatre), to extend the reach of performance (in theatre-in-education, theatre in prisons, reminiscence theatre), or to create new aesthetic forms

and extend existing genres (in *performance art). Devising also impacted on more conventional creative processes as some directors formed partnerships with playwrights, designers, or composers, and as some performers created companies to challenge the dominance of the *director and to celebrate the power of the ensemble.

These widespread trends signal the potentially radical force of devising. Besides its challenge to established processes in theatre it has become a rallying call to revolution in society. *Boal in the 1970s and 1980s devised what he called the theatre of the *oppressed, and his image theatre, forum theatre, and invisible theatre were designed for easy access to devising, so that anyone might participate in them as a 'rehearsal for revolution'. Boal's influence was enormous, especially in the rapid spread of theatre for *development in poorer countries. Devising became an international phenomenon and a small but important factor in the global struggle for democratic rights.   BRK

Devrient family Of Huguenot origins, the first and greatest member of the family, **Ludwig** (1784–1832), made his name acting leading roles at the Dessau and Breslau court theatres before being called to the Berlin National Theatre by *Iffland in 1815. Although his tragic roles were relatively few—Shylock, Lear, and *Schiller's Franz Moor were the most celebrated—he represented them so strikingly that he quickly acquired a national reputation. He played the unconscious of his *characters, not through the stark contrasts and transitions used by his exact English contemporary Edmund *Kean, but through quietly bringing to the surface impulses, emotions, and fears that undermined the stability of the character and led *audiences to feel the forces of pity and fear, for *villainous characters as for *tragic *heroes. He was equally skilled at *comedy, being one of the first German actors to give a successful representation of Falstaff, but his speciality was in plays that required him to appear as several different characters. The peak of his fame passed with his first season at the National Theatre, caused by the competing tragic style of *Wolff as well as by Devrient's chronic alcoholism. During his years in Berlin, he gradually acquired a legendary reputation as a *romantic *poète maudit*, stemming from his nocturnal drinking bouts with E. T. A. Hoffmann. Devrient's wild imagination may well have contributed to some of Hoffmann's last stories. After Hoffmann's death in 1822, Devrient's powers went into rapid decline. He continued to tour German theatres, occasionally with success, but his powers had left him completely before he died.

Ludwig's three nephews were all successful. **Carl** (1797–1872) had a solid career playing roles in the heroic *Fach*. **Eduard** (1801–77) was an actor and director at the Royal Theatre in Berlin and later at the Dresden Court Theatre; his *History of German Acting* (1848–74) is still a major resource. The most celebrated was **Emil** (1803–72), whose acting was diametrically opposed to his uncle. As leading actor of the Dresden Court Theatre between 1831 and 1868, Emil became the model of the virtuoso actor who developed a repertoire of roles. His lack of response to other actors and excessive vanity earned him much enmity. The latter part of his career involved an intense rivalry with Bogumił *Dawison, who adopted a more robust approach to acting and was, from 1852 to 1864, also a member of the Dresden Court Theatre. Later generations of the family produced more actors but none achieved the distinction and public recognition of the first two generations.   SJCW

Dewhurst, Colleen (1926–91) Canadian-born American actress, president of Actors' Equity (1985–91). A powerful actress with a commanding presence and a deep, resonant voice, at the start of her career Dewhurst was associated with Circle in the Square, and later frequently worked with *Papp's *New York Shakespeare Festival. Her performance as Josie in *O'Neill's *A Moon for the Misbegotten* (1973) remains one of the greatest in American theatre. She was awarded her second Tony for this role; her first was for her portrayal of Mary Follett in *All the Way Home* (1960). Other O'Neill plays in which she performed included *Mourning Becomes Electra, Ah, Wilderness!,* and *Long Day's Journey into Night.*   TFC

Dexter, John (1925–90) English director. In 1957 *Osborne introduced Dexter, a former factory worker and actor, to the *Royal Court. Here he subsequently directed an empathetic première of *Wesker's East End trilogy. As associate director of the *National Theatre (1963–6, 1971–5), he directed *Shaffer's *The Royal Hunt of the Sun* (1964) and *Equus* (1973). Dexter worked as *Olivier's assistant on *Othello,* and directed Olivier's final performance, *Griffiths's *The Party* (1973). His meticulous pre-planning and firm control within the *rehearsal room earned him a large reputation. With *opera Dexter demonstrated easy control of spectacle and crowd movement. His opulent *Benvenuto Cellini* (1966), designed by *Svoboda for *Covent Garden, established Dexter in this form; he frequently directed for the Ham-

burg State Opera, and was director of production at the Metropolitan Opera, New York, from 1974. Here he produced an acclaimed *Aida* (1976), Berg's *Lulu* (1977), and worked with designer David Hockney on *Parade* (1981). His dream of running the *Stratford Festival was shattered when he was denied a Canadian visa. Dexter produced highly acclaimed West End shows in the 1980s: *Gambon in *Brecht's *Galileo* (1980), *Rigg in *Heartbreak House* (1982), and *The Cocktail Party* (1986).   KN

Dhlomo, Herbert I. E. (1903–56) South African journalist, playwright, and poet. In 1937 he became the first African librarian at the Carnegie Bantu library in Johannesburg. After a series of disagreements with his employees he left for Durban in 1941 where he became assistant editor of *The Natal Sun*. Dhlomo's creative work focused on the African experience. He wrote at least nine plays (published 1985) and numerous poems from 1936 onward. His initial play, *The Girl Who Killed to Save* (1936), was the first English-language drama to be published by a black South African. It deals with events surrounding the vision of the Xhosa prophetess Nangquase, which led to a mass cattle killing and famine in 1857.   YH

Diaghilev, Sergei (1872–1929) Russian *manager, founder of the *Ballets Russes. After various starts in St Petersburg, Diaghilev mounted six exhibitions devoted to the 'world of art' group (1901–6). All his subsequent projects were realized abroad, beginning with an exhibition of Russian art at the Paris Salon. In 1907 he organized five Russian music recitals and, in 1908, supervised a production of Mussorgsky's *Boris Godunov* at the Paris *Opéra. The year 1909 saw the first season of the Russian ballets in Paris with *scenography by *Benois and *Bakst, among others. The next season saw five *ballets, including Stravinsky's *The Firebird,* which launched the composer's career, followed by *Petrushka* with decor by Benois. These 'seasons' lasted until 1913 and included famous first performances of Ravel's *Daphnis and Chloe* (1912), Debussy's *Prélude à l'après-midi d'un faune* (1912), and the *riot-provoking première of Stravinsky's *The Rite of Spring* (1913), in which Diaghilev's leading dancer, Vaclav Nijinsky, was soloist and choreographer. During the 1913 season the company *toured widely in London, Vienna, Berlin, and South America. As well as receiving a sound musical education in his youth and acquiring fluency in seven European languages, Diaghilev possessed entrepreneurial flair, acute artistic judgement, and a hypnotic personality which inspired the company with his belief in a composite art form where music, scenography, and movement coalesced.   NW

dialogue From the Greek *dialogos* ('words between', or discourse), dialogue normally refers to speech between two or more *characters that conveys information or tone to the *audience. While theatrical performance is made up of a large number of other elements, and while the *action of a drama can be accomplished by means ranging from *monologue to actors' movements and gestures to kinetic scenery and *lighting, it is usually dialogue that is at the centre of a play and the chief concern of the playwright. A dramatic text customarily comprises dialogue and stage directions—though there are cases where one is used exclusively—and contains at least two characters to be played by different actors who speak, most commonly to one another.

In ancient *Greek theatre, especially in *tragedy from *Aeschylus on, lengthy exchanges between two characters sometimes occurred in *stichomythia*, the actors each reciting a complete line of hexameter verse as if they were playing tennis with a live grenade. Frequently one of the actors would have exchanges with the *chorus. The conventions of *neoclassicism, looking back to Greek models, maintained that dialogue should obey the rules of decorum in *comedy and tragedy, an aristocratic notion of appropriateness that was sustained in French playwriting from the 1630s until the rise of *romanticism 200 years later. The rhyming alexandrines (six-beat lines, like those of the Greeks) of *Racine, *Corneille, and *Molière represented a purified form of the discourse expected in the King's presence, just as the formalized postures and movements of actors (and *ballet dancers) were based upon the body gestures of courtiers. *Early modern English writers, on the other hand, often used highly colloquial and sometimes extremely rude speech, even in tragedy, to develop character and theme. *Jonson's *satires present powerful dialogue from deviant characters that *parodies their own moral status. Shakespeare's mastery of dialogue ranged from the *Lyly-influenced formality of *Love's Labour's Lost* (*c.*1594-5) to the flexible blank verse, often close to ordinary speech, of *Twelfth Night* and *Hamlet* (both *c.*1600-1) to the psychotic dialogue of Leontes in *The Winter's Tale* (1609). But in England the French influence eventually proved the stronger in tragedy, and after the Restoration neoclassical principles of dialogue appeared in the heroic couplets of *Dryden and *Otway.

Dialogue has not always been used for direct communication or rational discourse. While the *realist and *naturalist movements tended to rely on stage speech that was immediately comprehensible and in some way mirrored the audience's own utterances, the *avant-garde reactions of the early twentieth century often proposed more abstract modes, using speech in a musical manner or to obscure or deny meaning; notable examples include *Jarry's *Ubu roi* (Paris, 1897), *Strindberg's *A Dream Play* (Stockholm, 1901), and *Marinetti's *futurist evenings. Those experiments, together with *Artaud's theoretical attempts to lessen the dominance of dialogue, reached a climax with the theatre of the *absurd in Paris in mid-century. In the early work of *Ionesco, language is unstable and thoroughly unreliable. Characters in *The Bald Soprano* (1950) utter nothing but hollow clichés, while the old man and woman in *The Chairs* (1952) prepare for suicide by engaging in banal conversations with invisible guests. *Beckett's dialogic exchanges, particularly in *Waiting for Godot* (1953) and *Endgame* (1957), are masterpieces of *music-hall turns that revolve in comically hideous circles. *Krapp's Last Tape* (1958), a monodrama in which the character converses through a tape recording with his decades-younger self, prepared the way for Beckett's late dialogue *in extremis*, where an onstage figure interacts with electronically mediated speech, as in *Footfalls* (1976), *Rockaby* (1981), and *What Where* (1983).

One result of modernist challenges to the communicability and virtue of language has been a wide acceptance that stage speech is rarely innocent of ulterior motives. Many of the *acting and *rehearsal techniques developed since *Stanislavsky have relied upon his notion that a *subtext of character desire lies under the written dialogue, and that the actor's job in rehearsal is to delve into the subconscious soup of the text to discover a deeper meaning. Some late twentieth-century writers in the realist mode—*Pinter, *Mamet, *Koltès, *Kane—have sought a poetry of inarticulateness for their characters, often adapting the coarsest street speech to craft dialogue redolent of menace, sexuality, and vulnerability. On a political level, the suspicion of language has been central to *feminist and *African-American theatre, where the need to fashion a vocabulary free of patriarchal or racial oppression has led to valuable insights. *Churchill's overlapping dialogue in *Top Girls* (1982) and her linguistic experimentation in *Blue Heart* (1997) propose woman-centred alternatives to the Western dialogic tradition. Anna Deavere *Smith's use of recorded interviews to generate speech that can be delivered in either monologue or dialogue offers an open-text approach appropriate to her democratic reflections on race riots in *Fires in the Mirror* (1992) and *Twilight: Los Angeles, 1992* (1993).   DK

diaspora From the Greek *diaspeirein*, meaning 'disperse' or 'scatter', diaspora refers to peoples who have settled, voluntarily or by force, outside their homelands or their traditional or ancestral homelands. Originally referring to the dispersion of the Jews after the Captivity, during the nineteenth century the term became more widely used in the context of Zionism to describe the situation of Jewish people living outside the biblical land of Israel. Today it is applied to numerous exiled communities all over the world.

Diasporic theatre Diasporic theatre is not a fixed concept. It embraces both emigrant culture and post-colonial structures. In a narrower sense it describes the theatre of people living outside their original homeland, but also can be used to designate a minority group's theatre in opposition to a majority culture. As a consequence diasporic theatre functions as a site of cultural self-reflection and self-assurance, and often becomes a surrogate for the home country and culture. This surrogation can gain an autonomous status, so that the efficacy of diasporic theatre lies less in the reliability of its representation of the original than in the successful presentation of a collective imagination.

The emergence of diasporic theatre is often a symptom of social change. While diaspora originally referred to religious or national groups, diasporic theatre will often signify an increasing loss of the authority of traditional institutions. Not all kinds of culturally displaced theatres can be described as diasporic, however. People living outside their homeland—especially in imperialist or colonialist circumstances—have imported their theatre to their new home. But the exportation of ancient *Greek and *Roman theatre to far-flung empires, or the introduction of *opera in South America in the nineteenth century, was part of a hegemonic strategy. In these instances theatre functioned as a bridgehead to the motherland for those who were serving abroad and cannot be considered diasporic, since a diaspora is determined not only by geographic distance but also by the exclusion of the immigrants from the dominant culture which surrounds them.

Immigrant theatre During the huge waves of migration from Europe to America at the end of the nineteenth century new traditions of theatre were established as a reaction to the novel situation. Yiddish theatre is the paradigm. The invention of an explicitly Jewish theatre was new because religious tradition prohibited any kind of professional theatre. From its beginnings in 1877 in Romania, professional Yiddish theatre was an international theatre of *touring troupes. *Goldfaden founded the first ensemble to function as a means of enlightenment as well as of entertainment. He used Yiddish, a vernacular based on Old High German with elements of Hebrew and the Slavic tongues, because it was the common language of most Eastern European Jews. Within a short time centres of Yiddish theatre emerged, in Vilnius, Warsaw, Kiev, and elsewhere. Although Jews thought of their existence in Europe as diaspora, Yiddish theatre in Eastern Europe can hardly be described as diasporic since it was based on a vibrant culture and community. Even inside the majority culture of Russia, Lithuania, or Poland, Yiddish theatre could rely on the Jewish community as a stable social unity; its *audience was familiar with its aesthetics and its language.

At the end of the nineteenth century huge numbers of Jews emigrated from Russia and Eastern Europe to the West due to political oppression and increasingly violent anti-Semitism. Some of them remained in Germany or Austria, others went to the Americas; between 1881 and 1903, 1,300,000 Yiddish-speaking Jews arrived in the USA. Most of those stayed in New York City, congregated on the Lower East Side, preserving the culture of their homelands and speaking their mother tongue. Yiddish theatre thus rose in New York as a diasporic immigrant theatre, its spectators those who spoke a language that marked them as separate. The main purpose of Yiddish theatre was to create an atmosphere of the lost homeland—which was not the Holy Land, but the *shtetl*, the Eastern European ghetto—helping to overcome the cultural displacement and radical alteration in daily life caused by migration. Performances often occurred in a café atmosphere, comparable to *vaudeville or *music hall. Most of the plays concerned the abandoned *shtetl* and used well-known songs; some also addressed the problems of exile and assimilation, offering advice on living in the New World. Though productions were harshly criticized on aesthetic grounds, even detractors admitted the value of the symbiotic community of actors and their audience.

Ultimately the increasing loss of coherence within the New York Jewish community caused a crisis for the Yiddish theatre. In addition to the spread of the Jewish population away from the Lower East Side, identification with an Eastern European Jewish identity primarily determined by the experience of loss naturally ceased with the ageing of the generations of immigrants and the assimilation of their children and grandchildren. A long-term integration into American society erased the diasporic basis of Yiddish theatre, and the *shtetl* became an imaginative place, deriving more from transfiguring nostalgia than from individual experience (as in *Bock's *musical *Fiddler on the Roof*, 1964).

The development of diasporic theatre cannot be removed from the context of the majority culture, as exemplified by the Irish diaspora in the USA. Irish immigration was caused by harsh political and catastrophic economic circumstances, especially during the Great Hunger (1845–51), when very large numbers of people left Ireland. Soon the Irish appeared in the US theatre. In the majority theatre the stage Irishman was one of two popular demeaning stereotypes—the other one being the black slave—and was used as a source of entertainment. This representation was produced by the majority (though the Irish diasporic playwright *Boucicault both exploited the stage Irishman and altered him), whereas the Irish themselves looked for positive images. One such was the figure of Kathleen Mavourneen, imagined as the incarnation of the former homeland of Ireland. When in 1852 the famous Irish singer Catherine Hayes visited New Orleans she was conceived as the embodiment of Kathleen Mavourneen. But this process of symbolic identification was the consequence of an elaborate campaign by her manager, *Barnum, who understood the need of Irish immigrants for emotional contact with their mother country. Thus emigrant theatre is determined by a complex bundle of functions. Primarily it serves the nostalgic desire of representing the abandoned home, yet it also engages in the process of developing or maintaining cultural identity in the face of the demands of the new society. It is intimately tied to migration but depends on the scope granted to immigrants by the majority culture. German immigrants in the USA, for example, had a vivid tradition of German theatre in New York that almost disappeared during the First World War, when German culture was devalued by the majority.

Diaspora as a programme A second type of diasporic theatre emerged in the mid-twentieth century. As a result of the increasing importance of the American civil rights movement and the decline of European colonialism, political discourse about cultural identity changed. In formerly colonized states, especially in Africa and India, a post-colonial theatre rose to deal with the sometimes convoluted issues connected to independence and the colonial legacy. At the same time in Western countries, a new kind of diasporic

theatre appeared whose paradigm can be considered the black arts movement in the USA (*see* AFRICAN-AMERICAN THEATRE). In the 1960s the long-held ideal of America as a 'melting pot' of numerous cultural groups was increasingly questioned: the concept of an American identity common to all was seen by some radical thinkers and activists as part of a hegemonic strategy of appropriation that refused to recognize the distinctiveness of differing social and ethnic groups. Defining their own situation as diaspora, African-American activists stressed that the immigration of their ancestors was not voluntary, nor forced by economic circumstances and the desire for a better life, but originated in violence, the slave trade, and an oppression that was ongoing.

In contrast to immigrant theatre, which was more or less based on the individual memory of spectators of the former home, or at least on sentiments concerning this home, the black arts movement had to invent its own cultural tradition. The reference point 'Africa' was taken not as a concrete geographic or historic point but rather as an imaginative place, and the theatre operated as an institution of collective memory or collective imagination. A landmark in this development was the Black Arts Repertory Theatre and School in Harlem, founded in 1965 by *Baraka. Although the group lasted only a few years, it began a search for a theatre with distinctive black American aesthetics. Baraka's ideal of a revolutionary theatre, proclaimed in 1964, represented an aggressive form of self-assertion by marking itself as separate from white American society. In this case diasporic theatre meant breaking with the concept of integration, which was seen as a disguise for prolonging racial discrimination. While immigrant theatre is situated between the 'old' (the lost home) and the 'new' (the strange home), programmatic diasporic theatre seeks to (re)draw the border between one's own community and the majority in order to redefine the status of the minority.

Programmatic theatre of diaspora can be found as a strategy in other subaltern groups. A powerful example in the USA is Chicano (or Mexican-American) theatre. In 1965 the playwright Luis *Valdez founded El Teatro *Campesino as a company of and for Chicano migrant farm labourers in California, and since 1968 the troupe has been a professional theatre dealing with the Mexican diaspora in the USA. Their style has been a mix of elements drawn from Italian *commedia dell'arte*, Mexican popular theatre, and vaudeville. Its main purpose is to intervene in the negotiation of the status of Chicanos, whose situation in the USA has been shaped by a double experience of exclusion:

they have been marked as non-authentic by official political discourse in Mexico, and dominant America has marginalized them as Mexicans. Chicano theatre became a realm to develop a new cultural identity. While other types of diasporic theatres chose their point of reference in the lost or ancestral home, Chicano theatre concentrated on a mythical place, called Aztlán, which in Aztec mythology was the original home of the Aztecs before they came to Mexico. By taking Aztlán as a point of reference, Chicanos can define themselves as descendants of the Aztecs, meaning that not they but white Americans are the immigrants. This invented tradition deals with diaspora in a double way: the loss of a homeland becomes the subject of the discourse as well as the status of the Chicanos, who are no longer seen as 'illegal' immigrants but rather as reclaiming their position as the original owners of the land.

While immigrant theatre disappeared because of the increasing integration of its target group, programmatic diasporic theatre maintains difference in order to improve the cultural status of the minority. The search for a new aesthetic originates from the need to create the group's own aesthetic language, since identity can no longer be achieved by borrowing the methods of the majority culture.

The two types of diasporic theatre are not mutually exclusive, and at the start of the twenty-first century both kinds can still be observed. Nonetheless after 1990 an observable increase of interest took place in the dominant Western theatre in specific national and traditional performances, such as Indian *kathakali* or Japanese *kabuki*, in a movement called *interculturalism. Mostly these forms have been part of a process of appropriation that does not consider them within their specific context but rather takes them as parts and signs of a 'world culture'. The diasporic origins of these elements disappear under the veil of social integration, and the elements of foreign culture inscribed in them are always in danger of becoming merely folkloric window dressing.

Diasporic theatre is mostly an expression of cultural and social change—it may be caused by migration but it can be also a symptom of a vanishing social concept like that of the melting pot in the USA. In the latter twentieth century, diasporic theatre could further be regarded as a counter-concept to the increasing globalization of theatre. While artists like *Mnouchkine, *Brook, or Robert *Wilson used alien elements to create productions that could be understood all over the world, diasporic theatre remained part of a localization of culture and art—maintaining the importance of the specific in creating and negotiating cultural identity.   PWM

Dickens, Charles (1812–70) English writer and performer. In 1832 Dickens planned to audition before Charles *Kemble. But Dickens caught a cold, the audition was cancelled, and he made his career in fiction and journalism. He was, however, an outstanding amateur actor. After the collapse of his marriage in 1858 Dickens undertook to read passages from his books in public. This venture produced reassuring profits and *applause but the strain probably shortened his life. His friend *Macready equated Dickens's rendering of the murder of Nancy (from *Oliver Twist*) with two *Macbeths. Dickens wrote little expressly for the stage but his novels have been a constant inspiration. They were dramatized by numerous contemporary playwrights, including W. T. *Moncrieff, *Boucicault, and *Gilbert. More recently their episodic construction has lent itself to radio and television serialization. They have been filmed with both human and animated performers, and have formed the basis for *musicals and *ballets and the remarkable *Royal Shakespeare Company version of *Nicholas Nickleby* (1980), adapted by *Edgar.   FD

Diderot, Denis (1713–84) French playwright and dramatic theorist. One of the most notable polymaths of his generation, chief editor of the *Encyclopédie*, Diderot pioneered the introduction on the French stage of *le drame*, which, drawing on the examples of *Lillo, established an intermediate form between *tragedy and *comedy. Diderot's theoretical writing was equally forward looking, and called for changes in staging and *acting. Neither of his plays, *The Natural Son* (published 1757, performed 1771) and *Father of the Family* (published 1758, performed 1761), was very successful, but his argument that conventional *characters should give way to 'conditions'—professions, social milieu, and family relationships—affected much subsequent thought. Although his ideas anticipated the serious drama of the nineteenth century, the idiom of *drame *bourgeois was soon handled more effectively by *Mercier and *Beaumarchais. Diderot's importance as a theoretician is assured by his *Paradox of the Actor* (not published until 1830), in which he argues cogently that the great actor depends on controlled technique rather than on sensibility; and by such occasional writings as his *Observations sur Garrick* (1770), in which he studied *Garrick as an illustration of the same thesis. *See also* NEOCLASSICISM.   WDH

difangxi (ti-fang hsi) Chinese regional opera. All but two of the over 300 forms of opera constituting the Chinese music-drama tradition known as *xiqu* (theatre [of] song) are classified as regional opera forms. The exceptions are the well-known Kun opera (**kunqu*) and Beijing opera (**jingju*), which are considered national forms, although both have their roots in regional opera. The geographic origin of most regional opera can be discovered in the title of the form. In many cases the first one or two written characters of a title refer to the place of origin, while the latter part of the title is generally the word for 'drama' (*ju* or *xi*), or a word indicating the style of music used. For example, *chuanju* means 'drama [of Si] chuan' while *Hebei bangzi* translates as the 'clapper opera [of] Hebei'.

While all regional forms share elements of the *xiqu* tradition, each also has distinguishing elements. The most important factor in determining form identity is aural signature; that is, the dialect and the type of music used in performance. Although Mandarin is now the official dialect of both the People's Republic of China and the Republic of China (Taiwan), local dialects, often incomprehensible elsewhere, are drawn upon for regional opera. Each form also employs one or more musical systems with specific melodic, modal, and rhythmic structures for the vocal and instrumental music of that tradition, along with a unique combination of melodic and percussion instruments for the orchestra.

Common to all regional forms are **character role categories and the four performance skills of song, speech, stylized movement or physical **acting, and martial movement or **acrobatics (*chang, nian, zuo, da*). All opera forms employ stylized make-up and **costumes, and rely on stories from China's historical, mythological, and religious past, but regional forms draw upon local folkloric, religious, and social customs for their material to deepen their idiomatic flavour. SPJ

Dingelstedt, Franz von (1814–81) One of the most important directors in nineteenth-century Germany, Dingelstedt's main contribution was in strengthening the position of the **director. Through a succession of important **management positions Dingelstedt was able to demonstrate that production required the coordination of textual and visual elements. His style, a historicist opulence aided by the designer W. von Kaulbach, suited **audience tastes of the mid-nineteenth century (*see* ANTIQUARIANISM). His greatest successes were Shakespearian cycles in Weimar (1864) and Vienna (1875). Dingelstedt was also known as the author of novellas, satirical verse, and the translator of Shakespeare's collected works (1877). CBB

Dionysia A generic name in **Greek antiquity for festivals dedicated to Dionysus. In Athens the term referred to the 'City Dionysia' or 'Great Dionysia', whereas festivals held in the townships (*demes*) of Attica are collectively known as 'Rural Dionysia'. Scholars have generally dated the creation of the City Dionysia at 534 BC, though some now place it soon after 508 in the early years of Athenian democracy. At the *Proagon* in late March, poets, accompanied by their uncostumed actors and **choruses, 'spoke about their compositions'. Religious festivities began next day with a procession in which the icon of Dionysus was taken from his shrine by his theatre to the Academy, a grove outside the city, and after hymns and sacrifice was returned to the theatre by torchlight. The official festival began two days later when an elaborate parade transported hundreds of sacrificial beasts, bread, cakes, and wine to the theatre. A carnival atmosphere was encouraged by drink, satyr **costume, and a series of large, decorated, and sometimes mechanically animated **phallus-poles, carried by men in erect-phallic costumes who **danced and sang suitably obscene lyrics.

The order of events may have varied but included twenty **dithyrambs performed by choruses of 50 boys and 50 men. The following three or four days were given over to competitions for five **comedies and three sets of three **tragedies. The tragedies were followed originally by a **satyr-play, later often by a fourth tragedy. The prize was for the production: a single judgement determined the victorious poet (who was usually also the director) and chorus. The prize for the chorus was honorific and given to the *choregus* (a wealthy citizen obliged to organize and pay for the chorus). Victorious poet-directors were crowned with ivy in the theatre but afterwards received substantial honoraria. A comic competition was added to the festival in 486 BC, while independent prizes for tragic actors were added around 449. Prizes for comic actors were not included until sometime between 329 and 312 BC. The evidence grows ever sparser with each succeeding century, but tragedy and comedy probably continued to be part of the Athenian Dionysia until the second century of the Christian era.

The Rural Dionysia were possibly celebrated by all 139 Attic *demes*, took place in December, and included phallic processions, sacrifices, communal drinking and eating, and dramatic competitions. The number of competitors was generally smaller than at the City Dionysia, but the evidence regularly attests to the participation of top performers. EGC

Dionysus, Theatre of Probably the world's first theatre (*c*.500 BC), built onto the south slope of the acropolis of Athens, north of the sanctuary of Dionysus Eleuthereus. Frequent rebuilding in later antiquity, stone-quarrying in the medieval to modern periods, and amateur archaeology in the early nineteenth century have destroyed nearly every trace of the earliest phases. The dating and architectural function of the remains are much disputed. The fifth-century BC orchestra measured some 30 m (100 feet) across, and an emerging consensus holds that it was rectangular. Rectilinearity would have facilitated the rebuilding of the **theatron's* 50 rows of bleachers, which held 10,000 to 15,000 spectators. (Contractors called '*theatron*-sellers' rebuilt the *theatron* regularly from wood, perhaps annually, and presumably dismantled it after each festival season to preserve the wood from damage by the summer sun.) The **skene* (stage building), in existence by 458 BC (the date of **Aeschylus' Oresteia*), was also wooden, and perhaps also temporary.

The statesman Lycurgus oversaw completion of the first stone theatre (338–326 BC). This *theatron*, which survives, surrounded more than half of a circular orchestra of 20 m (65 feet) in diameter, and sat 15,000 to 18,000 spectators. Later remodelling introduced a **Roman-style deep stage, reducing the orchestra to a semicircle. The theatre's demise is signalled by the conversion of the stage into a rostrum in AD 345 and the insertion of a Christian basilica in the fifth century.   EGC

diorama A painted scene that offered two views, developed by Louis Daguerre, a scenic artist at the Opéra in Paris, during the early 1820s. The technique involved sizing a thin canvas or calico scene drop with rabbit-skin size to provide overall translucency. The first scene was painted with transparent pigments, bound with spirit, on the front surface. The second scene (usually a variation or development of the first) was painted on the reverse of the canvas in opaque pigments. Cross-**lighting from front to rear magically changed the image. Dioramas were popular in their own right in exhibitions and in specially constructed buildings, such as Daguerre's and Charles Bouton's Diorama in London (1823). They also had a considerable fashion in the theatre during the 1830s. **Stanfield combined the technique of diorama painting with that of the panorama to create extended, spectacular travelogue scenes. Theatre dioramas involved backcloths up to 91m (300 feet) in length unrolling at the back of the stage with dioramic sections interspersed in them. Typical diorama scenes involved transitions from peaceful to stormy landscapes, and daytime scenes to romantic, moonlit scenes.   CLD

directing/director Directing is the process of governing preparation for a theatrical performance. In the twentieth century a single person normally exercised this power, now usually called in English the director (formerly called the **producer or the **stage manager, and in other European languages a variety of terms like *metteur en scène* in French, *Regisseur* in German). Theatre in the modern period has assumed that the complexity of production elements demands a final authority who ensures artistic unity and acts as the leader of the production team. In this sense the director is an expressive or enunciatory manager, centring the interpretation of the script and coordinating the many features of production (**scenography, casting, staging, **acting, **music, and supervising **rehearsal) before the first performance, after which the director's authority normally ceases. Directors vary greatly in the amount of aesthetic control they exercise, and rarely have unfettered dictatorial power; nonetheless they are at the centre of the process of mediation that occurs between the script and the **audience.

In earlier ages in the West theatrical production was generally in the hands of the playwright or the actors. The ancient **Greek dramatists taught or coached the actors in their texts, while the training and 'costuming of the **chorus were nominally in the hands of the *choregus*, the wealthy citizen who, out of civic duty, **financed the performance. In **medieval theatre a functionary usually called the bookkeeper tempts some historians to conclude that substantial management of rehearsals and performance was practised, especially for the large-scale **biblical plays and **Corpus Christi plays, which used amateur actors who would need considerable tutoring; similar claims are made for Elizabethan production. But it is unclear what authority such figures exercised, whether they were separate from the writer and actors, and—crucially—how much rehearsal time was allotted. In fact the rise of commercial theatre in the sixteenth century, with the attendant rise of competent and experienced professional actors, suggests a decline in the need for direction. In most periods of Western theatre the task of staging plays was made relatively simple by the existence of cultural assumptions regarding style shared by performers and spectators. Collective theatrical notions were expressed in rigorous conventions of casting, movement, voice, and scenography. Rehearsal time was extremely limited, and actor training was accomplished by an apprentice system, so that little value was granted to stylistic innovation.

Around the end of the nineteenth century in Europe theatrical style became more subjective and more self-conscious. Under the influence first of *realism and thereafter of *naturalism and *symbolism, an *avant-garde arose that favoured novelty of expression and scenic environment, artistic subtlety, and new narrative strategies. Since the techniques needed for naturalist and symbolist production did not exist among the traditional methods, the director emerged as a functionary separate from the playwright and the actor to supervise the particulars and nuances of performance. Much of the subsequent aesthetic experimentation of twentieth-century theatre was at the urging of stage directors, who commonly function as authors of productions.

Certain *actor-managers and playwrights in nineteenth-century England and America prefaced the director proper, while the Duke of Saxe-Meiningen (*see* MEININGEN PLAYERS) and his stage manager *Chronegk in Germany are often thought of as the first directors who were neither actors nor writers in the production. In Paris *Antoine, who founded the Théâtre *Libre in 1887, foregrounded directing by using detailed naturalistic settings and acting. His free theatre movement spread to Berlin (*Brahm opened the *Freie Bühne in 1889) and to London (*Grein started the *Independent Theatre two years later). Naturalism sought verisimilitude in acting and in scene. It achieved enormous influence through the acting and rehearsal theories of *Stanislavsky, whose early work at the *Moscow Art Theatre emphasized elaborately realized *costumes and scenery and, though relying on nineteenth-century mechanistic psychology, the inward emotional connection between actor and role. In many ways Stanislavsky established the dominant rehearsal practice in the twentieth century by encouraging actors to look beneath the surface of the written lines for a *subtext that was imagined to contain explanations and motivations for the *characters' speech and actions, and the director in the wide naturalistic tradition has assumed the task of guiding this exploration.

At the same time as naturalism was gaining force, symbolism promoted dreamlike states or abstract visions and had an almost equal influence through the scenographic theories of *Craig, whose concept of the actor as *Über-marionette* ('super puppet') in the director's control further elevated the director's authority. In Craig's view, the director/designer would take direct charge of all elements of production to create a distinctive performance. Many subsequent directors in the modernist tradition have drawn on one or the other of the opposing modes of naturalism and

symbolism, adapting them into movements or styles that are associated with directorial intervention (*see* EXPRESSIONISM; CONSTRUCTIVISM; SURREALISM; EPIC THEATRE; INTERCULTURALISM). It is clear that the passion for unity, interpretation, and innovation associated with modernism fortified the belief that only a single arbiter could properly organize a harmonious aesthetic experience. Some of the most notable directors of the twentieth century so operated, from *Reinhardt and *Meyerhold to *Brook and *Strehler.

In many Asian countries the faithful transmission of performance traditions has been the central feature of style and preparation and individualist aesthetic intervention for traditional forms would be considered improper. Under Western influence, however, modern theatre in Asia has tended to accept the director as necessary, as in Japanese *shingeki*, and powerful directors are now common in many Asian countries: *Ninagawa and *Suzuki in Japan, *Tanvir and *Thiyam in India, *Ong Keng Sen in Singapore.

The playwright's relationship to directorial intervention is complex and often problematic. Though the styles mentioned above were in many cases invented or supported by contemporary dramatists (*Zola and *Ibsen for early naturalism, for example, *Maeterlinck for symbolism), many of the most radical or innovative directors of the twentieth century made their marks using classic texts in the public domain. Living authors are a special case and the director's authority has often been challenged by writers or their literary estates, whose *copyright to the words of a play grants them a superior legal position. Most licences for performance of plays in copyright insist that the text may not be changed without approval, though directors (or actors) sometimes change the words anyway. Dramatic copyright in most countries, however, is ambiguous over matters of staging and thus there are often both legal and practical questions about the director's authority over the text, as has developed in the case of *Beckett.

Actors and critics have also objected to the director's authority at various times and attempted to subvert or bypass it—actors are especially aware of the power relationship they have with the director and can struggle onstage and off with its implications, sometimes in an environment charged with *gender questions or sexual politics. This matter has been intensified by the fact that until the latter part of the twentieth century most directors were men. Authoritarian modes of direction have been challenged through an increasing reliance on collaboration in preparing performances. But even under the influence of postmodernism, which retreats from ideas of mastery and unity, directors have retained much of their force; it is a great irony that the diversity, eclecticism, and cultural inclusion of some contemporary performance often seem to require even more aesthetic management, as in the productions of *Mnouchkine, Robert *Wilson, or *Lepage. *See also* COLLECTIVES AND COLLECTIVE CREATION; DEVISING; MANAGER.   DK

distancing effect *See* VERFREMDUNG.

dithyramb A choral song to Dionysus, originally associated with female devotees of the god. First given regular form by Arion at Corinth *c*.600 BC, it was admitted in 509 BC, as a strictly male affair, to the *Dionysia in Athens. An amalgam of poetry, *dance, and music, the dithyramb featured a circular *chorus of 50, before about 470 BC probably led and accompanied by the poet himself. Later, the poet withdrew, music and dance were elevated over poetry, lyric solo replaced choral song, and *mimetic elements were introduced. *Aristotle's opinion that *tragedy developed from the dithyramb is without warrant.   RWV

documentary drama and theatre Plays written, compiled, or even *improvised directly from 'documentary' sources became a feature of many theatre cultures during the twentieth century. Radio, film, and particularly television also developed documentary forms of drama, which characteristically deal with contemporary issues. 'Documents' used in such plays include official reports, trial transcripts, newspaper articles, newsreel footage. Although many dramas throughout history have been based on fact, documentary plays are much closer to their source material, often incorporating documents themselves directly into performance. The concept of documentary stems from the faith in facts that was a legacy of nineteenth-century positivism. Documents came to be regarded as unproblematic sources of facts and information, and information itself became a component in governments' control and organization of industrial nations. The camera's apparent capacity to record external reality added an important element, and resulted in the associated rise of documentary film and photography from the 1930s.

The USSR's Department of Agitation and Propaganda employed Blue Blouse theatrical troupes in the 1920s to create *touring and fast-moving entertainments that included the *zhivaya gazeta* (*living newspaper). These sketches, presenting facts and information about the progress of the revolution, were the first documentary dramas. The method spread to communist and proto-

communist groups in Europe in the 1920s and 1930s. In the USA, the *Federal Theatre Project had a Living Newspaper Unit whose plays were researched and produced by unemployed newspaper and theatre workers. Provocative analyses of the Great Depression included shows about agriculture (*Triple-A Plowed Under*, 1935), and housing (*One-Third of a Nation*, 1938). Other documentary dramas were developed through the experiments of major theatrical innovators such as *Meyerhold and *Piscator. Though *Brecht rarely used factual material directly, his use of film, slides, and placards significantly developed the ways documents could be incorporated into stage performance. The Second World War/Cold War period halted this developing tradition of political documentary theatre.

A new period of heightened political awareness (especially following the 1968 student uprisings) revived the form. In West Berlin, Piscator embarked on a new series of documentary productions, including plays about the Holocaust (*Hochhuth's *The Representative*, 1963; *Weiss's *The Investigation*, 1965). In Britain, *Theatre Workshop produced *Oh! What a Lovely War* (1963), an *epic theatre analysis of the Great War that provided a model for new political theatre troupes like *McGrath's 7:84 Company, and further inspired a brief spate of 'Theatre of Fact' plays including *Brook's 1966 *US* (about Vietnam) and *Mnouchkine's 1971 *Murderous Angels* (about post-colonial war in the Congo). Documentary forms are still in use both inside and outside the developed world, usually as part of political opposition (in, for example, *Boal's 'arena' and 'forum' theatre methodologies).

'Docudrama' became an important TV form. It differs from much documentary theatre in that contemporary social reality is usually portrayed through individual case studies in *naturalistic, not anti-*illusionist, performance and film styles. Periodically, such programmes cause controversy and celebrated examples have raised public awareness of important social and political issues (in Britain and America, for example, *Cathy Come Home* in 1966 and *Brian's Song* in 1971 raised housing and health issues respectively).   DJP

Dodin, Lev (1944–) Soviet/Russian director. Dodin graduated from the Leningrad Theatre Institute in 1965, and began his career as a director at the Leningrad Young Spectator's Theatre. He was appointed *artistic director of the Maly Drama Theatre in Leningrad in 1982, where he has created a fine repertoire, initially adapting prose for the stage. His trilogy based on Fyodor Abramov's rural tales (*The House*, 1980; *Brothers and Sisters*, 1985) caused a stir because of the outspoken treatment of human suffering during the purges. He adapted William Golding's *The Lord of the Flies* (1986), Yury Trifonov's *The Old Man* (1988), Sergei Kaledin's fiction (*Gaudeamus*, 1990), and Dostoevsky's *The Devils* (1991). His 1987 production of Aleksandr Galin's *Stars in the Morning Sky* underscored the theatre's role as an advocate of glasnost in staging a play about Moscow prostitutes. In the 1990s Dodin was inspired by a new group of actors he trained at the Theatre Institute for *Claustrophobia* (1994), based on études and improvisations of contemporary prose. *The Cherry Orchard* (1995) showed skilful psychological exploration, while *Chekhov's *Platonov* (1998), and Dodin's adaptation of Platonov's *Chevengur* (1999), displayed a preoccupation with grandiose stage constructions rather than traditional sets, concentrating on the imagery of water that appears to submerge the individual, actor and man. His production of Vasili Grossman's *Life and Fate* (2007) marked a return to the epic style of the 1980s, of which Dodin remains a master. BB

Donnellan, Declan (1953–) English director. In 1981 Donnellan founded *Cheek by Jowl with his regular collaborator Nick Ormerod. A small-scale company with a commitment to *touring classical theatre, Cheek by Jowl included a striking range of European drama in their repertory: from *Calderón to *Lessing, *Sophocles to *Corneille, as well as Shakespeare. Working on Ormerod's spare but effective set designs, the actors were pushed by Donnellan to explore social and sexual relationships in a precisely defined milieu. Success led the duo to the *National Theatre, where they directed a powerful version of Lope de *Vega's *Fuente Ovejuna* in 1989 and the British première of *Kushner's *Angels in America* in 1992. In 1998 Donnellan temporarily suspended Cheek by Jowl and worked mainly in Moscow until 2002 when he directed the only production of the *Royal Shakespeare Company's Academy. His recent productions have included *Pushkin's *Boris Godunov* (2001) and *Twelfth Night* (2003) with Russian actors, Racine's *Andromaque* with French performers (2007), and *Macbeth* with Cheek by Jowl (2009). PDH

Dorn, Dieter (1935–) German director. Dorn was educated in Leipzig and Berlin before moving to West Germany in 1958. He came to prominence in the early 1970s with a production of *Hampton's *The Philanthropist*. He was appointed director-in-residence at Munich's Kammerspiele in 1976 where he worked for 25 years,

becoming *artistic director in 1983. Aided by perhaps the finest *acting ensemble in Germany, Dorn developed the theatre into one of the most successful, finding a successful balance between classics and contemporary work by Botho *Strauss, *Dorst, and Herbert Achtenbusch. His most acclaimed productions were of Shakespeare (*A Midsummer Night's Dream*, 1978; *Twelfth Night*, 1980; *Troilus and Cressida*, 1986; *King Lear*, 1992; *The Tempest*, 1994). Most were recorded for television; his *Faust I* (1987) was filmed. Dorn productions chart a path between striking visual effects and respect for the text. In 2001 a disagreement with the municipal authorities led to his dismissal and almost immediate appointment as artistic director of the Residenztheater in Munich. CBB

Dorst, Tankred (1925–) German playwright. In the first phase of his career (1960–7), a strong influence of *absurdist drama is evident, but his major breakthrough came in the late 1960s with a shift to historical themes and *realist-*documentary plays. The *revue *Toller* (1968) dramatizes the playwright *Toller's involvement in the socialist Munich Republic of 1919. Dorst pursued the revue form in *Little Man, What Now?* (1973), and his preoccupation with history continued in the chronicle of the Merz family. This includes radio and television drama, theatre plays (*Auf dem Chimborazo*, 1974; *Die Villa*, 1980), and films (*Dorothea Merz*, 1976; *Klaras Mutter*, 1978) tracing the family during and after the Second World War. A radical break with both family and political history came with the monumental drama *Merlin; or, The Waste Land* (1981). In 97 scenes, which require two evenings to perform, Dorst dramatizes the Arthurian legends in an intertextual collage. He returned to a simpler style in work like *Korbes* (1988), *Fernando Krapp Wrote this Letter* 1992), and *Herr Paul* (1994). Since 1970 most of his plays have been co-written with his wife Ursula Ehler. CBB

Dorval, Marie (1798–1849) French actress, who made the most significant contribution to the establishment of *romantic drama in the 1830s. Dorval came from a background of itinerant players and the popular *boulevard theatres. Having gained experience by partnering *Lemâitre, she helped to consolidate the new theatrical idiom at the Porte-Saint-Martin Theatre, where she played with *Bocage in *Dumas *père's *Antony* in 1831, one of the great triumphs of romantic drama. The same year she was the *heroine in *Hugo's *Marion de Lorme*, but her greatest triumph was at the *Comédie-Française playing the tender, demure Kitty Bell in *Vigny's *Chatterton* in 1835. Her flexible *acting style, and lack of prejudice against the new drama, made a major contribution to the brief acceptance of romantic authors. Marie Dorval's personal life was unhappy, and she died in solitude and poverty.   WDH

Dotrice, Roy (1923-) English actor. Dotrice began acting in the unlikely surroundings of a German prisoner of war camp during the Second World War. After the war he worked in *regional repertory until joining the *Shakespeare Memorial Theatre in 1957 and stayed on for the founding of the *Royal Shakespeare Company, for a total of nine years in Stratford. He performed a wide variety of roles, including Father Ambrose in *Whiting's *The Devils* (1962) and the title role in *Julius Caesar* (1963). He doubled as Bedford and Edward IV in *Hall and *Barton's *The Wars of the Roses* (1963), and the following year contributed Gaunt, Hotspur, and Justice Shallow to the RSC's histories sequence. In 1968 Dotrice scored a hit with the one-person show *Brief Lives*, which *toured internationally. He relocated to America in the 1970s, doing much film and television work. He won a Tony award for his performance of *Moon for the Misbegotten* in New York in 2000.   MDG

Dowling, Joe (1948-) Irish director. Dowling joined the *Abbey Theatre acting company out of university, ran its studio theatre (1973–6), and became the youngest-ever artistic director of the Abbey in 1978, premiering to critical acclaim the work of *Friel (*Aristocrats*, 1979, and *Faith Healer*, 1980). He left the Abbey in 1985 to found the Gaiety School of Acting and to manage the Gaiety Theatre in Dublin. His extraordinary ability to capture *audiences' imagination was most visible in *O'Casey's *Juno and the Paycock* in 1996, hailed as definitive by critics in Dublin, London, and New York. Since 1995 Dowling has been artistic director of the *Guthrie Theatre in Minneapolis and has continued to engage with Irish theatre, such as in Friel's *The Home Place* in 2007.   BRS

drag shows *See* FEMALE IMPERSONATION; MALE IMPERSONATION.

Dragún, Osvaldo (1929–99) Argentinian dramatist. Author of more than 30 plays, Dragún was one of the first to introduce *Brecht to Latin America, developing his own *epic theatre, exemplified by *Eroica of Buenos Aires* (1966, unstaged in Argentina until 1984). He also utilized a device he termed 'animalization', '[deformed] man projected onto the reality of animals and things', the best-known example being *Stories to Be Told*. He effectively created his own genre, melding

Brechtian techniques, grotesque structures, and *absurdist-influenced 'committed' theatre. *Onward, Corazón!* (1987) evokes his Jewish upbringing, and his final play, *The Passenger on the Sun Boat*, was staged posthumously in Buenos Aires in 2000. Dragún also exerted enormous influence on Latin American theatre as a teacher and theatre administrator. In 1996 he assumed the direction of Argentina's National Theatre, where he remained until his death. One of the founders of the 1981 Teatro Abierto festival, he stayed with the project until its demise in 1985 and premièred three plays there: *Me and my Obelisk* (1981), *To the Violator* (1982), and *Today They Eat Skinny* (1983).   JGJ

Drake, Alfred (1914–92) American actor and singer. Born Alfredo Capurro, he made his professional debut in 1936 in *White Horse Inn*, followed by *Babes in Arms* (1937). He acted regularly in small parts until 1943, when his creation of Curly in *Oklahoma!* made him a star. From then on, the handsome baritone was the leading man of choice in *musicals for heroic roles requiring bravura *acting as well as excellent singing, notably in *Kiss Me, Kate* (1948) and *Kismet* (1953). An actor as much as a singer, he regularly appeared in non-musicals, from Shakespeare (Claudius to *Burton's 1964 Hamlet) to *Pirandello and *Wilder. In 1990 he was given a special Tony award for excellence in the theatre.   JD

Dramaten Swedish theatre company. Kungliga Dramatiska Teatern, or the Royal Dramatic Theatre, was founded in Stockholm by royal decree in 1788. King Gustav III was a passionate theatre enthusiast and encouraged the development of native drama. Initially only Swedish plays were performed, but soon the repertoire was extended to include the best of contemporary work from all over Europe. In 1908 the company moved into an impressive art-nouveau building on Nybroplan, opening with *Strindberg's historical drama *Master Olof*, and his plays have continued to occupy a key place in the theatre. Their complex *dramaturgy requires gifted interpreters, and Dramaten has promoted the work of outstanding directors as well as actors. The roll call of directors includes impressive figures such as *Sjöberg, *Molander, and *Bergman. At the start of the twenty-first century Dramaten consisted of six different venues ranging from the main house to studio theatres and a small space dedicated to theatre for *youth. The tradition of an eclectic repertoire has continued.   DT

dramaturgy/dramaturg Dramaturgy is the study of how meaning is generated in drama and performance. It can be understood as an attribute, a role, or a function. As an *attribute* it refers to a particular playwright or play, as in the dramaturgy of *Zola, *Brecht, or *Fornés, and describes the dramatic structure or conventions operating in the work, its *action, genre, characterization, and implied elements of production such as *costuming, scenery, or *lighting. Dramaturgy understood in this way intersects with dramatic theory and must include knowledge of the distinctions between periods, movements, or styles. So conceived dramaturgy might be called the architecture of the theatrical event, involved in the confluence of components in a work and how they are constructed to generate meaning for the *audience. But the term dramaturgy need not refer only to text-based performance. One could speak of the dramaturgy of a *dance piece by *Bausch or the dramaturgy of Buñuel and Dalí's film *Un chien andalou*, or the dramaturgy of a *ritual.

Dramaturgy as a *role* describes the person who carries the title 'dramaturg' on a performance programme or an established theatre, someone with knowledge of the history, theory, and practice of theatre who helps a *director, designer, playwright, or *actor realize their intentions in a production. The dramaturg—sometimes called a literary manager—is an in-house artistic consultant cognizant of an institution's mission, a playwright's passion, or a director's vision, and who helps bring them all to life in a theatrically compelling manner. This goal can be accomplished in myriad ways and the dramaturg's role often shifts according to context, and is always fluid. (In French the word *dramaturge* actually means 'playwright', but as the profession has developed the function of the dramaturg is separate from that of the dramatist.)

In Western theatre the position of dramaturg is usually considered to have begun with *Lessing's *Hamburg Dramaturgy* (1768), though the dramaturg in Britain and the USA only emerged in the 1960s. The tenor of the times caused theatres to look beyond the commercial fare typically offered, and the *regional theatre movement sought to bring theatre to areas far from the traditional theatrical centres of New York and London. A renewed interest in the classical repertoire and a vigorous advocacy of new work further prompted the development of the dramaturg. Jeremy Brooks with the *Royal Shakespeare Company, *Tynan at the *National Theatre, *Kott's influence on *Brook, and Francis Ferguson with the American Laboratory Theatre—all these pioneered the work of the dramaturg by helping to revise and reinvigorate classics or by reading and advocating the work of new playwrights. In Germany, with its much longer tradition of residential theatres, prominent dramaturgs have included *Tieck, *Grabbe, Brecht, *Palitzsch, Botho *Strauss, and Dieter Sturm of the *Schaubühne.

Dramaturgy as *function* refers to a group of activities necessary to the process of creating theatre. These activities, frequently involving the selection and preparation of material for production, are always being carried out—by *producers, directors, designers, or actors—whether or not someone carrying the title of dramaturg is involved. The functions might include the literary management necessary to select a theatre's season, collaboration with a director to create a new approach to a Shakespeare play, aid to a contemporary playwright in the gestation of a new work, writing programme notes or leading a post-show discussion, preparing a new translation of a play, or providing the visual, textual, or aural tools to stimulate a company's *rehearsal process. The dramaturgical sensibility begins by questioning received models of production or rehearsal, and seeks to enrich creation with critical, historical, sociological, ideological, and imagistic materials.   AV

drame, le See BOURGEOIS THEATRE; DIDEROT, DENIS.

Dressler, Marie (1869–1934) American actress, born Leila Marie Koerber in Ontario, Canada. Arriving in New York in 1892, she played supporting roles opposite Lillian *Russell before starring as the *music-hall singer in *The Lady Slavey* (1896). With successes in *musical comedy and *burlesque, she also triumphed in *vaudeville at Weber's Music Hall (1905–6) and at London's Palace Theatre in a 1907 *variety show. Her greatest theatrical success came with *Tillie's Nightmare* (New York, 1910), which featured Tillie Blobbs, the boarding-house drudge who sang 'Heaven will Protect the Working Girl', and launched Dressler into film with a Keystone Pictures series built around her signature *character. A wartime activist, Dressler then fought to establish Actors' Equity and was founding president of the Chorus Equity Association and a leader in the 1919 actors' strike. Her politics alienated her from theatre *managers, but she returned to stardom with MGM with *Anna Christie* (1930) and the Oscar-winning lead in *Min and Bill* (1930). Her autobiographies are *The Life Story of an Ugly Duckling* (1924) and *My Own Story* (1934).   KM

Drew family Louisa Lane (Mrs John Drew, 1820–97), the daughter of a provincial English actor, emigrated with her mother to America where she flourished as a child performer, playing with Junius Brutus *Booth and *Forrest. She made her New York debut in 1828, continued her career into adulthood, and in 1850 married Irish-born actor **John Drew** (1827-62). They settled in Philadelphia, co-*managing the Arch Street Theatre from 1853; John also co-managed the National Theatre in Washington shortly before his death.

Mrs Drew was a multi-talented performer, her parts ranging from Mistress Quickly to Lady Macbeth; her signature role was Mrs Malaprop. Her husband used his Hibernian background to great comic effect in plays such as *The Irish Immigrant, London Assurance,* and *The Rivals.* He was becoming a leading actor at the time of his sudden death. Mrs Drew took over sole management of the Arch Street and ran it well for three decades, though financial reversals forced her to give up management in 1892 and *tour for the final five years of her life.

Two of her children, **John** (1853-1927) and **Georgiana** (1856-93), had important stage careers, while a third, **Sidney** (1863-1919), was an early screen star. Georgiana quickly established herself as a great favourite and was becoming a major star when she died prematurely. In 1876 she had married Maurice *Barrymore, thus starting another acting dynasty. John was an accomplished classical comedian, frequently playing classics and contemporary works. His commanding presence carried him from his exciting debut in *The Masked Ball* (1873) to his final triumph in *Trelawny of the 'Wells'* (1927). In 1892 Frohman signed him at the unprecedented salary of $500 a week.   TFC

Drottningholm Court Theatre Built in 1766 by Fredrik Adelcrantz for Queen Lovisa Ulrika, at her summer palace on an island outside Stockholm, the *playhouse, which still operates, has an unusual T-shaped *auditorium. There are no galleries and only three small *boxes per side, which are screened by lattice grilles. The theatre still contains the chariot-and-pole system, four traps, and the cloud, thunder, wind, and wave machines. The theatre was at its height in the reign of Gustav III (1772-92), when French designer Jean-Louis Despez created much of the scenery, commissioned more by Carlo *Bibiena and Johann Pasch (over 30 of these settings still exist), and redesigned the foyer (1791). After the King's assassination (the subject of *Verdi's *A Masked Ball*), the theatre fell into disuse. It was rediscovered almost fully intact in 1921 by Agne Beijer and is now the home of an important

theatre museum and a summer season of early *operas.   FJH

Drury Lane Theatre Originally known as the Theatre Royal on Bridges Street in London, Drury Lane opened 1663 under the *management of *Killigrew, owner of the first theatre *patent issued by Charles II, who built it as the home of the King's Company of Players. Its design has been variously attributed to *Webb, Christopher Wren, and Richard Ryder (capacity 650-700). *Pepys was a regular visitor and Nell *Gwynn made her debut there in 1665. The theatre was destroyed by fire in 1672, and the second *playhouse opened in 1674, probably designed by Wren. It featured a pit (with ten benches), two levels of *boxes on each side, and one level of boxes surmounted by two galleries at the rear (capacity 2,000). Its apron stage was 5.5 m deep, and was entered by two *proscenium-arch doors on each side. It closed in 1676 but in 1682 became the home of the United Company under *Betterton. Christopher *Rich gained control in 1693, beginning a turbulent period ending with his expulsion in 1709. A triumvirate of actors (Colley *Cibber, *Wilks, and Thomas Doggett, replaced in 1713 by Barton *Booth) gained control in 1711 and managed it effectively until 1733, after which the theatre went into decline. *Garrick opened here in 1742 and returned in 1747 as *actor-manager with his partner James Lacey; together they made important innovations in *acting and *scenography.

In 1775 the theatre was renovated by Robert Adam (capacity 2,300), and *Sheridan became *manager when Garrick retired in 1776. Demolished in 1791, it was rebuilt by Henry Holland on Sheridan's orders in 1794 (capacity 3,611), and opened with a production of *Macbeth* starring John Philip *Kemble, Sarah *Siddons, and Charles *Kemble. Though it had the world's first fire curtain and was advertised as 'flame proof', it nonetheless burned to the ground in 1809. A fourth theatre was built in 1812 by Benjamin Dean Wyatt (capacity 3,060), modelled on the Grand Theatre, Bordeaux. Edmund *Kean made his debut here in 1814, and his son Charles *Kean in 1827. In 1817 Drury Lane joined *Covent Garden in introducing gas *lighting. A portico was added in 1820, a colonnade in 1831. The interior was remodelled many times, the present one created by F. Emblin-Walker and F. Edward Jones in 1922 (capacity 2,283). Since 1947 it has been primarily known for *musicals; *Lloyd Webber bought this theatre, along with nine others, in 2000.   FJH

Dryden, John (1631–1700) English writer. Dryden was quick to seize the opportunities offered by the Restoration of 1660, including the demand for new plays in the reopened theatres. Some of his first successes were collaborations: *The Indian Queen* (1664) with Robert Howard; an adaptation of Shakespeare's *Tempest* (1667) with *Davenant; and (probably) *Sir Martin Mar-all* (1667), based on two French comedies, with William Cavendish, Duke of Newcastle. Though he claimed to dislike *comedy as a form, Dryden was a successful writer in the 'Spanish' style, which balanced a central plot of court intrigue against the sexual warfare of a witty couple. The success of *Secret Love* (1667) led to a contract with the King's Company (1668–78). The subplot of his best comedy, *Marriage à la Mode* (1671–2), both exemplifies and ridicules the comedy of infidelity. His later comedies included the anti-Dutch propaganda of *Amboyna* (1673), the *satiric *Mr Limberham* (1678), and, at the height of the Popish plot, the anti-Catholic *The Spanish Friar* (1680).

The *heroic play, with its distinctive use of the rhyming couplet, was a form he made his own, a curious mixture of extravagant heroism, complex love intrigue, and intellectual discussion. Preferring plots about the conflict of cultures and religions, he created situations (like the Christian priest's attempt to convert Montezuma under torture in *The Indian Emperor*, 1665) where serious religious debate was inherent to the plot. The heroic couplet lent itself to the debate structure, and Dryden defended it effectively in his *Essay of Dramatic Poesy* (1667) and in his prefaces, *prologues, and *epilogues. The form was never altogether accepted: *The Rehearsal*, a collective burlesque of heroic plays by *Buckingham and others, focused particularly on Dryden ('Mr Bayes')—a natural target since in 1668 he had succeeded Davenant as Poet Laureate. Dryden's two-part *Conquest of Granada* (1670–1), with its noble savage hero Almanzor, came in for particular ridicule.

Whether or not affected by *The Rehearsal*, the prologue to Dryden's last heroic play, *Aureng-Zebe* (1675), expresses weariness with rhyme in drama and in the 1670s he turned toward different models. In 1677 he produced *All for Love,* his most successful work for the theatre: it largely replaced its original, Shakespeare's *Antony and Cleopatra,* until the nineteenth century.

Dryden did not write for the theatre during James II's short reign; having declared himself a Roman Catholic, he became heavily involved in religious controversy, and inevitably lost his court appointments after the Revolution of 1688. Despite his disgrace, some of his subsequent plays—*Don Sebastian* (1689) and an adaptation of *Molière's *Amphitryon* (1690)—were highly successful, as was *King Arthur* (1691), his 'semi-opera' written for the composer Henry Purcell. In the last months of his life he contributed *The Secular Masque* to *Vanbrugh's *The Pilgrim.* The sheer variety of his theatrical works, like that of his better-known poems and critical essays, is perhaps their most impressive feature, but their rare revivals have been successful enough to suggest that he deserves more theatrical attention.   LDP

Dubé, Marcel (1930–) Québec playwright. Few dramatists marked their era as indelibly as Dubé did French Canada from 1950. Over the next 25 years he wrote some 40 plays, along with many television and radio scripts. *Zone* (1953) was the first to attract national attention, especially in its TV adaptation. Dubé was in fact the first Québec playwright to realize fully the potential of the new medium, and all of his subsequent work is profoundly influenced by it, notably *Un simple soldat* (*Private Soldier*, 1957) and *Fine Sundays* (1965; film version 1974). Critics point out that Dubé's own upward socio-economic evolution is closely reflected in the plots and *characters to which he turned thereafter. Mainly tragic in inspiration and middle class in setting, plays such as *The Accounting* (1960) and *The White Geese* (1966) have now become part of the canon of Canadian theatre.   LED

Duchesnois, Mlle (Catherine-Joséphine Rafuin) (1777–1835) French actress. Protégée of Napoleon's wife Joséphine de Beauharnais, she was admitted to the *Comédie-Française on the same day in 1802 as Mlle *George, mistress of Napoleon. As ill-favoured as George was beautiful, Duchesnois was transfigured into a fine tragic queen by a sensibility and spontaneity reminiscent of Mlle *Dumesnil's. The press fuelled a bitter rivalry between the two actresses until, in 1808, George left for Russia. From then until her retirement in 1829, Mlle Duchesnois, who partnered *Talma for over twenty years, created a number of contemporary *tragedies, including Luce de Lancival's *Hector* (1809) and Étienne de Jouy's *Sylla* (1821).   JG

Ducis, Jean-François (1733–1816) French playwright. Ducis was the first to put Shakespeare on the French stage, adapting *Hamlet* (1769), *Romeo and Juliet* (1772), *King Lear* (1783), *Macbeth* (1784), and *Othello* (1792) according to a hybrid aesthetic that combined the decorous regularity of *neoclassical *tragedy with the mawkish sentimentality of eighteenth-century *drame* *bourgeois*. Having no English, his principal source was the reading translations of Pierre-Antoine de La Place (1745–9). Ducis's own most successful plays were *Oedipe chez Admète* (1778), which won him *Voltaire's chair in the Académie Française, and *Abufar; ou, La Famille arabe* (1795), which gave *Talma one of his finest roles. JG

Ducrow, Andrew (1793–1848) Belgian-English *circus entertainer who was an outstanding *mime, *acrobat, and equestrian. His great speciality was miming activities from life at sea or impersonating Greek statuary while standing on a galloping horse. Much of his early career was spent in France, though he came to fame in London in 1814 at *Astley's Amphitheatre, where he returned in 1824 and was *manager from 1830 to 1841. He staged *melodramas such as *Planché's *Mazeppa* (1831), but particularly promoted spectacular shows and *hippodramas such as *The Battle of Waterloo* (1824). JDV

Dukes, Ashley (1885–1959) Complete man of the English theatre, by turns critic, dramatist, translator, *producer, and *manager. He championed the innovative work of his contemporaries while acting as English editor for *Theatre Arts Monthly* and worked zealously to get staged in London the best of continental playwriting, translating extensively from French and German drama, especially work in the *expressionist style. His own plays, notably *The Man with a Load of Mischief*, are characterized by their thematic focus on social and racial tolerance. In 1933 he created the Mercury Theatre in Notting Hill, providing a platform for experimental verse drama; by bringing *Murder in the Cathedral* to London he launched *Eliot's theatrical career. Dukes consistently supported his wife Marie Rambert in working to establish her *dance company from 1931, also at the Mercury. RAC

Dullin, Charles (1885–1949) French actor, director, and teacher who worked briefly with *Copeau but left his company in 1918 to join *Gémier in a quest for a popular theatre. Dullin set up the Théâtre de l'Atelier in 1922 along the lines of Copeau's Vieux-Colombier, combining a company with a training school. In his revivals of the classics, Dullin starred in plays by *Aristophanes, *Molière, and Shakespeare, and championed the work of *Pirandello. He was influenced by *physical and popular forms of theatre, among them *commedia dell'arte* and *kabuki, making him the one director of the *Cartel des Quatre to come close to the notion of *total theatre. He had many notable disciples who had a significant impact on theatre in the twentieth century, among them *Barrault and *Artaud. He gave up the Atelier in 1940 to *Barsacq, but continued to direct, *produce, and influence future generations. His interest in *audience development resulted in a commissioned report for the Front Populaire government in 1937 which became the template for post-war decentralization of the arts in France. BRS

Dumas, Alexandre (Dumas *fils*) (1824–95) French writer, illegitimate son of *Dumas *père*. Regarded as leader of the '*école du bon sens*': writers with a firm moral tone about contemporary society, especially relations between the sexes. The son's first play, however, had more in common with the *romantic drama of his father, with its theme of passionate love defeated by the conventions of a hostile world. This was *La Dame aux camélias* (*The Lady of the Camellias*, sometimes known as *Camille*), adapted from the author's own novel, and based on his liaison with the courtesan Marie Duplessis. Initially banned by the *censor as an offence to public morality, the play was phenomenally successful in Paris in 1852, and was immediately adopted by *Verdi for *La traviata* (1853).

Thereafter, the moralist in Dumas progressively took charge, and a series of plays including *Le Demi-monde* (1855), *The Natural Son* (1858), and *The Friend of Women* (1864) show an increasingly didactic approach to problems of sexual morality. The best of his later plays is perhaps *Les Idées de Madame Aubray* (1867), in which dramatic action is persuasively linked to moral thesis. In terms of *dramaturgy, Dumas was content to endorse *Scribe and others who championed the *well-made play, though his ideas about a 'useful theatre', expressed in prefaces and pamphlets, show him to be a much more original thinker. WDH

Dumas, Alexandre (Dumas *père*) (1802–70) French novelist and playwright, father of *Dumas *fils*. Of major *romantic French dramatists—*Hugo, *Vigny, *Musset, and Dumas *père*—it was only the last who possessed a genuine sense of theatre. He was hugely stimulated by the visit of the English actors under J. P. *Kemble and Edmund *Kean in 1827; having begun writing *vaudevilles, Dumas now aimed at success in a literary theatre. His *Christine; ou, Paris, Fontainebleau, Rome*, a historical drama, though accepted at the Théâtre-Français (*Comédie-Française) in 1828, was performed in 1830 at the *Odéon; his prose play *Henri III et sa cour* became the first romantic drama to be staged at the Théâtre-Français

Napoléon Bonaparte (Odéon, 1831) was written to a very different formula: with six acts and 23 *tableaux, it aimed at an 'epic' presentation of history rather than a conventional dramatic construction, though its success was probably due to *Lemaître in the title role and to spectacular scenic effects.

Though Dumas continued to choose historical subjects—for instance *Catherine Howard* (1834) or *Lorenzino* (1842, with the same subject as Musset's *Lorenzaccio*)—his repertoire of historical plays was to become a list of dramatizations of his own successful historical novels, especially after he acquired the Théâtre-Historique in 1847. He had already produced *Les Mousquetaires* (1845) with the help of Auguste Maquet; *La Reine Margot* (1847), *Le Chevalier de Maison-Rouge* (1847), *Monte-Cristo* (1848), and *Les Girondins* (1848) were among plays created by the same collaboration. His plays on contemporary subjects provide the best representation of the romantic aesthetic. *Antony*, in which *Bocage played the Byronic *hero and *Dorval the sympathetic heroine torn between love and duty, was outstandingly successful in its appeal to spectators in 1831 as well as in frequent reprises, in part because of melodramatic *coups de théâtre. Richard Darlington* (1831) is pure *melodrama, but *Kean; or, Disorder and Genius* (1836), as well as offering a tribute to the English actor, provided a magnificent vehicle for a virtuoso performance by Lemaître as an unruly genius. The play was reworked by *Sartre in 1954.   WDH

du Maurier, Gerald (1873–1934) English *actor-manager. The son of George du Maurier (the author of *Trilby* and an artist), Gerald was better educated than most performers of his generation and became the quintessential gentlemanly actor. He *toured with *Forbes-Robertson in 1895, and later with *Tree; he then took a variety of largely upper-class parts, avoiding anything controversial, preferring undemanding contemporary plays for a fashionable London *audience. He was popular as Raffles (1906) and Bulldog Drummond (1921), and was much praised in the plays of *Barrie. His Captain Hook in *Peter Pan* (1904), greatly enjoyed by his novelist daughter Daphne, was much larger than life, and more effective for being the antithesis of his usual relaxed *acting style, which tended to conceal his careful preparation and skilled vocal technique. He was co-manager of Wyndham's Theatre (1910–25) and of the St James's (1925–9).   EEC

Dumesnil, Mlle (Marie-Françoise Marchand) (1713–1803) French actress. She made her debut at the *Comédie-Française in 1738 in passionate 'noble mother' roles such as *Racine's Phèdre and Clytemnestre—a *line of business she was to make her speciality. Rival of the more intellectual Mlle *Clairon, she relied on intuition and inspiration to give performances in which 'half the time she has no idea what she's saying, then she'll create a sublime moment' (*Diderot). One such moment occurred in *Voltaire's *Mérope* (1743), when, as the eponymous *heroine, she broke with conventions of tragic dignity and ran across the stage. Her *acting, by turns pathetic and terrifying, excited *audiences until she retired in 1776.   JG

Duncan, Isadora (1877–1927) American dancer and choreographer. A key forerunner of modern *dance, Duncan repudiated the artificiality of nineteenth-century *ballet, creating a new form of dance which she claimed was natural and would free women's bodies. She danced barelegged and barefoot in a neoclassical tunic. Drawing eclectically in her dance and writings from ancient Greek art, Nietzsche, and French and Russian revolutionary thought, Duncan influenced dress reform and inspired artists in every medium. She was both lyrical and powerful as a solo dancer, although she also created group dances. While her choreography was often simple—she skipped, walked, ran, paused, and gestured—her charismatic emotional power and profound musicality were intensely affecting to *audiences. She shared a spare, evocative aesthetic with *Craig (one of her lovers), whom she introduced to *Stanislavsky. She opened a series of schools for children in Europe, the last of which was in Moscow, where she lived for several years after the communist revolution.   SB

Dunlap, William (1766–1839) American playwright, *manager, painter, and historian. His early dramatic work, *The Father* (1789) and *Darby's Return* (1789), proved popular, but his major play *André* was hissed at its opening performance in 1798 because of its favourable portrayal of the British Major John André and its critical treatment of George Washington. Dunlap made some emergency modifications, and later rewrote it as a popular patriotic piece called *The Glory of Columbia: Her Yeomanry* (1803), portraying Washington as well as an ordinary American soldier as heroic figures. Dunlap became the manager of the newly opened Park Theatre from 1798 until he went bankrupt in 1805, then helped to manage it under the actor Thomas Cooper. He wrote numerous adaptations of *Kotzebue's *melodramas, including *The Stranger* (1798), *False Shame* (1799), and *Pizarro in Peru*

(1800). He also adapted French plays (*The Wife of Two Husbands* from *Pixérécourt, 1804) and continued to write original dramas about domestic subjects like *A Trip to Niagara* (1828). Considered the first major American dramatist, he completed more than 50 plays. He also published *History of the American Theatre* (1832), a biography of George Frederick *Cooke (1813), and *History of the Arts of Design* (1834).　　　SEW

Dunnock, Mildred (1901–91) American actress. A schoolteacher, Dunnock made her New York debut at the age of 30 in *Life Begins* (1932). She was acclaimed for her supporting role in the 1940 Broadway production of Emlyn *Williams's *The Corn Is Green* and as Lavinia in *Hellman's *Another Part of the Forest* (1946). But it was the role of Linda Loman in *Miller's *Death of a Salesman* (1949) that became a trademark. Her sensitive and dignified characterization was repeated in the Laslo Benedek film (1951) and in the television production (1966). A favourite actress of *Kazan, she played Big Mama in his staging of *Williams's *Cat on a Hot Tin Roof* (1955) and appeared in the Kazan films *Viva Zapata!* (1952) and *Baby Doll* (1956). Dunnock acted into her seventies, winning a Drama Desk award for her performance in *Duras's *A Place without Doors* (1970).　　　MAF

Durang, Christopher (1949–) American playwright and actor. Durang gained attention as a playwright in the late 1970s, with *regional and Broadway productions of *A History of the American Film*. *Off-Broadway, *Sister Mary Ignatius Explains It All for You* earned a 1979 Obie award while stirring protests about its anti-Catholicism. A humanist rage animates Durang's anarchic cartoon worlds, with their screwball debasements of religious dogma, psychobabble, and America's precious ideals of the nuclear family and its heterosexual inscription. Literary *parody and pop-culture *satire also have figured strongly in his work. Durang's savage thrust and crackpot logic has acquired a certain mainstream following with plays like *Beyond Therapy* (1981) and *The Marriage of Bette and Boo* (1985). His output since *Laughing Wild* (1987) has been more sporadic, but includes *Sex and Longing* (1996) and *Betty's Summer Vacation* (1999). Possessed of an affinity for performing since his Yale days, Durang has appeared in *cabaret, *revues, stage works (including his own), film, and television.　　　EW

Durante, Jimmy (1893–1980) American comic actor and singer. Durante worked as a ragtime piano player in New York saloons from the age of 17. In 1923 he opened a club in the Broadway district and became a favourite, moving into *vaudeville, film (*Roadhouse Nights*, 1930), and the 1930 Cole *Porter *musical *The New Yorkers*. With a comic personality built around his large nose, gravelly voice, and an underlying warmth and charm, Durante became a star of musical comedies and *revues in the 1930s and 1940s, including the spectacular Billy *Rose *circus musical *Jumbo* (1935) and Porter's *Red, Hot, and Blue* (1936). Aside from nightclub appearances, most of his work after 1940 was on radio, film, or television.　　　MAF

Duras, Marguerite (1914–96) French writer and director, who often transformed her novels into plays and her plays into films. Born in Indo-China, a post-colonial consciousness is evident throughout her work, as is her interrogation of representation itself. Duras's works are inter-textual, often revisiting the same material but continually reweaving it. Her first play, *The Square* (1955), is typically *absurdist. During the 1950s and 1960s her plays were often staged by *Barrault, notably *Days in the Trees* (1965), but in the 1970s she turned to director Simone Benmussa, whose spatial poetry accommodated Duras's search for ways to represent the feminine voice, and her rejection of a patriarchal style marked by rising suspense, climax, and Oedipal power struggles. *The English Lover* (1968) and *Eden Cinema* (1977) replay themes from her childhood in Indo-China, while her film scripts *Hiroshima mon amour* (directed by Alain Resnais, 1959) and *India Song* (which Duras directed, 1972) are also set in a remembered Asia, and reveal memory as unreliable and identity and time as fluid. Other plays include *The Viaducts of the Seine and Oise* (1963), *Véra Baxter* (1985), and *La Musica deuxième* (1985).　　　SBB

D'Urfey, Thomas (1653–1723) English playwright. Though later neglected, D'Urfey had at least 33 plays produced in London between 1676 and 1721, mostly *comedies. His satirical *farces and songs were popular with Charles II and James II and he continued to receive royal favour from subsequent monarchs and commercial success with the merchant *audience. D'Urfey earned his living by writing overtly theatrical pieces for the leading performers and sit uncomfortably in the literary tradition attributed to contemporaries, such as *Congreve. D'Urfey's three-part adaptation of Don Quixote (1694–5) attracted the unwelcome attention of the *anti-theatrical lobby, headed by *Collier, but was frequently revived until 1785. *The Marriage Hater Match'd* (1692) and *The Richmond Heiress* (1693), written for the acting partnership of Elizabeth *Barry and Anne *Bracegirdle, are typical D'Urfey comedies, containing a strong social commentary which reflects the shift toward the sentimental comedy of manners.   GBB

Dürrenmatt, Friedrich (1921–90) Swiss writer, one of the best-known German-language playwrights of the twentieth century. Dürrenmatt's early plays reflect his religious education, most notably *An Angel Comes to Babylon* (begun 1948, premièred 1953). Thereafter he began to adopt a lighter tone, as in *Romulus the Great* (1949), in which the Roman Emperor is more concerned about his chickens than about the invading barbarians from the north. Dürrenmatt achieved international fame with *The Visit* (1956), a characteristically grotesque *tragicomedy in which an old woman, Claire Zachanassian, constructed almost entirely from prostheses, returns to her home village to exact revenge on the man, significantly named Ill, who abandoned her in her youth. In an echo of the Nazi past, the villagers are gradually corrupted and conspire together to murder him. In 1960 *Brook directed *The Visit* in London and in 1963 Dürrenmatt's other major play, *The Physicists* (1962). Set in a mental hospital housing three homicidal inmates who claim to be famous physicists, the action reveals they are actually a scientist and two agents pretending to be mad so that potentially dangerous discoveries cannot be exploited by an evil world. However, the manager of the asylum is genuinely mad and has already stolen the nuclear secrets. Dürrenmatt shows a world in the grip of barbarian forces, of ruthless capital, or of the insane application of science, but the quiet courage of Romulus, Ill, and the three 'physicists' provides the only hope. Further work for the stage included adaptations of Shakespeare's *King John* (1968) and *Titus Andronicus* (1970), and domestic pieces, such as *Play Strindberg* (1969). After the 1970s Dürrenmatt concentrated on prose writing.   MWP

Duse, Eleanore (1858–1924) Italian *actor-manager. Born into a company of errant actors, Duse captured critical attention with her interpretation of Juliet in Verona's *amphitheatre (1875), and as the tormented Thérèse in *Zola's *Thérèse Raquin* (1879) in Naples. Over the next six years, she achieved fame as a member of Cesare Rossi's company, primarily due to the psychological *realism of her interpretations in *well-made plays (*Sardou, *Scribe, *Dumas *fils*) and in new Italian works, including Verga's *Cavalleria rusticana* (1884). She also proved herself a superb comedi-

enne in *Goldoni's *Pamela nubile* and *La Locandiera*.

When Rossi disbanded his company Duse became actor-manager of Compagnia Drammatica della Città di Roma (1887–94). She added to her repertory *Giacosa's *Tristi amori* (1887), Arrigo Boito's adaptation of *Antony and Cleopatra* (1888), *Praga's *Ideal Wife* (1890), *Ibsen's *A Doll's House* (1891), and *Sudermann's *Magda* (1892). Between 1889 and 1894 the company *toured widely. Her international renown led to comparisons with *Bernhardt, and in 1895 both performed Camille and Magda in London. *Shaw concluded that after seeing Duse's restrained *acting, Bernhardt seemed false, albeit charming.

By the early 1890s Duse was tiring of her realistic, mostly French roles as noble *heroine or sophisticated wife. Looking for poetic material to elevate Italian playwriting, for seven years she devoted herself to promoting the plays of the Italian poet, and her lover, *D'Annunzio. After premièring his dramatic poem *Spring Morning's Dream* in 1897 in Paris, she toured Italy and the USA with his *Francesca da Rimini, La Gioconda*, and *The Dead City*, though these were mostly unsuccessful. She broke from D'Annunzio when he allowed Irma *Gramatica to première *Daughter of Jorio* (1904) and, although she would continue to perform his work, she found new material in *Maeterlinck's *Monna Vanna* (1904), *Gorky's *Lower Depths* (1905), and particularly Ibsen: *Rosmersholm* (1906, *scenography by *Craig), *John Gabriel Borkman* (1908), and *Lady from the Sea* (1908). *Lugné-Poe served as director and *manager for some of her many tours between 1905 and 1909 throughout Europe, South America, and Russia. In 1909 Duse formally retired from the stage but continued to pursue projects and acted in her only film, *Cenere* (*Ashes*, 1916). Facing financial difficulties, she returned to the stage in 1921 with the help of *Zacconi and continued to be innovative. When she fell ill and died in Pittsburgh during her fourth US tour, she was mourned internationally and remains a legend.   JEH

Dutt, Utpal (1929–93) Bengali dramatist, director, and actor who worked with Geoffrey Kendal's *touring Shakespeariana company, became a convert to Marxism, and began writing plays in Bengali. With *Angar* (*Coal*, 1959), about a mining catastrophe, and *Kallol* (*Waves*, 1965), about the Indian Navy mutiny of 1946, he provided his Little Theatre Group with long-running productions. Dutt invented Bengali *documentary drama with *Manusher Adhikare* (*People's Rights*, 1968), on the 1931 trial of black youths in Scottsborough,

Alabama, specifically to encourage revolution among his working-class spectators.

Around this time he saw the potential of the folk genre of *jatra to communicate to a larger rural population, and prepared nineteen *jatra* with communist messages which travelled to villages. He also created what he called the 'poster play': *street-corner *agitprop in which the group read out and theatricalized factual accounts of class oppression. In 1969 he renamed LTG as the People's Little Theatre and staged some of his finest work: the richly *metatheatrical *Tiner Taloyar* (*Tin Sword*, 1971), *Barricade* (1972), and *Duhswapner Nagari* (*Nightmare City*, 1974) on police brutality, a production labelled seditious.

In his remaining years he directed, in addition to his 22 full-length *proscenium plays, another 40 or so productions, including work by Shakespeare, *Ghosh, and *Tagore. He translated Shakespeare and *Brecht into Bengali and wrote essays prolifically for his journal *Epic Theatre*, as well as books such as *Towards a Revolutionary Theatre*

(1982). He maintained a parallel career in film, acting in art and commercial movies in both Bengali and Hindi, though he tended to be typecast as the *villain or older buffoon.   AL

Duym, Jacob (1547–1612 or 1624) Flemish-born playwright. After serving in the army of William of Orange he settled in Leiden in the Netherlands, where he became a leading member of the immigrant Flemish *Chamber of Rhetoric called the Orange Lily. He was the author of two collections of six plays each, *Spiegelboeck* (*Book of Mirrors*, 1600) and *Ghedenckboek* (*Book of Memory*, 1606). Duym's work is in the allegorical, moralizing style typical of the Rhetoricians but at the same time also shows *early modern features. The plays in *Book of Memory* are political and propagandist, recalling great episodes from the struggle against Spain. Duym's elaborate stage directions are an important source for knowledge of the early Dutch stage, which still retained *medieval characteristics.   JDV

early modern period in Europe The early modern period includes overlapping epochs that have been variously called the Renaissance, the Reformation, the Restoration, the Enlightenment, the Age of Reason, and the Age of Revolution. Each of these terms designates specific intellectual, artistic, religious, economic, political, and scientific developments in Western culture. Influential cultural historians of the late twentieth century used the term 'early modern' to describe Europe and England from the fifteenth to the eighteenth centuries; for historians it encompasses a totality of cultural practices including, but not limited to, aesthetic production. Phenomena as diverse as guild memberships, plague effects, the formation of cities, enclosure acts, demographic migration, child-rearing practices, and material production are considered crucial to understanding the social history of the period. Scholars of the various arts, who used to be unconcerned about the term 'Renaissance', have become interested in the wider cultural context, and 'Renaissance' became the target of historicist and materialist critiques for its elitism, privileging of humanism, and narrow concern with aesthetic values. Consequently, it is now used with a degree of discomfort, regarded by some as an uncritical word that celebrates the revival of classical learning and the flowering of the arts at the expense of what was happening among the peasantry, the lower classes, and in women's lives. There is no satisfactory compromise available between the competing terms, but because 'early modern' is a more encompassing one, it has been preferred as the default term in this book, partly because the theatre of the time was particularly related to developing social, financial, and organizational issues. (The historical and intellectual ramifications are explained in detail in a lengthy essay in the parent volume, *The Oxford Encyclopedia of Theatre and Performance*.)   LC/DK

Ebb, Fred *See* KANDER, JOHN.

Echegaray, José (1832–1916) Spanish playwright, mathematician, and politician. His plays ranged from the effective social drama *The Great Galeoto* (1881) to neo-*romantic works with ex-cessive passions. *Ibsen's *Brand* was an influence on his *Madman or Saint* (1876), and *The Son of Don Juan* (1892) echoed the theme of *Ghosts* in a Spanish setting. Although his plays are seldom revived, he enjoyed immense esteem in Spain for three decades and was popular throughout Europe. In 1904, in the twilight of his career, he became the first dramatist to receive the Nobel Prize for Literature, an award that inspired protests in Spain.   MPH

Edgar, David (1947–   ) English dramatist, one of the socialist playwrights who emerged in the 1960s. Edgar's best-known work is an adaptation of *Nicholas Nickleby* (1980) for the *Royal Shakespeare Company, directed by *Nunn. Many of his plays have also been large-scale epics, seeking to capture a wedge of history or a socio-political contradiction in its unfolding. *Destiny* (1976), *Maydays* (1983), *The Shape of the Table* (1990), and *Pentecost* (1994) are representative. Working with smaller casts and more intense psychological scenes, *The Jail Diary of Albie Sachs* (1978), *Mary Barnes* (1978), and *That Summer* (1987) nevertheless take up critical political questions—apartheid in South Africa, R. D. Laing's controversial treatments for schizophrenia, the 1984–5 miners' strike. *Albert Speer* (*National Theatre, 2000) featured more than 25 actors and an elaborate *multimedia setting, showing that Edgar's dramatic imagination remains epic in scope and style. *Playing with Fire* (2005) deals with New Labour in the context of immigration. He has also published several books of essays and written widely for radio, film, and television.   JGR

Edinburgh International Festival One of the world's leading arts festivals, for three weeks in August Edinburgh hosts a selection of the best international theatre, *opera, *dance, and orchestral and other music in the city's major theatres and concert halls and other prestige venues. The festival was founded in 1947 as a symbol of postwar European reconciliation, a parallel to the *Avignon Festival of the same year. The first director was Rudolf Bing. It aimed to present a programme of work that would be representative of the highest possible artistic standards, presented by the foremost artists in the world. As with many international events the organizers have to balance the needs of Scottish *audiences with those of the significant tourist market drawn to the festival. Significant Scottish companies and artists that have been featured include the Glasgow *Citizens' Theatre, Scottish Opera, and Traverse Theatre. The Festival is programmed by an *artistic director, and artists and companies perform on invitation.

From its beginnings the festival also attracted to the city many more amateur and professional groups than those invited to the official events. It was not long before this peripheral activity was formalized as the Edinburgh Festival Fringe Society, and now many hundreds of shows are presented in its programme. Although there is a director, any company or individual who wants to perform, can locate a venue, pay the appropriate fee, and find a spot on the fringe. The range of work presented in this context is extraordinarily wide, from prestige productions to the eclectic and the bizarre. The Fringe in turn has spawned a series of satellite festivals, including the Military Tattoo, the International Film Festival, the Book Festival, and the Jazz and Blues Festival.   AS

educational theatre While all theatre might be construed to be 'educational' in the broadest sense (just as many have claimed that all theatre is political), the term is generally used (especially in Britain) to encompass three specific developments.

1. *Theatre-in-education.* TIE began in England at the Belgrade Theatre, Coventry, in 1965, when a team of 'actor-teachers' was established to take work into local schools, combining performance and participatory drama techniques. Funded by a partnership of local authority and the theatre, the team became the first of a series of such groups to be set up at various theatres across the country, some becoming independent companies in their own right, and the TIE movement went on to play an influential part in the development of progressive education, *community theatre, and theatre for *youth in Britain. TIE has spread widely beyond the UK, evolving in diverse ways in response to differing cultural needs.

2. *Theatre in health education,* a branch of TIE that emerged during the 1990s in direct response to the growing need for innovative approaches to educating young people in matters of sexual health, AIDS awareness, and drug abuse. The formats are similar to TIE programmes (for instance a play followed by interactive workshop) but the funding normally comes from health promotion agencies and the work must meet specific briefs and criteria. The best work tries to offer young people a rich dramatic experience rather than merely a vehicle for an all-too-predictable message.

3. *Theatre in museums.* During the last two decades of the twentieth century, as directors of museums and heritage sites endeavoured to find new and more appealing ways to interpret their collections, historic locations, and reconstructions, the use of theatre, TIE techniques and 'first-person interpretation', or *costumed role play, has gained increasing popularity. Notable examples are the extensive use of first-person interpretation at Colonial Williamsburg and Plimoth Plantation (USA), theatre-in-education programmes produced by the National Trust (UK), cameo performances presented as a regular feature of daily programming at London's Science Museum, the Royal Armouries in Leeds, the Science Museum of Minnesota, and a diverse array of site-specific performances at historic locations across Europe, from battle re-enactments to the intensive role-play days for schoolchildren in the nineteenth-century Apprentice House at Quarry Bank Mill in Cheshire.

In the USA, 'educational theatre' is often extended to include theatre for youth and other forms of dramatic activity with young people inside and outside the school curriculum, involving training in theatre skills and the production of school plays. In many other countries, especially in mainland Europe where the tradition of professional theatre for children is strong, the term 'educational theatre' does not translate well, having connotations of an inferior form, compromised by a supposed requirement to teach. Since good theatre for children will of itself be educational (for instance in inducting children into the classics, stimulating and enriching their imaginations, challenging preconceptions in its tackling of social problems), it is argued that education does not, and should not, have to be the primary goal. *See also* BOAL, AUGUSTO; DEVELOPMENT, THEATRE FOR; OPPRESSED, THEATRE OF THE.   ARJ

Edwardes, George (1852–1915) English *manager, *producer, and director. In 1881 Edwardes became manager of the new Savoy Theatre, and in 1885 *Hollingshead, who ran the Gaiety Theatre, hired him as co-manager; a year later Edwardes took control. For several years he continued to stage popular *burlesques featuring Kate Vaughan, among others. With *A Gaiety Girl* (1893), he developed a new kind of *musical comedy that came to dominate the London stage for two decades. Edwardes oversaw an empire of writers, composers, designers, musicians, performers, and several hundred staff members who helped him produce an almost unbroken string of long-running musicals. Expanding beyond the Gaiety, which featured the alluring 'Gaiety Girls' in fashionable *costumes, he began to use Daly's Theatre in 1895, purchasing it in 1899 when *Daly died. In 1903 he opened a new Gaiety Theatre, with Edward VII and Queen Alexandra in attendance. Throughout this period his productions *toured the world. Among his most successful shows were *An Artist's Model* (1895), *The Geisha* (1896), *San Toy* (1899), *A Country Girl* (1902), *The Cingalee* (1904), and *The Quaker Girl* (1910). His star performers included Marie *Tempest and Seymour *Hicks. TP

Edwards, Gale (1954–) Australian director, known for her bold, unapologetic, and challenging interpretations of the classics, and her work on *musicals, particularly those of *Lloyd Webber for whom she has directed revivals of *Aspects of Love* (1992), *Jesus Christ Superstar* (1996), and *Whistle down the Wind* (1998). Edwards's international career took off after working as *Nunn's associate director on the Australian production of *Les Misérables* in 1987. Her directing at the *Royal Shakespeare Company includes a controversial *Taming of the Shrew* (1995), which had a strong *feminist bite, and critically acclaimed productions of *Don Carlos* (1999) and *The White Devil* (1996). Edwards stresses clear storytelling and thrives in big spaces. Her use of violence onstage is also uncompromising, particularly notable in *The White Devil* and in a savage *Coriolanus* (Sydney, 1993). She directed *Jerry Springer: The Opera* in Sidney in 2009. EJS

Edwards, Hilton (1903–82) English actor and director. After seasons with Charles Doran at the *Old Vic, Edwards met Micheál *MacLíammóir in 1927, with whom he established the Gate Theatre, Dublin, a year later. He was a full-blooded, energetic performer with a studied concentration on stage that nicely offset his partner's romantic fervour. Edwards, a remarkably inventive director, took full advantage of current international innovations in *expressionist and presentational techniques of staging to bring a hugely diverse repertoire, classical and modern, to Ireland. This ensured that the Gate became a leading experimental art theatre, staging the best of new continental and American drama alongside works by Irish playwrights (*Johnston, Mary Manning, Maura Laverty) who favoured non-*naturalistic *dramaturgy. Edwards vividly described his productions and *rehearsal techniques in his autobiography *The Mantle of Harlequin* (1958). He excelled at establishing a precise dynamic rhythm for a production, choreographed crowd scenes to achieve ensemble sequences of great power, and placed his actors spatially within a design scheme to achieve effects of *total theatre unique in Irish practice. RAC

Effendi, Rustam (1903–79) Indonesian playwright, whose *Bebasari* (1926) was the first Indonesian scripted drama. Dutch-educated, he learned that drama in Europe could express political ideas, then took the kidnapping of Sita in the *Ramayana* for his theme. The title character Bebasari ('sweet freedom', that is, Indonesia) is a princess held captive by the demon Rawana (the Dutch), and is released by Bujangga (Indonesian youth). The text used the emergent language of Indonesian at a time when writing in what was a merchants' argot was considered a revolutionary act; Effendi and other nationalists abandoned ethnic languages to argue for a politically and linguistically unified nation-state. Performance was blocked by the Dutch and the self-published play was banned, but Effendi's model of political activism set the course for modern Indonesian drama. KFO

Efremov, Oleg (1927–2000) Soviet/Russian actor and director. Efremov became the prototype of the rebel hero of the 1960s, through his roles and as the founder of the Sovremennik Theatre in Moscow (1957). As a director of that brilliant company he combined stylized or abstract sets with grounded and *realistic performances in the *Stanislavsky tradition, as in *Rozov's *Alive Forever* (1956, 1961) and *Shatrov's *Bolsheviks* (1967). In 1970 he became *artistic director of the *Moscow Art Theatre, which had ossified after 30 years without genuine leadership. Efremov faced a huge challenge, which he surmounted by introducing the work of young dramatists that addressed the concerns and conflicts of contemporary *audiences. His main interest as a director lay with ethics and the individual conscience. He was the first to offer successful interpretations of the complex plays of *Vampilov: *The Duck Hunt* (1979) remains a landmark for the subtle investigation of the *hero's psychology. His interpretations of *Uncle Vanya* (1985) and *The Three Sisters* (1997) set new standards for staging *Chekhov with Stanislavsky's method. Alongside his work as a stage actor and director, Efremov played numerous roles in film. BB

Efros, Anatoly (1925–87) Soviet/Russian director. In 1963 Efros led the Theatre of the Lenin Komsomol, where he created a repertoire largely based on contemporary drama, provoking political controversy with a number of productions, including *Radzinsky's *104 Pages about Love* (1964) and *A Film Is Being Shot* (1965), criticized by the *censoring body for their sexual explicitness. *Arbuzov's *My Poor Marat* (1965), placing love above duty, did not please the authorities either, nor did Efros's interpretations of *Chekhov: *The Seagull* (1966) and *The Three Sisters* (1967) were condemned as forseeing Chekhov as a precursor of the theatre of the *absurd. Efros was sacked from the Lenin Komsomol Theatre and transferred to an inferior post at the Malaya Bronnaya Theatre, where he staged classical plays, enhancing the tragic dimensions in comic texts (such as *Gogol's *The Marriage*). In 1984 he was appointed *artistic director of the Taganka Theatre after *Lyubimov had been exiled. Efros had to face an ensemble only partly willing to cooperate, while trying to preserve his own style with productions such as *Gorky's *Lower Depths* and continuing Lyubimov's device of prose adaptations. BB

Eisenstein, Sergei (1898–1948) Russian/Soviet stage and film director and designer. He began his career with travelling theatre groups during the Civil War before joining Proletkult in 1920, moved to *Foregger's Workshop, where he experimented in *music hall and *circus techniques, before becoming assistant to *Meyerhold. In 1922 he assumed *artistic directorship of the Proletkult Theatre and staged a famous *avant-garde production of *Ostrovsky's *Wise Man* as a 'montage of attractions', breaking the play down into episodes staged as turns in a circus ring with actors dressed as *clowns, and incorporating *acrobatic stunts and a high-wire act. There followed productions of two works by *Tretyakov. His rejection by the Proletkultists caused him 'to drop out of the theatre into the cinema', as he put it. His first film, *Strike* (1924), put the theories advanced in his 1924 essay 'Montage of Attractions' into cinematic practice and also revealed his debt to Meyerhold's *biomechanics. Throughout his career, Eisenstein remained devoted to Meyerhold and during the period of Meyerhold's suppression as a 'non-person' helped to store and preserve his archive secretly. NW

Ekhof, Konrad (1720–78) German actor. One of the most respected performers of the mid-eighteenth century, Ekhof's *acting was analysed by *Lessing in *Hamburg Dramaturgy*. He worked with the finest troupes of the period (Schönemann, *Ackermann) and was the first German actor who tried to systematize his craft, founding a short-lived acting academy in 1753. He was admired particularly for his rich use of gesture

and subtle speaking voice, creating important roles in Lessing's plays such as Odoardo in *Emilia Galotti* and Tellheim in *Minna von Barnhelm*. He was director of the first permanent troupe at a German court theatre, in Gotha (1778). CBB

ekkyklema A large wheeled platform pushed onto the stage from the central doors of the stage building (*skene) in *Greek theatres. In *Sophocles and *Euripides the device normally presented interior scenes, particularly tableaux of murder victims, as if seen through opened doors. *Comedy used the device for tragic *parody and mock heroics. EGC

Ekster, Aleksandra (1884–1949) Russian *constructivist designer and cubist painter, who began her career at *Tairov's Kamerny Theatre with the designs for Annensky's *Thamira Kithar ides* (1916). The following year her concept of 'dynamic' or 'kinetic' staging was deployed in Tairov's production of *Wilde's *Salome*. Ekster believed that stage space should be organized so that setting and *costume played complementary and equal roles within an organically conceived *scenography. For Tairov's *Romeo and Juliet* (1921) costume merged with a setting of steps, arches, and bridges over which the actors swarmed at speed, especially in the fight scenes. For a time Ekster worked in film, designing futuristic costumes for Protazanov's *Aelita* (1924) before emigrating to Paris, where she became a friend of *Picasso. In 1925 she invented 'epidermic costumes' for a *ballet project where the dancers wore body paint and minimal costume. An admirer of *Appia, whose influence was apparent in *Thamira Kitharides*, Ekster also used *lighting in original and distinctive ways. NW

Elder, Lonnie, III (1927–96) *African American playwright, an early member of the Harlem Writers' Guild. He studied with Alice *Childress, with whom he performed in summer *stock. In the 1950s he roomed with Douglas Turner *Ward, who steered him toward playwriting. Elder appeared on Broadway in *Hansberry's *A Raisin in the Sun* (1959), and in 1965 took the role of Clem in Ward's *Day of Absence*. Elder's *Charades on East Fourth Street* was produced in Montréal in 1967. His major work, *Ceremonies in Dark Old Men*, was produced by the Negro Ensemble Company in 1969 and won the Drama Desk award. Elder has written a number of successful films about the African-American experience, including *Sounder* and its sequel (1972, 1976). BBL

Eliot, T. S. (Thomas Stearns) (1888–1965) Anglo-American poet, dramatist, and critic. His first dramatic work, *Sweeney Agonistes: Fragments of an Aristophanic Melodrama* (1932) was his most innovative, indebted to the *music hall and *minstrel show. In 1934 he provided text for a religious pageant, *The Rock*, to an outline by E. Martin *Browne, who directed all of Eliot's subsequent dramas. The theatrically effective *chorus in *The Rock* anticipated *Murder in the Cathedral* (1935), a historical verse drama about Thomas Becket first performed by amateurs in Canterbury Cathedral, then commercially in London (1935) and on Broadway (1938).

Eliot's religious preoccupations and sense of guilt stemming from his unhappy marriage pervaded his writing. Issues of conscience were central to his next play, *The Family Reunion* (1939), featuring Michael *Redgrave and based on *Aeschylus' *Oresteia*. Eliot's remaining plays, all premièred at the *Edinburgh Festival, also had classical models, hidden by a comedy-of-manners format, and the metre of the verse moved towards naturalistic prose. *The Cocktail Party* (1949), based on *Euripides' *Alcestis*, featured *Guinness and *Worth; *The Confidential Clerk* (1953), based on Euripides' *Ion*, and *The Elder Statesman* (1958), based on *Sophocles' *Oedipus at Colonus*, both featured Paul Rogers. Eliot's life and work have themselves spawned a play about his first marriage, Michael Hastings's *Tom and Viv* (1984, film 1994), and *Lloyd Webber's *musical *Cats* (1981), based on the poems from *Old Possum's Book of Practical Cats* (1939).   VRS

Elizabethan Stage Society London play-producing society like the *Independent Theatre. Founded by *Poel, the society was formed to serve 'the principle that Shakespeare's plays should be accorded the conditions of playing for which they were designed'. This meant Shakespearian playing spaces (imitated on fit-up stages or revisited in buildings where Shakespeare's company once played), *early modern *costume, cross-sex casting (usually females playing males, an inversion of Shakespeare practice), and Poel's notion of period pronunciation. Across ten years from its inaugural production, *Twelfth Night* (1895), the society presented a total of 33 productions, counting revivals. Although most of these were Elizabethan, plays from other periods were also staged: the only productions which did not incur losses were Milton's *Samson Agonistes* (1900) and the *morality *Everyman* (1901).   MOC

Elkunchwar, Mahesh (1939–) Marathi playwright. Elkunchwar's short play *Holi* (1970) was an aggressive exposition of the disillusionment of the younger generation. Since then he has written seventeen plays. Compassion entered his work with *Flower of Blood* (1980), and reached a peak in *The Stone Mansion* (1985), a finely nuanced *naturalistic play about the crumbling feudal order in rural Maharashtra. Two sequels followed—*Pensive by a Pond* and *End of an Age*—to complete a trilogy, staged in 1994. The versatility of Elkunchwar's dramatic imagination is testified by *Pratibimb* (1987), a witty fantasy that deals with a man's loss of his mirror reflection.   SGG

Elliott, Michael (1931–84) English director. A superb craftsman, Elliott's productions of *Ibsen were highly respected. He began his career in London by founding the 59 Theatre at the Lyric Hammersmith, directing Vanessa *Redgrave in *As You Like It* at Stratford in 1961, and running an acclaimed season in 1962 at the *Old Vic (*Peer Gynt*, *Merchant of Venice*, *Measure for Measure*). His production of *Little Eyolf* for the *Edinburgh Festival in 1963 was particularly lauded. He joined the *National Theatre in 1965, but refused to be *Olivier's assistant and instead founded the 69 Company in Manchester, which became the Royal Exchange. His in-the-round productions of *naturalist drama and Shakespeare in the old Corn Exchange building were often commended, and he managed to establish the Royal Exchange as a flagship *regional company. He directed extensively for television, most notably his award-winning *King Lear* (1984) with Olivier.   KN

Engel, Erich (1891–1966) German director. Initially an actor, Engel soon switched to *directing, first in Hamburg, and then in 1922 in Munich, where he met *Brecht and the designer *Neher. Their collaboration was to be crucial for the development of *epic theatre. In Munich Engel directed Brecht's *In the Jungle of Cities* (1923) before joining *Reinhardt in Berlin in 1925. Important productions there included *Coriolanus* (1925), which stressed the individual scenes as self-contained entities and decisively influenced Brecht's theories on episodic structure. Of Brecht's work, he directed the premières of *The Threepenny Opera* and *A Man's a Man* (both 1928), among others. During the Nazi period he worked at the *Deutsches Theater with Hilpert, and after the war he was *artistic director of the Munich Kammerspiele before joining Brecht at the *Berliner Ensemble, which he co-directed with *Weigel after Brecht's death in 1956. In keeping with the principles of epic theatre, Engel's productions were marked by analytic clarity and a distrust of all extraneous effects.   CBB

English Comedians Itinerant English theatre companies which *toured Germany from the late sixteenth to early seventeenth centuries. In many ways similar to the *commedia dell'arte* troupes, the Englische Komödianten differed in two important respects: they performed in German as well as English and they quickly included local actors. They were renowned for an exaggerated *acting style which may have been necessitated by language problems. They adapted English *clown *characters into the famous figure of Pickelhering, a mainstay of German itinerant theatre until the eighteenth century. They also introduced the Elizabethan and Jacobean repertoire to Germany, including the first performances of Shakespeare (probably), *Marlowe, and *Kyd on the Continent, albeit in crude adaptations. A troupe consisted of ten to fifteen actors plus several musicians. They were largely dependent on aristocratic patronage but also performed for local people in towns. The first troupe arrived in Germany via Denmark in 1586; the second, the ensemble of Robert Browne, came in 1592, probably because the London theatres were closed for the plague. The outbreak of the Thirty Years War in 1618 severely curtailed the English Comedians' activities, but their structure and organization formed the basis of the German itinerant companies of the second half of the seventeenth century.   CBB

English Shakespeare Company Troupe formed in 1986 by the director *Bogdanov and the actor *Pennington, chiefly in disillusion with the work of the *Royal Shakespeare Company and the *National Theatre. Seeking to make Shakespeare again the centre of a popular theatre, they *toured *1 and 2 Henry IV* and *Henry V* to the largest provincial theatres in England and Wales as well as to Germany, France, and Canada. Aggressively eclectic in style, the productions relished stirring up contemporary resonances, with Henry V's invading army as a bunch of football fans chanting "Ere we go, 'ere we go'. Further tours extended the cycle of histories to include *Richard II* and a three-part version of the first cycle, until by 1989 they were performing seven-play cycles amounting to 23 hours of theatre to excited *audiences largely new to Shakespeare. The withdrawal of Arts Council funding led to virtual collapse except for schools work.   PDH

English Stage Company Founded by George *Devine, Tony *Richardson, and the dramatist Ronald Duncan, the ESC became synonymous with the *Royal Court Theatre and the revival of British theatre begun in 1956. With Devine as *artistic director, the first season was dominated by the success of *Osborne's *Look Back in Anger*, which set the agenda thereafter for socially engaged new writing. The list of important play-

wrights championed by the ESC is enormous, from Osborne, *Wesker, and *Arden to *Ravenhill, *Kane, and *Crimp. *Gaskill, who succeeded Devine in 1965, premièred most of *Bond's early work and in the early 1970s fostered the new wave of left-wing political dramatists, including *Brenton and *Hare. *Stafford-Clark (director 1980–93) championed women playwrights like Louise *Page, Timberlake *Wertenbaker, Sarah *Daniels, and pre-eminently Caryl *Churchill. Thereafter Stephen *Daldry's tenure revived the company's tradition of radical new writing through Sarah Kane, Jez Butterworth, Joe *Penhall, and Nick Grosso, while companies like DV8 and Gloria widened the range. Daldry also saw the Court through major renovation in 1997–2000, during which time he was replaced by Ian Rickson, in turn replaced by Dominic Cooke in 2008.   DR

entremets/entremés *Entremets* (French) and *entremés* (Spanish), literally food served between main courses, or a side dish, came to indicate any diversion between courses, and in the late *medieval period referred to elaborate entertainments, usually performed by professionals, during a formal banquet. In Spain, *entremés* could also designate *biblical scenes in pageant processions. Like its English equivalent, *interlude, the Spanish *entremés* had by the sixteenth century become a common term for any short play of the popular repertory, an alternative to *paso*.   RWV

entries, royal The ceremonial entry of a royal personage or occasionally some other eminent person into a city. During the *medieval and *early modern periods, the celebration of coronations, royal weddings, visits of foreign royalty, the return of monarchs from exile, and the military victories of a royal commander frequently included a processional entry into one or more important cities. Typically, entries were civic events, financed and organized by local governments and trade guilds. The mayor (or his equivalent), accompanied by other civic officials, would meet the person to be honoured outside the city before escorting him or her in procession through city streets decorated with hangings and thronged with spectators. Along the processional route at suitable locations such as gateways, conduits, and entrances to major streets, there might be a series of pageants as complex and costly as any courtly entertainment. Elaborately constructed arches that distantly echoed the Roman triumphal arch, scenic devices, and stages (often multi-tiered) then offered the city's guest a series of spectacles involving some combination of emblematic images, banner texts and mottoes, *tableaux vivants, speeches, and even dramatic scenes. Subjects tended to derive from history, heraldry, mythology, or religion and were selected both to honour the person whose virtues were being celebrated and on occasion express particular concerns of the citizenry. ARY

environmental theatre

A term coined by *Schechner in 1968 to refer to the non-frontal, spectator-incorporative theatre he was then creating with the *Performance Group. The concept can be traced to the processional and church-based productions of *medieval theatre in Europe, as well as many forms of traditional Asian theatre and various folk performances. Whereas most representational theatre creates a frontal or oppositional relationship between the stage and *auditorium—and creates an aesthetic distance through an implicit or explicit separation of performer and spectator space—environmental theatre seeks to incorporate the spectator in some way within the performance and to diminish the sense of aesthetic distance. As a general rule, environmental theatre can be defined as any form of theatre in which a spectator cannot apprehend the total performance space within the normal frontal lines of vision.

*Audience incorporation may be achieved in several ways and in varying degrees. The stage or scenery may partially or completely surround the audience. Such approaches range from the merely atmospheric, as when an auditorium is decorated to enhance mood but the relationship to the stage does not change; to the structural, as with ring-like stages that surround the audience, or projecting stages such as the *hanamichi of *kabuki theatre, or the futuristic projects of artists such as Walter Gropius which placed audiences in the midst of spherical theatre; to totally enveloping environments as in some *happenings and some of the work of *Grotowski, *Kantor, and others in which all the space is potentially available to actors as well as spectators who may have to move about (sometimes called 'promenade performance'). Similarly, processional performances which move through a city, civic structure, or sacred or festival space—such as the medieval *biblical plays of England or Spain, royal *entries, the *Ram lila of India, or contemporary *parades and pageants—are environmental in that they traverse great distances that cannot be completely observed by a single stationary spectator, while at the same time implicitly transforming the urban architecture into a scenographic space.

Whereas religious, folk, and traditional performances around the world have evolved environmental strategies with little theory, much twentieth-century Western theatre has self-consciously experimented with non-frontal staging either as an attempt at greater *naturalism (as with the productions in Moscow of *Okhlopkov's Realistic Theatre or the *Living Theatre's staging of *Gelber's The Connection in New York). More often artists have used environmental staging as a means of thwarting conventional *illusion, as in various productions of *Meyerhold, *Barba, *Mnouchkine, the *Bread and Puppet Theatre, and others. Of more recent vintage is 'site-specific performance' in which a production is staged not in a *playhouse but in an existing structure or natural environment that is chosen either because of its theatrical qualities or its appropriateness for the theme of style of the production. In such cases the site becomes the theatrical environment and the spectator is surrounded by the *scenography whether the entire space is used for the performance or not. Several *performance artists, postmodern *dancers, and production organizations such as En Garde Arts (USA) and Forced Entertainment (UK) have presented works on beaches, railway stations, hotels, art galleries, city streets, factories, and the like. In site-specific work, as in much environmental theatre, the environment itself often becomes the central aspect of the performance and incorporates performer and spectator equally. AA

epic theatre

The term coined by *Piscator and *Brecht to describe their innovative theatrical principles, developed both collaboratively and independently from the 1920s until Brecht's death in 1956 and Piscator's in 1966. Piscator located the germane idea for epic theatre in his experience as a draftee in the German Front Theatre, where he acted in a production of Charley's Aunt amid bombed ruins, with shells exploding in the distance, a real-life 'estrangement effect': the juxtaposition of escapist entertainment on the stage framed by mass destruction and death. Brecht contrasted epic theatre with 'dramatic' or 'Aristotelian theatre', which he identified with *Aristotle's ideal climactic structure, noble *characters, and his rejection of the Homeric epic's representation of history in favour of *Greek *tragedy's representation of fate as beyond human control. More immediately, Brecht and Piscator were reacting against the conventions of *naturalism and *expressionism: neither naturalism's restricted slice-of-life picture nor expressionism's focus on the psyche of one individual could register, much less critique, the larger social, political, and historical realities beyond the theatre. Thus neither movement could comment on its own production of signs.

Although Brecht and Piscator worked together frequently in Berlin from 1918 to 1931, their concepts and practice of epic theatre differed. Piscator established the 'big picture' through a wealth of documentation via the old media of *actors and *dialogue and the new media of film, slides, loudspeakers, and life-size *puppets. Brecht, on the other hand, began with the parable as a microcosm of the social and economic system, through which the *audience could imagine and understand the larger world. Although Brecht also used projections, documentation, and titles, his focus remained on the characters' relations with each other. Both men followed the principle of the *Verfremdungseffekt; for them, the greatest power of art lay in its ability to challenge our habitual modes of perception and presumptions about what is normal in social relationships. Epic theatre became a medium for a Marxist critique of capitalism's economic and social power structure, insisting that the world can be changed.

The influence of epic theatre was spread first by the *Berliner Ensemble's *touring production of *Mother Courage* in Paris in 1954, and ever since has been taken up and adapted by succeeding generations of socially critical artists around the world. *See also* BOURGEOIS THEATRE; DOCUMENTARY DRAMA AND THEATRE; REALISM AND REALITY.   SBB

Epidaurus, Theatre of The best-preserved ancient theatre in Greece, frequently used for modern performances, seating about 11,000. Unlike the Theatre of *Dionysus in Athens, it was a cult theatre and not a city theatre, built before 300 BC for the pilgrimage sanctuary of Asclepius, the god of healing, and designed for its *ritual performances. Its high narrow stage was remodelled later but the present two tiers of seating probably represent the original design. While its general form may have been indebted to the Athenian theatre, which had been recently remodelled, its architectural mathematics are unique, being based on the so-called Pheidonic cubit, the pentagon, and the ratio known as the golden mean. As a result it seems likely that this 'most harmonious' theatre (so-called by the ancient writer Pausanias) owed its form to advanced Pythagorean ideas of mathematical-musical harmony, designed to provide a healing environment.   WJS

epilogue A speech or very occasionally a short scene at the conclusion of a play that comments on or draws conclusions from the presented action, offers reasons for deserving the *audience's approbation, or simply asks for *applause. Epi-

logues can therefore be either integral to the play or dissociated from it. They are commonly spoken by one of the *characters, although in some instances this is a mediating figure such as 'Chorus' or 'Doctor'. Because they are outside the fiction, epilogues serve to connect the world of the play with the world of the audience. Unlike the *prologue, the epilogue was not formally recognized in classical theory; like the prologue, it ran counter to the conventions of the *realistic theatre.   RWV

Erdman, Nikolai (1900–70) Soviet/Russian playwright. Erdman was a co-founder of the Theatre of Satire, Moscow. His first full-length play, *The Mandate* (or *The Warrant*), premièred in 1925, a biting *satire on the petty bourgeoisie in the context of the Party. *The Suicide* was completed in 1931 and rehearsed by *Meyerhold and *Stanislavsky before the *censorship board stopped *rehearsals in 1932. In the play the unemployed Podsekalnikov is mistakenly suspected of wanting to commit suicide and visited by representatives of different social groups who want him to die for their cause: the intelligentsia, women, Marxists, tradesmen, and the clergy. The play was not published in the Soviet Union until 1987, and received further attention through *Lyubimov's production of 1990. During the 1930s Erdman wrote a number of film scripts, including the *musical comedies *Jolly Fellows* and *Volga-Volga*. He was arrested in 1933 for anti-Soviet propaganda and exiled to Siberia. After his return to Moscow he wrote mainly scripts for animation and prose adaptations for the stage. He was formally rehabilitated in 1990, twenty years after his death.   BB

Ermolova, Maria (1853–1928) Russian actress. Daughter of a *prompter at the Maly Theatre, Ermolova first studied *ballet before becoming one of the outstanding tragic actresses of the Russian theatre. Her chance came in 1870 when *Fedotova fell ill before a benefit performance of *Lessing's *Emilia Galotti* and Ermolova took her place in the title role. Her success was instantaneous and she became a member of the Maly Theatre company the following year. In 1873 she acted Katerina in *Ostrovsky's *The Thunderstorm* and, in 1876, the role of Laurentia in Lope de *Vega's *Fuente Ovejuna*, where her interpretation of a common girl who becomes an inspired leader of a popular uprising was so powerful that the authorities rapidly removed it from the repertoire (*see* CENSORSHIP). Ermolova also scored successes as Shakespeare's Ophelia (1878) and Lady Macbeth (1896), *Schiller's Joan of Arc

(1884) and Mary Stuart (1886), and as *Racine's Phèdre (1890).   NW

Ervine, St John (1883–1971) Irish playwright and critic. Ervine briefly and contentiously *managed the *Abbey Theatre in Dublin (1915–16), where most of his plays also premièred, beginning with *Mixed Marriage* in 1911. Many of his plays concern Northern Ireland, including *The Magnanimous Lovers* (1912), *The Orangeman* (1914), *John Fergusson* (1915), and *Friends and Relations* (1941). Ervine also had several light *comedies staged in London, including *Anthony and Anna* (1926) and *The First Mrs Fraser*. His most successful play was *Robert's Wife* (1937), which provided a memorable role for Edith *Evans. He served as theatre critic for the *Observer* between the wars.   MDG

Escudero, Ruth (1945–) Peruvian actress and director. As the head of the National Theatre (1995–2001), she conducted an aggressive campaign to decentralize Peru's theatre by organizing regional conferences and establishing international networks in Minnesota, New York, Havana, Madrid, Paris, and Sofia. She worked for a higher standard of *acting through rigorous training and high-quality productions. Starting in 1973 Escudero's own *directing work has explored women, *gender, race, and social milieu in productions such as *Three Marías and a Rose, Isabel, Three Ships and One Actor, Scorpions Looking at the Sky, The Garden of the Cherries, The Day of the Moon, A Toy*, and, more recently, *Qoillor Ritti* (1999) and *The Rupertos* (2000).   LRG

Espert, Nuria (1938–) Spanish-Catalan actress and director. From her student days in Barcelona, she performed roles in both Spanish and Catalan from *Greek *tragedy to modern European and American playwrights. International attention came in 1971 when she portrayed *García Lorca's Yerma in a dynamic production directed by Víctor *García. In 1986 she made her directorial debut with a London staging of Lorca's *The House of Bernarda Alba*. Other important roles were Medea (1954) and Shen Te in *The Good Person of Setzuan* (1967) in the first production of *Brecht's play in Spain during the Franco period. More recently she appeared in *McNally's *Master Class* (1999), *Albee's *Who's Afraid of Virginia Woolf?* (2000), and Ventura Pons's film *Barcelona, a Map* (2006), based on a play by Lluïsa *Cunillé.   MPH

Estorino, Abelardo (1925–) Cuban playwright and director. *The Theft of the Pig* (1961) opened Cuban drama to issues emerging from the revolution after 1959, and *La casa vieja* (1964) showed for the first time on stage the contradictions generated by socialism. *Cain's Mangoes* (1965) marked Estorino's first incursion into a non-*realist aesthetic, to be expounded later in *The Sorrowful Tale of the Secret Love of Don José Jacinto Milanés*, about the fate of a nineteenth-century Cuban poet. Though written in 1974, official political doctrine prevented its production until 1985. The country's crisis of values following the disappearance of the international socialist bloc was the reference point of *She Does Look White* (1994). His other work includes *Times of Plenty* (1962), *Vague Rumours* (1992), and *The Dance* (2000). Estorino usually directed his own plays.   MMu

Etherege, George (1635–91) English playwright. The son of a royalist who died in France, Etherege probably spent time in that country before appearing in London in 1664 as the author of *The Comical Revenge*. The play's great success procured his entry into the inner circle of court wits, which included *Buckingham, Rochester, and *Wycherley. Following the production of *She Would If She Could* (1668) Etherege spent three years in Turkey as secretary to the English ambassador. Five years after his return he produced his masterpiece, *The Man of Mode* (1676). Knighted in 1679 and married the following year to a wealthy widow, he was posted to Bavaria in 1685 and did not return to England after the 1688 Revolution. Etherege was in many respects a typical Restoration figure, variously libertine, poet, courtier, and diplomat. His *comedies are similarly protean, brilliantly exploiting changing theatrical fashion.   RWV

Eulj, Ahmed Taieb al- (1928–) Moroccan songwriter, actor, playwright, and director, a highly visible figure in theatre since the 1950s. He was a member of the Moroccan Theatre Company from 1956 and its co-*manager from 1959, and remained important after its reorganization as Al-Maamoura. Among the 50 plays which constitute the repertory of that troupe, more than twenty were written or adapted by him. In his career he composed hundreds of songs, wrote about 50 plays, and adapted more than twenty. As an actor he created the majority of the roles in the *Molière plays he adapted, including *The Imaginary Invalid* (1958) and *Walyallah* (*Tartuffe*). Although he was versatile in a number of genres, and used formal Arabic in many of his plays, light *comedies remained his speciality, the Moroccan Arabic dialect his particular medium.   MMe

Euripides (c.480–407/6 BC) Athenian *tragic dramatist. The youngest and most problematic of the three great tragedians of *Greek theatre, Euripides wrote about 90 plays. He won only four victories at the *Dionysia, for reasons that are uncertain, but which scholars usually link to comic portrayals of him as *avant-garde and amoral. Many more of his plays survive than of his rivals: nineteen in all, though *Rhesus* is probably not his. One group (*Alcestis, Medea, Hippolytus, Andromache, Hecuba, Trojan Women, Phoenician Women, Orestes, Bacchae,* and *Rhesus*) was preserved by selection; the other (*Helen, Electra, Children of Heracles, Heracles, Suppliant Women, Iphigeneia at Aulis, Iphigeneia among the Taurians, Ion,* and *Cyclops*) seems to be part of an alphabetical collection of all his plays, and therefore represents a more random sample of his work.

Perhaps as a consequence of this, his work appears more varied than that of *Sophocles or *Aeschylus. His surviving plays include the only extant complete *satyr-play, *Cyclops* (a late work, from around 408 BC), and the extraordinary *Alcestis* (438 BC), performed fourth in its tetralogy instead of a satyr-play and apparently of intermediate genre. Among the *tragedies there is also considerable variety: some have seemed to critics more *melodramatic than tragic, like the 'escape' plays *Helen* and *Iphigeneia among the Taurians*; others have been criticized because they have more complex structures than most tragedies, like *Hecuba* and *Heracles*. The later plays are seen as most problematic, both in thought and in form. While there is no reason to endorse the old view of Euripides as an *enfant terrible* alienated from his society, it is true that in some respects, notably the manipulation of tragic conventions, Euripides genuinely (and not only in the imagination of *Aristophanes) seems to have been a compulsive innovator throughout his career. He delights in unexpected and theatrical entrances, as when Medea, having killed her children offstage, re-enters, not through the central door, but high up in the chariot of the Sun.

Euripides has often been said to use his stagecraft parodically: his Electra, married off to a peasant in a striking mythological innovation, enters bearing an urn in which she is fetching water, a 'realistic' action rather than a tragic one. This has been seen as a parody of the libation urns borne by Electra and the *chorus in Aeschylus' *Libation-Bearers*, which deals with the same story, and perhaps also of the urn in Sophocles' *Electra*, which she is falsely told contains Orestes' ashes. Certainly this is very different from Sophocles' connected use of significant properties—the urn is used to characterize Electra and her situation at her first appearance and then is discarded—but Euripides is not so much parodying other treatments of the myth here as marking out his own approach to the well-known story of Orestes' revenge. He sometimes does adopt a more Sophoclean use of significant objects when it suits him: in *Hippolytus*, a script framed by the appearance of two warring goddesses, Artemis and Aphrodite, the stage is similarly framed by their statues. The visual motif of veiling and unveiling is also used with great subtlety to underline the terrible choice between speech and silence faced by Phaedra, Hippolytus' hapless stepmother, whose unrequited love for him, imposed by Aphrodite, precipitates the *catastrophe. Phaedra, in other versions of the story a *villainess, is here a neurotic but infinitely pitiable victim of divine cruelty, one of a whole range of sympathetically drawn, and thus controversial, female tragic *characters for which Euripides was famous (Aristophanes travestied his interest in female psychology in *Women at the Thesmophoria*).

Especially in his later plays, Euripides does seem to have enjoyed pushing tragic convention to its limit, but only in order to make a tragic point. *Orestes* (408) is a play of extremes, but for a reason: the internecine struggles of the house of Atreus and the mythological deformations they undergo in this version are made more grotesque by the revolutionary staging. When Orestes, sentenced to death for killing his mother, attacks Helen inside the house, the outrage is described by a Phrygian slave who enters apparently by climbing over the *skene and dropping down onto the stage. The abandonment of normal tragic decorum is compounded by the actor's monody, a splendid example of the radical New Music of which Euripides was the most admired exponent and which was so splendidly parodied by Aristophanes in *Frogs*. The breakdown of the tragic conventions mirrors the breakdown of mythological norms, and of the family and the city in the play. And yet when we turn to *Bacchae*, it becomes very clear that novelty for Euripides was a tool, not a disease: nothing could be more conservative, not to say archaic, than his handling of the chorus in this posthumously performed play.

Euripides was highly popular in the *early modern period, but in the seventeenth and eighteenth centuries his innovative approach and his intellectualism made many of his plays lose popularity, first in the face of the *neoclassical taste for the *unities, then through *romanticism's distaste for rhetoric and for highly coloured

Euripidean violence. Some remained popular, though, especially *Medea*. *Corneille's *Médée* (1635) combined elements from Euripides and *Seneca; both Charpentier (1693) and later Cherubini (1797) wrote *operas called *Médée*; and *Medea* continues to be performed and adapted frequently. Notable modern productions include Robinson Jeffers's adaptation with Judith *Anderson and *Gielgud as Jason (New York, 1947); a remarkable all-male Japanese production directed by *Ninagawa, seen at the *Edinburgh Festival in 1986; a more traditional but powerful version directed by Jonathan Kent with Diana *Rigg (London, 1992); and an intense production by Deborah *Warner with Fiona *Shaw (Dublin and London, 2000–1). From having been popular in the seventeenth century as a play about love, *Medea* has become a political play, in its own way as timely as Euripides' *Trojan Women* (set the morning after the Sack of Troy) seemed during the inter-war years of the twentieth century.   JMM

Evans, Edith (1888–1976) English actress. After beginning her career with *Poel and then *touring with Ellen *Terry, she established herself in the 1920s as a distinguished London actress capable of a wide range of roles. For over five decades she performed in the canonical repertory, including Shakespeare, *Dekker, *Dryden, *Congreve, *Wycherley, *Farquhar, *Goldsmith, *Sheridan, *Ibsen, *Chekhov, *Wilde, *Shaw, *Kaiser, *Maugham, and *Coward. She often appeared at the *Old Vic in the 1920s and 1930s, and starred regularly in the West End theatres, often in modern plays by such dramatists as *Rice, Emlyn *Williams, *Bridie, and *Fry. During the Second World War she toured widely to entertain the military. She also appeared in films, including *The Importance of Being Earnest* (1952), *Tom Jones* (1963), and *The Chalk Garden* (1964). In *comedy she was peerless.   TP

Evans, Maurice (1901–89) English actor and director. After starting his career in 1926 as Orestes at the Cambridge Festival Theatre, Evans achieved his first London success in *Sherriff's *Journey's End* (1928). In the 1930s he appeared in Shakespeare, *Shaw, and Granville *Barker at *Baylis's *Sadler's Wells, where both his Hamlet and Richard II received praise. In 1935 he moved to the USA, and became an American citizen in 1941. He first *toured with Katharine *Cornell in *Romeo and Juliet*, then he appeared in Shakespeare productions directed by Margaret *Webster. During the war he entertained troops with his *GI Hamlet*. For the next three decades he performed in Shakespeare and Shaw, on tour and in New York, and had a Broadway success in

Dial M for Murder (1952). He appeared occasionally in film, including *Planet of the Apes* (1968) and *Escape from Planet of the Apes* (1969).   TP

Evreinov, Nikolai (1879–1953) Russian/Soviet theatre director, dramatist, theorist, and theatre historian. In the spirit of *Meyerhold, Evreinov was drawn to pre-Renaissance non-*realistic theatre and to popular forms such as *commedia dell'arte*. At the Theatre of Antiquity, which he founded in St Petersburg, he staged *mystery and medieval romance plays but his real impact was felt at the satirical 'theatre of small forms', the Krivoe Zerkalo (Crooked Mirror) Theatre, where between 1910 and 1917 he staged roughly 60 productions, including his own *Theatre of the Soul*, 'a monodrama in one act' (staged in London by Edith *Craig, 1915). Evreinov simultaneously published works of theory: his *An Introduction to Monodrama* appeared in 1909, followed by *The Theatre as Such* (1912), and *The Theatre for Oneself* (three volumes, 1915–17). Initially enthused by the events of the Russian Revolution, Evreinov staged a mass performance, *The Storming of the Winter Palace* (1920), as an example of 'theatre in life', a film of which survives. He emigrated to Paris in 1925, where he wrote an idiosyncratic history of Russian theatre (1946).   NW

executions, public From Roman crucifixion (*see* DAMNATIO) to contemporary Muslim fundamentalist beheadings, the agonies of death in public have assumed a para-theatrical significance. Although it might be seen as an emotional experience, the public execution is also a gruesome performance, incorporating all the elements of staging, *costume, text, *actors, and *audience. The death platform provides the stage: London's Tyburn Tree (now the site of Marble Arch) and Paris's Place de la Révolution (now the Place de la Concorde) were often compared to the theatre. Costume is particularly important for public executions. For beheading in England, the condemned were required to wear only enough to preserve their modesty: Mary Queen of Scots is reported to have said, with a smile, that she had 'never put off her clothes before such a company'. Before the passing of the Murder Act in 1752, the doomed could sell their bodies to a surgeon in advance so that they might buy presentable clothes for death.

The public demeanour of the condemned is a significant part of the performance as well, the reported cheerfulness of Queen Mary comparing alarmingly with the abject terror of some of America's death-row inmates. Charles I requested thicker underwear so that he would not shiver from cold and cause spectators to mistake this for fear. Timothy McVeigh's silence before his execution in 2001 for the Oklahoma bombings was regarded with surprise, given his unrepentant stance. Pamphlets recording death-row confessions, moralizings, or pleas of innocence survived well into the nineteenth century. Spectators have always been plentiful, witnesses to the state's ultimate power over its people. For the last public execution in Leeds in 1864, as many as 100,000 saw the hanging of James Sargisson and Joseph Myers, and some states in the USA in the early twenty-first century still permitted close relatives of the victims to observe the execution of their murderers, a ghastly indicator that vengeance remains a powerful rationale for capital punishment.

The death venue and the means of execution change according to cultural norms, from the overt theatricality of horror in the Roman Colosseum to the religious function of the medieval burning at the stake, from the personalized nature of hanging to the industrial efficiency of the guillotine, from the pseudo-scientific electric chair to the self-contradictory medical trappings of lethal injection. But the analogy to the theatre is hard to escape. *Dramaturgically speaking, a public execution is a battle between the *protagonist (the condemned) and the antagonist (the executioner); the plot moves implacably towards *tragedy, even though it may have comic elements; the *catastrophe and *denouement are predetermined. In turn the theatre has often drawn upon the scaffold for material. *Gay's *The Beggar's Opera* (1728), as well as its descendant, the *Brecht-*Weill *Threepenny Opera* (1928), both rely on last-minute reprieves for their *heroes, *parodies on the gallows of the *deus ex machina ending. Courtroom and police dramas, from *Aeschylus' *Eumenides* (458 BC) to numerous American television shows about lawyers and cops, often secure narrative intensity from the threat of capital retributive justice, while the photo-*realism of cinema has encouraged a subgenre of prison execution films. The theatre has tended to place execution offstage (Cawdor's reckoning in *Macbeth*, for instance), though there have been powerful representations of *characters' final moments: *Sellars staged the dual execution in Handel's oratorio *Theodora* as an American-style lethal injection (Glyndebourne, 1996). *See also* GLADIATORIAL CONTESTS; NAUMACHIA.   AF/DK

exposition The presentation of information necessary for the *audience's understanding of the dramatic situation and *action in a play. In traditional *dramaturgy, the exposition is identified with the introductory scenes preceding the rising action. In less rigid dramaturgy, the exposition might be scattered and extended throughout. Information is commonly presented through *dialogue, often among minor *characters, or between a *protagonist and *confidant; but it can also come through *soliloquy or narration, or through a *prologue-*chorus. In a wider sense, exposition is also a function of *scenography and *costume, and of publicity, reviews, and programmes.   RWV

expressionism A broad aesthetic term that has been applied to any portrayal of intense emotion, especially in the visual arts, but in the theatre refers more usefully to a movement originating in Germany in the early twentieth century. Reacting against the limited and untheatrical nature of *naturalism, the defining characteristics of expressionist theatre are, in addition to the depiction of powerful emotions: the rejection of individual psychology in order to penetrate to the essence of humanity; a concern with the contemporary social situation; episodic structures; generalized, often nameless *characters; strongly visual incidents in place of scenes dependent on linguistic exchange; a highly charged, often abrupt language (telegraphese); symbolic *scenography, *lighting, and *costumes; and powerfully theatrical performances. Major forerunners of expressionism were *Strindberg and *Wedekind, notably in *Spring's Awakening* (1906). The first truly expressionist play to be staged was *Hasenclever's *The Son* (1916), in which an oppressed and nameless son rebels against his father and goes off to an ill-defined freedom. *Reinhardt staged a similar piece in 1917: *Sorge's *The Beggar* (written in 1912). Here the *protagonist, a young poet, actually murders his technologically crazed father.

The best dramatist of the movement, and the only one to win *Brecht's respect, was *Kaiser, who succeeded in harnessing ecstatic emotion and despairing insights in a series of monumentally constructed dramas: *The Burghers of Calais* (1917) about an individual self-sacrifice for the sake of humanity; *From Morning to Midnight* (1917), which traces the progress of a nondescript bank clerk through the stations of one day; and the *Gas Trilogy* (1917–18). *Toller wrote a number of impassioned political pieces with a socialist bias: *Transfiguration* (1919), *Masses and Man* (1920), *The Machine Wreckers* (1922), and *Hinkemann* (1923). Some expressionist writers pushed the theatre to its limits, such as Hasenclever in *Humankind* (1920), where the *action takes on the quality of a dream, and whole scenes consist of one-word exclamations and questions. Apart from Kaiser, few plays survive in the repertoire, owing to the complexity of their staging, their political vagueness and naivety, and their imprecise and over-inflated language.

The true legacy of expressionism was to theatre practice. Using architectural sets, influenced by *Appia and *Craig, the new lighting technology, and vast ensembles, the theatre once again became a place of visual excitement and spectacle. While there were imitators elsewhere, most notably in America—*O'Neill's *The Emperor Jones* (1920) and *The Hairy Ape* (1922), *Rice's *The Adding Machine* (1923)—the biggest debtor to expressionism was the political theatre of the Weimar Republic that superseded it. From 1919, the Berlin director *Jessner employed expressionist methods in his political adaptations of classics like *Schiller's *William Tell* (1919) and Shakespeare's *Richard III* (1920). The episodic construction, generalized characters, and bold theatricality of expressionism laid the foundations for the theatre of Brecht.   MWP

Eyre, Richard (1943–) English director. Eyre's experience at the Royal Lyceum, Edinburgh, and the Nottingham Playhouse (1973–8) shaped much of his nine-year tenure as successor to *Hall in 1988 at the *National Theatre. Eyre's passion for new writing, shown through his association with *Hare, *Brenton, and *Griffiths at Nottingham, and as director for BBC television's *Play for Today* (1978–80), spilled into the National Theatre, most memorably through Hare's 'state of the nation' trilogy, a biting assessment of the Anglican Church, British law, and the Labour Party. Eyre's policies supported the production of *musicals (*Guys and Dolls*, 1982), encouraged internationalism (hosting *Lepage), and enabled special projects (an in-the-round season in the Olivier Theatre, 1997, with Theatre de *Complicité). He promoted new directors like *Daldry, *Donellan, *Hytner, and *Mendes, and writers like *Marber and *McDonagh. His own directing was often acclaimed, especially for Granville *Barker's *The Voysey Inheritance* (1989), *Richard III* (1991), and *King Lear* starring *Holm (1997, televised 1998). Eyre's other work includes the films *The Ploughman's Lunch* (1983), the highly acclaimed *Iris* (2002), *Stage Beauty* (2004), *Notes on a Scandal* (2006), and the controversial Falklands television drama *Tumbledown* (1988). After the NT Eyre combined the role of public figure with freelance directing of new plays. He wrote and presented a TV history of British theatre, *Changing Stages* (2000), and published his NT diaries as *National Service* (2003).   KN

Eysoldt, Gertrud (1870–1950) German actress. The original Lulu in *Wedekind's *Earth Spirit* (1903), Eysoldt was one of the most acclaimed actresses in *Reinhardt's troupe from 1902 to 1933, performing the part of Puck between 1905 and 1921 in his five productions of *A Midsummer Night's Dream*. Other important roles were the title parts in *Hofmannsthal's *Elektra* (1903) and *Wilde's *Salome* (1903). In her youth Eysoldt fascinated *audiences with her erotic presence; in her mature years she convinced with a clear, analytic approach to roles. The Eysoldt Ring, an annual award for actors, is named after her. CBB

Fabre, Jan (1958–) Flemish theatre and *performance artist, born in Antwerp. As a visual artist, author, choreographer, theatre and *opera director, Fabre represents the shift towards performance and the blurring of genres. His often enigmatic productions, which are reminiscent of Robert *Wilson, seem to be built on the tensions between reality and imagination, between order and chaos. His work is characterized by often extreme physicality and by repetitive elements. *This Is Theatre Like It Was Expected to Be and Foreseen* (1982) was an eight-hour production in which the actors performed with utmost precision activities such as dressing and undressing, or licking up yoghurt from the stage. Mere duration and repetition allowed reality (see REALISM AND REALITY) into the theatrical world. In *The Power of Theatrical Madness* (1984), which earned him international renown, the falsity of theatrical *illusion was the central theme. Fabre's most ambitious work is the opera trilogy *The Minds of Helena Troubleyn* (1990 and 1992). *Orgy of Tolerance* (2009), a mixture of dance and verbal theatre, was a critique of the world of excess.   JDV

fairground booths Early booths in Britain were simply temporary trading places, arranged in 'streets' and offering more substantial accommodation than straw or canvas stalls. As the entertainment aspect of fairs began to predominate in the seventeenth century, booths were adapted to house performances and exhibitions. A makeshift stage might be erected with a curtained area at the rear, or more elaborate structures could be built with an open parade and an indoor venue behind. Richardson's theatrical booth, reputedly one of the largest, was said to be 30 m (100 feet) long and 9 m (30 feet) wide, with an *audience capacity of about 1,500 people. According to *Dickens it offered 'a *melodrama (with three murders and a *ghost), a *pantomime, a comic song, an overture, and some incidental *music' (*Sketches by Boz*, 1835). At Bartholomew Fair in the eighteenth century, engagements in theatrical booths provided training for young performers and employment for regular actors when the London *playhouses were closed. Elsewhere fairground booths accommodated exhibitions of freaks of nature, *puppets, *operas, wrestling, and a temporary ballroom, complete with refreshment area and orchestra. The heyday of the fairground booth was the nineteenth century, and the decline of booth shows was rapid during the twentieth century as the increased mechanical sophistication of fairground rides provided the main attraction. Though the *freak show and novelty booth continued into the 1950s and 1960s, the demise of the booth was soon almost complete. *See also* BOOTH STAGE.   AF

Farag, Alfred (1929–2005) Egyptian playwright. Farag's experimentation with different forms and styles makes him difficult to categorize. His plays generally exhibit a blend of Western representational and folk-inspired performance strategies. He emulated his mentor *Hakim but wrote *dialogue in Fus'ha (literary Standard Arabic) that is more theatrically successful, as in *The Barber of Baghdad* (1964). His *Fire and Olives* (1970), written on a visit to Germany to study *Brecht and his successors, was the first Egyptian *documentary drama. Though written in prose, the poetic and tragic nature of his plays like *Sulayman of Aleppo* (1965) suggests Shakespearian influence.   HMA

farce A dramatic genre similar to *comedy, often with a happy ending, that is characterized by broad and at times cruel or crude physical antics, skits on pretention, or zany science fiction. The *protagonist of a farce is a born victim of bad luck and ill-treatment. As a *clown, he lacks protective skills. The *laughter that greets and sustains him springs from the wit of others and his own verbal ineptitude. Yet his *audience quickly shows affection towards him because he means them no harm. The most thoroughgoing farceur in history, *Aristophanes, mercilessly taunted his fellow Athenians for wasting their youthful limbs and capacities on the Peloponnesian War when they could have been feasting, drinking, dancing, and making love. After Aristophanes, farces can be shuffled into four groups.

1. *Knockabout*, in which servants and other menials are humiliated with a *slapstick. Knockabout

seems unrelentingly brutal, but is harmless. *Plautus' 21 surviving plays are filled with the comic *stock characters that have since peopled farce, smart slaves, foolish and gullible older men, lovesick youths, nagging wives, ever hungry parasites, and obliging courtesans. Plautus refurbished stories and roles which became staples for *commedia dell'arte* during the following millennium. Knockabout material was used in far continents, in Beijing opera's (*jingju*) acrobatic *wu* roles for men and the Japanese *kyōgen, which softens an otherwise stately *nō performance.

2. *Verbal farce*. Numerous playwrights drew upon the verbal traditions of farce for dialogue, from *Jonson and *Goldoni to *Goldsmith and *Sheridan. Through the nineteenth century verbal farce became the staple of playwrights such as *Labiche and *Gilbert. The twentieth century yielded British farceurs by the score, the more celebrated including *Barnes, *Churchill, *Frayn, *Pinter, *Orton, and *Travers. Paris acquired a special reputation for farce with *Feydeau.

3. *Tragi-farces*. The new century inaugurated a host of farcical novelties, from *Jarry's comic nightmares to the laugh-soaked *tragedies of *Pirandello. The theatre of the *absurd delighted in monstrous farce in the work of *Ionesco and *Beckett; mixing the serious with the hilarious, they squeezed mirth from cruelty. Many artists dipped freely into farce's new film language, especially Chaplin, Keaton, and Harold Lloyd. Film gave them new vehicles to conquer and be defeated by in nightmare scenarios.

4. *Farcical interruptions*. At the end of the sixteenth century Shakespeare compiled the most striking series of farcical roles: the two pairs of twins in *Comedy of Errors*, Bottom in *A Midsummer Night's Dream*, Dogberry in *Much Ado About Nothing*, Sir Andrew in *Twelfth Night*, and, most weightily, Falstaff in *1 Henry IV*. But long before Shakespeare, farce benefited from an air of corruption, sedition, and conspiracy, and long after him farce episodes took over the entire content of radio shows (*The Goon Show*), and television (*Monty Python's Flying Circus*). In the last example farce continually interrupted itself when a segment of dialogue, played by the actors, cut in on one of Terry Gilliam's weird illustrations, which itself ended when an oversized bare foot stamped the latest image out of existence.   ACB

Farnese, Teatro In 1618 Ranuccio I, Duke of Parma, commissioned a theatre on the first floor of the Palazzo della Pilotta, and named it after his Farnese dynasty. The architect, *Aleotti, was probably instructed to rival the indoor granducal theatres in Florence: this brief led to a firm division between stage and *auditorium by means of a *proscenium arch, diverging from the model of the Teatro *Olimpico. Behind the proscenium was a huge stage, 40 m deep and 12 m wide (131 by 39 feet), giving ample space for the elaborate concealed machinery which could produce the multiple surprise effects of baroque theatre. The horseshoe-shaped seating for the *audience also foreshadowed the structures of modern theatres; though since tournaments and even naval battles were to be mounted on the floor, there were also elements of an *amphitheatre in the design. The audience was seated on raked steps around the horseshoe, with a prominent central place for the Duke and his guests. Though there were no *boxes, the Teatro Farnese is seen as an important step towards the baroque theatre blueprint which became standard throughout Europe. Very few spectacles were staged there, however, the last one in 1732. Bombed in 1944, the Teatro Farnese can now be seen in a restored form. RAA

Farquhar, George (1678–1707) Irish playwright, the best comic dramatist of the eighteenth century in Britain. His plays achieved unprecedented runs, and two of them continue to be performed today, *The Recruiting Officer* (1706) and *The Beaux' Stratagem* (1707). He studied in Trinity College, Dublin, and started his career as an actor at *Smock Alley in 1696, where he met *Wilks. They became lifelong friends, and Wilks was the leading man in many of Farquhar's plays. Farquhar left for London, where he had the good fortune of staging his first play, the semi-autobiographical *Love and a Bottle* (1698). *The Constant Couple* (1699), which featured Wilks as Sir Harry Wildair, a good-natured, nonchalant, and exuberant *hero, was an incredible success, running 53 nights in its first season and remaining in the repertory throughout the century.

Success on the scale of *The Constant Couple* breeds envious detraction, and Farquhar was not immune. He responded to charges that the play was generically irregular (*see* NEOCLASSICISM) in *Discourse upon Comedy* (1702), asserting that the rules of *comedy are given by the *box, pit, and gallery. Although the sequel *Sir Harry Wildair* (1701) was unsuccessful, Farquhar scored another hit with *The Stage-Coach* (1701), a *farce. He adapted *Fletcher's *The Wild Goose Chase* as *The Inconstant* (1702) and tried to respond to Jeremy *Collier's criticisms of the morality of the stage in the surprisingly earnest *Twin Rivals* (1702; *see* ANTI-THEATRICAL POLEMIC). But his greatest successes came after a hiatus from the stage, during which he served in the army as a recruiting officer. *The Recruiting Officer* and *The*

Beaux' Stratagem exemplify the originality and good-natured humour characteristic of Farquhar's best work and mediate between the caustic *satire of the Restoration and the benevolent comedy of the eighteenth century.   MJK

Farr, Florence (1860–1917) English actress, gifted but untrained, associated with experimental ventures (1890–1912). *Shaw encouraged her to play Rebecca in *Ibsen's *Rosmersholm* (1891) and offered her *Arms and the Man* to salvage her ailing management of the Avenue Theatre (1894). *Yeats, considering her musicality in verse-speaking unrivalled, invited her to illustrate his lectures on the subject; she staged his *Countess Cathleen* for the inauguration of the Irish Literary Theatre (1899) and played Dectora in his *Shadowy Waters* (1905). Critical opinion was divided over her mannered Herodias in *Wilde's *Salome* (1906) and her Clytemnestra in Mrs Patrick *Campbell's Electra (1908).   RAC

Farrah, Abdelkader (1926–2006) Algerianborn designer, teacher, and self-taught painter. His first design was Saint-Saëns's *Samson and Delilah* (Amsterdam, 1953). He became head of design at the National Drama Centre in Strasbourg, working with Michel *Saint-Denis (1955–61), who brought him to the *Royal Shakespeare Company as associate designer, with responsibility for the experimental studio which Saint-Denis conducted (1962–4). With Tom Fleming, Farrah launched the Royal Lyceum Company, Edinburgh, and promoted the participation of thousands of children as designers (1965–9). He collaborated with *Kott on the *Mrožek double bill *Out at Sea and *Police* and designed the Edinburgh Royal Gala performance of *Brecht's *Galileo* (1966). Between 1962 and 1991 he designed over 50 RSC productions, including *Albee's *Tiny Alice* (1971) and *Genet's *The Balcony* (1972). His vision of England in the RSC's *Henry IV* and *Henry V* (1976–7) was created in a strong but simple emblematic style, without cumbersome scene changes. Colours and treated fabrics gave a painterly impression to the dramatic landscape.   PH

Fascism and theatre The term 'fascism' is used here to cover several ultra-nationalist and anti-liberal movements in the twentieth century that established dictatorial regimes, where their ideology of regeneration was translated into performance. This was achieved on a large scale in Italy and Germany, and to a minor degree in Spain and France.

Theatre under fascist regimes Mussolini's seizure of power in 1922 in Italy had little immediate impact on the theatre, which was almost entirely commercial in orientation and adhered to the *actor-manager system until the 1930s, providing the same type of entertainment as in previous decades. In 1930 Mussolini created a Corporation of Spectacles, promulgated a new *censorship law in 1931, and in 1935 instituted an Inspectorate of Theatre and Music in the Ministry for Press and Propaganda (later the Ministry for Popular Culture). Although Mussolini's functionaries reorganized the structures and economy of Italian theatre, authors, directors, and actors continued to produce shows with few signs of political engagement. State intervention was more successful outside traditional playhouses. In 1929 the *Carri di Tespi* (itinerant theatre companies) were instituted and reached an *audience that had rarely seen the inside of a theatre building. But their lack of enthusiasm for fascist drama meant that the repertoire was soon dominated again by *comedies and lightweight plays. Similarly, the open-air mass theatre (*teatro di ventimila*), which Mussolini opened in 1938 in the Terme di Caracalla in Rome and which was copied in 38 other cities, soon reverted to a traditionalist, mainly *operatic, repertoire.

The situation was markedly different in National Socialist Germany. Immediately after coming to power, Hitler ordered a reorganization of all cultural institutions and established the Reich Ministry for Enlightenment of the People and for Propaganda (13 March 1933). The Reich Theatre Act of May 1934 ushered in a draconian surveillance and censorship system, which ensured that every cultural activity was closely scrutinized and every artist vetted. The result was a mass exodus of some 4,000 theatre artists and 420 dramatists into exile. Although the new authorities had achieved complete control over the personnel and repertoire of 291 theatres, they were less successful in finding ways and means of creating the desired 'drama of the Third Reich'. In the second half of the 1930s new authors came to the fore who delivered plays that complied with Nazi political objectives, but they were extremely unpopular with audiences. The same can be said about the *Thingspiel* movement, another Nazi attempt at invoking (or inventing) ancient Teutonic culture. Consequently the repertoire of German theatre throughout the Nazi period was dominated by classical plays and innocuous *farces and comedies.

Fascist theatre aesthetics In the course of the 1920s and 1930s a number of critics, dramatists, and artists sought to develop a fascist aesthetic and practice of theatre. While they generally failed in traditional *playhouses, the large-scale spectacles of a cultic nature that gave symbolic representation to fascism as a secularized religion attracted mass audiences and proved to be a captivating force unequalled by propaganda in print. They shared with other *rituals the creation of communities out of isolated individuals, turning everyday anxieties into inner peace, providing desolate souls with self-confidence and a place of belonging. Whilst fascist mythology furnished the plot and politics furnished the dogma, the ritual celebrations became the liturgy and produced consensus and universal adherence to the New Order.

The great pageants and mass rallies were dramatically structured, narrating events with an overpowering emotive force that elicited profound responses and acted as an effective tool for binding the masses to the fascist leader. The most important were the Nuremberg Rallies. The ban on Hitler's public appearances in Bavaria had been lifted in 1927, and the National Socialist Party held the first rally there in 1929, which became an annual event. The Nuremberg festival alternated mass rallies and hours of commemoration, appeals and parades, military show-manoeuvres and public entertainment, and lasted at first four, then seven, and finally eight days. The heroic style and *dramaturgy of the rallies were fixed on celluloid by Leni Riefenstahl in her film *Triumph of the Will* (1934), which more or less provided a model for subsequent outdoor rallies until 1939.   GB

Fassbinder, Rainer Werner (1945–82) German director and dramatist. Best known for his internationally successful films, Fassbinder first came to attention as the co-founder of the small Munich theatre group antiteater, which he ran as a *collective together with others (1967–71). During this period he wrote and directed a number of controversial plays, such as *Cock Artist* (1968), *The Bitter Tears of Petra von Kant* (1971), *Pre-Paradise, Sorry Now* (1969), and *Bremen Coffee* (1971), which dealt with racism, lesbianism, and mass murder. Classical authors such as *Gay, *Goethe, and *Goldoni were presented in radically truncated textual collages. In the season 1974–5 he was appointed director of the Theater am Turm in Frankfurt but resigned when his play *The Refuse, the City, and Death* was banned over charges of anti-Semitism.   CBB

Faucit, Helen (1817–98) English actress. Thoroughly tutored by the older William Farren, she rose to prominence playing opposite *Macready during his *Covent Garden (1837–9) and *Drury Lane (1841–3) *managements, and at the *Haymarket in 1840. Faucit was a beautiful, poised, and elegant actress, admirable as Portia, Cordelia, Desdemona, Imogen, and Rosalind. She was not up to the great tragic parts like Lady Macbeth, which she played, but excelled in portraits of romantic love and tenderness; Pauline in *Bulwer-Lytton's *The Lady of Lyons* was one of her best. Her career was relatively short, since she married the well-connected writer Theodore Martin in 1851 and became Lady Martin when he was knighted. She returned to the stage infrequently, and published *On Some of Shakespeare's Female Characters* in 1892.   MRB

Favart, Charles-Simon (1710–92) French dramatist and *manager. The stage-struck son of a Paris pastrycook, Favart wrote comic *operas and *vaudevilles for the fairground theatres and the *Opéra-Comique. He became *stage manager of this theatre and married a young actress who was to act in many of his plays. On the closure of the Opéra-Comique, Favart became director of the company of Maurice, Maréchal de Saxe, who took Mme Favart as his mistress; when husband and wife absconded, they were imprisoned by *lettre de cachet*, being released only on the Maréchal's death in 1750. Thereafter, until her death in 1772, the couple enjoyed a highly successful theatrical partnership, Favart himself becoming director of the amalgamated Opéra-Comique and Théâtre-Italien in 1762. Much of his output was ephemeral, but the best plays are his first, *The Adventuress* (1741), *The Loves of Bastien and Bastienne* (1753), and *The English at Bordeaux* (1763). This latter, commissioned to mark the end of the Seven Years War, was the only play of Favart's to be performed at the *Comédie-Française. Favart's published correspondence provides valuable information for theatre history.   WDH

Fechter, Charles Albert (1824–79) French actor and *manager. Fechter acted in English, with a strong accent, as well as in French. He first appeared with the *Comédie-Française in 1840 and rapidly became a leading actor in Paris. In 1860 in London, he played the brave, handsome, and impetuous *hero in an English version of *Hugo's *Ruy Blas*. This was followed in 1861 by an unconventional new Hamlet, in which the Prince was the perfect Parisian gentleman who thought deeply and was capable of romantic tenderness. In 1862 Fechter undertook Othello, and then Iago, receiving more praise for the latter than the former, which was considered too close to French *melodrama. This kind of drama was indeed Fechter's strong point in his management of the Lyceum from 1863 to 1867, where he was the nonpareil of the dashing Gallic hero. He was a great success in *Bulwer-Lytton's *The Lady of Lyons* and as the *villain in *No Thoroughfare*, by *Dickens and Wilkie Collins. From 1870 to 1879 he was mostly in America, *touring and managing in Boston. He retired in 1876 and died in America.   MRB

Fedeli Of the second-generation Italian *commedia dell'arte* companies, the Fedeli were the most stable and long standing, simply because they can be identified with the career of their founder and director Giovan Battista *Andreini. The troupe was established in 1601 and taken into the patronage of the dukes of Mantua in 1604. The war which devastated Mantua in 1630 deprived Andreini and many other theatre professionals of their principal support; the title was resurrected as late as 1652, two years before Andreini's death. In their director's prime, and despite tensions and quarrels with leading figures such as Tristano *Martinelli, the company won notable successes all over northern Italy, were summoned to Paris no fewer than five times, and visited Vienna and Prague in 1628.   RAA

Federal Theatre Project Large-scale government-funded producing organization in the United States, 1935–9. The FTP represented a comparatively small part of the Works Progress Administration (WPA), a massive system of public works instituted by the Roosevelt administration as a means of restarting the Depression economy though short-term employment and government purchase of materials. While other WPA workers built bridges, schools, post offices, planted forests, or cleaned streets, the FTP employed theatre personnel to stage shows for free or at low cost to *audiences across the nation. The FTP employed more than 10,000 persons and operated in 40 states, offering more than 60,000 performances to nearly 30 million spectators. *Touring outside one's own region was discouraged, the purpose being to create and provide theatre by local people for local audiences. Units were organized by type of shows and included serious drama, classics, foreign language drama, *circus, 'Negro' theatre, *puppet shows, theatre for *youth, *musicals, and *opera. A separate Federal Dance Project was folded into the FTP in 1937. The first large-scale experiment in government-subsidized theatre in the United States, the FTP was from its beginnings a target of political criticism, and was shut down by Congress in 1939, disappointing many who had seen the Project as the best hope for a national theatre.

The FTP was directed by Hallie *Flanagan, who helped to launch many artists' careers, including *Houseman, *Welles, Joseph Cotton, John Huston, and Arthur *Miller. Though the vast majority of FTP productions had no discernible political bias, the left-wing perspective noticeable in some with highest visibility offended conservative Congressmen—especially *Living Newspapers such as *One-Third of a Nation* (1938).   MAF

Fedotova, Glikeria (1846–1925) Russian actress. Associated throughout her life with the Maly Theatre, Moscow, and the great *acting legacy of *Shchepkin, Fedotova first appeared there in 1858, playing leading roles from the outset. The Maly Theatre being known as the 'House of *Ostrovsky', it was not surprising that Fedotova was associated primarily with his plays, a total of 29 in all, including Katerina in *The Thunderstorm* and the Snow Maiden in the play of the same name. Fedotova also acquired a considerable reputation in Shakespearian roles, performing nineteen in all, including Beatrice (1865), Katherine (1871), Portia (1877), Lady Macbeth (1890), Mistress Ford (1890), the Queen in *Cymbeline* (1891), and Volumnia in *Coriolanus* (1902). In 1886 she acted opposite another great Maly actress, Maria *Ermolova, as Queen Elizabeth to the latter's Mary, Queen of Scots in *Schiller's *Mary Stuart*.   NW

féerie A spectacular story of the supernatural, associated almost exclusively with popular French theatre of the nineteenth century. Originating earlier in the fairground theatres, *féeries* shared the same black-and-white approach to morality as *melodrama, though the *action of the *féerie* invariably involved *magical effects, which were executed by increasingly versatile stage machinery, and extended beyond the purely human. *Féeries* could be seen in most of the major Parisian theatres, though the genre defied definition and was often aligned with the *pantomime and *operetta. Early *féeries* included Cuvelier de Trie's *Tom Thumb* (1801) and *Puss-in-Boots* (1802), and a spectacular *comedy with magic effects by Alphonse Martainville, *The Sheep's Foot* (1806). But the most celebrated was probably Anicet Bourgeois and Laurent's *The Pills of the Devil* (1839), in which the unfortunate *hero was subjected to every trick the scenic mechanist could devise. Toward the end of the century the *féerie* came to be regarded as suitable mainly for children and disappeared into other modes of spectacular performance.   SJCW

Fehling, Jürgen (1885–1968) German director. Fehling's breakthrough came in 1921 with acclaimed productions of *The Comedy of Errors*

and *Toller's *Masses and Man*. He joined *Jessner at the Berlin State Theatre, which remained his base. Strongly influenced by *expressionism, Fehling's productions were also marked by sensitivity to psychological nuances. In a sense he blended *Brahm's *naturalism and expressionism to find a new synthesis which enabled him to direct the whole gamut of dramatic literature as well as *opera. He directed over 100 productions at the State Theatre. Noteworthy were the premières of Barlach's work in the 1920s and his Shakespeare productions, particularly *The Merchant of Venice* in 1927 with *Kortner as Shylock and *Richard III* in 1936 with *Krauss. Fehling's career ended in 1944. He was unable to re-establish himself in the post-war period.   CBB

Felipe, Carlos (1914–75) Cuban playwright who—together with *Piñera and Rolando Ferrer—modernized national drama. Self-taught, an insatiable reader, his works adapted the methods of the *avant-garde: dreamlike atmospheres, ambiguities of identity, interplay of the *real and the imaginary, and a frequent resort to *metatheatre. His *characters, self-centred and solitary, pursue unachievable dreams in an environment marked by a lack of authenticity. When the revolution occurred in 1959 he had staged *The Chinaman* (1947), *Whim in Red* (1950), and *Mischievous Jimmy* (1951) on a small scale. He later attained critical and popular success with his *comedy *Like in a Film* (1963). His most important play, *Réquiem por Yarini* (1965), is a well-structured *tragedy in a popular setting, inspired by a mythical pimp with political connections who reigned in Havana's brothels in the 1920s. Other works include *The Lace Robe* (1962), *Los compadres* (1968), and *Ibrahim* (1968).   MMu

female impersonation With origins in folklore, mythology, and shamanism, female impersonation was often associated with religious *ritual and carnival, and has been a significant feature of theatre, East and West. Men played female roles in *Greek *comedy and *tragedy, and dramatic use of the device is prominent in *Euripides' *Bacchae* and *Aristophanes' *Thesmophoriazusae*. In England *boy actors played female roles until the closing of the theatres in 1642, and continued after their reopening in 1660, despite the introduction of actresses. Female impersonation as a plot device occurs in *Jonson's *Epicene*, and both Falstaff in *The Merry Wives of Windsor* and Sir John Brute in *The Provok'd Wife* (1697) resort to female disguise. Classical Asian theatre has relied widely on the device. In Japanese *nō male actors play female roles,

their femininity specifically defined by a *mask. *Kabuki was created by women, but after a ban on female performers in 1628, young men played female roles, to be replaced in 1652 by mature actors. A crucial aspect of the form was the *onnagata: male actors devoted their lives to playing female roles and were expected to live as women in everyday life also. Strict rules for dress, make-up, gesture, and deportment suggest the performance of the *onnagata* communicates a highly constructed notion of femininity (*see* GENDER AND PERFORMANCE). In both Beijing opera (*jingju) in China and *kathakali *dance-drama in India, highly stylised female impersonation is the norm.

Female impersonation in eighteenth- and nineteenth-century Europe often tended towards the grotesque, particularly in England, still to be seen in the *pantomime dame, and was found also in *music-hall, *minstrel, and *pierrot shows, *variety, and even the *circus. It was also common in armed services entertainment during the World Wars. Some all-male troupes continued to perform in peacetime *revues and variety shows, one such being the subject of *Nichols's *Privates on Parade* (1977). Female impersonation also had its detractors. Mae *West's *Pleasure Man*, which included impersonators among its *characters, was banned in 1928, while the phenomenon virtually disappeared from the homophobic Britain and Ireland of the 1950s.

From the late 1960s and 1970s female impersonation re-emerged in many guises. In the United Kingdom Danny *La Rue's combination of comedy and glamour proved effective in several shows, commencing with *Come Spy with Me* (1966), and re-established drag as potential family entertainment. In the 1970s *The Rocky Horror Show* broadened the parameters of female impersonation, as did Charles *Ludlam as Camille and in other roles at the Ridiculous Theatrical Company in New York, and Lindsay *Kemp in *Wilde's *Salome* (1977) and *Onnagata* (1992) in London. All-male revues featuring female impersonators attracted audiences from the 1950s in some countries. 'Radical drag' emerged in the 1970s through *gay groups such as Hot Peaches and the Fabulous Cockettes, while social and political *satire informed the performances of Barry *Humphries as the Australian Dame Edna Everage. The boundaries of female impersonation have been further extended by the cult *musical *Hedvig and the Angry Inch* (1998) and by the transsexual performer Kate Bornstein. *See also* MALE IMPERSONATION.   JTD

feminist theatre, UK Though significantly preceded by the *Ibsen and the suffragist movements at the turn of the twentieth century, feminist theatre in the UK developed more fully in the 1970s Women's Liberation Movement, using performance as a means of protest. Demonstrations against female discrimination and sexism in the late 1960s and early 1970s used performance as a means of protest. Feminist theatre had two main objectives: to raise consciousness of the social and political issues which concerned women and to improve the conditions of women working in the theatre. Taking the slogan 'The personal is political' as central, it aimed to educate *audiences about discrimination, working conditions, and equal rights, as well as explore relationships between private and public spheres of experience. Furthermore, women wanted to hold more authoritative positions in the institutions of theatre, and encourage positive and diverse representations of women on stage.

Early women's theatre adopted *agitprop styles of performance. In 1973 Ed Berman organized a season of women's work at the Almost Free Theatre, after which a series of feminist companies were set up, notably the Women's Theatre Group, an all-female company whose first play was *My Mother Says* (1974), and Monstrous Regiment, a socialist-feminist company whose first play was *Scum: death destruction and dirty washing* (1976) by Claire Luckham and Chris Bond. In 1975 Gay Sweatshop was founded as a company of *lesbians and *gay men. *Any Woman Can* (1976) by Jill Posner and *Care and Control* (1977) by Michelene Wandor focused directly upon *lesbianism. At the same time women playwrights began to work in subsidized theatre, notably Caryl *Churchill and Pam *Gems.

British feminist playwrights of the 1980s focused upon materialist feminism and the examination of historical contexts. Churchill's *Cloud Nine* (1979) and *Top Girls* (1982) analyse relationships between class and *gender by juxtaposing past and present, while Timberlake *Wertenbaker's *The Grace of Mary Traverse* (1985) examines women's oppression through the lens of the eighteenth century. This emphasis has supported feminist revision of history and the reclamation of a hidden past, including rediscoveries of earlier women writers, for example Aphra *Behn and Githa *Sowerby. Furthermore, women actors and directors have reworked classics in order to expose the sexism of the dramatic canon.

The influence of feminist theory in the 1980s has directed women's theatre towards the development of new representational aesthetics which cross the boundaries of *dance, theatre, and *performance art. Influenced by the work of women performance artists such as Bobby Baker and

Rose English, experimental theatre has attempted to release the representation of women from theatrical conventions. *See also* FEMINIST THEATRE, USA.   LT

feminist theatre, USA Performance as an articulation of feminist politics has been an important constituent of theatre in America, never more so than in the last 30 years of the twentieth century. In early manifestations, women used theatrical performance as well as theatricalized street protest, during the suffrage movement, for example, though it was not until the late 1960s and early 1970s that feminist theatre—that is performance for, by, and about women as a political and cultural category—emerged. The *Open Theatre, San Francisco Mime Troupe, and *Bread and Puppet Theatre are examples of companies that provided women artists with crucial exposure but also frustrated their attempts to create from and perform a feminist politic. Feminists came together across the country in a grass roots movement in order to convey women's experience both individually and collectively, to create performance from lived experience. Their stories were absent from the stage, feminists believed, and the only way they would appear was for feminists to create them. Topics of plays focused tightly on women's experiences overlooked by the larger culture— women's friendship and sexuality (*Voz de la mujer*, Valentina Productions, 1980; *Split Britches* by *Split Britches, 1981), mothers and daughters (*The Daughters Cycle Trilogy*, Women's Experimental Theatre, 1976–80), violence against women (*Rape-In*, Westbeth Feminist Playwrights Collective, 1971), race (*Chicana*, Las Cucarachas, 1974), history and myth (*Persephone's Return*, Rhode Island Feminist Theater, 1974; *Daughters of Erin*, Lilith, 1982), and spirituality (*Antigone Prism*, Women's Ensemble Theater, 1975–6). Groups usually preferred to perform for all-women *audiences. Most spectators experienced feminist theatre as affirming and supportive, although there were often lively, sometimes rancorous, debates about definitions of feminism and issues raised by the plays.

Production was also reinvented. A high value was placed on collectivity and collaboration, with power shared equally in decision making on questions ranging from creative material to managerial issues.

Connections among women and companies were crucial. Several groups collaborated on projects as well as on festivals. One of the most productive was the Women's One World Festival in New York in 1980. This led to the founding of the WOW Café in 1982, a performance space that launched and supported the careers of many feminist performers and groups, including Carmelita Tropicana, Holly *Hughes, and the Five Lesbian Brothers.

Race and sexuality were both divisive and uniting. As feminism was dominated by white heterosexual women, so too was feminist theatre. That is not to say that lesbians and women of colour were not influential and central participants, but that the problems of racism and homophobia were present in theatre companies. Women struggled to make coalitions across these divides, however, and plays often reflected these experiences. Playwrights Ntozake *Shange (*for colored girls . . .* , 1975) and Cherrie Moraga (*Giving up the Ghost*, 1986) were heavily influenced by the feminist theatre around them and brought many of those ideas into their influential work on race.

While most feminist theatre groups had disbanded by the late 1980s due to decreased funding, member burnout, and changes in the feminist movement, many members went on to create theatre in other ways. There was a proliferation of solo performers in the 1980s and 1990s (Marga Gomez, Robbie McCauley, Peggy Shaw, for example) and, in the twenty-first century, an explosion of plays performed in a variety of venues that have emerged from this work. *See also* GENDER AND PERFORMANCE; LESBIAN THEATRE.   CMC

Ferrari, Paolo (1822–89) Italian playwright. Ferrari resided in Milan for 30 years as a professor, leaving frequently to stage his plays. Skilled in delineating *character and expert in structuring plot, he often rewrote his plays in verse or adapted them from various dialects (Massese, Modenese, Venetian) into standard Italian for production by major troupes (*Bellotti-Bon, *Ristori). While his reputation rests on *Goldoni and his Sixteen New Comedies* (1852), he wrote additional *comedies based on the lives of Italians (Dante, *Alfieri) and patriotic historical dramas such as *La Satira e Parini* (1856) and *Fulvio Testi* (1888). Of particular note are his thesis plays, forerunners of *realism, that address current social problems: *Il duello* (1868), *Causa ed effetti* (1871), and *Il suicidio* (1875). He also wrote sparkling adaptations of works by *Goldoni and contemporary French dramatists (*Augier), *farces for young students, and lively dramas for the child actress Gemma Cuniberti.   JEH

Ferrer, José (1912–92) Puerto Rican-born American actor, producer, and director. He made his stage debut in 1934 performing nautical *melodramas on showboats cruising Long Island Sound. In New York Ferrer played in important works including *Spring Dance* (1936), *Brother Rat* (1936), *Missouri Legend* (1938), *Mamba's Daughters* (1939), *Key Largo* (1939), *Charley's Aunt* (1940), and the title role in *Cyrano de Bergerac* (1946). With his acclaimed performance of Iago to Paul *Robeson's Othello in 1943, Ferrer entered a new phase of his career as an actor and producer of classical drama. In 1948 he was appointed director of the New York Theatre Company at the City Center, where he appeared in *Volpone*, *The Alchemist*, and *Richard III*, in addition to plays by *Chekhov, *Čapek, and *O'Neill. In 1963 he created the role of the Prince Regent in the *musical *The Girl Who Came to Supper*. His extensive film career included *Moulin Rouge* (1953), *The Caine Mutiny* (1954), *Ship of Fools* (1965), and an Academy award for *Cyrano de Bergerac* (1950).   JAB

Feydeau, Georges-Léon-Jules-Marie (1862–1921) French dramatist, famed as a writer of well-crafted, swift-moving, *farce. Taking over where *Labiche had left off, Feydeau soon developed a distinctive formula, which he was very ready to acknowledge: 'When I sit down to write a play', he said, 'I identify those *characters who have every reason to avoid each other; and I make it my business to bring them together as soon, and as often, as I can.' He insisted that his characters be recognizable as inhabiting the same world as his spectators, with the same hypocrisies, marital infidelities, and sham respectability; through the latter part of his career, he was moving towards a more serious exposé of bourgeois marriage.

His plots should be seen as a nightmare sequence of events into otherwise unremarkable lives. A typical plot establishes in Act I the need for secrecy on which the subterfuge and duplicity of the leading characters will depend; in Act II we move to a public meeting place—most notoriously a hotel of not very savoury reputation, as in *A Little Hotel on the Side* (1894), or *A Flea in her Ear* (1907); while Act III restores things to a somewhat precarious status quo. The nightmare quality of Feydeau's middle acts is given visual expression not only by the frenzied comings and goings, but also by mechanical stage accessories such as the revolving bed in *A Flea*, which delivers characters on stage and whisks them off again, apparently with a will of its own. His plays were a mainstay of the *boulevard houses. Apart from curtain raisers, production at the *Comédie-Française had to wait until after the Second World War, when *Le Dindon* (1896) confirmed Feydeau's status as a classic. In Britain, *Coward first took up Feydeau, when *Occupetoi d'Amélie* (1908) was presented as *Look after

Lulu in 1959; while other successful adaptations into English are those of *Mortimer for the *National Theatre (*A Flea in her Ear*, 1966; *The Lady from Maxim's*, 1977; *A Little Hotel on the Side*, 1984).   WDH

Fialka, Ladislav (1931–91) Czech *mime, choreographer, and director. At the Theatre on the Balustrade, one of the few professional *repertory mime companies in the world, Fialka choreographed thirteen productions, ranging from a loose series of sketches (*Mime on the Balustrade*, 1959; *Études*, 1960) to attempts at coherent drama (*Button*, 1968; *Caprichos*, 1971) based upon his own texts. Most of his productions were kept in repertory for years and *toured abroad extensively. Impressed since his youth by French mime from *Deburau to *Marceau, Fialka created his modern version of *Pierrot, close to Marceau's Bip, showing a great variety of expression, from a tender melancholic to a tormented soul. At the same time he gave prominence to ensemble performance and technical ability   ML

Fichandler, Zelda (1924–) American director and *manager, one of the visionaries of America's *regional theatre movement. In 1950, in an abandoned cinema in Washington, DC, she founded *Arena Stage, the first racially integrated theatre in that city. She was *artistic director from 1952 to 1990, when she stepped down to be the director of New York University's graduate acting programme. Her interests in psychoanalysis, political activism, and Russian literature were evident in her directing, and in her philosophy that 'not-for-profit theatres do exist to generate a profit of a social nature, and a profit that is earned from the examination of reality by means of theatrical art'. Under her leadership, Arena won the first regional Tony Award in 1976, became the first American theatre to tour the USSR (1973), and, with her production of Howard Sackler's *The Great White Hope* (1968), starring Jane Alexander and James Earl *Jones, the first regional theatre to transfer a show to Broadway.   GAO

Field, Nathan (1587–1620) English actor and dramatist. As a boy Field was a member of the Children of the *Chapel and the Queen's Revels, and later appeared on stage in several *Jonson plays performed by the *Chamberlain's Men: *Cynthia's Revels* (1600), *The Poetaster* (1601), and *Epicene* (1609). Many of Field's roles are unknown although scholars suggest that he performed female *characters early in life. He was much celebrated in the title role in *Chapman's *Bussy D'Ambois* (published 1607) He may also

have played Littlewit in Jonson's *Bartholomew Fair* (1614). By 1613 he had joined Lady Elizabeth's Men, but by 1616 transferred to the King's Men. Field wrote two plays under his own name and collaborated on others with *Massinger and *Fletcher. Jonson compared him to Richard *Burbage, the most prominent actor in Shakespeare's company.   SPC

Fielding, Henry (1707–54) English writer and magistrate. Fielding is now known for his novels, but first he was the most successful dramatist of his generation. Beginning in 1728, he wrote 26 plays, all but five of them premièring before 1737. His early efforts were unremarkable *comedies, but he scored his first hit with *The Author's Farce* (1730), a high-spirited *farce that ridiculed the *patent houses and their rapacious managers. *Tom Thumb* followed (1730), a *burlesque of contemporary *tragedy, later revised as *The Tragedy of Tragedies*. He had some success with five-act comedies of serious purpose, notably *The Modern Husband* (*Drury Lane, 1732), but in general his patent house hits were the farces he wrote for Kitty *Clive, like *The Intriguing Chambermaid* (1734), or his adaptations of *Molière.

After the failure of *The Universal Gallant* (1735), Fielding turned again to the *Haymarket Theatre, which became critical of both the Walpole ministry and the patent theatres, scoring Fielding's most impressive triumphs, including *Pasquin* (1736) and *The Historical Register of the Year 1736* (1737). Partly in response to Fielding's *satire, the Walpole government engineered the 1737 theatre *Licensing Act, giving complete *censorship authority to the Lord Chamberlain, and putting Fielding out of business because he did not have a royal patent. He wrote a few more plays and briefly operated a *puppet show in the 1740s, but left the theatre entirely to write his great novels: *Joseph Andrews* (1742), *Tom Jones* (1749), and *Amelia* (1751). He also read for the law and had a simultaneous and effective career as an anti-corruption magistrate, attacking some of the same abuses that had provoked his dramatic satires.   MJK

Fields, Gracie (Grace Stansfield) (1898–1979) English *variety artist, singer, and actress. As a child she sang in local *music halls, juvenile troupes, and Pierrot shows in Blackpool. She met her first husband, comedian Archie Pitt, while *touring the *revue *Yes, I Think So* in 1915. In 1918 Pitt produced his own revue, *Mr Tower of London*, which, after touring the provinces with Gracie in the lead, achieved huge success in London. Stardom followed both in revues and variety

shows, as well as films such as *Sally in our Alley*
(1931). During the Second World War Gracie entertained British troops with songs like 'Wish Me
Luck as You Wave Me Goodbye', and raised considerable funds for the war effort. Her extraordinary ability to move from comedy to pathos,
*slapstick to sentiment, was demonstrated in
songs such as 'Walter', 'The Biggest Aspidistra in
the World', and 'Sally'.　　　　AF

Fields, Lew *See* WEBER, JOSEPH.

Fields, W. C. (William Claude Dunkenfield)
(1880–1946) American comic actor whose gravel
voice, vitriolic wit, and deadpan mutterings expressed disdain for authority, children, animals,
and teetotallers. Born in Philadelphia, Fields ran
away from home as a child and learned to *juggle,
his old-fashioned, frayed *costume saving him
money. He became a famous tramp juggler in
*vaudeville in America and Europe, receiving top
billing at the *Folies-Bergère in Paris and the
Hippodrome in London, and starred in several
editions of the *Ziegfeld Follies between 1915
and 1925. Fields patented his best skits, such as
the failed golf lesson and the fiasco of packing
a car for a vacation. As Eustace McGargle in
Poppy (1923), his first speaking role on stage, he
developed the *character of the disreputable
huckster he would repeat on film. He appeared in
The Earl Carroll Vanities of 1928 and as Q. Q.
Quayle in *Ballyhoo* (1930). He acted in several
cinema gems, most of which he wrote himself. FL

Fierstein, Harvey (1954–) American actor
and playwright. Fierstein performed in nightclubs
as a *female impersonator and played a corpulent
lesbian in Andy Warhol's *Pork* (1971). The semi-
autobiographical *Torch Song Trilogy* (1981) links
three one-act plays, originally performed at *La
Mama before moving to Broadway. Fierstein
played the leading role, Arnold, a comic drag
queen whose lover deserts him for a woman
(*The International Stud*, 1976); who joins this
couple in bed with Alan, his new lover (*Fugue in
a Nursery*, 1979); and who mourns Alan's murder
and raises their adopted son (*Widows and Children First*, 1979). In *La Cage aux Folles* (1983) a
mature homosexual couple try to gain a son's
approval; the commercially successful *musical
entertained without arousing controversy. *Safe
Sex* (1987) gave Fierstein's reactions to the AIDS
crisis. He has acted in over 70 stage productions
and frequently in film. His other plays include
Freaky Pussy (1976), *Spookhouse* (1983), and
Forget Him (1988).　　　　FL

Filippo, Eduardo de *See* DE FILIPPO,
EDUARDO.

finance Theatre has always been more than a
performance by people for people: someone has
to pay for the activity, with cash or its equivalent
in gifts of time and labour. When itinerant actors
perform in a public place, a hat will be passed
around during or after the show for the *audience to show its appreciation and contribute to
costs. For more elaborate productions financial
arrangements are far more complex, less direct,
and usually completed long before an actor steps
in front of an audience. Only the most popular
theatres have been financed entirely by their
audiences, notable among them *kabuki of
Japan in its original forms, *commedia dell'arte,
and *early modern Spanish and English theatres,
including the company and theatre in which
Shakespeare was a sharer, the *Chamberlain's
Men. Only theatres producing *melodramas and
popular *comedies have continued this direct dependence on the public at large through the nineteenth and into the twentieth centuries. Often
they have had to go on prolonged *tours to find
their audiences: for example, the *jatra theatres
that still thrive in India. Comedies written by
*Noda Hideki, who is also both actor and director,
were exceptional when they filled Tokyo theatres
for months on end in the 1980s and 1990s; this
was a sophisticated and technically ambitious
theatre able to sustain itself solely by public support and its own efforts. Towards the end of the
twentieth century, a number of mega-*musicals
originating in New York or London could also
show profit. Their producers ran the risk of huge
losses but, once acclaimed as popular successes,
the spectacular shows could be reproduced in the
biggest theatres around the world and make
millions for their *producers, directors, composers, designers, authors, and, to a lesser extent, a
few of their performing artists.

Down the centuries, the largest and most reliable sources of income for theatre have been
patrons, sponsors, state and municipal governments, and, occasionally, religious, ideological,
or communal organizations that have made it
their business to pay for the public to see theatre.
Plays written for the *Dionysia festivals at Athens
during the fifth century BC were part of official
civic and religious celebrations and a manifestation of the wealth and culture of the city-state.
Individual productions were paid for by leading
citizens and prizes given to those judged the best
in any one year. Throughout early modern Europe, princely courts supplied both finance and
the theatres in which to perform; in France,

Louis XIV (1643–1715) spent huge sums on productions that would boost his public image and gratify his taste for splendour, music, *dancing, and fine writing. In Italy especially, learned academies and other public bodies followed this lead while to this day, throughout Europe, government and municipalities have helped to finance theatre companies. On occasion, they subsidize tours to other countries and visits of productions from abroad. This support lends authority and a degree of permanence to a precarious profession.

Some governments resist this responsibility. Almost all theatre performances in Japan are self-financing, from ticket sales and sponsorship. In the United States, theatre has no supportive arts council, as in Britain and numerous Commonwealth countries, and no Ministry of Culture, as in Eastern Europe. The National Endowment for the Arts does give grants to individual artists and short-term projects, but takes no permanent responsibility for companies or buildings. Yet tax relief is given for donations made to theatres as charitable, 'not-for-profit' organizations and this, in effect, means that the state donates a very large subsidy that indiscriminately finances only those companies that please rich corporations and those citizens who have money to give away. By the end of the twentieth century, except for the few shows that appeal to large audiences and can be often repeated, theatre had become dependent on financial support from various external sources. Frequently ticket sales account for less than half of a company's yearly income, perhaps only 40 or 30 per cent; in Germany, where municipalities are traditionally generous, it may be as little as 20 per cent. In Turkey, the state has accepted responsibility for 'making art available to all citizens'; tickets are priced very low so that, although theatres are usually full, box office receipts are not a significant source of income.

In other than the very smallest scale, the cost of creating and running theatre productions has escalated because of increased labour costs and the large number of special skills involved, both big factors in the pricing of one-off, hand-crafted products in a mass-oriented consumer society. New and lavish buildings, provided by public funds, and the maintenance or modernization of old theatres have added to financial difficulties. So has recent technical elaboration in staging, often undertaken in an effort to rival the attractions of the spectacular and easily disseminated products of the film industry. Further costs have been incurred in pursuit of sponsorship: by the turn of the century, the fundraiser for a theatre company had often become the second highest-paid person, after the *artistic director.

One way of making theatre more financially viable has been to adopt ancient *Greek precedent and organize festivals in which productions share publicity costs, a holiday and communal spirit is encouraged, and audiences may more easily be lured from one show to another. In Australia, for example, over 1,300 festivals had been established by 1996, after attracting over 2.2 million paid attendances in the previous season. While promoting civic pride, the concentration of many exceptional events means that festivals are especially attractive to state organizations and commercial sponsors. For the first *Edinburgh Festival in 1947, the city corporation gave £22,000, the government-funded Arts Council £20,000, and donors £19,791; there was a deficit of £20,776. For the festival of 1995, the Edinburgh District Council contributed £950,000, the Lothian Regional Council £350,000, the Scottish Arts Council £747,000, and sponsors and donors £1,041,678; the deficit was £34,440.

By the turn of the century, few self-financed productions were to be seen on Broadway, the West End, or in commercially viable theatres around the world. By this time it was clear to everyone that films and spectator *sports, supported by exposure on television, were attracting by far the greater crowds and raising far wider interest. At the same time, finance from government and municipal sources had become less forthcoming because calls on the public purse from health, education, and pensions were all, simultaneously, increasing rapidly.

The financial difficulties of theatre are long-established and endemic. In one of his 'open letters' to members of the Intima Teatern, back in 1908–9, *Strindberg warned that, despite a conspiracy of silence, theatre attendance was poor and performances were being cancelled at the large theatres. At the same time Strindberg and his associates were starting a new theatre: time and again theatre has continued to outface financial difficulties with new artistic developments and new investment, loans, and donations.

Theatre history since then is full of independent innovators who started from nothing rather than attempt to reinvigorate existing establishments that were set in their ways. Annie *Horniman, the heiress of a tea merchant, funded a season of innovative plays at the Avenue Theatre in London in 1893; subsequently, with *Yeats and his associates in Dublin, she was instrumental in founding the *Abbey Theatre. In Moscow in 1897 *Stanislavsky, an amateur actor with private means, met with *Nemirovich-Danchenko, an actor-teacher, and together they founded what would become the *Moscow Art Theatre.

Barry *Jackson both financed and directed the *Birmingham Repertory Theatre in 1913. The *Provincetown Players in the US was started by a group of unpaid amateurs in 1915; later the company moved to New York, where it premièred works by *O'Neill and new translations of European classics.

Finance, for all its importance and necessity, is neither the source nor heart of theatre and, in many ways, a process of renewal continues. In 1964 *Mnouchkine and a few university friends started the Théâtre du *Soleil, a *collective that by 1970 had developed a distinctive style and would tour the world. In the 1990s, Simon *McBurney, again with some university friends and scarcely any money, started a very small company, Theatre de *Complicité, and within a few years it was performing in London at the *National Theatre and commercial venues. Increasingly, an alliance with educational institutions has provided the basis for new initiatives. In the USA several of *Bogart's early productions were staged by New York University's Experimental Theater Wing.

At the end of the twentieth century, the theatre most successful financially was started almost single-handedly by *Wanamaker, who dreamed of rebuilding Shakespeare's *Globe on Bankside in London. Slowly, over a period of 30 years, money was given, much of it by individuals more enthusiastic about Shakespeare than endowed with riches, authoritarian objections were removed, and construction started. In 1999, only a few years after the theatre had opened, the new Globe performed *Julius Caesar* to 95 per cent capacity, *The Comedy of Errors* to 93 per cent, and *Antony and Cleopatra* to 91 per cent. For all productions that year, including those of Elizabethan and Jacobean plays that no other theatre would dare, more than a quarter of a million tickets were sold. This is a theatre that is proud to be 'self-financing in operational terms and does not depend on public subsidy': even in adverse conditions, not all theatre is in financial crisis.   JRB

Finlay, Frank (1926–) English actor. Finlay was a member of the *English Stage Company at the *Royal Court, appearing in *Wesker's *Chicken Soup with Barley* (1958) and *Chips with Everything* (1962), and a member of *Olivier's *National Theatre, playing the First Gravedigger in the first production, *Hamlet* (1963). Subsequent appearances there included a celebrated Iago opposite Olivier's Othello (1964) and Dogberry in *Zeffirelli's *Much Ado About Nothing* (1965). In the 1970s he appeared at the National in *Griffiths's *The Party* (1973), *Brenton's *Weapons of Happiness*, and in *Blakemore's revival of *Travers's

Plunder (both 1976). Finlay reached a huge *audience through his roles in the television series *Casanova* (1971) and *A Bouquet of Barbed Wire* (1976), and as a flamboyant Porthos in Richard Lester's films *The Three Musketeers* (1973) and *The Four Musketeers* (1974). At the Palace Theatre, Watford, he appeared in *Harwood's *The Girl in Melanie Klein* (1980) and in the West End in Jeffrey Archer's *Beyond Reasonable Doubt* (1988). He was the monstrous patriarch Astley Yardley in Simon Nye's black sitcom *How Do You Want Me* (1998–9).   AS

Finley, Karen (1956–) American *performance artist. Trained as a visual artist, Finley began performing in 1979. She married and collaborated with Brian Routh of the Kipper Kids, a performance art duo known for its transgressive and scatological work. Finley's solo performances, which examine the objectification and abuse of women in patriarchal culture, are characterized by nudity, graphic language, and explicit imagery. Performed in a trance-like state, her pieces are neither directly autobiographical nor *character-based, comprised of disparate *monologues in both male and female voices, often directly political in focus and assaultive in tone. Food is a recurrent symbol, as in *The Constant State of Desire* (1986) and *We Keep our Victims Ready* (1989), in which she covered her nude body with substances such as raw eggs and melted chocolate to symbolize the abjectness of women's bodies. One of four artists singled out by the National Endowment for the Arts on charges of indecency, Finley became a central figure in the 'culture wars' of the 1990s. As a playwright, her works include *The Theory of Total Blame* (1988) and *The Lamb of God Hotel* (1992).   LW

Finney, Albert (1936–) English actor. One of the young, rough-edged regional actors of the English new wave theatre, Finney has proven to be a versatile performer in classical and comic roles. After work at the *Birmingham Repertory Theatre and the *Shakespeare Memorial Theatre, Finney achieved widespread recognition in the title roles of Hall and *Waterhouse's *Billy Liar* (1960) and *Osborne's *Luther* (1961). He joined the *National Theatre with notable roles in *Arden's *Armstrong's Last Goodnight* (1965) and *Shaffer's *Black Comedy* (1966). His production company, Memorial Enterprises, presented *Nichols's *A Day in the Death of Joe Egg* (1967), with Finney playing the lead in New York. After a stint as an associate director at the *Royal Court (1972–5), Finney became vital to the early years of *Hall's tenure at the National Theatre, playing

Hamlet, Macbeth, and Tamburlaine. In 1996 he formed part of the original London cast of *Reza's Art*. Finney has had a lengthy film career, performing memorably in *Saturday Night and Sunday Morning* (1960) and *Tom Jones* (1963) and in many other roles.   MDG

fireworks When gunpowder became available, fireworks became an expected part of the *medieval *biblical plays, particularly for *hell mouth. Stage directions before 1400 refer to fireworks. During the late Middle Ages and the *early modern period, four basic effects were possible: flames; smoke; 'squibs' (or 'fizzgigs' or 'serpents', tubes of gunpowder open at one end, which could either be released as rockets or held to spray sparks and flame); and firecrackers and bombs (enclosed gunpowder that made a report when it burst its container). Modern notions of safety were not a factor and many stunts would be unthinkable today—fireworks thrown into the *audience, worn on clothing, held in bare hands, and carried in the mouth. Burning, sparking devils emerging from a smoky, flaming hell were crowd-pleasers, and many plays until about 1680 incorporated fireworks. Technical improvements appeared throughout the early modern period. Small smoke-and-flame bombs in front of a trap, to cause actors to appear and disappear in a roar and flash, occurred as early as 1501 in France. Rockets and flame pots guided on wires, commonly signifying lightning, were in use in the 1550s in Italy. By 1600 the combination of flash-and-boom effects with the transformation trap, so that one *character could explosively become another, was standard stagecraft.

More controllable fireworks developed in Italy during the early sixteenth century. Adding a dash of the salts of certain metals to the powder could produce vivid colours. With the general movement of theatre indoors, fireworks focused more on quality of effect than on volume, whereas outdoor displays, with no specifically theatrical component, continued to grow bigger, louder, and more elaborate. This divorce between pure fireworks and stage pyrotechnics has continued to the present. By the early eighteenth century, the great rage for fireworks on stage was clearly over; only the *Comedié Italienne in Paris regularly featured indoor displays.

The early French *melodrama revived fireworks. The invention of a reasonably safe indoor cannon aided a vogue in the rue de Temple theatres in the 1790s for battle scenes, amplified with firecrackers and smoke bombs. *Féeries advertised new and improved fireworks, and the fashion spread rapidly across Europe. Technical

improvements resumed: gas burners for flames on cue, composite materials for indoor fire fountains, and smokeless powders so that technicians could choose rather than accept how much smoke should occur. By 1840 audiences had become accustomed to this new round of technical improvements, and fireworks again fell out of fashion (battle scenes excepted). In the twentieth century most technical improvements in stage fireworks were in safety. Concerns about injuries, hazardous substances, and fire predominated; the only significant innovation was electric firing. The most common firework effects in recent theatre have been simple fires, clouds of smoke, and bomb explosions.   JB

Fiske, Minnie Maddern (1865–1932) American actress, director, *manager, and playwright, who introduced the plays of *Ibsen to America and developed an approach to *realistic ensemble *acting. After a theatrical childhood she married Harrison Grey Fiske in 1890 and retired for several years, but returned to perform in and promote serious, intellectually challenging, and socially conscious drama. In addition to Nora, Hedda, and other major Ibsen characters, she created the title roles of *Tess of the d'Urbervilles, Becky Sharp, Mary of Magdala, Leah Kleschna*, and *Salvation Nell*. She established the Manhattan Theatre Company as a permanent ensemble in 1904. As a manager, Fiske fought the *Theatrical Syndicate, and was forced by the monopoly to use run-down halls; she remained defiant to the end despite great financial loss. She also performed in film, primarily in her famous stage roles, and wrote a number of one-act plays.   AHK

Fitch, Clyde (1865–1909) American playwright and director. Astoundingly successful, Fitch wrote 60 plays from 1890 to 1909, 36 original, the remainder adaptations. During the 1900–1 season he had ten plays in New York and on the road. *The City* (1909) was his greatest success (shocking *audiences with the line 'You're a God damn liar!'). Critic Walter Prichard Eaton said of him, 'Fitch's works correctly illustrated, would give future generations a better idea of American life than newspapers or historical records.' Most of Fitch's plays are conventional *melodramas; in 1899 he wrote one of the first cowboy dramas, *The Cowboy and the Lady*. His *Captain Jinks of the Horse Marines* (1901) made Ethel *Barrymore a star. Fitch's industry made him a hero to the public. He was seen as the ideal American writer: productive and primarily interested in his public, the embodiment of the Broadway 'show shop' playwright.   TFC

Fitzball, Edward (1792–1873) English playwright, who added his mother's maiden name, Fitz, to his own surname, Ball. A prolific author for a wide variety of major and minor theatres, Fitzball did his best work before 1840, especially in nautical, criminal, and supernatural *melodrama. *The Floating Beacon* (1824), *The Pilot* (1825, an adaptation of a Fenimore Cooper novel), *The Inchcape Bell* (1828), and *The Red Rover* (1829, another Cooper adaptation) are good examples of his nautical vein. Fitzball also knew about staging; he insisted on a setting for his popular crime melodrama *Jonathan Bradford; or, The Murder at the Roadside Inn* (1833) that would reveal *action in four rooms of the inn simultaneously. For *The Flying Dutchman* (1827) he suggested the back projection of magic lantern slides for the approach of the Dutchman's ship, rather than the usual costly building of a stage ship. Fitzball acted as reader of plays for both *Drury Lane and *Covent Garden, and his autobiography, *Thirty-Five Years of a Dramatic Author's Life* (1859), while deficient in chronology, is informative and entertaining.   MRB

Fitzgerald, Barry (1888–1961) Irish actor. Fitzgerald began acting in popular Irish *melodramas about 1914, joining the *Abbey Theatre in 1916. Projecting a roguish charm on stage, his broad *acting was in stark contrast to the static, incantatory style of the previous generation of Abbey actors; however, it was precisely what *O'Casey was looking for, casting him as Captain Boyle in *Juno and the Paycock* (1924). This led to a long association with the playwright, including Fluther Good in *The Plough and the Stars* (1926), and Sylvester Heegan in original London production of *The Silver Tassie* (1928). In 1929 Fitzgerald formed his own company to *tour the United States with O'Casey's work. He moved to Hollywood in 1937, and acted exclusively in films from 1941, winning an Oscar for *Going my Way* (1944).   ChM

Flanagan, Hallie (Hallie Flanagan Davis) (1890–1969) American teacher and administrator. Flanagan became a national figure in the 1930s as director of the *Federal Theatre Project, a Depression-era programme designed to employ theatre people and provide free or low-cost entertainment to the masses. A theatre instructor at Grinnell College, Flanagan studied with George Pierce *Baker at Harvard (1922–4). Inspired by European and Soviet theatre seen during a tour in 1926— and by her meetings with *Meyerhold, *Craig, and others—she built an innovative and respected theatre programme at Vassar College. Flanagan

was appointed in 1935 to head the FTP, and she succeeded in organizing a massive national theatre system that produced more than 1,000 plays, *operas, and other performances for more than 30 million spectators before funding was withdrawn in 1939.   MAF

Flanders, Michael (1922–75) English lyricist and performer, best known for his *revues with Donald Swann (1923–94) at the piano, *At the Drop of a Hat* (1956) and its sequel. Their witty and gently satirical songs usually dealt with domestic British matters (the weather, workmen, interior decorating), with an occasional distinctly sharp touch ('The Reluctant Cannibal', 'All Gaul'); the one most remembered is 'The Hippopotamus Song'. Despite his confinement to a wheelchair, Flanders played the Storyteller in *Brecht's *The Caucasian Chalk Circle* (*Royal Shakespeare Company, 1962).   EEC

flats and wings A flat is a large flat vertical surface forming part of a scene, kept rigid with a frame, supported by braces, jacks, poles, or fly lines. A wing is a flat whose offstage edge is beyond *audience sight lines, thus masking the backstage; or it may be a drape serving the same purpose. From the sixteenth century until the mid-nineteenth, many wings were movable on trucks or wheels in slots or grooves for very rapid scene-shifting. After 1840 the flat was the basic unit out of which *box sets were constructed. In 1950 flats were still the fundamental medium of the scenic artist; 50 years later, despite more three-dimensional scenery, they remained important. For centuries the paintable surface was canvas or muslin, which was light, took paint well, and improved with repainting, but was prone to waves and tears. Better, cheaper particle boards are replacing the traditional (or 'soft') flat with a fabric-surfaced board on a reinforcing frame ('hard flats'). Hard flats, though heavier, are tougher and not subject to ripples or waves. *See also* SCENOGRAPHY.   JB

flaw *See* HAMARTIA.

Fletcher, John (1579–1625) English dramatist who had a hand in more than 50 plays in a sixteen-year theatrical career. His first, the *pastoral *tragicomedy *The Faithful Shepherdess* (1609), was modelled after *Guarini's *Il pastor fido* and illustrates the interest in recent European literary movements. Fletcher may already have made minor contributions to *Beaumont's *The Woman Hater* (1606), and from 1609 they began to collaborate on a regular basis. The partnership lasted until Beaumont's retirement in 1613. During this period Fletcher also wrote his solo *comedy *The Woman's Prize* (1610): following a fashion for plays which countered, and apologized for, the misogyny of some earlier drama, it was a sequel to *The Taming of the Shrew* (the two comedies later played back to back in the King's Men's repertory), and it may have drawn him to the attention of Shakespeare. The fact that Shakespeare wrote his last three plays, the lost *Cardenio*, *Henry VIII*, and *The Two Noble Kinsmen*, in collaboration with Fletcher suggests that he was grooming the younger man as his successor, a role he assumed when Shakespeare retired around 1613. Fletcher's notable early contributions include two Roman tragedies about constructions of masculine honour, *Bonduca* (1613) and *Valentinian* (1614).

In 1619 a regular collaboration with *Massinger began with their *censorship-troubled *tragedy about Dutch current affairs, *Sir John van Olden Barnavelt*. The two men worked mainly together until Fletcher's death in the plague, though Massinger's contribution was effaced when the plays were published in 1647 under the 'Beaumont-and-Fletcher' trademark. Some of their plays, notably *The Sea Voyage* (1622), illustrate the dead Shakespeare's growing imaginative dominance in the work of his younger colleagues.

Sometimes Fletcher seems a complacent monarchist: his attention to aristocratic and gentry codes of behaviour, his interest in other world cultures in *The Custom of the Country* (1620) and *The Island Princess* (1621), and his slick management of *action in comedies like *The Pilgrim* and *The Wild Goose Chase* (1621) have been interpreted as a retreat from political seriousness. At other times, a pervading political unease appears beneath the polished surface. The plays held the stage through the eighteenth century, but have been rarely produced since. *The Chances* (*c*.1625), often considered Fletcher's best comedy, was revived for *Chichester Festival Theatre's inaugural season in 1962, but its commercial failure put the black spot on Fletcher for several decades.   MJW

Fleury (Abraham-Joseph Bénard) (1750–1822) French actor. Fleury, whose father had managed King Stanislas of Poland's court theatre, joined the *Comédie-Française in 1778. A natural elegance and courtier's polish equipped him well for leading roles in classical *comedy and his forte, *petits maîtres* (fops). His most successful role was that of Frédéric II in Ernest de Manteufel's *Les Deux pages* (1789). Director of Marie Antoinette's court theatre at Versailles, he was imprisoned in 1793 for anti-patriotic activities.

He escaped the guillotine, however, and in 1799 returned to the reconstituted Comédie-Française for a further nineteen years, the last of the courtier-actors.   JG

Flimm, Jürgen (1941–) One of the most influential German directors of the 1980s and 1990s, Flimm is a leading exponent of *director's theatre. As *artistic director of the city theatre in Cologne (1979–85) and the Thalia Theater in Hamburg (1985–99), he created productive environments for other directors. Under Flimm the Thalia became the German home for Robert *Wilson, originating many important productions. In his own productions Flimm ranged widely over the classical repertoire with a clear preference for Shakespeare and *Kleist. His best productions (Kleist's *Käthchen von Heilbronn*, 1979, *Chekhov's *Platonov*, 1989; *King Lear*, 1992) were characterized by bold visual metaphors as interpretative keys to the texts. Since 1990 he has directed *opera as well, including *Wagner's *Ring* at *Bayreuth (2000). In 1999 he was elected president of the Bühnenverein, the organization of German theatres.   CBB

Floridor (Josias de Soulas, Sieur de Primefosse) (1608–71) French actor, son of a minor aristocrat, who led a troupe to London, and played briefly in the French provinces, before making his debut in 1638 at the *Marais, where he soon established himself as a worthy replacement for *Montdory. In 1642–3 Floridor probably created the leading roles in Pierre *Corneille's *Cinna*, *Horace*, *Polyeucte*, and *La Mort de Pompée*. In 1647, perhaps by royal command, he transferred to the rival *Hôtel de Bourgogne, buying from Bellerose his position as troupe leader. There he rose to new heights, reviving Marais successes and adding new repertoire by both Pierre and Thomas *Corneille. His greatest triumphs in his latter years were in *Racine's *tragedies: as Pyrrhus (*Andromaque*) and Titus (*Bérénice*). Floridor appears to have been as highly regarded off the stage as on it, and in 1668 obtained a King's Council decree stating that a nobleman could be an actor 'without derogation'.   JG

Fo, Dario (1926–) Italian playwright, actor, director, and designer, who uses traditional Italian forms and *stock characters to produce contemporary political theatre. He has always despised the *avant-garde as elitist; *farce, reshaped to combine didacticism with *slapstick, has been the favoured genre throughout his career. He made his debut with one-person radio pieces, *Poer Nano*, in 1950, before moving into *variety theatre in Milan, where he met and subsequently married the actress Franca *Rame. In 1958 the couple staged two programmes of one-act farces by Fo with such success that they were invited to perform his longer, more complex, satirical *comedies in the main theatres of Italy. In 1968 he and Rame broke with *bourgeois theatre to establish a theatrical cooperative, Nuova Scena, with the purpose of performing popular, political theatre in alternative venues provided, initially, by groups close to the Communist Party. *Mistero buffo* (1969), the main work from this time, is a series of revised medieval sketches performed solo by Fo in the style of the medieval jester (*giullare*). The *satire of the thirteenth-century Pope Boniface VIII was also aimed at the contemporary pontiff and at the institutional Church as centre of power, but the work disconcerted comrades who demanded a more directly militant theatre.

He moved to the left of the Communist Party, and in 1970 established a second cooperative, La Comune, which produced *Accidental Death of an Anarchist* (1970), Fo's most successful venture in the style of hard-hitting but madcap political farce. In 1974, Fo and his associates took over the Palazzina Liberty in Milan, which became his base for the next decade. With the ending of the age of mass protest, he turned his attention to social problems, such as drugs (*Mum's Marijuana Is Best*, 1976), and, under the influence of feminism, to the dilemmas of women (*All Bed, Board and Church*, 1977). In the 1980s and 1990s, while continuing to write and act, he directed productions of *Molière and *Ruzante, whom he regards as predecessors. He was awarded the Nobel Prize for Literature in 1997, and ran unsuccessfully for mayor of Milan in 2006.   JF

Fokin, Valery (1946–) Soviet/Russian director who joined the Sovremennik Theatre (1971–85) in Moscow, where he staged numerous contemporary plays. In 1986 he became *artistic director of the Ermolova Theatre, where productions such as Ovechkin's *Speak!* (1986) and Nabokov's *Invitation to a Beheading* (1990) underscored his commitment to Gorbachev's reforms. After a split of the Ermolova Theatre (1991) he set up the Meyerhold Centre, where he produced Kafka's *Metamorphosis* (1995), and *A Room in a Hotel in the City of N* (1994, based on *Gogol's *Dead Souls*), set in the space of a small hotel room. From 2003 Fokin also ran the Alexandrinsky Theatre in St Petersburg, where he staged Gogol's *The Government Inspector* (2002) and *The Marriage* (2008). His production of *The Overcoat* in Moscow in 2004 garnered numerous awards.   BB

Fokine, Michel (Mikhail) (1880–1942) Russian dancer, choreographer, and *costume designer. He began his career at the Mariinsky Theatre in St Petersburg performing a range of roles with the distinctive grace and lightness which characterized his *dancing. His first *ballet was *Acis and Galatea* (1905), followed by Cherepnin's *Le Pavillon d'Armide* (1907) and Arensky's *Egyptian Nights* (1907–8), which revealed his talents as a reformer and innovator. He was generally opposed to traditional ballet and in tune with the modernist impulses of designers such as *Benois and *Bakst. His fame abroad began in 1909 with the first seasons of the *Ballets Russes, when his major successes as a choreographer included *Daphnis and Chloe, Petrushka, Prince Igor*, and *Le Spectre de la rose*. In 1919 he settled in New York, where he worked for the next ten years. *Drury Lane and *Covent Garden in London hosted some of his ballet productions in 1925, 1937, and 1938, including *Le Coq d'or*, based on a *Pushkin fairy tale, with designs by *Goncharova.   NW

Folies-Bergère Paris *music hall, opened in 1869 for productions of *operetta and *pantomime. The first *manager, Léon Sari, operated the hall until 1885; by allowing prostitutes into the large indoor promenade, he made the area a popular destination for young men and the venue became a fashionable spot. Between 1885 and 1918 various speciality acts appeared, and *audiences saw major performers such as Loïe *Fuller, *Chevalier, and *Guilbert. Paul Derval became manager in 1918 and created the internationally famous image of the Folies-Bergère as a showplace for naked or slightly clad women with huge plumed headdresses and sequinned trains. Although the stage was fairly small, Derval staged opulent *revues with grand staircases and tableaux. Additional acts included *jugglers, *acrobats, singers, *dancers, and comics. The Folies-Bergère still draws tourists, but its appeal has faded since its lush heyday between the wars.   FL

folk play (medieval) Folk drama appears worldwide, characterized by amateur actors who enact a plot and recite lines that have been passed down through generations. Commonly the performers wear traditional *costumes designed to disguise identity rather than to reveal character. Surviving mummers' troupes, for example, often wear costumes of multicoloured fabric or paper ribbons. They conclude their performance by demanding coins or drinks. Extant scripts date from the eighteenth century and later, but *mummers' plays, *Robin Hood plays, sword plays, and *morris dances were familiar fare in the late middle ages and probably earlier. While seasonal *ritual has been cited as the source of much of this activity, folk drama played a larger role in building or maintaining community, preserving or undermining social hierarchy, or channelling social disruptions into socially acceptable bounds. For example, the challenge to authority dramatized in the Robin Hood plays (in which disguise often figures in the action) eventually led to their outlawing by Episcopal decree. Performance traditions of folk plays differ by type and venue, but overall it appears that *costuming, scenery, delivery, and movement tended to be non-naturalistic, emphasizing the performance not as a simulation of *reality but as a disruption of the status quo. Performances were more likely to announce themselves than to take place at an expected time and place; mummers' troupes visited private and public houses during the Christmas season and demanded entrance whenever they arrived.   JCD

Fontanne, Lynn See LUNT, ALFRED.

Fonvizin, Denis (1745–92) Russian writer. Born into the gentry, Fonvizin worked as a translator in the Foreign Office and then as secretary to a cabinet minister. His first plays were translations from *Voltaire (*Al'zira; or, The Americans*, 1762) and Gresset (*Korion*, 1764), but Fonvizin is best known for two original plays, *Brigadier* (written 1766-9, produced St Petersburg, 1780) and *The Minor* (or *The Infant*, 1782). One further play, *The Selection of a Tutor* (1790), has been eclipsed by the other two. The major plays are didactic *satires set in Russia yet conform to the rules of *neoclassical *comedy by sticking closely to the three *unities and maintaining clear divides between the virtuous and vicious *characters. The language of *Brigadier* is strikingly contemporary to its period, discarding the rigid, elevated conformity of neoclassicism. A situation comedy, it targets the transparent morality and excessive Francomania of the provincial gentry, taking sideswipes at the corrupt Russian judicial system. The satirical tone is harsher in *The Minor*, which attacks the low moral and educational standards of the provincial gentry, in particular their maltreatment of serfs. Both have remained in the Russian repertoire. Fonvizin is regarded as precursor of *Griboedov and *Gogol.   CM

fool A comic entertainer, sometimes physically deformed, whose behaviour is the product of real or pretended mental deficiency. An Egyptian record of about 2200 BC mentions such a figure, and fools have been recorded in many cultures, vari-

ously associated with luck, religious sacrifice, poetic power, clairvoyance, and wisdom. In Europe, professional fools or jesters flourished from about 1300 to about 1500 as official household or court fools, or more generally as entertainers in taverns and brothels, or as civic functionaries. The conventional dress of a medieval fool consisted of a motley coat, often chequered red and green, a cowl-shaped hood with ears or coxcomb, and a sword, bladder, or bauble (called a marotte) carried in the hand. The fool also functioned as a theatrical creation, appearing as a *character type in ancient *mime and *farce (Bucco, Stupidus, Herakles), as a mask in the *commedia dell'arte (Arlecchino), as a *clown on the Elizabethan stage, as the German *Narr* and the French *sot*. The stage fool has replaced the motley fool, continuing in a number of guises, ranging from the Three Stooges to Chaplin's Little Tramp.   RWV

Foote, Samuel (1720–77) English actor, *manager, and dramatist who became known as the English *Aristophanes for his satirical portraits of eighteenth-century personalities. After the *Licensing Act of 1737, Foote evaded the restrictions on performance of drama by a satirical *revue entitled *The Diversions of the Morning; or, A Dish of Chocolate* (1747), in which *audiences were invited to tea at the Haymarket, and then offered a performance by the way; a similar event took place in 1748 called *The Auction of Pictures*. Foote's plays include *The Author* (1757), later suppressed by the Lord Chamberlain, and *The Minor* (1760), a controversial *satire on Methodism. Other works include *The Liar* (1762), *The Patron* (1764), and *The Mayor of Garratt* (1764), a satire on corrupt electioneering. After falling from the Duke of York's horse in 1766, Foote was compelled to have his leg amputated. As partial compensation, the Duke obtained for him the *patent of the Haymarket Theatre. Several of Foote's later plays cleverly transformed the actor's wooden leg into a source of laughter. Other plays included *The Nabobs* (1772) and *The Trip to Calais*, *censored in 1775.   JM

footlights Upward-pointed, lensless lights on the stage or below it, usually with a trough-shaped metal reflector, often called 'foots' or 'floatlights' or 'floats', since floating candles were used for fire safety and better reflection. Footlights were in use in Europe from *c.*1620 and throughout the West until early in the twentieth century, normally placed at the spectator edge of the forestage or in line with the *proscenium. Since no natural light sources shine on the human face from below, footlights create an effect that can be variously unattractive or eerie. But until electric lighting became practical, footlights remained crucial elements of *lighting because they were easy to reach, conceal, and dim (by lowering into a trap). They are rare today except in evocations of earlier theatrical styles, and in the received language of newspaper critics. JB

Forbes-Robertson, Johnston (1853–1937) English actor and *manager. Equally successful in *melodrama and Shakespeare, Forbes-Robertson was an elegant, handsome performer with excellent elocution and graceful movement. From the 1870s he acted with leading artists, including *Phelps (his mentor), Ellen *Terry, Geneviève Ward, the *Bancrofts, and Wilson *Barrett, and also performed Shakespeare with Mary *Anderson in the USA and London. In 1895 he created a company with Mrs Patrick *Campbell, featuring *Romeo and Juliet*, *Sudermann's *Magda*, and H. A. *Jones's *Michael and his Lost Angel*. In 1900 he appeared on *tour in *Shaw's *The Devil's Disciple*; Shaw wrote *Caesar and Cleopatra* (1906) for him. In 1908 he played the Stranger in Jerome K. Jerome's *The Passing of the Third-Floor Back*, a popular play that he revived often during the next five years, despite growing tired of the role. From 1900 forward his company, which also featured his wife Gertrude Elliott, balanced London performances with tours. He retired in 1913. TP

Ford, John (1586–*c.*1639) English playwright. Though a member of the Middle Temple, Ford's main interest was the theatre. He began collaborating with *Dekker on a number of plays, the best known of which is *The Witch of Edmonton* (1621, with *Rowley). He worked in close association with some of the most prominent dramatists of his time, including *Massinger, *Shirley, *Brome, and *Webster.

Ford's best-known solo works are the two *tragedies *'Tis Pity She's a Whore* and *The Broken Heart* (printed 1633), which portray impossible moral dilemmas that oppose self-asserting individuals against the conventions of society. A gory story of incestuous passion, often branded as morbidly sensational and a sign of the decline of the stage under Charles I, *'Tis Pity* was nonetheless successfully revived in the late nineteenth century and was by far the most successful of Ford's plays in the twentieth. Ford's historical drama *Perkin Warbeck* (printed 1634), a 'chronicle history' of the events leading to the defeat of the Yorkist pretender to the throne at the hands of Henry VII in 1495, provides a commentary on the ideology of kingship. PCR

Foregger, Nikolai (1892–1939) Russian/Soviet director and *ballet master. His work in experimental *dance technique, based on functionalist, mechanical principles, was influenced by *futurism and *constructivism and drew upon the work of *Meyerhold and *biomechanics. In 1918 Foregger established his Theatre of Four Masks, where he experimented with *circus-style entertainment before setting up the MASTFOR Workshop in Moscow, where a programme of revolutionary and satirical 'machine dances', based on industrial production processes and *acrobatics, were performed in a colourfully eccentric style using jazz and popular music, deriving partly from film techniques. *Eisenstein worked as a designer at MASTFOR during the 1922–3 season. The theatre also staged productions in styles which satirized those of the Bolshoi, the *Moscow Art Theatre, *Tairov, and Meyerhold. NW

Foreman, Richard (1937–) American experimental director, writer, and *manager. Foreman founded the Ontological Hysteric Theatre in 1968 in New York and has staged his plays under that banner at several different venues there and in Paris. Productions have included *Bad Boy Nietzsche* (2000), *Perminant Brain Damage* (1996), *I've Got the Shakes* (1995), *Film Is Evil, Radio Is Good* (1988), and *Rhoda in Potatoland* (1975). His *dramaturgical strategies have been influenced by Gertrude *Stein and her notion of a 'landscape play', which structures a continuous present beginning again and again. Traditional *action, narrative, and *character are elided and thus *audience identification and empathy are resisted in favour of performative moments which foreground the text's and the theatre's apparatus for producing meaning. Foreman has also written and directed works for the *Wooster Group and has directed other writers' works such as *Brecht and *Weill's *Threepenny Opera* at the *New York Shakespeare Festival, *The Fall of the House of Usher* by *Glass at *American Repertory Theatre, and *Strauss's *Fledermaus* at the Paris *Opéra. Foreman has published four collections of plays and theory. He continues to produce one show a year at his theatre. MDC

Fornés, Maria Irene (1930–) American playwright and director. Born in Cuba, she emigrated in 1945 to New York and was eventually caught up in the bohemian subculture of Greenwich Village. Fornés helped to define the *Off-Off-Broadway movement of the 1960s with a series of short, madcap plays, the most successful of which was *Promenade* (1965). In the 1970s she began to direct the initial productions of her plays, developing a precise, austere, formalist style. In 1977 she wrote her most significant and widely produced work, *Fefu and her Friends*, a landmark in *feminist drama which also revealed her interest in site-specific theatre. Fornés's most prolific period came in the 1980s, during which she wrote and directed such plays as *Mud* (1983), *Sarita* (1984), *The Conduct of Life* (1985), and *Abingdon Square* (1987). Each uses a series of short, snapshot-like scenes to trace a female *protagonist's wrenching passage from innocence to experience. Of Fornés's many prizes and commendations, the most telling are her nine Obies awards over 35 years, more than anybody except *Shepard. Despite neglect by the mainstream theatre, she is perhaps the most important American woman dramatist of the twentieth century.   STC

Forrest, Edwin (1806–72) The first native-born star of the US stage. Acclaimed for his patriotic heroics, Forrest's acting centred on his muscular build, booming voice, and strenuous *realism. Following several supporting roles with Edmund *Kean in 1825, Forrest gained stardom with Othello in 1826. To increase the number of his leading roles, Forrest organized several play contests and performed some of the winners throughout his career, adding *Metamora*, *The Gladiator*, *The Broker of Bogotá*, and *Jack Cade* to his mostly Shakespearian repertory. US critics celebrated King Lear and Metamora, a Native American *hero, as his best roles. Forrest blamed his lukewarm success with London critics on the intervention of *Macready and persecuted the English actor in the press, a rivalry that contributed to the Astor Place *riot in 1849. When Forrest and his English-born wife sued each other for divorce in 1851, the trial served as another lightning rod for social antagonisms, dividing the pro-English US elite from nationalistic working-class Americans who favoured traditional patriarchal values in marriage. Forrest amassed millions during his long career, which he prolonged as a platform speaker in the years before his death.   BMC

Forssell, Lars (1928–2007) Swedish writer. One of the most important literary voices in post-war Sweden, Forssell committed himself to an eclectic mix of serious and popular literary styles. He wrote popular verse, song lyrics, political ballads, and erudite poetry, the mix sometimes published in a single collection. A translator as well, Forssell introduced Ezra Pound to Swedish readers, and recast French *cabaret songs into national equivalents. His plays, including *The Jester Who Belonged to his Bell*, *Mary Lou*, *The Madcap*, and *The Sunday Promenade*, investigate *mask, role

playing, and identity. His politically conscious *Sweden, Sweden*, the Farce of the Bourgeoisie, *The Bourgeoisie and Marx* (a retelling of *Molière's *The Would-Be Gentleman*), and *The Hare and the Vulture* expose the emptiness of class-conscious social climbers. *Street-Lasse; or, Pirates* features *music, free verse, and rhymed couplets, while *The Dynamite Blaster and his Daughter Eivor* is a *naturalistic *tragedy.   DLF

Fort, Paul (1872–1960) French director and poet, famous for his support of the *symbolist movement. While still at school he formed the Théâtre Mixte (1890), and later that year he joined forces with Louis Germain's Théâtre Idéaliste, which opposed *naturalism, to found the *Théâtre d'*Art. Their early material would have found a home at *Antoine's Théâtre *Libre, which Fort strongly opposed, but over the course of some eighteen months between November 1890 and March 1892 he produced some of the most important symbolist dramas, most notably *The Intruder* and *The Blind* by *Maeterlinck. But Fort's programming was eclectic, and a mixture of short plays, poetry recitations, and silent *tableaux (along with gauze curtains, smells, and inaudible *acting) led to the outright hostility of critics. Fort's limitations as a *manager, together with poor programming and a narrow appeal of the repertoire, led to the theatre's demise. While the symbolist and *avant-garde baton immediately passed to *Lugné-Poe and the Théâtre de l'Œuvre, Fort continued his creative output as a poet. BRS

Fortune Theatre London *playhouse built in 1600 to replace the *Rose, when it acquired a new neighbour, the *Globe. *Henslowe and *Alleyn, its financiers, used the carpenter who had just completed the Globe. Located in Golding Lane in St Giles, the Fortune site was square, unlike the round Globe. The builder's contract, which survives in the Henslowe papers, specifies that it should be 24 m (80 feet) square, making the open yard a 17-m (55-foot) square, with three levels of surrounding galleries in twenty bays, and two stair towers for access to the galleries, and should have a stage 13 m (43 feet) wide reaching into the middle of the yard. Initially it housed the *Admiral's Men, until in 1603 they became the Prince's Men. The Fortune burned down in December 1621, at night-time, when—unlike the occasion when the Globe burned—nobody was around to save the properties and playbooks. Its company of players paid to replace it, possibly in brick, and it continued in service as 'a citizen playhouse', catering to the less affluent and still staging the famous old plays of the 1590s, until the closure of the theatres in 1642.   AJG

Fosse, Bob (1927–87) American choreographer, director, and dancer. Fosse's choreography exuded a slouching sexuality; his *dances, precise to the raise of an eyebrow or the tip of a hat, appeared almost anti-balletic in their angles and isolations but were capable of show-stopping spectacle. Fosse had performed on Broadway and in Hollywood *musicals by the early 1950s, when he was given a chance at Broadway choreography by director-writer *Abbott. His staging for *The Pajama Game* (1954), and particularly for the 'Steam Heat' number, became the talk of the town, defining his seductive, razzle-dazzle style. Fosse soon began directing as well as choreographing, and gained acclaim with, among others, *Sweet Charity* (1966) and *Chicago* (1975). The latter cast a cynical look at celebrity, which resonated anew in a hugely successful 1990s Broadway revival, spawning a number of international offshoots. Fosse directed several films, including *Cabaret* (1972) and *All That Jazz* (1979), a thinly veiled autobiographical rumination about an overdriven, chain-smoking, womanizing choreographer, which ironically foresaw his own death by heart attack.   EW

Foster, Gloria (1936–2001) *African-American actress. Foster first appeared *Off-Broadway in 1963 in the *documentary drama *In White America*, for which she won an Obie award, and later took roles in New York not tied to her race, including Medea (1965) and Yerma (1966). At the *New York Shakespeare Festival she performed with Morgan Freeman in *Coriolanus* (as Volumnia, 1979), in *Mother Courage* (1980), in Bill Gunn's *The Forbidden City* (1989), and as the mother in *Blood Wedding* (1992). On Broadway she played in Emily Mann's *Having our Say*, about the centenarian Delaney sisters. She appeared on television and in film, including the role of the oracle living in the projects in *The Matrix* (1999).   BBL

Fox, George W. L. (1825–77) American actor, pantomimist, and *manager. He was one of a family troupe ('The Little Foxes') that performed around New England and then moved to Troy, New York. Gaining renown especially in *burlesques of Shakespeare and *Sheridan, Fox in 1850 moved to New York City, where over the years he managed a series of theatres. In 1853 he scored a huge success by importing his family from Troy and presenting an adaptation of *Uncle Tom's Cabin* (fashioned by his cousin George Aiken), which ran for 325 performances (*see*

Tom show). A series of money-making *pantomimes (1864–7) led to the peak of his career when he premièred in 1868 Clifton Tayleure's *Humpty Dumpty*, the first full-evening pantomime on Broadway (1,286 performances), which he would *tour for sixteen months (1874–5) to 26 states. His grimacing and *slapstick clowning caused many to consider him the funniest performer of his day; and for some time he was the highest-paid entertainer in America. Insanity ended his career.   CT

Foy, Eddie (1856–1928) American actor and singer. Foy was born Edwin Fitzgerald in New York, where he was a sidewalk entertainer from the age of 8. At 16 he changed his surname and embarked on a series of jobs as singer, *dancer, and *acrobat. Teaming with James Thompson in 1877, he spent six years in *minstrel and *variety shows, mostly in western states. From 1888 to 1894 he worked for David Henderson in Chicago, starring in *The Crystal Slipper, Bluebeard Jr., Sinbad*, and *Ali Baba*. From 1898 to 1912 his comic talents enchanted New York *audiences in ten *musicals, including *Hotel Topsy Turvy, The Strollers, The Wild Rose, Mr Hamlet of Broadway*, and *Over the River*. His final years were largely spent with his children ('The Seven Little Foys') on the *vaudeville circuit, where he died on tour in Kansas City.   CT

Françon, Alain (1946–) French director. After mounting several noteworthy productions of *Vinaver in the 1970s and 1980s, Françon became director of the Centres Dramatiques Nationaux in Lyon (1989–92) and Annecy (1992–6). In 1996 he succeeded *Lavelli as director of the Théâtre National de la Colline, the newest of France's national theatres, noted for its attention to contemporary drama. There, after staging *Bond's *War Plays* at the *Avignon Festival (1992), he continued to champion Bond's later work, directing *In the Company of Men* (1994, 1997), *The Crime of the Twenty-First Century* (2001), and an often-reprised series of his shorter plays.   DGM

Frayn, Michael (1933–) English playwright and novelist. His commercial success derives from a deft sense of comic *character and construction, yet his philosophical training at university underpins all his work. *Alphabetical Order* (1975) farcically explores the relationship between order and chaos in the office of a provincial newspaper, while *Clouds* (1976) is set amongst journalists writing on Cuba after the revolution. *Make and Break* (1980) and *Benefactors* (1984) are more socially engaged, critiquing the values of commerce and community. *Copenhagen* (1998) investigates a mysterious encounter between two great nuclear physicists, Niels Bohr and Werner Heisenberg, during the Second World War, finally uncovering what might be the most significant misunderstanding of the twentieth century. His most famous play, *Noises Off* (1982, revised 2000) is a meticulously constructed *metatheatrical *farce, which depicts a disastrous production of a crude sex farce, *Nothing On*. Yet even here, the play addresses the relationship between chaos and order, using the metaphor of *acting to consider what happens to our sense of purpose and identity when the scripts of our lives fail us. Frayn is a fluent Russian speaker and his translations of *Chekhov's plays are widely acclaimed.   DR

freak show Public exhibition of the extraordinary body for pleasure and profit. Since the medieval period, the 'othered' body has been displayed, particularly at carnival occasions such as London's Bartholomew Fair. Dwarfs and giants were present in the royal courts of Europe; *fools and jesters and 'innocents' were royal companions. The cheapest freak shows in seventeenth-century England were in street or *fairground booths and rooms in coffee houses. Advertised on handbills with 'true likenesses' to whet the appetite, conjoined twins and dog-headed men were *toured and exhibited throughout the seventeenth and eighteenth centuries. By the nineteenth century the freak show often assumed a proto-scientific status. Showmen such as *Barnum exhibited their 'specimens' in 'museums', though at the same time parading them theatrically: General Tom Thumb (Charles Stratton) performed imitations of Napoleon Bonaparte, singing and reciting material specially devised for him. Less fortunate was Joseph Merrick, the Elephant Man; exploited by unscrupulous showmen, he was rescued and again exhibited for the medical establishment by Sir Frederick Treves. On film Tod Browning's *Freaks* (1932), the tale of the love of a *circus midget for a 'normal' trapeze artist and featuring actual sideshow performers, was banned in the United States until 1962, though it now enjoys academic cult status. As late as 1984, Otis the Frog Man, born with under-formed limbs, was earning his living in a sideshow in America.   AF

Freie Bühne (Free Stage) German theatre society. The Freie Bühne belonged to the European movement of 'free theatre' societies that began with *Antoine's Théâtre *Libre in Paris, established to promote the progressive drama of *Ibsen and others by avoiding direct *censorship through performances that were technically private. Set up in 1889 by *Brahm with a group of like-minded writers and actors, the Freie Bühne staged Ibsen's *Ghosts* in September 1889 and *Hauptmann's *Before Dawn* a month later. Other playwrights included *Tolstoy and Anzengruber. The society's periodical *Die Freie Bühne für modernes Leben* became an influential literary journal. The Freie Bühne never had its own theatre but contributed significantly to establishing *naturalism in Germany. Its activities came to an end when Brahm took over the *Deutsches Theater in 1894.   CBB

Frejka, Jiří (1904–52) Czech director, one of the leading figures of the Czech inter-war *avant-garde. Fascinated by *commedia dell'arte, *surrealism, and *constructivism, he rejected *realism utterly and advocated lyricism in drama and spontaneity in *acting. He founded the Liberated Theatre with Jindřich Honzl, which opened in Prague with an adaptation of *Molière's *Georges Dandin* in 1926. After a split with Honzl, Frejka founded the *Dada Theatre in 1927 and the Modern Studio in 1929. *Hilar invited him to establish a studio that year at the Czech National Theatre, and Frejka's artistry developed in spectacular productions of Lope de *Vega's *Fuente Ovejuna* (1935) and *Julius Caesar* (1936), both designed by František Tröster. Between 1945 and 1950 he was in charge of the Vinohrady Theatre, where his productions of Shakespeare were again the most memorable. Unable to comply with *socialist realism, he was dismissed and transferred to an *operetta theatre, and soon ended his own life.   ML

French, David (1939–) Canadian playwright. CBC-TV produced his first play, *Beckons the Dark River* (1962) and French became associated with the alternative theatre movement of the 1970s to promote and develop Canadian playwrights, especially at the Tarragon Theatre, Toronto. In Tarragon's Bill Glassco, French found the ideal director for *Leaving Home* (1972), and the subsequent plays, *Of the Fields, Lately* (1973), *Salt-Water Moon* (1984), and *1949* (1988), that form a tetralogy dealing with the complex problems of economic oppression and marginalized cultural values that afflict the Mercer family on their move from Newfoundland to Toronto. Other works directed by Glassco include *Jitters* (1979), a backstage *comedy which was French's greatest commercial success, *One Crack Out* (1975), a translation of *Chekhov's *The Seagull* (1977), *The Riddle of the World* (1981), and *Silver Dagger* (1993). French has received many major Canadian awards, and his works have been produced across

North and South America, Europe, and Australia, in English and in translation.   PBON

Friel, Brian (1929–) Irish playwright and short-story writer whose *Philadelphia Here I Come!* (Dublin 1964), became the longest-running Irish play on the New York stage, a lyrical meditation upon the protagonist's situation on the eve of emigration to America. Friel's characteristic preoccupation in succeeding works, *The Loves of Cass Maguire* (1966) and *Lovers* (1968), remained with the life of emotion and memory, often rendered theatrically with framing narrators, notable also in *Living Quarters* (1977) and *Aristocrats* (1979), the latter heavily influenced by *Chekhov, whose plays Friel has successfully adapted. One of his greatest plays, *Faith Healer* (1979), consists entirely of four *monologues. Events in Northern Ireland forced Friel into political drama with the polemic *The Freedom of the City* (1973), a fictionalized version of the Derry shootings of Bloody Sunday (1972). Together with the actor Stephen Rea he founded the Field Day Theatre Company in 1980 as a means of exploring issues of national identity behind the political crises in the North. Field Day opened in Derry with a triumphant production of Friel's *Translations* that toured in both parts of Ireland, and received equal acclaim in Dublin and London, an evocative expression of the colonial process. Though in 1980s Friel devoted to Field Day much of his energy and work, including *The Communication Cord* (1982) and *Making History* (1988), his next major success was *Dancing at Lughnasa* (1990, directed at the *Abbey by Patrick *Mason). Based on Friel's own 1930s memories of his mother's Donegal family, the piece resonates with Ireland's pre-Christian past and period nostalgia, which contributed to critical and popular acclaim in London and New York. If later plays, *Wonderful Tennessee* (1993), *Molly Sweeney* (1994), *Give Me your Answer Do* (1997), and the experimental *Performances* (2003) featuring an onstage string quartet, have been less successful, Friel, with the lyricism of his dramatic style, remains Ireland's most eminent contemporary playwright.   NG

Frigerio, Ezio (1930–) Italian designer. In 1955 Frigerio began a long and productive association with *Strehler, serving as his designer for many plays at Milan's Piccolo Teatro over the next four decades, including *House of Bernarda Alba*, *Threepenny Opera*, *Mountain Giants*, *King Lear*, *Servant of Two Masters*, *de Filippo's *Grand Magic*, *Strindberg's *Storm Weather*, and *Mozart's *Così fan tutte*. He was Strehler's designer for *operas at La Scala as well, including *Simon Boccanegra*, *Falstaff*, *Lohengrin*, *The Marriage of Figaro*, and *Don Giovanni*, and his designer at Théâtre de l'Europe in Paris for *Illusion comique*. Frigerio's international reputation took him all over Europe and to the United States for work in theatre, opera, *ballet, television, and film. His sets for Rudolf Nureyev's productions of Prokofiev's *Romeo and Juliet* and Tchaikovsky's *Sleeping Beauty* were typical: monumental in scale, with stable architectural elements that enabled different levels and planes of action, and movable pieces such as baroque columns (his signature), gates, curtains, painted backdrops, and chandeliers, which together created an atmosphere of magical beauty. Frigerio was nominated for an Academy award for his production design of *Cyrano de Bergerac* (1990).   JEH

Frisch, Max (1911–91) Swiss writer who first worked as an architect, influenced by *Wilder and *Brecht. His first play, *Now They Are Singing Again* (1945), grapples with the problems of guilt and war. *Don Juan; or, The Love of Geometry* (1953) revisits the mythical hero as a study of constructed identity. Frisch's best-known works are the parables *Biedermann und die Brandstifter* (*The Fire Raisers*, 1958) and *Andorra* (1961). In the former, a respectable bourgeois manufacturer takes in a trio of doubtful *characters despite his anxiety about a series of suspicious fires in the neighbourhood. Although the arsonists blatantly prepare their materials, Biedermann remains oblivious to the danger, despite warnings from a Greek *chorus of firemen. This *absurdist 'cautionary tale' gave rise to a plethora of political readings with the arsonists being seen on both sides of the Cold War divide. Explicitly ethical is the situation analysed in *Andorra*, where the inhabitants of a small town ostracize an inhabitant whom they consider to be Jewish. Although received as a study in anti-Semitism against the background of post-Holocaust Europe, the play is a much more generalized study of prejudice and xenophobia.   CBB

Frohman, Charles (1860–1915) American *manager. After a series of show business jobs, Frohman and his brothers Daniel and Gustave took over Steele *MacKaye's Madison Square Theatre in 1877. They devised a production system that changed American theatre, sending out full *touring companies with versions of successful New York shows. In 1883 Frohman's own producing career started with *The Stranglers of Paris*, but fame only came with his production of Bronson *Howard's *Shenandoah* (1889). By the century's turn he had co-founded the *Theatrical

Syndicate (1896) and was the leading *producer in New York and in London, introducing plays by *Barrie, *Pinero, *Wilde, and *Maugham. Frohman's ruthless reputation belies the fact that he died penniless and that stars such as Julia *Marlowe, Otis *Skinner, John *Drew, and Ethel *Barrymore were fiercely loyal to him throughout their careers. Maude *Adams was the emblematic Frohman performer: he had Barrie adapt *Peter Pan* as a vehicle for her. Frohman successfully manipulated his theatrical system for over two decades, creating stars who created *audiences for the works of his own playwrights, and ultimately produced over 500 plays. He went down on the *Lusitania*.   TFC

Fry, Christopher (1907–2005) English playwright, the most commercially successful writer in the revival of poetic drama in the mid-twentieth century. Unlike *Eliot, Fry pushed poetic language to the foreground, delighting in spiralling metaphors and verbal abundance. *The Lady's Not for Burning* (1948) is a romantic medieval *burlesque, set among witch-burners and satirically drawn petty officials. The lightness of his tone and the freedom of the verse proved an attractive antidote to the austerities of post-war London, and the darker themes of the play—which prefigure the *absurdists—are offset by a final affirmation of life and love. The poetic drama revival began in the 1930s, largely through the efforts of Canon George Bell at the Canterbury Festival, but Fry's non-doctrinaire Christianity was always worn lightly, even in the more overtly religious pieces like *The Boy with a Cart* (1938) and the pacifist *A Sleep of Prisoners* (1951). His linguistic exuberance has not come back into fashion, but revivals of *Venus Observed* (1950), and of his adaptation of *Anouilh's *L'Invitation au château* called *Ring round the Moon* (1950), have proved the continuing theatrical strengths of his work.   DR

Fuchs, Georg (1868–1949) German journalist, dramatist, and theatre reformer. His radically aesthetic understanding of theatre found its first practical manifestation in the festival play *The Sign* (1900), a homage to Nietzsche, staged for the artists' colony in Darmstadt. In *The Stage of the Future* (1904), Fuchs dreamed of a theatre free of commercial considerations, closer to *ritual and able to invoke a mystical union of spectators and performers. The performer would assume centre stage, together with generalized concepts such as rhythm, light, and space. Anti-*realistic in conception, his 'relief stage', with stylized backdrops, was intended to frame the performer like a

bas-relief. The theory was given architectural form in the Munich Art Theatre (1908), for which Fuchs worked until its closure in 1914. After this his ideas became increasingly nationalistic: during the First World War he promulgated the notion of national theatre festivals with *Passion plays as propaganda. His own contribution, *Christus* (1919), marked the end of his theatrical activity.   CBB

Fugard, Athol (1932–) South African playwright, actor, and director, his father an English immigrant of Irish descent, his mother from an Afrikaner pioneer family. With his actress wife Sheila Meiring, Fugard formed the Circle Players in Cape Town. In 1958 he made his first contacts in the black townships and the Fugards started the African Theatre Workshop in Sophiatown (1958–9), where they created *No-Good Friday* and *Nongogo*. *The Blood Knot* (1961) established Fugard as a playwright, and using his moderate fame he initiated an international writers' boycott of South Africa in 1963 to protest segregation legislation. From 1963 he worked with the Serpent Players, directing local adaptations of established plays, creating new work like *The Coat* (1967), and collaborating on plays with *Ntshona, and *Kani. His Port Elizabeth plays include *Hello and Goodbye* (1965), *People Are Living There* (Glasgow, 1968), and *Orestes* (1971).

The day after a performance of *The Blood Knot* on British television in 1967 his South African passport was withdrawn; it was not returned until 1971. In 1972 he opened the Space/Die Ruimte/Indawo, a theatre in a converted warehouse near the Cape Malay quarter, with Brian Astbury, *Bryceland's husband. There they premièred the plays he, Ntshona, and Kani had workshopped: *Statements after an Arrest under the Immorality Act* (1972), *Sizwe Bansi Is Dead* (1972), and *The Island* (originally *Die Hodoshe Span*, 1973). After the Black Consciousness movement made collaboration with black artists even more difficult, Fugard shifted to internal themes in *A Lesson from Aloes* (Market Theatre, Johannesburg, 1978), and *Dimetos* (*Edinburgh Festival, 1975). In 1982 he returned to engaged work with *Master Harold and the Boys* (Yale Rep, 1982). Later plays, which were widely performed internationally, include *Road to Mecca* (1984), *A Place with the Pigs* (1987), *My Children! My Africa!* (1989), *Playland* (1992), *My Life* (1994), *Valley Song* (1996), *The Captain's Tiger* (1997), *Sorrows and Rejoicings* (2001), *Exits and Entrances* (2004), *Victory* (2007), and *Coming Home* (2009). Fugard often directed his own work.   YH

Fukuda Tsuneari (1912–94) Japanese dramatist, translator, and literary critic. Shortly after the Second World War Fukuda became established as a dramatist through such plays as *Kitty Typhoon* (1950), *The Man Who Stroked a Dragon* (1957), and other *satires of post-war intellectual life. In 1954 he and other prominent playwrights of the period, such as *Kinoshita and *Mishima, joined the staff of the influential new magazine *Shingeki* (*New Theatre*), through which Fukuda's reviews and commentaries were widely disseminated. He long remained a leader in several prominent theatre companies which were devoted to artistic rather than political ends. Some of Fukuda's plays have been successfully produced in English translation in the United States, notably at the Milwaukee Repertory Theatre. Fukuda held a lifelong interest in English literature and translated the entire dramatic works of Shakespeare into Japanese. His translations have often been performed, replacing those created in the late nineteenth and early twentieth centuries by *Tsubouchi Shōyō. JTR

Fuller, Charles (1939–) *African-American playwright. *The Perfect Party* (1969) was Fuller's first play to attract critical attention, followed by *Off-Broadway productions of *In the Deepest Part of Sleep* (1974), *The Brownsville Raid* (1976), about black soldiers in a Texas town early in the twentieth century, and *Zooman and the Sign* (1980), about the accidental shooting of a young girl in a black neighbourhood. His most important work, *A Soldier's Story*, concerns the murder of a hated black sergeant in Louisiana in 1944, was performed by the Negro Ensemble Company in 1981, and became the second play by an African American to win the Pulitzer Prize; it was adapted into a film three years later. In the 1980s Fuller wrote *Sally*, which premièred at the National Black Arts Festival, *Prince under the Umbrella*, and *We. Jonquil* was produced in 1990, and a short play about Vietnam, *The Badge*, was seen on cable television in 1998. BBL

Fuller, Loïe (1862–1928) American actress, *dancer, and choreographer. In 1891, while performing a small role in a *burlesque-circuit *melodrama, Mary Louise Fuller created the Serpentine Dance by manipulating her silk skirt in and out of the gas stage *lighting. Encouraged by *audiences and reviewers, Fuller continued to experiment with the expressive possibilities of her own moving body by wearing layers of draperies, using wands to extend her limbs, and inventing coloured slides and gels to enlarge the lighting palette. In Paris her appearances at the *Folies-Bergères caught the attention of *symbolist poet Stephane Mallarmé, who called her 'La Loïe' and famously described her dancing as 'the dizzyness of soul made visible by an artifice'. Fuller remained based in Europe for the rest of her career, where she patented her lighting and *costume innovations and in 1908 founded her own school. LTC

Fura dels Baus, La Catalan theatre company founded in 1979. Although emerging from the same *street theatre tradition as *Comedians and Els *Joglars, La Fura embraced the language of urbanism in their fiercely paced, aggressive interdisciplinary spectacles which reinvented the language of performance. Working in abandoned or alternative urban spaces like morgues or warehouses, their visual and visceral productions like *Accions* (1983) and *Suz/o/Suz* (1985) merged the languages of *acrobatics, rock music, painting, and *dance to create fast and furious stagings which denied narrative cohesion in favour of episodic treatments of space that ruptured *audience/actor boundaries (*see* ENVIRONMENTAL THEATRE). Organizing the opening ceremony of the Barcelona Olympic Games in 1992, the company secured a wider audience. More recently they have made excursions into *opera with *The Martyrdom of St Sebastian* (1997), *DQ* (2000), a collaboration with architect Enric Miralles which reinvisaged the myth of Don Quixote for Barcelona's refurbished Liceu opera house, and Gyorgy Ligeti's *Le Grand Macabre* (Brussels, 2009). MMD

futurism Italian art movement founded in 1909 by *Marinetti, originally with a literary orientation but soon expanding into other disciplines. Futurism's entry into the theatre began with a series of controversial *serate* (evenings dedicated to the reading of manifestos, declamations of poetry, and presentations of paintings and musical compositions), followed in 1913 by a *tour by a professional Italian company that included several plays by futurist authors. In 1914 a second troupe toured a repertoire of exclusively *avant-garde and futurist plays. The central problem of the early futurist theatre was that none of the actors belonged to the movement and they did not find an adequate scenic language for the work. Marinetti and his colleagues soon realized that they would be unable to renew Italian theatre simply by writing innovative plays. They formulated their concepts of a new dramatic and theatrical style in a number of tracts: *Manifesto of Futurist Playwrights* (1911) to *Futurist Dance* (1917). Amongst the writers in the movement there was a tendency to seek inspiration from the popular traditions of theatre (*music hall, *circus), which led to several collaborations with stars of the *variety stage.

A different approach was taken by artists in Rome (such as *Prampolini), who proposed a mechanization of the stage, principally making use of three models: the *marionette, robot, and automaton; *costumes that imitated machines; and a mechanized body language aided by appropriate costume. Some of their ideas came to be realized in collaboration with the *Ballets Russes. A third line of development was explored in the *pomeriggi futuristi*, semi-public performances presented in the permanent futurist gallery of Giuseppe Sprovieri in Rome.

Marinetti, Emilio Settimelli, and Bruno Corra confronted the problems of a futurist *acting style on both theoretical and practical levels, but their proposals were not realized until the 1920s when the Futurist Mechanical Theatre produced a number of shows in which the performer was little more than the motivator of a machine-like costume. Prampolini again pursued a different route, in which the *dancer's body imitated the kinetic properties of a machine. These experiments led to the futurist pantomimes, first presented in Paris in 1927, and the 'aerodances' of the 1930s. In the course of the 1920s futurism entered mainstream theatre and made an impact on scenography and dramatic writing in Italy and abroad. In the 1920s Marinetti and company were no longer interested in the scandals, shock effects, and avant-garde gestures that had characterized the early performances. But the futurists had cleared the ground for other artists who were now becoming their competitors, among them *Betti and *Pirandello, a clear sign that futurism had a profound effect on the Italian cultural scene. At the same time it introduced ideas from the international avant-garde (*expressionism, *surrealism, *constructivism) into the otherwise stale theatre of *fascist Italy.   GB

G

Gabrielli family Italian actors in the sixteenth and seventeenth centuries. **Giovanni** (d. between 1603 and 1611) played the servant's role of Sivello, and was renownèd for his controlled non-scurrilous tone and his ability with *mime and bodily gesture. His son **Francesco** (1588–1636) played the liveried servant Scapino, which was later used as Scapin by *Molière. He was acclaimed by Niccolò Barbieri as 'the best *Zanni of his times', and was an accomplished singer and musician. Francesco's daughter **Giulia** played an Innamorata role as Diana. There is debate about whether later performers with the Gabrielli surname belong to the same family.   RAA

Gala, Antonio (1936–) Spanish poet, novelist, and playwright with a love–hate relationship with the theatre. Berated by many critics for their sentimentalism and, in the Francoist period, persecuted by the *censors, Gala's plays have nonetheless drawn large *audiences which responded favourably to their blend of social critique and emotional and lyrical intensity. His first success was *The Green Fields of Eden* (1963), often associated with the 'poetic' wing of the new Spanish *realism. The popularity of the play was matched a few years later by that of *Sunshine in the Ant's Nest*, a variation on the theme of the great theatre of the world, and *November and a Bit of Grass*, a daring indictment of the Spanish Civil War. After winning the Premio Nacional de Teatro in 1972 for *The Good Days Are Gone*, which ran for over 1,000 performances, Gala retired briefly from the stage only to return in 1979 with *Petra Regalada* and, six years later, *Samarkanda*, a semi-autobiographical piece which deals with the theme of repressed homosexuality.   KG

Galsworthy, John (1867–1933) English writer. Along with *Shaw and Granville *Barker, Galsworthy was a force for the New Drama in Edwardian England. In his breakthrough year of 1906, Galsworthy published *The Man of Property* (the first instalment of *The Forsyte Saga*) and had his first play produced, *The Silver Box*. Directed at the *Royal Court by Barker, it is a morality tale of the inequities of the legal system. His next, *Strife* (1909), about a strike at a tin works, was a minor

success. His most historically important play, *Justice* (1910), depicts the horror of solitary confinement with an *expressionist intensity, and prompted Home Secretary Winston Churchill to restrict the use of solitary confinement. After the war Galsworthy achieved his greatest commercial success with *The Skin Game* (1920) and *Loyalties* (1922), which both deal with social caste, and *Escape* (1926). While popular at the time, these post-war plays faded rapidly from critical esteem and his reputation as a playwright came to rest on his Edwardian dramas. Galsworthy, who won the Nobel Prize for Literature in 1932, remains better known for his novels.   MDG

Gambaro, Griselda (1928–) Argentinian playwright and novelist. Dismissed by the theatre establishment as apolitical and aestheticist, Gambaro's plays written before her political exile to Spain in 1977 dramatize Argentina's escalating social crisis. The *protagonists of *The Siamese Twins* and *The Camp* (1967) are passive, silent victims of a surrounding terror. Several plays were not staged until the junta's decline (including *Saying Yes*, 1973, produced 1981) and *Information for Foreigners* (1973) has still to be performed in her homeland. Gambaro's post-dictatorship works exhibit important changes: in *Bitter Blood* (1982), *From the Rising Sun* (1984), and Alberto Ure's 1984 restaging of *The Camp*, the female *characters, once relegated to passive or non-existent roles, rebelliously take centre stage. *Antígona furiosa* (1986) and *It's Necessary to Understand a Little* (1995) demonstrate a continued interest in the causes and consequences of authoritarianism, but with even more fury. The theme of the disappeared informed the 1992 chamber *opera *The House Not at Peace*. In *A Mother by Profession* (2000) a woman attempts to come to terms with her lesbian mother's earlier rejection. Gambaro has always written for an Argentine *audience, hence her inability to write plays during exile. 'One cannot confess alone,' she said.   JGJ

Gambon, Michael (1940–) Dublin-born actor whose career has been predominantly in London and in a series of hugely successful television roles, peppered with appearances in Hollywood films. Gambon joined the *National Theatre for its inaugural season in 1963 and has played regularly for it and the *Royal Shakespeare Company. He has had a long association with *Ayckbourn, appearing in *The Norman Conquests* (1974), *Just between Ourselves* (1977), *A Chorus of Disapproval* (1985), *A Small Family Business* (1987), and *Man of the Moment* (1990). Rather different work includes *Pinter's production of Simon *Gray's *Close of Play* (1979), *Dexter's production of *Brecht's *Galileo* (1980), and *Miller's *A View from the Bridge* (1987). In London in 1995 he appeared in the title role in *Jonson's *Volpone* and *Hare's *Skylight*. His most celebrated television role is Philip E. Marlow in *Potter's *The Singing Detective* (1987), and he was a monstrous thief in Peter Greenaway's film *The Cook, the Thief, his Wife and her Lover* (1989). In 2004 he played Falstaff in both parts of *Henry IV* for Nicholas *Hytner at the National. AS

gambuh Oldest surviving *dance-drama genre of Bali (Indonesia). It originated during the late Majapahit era (1293–1520) under influence from Hindu-Javanese court culture. *Gambuh* is considered the cradle of most classical Balinese performing arts, and for several hundred years constituted one of the main court-supported dance-dramas. It went into decline in the early twentieth century due to the sudden loss of court patronage during conflicts with the Dutch colonial forces. In 1906 this collision culminated in a ritual mass suicide (*puputan*) by the members of the eight royal houses of Bali. Following the demise of the courts, *gambuh* found a new system of support in village communities in the context of temple festivals, though performed in simplified and shorter versions. *Gambuh* consists of a synthesized form of dance, drama, language, and *music. The dramatic material (*lakon*) is drawn from the *Malat*, episodic stories about the mythical Javanese Prince Panji. The other personages are type characters with standardized movements and speaking styles. Refined characters speak in ancient Javanese Kawi, which is translated into contemporary Balinese for the *audience by attendant and *clown characters. KP

Ganassa, Zan The Italian *actor-manager Alberto Naseli (*c*.1540–84) adopted the stage role of 'Zan Ganassa', one of the earliest *Zanni roles in *commedia dell'arte*. The troupe which he managed for over twenty years was known by his name, rather than by a more allusive title. His first recorded appearance is in 1568 in Mantua. After a visit to France in 1571, the company worked in Madrid for ten years from 1574, where they played a crucial role in acquainting Spanish theatre with Italian models. RAA

Gandhi, Shanta (1917–2002) Actress and director from Gujarat, India. One of the founders of the Communist Indian People's Theatre Association, she performed in *dance-dramas like *Voice of Bengal*, *Spirit of India*, and *India Immortal*. In the early 1950s a chance involvement with tribal communities of southern Gujarat compelled her to create a method for educating underprivileged peoples and children by using their traditional performance. After 1960 she was a faculty member at the National School of Drama in New Delhi, where she taught production techniques and classical Indian drama. Her direction of *Bhasa's *Madhyam Vyayoga* (1965) was the first major step towards recovering classical texts and methods for their performance. Through her landmark production of *Jasma Odan* (1968), and her experiment with professional *nautanki* artists in a reinvented version of *Amar Singh Rathor* (1968), she established a method for adapting traditional forms in urban theatre. KJ

Ganz, Bruno (1941–) Swiss-born German actor. As the current bearer of the Iffland-Ring, Ganz can be officially considered the most important living German stage actor. He came to attention in 1969 in *Stein's Bremen production of *Goethe's *Torquato Tasso*, where he played the title *character as an 'emotional clown'. Throughout the 1970s and 1980s he was one of the leading actors at the *Schaubühne in Berlin, appearing in title roles in *Kleist's *The Prince of Homburg* (1972), *Empedokles* (1975), *Hamlet* (1982), and as Orestes in Stein's *Oresteia* (1979). He was the older Faust in Stein's monumental *Faust I and II* (2000–1). He has also worked extensively in film (*Knife in the Head*, 1978; *Nosferatu*, 1979; *Wings of Desire*, 1987; *The Reader*, 2008). CBB

Gao Ming (Kao Ming) (*c*.1305–70) Chinese playwright and native of Wenzhou, Zhejiang, the birthplace of southern drama (*nanxi*). Gao wrote *The Lute*, a foundational *nanxi*, sometime after he retired from service to the Mongol (Yuan) Dynasty in 1356. By 1368 Zhu Yuanzhang, founder of the Ming Dynasty, considered the work equal in importance to the Confucian classics. Gao substantially elevated the artistic level of *nanxi* in this play about a filial son, Cai Bojie, caught between the desire to care for his ageing parents and the duty to serve his ruler. Performances typically consisted of excerpts from the play's 42 scenes. Scenes depicting Cai Bojie's opulent life with his second wife Madam Niu in the capital might be performed at banquets, while arias sung by his first wife Zhao Wuniang, as she journeys there in search of him, were adapted for performance as *tanci*, a form of storytelling accompanied by lutes.   CS

Gao Wenxiu (Kao Wen-hsiu) (fl.1270) Chinese playwright. With over 30 *zaju* operas to his credit, Gao was popular and prolific enough to earn the nickname 'Little Hanqing' after the recognized master of the genre, *Guan Hanqing. Many of Gao's opera titles feature *heroes from the *Shuihu zhuan*, a popular story cycle about noble bandits fighting for loyalty, justice, and political legitimacy. One of only 30 cheaply printed, fourteenth-century *zaju* texts, Gao's *Zhao Yuan the Drunkard Meets the Emperor* embodies some of what might have appealed to Yuan audiences: robust humour, flawed yet likeable *characters, and a playful disregard for customary reverence and decorum. Yet for all their popularity in the Yuan Dynasty, Gao's operas were poorly transmitted. In dramatic and novelistic adaptations of the *Shuihu* cycle in the Ming period, the portrayals of the bandits became more overtly polarized and moralistic, militating against the earlier, less predictable alignments of male virtue, valour, and beauty.   PS

Gao Xingjian (Kao Hsing-chien) (1940-) Chinese playwright and novelist. After studying French at university, Gao became a pioneer in experimental theatre. As resident playwright for the Beijing People's Art Theatre, he wrote *Absolute Signal* (1982), *Bus Stop* (1983), and *Wilderness Man* (1985), *avant-garde, often *absurdist plays that marked a break from official *realistic theatre, bringing him critical and popular acclaim and official distrust. *The Other Shore* was banned from public performance in 1986 and the next year Gao went into exile in France. *Exile* (1990), about three people running from government pursuit after the 1989 Tiananmen incident, put him at odds with the Chinese government and the exiled Democracy Movement. His other dramas, including *Hades* (1988), *Between Life and Death* (1991), *Dialogue and Rebuttal* (1992), *Weekend Quartet* (1996), *Nocturnal Wanderer* (1999), and *Snow in August* (Taipei, 2002), have often been called modern Zen plays. Banned from production in China since 1990, his work has been widely staged elsewhere. His painting, done chiefly in black ink, has been much admired in France, and his philosophical novel *Soul Mountain* (1990; in English 2000) has achieved major recognition. He received the Nobel Prize in Literature in 2000 for his 'bitter insights and linguistic ingenuity, which have opened new paths for the Chinese novel and drama'.   SYL

García, Rodrigo (1964-) Argentine writer and director, based in Spain since 1986. His work, influenced by visual art, playfully questions the relationship between language and performance. With his company La Carnicería Teatro (The Butcher's Theatre) he created, in Madrid and elsewhere, a number of raw, angry, often brutally funny pieces in found spaces. Productions such as *Aftersun* (2000), *The Story of Ronald the Clown from McDonald's* (2004), and *Accidens* (2006)—in which a lobster was killed, cooked, and eaten on stage—have frequently prompted audiences to walk out in disgust or horror. García's texts produced by other directors include *Borges* (2003) and *Agamemnon* (2009).   MMD

García, Santiago (1929-) Colombian director, playwright, and actor. García was part of the university theatre movement until his staging of *Brecht's *Galileo* in 1965 prompted the authorities to remove him from the National University. This led eventually to founding the prestigious Teatro la Candelaria (1972) under his direction, where García's masterly use of Brechtian techniques, his creative designs, and his attention to detail have created memorable work. His playwriting alternates between adaptations of the classics and new social and political material. His works include *The Dialogue of a Rogue* (1982), *Wonderful to Be* (1986), and *El Quijote* (1999), a version of *Cervantes. From 1976 to 1980 he was the director of ENAD (the National School of Dramatic Art).   BJR

García, Víctor (1934-82) Argentine director. In his late twenties García went to Paris, studying alongside fellow Argentine *Lavelli. With a non-*naturalistic repertoire including *Claudel, *Valle-Inclán, *García Lorca, and *Arrabal, García soon demonstrated an architectural understanding of theatre space. Abandoning *realistic decor in productions like Arrabal's *The Automobile Graveyard* (Dijon, 1966) and *Genet's *The Balcony* (São Paulo, 1969), he created baroque imagery which juggled the *ritual with visceral impact. From 1968 to 1976 he directed three seminal productions with *Espert's Spanish company: *The Maids* (1969), *Yerma* (1971), and *Divine Words* (1975). Critics who had previously expressed unease at the dwarfing of actors in García's giant architectural structures were won over by the expressive physicality of the performers. Each production was dominated by a strong conceptual image—what the director referred to as the 'metallic spittoon' of *The Maids*, the womb-like trampoline of *Yerma*, the portable organ pipes of *Divine Words*—that undermined conventional ideas about the works. García's bold scenic creations paved the way for some of the most radical experiments in Spanish and French theatre in the latter decades of the twentieth century.   MMD

García Lorca, Federico (1898–1936) Spanish poet, dramatist, and director. Despite early success as a poet his first play, *The Butterfly's Evil Spell* (Madrid 1920, directed by *Martínez Sierra) was poorly received, and it was not until 1927 that he recovered with *Mariana Pineda*, presented by *Xirgu. During the 1930s García Lorca served as *artistic director of the student theatre company funded by the Second Republic, La *Barraca, taking the Golden Age canon to rural villages. These years were to produce his best-known works, the rural *tragedies *Blood Wedding*, 1933), *Yerma* (1934), and *The House of Bernarda Alba* (written 1936, performed 1945). Using poetic *realism and the Andalusian landscape of his birth as a backdrop, these social dramas investigate the claustrophobic frustration of women in an environment of stifling constraint and oppressive surveillance.

In the late 1920s and early 1930s García Lorca juggled the lyrical realism of the rural trilogy with a more elliptical *dramaturgy in work that went unstaged in his lifetime. Incomplete works like *Play without a Title* (written 1936) and *The Public* (c.1930), which celebrate sexual and political difference, suggest the directions he wished to pursue. During the 1980s revelatory productions by *Pasqual demonstrated this 'alternative' García Lorca, indicating a dramatist whose theatrical versatility defied attempts to pigeonhole him as a folkloric writer.

Although infused by his native Granada, the richness of his writing comes as much from the traditions of earlier generations of poets, from the *enfants terribles* of twentieth-century *surrealism, Luis Buñuel and Salvador Dalí, from his travels to New York and Cuba in 1929–30, and the pioneering work of his contemporaries like Ramón del *Valle-Inclán and Manuel de Falla.

Shot by nationalist troops in 1936, García Lorca was an early casualty of the Spanish Civil War. His name has stood as a potent symbol of a liberal era brutally brought down by an alliance of repressive elements keen to curb the changes begun by the (elected) left-wing Popular Front government. He now stands both as potent countercultural icon—the gay, martyred seer (a taboo topic during the Franco dictatorship)—and a national trademark of post-dictatorship Spain.   MMD

Gardner, Herb (1934–2003) American playwright. His career-making success was *A Thousand Clowns* (1962), which starred Jason *Robards, Jr., and was made into a popular film. *The Goodbye People* (1968), set on Coney Island and starring Milton Berle, failed, as did his one *musical, *One Night Stand* (1980, music by Jule *Styne). *Thieves* (1974) did better, but his biggest hit was *I'm Not Rappaport* (1985), a dark *comedy about ageing set in Central Park and starring Judd *Hirsch as an elderly Marxist Jew and Cleavon Little as his black companion. *Conversations with my Father* (1992), which also starred Hirsch, is an unsentimental study of an unbending Lower East Side immigrant bar owner. Gardner's best *characters are cantankerous, principled free spirits or throwbacks who wage spirited war with the present.   CR

Garneau, Michel (1939–) Québec dramatist, director, actor, translator, musician, and poet. Brilliantly eclectic, his career began in radio at the age of 15. His plays (more than 40 to date, many written to order) are characterized by intense social and political commitment (he was briefly imprisoned during Quebec's October Crisis in 1970), allied with an irreverence for everything previous generations considered sacred. They are usually in blank verse, and in popular Québécois idiom, yet they have had broad international success, notably *Quatre à quatre* (1973), dealing with four generations of Quebec women, and *Emily Will Never Again Feel the Breath of the Delphinium* (1981), a loose depiction of the life and works of the American poet Emily Dickinson. Garneau's translations/adaptations of Shakespeare (*Macbeth* and *The Tempest*, in particular) have been acclaimed by critics in their Montréal performances.   LED

Garrett, João Baptista de Almeida (1799–1854) Portuguese poet, novelist, and playwright. The leader of Portuguese *romanticism and the founder of modern Portuguese prose, one of Garrett's chief preoccupations as Inspector-General of Theatres was the professionalization of the national stage and the creation of a distinctly Portuguese dramatic repertoire. The first performances of the newly created Teatro Nacional D. Maria II (1846) included a selection of his own work, encompassing five *comedies, two historical dramas, and the groundbreaking *Um auto de Gil Vicente* (1838), a celebration of the *early modern Portuguese playwright *Vicente. In 1850 came *Frei Luís de Souza*, widely regarded as the most important play of Portuguese romanticism. Based on the true story of a Portuguese nobleman who, presumed dead in battle, returns to his homeland to the dismay of his daughter and wife, who has since remarried, this patriotic *tragedy was the most performed play of the first 100 years of the National's existence.   KG

Garrick, David (1717–79) English actor and *manager who dominated the eighteenth century. Raised in Lichfield, Garrick took a famous walk to London with Samuel *Johnson in 1737. In October 1741 he made a legendary London debut as Richard III, his success immediate and immense. The naturalness of his performance style contrasted markedly with the more formal, declamatory method of veterans like *Quin. Garrick gave his first performance at *Drury Lane in 1742 and quickly became the company's chief performer. After leading the failed actors' rebellion of 1743, Garrick left Drury Lane for Dublin in 1745–6 and *Covent Garden in 1746–7. In April 1747 he signed articles to become co-manager of Drury Lane with James Lacy, beginning a 27-year partnership that was amazingly profitable. Garrick made improvements to the theatre immediately by banishing gentlemen from going behind the scenes during a performance. In 1765–6 he installed wing lights similar to those he had seen in France, vastly improving the illumination of the stage.

In the 1770s he hired the Alsatian *scenographer Philip de *Loutherbourg, who combined scene painting, *lighting, and other media into a more compelling visual presentation. Garrick's instincts for song and spectacle were generally sound, although he badly miscalculated when he brought in French dancers to perform the *Chinese Festival* in 1755, on the eve of the Seven Years War, when anti-French sentiment was running high. *Rioting broke out, and the venture cost the theatre £4,000. Another costly fiasco was the Great Shakespeare Jubilee of 1769, which was Garrick's pet project. The multi-day celebration in Stratford-upon-Avon featured a horse race, *fireworks, torrential rains, and Garrick's 'Jubilee Ode', but no performances of Shakespeare. Garrick was roundly criticized for this exercise in vanity, and he reportedly lost £2,000 for his pains, but he began the vogue of bardolatry still flourishing in Stratford.

In dealings with actors and playwrights he was always diplomatic. He established a warm relationship with the volatile Kitty *Clive and was able to employ the mercurial Spranger *Barry for several seasons. As for authors, he politely dealt with the many entreaties he received to stage new plays, though he wrangled repeatedly with Arthur *Murphy and alienated John Home. An author

himself of light *farces and of dubious alterations of Shakespeare, Garrick was sometimes accused of stifling other playwrights while forcing his own work on the public.

He played an enormous variety of roles. In tragedy he had no rivals for Macbeth, Lear, and Richard III. Francis Gentleman praised Garrick's dizzying range of emotions in Macbeth, whom Garrick played as a sympathetic *hero-*villain, complete with a pathetic death speech of Garrick's invention. His portrayal of Lear avoided bombast and abstraction, emphasized a characteristic modulation of emotions, and exploited opportunities for pathos. But Hamlet was the *audience's favourite, and Garrick played it 90 times, from his second season to his last. Commentators were impressed by his melancholy demeanour and claimed that his skin actually grew paler upon seeing the *ghost. His great non-Shakespearian tragic roles included Lothario in *Rowe's *The Fair Penitent*, Jaffeir and Pierre in *Otway's *Venice Preserv'd*, and Lusignan in Aaron Hill's *Zara*.

In *comedy Garrick's most popular role was Abel Drugger in *Jonson's *The Alchemist*, a low comic role that he skilfully underplayed. Far different was his portrayal of the suave, rakish, but good-hearted Ranger in Benjamin Hoadly's *The Suspicious Husband* (1747). Although Quin scoffed at the young Garrick playing Sir John Brute in *Vanbrugh's *The Provok'd Husband*, the part became a mainstay of his repertory. Other great comic roles included Benedick in *Much Ado* and Don Felix in *Centlivre's *The Wonder*, the *character Garrick played for his final performance on 10 June 1776. Knowing that the emotion of actor and audience would be overpowering on the occasion, he wisely closed his unparalleled career on a comic note. And sensing that a rhyming *epilogue would detract from the dignity of the moment, he made a modest and emotional address in prose, bowed to all corners of the house, and walked slowly off the stage.   MJK

Garro, Elena (1920–98) Mexican playwright and novelist. Best known for her magical realist novel *Remembrance of Things Past* (1963), Garro began writing plays in the 1950s as a member of Poetry Out Loud. Known for her lyrical, often magical plays, she combined childhood memories with images of Mexico's indigenous culture and history. *A Solid Home* (1957) tinkers with the pre-Columbian belief that death is an extension of life by bringing together various generations of a Mexican family, all of them dead and buried in the same crypt. Other plays are *surrealistic, often violent encounters between men and women (*The Trace*, 1984), the rich and the poor (*The Tree*, 1983), the dead and the living (*The Lady on her Balcony*, 1966). While her plays have not always had the productions they deserve, her historical drama on the revolutionary hero *Felipe Angeles* (1979) won awards and enthusiastic *audiences.   KFN

Gascon, Jean (1921–88) French Canadian actor and director. He studied theatre in France 1946–51 and on return helped found the Théâtre du Nouveau Monde, becoming its *artistic director and leading actor. Notable for his performances of *Molière, he was responsible for introducing that author's work to the *Stratford Festival. He was Stratford's artistic director from 1968 to 1974 and was a major contributor to its national and international success, with tours of the USA, Europe, the Soviet Union, and Australia. Active in film and television, Gascon also served as director of Montréal's National Theatre School and of the National Arts Centre in Ottawa.   LED

Gaskill, William (1930–) English director. Gaskill was assistant director to George *Devine with the *English Stage Company (1957–9), where he forged strong ensemble work in plays by *Osborne and *Wesker, attracting invitations from the *Royal Shakespeare Company and to be associate director at *Olivier's new *National Theatre in 1963. Notable productions in this period included the RSC's *Richard III* (1961), *Cymbeline* (1962), and *Brecht's *The Caucasian Chalk Circle* (1963), and even a West End *Baal* (1963) starring Peter *O'Toole. In the National's first season he staged *Farquhar's *The Recruiting Officer* (1963), followed by Brecht's *Mother Courage* (1964) and *Arden's *Armstrong's Last Goodnight* (1965). He became *artistic director of the *Royal Court from 1965 to 1972, directing *Bond's *Saved* (1968), *Early Morning* (1969), *Lear* (1971), and *The Sea* (1973), as well as opening the studio Theatre Upstairs (1969). In 1972 he went freelance, and in 1973 with *Stafford-Clark he founded the cooperative *touring company Joint Stock, making it one of the leading fringe groups in England, with premières of scripts by *Hare, *Brenton, and *Churchill. Gaskill continued to work in the major theatres into the 1990s. His productions included *Oedipus the King* (Dubrovnik, 1976), *Hamlet* (Sydney, 1981), Osborne's *The Entertainer* (New York, 1983), *Shaw's *Candida* (Minneapolis, 1985), and *Pirandello's *The Mountain Giants* (National Theatre, 1993).   BRK

Gassman, Vittorio (1922–2000) Italian actor and writer. Gassman made his theatrical debut in 1943 and worked with the finest directors of his time, including in the 1940s *Visconti (*A Streetcar Named Desire* and *Troilus and Cressida*) and in the 1950s *Squarzina, his co-director in the Teatro d'Arte Italiano. Gassman's first film role in Italy came in 1946, but he did not find success in cinema until Mario Monicelli's *Persons Unknown* (1958) when he appeared alongside the Neapolitan actor Totò. He moved to Hollywood and shot films with King Vidor and Joseph H. Lewis, and in the 1970s with Robert Altman (*Quintet*, *A Wedding*). In 1974 he won the best actor prize at Cannes for his performance in *Profumo di donna*. A charismatic actor who felt his real métier was theatre, he was also successful as director, translator, especially of Shakespeare, and latterly as author of novels and autobiographical works.   JF

Gatti, Armand (1924–) French writer and director. Gatti at 17 was deported to a labour camp in Germany; the image of the concentration camp appears in several of his works. An ebullient self-styled anarchist, he had considerable success in the 1960s, starting with the semi-autobiographical *Imaginary Life of Auguste Geai* (1962), which showed his father at five different ages, played by five actors on seven stages, sometimes simultaneously. He wrote plays on the Chinese Civil War, the Guatemalan struggle for independence, the execution of Sacco and Vanzetti, and Vietnam, often presenting fragmented *characters and events, but reflecting his belief that the theatre could raise political consciousness. After the banning of *The Passion of General Franco* (1968, played 1976), he turned to a more directly 'engaged' form of *community theatre on politically sensitive subjects, involving whole communities for several months in events where the result was liable to appear in a wide variety of media rather than a published text. He has also made documentary films, and currently arranges events in Seine-Saint-Denis, such as *L'Internationale* (2001), on the Spanish Civil War.   EEC

Gay, John (1685–1732) English playwright, most famous for *The Beggar's Opera* (1728). The unprecedented run of that *ballad opera (it ran for 63 nights in its first season) and its experimental nature made it the most important and successful play of the eighteenth century, and became the basis of *Brecht and *Weill's *The Threepenny Opera* (1928). Gay's first success was *The What D'Ye Call It* (1715), a *burlesque afterpiece. *Three Hours after Marriage* (1717), which Gay co-wrote with Alexander Pope and John Arbuthnot, probably suffered from hostility to Pope. Gay's happy-ending *tragedy *The Captives* (1724) had a short run at *Drury Lane and brought the patronage of Princess Caroline; its blend of burlesque, *farce, and compelling *music was the culmination of his earlier works. Not merely an attack on *opera—after all, Gay wrote the libretto to Handel's *Acis and Galatea* (1718)—the ballad opera simultaneously exploited and ridiculed *musical theatre. That the play was seen as an attack on Robert Walpole's ministry was perhaps inevitable, given Gay's Tory friends and patrons, chiefly Pope and the Duke and Duchess of Queensberry. The political firestorm that erupted over its interpretation led to the suppression of the sequel, *Polly* (1729). MJK

gay theatre and performance Theatrical production conceived and performed by gay men for gay *audiences. In America, the movement is usually linked to the establishment of *Off- and *Off-Off-Broadway in the 1960s such as *Caffe Cino (1960), which often showcased gay playwrights, including Robert Patrick and Lanford *Wilson. The Judson Poets Theatre and *La Mama soon followed. Charles *Ludlam and his Ridiculous Theatrical Company (1967) began to mount a series of plays that helped popularize a new gay aesthetic: drag, exaggerated *acting, 'cheap theatrics', and camp treatment of production values. This highly *metatheatrical and anti-*naturalistic treatment was taken up by other gay companies. In 1968 Mart Crowley's *Boys in the Band* become an Off-Broadway hit, giving mainstream audiences an opportunity to observe gay men interacting with each other, uncensored and without apology. Political activism generated by the gay and lesbian liberation movement led to a wider, more visible community of gay men, thus creating a new audience, less closeted and eager to see itself portrayed. Newly formed companies dedicated to presenting exclusively gay and *lesbian theatre included Doric Wilson's TOSOS (1974) and John Glines's the Glines (1976). Gay theatre companies sprang up across the country. Comparable activity surrounded London's gay theatre, particularly after the Theatres Act of 1968 abolished *censorship. The Gay Sweatshop, founded in 1975, sought to present positive images of gays and lesbians in contrast to repressed and homophobic identities. In 1979, Martin Sherman's *Bent*, a play about the Nazis' brutal treatment of gays, opened in the West End and transferred the following year to Broadway. Gay activists soon appropriated the pink triangle as a recovered emblem of gay liberation. In 1981 the Glines' production of *Fierstein's Torch Song Trilogy* moved to Broadway, where it ran for several years, winning the Tony award for best new play.

The AIDS epidemic, while decimating the ranks of gay artists and audiences alike, stimulated work that reflected the anger, frustration, and loss felt by the community. *As Is* by William M. Hoffman and *The Normal Heart* by Larry Kramer (both 1985), were two early examples that dealt with the epidemic.

By the 1990s gay plays began to sound the call for integration and empowerment rather than opposition and separatism. *Kushner's two-part *Angels in America* (Broadway, 1992–3), while ostensibly dealing with the AIDS crisis and homophobia, made a prediction that 'we will become citizens'. Kushner won the Pulitzer Prize and the Tony for best play two years running. With a heightened awareness of ethnicity, race, and class within gay communities, the 1990s also brought more diverse voices. The work of *performance artists like Tim Miller, Ron Athey, and Eddie Izzard attested to the variety of identities and concerns that gay men possess beyond sexuality. By the early years of the new millennium, gay plays were mounted in theatres internationally. RN

geju (*ko-chü*) Chinese song-and-*dance dramas. The term can be applied to any full-length musical drama, and can even be used to denote Western *opera, but in the People's Republic of China *geju* normally connotes the communist-inspired, ideologically driven musical shows of the 1940s to the 1970s. *Geju* are still performed by government-sponsored troupes, but the genre itself, a product of a time when art was explicitly harnessed to the government's social objectives, lost focus in the more pluralist atmosphere at the turn of the twenty-first century. *See also* GEMING XIANDAI XI. KC

Gelber, Jack (1932–2003) American playwright and director. Gelber burst onto the New York scene in 1959 with the *Living Theatre's production of his first play, *The Connection*. Set to live jazz, this *naturalistic drama about a group of heroin-addicted musicians waiting for their drug dealer ran for 778 performances and received three Obie awards, including best new play. His screen adaptation appeared two years later. Gelber's subsequent work is characterized by a persistent exploration of dramatic form and theatrical presentation. *The Apple* (1961) experiments with *audience perspective as it portrays the life of a supposed madman. Other plays include *Square in the Eye* (1965), *The Cuban Thing* (1968), *Sleep* (1972), and *Rehearsal* (1976). In 1973 he received an Obie for his direction of Robert Coover's *The Kid*. JAB

Gélinas, Gratien (1909–99) French-Canadian playwright, actor, director. His contributions to Canadian culture span seven decades, from radio drama in the early 1930s through comic *monologues, sketches, and *revues, to social dramas for the stage, film, and television. For the revues he created Fridolin, initially an endearing street urchin, evolving into a good-humoured critic of social norms and individual foibles, then into the darker title roles of his two best plays, *Tit-Coq* (1948), a social drama from which the advent of modern theatre in Québec is usually dated, and *Bousille and the Just* (1959). *Bousille,* generally considered his best work, is a stinging indictment of Québec society just before its Quiet Revolution, while *Yesterday, the Children Were Dancing* (1966) deals with the stresses caused by that movement. Both were performed at La Comédie-Canadienne, founded by Gélinas in 1968, a much-needed venue for home-grown texts and players.   LED

Gelosi Probably the earliest named troupe of Italian *commedia dell'arte* actors, first recorded and identified in 1568. (Their name translates as 'Zealous', rather than 'Jealous'.) They visited France as early as 1571, and then later in 1603–4, thus beginning the process whereby Paris became a magnet for the best Italian theatre practitioners. In 1578 (it is thought) they were joined by Francesco and Isabella *Andreini, who together became a star attraction and provided the company's identity, to the extent that when Isabella died and Francesco retired in 1604 that identity became unsustainable. The Gelosi were renowned particularly for their ensemble teamwork and their versatility: whether or not they were the first performers of *Tasso's *Aminta,* their repertoire included all genres, both scripted and improvised. *See also* COMÉDIE ITALIENNE.   RAA

Gémier, Firmin (1869–1933) French actor and director. Acting extensively at the Théâtre *Libre before creating the title role in *Jarry's *Ubu roi* at the Théâtre de l'Œuvre (1896), Gémier began to direct in the footsteps of *Antoine, finally taking the directorial helm of the Théâtre Antoine from 1906 to 1922. Strongly committed to a people's theatre, he lay the groundwork for decentralized theatre. The founder of the Société Shakespeare, his productions of *The Merchant of Venice* (1916) and *The Taming of the Shrew* (1918) prefigured later innovators. For two years he made a bold (and financially disastrous) attempt to create a Théâtre Ambulant outside Paris, for which a 1,650-seat tent theatre travelled from city to city. He briefly took over the operation of the Cirque d'Hiver, which he saw as a model for the communal ethos of *Greek theatre, put to the test in his popular production of Bouhelier's *Oedipus, King of Thebes* (1919). During the 1920s, in addition to directing the *Odéon, Gémier directed the newly created *Théâtre National Populaire at the Palais de Trocadéro, an underfunded and impractical venture that would not be fully realized until after the Second World War.   DGM

***geming xiandai xi** (ko ming hsien tai hsi)* 'Revolutionary modern drama', Chinese plays with revolutionary themes, the only theatrical repertoire permitted during the Cultural Revolution. Mao was not pleased to see 'many Communists enthusiastic about promoting feudal and capitalist art instead of socialist art'. In 1963 Mao's wife Jiang Qing, a former film star in Shanghai, took an interest in developing revolutionary plays that 'help the masses to propel history forward'. Faced with resistance from the Cultural Ministry and the mayor of Beijing, Jiang found allies in younger *jingju (Beijing opera) actors and the mayor of Shanghai, who enthusiastically endorsed her plan in his opening speech to the East China Drama Festival in Shanghai that year. Although the two sides struck a temporary balance in 1964, Mao and Jiang did not win final victory until after the start of the Cultural Revolution.

Also called *geming yangban xi* (revolutionary model drama), the original eight model plays, performed in Beijing in 1967 to celebrate the 25th anniversary of Mao's *Yan'an Talks,* included five jingju (*The Red Lantern, Shajia Bang, Raid on the White Tiger Regiment, Taking the Tiger Mountain by Strategy,* and *On the Docks*), two *wujū or *dance-dramas (*Red Detachment of Women* and *The White-Haired Girl*); and the symphonic music from *Shajia Bang.* In the early 1970s several other revolutionary *jingju received permission for performance, often adapted locally by inserting different tunes into the original scripts. The model drama departed radically from traditional Chinese theatre. Aside from the revolutionary subject matter and highly simplified heroes of 'workers, peasants and soldiers', the model plays used Beijing dialect, much plainer make-up and *costumes, more complicated scenery and *lighting, act and scene divisions, and a symphonic orchestra. Banned from performance after the Cultural Revolution, *geming xiandai xi* were revived in the late 1980s and early 1990s as an attempt to boost the image of the Communist Party after the Tiananmen incident and the fall of communism in Europe and the Soviet Union. They were received with a mixture of suspicion and cynicism, but also with a sense of nostalgia by the generation who had grown up with them as their sole entertainment. SYL

Gems, Pam (1925–2011) English playwright. Gems came to playwriting at age 47, after raising a family. She found success with *Duse, Fish, Stas and Vi* (which premièred at the *Edinburgh Festival as *Dead Fish*) in 1976. Although the work solidified her reputation as a *feminist playwright. *Guinevere* (1976) began a series of feminist reworkings of well-known tales, followed by *Queen Christina* and *Piaf* for the *Royal Shakespeare Company in 1977–8 about the French singer, which garnered its star, Jane Lapotaire, both an Olivier and a Tony award for best actress. Through the next decade, Gems continued to review stories of women in *Camille* (1984), *La Pasionara* (1985), and *The Blue Angel* (1991), as well as writing adaptations such as *Przybyszewska's *The Danton Affair* (1986) and *Chekhov's *Uncle Vanya* (1991). She had another hit with the *National Theatre production of *Stanley* (1996) about painter Stanley Spencer, which won the Olivier award for best play and best actor (for Antony *Sher). In 1999 Sian Phillips starred as the elderly Marlene Dietrich in Gems's *Marlene*. MDG

gender and performance A concern with identity politics made issues of gender fundamental to contemporary culture. The significance of gender in determining social behaviour and in defining power relations between men and women has been a major part of cultural debates since the 1970s. Theatre, like other cultural practices, has developed ways of engaging with theories of gender and has devised critical approaches to performance which foreground gender identity and offer critiques of narrow representations of masculine and feminine ways of being. The term 'gender' refers to the socially constructed division between the sexes. It is concerned with the culturally determined group of attributes, including emotional and psychological characteristics, which differentiate masculinity and femininity. 'Sex', on the other hand, designates the biological and physiological differences between male and female. Culture ascribes particular gender qualities to maleness or to femaleness, and expectations of masculine or feminine social behaviour are assigned to the male and female child. Theories of gender, deriving from feminism and studies of masculinity and sexuality, attempt to clarify the distinction between sex and gender, opening up possibilities for change. From the separation of sex and gender comes the notion that although the child is biologically defined as

male or female at birth, it is society, rather than a process of nature, which shapes women and men.

From its early history, questions of gender have been significant for theatre. Theatre performance depends upon the construction of fictive roles which are separate from the actors' identities. In many historical forms, such as ancient *Greek, Japanese, and English *early modern theatre, where women did not appear on stage, female roles were created by male actors. The female role was produced through a set of coded visual signs (gesture, *costume, *mask, etc.) designed to convey 'woman' to the *audience. Whether the audience was made aware of the distinction between actor and role as in Japanese *nō theatre, or the male/female distinction was blurred as in *kabuki where the *onnagata aimed to impersonate the female in every detail, there was a tension between masculinity and femininity in the performance. In many of Shakespeare's plays, for example *Twelfth Night* and *As You Like It*, this tension was developed to create a critique of gender and sexuality dependent upon the ironic awareness of the gender split between *character and *actor, cross-dressing, and confused identities.

In modern theatre questions of gender have been raised in several ways. First, there have been revisions of Western theatre history and a reworking of the theatrical canon to reassess historical gender roles and to critique gender relationships in dramatic literature. The application of contemporary theories of gender and sexuality to canonical texts has produced radical performances which challenge traditional interpretations of texts. Furthermore, there have been rediscoveries of 'forgotten' writers, such as the seventeenth-century woman playwright Aphra *Behn, whose life and work challenge received notions of the ways women lived and were portrayed in theatre.

Second, issues of gender—historical, social, and political—have become major themes in the work of many late twentieth-century playwrights and theatre practitioners, exemplified by feminist playwrights Megan *Terry and *Gems, whose plays examine the role of women in society, and by Martin Sherman and *Rabe, whose plays focus on questions of sexuality and masculinity. Forms of theatre and performance have been developed which enable the deconstruction of gender roles in history and contemporary society. Drawing on models of practice developed by *Brecht, writers such as *Churchill in *Cloud Nine* (1979) have used the separation of actor and role to foreground the social construction of gender as separate from sex, and developed strategies of alienation

(*Verfremdung*) to draw attention to the political implications of the cultural construction of gender.

Third, using Lacanian psychoanalytic theory and feminist approaches derived from the French theoreticians *Cixous, Julia Kristeva, and Luce Irigaray, playwrights and performers have experimented with new forms of theatre aesthetics which dismantle traditional representational modes and offer new ways of delineating gender subjectivity. *Duras in *India Song*, Churchill in *A Mouthful of Birds*, and *Kushner in *Angels in America* disrupt traditional narrative structures and character coherence in order to foreground fluid gender identities. One effect of this emphasis is to focus on the body, for example in strategies of drag, cross-dressing, and *male and *female impersonation. The work of German choreographer *Bausch and the British *physical theatre company DV8 crosses the boundaries between *dance and theatre, using the physical skills of dancers in theatrical performances which centre on corporeal inscriptions of socially determined gendered behaviour.

Issues of gender have been a priority for live *performance artists such as Annie Sprinkle, Orlan, Karen *Finley, and Holly *Hughes, who are interested in examining questions of subjectivity. Rather than focusing on theatrical role play, this work uses the body of the artist as a site for exploring how sexual and gender identities are 'performed'. Postmodernism, feminism, and psychoanalysis have all theorized gender identity as performative. Developing the work of J. L. Austin, Judith Butler has described gender construction as proceeding through an endless process of citation and reiteration. While she does not ally this notion of performativity with theatre, Butler's theories have had an impact on the theory and practice of live art and theatre, since self-conscious performance can reveal the functioning of unconscious performativity. *See also* FEMINIST THEATRE; LESBIAN THEATRE; GAY THEATRE.   LT

Genet, Jean (1910–86) French playwright associated with the theatre of the *absurd. After the troubled early life of an orphan, spent in reformatories and as an itinerant and petty criminal, Genet's literary career began while in prison, where he wrote novels in a homoerotic and poetic language, focusing on themes of crime, homosexuality, and the marginalized in society. His subsequent plays present life as a series of transactions between masters and servants; the drama resides in the tensions between images of self and the fragility of their construction. *Ritual, transformation, and the interchangeability of identity are

all characteristics of his drama; so too is his rejection of plot and *character psychology. His first play, *Haute Surveillance* (*Deathwatch*, not performed until 1949), features the tensions and battles for supremacy of three prisoners in one cell, while another watches. *The Maids* (directed by *Jouvet, 1947) shows two servants acting a mistress-and-servant ritual, exposing their hatred of their oppression and of themselves for participating in it. Self-loathing carried on to *The Balcony* (directed by *Brook, 1956), which features pillar-of-society characters (bishop, judge, general) being 'enacted' in master-and-servant ritual games in various fantasy rooms in a brothel, while a revolution is raging outside to topple those very characters in real life.

Genet's final two plays *The Blacks* (directed by *Blin, 1959) and *The Screens* (written 1961; directed by Blin, 1966) added race to his theatrical ritual of power and domination. In the former, a troupe of black actors perform the ritualistic murder of a white woman before a jury of blacks wearing white masks. *The Screens*, Genet's most adventurous work, is a long investigation of the Algerian conflict—screens are used to point out how reality can never be essentialized, and that the images of a reality reflected on screens are always only images. Genet's work was vilified by the far right, and considered by many to be subversive. An outsider in his early life as a criminal, and throughout his life as homosexual, he was championed by the intellectual left, who secured a presidential pardon from a sentence of life imprisonment for recurrent theft. The greatest tribute was *Sartre's major study, *Saint-Genet, Actor and Martyr* (1952), in which Genet's appropriation of the label of *villain is seen as an act of resistance and defiance. From the mid-1960s he virtually gave up writing but continued to lecture and support radical causes, including the Black Panthers and Palestinian liberation groups. Numerous companies and directors have returned to Genet's work, from the *Living Theatre's *Maids* (1965) and Víctor *García's *The Balcony* (1969) to *Chéreau's *Screens* and *Stein's *Blacks* (both 1983).   BRS

George, Mlle (**Marguerite-Joséphine Weimer**) (1787–1867) French actress. Born into an acting family, she came to the notice of Mlle *Raucourt, who secured her entry to the *Comédie-Française. Making her debut in 1802, she partnered *Talma in many of the classical roles for which her queenly beauty and regal manner fitted her; a different kind of partnership was her liaison with Napoleon. After a successful spell in Russia, followed by a further period at the

Comédie, she helped to ensure the success of some of the more *melodramatic plays of the *romantic repertory. As the mistress of Harel, who *managed the *Odéon and then the Porte-Saint-Martin theatres, she created the roles of Marguerite de Bourgogne in *Dumas *père*'s *Tour de Nesle* (1832) and the eponymous *heroines of *Hugo's *Lucrèce Borgia* and *Marie Tudor* (both 1833). Ending her career at the Comédie-Française, she gave her farewell performance as Rodogune in *Corneille's play of that name in 1853.   WDH

Gershwin, George (Jacob Gershvin) (1898–1937) and **Ira Gershwin (Israel Gershvin)** (1896–1983) American composer and American lyricist. Their early influences included Irving *Berlin, ragtime, and *Kern's Princess Theatre *musicals. In 1919 George wrote his first hit song, 'Swanee' (lyrics by Irving Caesar), and his first Broadway score, *La La Lucille* (lyrics by Howard Jackson and Buddy DeSylva). Up to 1924 Ira wrote lyrics under the pseudonym Arthur Francis, but subsequently he worked under his own name and almost exclusively with George.

Their first hit show, *Lady, Be Good* (1924), carried forward Kern's witty style and infused it with a solid jazz feel and snappy, conversational lyrics. Gershwin musicals up to 1930, including *TipToes* (1925), *Oh, Kay!* (1926), *Funny Face* (1927), and *Girl Crazy* (1930), showcased major stars including *Astaire, *Merman, and Gertrude *Lawrence. When the Great Depression arrived, the frivolous musical comedies of the 1920s lost much of their appeal. The Gershwins responded with *Strike up the Band* (1930), an anti-war *satire, and *Of Thee I Sing* (1931), a political spoof that won the Pulitzer Prize. Its integration of *music, song, and *dialogue revealed a sophistication of technique and content then rare on Broadway. The sequel, *Let 'Em Eat Cake* (1933), had an even stronger satiric tone. The Gershwins' theatrical career culminated in the ambitious *Porgy and Bess* (1935), an *opera based on Dubose Heyward's short novel *Porgy*, set in a black neighbourhood in Charleston.

George's untimely death cut short one of the century's great musical talents. No other American composer more successfully straddled the worlds of 'serious' and popular music or more completely embodied the spirit of the Jazz Age. From *cabaret to the world's concert halls, the Gershwins made American popular music the world's popular music. Ira went on to write lyrics with Kern, *Weill, *Arlen, and others. The last show on which he worked, *My One and Only* (1983) ran for 762 performances.   SN

Ghelderode, Michel de (Ademar Martens) (1898–1962) Belgian playwright. Though he wrote in French, Ghelderode's work is markedly Flemish in spirit, characterized by a combination of popular, folkloric, fantastic, and strongly visual elements. His early work did not appeal to French-speaking *audiences but matched the style of the Vlaamse Volkstoneel, the popular Flemish company with a highly *expressionist code. Ghelderode's plays written for the company include *Pictures from the Life of St Francis* (1927), a *burlesque spectacle; *Escurial* (1927), in which the Spanish sovereign and his Flemish *fool exchange roles; and *Barrabas* (1928), a *Passion play seen from the point of view of an anarchist. Of particular interest is *Pantagleize* (1929), whose eponymous (anti-)*hero becomes unknowingly involved in a revolution and is executed. Ghelderode considered *Mademoiselle Jaïre* (1934) his most characteristic work, a quasi-*mystery play in which a young girl is resuscitated from death but continues to long for the other world. It was not until the late 1940s and early 1950s that Ghelderode's work was discovered in France. The postwar *avant-garde recognized him as a kindred spirit, sharing elements with the theatres of the *absurd and *cruelty.   JDV

Ghosh, Girish Chandra (1844–1912) Bengali *actor-manager and dramatist, the father of Bengali theatre, who established the idiom for the Bengali stage by combining spectacular entertainment and stylized declamatory acting, equally influenced by folk and Western models. The author of approximately 80 plays, Ghosh tried his hand at many genres: mythological, historical, social, nationalistic, *musical, and comic. Many of the mythological works, like *Bilwamangal Thakur* (1886), proved commercially successful, but critics rank the social *melodrama *Praphulla* (1889) as his best. In the final decade of his life, some of his patriotic plays, all of which did well at the box office, brought him into conflict with the British administration, who banned *Sirajuddaula* (1905), about the last nawab of Bengal. Ghosh also translated or adapted classics by Shakespeare and *Molière.   AL

ghost Stage figure of *revenge tragedy, who predicts or demands retribution for a past wrong. Rare in *Greek *tragedy, the figure was firmly established by *Seneca, whose bloodthirsty shades were models for *early modern dramatists, especially in Italy. Brilliantly exploited by Shakespeare in *Hamlet*, the figure was a staple of Jacobean tragedy as well.   RWV

Giacometti, Paolo (1816–82) Italian playwright. Influenced by *romanticism, Giacometti believed in a national, popular theatre with humanitarian and educational goals. From 1848 to 1852 he was resident poet of Turin's prestigious Reale Sarda Company. Thereafter his works—numbering over 80, many of them *melodramatic historical dramas—served as vehicles for prominent *actor-managers (*Bellotti-Bon, *Ristori, *Salvini, *Zacconi). *La Morte civile* (1861), considered his finest problem play, addresses the theme of divorce when the husband is a convicted murderer. It afforded actors the opportunity to horrify *audiences with *realistic portrayals of a man suffering the agonies of suicide by poison. JEH

Giacosa, Giuseppe (1847–1906) Italian dramatist and librettist. Best known as the librettist, with Luigi Illica, of *Puccini's *operas *La Bohème* (1896), *Tosca* (1900), and *Madama Butterfly* (1904), Giacosa also enjoyed significant success as a dramatist of 32 plays. His early plays, including the popular *Game of Chess* (1871) and *Triumph of Love* (1872), are late *romantic works with poetic charm but little dramatic vigour. After several historical dramas and light *comedies, Giacosa came under the influence of *realism in the work of *Ibsen, *Zola, and *Becque. His finest verismo dramas are *Unhappy Love* (1889), a tense and tautly structured play on an adulterous triangle, and *Like Falling Leaves* (1900), in which a rich family falls upon hard times. SJCW

Gide, André (1869–1951) French writer whose plays had less critical success than his other works, but paved the way for *Camus and *Sartre through an original style with little connection to *symbolist, *neoclassical, or *naturalist theatre. Thoughtful and ambiguous, they lack climactic plots and emphasize ideas over *action. *Saul* (produced 1922, written 1903) concerns a love triangle among King Saul, David, and Jonathan. In *The Return of the Prodigal Son* (1928; written 1907), the prodigal persuades his brother to run away with him. *Oedipe* (1932) changes *Sophocles' play to a battle between individuality and submission to religious authority. Gide translated *Antony and Cleopatra* (1920), and his *Hamlet* (1946) opened the *Renaud-*Barrault company's first season. He also wrote an adaptation of Kafka's *The Trial* for Barrault. Other plays include *Philoctète* (1919), *Persephone* (1934; later a Stravinsky *opera, 1950), and *Robert; or, The General Interest* (1946). FL

Giehse, Therese (1898–1975) German actress. Born in Munich, Giehse balanced throughout her career the popular Bavarian with the intellec-

tual *Brechtian tradition. Forced into exile by the Nazis, she emigrated to Zurich where she founded a political *cabaret and played the original Mother Courage (1941), a role she repeated in a number of productions. She joined Brecht at the *Berliner Ensemble from 1949 to 1952, and thereafter divided her time between Zurich and Munich. Her last major role was in *Stein's production of Brecht's *The Mother* (1970), a living link with the Brechtian tradition that the *Schaubühne endeavoured to demonstrate in its inaugural production. CBB

Gielgud, John (1904–2000) English actor and director. Longevity as well as achievement made Gielgud into the icon of traditional values in English *acting in the twentieth century. But his respect for the text and for the skills he epitomized often overshadowed critics' understanding of the quirky brilliance of his performances, his fascination with new forms of theatre, and his surprising ability to remake himself to suit successive models of performance. Gielgud came from the *Terry family: Ellen *Terry was his great-aunt. By 1924 he was playing leading roles in London, including Romeo (the first of four times) but also in *Ibsen, *Chekhov, and *Shaw. With his Richard II (1929) and Hamlet (1930, a role he would play in over 500 performances in six different productions up to 1946), he was established as the greatest lyric actor of his generation, his voice praised for its musicality and its romantic potency. Above all, he spoke with an overwhelming awareness of the verse line, rejecting *naturalism in delivery while never losing sight of his *characters' reality. Gielgud also proved himself the consummate master of classical *comedy in *Congreve, *Sheridan, and especially as John Worthing in *The Importance of Being Earnest* (1930, 1939, 1942, 1947).

In the 1930s he used his prestige as an actor to become a director, working frequently with the three then unknown designers who formed *Motley to find a new style for Shakespeare production that used permanent sets to bring speed to the flow of scenes. At the New Theatre (1934–7) and the Queen's Theatre (1937–8) in London, Gielgud found a new *managerial style, creating a genuine ensemble of superb actors to explore the classical repertory, a combination of what he sought in Shakespeare and had learned from Chekhov. His own performances continued to gain almost unstinting praise, especially as Richard in Daviot's *Richard of Bordeaux* (1932), which made him even more of a popular star. His roles included Shylock, Romeo, Mercutio (when *Olivier took over as Romeo), an icily manipulative Joseph Surface in *Sheridan's *School for Scandal*, and Benedick in *Much Ado About Nothing*, often playing opposite *Ashcroft.

The first years after the war were difficult. Gielgud was less admired than *Richardson and Olivier, but in 1950 his work at Stratford, including Angelo (his first role for *Brook), Cassius, and Leontes, showed how his understanding of a role—especially when encouraged by a great director—could lead to simplicity and shocking power in exploring neurotic emotions. He was knighted in the coronation honours list of 1953 (and arrested the same year for homosexual importuning) but his career seemed to have lost direction. In 1957 he began ten years of *touring a one-person Shakespeare show, *The Ages of Man*, which was admired but also seemed irrelevant to English theatre culture.

In Brook's production of *Seneca's *Oedipus* for the *National Theatre in 1968, Gielgud looked like a relic from a lost theatrical world; yet his fear of Brook's new methods was balanced by his awareness of how necessary it was for him to work in a radically different kind of theatre. As the Headmaster in *Bennett's *Forty Years On* (1968), Harry in *Storey's *Home* (1970), Shakespeare in *Bond's *Bingo* (1974), and Spooner in *Pinter's *No Man's Land* (1975), Gielgud showed an unexpected sympathy for new forms of drama and wholly new ranges in his own performance style. He played Prospero in 1974, looking deliberately and remarkably like Shakespeare, and Caesar in 1977, but, barring a brief return to the West End in 1988, he left the stage. He had often acted in films but in his last years he appeared in an inordinate number (100 from 1970 until his death), gaining an Academy award for his very English butler in *Arthur* (1981). In 1991 he played Prospero again, over 60 years after his first *Tempest*, in Peter Greenaway's film *Prospero's Books*, where he spoke all the parts and became explicitly the playwright and director as well. In this merging of roles and unique act of ventriloquism, Gielgud became the embodiment of Shakespearian theatre, the centre of tradition in an experimental film (and brave enough to be naked on screen at 86). He was made a Companion of Honour in 1977 and appointed to the Order of Merit in 1996 but perhaps the most significant honour was that London's Globe Theatre, where he had often performed, was renamed the Gielgud Theatre in 1994. Of his six books and memoirs, *Early Stages* (1939), *Stage Directions* (1963), and *An Actor and his Time* (1979) are notable.   PDH

gigaku An ancient Japanese genre of *masked *dance, pantomime, and music, of a comic and often erotic nature, also sometimes known as *kuregaku* or in ancient times as *kure no utamai* (dance-music from Wu). Though originally a Chinese art, *gigaku* was transmitted to Japan from Korea. According to the *Nihon shoki*, in AD 612 Mimashi of Paekche (Korea), who had studied *gigaku* in Wu, emigrated to Japan and taught this art to young people there (*See* KIAK). A large number of painted wooden *gigaku* masks, most dating from the Nara Period (710–84), are preserved at the Hōryūji and Tōdaiji temples and the imperial treasure house (Shōsōin), all in Nara. Many of these masks depict semi-mythical beasts, legendary warriors or kings, gods, or other *stock figures. Nara-period *gigaku* dancing was accompanied on hand gongs, hip-drums, and flutes; later cymbals apparently replaced the hand gongs. After the thirteenth century, *gigaku* declined rapidly in popularity, becoming more or less extinct in the following centuries. *Gigaku* masks may, however, have influenced the development of the *nō mask.   GG

Gilbert, W. S. (William Schwenck) (1836–1911) English playwright and librettist. Gilbert began as a barrister in 1863, but found it more interesting and profitable to write verse for comic periodicals like *Fun* and *burlesques for the stage. By 1869 Gilbert had begun a series of 'fairy' *comedies, including *The Palace of Truth* (1870) and *The Wicked World* (1873). His best comedy, *Engaged* (1877), is a revolutionary and anti-idealistic play in which his irony deals destructively with Victorian stage icons: romantic love, friendship, filial and paternal affection. By 1877 Gilbert was well embarked upon his collaboration with Arthur *Sullivan, leading to their business partnership with the impresario Richard D'Oyly Carte. Thirteen works, representing collectively the very best of English comic opera (*see* OPERETTA), were the fruit of this collaboration, of which the first, *Thespis* (1871), is now lost. The last eight were produced at the Savoy Theatre. The collaboration was busy and fruitful; the list comprises *The Sorcerer* (1877), *HMS Pinafore* (1878), *The Pirates of Penzance* (1879), *Patience* (1881), *Iolanthe* (1882), *Princess Ida* (1884), *The Mikado* (1885), *Ruddigore* (1887), *The Yeomen of the Guard* (1888), *The Gondoliers* (1889), *Utopia Limited* (1893), and *The Grand Duke* (1896). Gilbert's wit is playful, but also mocking; his somewhat bilious view of mankind and his satirical fantasies are transformed by Sullivan's music into something softer, kinder, more charming, and remain the mainstay of amateur operatic societies all over the English-speaking world.   MRB

Gill, Peter (1939–) Welsh director and playwright, who established his reputation with productions in 1968 of three little-staged *Lawrence plays at the *Royal Court Theatre, where he had acted since 1959. The Court premièred two of his plays in 1969, *The Sleepers' Den* and *Over Gardens Out*, and in 1976 *Small Change*, which captured the textures of everyday life with impressionistic lyrical grace. He left to run the Riverside Studios in 1977, directing productions of *Chekhov's *Cherry Orchard* (1978), *Middleton and *Rowley's *The Changeling* (1978), and *Measure for Measure* (1979). Peter *Hall made him associate director at the *National Theatre (1980–97), where he was founder director of the Theatre Studio (Cottesloe). At the National he continued to champion new writing, with a notable season in 1985, and to stage impressive productions such as *Turgenev's *A Month in the Country* (1981) and Büchner's *Danton's Death* (1983). He later directed his own *Cardiff East* (1997), *Friendly Fire* (1999, *youth theatre), and revived *Small Change* (2008). BRK

Gillette, William Hooker (1853–1937) American actor and playwright. His first acting and writing success came when he took the lead in his own play, *The Professor* (1881). Subsequently his original plays provided him with a series of notable parts: Blane in *Held by the Enemy* (1886), Billings in *Too Much Johnson* (1894), and Thorne/Dumont in his Civil War spy *melodrama *Secret Service* (1895). His signature role, one he played more than 1,000 times over 30 years, came from his adaptation of Arthur Conan Doyle's stories as *Sherlock Holmes* (1899). His impersonation of the famous detective defined the *character for generations of American and English theatregoers. When his own writing no longer found public favour, Gillette still enjoyed acting success in many plays, including *Barrie's *The Admirable Crichton* (1903) and *Dear Brutus* (1918). While limited in range, Gillette perfected a cool, detached *acting style that perfectly matched the characters he assumed. GAR

Gilpin, Charles (1878–1930) *African-American actor who originated the title role of *O'Neill's *The Emperor Jones* (1920). A founding member of the Pekin Company and the Lafayette Players, to sustain his career he took a series of ordinary jobs. He came to attention on Broadway as the minister in John Drinkwater's *Abraham Lincoln* (1919), and was cast in O'Neill's play the following year. O'Neill considered Gilpin a brilliant actor, one of the best to appear in his plays. But when Gilpin objected to some of the lines he changed them in performance, part of the reason why *Robeson

was chosen to replace him later, on stage and in the film (1933). Gilpin suffered from racial prejudice and the difficulty of sudden fame, and he drank his career away. BBL

Giraldi, Giovan Battista ('Cinthio') (1504–73) Ferrarese humanist, author, and dramatist. The plots of his short stories, or *Hecatommithi* (1565), became an important source for European drama and literature, including Shakespeare. More significantly, Giraldi's *Orbecche* was the first original classical-style *tragedy performed in Italy, in 1541: its plot was related to Boccaccio's *Decameron*, but its theatrical inspiration was the bloodthirsty tragedies of *Seneca. After two more plays, Giraldi began to put theoretical ideas on paper, and his *Discourses on Composing Romances, Comedies, and Tragedies*... was published in 1554. In this work, and in most of his nine tragedies, he struck a balance between *Aristotelian precepts and real contemporary demands. His most striking decision was that the ferocious Senecan *catastrophe should be replaced by something more emotionally and morally satisfying; so his plays after *Orbecche* are 'tragedies with happy endings', in which virtuous *heroes and heroines, although severely threatened, emerge unscathed, and lurid punishments are reserved for the *villains who deserve them. In this way Giraldi reconciled classical *catharsis with Christian poetic justice and paved the way for the genre later designated as *tragicomedy. RAA

Giraudoux, Jean (1882–1944) French writer. A career diplomat until 1940, Giraudoux published short stories and novels in his spare time, turned to theatre when 46, and became the leading French dramatist between 1928 and the Second World War. This was largely due to his collaboration with *Jouvet, who reworked and cut the plays extensively in *rehearsal, and staged them inventively in fashionable Paris theatres with leading actors and little or no subsidy. Giraudoux was essentially a literary dramatist, with a distinctive, subtle, poetic style; his *characters use complete sentences, long speeches, and *monologues, and his success depended on a regular *audience of well-educated, middle-class Parisians. In his first play, *Siegfried* (1928), the *protagonist is a French soldier who lost his memory and was re-educated as a German, reflecting Giraudoux's recurring preoccupation with relations between the two countries, shown most clearly and pessimistically in the debates on war in his greatest success *La Guerre de Troie n'aura pas lieu* (translated by *Fry as *Tiger at the Gates*, 1935).

Other plays treat twentieth-century preoccupations through Greek myth (*Amphitryon 38*, 1929; *Électre*, 1937) or biblical sources (*Judith*, 1931); *Intermezzo* (1933) has a lighter and more fairytale atmosphere; and the posthumous *The Madwoman of Chaillot* (1945) is a whimsical attack on capitalism. *L'Impromptu de Paris* (1937), in the tradition of Molière, shows Jouvet and his leading actor Pierre Renoir discussing the function of the theatre, and paradoxically deciding that a play should appeal to the senses and imagination of the audience rather than to its understanding. Giraudoux's plays were frequently produced in London until the 1950s, but fashion has moved against them. EEC

gladiatorial contests Gladiatorial displays originated at aristocratic funerals at Rome in the third century BC to honour the deceased. The funerary context persisted throughout the republic, but politicians began to exploit this practice as an opportunity to buy popularity by staging memorial games in honour of relatives some years dead. The first such opportunist was Julius Caesar; as aedile in 65 BC he staged a gladiatorial show (*munus*, or *munera* in the plural) in honour of his father, who had died twenty years previously. The transition from memorial to entertainment was completed by Caesar's heir Augustus. As Rome's first *princeps* (emperor) he established the *munus legitimum*, combining beast-hunts or *animal fights (venationes) and *munus*. To keep potential rivals from cultivating popularity by staging *munera* he passed legislation requiring the Senate to authorize each *munus* and limiting sponsors to two *munera* annually. The imperial cult that he established was staffed in every municipality by priests who were responsible for staging gladiatorial displays on the Emperor's birthday. Gladiators originally competed in the local forum, which continued to be used ad hoc in communities where no *amphitheatre was ever built. Amphitheatres are largely confined to the west; in the east, Greek theatres and stadiums were usually adapted for gladiatorial shows and beast-hunts.

Gladiators were trained combatants comprising two broad categories: slaves, and freeborn persons who had sworn to subject themselves to physical coercion, thereby acknowledging a servile relationship with their owner/trainer (*lanista*). Freeborn gladiators forfeited their social status and were technically *infamis* (unspeakable); in exchange they received a cash payment. Gladiators were highly trained and well fed. They fought in numerous distinctive styles characterized by special equipment that may originally have been as-

sociated with specific ethnic groups. Most wore helmets and heavy armour. Opponents might fight in the same style, or else advantages and disadvantages might be balanced in a mixed pair. One example of such pairing was the contest between the *retiarius* (netter) and the *murmillo* (sporting the emblem of a fish on his helmet). The *retiarius* was fast but vulnerable, unprotected except for a shoulder-guard and equipped with a net, trident, and dagger. The *murmillo* was heavily armed, hence well protected but encumbered. The different styles attracted loyal supporters. The capacity to fight in more than one style was a prized accomplishment. Female gladiators are occasionally attested.

A *lanista* might put on a show himself and charge admission. More often he rented gladiators to a magistrate sponsoring a gladiatorial show, or a private individual commemorating a deceased relative. The number of pairs was advertised in advance, and sponsors often recorded in their epitaphs how many they had displayed. In small communities in Italy and the provinces as few as three or four pairs might fight on a single occasion. At Rome under Augustus (27 BC–AD 14) the Senate passed legislation making 60 pairs the limit for one *munus*, although Augustus himself displayed 10,000 pairs in eight *munera*. The pairs fought separately. An umpire presided over the fight, a band supplied musical accompaniment, and spectators chanted slogans. Though a contest often ended in unambiguous victory or defeat for the participants, gladiators were seldom killed in combat. A defeated party could appeal for a reprieve, and spectators indicated their verdict by gesturing with the thumb. In the case of a draw, both opponents were declared 'reprieved standing'. Gladiatorial schools recorded the performance of individual gladiators, and these details reappear in gladiators' epitaphs commissioned by their relatives or fellow gladiators. Gladiatorial combat survived the advent of Christianity and did not cease until early in the fifth century. KMC

Glaspell, Susan (1876–1948) American playwright. Spending the summer of 1915 with a group of artists, writers, and political radicals in Provincetown, Massachusetts, Glaspell and her poet husband George Cram Cook staged *Suppressed Desires*, their short *comedy on the fad for Freudianism. Glaspell's *Trifles*, a deftly structured short play in which two women cooperate in concealing evidence to assist an absent woman, was one of eight works staged the second summer, when the group formalized as the *Provincetown Players. Soon beginning a winter operation in Greenwich Village, the Players would stage nine more Glaspell plays, including the full-length works *Bernice* (1919), *Inheritors* (1921), and *The Verge* (1921). Glaspell and Cook moved to Greece in 1922, where she returned to fiction writing, but experienced a period of low creativity after Cook's death in 1924. She won the Pulitzer Prize for her last play, *Alison's House* (1930), but *Trifles* has been most widely produced and *The Verge*, which uses *expressionist and *symbolist techniques, rediscovered as formally innovative.   MAF

Glass, Philip (1937–) American composer. His encounter with non-Western *music in Paris led him to renounce his previous efforts in favour of minimalist composition. In 1970 Glass co-founded *Mabou Mines, an *avant-garde performance *collective that included *Akalaitis and *Breuer, sparking a series of collaborations with performing artists in theatre, *dance, *opera, film, and *performance art. Glass is probably most famous for his work with Robert *Wilson. *Einstein on the Beach* (1976), a four-hour opera that combines the trance-inducing repetition of musical phrases with Wilson's non-narrative collage of texts and dream imagery, is a landmark of twentieth-century performance. Other notable musical-theatre creations with Wilson include *White Raven* (1991), *the CIVIL warS* (1994), *Monsters of Grace* (1997), and an adaptation of *Büchner's *Woyzeck* (2001). Glass has also written music for choreographers Twyla Tharp and Susan Marshall.   JAB

Globe Theatre Shakespeare's Globe was a second-best option as a *playhouse. Its builders, the brothers Cuthbert and Richard *Burbage, lacked enough money to complete it, since their inheritance from their father James *Burbage was locked up in the Blackfriars, which they could not use. In 1599 they had the *Theatre, their former playhouse, dismantled and took its timbers for the new theatre, cutting in five of the players in the company, the *Chamberlain's Men, to help finance the construction. In the next ten years, staging Shakespeare's new plays along with his existing repertoire, the Globe became the most celebrated playhouse in London. In 1608 the Burbages retrieved the Blackfriars for winter use. In 1613 the first Globe burned down, thanks to a smouldering wad from a cannon which lodged in the thatch roofing the galleries. The company rebuilt it more lavishly than before, this time with a tiled roof, on the same foundations. It continued to serve the King's Men (as they were now called) as a summer playhouse until all the theatres were

closed in 1642. In 1644 the second Globe was pulled down to make way for tenement housing.

In 1970 Sam *Wanamaker, an American actor, conceived the idea of rebuilding the Globe in Southwark. His first concept was a modern structure, with a glass roof, electric light, and other conveniences, on the original site. He soon saw the value of constructing as exact a replica of the first Globe as scholarship could devise, in order to replicate the conditions in which Shakespeare and his fellows performed. Using the original site proved impossible, since it would have destroyed the original foundations, some of which were excavated nineteen years later. A site alongside the Thames was secured from Southwark Council, and building commenced in 1986. The discovery of sections of first the *Rose and then the Globe by archaeologists in 1989 caused some modifications to the design, which was completed in 1997 and became an extremely popular attraction under the *artistic direction of Mark *Rylance.   AJG

Głowacki, Janusz (1938–) Polish writer. A student of *Kott's in Warsaw, Głowacki worked for important film directors including *Wajda. *Adultery Punished* (1971) began his playwriting career. In London when martial law was imposed in Poland in 1981, he moved to New York. *Hunting Cockroaches* was produced *Off-Broadway (1984) and had a successful life in American *regional theatres. *Antigone in New York*, a version of Sophocles in which the *characters are immigrants from Puerto Rico, Poland, and Russia, had major productions in Washington and New York. His works were again published and produced in Poland after the changes of 1989; *Antigone in New York* opened in Warsaw in 1993, and soon was staged in six other theatres. Głowacki's other plays include *Cinderella* (1979), set in a girls' correction home, *Fortinbras Gets Drunk* (1986), a footnote to *Hamlet* full of political allusion, and *The Fourth Sister* (1999), an ironic continuation of *Chekhov. In general his work combines *realism with the grotesque, creating a dark but hilarious pastiche.   KB

Godber, John (1956–) English playwright and director. A Yorkshire miner's son, in 1984, after a string of award-winning *youth plays, he gave up teaching to run Hull Truck Theatre, a *touring company based in Hull. In 1993 he was the third most produced playwright in Britain. His first production at Hull Truck, the Olivier award-winning *Up 'n' Under*, typifies his style. The play is accessible to northern working-class oral culture, utilizes a small ensemble who play multiple *characters, has physical gags, and mocks the establishment. Other work includes *Bouncers* (1985), *Teechers* (1987), *Salt of the Earth* (1988), *On the Piste* (1990), and *Fly Me to the Moon* (2003). Godber's detractors—mainly from the south of England—claim that his plays are stereotypical and shallow, but he reached the *Guinness Book of Records* in 1982 when 47 amateur companies simultaneously performed *Happy Families*. Godber fuelled debate in 1998 when he said 80 per cent of theatre productions were tedious.   KN

Goering, Reinhard (1887–1936) German dramatist. An influential *expressionist, Goering turned his war experiences as a medical officer into a series of plays. Most successful was *Sea Battle* (1917) which depicts seven nameless sailors 'imprisoned' in the gun turret of a battleship. The form of verse *tragedy stands in strange contrast to the modern technological warfare represented—combat is heard but not seen. Goering was responding to reports of the battle of Skagerrak (1916) which took place without the ships ever sighting one another. The use of types rather than *characters, the interweaving of dream and reality, *action and vision, and the extensive use of *monologues all belong to the repertoire of expressionist technique. *Reinhardt's production (Berlin, 1917) was an important breakthrough for expressionist theatre. Goering's only other success was *Captain Scott's Expedition to the South Pole* (1930) directed by *Jessner. Both plays explore fate in a modern world.   CBB

Goethe, Johann Wolfgang von (1749–1832) The major literary figure in the German language, who was also a scientist, director, and court official. Influenced by *Lessing's admiration for Shakespeare, he became a leading exponent of *Sturm und Drang, notably in *Götz von Berlichingen* (1773), a sprawling play in prose about a medieval knight in revolt against corrupt rulers. In 1775 he was invited to the court of Weimar, where he became involved with the flourishing amateur theatre, writing and directing plays and *Singspiele. In 1780 he was appointed privy counsellor and was ennobled two years later. By now he had left behind his wild youth and was committed to moderation and renunciation, not least because of his unconsummated love for Frau von Stein, the wife of a fellow courtier. Significantly, his *Iphigenia on Tauris* (1779) reveals the humanizing quality of a noble woman in a rewriting of *Euripides' play. There followed *Egmont* (1789), a prose *tragedy most familiar from Beethoven's overture. Egmont, a leader of the revolt by the Netherlands against Spanish misrule, is captured and executed mainly as a result of his blind conviction in his own invincibility.

In 1791 Goethe became director of the newly founded professional court theatre at *Weimar, where he undertook to reform the state of German theatre. Goethe introduced a respect for the text and worked with his actors as a disciplined ensemble in place of the self-indulgent attitudinizing he described in his novel *Wilhelm Meister's Apprenticeship* (1796). He trained his actors in the skills of verse speaking and had a painter's eye for pleasing visual arrangements. He insisted on careful *rehearsals, and demanded that actors be word-perfect in performance, unusual for the period. His *Rules for Actors* (1803) are full of pragmatic advice about good vocal delivery, verse speaking, positions on stage, gesture, and *costume. He treated his actors well, and they became accepted members of court society, a remarkable change from the common eighteenth-century perception of performers as vagabonds. Far from promoting his own work (performances of his plays represented only 7 per cent of the total repertoire), Goethe, together with a majority of lighter theatrical fare, presented Shakespeare, the *operas of *Mozart, and the great verse tragedies of *Schiller. In 1807 the court theatre staged Goethe's other major verse play, *Torquato Tasso*, dealing with the court poet at Ferrara finding himself torn between his creative passion and the demands of court life, similar to Goethe's experiences as a young arrival in Weimar.

The avoidance of the tragic is also at the core of Goethe's major drama, his reworking in two parts of the Faust legend. His *Faust*, more a long dramatic poem than a piece for the stage, was begun in 1773 and not completed until 1831. The core of the legend is retained: the learned doctor who, anxious to live life to the full, pledges his soul to Mephistopheles. In Part I he woos and impregnates an innocent young girl, Gretchen, and abandons her when she faces execution for the murder of her baby. In Part II his adventures range far wider, including a liaison with Helen of Troy. Finally, when Mephistopheles comes to claim Faust's soul, Faust is saved by the 'Eternal Womanly', with the angels declaring that 'Whoever strives endlessly can be saved.' Usually only Part I of *Faust* is performed, although *Reinhardt staged both parts (1909 and 1911). It was famously directed by *Gründgens, who also played Mephistopheles, throughout the 1930s and 1940s, and can now be read as a metaphor for Gründgens, like Faust, allying himself with the forces of Nazi evil. In 2000 Peter Stein directed both parts with success, with Bruno *Ganz as

Faust. In 1817, when the Duke's mistress insisted on having a performing dog in a court theatre production, Goethe resigned from his directorship. Though his dramas lack the theatricality of Schiller's plays, they remain a staple of the German repertoire.   MWP

Gogol, Nikolai (1809–52) Russian writer. Early success came with his short stories, eclipsing his first dramatic efforts. Gogol's theatrical reputation rests primarily on his masterpiece *The Government Inspector* (1836, with *Shchepkin as the Mayor), with *Marriage* (1842) a strong but lagging second. A final play, *The Gamblers* (1843), has not had the same success. His two major plays respond to Gogol's desire to create a national repertoire. *The Government Inspector* brought him notoriety, evoking wildly differing reactions. The play turns on the dignitaries of a small town mistaking the identity of a passing adventurer, Khlestakov, for a government inspector; its splendidly comic treatment of the serious theme of state corruption and oppression sets it apart from most other *satires. It also exploits *acting and the theatre as thematic metaphors, as Khlestakov creates and performs a fantasized version of himself and the officials perform ideal versions of themselves, but reveal their true personalities through exaggeration and corruption. *Marriage* comically satirizes the matchmaking market, but the twist is that the *hero Podkolyosin, disturbed by the concept of marriage itself, escapes betrothal by leaping through a window.

In these plays, as well as in his novel *Dead Souls* (1842), the inexplicable and the unexpected lurk just beneath the *comedy and social comment. Gogol's vitality as a dramatist was maintained in the Soviet period. *The Government Inspector* has attracted major directors and landmark productions, including those by *Meyerhold (1926) and *Tovstonogov (1972). *Efros's *Marriage* (1975), *Lyubimov's composite portrait of Gogol's work (*Inspectorate Fairy Tales*, 1978), various adaptations of *Dead Souls*, including the *Moscow Art Theatre's (1932) and another composite by Efros (*Road*, 1979), are signs of his continuing significance.   CM

Goldfaden, Abraham (Avrom Goldfadn) (1840–1908) Ukrainian dramatist and composer, considered the father of the modern Yiddish stage. Goldfaden mounted full-fledged *operettas, some of which—*The Witch* (1879), *The Two Kuni-Lemls* (1880), and *Shulamith* (1880)—became Jewish classics, with the names of their characters entering the Yiddish lexicon. He wrote, composed, directed, and designed his productions,

which by 1880 were *touring throughout Russia. But wandering troupes had little regard for *copyright laws, so that his popular plays and tunes were stolen and plagiarized and soon Goldfaden's work was the mainstay of numerous Yiddish companies. He came to New York in 1887, hoping to capitalize on his fame, but returned to Europe after a cold welcome. He was back again in America in 1903 but he never regained his earlier position. Goldfaden wrote about 60 *musical plays; his last work, the Zionist-inspired *Ben-Ami* (*Son of my People*), premièred in New York a few days before his death. *See* DIASPORA.   EN

Goldoni, Carlo (1707–93) Italian playwright. Goldoni was born in a Venice which had lost its empire and discovered a role as the Las Vegas of the age; the city had sixteen theatres when London had four. He was a sharp, critical observer, too genial to jeer but too intelligent to fail to chronicle and mock the vice, folly, and hypocrisy of his own time. Goldoni studied law and his work in theatre was interspersed with periods of practice as lawyer or prosecutor in several cities. In 1731 he fled to Milan to escape an unwished-for marriage, and there underwent the embarrassment of seeing his first theatrical work, a *melodramma* (a *musical drama in heroic style) entitled *Ammalasunta*, derided by actors and salon intellectuals for its failure to comply with the rules of *neoclassicism. He returned to the law in Pisa in 1745, although he wrote *The Venetian Twins* and *Servant of Two Masters* during this period, and was enticed back to Venice three years later, remaining there until, nauseated by the endless disputes with playwrights *Gozzi and Pietro Chiari, he moved to Paris and the *Comédie Italienne. His life there was made difficult by recalcitrant actors who abominated his reform programme. He wrote his *Memoirs*, dedicated to Louis XIV, in 1784 and died in poverty in Paris after the revolution.

Goldoni represents a kind of artist who emerged only in the eighteenth century, one who settled for the position of hired hand, producing goods as required by contract, not in accordance with the promptings of some nobleman or demiurge. Classical *heroes, subjects from myth or religion, were not for him; he preferred domestic or social themes. He produced around 150 *comedies as well as *melodrammi*, *tragedies, *tragicomedies, and *opera librettos. In 1750, for a wager, he turned out sixteen plays, including such masterpieces as *The Coffee House* and *The Liar*. His writing was designed for that evening's performance, not for posterity, and he adapted his work to meet public taste and the requirements of a contracted cast. Goldoni preferred *realist drama and had no truck with fantasy, but when the public taste demanded exotic work he turned his hand to *The Persian Woman* (1753) and *Ircana in Julfa* (1755). For all his surface bonhomie, there was a dark side to Goldoni, sometimes hidden by the reworking of his plays for publication, though brought to the surface for twentieth-century directors like *Strehler.

In Goldoni's years with the Imer company at San Samuele Theatre he grew dissatisfied with the restrictions placed on the writer by actor-dominated *commedia dell'arte*, and irritated by the virtuosity or coarseness and ribaldry to which the genre had declined. He achieved his reform in Sant'Angelo, with the Medebac company. The play *Il teatro comico* (1750) can be regarded as a manifesto for a multifaceted programme which involved conferring on the author that primacy in theatre, compelling the actors to learn parts rather than rely on *improvisation and the recall of standard situations, removing the *masks, and converting the *stock characters into individuals with a psychological structure of their own. The positive hero of his theatre was the industrious, morally irreproachable bourgeois, such as the coffee-house owner, or Mirandolina of the *Inn Keeper* (1752), and the butt of his humour often the socially redundant nobleman. The reform programme encountered the opposition of the *acting profession, and both his hostility to traditional Italian theatre and his allocation of the central role to bourgeois characters enraged Gozzi, who saw Goldoni as the proponent of Enlightenment ideas. But Goldoni was not an ideas playwright, and espoused no explicit programme. He consolidated his reforms with his output at Antonio Vendramin's San Luca (1753–62), where he staged such late works as *The Lovers* (1759), a dissection of love and jealousy worthy of *Chekhov, and *Il campiello* (1755) and *The Chioggia Quarrels* (1761), the only works in which working people feature. Work with the Comédie Italienne required him to abandon his reforms and return to *commedia* styles, but his reforms of Italian theatre endured.   JF

Goldsmith, Oliver (*c.*1730–1774) Irish writer. Educated at Trinity College, Dublin, he settled in London and became astonishingly prolific, turning out a continuous flow of journalism, biographies, and histories in an ineffectual struggle to order his ramshackle financial affairs. 'No man was more foolish when he had not a pen in his hand', commented *Johnson, 'or more wise when he had.' Goldsmith's major writings for the theatre are few in comparison to his prodigious out-

put: two plays and an essay. However, those two plays—*The Good Natur'd Man* (1768) and *She Stoops to Conquer* (1773)—and the essay 'A Comparison between Laughing and Sentimental Comedy' (1773) were to have a lasting influence on English theatre. '*Comedy', Goldsmith argued, 'should excite our *laughter by ridiculously exhibiting the Follies of the Lower Part of Mankind'; it should not, he insisted, 'expose the Virtues of Private Life' by making us applaud *characters with 'an abundance of Sentiment and Feeling'. *She Stoops to Conquer*, a comedy of confused class identities, puts this theory into practice. It was an immediate success when first staged at *Covent Garden, and has held the stage ever since.   ChM

Gombrowicz, Witold (1904–69) Polish novelist, playwright, and essayist. In 1939 he left Poland never to return, first for Argentina, then for France in 1964. Most of his work was banned in Poland until the 1980s. He attracted attention with his first play, *Ivona, Princess of Burgundy* (1938); *The Wedding* (1953) and *Operetta* (1968) followed. His novels include *Ferdydurke* (1937), *Trans-Atlantic* (1953), *Pornography* (1960), and *Cosmos* (1965). Gombrowicz wrote about the psychological, intellectual, social, and national structures and conventions that identify, shape, and limit individual freedom, emphasizing that what he called 'immaturity' is a source of beauty, curiosity, and rebellious energy. The plays have been widely translated and produced internationally.   KB

Gómez de Avellaneda, Gertrudis ('Tula') (1814–73) Spanish playwright, poet, and novelist. Born in Cuba, she emigrated to Spain and became that nation's best-known woman dramatist of the nineteenth century and a staunch defender of women writers as well. After the Madrid première of *Munio Alfonso* in 1844, she wrote fifteen other full-length plays that usually reflect *romantic motifs and focus on religious sentiment or conflict. Two of her greatest successes were the biblical drama *Saul* (1849), staged in lavish settings at the Teatro Español, and the pseudo-historical *Baltasar* (1858). A different side of her talent was revealed in the equally popular *The Daughter of the Flowers* (1852), a three-act verse *comedy that dealt more with middle-class social values than romantic passions.   MPH

Gómez-Peña, Guillermo (1955–) *Performance artist and cultural theorist. Born in Mexico City, he began working in the United States in 1978, and came to international attention in 1989 with his solo performance *Border Brujo*, a bilingual, narratively fractured piece in which he embodied various archetypal *characters associated with the US–Mexican border. His performance projects include poetic *monologues, interactive gallery installations that subvert the colonial format of the living diorama, experimental *opera, and large-scale *multimedia works for the *proscenium stage. Gómez-Peña's publications include *Warrior for Gringostroika* (1993), *The New World Border* (1996), and *Dangerous Border Crossers* (2000), as well as *The Temple of Confessions* (written with Roberto Sifuentes). Recipient of numerous awards, including a MacArthur Fellowship (1991) and an American Book award (1999), Gómez-Peña epitomizes the role of the artist as citizen diplomat and public intellectual, using performance as a tool to initiate dialogue on a range of issues, including immigration, global capitalism, and Anglo-American attitudes toward Latinos and indigenous peoples.   LW

Goncharova, Natalya (1881–1962) Russian/Soviet painter and designer. Her first significant works for the theatre were *scenography in 1914 for *Tairov's production of *Goldoni's *The Fan* at the Kamerny Theatre, and for *Diaghilev's production in Paris of *Le Coq d'or*. For the second she supplied sumptuous backdrops and *costumes in stylized colour combinations which drew on traditional peasant costume, handicrafts, and ornaments. She later produced plain designs in white and maroon for Stravinsky's *Les Noces* (Paris, 1923), with costumes based on the *dancers' own work clothes. Her designs for a refurbished production of *The Firebird* (1926), first seen in London, were in a style reminiscent of ancient Russian icons. Her association with the *Ballets Russes continued in Monte Carlo but she also worked in New York in 1933 and in London during the 1950s.   NW

González-Dávila, Jesús (1940–2000) Mexican playwright. Relentlessly pessimistic, González-Dávila's plays capture the sordid reality of a lost generation, as in his highly successful *Of the Street* (1987), which gives an unsentimental but sympathetic look at street urchins surviving in the underbelly of Mexico City. Many of his plays are pieced together with episodes that move the *characters from one seamy urban space to another. In other plays the dramatic world is claustrophobic, enclosing families and lovers in rooms with no exit except violence, such as the shabby hotel rooms and apartments of *A Delicious Garden* (1984) and *Amsterdam Boulevard* (1986).   KFN

Goodbody, Buzz (1946–75) English director. Goodbody (born Mary Ann) joined the *Royal Shakespeare Company in 1967 and became the first woman to direct for the company. A committed *feminist and communist, she worked with Theatregoround, the RSC's educational outreach programme, and did much to develop the studio venue the Other Place in Stratford. Her controversial 1970 *King John*, featuring Patrick *Stewart, was unashamedly political, *farcical, and irreverent, though her mainstage *As You Like It* (1973), which included rock songs and hippie *costumes, received a critical mauling. In 1974 Goodbody became *artistic director of the Other Place, where she directed *King Lear* (1974) and a modern-dress, fast-paced *Hamlet* (1975). Starring Ben Kingsley, *Hamlet* gained stunning reviews but Goodbody had committed suicide before it opened. Her influence on the RSC can be seen in the large number of Other Place Shakespeare productions in the years following her death, which successfully exploited the intimate space as her *Hamlet* had done.   EJS

Gordin, Jacob (1853–1909) Ukrainian Yiddish playwright. Immersed in Russian culture, Gordin arrived in New York in 1892 and was soon commissioned by Jacob *Adler to write *Siberia*, a *melodrama that marked the beginning of serious Yiddish drama. He wrote dynamic plays with strong parts for Yiddish stars, including Adler, David Kessler, Bertha Kalich, and Keni Liptzin. Much of his best-known work was inspired by Shakespeare, *Tolstoy and *Goethe, and focused on themes such as intergenerational conflict, the rights of women, and the pursuit of wealth. His plays—*The Jewish King Lear* (1892), *Mirele Efros* (1898), *God, Man and Devil* (1900), and *The Kreutzer Sonata* (1905)—have been revived, translated, and filmed. Gordin was instrumental in introducing a more *natural stage language and insisted on strict adherence to a playwright's text. *See* DIASPORA.   EN

Gordon, Ruth (1896–1985) American actress and playwright. After years of *touring in stock productions (often in the roles performed on Broadway by Helen *Hayes, with whom she was frequently compared), Gordon became a Broadway star when cast by *McClintic in Maxwell *Anderson's *Saturday's Children* (1927). In *They Shall Not Die* (1934), she shattered her usual type by playing a prostitute. She was invited by *Guthrie in 1936 to play Mrs Pinchwife in *The Country Wife* at London's *Old Vic, in a cast including Michael *Redgrave and Edith *Evans. Major roles followed in London and New York, including Nora in *A Doll's House* (1937) and Natasha in McClintic's 1942 production of *Three Sisters*. *Wilder adapted the role of Dolly Levi for her in *The Matchmaker*, an international success in 1954–5. Married to writer *Kanin in 1942, the pair wrote numerous plays and screenplays, including *Adam's Rib* (1949).   MAF

Gordone, Charles (1925–95) *African-American actor and playwright. His New York career began with *Climate of Eden* (1957). Two years later he played in *Genet's *The Blacks*, performing along with Maya Angelou, James Earl *Jones, and Cicely Tyson. He *managed the Vantage Theatre in Queens, and also worked in a Greenwich Village bar named Johnny Romero's, which became the setting of his play *No Place to Be Somebody*. Produced in 1969 at the *New York Shakespeare Festival, *No Place* was transferred to Broadway by Ashton Springer, a black producer, and became the first play by an African American to win the Pulitzer Prize. For the next seven years Gordone was occupied with national *tours, and in the 1980s he co-founded the American Stage in Berkeley, California.   BBL

Gorelik, Mordecai (1899–1990) American *scenographer and theorist. Born in Russia, Gorelik emigrated to New York with his parents and graduated from Pratt Institute in 1920, having studied with designers Serge Soudeikine, *Bel Geddes, and Robert Edmond *Jones. In contrast to the poetic interests of Jones or Jo *Mielziner, Gorelik showed the influence of *constructivism and *epic theatre. He called the production 'a machine-for-theatre'. His industrial, collage-like setting for *Processional* (*Theatre Guild, 1925), the sliding panels and wagon stage for the *Group Theatre's *Men in White* (1933), and the room suggestive of a boxing ring for the Group's *Golden Boy* (1937) typified Gorelik's technique. Exposed to *Brecht through reading and while designing *The Mother* in 1935, Gorelik's book *New Theatres for Old* (1940) introduced Brecht's theories into the United States.   MAF

Gorky, Maxim (Aleksei Peshkov) (1868–1936) Russian writer. Persuaded to write for the theatre by *Chekhov and *Nemirovich-Danchenko, the first two of his sixteen plays, *Philistines* and *The Lower Depths*, were staged by the *Moscow Art Theatre in successive seasons in 1902. *Philistines* is an attack on the capital-driven bourgeoisie, while in *The Lower Depths* Gorky portrayed the down-and-out inhabitants of a doss-house. Apart from political themes, his work treats the meaning of art, the status of women, the destructiveness of vengeance, and the dynamics of the family. Gorky wrote plays about different social groups: *Summerfolk* (St

Petersburg, 1904) and *Barbarians* (Riga, 1906) are about the intelligentsia; while *Enemies* (Berlin, 1907) is about the class struggle.

Exiled after his involvement with the 1905 Revolution, most of his later plays were written in Italy. A work about police corruption, *The Last Ones* (1908), was followed by *Eccentrics* (1910) and by two about the rapacity of the merchant class, *Vassa Zheleznova* (1910) and *The Zykovs* (1918), then another about the bankruptcy of the urban petty bourgeoisie, *Counterfeit Coin* (1913). Gorky returned to Russia under amnesty that year, but the comic treatment of political, verbal diarrhoea in the one-act *Workaholic Slovotekov* (1920) irritated the Party leaders, and he again went into exile in 1921, ostensibly for his health. To recapture the heroic spirit of the 1917 Revolution, in the late 1920s he wrote the masterly *Egor Bulychov and the Others* (Moscow, 1932), followed by *Dostigaev and the Others* (Leningrad, 1933). The antagonism of the early work was replaced by engagement with the new Bolshevik *hero. Gorky finally returned to Russia in 1933. Fêted as a master, engaged in the formulation of *socialist realism (1934), he remodelled *Enemies* and *Vassa Zheleznova* to fit the new requirements. He protected as many people as he seemed to betray by his closeness to Stalin, but it is almost certain he was poisoned on Stalin's orders.   CM

Gorostiza, Carlos (1920–) Argentinian playwright, novelist, and director. Gorostiza was a constant presence in Buenos Aires theatre for 50 years, from his early days as *puppeteer and independent theatre actor to his service as national Secretary of Culture (1983–5), and especially for his nearly 30 plays. Gorostiza's realistic theatre has evolved over the years, beginning with *The Bridge* (1949, heralding a national *realism on a par with US and European theatre), continuing with *Our Fellow Men* (1966), and finally the more theatricalized realism of *The Accompaniment* (1981) and *Aeroplanes* (1990).   JGJ

Gorostiza, Celestino (1904–67) Mexican playwright, director, and translator, a pivotal figure in the development of the modern professional stage. In 1932 Gorostiza created the Teatro de Orientación, which for three years was an energetic site of experimentation and renovation, mounting plays by established European playwrights and, more importantly, by contemporary Mexicans who did not have easy access to production. Gorostiza began by writing plays in the manner of *Cocteau and Lenormand, but is best remembered for *The Color of our Skin* (1952), a powerful, *realistic study of the subtle but destructive forces of racism in Mexico.   KFN

Gotanda, Philip Kan (1951-) American playwright. While working for North Beach Chinatown Legal Aid in San Francisco, Gotanda wrote his first play, *The Avocado Kid* (1980), a *musical inspired by the Japanese children's story 'Peach Boy', which premièred at East West Players, the first Asian-American theatre company. His second play, *A Song for a Nisei Fisherman* (1981), examines the life of a physician who is mentally damaged by the internment of Japanese Americans during the Second World War. Subsequent plays include *Bullet Headed Birds* (1981), *Dream of Kitamura* (1982), *American Tattoo* (1983), *The Wash* (1985), *Yankee Dawg You Die* (1988), *Fish Head Soup* (1991), *Day Standing on its Head* (1994), and *Ballad of Yachiyo* (1996). Throughout his career as filmmaker, director, and playwright Gotanda has remained steadfast in his attempts to provide sensitively written, realistic alternatives to the Asian stereotype. *See also* DIASPORA.   JSM

Gottsched, Johann Christoph (1700-66) German dramatist and critic. While professor of literature in Leipzig he formed a close acquaintance with Caroline *Neuber and her acting troupe in the 1730s. Together they vigorously opposed the improvisational practices and taste for low *comedy that characterized most German itinerant troupes. In his influential work *Critique of Poetry for the Germans* (1730) he laid down rules for drama based on French *neoclassical principles. His *tragedy *The Dying Cato* (1732) is an attempt to follow them and had some success when performed.   CBB

Gozzi, Carlo (1720-1806) Italian writer. Gozzi was born into the ancient Venetian aristocracy which Carlo *Goldoni, his lifelong adversary, satirized as a set of impecunious drones. Gozzi was author of many verses and pamphlets, mainly polemical in purpose, and from them he emerges as a bilious defender of the nobility, Church, and state against the encroachment of Enlightenment thought, and indeed as an opponent of reform of all types. He was every inch the patrician, dilettante man of letters, out of sympathy with the new breed of professional artist emerging in the proto-capitalist Venice of his day.

Gozzi made himself champion of *commedia dell'arte*, eviscerated by Goldoni's reform programme. It was a spirit of rivalry and bravado which drove him to compose the ten fables (1761-5) that were intended to restore traditional Italian drama to its pristine vigour. These fables represent a

world of fantasy, magic, and *illusion which stands at the opposite extreme from Goldoni's theatre of *realism and observation, but Gozzi incorporated into his fables, especially *The Beautiful Green Bird* (1765), his continuing struggle against the new philosophy. He had a role for the *stock characters of *commedia* alongside freshly created *characters, but he deluded himself over his ability, or willingness, to restore *improvisation to Italian *comedy and to undo Goldoni's reforms. His Pantaloon was the same wise counsellor who appeared in Goldoni's reformed theatre, not the lecherous goat of late *commedia*, and only the first play, *The Love of the Three Pomegranates* (1761) was written as a *commedia* script affording actors the old freedom to improvise *dialogue and *action. From *The Crow* (1761) onwards, Gozzi produced fully written scripts, including *The Stag King*, *The Serpent Woman* (both 1762), and *The Green Bird* (1765). *Turandot* (1762), a hauntingly exotic tale with elements of the misogyny which recurs in his work, remains his most powerfully imagined work (and the basis for *Puccini's *opera, 1926). Gozzi's taste for fantasy has attracted unexpected admirers from *Goethe to *Brecht, but it is no accident that his work has had most success when adapted for *ballet and opera.   JF

Grabbe, Christian Dietrich (1801-36) German dramatist. The author of historical dramas on a grand scale, Grabbe remained largely unperformed in his short lifetime. Works such as the two-play cycle *The Hohenstaufens* (1827), *Napoleon; or, The Hundred Days* (1831), and *Hannibal* (1835) focus on great military leaders and historical figures in an epic form that was considered unproduceable. In his fascination with the failure of great leaders Grabbe outlines a pessimistic view of history, occasioned by the restoration of the monarchy after 1815. *Don Juan und Faust* (1829), the only work he saw performed, explores the two figures as indicative of the principles sensuality and spirituality. Best known today is the *comedy *Joke, Satire, Irony, and Deeper Meaning* (1827) in which he takes issue with the literary pretensions of his fellow *romantic writers and the small-town provincialism he suffered. Grabbe's work became influential after 1900 when he was seen as a precursor of both *expressionist and *epic drama.   CBB

Graham, Martha (1894-1991) American dancer, choreographer, teacher, and company director. A pioneer of American modern *dance, she developed a technique of contraction and release that was angular and percussive, stressing the body's weight and giving in to gravity with falls to the floor. She taught at her own school and also for many years trained actors at the Neighborhood Playhouse in New York. Her choreography was dramatic and expressive, making use of modern literary and cinematic techniques such as flashbacks and interior *monologues. Graham frequently collaborated with Isamu Noguchi, whose stark, symbolic sculptures captured the essence of her dramas, and with American composers, including Aaron Copland. Though she choreographed for nearly 70 years, she is best known for her *Greek *tragedies of the 1940s, often told from the point of view of a sexually anguished mythical *heroine, such as Jocasta in *Night Journey* (1947), Graham's adaptation of the Oedipus story. SB

Gramatica, Emma (1872–1965) and **Irma Gramatica** (1867–1962) Italian actresses. Emma played Sirenetta in *D'Annunzio's *Gioconda* (1899), acted in top *touring companies with *Duse, *Ruggeri, and her sister Irma, and formed her own troupes. She helped introduce *Hauptmann, *Ibsen and *Shaw to Italy. Irma was a lyrical performer with an excellent voice, and made her name in the popular French repertory of the 1890s, especially in *Zola's *Nana* and *Thérèse Raquin*. She then became lead actress for *Zacconi and Virgilio Talli. In her vast repertory—Shakespeare, *Schiller, *Pinero, *Sardou, *Hauptmann, *Giacosa, *Praga, *Sudermann— she originated many roles, including Mila in D'Annunzio's *The Daughter of Jorio* (1904). JEH

Grand-Guignol, Théâtre de Paris *playhouse dedicated to portrayals of dread and torture. Oscar Méténier founded it in 1895; in 1899, under the direction of Max Maurey, it moved to a building that had been a convent (and kept its wooden angels). Aficionados claimed they heard ghosts of nuns moaning above the 285-seat theatre. At first *naturalist slices of life were interspersed with *comedies, but the genre changed to horror, especially under the direction of André de Lorde, known as the 'prince of terror'. He wrote over a hundred thrillers modelled upon the stories of his idol Edgar Allan Poe. Although de Lorde favoured psychological distress, he also wrote shockers with believable depictions of ripped skin, gouged eyeballs, burning flesh, and other disasters. Actors judged success by the number of spectators who fainted or vomited. Evenings began with a comic curtain raiser, showed two horror plays, and ended with a sex *farce. By the 1940s detective stories dominated the offerings, and in the 1950s *audiences found

the plays camp rather than chilling. The theatre closed in 1962. FL

Granville Barker, Harley *See* BARKER, HARLEY GRANVILLE.

Gray, John (1946–) Canadian playwright and composer. His best-known play, *Billy Bishop Goes to War* (1978, Broadway 1980), is a two-person *musical that examines the ambiguous attitudes of Canada's most famous flying ace of the First World War. Other major musicals include *18 Wheels* (1977), about long-distance truckers; *Rock and Roll* (1981), about a small-town Canadian rock band; and *Don Messer's Jubilee* (1985), about a one-time cultural icon of Gray's native Nova Scotia. Another musical, *Health* (1989), was not so well received. DWJ

Gray, Simon (James Holliday) (1936–2008) English playwright. Gray began an academic career in Vancouver and continued it in London while his writing career flourished. His plays frequently reflect the quixotic and sometimes exclusive worlds of academia and publishing, but nonetheless contain violent and abusive sexual relations, emotional betrayal, and complex relationships, often concerning men forced into destructive isolation by confused sexual identity or crippling shyness. In his first West End play, *Wise Child* (1976), the central *character is a transvestite, played by *Guinness. In *Butley* (1971), *Bates appeared as the savagely witty but appallingly self-destructive *hero, a university lecturer whose affair with a male student hastens the collapse of his sham marriage. *The Common Pursuit* (1984) follows a group of university friends over twenty years, ending with a reported suicide. *Melon* (1987) provided Bates with a complex role of a successful literary publisher in the face of psychological collapse, similar to his character in *Otherwise Engaged* (1975). *Quartermaine's Terms* (1981), with its *Chekhovian overtones, and the television play *After Pilkington* (1987), are perhaps Gray's most assured works of emotional regret, intellectual failure, and social alienation, poignant and acerbic accounts of educated England and the masculinities it restrains, excludes, and ultimately destroys. AS

Gray, Spalding (1941–2004) American actor and writer. Gray moved to New York in 1967 with his then-girlfriend, the director Elizabeth *LeCompte. His mother committed suicide that year, an event that became material for some of his and LeCompte's theatrical experiments with the *Wooster Group, which they formed in 1980 after having worked with the *Performance

Group. The Wooster Group created *Three Places in Rhode Island*, multi-*character pieces in which Gray played himself and used his own experiences as material. His best-known monologue is *Swimming to Cambodia* (1985), about acting in the film *The Killing Fields* (1984). When performing Gray sat behind a desk in street clothes with a notebook and seemed to talk quite casually, but his monologues were closely scripted and continually reworked over many years. His subsequent pieces charted his life in detail, including his experiences of writing a book (*Monster in a Box*, 1990), suffering illness (*Gray's Anatomy*, 1993), leaving his wife for another woman (*It's a Slippery Slope*, 1996), and fatherhood (*Morning, Noon, and Night*, 1999). He suffered severe injuries in a car accident in Ireland in 2001 and later committed suicide.   KF

Gray, Terence (1895–1986) Irish director and *manager. An avid experimental modernist, Gray evolved a system akin to building blocks for easily movable architectural scenic units. Acquiring a theatre, which he renamed the Cambridge Festival, he put his experimenting into practice (1926–33) in a series of iconoclastic productions, inspired by innovations. Gray proved how readily adaptable the *expressionist methods of *Jessner and *Fehling were to the repertoire of classics. He staged *Aeschylus, *Sophocles, *Aristophanes, *Terence, Shakespeare, *Wilde, *Yeats, *Shaw, *Strindberg, *Čapek, *Pirandello, and contemporary German and American political drama. Gray appreciated that expressionist stagecraft required significant changes to *lighting design, and that the resulting style necessitated changes in actors' modes of delivery, stance, and movement too. To meet this last need, Gray brought in his cousin Ninette de Valois as movement director, offering her in return a stage for her choreography. Gray's remarkable achievements were possible because of his predominantly Cambridge undergraduate *audiences.   RAC

Greek theatre, ancient *Aristotle argued for an *origin for drama in three genres of Dionysiac song and *dance: he derived *tragedy from 'those who led the *dithyramb' and from 'a *satyr-play like performance'; *comedy he derived from 'leaders of the phallic songs'. So far as we know drama in Classical Athens was performed only at festivals of the god Dionysus, but this was not true elsewhere or in later periods. Outside Athens, even in the fifth century, theatres were built in the sanctuaries, and dramas performed at festivals, of other gods. In later centuries drama's link with Dionysus appears still more tenuous. One might

then freely doubt that drama originated in exclusively Dionysiac *ritual, especially as *costumes, *masks, and mythological pageants are also attested for the cults of the goddesses Artemis and Demeter, and minor mystery gods, called the Cabeiri. But the evidence we possess shows that Aristotle's claim is in outline correct, if over-schematic. Drama's most immediate antecedent was ritual entertainments at festivals of Dionysus, and particularly those entertainments in which a *chorus interacted with a 'leader', singing refrains, to what, in origin, was probably improvised verse.

Archaic and Classical Greek theatre (508–317 BC) Ancient scholars claimed that one Thespis first performed a tragedy in Athens around 534 BC, during the reign of the tyrant Pisistratus. But the first certain evidence of drama comes from the earliest years of the Athenian democracy which ousted the Pisistratid tyranny in 508 BC. A fragmentary inscription (*Fasti*), thought to rely on official archives, begins a list of productions from this date. The end of the sixth century BC also saw the building of the first Theatre of Dionysus in the city and the earliest *deme* theatre (at Thorikos). Many scholars now think that, despite ancient tradition, drama was a creation of the Athenian democracy.

Clearly the democracy found theatre suited to its ends. The occasions for theatrical performance soon multiplied and spread through the territory of Athens (Attica). Originally, drama may have been performed only at the urban festival of Dionysus (City *Dionysia). From about 508 BC there were competitions for dithyramb and for tragedies (followed by satyr-plays). In about 486 BC a contest for comedy was added. A second major festival, the *Lenaea, assumed competitions for both tragedy and comedy in about 440 BC. At this time the larger village festivals (Rural Dionysia) began to incorporate dramatic competitions, and the Anthesteria added comedy by 326 BC. Before the collapse of the democracy in 322 BC, there were at least fourteen annual dramatic festivals in Attica, all crammed into the four winter months, some lasting several days.

One democratic (also Dionysiac) feature of the theatre was its inclusivity. The earliest Athenian theatre held perhaps 10,000 to 15,000 spectators, and, like later theatres, it constituted the largest place of assembly in the state. The figure represents only 3 to 5 per cent of the estimated total population of mid-fifth-century BC Athens, but indicates a spectatorship rivalled only by the athletic games of the large pan-Hellenic sanctuaries. Slaves, foreigners, and children were freely admitted in the *audience, and probably women (though their attendance is still debated).

A second democratic feature was drama's openness to citizen participation. By law membership in the dramatic chorus was restricted to Athenian citizens, though the Lenaea and lesser festivals admitted also resident foreigners (*metics*). Chorus members received maintenance and probably monetary compensation for the training period. The chorus was officially identified with the production and the competition was notionally for the best chorus. The chorus was the focal point of audience sympathy both in the drama and in the festival competition: in the narrative the chorus generally represented a group of ordinary citizens, relatively disempowered in contrast to the *characters played by the actors; in the theatre competition chorus members, insofar as they were ordinary citizen amateurs, were personally known to many in the audience. A great many in the audience had performed in choruses at some times in their lives—a very conservative estimate of the annual demand for dramatic chorus members in Athens by the later fourth century BC is 1,332, and probably closer to 6,000 if we include dithyramb (about 17 per cent of the estimated citizen male population, or indeed closer to 50 per cent of all eligible male citizens, since chorus duty was considered too strenuous for anyone over 30). This also helped make the chorus a focal point of audience identification. Public participation was also encouraged by the judging process. Although a panel of judges was selected from the audience, in the final instance by lottery, our sources make it clear that judges were expected to take audience reaction into account—we even hear of the people prosecuting judges at the Dionysia for 'incorrect judgement'. The notion that the audience determined the outcome of the competition was at least shared by the comic poets who make frequent appeals for audience support, and who eventually developed *claques to stimulate audience response. Athenian audiences were anything but passive. They drove many plays out of the theatre by prolonged clucking, heel banging, and whistlings.

A third democratic feature, mainly affecting comedy, was poetic outspokenness. *Old Comedy, and especially the comedy of the 'radical democracy' (430-405), freely abused politicians and prominent public figures, or was outspoken in its ridicule of social and political policy. The public encouraged such behaviour, and libel laws, prosecutions, and attempts at *censorship had little or no effect, not only because comedic licence was consistent with the licence of the Dionysiac festival, but because it conspicuously affirmed the rights of equality and free speech which were fundamental to the democracy.

A fourth democratic feature was strict *financial and administrative control of theatre by public officials. The chief responsibility was assumed by the 'Eponymous Archon', an ordinary citizen, selected by lot. In addition to general *management of the festival, the archon appointed sponsors (*choregi*), selected poets, and, by the later fifth century, made contracts with actors and probably pipers. The large scale of theatrical festivals at Athens required a complex mixture of private patronage, volunteer and paid labour, user fees, private enterprise, and public money. Wealthy elites were appointed by the archon to serve as *choregi*, which meant they were compelled to pay for the costuming, training, and maintenance of the chorus. In return they received a purely symbolic prize on behalf of the chorus, together with considerable prestige if they were successful. Private entrepreneurs called '*theatron*-sellers' bought contracts from the state to manage the theatres, and in particular to rebuild the wooden benches in the *theatron for each festival season. In return they received not inconsiderable entrance fees (charged for the first time at any religious festival in Greece). Since entrance fees excluded many poorer citizens, the public treasury distributed a 'festival-dole' (*theorikon*) to all citizens to defray entrance costs sometime between 450 and 343 BC. Public funds also went to sacrifices for the festival and fees and prizes for the professional performers.

Greek drama was not, however, uniquely Athenian nor inherently democratic (though it would certainly have appeared in a different form, if at all, in a less democratic age). Other cities claimed to be the birthplace of tragedy, comedy, and satyrplay. Moreover, an independent comic tradition developed in Syracuse in mainland Megara, and its colony, Sicilian Megara. Indeed, far from adapting Athenian drama, the influence seems to have run in the other direction: Aristotle claims that Athenian comic poets learned to 'write plots' from the Sicilian Epicharmus.

We have little evidence for the spread of theatre beyond Syracuse and Attica until the last decades of the fifth century BC, when the Macedonian tyrants Perdiccas and Archelaus collected dithyrambic and dramatic poets, including *Euripides, and instituted a dramatic festival. Artefacts or remains of theatres make drama probable for at least half a dozen other cities in southern Italy and mainland Greece. In the fourth century tragedy and comedy in the Attic style were disseminated rapidly through the Greek world. Within the first two decades an active trade in terracotta figurines of actors demonstrates interest in theatre from the Greek colonies on the Black Sea to as far away as North Africa and Spain. By the 370s BC poets and actors come from all parts of the Greek world. By 350 theatres in Greece were plentiful, and by 300 ubiquitous. Actors were adroitly employed as ambassadors and negotiators. Philip conspicuously cultivated theatre in order to assert Macedon's (otherwise dubious) place within Greek culture. Alexander punctuated his voyage of conquest across Asia by producing massive theatre festivals which attracted thousands of artists from all over the Greek world. His policy in doing so was to attract the attention of the refractory Greek states to his unbroken string of conquests, while at the same time advertising his growing empire as a triumph for 'Greek' (not 'Macedonian') culture. The theatre industry was indeed Alexander's principal beneficiary.

The large-scale economics of the theatre industry permitted a degree of specialization and professionalization never before seen in Greece. In the early fifth century most aspects of dramatic production were firmly in the control of the poet: he took the role of *music director, dance instructor, and even *actor, all functions which belonged to separate specializations by the fourth century. We are also told that in early drama the poet himself hired the actors and the piper. Official recognition of the importance of the acting profession comes first in about 449 BC with the creation of a tragic actor's prize independent of the success of the performance, and a decade later with the creation of both tragic and comic actors' prizes at the Lenaea.

From the 420s BC theatre artefacts indicate a shift in popular interest from a nearly exclusive focus upon the (volunteer) citizen chorus, to a nearly exclusive focus upon the (professional) actors and pipers. Theatre pipers began to achieve wealth, fame, and stardom by developing a new level of virtuosity and expanding the range and dexterity of their instrument through technical innovation. In the later 420s Euripides began to incorporate their more complex music into his tragedies and to transfer the burden of musical delivery from the amateur chorus to the professionally trained voice of the actor. Comic poets and elite philosophers condemned the more liberated, professional, emotional, and, frankly, more mercenary 'New Music' as decadence caused by mercenary interests catering to the tastes of vulgar audiences. The same sources indicate that actors too had begun to develop the power of their voice and gestures to reach much higher standards of mimetic *realism. The more popular the new styles in music and acting became, the

more vehemently elitist critics decried them as affronts to traditional tragic dignity and propriety.

With just such reactionary gloom Aristotle observed that actors in the fourth century were more important than poets. The rapid spread of theatre created the conditions for the emergence of professional superstars. Organizers were forced to advance huge deposits to encourage actors to appear at their festivals, and to levy huge fines when they failed to do so. Even the Athenian Dionysia might be passed by, as it was by the actor Athenodorus in 331 BC. By 341 BC star actors so completely determined the success of a performance that the archon was forced to require each team of actors to perform in one play of each competitor. Over the century the income of top actors rose from large to legendary: Theodorus, the most famous tragic actor of his day, was able to contribute four times more to the rebuilding of the temple of Apollo at Delphi than any other private individual; Neoptolemus could afford to give substantial monetary gifts to Athens in exchange for public honours; Aristodemus and Polus are said to have charged 'appearance fees' of a talent or five talents (roughly 6,000 to 30,000 times the average daily wage for even a skilled labourer). An inscription shows that Polus charged so much for an appearance that the medium-sized state of Samos, desperate in 306 BC to celebrate its new kings with due magnificence, heaped fulsome honours upon him when he agreed to accept reduced fees and deferred payment in exchange for all the box-office proceeds.

In 322 BC Antipater, the Macedonian viceroy, crushed a Greek revolt stirred up by the Athenian democracy. He exiled or disenfranchised the poorest Athenians and in 317 BC instituted an oligarchy under the regency of Demetrius of Phaleron. Demetrius abolished the festival dole and the choregic system. Drama was now organized, in the city, by an 'Arranger of Contests' (*agonothetes*), which probably brought the first professional choruses to the Athenian orchestra. Public participation came to an end. In the plays of *Menander (mostly after 317 BC) choral entertainments were mere entr'actes with no connection to the drama. Thus, while the drama of the democracy was a drama of symbolic inclusion focused on the chorus, *New Comedy sooner expressed the community's exclusion. Where once Old Comedy invited the world of the theatre into the drama (so often that some scholars reject the utility of the word *'illusion' altogether), New Comedy erected a 'fourth wall' that was rarely breached. Where once Old Comedy offered radical solutions to political problems, New Comedy's problems were private, deliberately trivialized, morality plays. Aristophanes' lower-class *heroes, whose triumphs over the establishment satisfied the wish-fulfilment fantasies of the powerless, were now replaced by Menander's naive, ironically distanced, well-meaning, upper-class heroes, all struggling to maintain their proper niche within a given social order.

Greek theatre after 317 BC The conquests of Alexander brought with them an immediate dissemination of theatre to all corners of his empire, where new theatres, along with gymnasia, could be regarded as one of the central elements of the Hellenization of non-Greek peoples. Only among some parts of the population of Judaea was there strong opposition to heavy-handed implementation of the new cultural policies. The dominance of the theatre was undoubtedly supported both by the creation of an educational system in which Greek Classical drama was studied and even acted, and also by the well-organized association of the *Artists of Dionysus; these had both close personal connections to the Hellenistic rulers, and the ability to staff the festivals that sprang up in the newly prosperous cities of Asia Minor, Syria, and Egypt, not only celebrating the old gods but also the new semi-divine members of the ruling families. Regrettably, we have almost no surviving evidence for these dramas after Menander. The programmes of these festivals, known to us from many victor lists and other inscriptions, show remarkable consistency in their dramatic components, following the fashion at Athens. Even at small festivals there could be prize competitions for the writers of new comedy, new tragedy, and sometimes even new satyr-play. The other division of drama, the performance of Classical plays, was undoubtedly more prestigious, as we can tell from the prizes awarded.

Before the first century BC there had been numerous Greek festivals in honour of Rome, and festivals for Roman generals were founded. As the Greek world under Augustus recovered from the ravages of Roman armies, cities and provinces naturally established formal worship of the emperors with attendant local and provincial festivals. These were celebrated by local magnates who had been appointed chief priests of the imperial cult, both in the east and west, and who helped to establish the hierarchy of empire and ties with Rome. Such festivals, therefore, some linked to older celebrations, soon become significant as a visible representation of Roman power, and as such were early distinguished by the additional appearance of Roman entertainments given in the name of the emperor. These consisted not only of the expensive Roman programme of *gladiators, *animal fights, and even judicial execution (**damnatio*), which were associated in the east only with the imperial cult, but also of mimes and *pantomime spectacles, which were especially popular in imperial Rome (see ROMAN THEATRE). But these mimes and dances were not prize competitions, and so they appear only very rarely in the programmes of regular Greek prize festivals after AD 170. Soon after AD 200 our real inscriptional evidence for imperial drama disappears, though mimes and pantomimes certainly continued for several centuries in the chief cities, especially Antioch, Alexandria, and Constantinople.

The actors of Greece were all free citizens, but their associations found it easy to adapt to the installation of the warlords who followed Alexander, whose pro-theatrical views they could only encourage. Greek Artists had assisted in Macedonian Amphipolis at the Greek festival with which Aemilius Paulus celebrated his Macedonian victories in 167 BC, and in Rome itself at the triumphal festivities of Anicius Gallus the next year. The adjustment to the arrival of the Romans was not without difficulty, and their headquarters in Athens was destroyed by Sulla in the siege of 86 BC. Nonetheless the Artists took care to have their privileges confirmed by Sulla soon after, and since the Emperor Claudius is known to have confirmed the privileges of the Artists, it is likely that earlier emperors had done the same, and assured their patronage (and perhaps eventually control) of the association. Claudius' successor Nero was certainly a strong supporter of Greek theatre, and under Hadrian there was a well-endowed chapter of the Artists in Rome itself. The fundamental difference between Rome and Greece is that acting for money on the public stage was never officially acceptable to Roman society, though private acting probably was. As a result the Greek Artists did not have a Latin-speaking branch, and festivals with programmes of the Greek type were very rare in the west save in the Greek areas of Africa and Gaul.

The influence of Greek Egypt was famously in scholarship and science, but almost certainly also in political mime and pantomime dance. Scurrilous nicknames for emperors, originating in Egypt, were soon known in Rome. The art of rhythmic handclapping (see APPLAUSE) came from Alexandria to Rome under Nero, and from there and Syria the great pantomimes arrived in Augustan Rome. From Alexandria too we have our most detailed description of the organization of theatre claques for the purposes of acclamations and even rioting, both of which played such an important role in

Rome itself. The Greeks of Alexandria chose the theatre to carry out publicly an ugly persecution of the Jewish minority. Obviously the Greek theatre continued to maintain its social significance, while its influence via Alexandria on Roman theatre behaviour must have been considerable.

Theatres had always been places for the people to see their leaders. The people soon learned to express their opinions not only of the performance but of these leaders by concerted rhythmic shouting and clapping. Theatre claques, or paid supporters of actors, which Greeks called choruses, are first known from *Plautus in c.200 BC, but must be earlier in Greece; soon afterwards the theatre was the place for any well-known figure to discover if he was popular or not. Naturally emperors and their officials sought to control these expressions, not always successfully, by placing soldiers and police in the theatre, but especially by their own claques, organized in quasi-military manner; Nero's numbered 4,000. The shouts of the theatre were formally noted from the beginning of the empire as a political statement, since indeed there was no other place for popular expression, just as the silversmiths of Ephesus protested in the theatre against the visit of St Paul (Acts of the Apostles 19), or the people of Antioch protested there against high taxes to the annoyance of the Emperor Julian. None of this was necessarily spontaneous, and we know that the main professional claque in Antioch in the third century AD was 300 strong, and did not respond even to emperors unless paid; in Christian Alexandria it was 500 in number. The repeated shouting was accompanied by complex handclapping and the waving of banners and clothing. The *agonothetes* of the Greek world expected to be applauded formally by the theatre crowd for their generosity, just as the victors in competition were for their skill.

Apart from some mime fragments, nothing of Greek drama from this period survives, and it may never have left the hands of the professional Artists. But inscriptions demonstrate that it was still performed after AD 200, and Classical drama continued to be studied in schools and performed privately for centuries afterwards. But a deconstruction of Classical tragedy into solos and choral works is also evident; these artists 'sing tragedy' in imperial times. As mime replaced comedy, so tragedy was replaced by danced pantomime, and its Greek artists called themselves not 'pantomimes' (that is, 'all-mimes') but 'actors of tragic rhythmic movement', which makes evident their claim to be cultural descendants of tragedy and the gymnasium. They 'danced tragedy', and they were by far the most popular artists of late an-

tiquity, becoming attached to the powerful circus factions of Constantinople. Thus Greek myth continued to maintain its cultural appeal even in the multicultural world of early Greek Christianity, while scenes from Menander's comedies decorating the living room floor of a fourth-century gentleman still served as a sign of antique taste. As Plutarch had said 200 years earlier, a dinner would be as incomplete without Menander as without wine.

Surviving texts Thanks to a continuous copying tradition, 44 ancient Greek plays survive virtually complete, including 32 tragedies, eleven comedies, and one satyr-play. Six of the tragedies are by Aeschylus, seven by *Sophocles, seventeen by Euripides, and two by unknown authors (*Prometheus Bound* and *Rhesus*, though attributed to Aeschylus and Euripides). The eleven comedies are by Aristophanes and the satyr-play (*Cyclops*) by Euripides. Drama is the best-represented Greek literary genre before the late fourth century BC, yet the remains constitute only 13 per cent of the total output of the four named dramatists, and a minuscule fraction of the drama performed at antiquity's major festivals.

Papyri and ancient quotations add fragments of about 2,000 plays and another 470 playwrights. The fragments vary in size from mere titles to nearly complete plays. They particularly enhance our knowledge of antiquity's two most popular playwrights: another sixteen Euripidean tragedies are represented by substantial fragments, while papyrus finds since 1896 have restored several large fragments of Menander, including one virtually complete comedy (*Dyscolus*), and extensive fragments of another six. The papyri also permit us to make reasoned judgements about the extent to which the Roman comic poets followed Greek models, and so add the evidence of 27 surviving Roman comedies to our information about Greek New Comedy. The comedies of *Plautus and *Terence adapt plays by at least six or seven Greek authors, all of the late fourth and early third centuries BC.

Papyrus fragments of some two dozen subliterary Greek mimes survive entirely by chance. But ancient selection had something to do with the survival of most other remains, leaving our knowledge of Greek dramatic literature spotty and uneven. Our texts and fragments come mainly from tragedies of 480–330 BC, and especially 430–405 BC, and from comedies of 430–388 and 317–263 BC. Because considerations other than quality or theatrical success sometimes played a determining role in the formation of the ancient canon, we cannot assume that our preserved texts are typical or representative of dramatic production in their respective periods.   EGC/WJS

Green, Adolph *See* COMDEN, BETTY.

Green, Paul (1894–1981) American playwright who came to public attention in 1926 when the *Provincetown Players produced *In Abraham's Bosom*, a *tragedy about an African-American teacher lynched by the Ku Klux Klan. The *Group Theatre selected *The House of Connelly* as their first production (1931) and commissioned Green's collaboration with *Weill on *Johnny Johnson* (1936), an anti-war *musical. In 1941 Green's adaptation of Richard Wright's novel *Native Son* was directed by *Welles. But Green was unenthusiastic about New York success and spent the majority of his career developing regional pageant-dramas based on historical or legendary materials. Beginning with *The Lost Colony* in 1937, he pioneered the 'symphonic drama', blending play, pageant, and regional lore in spectacles intended for large-scale production in outdoor *amphitheatres. In addition to *The Lost Colony* (produced annually on Roanoke Island in North Carolina), Green was commissioned to craft outdoor dramas for sixteen sites. Several, such as *Trumpet in the Land* (New Philadelphia, Ohio) and *The Stephen Foster Story* (Bardstown, Kentucky), continue annually to large audiences. MAF

Greene, Graham (1904–91) English novelist and playwright. The exotic settings and formal innovation of his novels were not reflected in his plays, which were *well made in form even when their content was mysterious in nature. Greene's recurring theme was the tension between divine law and human desire in a Roman Catholic context. In *The Living Room* (1952) an orphaned girl is driven to suicide by the guilt of an adulterous affair. In *The Potting Shed* (with *Gielgud and *Worth, 1958) an atheistic family deals with a terrifying miracle. *The Complaisant Lover* (with Ralph *Richardson, 1959) provocatively explores marriage conventions. Greene's reputation as a playwright suffered by comparison to *Osborne after 1956. Greene's screenplays include *The Third Man* (1949) and *Our Man in Havana* (1959, based on his 1958 novel).   GAO

Greene, Robert (1558–92) English playwright and pamphleteer. As a graduate of both Cambridge and Oxford, Greene was one of the so-called university wits whose dramatic experiments dominated the *public theatres in the 1580s. His contribution to the theatre has sometimes been overshadowed by his unflattering reference to Shakespeare in *Greene's Groats-worth of*

Wit (1592) as 'an upstart crow', and by Gabriel Harvey's report that his death resulted from a surfeit of Rhenish wine and pickled herring. The five plays attributed to Greene exhibit considerable variety. *Alphonsus* (*c.*1587) and *Orlando Furioso* (*c.*1591) imitate, or *parody, *Marlowe's *Tamburlaine*. *A Looking-Glass for London and England* (*c.*1590) dramatizes the biblical story of Nineveh as a warning to London. *James IV* (*c.*1591) unites Italian romance and Scottish history. *Friar Bacon and Friar Bungay* (*c.*1589), Greene's finest play, successfully integrates sorcery and *farcical *comedy with a story of true love.   RWV

Greet, Ben (1857–1936) English actor, *manager, and director. Reputedly born on a training ship on the Thames and destined for a naval career, Greet was a schoolmaster before an actor. He formed his own provincial *touring troupe, and by 1907 had between ten and fifteen companies travelling in England and America. His open-air productions of Shakespeare at Kew Gardens were paralleled by his promotion of the Shakespearian repertoire in America. With *Poel he revived the *morality play *Everyman* (1902), touring it successfully in England and America. At the *Old Vic he was a prominent director of over twenty Shakespeare productions between 1915 and 1918.   AF

Gregory, Andre (1934–) American director and actor. After studying at the *Actors Studio, Gregory began his directing career with a popular *Off-Broadway production of *Genet's *The Blacks* (1962). By the late 1960s he was closely associated with *Grotowski, and in 1968 founded the Manhattan Project, a *collective dedicated to creating 'poor theatre', which produced *Beckett, *Chekhov, and *Our Late Night* (1975) by Wallace *Shawn. The group's best-known work was their adaptation of *Alice in Wonderland* (1968) set in a mental asylum, which they *toured for five years. During the late 1970s, Gregory left theatre to explore para-theatrical experiments in the Grotowski manner. This formed the background to his return in a film co-written with Shawn, *My Dinner with Andre* (1981); a second film, *Vanya on 42nd Street* (1994), began as a theatre workshop; both were directed by Louis Malle. Gregory directed the American première of Shawn's *The Designated Mourner* (1999) and *Grasses of a Thousand Colors* in London (*Royal Court, 2009).   JAB

Gregory, Augusta (Lady) (1852–1932) Irish playwright, *manager, and leading figure in the Irish renaissance. Born into the Anglo-Irish ascendancy, in 1880 she married Sir William

Gregory (aged 63). On his death in 1892, she established her house at Coole Park as a meeting place for writers and activists in the nationalist cultural project. With *Yeats and Edward Martyn she conceived in 1897 the idea of a national theatre, which in 1904 became the *Abbey Theatre. She wrote prolifically for the Abbey: skilfully constructed *comedies like *Spreading the News* (1904), *The Workhouse Ward*, and *The Rising of the Moon* (both 1907), folk history plays like *Dervorgilla* (1907), *Kincora* (1904), *Grania* (1911), and 'wonder' plays. She made translations of *Molière, *Sudermann, and *Goldoni. *The Gaol Gate* (1906), a brief tragic threnody, is a masterpiece of condensed form. She was a dynamic manager of the Abbey Theatre, confronting and quelling powerful opposition to *Synge's *Playboy* on the company's *tour to the USA (1911–12), and defending *O'Casey's *The Plough and the Stars* (1926) against cuts and public outcry.   CAL

Greig, David (1969–) Scottish dramatist, who marks a shift away from *naturalism and *melodrama to global and historical themes, and places questions about Scottish national identity in a wider European context, in pieces like *Europe* (1994) and *The Cosmonaut's Last Message to the Woman He Once Loved in the Former Soviet Union* (1999). His early plays dealt with war guilt (*And the Opera House Remained Unbuilt*, 1992), the collapse of the communist bloc (*Stalinland*, 1992), and German reunification (*One Way Street*, 1993). He displays the influence of *Vinaver in his playfulness with narrative, particularly in work for his own company, Suspect Culture, such as *Timeless* (1997) and *Mainstream* (1999). For the Traverse Theatre he wrote *Europe* (1994), *The Speculator* (1999) and *Outlying Islands* (2002), and *Victoria* (2000) was for the *Royal Shakespeare Company. His work is deeply, if inexplicitly, political, displaying an acknowledgement of the damage caused by a society of consumerist individualism, and a yearning for utopian forms of connection. More recently he has been concerned with environmentalism and the politics of the Middle East, as in *The American Pilot* (2005), *Futurology* (2007), and *Damascus* (2008).   DR

Grein, J. T. (1862–1935) Dutch journalist, playwright, and *manager, later a British citizen. Grein spent 50 years promoting the cause of English drama and writing dramatic criticism. The highlight of his long career was the founding of the *Independent Theatre Society in London in 1891 as a subscription theatre, on the model of *Antoine's Théâtre *Libre, to produce worthwhile non-commercial plays, some of which had been banned (*see* CENSORSHIP). The first production, *Ibsen's *Ghosts*, caused such a scandal that no manager would thereafter risk an unlicensed play; but in seven years' existence Grein's society mounted two plays by Ibsen, two by *Zola, one by *Brieux, and thirteen new English works, including *Shaw's first play, *Widowers' Houses* (1892). Unlike Antoine, Grein was not a director, never had a permanent company or theatre, never acted himself, and rarely attended *rehearsals; and his hopes of a stream of new English plays were dashed. During the rest of his life he supported many causes, including the *Stage Society and a German Theatre in London.   EEC

Grenfell, Joyce (1910–79) English actress and entertainer, who made her debut in *The Little Revue* (1939). She *toured hospitals in concert parties during the Second World War and continued to appear in *revues until the early 1950s when she began her one-person show *Joyce Grenfell Requests the Pleasure*. Her métier was the comic *monologue in which she described and gently mocked the habits and foibles of middle-class English spinsters, schoolmistresses, and other assorted eccentrics: the very type of role she played in several British films directed by Frank Launder, including *The Happiest Days of your Life* (1950), *The Belles of St Trinians* (1954), and *Blue Murder at St Trinians* (1957).   AS

Griboedov, Aleksandr (1795–1829) Russian dramatist and poet whose reputation rests on a single play, *Gore ot uma*, most commonly translated as *Woe from Wit*. The play owes a debt to *Molière's *The Misanthrope* and concerns the return to Moscow, after a sojourn in the West, of a young rebellious nobleman, Chatsky, charting the course of his disillusionment with his unfaithful girlfriend and her father. It offers wonderful opportunities for *character actors. *Shchepkin and *Stanislavsky were famous Famusovs and *Meyerhold staged two productions of a play whose language has become part of everyday Russian expression. Banned before being performed in a heavily *censored version in 1833, it was published in its entirety in 1861.   NW

Grieve family English scene painters. The Grieve dynasty, pre-eminent among nineteenth-century stage designers, spanned three generations: the scion, **John Henderson** (1770–1845); his sons **Thomas** (1799–1882) and **William** (1800–44), and **Thomas Walford** (1841–82), son of Thomas. For almost a century they were principally associated with *Covent Garden, where John Henderson created picturesque designs under *Kemble's *management. In 1835 William joined *Drury Lane but returned to Covent Garden in 1839 under the new management of *Vestris and *Mathews. Thomas is best remembered as one of the principal scenic artists for Charles *Kean's lavish *antiquarian stagings of Shakespeare in the 1850s. Given the diversity of the nineteenth-century theatrical repertoire, the Grieves created scenery for everything from Shakespeare to *ballet to *pantomime. Like *Stanfield, they incorporated the *diorama into theatrical scenery, thus linking performance even more closely with the prevailing popular culture of spectacle and display. *See also* SCENOGRAPHY. RWS

Griffin, Hayden (1943–) Beginning in the late 1960s he worked with the *Royal Court, designing the premières of *Bond's *Narrow Road to the Deep North* (1968) and *Bingo* (1974). In the mid-1970s Griffin began working with the *National Theatre, particularly with director *Bryden, for whom he designed *Playboy of the Western World* (1975), *The Plough and the Stars* (1976), *The Madras House* (1977), *The Crucible* (1981), *Don Quixote* (1982), *A Month in the Country* (1994), and *The Good Hope* (2001). Other National Theatre designs include *Watch It All Come Down* (1976), *Weapons of Happiness* (1976), and *Plenty* (1978). Griffin has also worked for the *Royal Shakespeare Company, the Birmingham Royal Ballet, the *Chichester Festival Theatre, and the Metropolitan Opera in New York. MDG

Griffiths, Trevor (1935–) English playwright and director who developed a political theatre that drew upon European models with British inflections. *Occupations* (1970), set in Turin in 1920, presents a debate between a pragmatic Soviet envoy and the idealistic intellectual Gramsci whose emotional politics is a powerful corrective to emergent Stalinism. *Thermidor* (1971), set in a Soviet interrogation room during the 1930s purges, considers the relationship between conscience and revolutionary commitment. *The Party* (*National Theatre, 1973, starring *Olivier) is a debate between fashionable radicals against the backdrop of the French insurrection of 1968, while *Comedians* (1975) dramatizes the possibilities and betrayals of post-war working-class politics through the performances of would-be stand-up comics.

His first television play, *All Good Men* (1974), deals with familiar themes of the struggles and betrayals of post-war socialism. Subsequently, *Bill Brand* (1976) developed these concerns in an eleven-part serial, and *Country* (1981) returned to an examination of a revolutionary moment,

here the 1945 general election. *The Last Place on Earth* (1985) studies nationalism through the Antarctic explorer Captain Scott, and the screenplay *Reds* (1981) is set during the Russian Revolution. Griffiths's later work has again been for the theatre and includes *Real Dreams* (1984), *The Gulf between Us* (1992), and *Thatcher's Children* (1993). *Food for Ravens* (1997) is a television film about the Labour politician Aneurin Bevan. SF

Grillparzer, Franz (1791–1872) The most important Austrian dramatist of the nineteenth century, Grillparzer managed to synthesize the legacy of Spanish baroque drama and the practice of Viennese popular theatre with German *neoclassicism and *romanticism. The director of the *Burgtheater, Joseph Schreyvogel, arranged premières. His first success was *The Ancestress* (1817) an exercise in the fate tragedy popular at the time. It was followed by a classical *tragedy, *Sappho* (1818), which dramatized the poet's life as a conflict between life and art. An important work is the *Golden Fleece* trilogy (1821) exploring the Jason and Medea story as a clash of cultures and sexuality. *Waves of the Sea and Love* (1829), on Hero and Leander, proved his most popular play. Grillparzer's interest in the Spanish baroque led to a reformulation of *Calderón's *La vida es sueño* as *A Dream of Life* (1832), a dramatic fairy tale in the Viennese popular style. The failure of his *comedy *Woe to Him Who Lies!* (1838) led Grillparzer to forsake the theatre. Other major works, such as *Family Strife among the Habsburgs* and *The Jewess of Toledo*, were performed posthumously in 1872. CBB

Grimaldi, Joseph (1778–1837) English *pantomime *clown. Grimaldi was from a family of Italian dancers, though born in London. After Grimaldi, clowns were called 'Joey', and it was Grimaldi who devised the make-up that became traditional: a white face with a red half-moon (or spot later) on each cheek. The talented Joey was performing at *Sadler's Wells Theatre when he was little more than an infant, and became a regular member of that company, appearing also at *Drury Lane and then settling at *Covent Garden, where he was a huge success in 1806 in *Harlequin Mother Goose*, which was acted 92 times, and *Harlequin and Padmanaba* (1811) and *Harlequin and the Red Dwarf* (1812). Worn out and crippled by extreme exertions on stage—at one time or another he broke almost every bone in his body—he retired in 1823, making two brief farewell appearances, with great difficulty, in 1828. Grimaldi's Joey defined the nineteenth-century clown and took the focus away from the previously dominant *Harlequin. Additionally, Grimaldi was a trained *dancer and *acrobat, a superb singer of comic songs, a parodist of contemporary dress and behaviour, and an ingenious inventor of trick scenes and stage transformations.   MRB

Grock (Charles Adrien Wettach) (1880–1959) Swiss *clown. The 'king of clowns' was born in France and performed professionally at 14. His own speciality was as a musical clown, a routine he learnt while on an extended tour to South America in 1903. By 1907 he had a successful solo programme in which he played a multitude of musical instruments 'badly'. As his numbers grew in length they became unsuitable for *circuses and he performed in *music halls and *cabarets throughout Europe. In a career spanning 60 years he became the most successful (and probably the richest) clown of the twentieth century. His trademarks were a white face, bald head, and ill-fitting clothing. He often appeared with a comic foil whose only function was to highlight Grock's own zaniness. Towards the end of his career he owned his own travelling circus (1951–4).   CBB

Gros-Guillaume (Robert Guérin) (d.1634) French actor. A member of various troupes that acted at the *Hôtel de Bourgogne as early as 1598, he headed the Comédiens du Roi from 1622 until his death. For nearly two decades he, the rail-thin Gaultier-Garguille, and the knavish *Turlupin formed an inimitable trio in *farce. He played rustic and naive *characters, dressed in a flat cap, striped trousers, and a loose tunic; his impressive belly was set off by two belts above and below, and his open, trusting moon-face was heavily floured, in contrast to his two companions who wore *masks. His persona was also incorporated into *pastorals and *tragicomedies; when performing *tragic roles he used the name La Fleur. A favourite of Henri IV and of the general public, his popularity did much to establish the viability of commercial theatre in Paris.   RWH

Grotowski, Jerzy (1933–99) Polish director and theorist. Grotowski studied directing in Moscow and completed his education in Cracow, where his earliest productions displayed traces of *constructivism. In 1959, *dramaturg Ludwig Flaszen was given charge of a small theatre in Opole, Poland, and hired Grotowski as *artistic director. Grotowski established a stable company with a commitment to ongoing training and rigorous research into the fundamental bases of *acting. He was assisted in early productions by Eugenio *Barba, who played a crucial role in dis-

seminating the theories and principles of what became known as the Polish Laboratory Theatre. The company gained international renown for its highly unconventional stagings, which emphasized the encounter between actor and *audience as the core of the theatrical exchange, stripping away *costume and scenery to focus on the actor's ability to create transformation by means of craft alone. Grotowski's contributions to performance, as detailed in his manifesto *Towards a Poor Theatre* (1968), include an investigation of the possibilities of *environmental staging, an approach to textual montage that posited the *director's role as *auteur* rather than executant, and an emphasis on the performer's obligation to daily physical and vocal training, as well as the methodical investigation of a performance technique rooted in the principles of *Stanislavsky's 'method of physical actions'.

Grotowski rejected theatre as entertainment, seeking to revitalize the *ritualistic function of performance as a site of communion. Central to his precepts was the notion of the 'holy actor', one able to use the dramatic role as a surgical instrument, peeling away the daily mask of social behaviour. Grotowski believed that this act of testimony could serve as a provocation for the spectator, inviting the viewer to conduct a similar act of self-penetration.

The first of the Laboratory Theatre's productions to gain critical attention outside Poland was *Dr Faustus* (1963), an adaptation of *Marlowe that unfolded during the final hour of the *protagonist's life, with spectators seated around a table on which the action took place. Grotowski's staging of *Wyspiański's *Akropolis*, a play which celebrates the achievements of human civilization through depiction of classical and biblical vignettes, was starkly recontextualized in a concentration camp. *The Constant Prince* (1965), departing from *Słowacki's adaptation of *Calderón, positioned the spectators as voyeuristic observers of a process of torture and martyrdom. *Cieślak's performance in the central role was viewed as the complete realization of Grotowski's vision of the 'total act' and the pinnacle of the Laboratory Theatre's achievement. The company's final production, *Apocalypsis cum Figuris* (1969), cast Cieślak as a village idiot/Christ figure, rejected by the modern world. During the run of the production, the company worked to minimize all traces of theatricality and moved toward a progressively more intimate spatial relation between actors and spectators.

With his staging of *Apocalypsis* Grotowski felt that he had accomplished everything he could within the realm of theatre. From 1969 to 1978 the Laboratory Theatre investigated a range of para-theatrical activities, exploring circumstances in which a more authentic meeting between actors and spectators could occur. Beginning in 1976, he shifted his attention to examining *ritual performance practices of various world cultures, a project he described as 'theatre of sources'. His intent was to discern whether these performative elements could exert a tangible, psycho-physical impact on participants, regardless of culturally conditioned structures of belief.

Grotowski fled Poland in 1982 following the declaration of martial law. He received political asylum in the USA, and was eventually given the opportunity to continue his research at the University of California–Irvine. Diagnosed with leukemia in the early 1980s, his awareness of mortality became more urgent after he suffered two strokes in the early 1990s. He became preoccupied with questions of transmission. Beginning in 1986, Grotowski took up residence at a secluded centre in Pontedera, Italy, where he initiated 'art as vehicle', the culmination of his life work. Built around performance of traditional songs, primarily from the African diaspora, art as vehicle examined the potential of ritual instruments to trigger a process of energetic transformation. While the work was conceptualized as a form of meditative practice for the doers rather than observers, the performance structures were made accessible to spectators in small groups and can be received and appreciated as theatrical events.   LW

Group Theatre New York ensemble active from 1931 to 1941. Asked in 1931 by the Board of Managers of the *Theatre Guild about the rebel 'Group' among the Guild's younger staff, *Clurman answered, 'We want to establish a theatre, not merely a production organization.' The Guild responded by giving money, two salaries, and their option on *Green's *The House of Connelly* to launch the Group. Influenced by *Copeau and the *Moscow Art Theatre, Clurman was the intellectual inventor who 'talked the Group into being'. *Managed by a triumvirate of Clurman, Cheryl Crawford, and *Strasberg, its initial membership included 27 actors. Crawford took charge of business affairs and was a valuable mediator between Clurman and Strasberg, whose *acting *Method was to provide an ensemble unified by technique as well as philosophy. The opening of *The House of Connelly* in 1931 was a sensation, the Group praised as the inheritor of the ensemble tradition of the Moscow Art Theatre.

Severing connections with the Guild, they began their continual search for plays which were new,

American, and optimistic. The Group's peak year was 1935, when *Odets, a minor actor in the Group, brought forward *Waiting for Lefty* and *Awake and Sing!*, which ran simultaneously in packed Broadway theatres. By 1937, the Group had suffered multiple *financial failures, Strasberg had resigned, and Odets had followed some Group actors to Hollywood. The Group reorganized during the late 1930s under Clurman and *Kazan, but the original idea of shared consciousness ended in 1937. Its influence was felt for many years, however, through the *Actors Studio and the studios of Stella *Adler, Morris *Carnovsky, Robert *Lewis, and Sanford Meisner.   MAF

Grüber, Klaus Michael (1941–2008) German director. Grüber, who began as an assistant to *Strehler, was one of the most uncompromising and idiosyncratic contemporary German directors; his intense personal vision created radical readings of classical texts. Highly controversial was his *Faust I* at the Berlin Freie Volksbühne (1982), which he reduced to just three *characters: Faust, Mephisto, and Gretchen, the latter played by an amateur. In Germany he worked almost exclusively at the *Schaubühne. Important productions included *Horváth's *Tales from the Vienna Woods* (1972), which he staged as the nightmarish recollections of one of the characters; *Euripides' *The Bacchae* (1974); and *Winterreise*, a staging of Hölderlin's epistolary novel *Hyperion* in the Berlin Olympic stadium. During the Schaubühne's early political phase Grüber insisted on aesthetic autonomy for the theatre. Seven of his productions were invited to the Berlin *Theatertreffen. In the 1990s he directed mainly *opera.   CBB

Gründgens, Gustaf (1899–1963) German actor and director. From 1923 he acted and directed at Hamburg, came to the attention of *Reinhardt, joined the *Deutsches Theater in 1928, and rapidly became a leading actor. Gründgens directed *comedies, performed in *cabaret, *opera, and film (for instance, the ruthless underworld boss in Fritz Lang's *M*, 1931). In 1932 he moved to the Staatstheater where his Mephisto in *Faust I* was highly praised. In 1934 Hermann Göring appointed Gründgens director of the Staatstheater. Thus began the most controversial period in his career, as he tried to balance connivance with and resistance to the Nazi regime. This balancing act is analysed by Klaus Mann in his novel *Mephisto* (1936) and was dramatized by *Mnouchkine for the Théâtre du *Soleil in 1979. After his denazification in 1946 his most important posts were the directorships of the

Düsseldorf Schauspielhaus (1951–5) and the Hamburg Schauspielhaus (1955–63). Here he directed *Faust* and performed Mephisto once again (1957; filmed 1961). In his final years Gründgens vociferously opposed the emergence of *director's theatre and defended the pre-eminence of the author.   CBB

Grundy, Sydney (1848–1914) English playwright. From 1869 to 1876 Grundy was a barrister in Manchester. His first play, a *farce, *A Little Change* (1872), appeared at the *Haymarket in London, and he wrote some 60 more, including many adaptations from French and German. Grundy's most popular play was the fairy-tale *comedy from the French, *A Pair of Spectacles* (1890), which ran for 335 performances and provided a fine part for John *Hare, the *actor-manager, as the philanthropist Benjamin Goldfinch, who takes on his brother's flinty and miserly *character when he breaks his spectacles and borrows his brother's. Grundy was a social conservative and a bitter opponent of both *Ibsen and *feminism; his comedy *A New Woman* (1894) reflects some of these prejudices.   MRB

Guan Hanqing (Kuan Han-ch'ing) (*c.*1240–*c.*1320) Chinese playwright. The most versatile and prolific Yuan Dynasty dramatist, Guan has traditionally been considered the originator of *zaju* as a literary form. Neither a landed scholar nor a court-appointed official, Guan represented a new breed of writer. Nearly a third of his more than 60 known *zaju* are extant and exhibit a prodigious imagination. Using military, political, courtroom, domestic, romantic, and lyrical themes, Guan's range was wide and his lively vernacular rich. Such thematic and linguistic breadth did not endear him to the Ming court and to the Ming literati, but did grant him pre-eminence with modern critics. Even in their redacted incarnations, the resourceful women *protagonists of Guan's five romantic *comedies, including *Rescuing One of the Girls*, defy the clichés of female virtue and vice. Of the courtroom plays, *Injustice to Dou E* entered the Qing Dynasty operatic repertoire and became recognized in the early twentieth century as a *tragedy. In the early decades of the People's Republic of China, Guan gained a new reputation as an articulate spokesman for the oppressed. His plays were enlisted in the service of political campaigns, biographical details were invented, and he became known as the Chinese Shakespeare.   PS

Guare, John (1938–) American playwright. Many of his plays deal with *characters distanced from an affluent society, a theme present in his first major success, the *Off-Broadway *The House of Blue Leaves* (1971), in his most popular later play, *Six Degrees of Separation* (1990; film, 1993), and in the *Lydie Breeze* trilogy tracing the failure of a nineteenth-century utopian experiment. Other plays explored familial relations (*Bosoms and Neglect*, 1979; *Lake Hollywood*, 1999). Guare experiments with dramatic structure, often purposefully shattering the conventions of *realistic theatre, and frequently employing direct *audience address. His libretto for a rock *musical version of *Two Gentlemen of Verona* was produced by the *New York Shakespeare Festival. A screenplay for Louis Malle's *Atlantic City* (1980) was highly praised, but Guare has focused his energies on the live theatre. *Chaucer in Rome* (2001) is a sequel to *House of Blue Leaves*.   AW

Guarini, Battista (1538–1612) Ferrarese courtier, teacher, and playwright. He was the author of the internationally successful *pastoral play *Il pastor fido* (*The Faithful Shepherd*), first drafted in the 1580s and published in Guarini's own definitive edition in 1602. This work established a model for the pastoral genre of theatre all over Europe, and was translated and imitated for many generations. Equally important were his own glosses to the play and other theoretical writings which argued for the legitimacy of pastoral drama, and for the mixed genre of *tragicomedy, despite the absence of both from the standard classical authorities such as *Aristotle and Horace.   RAA

Gubenko, Nikolai (1941–) Soviet/Russian actor and director. Gubenko trained at the State Institute for Cinematography and joined the Taganka Theatre in 1964. He played a number of lead roles before he turned to filmmaking, but returned to the Taganka in 1980, where he played the main part in *Boris Godunov* (banned 1982, produced 1988), giving a most powerful portrayal of the conscience-stricken Tsar. Gubenko took over *artistic directorship of the Taganka (1987–91) and revived several previously banned productions. From 1988 to 1991 he was the Soviet Minister of Culture; since then he has headed the theatre called Comradeship of Taganka Actors, which broke away from *Lyubimov.   BB

Guerrero, María (1868–1928) Spanish actress. Following her theatrical debut in 1886 in *Echegaray's *Sin familia* (*No Family*), Guerrero trained in Paris under the guidance of *Coquelin and went on to act alongside *Bernhardt. In 1896 she married Fernando Díaz de Mendoza, with whom she formed a successful company which acted in Spain, France, Italy, and South America, and was instrumental in the construction of the Teatro

Nacional Cervantes in Buenos Aires. Her repertoire included plays by classical and modern Spanish authors such as Lope de *Vega, *Calderón, Echegaray, and *Guimerà, but also a number of foreign playwrights, notably *Rostand, *Schiller, and *Maeterlinck. A graceful and highly expressive actress, Guerrero specialized in the role of the witty and resourceful woman, performing in more than 150 plays over a 40-year span. Madrid's Teatro Nacional María Guerrero is named after her. KG

Guignol Generic name for a glove *puppet in France. The *character was invented in Lyon around 1808 by Laurent Mourguet. With his drunken cobbler friend Gnafron, Guignol delighted drinkers in cafés. The first Guignol repertoire was purely oral, with *scenarios based on well-known plays, but social and satirical comments attracted the attention of the *censors in 1852. In 1878 Pierre Rousset at the Café Condamin (Lyon), created a new repertoire of dramatic and *operatic *parodies. By 1900 puppets were perceived as children's entertainment, and the character of Guignol became younger and politer. JMCC

Guilbert, Yvette (c.1867–1944) French singer and *cabaret monologist (*diseuse*). Guilbert began in Paris as a model, actress, and singer, and became the rage in the 1890s, singing at the Chat Noir, the Divan Japonais, and the *Moulin-Rouge, and inspiring many lithographs and posters by Toulouse-Lautrec. She performed witty, mildly risqué songs (such as 'Madame Arthur', the lady with the famous 'je ne sais quoi'), presented as mini-dramas, some written especially for her by Aristide Bruant. She was tall, red-haired, and angular, with a slightly raucous but mobile voice and clipped clear diction, and wore trademark long black gloves. In a long career she appeared in London, many European countries, and New York. After 1900 she developed a larger repertoire of historical songs, both secular and religious; she also appeared in *revues and plays and in Murnau's film of *Faust* (1926). EEC

Guimerà, Àngel (1845–1924) Catalan poet and playwright. Already a prizewinning poet, Guimerà turned in the late 1870s to the theatre. *Gala Placídia* (1879) and *Judith de Welp* (1883) were his first incursions into verse drama; they revitalized the outmoded form of historical *romanticism. This romantic phase was soon superseded by a more *naturalistic theatre, exemplified in the immensely popular and frequently revived *Sea and Heaven* (1888), *Maria Rosa* (1894), and the internationally acclaimed *Lowlands* (1897). A confirmed Catalanist, Guimerà's love of his local

language was crystallized in the dramatic *monologues of the 1890s, *Mestre Oleguer* and *Death of Jaume d'Urgell*. His unsuccessful flirtation with psychological drama was followed by a return, at the very end of his career, to the historical plays of his youth. KG

Guinness, Alec (1914–2001) English actor and director. After initial difficulties at the *Old Vic, struggling to meet the expectations of *Gielgud and *Guthrie, he developed into an accomplished actor in the 1930s, notably as Aguecheck in *Twelfth Night* (1937) and as Hamlet in Guthrie's modern-dress production (1938). During the war he served in the Royal Navy, after which he excelled on stage and screen for five decades. He continued to act in a wide range of plays, from *King Lear* (the Fool, 1946) and *Gogol's *The Government Inspector* (1948) to *Eliot's *The Cocktail Party* (1949) and Simon *Gray's *Wise Child* (1967). He also adapted Dostoevsky's *The Brothers Karamazov* for the stage (1946), directed occasionally (*Twelfth Night*, 1949; *Hamlet*, 1951), and starred in the initial season of the *Stratford Festival in Canada. In cinema he played comic and serious roles with equal brilliance. He starred in the famous Pinewood Studios *comedies *Kind Hearts and Coronets* (1949, in which he played eight roles), *The Lavender Hill Mob* (1951), and *The Lady Killers* (1955), while his serious films included *The Bridge on the River Kwai* (1957, Academy Award), *Tunes of Glory* (1960), *Lawrence of Arabia* (1962), *A Passage to India* (1984), and *A Handful of Dust* (1988). He achieved cult standing for his portrayal of Obi-Wan Kenobi in *Star Wars* (1977). He also acted on television, notably in adaptations of John Le Carré's spy novels (1979, 1982), and he regularly did radio programmes. TP

Guitry, Sacha (1885–1957) French actor, writer, filmmaker, and boulevardier, the son of France's finest *fin de siècle* actor, Lucien Guitry. Sacha made his stage debut at 5 in a court performance with his father for Tsar Alexander II. After his parents' divorce, Sacha was raised in France, ardently patriotic and obsessed with theatre. From the 1910s to 1930s, Guitry had at least two *comedies of sexual intrigue playing each season in Paris. He also wrote bio-dramas, including *Pasteur* (1919), which featured his father's commanding presence in the title role. Guitry directed most of his 125 plays, usually playing the leading role opposite his current wife. He married five times. His stage *character was usually a bon vivant or a detached seducer, but later he enjoyed playing multiple roles with make-up changes. His frequently revived *N'écoutez pas, mesdames!*

(*Do Not Listen, Ladies*, 1942) heartened French *audiences during the Paris occupation. He also wrote and directed 30 films, and published about twenty books of memoirs and sketches. Legendary for his ready wit, Guitry is often compared to *Molière in impact on his time.   FHL

Gunter, John (1938–) English designer. Trained at the Central School of Art and Design, he was head of theatre design at Central St Martin's, London, for eight years. He has designed for the *Royal Court, *Royal Shakespeare Company, the Peter *Hall company, and the West End. Gunter maintains that stage design should be 'evocative, suggestive of ambience' to set *audiences 'off on a visual journey that they complete for you'. Head of design at the *National Theatre under *Eyre, he won Olivier awards for *Guys and Dolls* (1982) and *Wild Honey* (1984). He has designed for *opera in Europe, Australia, and the Americas.   RVL

Guo Muoruo (Kuo Mo-jo) (1892–1978) Chinese playwright and scholar. One of the most prominent cultural figures in twentieth-century China. At the time of his return from Japan in 1923, he was already well known for his poetry, translations, and romantic historical plays. In the following years he wrote three plays with historical heroines that advocated women's liberation: *Zhuo Wenjun* (1924), *Wang Zhaojun* (1924), and *Nie Ying* (1925). In 1937, after ten years of self-exile in Japan to avoid government persecution, Guo returned to China to lead the literary resistance movement in the Sino-Japanese War, completing six historical plays in eighteen months between 1941 and 1943. Four of them were about tragic *heroes of the era of the Warring States (770–221 BC), and again utilized a thematic correspondence to the present. After the communist victory in 1949 Guo held a series of high-ranking government posts relating to the arts. He wrote two highly influential historical plays in his last period: *Cai Wenji* (1959), about a great woman poet, and *Wu Zetian* (1960), about the only empress in Chinese history.   SYL

Gurik, Robert (1932–) Québec playwright. Born in France, he emigrated to Montréal in 1950. He first attracted attention with the cleverly parodic *Hamlet, prince du Québec* (1968), lampooning the principals in the heated confrontation between Ottawa and Québec caused by the visit of Charles de Gaulle in 1967. Thereafter his plays reflect growing concern for the marginalization of individuals in modern mechanized, consumerist society. Typical is *Api 2967* (1971), portraying a sterile, Orwellian future where human values no longer exist. *The Trial of Jean-Baptiste M.* (1972),

based on a real-life occurrence, presents an individual who, pushed to the limit, decides to murder all three of his capitalist employers 'on principle'. *Jacques' Bay* (1976), inspired by *Brecht's *Mahagonny* and set in Québec's remote north, develops similar themes. Many of his twenty-odd plays have been translated and staged in several languages.   LED

Gurney, A. R. (Albert Ramsdell) (1930–) American dramatist, identified with the north-eastern affluent culture where he locates most of his plays. His wry *comedies foreground wit and social form, while he presents time as fluid and personality as fragmentary. In both *The Wayside Motor Inn* (1977) and *The Dining Room* (1982), vignettes overlap in the same space while the *characters are oblivious to each other. Gurney explored theatricality more topically than structurally in such plays as *The Perfect Party* (1986) and *The Fourth Wall* (1992), which involves a dramatist asking his family's permission to base a play on their experiences. He took unusual approaches to character in *Sweet Sue* (1982), doubling each of the two roles in order to sketch them from multiple perspectives, and in *Sylvia* (1995), whose title role is ostensibly a man's pet dog but played as (and by) a witty, alluring young woman. Perhaps the quintessentially disengaged Gurney play is *Love Letters* (1988), an epistolary romance in which interaction is limited to correspondence and the seated actors read the text to the *audience.   JDM

Guthrie, Tyrone (1900–71) Anglo-Irish director. Guthrie was appointed director at the *Old Vic in 1933 and 1936, and administrator of the Old Vic and *Sadler's Wells theatres (1939–45), when he earned a reputation for staging *opera as well as drama. His notable productions over these years included *Tobias and the Angel* (1930) and *The Anatomist* (1931) by *Bridie, *Hamlet* with *Olivier (1937), and *Peer Gynt* with Ralph *Richardson (1944). After 1948 his career became increasingly international, largely in consequence of his staging *Lindsay's *A Satire of the Three Estates* in the old Assembly Hall at the *Edinburgh Festival. This non-theatrical space allowed him to develop further his interest in non-*proscenium venues, which had been sparked in 1937 when a performance of *Hamlet* at Elsinore Castle had, because of storms, to be redesigned in-the-round within a nearby hotel ballroom.

The years in which Guthrie directed the *Stratford Festival (Canada, 1953–7) allowed him to develop with the designer, *Moisewitsch, a form of thrust stage which carried the action into the *audience. The thrust emerged from a permanent structure allowing for the use of an upper and a lower playing area with multiple entrances, reminiscent of both the *skene* of ancient theatres and the tiring house wall backing Elizabethan *public theatres. The concept was further refined with the creation of the *Guthrie Theatre in Minneapolis in 1963, a stage which became the prototype for many built in England in the ensuing decade including the *Chichester Festival Theatre.

In later years Guthrie's directing focused almost entirely on *Greek or *early modern plays, though his approach was never orthodox. Several times he essayed modern-dress productions (*Hamlet* with *Guinness and *Jonson's *The Alchemist*), while in *Volpone* with Colin *Blakely at the new *National Theatre he experimented with movements inspired by the creatures after which the *characters are named. His excellence at choreographing crowd scenes was seen at its best in *Marlowe's *Tamburlaine* with *Wolfit for the Festival of Britain (1951).   RAC

Guthrie Theatre American *regional theatre in Minneapolis. Conceived in 1959 by Tyrone *Guthrie, Oliver Rea, and Peter Zeisler, it opened in 1963 as the Minnesota Theatre Company in a new *playhouse adjacent to the Walker Art Center. To achieve actor-*audience intimacy, the facility featured a steep *auditorium and a deep, asymmetrical thrust stage designed by *Moisewitsch, based on her experience with Guthrie at the *Stratford Festival. In its commitment to establish a permanent resident theatre that brought a classical repertory to America's heartland, the company became a flagship of the regional theatre movement. Guthrie stepped down as *artistic director in 1966 and was replaced eventually by *Langham (1971-8). Other artistic directors include Alvin Epstein (1978-80), *Ciulei (1980-6), *Wright (1986-95), and *Dowling (from 1995), former head of Dublin's *Abbey Theatre. Dowling spurred a major increase in attendance and a new three-theatre complex on the Mississippi River, opened in 2006.   STC

Gwynn, Eleanor 'Nell' (*c.*1642-87) English actress and *dancer. Nell Gwynn's fame for her offstage role as Charles II's mistress has largely obscured her onstage success as an accomplished comedienne. She first joined the King's Company at *Drury Lane around 1663 and by 1665 was playing leading roles opposite the *actor-manager Charles Hart, reputed to be one in a line of influential lovers. The rags-to-riches story of Nell, the orange girl, rising to become a popular *prologue and *epilogue speaker who attracted the attentions of the King, epitomizes traditional notions of the actress as whore. *Pepys's *Diary* includes several references to Nell's offstage attractions but also praises her onstage performances, particularly as Florimel in *Dryden's *Secret Love* (1667), a comic *breeches role in which she excelled. Nell retired from a relatively short acting career in 1670, following the birth of her first son by the King. She maintained her connections with the *playhouse and in 1679 Aphra *Behn dedicated *The Feign'd Curtizans* to 'the fair, witty and deserving' Nell Gwynn.   GBB

Hacks, Peter (1928-2003) German dramatist. After studying at Munich, Hacks moved to East Berlin in 1955 where he worked as a *dramaturg at the *Deutsches Theater until 1963. His first plays and essays were heavily influenced by *Brecht. In *Anxieties and Power* (1960) he examined problems of production in the German Democratic Republic, and in *Moritz Tassow* (1965) the debate between pragmatic and idealistic versions of communism. His indirect, ironic style did not always find the approval of East German authorities, which led him to turn to translations and adaptations. Particularly successful were *Peace* (*Aristophanes, 1962), *Helen of Troy* (*Meilhac and Halévy, 1964) and *Polly* (*Gay, 1966), in congenial productions by *Besson. In the 1970s he treated a number of literary subjects and achieved a major success with the witty monodrama *A Conversation in the Stein Household about the Absent Herr von Goethe* (1974). Although considered the most important GDR dramatist after *Müller, with the exception of his plays for *youth he has been much less performed.   CBB

Hagen, Uta (1919-2004) American actress and teacher. Born in Germany, Hagen made her debut as Ophelia in Eva *Le Gallienne's *Hamlet* (1937) and her first Broadway appearance as Nina in the *Lunts' production of *The Seagull* (1938). She played Desdemona opposite *Robeson's Othello (1945). Through *Clurman and *Berghof, Hagen learned the *Stanislavsky system and began to teach in 1947. Despite acclaim for her performances of Blanche in *Williams's *A Streetcar Named Desire* (1948), Georgie in *Odets's *The Country Girl* (1950), Natalia in *Turgenev's *A Month in the Country* (1956), and especially Martha in *Albee's *Who's Afraid of Virginia Woolf?* (1962), Hagen subordinated her *acting career to teaching. As a performer, she was clear and understated, with a strong presence and deep voice. In her teaching, she supported the *Method but opposed its tool of emotional memory. Her *Respect for Acting* (1973) and *A Challenge for the Actor* (1991) offer pragmatic and theoretical advice.   FI

Hakim, Tawfiq el- (1898-1987) Egyptian playwright. Hakim's *The People of the Cave* (1933) was the first original Egyptian drama—as distinct from translated or adapted ones—to be considered serious literature. He subsequently drew on various indigenous and French traditions, as well as on Egyptian social themes. He also undertook daring experiments in language and genre. These include *The Deal* (1956), which uses a third language halfway between colloquial Egyptian vernacular and the more literary Standard Arabic (Fus'ha); *The Tree Climber* (1963), an attempt at an Egyptian *absurd theatre; and *Bank of Anxiety* (1968), a combination of novelistic and dramatic forms. His tendency to foreground *dialogue and philosophy suggest that his work is intellectual *closet drama,' but many of his plays have been successfully staged at home and abroad.   HMA

Hall, Peter (1930-) English director and *manager. Energetic in directing undergraduate productions at Cambridge, Hall soon became director of the Arts Theatre in London where he mounted the first British production of *Waiting for Godot* (1955). After success at the Stratford *Shakespeare Memorial Theatre, he became its artistic director in 1960 and transformed the company into the *Royal Shakespeare Company in 1961 as a permanent ensemble playing in Stratford and London. The repertory included Shakespeare and his contemporaries rescued from neglect, major European and American plays, and a firm commitment to new work. The RSC became the major national company and its Shakespeare productions were marked by an often politicized modernity balanced by scrupulous attention to the text and verse speaking. Hall's best work at this time included *The Wars of the Roses* (1963) which made the neglected *Henry VI* plays and *Richard III* into a trilogy investigating power-politics, and *Hamlet* (1965), with David *Warner as a contemporary student prince. Hall also directed the premières of a number of *Pinter's plays.

Resigning from the RSC in 1968, Hall briefly became director of productions at the Royal Opera House, but complained about *Covent

Garden's extravagant budgets (though he continued to direct *opera, including *Wagner's *Ring* at *Bayreuth in 1983). He succeeded *Olivier as director of the *National Theatre in 1973, surviving strikes, boardroom battles, and perennial fights for sufficient funding. He supervised the company's move from the *Old Vic to its own home on the South Bank and programmed its three theatres with an immense range, epitomized by his productions of *Marlowe's *Tamburlaine* (1976), *Shaffer's *Amadeus* (1979), and a *masked, all-male version of *Aeschylus' *The Oresteia* (1981) in Tony *Harrison's translation. Leaving the National in 1988, he established his own company in West End theatres, the Old Vic, and New York.

A powerful advocate for British theatre, Hall often returned to a play he had explored before (for instance *Hamlet* in 1965, 1975, and 1994). His productions of *Greek drama, including *Lysistrata* (1993) and the Oedipus plays (NT, 1996), kept it vital in Britain and led to his flawed but bold adaptation of the *Tantalus* sequence (2000) by his colleague from Cambridge onwards, *Barton.

                                                                    PDH

Hall, Roger (1939–   ) British-born New Zealand playwright. The spectacular success of *Glide Time* (1976), an office-based civil service *comedy of circumscribed middle-class lives, launched Hall's career as the most performed playwright in New Zealand. It also secured a place for locally written plays in theatres which had until then relied on London and New York hits. *Middle-Age Spread* (1977) had a similar success in New Zealand, won the London Comedy of the Year award for its long West End run, and was subsequently filmed. Twenty years after *Glide Time* almost all its original cast appeared in *Market Forces* (1996) to show how the same *characters (now household names from Hall's radio and television series) were coping (or not) with a restructured public service in a deregulated economy. In addition to his many comedies, Hall has written *musicals, *pantomime, children's shows, *revues, serious drama, and British television sitcom. He is a major force in teaching and supporting young playwrights.   DC

Hall, Willis *See* WATERHOUSE, KEITH.

Hallam family The Hallams were a well-known theatrical family in early eighteenth-century London. Adam Hallam regularly maintained a *booth in Bartholomew Fair and appears as a character tumbling from a platform in Hogarth's 1733 painting *Southwark Fair*. Adam's sons **William** (d. 1758) and **Lewis** (1714–55) continued

the family tradition; in 1751, after a financially disastrous turn as *manager of the Goodman's Fields Theatre, William took the extraordinary step of sending part of his company to the New World.

Led by Lewis, the troupe opened their eleven-month season in 1752 in Williamsburg, Virginia, with *The Merchant of Venice* and *The Anatomist*. For the next two years, they toured the colonies, building theatres and playing an ambitious repertory of *Lillo, *Congreve, *Gay, and Shakespeare, before retreating to Jamaica as the French–Indian War expanded. Lewis died in Jamaica; his widow married David Douglass, an itinerant actor of uncertain origin. **Mrs Hallam** (d.1773) had been a performer of some note on the London stage before accompanying her husband to America. With Douglass in charge, the American Company, as it was now known, returned to the northern colonies in 1758. Lewis's son **Lewis Jr.** (1740–1808) was elevated to his father's leading roles.

From then until 1774 the Hallam/Douglass company remained the dominant troupe in the colonies. Among their many accomplishments was the first professional staging of a script by an American playwright, Thomas Godfrey's *The Prince of Parthia* (1767). Lewis Jr. also holds the distinction of being the first actor in America known to have performed Hamlet. After waiting out the Revolutionary War in the West Indies, Lewis Jr. returned to reorganize the company, assuming full management after Douglass's death in 1786. Eventually joining forces with *Dunlap and others, Lewis rebuilt the Southwark Theatre in Philadelphia and the John Street Theatre in New York. Although he relinquished his managerial duties in 1798, he continued to act and occasionally to tour the major east coast cities until his death.   PAD

hamartia Literally 'a missing of the mark', *hamartia* could in ancient Greek range in meaning from innocent mistake to wilful evil. *Aristotle's tragic *protagonist is somehow responsible for an act he performs in ignorance of its true nature; and in some *tragedies he undergoes a change in fortune (*peripeteia*) because of some *hamartia*. The traditional debate about *hamartia* as moral flaw or intellectual error makes it an attribute of *character, but it is equally possible to see it as part of the plot, an *action rather than a character flaw. We might also see it as ignorance itself, the human condition that renders the act tragic. RWV

Hammerstein, Oscar I (1846–1919) American impresario and *manager. Born in Berlin, Hammerstein ran away and emigrated to New York in 1863. A series of patented inventions enriched him sufficiently to build eight theatres that culminated with the Manhattan Opera House (1906), where he introduced such *opera stars as Mary Garden, Nellie Melba, and Luisa Tetrazzini. In 1908 Hammerstein opened the Philadelphia Opera House, and then the London Opera House in 1911. He wrote several *musicals himself, notably words and music for *Santa Maria* (1896). His most successful Broadway show, however, was Victor *Herbert's *Naughty Marietta* (1910). He was the grandfather of the renowned lyricist Oscar *Hammerstein II.   CT

Hammerstein, Oscar II (1895–1960) American lyricist, author, and *producer. Along with Richard *Rodgers, Hammerstein revolutionized *musical theatre. Hammerstein came from a theatrical background—his grandfather, Oscar *Hammerstein I, was an *opera impresario and his father a *vaudeville theatre *manager—and studied law at Columbia University. His first experience writing lyrics was for Columbia Varsity shows, on which he collaborated with *Hart and Rodgers. Hammerstein began in *operetta, breathing new life into a near moribund genre with Rudolf Friml (*Rose Marie*), *Romberg (*The Desert Song*, *The New Moon*), and *Gershwin (*Song of the Flame*). He then worked with *Kern on a number of musicals including their masterwork about the American south, *Show Boat* (1927). Hammerstein also wrote the acclaimed 1943 musical *Carmen Jones*, an all-black retelling of Bizet's *Carmen*.

Rodgers and Hammerstein's first collaboration, *Oklahoma!*, was a huge success. Their shows combined accessible and entertaining music with involving, often serious stories, and broached such difficult subject matter as domestic abuse (*Carousel*, 1945), racism (*South Pacific*, 1949), and Nazism (*The Sound of Music*, 1959). Hammerstein is noted for his simple, heartfelt lyrics. The partners formed their own music publishing firm in 1949 and from that year produced their works and many others, including *Van Druten's *I Remember Mama* (1944) and Irving *Berlin's *Annie Get your Gun* (1946). The duo wrote one musical directly for film, *State Fair* (1945), and one for television, *Cinderella* (1957). Hammerstein's personal honours included two Pulitzer prizes, two Academy awards, and five Tony awards.   KF

Hampden, Walter (1879–1955) American actor and *producer. Born in Brooklyn and educated at Harvard, Hampden apprenticed in England with *Benson's company, performed under *Irving and Granville *Barker, and ap-

peared in America in 1907 opposite Alla Nazimova in her *Ibsen repertory. He played Manson, a reincarnation of Jesus, in Charles Rann Kennedy's *The Servant in the House* (1908), a role which fed his Shakespearian ambitions; in 1918 he *financed a series of Shakespeare matinées on Broadway. Hampden triumphed in 1923 with *Rostand's *Cyrano de Bergerac*, which ran for over 1,000 performances. He assumed *management of the Colonial Theatre and led his own company there (1925–30), frequently reviving *Cyrano* to boost receipts, but focusing on Shakespeare. His romantic *acting style and script choices failed to keep the theatre afloat during the Depression, though he performed Shakespeare on *tour. As a member of the American Repertory Theatre in New York, he played Cardinal Wolsey in *Henry VIII* (1946). His final role was Danforth in *Miller's *The Crucible* (1953).   FL

Hampton, Christopher (1946–) English playwright. The *Royal Court produced Hampton's first play before he left Oxford (*When Did You Last See my Mother?*, 1966). *Total Eclipse* followed (1968), then *The Philanthropist* (1970), *Savages* (1973), and *Treats* (1976), all for the Royal Court. The most 'continental' of his English contemporaries, Hampton has translated *Chekhov, *Ibsen, *Molière, *Reza's *Art* (1996), and Choderlos de Laclos's novel *Les Liaisons dangereuses* (1985), which was a huge success for the *Royal Shakespeare Company. Hampton also promoted the work of Ödön von *Horváth, translating *Tales from the Vienna Woods* (1977) and *Don Juan Comes back from the War* (1978). Horváth inspired Hampton's *Tales from Hollywood* (1982), about the émigré literary community in California during the war. He contributed another tale of Hollywood with the book for *Lloyd Webber's musical *Sunset Boulevard* (1993), for which he won a Tony award. Hampton has written a number of films including the (retitled) *Dangerous Liaisons* (1988, Academy Award), *Total Eclipse* (1995), and *Atonement* (2007).   MDG

hanamichi The 'flower path' in Japanese, a characteristic feature of the *kabuki stage, is a platform a little less than a metre wide, the same height as the stage, running from stage right to the back of the *auditorium. The audience is seated on both sides of this ramp, which is used primarily to give impact to entrances and exits. Important action usually takes place seven-tenths of the way from the back of the auditorium at a spot known as the *shichi-san* (seven-three), where a trap is located for magical appearances and disappearances. Most contemporary kabuki theatres have a motorized cable system rigged to allow flying exits from the *shichi-san* to the top balcony. The origins of the *hanamichi* are in dispute, but the term may have referred originally to the place where fans could step onto the stage and present gifts to the actors (*hana* means 'flower' and thus 'gift'). During the seventeenth century kabuki was most often presented on a stage resembling that of the *nō* theatre, with entrances and exits played on the *hashigakari* bridgeway parallel to the stage at the right. But beginning in the 1680s the bridgeway was gradually expanded, until by the 1730s the permanent *hanamichi* came into common use. LRK

Hancock, Sheila (1933–) English performer. An assured comedienne and fine dramatic actress, Hancock first made her name in television in the sitcom *The Rag Trade* (1961–3). She appeared in the West End in *The Anniversary* (1964), on Broadway in *Orton's Entertaining Mr Sloane* (1965), was a wicked Miss Hannigan in the West End revival of *Annie* (1978), an ebullient Mrs Lovett in the London première of *Sondheim's Sweeney Todd* (1980), and a spurned Lady Wishfort in *The Way of the World* at the Lyric Theatre Hammersmith (1992). In 1985 she directed Ian *McKellen in *Sheridan's The Critic* at the *National Theatre. She was Anne, a middle-aged teacher awakening to love, in David Eldridge's *Under the Blue Sky* at the *Royal Court (2000). AS

Handke, Peter (1942–) Austrian playwright and novelist. His literary career began with prose works, but his controversial *Publikumsbeschimpfung* (*Offending the Audience*, 1966) became one of the most widely performed 'anti-plays' of the 1960s. The plotless, *characterless torrent of offensive sentences went far beyond the confines of *absurd theatre. Handke rejected overtly political drama of the *Brechtian mould and instead sought to uncover the deficiencies of society by critiquing its language. His interest in Wittgenstein informed his 'speech plays' *Prophecy* (1966), *Self-Accusation* (1966), and *Calling for Help* (1967). In *Kaspar* (1968) the language of the civilized world imposed on a 'wild child' foundling is a tool of both socialization and victimization, which pushes the boy from a state of natural existence into madness. However, for the actors the 'speech-torture' has a liberating effect as it shifts the emphasis away from word-centred drama to *physical theatre. In the play without words *My Foot my Tutor* (1969), a ward and his guardian are locked in a power struggle, but the precise description of their actions is regularly interrupted by the indeterminable movements of

a cat on stage. Handke considered *Quodlibet* (1970) a prelude to *The Ride across Lake Constance* (1971) where the same characters, now given the names of famous actors of the Weimar Republic, engage in highly cryptic *dialogues. This and his later plays, *They Are Dying Out* (1974), *Across the Villages* (1982), *A Play about Questions* (1990), and *The Hour We Were Ignorant of Each Other* (1992), are large-scale works for major *playhouses and have not seen many productions. He continues to court controversy, as when in 2006 he spoke at the funeral of Slobodan Milošević. GB

Hands, Terry (1941–) English director. Hands co-founded the Liverpool Everyman Theatre in 1964 but moved in 1966 to run the *Royal Shakespeare Company's small-scale *touring company Theatregoround. For the main company, his *The Merry Wives of Windsor* (1968) showed the town world of Windsor with comic affection. Hands extended the RSC's repertory with *Genet (*The Balcony*, 1971) and other new work, and he directed Shakespeare at the *Comédie-Française (for example, *Richard III*, 1972), becoming a consultant director there in 1975. He directed notable productions of Shakespeare's history plays for the company with Alan *Howard as Hal and Henry V (1975) and as Henry VI (1977). In 1978 he became joint artistic director with *Nunn and sole artistic director from 1986 to 1991. At his best, in *Much Ado About Nothing* (1982) and *Cyrano* (1983), both starring *Jacobi, he could create a subtlety and individuality rarely seen in his larger-scale productions. He became artistic director of Theatr Clwyd in 1997. PDH

Hankin, St John (1869–1909) English playwright and journalist. Hankin wrote four major plays between 1905 and his suicide, produced in London by the *Stage Society or at the *Royal Court, and were popular with the provincial *repertory theatres before 1914, but were overshadowed by the fame of other Court dramatists and did not reach the West End until *Gielgud mounted *The Return of the Prodigal* in 1948 (originally directed by Granville *Barker, 1905). Hankin's plays, *well made but unsentimental and deterministic, have a disillusioned humour that found favour with *Shaw. *The Cassilis Engagement* (1907) was successfully revived at the Orange Tree Theatre in 1999. EEC

Hansberry, Lorraine (1930–65) *African-American playwright who broke the Broadway colour line for women with *Raisin in the Sun* (1959). Taking its title from a line in Langston *Hughes's poem 'Harlem', *Raisin* won the Drama

Critics' Circle award and launched a new era in African-American theatre. Directed by Lloyd *Richards, the cast, all unknowns at the time, included Ruby *Dee, Louis Gossett, Douglas Turner *Ward, and Sidney Poitier. (Because white audiences flocked to see *Raisin*, several black militants charged that her work was racially conciliatory.) *The Sign in Sidney Brustein's Window*, about a Jewish couple, also premièred on Broadway (1964). In 1960 NBC commissioned Hansberry to write a television drama honouring Abraham Lincoln, but declined to produce it because of its strong racial position. *To Be Young, Gifted and Black*, completed and arranged by her former husband, was produced in 1969 after the playwright's early death from cancer. The next year, *Les Blancs*—the title an inversion of *Genet's Les Nègres (The Blacks)*, the play about the ending and after effects of European colonialism in Africa—was produced at the Longacre. Hansberry's last published play was *What Use Are Flowers* (1972).   BBL

happenings A performance genre developed by Allan *Kaprow towards the end of the 1950s. Starting off with action paintings, action collages, assemblages, and then environments, Kaprow began to add flashing *lights and audible elements, and finally integrated visitors as mobile components into the structure of his exhibitions. This led in 1959 to *18 Happenings in 6 Parts*, performed at the Reuben Gallery in New York. Parallel developments took place in Paris by the Nouveau Réalisme group organized by Pierre Restany, in Vienna amongst a group of painters later known as Viennese Actionists, and in the Rhineland amongst the Zero group. These artists worked entirely independently of each other and were only united by their interest in exploring time-based structures in their works and introducing aspects of everyday life. The integration of materials not commonly associated with high art extended to the use of human beings. Some of the resulting 'events' were *improvised, but usually happenings were premeditated or even scripted. This structuring and planning aimed at offering a concentrated experience of life and focused attention on aspects of reality usually considered unworthy of artistic attention. A more minimalist version with stronger musical direction was advocated by the Fluxus movement directed by George Maciunas, active chiefly between 1962 and 1966 in various European locations and in New York. *See also* PERFORMANCE ART.   GB

Hardy, Alexandre (*c.*1570–1632) Almost certainly France's first full-time professional

dramatist, Hardy began his prolific career about 1592. He was attached to Valleran Le Conte's itinerant troupe, possibly from 1598, as salaried author, and later at the *Hôtel de Bourgogne (1622–6). In 1627, in exchange for a company share, he contracted to supply 36 plays over six years to the troupe of Claude Deschamps de Villiers; fifteen figured in the Bourgogne's repertory in the 1630s. Of the '600 plays and more' Hardy estimated he wrote, only 54 are known. Forty-one survive in print, mostly *tragicomedies, though he drew little generic distinction between *tragedy, tragicomedy, and *pastoral. Composed with total disregard for the *neoclassical unities, Hardy's structurally chaotic dramas were intended for a simultaneous staging system. He plundered sources as disparate as Homer and Heliodorus, Lucian and Lope de *Vega, *Giraldi and *Cervantes, to devise plays whose titles betray the extravagant baroque subject matter his *audiences enjoyed: *The Rape of Proserpine* (1626), *Lucretia; or, Adultery Punished* (1628), *Turlupin's Madness* (1621/32). While his obscure verse makes them inaccessible today, Hardy helped effect a transition from the stilted, *Senecan academic drama of the sixteenth century to the lively professional theatre of the seventeenth.   JG

Hare, David (1947–) English playwright, screenwriter, and director. Hare quickly established himself as a political theatre practitioner, founding Portable Theatre (1968) with Tony Bicât and Joint Stock Theatre (1973) with *Stafford-Clark and David Aukin. His early plays include *How Brophy Made Good* (1971) for the Portable, *Slag* (1971), and *The Great Exhibition* (1972), *Knuckle* (1974), and *Fanshen* (1975) for Joint Stock. He also directed plays by colleagues *Brenton, Snoo Wilson, and *Griffiths, including such collaborative efforts as Hare and Brenton's *Brassneck* (1973) and the multi-authored *Lay-By* (1975).

In 1975 Hare wrote and directed *Teeth and Smiles* starring *Mirren. Produced at the *Royal Court, both it and *Brassneck* were televised by the BBC, and *Knuckle* televised in America. Over the next five years, Hare enjoyed sustained productivity and wide recognition as one of the most important writers and directors of his generation. He directed Brenton's *Weapons of Happiness* as the first new play staged at the new *National Theatre in London in 1976, and wrote and directed *Licking Hitler* (1978) and *Dreams of Leaving* (1980) for television. Perhaps the best play of the decade, *Plenty* (1978), directed by Hare and starring Kate Nelligan, also opened at the National.

In the 1980s Hare frequently featured a woman *protagonist who negotiates issues of personal ethics and agency against a political backdrop. His best-known works include *A Map of the World* (1982), *Pravda* (1985) with Brenton, and *The Secret Rapture* (1988). He also wrote and directed the films *Wetherby* (1985), starring Vanessa *Redgrave, and *Paris by Night* (1989). Fred Schepisi's film version of *Plenty* starred Meryl Streep (1985). During the 1990s Hare conceived of a trilogy of plays on national institutions for *Eyre, *artistic director of the National. *Racing Demons* (1990) about the ministry and religion was extremely successful; *Murmuring Judges* (1991) and *The Absence of War* (1993) were only slightly less so. Hare continued to write and direct with *Skylight* (1995), *Amy's Room* (1997), and *The Blue Room* (1999), appearing himself in a solo piece about the Middle East (*Via Dolorosa*). In 2000 *The Zinc Bed* joined the first season of the remodelled Royal Court. Since then his plays include *Stuff Happens* (about the Iraq war, 2004), *Gethsemane* (about the Labour Party, 2008), both at the National, and *The Vertical Hour* (again concerning Iraq, New York, 2006). His later film scripts include *The Hours* (2002) and *The Reader* (2008), both directed by *Daldry.   JGR

Hare, John (1844–1921) English actor and *manager. Hare obtained a position in 1865 with Marie *Wilton at the Prince of Wales's in London, playing in all six *Robertson *comedies, specializing in old men. In 1875 he assumed management of the *Royal Court, with a strong company containing Ellen *Terry and the *Kendals. He then joined the Kendals in the management of the St James's in 1879, taking over the new Garrick Theatre in 1889, the Globe in 1898, and *touring extensively. Hare was a polished actor in refined comedy and society drama, like *Pinero's *The Profligate* (1889) and *The Gay Lord Quex* (1899) which he first produced, and one of the leading West End *actor-managers of the day.   MRB

Harlequin Also known as 'Arlechino' and 'Harlechino', a *stock character of *commedia dell'arte said to have originated in Bergamo. *Riccoboni states that before the seventeenth century Harlequin was a proficient tumbler and an inveterate trickster. Tristano *Martinelli was the earliest acclaimed Harlequin, while Dominique, in Louis XIV's reign, developed the *character's wit. Always undertaking intrigues for his master and getting into scrapes, by the second half of the seventeenth century his *costume consisted of patches of blue, red, and green triangles joined with yellow braid, later replaced by diamond-shaped lozenges. He wore a short jacket, a double-pointed hat, and a half-*mask and black chinpiece: his arched eyebrows and beard were bushy with stiff bristles; his forehead lined with wrinkles; and tiny holes represented eyes. He often commented on topical events and parodied the serious drama. In English *pantomime he was a silent character, a *dancer, and tumbler, leaping through traps to evade Pantaloon and *Clown, and empowered by a magic bat.   JTD

harlequinade See PANTOMIME, BRITISH.

Harrigan, Edward (1844–1911) and **Tony Hart** (1855–91) The most popular American comedy team from 1871 to 1885. Beginning separately as *minstrel performers, in 1871, Harrigan and Hart formed an act whose *character songs, *dancing, and *clowning soon propelled them to the heights of the *variety circuit. Opening Manhattan's Theatre Comique in 1875, they initially replicated their variety act, but eventually Harrigan began writing longer pieces. For example, working in 1872 with his future father-in-law, composer David Braham, Harrigan wrote 'The Mulligan Guard', a song that achieved international fame. By 1873 the song had evolved into a ten-minute sketch satirizing New York's pseudo-militias, and by 1878 had become *The Mulligan Guard Picnic*, the first of several full-length plays dealing with Irish, German, and Italian immigrants and the *African-Americans who shared the lower rungs of New York life. Harrigan and Hart served as a bridge between minstrelsy and American *musical theatre.   GAR

Harris, Audrey See MOTLEY.

Harris, Jed (1900–79) Austrian-born American director-*producer. Harris came to prominence in the 1920s when he produced a series of Broadway *melodramas and fast-paced *comedy hits, including *The Royal Family* (1928) and *The Front Page* (1928). His shows were known for their smooth pacing, expert casting, psychologically truthful *acting, and tasteful decor. Even when not credited as director, Harris participated closely in the staging and script revisions. He often quarrelled with dramatists over his claims to co-authorship, and had an abusive disposition that helped foster his image as a ruthless tyrant. Despite many flops, Harris maintained a reputation with the homosexually themed *The Green Bay Tree* (1933), a revival of *A Doll's House* (1937) starring Ruth *Gordon, and, most notably, *Our Town* (1938), for whose famed minimalist staging Harris claimed responsibility. His later successes included *Dark Eyes* (1943), *The Heiress* (1947), and *The Crucible* (1953), although this last was marred by differences with playwright *Miller. Harris's Broadway career ended in 1956.　　SLL

Harris, Margaret *See* MOTLEY.

Harris, Rosemary (1927–) English actress who made her New York debut in *The Climate of Eden* (1952) and appeared the following season in London in *The Seven Year Itch*. She worked at the Bristol Old Vic and the *Old Vic, returning to New York as Cressida in the Old Vic's *Troilus and Cressida* (1956). She has been a prominent member of numerous transatlantic companies: the *Chichester Festival Theatre, the *National Theatre, Lincoln Center, the American Shakespeare Festival, and the Williamstown Festival. Stunning and graceful, she has achieved distinction in classical and contemporary roles, making the transition from youthful to mature and older roles with elegance and ease. In 2008, at age 80, she was touring the US in a one person show, *Oscar and the Pink Lady*.　　TFC

Harrison, Rex (1908–90) English actor, who began in 1924 at the Liverpool Playhouse. Harrison appeared in London from 1930, quickly establishing himself as a stylish comic actor, adept in the plays of *Rattigan and *Coward. In the 1930s he also appeared regularly in films. During the war he served in the Royal Air Force, then resumed his career in England and the USA. On stage he performed in *Van Druten's *Bell, Book and Candle* and *Fry's *Venus Observed*, but his major stardom was achieved as Henry Higgins in *Lerner and Loewe's *musical *My Fair Lady* (1956); he also played the role in the film version (1964). For the rest of his career he alternated between stage and screen. On stage in London or New York he appeared in *Anouilh, *Chekhov, *Pirandello, Rattigan, and *Shaw.　　TP

Harrison, Tony (1937–) English dramatist, poet, and director. His first dramatic work, a translation of Molière's *The Misanthrope* (1973), initiated a relationship with the *National Theatre which produced *The Oresteia* (1981), a translation of *Aeschylus's trilogy, and *The Mysteries* (1985), a version of medieval *mystery plays, both inflected by speech from the north of England. Harrison's interest in the relationship of classical and contemporary culture, and his commitment to a demotic poetic drama, have marked his theatrical work. *The Trackers of Oxyrhynchus* (1990) is a version of *Sophocles' *satyr-play, while *Square Rounds* (1992) is a mordant account of the inventors of the machine gun and poison gas using *mime and *clowning. *Black Daisies for the Bride*

(1993) is a television *documentary drama concerning Alzheimer's disease, and *The Kaisers of Carnuntum* and *The Labourers of Herakles* (both 1995) were written for *amphitheatres in Austria and Greece. Harrison wrote and directed the epic film *Prometheus* (1999) which again blends classical myth and contemporary locations. *Fram* (2008) is a large-scale drama based on the life of the Arctic explorer Fridtjof Nansen.　　SF

Hart, Lorenz (1895–1943) American lyricist. With composer Richard *Rodgers, Hart contributed to many successful *musicals from 1925 to 1943. Noted for bittersweet love songs, he was one of Broadway's most gifted lyricists. Hart's talent first emerged at Columbia University where he and Rodgers wrote college shows. Their first hit song, 'Manhattan' (in *The Garrick Gaieties*, 1925), was followed by a string of popular shows, including *Dearest Enemy* (1925) and *A Connecticut Yankee* (1927). After writing for Hollywood musicals in the early 1930s, Rodgers and Hart returned to Broadway with such distinguished shows as *On your Toes* (1936), with an innovative *ballet by *Balanchine, and *Babes in Arms* (1937), which included the songs 'My Funny Valentine' and 'The Lady Is a Tramp' (two numbers that found their way into the 1957 film of *Pal Joey* starring Frank Sinatra). In its original stage version, *Pal Joey* (1940) departed from romantic musicals with its cynical main *character and shady nightclub setting. Though vastly talented, Hart was a troubled man. His descent into alcoholism ended both his partnership with Rodgers and his life.　　SN

Hart, Moss (1904–61) American playwright and director. Hart achieved fame when he collaborated with *Kaufman on the Hollywood *satire *Once in a Lifetime* (1930). Among his eight collaborations with Kaufman were the *comedies *You Can't Take It with You* (1936, Pulitzer Prize) and *The Man Who Came to Dinner* (1939), as well as the *musical satire of F. D. Roosevelt *I'd Rather Be Right* (1937, music by *Rodgers, lyrics by Lorenz *Hart). Moss Hart wrote and staged the musical on psychoanalysis *Lady in the Dark* (1941, music by *Weill, lyrics by Ira *Gershwin). Hart's outstanding solo work was the backstage comedy *Light up the Sky* (1948). As a director Hart created some of the most admired stagings of twentieth-century Broadway, especially the unified visual palette and balletic crowd scenes in *My Fair Lady* (1956), which ran for nearly 3,000 performances. Hart's memoir of his career up to 1930,

Act One (1958), has endured as an archetypal rags-to-riches theatrical story.   MAF

Hart, Tony *See* HARRIGAN, EDWARD.

Harwood, Ronald (1934–) South African playwright. Harwood moved to Britain in the early 1950s and joined *Wolfit's company as an actor, an experience which would inform his best-known play, *The Dresser* (1980, filmed 1983), which centres on the relationship between a barnstorming *actor-manager and his quietly efficient dresser. The play shows a wry fondness for the world of the theatre also found in *After the Lions* (1982) and *Reflected Glory* (1992). Harwood's career has mostly unfolded in the commercial sector, which has contributed to his being critically underrated. Plays like *J. J. Farr* (1987) and *Taking Sides* (1995) are serious and complex pieces. Their themes of resistance and oppression, and of faith and politics, are explored further in his autobiographical work like *Tramway Road* (1984) and *Another Time* (1989), and the overtly political *The Deliberate Death of a Polish Priest* (1985). His screenplays have been highly successful, especially *The Pianist* (2002, Academy Award) and *The Diving Bell and the Butterfly* (2007).   DR

Hasenclever, Walter (1890–1940) German dramatist. The première of *The Son* (1916) marked the beginning of *expressionism on the German stage. The play's exalted language, episodic structure, and eponymous figure who rebels against a tyrannical father are prototypical of the movement. *Antigone* (1919) displays an expressionist utopia of a new society. Hasenclever changed track in the mid-1920s and wrote sophisticated *comedies. *A Man of Distinction* (1927), featuring a marriage swindler, was a runaway success, while *Marriages Are Made in Heaven* (1928), a widely performed *succès de scandale*, attracted charges of blasphemy. His exile plays *Münchhausen* (1934) and *Scandal in Assyria* (London, 1939) were less successful. He committed suicide after the German invasion of France.   CBB

Hashmi, Safdar (1954–89) Indian playwright, actor, director, and lyricist. He was a founding member of Janam in 1973. Initially performing open-air plays for mass *audiences, Janam took to *street theatre in 1978 with *Machine*, which was written collaboratively, with Safdar (as he was generally called) making a large contribution. His contribution grew in later plays, though none is attributable entirely to him. He was the de facto director of Janam, which gave about 4,000 performances of 24 street plays until his

death. Hashmi's output includes two proscenium plays—an adaptation of *Gorky's *Enemies* (1983), and *Moteram ka Satyagraha* (with *Tanvir, 1988)—many songs, a television series, poems and plays for children, and documentary films. While committed to radical, popular, and left-wing art, Hashmi refrained from clichéd portrayals and was not afraid of formal experimentation. Janam was attacked by political hoodlums while performing *Halla Bol* (*Attack!*) in an industrial area near Delhi on 1 January 1989. Hashmi succumbed to his injuries the following day, and became for many a symbol of cultural resistance against authoritarianism.   SD

hasta Hand gesture, as delineated in the diverse vocabularies of classical *dance-theatre traditions in India. The different gestural ideograms created through the fingers and the hands constitute one of the most highly codified sign languages in world theatre. Depending on the direction of the palm (up, down, slanting), the particular positioning of the fingers, the elevation of the gesture, and the speed with which it is represented, *hastas* are divided into different categories. The *Natyasastra* specifies 64 *hastas*, 24 of which are shown by a single hand (*asamyuta*), though sometimes both hands show the same gesture. There are thirteen *hastas* shown by both hands (*samyuta*), and 27 are specifically delineated for dance (*nritta*). Drawing on treatises like the *Abhinayadarpana* and the *Hastalakshanadeepika*, the actors of *kathakali* have refined their storytelling skills through their elaborate use of *hastas*. In *kutiyattam*, hand gestures are used to convey grammatical shifts in registering the tense, number, and case of particular sentences in the drama. In their more iconographic usages, particularly in sculpturesque poses, *hastas* are also referred to as *mudra*.   LSR/RB

Hauptmann, Gerhart (1862–1946) German playwright, poet, and essayist. His first play, *Before Dawn* (1889), a *naturalist piece with brutish peasant *characters, caused an uproar at its première at the *Freie Bühne. Precipitated into becoming the leader of the German *naturalist movement, Hauptmann continued to write plays about ordinary people. Originally written in Silesian dialect, his best play, *The Weavers* (1894), describes the weavers' Luddite revolt against their paymasters in 1844. Together with *Büchner's *Woyzeck*, it is the most powerful social drama in German and is distinguished by the fact that the community of weavers forms a collective *hero. In *Rose Bernd* (1903) a desperate young girl strangles her newborn baby, and *Carter*

Henschel (1898) and *The Rats* (1911), a 'Berlin *tragicomedy', both end in suicide. At the same time Hauptmann was writing *comedies, most notably *The Beaver Coat* (1893), and a historical piece, *Florian Geyer* (1896), set during the Peasants' Revolt. He was also gradually turning towards *symbolism, with *The Sunken Bell* (1896) and *And Pippa Dances* (1906). Awarded the Nobel Prize for Literature in 1912, Hauptmann's prolific output of later plays, including a reworking of the *Atridean Tetralogy* (1944), never quite matched the excitement of his early naturalist work. He died at the age of 84, just in time to witness the defeat of Germany, where he had remained under the Nazi regime.   MWP

Haussmann, Leander (1959–   ) German director. Haussmann worked first as an actor at regional theatres. His breakthrough as a director came in 1990 with a production of *Ibsen's *A Doll's House* in Weimar, and he was voted best new director in 1991. From 1991 to 1995 he worked freelance at major German theatres and established a reputation for unorthodox productions, especially of Shakespeare. Perhaps most successful was his *Romeo and Juliet* (Munich, 1993). Haussmann is particularly renowned for mixing classics with elements of contemporary pop culture. From 1995 to 2000 he was *artistic director in Bochum, and in 2003 directed *The Tempest* for the *Berliner Ensemble. His film *Sonnenallee* (2000), a nostalgic look at youth in East Germany, has been followed by many others.CBB

Havel, Václav (1936–   ) Czech playwright, essayist, politician; President of Czechoslovakia (1989–1992) and of the Czech Republic (1993–2003). Havel was assistant director and *dramaturg of the Theatre on the Balustrade in Prague, where his plays *The Garden Party* (1963), *Memorandum* (1965), and *The Increased Difficulty of Concentration* (1968) were premièred. In the *absurdist vein, they exposed the distortions of human behaviour and communication under the communist regime. On a deeper level the subjects of human manipulation, the relationship between the individual and a dehumanized system or institution, and of the temptation to give up freedom in exchange for material welfare or collectivist ideology, remained Havel's preoccupation. In the late 1960s he was increasingly explicit on these issues; after the Soviet invasion of 1968, Havel was persecuted and repeatedly jailed. In the 1970s and 1980s his work—including *Largo Desolato* (1984), *Temptation* (1985), and *Urban Renewal* (1987), the three highlights of his dramatic career—was banned in Czechoslovakia but

published and staged abroad. In November 1989 Havel was the architect of the Czech Velvet Revolution and a month later was elected President.   ML

Havergal, Giles (1938–   ) English director, writer, and actor, *artistic director of the Glasgow *Citizens' Theatre 1969–2003. With director-designer Philip *Prowse and playwright Robert David MacDonald, Havergal created a 'people's theatre' with low-priced tickets and equal billing for actors. His fare of literary adaptations (for example, a version of *Nicholas Nickleby* in 1969), classic and twentieth-century drama, and extravagant campy *pantomimes was highly popular. He directed, wrote, or acted in a number of striking productions, most notably accomplishing all three functions in *Travels with my Aunt* (1989). He also guest directed for Shared Experience (1985–7).   KN

Hawtrey, Charles Henry (1858–1923) English *actor-manager who began his career in 1881 at the Prince of Wales's Theatre and his long managerial career with the lease of Her Majesty's in 1885. Although extraordinarily active in both capacities (he managed more than sixteen London theatres), his range as a performer was narrow. He preferred to identify himself with *characters that reflected aspects of his own personality and were palatable and recognizable to his society *audiences. In this he was eminently successful, playing a sequence of likeable upper-class rogues with effortless ease within a *farcical framework. He was especially noted for his performances in *The Private Secretary* (1883), *A Message from Mars* (1899), *The Man from Blankley's* (1901), and the plays of H. V. Esmond, Charles Brookfield, and Comyns Carr. He *toured the United States extensively (1901, 1903, 1912) with equal success. As a personality actor in *comedy he inherited the mantle of Charles *Mathews and anticipated the qualities with which *Coward and Rex *Harrison were later associated—charm, knowing detachment, and elegance.   VEE

Hayes, Helen (1900–93) American actress, sometimes called 'the First Lady of the American Theatre'. Discovered at the age of 5 among a Washington, DC, *stock company, Hayes performed in numerous Broadway plays and *musicals for producer Lew Fields. Her small physical stature and wide-set eyes gave her an appearance that, as Hayes said, led people to 'coddle and care' for her. During the years 1917–23, she personified the plucky *ingénue, performing in a series of light *comedies. She broke this pattern in 1924, playing Cleopatra in *Shaw's *Caesar and Cleopatra*. During the long run of *Coquette* (1927-9), she married playwright *MacArthur. Hayes was admired for her transformative *illusion from youth to old age in the long-running *Victoria Regina* (1935-9) and, though the playwright disliked her performance, critics praised her Amanda Wingfield in the 1948 London première of *Williams's *The Glass Menagerie*. Hayes acted almost continuously until 1985. MAF

Haymarket, Theatre Royal Located in the centre of the West End, the Haymarket remains one of the oldest and most successful *playhouses in London. The first theatre was built in 1720. The political *satires of *Fielding produced there led directly to the passing of the *Licensing Act of 1737, which brought about *censorship and the monopoly of *legitimate drama by the *patent theatres. In 1766, the Haymarket's *manager, *Foote, obtained a patent licence for the summer months, which remained the basis of operation until the Theatre Regulation Act abolished the monopoly in 1843. The venue's identification with comedy was continued by the *Colman family from 1776 to 1817.

The second theatre opened in 1821 immediately adjacent to the old site. Benjamin *Webster managed it from 1837 to 1853; he had it lit by gas (*see* LIGHTING) and introduced orchestra stalls. The house's nineteenth-century heyday coincided with the management (1853-78) of *Buckstone, himself a 'low comedian'. Squire and Marie *Bancroft it took over for five years from 1880 and transferred many of their successful productions, consisting largely of the plays of *Robertson. *Tree's tenure (1887-96) was marked by *Wilde's *A Woman of No Importance* (1893) and *An Ideal Husband* (1895), while Cyril *Maude and Frederick Harrison bought the theatre's lease in 1896 and produced the plays of *Jones, *Barrie, and *Grundy. In 1904 the theatre was given a major refurbishment, including the re-establishment of the pit (*see* BOX, PIT, AND GALLERY), and from 1905 to 1981 remained in the hands of Harrison and his estate. The lease was then acquired by the Louis Michaels company and in 1994 the Haymarket was completely redecorated at a cost of £1.3 million. VEE

heavens A 'mansion' structure or 'house' representing heaven often appeared in the simultaneous settings of cycle *biblical plays in *medieval theatre, and was traditionally located to stage right in opposition to *hell mouth on stage left, or to the east of any open acting area. It could be crowned with rings of painted angels surrounding a heavenly throne, and Christ sometimes ascended into it by means of a concealed pulley and tackle. It could also be found on some of the pageant wagons, where it took the form of a small upper balcony where angels stood, and from which God could descend.

In the Elizabethan theatre the 'heavens' was an upper room located above the rear part of the stage, supported by pillars resting on the stage (as at the *Swan Theatre) or by beams running forward from the roof (as at the *Hope). It contained a winch for lowering actors and objects to the stage, and its lower surface was usually decorated with paintings of the sun, moon, and stars. JWH

Hebbel, Christian Friedrich (1813-63) German writer. Arguably the most important German dramatist of the mid-nineteenth century, Hebbel draws on the Old Testament, Roman history, ancient myth (*Gyges und sein Ring*, 1856), Germanic saga, the Middle Ages (*Genoveva*, 1843; *Agnes Bernauer*, 1852), and his own time. The plays employ both verse and *realistic prose. The *tragedy *Judith* (1841) brought Hebbel his first success. He provides the Judith–Holofernes story with an original psychological motivation that anticipates Freudian theories of the unconscious. Mistrust and sexual conflict also motivate the blank verse tragedy *Herodes und Mariamne* (1849), which combines individual psychology, historical setting, and religious overtones. Hebbel's most popular work in his lifetime was the *Nibelungen* trilogy (1855-60); recent revivals (*Heyme in Stuttgart, 1973, *Flimm in Hamburg, 1988) have concentrated on the mythic world and the *character conflicts. His most successful play remains the *bourgeois tragedy *Maria Magdalene* (1846), which marks an important step towards the social drama of *Ibsen and *Hauptmann. CBB

Hecht, Ben (1894-1964) American playwright. Most of Hecht's notable work in theatre was written in collaboration with Charles *MacArthur, with whom he shared a background as a Chicago newspaperman. *The Front Page* (1928), a *melodrama-*farce about the newspaper business, was a major success and was followed by another successful collaboration, *Twentieth Century* (1932), a similarly antic- and plot-driven play about theatre. Hecht and MacArthur wrote the book for the *musical extravaganza *Jumbo* (1935, with *Rodgers and *Hart) and collaborated intermittently up to *Swan Song* in 1946. Both turned mostly to screenwriting after 1933. Hecht wrote or co-wrote more than 60 Hollywood films (including *Nothing Sacred*, 1937, and Hitchcock's *Notorious*, 1946), published fifteen novels and fourteen volumes of short fiction, and a biography of his former collaborator. MAF

Heijermans, Herman (1864–1924) Dutch playwright and critic. Although Heijermans's early plays were influenced by the *naturalism of *Ibsen and *Hauptmann, he found determinist philosophy too pessimistic. His tragic dramas, set among the working and middle classes of the Netherlands, have frequently been compared to the Dutch domestic paintings of the seventeenth century. Heijermans's socialist beliefs in the possibility of utopia on earth endowed his plays with some optimism. *The Good Hope* (1900), about the loss of a fishing vessel at sea, is generally acknowledged as his masterpiece, but *Ghetto* (1889), *Ora et Labora* (1902), *The Maid* (1908), and *The Devil to Pay* (1917) powerfully dramatize class tensions in Dutch society and display compassion for the underprivileged, even when they engage in acts destructive of the happiness of wealthier people. Heijermans was the only Dutch playwright of the twentieth century whose plays were regularly staged outside his native country. SJCW

Hellman, Lillian (1905–84) Often ranked with *O'Neill, *Williams, *Miller, and *Wilder as one of America's outstanding playwrights, Hellman built an impressive body of serious *realistic drama over the course of three decades. Inspired by Dashiell Hammett, with whom she had a long relationship, Hellman turned to playwriting in 1934 with *The Children's Hour*, based on a Scottish libel case concerning a female student's accusation of lesbianism against two teachers. It ran for 691 performances and had countless revivals. After the failure of the labour drama *Days to Come* (1936), Hellman returned to success with *The Little Foxes* (1939), at once a realistic depiction of the power struggle within an antebellum southern white family and a parable about the corrosive effects of capitalism on moral character. Hellman's string of realistic, family-centred dramas continued with the anti-fascist *Watch on the Rhine* (1941); *The Searching Wind* (1944), a morality tale about the causes of the Second World War; *Another Part of the Forest* (1946), a prologue to *The Little Foxes*; *The Autumn Garden* (1951); and *Toys in the Attic* (1960), about incestuous desire and race consciousness. After the failure of a 1963 adaptation, Hellman withdrew from theatre and focused on her memoirs, *An Unfinished Woman* (1969), *Pentimento* (1973), and *Scoundrel Time* (1976). MAF

hell mouth A 'mansion' structure or 'house' representing hell often appeared in the simultaneous settings of cycle *biblical plays in *medieval theatre, and was traditionally located to stage left in opposition to *heaven on stage right, or to the west or north-west of any open acting area. It took the form of a monstrous dragon's head with gaping jaws, inside which the damned could often be seen being boiled in a cauldron. JWH

Helpmann, Robert (1909–86) Australian *dancer, choreographer, and actor. He began his career assisting Pavlova on her *tour of Australia (1926) and later Margaret Rawlings who, encouraging his coming to London in 1931, introduced him to Ninette de Valois in whose *Sadler's Wells Ballet he starred (1933–50), rapidly proving a worthy partner to Markova and Fonteyn and a brilliant *mime, a quality de Valois exploited when creating Tregennis (*The Haunted Ballroom*), the Rake (*The Rake's Progress*), and the ailing Red King (*Checkmate*), a role he was still playing six weeks before his death. Helpmann's own choreography was narrative based and theatrical: *Comus* and a *surreal *Hamlet* (both 1942), *Miracle in the Gorbals* (1944), *Adam Zero* (1946), *Elektra* (1963). During this period he also acted, chiefly in Shakespeare (Oberon, Hamlet, Shylock, King John, Richard III) and directed (*Antony and Cleopatra*, *Madame Butterfly*, *The Soldier's Tale*). From 1965 to 1976 he was director of the Australian Ballet, for whom he created *The Display*, *Yugen*, and a revised *Elektra*. RAC

Heminges, John (1556–1630) English actor. Heminges probably began his career in the late 1580s with the *Queen's Men, but moved fairly soon to Strange's Men and the *Chamberlain's Men, remaining when they became the King's Men. His roles as an actor are unknown, though he is listed in many cast lists for *Jonson's plays. He held many business interests, theatrical and non-theatrical, and apparently served as the company's business *manager and payee for court performances. With Henry *Condell, Heminges was responsible for the compilation of the First Folio of Shakespeare's plays (1623). SPC

Henley, Beth (1952–) American playwright. Mississippi-born Henley's first full-length play, *Crimes of the Heart* (*Actors Theatre of Louisville, 1979), was the first play to win a Pulitzer Prize before a Broadway run (1981), and the first Pulitzer given to a woman since 1958. It signalled the arrival of a new generation of women playwrights, including Marsha *Norman and *Wasserstein. The play typifies Henley's use of the southern idiom, quirky *comedy, female perspective, and movement towards understanding instead of resolution. Other plays include *The Miss Firecracker Contest* (1980), about a dark horse in a southern beauty pageant, *Abundance* (1990), about mail-order brides in the Old West, *L-Play* (1995), made up of six scenes in six styles, all titled with L-words, *Impossible Marriage* (1998), *Family Week* (2000), and *Ridiculous Fraud* (2006). Henley wrote the screenplays for Hollywood films of *Crimes of the Heart* (1986) and *The Miss Firecracker Contest* (1998). GAO

Henry, Martha (1938–) Canadian actor and director, born Martha Buhs in Michigan. She moved to Canada in 1959 and appeared at the *Stratford Festival in 1961 as Miranda in *The Tempest*. During twenty seasons at Stratford, she portrayed women of strong convictions, such as Cordelia (1964), Titania (1968), and Lady Macbeth (1999). She made her directorial debut at Stratford with *Brief Lives* (1980), and abandoned *acting in 1986 to focus on *directing. Henry served as the *artistic director of the Grand Theatre, London, Ontario (1988–95). Returning to Stratford in 1994, she acted Mary Tyrone in *O'Neill's *Long Day's Journey into Night* (1994) and Linda in *Miller's *Death of a Salesman* (1997), and directed *Ibsen's *Enemy of the People* (2001). She has also acted in London, New York, and in theatres across Canada. PBON

Henslowe, Philip (*c.*1555–1616) English *manager and financier. Originally a dyer by trade, Henslowe became part-owner of the most successful theatre entrepreneurship in *early modern London, eventually holding several court positions as well. In 1587 he decided (for reasons that are unclear) to build the *Rose Theatre in Southwark. In 1592 he undertook substantial renovations, and in the same year his stepdaughter married the actor Edward *Alleyn. The two men formed a partnership that eventually included three playhouses (the Rose, *Fortune, and *Hope), and the Bear Garden, a *baiting arena rebuilt as the Hope in 1613, and held the patent to the Mastership of the Bears, Bulls, and Mastiff Dogs.

Many players and several companies performed in Henslowe's theatres, but he was primarily connected to them as a financier, for which he collected a portion of their profits. He and Alleyn also arranged dramatic contracts with playwrights, paid for licences for performances, and authorized payments for *costumes and other necessities. Henslowe's 'diary'—a memorandum book recording many of his *financial dealings (1593–1603)—is a major document of the London theatre. In it Henslowe noted payments to dramatists, the titles of plays and the days on which they were performed, costume purchases, loans to actors, performance receipts,

and contracts with players. It also provides information on the repertory of the *Admiral's Men and the scheduling of plays. His estate and manuscripts passed to Alleyn, who preserved them, along with his own papers, at Dulwich College. SPC

Herbert, Jocelyn (1917–2003) English designer, who designed over 70 productions for drama, *opera, and film since she joined the *English Stage Company in 1956. Influenced by *Brecht's designer, *Neher, she rapidly devised an innovative minimalist style, remarkable for its concise but poetic functionalism, achieving atmosphere and place by sculptural rather than painterly means. She showed a profound affinity with *Ionesco (*Exit the King*), *Beckett (*Krapp's Last Tape, Happy Days, Not I, Footfalls, That Time*), *Wesker (*Roots, I'm Talking about Jerusalem*), *Osborne (*Luther, A Patriot for Me*), and *Storey (*Home, The Changing Room, Life Class*). For the *National Theatre she designed Brecht's *Mother Courage* and *Galileo* and many of Tony *Harrison's stage works, notably his translation of *The Oresteia*. Opera designs included Berg's *Lulu* and Birtwistle's *The Masks of Orpheus*. RAC

Herbert, Victor (1859–1924) American composer. Irish born, trained in Germany as a cellist, he came to America in 1886, playing in the pit of the Metropolitan Opera and serving as a part-time military bandmaster. He soon became an American citizen and set out to learn the popular American musical idiom. All of these influences would affect the style of the man who was America's first theatre composer of lasting note. In 1894 he began writing *music for the stage, and in 1898 he had his first hit, the gypsy-flavoured *The Fortune Teller*. Now in demand, he cranked out stage works with rapidity until he scored a huge success with *Babes in Toyland* (1903), a spectacular children's story bathed in music ranging from marches to ragtime to the Irish-flavoured 'Toyland'. A series of popular *operettas followed, culminating in *Naughty Marietta* (1910), a work which set the standard for American operetta. He wrote the music for more than 40 stage works, becoming the grand old man of American theatre music. He was also a founder of ASCAP, the music licensing firm protecting *copyright. JD

Herman, Jerry (1933–) American composer and lyricist. During the 1950s he wrote words and *music for several *Off-Broadway *revues, cracking Broadway in 1961 with *Milk and Honey*, a tuneful romance set in Israel with Yiddish theatre veteran Molly Picon. This focus on an older central *character would mark Herman's next several *musicals, notably his greatest hit, *Hello, Dolly!* (1964), and its successor, *Mame* (1966), both exuberant, highly traditional, but irresistibly appealing scores with songs that repeatedly emphasized the shows' titles. A more adventurous score still emphasizing older women, *Dear World* (1969), was less successful, as were *Mack and Mabel* (1974) and *The Grand Tour* (1979). But in *La Cage aux Folles* (1983), he re-established his formula of an energetic traditional score framing an untraditional situation, with the first *gay-themed Broadway blockbuster. Herman has seen several revues of his popular tunes—*Jerry's Girls* (1985), *The Best of Times* (1995), *An Evening with Jerry Herman* (1998)—and written a television musical, *Mrs Santa Claus* (1996).   JD

Hernández, Luisa Josefina (1928–   ) Mexican playwright, novelist, and educator. The first woman to achieve an equal place in the male-dominated Mexican theatre world, Hernández has guided generations of aspiring playwrights through her professorship at the National Autonomous University of Mexico. *The Fallen Fruit* (1957), written when she was a student of *Usigli and directed by the Japanese émigré Seki Sano, who introduced *Method acting into Mexico, established Hernández as a master of psychological *realism with a keen insight into the hypocrisy of the middle class, especially in relation to sexuality. Her *History of a Ring* (1967) and *The Mulato's Orgy* (1970) are *Brechtian critiques of political corruption and economic oppression. Hernández also has written historical plays such as *Popol Vuh* (1967), based on the holy Mayan text, as well as numerous short plays for a variety of student activities. Translated into English and various European languages, Hernández has won important national awards for playwriting, although her works are not often given professional stagings in Mexico.   KFN

Herne, James A. (1839–1901) American *actor-manager and playwright. With no formal education past the age of 13, Herne built a lifelong career as a popular performer in romantic *melodrama, after several years with barnstorming troupes on America's east coast. He eventually settled in San Francisco, and began writing plays with *Belasco. With *Hearts of Oak* (1879) and *Drifting Apart* (1888), Herne developed a strength for rural dramas, with *dialogue reflecting *Ibsen and other early *realists. Herne attempted a serious social drama with *Margaret Fleming* (1890). Herne's major popular success was *Shore-Acres* (1892), his signature role for the rest of his life. Although a romantic melodrama with a rural

Maine setting, it features such realistic elements as the preparation, serving, and eating of a Thanksgiving dinner on stage, and an astonishing ending, performed entirely in silence, with Herne on stage puttering about closing the family home for the evening, while reflecting on events, the first clear use in American drama of what *Stanislavsky would later call *subtext.   AW

hero and antihero (heroine) Terms used to denote the *protagonist of a dramatic *action. In drama prior to *romanticism, hero described a figure in either *tragedy or *comedy. Heroes were distinguished by admirable personal qualities, by the sense that they often had access to sources of energy and insight denied the common man, and by their status as representatives of the social community. Romanticism, however, posited the hero as one who was alienated from society and highly critical of it. The 'antihero', as this figure could be called, often stood at the centre of the action in the *realistic dramas of *Ibsen, *Strindberg, *Chekhov, and *Shaw, and became the icon of the 'angry young man' English drama of the 1950s. Several of the central *characters in tragedies by playwrights as diverse as *Euripides, Shakespeare, and *Calderón now appear to be more antiheroic than heroic. Yet nineteenth-century *melodrama, and its numerous descendants on stage and in Hollywood action films, relied on the heroic qualities of the protagonist for the successful resolution of the action, usually pitting him or her against an evil *villain in order to clarify the hero's morally superior status.   SJCW

heroic tragedy A form of serious drama which flourished briefly in England during the Restoration. Heroic tragedy, in rhymed couplets, featured a titanic *protagonist, spectacular action in an exotic setting, bombast and overwrought emotion, and themes of love and honour. A tragic *denouement was not a requisite. It had affinities with *Corneille's *tragedies, but its immediate progenitor, according to its most prominent advocate, *Dryden, was *Davenant's *Siege of Rhodes* (1656). Dryden, with Robert Howard, inaugurated the vogue with *The Indian Queen* (1664), but after *Aureng-Zebe* (1675) he turned to blank verse tragedy and by the early 1680s heroic tragedy had run its course.   RWV

Heron, Matilda (1830–77) American actress. Born in Ireland, Heron came to the United States at an early age. She made her stage debut in 1851, at Philadelphia's Walnut Street Theatre, then *toured California and appeared in New York. Her greatest success came in the role of Camille, in the *Dumas play she adapted and virtually made her own. Heron's version ran for 100 nights at Wallack's in New York, in 1857, after which she toured it with phenomenal success. Her style of *acting, which was noted for its emotional *naturalism and power, greatly influenced other actors of the late nineteenth century. Aspects of her style that were new to American *audiences included using a conversational tone for *dialogue, turning her back on the audience, and portraying illness and suffering without refinement or sentimentality.   AHK

Herrmann, Karl-Ernst (1936–   ) German designer and director. One of the most important stage *scenographers of the post-war period, in 1969 Hermann began an association with *Stein and was a founding member of the Berlin *Schaubühne, working on practically all the best-known productions. Most notable were *Peer Gynt* (1971), where he constructed a square arena stage with the *audience on both sides; *Gorky's *Summerfolk* (1974) featuring real birch trees; the *environmental staging in *Shakespeare's Memory* (1976); and *Chekhov's *Three Sisters* (1984) with a reconstruction of the set of the original Moscow Art Theatre production. Since 1982 Herrmann has worked as a director and designer of *opera. Important productions (especially for Brussels) include *Mozart's *La clemenza di Tito* (1982; *Salzburg Festival, 1992), *La finta giardiniera* (1986), and *Don Giovanni* (1987); *Verdi's *La traviata* (1987); and Gluck's *Orpheus and Eurydice* (1988). In 2005 he designed Botho *Strauss's *Die eine und die andere* for the *Berliner Ensemble.   CBB

Hewett, Dorothy (1923–2002) Australian writer. One of the country's most acclaimed playwrights, Hewett first came to notice with *This Old Man Comes Rolling Home* (1966), a drama of Sydney working-class family life. A controversial and distinctive writer, her partly autobiographical and intensely personal style emphasized sexual and family relations in plays such as *The Chapel Perilous* (1971). Later work, such as *The Man from Muckinupin* (1979) and *The Fields of Heaven* (1982), chronicled the need to value cultural heritage and cherish landscapes. A radical writer with a free-ranging style, Hewett remains a figure who polarizes *audiences and critics.   SBS

Heyme, Hansgünther (1935–   ) German director. Heyme became assistant to *Piscator in Berlin and Mannheim in 1956. From 1958 to 1963 he was director-in-residence in Heidelberg where he directed among other works *Toller's *Hinkemann* (1959) and *Camus's *The Possessed*

(1960). Heyme's first production to attain national recognition was *Weiss's *Marat/Sade* in Wiesbaden, where he was director from 1964 to 1968. As *artistic director of Cologne's municipal theatre (1968–79), he experimented remarkably with *Greek *tragedy and *comedy. The central focus, however, was the German classical tradition of *Goethe, *Schiller, and *Hebbel, and a number of productions were invited to the Berlin *Theatertreffen. His farewell production in 1979 was a controversial *Hamlet* designed by the *performance artist Wolf Vostell which made extraordinary use of television monitors and other electronic mediation of the stage events. He held subsequent posts in Stuttgart and Essen. An important representative of German *director's theatre, which established itself as the dominant aesthetic trend in the 1960s and 1970s, his productions were based on intensive cooperation with *dramaturgs and fused scholarly research with radical reinterpretations of the classics. CBB

Heyward, Dorothy (1890–1961) and **Dubose Heyward** (1885–1940) American playwrights. Though they occasionally worked apart, as in Dorothy's *Cinderelative* (1930) or Dubose's *Brass Ankle* (1931), the Heywards' major works were written as a husband-and-wife team. The process typically involved field research, then a novel by Dubose dramatized by Dorothy and polished together. Their three successes were based upon research into folkways of African Americans in South Carolina. *Mamoulian's *ritualistic and semi-musical staging of *Porgy* (1927) contributed to the interest in folk drama in the 1920s seen also in plays by Paul *Green, who—like the Heywards—was a sympathetic white intellectual observing black culture. *Porgy* was reworked as the hugely successful *opera *Porgy and Bess*, with *music by George *Gershwin, book by Dubose Heyward, and lyrics by Heyward and Ira *Gershwin. The Heywards' other success was *Mamba's Daughters* (1939), a violent and eventful *tragedy which featured Ethel *Waters.   MAF

Heywood, John (c.1497–1579) English playwright, musician, and poet. From 1520 Heywood was active at the court of Henry VIII as a 'singer and player of virginals' and later as master of an acting troupe of boy singers. He apparently continued to produce pageants and entertainments during the reigns of Edward VI and Mary Tudor. In 1564 he fled to Flanders, where he died. Five of Heywood's six plays (all written before 1533) take the form of comic debates, which poke fun at academic chop-logic while simultaneously making a didactic point: *The Play of Love*,

Witty and Witless, The Play of the Weather, The Four PP, The Pardoner and the Friar. The scatological humour and *farce in the last two are central to Heywood's best play, *John John, Tib, and Sir John,* a brilliant adaptation of a French farce. Heywood wrote for his *boy actors, but his more ribald plays were also suited to the popular repertory.   RWV

Heywood, Thomas (*c.*1574–1641) English playwright, actor, and pamphleteer. In 1598 he was contracted as an actor with the *Admiral's Men, for whom he also wrote a couple of plays. About 1600 he began a twenty-year association with the Earl of Worcester's (later Queen Anne's) company at the *Rose (1602-3), the *Curtain (*c.*1603–1606), and the Red Bull (*c.*1606–17). Between 1624 and 1634 he wrote plays for *Deeston's companies. In 1631 he produced the first of seven pageants for the annual Lord Mayor's Day. Of the more than 220 plays that Heywood claimed to have written or collaborated on, approximately two dozen are extant. *A Woman Killed with Kindness* (1603), a domestic *tragedy, is his finest, but several others are worthy representations of Elizabethan popular taste: *If You Know Not Me, You Know Nobody* (1605–6) and *The Fair Maid of the West* (two parts, 1610, *c.*1630). One of Heywood's last plays, the *masque-like *A Challenge for Beauty* (1634–6), was a great success at court as well as at the Phoenix. Heywood's defence of players in *An Apology for Actors* (1612) is good natured and informed.   RWV

Hibberd, Jack (1940–) Australian playwright. He practised as a physician from 1964 until 1973, when he resigned to devote himself to the theatre. Until 1977 he was closely associated with the Australian Performing Group in Melbourne, who presented ten of his early plays, including *White with Wire Wheels* (1967). Hibberd's work presents distinctly Australian attitudes in an extravagant theatricality, demonstrating an increasing distancing from *realism, with *music and song reminiscent of *Brecht. *Dimboola* (1969) is typical, seeking *audience involvement and requiring the serving of food. Others, such as *A Toast to Melba* (1976), ironically celebrate famous Australians, and *A Stretch of the Imagination* (1972) is the best known of his monodramas. Hibberd returned part time to medical practice in 1986 but has also published novels, translated poetry, and continued writing for the theatre.   SBS

Hicks, Edward Seymour (1871–1949) English *actor-manager and dramatist. He first appeared at the Grand, Islington (1887), subsequently *toured America with the *Kendals, and

co-produced *Under the Clock* (1893), the first *revue staged in London. Early successes included *Walker London* (1892) and *Barrie's *Quality Street* (1904). He wrote light *comedies and Christmas plays (such as *Bluebell in Fairyland*). He built the Aldwych Theatre (1905), the Globe (1907)—opening both with his own plays—and took over Daly's (1934). During both world wars he took performers to France.   JTD

Highway, Tomson (1951–) Canadian writer. Born to a Cree family in northern Manitoba, Highway became a major new voice in Canadian theatre on the strength of two award-winning plays, *The Rez Sisters* (1986) and *Dry Lips Oughta Move to Kapuskasing* (1989). The plays, both set on the fictional reserve of Wasaychigan Hill on Manitoulin Island in Lake Huron, are structured as a diptych: the former with seven female *characters plus a male Nanabush (the traditional Native 'trickster' figure), the latter with seven male characters plus a female Nanabush. Highway sprinkles Cree and Ojibway *dialogue, often untranslated, in these mostly English-language scripts. Other works include a novel *Kiss of the Fur Queen* (1998), a musical *Rose* (2000), and three children's books written in Cree and English.   DWJ

Hijikata Tatsumi (1928–86) Japanese dancer and choreographer, one of the originators of *butoh. His *Forbidden Colours* (1959), a *dance based on *Mishima's novel of homosexuality, was a *succès de scandale,* and is generally acknowledged to be the first genuine butoh performance. A seminal figure in the cultural ferment of 1960s Japan, Hijikata was friend and collaborator with major writers, artists, and composers. He worked extensively with *Ono Kazuo and Ono's son Yoshito on dances such as *Notre Dame des fleurs* (1960) and *Rose-Coloured Dance* (1965). His own work demonstrated a taste for the decadent, the violent, and the anarchic—*Genet, Sade, Lautréamont, and Beardsley were early influences—but *kabuki and the folkways of his native Tōhoku were instrumental in creating his unique style. Representative pieces include *Revolt of the Flesh* (1968) and *A Tale of Smallpox* (1972). For the last decade of his short life, Hijikata worked chiefly as director and choreographer for large dance ensembles.   CP

Hijikata Yoshi (1898–1959) Japanese director. In 1920 Hijikata met *Osanai and became one of his most ardent disciples. Living in Berlin in 1922, Hijikata then fell under the influence of *expressionist playwrights *Toller and *Kaiser. On his way back to Japan immediately after the 1923 Tokyo earthquake, while waiting in Moscow for rail connections, he first saw *Meyerhold's productions and was deeply impressed by the ideals and accomplishments of Soviet theatre. Hijikata was active in the establishment of the Tsukiji Little Theatre in Tokyo, directing plays by *Goering, *Rolland, and others. After Osanai's death in 1928, Hijikata formed the New Tsukiji Troupe, dedicated to the principles of *socialist realism. In 1933 he was invited to the Soviet Union where he remained until 1941; on his return he was immediately arrested and jailed until 1945. In the last decade of his life he was permanently in poor health, but managed to direct occasionally. Hijikata has remained a hero of the Japanese theatrical world for his resistance to *fascism and for helping to create the Tsukiji Little Theatre.   JTR

Hilar, Karel Hugo (1885–1935) Czech director, critic, and poet. He was the *dramaturg, then director of the Vinohrady Municipal Theatre, Prague, from 1911 to 1921; between 1921 and 1935 he was head of the Czech National Theatre's drama company. An early admirer of *Reinhardt, his later style was closer to *Jessner's, sometimes even anticipating him. Hilar used the script to present a vision of the contemporary world, with original *scenography, commissioned music, and stylized *acting as instruments. In the National Theatre his style changed to sober matter-of-factness, close to the German 'new seriousness' of the same period. Amongst his Shakespearian productions, his antiheroic *Hamlet* (1926) was acclaimed by the young generation. His version of *expressionism well suited *The Insect Play* (1921) by Karel and Josef *Čapek. His last significant production was *Mourning Becomes Electra* (1934) by *O'Neill.   ML

Hildegard of Bingen (1098–1179) Benedictine abbess and mystic, founder of the Abbey of Rupertsberg near Bingen, Germany. Hildegard's religious visions and insights are recorded in three major works: *Knowledge, Book of a Life of Merit, Book of Divine Works*; her theology in two treatises; and an unexpectedly sophisticated knowledge of the human body in two medical texts. She also wrote 77 *carmina* (songs) besides a number of songs incorporated into *Knowledge* and used in her musical play *Ordo Virtutum* (*c*.1155). The *Ordo* is an early example of a *morality play. Based on Prudentius' *Psychomachia* (fourth century), it features a struggle between sixteen personified virtues and the forces of the devil for the Christian soul. The play was possibly intended to be played by the nuns of Hildegard's

convent. The success of performances and recordings since 1980 attests to its theatricality. RWV

Hill, Jenny (1851–96) English *music-hall performer, 'the Vital Spark' of the first generation of stars of the halls. She excelled in *characterizations of women of her own working-class background, moving over time from rude acrobatic *dancing in songs like 'The Coffee-Shop Gal' to sympathetic and caustic representations of abused wives 'determined no longer to stand it'. Her *male impersonations included a version of 'Arry' the flashy cockney stereotype who asserted his superiority to idle upper-class men. In later years she used brief *melodramas with elaborate scenery and supporting casts to ease the demands of solo work. A prominent member of music-hall society, known for her readiness to speak up for herself from the stage and at celebratory dinners and formal functions, she repeatedly tried and failed to break into the male monopoly of music-hall *management.   JSB

Hiller, Wendy (1912–2003) English actress. Hiller became a success in London in 1935 in *Love on the Dole*. In 1936 at the Malvern Festival she played the title role in *Shaw's *St Joan* and Eliza in *Pygmalion*, then did the film versions of *Pygmalion* (1938) and *Major Barbara* (1941). After the war she featured in Shakespeare at the *Old Vic and in several plays adapted from the novels of Henry *James, Thomas Hardy, and H. G. Wells. Additional roles included Josie in *O'Neill's *A Moon for the Misbegotten* (New York, 1957), Carrie Berniers in *Hellman's *Toys in the Attic* (London, 1960), and Queen Mary in Royce Ryton's *Crown Matrimonial* (London, 1972). In 1975 she appeared with Peggy *Ashcroft and Ralph *Richardson in *Ibsen's *John Gabriel Borkman* at the *National Theatre. Selectively, she continued to do films, including *A Man for All Seasons* (1966) and *The Elephant Man* (1980); she won Academy awards for *Pygmalion* (1938) and *Separate Tables* (1958).   TP

hippodrama A theatrical form employing specially trained horses as major performers, dating from the beginning of the nineteenth century. The Cirque Olympique in Paris and *Astley's Amphitheatre in London produced spectacle *melodramas in a space that evolved into a strong, large stage connected by ramps to a *circus ring. The *action could take place in both areas and frequently involved large numbers of horses and hundreds of performers. Patriotic military spectacle was the principal material of hippodrama. At Astley's, *The Battle of Waterloo* was given four times, as well as many battles from the

Napoleonic and later wars. Hippodrama was also staged at other venues, like Vauxhall Gardens in London and the Roman *amphitheatre at Nîmes, and was even welcomed at *Drury Lane and *Covent Garden. The notorious Ada Isaacs Menken flaunted her curvaceous figure in *Mazeppa*, and there was a brief vogue for equestrianized Shakespeare at Astley's in 1856 and 1857. Racing melodramas and the chariot-filled *Ben-Hur* (1899) were the last refuge, outside circus, of equestrian drama. *See also* ANIMALS.   MRB

Hirata Oriza (1962–) Japanese playwright, director, and critic, a leading exponent of the 'quiet theatre' (*shizuka na engeki*) movement of the 1990s. In a hyper-realistic and understated dramaturgy, Hirata's plays dissect the ways Japanese interact with themselves and the world. He has written close to 40 plays for his company Seinendan (Youth Group) and for major *shingeki companies. Past President of the Japan Playwrights Association and the Japan Society for Theatre Research, Hirata is also a major spokesperson on theatre education and cultural policy, leading workshops for students, doctors, politicians, and others exploring the bridges and barriers to communication in contemporary society. His most famous work, *Tokyo Notes* (1994) has toured abroad almost annually. Recently he has moved into multilingual drama, in French and Korean, and comic parodies of Japanese history.   CP

Hirsch, John (1930–89) Canadian director. Born in Hungary, Hirsch emigrated to Winnipeg in 1947. In 1957 he founded Theatre 77, which the next year merged to form the Manitoba Theatre Centre. As its first *artistic director (1958–66) he staged, most notably, *Mother Courage* with Zoë *Caldwell (1964). In 1965 he directed *The Cherry Orchard* at the *Stratford Festival, followed by *Richard III* with *Bates (1967), *A Midsummer Night's Dream* with *Newton (1968), and *The Three Sisters* with Maggie *Smith (1976). In 1967 he was named associate artistic director of the festival, but left two years later following his controversial production of a new *musical play *The Satyricon*. He then directed extensively in the USA, including seven productions at Lincoln Center in New York, and won an Obie award for *AC/DC* by Heathcote Williams. He also served as head of CBC television drama (1974–7). Hirsch returned to Stratford as artistic director from 1981 to 1985, mounting several memorable productions including *The Tempest*, *As You Like It*, and *Tartuffe*.   DWJ

Hirsch, Judd (1935–) American actor. He created the roles of Bill in *The Hot l Baltimore* (1973)

and Matt in *Talley's Folly* (1980), both for Lanford *Wilson, and he won Tony awards for *I'm Not Rappaport* (1985) and *Conversations with my Father* (1991) by *Gardner. He also appeared in *Scuba Duba* (1968), *Knock Knock* (1976), and *Art* (1998), and he played the role of Murray in *A Thousand Clowns* (1996). He won two Emmy awards as cab driver Alex Rieger in the television series *Taxi* (1978–83) and appeared from 2005 in *Numb3rs*. His film roles include Dr Berger in *Ordinary People* (1980) and Julius Levinson in *Independence Day* (1996).   JDM

Hispanic theatre, USA *See* DIASPORA.

Hochhuth, Rolf (1931–) German playwright. Hochhuth came to international prominence in 1963 with the *documentary drama *Der Stellvertreter* (*The Representative* or *The Deputy*) in a production by *Piscator, subsequently widely produced internationally. This controversial play, in which the relationship between Pope Pius XII and the Nazis is critically examined, provided Hochhuth with his overriding theme, the exploration of moral responsibility and political action, and his formal approach, historical debate based on extensive documentary research. In *Soldiers* (1967) he accuses Churchill of the unnecessary bombing of German cities and other war crimes; its production at the British *National Theatre was cancelled before opening. *Guerillas* (1970) was the first of a number of plays in which individuals go beyond the law for moral reasons. In *The Midwife* (1972) a young woman resorts to illegal means in order to publicize the plight of the homeless; in *Judith* (1984) an assassination attempt on Ronald Reagan is morally justified as 'rebellion of the powerless'. *Lawyers* (1979) returns to documentary drama in an exposé of a leading German politician's Nazi past, and in *Women Doctors* (1980) the target is the pharmaceutical industry. *Westies in Weimar* (1993) critically examines reunification. His latest play is *Heil Hitler* (Berlin, 2007).   CBB

Hofmannsthal, Hugo von (1874–1929) Austrian poet, playwright, and librettist. Hofmannsthal first came to attention as a teenager with his verse play *Yesterday* (1891) and quickly became an important figure in Viennese literary circles. Although he wrote several verse dramas in the 1890s, his first performed work was *The Woman at the Window* (1898), a verse *tragedy set in Renaissance Italy. He grew increasingly fascinated by the theatre and formed a close acquaintance with *Brahm and *Reinhardt. The latter staged Hofmannsthal's one-act *Elektra* in 1903, which formed the basis for the *opera by

Richard Strauss (1909). Their operatic collaboration intensified with *Der Rosenkavalier* (1911), *Ariadne auf Naxos* (1912), *Die Frau ohne Schatten* (1919), and others. Few of Hofmannsthal's stage plays have stood the test of time. His *comedy of manners *The Difficult Man* (1921), loosely based on *Molière's *The Misanthrope*, is a sophisticated analysis of pre-First World War Viennese society. His most famous play remains *Jedermann* (*Everyman*, 1911), an adaptation of the medieval *morality play, which is still performed every year during the *Salzburg Festival. The idea for the festival was developed by Hofmannsthal in 1917, together with Reinhardt and Strauss, and in the *1920s became a major European cultural event.   CBB

Holberg, Ludvig (1684–1754) Danish dramatist. From 1717 Holberg occupied a succession of professorships at the University of Copenhagen, publishing a series of philosophical works stressing the importance of reason. Because of his success as a satirical poet (including the mock epic *Peder Paars*, 1720) Holberg was invited to write *comedies for Denmark's first public theatre. In great haste, he wrote five volumes of comedies for the enterprise between 1722 and its closure six years later. All offer larger-than-life *satires of contemporary individuals who have forsaken the light of reason out of obsession or brute stupidity. In *The Political Tinker* Holberg mocked the political arrogance of ordinary folk; in *Erasumus Montanus* he satirized a bumptious undergraduate; in *Jeppe of the Hill* he drew a satirical portrait of a drunken peasant; and in *Jean de France* he satirized a local lad aping French fashion. The theatre reopened in 1746, when Holberg provided it with further plays. Although influenced by *Molière, Holberg's comedies are distinctively Danish in tone and content.   DT

Holbrook, Hal (1925–) American actor. Holbrook developed a one-person show on the writings of Mark Twain while a college student. *Mark Twain Tonight!* became his professional debut in 1954; by 2001 he had performed Twain over 2000 times, and spawned a virtual industry of solo performers re-creating historic figures. Holbrook's success was due to the skill with which he wove together Twain's writings, and his ability to play convincingly, in his late twenties, a man in his seventies. Holbrook created a series of effective performances on Broadway and in *regional theatres, also appearing frequently on film and television. He played major roles in *Miller's *After the Fall* (1963) and Robert *Anderson's *I

Never Sang for my Father (1968), *King Lear* (1990), and in *Wasserstein's *An American Daughter* (1997). Holbrook's Midwestern roots and commonsense approach allowed him to play *characters ranging from honourable politicians (*The Senator*, television series, 1970), to a less honourable financier (the film *Wall Street*, 1987), and martyred presidents (*Abe Lincoln in Illinois*, 1963 on stage; *Sandburg's Lincoln*, television, 1976).   AW

Holcroft, Thomas (1745–1809) English actor and author. Holcroft began his stage career as a comic actor and singer but his greatest contributions are his plays. His first was a comic *opera, *The Crisis* (1778), followed by a popular translation of *Beaumarchais's *Le Mariage de Figaro* called *The Follies of a Day* (1784). Treading the line between sentiment and social commentary, works like *Duplicity* (1781) and *Seduction* (1787) chastise the bad habits of social elites, such as gaming and sexual promiscuity. *The Road to Ruin* (1792) characteristically exposes the vices of the rich but ends in repentance and sentimental reconciliation. In the 1790s, Holcroft's radical sentiments required that some of these plays be published anonymously, and in 1794 he was briefly imprisoned on charges of high treason (he was released without trial).   MJK

Hollingshead, John (1827–1904) English *manager. In 1868 Hollingshead abandoned journalism, and with borrowed money took over the newly built Gaiety Theatre in London. He presented a popular repertory based on *burlesque until 1886, when he disposed of the theatre to George *Edwardes. By 1880 Gaiety burlesques had a three-act structure, a greater elegance of dress and decor, and more *music than previously. Hollingshead also staged the occasional serious work, such as the first English version of an *Ibsen play, by William *Archer: *Quicksands; or, The Pillars of Society* (1880).   MRB

Holm, Celeste (1919–) American actress and singer. Holm made her Broadway debut in *Saroyan's *The Time of your Life* (1939). Eventually she was cast as the irresistibly naughty Ado Annie in the original production of *Oklahoma!* (1943), which led to her first starring role in *Bloomer Girl* (1944). Holm soon had a Hollywood contract, appearing in a few films before her Oscar-winning performance in *Gentleman's Agreement* (1947). She returned to New York to star in productions of *She Stoops to Conquer* (1949) and *Anna Christie* (1952), remaining connected to the stage in Broadway productions like *Candida* (1970) and *I Hate Hamlet* (1991), while occasionally appearing on television and film.   EW

Holm, Ian (1931–) English actor who joined the *Shakespeare Memorial Theatre in 1954. In 1956 he made his London debut in *Love Affair*, and *toured Europe with *Olivier in *Brook's *Titus Andronicus* in 1955. From 1957 to 1967 he was a member of the *Royal Shakespeare Company, where he played Hal, Henry V, and Richard III in the *Hall–*Barton *The Wars of the Roses* (1963–4), as well as Romeo (1967). In the modern repertoire he appeared in *Pinter's *The Homecoming* (1965) and *Bond's *The Sea* (1973). In 1976 he left the theatre after suffering stage fright during *rehearsals for *O'Neill's *The Iceman Cometh*, only returning to stage *acting in 1993 in a production of Pinter's *Moonlight*, subsequently appearing as Lear under *Eyre at the *National Theatre (1997). His repertoire of screen roles is substantial and hugely diverse: *Alien* (1979), *Chariots of Fire* (1981), *Dance with a Stranger* (1984), *The Sweet Hereafter* (1997), and *The Lord of the Rings* (2001–3).   AS

Home, William Douglas (1912–92) English playwright. From the 1940s to the 1970s, Home crafted a number of comic star vehicles for the West End stage, which took little notice of the new wave theatrical revolution of 1956. He drew on his family life (son of an earl and brother to Prime Minister Alec Douglas-Home) to write sentimental *satires of upper-class political manoeuvrings, notably in his first hit, *The Chiltern Hundreds* (1947). Other *comedies include *The Manor of Northstead* (1954), *The Reluctant Peer* (1964) with Sybil *Thorndike, *The Jockey Club Stakes* (1970) with *Sim, *Lloyd George Knew my Father* (1972) with Ralph *Richardson and Peggy *Ashcroft, and *The Kingfisher* (1977) starring Richardson again. Home occasionally approached other dramatic styles in plays such as *Now Barabbas...* 1947), about a condemned man awaiting execution, and *The Thistle and the Rose* (1949), a historical drama about the battle of Flodden.   MDG

Hong Sheng (Hung Sheng) (*c*.1646–1704) Chinese author of *Changshengdian* (*Palace of Lasting Life*), a Kun opera in 50 scenes. Equated with *Kong Shangren as an influential Qing Dynasty playwright, Hong, like *Liang Chenyu a century earlier, historicized a traditional love theme and examined how love and politics become entwined. In the play, the infatuation of the Tang Emperor Xuanzong (ruled 712–56) with his 'Precious Consort' Yang Guifei leads to the usurpation of his throne by An Lushan and his barbarian allies. Despite its veiled references to the turbulent early Qing period, the Kangxi Emperor en-

joyed *Changshengdian* when it was performed in Beijing in 1689. It took three days and nights to perform all 50 scenes, and a 28-scene abridgement was made by Hong's friend Wu Shufu (*c*.1657–?), whose commentary on the text addresses aspects of performance. *Changshengdian* was most commonly performed as *zhezixi* (highlights), though it is now sometimes staged in a version consisting of eight to ten scenes.   CS

Hooft, Pieter Corneliszoon (1581–1647) Dutch playwright, poet, and historian. Hooft was a typical *early modern artist who joined Samuel Coster when he established the Duytsche Academie in Amsterdam (1617), the forerunner of the *Schouwburg (1638). Hooft wrote a number of *tragedies in the classical style. *Achilles and Polyxena* and *Theseus and Ariadne* (published 1614, written earlier) show features of *Senecan drama. *Geeraerdt van Velsen* (1613) is a tragedy about the conspiracy against Count Floris, the national historical episode which *Vondel was to dramatize in *Gijsbrecht van Aemstel* (1637). Hooft also wrote a *pastoral play, *Granida* (1605), partly inspired by *Guarini and *Tasso. The play for which Hooft is best known and which still holds the stage is his *comedy *Warenar* (1617), an adaptation of *Plautus' *Aulularia*.   JDV

Hope Theatre Built by *Henslowe in 1614, when there were more playing companies in London than licensed *playhouses, the Hope was designed to double as a theatre and a bear-*baiting arena for Henslowe's other main business. Plays were to be staged on Mondays, Wednesdays, Fridays, and Saturdays, and bears were to be baited on Tuesdays and Thursdays. It was built as a playhouse, like its neighbour the *Swan, but its stage had no posts, the *heavens covering the stage being supported from the gallery roofing. This allowed the stage itself to be removed to make more space when the *animals had to use it. The players, however, objected to the smells and rubbish produced by the bears and dogs. In *Jonson's *Bartholomew Fair*, one of the first plays staged there, they claim that it was 'as dirty as Smithfield, and as stinking every whit'. From 1616 the only entertainment offered was the bears. AJG

Hopkins, Anthony (1937–) Welsh actor. Perhaps the most internationally recognized British performer of his generation, Hopkins's success on screen has come to overshadow his earlier career on the stage. His first professional role was in *Julius Caesar* (London, 1964), and in 1965 he joined the *National Theatre, where he achieved great successes, playing in *Strindberg's *Dance of Death* (1967) and *Shaffer's *Equus* (1974). Later roles at the National include the media monster Lambert LaRoux in *Brenton and *Hare's *Pravda* (1985), and the leads in *King Lear* (1986) and *Antony and Cleopatra* (1987). In 1991 Hopkins won an Academy award for his performance as Hannibal Lecter in *The Silence of the Lambs*. Its critical and popular success established him as a major star and led to a series of high-profile, critically praised film roles, including Henry Wilcox in *Howards End* (1992), Stevens in *The Remains of the Day* (1993), C. S. Lewis in *Shadowlands* (1993), the title role in Julie *Taymor's *Titus* (1999), and many others.   AS

Hopkins, Arthur (1878–1950) American director and producer. Influenced by the writings of *Wagner and *Craig and productions of *Reinhardt, Hopkins was instrumental in introducing the 'New Theatre' and—in his collaborations with designer Robert Edmond *Jones—the 'New Stagecraft' onto Broadway in the 1910s and 1920s. Hopkins's theory of 'Unconscious Projection' saw the stage-work communicating directly with the unconscious mind of the *audience. He sought a simple, unified stage and clear, unmannered performances to still the conscious mind and open the pathways to the unconscious. His first Broadway production, *Poor Little Rich Girl* (1916), employed *symbolist techniques of fantasy and suggestion. His 1922 collaboration with Jones on *Macbeth* shocked New York as the first major *expressionist production seen there. Equally adept at *realism, Hopkins's productions of *Holiday* (1928) and *The Petrified Forest* (1935) were among his many commercial successes. His last production was *The Magnificent Yankee* (1946).   MAF

Hordern, Michael (1911–95) English actor who made his professional debut in *Othello* in 1937. After the war he worked at the *Shakespeare Memorial Theatre (1952), and at the *Old Vic (1953–4) he appeared in a range of classical roles including Polonius, King John, Prospero, and Malvolio. He was later in *Pinter's own production of *The Collection* (1962), was a touching and closely realized Lear for Jonathan *Miller at the *National Theatre (1969), was in *Stoppard's *Jumpers* (1972), Howard *Barker's *Stripwell* (1975), and played Sir Anthony Absolute in *The Rivals* (1983). He specialized in ageing eccentrics, sometimes amiable and slightly dotty, sometimes dark and manipulative. Extensive film credits include *Passport to Pimlico* (1949), *A Funny Thing Happened on the Way to the Forum* (1966), *The Slipper and the Rose* (1976), and *The Missionary* (1981). He made many television

appearances, including *Mortimer's *Paradise Postponed* (1986).   AS

Horniman, Annie E. F. (1860–1937) English *manager. The daughter of a Quaker tea merchant, she studied art and then spent much of her modest fortune on the emerging *regional repertory movement. She helped to finance *Farr's 1894 season at the Avenue Theatre, which presented *Yeats's *Land of Heart's Desire* and *Shaw's *Arms and the Man*; she greatly admired Yeats's work, and later offered to buy the Irish National Theatre Society its own building. This opened as the *Abbey Theatre in December 1904, and she continued to support it financially until 1907, in spite of strained relations. She was much happier with her next venture, at the Gaiety Theatre, Manchester, which she bought in 1908, taking *Payne with her from Dublin as artistic director. Here she stayed until 1917, establishing a company committed to short runs, *naturalistic *acting, and serious plays, including those of the 'Manchester school' (*Brighouse, *Houghton, Monkhouse). She mounted more than 200 plays between 1908 and 1917, over half of them new writing, and encouraged *tours to London, Canada, and the USA.   EEC

Horovitz, Israel (1939–) American playwright and screenwriter. A prolific and Procrustean playwright, Horovitz focuses on betrayal, passion, and violence. He achieved national prominence in 1968 with his *Off-Broadway double bill of *The Indian Wants the Bronx*, in which a Bengali is gratuitously mugged, and *It's Called the Sugar Plum*, wherein a Radcliffe student allows her fiancé's killer to seduce her. He continued to find success with short plays such as the *absurdist *Line* (1968), still running in New York in 2010, and an uncharacteristically uproarious *comedy, *The Primary English Class* (1976). Horovitz's later, longer works evince a stern proletarian work ethic. Outstanding are *Henry Lumper* (1985), a reworking of Shakespeare's *Henry IV*, and *North Shore Fish* (1986), a gritty survival drama of working women. He has won numerous awards and is one of the most frequently produced American playwrights in France.   TFC

Horváth, Ödön von (1901–38) Austrian playwright. The son of an Austro-Hungarian diplomat, Horváth received a German education. Arguably the most important twentieth-century German playwright after *Brecht, Horváth's fame and influence rest essentially on four plays written between 1929 and 1932: *Italian Night* (1931), *Tales from the Vienna Woods* (1931), *Kasimir and Karoline* (1932), and *Faith, Hope, and Charity* (produced 1936). In these works Horváth unmasks the consciousness of the German petty bourgeoisie towards the end of the Weimar Republic. He analyses *characters through their language—a mixture of half-understood literary quotations, proverbs, dialect, and media clichés. In 1933 Horváth was forced into exile and his writing shifted to more 'universal' themes as he struggled to find an *audience. His most important works from this period, *Don Juan Comes back from the War* (1936) and *Figaro Gets Divorced* (1936), explore the predicament of exile. After his death in Paris (he was struck by lightning), Horváth was forgotten, but in the mid-1960s a renaissance began which focused on the social critical plays of the Weimar period. More recently lesser-known works such as *Zur schönen Aussicht* (*Bellevue*, 1926) and *Judgement Day* (1937) have been successfully revived.   CBB

Hôtel de Bourgogne The first public theatre in Paris was built by the *Confrérie de la Passion in 1548, on property once owned by the dukes of Burgundy. That year, to compensate for a ban on religious plays, the Confrérie were granted a monopoly on all drama in Paris. They turned to *farces and other secular pieces, until in about 1570 they gave up acting and concentrated on *management, leasing their theatre to itinerant and foreign companies. From 1629, the Comédiens du Roi became the Confrérie's permanent tenants. The Confrérie was dissolved in 1677 and from 1680, when the *Comédie-Française was established at the Hôtel Guénégaud, Tiberio Fiorilli's Italian troupe was granted occupancy of the Bourgogne. From then until its final closure in 1783—except for the period 1697-1716, when it stood dark—the *Comédie Italienne, as it became known, remained the Italians' home in Paris.

The theatre's original design was probably inspired as much by the great hall of the Hôpital de la Trinité (where the Confrérie had played until 1539) as by the traditional *tennis court, to which its dimensions bore a marked similarity. The *auditorium was dominated by a pit for standing spectators, on three sides of which, parallel to the walls, were two tiers of *boxes, seven along the side walls and five facing the stage. The Bourgogne was refurbished many times during its long life.   JG

Houdini, Harry (**Ehrich Weiss**) (1874–1926) Hungarian escape artist. Starting as a *magician in American dime museums in the early 1890s, in 1899 Martin Beck booked him on the Orpheum *vaudeville circuit as an escape artist, and he was soon known as 'The King of Handcuffs'. In 1900

he executed his first jail cell escape, and in 1906, he first leapt from a bridge into deep water and freed himself from manacles before surfacing. Responding to challenges, he escaped from a submerged crate, an iron boiler, a rolltop desk, a diving suit, a mail pouch, a titanic rope-fibre manila envelope, a gigantic football, an oversized milk can, a coffin, and the innards of a dead creature reported as a 'whale-octopus'. In 1912 he introduced the Water Torture Cell, escaping from a small cabinet filled with water after being suspended from his ankles and locked in, and in 1916 he first released himself from a straitjacket while hanging upside down over a city street filled with spectators. Houdini combined meticulous skill with showmanship and a keen eye for publicity, responding to the public fascination with crime and playing on spiritualist expectations even while debunking the tricks of mediums and psychics.   JDM

Houghton, Stanley (1881–1913) English dramatist, one of the 'Manchester school' of playwrights closely associated with *Horniman and her pioneering *regional repertory company at the Gaiety in Manchester. His plays include the one-act Lancashire *comedy *The Dear Departed* (1906), *Independent Means* (1909), *The Younger Generation* (1910), and most famously *Hindle Wakes* (1912), a *satiric comedy about a working-class girl who causes a scandal by refusing to marry the son of the wealthy local mill owner, believing that a mere fleeting affair should not condemn her to marrying a man she does not love. This controversial twist gained the play rapid notoriety and popularity. First presented by the company in London, it soon transferred to the Gaiety and was taken on successful *tours in both Britain and America.   ARJ

Houseman, John (1902–88) American *manager and director. Born in Bucharest as Jacques Haussmann, he worked throughout the 1920s as an international grain-trader. When business collapsed in 1929, Houseman found success as a director with the Gertrude Stein–Virgil Thomson *Four Saints in Three Acts* (1934). In 1935 Houseman was named director of the 'Negro Theatre' unit of the *Federal Theatre Project in Harlem, where he met Orson *Welles. Their acclaimed production of a Haitian-inflected *Macbeth* launched a sustained collaboration, with Houseman *producing and Welles directing. In 1936 they founded a classic-based unit for the FTP, staging inventive productions of *Horse Eats Hat* (from *Labiche's *An Italian Straw Hat*) and *Marlowe's *Dr Faustus* (1937). Political pressure over their production of *Blitzstein's *The Cradle Will Rock* (1937) forced

Houseman and Welles to leave the FTP and found the Mercury Theatre. Their modern-dress *Julius Caesar* (1937) set in a fascist state was a landmark in reinterpretation.

Splitting with Welles after the 1941 production of *Native Son*, Houseman worked as a film producer in California and continued as stage director. He was *artistic director of the American *Shakespeare Festival (1956–9). Along with Michel *Saint-Denis, Houseman founded the drama division at the Juilliard School (1968) and the Acting Company, a *touring company of Juilliard graduates, in 1972.   MAF

Housman, Laurence (1865–1959) English playwright. An unlikely figure in the struggle against theatre *censorship, Housman frequently found his quaint, reverential plays banned for depicting sacred or royal figures on stage. Refused by the Lord Chamberlain, *Nativity* (1902) was staged by *Craig in a private performance. Housman collaborated with Granville *Barker on *Prunella; or, Love in a Dutch Garden* (1904), in which Barker played Pierrot. Banned from public performance, his best-known works, often chronicle plays, initially appeared as *closet dramas. *Little Plays of St Francis*, first published in 1922, became a Christmas staple of amateur theatre. His most famous piece, *Victoria Regina*, was a selection of ten vignettes (out of an eventual 50) on the life of Queen Victoria (New York, 1935, starring Helen *Hayes; London, 1937).   MDG

Houston, Velina Hasu (1957–) American playwright. The child of a Japanese mother and a father of mixed *African-American and Native American heritage, Houston's first three plays, *Asa Ga Kimashita* (*Morning Has Broken*, 1981), *American Dreams* (1984), and *Tea* (1987), examine the politics of multiracial life in America. She has since written over twenty plays, including *Necessities* (1991) *The Matsuyama Mirror* (1993), and *Kokoro* (*True Heart*, New York, 1994). She has also written numerous screenplays. Her work questions the myth of solidarity among racial groups in America, creating a complex and troubling view of race relations. *See also* DIASPORA.   JSM

Howard, Alan (1937–) English actor who began a long association with the *Royal Shakespeare Company in 1966. He rose rapidly to play Edgar in *King Lear* and Benedick in *Much Ado About Nothing* (1968), Hamlet (1970), and the remarkably doubled Oberon and Theseus in *Brook's famous *A Midsummer Night's Dream* the same year. He was Hal and Henry V in 1975, beginning a fruitful association with Terry

*Hands, who directed him in most of Shakespeare's history plays including *Henry VI* (1977), *Richard II*, and *Richard III* (1980). He played Halder in the première of C. P. *Taylor's *Good* (1981). Following a break from stage work he appeared at the *National Theatre as Higgins in *Pygmalion* (1992) and George in *Cocteau's *Les Parents terribles* (1994). For Peter *Hall he was Vladimir in *Waiting for Godot* and Lear (both 1997). More recently he was Teiresias in *Oedipus* at the National (2008). Howard's film career includes the lover in Peter Greenaway's *The Cook, the Thief, his Wife and her Lover* (1989).   AS

Howard, Bronson (1842–1908) American playwright. His first major success was *Saratoga* (1870), a satiric examination of the stylish resort. After a series of lacklustre plays, Howard caught the public imagination with *The Banker's Daughter* (1878). With his next major success, *Young Mrs Winthrop* (1882), Howard moved toward a more *realistic examination of contemporary American society. He continued in this vein in *The Henrietta* (1887) and *Aristocracy* (1892), both of which examined an emerging American type, the business tycoon. Howard's greatest popular triumph was *Shenandoah* (1888), a spectacular Civil War *melodrama. He sought to elevate playwriting in America to a profession, and successfully lobbied for revisions in the *copyright laws to prevent piracy.   GAR

Howard, Pamela (1939–) English *scenographer and director who has realized over 200 productions. She designed a Venetian-inspired *Othello* (*Royal Shakespeare Company, 1979), an intriguing set of torn and crumpled shrouds, sails, and projected images for Ted Tally's *Terra Nova* (*Chichester, 1980), and a bleak version of *Shaw's *On the Rocks* (Chichester, 1982). Howard's scenography plays with manipulating space, as in the site-specific set for *Border Warfare* (Glasgow, Old Museum of Transport, 1988), where the forest primeval later metamorphosed into a football pitch. Her design for *Hedda Gabler* received the best *touring production award. She has also designed *Yerma*, *The School for Wives*, and *Happy Birthday Brecht* for the *National Theatre, and a fascinating touring production by Di Trevis of *The Taming of the Shrew* (RSC, 1985). She co-directed *Concierto barroco* (1999) for Opera Transatlántica, for which she is *producer. She directed and designed *Rojas's *La Celestina* in the USA (2002), and designed *The Great Game* (London, 2009), twelve new half-hour plays about Afghanistan commissioned for the Tricycle Theatre. At Central St Martin's College of Art and

Design in London, she developed the highly successful international MA in scenography. She has advanced the critical debate on design through Scenofest (an international scenography festival), work with the Prague Quadrenniale, and through her widely read book *What Is Scenography?* (2001, 2009). RVL

Howard, Sidney (1891-1939) American playwright. Howard studied playwriting with George Pierce *Baker at Harvard (1915-16) and achieved wide recognition in 1924 with the *Theatre Guild production of *They Knew What They Wanted*. This drama about an older man's pursuit of a younger woman was admired for its maturity and rationality. This success was followed by such dramas as *The Silver Cord* (1926), in which a son rejects his mother's possessiveness, and *Yellow Jack* (1934), a *documentary historical drama about the fight against yellow fever. Howard was a skilled adapter of the work of others, crafting *The Late Christopher Bean* (1932) from a French source and *Dodsworth* (1934) from the Sinclair Lewis novel, and as a screenwriter won Academy awards for *Arrowsmith* (1931) and *Gone with the Wind* (1939). MAF

Howe, Tina (1937-   ) American playwright. Her anarchic sources are *Ionesco, *Beckett, and the *Marx Brothers, but her plays are *feminist comic fantasies that deal with food, art, family, and loss. The savage *Birth and After Birth* (published 1973, produced 1995), dives into the turmoil of motherhood, with a hairy adult toddler who dominates his parents. When *producers rejected the script, Howe turned to public settings fraught with ludicrous mayhem: an art gallery in *Museum* (1976), a restaurant in *The Art of Dining* (1979), a fitting room in *Appearances* (1982). In *Painting Churches* (1983), an artist faces the decline of her ageing parents, while *Approaching Zanzibar* (1989) follows a fractious family road trip toward a dying aunt. *One Shoe Off* (1993) reveals a house devoured by indoor vegetables as five adults attack each other with literate quotations. *Pride's Crossing* (1998) travels through time, seven actors playing twenty *characters in the life of an aristocratic old woman, a former Channel swimmer. Other work includes *Coastal Disturbances* (1986) and *Swimming* (1991). FL

Hoyt, Charles (1860-1900) American playwright, director, and *manager. Hoyt began writing for the stage in 1881, and had penned some twenty stage works by his early death, chiefly *satirical *farces on contemporary issues: hotel management (*A Bunch of*, 1883), city life (*A Tin Soldier*, 1885), railways (*A Hole in Ground*, 1887), fetishism (*A Brass Monkey*, 1888), rural life (*A Midnight Bell*, 1889), political corruption (*A Texas Steer*, 1890), baseball (*A Runaway Colt*, 1895), women's suffrage (*A Contented Woman*, 1897). He normally directed his own shows, sometimes in his own theatre. His biggest hit was the *musical *A Trip to Chinatown* (1891), whose 657 performances held the Broadway record for nearly three decades; it *toured the country for more than twenty years. CT

Hrotsvitha of Gandersheim (*c.*935-973) German poet and playwright. Hrotsvitha was a member of a religious community of women, 'secular canonesses', at the Abbey of Gandersheim in Saxony. Such communities were usually restricted to the nobility and did not require the renunciation of private property. Hrotsvitha's body of written work, discovered by the humanist Conrad Celtis in 1494 and published in 1501, reveals an author well versed in classical literature as well as scripture and the Christian fathers. Her writings, in Latin, included eight saints' legends and six plays. By her own account, Hrotsvitha modelled her plays on those of the *Roman playwright *Terence, 'so that in that self-same form of composition in which the shameless acts of lascivious women were phrased | The laudable chastity of sacred virgins be praised'. Constancy, conversion, and martyrdom are the themes of *Gallicanus, Dulcitius, Calimachus, Abraham, Pafmutius*, and *Sapienta*, but Hrotsvitha extends the emotional range with scenes of *burlesque (*Dulcitius*) and of homoeroticism and necrophilia (*Calimachus*). There is a considerable amount of *action, the *dialogue is lively, the settings varied and specific—all evidence of their performability, although semi-dramatic recitation is the most likely mode of any original performance. There have been a number of successful modern productions. RWV

huajü (hua chü) 'Spoken drama', the Chinese term for Western-style drama with *realistic *dialogue. In 1907 in Tokyo a group of Chinese students, calling themselves *Chunliu She (the Spring Willow Society), performed *The Lady of the Camellias* and *Uncle Tom's Cabin*, marking the beginning of Western-style theatre in Chinese. The first form of new drama was *wenming xi* ('civilized drama'), which flourished in Shanghai in the 1910s. Most were *mubiao xi* (outline plays), *scenarios that relied heavily on *improvisation. The performance style was a mixture of Japanese *shimpa* and traditional Chinese theatre. To counter commercial tendencies, *aimei jü* (amateur drama) became popular in the 1920s, emphasizing direct translations of modern

European plays. At the same time plays by Chinese playwrights, mostly educated in Japan, Europe, and the USA, were beginning to draw national attention. The term *huajü* was first adopted by *Tian Han in 1927 and the form had matured by the next decade, with a repertoire of quality plays and diversified performance styles as more directors returned from abroad. During the Sino-Japanese War (1937–45), *huajü* became a powerful propaganda weapon, with almost all theatre people enthusiastically involved in the anti-Japanese effort. In the 1950s the close Sino-Soviet relationship ushered in the *Stanislavsky system, even though the idea of the 'self' was eliminated because of its bourgeois individualism. Banned as a capitalist 'poisonous weed' during the Cultural Revolution, *huajü* later returned and remains a major theatrical form.   SYL

hubris In ancient Greece hubris was originally a legal term denoting an illegal action, one overstepping the boundaries of justice. It later came to include the religious notion of trespassing the boundary between human and divine. It could also refer to the human attribute that causes the transgression and thus came to mean the presumptuousness or arrogance that leads to the overstepping of legal or divine boundaries. Hubris, sometimes rendered less pejoratively as 'pride', has often been seen as the *sine qua non* of the *tragic *protagonist, whose presumptuousness in pursuing his own destiny provokes an inevitable retribution.   RWV

Hughes, Barnard (1915–2006) American actor. Hughes made his professional debut in 1934, becoming a solid Broadway supporting actor in *The Teahouse of the August Moon* (1956), *Advise and Consent* (1960), *Gielgud's *Hamlet* (1964), and *Hogan's Goat* (1965). Maturing into a powerful character actor with a burly, gravel-voiced intensity and eyes that could twinkle or glower, he excelled as Dogberry, Serebriakov, and Falstaff. Stardom and many awards came with his signature role, first in New York (1978), later in Dublin, as the irascible title *character in *Leonard's *Da*. Later Broadway leads included *Angel's Fall* (1983), *The Iceman Cometh* (1985), and *Prelude to a Kiss* (1990). He and actress Helen Stenborg celebrated their 50th wedding anniversary in 2000, fêted on stage by Lauren Bacall and Rosemary *Harris, while they were all appearing in the New York première of *Coward's *Waiting in the Wings*.   GB

Hughes, Holly (1955–) American playwright and *performance artist. Her plays such as *The

Well of Horniness (1983) and *The Lady Dick* (1985), darkly comic ensemble pieces that foreground *lesbian sexuality and *parody conventions of *film noir*, were developed at WOW Café in New York. After writing *Dress Suits to Hire* (1987) for Peggy Shaw and Lois Weaver of *Split Britches, Hughes shifted to solo work. Her solo pieces are primarily autobiographical, recounting memories of her mother, her sexual identity, and her suburban childhood. While she celebrates women's sexuality, her style is by no means graphic. Nonetheless she was one of four artists singled out by the National Endowment for the Arts on charges of indecency. Ironically, the piece for which funding was denied, *World without End* (1989), had only peripheral lesbian content and little that could reasonably be construed as indecent. *Preaching to the Perverted* (1999), examined how queer identity is excluded from constructions of American citizenship.   LW

Hughes, Langston (1902–67) *African-American writer, considered the poetic voice of the Harlem Renaissance. His play *Mulatto* (1935), the story of the white patriarch and the long-suffering maid who bears his children, was the first full-length drama by an African American to appear on Broadway. Prior to this Hughes had collaborated with *Hurston on a folk play called *Mule Bone*, based on her short story; the partners quarrelled, and the work was not produced until 1991. Hughes worked with Cleveland's Karamu House in 1936, then founded the Suitcase Theatre in Harlem, which staged his *Don't You Want to Be Free*. In the 1940s he collaborated with *Weill and *Rice on *Street Scene*, and with William Grant Still on *Troubled Island*, an *opera set in Haiti. In 1957 Hughes wrote the libretto for *Simply Heavenly*, and his *Tambourines to Glory*, a gospel *musical, was on Broadway in 1963.   BBL

Hugo, Victor-Marie (1802–85) French writer, the outstanding exponent of *romanticism in French drama. Hugo achieved early distinction as a poet and a novelist; his fascination with the theatre was sparked by repeated visits to a *Pixérécourt *melodrama. His first mature play was a vast, unplayable historical verse drama, *Cromwell* (1827), accompanied by a forceful preface. The impact of the *Préface de Cromwell* was tremendous, calling for the abolition of the *unities, a rounded approach to *character, and versification freed from *neoclassical metre and vocabulary.

The theoretical challenge received practical shape in *Hernani* (1830), whose innovations of form and content provoked the famous 'battle' in the *auditorium of the *Comédie-Française night after night (*see* RIOTS). *Marion de Lorme* had a less turbulent reception (1832), running for 68 performances, with *Dorval and *Bocage as the ill-starred romantic couple; while *Le Roi s'amuse* (*The King's Pleasure*, 1832) was suspended by government order after the first night, to receive its second performance exactly 50 years later. *Ruy Blas* (1838) was the most successful, with *Lemaître in the title role. Hugo tried romantic drama in prose, with mixed success, in *Lucrèce Borgia* and *Marie Tudor* (1833) and *Angelo* (1835). *Les Burgraves* (1843) is regarded as marking the end of romantic drama; and although it ran for over 30 performances at the Comédie-Française, Hugo's genius had by now moved away towards an epic and visionary imagination ill-fitting the stage. Disappointed in his political ambitions after the 1848 Revolution, Hugo spent most of the rest of his life in Guernsey, where he wrote the verse *satires *Les Châtiments*, the philosophical collection *Les Contemplations*, and composed poems for *La Légende des siècles*, as well as writing the novels *Les Misérables* (1862), *Les Travailleurs de la mer* (1866), and *L'Homme qui rit* (1869). The only drama texts of note to have survived from this period are *Torquemada*, a powerful verse play indicting religious fanaticism, and in quite a different vein *Mangeront-ils?* (*Shall They Be Fed?*), an allegorical fantasy with something of the lightness and spontaneity of Shakespearian *comedy. None of Hugo's verse plays of the 1830s ever achieved major success in the theatre, but *Hernani* and *Le Roi s'amuse* still flourish, thanks to *Verdi, as *Ernani* and *Rigoletto*.   WDH

Humphries, Barry (1934–) Australian performer who first unleashed his most famous cross-dressed creation, Edna Everage, in 1955. The *character of this mousey suburban housewife, who satirizes the middle-class Melbourne environment of Humphries's upbringing, evolved into a flamboyant television megastar famous for her ability to humiliate people, and for her surreal wardrobes and spectacle frames. Humphries moved to London in 1959 and since then has made a career out of ridiculing Australian lifestyles. His strip-cartoon character Barry McKenzie, the innocent Australian abroad, appeared in *Private Eye* and resulted in two feature films. Other famous Humphries characters include the slob Australian cultural attaché Sir Les Patterson, and Sandy Stone, a faded, Melbournian suburban man, later a ghost. Humphries continues to combine an international TV career with the cut and thrust of live performances, where he is willing to say the unsayable, and to insult anyone and everyone. *See* FEMALE IMPERSONATION.   FJS

Hunt, Hugh (1911–73) Welsh director. After Oxford a production of *King John* (London, 1933) gained him provincial appointments. From 1935 to 1938 he was *producer at the *Abbey Theatre, Dublin, where he directed 33 productions, among them the premières of *Ervine's *Boyd's Shop*, *Shiels's *The Passing Day*, and *Yeats's *Purgatory*, all revived many times. At the Abbey he collaborated fruitfully with the designer *Moisewitsch and the author Frank O'Connor. Following military service, he became director at the Bristol Old Vic in 1945, working mainly in Shakespeare and other established playwrights. In 1949 he moved to the *Old Vic in London, consolidating his reputation as a Shakespearian interpreter. He returned to the Abbey as part-time artistic director, when his most memorable productions were revivals of *O'Casey's *The Silver Tassie* and *Red Roses for Me*.   CFS

Hunter, Kathryn (1957–) Dynamic and versatile English actor and director who came to prominence with Theatre de *Complicité. Celebrated appearances include *Dürrenmatt's *The Visit* (1991) for that company, Lear at the Leicester Haymarket and Young Vic (1997), and Galactia in Howard *Barker's *Scenes from an Execution* (1999). One of her more extraordinary roles came in *Spoonface Steinberg* (1999). Lee Hall's drama, originally a radio play, was adapted for stage with Hunter as the eponymous *opera-loving, autistic, Jewish child of 7, struggling to come to terms with cancer. Hunter's directing credits include *Brecht's *Mr Puntila and his Man Matti* (1998), *Bernhard's *Destination*, and Rebecca Gilman's *The Glory of Living* at the *Royal Court (both 1999).   AS

Hunter, N. C. (Norman Charles) (1908–71) English playwright. Although he had been writing plays since the 1930s, Hunter found commercial success in the West End only in 1951 with *Waters of the Moon*. Chosen for the Festival of Britain, the play served as a vehicle for *Thorndike, *Hiller, and Edith *Evans. Its success spurred similar star-studded productions, like *A Day by the Sea* (1953) with *Gielgud, *Richardson, *Worth, and Thorndike, and *A Touch of the Sun* (1958) with Michael and Vanessa *Redgrave. Hunter's genteel plays are mood pieces whose bittersweet melancholy prompted comparisons at the time to *Chekhov, a plaudit they hardly seem to warrant in hindsight. Like *Rattigan's work, Hunter's plays have come to represent the glamorous, 'quality' West End drama of their producer, *Beaumont, that was supposedly rendered obsolete by the new wave drama issuing from the *Royal Court and *Theatre Workshop. MDG

Hurston, Zora Neale (1891–1960) *African-American writer, best known for her fiction. She began writing plays at Howard University; *Color Struck* took second prize in an *Opportunity* magazine contest judged by Fannie Hurst and *O'Neill (1925). From 1930 to 1935 Hurston tried to establish a theatrical career, writing over a dozen works, including *The Great Day* (Broadway, 1932). In 1931 she began a dramatic adaptation of one of her short stories with Langston *Hughes, but the collaborators fell out and *Mule Bone* did not see the stage until 1991. Thereafter she wrote for *Fast and Furious*, a Broadway *revue with comedian Moms Mabley and Hurston herself in the cast, and coached actors at the Harlem unit of the *Federal Theatre Project, but was unsuccessful in achieving productions of her plays. Ten Hurston plays were discovered at the Library of Congress in 1997; one of them, *Polk County*, was produced at *Arena Stage in Washington in 2002. BBL

Husain, Shaharom (1919–2008) Pioneering playwright of modern drama in Malaysia. Dedicated to promoting Malay language and literature, he was a central figure in its growth and development, especially during his tenure at Sultan Idris Training College in Kuala Lumpur. His plays were engaged with the social realities of the time—particularly the Malay struggle for independence from the British—although the majority of his plays (*sandiwara*) were set in feudal times and were not historically accurate. His best-known work, *The Hunchback of Tanjung Puteri* (1956), tackled the theme of loyalty versus personal freedom. CRG

Hussain, Fida (1899–2000) Indian singer, actor, and director in the *Parsi theatre tradition. As a young man Hussain joined the New Alfred Theatrical Company of Bombay, the most popular company in the 1910s and 1920s all over India. 'Master Fida Hussain', as he was known, played *female roles for many years, achieving particular popularity as the melodious *heroine in *Parivartan*. He assumed the male role in *Laila Majnun* in 1930, and after the break-up of the New Alfred in 1932 joined the film industry in Calcutta. In the 1930s and 1940s he continued his theatrical work as a member of several companies. In 1950 he joined the Moonlight Theatre of Calcutta where he worked as lead actor and director until his retirement in 1968. With his deep voice, artful enunciation of Hindi and Urdu, and commanding physical presence, Hussain became

a mentor to young actors at the National School of Drama. KH

Hussein, Ebrahim (1943–) Tanzanian playwright and poet. His first play, *Kinjeketile* (1969), is a deep and original meditation on power and on traditional religion: can magic repel guns? After a successful performance at home it was chosen to represent Tanzania at African festivals abroad, and was translated from Swahili into English by the author. His other plays, *Devils* (1971), *Wedding* (1980), and *Kweneye ukingo wa thim* (1988, translated as *At the Edge of Thim*, 2000), were published in Nairobi and became set books for exams, but were considered too sophisticated and too complex by Tanzanian critics. Hussein became the first professor of drama at the University of Dar es Salaam. He resigned in 1986 and withdrew from theatre work. AIR

Hutt, William (1920–2007) Canadian actor and director who established his career in regional summer *stock. A member of the inaugural *Stratford Festival company in 1953, he was greatly influenced by *Guinness, who starred in that season. With the Canadian Players between Stratford seasons, Hutt performed such major roles as Macbeth (1955), Hamlet (1956), and King Lear (1960), and earned his first major role at Stratford as Prospero in *The Tempest* (1962), where he played King Lear (1972, 1988, 1996), *Wilde's Lady Bracknell (1975, 1976, 1979), Falstaff (1978, 1995), the Fool opposite *Ustinov's Lear (1980), Titus Andronicus (1980), and James Tyrone in *O'Neill's *Long Day's Journey into Night* (1994). Although he performed on Broadway and in London, he remained 'the great Canadian actor who stayed in Canada', playing more Shakespearian roles than *Olivier and *Gielgud combined. He retired from Stratford in 2005 with a reprise of Prospero. The first member of the Stratford company to direct at the festival, his *Waiting for Godot* (1968) was followed by *Much Ado About Nothing* (1971), *St Joan* (1975), and *Hamlet* (1976). PBON

Hwang, David Henry (1957–) American playwright. Hwang wrote *FOB* ('fresh off the boat') in 1978, while still a student at Stanford. It was produced *Off-Broadway in 1980. He subsequently wrote *The Dance and the Railroad* (1981), *Family Devotions* (1981), *House of Sleeping Beauties* (1983), and *The Sound of a Voice* (1983), plays which featured *characters of Asian ancestry. His most important work, *M. Butterfly* (1988), won numerous awards; the play reworks the Madame Butterfly myth and attacks Western stereotypes of Asia. Since then, Hwang has written two *musicals (*One Thousand Airplanes on *the Roof*, 1988, music by *Glass; and *The Silver River*, 1997, music by Bright Sheng), two *operas (*The Voyage*, 1992, music by Glass; *Aida*, 2000, music by Elton John), *Bondage* (1992), *Face Value* (1993), *Golden Child* (1996), and new adaptations of *Ibsen's *Peer Gynt* (1998), *Rodgers and *Hammerstein's *Flower Drum Song* (2001), and the film *The Fly* (2008). *Yellow Face*, an autobiographical play, opened in Los Angeles in 2007. *See also* DIASPORA.   JSM

Hyman, Earle (1926–) American actor, who may have undertaken more Shakespearian *characters than any other contemporary *African-American. One of his earliest roles was the young boy in *Anna Lucasta* (1944), an American Negro Theatre production that started in Harlem and travelled to Broadway and London. In the 1950s, when he was also studying at Howard University, he was cast primarily in classical roles, including *Hamlet* and *Othello*, which he has played many times; in Oslo he was knighted when he performed *Othello* in Norwegian. He has also played Macbeth and King Lear. In 1988 Hyman was the solicitous chauffeur in the stage version of *Driving Miss Daisy*. Despite his classical work, he is more widely known for his role on *The Cosby Show* as Russell Huxtable, Cosby's father.   BBL

Hynes, Garry (1953–) Irish director. Hynes co-founded Druid Theatre Company in Galway in 1975. Her work with Druid was interrupted when she became *artistic director of the *Abbey Theatre (1991–4), and she has also directed for the *Royal Shakespeare Company and the *Royal Court. Her compelling productions of Tom *Murphy, Martin *McDonagh, and Marina *Carr

established the reputations of these writers. Her revivals of *Synge's *Playboy* and of *O'Casey's *The Plough and the Stars* challenged received opinions of *audiences and critics, proposing new performance energies in the Irish canon. She won the Tony award for best direction (for McDonagh's *The Beauty Queen of Leenane*) in 1998. 'Druid/Synge', her production of all six of Synge's plays (2005), has *toured widely to high praise.   CAL

Hytner, Nicholas (1956–) English director. Hytner's exuberant, moving, clear, and visually rich productions secured his reputation early. His highly acclaimed debut for the *Royal Shakespeare Company (*Measure for Measure*, 1989), and the next year for the *National Theatre (*Sobol's *Ghetto*), followed regional directing and work in *opera. His productions demonstrate considerable versatility: *musicals such as *Miss Saigon* (*Drury Lane, 1989) and *Carousel* (RNT, 1992); *operas such as *The Turn of the Screw* when he was 20, and *Mozart's *La clemenza di Tito* (Glyndebourne, 1991 and 1995). An associate director of the NT from 1989, his direction of Alan *Bennett's *The Madness of George III* (1991) led to Oscar nominations for the subsequent film. Other film credits include *Miller's *The Crucible* (1997). Hytner returned to the stage with productions of Shakespeare, *Williams, and new writers *Ravenhill and *McDonagh. In 2001 he was appointed director of the NT where he has extended the range: introducing £10 seats, a production of *Jerry Springer—The Opera* (2003), an adaptation of Philip Pullman's *His Dark Materials* (2003–4), and attracting black audiences through Kwame Kwei-Armah's *Elmina's Kitchen* (2003).   KN

Ibsen, Henrik (1828–1906) Norwegian playwright. Born in Skien, the son of a wealthy merchant whose business empire collapsed in 1835, Ibsen left home in 1843 to work as an apothecary's assistant in Grimstad, where he drafted his first play, *Catiline* (1849). When he left Grimstad in 1850 to enrol as a student in the capital (then called Christiania), he paid his last visit to his parents. Though he never contacted them again, refracted images of his parents appear in several of his later works, notably *The Wild Duck* and *John Gabriel Borkman*.

The Warrior's Barrow was performed by the Christiania Theatre in 1850. In 1851 he gave up his studies to become assistant director at the newly founded National Theatre in Bergen, and during his six years there learnt how to make effective use of stage space. He continued writing plays in a national *romantic tradition, the most important being *Lady Inger of Østraat* (1855) and *The Feast at Solhaug* (1856). In 1857 Ibsen became *artistic director of the Norwegian Theatre in Christiania, and in the following year married Suzannah Thoresen. His years in the capital were a time of poverty and despair. His own theatre went bankrupt in 1862, after which he eked out a living as a literary adviser for a rival theatre. Despite these setbacks, he managed to write a light-hearted *satire, *Love's Comedy* (1862), and the last of his national romantic plays, *The Pretenders* (1863).

With the help of a state grant, Ibsen left Norway in 1864 for Rome, the beginning of a period of exile that was to last 27 years. His relief in leaving a country and a life that had brought personal defeats unlocked his creative energies. In swift succession he wrote two magnificent verse plays that brought him international recognition: *Brand* (1866) and *Peer Gynt* (1867). Both explore recurring concerns: the tension between environmental determinism and human agency, and the demands of vocation juxtaposed with those of love. In 1868 Ibsen moved to Dresden, where he completed an edition of poems and a lengthy philosophical play, *Emperor and Galilean* (1873), in which he attempted to dramatize the clash between Christian and pagan thought centred around the *character of Julian the Apostate.

During the late 1870s he embarked on a new and decisive phase, aiming to address contemporary social issues in his work (*see* REALISM). The first of these plays, *The Pillars of Society* (1877), is a caustic critique of contemporary capitalist entrepreneurs. In *A Doll's House* (1879) and *Ghosts* (1881) Ibsen subjected middle-class marriage to a remorseless deconstruction. He denied that he was a *feminist but he nevertheless highlighted the exploitation of women in a society that deprived them of any legal, property, or democratic rights. In response to the outrage these plays caused, Ibsen offered an ironic portrait in *An Enemy of the People* (1882) of an individual who is hounded for telling the truth.

With *The Wild Duck* (1884) he began to exploit *symbolist techniques. The central symbol of the wild duck is associated with a number of the characters in the play, but above all with the young adolescent girl Hedvig who is driven to shoot herself by the selfish and inadequate behaviour of her father Hjalmar. After a brief visit to Norway in 1885, Ibsen wrote *Rosmersholm* (1886) and *The Lady from the Sea* (1888). The last play of his exile, *Hedda Gabler* (1891), caused consternation by its comic effects in treating the serious issue of a woman trapped in a stifling middle-class marriage.

In the final group of plays, which Ibsen wrote after his return to Norway in 1891, he embraced elements of *expressionism in order to subject his own life as a creative artist to critical scrutiny. In *The Master Builder* (1892), *John Gabriel Borkman* (1896), and *When We Dead Awaken* (1899), he explored the conflicting demands of art and life, vocation and personal happiness, in ways which brought together realist and dream-play techniques. All three express his own harsh judgement of himself as a man and artist. In 1900 Ibsen suffered the first of two strokes, which left him unable to write and increasingly paralysed and helpless.

Ibsen's plays do not provide neat solutions, and often leave questions provocatively unresolved. They are full of hidden resonances and richly layered *subtextual meanings, but a moral framework is implied in the *action and *audiences are invited to judge the behaviour of the characters. They had a profound impact on twentieth-century playwrights concerned with social issues, notably *Miller, but also writers as diverse as *Bond and *Hare.

Ibsen's plays effectively launched the *naturalist movement in the theatre, with *Antoine in Paris, *Brahm in Berlin, and others presenting detailed naturalist stagings. In 1906, a new generation presented symbolist and expressionist readings: *Meyerhold in St Petersburg (*Hedda Gabler*), *Craig in Florence (*Rosmersholm*), and *Reinhardt in Berlin (*Ghosts*). From the 1960s leading European directors offered a series of challenging interpretations. *Bergman's 1964 *Hedda Gabler*, *Stein's 1971 Marxist *Peer Gynt*, Peter *Hall's 1975 emblematic *John Gabriel Borkman*. The 1980s and 1990s sparked productions based on ironic deconstruction of Ibsen's texts (particularly in Germany), juxtaposed with some finely judged acting of a more traditional kind (notably in England and the USA). Thomas *Ostermeier's updated *Hedda Gabler* for the *Schaubühne (2005) contained both elements, and *toured widely to high praise.   DT

Ichikawa Danjūrō IX (1838–1903) *Kabuki actor, the fifth son of *Danjūrō VII and the leader of kabuki during the Meiji Period (1868–1912) in the transition from feudal to modern Japan. An actor impressive in both voice and stature, he played a wide range of roles. In early Meiji he became a leader of kabuki reform, particularly with the Living History Play movement, for which he applied notions of psychological *realism to the interpretation of *characters. Later he and Onoe Kikūgorō V formed a popular acting combination and in 1887 they starred in the first kabuki plays to be seen by an emperor, part of Danjūrō's campaign to improve the social status of the art. From the late 1880s he emerged as a leader of a conservative movement, successfully preserving the authority of old families over upstart actors. When Living History Plays proved unpopular Danjūrō returned to the classics and enjoyed great success in both *dance pieces and dramatic plays, establishing his own 'New Eighteen Great Plays'.   LRK

Idris, Yussuf (1927–91) Egyptian writer. Outstanding among his eight plays is *Al-Farafir* (*The Flipflaps*, 1964). With it and a series of articles entitled 'Towards an Egyptian Theatre' he rejected *illusionist European drama in favour of 'authentically Egyptian' performance traditions with more vigorous performer–*audience interaction. As alternatives Idris proposed *shadow theatre, *Karagöz, folk *rituals, and *al-sāmir (a peasant theatre in the round consisting of *acting, *music, and *dance). Though it now seems that *Al-Farafir* owes as much to *avant-garde European models as to any exclusively Egyptian tradition, Idris's contribution nonetheless paved the way for the post-1967 trends in Egypt that sought to rediscover indigenous art forms. *Al-Farafir* also occasioned the first Egyptian public dispute between a playwright and a director over the artistic control of production.   HMA

Iffland, August Wilhelm (1759–1814) German *actor-manager and dramatist who began his career at the Gotha Court Theatre under the tutelage of Konrad *Ekhof. He moved to Mannheim in 1779 where he came to prominence as a major exponent of *realistic *acting (the 'Mannheim school'). During this time he began writing highly successful moralistic *comedies and *melodramas which rivalled those of *Kotzebue in popularity. In 1796 he assumed the directorship of the Berlin Royal Theatre which he managed until 1813. He oversaw the building of the new Theater am Gendarmenmarkt (1802) and established Berlin as a centre for German-speaking theatre, rivalling Vienna's *Burgtheater. Following *Goethe's example at *Weimar, he performed a mixture of classical (Goethe, *Schiller, *Molière, *Voltaire, Shakespeare) and popular drama. He involved himself in all aspects of production from *dramaturgical adaptation to supervision of *rehearsals. As an actor he was particularly renowned for his Shakespearian roles, as a director for his productions of Schiller's plays.   CBB

Ilinsky, Igor (1901–87) Russian/Soviet actor who began his career in Moscow with *Komisarjevsky and *Foregger before joining *Meyerhold, with whom he worked, on and off, until 1935. A great comic actor, Ilinsky was an expert interpreter of Meyerhold's *acting techniques, seen to startling effect as the frenetically jealous Bruno, in Crommelynck's *The Magnanimous Cuckold* (1922), as the comic actor Schastlivtsev in *Ostrovsky's *The Forest* (1924), as the naive, bourgeoisified Prisypkin in *Mayakovsky's *The Bedbug* (1929), and as the pathetic Raspluyev in *Sukhovo-Kobylin's *Krechinsky's Wedding* (1933). The rest of his career was spent at the Moscow Maly Theatre, where in his 80th year he gave a three-hour performance as *Tolstoy. Ilinsky was an actor of extraordinary versatility, charm, and energy.   NW

illusion The aesthetic experience which is generated when a representation has the appearance of being true or real and when recipients respond to it as such. Illusion is thus the product of an interaction influenced by a range of variables, including the artistic media and social context involved.

Renaissance (*early modern) architects fostered pictorial illusion by means of optical tricks such as *perspective settings, borders, flats and wings, and the *proscenium arch, which masked the offstage space and its machinery (*see* SCENOGRAPHY). Due to the development of a materialist conception of reality, embodied in nineteenth-century *realism, illusion became increasingly characterized by an emphasis on historically accurate replication and the further removal of features, including visible *footlights and spectators, which drew attention to the artifice of the stage event.

Despite its prominence in the age of reproductive technology, empiricist replication is not the only mode of illusion. According to the *neoclassical idea of *vraisemblance*, believable drama represented what ought and what was normally (or socially) expected to happen. In line with *romanticism, S. T. Coleridge gave greater emphasis to the role of imagination, famously claiming that illusion requires 'a willing suspension of disbelief', the recipient voluntarily relinquishing the impulse to judge and compare with external reality. By contrast, commentators such as *Diderot have regarded the spectator's participation as an involuntary response to sensory and emotional arousal. The spectator's identification with *character is a major source of such arousal, one supposedly enhanced when the actor maintains the illusion of a fourth wall by performing as if sealed in the character's world and unaware of the *audience beyond the playing space.

Since the advent of realism, there have been numerous challenges to the modes of illusion associated with it. While the *symbolists replaced detailed attention to surface appearance with abstract expression of an ideal essence, *Brecht used *Verfremdung (distancing) to expose imitation and fourth-wall illusionism as tools for preserving the bourgeois status quo (*see* EPIC THEATRE; BOURGEOIS THEATRE). Brecht argued that a focus on character-centred identification and linear plot encouraged a passive self-indulgent spectator with a fatalist outlook, one whose ability to reflect critically on social reality was inhibited. While his self-reflexive use of *Verfremdung* is sometimes described as anti-illusionist, to draw attention to the process of illusion making is itself an attempt to give the appearance of being true or real. Whenever makers of representation engage with conceptions of reality and art's relation to it, they by definition contribute to the constitution of illusion.   MM

imitation *See* MIMESIS

Immermann, Karl Leberecht (1796–1840) German director, dramatist, and novelist. As a

Prussian official in Düsseldorf, Immermann established the first municipal theatre there, pursuing a literary repertoire based on *Goethe's model at the *Weimar Court Theatre. Preferred dramatists were Shakespeare, *Calderón, Goethe, *Schiller, and *Kleist. Although this undertaking was short-lived (1835–7) and closed for financial reasons, Immermann's philosophy of theatre was influential. His approach to production called for a cohesive vision of the textual and *scenographic, which enhanced the status of the *director. He stressed ensemble playing over virtuoso *acting and insisted on extensive *rehearsals. In 1840 he mounted *Twelfth Night* on a stage built to his specifications that combined elements of the Elizabethan open stage with an Italian pictorial one. His dramatic output is largely derivative; only *Merlin* (1832) and *Andreas Hofer* (1834) have been revived.   CBB

improvisation Unscripted *acting in which the performers collectively make up the story or situation as they go, or collectively try to carry out a specified difficult performance in the presence of the *audience. There have been many kinds of improvisational theatre through the centuries. *Commedia dell' arte* is probably the best known among the Western traditions, but most comic or *clown traditions have allowed the performer to establish rapport through improvised jokes and patter, as Hamlet complains in his instruction to the Players to speak only what he wrote for them. Almost any performance involving direct interaction with the audience must have an improvisational content. But improvisation as a separate form of theatre was formalized through acting exercises in the United States and Britain in the mid-twentieth century, especially as popularized by Viola Spolin's *Improvisation for the Theater* (1963). In general the form relies on structuring the *action into games or conventionalized rules that somewhat resemble *commedia* *scenarios or the old *lines of business. For example, actors may be required to begin all lines of *dialogue with successive letters of the alphabet, working from a specified A to a specified Z, while trying to maintain a coherent story; or a scene may start with two *characters, with more added progressively, each character bringing some additional *exposition or complication for the others to cope with.   JB

Inchbald, Elizabeth (1753–1821) English actress and author. Despite a lifelong stutter, at the age of 19 Inchbald began acting on the provincial stage, establishing a large and diverse repertory of roles, such as Fanny in *Colman and *Garrick's *The Clandestine Marriage*, Hermione in *The*

Winter's Tale, and Louisa Dudley in *Cumberland's The West Indian*. She acted at *Covent Garden throughout the 1780s, adding important roles like Mrs Fainall in *Congreve's *The Way of the World* and Imoinda in *Oroonoko*. She was tall, beautiful, and (although self-taught) highly intelligent. Realizing that she could not achieve great fame on the London stage, she left off acting at the age of 37 and devoted herself to writing. Her original plays, such as *The Child of Nature* (1788) and *Everyone Has his Fault* (1793), and her translations of *Kotzebue, often explore important social issues, eschewing easy sentimentality while expressing great sympathy for the oppressed. She edited collections of plays, Bell's *British Theatre* (25 volumes, 1806-9), and *The Modern Theatre* (10 volumes, 1809).   MJK

Independent Theatre Private society founded by *Grein in London in 1891. Its name advertised imitation of *Antoine's Théâtre *Libre (1887) in Paris and *Brahm's *Freie Bühne (1889) in Berlin. Like Brahm, the Independent Theatre chose *Ibsen's *Ghosts* for its inaugural production, a single performance at the Royalty Theatre in 1891. The society's 22 productions included English premières of two further plays by Ibsen (*The Master Builder* in 1893, *The Wild Duck* in 1894) and *Shaw's first play (*Widowers' Houses*, 1892). Aiming 'to give special performances of plays which have a *literary* and *artistic*, rather than a commercial value', the Independent Theatre was organized as a producing society: membership subscriptions, paid in advance of production, provided capital and permitted performances to be deemed private (and thus disregarded by the Lord Chamberlain's Examiner of Plays). Similar organization was adopted by others determined to present plays which, being restricted in appeal or controversial in subject matter, were unlikely to be staged in a commercial theatre economically driven by long runs and legally subject to pre-*censorship. *See also* STAGE SOCIETY.   MOC

Inge, William (1913-73) American playwright. Encouraged by *Williams, Inge completed *Farther off from Heaven* (produced in 1947 by Margo *Jones in Dallas). When staged on Broadway in 1950 as *Come Back, Little Sheba*, it secured Inge's position as a talented *realist, bolstered by the film version (1952) with Burt Lancaster and Shirley *Booth. Three more successful plays of small-town Midwestern life followed: *Picnic* (1953), *Bus Stop* (1955), and *The Dark at the Top of the Stairs* (1957). Inge was awarded the Pulitzer Prize for *Picnic* and an Academy award for his screenplay for *Splendor in the Grass* (1962). After the failures

of *A Loss of Roses* (1959), *Natural Affection* (1963), and *Where's Daddy?* (1966), he grew increasingly depressed, struggled with alcoholism, and committed suicide in Los Angeles. With the growth of the *regional theatre movement in the 1970s, Inge's four successful plays from the 1950s became staples of the American repertory.   MAF

Ingegneri, Angelo (1550-1613) Italian poet and dramatist who led a peripatetic life at a variety of Italian courts. He was a member of the Olympian Academy in Vicenza, for whom he directed a magnificent production of *Oedipus the King* (1585), which inaugurated the Teatro *Olimpico designed by *Palladio. Ingegneri's *pastoral drama *Danza di Venere* (*Dance of Venus*) was produced at the court of Parma in 1583, though the *tragedy *Tomiri* (1607) remained unperformed. From 1586 to 1592 he served as theatrical adviser of Ferrante Gonzaga at the court of Guastalla. He is best known for his two treatises *On Dramatic Poetry* and *How to Produce Stage Plays* (Ferrara, 1598).   GB

ingénue A term from French denoting a youthful actress who played significant parts. In the English theatre 'female juvenile lead' meant the same, and she would have played opposite her *stock company counterpart, the male juvenile lead. *Heroines fell into this category, if they were young and not played by the company's leading lady. Qualities of innocence and simplicity (abundant in the heroines of *melodrama) were essential. From the Shakespearian repertory, Ophelia, Desdemona, and Cordelia would have fallen to the ingénue. *See also* LINES OF BUSINESS.   MRB

Inoue Hisashi (1934-2010) Japanese playwright and novelist. Inoue's first stage play was *The Japanese Navel* (1969); he has since written dozens of plays and novels that have won both popular and critical acclaim. Many of his best dramas, such as *Dōgen's Adventures* (1971), *Kobayashi Issa* (1979), and *Headache, Stiff Neck, Higuchi Ichiyō* (1984), are satirical biographies or *parodies of historical events. His light, comedic approach to serious subjects, such as social or regional discrimination, injected new energy, wit, and inventiveness into contemporary mainstream Japanese theatre. Since 1983, his own theatre troupe, Komatsuza, staged most of his plays. *The Great Doctor Yabuhara* (1973) and *Make-up* (1982) were well received in Europe and North America.   CP

interculturalism One of the most controversial of contemporary performance practices, characterized at its best by a sharing and mutual borrowing of the manifestation of one theatre practice by another. At worst it features the appropriation and annihilation of indigenous, premodern practices in traditional societies by a rapacious 'First World' global capitalism. Interculturalism has its roots in orientalism, a term used to describe a European art movement of the mid-nineteenth century obsessed with both *realism and a fascination with the unknown, the tribal, non-Christian, and seemingly unregulated societies at the far side of the Mediterranean, from Morocco to the Near East. This artistic practice came at a time of European colonialism and expansion into the Far East. New trade routes permitted the shipping back of foreign goods and artefacts, as well as an obsession with what was not understood or not permitted for the Westerner, namely the harem and the temple or mosque.

In the first half of the twentieth century modernist European theatre practitioners, from *Yeats to *Artaud, sought to overhaul their work and produce ever stimulating novelty by seeking out oriental practices and holding them up as templates for the theatre of the future. Yeats's plan for a new indigenous Irish theatre looked to Ireland's pre-colonial myths and legends for his subject, but also to the classical *nō plays of Japan for its *dramaturgy. *Cathleen Ní Houlihan* (1902) features the restless soul of an Old Woman who is ritually transformed into a young girl by the blood sacrifice of Ireland's volunteer revolutionaries; like the *shite* *protagonists of nō she is appeased through *ritual performance. Artaud's experience of oriental cultures was in tourist versions of Balinese and Cambodian *dancing, but the codified movements he saw as unleashing mystical powers and their formalism came to represent for him a template for European theatre of the future. The interculturalism of these two major figures was abetted by geographical distance, as they lived in a colonial world that separated them from the cultural Other. Their experience of other cultures came from imported and sanitized versions brought to Europe in the Great Exhibitions as triumphalist trophies of European dominion. *Orientalism* (1976), the seminal work by the Palestinian cultural historian Edward Said, mapped out the politics of this cultural practice, particularly the hegemonic imperialism inscribed within it, and has been used as the theoretical touchstone for the analysis of Western intercultural theatre.

A post-1960s generation of directors—*Brook, *Mnouchkine, and *Barba, among others—came under the spotlight as they sampled the cultures of Africa and Asia in their search for a form to break with realism. Brook's version of the Hindu epic *The Mahabharata* (1985), featuring actors from the four corners of the globe in a production which *toured the world, set alight the debate on the ethics of such practice. The social, cultural, and most importantly religious context of the work was deemed by some to be lost in an aestheticized package for global consumption. Removed from its religious and devotional context and placed in a new European setting of non-believers, the text lost its third dimension, namely its *audience of the gods.

Mnouchkine's intercultural work of the 1980s and 1990s largely escaped the critical wrath directed at Brook, since her direction was an imagined oriental practice layered on the textual heritage of Europe. The most famous of her productions, three plays by Shakespeare (1981–4), and four ancient *Greek texts called *Les Atrides* (1990–3), featured multinational troupes of actors who trained in the forms of oriental theatres and created their own form. Mnouchkine thought that the surviving classical theatres of the Far East were suitable templates for constructing new forms for the presentation of ancient or medieval histories of Europe, given that European theatre has no such equivalents. *Costumes were eclectic mixes of both European heritage and oriental samples, while the *mise-en-scène (like its Eastern models) broke all the bounds of realism.

This brand of interculturalism feeds into the practice of modernist orientalism in its nostalgic search for a formalism with which to reinvigorate theatre practice and to produce novelty. It seems to suggest that European theatre has been exhausted and that the classical forms of oriental cultures are to be quarried for the Western palate. Alongside these productions of European classics Mnouchkine also worked with playwright Hélène *Cixous in productions of contemporary Asian history. *The Terrible But Unfinished History of Norodom Sihanouk, King of Cambodia* (1985) pitted *Brechtian distancing (*see* VERFREMDUNG) against images of Pol Pot's killing fields and disastrous US foreign policy decisions in the region. *The Indiade; or, India of their Dreams* (1997) similarly charted the struggle for independence in India. The proximity, and familiarity through media representation, of these histories and the real-life figures meant that a theatrical formalism could not be applied; the productions faltered with images of a white French actor playing King Sihanouk and Ghandi. Mnouchkine's production of Cixous's *Drums on the Dyke* (1999), however, presented an imagined version of a real event, namely the flooding of a valley in China in order to create a dam, thus wiping out communities and cultures. It was a groundbreaking experiment of live actors being manipulated as *bunraku puppets, challenging Western notions of *character.

Perhaps Eugenio Barba's Odin Teatret of Denmark comes closest to the concept of interculturalism in its strictest sense, in that he and his actors, though touring the world, engage in a bartering process with the other culture, as hosts and guests present work to each other. But this kind of exchange is forever lopsided, as the traditional theatre forms that Odin Teatret encounters have a history and a constituency within their cultures and societies. That is not true of Barba's troupe, which can be seen as a band of high-art experimenters attempting to establish an essentialism of performance in order to discover the commonalities of all cultures.

But interculturalism quite clearly does not operate solely on a unidirectional East/West, Asian/European axis. Throughout the twentieth century Asian practitioners have sought inspiration in European practices. For instance, the Japanese *shingeki movement modelled itself on the new drama of Europe, inspired by the plays of *Ibsen, while the popular female *musical-theatre form *Takarazuka has always invested heavily in pastiches of Western culture, from nineteenth-century *opera to classical Hollywood film. Further, the post-shingeki *dance form *butoh, though it draws on pre-modern mysticism, owes a debt both to Artaud's Theatre of *Cruelty and the choreography of Mary Wigman. More recently, directors such as Japan's *Ninagawa and Singapore's *Ong Keng Sen have sought not to reinvigorate their own national theatre practices but to reject authenticity and embrace hybrid multiple realities. Thus one of the reasons why First World interculturalism has become a global phenomenon is that it purloins the surfaces of other cultures in order to attain the greatest market share, by reaching out for the largest common denominator of mythologized cultural icons. Ninagawa and Ong are very much part of the transnational circus of the supra-cultural festival circuit, whose constituency has no real national or social hinterland other than the globalized community of high-art consumers, many of whom experience theatre as cultural tourists.

What place then for the local and indigenous? Points of resistance to such practices can be found in various national and post-colonial agendas. Instead of relying on the method of global iconicity to fill the void left by colonial policies which erased indigenous culture, in many locations practitioners seek a rediscovery

and reassembly of pre-colonial practices. The asymmetric power relations between colonizer and colonized can now sometimes give way to indigenous discourses within globalized cultural markets, which treat the pre-modern local traditions as raw materials to be repackaged for export, rather than as historical entities to be respected and protected. Ghana's Efua *Sutherland, Nigeria's Wole *Soyinka, and India's Kavalam Narayana *Panikkar are representative post-colonial playwrights who have imagined and reconstructed indigenous performances which resist the transnational trends of interculturalism. These practices are known as 'intracultural': the pre-colonial cultural practices are first recognized as temporal, though not cultural, 'others', and then are mastered and assimilated into a contemporary idiom.

What interculturalism often leaves behind in traditional societies is a desire to transform indigenous performance in order to suit the palate of the Western consumer. The intercultural Western project swapped the material produce of empire for its own ideologies of capitalism and Christianity. Interculturalism thus becomes a means by which everything which is wished for in Western or First World culture can be fantasized, created, and played out. The quest for appropriation is fuelled by a vision of the Orient as a nostalgic space of lost ritual, formalism, and religion, a nostalgic space for the authentically pure, sometimes barbarian, for everything the Westerner is not: his or her opposite in cultural fixity, morality, devotion, tradition, and belief. Whether the interculturalist is in Tokyo, London, or New York, she or he is performing from a single ruling perspective that defines itself as West.

Interculturalism thus is paradoxical, since it stems from both a self-belief and an anxiety. It is a means of imagining culture as a landscape which, when occupied, produces, transmits, and substitutes for a once authentic culture. Rather than a mutual meeting in a space between cultures, intercultural performance is most often a practice of the desire, imagination, and anxieties of the one cultural system which looks to the other culture for formalist or aesthetic templates for the renovation of itself. Intercultural theatre thus operates in the space between two or more cultures, but those cultures themselves rarely, if ever, meet, let alone interact. But not all intercultural practices operate within a dichotomized structure of cultural exchange, where one dominant First World practice feeds off its Third World other. Some movements in Asia, for example, such as the Indian *Parsi theatre, modelled themselves on the performance practices of their nineteenth-century colonial masters, a sign of the practitioners' aim to single themselves out as a home-ruling cultural elite. Many of the aforementioned practices of both modern and postmodern Western theatre, what is more, although seemingly rooted in orientalist drives for self-regeneration, in fact exist less on a material plane and more on a theoretical level or within only one geographical region and economic system. Such trajectories of exchange break down the East-West dichotomy and were not mediated by colonialism at all.

Yeats's borrowings of nō dramaturgy, for example, though rooted in modernism's obsession with novelty, were formulated at a philosophical level and from a desire to create a new Irish idiom beyond available contemporary realities. Thus his interculturalism did not replicate the surface of an Asian culture, since there was no actual exchange of anything, but was simply a means of imagining a new drama, with a medieval oriental ritual theatre (such as nō) providing the allegorical and dramaturgical framework for revolutionary political drama for which realism was inappropriate. Similarly, the influence of the Beijing opera (*jingju*) performer *Mei Lanfang on *Brecht's notion of *Verfremdung* represents more of a conceptual borrowing of a theatrical form for political reformation than an orientalist appropriation.

So, although rooted in the drives of orientalism, many modernist innovations differ from the late twentieth-century's obsession with speaking for and materially representing their desired Asian others. Complicating the interculturalism of early modernism further is the knowledge that intercultural influences roam intercontinentally, beyond the trade routes of cultural exchange. For example, Yeats also acknowledged a debt to the Indian poet *Tagore, who himself was influenced by Japanese philosopher Okakura Tenshin; and the form of nō that provided Yeats with his template had its roots in rural ritual songs and dances with origins in China. This ideational interculturalism is a less problematic form of exchange than the materiality of colonial and/or imperialist representation. Further, the digitized possibilities of new technologies in the twenty-first century abet ideational roaming, but also call into question the notion of culture as a property, of the nation with confined borders, and the old intercultural binaries of self/other, colonizer/colonized, and West/East. BRS

interlude In the *early modern period an interlude was a short *farce or a light-hearted moral piece which was 'played between' (its Latin meaning) the courses of a meal, or at its end. In other contexts it can mean a piece played between the acts of another drama or *opera, like the Italian *intermezzo*. In sixteenth-century England the term often meant simply a short play. *See also* MORALITY PLAY. JWH

International Centre for Theatre Research *See* BROOK, PETER.

Ionesco, Eugène (1912–94) Born in Romania, Ionesco became a major playwright of the French *absurdist theatre, rejecting *realism, psychologism, causal action, and the Marxist theatres of *Brecht and *Sartre. Sharing the absurdists' existential themes and the *surrealists' use of dreams, he attempted to create verbal and visual language to express a reality beyond the objective. In Ionesco's view, society uses language not to communicate meaning but to bury it in clichés, propaganda, and banalities. His *characters are often puppet-like and live in a present from which they cannot escape. The cultural alienation in Ionesco's characters was also present in his life. His lifelong sense of being split between two cultures infused all of his plays, beginning with *La Cantatrice chauve* (1950, known in English as *The Bald Prima Donna* and *The Bald Soprano*), which he described as 'a *tragedy of language' until the Paris *audience reacted to it as a powerful *comedy. Several more one-acts followed, including *The Lesson* (1951) and *The Chairs* (1952), for which his term 'tragic *farce' is appropriate. The early plays appeared in small experimental theatres in the Latin Quarter, often playing to nearly empty houses. Yet *The Bald Soprano* and *The Lesson* have played continuously since 1957 in La Huchette, a living museum for generations of students and scholars.

The next plays were full-length, including *Amédée* (1954) and *The Killer* (1959), and drew larger audiences as Ionesco's reputation rose to the point where *Rhinoceros* was directed by *Barrault at the *Odéon Théâtre (1960). Here the character Bérenger, who also appears in *The Killer*, *A Stroll in the Air*, and *Exit the King* (both 1962), struggles in vain against an 'epidemic' of ideological conformity.

Ionesco came to see his anti-leftist plays like *Hunger and Thirst* (1966) as too politically explicit, but soon effectively combined politics with *slapstick, dream, and *Artaudian violence in *The Killing Game* (1970) and *Macbett* (1972), a *Jarryesque *parody of Shakespeare. Even more autobiographical than the Bérenger plays is *The Man with the Luggage* (1974), and his last play, *Journeys among the Dead* (1983), achieved the hallucinatory quality of his early works. Its première at the *Théâtre National Populaire in Villeurbanne was directed by *Planchon, who retitled it *Ionesco* and included other writings by the author, transforming it from Ionesco's personal journey into a monumental production of his life and times. Responding to the controversy this caused, Planchon argued that Ionesco's work and life should be re-evaluated as part of the 'chronicle of damage' done to Western humanism by the Cold War. Besides his twenty major plays, Ionesco published poetry, film scripts, short stories, literary criticism, memoirs, and children's tales, and in 1970 was elected to the Académie Française.   SBB

Irish Literary Theatre *See* ABBEY THEATRE.

Irving, Henry (1838–1905) English actor and *manager. Born John Henry Brodribb, he took the name Irving for his professional debut in *Richelieu* at Sunderland in 1856, thereafter working hard as a provincial actor; in his first three years he played a total of 451 different parts. From 1867 he played in several London theatres until his Digby Grant in *Albery's *Two Roses* in 1870 led to a Lyceum engagement as leading man with Colonel *Bateman. In 1871 Irving was immediately propelled into the front rank of actors by his extraordinary performance of the haunted Burgomaster Mathias in Albery's *The Bells*, a good family man who twenty years before had robbed and murdered to lay the foundations of his prosperity. Irving played Hamlet in 1874 for an astonishing 200 performances. In 1879 the Batemans' star actor took over the Lyceum himself as *actor-manager, and immediately engaged Ellen *Terry as his leading lady.

During his 23-year tenure, Irving made the Lyceum a place of pilgrimage for the famous and the artistic: it was both popular and fashionable. Eight company *tours to North America extended his reputation, and regular provincial touring made him a household name in Britain. His repertory was principally Shakespeare (twelve plays) and poetic, *romantic, and historical drama, and his company was remarkably stable. The Lyceum was large, holding 1,700–1,800 spectators, with a backstage staff of well over 100; during *Faust* (1885) it employed, altogether, over 350, for *Robespierre* (1899) over 600. Thus it required a grand style of production and big *acting. Neither Irving nor Terry were modern psychological actors, and Irving, much to the disgust of *Shaw, was not interested in the modern experimental repertory. Irving controlled and supervised everything: employment of actors, wages, the *music, the repertory, *rehearsals, and the *lighting system, his personal creation. Productions were pictorially beautiful in the best Victorian tradition.

Years of overwork and financial difficulties combined to push Irving out of the Lyceum in 1902, and he spent most of his last years traversing the provinces once more, old, sick, and weary. His funeral in Westminster Abbey was appropriately theatrical.

As an actor Irving took a long time to reach greatness; once there, he easily dominated his profession and the English theatre as a whole. Having played hundreds of roles in such a long apprenticeship to stardom—he had, for instance, played seven parts in *Hamlet* before he played the prince—Irving brought both enormous experience and a discriminating intelligence to the art of acting. Despite physical faults in speech and movement, he was an intense, magnetic, haunted actor who could almost hypnotize an *audience. He was equally powerful at playing nobility and goodness on the one hand, and malignity and evil on the other. Irving was knighted in 1895, the first actor to be so honoured.   MRB

Irwin, Bill (1950–) American *clown, *dancer, actor, and director. Irwin's marriage of physical virtuosity and mischief-making has appealed to critics and mass *audiences alike. His self-effacing persona and seemingly boneless body have served as comic centrepieces for several full-length shows, including *The Regard of Flight* (1982) and *Largely New York* (1989). These *surreal concoctions drew on traditional clowning strategies in satirizing hi-tech culture, the *avant-garde, and other contemporary targets, serving to associate him with the New Vaudeville movement. *Fool Moon*, his clown *revue with David Shiner, merited several incarnations in the USA and Europe from 1993 to 2001. Irwin has been as likely to show up on children's television as in stage roles like Galy Gay in *Brecht's *A Man's a Man* (1985). He has also appeared in plays by *Fo, *Molière, and Shakespeare. His direction for the stage includes his own one-person performance of *Beckett prose pieces, *Texts for Nothing* (2000). In *Waiting for Godot* in New York, he played Lucky in 1988 and Vladimir in 2009.   EW

Isherwood, Christopher (1904–86) English writer. Best known as novelist and writer of short stories, he collaborated (1934–8) with *Auden on three plays to be staged by the Group Theatre in London: *The Dog beneath the Skin* (1935), *The Ascent of F6* (1937), and *On the Frontier* (1938). Precisely which was responsible for which elements in the composition is not clear, but presumably Isherwood conceived the overall *scenario and then developed the plot and (somewhat thin) characterization in the *expressionist manner required. Isherwood had experienced expressionist drama during his lengthy stay in Germany (1930–3); none of his fictional writings of the time demonstrates the profound moral and social *satire found in the plays, nor the developed Marxist political critique that underpins them. The plays are vigorous, yet beneath them lies a deep-rooted anger and disgust, the product of Isherwood's time in Berlin, with Europe succumbing to *fascism while pursuing an endless round of fun. RAC

Ivanov, Vsevolod (1895–1963) Russian/Soviet dramatist and prose writer, one of whose early occupations was as a *circus *clown, his experiences being later recorded in the autobiographical *We're Going to India* (1960). Influenced by *Gorky, Ivanov's own subject matter, couched in an ornamental style, tends to be grim and rather brutal. He adapted his novel about Siberian partisan activity, *Armoured Train 14–69* (1922), as a play for the *Moscow Art Theatre (1927). The production, which was directed by Ilya Sudakov, listed *Stanislavsky as an adviser and its optimistic, if melodramatic, revolutionary message became a turning point in the Art Theatre's relationship with the Soviet regime. Ivanov's play about the Kronstadt sailors' rising of 1921, *Blockade*, was also staged at the Art Theatre (1929). NW

Izumi Kyōka (1873–1939) Japanese novelist and playwright. Starting in 1894, much of his early melodramatic fiction was adapted for the *shimpa stage, but Kyōka (he was usually known by that assumed 'art' name) became increasingly dissatisfied with adaptations of his work. In contrast to the *shimpa* *melodramas, his own plays were more fantastic and *surrealistic in style, like his best fiction. His 1907 translation of *Hauptmann's fairy play *The Sunken Bell* was a guide for the *dramaturgy of fantasy, but he also had *nō and *kabuki for models. Ahead of their time, his best plays—*The Sea God's Villa* (1913), *The Castle Tower* (1917), and *The Wild Rose* (1923)— were not staged until after his death. Kyōka's works have enjoyed something of a revival since the 1960s, thanks largely to adaptations by *Kara, *Terayama, *Suzuki, and *Ninagawa. The popular kabuki *onnagata *Bandō Tamasaburō V frequently starred in *shimpa* productions of his plays, and has directed two films based on Kyōka's work, *The Surgery* (1990) and *The Castle Tower* (1995). CP

Jackson, Barry (1879–1961) English director and *manager. Trained as an architect, Jackson was heir to a fortune derived from one of the leading grocery firms in the Midlands. In 1907 he founded an amateur group in Birmingham, the Pilgrim Players, which went professional in 1913 as the *Birmingham Repertory Theatre, one of the first examples of the *regional repertory movement. Jackson funded a new *playhouse that year, and despite a number of *financial crises maintained the venture out of his own pocket for 22 years. (After 1935 the theatre was administered by a trust, with support from subscription holders.) A close associate of *Shaw's, Jackson was also the prime mover of the Malvern Festival, which he directed from 1927 to 1939. In 1945 he succeeded Robert *Atkins as director of the *Shakespeare Memorial Theatre in Stratford, where he attempted to break out of the provincialism that had bedevilled the annual festivals. Among his successes were *Brook's *Love's Labour's Lost* (1946) and *Romeo and Juliet* (1947) and *Benthall's *Hamlet* (1948) with *Helpmann and *Scofield alternating the lead. But Jackson's policies of higher spending and more adventurous productions did not accord with the conservatism of the governors, and he was replaced in 1948 by Anthony *Quayle. He continued to direct the Birmingham Rep until his death.   RJ

Jackson, Glenda (1936–) English actress. Jackson came to critical notice in *Marowitz and *Brook's Theatre of *Cruelty season in London (1964), which led to a starring role as Charlotte Corday in Brook's production of *Weiss's *Marat/Sade* (1965), a sexually knowing Ophelia to David *Warner's angry Hamlet in *Hall's production for the *Royal Shakespeare Company (1965), and Masha in the *Royal Court's production of *Chekhov's *The Three Sisters*. Other notable performances include *Mortimer's *Collaborators* (1973), *Hedda Gabler* (1975), Hugh Whitemore's *Stevie* (1977), and *O'Neill's *Strange Interlude* (1984). Having appeared in over 30 movies, she garnered two Academy Awards, for *Women in Love* (1969) and *A Touch of Class* (1973). She reached a popular *audience playing Elizabeth I in the television mini-series *Elizabeth R* (1971), a role which exploited her ability to project a powerful intelligence and sexuality. Jackson retired from acting in 1992 and was elected to Parliament. She was appointed Under-Secretary of State for Transportation in the Tony Blair government, and later campaigned (unsuccessfully) to be the Labour Party candidate for Mayor of London.   MDG

Jacobi, Derek (1938–) English actor. Starting at the *Birmingham Repertory Company, Jacobi joined the fledgling *National Theatre in 1963, playing Laertes to Peter *O'Toole's Hamlet. He also appeared in *Othello* with *Olivier (1964), *Coward's *Hay Fever* (1964), *Shaffer's *Black Comedy* (1966), and Clifford *Williams's all-male production of *As You Like It* (1967). In 1972 Jacobi joined the Prospect Theatre Company, playing the leads in *The Lady's Not for Burning* (1978) and *Hamlet* (1977), which *toured internationally. From 1982 to 1985, he worked with the *Royal Shakespeare Company, playing Peer Gynt, Prospero, Benedick, and Cyrano, for which he won an Olivier award. In 1986 he originated the role of Alan Turing in Hugh Whitemore's *Breaking the Code*. Jacobi also appeared in a number of starry West End revivals, served for two seasons as *artistic director of the *Chichester Festival Theatre, taking the lead in *Uncle Vanya* in 1995, and recently partnered with director Michael Grandage on several productions, most notably Schiller's *Don Carlos* (2004) and *Twelfth Night* (2008). Jacobi is best known for playing the title role in television's *I, Claudius* (1976).   MDG

Jacobs, Sally (Sally Rich) (1932–) English designer. Her first job was for British Feature Films, but she became *Brook's favourite designer at the *Royal Shakespeare Company, collaborating on the Theatre of *Cruelty season (1964), *The Screens* (1964), *US* (1966), and the film and stage versions of *Marat/Sade* (1964), where inmates in grubby white tunics cavorted like Daumier caricatures in a brick-walled asylum littered with sunken pits. For Brook's *A Midsummer Night's Dream* (1970), Jacobs created a galleried white cube with iron ladders, trapezes, and scarlet-feathered trampoline; stilt-walking, plate-spinning fairies stalked woodland glades of coiled wire, which dropped upon the unwary lovers. In 1973, following Brook's research tour of West Africa, she designed *The Conference of Birds* and his film *Meetings with Remarkable Men* (1976). In 1982 Jacobs returned to London; her 1984 collaboration with director *Șerban on *Turandot* gave rise to a flourishing career with the Royal Opera at *Covent Garden and the *Royal Court.   RVL

James, Henry (1843–1916) American novelist. Hoping also for a career as playwright in London, the expatriate completed some fifteen plays, though only four of these were staged: *The American, Guy Domville* (a historical *tragedy written for George *Alexander which met a hostile reception in 1895), *The High Bid*, and *The Saloon*. James, profoundly observant of the *acting techniques of French theatre, which he deemed superior to English styles, became a shrewd critic of performance; his collected reviews were published in *The Scenic Art* (1949). These and his detailed advice about her roles to Elizabeth *Robins (chiefly in *Ibsen's plays) offer considerable insight into turn-of-the-century practice. *The High Bid* (1907), revised from a one-act drama (*Summersoft*) created for Ellen *Terry in 1895, shows James's *dramaturgical principles at their best. The *dialogue teems with directions, determining not movement but the meticulous tonal placing of words and phrases.   RAC

Jaques-Dalcroze, Émile (1865–1950) Swiss teacher and composer. As professor at the Geneva Music Conservatory (1892–1910), he found that his students could read music but lacked listening skill, so he developed an innovative approach, called eurhythmics, that used the human body to appreciate music. From the basic elements of walking, singing, breathing, and beating time, he turned to bolder methods: barefoot skipping, running, lunging, jumping, cooperating with partners. From 1911 to 1914 he taught in the garden city of Hellerau near Dresden, where he attracted international interest. *Appia designed the performance space, an enormous hall seating over 700 in movable raked seats; steps and platforms could be changed easily, and fabric hid banks of dimmable electric lights. Among the artists who visited were *Reinhardt, *Stanislavsky, *Shaw, *Claudel, *Diaghilev, *Laban, Mary Wigman, and Marie Lambert, some of whom witnessed an influential student recital of Gluck's *Orpheus (1913) which used Appia's stage and *lighting designs. The First World War ended the Hellerau experiment, and Jaques-Dalcroze returned to Geneva to teach until just before his death. By 1935 he had published 25 volumes on eurhythmics, which continues to be taught around the world.   FL

Jardiel Poncela, Enrique (1901–52) Spanish playwright and novelist. After an early success with a clever but traditional *comedy, *A Sleepless Spring Night* (1927), he developed a personal style of *absurdism in plot and language that is often described as 'jardielesco'. During the Spanish Republic and early years of the dictatorship, he became Spain's most innovative comic writer and reached his peak of popularity with *A Round-Trip Husband* (1939) and *Eloise Is under an Almond Tree* (1941). In 1933–4 he worked as a scriptwriter in the Spanish division of Fox Studios and later based one of his most ambitious plays, the darkly parodic *Love Only Lasts 2000 Metres* (1941), on his impressions of Hollywood. Renewed interest in his plays came with a new production of *Eloise* at Spain's National Theatre Centre in 1984 and a major revival of his *operetta spoof *Carlo Monte in Monte Carlo* (1939) in 1996.   MPH

Jarry, Alfred (1873–1907) French playwright, most famous for *Ubu roi* (1896), performed by the champion of the *symbolists, *Lugné-Poe, when Jarry was 23 years old. The play, which began life as a schoolboy send-up of Jarry's physics teacher, caused a scandal in the theatre with its scatological and theatrical irreverence. The play essentially is a *satire on *Macbeth and features a *Punch-and-Judy-like king and his wife who are motivated by avarice or whim. Accused of puerility, the play broke every convention of nineteenth-century theatre with its anti-*realism and *metatheatrical self-consciousness. It features one of the most notorious opening lines of the theatre: 'Merdre!' ('Crrrap!'). Jarry invested heavily in the production, dictating everything from scenery to actors' delivery. From then on Ubu became his obsession and in his personal life he took on Ubuesque characteristics which led to some extreme antisocial behaviour. He wrote three further unsuccessful Ubu plays (*Ubu cocu, Ubu enchaîné*, and *Ubu sur la butte*). But his influence spread throughout the twentieth century: *Ubu roi* was accepted as a precursor of *surrealism and the theatre of the *absurd, Jarry's name headed *Artaud's first theatrical enterprise, and his spoof philosophy, 'Pataphysics' (described as upsetting 'the balance of waking logic'), inspired a literary movement after the Second World War. Alcoholism contributed largely to his premature death.   BRB

jatra Bengali theatre form in Bangladesh and West Bengal in India, performed all night by large companies travelling to villages and small towns. *Jatra* is usually given in the open under a temporary canopy, the musicians sitting on opposite sides of an elevated stage, the spectators arranged on three sides; in urban areas *jatra* is also performed on *proscenium stages. Often disdained by the urban middle class, *jatra* enjoys immense popularity among ordinary people of all religions and castes. *Jatra* (literally, 'act of setting out on a journey') performances are based on written texts, composed mostly in prose interspersed with a few lyrical passages. The plays fall into three broad categories, though heightened conflict and high emotion are common to all. In social plays, which have the widest popularity, the *characters and stories are drawn from contemporary life. Historical plays enact fictional accounts of past events in order to promote heroism, patriotism, nationalism, or harmony between Hindus and Muslims. Biographies of important personalities such as Gandhi, Hitler, Ho Chi Minh, and Che Guevara have recently become important materials for a third variety of *jatra* plays. In addition, a few devotional plays use religious legends drawn from the *Ramayana*, the *Mahabharata*, and various Puranas. No matter the category, the plays are eventful and fast moving, built on principles of European *dramaturgy, and tend to rely on type characters who are clearly divided into the virtuous and the vicious.   SJA

Jefferson family Anglo-American actors. **Thomas Jefferson** (1732–1804) was a minor actor under *Garrick at *Drury Lane, *toured the provinces, and became a *manager in Plymouth. His son **Joseph I** (1774–1832) began with his father, but was brought to New York as a comic actor in 1795, moving in 1803 to Philadelphia. His son **Joseph II** (1804–42) was less regarded as an actor than as a scenic artist. His son **Joseph III** (1829–1905) became the most famous comic actor in nineteenth-century America. After his father's death, he toured the south with his mother and soon was playing supporting roles for such leading stars as Junius Brutus *Booth and Edwin *Forrest. For a short time he managed theatres in Baltimore and Richmond before joining Laura *Keene's company in New York. His comic talents were quickly recognized, and he gained popular acclaim for his portrayals of Dr Pangloss in *The Heir at Law* and Ase Trenchard in Tom *Taylor's *Our American Cousin*. He moved to the Winter Garden Theatre in 1858 where he began a pivotal association with *Boucicault. After a failed attempt at playing the title role in his own version of *Rip Van Winkle* in 1859, Jefferson convinced Boucicault to revise the play. In 1865, while in London, Jefferson perfected the *character that

would define his life and career for the next 40 years in America. Although he played other comic leads on occasion, Rip Van Winkle remained primary until his retirement in 1904.   PAD

Jefford, Barbara (1930–) English actress who played almost all of Shakespeare's *heroines at the *Shakespeare Memorial Theatre (1950–4), *Old Vic (1956–62), and Prospect Theatre (1977–9). At Stratford her roles included Isabella, Desdemona, Rosalind, and Helena in *A Midsummer Night's Dream*, while at the Old Vic she appeared as Imogen in *Cymbeline*, Beatrice, Portia, Viola, Ophelia, Lady Anne in *Richard III*, Queen Margaret in *Henry VI*, Isabella, Regan, Ophelia, Rosalind, and Lady Macbeth. At the *National Theatre she was Gertrude (1976) and, returning to Stratford for the *Royal Shakespeare Company, was Volumnia in *Coriolanus* (1989), the Countess in *All's Well That Ends Well*, and Mistress Quickly in *The Merry Wives of Windsor* (1992).   AS

Jellicoe, Ann (1927–) English playwright and director who became the only woman in the *Royal Court's stable of angry young men, co directing her *The Sport of my Mad Mother* with Keith Johnstone in 1958, a *surrealistic fantasia on violence which broke from the Court's kitchen sink *realism and was coolly received. Her next play, *The Knack* (1962), was a commercial and critical success. This lightly *absurdist piece with its freewheeling plot about youthful sexual games looks forward to Swinging London later in the decade. After spending several years in the early 1970s as the literary manager for the Court, Jellicoe founded the Colway Theatre Trust and concentrated her energies on *community theatre, writing and directing the massive history play *The Reckoning* (1978).   MDG

Jerrold, Douglas (1803–57) English dramatist and journalist. Born into a family of strolling players, he served for two years in the navy as a boy. He wrote many *farces and *melodramas for the minor theatres from 1818 to 1832, and scored a huge success with a nautical melodrama, *Black Ey'd Susan* (Surrey Theatre, 1829), which held the stage for the rest of the century but made him no money. His first success in the *legitimate theatre was a domestic drama, *The Rent Day* (*Drury Lane, 1832). He moved to *satirical high *comedies palely reminiscent of *Congreve (without the sex) and *Sheridan, such as *Bubbles of the Day* (*Covent Garden, 1842) and *Time Works Wonders* (*Haymarket, 1845). They were often favourably noticed, but weakness in dramatic structure and cardboard *characters condemned them to speedy oblivion. Jerrold channelled his energies more and more into journalism, especially for *Punch*. His career as a playwright came to a dismal end with a bitter wrangle with Charles *Kean over the production of Jerrold's last play, *A Heart of Gold* (1854). MDS

Jessner, Leopold (1878–1945) German director who came to prominence in 1919 as the first director of the newly reformed Staatliches Schauspielhaus in Berlin, the former court theatre of the Kaiser. He welcomed the new Weimar Republic by opening his programme with a production of *Schiller's *William Tell*, a celebration of republican freedom. In place of traditional Alpine scenery, he used a construction of wooden ramps, stairs, and bridges. So incensed was the *audience at this treatment of a beloved classic that the actor *Bassermann reprimanded the hecklers, and the police had to be called. *Tell* established Jessner's method of appropriating the classics for political ends and, in the manner of *expressionism, using symbolic settings and *lighting in place of *realistic *scenography. Jessner's *Richard III* with *Kortner, a prophetic warning of the danger of a tyrant seizing power, possessed the clarity of a *morality play. Played on an almost bare stage, it introduced a flight of steps, for which Jessner became renowned (the *Jessnertreppe*). In 1921 he directed *Othello*, again using a permanent architectural set with different levels. Most other productions contained a political theme: Schiller's *The Conspiracy of Fiesco in Genoa* (1921) and *Don Carlos* (1922); *Grabbe's *Napoleon* (1922); *Hamlet* (1926), which he set in the court of Kaiser Wilhelm; *Hauptmann's *The Weavers* (1928); and *Kaiser's *Gas I* (1928). Under increasing pressure from right-wing elements, Jessner resigned his directorship in 1930, and, as a Jew and a socialist, was forced into exile by the Nazis in 1933, to London and the USA. MWP

jig The English jig was a sprightly *dance, related to the hornpipe, that featured heel stamping and rapid footwork with little movement of the torso. As an element of Elizabethan stage entertainment it became associated with *clowns such as Richard *Tarlton and Will *Kempe. The jig was introduced to the Continent by the *English Comedians. Robert Reynolds, known in Germany as Pickelhering, performed 'Nobody's jig' in *Nobody and Somebody* (c.1592). While the jig could be incorporated into the performance of plays, it was more popularly performed as an independent afterpiece. Words and farcical *action were added to the dance to provide a broad and bawdy entertainment. (An Order of 1612 refers to the 'violence or outrage' that accompanied the performance of jigs.) The singing of doggerel verse to popular tunes, interspersed with lively dances, anticipated the later *ballad opera. RWV

***jingju* (*ching chü*)** Beijing (or Peking) opera, an indigenous Chinese theatrical form. Its beginnings are traced to 1790 when actors and musicians from around China gathered in Beijing for the celebration of Emperor Qianlong's eightieth birthday. Troupes from Anhui province, who specialized in *xipi* and *erhuang* music, provided the basis for the new musical system. Its current name means literally 'capital drama', referring to Beijing. As with other genres of Chinese opera, *music gives Beijing opera its unique identity. The traditional orchestra is made up of two parts. The melodic portion (*wenchang*) consists primarily of bowed and plucked string instruments; the percussion portion (*wuchang*) includes a large and a small gong and hand-held cymbals, led by the player of a small single-headed drum and clappers. Starting in the mid-twentieth century the orchestra was gradually expanded with additions from Chinese folk and classical instruments, but it was not uncommon to hear cello, double bass, and timpani in late twentieth-century productions.

The performative elements of *jingju* are highly synthesized: the story is told through song, stylized speech, pantomime, *dance, and sometimes *acrobatics. Beijing opera singers frequently dance, perform complicated *mime routines, or even engage in combat while singing. The traditional stage is sparse, with only a carpet, a table, several chairs, and no backdrop. The form makes use of a rich vocabulary of convention and symbolism; a stylized whip held in a performer's hand, for instance, signals the presence of a horse. Dance-acting movements communicate whether the character has mounted or dismounted, or if the horse is stuck in mud. Meaning is also encoded in percussion patterns and certain melodies: the pattern played when a character enters may reveal whether he is dignified or unscrupulous.

Imperial patronage from the mid-1800s promoted *jingju*'s status, drawing the interest of wealthy patrons and talented performers. Its golden age was in the first several decades of the twentieth century, when it was the most pervasive and popular of all entertainments in China. The work of actors, musicians, and librettists of the early republic (c.1911–49) remains unsurpassed in terms of volume, innovation, and frequency of performance. Among the many important works from this period are *Mei Lan Fang's *Farewell my Concubine*, *Cheng Yanqiu's *Snow in Midsummer*, and Zhou Xinfang's *Four Advancing Officials*.

Mao Zedong's ideology became the guiding principle for Beijing opera reform with the founding of the People's Republic of China in 1949. New operas on contemporary themes were composed and traditional operas were revised to emphasize themes such as equality between the sexes and patriotism. During the Cultural Revolution (1966–76), traditional Beijing opera was banned and numerous top performers were tortured or killed. 'Revolutionary modern drama' (*geming xiandai xi*), whose themes were revolutionary and presented with *realistic *costumes and staging, was the only form permitted. The traditional repertoire and performance style slowly returned after 1976. Now *jingju*'s future as a living tradition is uncertain. Following its economic reform policy, the state has withdrawn substantial funding from companies and training schools; some talented performers have turned to more profitable professions; and young people's interest in the traditional arts is waning.   NGu

Joaquin, Nick (1917–2004) Filipino writer. His plays, written in English and set in various Philippine historical eras, have been the most frequently produced dramatic works in the country. In *A Portrait of the Artist as Filipino*, two impoverished spinster sisters guard an old painting by their sick father as they reminisce about bygone grandeur. First staged in 1955, it has been translated into Filipino (1969), adapted for film, and turned into a *musical. Other plays include *The Beatas*, *Tatarin* (1978), *Fathers and Sons* (first produced in Filipino, 1976), *Camino Real*, and a domestic drama set in the Marcos years, *Pinoy Agonistes* (both 2001). He also wrote fiction, essays, and a considerable amount of journalism.   RV

Jodelet (Julien Bedeau) (c.1600–60) French actor. A member of *Montdory's troupe on its arrival at the *Marais in 1634, Jodelet was transferred to the *Hôtel de Bourgogne for a few years but returned to the Marais and was the mainstay of that theatre for most of his career. He arrived in Paris just as the period of *Gros-Guillaume and the other great *farce players was coming to an end, and died just as *Molière's career was beginning; for an entire generation he was the one performer who kept the farce tradition alive. He created the role of Cliton, the valet in *Corneille's *comedy *Le Menteur* (1643), and played scheming, cowardly, or naive valets named Jodelet in comedies by *Scarron and others. His trademarks were his floured face and his nasal voice. He joined the newly arrived company of Molière for the last year of his life. His brother François,

known as L'Espy, acted with him throughout his career.   RWH

Jodelle, Étienne (1532–73) French poet and dramatist, who broke from the declamatory models of *Senecan *tragedy. His tragedy *Cléopâtre captive* and *comedy *Eugène* made history in 1552 when they were played by the 20-year-old author and his young friends before Henri II at court, earning a payment of 500 crowns. Though static and lacking in dramatic structure (Jodelle's five acts correspond to Act 5 of Shakespeare's *Antony and Cleopatra*), *Cléopâtre captive* was an important first response to Du Bellay's call in 1549 for an indigenous French tragedy. Yet *Eugène* still bears the mark of medieval *farce tradition; its subject matter—the cuckolding of a simple-minded husband and a satirical portrayal of the clergy—owes little to classical influence. Jodelle's other surviving tragedy, *Didon se sacrifiant* (1558), is almost as static, consisting largely of lament over a predictable outcome. Its merit is that it was written entirely in alexandrines (*Cléopâtre* had been in a mixture of verse forms), thus establishing a model for verse tragedy to come.   WDH

Joglars, Els Catalan theatre company formed in 1962 by Anton Font, Carlota Soldevila, and Albert Boadella, influenced by their training with *Lecoq. Moving away from conventional theatre, the company (the name means 'jesters') embraced *mime to form a vocabulary able to defy the Francoist *censor. Under Boadella's artistic direction since 1966, Els Joglars was at the forefront of the cultural fight against Francoism, collaborating with innovative designers like Iago Pericot on *Mary d'Ous* (*Egg Mary*, 1972) and Fabià *Puigserver on *Àlias Serrallonga* (1974). In the post-Franco era they continued experimentation with a series of productions which interrogate contemporary myths. These include *I Have an Uncle in America* (1991) and a corrosive trilogy on Catalonia which began in 1995 with the audacious *Ubu president*, an acerbic critique of the extreme Catalan nationalism promoted by President Jordi Pujol, and concluded in 1999 with *DAAALÍ*, a delicious spectacle on the painter's extraordinary life and death.   MMD

Johnson, Bob (1904–85) Ghanaian entertainer. Born in Saltpond, Gold Coast, Johnson and some friends established the Versatile Eight in 1930, building on tradition and the cinema to create *comedies of domestic discord. The group eventually shrank to become 'The Two Bobs and their Carolina Girl', with E. K. Dadson as the *female impersonator and Johnson as the bizarrely dressed, mischief-making houseboy, the joker, or 'Bob'. Their work, which incorporated *satire, of recognizable types and a medley of musical interludes, was extensively *toured and highly popular. During the 1930s the patterns of publicity, business practice, and performance emerged for what became known as *concert party, and continued evolving for three decades. Johnson grew with the tradition, the pioneer and father-figure of a form closely wedded to popular taste. The demands on him as a stage instructor in Nkrumah's socialist propaganda group were curiously at odds with the capitalist ethos of the concert parties. JMG

Johnson, Samuel (1709–84) English writer. Though Dr Johnson was the literary arbiter of Britain, he never found the fame as a playwright that he desired. He carried his *tragedy *Irene* on his famous walk to London in 1737 with his pupil *Garrick. The play was ultimately produced at *Drury Lane in 1749, but only because Garrick was co-*manager. Although it ran for a respectable nine nights, it could not be considered a success. Garrick's management was inaugurated in the autumn of 1747 with Johnson's famous *prologue that declared

The drama's laws, the drama's patrons give,
For we that live to please, must please to live.

This attitude toward the rules of drama found even more famous expression in the preface to Johnson's edition of Shakespeare (1765), in which he attacked the *neoclassical *unities and eloquently defended Shakespeare's 'irregular' *dramaturgy. A revised edition of Shakespeare was published by Johnson and George Steevens in 1773. MJK

Johnston, Denis (1901–84) Irish dramatist, actor, and radio and television director. Johnston conceived a number of plays adhering to an *expressionist style: *The Old Lady Says, 'No!'* (1928); *A Bride for the Unicorn* (1933), and *The Dreaming Dust* (1940), all staged by Hilton *Edwards at the Gate Theatre in Dublin. Other works pursued a strict attention to *realism, making them of greater appeal to the *Abbey: *The Moon in the Yellow River* (1931), situated in the aftermath of the civil war, and *The Scythe and the Sunset* (1958), which tackles the same territory as *O'Casey's *The Plough and the Stars*. It is not surprising that, having trained as a barrister, Johnston devised two plays which criticize the inadequacy of legal processes: *The Golden Cuckoo* (1939) and *Blind Man's Buff* (1936). Interestingly, this drama, a creative adaptation of an expressionist play by *Toller, was later reworked in the realist mode as *Strange Occurrence on Ireland's Eye* (1956). His plays are notable for

their games with time, style, verbal register, and dramatic form. RAC

Jolson, Al (1886–1950) American performer. Born Asa Yoelson in Lithuania, Jolson was one of the most popular stars in America in the 1920s and 1930s. The son of a rabbi, Jolson ran away at the age of 13 to *tour in *vaudeville and *burlesque, becoming known for his blackface performances with Lew Dockstader's Minstrels (*see* MINSTREL SHOW). His first Broadway *musical, *La Belle Paree* (1911), began a thirteen-year association with the *Shuberts, who built Jolson's 59th Street Theatre in 1921. Jolson's warmth and sentimentality endeared him to *audiences; his charismatic performances introduced such songs as 'Mammy', 'Sonny Boy', 'Swanee', and 'Toot, Toot, Tootsie'. In *The Jazz Singer* (1927), the story of a cantor's son who goes on the stage, Jolson became the first speaking actor in a feature-length talking film with the words 'you ain't heard nothing yet'. *Hold on to your Hats* (1941) was his final Broadway show. He entertained troops during the Second World War and the Korean War, and the film *The Jolson Story* (1946) resurrected his recording and broadcasting career. GAO

Jones, David (1934–2008) Anglo-American director. His work was characterized by a self-effacing directorial style and a close association with certain playwrights. Jones joined the *Royal Shakespeare Company in 1964, later becoming company director for London, directing Shakespeare, *Gorky, and David *Mercer, as well as Graham *Greene's theatrical swansong, *The Return of A. J. Raffles* (1975). Less happy was *Arden and Margaretta D'Arcy's Arthurian trilogy *The Island of the Mighty* (1972), a famously troubled production that was picketed by its authors. In 1979 Jones became *artistic director of the Brooklyn Academy of Music theatre in New York, appointing Richard *Nelson as literary manager (*see* DRAMATURGY/ DRAMATURG). Jones went on to direct several of Nelson's plays in Britain and the USA, and to collaborate with him on *Making Plays* (1995), a book on the author–director relationship. CDC

Jones, Henry Arthur (1851–1929) English playwright. After *A Clerical Error* in 1879, he wrote nine plays in the three years before his first real success, *The Silver King* (1882), written in collaboration with Henry Herman for Wilson *Barrett. It was less sensational and more natural in *dialogue than most *melodramas, and it withstood revivals in the 1990s at *Chichester and the *Shaw Festival in Canada. Jones was a natural anti-Ibsenite, and he and Herman wrote a version of *Ibsen's *A Doll's House* called *Breaking a Butterfly*

(1884) in which Nora recognizes the error of her ways and returns to her family. Jones's writings and lectures on the theatre were extensive and often advanced, but his many serious plays suffer from conventional morality. Unusually for the time, he used religion as a theme, depicting the dissenters he was brought up with, treating faith healing, and even staging a church service in work such as *Saints and Sinners* (1884), *Judah* (1890), and *Michael and his Lost Angel* (1896). His *comedies, such as *The Liars* (1897) and *The Case of Rebellious Susan* (1894), deal with marital difficulties but end with a return to the status quo. *Mrs Dane's Defence* (1900), his last real success, has a fine interrogation scene in Act III, though, as usual, the fallen woman has to pay.   EEC

Jones, Inigo (1573–1652) English architect and *scenographer who designed scenery and *costumes for many of the major Jacobean and Caroline court *masques. His first commission was in 1605 for the Queen's Twelfth Night masque, *The Masque of Blackness* (libretto by *Jonson); he continued to work on these entertainments until they ended in 1640 with *Salmacida Spolia* (libretto by *Davenant). Jones was appointed successively Surveyor of the Works to Prince Henry (1610–12) and to the Crown (from 1615), and in this capacity he designed a new *Whitehall Banqueting House (1622) and converted Henry VIII's Whitehall cockpit into a *playhouse, the *Cockpit-in-Court (1630); these two buildings were the regular venues for Charles I's court performances.

Jones was already 'a great traveller' by 1605, and he spent an extended period on the Continent in 1613–15. His work was heavily influenced by Italian sources, and his study of the theatre designs of *Serlio revolutionized English stage technology. *The Masque of Blackness* saw the first use of *perspective scenery in England. At court he developed scenery which would transform itself on a revolve or pivot (*machina versatilis*), and in *Oberon the Fairy Prince* (1611, libretto by Jonson) successive scenes were painted on movable shutters (*scena ductilis*). His masques were also notable for their extensive use of flying characters.

Jones's creative tension with Jonson was valuable, until it provoked a bitter personal quarrel after the production of *Chloridia* (1631). Jones won: Jonson was never again employed at court, and took revenge by *satirizing Jones on stage in *A Tale of a Tub* (1633) and *Love's Welcome at Bolsover* (1634). During the 1630s the masques' non-literary elements became central to their allegorical meaning.   MJW

Jones, James Earl (1931–) *African-American actor. Jones first appeared on Broadway in *Sunrise at Campobello* (1958) and worked at the *New York Shakespeare Festival in the early 1960s. Howard Sackler's *The Great White Hope* (1968) brought him fame and a Tony award as the black boxer Jack Jefferson who becomes heavyweight champ in 1910 but is ruined through an affair with a white woman (filmed 1970). He has frequently played the Shakespeare tragic *heroes (Lear, Coriolanus, Macbeth, Othello), and played Paul *Robeson in Philip Hayes Dean's play of that title (1979). In 1987 Jones was awarded another Tony for his portrayal of the might-have-been baseball star Troy Maxson in August *Wilson's *Fences*, and he appeared in a number of *Fugard's works directed by Lloyd *Richards. He played Big Daddy in an all-black production of *Williams's *Cat on a Hot Tin Roof* (Broadway, 2008). He has become a Hollywood fixture in such films as the *Star Wars* sequence (as the voice of Darth Vader), *Field of Dreams* (1989), and the Tom Clancy series (*The Hunt for Red October*, 1990; *Patriot Games*, 1992; *Clear and Present Danger*, 1994).   BBL

Jones, Joseph S. (1809–77) American actor, *manager, playwright, and doctor. The quintessential Jacksonian-era playwright, Jones wrote well over 100 plays encompassing a wide range of subjects and styles. At the start (*The Liberty Tree*, 1832) and at the end (*Paul Revere and the Sons of Liberty*, 1875), he held an abiding interest in patriotic themes. On the other hand, he was also adept at *character portraits, often of Yankees or rural innocents, such as those found in *The Green Mountain Boy* (1833), *The People's Lawyer* (1839), and his most successful play, *The Silver Spoon* (1852). Finally, he wrote numerous *melodramas, including *The Surgeon of Paris* (1838) and *The Carpenter of Rouen* (1840). He managed Boston's Tremont Street and National theatres, but, except for brief periods, retired from the stage when the Tremont was forced to close in 1843, the same year he received a medical degree from Harvard.   GAR

Jones, LeRoi See BARAKA, IMAMU AMIRI.

Jones, Margo (1913–55) American *producer and director. Jones achieved national celebrity as the founder and *artistic director of Theatre '47 (later the Margo Jones Theatre) in Dallas. The theatre and her book *Theatre-in-the-Round* (1951) offered fresh models for the successful *management of a *regional theatre and emphasized the artistic and economic advantages of arena staging. Closely associated with *Williams, she co-directed the original production of his *The*

Glass Menagerie (1945) and in Dallas directed the première of *Summer and Smoke* (1948), pioneering the regional theatre as a venue for new play development. She went on to direct the New York production of *Summer and Smoke* as well as works by other writers before her early death. MAF

Jones, Marie (1951–) Irish playwright and actor. Co-founder of Charabanc Theatre Company, Belfast, her work as actor and resident writer from 1983 to 1990 included *Somewhere over the Balcony* and *Girls in the Big Picture*. She co-founded the company DubbelJoint in 1991. Her plays use vibrant humour to challenge forms of discrimination and prejudice. *A Night in November* (1994), *Women on the Verge of HRT* (1997), and *Stones in his Pockets* (1999) *toured Ireland and transferred to London and New York in commercial productions. She has written for radio, television, *educational theatre, and *community theatre. AEM

Jones, Robert Edmond (1887–1954) American *scenographer. Primarily responsible for the introduction of the 'New Stagecraft', Jones was central to modernism in American theatre between 1915 and 1930. He spent a life-changing year in Germany, studying with *Reinhardt. In New York in 1914 he designed *Maeterlinck's *Interior* for the Washington Square Players (1914–15) and two short plays for the *Provincetown Players (1915). Jones's first mainstream attention was for a non-representational design for Anatole France's *The Man Who Married a Dumb Wife* (1915), directed by Granville *Barker. Jones's major collaborator became Arthur *Hopkins, an artistically driven *producer-director working—most unusually—on Broadway; Jones would design 40 Hopkins productions in twenty years. For Hopkins's *Macbeth* in 1920 Jones featured gigantic *masks above the stage, suggesting their omnipresence, the first major *expressionist design in New York.

Jones's importance was reinforced with *Continental Stagecraft* (1922) by Jones and *Macgowan. Jones's 40 illustrations of theatres and settings reinforced the call for a theatre that eschewed material *realism for spiritual reality, to be evoked through techniques of *Appia, *Craig, Reinhardt, *Stanislavsky, *Jessner, *Copeau, and *Jouvet. At the same time, Jones's designs for *O'Neill's *The Hairy Ape* (1922), *The Emperor Jones* (1924), and *Desire under the Elms* (1924) demonstrated creative use of scrims, empty space, shadow, and *light. After 1930 Jones was seen as a talented and creative mainstream designer, producing satisfying work for Broadway, the Metropolitan Opera, and the *Theatre Guild, designing O'Neill's

Ah, Wilderness! (1933) and *The Iceman Cometh* (1946). Jones's 1941 *The Dramatic Imagination* exerted wide influence in its call for the self-abnegation of the designer in service to the universal and eternal truth in the play. MAF

Jonson, Ben (1572–1637) English dramatist and poet, born in London, the posthumous son of a minister. He was educated at Westminster School, but left when his stepfather set him to work as a bricklayer. He began his long theatrical career as a *touring actor, and by 1597 he was back in London writing plays for Pembroke's Men; from this period there survives only his *Plautine *comedy *The Case Is Altered*. In the later 1590s he worked for both the major adult companies, the *Chamberlain's Men and the *Admiral's Men, though he abandoned the latter (and chose not to preserve anything he wrote for them) when the boys' companies reopened at the turn of the century. One strand of Jonson's career was a model of progressive success, affluence, and social standing. He came to the Chamberlain's Men with *Every Man in his Humour* (1598), a comedy of humours which remained in their repertory for decades, and after their elevation as the King's Men he wrote them two more bankable classics in *Volpone* (1605) and *The Alchemist* (1610). The move to the Children of the *Chapel, with their indoor theatre and elite *audiences, was also a step up, and 1605 saw the first of his court *masques, *The Masque of Blackness*. Throughout James I's reign he was a prominent contributor to the dramatic entertainment offered at high-profile state occasions (37 of his scripts are extant), which brought him recognition, status, and, in 1616, a royal pension which enabled him temporarily to give up commercial stage writing.

However, there was also an underside of failure and misjudgement, driven by his difficult personality, his fussy sense of his own literariness, his equivocal attitude to authority, and partly also by sheer bad luck. In 1597 he was imprisoned after the Privy Council took exception to satirical material in his collaborative play with Thomas Nashe, *The Isle of Dogs*. Later brushes with power concerned his representation of Queen Elizabeth in *Every Man out of his Humour* (1599), a piece of gossip about Lady Arabella Stuart in *Epicene* (1609), and offence taken by a courtier at *The Devil Is an Ass* (1616). In 1600–1 he engaged in the 'War of the Theatres': when *Marston, probably intending a compliment, represented him on stage, he took offence and retaliated with the devastating personal *satire of *Poetaster*. If he gave the King's Men success with his comedies, his *tragedies were less fortunate: vocal audience displeasure forced the players to abandon both *Sejanus' Fall* (1603) and *Catiline's Conspiracy* (1611) in the middle of their first public performances, and Jonson was questioned by the Privy Council about the political content of *Sejanus*. If in 1605 he pleased the court with his Twelfth Night masque, only months later he was back in jail, having offended the King with anti-Scots satire in *Eastward Hoe* (written with *Chapman and Marston).

Jonson was difficult because, for all his success, he was insecure: the premature end of his formal education made him the more proud of his scholarly attainments and anxious for his work to be adjudged worthy by the accepted standards of *neoclassical aesthetics. This meant that he would often downgrade the theatrical side of his work. It is typical that in the 1630s he quarrelled with Inigo *Jones, the producer of his court masques, over the relative status of his scripts and Jones's *scenography. Characteristically, Jonson was the first English dramatist to assert the literary value of his plays by including nine of them alongside his poems and masques in a Folio collection of his *Works* in 1616.

In the induction to *Bartholomew Fair* (1614), he had proclaimed a straightforward modernity for his work, drawing a contrast with the old-fashioned barnstormers *Titus Andronicus* and *The Spanish Tragedy*. In his next two comedies, *The Devil is an Ass* and *The Staple of News* (1626), he explored the differences and continuities between the old drama and the new. Jonson spent his final years confined to one room. Some contemporaries assumed that he had died; in fact, he had suffered a stroke in 1628 and the following year, annoyed by the failure of *The New Inn*, resolved to give up writing for the stage. It was a promise he was unable to keep: he completed *The Magnetic Lady* (1632) and *A Tale of a Tub* (1633); a *pastoral, *The Sad Shepherd*, remained unfinished.

Jonson's core comedies were regularly in production after the Restoration and through the eighteenth century: *Garrick made notable appearances in *The Alchemist* (from 1743) and *Every Man in his Humour* (from 1751), in roles later taken by Edmund *Kean (1814-16). By then, however, the plays had begun to lose their popularity: 'coarse' elements were removed from *Volpone* when it was staged in the 1770s, and it dropped from the repertory altogether, along with *Epicene*, in the 1780s; only *Every Man in his Humour* reached the Victorian stage, with notable productions by *Macready (1838) and *Dickens (1845). The plays returned to production at the end of the nineteenth century, rediscovered by antiquarians like *Poel, and the twentieth saw a

wider range of his work on the stage. *Volpone* and *The Alchemist* appear regularly, *Batholomew Fair* on occasion; in 1987, the *Royal Shakespeare Company even revived *The New Inn*.   MJW

Jordan, Dorothy (1761-1816) English actress. 'Dora' Jordan was the most famous comic actress of the late eighteenth and early nineteenth centuries. She began in Dublin in 1779 as Dorothy Bland, fleeing in 1782 when pregnant by the unscrupulous *Smock Alley *manager Richard Daly. She acted in Tate *Wilkinson's company for several seasons, establishing a wide comic repertory under her new name, Jordan, given by Wilkinson because she had 'crossed the water'. Her London debut came in 1785 at *Drury Lane. She quickly became a favourite, and throughout her long career she was especially praised for her rich voice, her engaging laughter, and her pathos. Among her most famous roles were Viola, Ophelia, and (improbably) Young Pickle in *Bickerstaffe's *The Spoiled Child* (1790). Her long affair with the Duke of Clarence inspired a great deal of gossip, but it did not prevent her acting throughout Britain. She was a national institution by the time of her death in Paris.   MJK

Jory, Jon (1938-) American director and *producer. Jory studied playwriting at the Yale School of Drama but left in 1965 to found the Long Wharf Theatre. In 1969 he became the producing director of *Actors Theatre of Louisville. Over the next three decades he fashioned ATL into a pre-eminent *regional resident theatre. He brought a pragmatist's common sense and an impresario's bravado to his position, forging ties with civic and business leaders and creating programming that drew international attention to a city better known for its alcohol and tobacco industry. His most important initiative was the Humana Festival of New American Plays, but he also created festivals around short plays, solo performances, and modern classics. Jory is widely assumed to be the pseudonymous playwright Jane Martin, all of whose plays premièred at ATL under his direction. After 1,500 productions, 141 of which he directed, he left ATL in 2000.   STC

Jouvet, Louis (1887-1951) French director and actor. Jouvet began his career, together with *Dullin, in *Copeau's first company of the Théâtre du Vieux-Colombier as *lighting designer and actor (most notably Sir Andrew Aguecheek in a famed *Twelfth Night*, 1914). He left Copeau in 1922 for the Comédie des Champs-Élysées, where one of his earliest critical and commercial successes was as director of *Romains's *comedy *Knock*, in which he played the lead role in over 1,400 performances. In 1927, together with *Baty, *Pitoëff, and Dullin, Jouvet formed the *Cartel des Quatre. His greatest triumph was with Jean *Giraudoux. At the end of his lease Jouvet moved to the Athénée, where he staged with enormous success Giraudoux's *La Guerre de Troie n'aura pas lieu* (1935, translated by *Fry as *Tiger at the Gates*). Jouvet maintained his film career up to and beyond the war but kept his theatre dark during the Occupation and *toured South America. Upon his return he directed notable premières, including Giraudoux's last play, *The Madwoman of Chaillot* (1945), *Genet's *The Maids* (1947), and *Sartre's *The Devil and the Good Lord* (1951), and continued to tour the world. BRS

Juana Inés de la Cruz, Sor (1651–95) Mexican poet and dramatist. Self-educated, she became lady-in-waiting at the viceregal court of New Spain and later entered a convent as Sor Juana. Writing on both religious and secular themes, she composed *comedias*, *autos sacramentales*, a variety of shorter sketches, and dramatic poems to be sung in church that incorporated roles for Africans, Aztecs, Moors, and Basques. Sor Juana's plays, which were performed at court in Mexico City and in churches throughout New Spain, generally conform to the style of *early modern Spain, showing particular similarity to the work of *Calderón, but she often arranged plots and reversed roles to emphasize *gender issues and the circumstances of the New World. *The House of Trials* (1683) presents the difficulties of a noblewoman much like Sor Juana herself. *The Divine Narcissus* (1689), considered to be her masterpiece, transforms myth into a *pastoral love story with theological significance. The *Royal Shakespeare Company included her *The House of Desires* in a Golden Age season (*Swan, 2004). JuJ

juggler The almost supernatural skill of juggling —'the dextrous manipulation of objects'—was probably recognized before the ancient Egyptians, but around 2000 BC they were the earliest to depict (women) jugglers, in the Beni-Hassan tombs. Juggling figures later appeared on Greek pottery and Roman wall reliefs. Tagastus Ursus (AD 53–117) claimed to have been the first to juggle with glass balls. The fifth-century Irish hero Cuchulain juggled nine apples and, more spectacularly, Tulchinne, the jester at the court of King Conaire, is described as juggling nine swords, silver shields, and balls of gold. The juggling of large numbers of objects is not unusual;

the world record in 2001 was twelve rings, eleven balls, and eight clubs.

The association of juggling with *magic and sleight of hand is of long standing. The Roman term *praestigiator* referred to the trickster-magician as well as the juggler, and in the West suspicion has always been mixed with admiration. For the ancient Chinese, on the other hand, juggling was allied with the skills of hunting and fighting. The 'Hundred Entertainments' of the Han Dynasty combined the exhibition of jugglers with *acrobats, *animal tamers, equestrians, and other *circus trades. In the nineteenth-century popular mind, juggling was located in the East, particularly in India and Japan, and overlaid with the exoticism of fire-walking and sword-swallowing; to attract an *audience the German juggler Karl Rappo was forced to wear a turban and appear as an Indian. The *music hall claimed many jugglers from the circus. Paul Cinquevalli juggled billiard balls and caught a cannon ball on his neck. Kara, who performed in evening dress, juggled a hat, a cigar, gloves, a newspaper, matches, and a coffee cup. It was not until the first part of the twentieth century that the specialized talents of jugglers such as Enrico Rastelli and Bobby May were appreciated. Whilst balancing on a board, itself on a rolling cylinder, Rastelli juggled seven balls, twirled three rings on one leg, and spun balls on a mouthpiece. AF

Julia, Raul (1940–94) Puerto Rican actor. Julia played five roles in San Juan before he appeared in New York in a Spanish-language production of *Calderón's *La vida es sueño* (1964). From 1966 onwards he performed with *Papp and the *New York Shakespeare Festival, winning praise for Proteus in the *musical adaptation of *Two Gentlemen of Verona* (1971), Osric in *Hamlet* (1972), and Orlando in *As You Like It* (1973), and appearing twice as Othello (1979 and 1991). He had success as Mack the Knife in the *Weill-*Brecht *Threepenny Opera* (1976) and as Charles Wykeham in the *Loesser-*Abbott musical *Where's Charley?* (1974). He played Lopakhin in *Chekhov's *Cherry Orchard* (1977) and Jerry in *Pinter's *Betrayal* (1980). In addition to over 100 stage productions, Julia also played in films such as *Kiss of the Spider Woman* (1985) and gained popular renown for *The Addams Family* (1991). He won a posthumous award for a television movie about Brazilian martyr Chico Mendez, *The Burning Season* (1994). FL

Juvarra, Filippo (Filippo Juvara) (1678–1736) Italian architect and designer. Born in Messina, he studied architecture in Rome with Carlo Fontana. Juvarra's architectural works can be seen in Italy, Spain, and Portugal. The sets he designed for *operas include *Giunio Bruto*, commissioned by the Emperor Josef I of Austria, and *Ciro*, scored by Alessandro Scarlatti. Juvarra's theatre designs influenced his buildings, and the definition of space in his later works is marked by a theatrical fluidity and elegance, exquisite examples of early Italian rococo.   ATS

juvenile theatre *See* TOY THEATRE.

kabuki Lavish Japanese stage performance that includes *dance, music, and dramatic *acting, now the nation's most popular form of classical theatre. Kabuki was founded in Kyoto around 1600 by the female temple dancer Izumo no *Okuni. At that time 'kabuki' referred to persons or styles that were chic, suggestive, or eccentric. Okuni often dressed on stage in men's clothing and wore a rosary and items of European dress. Okuni's kabuki included dances by women, playlets about contemporary dandies and prostitutes, and sideshow acts. Her kabuki was soon imitated by troupes of prostitutes who added the three-stringed *shamisen* to the *nō flute and drums used in Okuni's musical ensemble. Travelling troupes created a kabuki boom that swept the country. The lawlessness and social inversion that accompanied kabuki performances led to numerous local prohibitions and finally to a national ban of women's kabuki in 1629. Early kabuki was also performed by young men (*wakashū*), many of whom were homosexual prostitutes. When *wakashū kabuki* was banned in the 1650s, mature men became the main performers and kabuki began its development away from *vaudeville-like performance into drama. Producers looked to the more highly developed *puppet theatre (*bunraku) for inspiration. Actors began to specialize in role types—there were women's role specialists (*onnagata), male leads (*tachiyaku*), *villains (*katakiyaku*), and so on.

In the late seventeenth century great actors turned kabuki into an art of breadth and sophistication. Permanent licensed theatres were located in Kyoto, Osaka, and Edo (Tokyo). In Kamigata (Osaka and Kyoto) *Sakata Tōjūrō I perfected the art of the romantic male lead (*wagoto*) and was kabuki's first stage idol, attracting women fans to the theatre in record numbers. He experimented with psychological approaches to acting. Kamigata was the breeding ground for great onnagata. *Yoshizawa Ayame advocated living offstage as a woman so that the slightest onstage gesture and nuance might be convincingly feminine even to women in the audience. Actors in Edo took a different approach. Ichikawa *Danjūrō I (1660–1704) created the bravura style (*aragoto*), featuring superhuman feats by martial *heroes who are given their powers by the gods they revere. Danjūrō wrote his own plays, and made the deities he worshipped heroes in many of them. His descendants dominated kabuki in Edo for the Tokugawa Period.

By the early 1700s kabuki's calendar of events was set. Most important was the *kaomise* (face-showing) production in the Eleventh Month, which showcased actors. Festive New Year's productions, spring plays about romance, and summer productions featuring ghosts and monsters were other seasonal favourites. When plays drew poorly, they were quickly replaced by new ones. From the outset kabuki was commercial theatre, intended primarily for urban commoners. From the 1690s on kabuki relied on published plays and actor critiques, and *ukiyo-e* posters, prints, and advertisements to publicize its actors and shows. By the mid-1700s leading actors, especially *onnagata*, supplemented their already generous salaries by endorsing products decorated with their personal crests and designs. Product placement in plays began in the 1710s.

Until the late 1600s playwriting was relatively unimportant in kabuki. Plots were chosen by leading actors and lines were written down, but actors were free to change them. By the 1680s it was clear that long, integrated scripts were necessary to stage successful plays. *Chikamatsu Monzaemon (1653–1724) became the first specialist playwright, and by the 1700s teams of staff playwrights worked under a leading actor-producer, crafting plays as vehicles for leading actors. Plays were divided into two broad categories: history plays (*jidaimono*) about samurai conflicts of the pre-Edo era, and domestic plays (*sewamono*) about the contemporary commoner class.

Initially kabuki was performed on nō stages, but over the years the bridgeway expanded into an extension of the main stage. The *hanamichi* runway leading from the stage to the back of the *auditorium came into use in the early 1700s. Today this feature distinguishes the kabuki stage from any other variety. Around the late 1600s painted backdrops started to appear and large properties were employed. Various traps, lifts, revolves, and flying harnesses were devised for special effects, and the full-stage revolve was in use by 1758, long before it was introduced into Europe. In the mid-eighteenth century actors began to eschew narrow role specialization in favour of broader acting skills. Dance-dramas, hitherto the speciality of *onnagata*, were written to include *tachiyaku*. Many new dances featured magical transformations by spirits and required one performer to dance multiple roles. In the early nineteenth century the playwright *Tsuruya Namboku IV pioneered a new genre, the 'raw domestic play', featuring heroes from Japan's lowest classes—criminals and outcasts—and more brutality, violence, and terrifying scenes of the occult than in previous plays. Later in the century *Kawatake Mokuami created a new genre of plays about gallant outlaws. Other innovations were pioneered by actors. In 1832 Ichikawa *Danjūrō VII (1791–1859) canonized his family's *aragoto kabuki* heritage by publicizing the 'Eighteen Great Plays', inspiring others to do the same with their family acting traditions. In 1840 he devised a new genre of dance-drama based on nō and *kyōgen plays; the first and most popular of these is the *aragoto* classic *The Subscription List*.

In 1840 the central government ordered Edo's theatres torn down and relocated to a north-eastern suburb and in 1842 it banished Danjūrō VII from Edo for infraction of sumptuary laws. These were among the more drastic measures taken by the shogunate in its two-and-a-half-century-long battle with kabuki. The government attempted to suppress the baleful influences of the form by restricting attendance, theatre size, and design, the sumptuousness of productions, actors' salaries, and housing. After a major scandal in 1714 involving a love affair between a senior lady-in-waiting and a leading actor, the government permanently liquidated one of Edo's four theatres. Nevertheless, no government policy ever managed to deter the commoners' beloved kabuki theatre. Japan's modernization presented greater challenges. In the Edo period kabuki had set fashion trends and enacted contemporary issues and scandals, but *buyō* dance-based acting made no sense when performers wore Western clothes. After several fruitless modernization attempts in the late 1800s ('living history plays', 'cropped-hair plays'), kabuki found its niche in modern Japan as classical drama. Productions were redesigned to present great acts from unrelated master works. Certain twentieth-century innovations did succeed, including 'new kabuki'—historical dramas featuring psychologically complex *characters delineated through *dialogue and modern, *realistic acting. Fine playwrights emerged to write new

works, *Mishima among them. In 1986 Ichikawa Ennosuke III (b. 1939) created Super Kabuki—spectacular, hi-tech plays with scripts in modern Japanese. They have enjoyed great commercial success. Today the Shōchiku Corporation runs kabuki as a profit-making venture in Japan's major cities. The federal government assists with productions in Tokyo's National Theatre. Acting remains very much a family business—the great names pass from father to son—but supporting actors are trained by the National Theatre and by Shōchiku. Some leading actors work to revive lost plays, and others use their kabuki skills in television, film, and experimental dance and drama.   LRK

Kachalov, Vasily (1875–1948) Russian/Soviet actor who joined the *Moscow Art Theatre in 1900 and became the company's romantic lead. Possessing superb vocal qualities, Kachalov was a natural tragedian but also proved extremely successful in *Chekhov roles. He played Tuzenbach in *Three Sisters*, inheriting the part from *Meyerhold, Trofimov in *The Cherry Orchard* (1904), and the eponymous Ivanov (1904). He starred as Hamlet in the *Stanislavsky–*Craig production (1911) and performed leading roles in productions directed by *Nemirovich-Danchenko, appearing as the Baron in *Gorky's *The Lower Depths* (1902), as Julius Caesar in 1904, as *Ibsen's Brand in 1906, and Ivan Karamazov (1910).   NW

Kahn, Michael (1937–) American *producer, director, and educator. *Artistic director since 1986 of the Shakespeare Theatre in Washington, DC, Kahn was also head of drama at the Juilliard School in New York (1992–2006). In directing on Broadway, *Off-Broadway, in *regional theatre, and *opera, he specialized in the classics, wielding an eclectic vigour that has attracted many important actors (such as *Carnovsky, *Le Gallienne, Glenn *Close, *Von Sydow, Eileen *Atkins, *Ferrer). At the Shakespeare Theatre, his stars included Fritz Weaver, *Holbrook, and Pat Carroll, who played both Falstaff and Volpone, certainly a professional first for a woman. Kahn's directorial freshness and use of stars expanded American interest in Shakespeare, and he was a key figure in the growth of non-commercial theatre, having previously led the American Shakespeare Festival in Connecticut, the McCarter Theatre in Princeton, and the Acting Company in New York.   CR

Kailasam, T. P. (1884–1946) Indian playwright and director whose interest in theatre developed in London (1908–15). After his return to Bangalore, he wrote his first play *Tollu Gatti* in 1918. It inaugurated his typical theme, the tension between the brahmanical tradition and the modernity of the emerging upper middle class in southern Karnataka. He wrote twenty plays in Kannada (for example, *Poli Kitty*, *Home Rule*, *Nam Kampni*) and four in English (including *Karna* and *Purpose*). All feature a highly stylized range of *characters, representing the two contending social classes. Kailasam invented a hybrid composite of English and Kannada that is both witty and farcical. He vehemently opposed the standard *melodrama of the professional theatre. Although he had several imitators in Kannada theatre, because of their intricate language his plays have largely remained inaccessible outside southern Karnataka.   KVA

Kainz, Josef (1858–1910) Austrian actor. The most acclaimed German-speaking actor of the late nineteenth century, Kainz left school at 15 to join a *touring company in Austria. From 1877 to 1880 he performed leading roles for the *Meininger; he left to join the Munich Court Theatre, where became a favourite of King Ludwig II. His international fame began after 1883 when he moved to Berlin, performing first at the new *Deutsches Theater, then at the Berlin Theatre, where he soon broke contract. This resulted in a ban at all theatres belonging to the German Stage Organization, which he overcame with extended tours in Europe and the USA. In 1892 he returned to the Deutsches Theater and performed for a short time with *Brahm, but his virtuosic style was incompatible with Brahm's *realism. In 1899 he had his debut at the *Burgtheater in Vienna, where he remained until his death. Kainz retained throughout his career a youthful appearance and dynamism which electrified *audiences. His greatest asset was his voice, which he used in an almost operatic manner.   CBB

Kaiser, Georg (1878–1945) German playwright. Although the best dramatist of German *expressionism, his reputation rests primarily on only six of his 70 plays. He achieved a breakthrough with *The Burghers of Calais* (written 1913, premièred 1917). The play is characteristically expressionist: there is no attempt at historical authenticity, the action is generalized and depersonalized, the language is strongly rhetorical, above all there is the optimistic conclusion that individual sacrifice can lead to universal regeneration. In *From Morning to Midnight* (written 1912, premièred 1917) a nondescript clerk steals money from his bank, tries to buy excitement, and, disillusioned by his greed, throws it away and shoots himself. From this indictment of capitalism, Kaiser passed on to attack industrialism in

the *Gas Trilogy* (1917–20). *Gas I* describes how a devastating gas explosion in a factory might be used as the opportunity to turn away from technology to create an idyllic rural lifestyle, but the visionary *hero, the Millionaire's Son, is defeated by the workers' resistance to change. Compared with *Gas*, which strongly influenced Fritz Lang's film *Metropolis* (1926), most of Kaiser's later dramas seem either trivial (*Side by Side*, 1923), or reflect his obsession with his own privileged status as an artist, as in his reworking of *Pygmalion* (1944). In 1933 the Nazis banned his plays, and in 1938 he emigrated to Switzerland.   MWP

Kakul, I Nyoman (1905–82) Balinese performer and teacher, the leading *topeng* (masked dance) performer of his generation. By the age of 13 he had joined a travelling *dance-theatre troupe, later becoming known as an exceptionally versatile performer, and being employed by several regional courts. In 1953 Kakul toured Europe and America as featured performer in an all-star troupe. Upon his return, he won further renown as a solo performer of remarkable grace, knowledge, and humour; started a *topeng* troupe; and helped revive the venerable form of *gambuh*. When formal conservatory programmes were established in the late 1960s, Kakul became a master teacher of *topeng*, profoundly influencing the next generation of Balinese artists and teachers.   JE

Kalidasa The greatest Sanskrit poet and playwright of India. His dates are controversial (suggestions range from the first century BC to the fifth century AD). It is believed that he was an unlettered cowherd by birth, who by the grace of the goddess Kali was transformed into a great literary figure. Hence the name Kalidasa (the devotee of Kali). Three plays are ascribed to Kalidasa. *Malavikagnimitra* is a court *comedy depicting the love of King Agnimitra for a maid in the service of one of his Queens. In *Vikramorvasiya*, based on an ancient legend in the *Rigveda*, the mortal king Pururavas falls in love with the celestial nymph Urvasi. The most mature work is *Abhijnanashakuntala*, from a story in the *Mahabharata*. Kalidasa's play focuses on the meeting between King Dushyanta and Shakuntala; their subsequent consummation of love; his loss of memory due to the curse of Durvasa; the birth of a child to Shakuntala while she is abandoned; and Dushyanta's reunion with Shakuntala.

*Goethe acknowledged his debt to Kalidasa in his *prologue to *Faust*, while the German *romantics envisioned in Shakuntala the embodiment of femininity. At the outbreak of the First World War, *Tairov opened his season at the Kamerny Theatre in Moscow with a *symbolist translation of

Shakuntala. In 1960 *Shakuntala* received another *avant-garde interpretation by *Grotowski, who sought to create new psychophysical models of gesture and behaviour. KNP

Kambanellis, Iakovos (1922–) Greek playwright. His first play, *To Dance on Wheat*, was produced in 1950. *The Seventh Day of Creation*, produced by the Greek National Theatre in 1956, began a trilogy that continued with *Yard of Wonders* (1957), directed by Karolos *Koun, and ended with *The Age of Night* (1959). Kambanellis's trilogy marked the beginning of a new era for modern Greek theatre. He took the *realistic tradition of the nineteenth and early twentieth centuries a step further, not only by re-creating the everyday reality of post-war Greece, but also by criticizing this reality and attempting to explain its complex social structure. His other plays include *Tale without Title* (1959), *Odysseus, Come Home* (1966), and *Our Dad the War* (1980). KGO

Kambar, Chandrasekhar (1938–) Indian playwright, poet, and folklorist who writes in Kannada. Born in north Karnataka, he began writing short modernist plays before his first major poem *Listen, I Will Narrate* (1964) established him as an indigenous talent. This led him to explore folk theatre; he co-edited the text of *Sangya Balya*, a popular Karnataka folk play, which became the prototype for most of his own work. His first success was *Jokumaraswami* (1973), about a rebellion against a feudal lord; interspersed with the *ritualistic slaying of the phallic god Jokumara, it relies on song, *dance, and witty *dialogue. Its huge success prompted a number of imitations. Kambar continued to explore folk themes as metaphors of contemporary experience in plays such as *Alibaba* (1980) and *Huliya Neralu* (1988). Since then his work has shifted towards a more symbolic exploration of folk mythology, the best example being *Sirisampige* (1992), about a prince who divides himself into a serpent and a human self. Kambar's plays have been translated into several Indian languages and into English. KVA

kamyŏngŭk *Masked *dance-drama in Korea, the country's most pervasive form of traditional performance. Probably developed from ancient religious ceremonies, *kamyŏngŭk* can be classified into two main types: various masked dance styles, collectively known as *sandaegŭk* (mountain play), which are regional; and village-festival masked dance forms. Of the village festival masked dramas, the *pyŏlsingŭt* play of Hahoe is the best known. The performance traditionally occurs on the Tano festival, supplicating the prosperity of the village, expulsion of evil spirits, and the prevention of demons. The structure of the performances is orally transmitted from generation to generation. The play consists of scenes held together by themes: *satires of transgressing monks, for example, or of corrupt upper classes or insensitive local officials. Despite regional differences, performance elements common to all *sandaegŭk* styles include masks, dance, song, music, pantomime, and *dialogue. The plays are anonymous and transmitted orally, though since the 1960s performances have been recorded, transcribed, and published. Content varies according to region, but most plays can be divided into the following scenes: a scene of conflict between a nobleman and a servant; a scene of argument between an old woman and her husband about his concubine; a scene of argument between a monk struggling with worldly desires and a troublemaker around the markets. The *characters tend to reflect the villagers' point of view, and the dialects are regional. Performances are traditionally held at night in an outdoor space, lit by torches, with the *audience sitting in a circle. *Costumes for servants and women are bright and gaudy. The masks, made from gourds, paper, and other materials, were traditionally burned at the end of each performance. Comic, grotesque, and exaggerated, they have established standard features, though the performers add characterization through gestures and dance. Performances of *kamyŏngŭk* today are presented as government cultural events or as tourist entertainments. JOC

Kan'ami (Kannami, Kanze Kiyotsugu) (1333–84) Japanese *nō playwright, *manager, and actor, the father of *Zeami. Kan'ami headed the Yūzaki troupe (renamed Kanze) in Ise. Later he moved to Yamato, where he won the patronage of the shogun Ashikaga Yoshimitsu in 1374. Despite his success in the capital, however, Kan'ami continued to *tour the countryside and died after a performance at Sengen temple in Suruga (modern Shizuoka). He combined the best elements of various *sarugaku* performers and adopted the rhythms and materials of *kusemai* (a medieval song-and-dance form) into nō, thereby helping to transform it into a highly successful theatrical form. Zeami writes admiringly of Kan'ami's *acting skills and musical abilities and claims that his own earliest writings express his father's ideas. As Zeami reworked most of Kan'ami's plays, it is difficult to evaluate the father's skills as a dramatist, but many plays connected with him are still considered masterpieces, including *Matsukaze, Motomezuka, Sotoba Komachi, Kayoi Komachi*, and *Eguchi*. KWB

Kander, John (1927–) and **Fred Ebb** (1932–2004) American composer and lyricist. Under the aegis of Harold *Prince they collaborated on *Flora, The Red Menace* (1965), and *Cabaret* (1966), scores which displayed their ability to combine traditional Broadway sounds with an evocation of a historical period. The extraordinary success of *Cabaret* established Kander and Ebb as a major team in *musical theatre, and they maintained an exclusive collaboration for more than 35 years and eleven Broadway (or Broadway-bound) musicals, in addition to club acts for specific performers, notably Liza Minelli, who starred in both *Flora* and the film version of *Cabaret* (1972) and for whom they wrote the award-winning television special *Liza with a Z*. Their work regularly included both traditional and innovative shows; among the latter are the geriatric musical *70 Girls 70* (1971) and *The Rink* (1984), a Broadway-sized musical with three principals and a *chorus of six men who play all the other roles, male and female. They demonstrated the ability to write for stars—as in the case of *Woman of the Year* (1981), a vehicle for Lauren Bacall—and for conceptualist directors such as Bob *Fosse, with whom they wrote *Chicago* (1975). In addition to *Cabaret*, their films include *Funny Lady* (1975) and *New York, New York* (1977).   JD

Kane, Sarah (1971–99) English playwright. *Blasted* (1995) brought Kane to attention in a disturbing way. A middle-aged journalist and a young girl spend the night in a British hotel room; an explosion rips the room apart, and the *characters endure a horrific series of violent encounters and sexual violations. That this disorienting structure mimicked the uprooting of life during the Bosnian genocide was lost on the critics, but its influence was strong. Her subsequent plays, notably *Cleansed* and *Crave* (both 1998), continued to investigate the extremes of human experiences, the second a delicate, elliptical piece that affirms suicide as an act of liberation. Feeling herself sinking once again into profound depression, Kane took her own life. Her final play, *4.48 Psychosis* (2000), was posthumously performed at the *Royal Court, where most of her other work had been seen. It is a bleak piece of scattered poetry, with almost no textual indications for staging, tracing the contours of a mind in the deepest state of despair. DR

Kanhailal, Heisnam (1942–) Director and writer from Manipur, India. Kanhailal has explored non-verbal, *physical, ensemble *acting in numerous theatre pieces, steeped in the indigenous myths and conventions of Meitei culture.

After experimental plays like *Haunting Spirits* and *Half-Man, Half-Tiger*, Kanhailal created a sensation with his sharp and lyrical retelling of a popular folk tale *Pebet* (1975), in which Mother Pebet, a mythical bird, succeeds through subterfuge in re-uniting her children, who have been abducted by the Cat. Thinly disguised as an allegory of neocolonial domination, with the Cat masquerading as a Vaishnavite monk, the play was condemned as 'anti-Hindu' and 'anti-Indian', even as it was hailed as a theatrical masterwork.

Kanhailal dramatized L. Samarendra Singh's poem *Africagee Wakhanda Gee* in another memorable evocation of the survival of the human spirit in *Memoirs of Africa* (1985). More recently, his plays have moved from lyrical resilience towards a more verbal, layered, and ironic reading of myth and history, as in his reinterpretation of *Karna* (1997), the tragic warrior from the *Mahabharata*, and his adaptation of Mahasweta Devi's story *Draupadi* (2000).   RB

Kani, John (1943–) South African actor and writer. He was a janitor in the Ford factory when he joined the Serpent Players (1965), acting Creon in *Antigone*. His first major production was *Camus's *The Just* (retitled *The Terrorists*, Cape Town, 1972), after which he and Winston *Ntshona became full-time artists. Within months they collaboratively produced *Sizwe Bansi Is Dead* (1972) and *The Island* (1973) with *Fugard. Kani originated the lead roles in a number of other Fugard plays, locally and abroad, including *Statements after an Arrest . . .* (1972) and *Master Harold and the Boys* (1982), and appeared in a revival of *The Blood Knot*. He has played a number of racially controversial roles: he was the first black Othello opposite a white Desdemona in South Africa (in *Suzman's 1987 production, Market Theatre, Johannesburg), and was the servant Jean in *Strindberg's *Miss Julie* opposite Sandra Prinsloo (1985). He became director of the Market Theatre after Barney *Simon's death in 1995. His play *Nothing but the Truth* was at the Market in 2002.   YH

Kanin, Garson (1912–99) American actor, playwright, director, and screenwriter. Kanin left acting to become George *Abbott's assistant, working on *Room Service* (1937), and made his directing debut with *Hitch your Wagon* (1937). Discovered by Samuel Goldwyn, he moved to Hollywood to direct films, and continued during his war service (1941–6). Kanin's greatest stage success came with his hit *comedy *Born Yesterday* (1946), a Pygmalion-like story about a young man hired to tutor a tycoon's girlfriend. Kanin married actress-writer Ruth *Gordon in 1942, and together they wrote a series of successful film comedies in the 1940s and 1950s, most directed by George Cukor—among them *Adam's Rib* (1949) and *Pat and Mike* (1952). Kanin staged other Broadway productions, including *The Diary of Anne Frank* (1955) and *Funny Girl* (1964). MAF

Kantor, Tadeusz (1915–90) Polish director, designer, visual artist, and theorist. During the Nazi occupation he founded the Independent Theatre, for which he directed *Słowacki's Balladyna* (1942) and *Wyspiański's The Return of Odysseus* (1944). After the war Kantor worked as a designer. After a year in Paris, he organized the first post-war exhibition of modern Polish art. In 1949 he publicly refused to participate in the official culture of *socialist realism; his professorship at the Cracow Academy was revoked, though he continued to work as a designer and painter.

At the end of the Stalinist period Kantor co-founded CRICOT 2, named after the 1930s theatre created by visual artists. The opening event was his production of *Witkiewicz's The Cuttlefish* (1956), which developed his notions of Autonomous Theatre (independent of any external reality) and Annexed Reality (reality which could not be appropriated by prevailing conventions or assigned a use-value). Subsequent productions of texts by Witkiewicz marked the stages in Kantor's development: *The Country House* (1961: 'Informel Theatre'), *The Madman and the Nun* (1963: 'Zero Theatre'), *The Water Hen* (1967: 'Theatre-Happening', an outgrowth of his experiments with *happenings from 1965), and *Dainty Shapes and Hairy Apes* (1973: 'Impossible Theatre'). All these sought to depreciate the value of reality by exploring its unknown, hidden, or everyday aspects and challenged traditional notions of representation. 'The Theatre of Death' manifesto (1975) marked a major shift, and productions which followed explored notions of memory, history, myth, artistic creation, and the artist as the chronicler of the twentieth century. *The Dead Class* (1975), presented memories taking place behind an impassable barrier, and other productions dealt with similar themes—*Wielopole, Wielopole* (1980) introduced the concept of the room of memory; *Let the Artists Die* (1985) explored a place where memories are superimposed upon each other, using the theory of negatives; *I Shall Never Return* (1988) put forth the concept of the inn of memory, which existed beyond the confines of time and space, where Kantor encountered his own past creations; and *Today Is my Birthday* (1990) focused on crossing between illusion and reality. A characteristic feature of Kantor's perfor-

mances was his presence on stage observing, and often correcting, his actors. MAK

Kanze Hisao (1925–78) Japanese actor. The eldest son of Kanze Gasetsu, the seventh Tetsunojo (1898–1988), Kanze Hisao was the most influential *nō actor and theorist of the mid-twentieth century. His talent as a performer was recognized in his youth, and after the Second World War he helped reinvigorate nō, giving new life to old ideas and practices without resorting to the fashionable lure of *realistic drama (*see* SHINGEKI). In 1962 he went to France where he studied theatre with *Barrault, and in the 1960s and 1970s he participated in various forms of modern theatre. He also founded study groups for *Zeami's theories. A superb, traditional nō actor, Kanze was interested in new approaches to staging plays, exemplified in his *music and choreography for *Hawk Princess*, a 'new' nō play based on *Yeats's *At the Hawk's Well*. KWB

Kapoor, Prithviraj (1906–72) Scion of India's leading film family, actor in over 50 silent and sound films, and *actor manager of Prithvi Theatres, a professional Hindi–Urdu drama company. Born into a middle-class family of Peshawar, Kapoor began acting while in school. He left law school for Bombay and appeared in nine silent films. He next *toured India with the Grant Anderson Theatre Company, performing Shakespeare in English. Between 1933 and 1944 he returned to cinema and starred in the epic *Sikandar* and other early sound films. In 1944 he established his own repertory theatre group and toured India extensively for sixteen years. Prithvi Theatres was known for its *naturalistic stagecraft and the political thrust of dramas such as *Deewar* (*Wall*), *Pathan*, and *Gaddar* (*Traitor*), which opposed Partition and promulgated communal harmony. Travelling with a company of 100, Kapoor sought to establish a national theatre movement in India on the tumultuous eve of independence. In the 1950s and 1960s, Kapoor made many well-known films, including *Mughal-e Azam, Dahej*, and *Awara*. KH

Kaprow, Allan (1927–2006) Painter, critic, and performer, the inventor of *happenings. Inspired by Jackson Pollock's Action Paintings he developed a technique of 'action-collage' in the mid-1950s. When he introduced flashing *lights, audible elements, and thicker chunks of material, these assemblages turned into environments, which could incorporate viewers as part of their structure. This led to *18 Happenings in 6 Parts* at the Reuben Gallery in New York (1959). The gallery had been divided into three compartments, where six sequences of events occurred simultaneously. The *actions had been fixed in a *scenario and *rehearsed by friends of the artist. Visitors at the exhibition were given precise instructions that allowed them to carry out actions within clearly defined parameters of time and space. In the following years he organized over twenty major happenings. After 1970 he focused on much simpler events, activities, and self-performances, which became barely distinguishable from occurrences in everyday life. *See also* PERFORMANCE ART/ART PERFORMANCE.   GB

Karagöz Popular Turkish *shadow puppet, which once covered an area from Romania to the Maghrib. The show centres on the solo puppeteer's improvised comic and topical repartee between Karagöz (Black Eye) and his friend Hacivat. A series of familiar social types also appears. Performances occurred mainly during Ramadan and in cafés, with special shows at court or for circumcisions or marriages. The figures are made out of translucent dyed camel skin. Jointed at the neck or waist (Karagöz also has a jointed arm), they are held against the screen with horizontal rods. In Egypt the name passed to the glove puppet Aragoz. In nineteenth-century Greece Karagöz evolved into Karaghiozis and rose on a tide of nationalism, holding his own until the last quarter of the twentieth century. He was also popular as a strip-cartoon figure. *See also* PUPPET THEATRE.   JMcC

Kara Jūrō (1940–) Japanese playwright, director, actor, and novelist. With *Terayama Shūji he was one of the spearheads of the underground (*angura) theatre movement in Japan. The productions of his Situation Theatre (Jōkyō gekijō, established 1963) in a red tent were a symbol of 1960s counter-culture and a tribute to the carnivalesque spirit of early *kabuki. Like *Hijikata, Kara attempted to revive the native, erotic energies of traditional Japanese theatre by emphasizing the actor's physical presence. His complex plays are lyrical, *surrealistic, shocking, funny, even baffling. He came into his own as a playwright with such 1970 works as *John Silver* and *The Virgin's Mask*, and *toured Korea with *A Tale of Two Cities* (1972), Bangladesh with *Bengal Tiger* (1973), and Palestine with *Matasaburō of the Wind* (1974). He disbanded the Situation Theatre in 1985 and founded a new company of younger actors, the Kara Gang (Kara-gumi), in 1987. Later plays include *Invisible Man* (1990). He continues to tour Japan with his red tent.   CP

Karanth, B. V. (1928–2002) Indian director and composer. Born in Karnataka, Karanth joined the famous Gubbi Theatre Company (*see* VERANNA,

GUBBI) as a child actor. Between 1967 and 1972 he produced a phenomenal number of plays in the Kannada language, often at a feverish pace, and soon established himself as a major director. His vigorous celebration of *music, *dance, and visual theatricality inspired the amateur theatre movement in Karnataka, and by 1978 he was known widely in India for his experimentation with indigenous theatrical forms in a contemporary idiom. From the late 1970s he headed a number of important theatre organizations in India, including the National School of Drama. His major productions include *Evam Indrajit* (1969), *Jokumaraswami* (1972), *Hayavadana* (1973), *Sattavara Neralu* (1975, all in Bangalore), *Barnam Vana* (an adaptation of *Macbeth*, Delhi, 1979), *Ghashiram Kotwal* (Bhopal, 1982), and *Gokula Nirgamana* (Heggodu, 1993).   KVA

Karatygin, Vasily (1802–52) Russian actor. Raised in the tradition of *neoclassicism, his stylized deportment and declamatory style lent themselves well to *Corneille's Le Cid (1822) and Hippolyte in *Racine's *Phèdre* (1823), and when the Aleksandrinsky Theatre opened in St Petersberg in 1832, Karatygin became the company's leading tragedian. Here he performed in works by Russian dramatists but also made his mark in Shakespeare, following the first translations by Nikolai Polevoy in the 1830s, including Othello (1836), Hamlet (1837), and King Lear (1838). He appeared as Karl Moor and as Ferdinand in *Schiller's *The Robbers* and *Love and Intrigue* respectively, and was the first to perform the roles of Chatsky in *Griboedov's *Woe from Wit* (1831) and Arbenin in *Lermontov's *Masquerade* (1852). NW

Karnad, Girish (1938–) Indian playwright, filmmaker, and actor. Though his early plays were inspired by existential modernist drama, the themes focused primarily on Indian myths, history, and folklore. His first play, *Yayati* (1960), tells of a king who borrows youth from his son. His second, *Tughlaq* (1964), is concerned with the fourteenth-century king Muhammad-bin-Tughlaq, who in his apparent madness becomes increasingly more violent in order to bring about an ideal state; critics noted the oblique similarity to Nehru's dreams of an ideal India. *Hayavadana* (1971) is based on a folk story about the exchanging of heads between two friends, and dramatizes the modernist opposition between mind and body. Karnad's other important works include *Naga-Mandala: Play with a Cobra* (1980), *Taledanda* (1990), and *The Fire and the Rain* (1994).   KVA

Kasper (Kasperl, Kasperle) A traditional role of the old Viennese popular theatre and the

German *puppet theatre, derived from the Italian Arlecchino (*see* COMMEDIA DELL'ARTE) and the German Hanswurst. After Caroline *Neuber's symbolic expulsion of *Harlequin *farces from the German stage in 1737, the comic figure found a new home in the Austrian theatre and was performed under different guises by *Stranitzky and Gottfried Prehauser. Towards the end of the eighteenth century, Kasper was given a 'classic' form by Johann Laroche, and his main stage, the Leopoldstädter Theater, was thereafter referred to as 'Kasperletheater'. The coarse humour of this proletarian figure particularly appealed to the tastes of lower-class *audiences, and around 1800 he entered the repertoire of German puppet theatres, where he expressed the children's hatred of the regimented world of adults. Franz Graf von Pocci elevated him to a literary status, but also romanticized the figure and defused his oppositional quality. In the twentieth century various authors rediscovered the figure's anarchic, subversive quality and gave his cudgelling and anti-authoritarian rebellion a distinctly political character.   GB

Kataev, Valentin (1897–1986) Russian/Soviet writer. His novel *The Embezzlers* (1927), an adventure story set during the New Economic Policy period, concerns two corrupt Soviet officials in search of 'high society'. It was adapted and performed at the *Moscow Art Theatre in 1928. *Squaring the Circle*, an engaging *comedy about the accommodation shortage in 1920s Moscow, was also staged at the Art Theatre in 1928 and proved popular with English and American *audiences during the 1930s. Kataev also dramatized his Five-Year Plan novel *Time, Forward!*, which depicts the construction of a metallurgical plant, where a group of workers set a world record for pouring concrete (1932). Other stage adaptations of his work include *I Am the Son of Working People* (1937) and *For Soviet Power* (MAT, 1954). Kataev also made stage versions of his books for children *A White Sail Gleams* (1937) and *Son of the Regiment* (1945).   NW

kathakali Literally, 'story play', *kathakali* emerged as a new genre of performance in the late sixteenth and early seventeenth centuries in Kerala, India. Under the patronage of regional rulers, it was created from a confluence of arts including the martial art (*kalarippayattu*) whose Nayar practitioners provided the first actor-dancers, Sanskrit temple drama (*kutiyattam*), the devotional *dance-drama sacred to Lord Krishna (*krishnattam*), and *ritual performances (*teyyam*).

A highly physical dance-drama staging stories written in Sanskritized Malayalam and based on Indian epics (*Ramayana, Mahabharata*) and Puranas, *kathakali* is performed on a bare stage with only stools and occasional properties, by three groups of performers: actor-dancers, percussionists, and vocalists. With a few exceptions, all-male companies of actor-dancers use a highly physicalized performance style embodied through years of training to play kings, *heroines, demons, demonesses, gods, animals, priests, and a few *characters drawn from everyday life. Each role is easily identifiable to a local *audience as a particular character type. Roles are created by using a repertory of dance steps, choreography, a complex language of hand gestures (*hastas*) for 'speaking' their character's *dialogue with their hands, make-up, *costume, and a pliable use of the face and eyes to express the internal states (*bhava*) of the character. The percussion orchestra includes three drums, each with its own distinctive sound, and brass cymbals, which keep the basic rhythmic cycles around which the dance-drama is structured. Two onstage vocalists keep the basic time patterns on cymbals and sing the text, including both third-person narration and first-person dialogue, in an elaborate, repetitious vocal style. Performances traditionally begin at dusk, and end at dawn.

Kathakali playtexts consist of third-person metrical verses (*slokas*) which, often composed completely in Sanskrit, narrate what happens in the ensuing dialogue or *soliloquy. *Padams* (songs) are composed in the first person in a mixture of Sanskrit and Malayalam, and are interpreted onstage by the actor-dancers. *Slokas* and *padams* are set to specific musical ragas appropriate to the mood and context; *padams* are also set in specific rhythmic patterns (*tala*) and tempos (*kala*). Successive generations of performers have modified *kathakali* playtexts by handing down techniques and styles of performance for specific plays. In keeping with the *rasa aesthetic, which encourages elaboration to enhance aesthetic pleasure, interpolations (*ilakiyattam*) are added to the performance. Lasting up to an hour, the best known are opportunities for senior performers to display one or more aspects of their virtuosic abilities, such as the choreographic *tour de force* of Arjuna's interpolation in *Kalakeya Vadham*, in which he describes the sights of the heavenly abode. What distinguishes interpolations from the literary text is that they are not sung, but simply enacted without repetition by the actor or actors, through action and hand gestures.

Many plays still in the active repertory have been edited to three- to four-hour performances. It is commonplace for an all-night performance to include three shortened plays focusing on scenes of most interest to connoisseurs. Since 1930 when the Malayali poet, Mahakavi Vallathol Narayana Menon, founded the Kerala State Arts School, Kerala Kalamandalam, *kathakali* has been adapted both by practitioners from within the tradition and by artists and entrepreneurs from without. These experiments have included *kathakali* for tourist audiences, writing and staging new plays based on traditional epic/puranic sources, transforming *kathakali* techniques into modern Indian dance or dance-drama, and writing and staging new plays based on non-traditional sources or current events, such as the 1987 leftist production of *People's Victory* which pitted the personified hero (World Conscience) against the personified *villain (Imperialism). Non-Hindu myths or non-Indian plays have also been adapted for *kathakali* style productions, such as the stories of Mary Magdalene, the Buddha, Faust, as well as the *Iliad* and *King Lear*.   PZ

Katona, József (1791–1830) Hungarian actor and playwright. In 1808, while still a student, Katona joined the company of the celebrated actress Madame Déry, with whom he was in love, using the stage name Békesi. He translated several plays for the company and adapted prose works for the stage. The performance of his masterpiece, the historical drama *The Viceroy* (written 1815), was banned (*see* CENSORSHIP). Published in 1820, it was presented posthumously in 1833. Katona had been influenced by the *Sturm und Drang* movement and his play is full of the national ardour of *romanticism; it was revived at the National Theatre of Budapest on the eve of the Hungarian Revolution of 1848. Ferenc Erkel, the composer of the Hungarian national anthem, transformed *Bánk bán* into an *opera in 1861, and his version has remained in the repertoire. Katona returned to his home town, Kecskemét, in 1826 and worked as a district attorney. He attempted unsuccessfully to establish a theatre there, after which he retired from artistic activity.   HJA

Katrakis, Manos (1908–84) Greek actor, whose career began in the 1927 silent film *The Banner of 1821*, followed by a stage debut the next year. After performing with the Greek National Theatre, he starred in Shakespeare's *Tempest* and *Schiller's *Don Carlos* (1945–6). After imprisonment for leftist politics he was back on stage in 1952 to play *Prometheus Bound* in Delphi to international acclaim for his stage presence, voice, and artistic sensitivity. In 1955 he founded the People's Theatre in Athens where he produced numerous plays, including Lope de *Vega's *Fuente Ovejuna* and *Kambanellis's *Yard of Wonders*. Katrakis also starred in several films, including

George Tzavella's *Antigone* and Theo Angelopoulos's *Voyage to Cythera* (1984).   KGO

Kaufman, George S. (1889–1961) American playwright and director. Known as 'the great collaborator', Kaufman wrote only one solo play, *The Butter and Egg Man* (1925). Between 1917 and 1930 he was drama editor for the *New York Times* and between 1921, with the success of *Dulcy* (with Marc *Connelly), and 1953, with a comeback hit, *The Solid Gold Cadillac* (with Howard Teichmann), he was among the most prolific and sought-after comic writers and directors in the United States. Kaufman collaborated with Connelly on ten plays (some one-acts) between 1921 and 1924, including *Merton of the Movies* (1922), which ran for nearly 400 performances, and *Beggar on Horseback* (1924), an *expressionistic *satire of business culture. He collaborated on six plays with Edna Ferber, including the dark *comedy *Dinner at Eight* (1932), and with other writers such as Dorothy Parker, Ring Lardner, and the composers *Gershwin, *Rodgers, and *Porter. Kaufman's enduring comic successes came with Moss *Hart: *Once in a Lifetime* (1930), *You Can't Take It with You* (1936, Pulitzer Prize), and *The Man Who Came to Dinner* (1939). Kaufman was in high demand as a play doctor during the 1930s. He directed most of the plays he wrote as well as other work, including *The Front Page* (1928) and *Of Mice and Men* (1937). The satire *Of Thee I Sing* (1931, with Morrie Ryskind and the Gershwins) was the first *musical to be awarded the Pulitzer Prize.   MAF

Kawatake Mokuami (1816–93) Japanese *kabuki playwright. Mokuami (his stage name) worked with, but subordinate to, actors in the kabuki theatre all his creative life, but the range of his production has elevated him with the very few playwrights who have left their mark on the form. He came into his own in the 1870s and 1880s, when kabuki took some hesitant steps towards modernization; he wrote for all the most famous actors of his day and was chief playwright at the Shintomi-za, a theatre which reformed many aspects of kabuki theatregoing. Not a natural innovator himself, Mokuami raised the general artistic level by judicious and sustained use of musical background, by paying much more attention to *dialogue than his predecessors had done, and by adapting *nō plays for kabuki. He responded to calls for plays more in tune with the age by writing *katsurekigeki* (plays of living history), in which there was some observance of historical fact, and *zangiri-mono* (cropped-hair pieces), featuring characters from contemporary Japan.   BWFP

Kazan, Elia (1909–2003) American director. A veteran of the *Group Theatre and co-founder of the *Actors Studio (1948), Kazan's direction of *Miller and *Williams epitomized the *naturalistic *acting and poetic staging associated with serious post-war American theatre. Of Greek heritage, Kazan emigrated with his family from Turkey at the age of 4. In 1932 he left Yale to accept an unpaid apprenticeship with the Group Theatre. The Group's social consciousness, *Method acting, and emphasis on ensemble left indelible marks. Kazan became adept at the close reading of texts and psychological analyses of *character. 'Direction', he later said, 'finally consists of turning psychology into behavior.' He emerged as an actor in *Odets's *Waiting for Lefty* (1935) and as director with two plays by Robert Ardrey: *Casey Jones* (1938) and *Thunder Rock* (1939). After the Group's collapse (1941), his productions of Miller's *All my Sons* (1947) and *Death of a Salesman* (1949), and Williams's *A Streetcar Named Desire* (1947), *Camino Real* (1953), *Cat on a Hot Tin Roof* (1955), and *Sweet Bird of Youth* (1959) were inflected by a poetic delicacy derived partly from Kazan's frequent collaboration with designer Jo *Mielziner. Despite Kazan's artistic sympathy with Miller, their relationship was put under great strain by Kazan's 1952 testimony before the House Un-American Activities Committee, during which Kazan named as communists eight former Group Theatre associates. Kazan served as director of the *Lincoln Center Repertory Company in New York from 1962 to 1964, but thereafter devoted his energies to film and writing.   MAF

Kazantsev, Aleksei (1945–2007) Soviet/Russian playwright who emerged during perestroika (notably with *And the Silver Rope Snaps*), but built his reputation in the 1990s. *This Other World* (1993), staged in both Moscow and St Petersburg, suggested that film is more real than life, and only when life is treated like a film is self-recognition possible. *Running Wanderers* (1996) dealt with the effects of change. With Mikhail Roshchin, Kazantsev established a centre for young playwrights and directors, and he was editor of the journal *Dramaturg*, which he launched in 1993 to promote new plays.   BB

Kazantzakis, Nikos (1883–1957) Greek writer. Best known for his novels, particularly *Zorba the Greek* (1946), and for his 33,333-line epic poem *Odyssey* (1938), he also wrote several *tragedies, some in verse, whose *characters were largely based on Greek myth and history. His first play, *It Is Dawning* (1907), was followed by the *absurdist *Comedy* (1908), *Christ* (1921), *Odysseus* (1922), *Nikiforos Fokas* (1927), *Melissa* (1937), *Julian the Apostate* (1939), *Prometheus* (1943), *Capodistria* (1944), *Sodom and Gomorrah* (1948), *Kouros* (1949), *Christopher Columbus* (1949), *Constantine Paleologos* (1951), and *Buddha* (1956). His work was philosophical in nature and greatly influenced by his teacher Henri Bergson, Nietzschean theory, and Buddhism. Kazantzakis emphasized poetic elements and often disregarded the practical demands of staging. There were, however, several productions of his plays worldwide, including the Greek National Theatre's *Capodistria* (1976) and *Buddha* (1978), both directed by Alexis Solomos.   KGO

Kean, Charles (1811–68) English *actor-manager. The son of Edmund *Kean, he was raised to be a gentleman but became an actor against his father's wishes. He made his debut at the age of 16 in *Drury Lane, then learned his craft in provincial theatres. He returned to Drury Lane as Hamlet in 1838, receiving triumphant reviews and the princely sum of £50 per night. Throughout the 1840s Kean played leading roles at *Covent Garden, Drury Lane, and the *Haymarket. In 1842 he married the actress Ellen *Tree. Kean's celebrity was enhanced in 1848 when Queen Victoria asked him to produce private theatricals at Windsor Castle, a task which he undertook for the next ten years. In 1850 Kean assumed joint *management of the Princess's Theatre with the comedian Robert Keeley. He became sole lessee after two years, supervising productions of Shakespeare, *melodrama, *comedy, and *pantomime. Despite its moderate size and unassuming shopfront exterior, the Princess's became one of London's most fashionable *playhouses, patronized by Victoria and Prince Albert, *Dickens, and Gladstone. Kean relinquished the managerial reins in 1859 and spent the remaining nine years of his life performing throughout Britain, America, and Australia.

Never widely praised as a tragedian, Kean nonetheless excelled in cape-and-sword melodramas. As a manager he is remembered for staging lavish historical spectacles. Between 1852 and 1859 he re-created the medieval and Tudor England of Shakespeare's chronicle plays, Assyria (*Byron's *Sardanapalus*, 1853), Peru (*Sheridan's *Pizarro*, 1856), Periclean Athens (*A Midsummer Night's Dream*, 1856), and Renaissance Italy (*The Merchant of Venice*, 1858). Kean's *antiquarian revivals were celebrated—and censured—for their sets, *costumes, and properties of unprecedented historical precision; re-enactment of events not dramatized by Shakespeare (such as the return of Henry V to London after the battle of Agincourt); interpolation of *dialogue and music of presumed authenticity (such as insults hurled at the captive Richard II); and playbill essays on his historical research. So fastidious was Kean's insistence upon authentic stage accessories that *Punch* dubbed him not the 'Upholder' of Shakespeare, but the 'Upholsterer'. RWS

Kean, Edmund (c.1787–1833) English actor, the leading tragedian of the *romantic age. His violent *acting style, full of energy and passion, displaced the cold, declamatory *neoclassicism of John Philip *Kemble. Kean's most famous roles also played a crucial part in transforming established critical views about Shakespearian *characters, notably Richard III, Iago, and Shylock. Kean was the illegitimate son of a minor actress; as a young man playing the provincial circuit, he was acclaimed for his performances as *Harlequin and in noble savage roles. He and his family were in a state of abject poverty when he finally secured an engagement at *Drury Lane Theatre. In 1814 Kean astonished fellow actors and *audience with a performance more powerful, Hazlitt wrote, 'than any we have almost ever witnessed'.

Kean's unprecedented popularity saved the ailing Drury Lane from bankruptcy. His performances were celebrated for their frenzied, tempestuous emotion and for sudden, unexpected transitions between contrasting moods. In Richard III, perhaps his finest role, Kean was full of ironic contempt and sardonic humour; as Hamlet, he returned at the end of the nunnery scene to press his hand tenderly to Ophelia's lips. Other roles included Macbeth and a leaden Romeo (both 1815), a bitter, sceptical Timon, and the *villainous Sir Giles Overreach in *Massinger's *A New Way to Pay Old Debts* (both 1816). Kean also portrayed the wild and yet pathetic Oroonoko in *Southerne's eponymous drama (1817), as well as King John (1818), Coriolanus (1819), and King Lear (1820).

Kean became one of the great celebrities of the Romantic era at home and abroad. But the actor's dissipated lifestyle and addiction to alcohol rapidly destroyed him. In 1825 he was successfully prosecuted by Robert Cox, a member of the Drury Lane committee (Kean had been conducting a long and scandalous affair with Cox's wife Charlotte). Violent opposition greeted Kean's appearance at Drury Lane in the aftermath of this conviction; soon afterwards, Boston *audiences hounded him from the stage. On his return to London, Kean gave only occasional performances.

In March 1833, he played Othello to the Iago of his son Charles *Kean, but collapsed on stage during the third act and died a few weeks later. JM

Keane, John B. (1928–2002) Irish playwright. His first play *Sive* caused a sensation at the 1959 All-Ireland Drama Festival. At once a *realistic and *ritualistic drama of rural cruelty and hypocrisy, *Sive* was declined by the *Abbey Theatre. The Abbey produced *Hut 42* in 1962, by which time Keane's work had entered the national repertoire. The land and people of north Kerry, with their idiosyncratic customs and language—in which pithy Gaelicisms abound—are at the centre of Keane's work. Among his best plays are *Sharon's Grave* (1960), *Many Young Men of Twenty* (1961), *The Year of the Hiker* (1963), *The Field* (1965), and *Big Maggie* (1969). Productions of *Sive, The Field*, and *Big Maggie* at the Abbey in the 1980s put an end to the metropolitan perception of Keane as a 'talented provincial'. He also wrote short stories, novels, and reminiscences. CFS

kecak (cak) Indonesian *dance-drama created in the Gianyar province of Bali in the 1930s by Balinese performers, in collaboration with Western artists and anthropologists Walter Spies and Beryl de Zoete. With the steep increase in tourism since then, *kecak* has become a popular and standardized entertainment component of tourist performances, also advertised as 'Monkey Dance'. *Kecak* is famous for its large male *chorus of over 100 chanters, seated in dense concentric circles surrounding a small playing area illuminated by a single, large oil lamp. While chanting highly complex, interlocking rhythmic patterns of 'cak cak cak', directed by the lead chanter, they wave their arms and torsos in time to the chanting. The dance sequences are based on episodes from the *Ramayana* and resemble the Balinese *wayang wong* in most of their performance convention, including dance style, *acting, and *costuming. No *masks are used. The leading refined *characters, such as Rama, Sita, and Laksmana, use Kawi (the ancient Javanese court language), while less refined characters and *clown servants use colloquial Balinese. KP

Keene, Laura (1826–73) American actress and *manager. Born in England, she went on the stage after an early marriage failed, apprenticing with *Vestris before emigrating to the United States in 1852. She achieved immediate success playing romantic roles opposite Lester Wallack, and subsequently *toured California and Australia with the young Edwin *Booth and managed the American Theatre in San Francisco before returning to New York. In 1855 she opened Laura Keene's Varieties, moving to a new theatre in 1856. Though her own magnetism was an element in the theatre's popularity, she also built a strong ensemble, used publicity well, and closely supervised all aspects of production. At her performance of *Taylor's *Our American Cousin* at Ford's Theatre in 1865, Abraham Lincoln was assassinated by John Wilkes *Booth.   AHK

Keith, B. F. (Benjamin Franklin) (1846–1914) American *vaudeville *producer. Keith ran away from his family's New Hampshire farm to join the *circus, working for several major companies including *Barnum's. By the mid-1880s he was *managing the Boston Gaiety Musée, where he claimed he developed the form of continuous entertainment that would become known as vaudeville. He formed a partnership with Edward F. Albee (1857–1930) in 1885 and opened the Bijou Theatre in Boston, beginning the great Keith-Albee vaudeville chain. For the small fee of ten cents, they offered a non-stop line of performers, comics, singers, and *dancers that ran from 10 a.m. to 11 p.m. The firm grew to a national chain of more than 400 houses by 1920. While Albee handled the business side, Keith focused on day-to-day management and insisted on maintaining a moral code on stage that forbade profanity or innuendo, appealing to Victorian sensibilities.   PAD

Kellar, Harry (1849–1922) America's most popular magician from 1898 to 1908. He learned *magic in his teens, and in 1873 Kellar and Bill Fay established a mix of magic, escape, and spiritualist acts. After years of *touring the world, Kellar opened his own show in 1884 in New York and quickly became the rival of Alexander Herrmann, then the most popular, competing for the greatest illusions and best bookings until Herrmann's death in 1898. Kellar was a perfectionist, with every word and movement carefully prepared. At the end of his final tour (1907-8), he turned his show over to Howard Thurston. Kellar performed one last time in 1917 in a benefit organized by *Houdini.   WFC

Kelly, Dennis (1968–) English playwright whose tautly observed dialogue creates estranged and nightmarish visions of the contemporary world. *Love and Money* (2006) used a fragmented and temporally disordered structure to explore the brutal decline of a relationship in a world in moral disarray, while *Taking Care of Baby* (2007) investigated the complexities of truth, guilt, and emotion in *documentary drama form. Other plays include *Debris* (2003), *Osama the Hero*, and *After the End* (2005).   DR

Kemble family English actors, *managers, and writers. **Roger and Sarah Kemble**, itinerant actors, had twelve children, the eldest of whom was Sarah *Siddons. The next child, **John Philip** (1757–1823), made his London debut as Hamlet at *Drury Lane in 1783 shortly after his sister's triumph. His appearance fitted him for classical *characters, such as Shakespeare's Brutus and *Addison's Cato, but he could also embody romantic *heroism, as Rolla in *Sheridan's *Pizarro*. The leading roles of the 1790s suited him well, such as Penruddock in *Cumberland's *The Wheel of Fortune* and Count Waldbourg in *Kotzebue's *The Stranger*. He was a studious actor, a buyer of books, and an editor and adapter of plays. He had no gift for *comedy. Not being inclined to mimicry and gossip proved a decided advantage when he mingled socially with well-born men who like himself had a traditional education, polished manners, collecting habits, and a formidable capacity for drink. While he was manager of *Covent Garden Kemble's high connections intensified hostile feelings sparked by a rise in seat prices and in the number of private *boxes. His dignity, prestige, and private fortune suffered as a result of the OP (Old Price) *riots which disrupted performances from September to December 1809. From 1814 Kemble's *acting was insistently contrasted with that of the newcomer Edmund *Kean, and the *neoclassicism of the older actor described as either a standard of excellence from which the *romanticism of Kean had deviated or a pompous stateliness which had had its day. At his best Kemble had ample power to play the most taxing roles, but he was increasingly troubled by asthma and gout and in 1817 gave his last performance in his favourite character of Coriolanus.

He made over his share in Covent Garden to his brother **Charles** (1775–1854), who was for many years London's leading fine gentleman in comedy, renowned for his insinuating charm and the elegance of his demeanour. He retired in 1836 and became Examiner of Plays (*see* CENSORSHIP) but three years later played four leading roles by royal command so that Prince Albert might see him act.

Frances Anne ('Fanny') (1809–93), daughter of Charles, emerged from a comparatively secluded girlhood to play Juliet at Covent Garden in 1829 as a desperate measure to save her father from bankruptcy. She was successful, and went on to play many of the parts associated with Mrs Siddons. She followed her father into high comedy in roles such as Lady Teazle and Kate Hardcastle, and continued the family's literary tradition by writing plays, memoirs, and poetry. Her younger sister **Adelaide** (1815–79) enjoyed a brief but glorious career as an *opera singer and performed for Queen Victoria, at whose court Fanny was presented.   FD

Kemp, Lindsay (1938-) Scottish *mime, dancer, actor, and director, whose company, founded in the early 1960s, has throughout fifteen productions explored the boundaries between the media for live performance, incorporating influences from *ballet, *nō, *butoh, and *kabuki, modern *dance, *Marceau-trained mime, *opera, and *physical theatre. Kemp's productions include the much revived *Flowers* (1974-94), based on themes from *Genet's novels; a version of *Wilde's *Salome*; *Mr Punch's Pantomime*; *A Midsummer Night's Dream*; *Duende*; *Nijinsky*; *The Big Parade*; *Onnagata*; and *Cinderella*, staged as a Gothic *operetta. All Kemp's stage work is notable for its powerful imagery, achieved by innovatory *lighting, scenery, and *costume design, which together create an erotic visual poetry. For Ballet Rambert he created *The Parade's Gone By* (1975) and *Cruel Garden* (1978) inspired by *García Lorca's life and works. Some seven film appearances include *Savage Messiah* (1971) and *Valentino* (1977) for Ken Russell and *Sebastiane* (1974) and *Jubilee* (1977) for Derek Jarman. For David Bowie he directed the 'Ziggy Stardust' concerts in 1972.   RAC

Kempe, William (d.1603) English comic actor. Kempe, a highly physical performer celebrated for his *dancing, was perceived as the natural successor to the *clown Richard *Tarlton, whom he may have replaced as principal comedian with Leicester's Men as early as 1583: his style was sufficiently non-verbal for his popularity to have extended to the Continent, which he *toured in the 1580s and again around 1601. He joined Strange's Men in 1592 and then served with the *Chamberlain's Men between 1594 and 1599, where he created the role of the servant Peter in Shakespeare's *Romeo and Juliet* in 1595. After this his Shakespearian roles increased in prominence, from Bottom (probably) via Lancelot Gobbo (probably) to Dogberry (certainly) and Falstaff (probably). For whatever reasons, however, Kempe went solo (and was replaced by Robert *Armin) soon after the company moved to the *Globe, performing a marathon publicity-stunt *morris dance all the way from London to Norwich (described in his pamphlet *Kempe's Nine Days Wonder*, 1600). Hamlet's attack on clowns who speak more than is set down for them has suggested to many that Shakespeare and Kempe had quarrelled over his ad libbing.   MD

Kempinski, Tom (1938-) English playwright. His plays usually deal with individuals

who are cut off from mainstream life. *Duet for One* (1980), loosely based on the life of cellist Jacqueline du Pré, focuses on a concert violinist suffering from multiple sclerosis and in psychotherapy. The nature of the artist and the nature of communication are at the root of *Separation* (1987), which enacts an odd long-distance relationship between a reclusive writer in London and an ailing (perhaps dying) actress in New York. The theme of analysis, Freudianism, and a structure based on conversation and even interrogation lie at the heart of *When the Past Is Still to Come* (1992), which reworked his own experiences of therapy in attempting to deal with family memories of the Holocaust.   AS

Kendal, Madge (Margaret Robertson) (1848-1935) and **William Hunter Kendal** (1843-1917) English actors. Before their marriage in 1869, Madge Robertson made her London debut as Ophelia in 1865, and subsequently played Desdemona to Ira *Aldridge's Othello (1865), Edith in the spectacular *Drury Lane *melodrama *The Great City* (1867), and Lilian Vavasour in *Taylor's *New Men and Old Acres* (1869). She had already established her signature style: a combination of arch vivacity in *comedy and dignified pathos in adversity. William Kendal developed his abilities as part of the *Haymarket comedy company (1866-74), playing roles like Harry Lester in *Lewes's *The Game of Speculation*, Charles Surface in *Sheridan's *The School for Scandal*, and Orlando in *As You Like It*. After marriage he undertook secondary roles while proving himself to be an astute *manager at the *Royal Court and the St James's together with John *Hare. The Kendals made five consecutive *tours of North America (1889-96), where they introduced *Pinero's *The Second Mrs Tanqueray*. Often compared with the *Bancrofts, they epitomized the respected position to which Victorian actors aspired.   VEE

Kennedy, Adrienne (1931-) *African-American playwright. Participation in *Albee's workshop led in 1964 to *Funnyhouse of a Negro* and her involvement *Off-Off-Broadway. Her plays of that period, which include *The Owl Answers* (1965) and *A Movie Star Has to Star in Black and White* (1976), are quasi-autobiographical explorations of a troubled consciousness, female and black, divided against itself and at odds with the world around it. The imagery is private and visceral, the form subjective and fragmented, and the situations often violent. On the surface, her later work is more serene and narrative in form but just as concerned with racial injustice and identity. Her plays are more widely studied than performed, but in 1992 Great Lakes Theatre Festival in Cleveland premièred *The Ohio State Murders*. The 1995–6 season of the Signature Theatre in New York was devoted to her work and included the world première of *Sleep Deprivation Chamber*, written with her son Adam and directed by Michael *Kahn, who also staged many of her earlier plays. She is the recipient of three Obie awards.   STC

Kente, Gibson (1932–2004) South African actor, composer, and *producer of township *musicals. His early productions, which he wrote, directed, and played in, include *Manana, the Jazz Prophet* (1963) and *Sikalo* (1966). He broke with Union Artists to form his own company with Sam Mhangwane, creating *Lifa* (1968) and *Zwi* (1970), and by 1974 he managed three companies, in which the performers earned four times a factory worker's wage. Although not overtly political, Kente's work was influenced by the Black Consciousness movement; his film *How Long?* (1974) and the plays *I Believe* and *Too Late!* (1975) were banned (*see* CENSORSHIP). Later productions that he wrote and directed include *Can You Take It* (1977), *La Duma* (1978), and *Mama and the Load* (1980). Kente's use of narrative, *mime, movement, voice, *music, and *dance blended established forms of theatre with traditional African oral performance to create 'township *melodrama', relying on urban experience and culture. YH

Kern, Jerome (1885–1945) American composer. Kern's insistence on *musicals that fully integrated *dialogue, *character, song, and staging had a profound impact on the development of twentieth-century musical theatre. His masterpiece, *Show Boat*, is arguably the most important and influential stage musical ever written. Between 1915 and 1918 Kern wrote a series of musicals with lyricist *Wodehouse and librettist Guy *Bolton. In 1927, *Show Boat* (lyrics and libretto by Oscar *Hammerstein II) achieved a more complete unification of song and story. Touching on sensitive social issues (interracial marriage, spousal abuse, abandonment, and alcoholism), a rich score, and the first racially mixed cast on Broadway, it was a major advance. Kern also composed for Hollywood, including two films for Fred *Astaire (*Roberta*, 1935; *Swing Time*, 1936) and a bevy of standards such as 'Smoke Gets in your Eyes', 'The Way You Look Tonight', and 'Long Ago and Far Away'. Kern died in New York while preparing to write music for *Annie Get your Gun* (1946), a project ultimately undertaken by Irving *Berlin   BN

Kerr, Walter (1913–96) American critic, playwright, and director. Kerr was one of the most influential theatre critics of his generation, and also an accomplished theatre artist. A number of plays and *musicals which Kerr wrote, co-wrote, or adapted transferred to Broadway, including *Count Me In* (1942), *Stardust* (1943), and *Song of Bernadette* (1946, with his wife Jean Kerr). He moved to New York in 1949 to become theatre critic for *Commonweal*, moving in 1951 to the *New York Herald Tribune* and then the *New York Times* (1966–83). Kerr was noted for the intelligence of his criticism and his strong sense of principle. In 1990 the Ritz Theatre on Broadway was renamed in his honour.   KF

khon Masked *dance-drama of seventeenth-century Thailand, which began as a royal pageant in the fifteenth century. Deriving from the *nang yai* *puppet theatre, *khon* was originally performed by male dancers who portrayed four type *characters—*hero, heroine, demon, and monkey—each wearing a different *mask. Today, however, female roles are usually played by women and only the demons and monkeys wear masks. The play, taken from an episode in the *Ramayana*, represents the battle between Ravana and Rama through dance. It normally ends with the defeat of Ravana's general, though the death scene is never portrayed.   SV

kiak Ancient Korean music and *dance, originally designed for Buddhist religious services. *Kiak* probably originated from simple dances performed before the statue of Buddha in India and was brought into China where it was shaped into a broader art form. At about the start of the seventh century it reached Korea where it was again altered and was performed at Buddhist temples as a didactic *masked dance-drama for a general *audience. *Kiak* travelled from Korea to Japan where it was called *gigaku*. Though the dance became extinct in Korea and Japan around the thirteenth century, the Japanese *Kyōkunshō* (1223) describes an actors' procession, a lion dance, a priest, an old woman, a nobleman, and a story of a love triangle. *Kiak* was performed with large masks entirely covering the performers' heads. It is possible that it influenced the Korean masked dance-drama (*kamyŏngŭk*) which survives today.   JOC

Kidd, Michael (1919–2007) American director and choreographer. Born Milton Greenwald, he began in *ballet, working with several companies marked by an interest in stylized Americana, which drew him to Broadway. His first assignment was to choreograph *Finian's Rainbow* (1947). Other major assignments followed, including *Guys and Dolls* (1950) and *Can-Can* (1953). He also choreographed for films, including *Seven Brides for Seven Brothers* (1954). He featured a special brand of dance—highly athletic and technically demanding. In 1956 he became a director/choreographer for *Li'l Abner*, a practice he would continue throughout the rest of his stage career, although without great success. He continued to choreograph for film (*Star!, Hello, Dolly!*).   JD

Killigrew, Thomas (1612-83) English playwright and *manager. *Pepys reports that as a child Killigrew volunteered to play devils at the Red Bull in order to see plays for free. Two of his courtly romances, *The Prisoners* (1632-5) and *Claracilla* (1636), were acted at the Phoenix by Queen Henrietta's Men. A third romance, *The Princess* (*c.*1636-7), and a *comedy, *The Parson's Wedding* (1639-40), were probably played by the King's Men at *Blackfriars. Killigrew spent the Interregnum on the Continent in the service of the royal family. At the Restoration in 1660, Killigrew, together with *Davenant, was granted a monopoly on the London stage, and Killigrew launched an unsuccessful career as manager of the King's Men at the Theatre Royal and then at *Drury Lane. Unable to adapt to changing theatrical tastes, and lacking business sense, by 1676 he had ceded control of the company to his son Charles. He succeeded Sir Henry Herbert as Master of the Revels in 1673 and held the post until 1677.   RWV

Kilroy, Thomas (1934-   ) Irish playwright, novelist, literary critic. Born in County Kilkenny, Kilroy has had an academic as well as a writing career. *The Death and Resurrection of Mr Roche* (Dublin 1968), was significant as the first explicit exploration of homosexuality in Irish theatre. Kilroy has often been drawn to historical settings and biographical material. One of his most innovative plays was *Talbot's Box* (*Abbey and *Royal Court, directed by Patrick *Mason), which dramatized the inner psychology of Dublin's worker saint Matt Talbot with five actors in an all-purpose stage box that figured at once mind and society. *Double Cross* (1986) evoked the lives of Irishmen Brendan Bracken, British loyalist, and William Joyce, the traitor Lord Haw-Haw, both played by Stephen Rea. Kilroy's capacity for combining conceptual rigour with dramaturgical innovation was again displayed in *The Secret Fall of Constance Wilde* (1998), while *The Shape of Metal* (2003) was less successful.   NG

Kim U-jin (1897-1926) Korean director, producer, theorist, and playwright. Despite his brief career, Kim had a remarkable influence upon modern theatre in Korea, writing five plays, numerous essays on Western theatre and drama, and three translations of foreign plays. As a student at Waseda University in Tokyo, Kim saw Japanese modern theatre (*shingeki*), and in 1921 he used the Tongwuhoe (Society of Comradeship) to introduce Western theatre in Korea. He was the first Korean playwright to be influenced by the work of *Ibsen, *Shaw, *Strindberg, and *O'Neill, and through his essays also introduced Lord Dunsany, *Čapek, and *Pirandello to Korea. He experimented with *realism, *naturalism, and *expressionism, writing about conflict between old customs and new ideas, including the difficulties women endured under the old ways. His representative plays, written between 1924 and his suicide, are *High Noon, Yi Yŏng-nyŏ, The Disillusion of Poet Tudugi, Shipwreck*, and *The Boar*.   JOC

King, Thomas (1730-1805) English actor and *manager, the foremost comic actor during the *Garrick era. He created such roles as Lord Ogelby in the Garrick-*Colman *Clandestine Marriage* and Sir Peter Teazle in *Sheridan's *The School for Scandal*. Discovered by Garrick in 1748, King spent the majority of his career at *Drury Lane, though he acted and *danced in many provincial theatres and had a managerial interest in Bristol and *Sadler's Wells. He was also Sheridan's *stage manager at Drury Lane.   MJK

Kingsley, Sidney (1906-95) American playwright and director. Kingsley's dramatic output was small—only nine plays over 30 years—but his works were exceptionally well crafted and raised the standard for social drama. He won the Pulitzer Prize for his first play, *Men in White* (1933). A tautly constructed *melodrama that dealt matter-of-factly with abortion and racial prejudice, it was exquisitely staged by *Strasberg for the *Group Theatre. *Dead End* (1935), a *naturalistic drama set outside a New York tenement, ran for nearly 700 performances. Kingsley directed that and all his later plays with the exception of *The Patriots* (1943). *Detective Story* (1949) and *Darkness at Noon* (1951, from Arthur Koestler's novel) saw long Broadway runs and film adaptations.   MAF

King's Men *See* CHAMBERLAIN'S MEN, LORD.

Kinoshita Junji (1914-2006) Japanese playwright. Active in the *shingeki* (new drama) movement since 1939, Kinoshita both wrote within its *realistic mode and consciously moved outside it. His search for dramatic form appropriate to modern Japan focused on language, consciousness of sin, and fate. *Twilight Crane* (1949), the most famous of his folk tale plays, makes innovative use of language to suggest different moral and ideological worlds. An underlying recognition of ineradicable sin is an organizing concept in several plays about recent Japanese history, such as *Okinawa* (1961). Kinoshita's greatest work is *Requiem on the Great Meridian* (1978). In this monumental play the rhythmic language of a thirteenth-century war tale is blended with Kinoshita's contemporary version in seamless transitions from group chanting to *dialogue between individuals. *Characters step out of the group, symbolizing collective historical consciousness; cosmic forces and fate, the latter recognized clearly by the *hero, bring about his and his clan's destruction.   BWFP

Kipphardt, Heinar (1922–82) German playwright. Kipphardt's name is synonymous with the *documentary theatre to which he (and *Hochhuth) made a decisive contribution. His play *In the Matter of J. Robert Oppenheimer* (1964) relied heavily on the trial transcripts of the nuclear physicist during the 1950s, which *Piscator's Berlin production further visualized with slide projections and film clips (*see* MULTIMEDIA). It was an international success with productions in Paris by *Vilar and in Milan by *Strehler, both in 1964. *The Story of Joel Brand* (1965) draws on documents to dramatize a deal made between Eichmann and Hungarian Jews. Both plays were originally written for television. Other successful plays include *März* (also a novel and TV play, 1980) and the posthumous *Brother Eichmann* (1983), a complex collage of scenes which draws parallels between the Vietnam War, the Baader-Meinhoff terrorists, and the Adolf Eichmann trial.   CBB

Kirshon, Vladimir (1902–38) Russian/Soviet writer who became known in the West when his first play, *Red Rust* (1926), was performed in New York by the *Theatre Guild (1929), as well as elsewhere. The play centres on social problems of post-revolutionary Soviet youth, just as *Bread* (1930) centres on the problem of the kulaks (rich peasants) during collectivization, and *The Rails Are Humming* on the 'heroic task' of industrialization. His *comedy *The Miraculous Alloy*, about research in the aircraft industry, proved extremely popular. Kirshon fell foul of the regime and became a victim of Stalin's purges.   NW

Kishida Kunio (1890–1954) Japanese playwright, director, and critic. Kishida's love of French literature led him to Paris in 1919, where he studied with *Copeau at the Vieux-Colombier. Back in Japan in 1923, he determined to create a modern Japanese theatre with high artistic standards. Kishida's interests remained with the poetic and psychological, for which his early one-act plays provided a congenial format, and he took no interest in the socialist theatre then in the ascendancy. Of his longer plays, the strongest is *The Two Daughters of Mr Sawa* (1935), which chronicles complex and nihilistic personal family relations. In 1938 Kishida and others formed a new troupe entitled Bungakuza (the Literary Theatre), which upheld literary rather than political ideals. Kishida joined in the war effort and was severely treated afterwards by his colleagues. His few postwar plays are subdued but effective.   JTR

kkoktukaksi norŭm Traditional *puppet theatre of Korea, its precise origin unknown. The central *characters enact familiar tales that deal satirically with the corruption of Buddhist monks, domestic problems, and the malfeasance of the ruling classes. Traditionally performed by three or four puppeteers on a simple portable stage in any open space, with three or four musicians in attendance, a puppeteer manipulated a single puppet at a time, speaking the *dialogue and singing songs to music. *Kkoktukaksi norŭm* is still performed today as government cultural events or tourist entertainments.   JOC

Kleist, Heinrich von (1777–1811) German writer. In Paris in 1803 he tried to join the French army to fight against England, but was deported to Germany, where he had a breakdown. His first extant drama, *The Schroffenstein Family* (1804), is a dark *tragedy of fate in verse, in which lovers from rival families are destroyed. After settling in Königsberg, he began three of his best-known plays: *Amphitryon* (1807), *Penthesilea* (1808), and *The Broken Jug* (1808), one of the few classic German *comedies that survives in the repertoire. In 1807 Kleist was arrested in Berlin by the invading French forces and taken to France, unsettling him even further. In 1811 he shot himself. His plays met with little success in his own lifetime: *Amphitryon* was not performed until 1898, *Penthesilea* in 1876, *The Broken Jug*, after an unsatisfactory première at the *Weimar Court Theatre in 1808, was first successfully staged in 1820. His best work, *The Prince of Homburg*, was not published and performed until 1821. A young Prussian officer wins a battle by defying orders. In order to remind him of the need for discipline, he is sentenced to death and undergoes a mock execution. Kleist was also the author of a seminal essay, 'On the Marionette Theatre' (1810), which argues that the *puppet is graceful because it is free of self-consciousness, a prototype of *Craig's de-individualized Über-marionette. MWP

Kline, Kevin (1947–) American actor. He made his Broadway debut in 1972 as a founding member of *Houseman's Acting Company. With the *New York Shakespeare Festival he played various roles, including two renditions of Hamlet, first directed by *Ciulei (1986) and then under his own direction (1990), Trigorin in *Chekhov's *The Seagull* (2001), and King Lear (2007). He won Tony awards for Bruce Granit in *On the Twentieth Century* (1978) and the Pirate King in *The Pirates of Penzance* (1981); other Broadway credits include *Loose Ends* (1979), *Arms and the Man* (1985), and *Ivanov* (1997). He made his film debut as Nathan in *Sophie's Choice* (1982) and went on to a major career that includes *A Fish Called Wanda* (1988), *Chaplin* (1992), the title role in *Dave* (1993), *In & Out* (1997), Bottom in *A Midsummer Night's Dream* (1999), and Jaques in *As You Like It* (2006). He returned to NYSF for *Mother Courage* with Meryl Streep, directed by *Wolfe (2006). JDM

Knipper-Chekhova, Olga (1868–1959) Russian actress, who married *Chekhov in 1901. Having studied under *Nemirovich-Danchenko from 1895, Knipper was one of several prime candidates for the *Moscow Art Theatre which Nemirovich-Danchenko set up with *Stanislavsky in 1897. Knipper created a remarkable series of classic roles, beginning with Chekhov's major heroines: Arkadina (*The Seagull*, 1898), Elena (*Uncle Vanya*, 1899), Masha (*Three Sisters*, 1901), Ranevskaya (*The Cherry Orchard*, 1904), and Sarah (*Ivanov*, 1904). She also played major roles in MAT productions of plays by *Hauptmann, *Ibsen, and *Gorky, and was significantly instrumental in creating the core of the MAT repertoire. Her style of playing suited these contemporary works in *naturalistic productions, and she was recognized for her ensemble skills, her penetrating and detailed study of *character, her natural grace on stage, her discipline, and her exacting standards. Knipper's lifelong career at MAT called for adaptability: after the revolution she continued to play the favourite roles but also created memorable characters in a vastly different political situation, notably Polina in Gorky's *Enemies* (1935). CM

Knowles, James Sheridan (1784–1862) Irish playwright. Knowles was immensely popular in his time, and hailed as a second Shakespeare for his *tragedies and *comedies written in blank verse and prose imitative of the Elizabethan manner but thoroughly imbued with the domestic spirit of the nineteenth century. Starting in Ireland as an actor, Knowles attained fame with *Virginius* (1820), a tragedy staged at *Covent Garden by *Macready, who played a Roman patrician who kills his own daughter to keep her out of the *villain's clutches. *Virginius* provided star actors with a leading role for the rest of the century. The father–daughter and father–son relationship is also the heart of other dramas such as *William Tell* (1825), *The Daughter* (1836), and *The Rose of Aragon* (1842). *The Love-Chase* (1837), reminiscent of *Much Ado About Nothing*, is his most stylish and witty comedy. Knowles was fortunate in having the best actors of the day in his principal *characters, but his work, now unplayable, represents the last twilight of the legitimate Elizabethan-influenced verse tragedy and comedy. MRB

Kokkos, Yannis (1944–) Greek *scenographer and director whose work has been chiefly in France. Instrumental in Antoine *Vitez's deconstructive visions of plays such as *Racine's *Britannicus* (1981), *Hugo's *Hernani* (1985), and *Claudel's *The Satin Slipper* (1987), Kokkos often presented a stark minimalism and experimented with reverse *perspective and other techniques designed to reorient spectators' perceptions of space. He has designed *operas and *ballets at many of the world's great houses, including the Paris Opéra, the Vienna Staatsoper, *Covent Garden in London, La Scala in Milan, the Grand Théâtre in Geneva, the San Francisco Opera, and the Hamburg Ballet. His directing credits include Racine's *Iphigénie* (1991) and *La Thébaïde* (1995) at the *Comédie-Française, as well as several ambitious opera productions for which he served as both director and designer. DGM

Kokoschka, Oskar (1886–1980) Austrian painter, designer, and dramatist. Although Kokoschka is best known as a painter and major exponent of German *expressionism, he was actively involved in the theatre around the time of the First World War. His best-known play is *Murderer Hope of Womankind* (1910), a prototypical expressionist work in its combination of sound, colour, and expressive language. Other plays are *The Burning Bush* (1913), *Job* (1917), and *Orpheus and Eurydice* (1919), some of which he directed and designed at the Albert Theater in Dresden. Kokoschka returned to the theatre in his later years, working mainly as a designer. CBB

Koltai, Ralph (1926–) Designer, born in Berlin, who emigrated to England in 1939. In 1945 he was attached to British Intelligence at the Nuremberg trials and subsequently to the War Crimes Interrogation. Thereafter he studied theatre design at the Central School of Art in London, his first production being the *opera *Angélique* (1950). He has since designed over 200 productions of opera, *dance, *musicals, and drama around the world. As associate artist of the *Royal Shakespeare Company he designed over 27 plays from Shakespeare and *Beckett to Solzhenitsyn and *Brecht, including the world première of *Hochhuth's *The Representative*. Koltai directed and designed *La traviata* and *The Flying Dutchman* for the Hong Kong Arts Festival (1987), and *Williams's *Suddenly Last Summer* for Nottingham Playhouse. In 1997 a major retrospective of his work was seen in London, Beijing, Hong Kong, Taipei, and Prague. He is acknowledged as an innovator in the use of materials, notably mirrors, but he sets out to focus on the actor, 'without whom', he said, 'the stage is dead'. PH

Koltès, Bernard-Marie (1948–89) French playwright and novelist. Koltès came to prominence with *Struggle of the Dogs and the Black* (1983) directed by *Chéreau, who thereafter staged most of his plays at the Théâtre des Amandiers in Nanterre. Koltès's work features multiracial *characters and narratives in marginal, contested territories such as colonial West Africa and an abandoned American docklands warehouse. Most famous are *Quay West* (1985), *In the Solitude of the Cotton Fields* (1986), and *Roberto Zucco* (staged posthumously by *Stein at the *Schaubühne, Berlin, 1990). In these works Koltès combined the antithetical ideologies of rich and poor, natives and immigrants, the collective and the individual, transnational capitalism and community, creating dramas of violence, crime, fear, and racism. His characters are presented without apology, but with an intense compassion that matches the playwright's hatred of the establishment. His plays quickly received international attention and continue to be performed all over the world. BRS

komedya Play in verse from the Philippines depicting the Christian saints, real events, or imaginary kingdoms. The last, also called *moromoro*, dramatizes the conflict between medieval Christian kingdoms and the Moorish empire. Scripts are usually adapted from metrical romances involving European heroes, such as Gonzalo de Cordoba or Charlemagne and the twelve peers of France. Indebted to the Spanish *comedia, the typical *komedya* takes about three days or nights to perform, mounted during the town fiesta on an open-air stage denoting a tiered palace façade. Christian royals—civilized, loyal, and noble—are fair-skinned like Europeans; Muslim princes—uncouth, selfish,

and cowardly—are dark like Filipino natives. From 1598 to 1898 *komedya* contributed in no small measure to colonization by converting Filipinos to Spain's religion, by teaching them to obey authorities, by imposing European standards of beauty, and by fomenting enmity between Christianized natives and the Muslims of the southern Philippines who resisted colonization to the end of the Spanish regime. Since then *komedya* has gradually declined and now survives only in a few rural towns where a Hispanized feudal culture continues to hold sway. NGT

Komisarjevsky, Theodore (Fyodr **Komissarzhevsky**) (1882–1954) Russian director and designer, half-brother to Vera *Komissarzhevskaya. 'Komis', as he became known in England, began his career at his sister's theatre in St Petersburg (1906) before moving to Moscow, where he directed plays and operas. He emigrated to England in 1919, staging Borodin's *Prince Igor* at *Covent Garden that year and *The Government Inspector* with Claude Rains (1920). Komisarjevsky's productions of *Chekhov proved revelatory for British *audiences, his first (*Uncle Vanya*) staged at the *Royal Court in 1921, followed by *Ivanov* at the Aldwych Theatre in 1925. But his tenure of the Ranelagh, a tiny theatre in Barnes (1925–6), produced the greatest impact. Here he staged *Vanya*, *Three Sisters*, and *Cherry Orchard* with casts which included *Gielgud, *Laughton, and *Ashcroft. Hitherto English productions had tended to stress Chekhov's mournful and lyrical side; Komisarjevsky brought out the lightness and sense of the absurd.

At the *Shakespeare Memorial Theatre in Stratford, he staged groundbreaking productions of *The Merchant of Venice* (1932), *Macbeth* (1933), *The Merry Wives of Windsor* (1935), *King Lear* (1936), *The Comedy of Errors* (1938) and *The Taming of the Shrew* (1939). Having settled permanently in the USA in 1939, Komisarjevsky opened a drama school in New York which he ran until his death. He staged his own play *Russian Bank* (1940) and a version of *Crime and Punishment* with Gielgud (1947). He married Peggy Ashcroft in 1934 (annulled 1936). NW

Komissarzhevskaya, Vera (1864–1910) Russian actress and *manager, half-sister of Theodore *Komisarjevsky. She made her mark as the first Nina in *Chekhov's *The Seagull* (St Petersburg, 1896), giving a memorable performance in an otherwise ill-fated production. She founded her own theatre there in 1904, where she appeared in productions of Chekhov—*Ivanov* and *Uncle Vanya*—and as Desdemona, Ophelia, and Nora

Convinced of theatre's idealistic role, and tired of theatrical routine and the dominant *naturalistic trends, Komissarzhevskaya boldly extended an invitation to the young *Meyerhold to join her company, fresh from his unsuccessful attempts to stage *symbolist plays at the *Moscow Art Theatre. Meyerhold proved to be more interested in staging methods than in providing vehicles for a great actress and, apart from appearances as Hedda Gabbler and as Sister Beatrice in *Maeterlinck's play (both in 1906), the collaboration proved unfruitful, and Meyerhold was dismissed in 1907. The remainder of Komissarzhevskaya's career was spent *touring, but her fame was such that when she died of smallpox in 1910, her funeral was attended by vast crowds of mourners.   NW

Komparu Zenchiku (Ujinobu) (1405–*c.*1470) Japanese *nō playwright, actor, *manager, and theorist, active mostly in the Nara region. Disciple, son-in-law, and artistic successor of *Zeami, Komparu headed the Emman'i troupe (modern Komparu school) and was in competition with On'ami, head of the Kanze troupe. He composed over ten poetic nō plays that are still admired today, including *Bashō, Kamo, Tamakazura, Teika, Ugetsu,* and *Yokihi.* His critical treatises, such as *Six Circles, One Dewdrop* (1455) and *The Essence of Song and Dance* (1456) combine Buddhist and Confucian philosophy, poetics, musical theory, and nō aesthetics.   KWB

Kong Shangren (K'ung Shang-jen) (1648–1718) Chinese dramatist, best known as the author of the *chuanqi* drama *The Peach Blossom Fan* (1698). The play deals with the last days of the Ming Dynasty, directly addressing the literati who still mourned its end. The most *metatheatrical of Chinese plays, Kong relied on the metaphor of the world as stage to propose that all worldly attachments, including those to family and nation, are but illusion. Kong's pedigree as a linear descendant of Confucius (Kong zi) in the 64th generation granted him the opportunity to lecture on the Confucian classics to the Qing Emperor Kangxi and act as guide when the Emperor toured Qufu, the site of the national shrine to Confucius. Kong was also an expert in *ritual, and wrote several treatises on the subject.   SYV

König, Michael (1947–) German actor. König made his debut at the Munich Kammerspiele in 1966 where he met Peter *Stein and appeared in his production of *Bond's *Saved* (1967). He followed Stein to Bremen, playing Ferdinand in *Schiller's *Kabale und Liebe* (1968), and was a founding member of the Berlin *Schaubühne. His most notable roles there include the

young Peer Gynt (1971), Alfred in *Tales from the Vienna Woods* (1972), Dionysus in *The Bacchae* (1973), and Orlando in *As You Like It* (1977). He also directed Achtenbusch's *Ella* (1978) and *Büchner's *Woyzeck* (1981) at the Schaubühne. He left in 1999, one of the few members of the original ensemble to remain so long.   CBB

Koonen, Alisa (1899–1974) Russian/Soviet actress and wife of Aleksandr *Tairov, with whom she established the Kameny (Chamber) Theatre in 1914 and where, for the next 30 years, she performed leading roles in productions directed by her husband. Excellent in both *tragedy and *comedy and blessed with physical beauty, grace, and an expressive voice, Koonen numbered among her outstanding roles *Kalidasa's Shakuntala (1914), *Wilde's Salome (1917), *Scribe's Adrienne Lecouvreur (1919), *Racine's Phèdre (1922), *Shaw's St Joan (1924), Abbie in *O'Neill's *Desire under the Elms* (1926), Ellen in *Treadwell's *Machinal* (1933), the woman commissar in *Vishnevsky's *Optimistic Tragedy* (1933), Cleopatra (Shaw/Shakespeare, 1935), and Emma Bovary (1940).   NW

Kopit, Arthur (1937–) American playwright. Kopit scored his first *Off-Broadway success with *Oh Dad, Poor Dad, Mamma's Hung You in the Closet and I'm Feelin So Sad* (1962). This Oedipal tale about an overbearing woman who keeps her husband's corpse in the closet and tyrannizes her son became characteristic of Kopit's early enthusiasm for madcap *characters and situations. *Indians* (1968) is a *tragicomedy about the nineteenth-century American frontier scout and showman Buffalo Bill *Cody and a political parable about the Vietnam war. *Wings* (1978) depicts a woman who struggles to reclaim her ability to speak after two debilitating strokes. Kopit returned to satire with *End of the World* (1984). His next work, originally entitled *Bone-the-Fish,* is a blistering and controversial spoof of *Mamet's satire on Hollywood, *Speed-the-Plow,* revised as *The Road to Nirvana* (1991). *Y2K* is an anti-technology parable that portrays a couple whose privacy is invaded by a computer hacker (1999; published as *BecauseHeCan*).   JAB

Kornfeld, Paul (1889–1942) German dramatist. Kornfeld grew up in Prague where he was associated with Franz *Werfel and Franz Kafka. Kornfeld first came to prominence during the First World War with *expressionist dramas (*The Seduction,* 1918), and essays such as 'The Man of the Soul and the Psychological Man' (1918), a central manifesto of the expressionist movement. His greatest success was the *tragedy *Heaven and Hell* (1920) at the *Deutsches Theater in Berlin.

He then turned to psychological *comedies (*Killian; or, The Yellow Rose*, 1926) and historical plays (*Jud Süss*, 1930). In the 1920s he worked as a *dramaturg for *Reinhardt, and returned to Prague in 1933. After the German invasion he was deported to Łódź in Poland, where he was killed in a concentration camp.   CBB

Kortner, Fritz (1892–1970) German actor and director. Kortner quickly established himself as a major talent in Berlin and Vienna. He played the main role in *Toller's *Transfiguration* (1919), his breakthrough in Berlin, and in many of *Jessner's most important productions. Particularly noteworthy were his performances in *Schiller's *William Tell* (1919), Shakespeare's *Richard III* (1920), and *Wedekind's *Marquis von Keith* (1920). In this period he came to be regarded as the prototypical *expressionist actor in both contemporary and classical plays. At the same time he established himself as a major film actor. His performances in the late 1920s were informed by a more restrained, *realistic style. His Shylock in *Fehling's *Merchant of Venice* (1927) introduced new complexity to the *character in a time of growing anti-Semitism. In 1933 Kortner was forced into exile, moving from Vienna to London, New York, and finally to Hollywood, where he established himself as an actor and scriptwriter. In 1949 he returned to Germany and worked mainly as a director. In protracted, intensive *rehearsals he demanded absolute precision from actors, developing a distinctive style characterized by a search for realism in contrast to the prevailing abstract classicism.   CBB

Kott, Jan (1914–2001) Polish scholar and critic. His major work, *Shakespeare our Contemporary* (1961), interprets Shakespeare's plays as emblematic of the modern world. Other works include *The Eating of the Gods* (1973), *The Theatre of Essence* (1984), and *The Memory of the Body* (1992). Greatly affected by Cold War conditions in Eastern Europe, Kott converted historical knowledge into living experience, reading old literary works with contemporary consciousness. His famous analysis of *King Lear* as an example of the theatre of the *absurd compares it to the comic grimace of *Beckett's *Endgame*. *Shakespeare our Contemporary* was enormously influential in criticism and production, most notably affecting *Brook's *King Lear* for the *Royal Shakespeare Company in 1962.   KB/DK

Kotzebue, August Friedrich von (1761–1819) German dramatist who worked in St Petersburg in the Russian state service. His staunchly monarchist stance led to tension with liberal stu-

dents in the post-Napoleonic period, and he was assassinated by one in 1819. His sentimental drama of adultery *Misanthropy and Repentance* (1789) made him famous overnight and established the basic formula he varied across genres approximately 200 times: skilfully constructed dramatic tension, mixed with comic relief, sentimental endings, and moral didacticism. Like many of his works, this play was widely translated into other languages. In England Benjamin Thompson adapted it as *The Stranger* (1798), one of the most successful plays of the nineteenth century. Kotzebue particularly favoured exotic settings, which he combined with love interests in *Pizarro* (1794, adapted in English by *Sheridan, 1799) and *La Peyrouse* (1797), a topical treatment of the lost French expedition to the South Seas, which was adapted into a *pantomime (London, 1799), a *ballet (Naples, 1822), and a drama (Paris, 1859).

Kotzebue was acutely aware of social issues, not afraid of controversy, and part of his success lay in the ability to present current social questions. *Kind der Liebe* (1796, known in English as *Lovers' Vows*, a performance of which is banned in Jane Austen's *Mansfield Park*) was castigated for sexual and political frankness. Nevertheless, the overwhelming success of his plays made them a mainstay of theatre for over 30 years, and his successful *dramaturgical formula had a seminal influence on the development of Anglo-American *melodrama. Hugely prolific, his plays featured prominently throughout Europe and America until the mid-nineteenth century, though few have remained in the repertory.   CBB

Koun, Karolos (1908–87) Greek director. He founded the People's Stage in 1934 with the artist Yannis Tsarouhis, where Koun directed an acclaimed production of *Euripides' *Alcestis*. He founded the Art Theatre in 1942 in order to explore international dramatic styles using a psychological method. Among his most innovative productions were *Ibsen's *The Wild Duck* (1942) and *Rosmersholm* (1943), *Chekhov's *Cherry Orchard* (1945), *Williams's *A Streetcar Named Desire* (1949), *Brecht's *The Caucasian Chalk Circle* (1957), *Kambanellis's *Yard of Wonders* (1957), and *Ionesco's *Rhinoceros* (1963). Koun made his mark on the staging of *Aristophanic comedy as well, emphasizing *expressionistic elements of Greek popular culture in the *characters and situations. He also directed for the Greek National Theatre and *toured Europe with several of his productions, including *Birds* (Paris, 1962; London, 1964).   KGo

Krauss, Werner (1884–1959) Austrian actor whose breakthrough came in 1914 in *Reinhardt's cycle of *Wedekind plays in Berlin. Krauss's virtuosic style and uncanny ability to change appearance made him a prototypical 'new actor' for *expressionism, and he is best remembered for his title role in the expressionist Robert Wiene's film *The Cabinet of Dr Caligari* (1919). In the 1920s Krauss worked for both *Jessner and Reinhardt in Berlin, playing Macbeth, Richard III, Julius Caesar, Lear, and modern roles. He attained notoriety under the Nazis for his racist rendition of Shylock at the *Burgtheater in 1943 and for his part in Veit Harlan's anti-Semitic propaganda film *Jud Süss* (1940), which got him banned from work after the war until 1948.   CBB

Krejča, Otomar (1921–2009) Czech actor, director, and *manager. Krejča entered the Czech National Theatre in 1951, becoming the head of its drama company between 1956 and 1961. The highlights of his acting career were Don Juan in 1957 and Malvolio in 1963. In these years, however, he was already an established director devoting himself mainly to modern Czech drama (Kundera, *Havel) and exploring, with *Svoboda as *scenographer, the possibilities of simultaneous *action, kinetics, and *light on stage. In the Theatre beyond the Gate, established for him in 1965, emphasis on the actors' performances became more prominent, and the playwright's scripts were sometimes dismantled and rearranged. In 1972 the Theatre beyond the Gate was closed and Krejča banished to a suburban theatre; between 1976 and 1989 he was permitted to work only abroad. Shortly after the Velvet Revolution in November 1989, the Theatre beyond the Gate was re-established, though it closed again in 1994. In 1997 Krejča's adaptation of *Goethe's *Faust*, with Svoboda's ingenious sets, opened at the National Theatre.   ML

krishnattam A religious *dance-drama in eight parts celebrating the life of Lord Krishna, performed in the Guravayur temple in Kerala, India. Inspired by the 'play' of Krishna (as the word *attam* suggests), this form is generally attributed to Prince Manaveda, the Zamorin of Calicut (1655–58, who apparently saw the child Krishna dancing in the temple courtyard with a peacock feather stuck in his hair. Through almost 350 years of a slowly evolving *dramaturgy and choreography, almost entirely undocumented, *krishnattam* has emerged as an intimate representation of Manaveda's chaste Sanskrit composition of *Krishnageeti*. In earlier times a solitary troupe of *krishnattam*, based in Calicut, would travel to Guruvayur every year, performing at various temples *en route*. This tour would culminate in the performance of all the eight plays in the *krishnattam* cycle. Since it was considered inauspicious to end the cycle with Krishna's death in *Swargarohanam* (ascension to heaven), it was obligatory to follow this performance with the opening play of *Avatharam* (incarnation), which deals with Krishna's birth. The other six plays in the cycle deal with Krishna's love-play with the *gopis* (milkmaids) in *Rasakreeda*; the celebration of marriage in *Swayamvaram*; and the defeat of arrogant and *villainous *characters in *Kamsavadham, Banayuddham, Vividavadham*, and *Kaliyamardanam*. Each of these plays is performed as a *ritual offering every night between 9 pm and 3 am in the north-eastern courtyard of the Guruvayur temple. The pilgrims who pay for each performance select the play on the basis of specific desires and needs—for instance, if one seeks blessings for a child, then one can sponsor a performance of *Avatharam*; likewise, *Swayamvaram* is offered for marriage.   LSR/RB

Kroetz, Franz Xaver (1946–   ) German playwright. Kroetz came to attention in the late 1960s as one of a group of Bavarian and Austrian playwrights dedicated to regenerating dialect and local themes. In *Work at Home* (1971), *Request Concert* (1972), and *Stallerhof* (1972), Kroetz portrays both petit bourgeois and rural existence in brief scenes. The language of the characters (the unemployed, trades people, shop assistants, farm workers) is an impoverished artificial dialect punctuated by pauses—communication is primarily non-verbal. During the 1970s Kroetz was the most performed playwright in Germany after *Brecht. Plays such as *Nicht Fisch nicht Fleisch* (1981) and *Max Strong* (1980) examined the effects of unemployment and technological change on the lives of skilled workers. In these and later works like *The Urge* (1994), which include *surrealistic scenes and highly explicit sexual language and actions, Kroetz tested the last taboos in German theatre. Although he has written over 30 plays, his output in recent years has declined. He became a household name in Germany playing the society journalist Baby Schimmerlos in the satirical television series *Kir Royal*.   CBB

Ksentini, Rachid (1887–1944) Algerian actor, singer, playwright, and director. He began his career acting in *Allalou's Zahia Troupe in 1926 and finished it in 1944 with *Bacheterzi's company; between these two dates he created a company that produced his own plays. A wide traveller, Ksentini viewed Algerian society with a satiric eye. He recorded more than 200 comic songs, composed and played about 30 sketches, and wrote and directed 25 *comedies (including *Hole in the Ground*, 1931; *Hold Tight*, 1935; *What Was Said*, 1938). He ridiculed the conservatism and superstition prevalent in Algerian society through typically Algerian comic *characters, in plays such as *Bouborma* (1928) and *Bousebsi* (1932).   MME

Kubo Sakae (1900–58) Japanese playwright and director. While studying German literature at Tokyo University, Kubo became a disciple of *Osanai Kaoru at the Tsukiji Little Theatre. After Osanai's death in 1928, Kubo, now a committed Marxist, chose to work with *Hijikata's New Tsukiji Troupe. Both as a director and as a writer Kubo became a respected spokesman for the importance of historical *realism in the theatre. His most fully accomplished work, the lengthy *Land of Volcanic Ash* (1937), remains a masterpiece of socially committed drama. Drawing on his childhood knowledge of the difficulties of colonizing Japan's cold northern island of Hokkaido, Kubo created in Amamiya a tragic figure who attempts to combine his humanism with his scientific knowledge. Under house arrest during the Second World War for his left-wing politics, Kubo never fully recovered his health and committed suicide in 1958.   JTR

Kukolnik, Nestor (1809–68) Russian dramatist and poet. A reactionary *romantic, Kukolnik's first play, *Torquato Tasso*, consists mainly of verbose speeches of inordinate length. He followed this with one of the most famous 'hurrah-patriotic' plays of the nineteenth century, *The Almighty's Hand the Fatherland Hath Saved*, staged for *Karatygin's *benefit in 1834 and celebrating the arrival on the scene of the Romanov dynasty in the early seventeenth century. When in 1866 an unsuccessful assassination attempt was made on Alexander II, the fifth act was performed in Moscow as a rallying cry and act of thanksgiving. Of the many other dramas Kukolnik composed, almost all have been forgotten, with the possible exception of *Prince Mikhailo Vasilevich Skopin-Shuisky* (1835). Set during the same period as *The Almighty's Hand*, the play is partly an attempt to create a Russian Lady Macbeth in the person of one Katerina, who poisons a prince but who is then herself forcibly poisoned with the drink she has administered.   NW

kunqu (*k'un-ch'ü*) One of the dominant musical styles of Chinese opera of the late imperial and modern periods. Traditional Chinese theatre is essentially *opera with lyrics that can be sung in any number of musical styles. Considered particularly elegant and subtle, *kunqu* was most popular among the gentry from the late sixteenth to the late eighteenth centuries. It originated in the Kunshan area of Wenzhou, and is a refinement of the regional style of singing popular there during the fifteenth century. The scholar *Wei Liangfu is credited with combining the northern and southern musical styles to create *kunqu* (the term condenses the words *kunshan quiang*, 'music of Kunshan'). Wei based the new style on Kunshan's regional music that blended the flute, reed pipes, small drum, and clapper. In his time *kunqu* was used only for song suites or for art songs (*sanqu*). The writer *Liang Chenyu, after experimenting with setting northern *zaju* plays and art songs to *kunqu* music, wrote the first *kunqu* play, *Huan Shaji* (*Washing Silk*), around 1579, a sensational success that popularized the *kunqu* style.

In fact *kunqu* is better suited to the performance of individual songs than to the stage. A particularly slow style, it lends itself to great clarity of pronunciation. The music is also softer and more delicate than that of the other styles popular during the late imperial period; its most important instrument is the flute, and it uses no big drums or gongs. For these reasons, *kunqu* lent itself to performances in enclosed, intimate settings, such as the banquet halls of the scholarly elite. The other dominant style at the time, *yiyang*, which originated in Jiangxi, was faster and noisier, incorporating drums and cymbals, and thus better suited to the open air performances favoured by the common people. The growing popularity of Beijing opera (*jingju*) in the eighteenth century, and the devastation wrought by the Taiping rebellion upon southern China in the mid-nineteenth century, contributed to the end of *kunqu's* dominance of the Chinese stage. It is kept alive today by professional troupes in China and Taiwan and amateur singers the world over. The current repertoire consists mainly of plays from the late imperial period, though in the last decades of the twentieth century a divide opened between traditionalists and reformers.   SYV

Kurbas, Aleksandr (Les Kurbas) (1887–1937) Ukrainian/Soviet director whose career began as an actor in 1912. His first directorial experiments were in Kiev (1917), where he anticipated the *avant-garde innovations of *Meyerhold. The establishment of the Berezil Theatre in 1922 was part of an attempt to unify the proliferating studio groups inspired by Kurbas's example, the fourth and most radical of which described itself as 'a new type of revolutionary theatre'. The range of Kurbas's work, at both the studios and the Berezil, included *constructivist versions of *Kaiser's *Gas* (1922) and *Jimmy Higgins* (1923, after Upton Sinclair, which Meyerhold invited to

Moscow), a version of *Macbeth* as *Grand Guignol (1924), highly *expressionistic versions of Prosper Mérimée's *Jacquerie* (1925), and *Sadie Thompson* (after *Maugham, 1927). The attempts of the authorities to exert control over Kurbas led to the Berezil Theatre being relocated to Kharkov in 1926. Kurbas's last work was as assistant to *Mikhoels and *Radlov on *King Lear* at the Moscow State Yiddish Theatre, before he was arrested in 1934 and 'disappeared'.   NW

Kushner, Tony (1956–) American playwright. Kushner had been writing plays for a decade before *Angels in America* catapulted him to international fame. Of its two parts, *Millennium Approaches* (London, 1992, Broadway, 1993) won the Tony award and the Pulitzer Prize; *Perestroika* (1993) also won the Tony. Subtitled 'A Gay Fantasia on National Themes', the two parts form an epic *comedy that sets the millennial anxiety of the AIDS epidemic against the backdrop of the Reagan era and a more general American restlessness. A television all-star mini series of the play (2003) was directed by Mike *Nichols. Kushner followed with a 'coda' about the collapse of the Soviet Union, *Slavs!* (1995); several shorter, occasional pieces; adaptations of *Brecht's *The Good Person of Setzuan* and Anski's *The Dybbuk* (both 1997); and a book of essays, *Thinking about the Longstanding Problems of Virtue and Happiness* (1995). Earlier works include *A Bright Room Called Day* (1987) and an adaptation of *Corneille's *L'Illusion comique* (1988). *Homebody/Kabul* (2001) took up the subject of Afghanistan, and *Caroline, or Change*, a musical (New York, 2002), played at the *National Theatre in London (2006). *The Intelligent Homosexual's Guide to Capitalism and Socialism with a Key to the Scriptures* premiered at the *Guthrie Theatre as part of a Kushner festival (2009).   STC

kutiyattam A highly elaborate performance tradition of Sanskrit drama. In an unbroken tradition of more than ten centuries, it is enacted by the temple-serving caste of the Cakyar community in the south-western state of Kerala in India. *Kutiyattam* literally means the combined acting of more than one person. Other participants in this rarefied tradition controlled by approximately six families include the Nambiars, who provide the rhythmic background for the performance by beating on a large pot-drum (*mizhavu*), and the Nangyars—the women of the Nambiar community—who enact the female roles. As a Hindu temple-based art, usually performed in temple theatres (*kuttampalam*) or in the inner hall of the temple complex itself, the performance begins

with *rituals drawn from the *purvaranga* as delineated in the *Natyasastra*. A *character is introduced from behind a hand-held half-curtain, his painted face resembling the more elaborate *kathakali* conventions of *costume and make-up influenced by *kutiyattam*. While the introduction lasts around two to three hours, a *kutiyattam* performance can stretch to eight hours, extending over several nights. On the second day the actor provides *exposition, improvised by physical and gestural means, using codified hand gestures (*hastas*). Countering this virtuosic physical enactment, the *vidushaka* (*clown or jester) entertains the spectators with vocal improvisations on the joys of food, sex, deception, and good living.

The dramatic text is always enacted in the final days of the performance. Drawing from a rich repertoire of Sanskrit classics (including the plays of King Kulasekharavarman, the earliest patron and reformer of *kutiyattam*), the repertoire draws extensively on *Bhasa, whose plays existed in the manuals of *kutiyattam* long before they were discovered as dramatic texts in 1910.

Despite its literary inputs, the fundamental challenge in the performance of *kutiyattam* is not to tell the story of the play, which is already known to its relatively small coterie of spectators, but to elaborate on the character's innermost feelings and sentiments through subtle tremors of the lip, eyes, eyebrows, and even the cheek. This histrionic regimen, which demands a psychophysical understanding of breathing and energy, is nurtured through hereditary modes of training. Shortly after India's independence in 1947 *kutiyattam* was on the verge of extinction, but has been revived through the patronage of institutions like the Sangeet Natak Akademi and the dedicated intervention of scholars and connoisseurs, and is now recognized by UNESCO as part of the world's 'intangible heritage'.   LSR/RB

Kyd, Thomas (1558–94) English dramatist. Kyd's only surviving plays are *The Spanish Tragedy* (*c.*1586) and *Cornelia* (1594), though he may also have written a play based on the Hamlet story. In 1593, heretical writings were found amongst his papers and he was arrested; he later claimed that the documents belonged to *Marlowe, with whom he had shared accommodation a few years earlier. Though he was eventually released, his prison experiences may have hastened his death.

In the late sixteenth century, people regarded *The Spanish Tragedy*, along with Marlowe's *Tamburlaine*, as the beginning of 'modern drama'. Set in a fictitious modern European court, it is striking for its intricate, layered architectonics and its use of intrigue and dramatic irony as tragic devices, but sixteenth-century *audiences found it most compelling for the stark, powerful rhetoric which expresses the leading *character Hieronimo's psychological disintegration after the murder of his son. The play was frequently performed in 1590s England (notable Hieronimos included Richard *Burbage and the young *Jonson), and generated several spin-offs. It inaugurated English *tragedy's preoccupation with the social, ethical, and political dilemmas of *revenge which were ultimately addressed in *Hamlet*. Its stage life continued well into the seventeenth century, and twentieth-century productions by the *National Theatre (1982) and the *Royal Shakespeare Company (1997) demonstrated its durability.　　　　　　　　MJW

Kyle, Barry (1948–　) English director. Kyle was an associate director of the *Royal Shakespeare Company from 1978, and was made honorary associate in 1991 after directing nearly 40 plays for the company. His fascination with Jacobean texts led him to produce, with John *Barton, John *Ford's rarely staged *Perkin Warbeck* (1975). He also collaborated with Barton on *King John* (1974) and *Cymbeline* (1974), and wrote and directed *Sylvia Plath* (1973). His socialist views were exemplified in productions like *Brenton's *The Churchill Play* (1988). Kyle's other productions for the RSC include *The Taming of the Shrew* (1982), *Love's Labour's Lost* (1984), and Louise *Page's *The Golden Girls* (1984). In the 1990s he directed Shakespeare abroad, most successfully in New York with award-winning productions of *Henry V* (1994, with Mark *Rylance), and *Henry VI* (1996). He directs freelance in England, including *King Lear* (2001) and *Richard III* (2003) for the *Globe Theatre.　　　　　　　　　　　　　　KN

Kynaston, Edward (1643–1712) English actor. One of the few *boy actors to continue playing female roles after the Restoration, Kynaston's offstage performances extended to appearances in Hyde Park, where fashionable women vied to be seen with the cross-dressed actor in full female *costume. A sharing member of the King's, United, and *Lincoln's Inn Fields companies, Kynaston's talent for mimicry made him some enemies but brought him success in a variety of leading male roles.　　　　　　　　　　GBB

kyōgen Japanese short *farces performed between *nō plays; also, actors who play kyōgen roles; also, a term used after the 1650s for *kabuki performances or texts. The characters *kyōgen* mean 'mad words'. Kyōgen farces are Japan's oldest *dialogue drama. Humorous skits were part of early *sarugaku* (*see* nō), and kyōgen plays were differentiated from nō plays by the mid-1300s. Medieval kyōgen actors were members of nō troupes, but in the seventeenth century they left to form three kyōgen schools: Okura, Izumi, and Sagi. Pre-seventeenth-century kyōgen plays were simple plots performed extemporaneously, and the names of authors are unknown. Full playtexts were first published in 1623, and the first treatises on the art were written in the 1630s.

Kyōgen actors perform two primary functions. First, they play minor roles in nō plays, often during the interval when the *shite* changes *costume; such intervals are called *ai-kyōgen*. Second, they perform in discrete kyōgen plays (*hon-kyōgen*), which present humorous conflicts between *stock characters: masters and servants, lords and retainers, samurai and commoners, husbands and wives, deities and mortals, etc. Usually the socially inferior party emerges victorious, and many plays *parody authority figures such as samurai, priests, and gods. While dialogue is central, many examples contain short dances and/or songs which resemble nō in rhythm and timbre, but are light-hearted in content. The posture and gait of kyōgen actors closely resemble their counterparts in nō. Speech in kyōgen is much livelier, however, and contains substantial amounts of onomatopoeia. Contemporary *audiences easily understand kyōgen speech.

Today's leading kyōgen actors are members of families that have been performing for many generations. Training begins at about 5 years of age, and actors pass through a series of progressively more difficult graduation pieces during the course of their careers. Almost all professional kyōgen actors are men. Kyōgen *masks are used for deities, demons, and animals, and exhibit grotesque, exaggerated expressions. Most kyogen costumes are made of relatively inexpensive materials and feature large, bold, earthy designs. Today the major acting families among the two surviving schools (Okura and Izumi) stage all-kyōgen shows in addition to performing in nō productions. Since the Second World War a few new kyōgen plays have been written and staged, based on sources as diverse as French farce, Shakespeare, and Japanese folklore.　　　LRK

Kyōka *See* Izumi Kyōka.

Kyveli (Adrianou) (1887–1978) Greek actress and *manager. Kyveli made her debut in 1901 with Constantine Christomanos's New Stage, where she acted in plays by Shakespeare, *Ibsen, and *Sophocles until she formed her own company in 1906. She played the leads in *Ibsen's *A Doll's House* and *Strindberg's *Miss Julie* to critical acclaim, and in 1908 she appeared as Lord Byron in Spiros Potamianos's play of that title. After acting in a large number of Greek and European dramas, in 1932 she was notable as Mary Stuart in *Schiller's play, opposite Marika Kotopouli's Elizabeth. Her third marriage was to the politician George Papandreou in the late 1930s. In 1958, at the age of 70, she gave one of her most memorable performances in *Brecht's *Mother Courage*.   KGO

Laban, Rudolf (1879–1958) German choreographer, dance theorist, and educator. Laban was a key influence upon European modernist *dance in the 1920s and 1930s. His schools in Germany emphasized improvisation and expressive plastic rhythms, as demonstrated in his 'movement choirs', which involved amateur and professional dancers. At the height of his popularity, his *Vom Tauwind und der neuen Freude* was performed at the 1936 Berlin Olympics, but Goebbels's disapproval ended his career in Germany. His former pupil Lisa Ullmann enabled him to continue his work in England, where Laban analysed the organizing principles of human movement: space, time, weight, and flow. Employed by Frederick Lawrence to work on time–motion efficiency, Laban adapted his methods to serve the war effort. His Labanotation system enabled precise recording of choreography. His principles have been extended by former pupils: Mary Wigman and Kurt Jooss founded their own dance companies; Jean Newlove worked with *Littlewood's *Theatre Workshop; Yat Malmgren developed a Laban-based system of actor training. RVL

Labiche, Eugène (1815–88) French playwright. Taking over from *Scribe and his contemporaries the formula of *comédie-vaudeville*, Labiche wrote most of his plays in collaboration with other talented dramatists. Fifty-seven of his 175 plays are included in the ten volume edition of his *Théâtre* (1879). The blend of fast-moving *farce and literary *comedy makes *An Italian Straw Hat* (1851), *The Misanthrope and the Man from Auvergne* (1852), *Le Voyage de Monsieur Perrichon* (1860), or *Dust in the Eyes* (1862) a joy to read as well to stage. In Labiche everything depends on chance, *character is minimal or fixed, *action is swift moving, and *laughter is abundant. His treatment of the *bourgeois of Second-Empire Paris, who also made up his *audience, is gentle and socially observant. *See also* WELL-MADE PLAY. WDH

Labou Tansi, Sony (Ntsoni za Buta Marcel) (1947–95) Dramatist and novelist from ex-Belgian Congo. Labou Tansi is best known for his fourteen plays. *Conscience de tracteur* (1979), *La Parenthèse de sang* (1981), *La Résurrection en rouge*

et en blanc de Roméo et Juliette (1990), and *Antoine m'a vendu son destin* (1997) are mostly concerned with the dictatorial abuse of power and notable for their ferocious *satire, their use of fantasy and the grotesque, and their nightmarish atmosphere. To him the modern theatre should aspire to the condition of the *mbongi*—the public space in Congolese villages where meetings and feasts are held and the affairs of the community transacted. To this end he often took his troupe to traditional, rural occasions like the *matanga*—feasts of remembrance of the dead—where his contribution, in the midst of a liberal flow of alcohol, took the form of a performance of a piece entitled 'A Legend on the Invention of Death'. His troupe, the Rocado Zulu Theatre, was well known for innovative productions in Congo and France. PNN trans. JCM

LaBute, Neil (1963–) American playwright, screenwriter, and film director. LaBute's first play, *In the Company of Men* (1993), a moralistic and misanthropic tale of two men and a deaf woman, opened at the Mormon Brigham Young University in Utah, and was the basis of his independent film of that title (1997) which won numerous awards. *Bash: Later-Day Plays* (2000), a sequence of three short plays about violent Mormons (Latter-Day Saints), got him expelled from the church. *The Mercy Seat* (New York, 2002) depicts a worker at the World Trade Center thought dead by his family, who actually was with his mistress (and boss) at the time of the September 11th attacks. Such gruesomely comic situations characterize more recent plays as well, such as *This Is How It Goes* (2005), *Wrecks* (2006), *In A Dark Dark House* (2007), and *reasons to be pretty* (2008; Broadway, 2009). LaBute's films, often with celebrity casts, include *Your Friends & Neighbors* (1998), *Nurse Betty* (2000), *Possession* (2002), *The Shape of Things* (2003), *The Wicker Man* (2006), and *Lakeview Terrace* (2008). DK

La Chaussée, Pierre-Claude Nivelle de (1692–1754) French playwright. La Chaussée pioneered *comédie larmoyante* in the 1730s and 1740s, holding that *comedy, however amusing, must have a clear moral end. His career met with early success, his first play *False Antipathy* (1733) being followed by *Le Préjugé à la mode* (1735), in which the 'modish prejudice' was an aristocratic scorn for the marriage tie. Next came his masterpiece, *Mélanide* (1741). These plays were all strongly supportive of conjugal love, with *heroes—and more particularly heroines—surviving the challenge of prejudice and adverse circumstance in order to win a happy ending in a welter of sentimental clichés. The idiom of these verse plays often reflected that of *Corneille's heroic *tragedies rather than the robust language of *Molière. La Chaussée was the butt of constant criticism from *Voltaire, who scornfully dismissed *comédie larmoyante* as 'the tragedy of chambermaids', but he occupies an influential place in the development from *character comedy to the sentimental *drame *bourgeois* of *Diderot and his followers. His later plays include *Paméla* (1743), based on Richardson's novel.   WDH

Lacy, John (*c.*1615–81) English actor and playwright. Lacy was apprenticed as a dancer and acted with *Beeston's Boys at the Cockpit before the closing of the theatres. After the Restoration he achieved prominence as a member of *Killigrew's company at the Theatre Royal (*Drury Lane); his acting and dancing were much admired by *Pepys. Besides major roles in revivals of *Jonson, *Fletcher, and *Shirley, Lacy also adapted *The Taming of the Shrew* as *Sauny the Scot* (1667), and wrote three successful but undistinguished *comedies.   RWV

Ladipo, Duro (1931–78) Nigerian performer and playwright. After some early plays, he founded the Mbari Mbayo Club in Oshogbo (1962) and was soon performing there with his travelling theatre group, later known as the Duro Ladipo Players. Moving away from Christian sources and from the preoccupations and 'glees' of Hubert *Ogunde, Ladipo selected episodes from the history of the Oyo kingdom as the basis for plays, which were sometimes called *Yoruba folk operas. Productions of *The King Did Not Hang, The King Is Dead,* and *Moremi* were enriched by extensive research and proved popular on *tours to Berlin (1964) and Britain (1965). A performer with an imposing stage presence, Ladipo generally played the charismatic central roles that were a feature of his *dramaturgy. During the 1970s his plays and productions moved closer to the populist style appreciated by the public in western Nigeria.   JMG

Lagerkvist, Pär (1891–1974) Swedish writer who received the Nobel Prize in 1951. The quest for existential meaning preoccupied him as a young poet, as it did in his late novels. His *expressionist play *The Secret of Heaven* (1919) showed a group of grotesque figures living isolated lives on a huge blue sphere; it was given a striking production at Nya Intima Teatern. *The Man Who Lived his Life Over Again* was a less abstract *morality play, reflecting the new *realism of the period (*Dramaten, 1928). As the Nazis swept to power in Germany, Lagerkvist expressed passionate opposition to totalitarian violence. His anti-Nazi play *The Hangman,* directed by Lindberg in 1934 with Gösta Ekman in the lead role, was warmly received in Norway but caused some embarrassment in a Sweden that had many Nazi sympathizers. Lagerkvist's remaining plays were mainly concerned with terrorism, *The Man without a Soul* (1936), and the struggle between democracy and Nazism, *Victory in the Dark* (1939).   DT

La Grange (Charles Varlet) (1635–92) French actor. The most important of *Molière's colleagues, he joined the troupe shortly after it arrived in Paris, held it together after Molière's death, published his last plays, and was a mainstay of the *Comédie-Française. His *Registre,* a day-by-day accounting for 26 years of the troupe's repertory, receipts, expenditures, and personnel actions, is an unparalleled source of information. His gracious, charming, self-assured stage image destined him initially for young-lover roles, but this image soon became the essential foil to Molière's own comic performance: Molière played far more scenes with La Grange than with any other actor, and the list of the pairs they undertook—Alceste-Philinte, Arnolphe-Horace, Sganarelle-Don Juan, Jourdain-Dorante —suggests how essential La Grange was to the development of Molière's comic vision.   RWH

Lahr, Bert (1895–1967) American comic actor. Born Irving Lahrheim in New York, Lahr entered *burlesque at 15. He began in a series of 'Crazy Kid' acts and stepped into *vaudeville in 1921 with a sketch featuring his wobbly, mock-heroic singing and rubbery physical presence. The 1927 Broadway revue *Harry Delmar's Revels* led to featured casting in *Hold Everything* (1928) and his first film appearance in 1930. Despite international success as the Cowardly Lion in *The Wizard of Oz* (1939), Lahr was rarely used effectively by Hollywood. His greatest stage success was also 1939 in the Cole *Porter *musical *Du Barry Was a Lady,* playing a men's room attendant who dreams he is Louis XV. In addition to roles in musicals, *revues, and classical *comedies, Lahr played Estragon in the American première of *Beckett's *Waiting for Godot* (1956).   MAF

Lai, Stan (1954–) Taiwanese playwright, director, and *producer, born in the US. In 1984 he founded his own theatre group, Performance Workshop, and since then has consistently staged some of the most exciting theatre in the Chinese-speaking world. He makes extensive use of *collective *improvisation and is particularly adept at *comedy. His innovative blending of high art and popular Taiwanese culture makes his productions—mostly about life in contemporary Taiwan—attractive even for the international *audience. In addition to over 200 episodes of a groundbreaking television comedy, Lai has created numerous original plays, some of which have gone on overseas *tours, and directed many more. Especially popular are *Plucking Stars* (1984), and *Pining . . . In Peach Blossom Land* (1986). The latter was made into the award-winning film *The Peach Blossom Land* (1992), with Lai as director. The new millennium witnessed a more reflective mood in Lai, as he explored the themes of death, compassion, and religion, such as his seven-hour *Dream-like Dream* (2000) and *Stories for the Dead* (2007).   MPYC

lakhon (*lakon*) Dramatic term used in South-East Asia. In **Cambodia** *lakhon* means drama or theatre, and variously includes court or classical *dance, all-male *masked dance-drama, folk opera with stylized movement, *lakhon niyey* or Western-influenced spoken drama, and forms of *shadow puppet theatre. In **Laos** *lakhon fon* describes a dance-drama, part of a shared cultural tradition with Thailand and Cambodia, in which *costumed dancers with elaborate headpieces, and sometimes masks, act out a story through dance and *mime, accompanied by a classical music ensemble. Today taught at the national school, *lakhon fon* is promoted for the international community. Short dance-dramas are performed for diplomats and tourists in major cities of Vientiane and Luang Prabang and at international festivals. In **Thailand**, *lakon* first appeared in the early fifteenth century. There are four main styles. (*a*) *Lakon chatri* is the oldest and simplest dance-drama form with links to animistic practices and spirit worship, traditionally done by an all-male troupe. The repertoire is based on *jataka* (tales of Buddha's incarnations) and local stories. (*b*) *Lakon nok* developed as a refinement of *lakon chatri*. While the performers do not sing, they still improvise dialogue and dance to lyrics from off-stage singers. *Lakon nok* went into decline in the early twentieth century and is now rarely performed. (*c*) *Lakon nai* developed around the early eighteenth century from court *ritual dances and short dance-plays which were combined with elements from *khon and *lakon nok*. Similarities

to Khmer court dance forms are apparent. It is considered the finest form of Thai theatre as it incorporates literature, music, dance, and costume, and uses dancers who were once ladies at court. Now presented only by women, in the past it was performed by men as well. Based on the Javanese legend of *Inao*, *lakon nai* is chiefly dance with a few verse lines. (*d*) *Lakon pantang*, emerging in the mid-nineteenth century, is a *variety theatre whose stories, characters, songs, and dances were greatly influenced by the mosaic of cultures brought by early migrants to Bangkok. Seen as a departure from earlier traditions, it is a derivation of *lakon nok* and relies upon the same structure as the traditional form.   SV

La Mama Experimental Theatre Club Founded in New York by Ellen Stewart (1920–2011) in 1961 as a basement gallery by day and shoestring performance venue by night, within five years La Mama was at the centre of the *Off-Off-Broadway movement. Its first production was an adaptation of a *Williams short story about a male prostitute entitled *One Arm* (1962). After a period of plays by *O'Neill, *Pinter, *Arrabal, *Ionesco, and other established playwrights, La Mama began nourishing most of the important *avant-garde artists of the 1960s. Stewart helped launch the careers of a generation of American playwrights, including Lanford *Wilson, *Shepard, *Terry, *Van Itallie, *Bullins, and *Ludlam. Wilson's *Balm at Gilead* (1966), a hyper-*realistic portrait of the emergent New York counter-culture, quickly established La Mama at the forefront of controversial, 'hip' theatre. The following year wider *audiences could see the film *Three Plays from La Mama* (1967) which showcased Van Itallie's *Pavane*, Shepard's *Fourteen Hundred Thousand*, and Paul Foster's *The Recluse*.

La Mama also fostered the work of innovative directors and actors. Tom O'Horgan, who directed many of the company's early productions, including an all-male version of *Genet's *The Maids* (1964), transplanted the La Mama style to Broadway with the *musical *Hair* (1968). *Chaikin's *Open Theatre staged several productions, including Megan Terry's *Viet Rock* (1966), and the company created shock waves with the first American showing of *Grotowski's Polish Laboratory Theatre in 1969. Since then, La Mama has supported pioneering work by *Şerban, *Mabou Mines, Spiderwoman Theater, the Pan Asian Repertory Theatre, *Split Britches, Ping *Chong, Ubu Repertory Theatre, and others. Despite dwindling support from the National Endowment for the Arts after the culture wars of the 1990s, by the end of the decade La Mama had staged almost 2,000 productions and received numerous awards for its development of playwriting and performance. It has since received a major grant and continues in operation. JAB

Lampe, Jutta (1943–) German actress. After training in Hamburg she joined the Bremen Theatre in the late 1960s. Here she met *Stein, playing Leonore in his legendary production of *Goethe's *Torquato Tasso* (1969). She was a founding member of the Berlin *Schaubühne and became one of its most important actors. Significant roles in Stein productions include Solveig in *Peer Gynt* (1971), the Doctor in *Gorky's *Summerfolk* (1972), Rosalind in *As You Like It* (1979), Masha in *The Three Sisters* (1984), and *Racine's *Phèdre* (1987). In 1990 she played the title role in Robert *Wilson's production of *Orlando*, for which she was voted best actress of the year (for the second time). Cinema work includes two films with Margarete von Trotta. Lampe's *acting ranges from finely observed psychological *realism to highly stylized classical declamation. CBB

Langham, Michael (1919–2011) English director who began his career while a prisoner of war in Europe. After the war he served as *artistic director of the *Birmingham Rep and the *Citizens' Theatre. Freelance assignments included *Julius Caesar* at the *Shakespeare Memorial Theatre (1950) and *Othello* at the *Old Vic (1951). In 1955 *Guthrie invited Langham to Canada's *Stratford Festival, and the next season Langham succeeded him as artistic director. Langham gradually won the company's admiration and built its reputation internationally. His productions there, admired especially for their mastery of movement on Stratford's thrust stage, included *Henry V* (1956), *Romeo and Juliet* (1960), *Coriolanus* (1961), *Love's Labour's Lost* (1961), *Cyrano de Bergerac* (1962), *Timon of Athens* (1963), *King Lear* (1964), and *The Government Inspector* (1967). Langham served as artistic director of the *Guthrie Theatre in Minneapolis (1971–7), where he restored that company's flagging fortunes, and headed the drama division of New York's Juilliard School (1978–92). His busy freelance career included productions with the *Chichester Festival, *Royal Shakespeare Company, and *National Theatre. DWJ

Langner, Lawrence See THEATRE GUILD; WASHINGTON SQUARE PLAYERS.

Langtry, Lillie (1853–1929) British actress. In 1881 she separated from her husband, and in the same year became one of the first society ladies to appear on the professional stage when she played Kate Hardcastle in *Goldsmith's *She Stoops to Conquer*. She briefly joined the *Bancroft company, after which she founded her own company and made her New York debut in 1883 in *Taylor's *comedy *An Unequal Match*. She *toured America with great success. Although a limited actress, Langtry was a shrewd entrepreneur and self-publicist. Her role as Mrs Trevelyan in *Grundy's *The Degenerates* (1899), a story of scandal in high society, reflected her personal life which involved a number of public love affairs, including a long-standing liaison with the Prince of Wales, the future Edward VII. Langtry's other celebrated roles included Rosalind and Lady Teazle. SF

Lansbury, Angela (1925–) Anglo-American actress. English born, sent to America to escape the Blitz, she began her acting career with the film *Gaslight* (1944), for which she received an Academy award nomination, her first of three. She made 21 films before her 1957 Broadway debut in *Hotel Paradiso*, followed by *A Taste of Honey* (1960). She reached stage stardom in a series of *musicals in the 1960s and 1970s—*Anyone Can Whistle*, *Mame*, *Dear World*, *Gypsy*, and *Sweeney Todd*—winning Tony awards for the last four. In 1984 she began a twelve-year run as Jessica Fletcher in the television series *Murder, She Wrote*, all the while continuing her film work. In a career stretching from ingénue to dowager, from elegant *heroine to depraved *villainess, she has displayed durability and flexibility, as well as a highly admired work ethic. JD

Lao She (1899–1966) Chinese novelist and playwright, pen-name of Shu Sheyu. By the time Lao She turned to plays he was one of the best-known writers in China, having started his career in 1926 while teaching Chinese at the University of London. His first play, *The Remaining Fog*, was written in 1939 as a *satire of the corruption in the Chinese-controlled south-west during the war. Although immature in dramatic technique, the play received wide acclaim for its *dialogue and satire, trademarks Lao had exhibited in his novels. This was followed by about ten more plays written during the war. Between 1946 and 1950 he lived in the USA, where he wrote and supervised the translation of several of his novels. His best plays, including *Dragon Beard Ditch* (1951) and *Teahouse* (1957), were written after his return to China. Using a teahouse as the backdrop to life in Beijing between 1910 and the 1940s, the latter has become a classic of modern Chinese theatre. Abused by Red Guards during the Cultural Revolution, he drowned himself in a Beijing lake. SYL

Larivey, Pierre de (c.1540–1619) French playwright. Italian by birth, Larivey was the most significant comic dramatist before Pierre *Corneille and the author who acclimatized Italian *commedia erudita* to Gallic culture. Inspired by performances of the *touring *Gelosi troupe, he published a collection of six *comedies in 1579 and a further three in 1611. Adapting Italian models, Larivey relocated these plays in France and created an original colloquial Gallic comic prose style for them. Whether his work reached the public stage in its own day is uncertain, but it was widely read: five new editions of the 1579 collection appeared during his lifetime. In his best-known comedy, *The Ghosts* (1579), Larivey transposes to a bourgeois Paris context Lorenzino de' Medici's *Aridosia* (1536), a play in turn adapted from two Plautine comedies *Aulularia* and *Mostellaria*, and *Terence's *Adelphi*. There is evidence of both Larivey and *Plautus in *Molière's *The Miser* (1668).   JG

L'Arronge, Adolf (Adolf Aronsohn) (1838–1908) German *manager and dramatist. L'Arronge trained as a musician and worked as a composer and conductor at various theatres. In 1881 he purchased the Friedrich-Wilhelmstädtische Theater in Berlin, which he managed from 1883 to 1894. Under the name *Deutsches Theater he established it as a leading forum for dramatic literature, both classical and contemporary, with star actors such as *Kainz and *Sorma. L'Arronge was also a highly successful author of sentimental *comedies, the best known of which is *Mein Leopold*.   CBB

La Rue, Danny (Daniel Patrick Carroll) (1927–2009) Irish *female impersonator and popular entertainer. He began performing in troop entertainments while in the Royal Navy before working in British *regional repertory and *variety theatre. He made his London debut in *revue at the Irving Theatre, and by 1955 was a *cabaret star at Winston's Club. In 1964 he opened his own nightclub, the Danny La Rue Club, in Hanover Square. On stage he appeared in *Danny La Rue at the Palace* (1970), as Dolly Levi in *Hello, Dolly!* in the West End and on Broadway, and as numerous *pantomime dames, notably in *Queen Passionella and the Sleeping Beauty* (1969). Bob Hope described him as 'the most glamorous woman in the world'.   AS

Laterna Magika Czech performance organization, a *multimedia combination of theatre and film rhythmically organized and synchronized. Relying on a complex structure of music, sound, and visual images, and the interaction of the bodies of performers with their ephemeral images, it was conceived by the director Alfréd *Radok and the *scenographer *Svoboda. The first Laterna

Magika programme was shown at the Expo 58 in Brussels as an entertaining piece of state publicity. A more ambitious second programme was banned and Radok forced out. Self-supporting and headed by Svoboda after 1973, Laterna Magika was one of the Czech National Theatre companies between 1973 and 1992. Its live performers are *dancers.   ML

Laube, Heinrich (1806–84) German dramatist, critic, and director. Laube came to prominence as a journalist and member of the radical writers' group Junges Deutschland. He was imprisoned in 1837 for political activities and his writings were banned. By the time he became a member of the 1848 Frankfurt National Assembly, his views had mellowed and his interests chiefly focused on the stage. From 1849 to 1867 he was *artistic director of the *Burgtheater in Vienna, where he was a proponent of *realistic staging and paid utmost attention to textual fidelity. He combated virtuoso *acting, encouraging actors to play to each other rather than the *audience. He discouraged the opulent scenery popular at the time, considering it a distraction from the text. He also wrote many plays, the most interesting of which is *Die Karlsschüler* (1846), dealing with *Schiller's school years and the writing of *The Robbers*. His writings on the theatre were also influential.   CBB

Lauder, Harry (1870–1950) Scottish actor. Lauder became the highest-paid performer of his time as an international *music-hall star. He created a sensation in London in 1900, perfecting *monologues, a wide variety of broadly drawn Scottish caricatures, and singing Scottish songs. Some of the songs he wrote himself, including his signature tunes 'Roamin' in the Gloamin' and 'I Love a Lassie'. Knighted in 1919 for his part in organizing troop entertainments during the First World War, Lauder's act appealed not just to the domestic market but to the Scottish *diaspora and beyond, and he *toured the USA, Canada, and Australia almost annually from 1907.   AS

laughter Indication, by sound or action, of amusement. Laughter is the expected response of the *audience to a comic moment or scene and evidence that the *comedy has been successful. Dramatic theories of comedy have necessarily paid attention to laughter. Cicero provides discussion of the rhetorical strategies that might stimulate laughter through language. The *Tractatus Coislinianus* (generally believed of late Greek or early Roman origin) considers laughter to be the *cathartic effect of comedy, purging the emotions. Laughter at the expense of the wrongdoer or fool is the means of restoring appropriate social decorum in a comedy.

Early eighteenth-century dramatic theorists debated laughter following from Thomas Hobbes's claim that comic pleasures came from a sense of intellectual security relative to the experience of others. Thus comedy was seen as morally bankrupt and laughter merely the result of ridicule. Instead of the ridicule of comic *characters, *Steele argued for more sober and polite 'mirth'. With the comedies of *Terence as his examples, Steele suggested a reform of comedy that would take as its goal sympathy and admiration rather than ridicule, sentiment rather than laughter. George Meredith's essay 'On the Idea of Comedy' (1877) categorizes the 'powers of laughter' into various sub-groups: *satire, irony, and humour. Satire is the cruellest because it affords so little sympathy with the object of the laughter, whereas humour is the kindest and the pity it can evoke may even be strong enough to dispel laughter altogether.

Henri Bergson's discussion of laughter in 'Le Rire' (1900) has been particularly influential, proposing that laughter is a weapon used by society to intimidate others. He concludes by describing it as 'a froth with a saline base'—initially pleasurable but ultimately bitter-tasting. Laughter occasionally takes place on stage as a reaction to moments of extreme *tragedy and horror (what Freud might describe as a defence mechanism). Some of the most famous examples appear in *early modern plays—in Shakespeare's *Titus Andronicus*, confronted with the severed heads of two of his sons, the rape and mutilation of his daughter, as well as his own severed hand, Titus responds to his brother's threats with the line 'Ha, ha, ha!' Asked by Marcus (his brother) why he laughs, Titus responds, 'Why, I have not another tear to shed.' *See also* APPLAUSE.   SBe

Laughton, Charles (1899–1962) English actor and director. He worked with *Komisarjevsky in his groundbreaking seasons of Russian plays in 1926, and made his first appearance in New York in 1931 as Hercule Poirot in an adaptation of *Christie's *The Alibi*. He returned to England in 1933 to act at the *Old Vic under *Guthrie, playing Angelo in *Measure for Measure*, Prospero, Macbeth, and Canon Chasuble in *Wilde's *The Importance of Being Earnest*. From 1932 he spent most of his time in America creating the roles on film for which he became famous, including Bligh in *Mutiny on the Bounty* (1935) and Quasimodo in *The Hunchback of Notre Dame* (1940). In later life he collaborated with *Brecht on the first production in English of *Galileo* (Los Angeles, 1947), and

his own production of *The Caine Mutiny Court Martial* (New York, 1954). Laughton revelled in fleshy, often cruel parts which allowed him to demonstrate his abilities as a *character actor oscillating between sensuality and vulnerability.VEE

Laurents, Arthur (1918–2011) American playwright, librettist, and director. Laurents reached Broadway with his first play, *The Home of the Brave* (1945). Subsequent successes included *The Time of the Cuckoo* (1952) and *A Clearing in the Woods* (1957). At the same time he was writing screenplays for Hollywood, including *Rope* (1948) and *Anastasia* (1956). His career took yet another direction when he wrote the libretto for two successful *musicals: *West Side Story* (1957) and *Gypsy* (1959). He also began to direct, starting with his own play, *Invitation to a March* (1960). In 1962 he began directing musicals with *I Can Get It for You Wholesale*, continuing with *Anyone Can Whistle* (1964), for which he also wrote the libretto. Further screenplays include *The Way We Were* (1973) and *The Turning Point* (1977), while additional plays are *The Radical Mystique* and *My Good Name* (both 1997). He directed a revival of *West Side Story* on Broadway in 2009.   JD

Lavelli, Jorge (1931–) Argentinian director. Trained as an actor in Buenos Aires' independent theatre movement, Lavelli went to Paris on a scholarship in 1960, winning recognition three years later for his staging of *Gombrowicz's *The Wedding*. His name has since been associated with highly visual, *ritualistic productions of plays by *Arrabal, *Ionesco, Shakespeare, and *Goethe, but also the works of fellow Argentinian expatriate *Copi (including *Diary of a Dreamer*, 1967, and *An Inopportune Visit*, 1988). In the 1970s Lavelli began staging *operas. He relies on an aesthetic closer to *Beckett than *Brecht, privileging situations over words, truth over verisimilitude, and theatricality over text. After 25 years of nomadic freelancing, Lavelli directed France's new Théâtre Nationale de la Colline from 1987 until his retirement in 1997. He continues to work in Buenos Aires and other major cities and to direct his long-lived troupe Méchant Théâtre.   JGJ

Lawrence, D. H. (David Herbert) (1885–1930) English writer. Only two of Lawrence's eight plays were produced in his lifetime, *The Widowing of Mrs Holroyd* (1910, produced 1920), a *realist study of a mining community, and his last play *David* (1927), a biblical epic. Five of the others were written before 1914 and explore concerns similar to his autobiographical novel *Sons and Lovers* (1913), while *Touch and Go* (1919) drew upon and anticipated the publication of his novel *Women in Love* (1921). Lawrence's plays were revived after a successful performance of his first play *A Collier's Friday Night* (1906) at the *Royal Court in London in 1965. Two years later the same company produced *The Daughter-in-Law* (1912), and in 1968 presented a season of these two plays with *The Widowing of Mrs Holroyd*. The *comedies *The Merry-Go-Round* (1910) and *The Fight for Barbara* (1912) were first performed in 1973 and 1967 respectively.   SF

Lawrence, Gertrude (1898–1952) English singer, dancer, and comedy actress who had a glittering career, chiefly in the USA. She appeared in *musicals, plays, and minor *revues in London before she joined André Charlot's revues in 1916, making her Broadway debut in 1924 in one of these. In 1926 she starred in George and Ira *Gershwin's *Oh, Kay!* (1926), which transferred to London the next year, and in 1928 appeared in their *Treasure Girl*. Her signature performance was as Amanda in *Coward's *Private Lives* (1931), a role written for her, which she played opposite Coward's Elyot and *Olivier's Victor. Her greatest triumph was as Liza Elliot in the Moss *Hart-Kurt *Weill musical *Lady in the Dark* (1941). Her last stage role was in *The King and I* (1951). She appeared in a handful of films, including a memorable performance as Amanda Wingfield in *The Glass Menagerie* (1950).   AS

Lawrence, Jerome (1915–2004) and **Robert E. Lee** (1918–94) American playwrights. Lawrence and Lee formed a writing partnership in 1942. Prominent in writing for radio, they made their Broadway debut with the *musical *Look, Ma, I'm Dancin'!* (1948). Their next theatrical work was *Inherit the Wind* (1955), presented at Margo *Jones's Theatre '55 in Dallas and quickly produced on Broadway. They scored another success in their adaptation of *Auntie Mame* (1956), and a major triumph in 1966 with the musical *Mame*. Their anti-war play *The Night Thoreau Spent in Jail* (1970) was widely produced across the United States through the American Playwrights Theatre, founded by Lawrence and Lee in 1966 as an alternative to the commercial theatre. Their final success was *First Monday in October* (1978). A strong social consciousness is apparent in all their plays: freedom of speech and thought in *Inherit the Wind* and *The Night Thoreau Spent in Jail*, *censorship issues in *First Monday in October*.   AW

lazzo (plural: *lazzi*) Italian jargon term from *commedia dell'arte*, possibly derived from a word meaning a 'lace' or 'link': its meaning might be rendered in English as 'gag', 'number',

'act', or 'routine'. The word emerged during the seventeenth century, and is found in manuscript collections of *scenarios denoting some form of prepared joke. Either a particular mask was given the opportunity to come up with material from his/her own repertoire ('*Zanni does his *lazzi...*'); or a brief shorthand reference (such as 'the *lazzo* of the sponge...') was enough to remind performers of what was involved. Such evidence as we possess suggests that a *lazzo* could be anything from a one-line gag to a complex physical or verbal routine involving many players, which would need separate *rehearsal; but all cases would have implied drawing on a stock of items already stored in the memory, rather than inventing something while on stage.   RAA

LeCompte, Elizabeth (1941–) American director. As *artistic director of the *Wooster Group, LeCompte is a major figure in international theatre practice. She studied painting at Skidmore College and considers herself as much a visual artist as a theatrical one. With Spalding *Gray she moved to New York where Gray's connection with the *Open Theatre under *Chaikin spurred LeCompte's interest in theatre; in 1970 both joined *Schechner's *Performance Group. LeCompte was heavily influenced by Schechner's use of multiple materials and sources, from books and films to the actors' own experiences. Growing disillusioned with Schechner, in 1974 LeCompte, Gray, and other Performance Group members started creating their own work and in 1980 formed the Wooster Group. Non-linear and sensorially dense, LeCompte's productions emphasize process over a finished product—she banned reviews of Wooster Group shows until the late 1990s—and have generated significant controversy. She directs all Wooster Group productions.   KF

Lecoq, Jacques (1921–99) French teacher and theorist. Beginning as a teacher of physical education, Lecoq became one of the world's most influential theatre teachers in the second half of the twentieth century. Continuing the work of *Copeau's École du Vieux-Colombier (which he learned from Jean *Dasté), Lecoq emphasized the use of *masks in actor training. He taught for eight years in Italy, first in Padua, and later in Milan, where he founded (with *Strehler) the school of the Piccolo Teatro. Lecoq's school in Paris was a magnet for students of *mime, *physical theatre, and masks from 1956 until his death. There he developed the use of the 'neutral mask', a concept he learned from Dasté and, still following Copeau's example, brought the *clown back into the theatre. While not primarily a performer, Lecoq's work demonstration entitled 'Everything Moves' was considered by many to be a brilliant piece of theatre. His influential students included *Mnouchkine, Simon *McBurney, and the Swiss masked troupe Mummenchanz. TL

Lecouvreur, Mlle (Adrienne Couvreur) (1692–1730) French actress. Lecouvreur played at the court of the Duc de Lorraine before being admitted to the *Comédie-Française in 1717. She turned her slight build, frail constitution, and limited vocal range to advantage, developing a playing style in which emotional sincerity and simplicity of expression supplanted the traditional sing-song artificiality and howling. Seeing in her a kindred spirit anxious to emphasize the emotional content of a text rather than form, *Baron emerged from retirement in 1720 to act with her for eight years. Although she played regularly in *comedy her real talent was for the *tragedies of *Racine, Pierre *Corneille, and *Voltaire. She died in the arms of Voltaire, a fervent admirer whose Artémire (1720) and Mariamne (*Hérode et Mariamne*, 1724) she had created, and the Maréchal-Comte Maurice de Saxe, who had been her lover since 1720. JG

Lee, Canada (Leonard Conegata) (1907–52) *African-American actor, who was a boxer and musician before turning to the stage. While leading a band in 1934, he auditioned for a Harlem production of *Brother Mose*, and later played Banquo in *Welles's *'voodoo' *Macbeth* (1936). Several other New York roles followed, including one in *Stevedore*, as the Emperor Christophe in *Haiti* (1938), and, on Broadway with Ethel *Waters, in *Mamba's Daughters* (1939). Two years later he achieved great critical success as Bigger Thomas in the stage version of Richard Wright's *Native Son*, a role that stands as an indicator of Lee's commitment to political theatre and social causes. In classical works he was Caliban in Margaret *Webster's production of *The Tempest* (1945) and Bosola (in whiteface) in *The Duchess of Malfi* (1946). His last great role was on film, as the lead in *Cry the Beloved Country* (1951). BBL

Lee, Eugene (1939–) American *scenographer. Lee began a career-long partnership with director Adrian Hall as resident designer at Trinity Repertory Company, at Dallas Theatre Centre, and elsewhere. Among their dozens of collaborations was *Baraka's *Slave Ship* (1969) in New York. Lee pioneered an iconoclastic and innovative approach to design that rejected *illusionistic scenery in favour of rough-hewn environments that emphasized intimacy. His designs use raw, natural materials—unpainted wood, scrap metal, dirt—and ramps, catwalks, scaffolding, and platforms to create multiple playing areas that penetrate or surround the *auditorium. For *Brook, he designed *Orghast* (1971) at the Shiraz Festival in Iran and *Handke's *Kaspar* (1980) in Paris. He won Tony awards for *Candide* (1974) and *Sweeney Todd* (1979), both directed by Harold *Prince, and designed the *Boublil and Schönberg *musical *The Pirate Queen* (2006). In television, Lee created the industrial set for *Saturday Night Live* and served for many years as the show's production designer. STC

Lee, Hugh (1955–) Taiwanese playwright, director, and actor. After a successful early career on stage and television, Lee founded the Ping-Fong Acting Troupe in 1986 and started directing his own work. He has written over 40 plays and 100 television scripts. Most of his plays are *satirical *comedies about urgent social and political issues. Zany in argument, irreverent in tone, stirring in effect, and with the *dialogue and *action criss-crossing the realms of *farce and the *absurd, Lee's productions—at once prizewinners and box-office successes—have popularized theatre in Taiwan. With the profits Lee set up Ping-Fong branches outside Taipei and runs training courses. Lee has taken his productions on overseas *tours since 1992. Particularly well received have been *National Salvation Corporation Ltd.* (1991), *The Classified* (1992, in which he played 22 *characters), *West of Yangkuan* (1994), and *Shamlet* (1994, 1996), a *parody of Shakespeare. MPYC

Lee, Ming Cho (1930–) American designer. Born in Shanghai, Lee entered America as a student in 1949, eventually moving to New York as apprentice in Jo *Mielziner's studio. His first credits were in *regional theatre and *Off-Broadway. In 1962 he became resident designer for the *New York Shakespeare Festival, a position he held for more than a decade. With low budgets for scenery, Lee created sets that were sculptural and textural, using natural materials consciously and forcefully, avoiding the painted pictorial in favour of *environmental settings. His style broke new ground, particularly in classic plays and *opera. Lee moved easily from Broadway to noted regional theatre and important opera companies in America and Europe. As a teacher since 1968 at the Yale School of Drama, he has influenced a generation of young American designers. Among the high achievements of his career have been his designs for *Little Murders* (1967) and *K2* (1983) on Broadway; *Electra* (1964) and *Hair* (1967) for the

New York Shakespeare Festival; *Angels in America* (1996) for the Dallas Theatre Center; and *Khovanschchina* (1985) for the Metropolitan Opera.   MCH

Lee, Nathaniel (*c.*1648–1692) English playwright. After a brief acting career (1672–3), Lee turned to playwriting and between 1674 and 1683 produced, besides two plays in collaboration with *Dryden, eleven *tragedies marked by rapid and bloody *action, emotional tension, and spectacular stage effects. Failures were equally interspersed with popular successes. *Lucius Junius Brutus* (1680), arguably his finest play, was banned on political grounds after six performances. *The Princess of Cleve* (1680–3) was a savage attack on *heroic drama and sex *comedy. *The Rival Queens* (1677), Lee's greatest success, is a relatively restrained blank verse tragedy whose contrasted female *characters, acted among others by Elizabeth *Barry and Anne *Bracegirdle, were echoed in Dryden's *All for Love* (1677), and became a dramatic stock-in-trade. Lee spent four of his last six years insane and died in obscurity.   RWV

Lee, Robert E. *See* LAWRENCE, JEROME.

Le Gallienne, Eva (1899–1991) American actress, director, *producer, and translator. Born in London and trained at *Tree's *acting academy, Le Gallienne went to the United States in 1915. She achieved fame in the *Theatre Guild production of *Molnár's *Liliom* (1921) and continued as a leading Broadway actress until founding the Civic Repertory Theatre in 1926. This ambitious company, often featuring Le Gallienne in leading roles, her *direction, or her translations of *Ibsen and *Chekhov, presented 37 plays between 1926 and 1936 when its chronic financial shortfalls forced closure. Le Gallienne went on to co found two other short-lived *repertory companies, to act in *regional productions and *tours, and to perform on Broadway in star vehicles such as the 1961 revival of Maxwell *Anderson's *Elizabeth the Queen* (1930). Her last appearance was in a 1982 revival of her adaptation of *Alice in Wonderland* (1932).   MAF

legitimate drama A term applied in the first half of the nineteenth century to English 'traditional' drama. The 1737 *Licensing Act specified that only *Drury Lane and *Covent Garden could perform spoken drama. By the late eighteenth and early nineteenth centuries other London theatres had sprung up which were permitted to play 'illegitimate' drama: *melodrama, *musical pieces, *burletta. The 'legitimate' meant, in contrast, Shakespeare, *Jonson, and the older drama

tists, and new *tragedies, *comedies, and *farces, all 'regular' forms with traditions back to the sixteenth and seventeenth centuries. Conservative critics considered it to be the true English drama, and the 'illegitimate' was decried as debasing the heritage of Shakespeare, Jonson, and *Sheridan. After 1843 and the Theatres Regulation Act, whereby any theatre could play any kind of drama it wished, subject to the *censorship powers of the Lord Chamberlain, the distinction between 'legitimate' and 'illegitimate' ceased to have any meaning. *See also* PATENT THEATRES.   MRB

legong Classical Balinese dramatic *dance performed by two or three pre-pubescent girls. According to court chronicles, it was created by royal commission in the late eighteenth century. It combines elements of older traditions, taking music, choreography, and story material from *gambuh, and movement vocabulary from the trance dance *sanghyang dedari. The story typically centres on the tale in which Princess Rangka Sari is kidnapped by King Lasem. The dancers do not speak; the text is delivered by singers, accompanied by the gamelan orchestra. Dancers are dressed in tightly wrapped skirts and elaborate headdresses. Outstanding features are expressive eye movements and the use of fans with the fast, precise dance movements. Originally a court tradition, it became popular in the villages in the twentieth century and is performed during temple festivals. Shorter versions of *legong*, often performed by adult women, have become popular for tourist entertainment.   KP

Leigh, Mike (1943–   ) English dramatist and director, famed for his *improvisatory work with actors. His first original play, *The Box Play*, grew out of improvisations at the Midland Art Centre in Birmingham. His television plays for BBC include *Hard Labour* (1973), *Nuts in May* (1975), *Grown Ups* (1980), and *Four Days in July* (1984). He has made several films for Channel 4, including *High Hopes*. An earlier feature film, *Bleak Moments*, was developed from a play originally performed at the Open Space Theatre, London; other stage plays include *Babies Grow Old* (*Royal Shakespeare Company, 1974), *Abigail's Party* (1977), *Ecstasy* (1979), *Goose-Pimples* (1981), *Smelling a Rat* (1988), *Greek Tragedy* (Sydney, 1989), and *Two Thousand Years* (*National Theatre, 2005). Other films include *Life Is Sweet* (1990), *Naked* (1993), *Secrets and Lies* (1995), *Career Girls* (1997), *Topsy-Turvy* (1999), *Vera Drake* (2004), and *Happy-Go-Lucky* (2008).   JTD

Leigh, Vivien (Vivian Mary Hartley) (1913–67) English actress. Best known for winning an Academy award for Scarlett O'Hara in *Gone with the Wind* (1939), and for her troubled marriage of two decades to *Olivier, Leigh's first major success was her portrayal of Henriette in *The Mask of Virtue* in London. At the *Old Vic she was Ophelia (1937), Titania (1937), Lady Teazle in *The School for Scandal* (1949), and Lady Anne in *Richard III* (1949). In 1949 she also appeared as Blanche Dubois in the London production of *A Streetcar Named Desire* and won her second Academy award for the film version (1951). Her performance as Lavinia in *Brook's *Titus Andronicus* at Stratford (1955), opposite Olivier, was striking and unforgettable.   TK

Leighton, Margaret (1922–76) English actress who had a successful career as a leading lady in stage plays and films and later easily adapted to roles of older eccentric and utterly knowing women. In the 1940s Leighton joined the *Old Vic under *Olivier and *Richardson. She was in their première production of *Priestley's *An Inspector Calls* and in *Henry IV, Uncle Vanya, The Critic,* and *Oedipus* on Broadway, all in 1946. Later she returned to Broadway to appear in *Rattigan's *Separate Tables* (1956) and *Williams's *Night of the Iguana* (1961), winning Tony awards for each production. Again on Broadway she appeared in *Slapstick Tragedy,* two one-act plays by Williams (1966), and in Mike *Nichols's revival of *The Little Foxes* (1967). Leighton married three times: first to *Reinhardt, then to Laurence Harvey, and finally to Michael Wilding. Her screen career began in 1948 with *The Winslow Boy* and she was nominated for an Oscar for *The Go-Between* (1971).   AS

Leivick, H. (Halpern) (1886–1962) Russian-American poet and dramatist. After seven years in the Tsar's prisons for revolutionary activity, Leivick escaped in 1913 to settle in New York, where he became a leading Yiddish writer. Two of his major plays are situated in the garment district: *Rags* (1921), and *Shop,* produced by Jacob *Ben-Ami (1926); both became Yiddish classics. His plays on revolutionary themes include *Hirsch Leckert* (1928) and *Chains* (1930), but his best-known work is *The Golem,* about a medieval clay robot made by a Prague rabbi, which premièred in Hebrew translation at the Habima Theatre (Moscow, 1925). Plays written after the Second World War include *In the Days of Job, A Wedding in Fernwald,* and *The Miracle in the Warsaw Ghetto. See* DIASPORA.   EN

Lekain (Henri-Louis Cain) (1729–78) French actor. Lekain was *Voltaire's protégé: his first and last performances, as a young amateur in 1748 and as the century's leading tragedian in 1778, were in plays by the philosopher-playwright. During a 28-year career at the *Comédie-Française he played 178 roles in plays by 65 different authors. But Lekain—short, bow-legged, unattractive, with a harsh voice—was neither shaped for heroic or romantic roles, nor particularly inclined to comic ones. Rather his passionate, gestural playing style, marked by powerful pauses and eloquent business, drew him towards Voltaire's *melodramatic *tragedies, and he played in twenty of them, scoring spectacular successes as Gengis-Kan (*The Orphan of China,* 1755), Arsace (*Sémiramis,* 1748), and Orosmane (*Zaïre,* 1732). In the 1750s, with Mlle *Clairon's support, Lekain pioneered the introduction of a 'new *realism' in several aspects of stage production. He sought to replace conventional tragic skirts, wigs, and gloves with *costumes that offered novel hints of local colour. In 1756 he was the first to argue a case for the establishment of a national *acting school.   JG

Lemaître, Frédérick (1800–76) French actor. Frédérick (from early in his career he used the single name) started in the *boulevard theatres, where he contributed to the success of popular *melodrama. He had higher aspirations, especially with the *romantic dramatists. At the *Odéon and the Porte-Saint-Martin, he created the roles of Napoleon in *Dumas *père's *Napoléon Bonaparte* (1830), Concini in *Vigny's *La Maréchale d'Ancre* (1831), Richard Darlington in Dumas's play of that name (1831), and Gennaro in *Hugo's *Lucrèce Borgia* (1834), before undertaking the two roles which constitute the peak of his achievement. In 1838 he played the title role in *Ruy Blas,* the most successful of Hugo's plays; but although the valet loved by the Queen of Spain provided plenty of scope for Frédérick in terms of temperament, he was probably less happy with the alexandrine verse medium than with prose. The success of *Ruy Blas* was compromised by a quarrel between the co-*managers of the Renaissance Theatre, and the play was taken off after 50 performances. In 1836, however, at the Variétés, he had been able to create, in Dumas's *Kean,* the part of the great English actor who had died only three years earlier, a part written specifically for him, and in which he was to score an unqualified triumph. Dumas's play is subtitled 'Disorder and genius', a label which is just as appropriate to the French actor's life as to that of the Englishman he was portraying. Gautier praised Frédérick's performance by saying that Edmund *Kean 'couldn't have played his own part any better'. The decline in popularity of romantic drama and of old-fashioned melodrama by the middle of the century signalled the decline of Frédérick's success in the theatre, and he died in poverty. WDH

Lenaea Festival of Dionysus at Athens celebrated in Gamelion (late January). To this ancient festival (dated to before 1000 BC) competitions for *tragedy, *comedy, tragic actors, and comic actors were added around 440 BC. The programme included two or three sets of two tragedies, and five comedies.   EGC

Leñero, Vicente (1933–) Mexican writer. A major figure in contemporary letters, Leñero began with *documentary plays which combined his background in journalism with lucid criticism of Mexico's social ills; *Rejected People* (1968) censures religious intolerance and *The Trial* (1971) looks at political assassination and judicial corruption. *The Martyrdom of Morelos* (1982) is a critique of official historical discourse that passes as truth. *The Night of Hernan Cortés* (1992) is a hallucinatory trip back to the horrors of the Spanish Conquest of Mexico as remembered by the conquistador on the eve of his death. Consistently inspired by current events, Leñero took a cue from the 1994 Zapatista Indian rebellion in Mexico's southern state of Chiapas for *We Are All Marcos* (1995). *Nobody Knows Anything* (1988) is a political thriller that was staged simultaneously in nine contiguous spaces. In addition to his original texts, Leñero has adapted Dostoevsky and Dante, as well as his own award-winning novel *The Bricklayers* (1963). *How Quickly It Becomes Late* (1997) and *As the Years Pass* (2000) are bittersweet explorations of ageing.   KFN

Leno, Dan (1860–1903) British comedian, actor, and *dancer. Victorian England's most feted *music-hall comedian and best-loved *pantomime dame started performing at the age of 4. His first adult successes were as a dancer but became associated with comic songs incorporating large amounts of patter, and strongly reliant on the creation of *characters: 'The Grass-Widower', 'The Shopwalker', 'The Recruiting Sergeant', 'The Huntsman', and the determined woman of 'I'll Marry Him', one of his many *female impersonations. He first appeared in pantomime as Dame Durden in *Jack and the Beanstalk* (1886), and starred every Christmas at *Drury Lane between 1888 and 1903, usually as the dame, opposite performers like Marie *Lloyd, Vesta *Tilley, and his most frequent accomplice, Herbert Campbell, whose Falstaffian frame contrasted with the tiny Leno. Scripts were written by the theatre's *manager, Augustus Harris, and later by J. Hickory Wood, who created Leno's most

famous vehicle *Mother Goose* (1902). Leno also appeared in the comic plays *Orlando Dando* (1898), *In Gay Piccadilly!* (1899), and *Mr Wix of Wicknam* (1902). His last years were affected by ill-health and alcoholism, leading to a premature death.   CDC

Lenya, Lotte (1900–81) Austrian actress and singer. Born Karoline Blamauer in Vienna, she moved to Berlin in 1927 where she met and married Kurt *Weill. Her breakthrough came in 1928 with the role of Polly in Weill's collaboration with *Brecht, *The Threepenny Opera*. She advanced to significant roles in productions such as *Oedipus* (1929) and *Danton's Death* (1931) at the Berlin Staatstheater, and a major success was Jenny in the Brecht-Weill *opera *Mahagonny* (1931). Her career in Germany ended in 1933 when she accompanied Weill into exile, performing Anna in the Brecht-Weill *Seven Deadly Sins* in Paris (1933). They divorced shortly afterwards but reunited in 1938 when Weill emigrated to the United States. Lenya launched a second career after Weill's death in 1950 when she devoted herself to popularizing her husband's work in the USA and Europe in concerts and recordings. She also performed in many films (most curiously in the second James Bond adventure, *From Russia with Love*, 1963) and on Broadway (*Cabaret*, 1968). With her highly expressive, if not particularly melodic voice, she defined the tradition of performing Brechtian songs.   CBB

Lenz, Jakob Michael Reinhold (1751–92) German dramatist. A key figure in the *Sturm und Drang* movement, Lenz's first efforts were adaptations of *Plautus which remained unperformed in his lifetime. More important are his plays *Der neue Menoza*, a grotesque *comedy (1774); *The House Tutor* (1774); and *Die Soldaten* (1776). His reputation rests mainly on the latter two works. Both are critical of aspects of the feudal system: private tutors in the one, and the officer caste in the other. Formally, the plays reveal the influence of Shakespeare in the use of short scenes, indifference to the *neoclassical *unities, and rich characterization. His 1774 essay *Notes on Theatre* is an important manifesto of *Sturm und Drang*, particularly in its espousal of individual genius over rationalism and an anti-*Aristotelian preference for *character over *action. Lenz was an important influence on *Büchner, *Grabbe, *Wedekind, and *Brecht. CBB

Leonard, Hugh (1926–2009) Irish playwright and journalist. The adopted son of a gardener in Dublin's suburb of Dalkey, Leonard (pseudonym of John Byrne) had a prolific career writing for television as well as the theatre, in Britain and Ireland. He was a notably skilful adapter, for example in *Stephen D*, his 1962 version of Joyce's *A Portrait of the Artist*. Breaking with the Irish dramatic tradition of rural or small-town settings, Leonard concentrated on the urban and suburban middle classes, as in his *satiric *farce *The Patrick Pearse Motel* (1971). His major international success came with *Da* (1973). Autobiographically based, it centres on the remembered figure of the father who haunts the mind of the returning Irish writer, played on stage both in his older and younger selves. This split time and double casting were repeated in the sequel *A Life* (1979), produced at the *Abbey with a notable central performance by Cyril *Cusack.   NG

Leonov, Leonid (1899–1994) Russian/Soviet novelist and dramatist. His first play, *Untilovsk* (1928), about a Siberian scientist's conversion to Bolshevism, was staged at the *Moscow Art Theatre in 1928, and a dramatization of his novel *The Badgers*, about the ideological contrasts between city and village, had been staged at the Vakhtangov Theatre in 1927. Following a further dramatization of a novel about another scientist, *Skutarevsky* (1934), Leonov composed a Soviet response to *Chekhov's *The Cherry Orchard* in the shape of his quasi-symbolic play *The Orchards of Polovchansk*, in which the sounds of approaching war are heard (MAT, 1939). The same year saw his play *The Snowstorm* banned for ideological incorrectness. His best-known play outside Russia is the war drama *Invasion*, about a released political prisoner who becomes a staunch defender of the Soviet Union (1943). *The Golden Carriage*, set in post-war Russia, was staged at the MAT in 1957, and his novel *The Russian Forest* (1953) was adapted for the stage in 1959. Another play, *An Ordinary Man*, was filmed by Mikhail Romm that year.   NW

Lepage, Robert (1957–) Canadian (Québécois) director, writer, performer, and filmmaker. Lepage's productions combine *physical and visual elements with text and performance and are rich in imagery and sensory appeal. Born in Québec City and trained as an actor there, Lepage joined the experimental troupe Théâtre Repère in 1982, which created its productions collaboratively through *improvisation. Lepage spearheaded an epic, six-hour production, *The Dragon's Trilogy* (1985, revised 2003), which depicted life in three Canadian Chinatowns over the span of 70 years. The show was highly successful internationally. Lepage went on to create a number of *devised pieces, including

Polygraphe and *Tectonic Plates* (both 1988), and solo pieces for himself: *Vinci* (1986), about a young Quebecker on his first trip to Europe, *Needles and Opium* (1991), which drew on Miles Davis and *Cocteau, and *Elsinore*, a version of *Hamlet* (1995). Lepage's productions involve concepts of searching and connecting: his *characters are often on quests for identity and for ideas or experiences which will give them a sense of connectedness. As his career has developed his subject matter has become increasingly international and cross-cultural (*see* INTERCULTURALISM).

Lepage served as *artistic director of the National Arts Centre of Canada from 1990 to 1992. He formed a company to develop and produce his work, Ex Machina, in Québec City in 1994. Ex Machina's projects have included *The Seven Streams of the River Ota* (1994), seven interconnected, hour-long acts which focused on the ideas of devastation and rebirth; *Geometry of Miracles* (1998), about the unlikely overlapping of ideas in the careers of architect Frank Lloyd Wright and mystic Georgi Gurdjieff; and *The Far Side of the Moon* (2000), a solo piece which sets the story of two Québécois brothers forced to confront their differences set against the story of the space race. Recent projects include *La Celestina* in Spanish (Barcelona, 2004) and *The Blue Dragon* (2008). Lepage has directed *operas and plays in many international venues and festivals, and has made several films, including *Le Confessional* (1995), *Possible Worlds* (2001), and *The Far Side of the Moon* (2004).   KF

Lermontov, Mikhail (1814–41) Russian writer. Best known as a poet and for his novel *A Hero of our Time*, Lermontov wrote five plays, none of which was staged in his lifetime, partly because he was exiled to the Caucasus for his poem *Death of a Poet* (1837). Like *Pushkin, the subject of that poem, Lermontov was killed in a duel. Early attempts at playwriting show strong influence of Shakespeare and *Schiller: *The Spaniards* (1830), *People and Passions* (1830), and *The Strange Man* (1831), and his best-known work, *Masquerade* (1835–7). The unfinished *Two Brothers* (1836) was based on autobiographical material. Set in St Petersburg high society, *Masquerade* *melodramatically charts the mounting jealousy of Arbenin towards his innocent wife Nina. The only one of the plays to achieve a stage life, *Masquerade* was finally performed in 1852. A production by *Meyerhold, in 1917 on the eve of the February Revolution, turned the enigmatic *hero and the nightmarish world he inhabits into a metaphor for the uncertainty of the times. Other notable twentieth-century performances retained the richness and controversy which seemed attached to this play, such as at the Vakhtangov Theatre in 1941, and *Vasiliev's controversial version for the *Comédie-Française (1993).   CM

Lerner, Alan Jay (1918–86) and **Frederick Loewe** (1901–88) American lyricist and librettist, and American composer, along with *Rodgers and *Hammerstein the pre-eminent *music-theatre songwriting team of the post-war era. Loewe, born in Germany, the son of an *operetta tenor, was a classically trained piano prodigy who moved to New York in 1924 and learned English while playing piano in clubs. He first reached Broadway in 1938 when he wrote the music for Great Lady, a flop that sent him back to the clubs. A few years later he met Lerner, a wealthy New Yorker who was himself a competent pianist. They first collaborated on What's Up? (1943), a conventional *musical that quickly failed. Their next effort, The Day before Spring (1945), was far from conventional: it investigated the psychology of nostalgia. Encouraged, the team struck gold with Brigadoon (1947), a fantasy of a 200-year-old Scottish town that comes to life for one day every hundred years.

In a pattern which would haunt their collaboration, Loewe, unused to wealth, took time off to enjoy success. Lerner, however, wanted to work, and he teamed with *Weill to write the innovative Love Life (1948). When Loewe was ready to resume, they turned to period Americana with Paint Your Wagon (1951). Their next effort was My Fair Lady (1956), whose early twentieth-century setting and swirling waltzes suited Loewe perfectly, while Lerner, basing his libretto on *Shaw's Pygmalion, had a ready-made structure. My Fair Lady was the biggest hit of the 1950s, setting a long-run record, but Loewe would collaborate with Lerner only twice more. The film Gigi (1958) offered Loewe another opportunity to write in the idiom with which he was most comfortable, but Camelot (1960) was an unpleasant experience for all concerned, and Loewe retired to enjoy his wealth. Lerner continued writing with a string of collaborators, including *Bernstein, but he would never again find the same success. Only one of his six subsequent musicals—On a Clear Day You Can See Forever (1965)—could be called a hit.   JD

Lesage, Alain-René (1668–1747) French playwright and novelist. Lesage went to Paris about 1690, writing *comedies adapted from Spanish plays by *Rojas and Lope de *Vega. His first real successes came in 1707, with The Devil of Crutches, a satirical novel, and a one-act comedy for the *Comédie-Française, Crispin, Rival of his

Master. His next play, Turcaret (1709), is a comic masterpiece, in which the *hero, a nouveau riche tax farmer, finds himself exploited as heartlessly as he exploits others. It is a cynical *satire exposing the self-obsessed materialism of Regency society. Turcaret met with powerful political opposition and was quickly suppressed; reinstated in 1730, it remains a fixture in the repertory. A quarrel with the actors, however, caused Lesage to forsake the Comédie-Française for the Paris fairground theatres, and between 1712 and 1737, either alone or with collaborators, he penned over 100 pieces for them, *opéras-comiques, placard-plays, and *vaudevilles, liberally spiced with sexual innuendo, physical buffoonery, song, and *dance. Lesage continued to write fiction, especially his most famous work, Gil Blas (1715–35).   JG

lesbian theatre Although history contains many examples of women who displayed homoerotic attachments both on and off the stage, the social category 'lesbian' did not emerge until the late nineteenth century. Theatre created by self-identified lesbians and intended primarily for lesbian, *feminist, or *gay *audiences dates to the early 1970s in both the United States and Britain, following the second wave of feminist and gay liberation movements. The form and content of early lesbian theatre was a concurrent, geographically fragmented *community theatre, rather than an organized or centralized movement. Performance texts were largely autobiographical, first-person narratives of the author's struggle to overcome oppressive gender and sex roles. Another popular narrative included a performer's 'coming out' story. In most instances performers assumed an intimate audience of lesbian, gay, or feminist spectators, and the object was to project positive representations of lesbians on stage.

Lesbian theatre in Britain rose out of the fringe theatre movements of the 1960s. Women played a significant role in founding and sustaining London's Gay Sweatshop during the early 1970s, which was a critical moment in this history. Although decentralized and poorly funded, lesbian troupes maintained a fringe presence in Britain through the 1990s. The American equivalent was the WOW Café. Operating on spartan resources, the self-producing artists of WOW included Holly *Hughes, Five Lesbian Brothers, Carmelita Tropicana, Reno, and *Split Britches. The members of Split Britches (Peggy Shaw, Lois Weaver, and Deb Margolin) became the bellwether for feminist and lesbian performance in the late twentieth century, due largely to the lesbian-feminist scholars who claimed WOW Café and its artists as a paramount site of progressive lesbian representation. Performance practices include butch/femme role playing, campy formal elements such as lip-synching *satire and *vaudevillian shtick, an aesthetic shaped by marginalized, cash-poor conditions, and content drawn from current lesbian and feminist politics.

Lesbian representations are now more available in mainstream venues. A number of lesbian playwrights write plays with identifiable lesbian characters, which are produced in America in *regional and *Off-Broadway theatres, starting with Jane Chambers's *Last Summer at Bluefish Cove* (1985) Off-Broadway. Other contemporary lesbian playwrights include Paula *Vogel, Joan Schenkar, Susan Miller, and Carolyn Gage. *See also* GENDER AND PERFORMANCE.   SBM

Lessing, Gotthold Ephraim (1729–81) German dramatist and critic, one of the first German writers to make a living from his pen. Friendship with the philosopher Moses Mendelssohn caused him to write the play *The Jews* (1775). At the same time, in *Theatrical Library* (1754–8) Lessing developed the concept of 'domestic *tragedy' which advocated the use of middle-class *characters as tragic *heroes, and with *Miss Sara Sampson* (1755) he produced one of the most successful examples of this new genre. His *Letters Concerning the Latest Literature* (1759–65) attacked *neoclassical interpretation of the *Aristotelian *unities. By using Shakespeare as a role model, he suggested replacing rigid French aesthetics with a more natural language and freer *dramaturgy, which would focus on the *audience's emotional responsiveness and moral improvement. In 1760 *The Theatre of Mr Diderot* introduced *Diderot to Germany, and his 'Laokoon' essay of 1766 was one of the most important formulations of an Enlightenment aesthetic internationally. In 1767 he became literary adviser of the Hamburg National Theatre, a short-lived *repertory company, writing *Hamburg Dramaturgy* (1767–9), which set the concept of genius against neoclassical dogma, discussed the latest trends in French and English *bourgeois drama, and redefined many central categories of theatre. His critical theories were put into practice in *Minna von Barnhelm* (1767), *Emilia Galotti* (1772), and *Nathan the Wise* (1783), which became his most enduring plays.   GB

Levin, Hanoch (1943–99) Israeli dramatist whose plays are characterized by biting *satire and vivid theatricality. Recurrent themes in his *absurdist *tragicomedies are the shabbiness of everyday life and the vulgarity of human exis-
tence; his *characters, either oppressors or oppressed, are mostly stupid, inept, and cruel. Levin wrote 50 plays, 34 of them staged from 1969 on, mostly directed by him. Much of Levin's work is associated with the Cameri Theatre, where he served as resident playwright. His best-known work includes *You, I, and the Next War* (1970), a sharp political satire that stirred enormous controversy, *Yaacobi and Leidental* (1972), *The Rubber Merchants* (1978), *The Passion of Job* (1981), *The Suitcase Packers* (1981), *The Labour of Life* (1988), *Murder* (1998), and *Funeral* (1999), which he directed from his hospital deathbed.   EN

Lewes, George Henry (1817–78) English playwright and critic. Lewes was a polymath whose professional interests extended to philosophy, physiology—he was professor of physiology in the University of London—sociology, and psychology, as well as biography and literature. From 1854 until his death he was the partner of the novelist George Eliot. Lewes acted with the *Dickens amateurs and in his own *tragedy *The Noble Heart* (1849). He was the drama critic of the *Leader* in the 1850s and wrote essays on drama for the *Pall Mall Gazette*. His *On Actors and the Art of Acting* (1875) is the best book in English on nineteenth-century *acting. Lewes wrote thirteen plays, most of them for the *Vestris–*Mathews *management at the Lyceum. The most interesting is *The Game of Speculation* (1851), adapted from French and containing the popular Victorian dramatic themes of money, social ambition, speculation, and ruin.   MRB

Lewis, Robert (1909–97) American actor and director. Lewis joined the *Group Theatre, becoming known for his eccentric roles. He advocated *Stanislavsky's *acting theories, shifting from *Strasberg's emphasis on emotional memory to *Adler's when circumstances warranted. Eventually he became a leading acting teacher, and with *Kazan and Crawford founded the *Actors Studio in 1947. He also created the Robert Lewis Acting Company in Westchester, New York. His *directing style was called 'poetic *realism', first noted in *My Heart's in the Highlands* (1939). He directed many plays and *musicals, on Broadway and elsewhere, but rarely attempted classical material. His best-remembered Broadway shows are *Brigadoon* (1947), *The Happy Time* (1950), *Miller's version of *Ibsen's *An Enemy of the People* (1950), *Teahouse of the August Moon* (1953), *Witness for the Prosecution* (1953), *Jamaica* (1957), and *On a Clear Day You Can See Forever* (1965).   SLL

Liang Chenyu (Liang Ch'en-yü) (1520–*c*.1593) Chinese playwright, author of *Washing Silk*, the first southern drama (**chuanqi*) written for the newly refined Kunshan musical style. Though he did not enjoy the same high regard as his teacher *Wei Liangfu, Liang broadened Kunshan's appeal by using it in a work that was staged, not simply sung to musical accompaniment. Set in Suzhou in the fifth century BC, *Huansha ji* links its love theme to the theme of national survival, drawing on historical accounts of rivalry between the ancient kingdoms of Wu and Yue to allude to contemporary events, in a manner subsequently imitated by the early Qing playwrights *Hong Sheng and *Kong Shangren. Liang's poignant depiction of the beauty Xi Shi and her lover Fan Li, who forgo personal fulfilment out of devotion to king and country, remained popular onstage until the modern era. CS

Libre, Théâtre Private French company opened in 1887 by Antoine. The Théâtre Libre (Free Theatre) became the home and testing ground of Europe's new drama and the model for independent theatres elsewhere, such as *Brahm's *Freie Bühne (1889), *Grein's *Independent Theatre (1891), and *Yeats's and Lady *Gregory's *Abbey Theatre (1904). More by accident than design, Antoine's theatre became associated with *naturalist drama, although the director himself was more concerned with *realism. He was inspired by the work of the *Meiningen company, particularly in their ensemble *acting and historical exactitude. Antoine's artistic policy was eclectic, and included verse drama, naturalism, *symbolism, and the translation of foreign works (*Strindberg, *Ibsen, *Bjørnson, and *Hauptmann). New writers and new plays by established writers featured heavily but Antoine was unwilling to give authors a second chance, such was his desire for novelty. The company's trademarks included the darkening of the *auditorium, the abolition of *footlights, overhead and side *lighting, three-dimensional scenery, authentic *costumes, and truthfulness of acting. From the outset Antoine's company was privately funded through subscriptions to avoid *censorship. But the rapid turnovers, the burdens of realism, *touring, and the lack of a permanent home (the company moved three times in seven years, crossing the Seine with each move) led to *financial collapse, leaving the company stranded in September 1894 on *tour in Rome. BRS

licensing acts The Stage Licensing Act (1737) transformed the regulation of theatre in Britain and established a system for dramatic *censorship which lasted until 1968. Before this Act, Masters of the Revels had exercised some authority over the licensing and correcting of plays. This authority, however, was compromised by granting theatrical royal *patents for London to *Killigrew and *Davenant at the Restoration of 1660, because the patents holders themselves censored plays performed by their companies. During the early 1730s, moral, religious, and economic opposition to theatres intensified: commentators and pamphleteers denounced *playhouses as nurseries of vice and debauchery which encouraged indiscipline and distracted the lower classes from their work (*see* ANTI-THEATRICAL POLEMIC). But the most immediate catalyst for the Licensing Bill was the determination of Robert Walpole, the Prime Minister, to quash the political *satires at the Little Theatre in the *Haymarket by *Fielding. At a time of great anxiety over public disorder and fears of impending revolution, playhouses became an easy target.

The Licensing Act sought to control theatre in Westminster by limiting performances to those theatres acting under the authority of letters patent or licence from the Lord Chamberlain. In practice, this meant that performances became restricted to the London patent theatres and to the provincial theatres royal in cities such as Bristol, Norwich, and York. Performers at unlicensed playhouses were now treated in accordance with the Vagrancy Act, that is, as rogues and vagabonds. The new legislation effectively outlawed theatres such as Goodman's Fields and Fielding's Little Haymarket: Fielding soon gave up theatrical management to write novels.

The most striking feature of the Licensing Act was the comprehensive system it introduced for the censorship of playscripts. The Act stipulated that all new plays had to be submitted to the Lord Chamberlain's office at least fourteen days before first performance. (In practice, the reading of scripts was undertaken by the Examiner of Plays and his deputy.) *Managers who failed to submit a play were fined £50. The Licensing Act allowed the Lord Chamberlain to forbid any dramatic piece acted 'for hire, gain or reward' anywhere in Great Britain. Successive Lords Chamberlain did indeed ban some plays outright; in many cases, the Examiner insisted on the deletion of particular speeches or entire scenes.

Some managers became adept at circumventing the rules and new places of entertainment opened on the south bank of the Thames and around the East End near the end of the eighteenth century, regulated not by the Lord Chamberlain but rather by annual licence from local magistrates, according to the provisions of the Disorderly Houses Act of 1752. This system unwittingly created a legal loophole which enabled the 'minor theatres' beyond Westminster to stage plays without submitting their play texts for censorship. By the late 1820s the division between the patent theatres and the minor playhouses had all but collapsed, and several controversial productions had drawn attention to the freedom enjoyed by the uncensored theatres beyond Westminster. In 1843, the Theatre Regulation Act, which superseded the Act of 1737, abolished the patent theatres' monopoly over spoken drama. It gave legal recognition to all the London minor theatres, which were henceforth required to submit playscripts for censorship to the Lord Chamberlain's Office, a condition that continued until 1968.   JM

licensing of plays *See* COPYRIGHT.

Liera, Oscar (1946–90) Mexican playwright, director, and actor. Born Jesús Cabanillas Flores, he gained notoriety with his anticlerical *satire Cúcara and Mácara* (1981), which incited violent protests by groups who (erroneously) read into it a defamation of the Virgin of Guadalupe. Beginning as a *realist, Liera ended as a visual and playful playwright whose *characters often travel seamlessly from the real to the magical. In the trilogy · *The Horseman of the Divine Providence* (1984), *The Perverse Fables* (1985), and *The Red Road to Sabaiba* (1986), history, legend, and myth function as an effective means of escape from social injustice.   KFN

lighting The very word theatre, a 'seeing place' (*theatron*), implies that a stage will be lighted somehow. Stage lighting began with simple visibility, but a complex interaction of technical advance, theatrical convention, and aesthetic theory has made light a fully plastic medium, and lighting an art.

Pre-optical lighting The pre-industrial scripted performance traditions about which we know anything—China, India, *Greece, *Rome, *medieval Europe, Korea, Japan, Indonesia—contain many brief accounts of mostly unsuccessful experiments in stage lighting: colouring with reflectors or media, *fireworks, use of natural light (such as the sunrise in *Agamemnon*), rearprojected shadows, and chiaroscuro. But until very recently in theatre history, the main issue regarding light was visibility. Plays were performed during the daytime, outdoors or in covered spaces with large windows. If social circumstances forced theatre indoors or into the night, plays were performed with candles, torches, and lamps as close to the stage as possible. Lighting in these periods was about how per-

formance adapted to the light, not how light was designed for performance.

Early modern discovery of light, 1500–1680 The *early modern period was fascinated with light. *Perspective illustrates the geometry of light: objects in the field of vision have their apparent shapes and sizes because light travels in straight lines through the tiny aperture of the iris. Renaissance painting famously developed the means to depict light, proposing that the kind of light striking an object strongly influenced what it looked like, and noting the visual implications resulting from the fact that sunlight is naturally highly collimated. (The collimation of a beam of light is the extent to which its rays form parallel lines.) The sun is so far away that for practical purposes all light coming from it to the earth is parallel. The results are familiar: sharp, unidirectional shadows in uniform proportion. Although the late Renaissance scene painters did not know how to make bright collimated beams that would mimic sunlight, they understood their desirability. In a fashion analogous to Leonardo's flying machines for which no engines existed, *scenographers between 1545 and 1595 wrote about and drew what stage light ought to be, imagining light for accent, contrast, time of day, and mood, and providing an analytic technique for imitating natural light, for focused and directed coloured beams, the darkened house, concealed sources, dimming, translucent gauze effects, and shuttering in the manner of a modern spotlight.

In his *Second Book of Architecture* (1545), *Serlio not only discusses the use of *bozze*—hollow glasses flat on one side and curved on the other, filled with coloured water or oil, crude versions of the plano-convex lens—but even describes the placement of a torch between a polished barber's basin and *bozze*, very similar to the mid-twentieth-century plano-convex spotlight. *Ingegneri described a flying batten of lamps, that is, the borderlights of a century after; Sabbatini proposed a system for lowering and raising open-ended cylinders over candles for dimming at a distance. *Bozze* were common in Italian theatres; the surviving *bozze* at the Teatro *Olimpico are hemispheric, about 7 cm (2.75 in) in diameter, and are mounted on the backs of painted wings to illuminate scenery further upstage.

The enlightenment discovery of optics, 1680–1820 The lens-grinding industry developed in the seventeenth century, but lenses were small, and thus gathered little of the light around a flame. Theatre lighting practice remained oriented almost entirely toward visibility. It is often asserted that in the Restoration theatre, audience and actors were in equal light. This is an exaggeration. The basic source, a chandelier over the forestage which could be moved on a pulley, was closer to the backcloth than to the galleries when lowered for performance, making the stage somewhat brighter than the house. This effect was increasingly enhanced with *footlights, borderlights, and scene ladders, vertical columns of candles or oil lamps attached to the inside edges of the wings to light the playing area and the wing or drop immediately upstage. By the 1720s many scene ladders were equipped with scene blinds, reflector shades consisting of two nested rotating partial cylinders, usually of tin, surrounding the candle or lamp. The cylinder created an opening which could be aimed, narrowed, or widened, allowing crude direction and dimming. Because self-consuming wicks had not yet been developed, candles required constant snuffing (wick cutting) while they burned, to prevent guttering, in which a too-long wick fell over and melted through the lip, sending the molten wax running uselessly away into a dangerous flammable puddle. Snuffers were vital personnel in a candlelit theatre, and took priority over everything for safety's sake, and guttering candles provoked loud shouts of 'Snuffers!' during performance. While the play continued, snuffers walked onto the stage to trim footlights or to reach for borders and chandeliers with long-handled tools, and crossed between wings upstage as they tended scene ladders and sconces.

The major innovations of the period were the work of scientists in general illumination. Antoine-Laurent Lavoisier (1743–94), known for his work in chemistry, created the *réverbère*, the first conic-section reflector, doubling the delivered light of any one source. Trough-shaped *réverbères*, installed as footlights and borders, considerably brightened the stage, especially relative to the house, and would later form the basis for many of the safety footlights of the gas era. In 1780 Aimé Argand introduced an oil burner that was a threefold improvement in brightness. *Loutherbourg, brought to London as a scene painter by *Garrick, developed a sophisticated display he called the *Eidophusikon* (1781), painted scenes presented under controlled light on a model stage, with Argand lamps, ellipsoidal and parabolic reflectors, and mechanical dimming.

Gas and controllable light, 1790–1890 Some spectators who saw *Beaumarchais's *comedies by candle saw *Scribe's by gas, a tenfold increase in brightness. *Coal gas was a varying, dirty mixture of three flammable gases plus flammable

hydrocarbons, smelled badly, deposited greasy black carbon above the burner, corroded pipes and burners dangerously, but burned eight times more brightly than oil, could be shut off from a distance in a fire, and its already low price was subsidized by the sale of coke and coal tar, the other products of coal distillation. Gasification of stage lighting was complete in London by early 1822, and spread to every other city, worldwide, as soon as there was a gasworks.

At first gas burners simply replaced oil lamps in the same fixtures. By 1830 instruments specific to gas were manufactured, and before 1840 they had nearly reached their final forms. The gas era was also the era of *limelight, which permitted experiments with lensed instruments, but limelight was bright enough to shine through coloured media, enabling colour mixing. Limelight was expensive however, and the limes required much maintenance by skilled labour, sharply limiting its use.

The availability of lighting effects, even the very simple ones of the time, required fading from one set of gaslights to another, which prompted the first unified control systems. Gaslights are brighter depending on how much gas they receive; thus a valve that partially closes a line can be used to dim a light, and for effects, it was most convenient if all the valves were in a central location backstage, called the gas table. By the mid-1860s, new theatres were built with centralized gas tables, but control was difficult and unsophisticated. For safety's sake, no light could be dimmed to black and then reused. Operators had to rely on hand signals or speaking tubes to know what was happening on stage.

Beginning in 1878 at the Lyceum, *Irving introduced a very modern look: a fully darkened house, selective area lighting, routine use of gauzes, colour media, and mixing in limelight, masking by the use of black velvet hung in the dark, colour grouping of footlights, and lacquered-glass colour media. A single gas table cued by the *prompter, and much brighter light everywhere from the new Siemens burners, gave more control over light than ever before.

Electricity and controlled light, 1880–1950 From its first practicality in 1879, the electric incandescent filament was superior to gas. Electricity was intrinsically cleaner (coal gas did not illuminate if it did not emit soot), and had a far better light-to-heat ratio than either gas or limelight. It was also far safer.

In October 1881 Richard D'Oyly Carte reopened the Savoy in London as the first theatre with all-electric lighting. There were immediate complaints that electric light was 'harsh' or 'cold',

But since the light was also much brighter than gas, it could be 'cut down' with red or yellow media without making the stage too dark. Coloured media, either gelatine or glass, thus became much more important, and by 1920 it was rare to see an uncoloured instrument; with electricity colour went from optional to mandatory. When 1,000-watt electric lamps became commercially available in 1913, limelight too vanished. But the habits of gas lingered longer; at first electricity was used mainly to provide a cheaper and brighter version of what had been done with gas.

Until electricity, sources had always been inadequate. Electric lighting made it finally possible to make every part of the stage brilliant and shadowless. *Appia, in *Music and the Art of the Theatre* (1899), stated that colour mixing and contrast were the keys to improved visual acuity, and gave a detailed example applied to *Tristan and Isolde*, the first true lighting concept in published form. Appia was more right than he knew. Experiments by Stanley McCandless in the 1920s revealed that an object surrounded by darkness and lighted by differently coloured collimated beams at plan angles is perceived with greater acuity than in real life. The visual cortex responds to difference rather than to absolute brightness, both for colour and for shape. Visual acuity will be optimal where difference is maximized, that is, where the instruments are at plan angles and gelled in complementary colours at different saturations. Such light, blended by adding a top light, is called 'McCandless lighting', and is used in nearly all theatrical productions worldwide today, enabled by highly specialized directional lamps.

Besides collimated front light, the new lighting required many quick cue changes. In 1900 the only practical form of dimming was to put lamps in series with a variable resistor, a small tank of salt water within which resistance was varied by changing the distance between upper and lower electrodes through cumbersome mechanical cranks. Nonetheless, a small team of technicians could produce the smooth and graceful transitions and seemingly infinite flexibility of *Reinhardt's seminal *Midsummer Night's Dream* (Berlin, 1905), which, with its very large number of smooth light cues, front-of-house lighting, and *cyclorama, was a visual wonder to audiences and finally established the superiority of electricity, for an army of gasmen could not have accomplished anything like it. Extensive experimentation in dimming occurred in the 1920s and 1930s. The all-electric board built by General Electric for Radio City Music Hall permitted a set up four cues ahead, so that very complex transitions of

hundreds of instruments simultaneously changing levels in a few seconds could be accomplished by a single operator.

Art of controlled light, 1950–present After the Second World War, works like *Miller's *Death of a Salesman* and *Williams's *A Streetcar Named Desire* relied upon lighting to make a realistic unit set flexible. Other plays were written that specified lighting designs, and the lighting designer was no longer 'a bloody electrician with notions', as Jean *Rosenthal was called early in her career, but a necessary artist among artists. Significant advances were made in instruments, but the real revolution was in how they were controlled. Though a technician of 1950, if transported to a theatre 50 years later, would recognize nearly everything hanging overhead, the control and dimming system would be an utter enigma, both in what it can do and how it does it. The best computer-driver lighting boards now allow a single operator to preset and control an entire complicated show, the number of light cues theoretically unlimited, the changes effected by touching a button.

Like all design, lighting design is a mixture of art and craft; uninspired but serviceable designs which merely follow the rules abound, but the best modern designers are able to step far beyond, based on a grasp of space, light, script, and production. Ideally the designer takes extensive notes during *rehearsals to identify acting areas and special cues, acquires and analyses copies of the set and *costume renderings for colour, and accumulates extensive pictorial research on the appearance of the light in the locations and times in which the play is set. The designer then draws diagrammatic plans for imitating the real light while modifying it to support visibility, actor and director choices, and set and costume designs.

There is still much remaining to be accomplished. Stage lighting rarely reaches perfect acuity and never does so over the whole area of a stage; colour mixing still is mostly worked out in trial and error after a first rough guess; many cues are still sharply limited by what control systems can accomplish. True perfect lighting over the whole area of a stage, so that the designer's imaginings were executed exactly at every point and acuity was maximal, would require the replacement of large instruments with many thousands of tiny, aimable apertures, covering much of the ceiling of the theatre. Interestingly enough, the hardware for all of this existed at the beginning of the twenty-first century, either in industrial laboratories or off-the-shelf, though usually too expensive for most theatres. Perhaps the lighting revolution that has been nearly continual since 1550 is far from over; perhaps the next phase will see a return to greater simplicity, as the work of some performance experiments suggests. *See also* MULTIMEDIA PER-FORMANCE.   JB

Lillie, Beatrice (Lady Robert Peel) (1894–1989) Canadian comedienne. Born in Toronto, Bea Lillie made her English stage debut in 1914 and her American debut in 1924, dividing a career of some 50 shows between the two countries. Her forte lay in the *revue and solo *cabaret, with a handful of *musicals and plays. Slender and short, she had a long, expressive face, and enjoyed a widespread reputation as the funniest woman in the world. In the 1950s she *toured her award-winning *An Evening with Beatrice Lillie* around the world for several years. Her triumphant stage farewell came on Broadway in 1965 as Madame Arcati in a musicalized version of *Coward's *Blithe Spirit.*   CT

Lillo, George (1693–1739) English author, most famous for his *bourgeois *tragedies *The London Merchant* (1731) and *Fatal Curiosity* (1736). Lillo revolutionized domestic tragedy by eschewing royal courts for the world of masters and apprentices in *The London Merchant*, the story of a good apprentice gone bad. The play was a runaway success during the eighteenth century (it inspired Hogarth's *Industry and Idleness*) and was noted for its psychological power. Criticized more recently for its pious morality and faith in the virtues of bourgeois capitalism, the play expresses widely held beliefs of its day and became a favourite of London masters, who sent their apprentices to the theatres to see its annual performances. *Fatal Curiosity* was not a great success initially but became very popular later in the century, adapted by *Colman the Elder in 1782. It is the story of impoverished parents who kill a lodger for money, only to discover that he was their rich son, returning home incognito. Even with the *ballad opera (*Silvia; or, The Country Burial*, 1730), historical play (*The Christian Hero*, 1735), or Shakespearian romance (*Marina*, 1738), Lillo's interest in temptation and Christian fortitude are evident. *See also* VOLTAIRE.   MJK

limelight When calcium oxide (lime) is heated to incandescence, it gives off bright, almost perfectly white *light. Instruments designed to project that light, the light they cast, and the attention thus created were all called limelight, and term survives in the last sense today. Invented in England in 1816, it was in standard use in the West by about 1855. Though the light could not be sharply focused, its brilliant, warm glow was flattering to

most actors and was sentimentalized after it was replaced by the colder, bluer electric spotlight. JB

Lincoln Center for the Performing Arts An urban renewal project for the upper west side of Manhattan in New York, promoted by John D. Rockefeller III and constructed between 1959 and 1972. Its centrepiece is the Metropolitan Opera House. Among its many other venues for *dance, *music, *opera, theatre, and education is the New York State Theatre (capacity 2,779), designed by Philip Johnson and John Burgee, which opened in 1964 and hosted a number of important *musicals until the renovations of 1982. It is now the home of the New York City Ballet and the New York City Opera. Lincoln Center's two primary *playhouses, the Vivian Beaumont (capacity about 1,100) and the Mitzi E. Newhouse (called the Forum until 1973; capacity 299), were designed by Eero Saarinen and Jo *Mielziner and opened in 1965. The Beaumont featured a steeply raked *auditorium with a large stage that was to be easily changed from thrust to *proscenium. The theatres were built for the Repertory Theater of Lincoln Center, headed by *Kazan and Robert Whitehead, both of whom resigned before the buildings opened. A succession of co-directors and directors—*Blau (1965–7), Jules Irving (1965–73), *Papp (1973–7), and Richmond Crinkley (1979–84)—failed to make the *repertory a success. In 1980–1 the Vivian Beaumont stage was converted to a proscenium arch and the rake of the seating was reduced. In 1985 the not-for-profit Lincoln Center Theatre corporation was established under *artistic director Gregory Mosher, who ran it until 1992. With the motto 'Good Plays, Popular Prices', the LCT finally made the Beaumont one of the pre-eminent theatres in the country. Lincoln Center also houses a library of performing arts.   FHJ

Lincoln's Inn Fields Theatre *Davenant's conversion in 1660–1 of Lisle's indoor *tennis court in Portugal Street in London established the spatial arrangement used in British theatres for some 150 years. The *proscenium arch created two stage spaces: an upstage scenic stage with painted shutters drawn to meet in the middle, and a deep thrust forestage which was entered by pairs of doors on either side of the stage. Rows of side *boxes (some on the forestage itself), the pit, and gallery permitted the *audience to enjoy scenic spectacle (although many areas had limited sight lines) while retaining an intimacy with the players which was central to Restoration theatre. Davenant's Duke's Company occupied the theatre until 1671 when they moved to Dorset

Garden Theatre. The intimate 'Little Theatre' of Lincoln's Inn Fields was later home to the Players' Company managed by *Barry, *Bracegirdle, and *Betterton (1695-1705). Successfully refurbished by John *Rich in 1714, it fell into disrepair and ceased to be a regular *playhouse after 1732. GBB

Lindsay, David (c.1486-1555) Scottish dramatist and courtier. His diplomatic missions to Europe in the 1530s and 1540s probably exposed him to French dramatic forms, notably the mock sermon, which he later incorporated in his own work. Involved in Edinburgh court theatricals from 1511, he was probably the author of a lost allegorical play performed at Linlithgow Palace in 1540, which attacked clerical abuses; the material was later extensively reworked into his day-long epic about the government of the realm, *A Satire of the Three Estates* (1552). Its juxtaposition of trenchant social commentary with scatological *farce remained potent in several twentieth-century revivals, notably that of *Guthrie at the *Edinburgh Festival in 1948. MJW

lines of business A system of *character specialization within an *acting company, which enabled each member to play a large number of roles within the bounds of his or her own speciality. The Elizabethan acting company offered this kind of specialization; by the late eighteenth and early nineteenth centuries and especially with the advent of *melodrama, the system was firmly established. An actor was hired to fill a vacant line of business. The leading man and lady did not act lines of business, since each simply assumed the principal male or female part in a play. The main lines of business were juvenile lead, female juvenile lead (*ingénue), heavy man, character actor, low comedian, light comedian, old man, old woman, walking gentleman (a *confidant of the leading man) and utility (in America, responsible). Such a company, with additions and omissions and the extensive doubling or trebling of parts, could handle anything in the repertory: *tragedy, *comedy, *farce, or melodrama. Almost every male line of business had its female counterpart. Each actor with a line of business built up a stock of *characters within his or her own line, fully aware of the essential characteristics of a melodramatic *villain or *heroine, but also able to handle variations in personality, manner, and social type, since all villains and heroines were not the same. MRB

Linney, Romulus (1930-2011) American playwright and director. Linney's work has the unadorned poetic quality of a testament. Best known for his plays about Appalachia—including

Holy Ghosts (1976), about snake-handlers, and *Sand Mountain* (1981), based on Appalachian folklore—his historical dramas include *The Sorrows of Frederick* (1967), *Childe Byron* (1978), and *2* (1990), about Hermann Goering. Adaptations include *Gint* (1998) and *A Lesson before Dying* (2000), from the novel by Ernest Gaines. The lyric southern language in Linney's plays is derived, he said, from the rhythms of the King James Bible. Linney often directed his own work. GAO

Lin Zhaohua (Lin Chao-hua) (1936-) Chinese director. After graduation from the Central Academy of Drama in 1961, Lin worked regularly as an actor at the Beijing People's Art Theatre and became the most all-round stage director in China. His productions of *Gao Xingjian's *Absolute Signal* (1982) and *Bus Stop* (1983) are considered by critics to have initiated the 'Little Theatre movement' (experimental productions in studio theatres) on the Chinese mainland. He excels, too, in handling slice-of-life drama, which represents the mainstream tradition in China. Celebrated productions that were also box-office hits include Guo Shixing's *Birdmen* (1996) and *Lao She's classic *Teahouse* (1999). He is just as inspiring in directing plays with complex *characters, such as Jin Yun's *Uncle Doggie's Nirvana* (1986) and *Hamlet*, which he adapted in 1990. Beijing opera (*jingju) fascinates him, and his production of *Prime Minister Liu Luoguo* (2000, co-director Tian Qinxin) opened up new possibilities of development for the form. His further productions of Shakespeare at the People's Art Theatre received considerable attention: *Richard III* (2000) and *Coriolanus* (2007, in a new translation by *Ying Ruocheng). MPYC

Lipman, Maureen (1946-) English actress, best known for her work in *comedies and *musicals. She was a member of the *National Theatre at the *Old Vic (1971-3) and played Celia with the *Royal Shakespeare Company (1974). London productions have included *Shaw's *Candida* (1976), *Bernstein's *Wonderful Town* (1986), *Simon's *Lost in Yonkers* (1992), *Wasserstein's *The Sisters Rosensweig* (1994), and her one-person celebration of the work of Joyce Grenfell, *Re: Joyce* (from 1988). She was in *Nunn's revival of *Oklahoma!* for the National (1998) and joined the expanding list of actresses to appear in Eve Ensler's *The Vagina Monologues* (2001). Many of her television roles were written by her husband Jack Rosenthal, including those in *The Evacuees* (1975) and *The Knowledge* (1979). AS

Liston, John (1776-1846) English actor, the best low comedian of the *romantic era. He spent most of his career at *Covent Garden, acting there from 1805 to 1822 when he left for *Drury Lane, where Liston became the highest-paid comic actor. Given his great success at the established *patent houses, his move to *Vestris's Olympic Theatre in 1831 is surprising; perhaps he sought the intimacy of a smaller *playhouse. Liston specialized in buffoon roles and was physically suited to them, being corpulent and red faced. While a physically expressive performer, he was nonetheless admired for underplaying roles that others tended to exaggerate. His most memorable role was Paul Pry in John Poole's play of that name (1825). His Shakespearian roles include Ophelia in Poole's *Hamlet Travestie* (1813) and Sir Andrew Aguecheek.   MJK

Little Theatre movement The wave of small amateur companies founded in the United States from 1909 to 1929. Professional theatre production in the USA had by 1890 been consolidated under the *Theatrical Syndicate (and later the *Shuberts): a handful of New York businessmen dictated play selection and production styles for country, because local *playhouses had been bought up and local companies liquidated. American intellectuals despaired at the standardized, industrialized condition of the theatre, as the *touring system favoured the lowest common denominators in playwriting and conventional scenery selected for ease of shipping. The Little Theatre movement arose from the desire of small groups of intellectuals and aesthetes to restore American theatre as an art and provide meaningful leisure activity for a middle class. While organizations such as the Drama League (founded 1909) pointed to European companies such as the *Abbey Theatre as models of socially relevant art, playwright and *producer Percy *MacKaye in his book *The Civic Theatre* (1912) argued for theatre as a means of 'constructive leisure' by which Americans could find meaning, forge relationships, and improve their communities.

Maurice *Browne's Little Theatre in Chicago (1911) was often cited as an early model, though others pre-dated it, such as the Hull-House Players in Chicago (1901) and the Players in Providence, Rhode Island (1909). Irene and Alice Lewisohn began their community-based theatre work with immigrants in New York in 1902 and founded the Neighborhood Playhouse in 1912. The *Washington Square Players and *Provincetown Players (both 1915) propelled the Little Theatre idea to national prominence with their discoveries of provocative new playwrights—especially *O'Neill and *Glaspell—and the introduction of European staging techniques derived from

*symbolism and *expressionism. Little theatres began to spring up around the country and, while no exact programme was followed, tended toward short plays, often European, new American plays, often written locally, experimentation with European *avant-garde techniques described in *Theatre Arts* magazine (founded 1916), and a preference for studio venues seating less than 100. The outstanding little theatres founded in the 1910s included those in Indianapolis (1915), Detroit (1915), the Cleveland Play House (1916), and the Little Arts Theatre of Los Angeles (1916). While some of these groups transformed themselves into professional theatres, others continued deliberately as amateur operations and formed the basis of the *community theatre movement.   MAF

Littlewood, Joan (1914–2002) With Theatre of Action, Theatre Union, and finally *Theatre Workshop (London, from 1953), Littlewood became famous for her anti-establishment, risk-taking, collaborative theatre. Her developmental approach, called 'work-shopping', was applied to the classics and living authors alike. Some distressed dramatists found their plays work-shopped beyond recognition, but the scripts of *Behan and *Delaney, among others, were successfully produced by this method. Littlewood was always opposed to the *bourgeois theatre of *illusion; she advocated anti-*realistic theatre, often based in popular styles such as the *music hall, and she worked extensively with *physical theatre techniques derived from *Meyerhold, *Stanislavsky, and *Laban. Littlewood's irrepressible, entertaining, and yet politically serious style was epitomized by *Oh! What a Lovely War* (1963), a *satire on the First World War, which had profound influence in Britain and abroad. As recognition grew, the company transferred several productions to the West End; this was financially rewarding but overextended the enterprise. Worn out by running several companies simultaneously, Littlewood became increasingly disenchanted and retired from active theatre work in the early 1970s.   EJS

liturgical drama A term normally applied to approximately 1,000 Latin texts, extracted from a variety of *medieval ecclesiastical service books, which modern scholars have identified as dramatic scripts. This 'drama', performed as part or in the context of the official public worship of the Christian Church, shares most of its dramatic and theatrical characteristics—symbolic gesture, movement, and *costume; antiphonal singing; role playing—with the mass itself, and it has proved difficult always to distinguish adequately between a liturgical and a dramatic performance. Any distinction must be based less on the formal qualities of a performance than on its status and function. A liturgical *ritual performance is primarily a form of worship sanctioned by ecclesiastical authority; a drama is a non-essential elaboration of the liturgy. Nevertheless, medieval liturgy and liturgical drama are formally and functionally on a performance continuum that precludes sharp distinction. Although the longest and most complex texts date from the twelfth and thirteenth centuries, there is no discernible pattern of development reflected in the texts and no question of more elaborate texts replacing simpler ones. Performances can, however, be roughly categorized in terms of the closeness of their connection to the liturgy proper.

Besides the mass, the theatrical qualities of which were recognized by ecclesiastics as early as the twelfth century, certain other ceremonies not essential to the liturgy but firmly based in it, approach dramatic status and may sometimes have been detached from the liturgy altogether. The traditional ceremonies of Holy Week remained liturgical actions, but other ceremonies commemorating the Annunciation, the Purification, the Assumption, and the Presentation in the Temple were more loosely connected to the liturgy.

The bulk of the liturgical drama, however, developed from elaborations on the 'Te Deum' at Christmas and especially Easter. The *Quem Quaeritis* trope, dating from the tenth century, which presents the visit of the three Marys to Christ's empty tomb and their short dialogue with the angel, gave rise to the *Visitatio Sepulchri*, which appears in nearly 800 texts from the tenth to the twelfth centuries. Both Christmas and Easter plays were subject to extra-biblical elaboration.

Approximately twenty religious plays in Latin, most dating from the twelfth century and later, though showing signs of their liturgical origins, are frequently designated as *ludus, jeu,* or *spiele,* 'play' rather than the liturgical *ordo* or *officium,* and were not limited to Easter or Christmas seasons. The so-called *Fleury Playbook* (twelfth- or thirteenth-century) contains ten texts that appear to have been consciously collected as dramas.

Liturgical drama used the resources of the church itself in its staging. The church building functioned as *playhouse, providing defined spaces for performers (clerics) and *audience (congregation). Dramatic costume was an augmented version of liturgical vestments; dialogue was a development of chanted antiphons; setting and scene were provided by the nave, altar,

sepulchre, cross, and ambo of monastic churches, as well as by specially constructed mansions.RWV

living newspaper A species of *documentary theatre pioneered by the Blue Blouses in the Soviet Union and by *Piscator in Berlin in the 1920s, adapted in the 1930s by the Unity Theatre and Theatre of Action in Britain and the *Federal Theatre Project in the United States. Living newspapers tend to combine live *action, often based upon actual documents, with large-scale projections of photographs or films of actual events. The American productions were elaborate, intended by FTP director *Flanagan as a means of employing large numbers of theatre people and journalists (1935–9). She and Elmer *Rice, along with Morris Watson, vice-president of the American Newspaper Guild, created the Living Newspaper Unit. Rice resigned when the first Living Newspaper—*Ethiopia* (1936)—was prevented from opening due to pressure from the US State Department. The unit produced numerous successful works, often magnets for controversy in their advocacy of land redistribution (*Triple-A Plowed Under,* 1936), government ownership of utilities (*Power,* 1937), and housing (*One Third of a Nation,* 1938). Productions made creative use of projected silhouettes, life-sized *puppets, and *naturalistic stage effects, such as the simulated tenement fire in *One-Third of a Nation.* MAF

Living Theatre American theatre *collective. Founded in 1947 by Julian *Beck and Judith *Malina, the company was instrumental in the development of *Off-Broadway in the 1950s, promoting new American and European drama and experimental performance techniques of collectivity, abstraction, and *improvisation. The first performances were in small spaces throughout New York, producing the *avant-garde plays of Gertrude *Stein, William Carlos Williams, *Cocteau, *Brecht, and *Pirandello. In the company's first permanent home on 14th Street and Broadway, the Living Theatre gained national prominence with a series of politically charged provocative productions, including *The Connection* by *Gelber (1959), *A Man's a Man* by Brecht (1962), and *The Brig* by Kenneth Brown (1963). The performances developed a violent *realism inspired in part by *Artaud's notions of a theatre of *cruelty. A primary meeting place for radical artists and politics in the early 1960s, the company collaborated with John Cage to produce an evening called 'Theatre of Changes' which utilized Cage's strategies of chance operations in art creation. In 1963 the Internal Revenue Service closed the theatre for back taxes. The company undertook a voluntary exile in Europe in 1964, where they began experimentation in collective creation influenced by alternative lifestyles of the 1960s, and produced *Mysteries and Smaller Pieces* (1964), *Frankenstein* (1965), *Antigone* (1967), and *Paradise Now* (1968). Each of these *devised works attempted a marriage of radical politics with a new aesthetics of improvisation and confrontation, in a reconfigured *audience–actor relation. In *Paradise Now* audience members were engaged in direct *dialogue on issues of the day, invited to discard their identification papers and clothes, turn on to drugs, and join the performance in some manner.

During a *tour of the USA in 1968, the company moved away from middle-class audiences to focus on radical theatre for working-class participants in Brazil (1970) and later with steel mill workers in Pittsburgh. After Beck's death in 1985, the company continued under the direction of Malina and Hannon Reznikov and continues to perform   MDC

Li Yu (Li Yü) (1611–c.1680) Chinese writer, author of 'southern style' *chuanqi operas. Li Yu wrote ten *comedies to entertain and amuse rather than instruct his *audience. He trained and directed his household troupe of actresses and *toured with them, giving performances in the homes of wealthy patrons. Several plays adapt his own stories, and in all of these respects Li Yu broke with existing conventions for southern drama. His largest contribution was as a theorist. Two chapters in his *Casual Expressions of Idle Feeling* are the first systematic treatise on drama in Chinese. In them Li emphasized performability rather than prosodic skill, and instructed playwrights to write shorter plays (about 30 scenes) centred on 'one *character and one *action', with equal importance given to arias and *dialogue. He found fresh subjects for his own plays. In *Women in Love*, two women in love unite by marrying the same man. *Woman in Pursuit of Man* inverts a familiar plot when three women compete for one man, and in *You Can't Do Anything About Fate* three beautiful women cooperate and make bearable life with an ugly husband.   CS

Lloyd, Marie (Matilda Victoria Wood) (1870–1922) English *music-hall performer. As Bella Delamare, her first professional engagement was in Hackney. Changing her name to Marie Lloyd, her first success, as vocalist and *dancer, was with 'The Boy I Love Is up in the Gallery'. Her popularity increased with saucy songs such as George Le Brun's 'Among my Knick-Knacks' and 'What's That for, Eh?' As she said, people 'don't pay their sixpences and shillings at a music hall to hear the Salvation Army'. She played *pantomime throughout her career, notably at *Drury Lane in *Robinson Crusoe* with Little Tich and George *Robey, and had successful *tours of America, South Africa, and Australia. Her private life was dogged by a succession of violent and miserable marriages, but she was unfailingly generous, contributing large sums to the Music Hall Strike Fund in 1907. At the Edmonton Empire, whilst singing 'It's a Bit of a Ruin That Cromwell Knocked about a Bit', she was taken ill, the *audience convinced that her staggering and swaying was part of the act. Her funeral attracted over 50,000 people. AF

Lloyd Webber, Andrew (1948–   ) English composer. While still in school, he teamed with lyricist Tim *Rice to write *Joseph and the Amazing Technicolor Dreamcoat* (1968), a gentle biblical tale with a soft-rock score that attracted a good deal of attention. It was followed by the controversial *Jesus Christ Superstar*. Released as a record album in 1970, orchestrated for rock band and symphony orchestra, it mixed contemporary rock and old-fashioned *music-hall turns. Subsequently staged in New York and London, it made Lloyd Webber a household name. The team's *Evita* (1978), another 'pop opera' which cemented their reputation, also marked the end of their collaboration. In subsequent years, Lloyd Webber has had varying success with *musicals on sometimes unlikely subjects. His two greatest hits, *Cats* (poems by *Eliot, directed by Trevor *Nunn, 1981) and *The Phantom of the Opera* (directed by Harold *Prince, 1986), have achieved record-breaking long runs, and his roller-skating parable of trains, *Starlight Express* (Nunn, 1984), while a failure in New York, was still running in London in 2010. Less triumphant have been *Aspects of Love* (1989), *Sunset Boulevard* (1993), and *Whistle down the Wind* (1996). An extravagant sequel to *Phantom* called *Love Never Dies* opened in London in 2010. While many associate his musicals with gaudy spectacle—dancing cats, falling chandeliers—Lloyd Webber has never shied away from smaller-scale, human-interest musicals, such as *Song and Dance* (1982) and *The Beautiful Game* (2000). While some have deplored his economy in building an entire score around a few melodies and for recycling songs, his melodic gifts, typically wrapped in lush, inventive orchestrations, have endeared him to *audiences. Musicals have made him one of the wealthiest men in England, and at one time he owned thirteen West End theatres. Knighted in 1992, he was made a life peer in 1997.   JD

Lochhead, Liz (1947–) Scottish playwright. Lochhead first received recognition as a poet, and performing her own poetry led to writing for the stage. Her first produced play, *Blood and Ice*, premièred in 1982 at the *Edinburgh Festival. In 1988 she was writer-in-residence for the *Royal Shakespeare Company. Notable plays since then are *Dracula* (1985), *Mary Queen of Scots Got her Head Chopped Off* (1989), and *Perfect Days* (1998). She has also translated *Tartuffe* (1986) and the York Mystery Cycle (1992), adapted *The Tempest* as a play for children (*The Magic Island*, 1993), and written several scripts for radio and television. Her work addresses issues of history, myth, and *gender, and has been praised for its strong narrative, connections with popular memory, and poetic language.   AHK

Loesser, Frank (1910–69) American composer-lyricist. The most versatile Broadway songwriter since Irving *Berlin, Loesser began his career in Hollywood and from 1936 to 1942 wrote film lyrics, producing a string of hits including 'Heart and Soul', 'Two Sleepy People', and 'I Don't Want to Walk without You'. In 1942 he wrote music and lyrics to 'Praise the Lord and Pass the Ammunition', one of the Second World War's biggest hits, and thereafter wrote his own music. In 1948 he composed *Where's Charley?*, his first Broadway score, and followed it in 1950 with *Guys and Dolls*, a masterpiece of *musical comedy. The show, based on the fiction and *characters of Damon Runyon, featured a rare balance of comic and romantic elements. His other successes include *The Most Happy Fella* (1956) and *How to Succeed in Business without Really Trying* (1962), for which he and director/librettist Abe *Burrows received the Pulitzer Prize. Loesser's gift for novelty and character songs, especially the contrapuntal duet, was unsurpassed.   SN

Loewe, Frederick *See* LERNER, ALAN JAY.

Logan, Joshua (1908–88) American director and playwright. After studying with *Stanislavsky in Moscow, before the Second World War Logan had directed more than a dozen Broadway plays and *musicals. His post-war success began with *Annie Get your Gun* (1946) and continued with *Mister Roberts* (1948) and *South Pacific* (1949), both of which he co-authored as well as directed, winning a Pulitzer Prize for the latter. Continuing to direct and sometimes *produce on Broadway, he began directing Hollywood films as well, beginning in 1955 with *Mister Roberts* and *Picnic*. His success in film was not surprising, as his stage direction had been noted for its cinematic fluidity. Logan's career on both stage and screen declined following the failures of his film versions of *Paint your Wagon* (1960) and *Camelot* (1967).   JD

Lonsdale, Frederick (1881–1954) English playwright and librettist. Lonsdale began his theatrical career as a librettist for Ruritanian *musical comedies such as *The King of Cadonia* (1908), *The Balkan Princess* (1910), and *The Maid of the Mountains* (1917), which ran for 1,352 performances. In the 1920s he began writing the social *comedies for which he is chiefly remembered, including *Aren't We All* (1923), *The Last of Mrs Cheney* (1925), *On Approval* (1927), *Canaries Sometimes Sing* (1929), and *Once Is Enough* (1938). Lonsdale's success rested primarily on his lightly ironic style and witty *dialogue, combined with well-constructed plots.   MDG

Loos, Anita (*c.*1893–1981) American playwright and screenwriter. Loos was a professional film scenarist from the age of 19. The spectacle of sexually attractive young women competing to marry wealthy if unperceptive older men was presented as comic sport in her best-selling novel *Gentlemen Prefer Blondes* (1925). This material and its *protagonist Lorelei Lee came to define Loos's career, as she and her husband (John Emerson) adapted the novel for the stage in 1926, and she collaborated with Joseph Fields and composer Jule *Styne to create the 1949 *musical—a production centred upon a career-making performance by Carol *Channing. Loos's *Happy Birthday* (1946), a Helen *Hayes vehicle, and *Gigi* (1951, adapted from stories by Colette) were also commercial successes.   MAF

Lope de Rueda *See* RUEDA, LOPE DE.

Lope de Vega *See* VEGA CARPIO, LOPE DE.

Loquasto, Santo (1944–) American designer. Moving among stage, film, and *dance, Loquasto built a reputation for sculpturally striking and exquisitely detailed design. His work for *regional theatre and Broadway includes the conceptual design for Andrei *Şerban's 1977 production of *Cherry Orchard*, and the evocation of a 1940s restaurant in the 1989 revival of *Café Crown*. Since his first Broadway sets in 1972 for *Sticks and Bones* and *That Championship Season*, Loquasto's prolific output has included designs for *Bent* (1980), *Lost in Yonkers* (1991), and *Fosse* (1999), *Ciulei's *Peer Gynt* (1983) at the *Guthrie Theatre, and *Waiting for Godot* (New York, 2009). In dance, Loquasto's work for American Ballet Theatre in New York began with *costumes for Twyla Tharp's *Push Comes to Shove* (1976), and has included collaborations with Jerome *Robbins, Agnes *de Mille, and Mark Morris. His long-time association with Woody Allen has included *Bullets over Broadway* (1994), *Melinda and Melinda* (2004), and *Whatever Works* (2009). EW

Loraine, Robert (1876–1935) English *actor-manager. Loraine's career began in 1889 when he performed in the companies of *Tree and *Alexander. He soon established himself as a popular star in *melodramas, from *The Three Musketeers* (1899) to *The Prisoner of Zenda* (1923). He also performed regularly in Shakespeare and *Shaw, and in 1905 he played John Tanner in *Man and Superman* in New York. Back in London, he appeared in several of Shaw's plays in 1907 and 1908; during the next few years he worked in plays by *Sheridan, *Goldsmith, Shakespeare, and *Maugham, and in 1911 took over the lease on the Criterion Theatre in London, reviving *Man and Superman*. During the war he served in the Royal Flying Corps and was wounded in action. In 1919 he was a success in a revival of *Cyrano de Bergerac*, then returned to actor-management in the 1920s, performing not only plays by Shaw, *Barrie, *Strindberg, *Congreve, and Shakespeare but also romantic melodramas. TP

Lorca, Federico García *See* GARCÍA LORCA, FEDERICO.

Lord Chamberlain *See* CENSORSHIP; LICENSING ACTS

Lourenço, João (1944–) Portuguese actor and director. His acting career began in 1952 in radio, included notable roles at the Teatro Nacional D. Maria II, and extended to television and film. His discovery, during a *tour, of the new theatre in Brazil led to the foundation in 1966 of a society of actors, Grupo 4, a pioneering step in a movement for independent theatre, of great significance after the 1974 Revolution. A year later Lourenço began directing authors previously banned by the *censors (*Kopit, *Weiss, *Mrożek, and *Fo) and promoting contemporary Portuguese playwrights. An enthusiastic director of *Brecht (his most admired production remains *Mother Courage*, 1986), Lourenço turned his attention to contemporary German and English-speaking drama in the 1990s. *Opera and *musicals also feature in his long directing career, characterized by a sober inventiveness in *scenography and a socially responsible repertoire. MJB

Loutherbourg, Philip James de (1740–1812) Alsatian designer. A fashionable painter in Paris during the 1760s, on a visit to London he intrigued *Garrick with ideas for new scenes and stage machinery and was employed at *Drury Lane from 1772 to 1781 with total *scenographic

authority. Loutherbourg sought a harmony of scenographic elements, a visual unification of scene and performer, and an involvement of the *audience that predicted the *romantic *realism of the following century. Loutherbourg designed for *pantomimes, spectacular *tragedies, and topical entertainments; it was assumed he would not replace the stock scenery used in *comedies. He remained when Garrick retired in 1776 and in 1779 he created a 'travelogue' pantomime, *The Wonders of Derbyshire*, for the new *manager, *Sheridan. As a newly elected member of the Royal Academy, he left Drury Lane in 1781 to pursue his career as an easel artist. Painting tours to Derbyshire, the Lake District, and Snowdonia effectively created these districts as topics for art. Concurrently, he created a large model theatre the *Eidophusikon* that showed views of scenic spectacle to small audiences. Building upon the excitement created by Captain Cook's South Sea explorations, Loutherbourg worked with *O'Keeffe to prepare *Omai; or, A Trip round the World* at *Covent Garden Theatre in 1785, probably his final stage work, after which he focused upon landscape, naval, and his late mystical canvases. CLB

Lovelace, Earl (1935–) Trinidadian novelist and playwright, particularly associated with the theme of the clash of city and country. His first play, *The New Boss* (1962), used the metaphor of the island as an estate left to its workers after independence. *My Name Is Village* (1976), a *musical with folk themes, followed his emergence as an accomplished novelist, and was staged as part of Trinidad's Best Village Festival, involving the whole village of Matura in the production. *Jestina's Calypso* (1978) is a witty exploration of sexism in Trinidadian culture, while *The New Hardware Store* (1980) relies on elements of carnival. Lovelace's celebrated novel *The Dragon Can't Dance* was dramatized by the Trinidad Theatre Workshop in 1978, and a later novel, *The Wine of Astonishment*, was staged as a play in Trinidad a decade later. ES

Lowin, John (*c.*1576–*c.*1659) English actor and *manager. Lowin made his career with the King's Men (*see* CHAMBERLAIN'S MEN) whom he joined by 1603 when he appeared in the cast list for *Jonson's *Sejanus*. Many other highly versatile parts for that company followed, including Bosola in *Webster's *The Duchess of Malfi*. He became one of the company's *managers, as well as a housekeeper in the *Globe and *Blackfriars *playhouses. John Downes claimed in 1708 that *Betterton excelled in the lead of Shakespeare's *Henry*

VIII because he had been instructed in the role by *Davenant, who had, in turn, been taught by Lowin. SPC

Lucas, Craig (1951–) American playwright. Starting his career in the *choruses of several Broadway *musicals, Lucas produced a steady stream of plays, primarily *Off-Broadway and *regionally, beginning with *Missing Persons* in 1981. Lucas's career coincided with the AIDS epidemic, and many of his plays deal with *characters—whether gay or straight—coping with cataclysmic change. He collaborated with director Norman Rene on *Reckless* (1983), *Blue Window* (1984), *Prelude to a Kiss* (1988), and *God's Heart* (1993). After Rene's death in 1996, Lucas's work often centred more directly on AIDS, a central element in *The Dying Gaul* (1998). Individual cruelty is the subject of *Stranger* (2000). He wrote the book for the *musical *The Light in the Piazza* (2005). AW

Lucie, Doug (1953–) English playwright who holds up the illusions and delusions of Thatcherite and post-Thatcherite Britain to unflinching ridicule. Whether he is dealing with political advertising in *Fashion* (1987) or journalism in *The Shallow End* (1997), his plays are characterized by cruel humour and passionate moral polemic. He shows an indebtedness to *Osborne in his scabrous articulacy, and he has turned his fire equally on the delusions of the left in *Progress* (1984) and right-wing evangelism in *Grace* (1992). *Fashion* (1988) most precisely places his *satire within a fully worked narrative, dealing hilariously and shockingly with the influence of advertising and spin doctors in British politics. DR

Ludlam, Charles (1943–87) American playwright, actor, and *manager. In 1966 Ludlam joined the company of the Playhouse of the Ridiculous, formed by Ronald Tavel and Jon Vacarro. The *gay camp style was marked by *parodies of historical dramas and classic Hollywood formulas, sexual wordplay (primarily homosexual references), scatological humour, and allusions to popular entertainment. Ludlam developed the 'Ridiculous' aesthetic further in his own troupe, the Ridiculous Theatrical Company, in which he was the lead actor, playwright, and director. His dramas construct a labyrinth of allusions and pastiche of earlier forms through textual appropriations that strive to elicit a *laughter not of moral judgement but of the absurdity of action and belief. Ludlam's performances of the central women of his plays, especially Camille, won him much praise as an actor. His 29 plays include *Bluebeard* (1970), *Camille* (1973), *Stageblood* (1975), and *The Mystery of Irma Vep* (1984). MDC

ludruk Regional theatre popular in east Java (Indonesia). Its origins are obscure, believed to reach as far back as the thirteenth century as *ritual *ludruk bandan* and *ludruk lyrok*. The first written evidence dates from 1822. Main features were *female impersonators (*waria*) who perform songs and *dances, and *clown characters. Since the 1920s more complex dramatic stories have been added under the influence of *bangsawan* theatre. These *melodramas and *farces feature mostly contemporary domestic stories or, less frequently, legendary or historical and political material. Scenes are *improvised based on short *scenarios, presented in a *realistic acting style in contemporary dress, and performed in local dialects. A gamelan orchestra accompanies the entire performance. Clowns are central characters in *ludruk*, as they voice criticism, subvert power structures, and speak for common people. The form has become commercial entertainment popular with urban and rural working-class *audiences. KP

Lugné-Poe, Aurélien-Marie (1869–1940) French actor and director. His early acting career was inauspicious, in *Antoine's Théâtre *Libre and *Fort's Théâtre d'*Art; but at the latter he encountered the work of *Maeterlinck, with whom he became closely associated. After the demise of Fort's theatre in 1893, Lugné-Poe set up a company which would perform the work of great foreign dramatists and the young *symbolists. He directed Maeterlinck's *Pelléas and Mélisande* before naming this new venture the Théâtre de l'Œuvre. The early seasons were composed of a mixture of Scandinavian drama (including *Ibsen, *Strindberg, and *Bjørnson), and in this he differed little from Antoine. But his aim was to turn actors into instruments of the *director or give precedence to poetry in 'mood plays'. One notable exception was the première of *Jarry's *Ubu roi* in 1896. A year later Lugné-Poe announced a break with symbolism. He never managed to secure a permanent troupe of actors, and his move to the 1,000-seat Nouveau-Théâtre, an annexe of the Casino de Paris, was hardly appropriate for an *avant-garde programme. He managed to fill the seats nonetheless, with only 10 per cent of them going to paying subscribers, 30 per cent to journalists, and the remainder given away free. The small subscription base, a reputation for trouble in the *auditorium, the snub to young French authors, and mounting debts led to the theatre's demise in 1899. Lugné-Poe reopened the theatre in 1912, but though he is now recognized as the champion of Maeterlinck and the director of influential modernist drama, he lived near to the breadline for most of his life.   BRS

Lully, Jean-Baptiste (Giovanni Lulli) (1632–87) Italian composer, musician, and dancer in the service of Louis XIV from 1652. Lully was the most influential of Louis XIV's court musicians. As a composer, his output was tremendous: eleven *comédies-ballets*, thirteen *tragédies-lyriques* (a form of opera), over 30 *ballets de cour*, instrumental music, and twenty motets. He collaborated with important figures in music, dance, and theatre, including *Molière, *Quinault, and *Corneille. He established the French opera as an independent form which incorporated not only song and dance, but a unified plot and poetic recitative. At a *rehearsal in 1687, he banged his big toe with a cane: a few weeks later he died of gangrene.   GES

Lunacharsky, Anatoly (1875–1933) Russian/Soviet dramatist, critic, and the Soviet Union's first cultural commissar (1917–29). Lunacharsky's tastes were cosmopolitan; in a book of essays (1908), he rubbed shoulders with leading *symbolists, including *Meyerhold, whom he appointed head of the theatrical section of the Cultural Commissariat in 1919, before growing alarmed at some of his protégé's innovative excesses and dismissing him. In 1923 he coined the slogan 'Back to *Ostrovsky', as part of an attempt to curb the tendencies of the *avant-garde to distort the classics in the name of revolutionary innovation. During the latter years of his cultural leadership, however, Lunacharsky did his best to protect theatrical practitioners such as Meyerhold and *Tairov from persecution, despite his own predilection for a specifically proletarian culture. Throughout the 1920s he polemicized at public meetings, in newspapers and journals, while continuing to write plays. These are large scale and include some in verse drawing on themes from Russian folklore or, like *Oliver Cromwell* (1920) and *Faust and the City* (1918), bring together themes from the past with those of the Revolution.   NW

Lunt, Alfred (1892–1977) and **Lynn Fontanne** (1887–1983) American actors. The Lunts first appeared together in 1919, married in 1922, and made an indelible impression in the *Theatre Guild production of *Molnár's *The Guardsman* in 1924. Both were well-known in their own right but after 1929 they declined to act separately. They excelled in *comedy. Plays such as *Sherwood's *Reunion in Vienna* (1931) and *Idiot's Delight* (1935), or *Behrman's *Amphitryon 38* (1937) were specially crafted to exploit the

rapid-fire overlap of their *dialogue and the precise physical collisions that appeared spontaneous. Perfectionists about their work, the Lunts were said to *rehearse almost non-stop, even taking scripts to their bed. The couple developed a close friendship with *Coward; he wrote *Point Valaine* (1934) and *Quadrille* (1952) for them, and appeared with them to complete the romantic threesome in his *Design for Living* (1933). The Lunts appeared in Sherwood's anti-totalitarian drama *There Shall Be No Night* from 1940 to 1944, *touring the USA and Britain. Their longest Broadway run was in *Rattigan's *O Mistress Mine*, which had 451 performances in 1946–7. In 1958 they made a farewell appearance in *Dürrenmatt's *The Visit* at the newly named Lunt-Fontanne Theatre.   MAF

Lupino family The family story begins with Georgius Luppino, a refugee from Bologna who arrived in Plymouth in 1634 with only his skills with *puppets, and goes on to unverified tales of Bartholomew Fair performers. The family members were leaders in traditional and innovatory skills—scene painters, *acrobats, *dancers, animal impersonators, singers, *music-hall comedians, film and television makers—hard-working stars of entertainment. In the ninth generation, **George Hook Lupino** (1820–1902) and **Rosina Proctor**, both acrobatic dancers, had sixteen theatrical children, including **George** (1853–1932), 'the last of the old-time clowns', **Arthur** (1864–1908), a famous 'skin' performer who played the dog Nana in *Peter Pan*; and **Harry Charles** (1865–1925), who with Arthur formed a music-hall act as the Brothers Lupino. These three had many children and grandchildren in the profession, including **Lupino Lane**, famous for the dance the Lambeth Walk, as well as **Stanley** (1893–1942), **Mark**, and **Barry** (1882–1962), all working comic actors on stage and screen. **Barry Jr.** was a BBC TV director, and **Richard** and **Ida** (b. 1914) went to Hollywood; Ida, 'Queen of the Bs', became a star actress and a director. The family renewed itself in each generation by marriages to talent, often linking to other theatrical families. It was the Lupinos' boast that every boy and girl was trained to the profession, and no true Lupino ever left it.   JSB

LuPone, Patti (1949–   ) American actress and singer. Although she has appeared in numerous non-musical plays, including many by *Mamet, she is best known for *musicals. She won Tony awards for the title role in *Evita* in New York and for Reno Sweeney in the 1988 revival of *Anything Goes*. In London, she created the roles of Fantine in *Les Misérables* and Norma Desmond in *Sunset

Boulevard, although composer *Lloyd Webber controversially had her replaced in the latter. She has also performed extensively in film and on television. She has recently been much hearalded for Mrs Lovett in John Doyle's revival of *Sweeny Todd* on Broadway (2005; in which she also played the tuba) and as Rose in *Gypsy* (2008).   JD

Lyly, John (*c.*1554–1606) English dramatist. Lyly was already established as a writer of prose fiction when his patron, the Earl of Oxford, made him a partner in the first *Blackfriars Theatre in the early 1580s. For the rest of the decade he *managed the associated company of *boy actors and wrote many of the *comedies in their repertory, beginning with *Campaspe* (1583). His comedy of cross-dressing and metamorphosis, *Galatea*, was eventually produced at a theatre at St Paul's; other productions there included *Endymion* (1588) and *Midas* (1589). In the late 1580s, he was drawn into the Marprelate controversy, and wrote satirical pamphlets in support of the government. His company collapsed in disarray soon afterwards. For the rest of his life, Lyly hoped for court advancement, but repeatedly failed to achieve it, and he died in poverty. Performing at upmarket theatres and often at court, Lyly's boy company served a socially elevated clientele, and his plays reflect this in style, their use of prose, and a kind of knowing and polite self-deprecation.   MJW

Lyttelton Theatre *See* NATIONAL THEATRE OF GREAT BRITAIN.

Lytton, Edward Bulwer, Lord *See* BULWER-LYTTON, EDWARD.

Lyubimov, Yury (1917–   ) Soviet/Russian director. Lyubimov joined the Vakhtangov Theatre after the war and became *artistic director of the Taganka Theatre in 1964 where he developed a repertoire of prose adaptations and montages of poetry and other texts, the director effectively authoring the production. *Listen!* (1967), for example, was based on *Mayakovsky's poetry and integrated the poet's biography into the production with the presence of five Mayakovskys, each representing a different facet of his personality. Lyubimov's synthetic theatre drew on *music hall, *circus, and *shadow play, involving well-known composers and set designers such as Edison Denisov and *Borovsky. In the 1960s his work promoted confidence in independent action, as with *Ten Days That Shook the World* (1965), where the *audience's opinion on the production was polled at the end. In the 1970s, as Lyubimov's position became more vulnerable and his productions increasingly subjected to *censorship, the tone changed to doom and despair about the individual in society. In *Hamlet* (1971) the main part was played by the bard Vladimir *Vysotsky, reciting Pasternak's unpublished poem 'Hamlet' to the guitar. Vysotsky's *costume—a black sweater and jeans—made him a man of the people rather than a prince. Lyubimov was exiled in 1983 during a stay in London, where he directed *Crime and Punishment*. He was allowed to return for a visit in 1988, and permanently in 1989; he resumed the artistic direction of the Taganka in 1991 and continued to apply his aesthetics in work such as *Doctor Zhivago* and *Marat/Sade*.   BB

Mabou Mines New York experimental company, formed in 1970 by JoAnne *Akalaitis, Lee *Breuer, Philip *Glass, and Ruth *Maleczech. (The company was named after a small town in Nova Scotia where the founders created their first piece). Mabou Mines developed a style of psychological *acting within a highly imagistic stage. Although the performance aesthetics of the company are diverse, unifying elements include mixed media and new technologies including holograms in *Imagination Dead Imagine* (1985) and televisual performers in *Hajj* (1983). Text development includes playwriting by company members, *collective *devising, and adaptations. Major productions have included Breuer's *The Red Horse Animation* (1970), *Dressed Like an Egg* (1977), *Dead End Kids* (1982), *Kroetz's *Through the Leaves* (1984), *The Gospel at Colonus* (1988), *Lear* (1990), and *Peter and Wendy* (1996). Mabou Mines has produced numerous works by *Beckett, some of which have been world premières of texts not originally written for the theatre. *A Song for New York*, directed by Maleczech, a 'delayed' response to September 11th, was set on a barge in Staten Island (2007). MDC

MacArthur, Charles (1895–1966) American playwright, married to Helen *Hayes. MacArthur's best work was in collaboration with Ben *Hecht, with whom he shared a background as a Chicago reporter. Their *farce-*melodrama *The Front Page* (1928) brought them wide attention and invitations to Hollywood. Though much of their work (together and separately) would thereafter be in film, they collaborated on five more stage works, including the farce-melodrama *Twentieth Century* (1932) and the *circus *musical extravaganza *Jumbo* (with *Rodgers and *Hart), produced at New York's Hippodrome in 1935. MacArthur's outstanding solo work for theatre was the 1942 political *satire *Johnny on a Spot*. His later years were marred by a long struggle with alcoholism. MAF

McBurney, Simon (1958–) English director, actor, and writer. McBurney developed an early interest in comedy and in 1983 founded the *collective *devising company Theatre de *Complicité, with classmates from *Lecoq's school. Early on they were a hit at the *Edinburgh Festival with *More Bigger Snacks Now* (1985). McBurney's abilities as a physical performer were evident in text-based work at the *National Theatre, *The Street of Crocodiles* (1992) and *Brecht's *Caucasian Chalk Circle* (1997), which he directed. Since 1992 he has been the sole director of Complicité (renamed in 2000), where his directing work has become increasingly international, combining *physical devising, literary adaptation, and *multimedia in productions such as *The Elephant Vanishes* (2003) and *A Disappearing Number* (2007). McBurney played the choirmaster in the BBC television series *The Vicar of Dibley*, directed comedy duo French and Saunders, and has acted in the films *Morality Play* and *The Furnace*. KN

McCann, Donal (1943–99) Irish actor. Early successes included Vladimir in *Beckett's *Waiting for Godot* at the *Abbey Theatre with Peter *O'Toole. McCann excelled in subtle and ambivalent roles and played in Irish and European classics as well as in contemporary work. The depth of his concentrated presence onstage reflected his complex and troubled personality. He embodied the intelligence, spirituality, excessiveness, and dangerous sensitivity of Frank Hardy in *Friel's *Faith Healer* (1980), and his Captain Boyle in *O'Casey's *Juno and the Paycock* was full of complexity and bravado. On film he worked several times with the director John Huston, most notably playing Gabriel in the adaptation of Joyce's 'The Dead'. McCann's last, and to many his most moving performance before his death from cancer, was in Sebastian *Barry's *The Steward of Christendom* (1995) in London and Dublin. CAL

McCarthy, Lillah (1875–1960) English actress and *manager. After eight years of world *touring with Wilson *Barrett, she created the role of Ann Whitefield in *Shaw's *Man and Superman* at the *Royal Court in 1905, playing opposite Granville *Barker, whom she soon married. She became central to Barker's reforming project, excelling in roles for passionate, dominating women, including some Shaw wrote for her. She also went into management with her husband at a number of

London theatres. Shaw thought she gave 'performances of my plays which will probably never be surpassed'; she was also notable as Jocasta in *Reinhardt's monumental *Oedipus the King*, in Barker's revivals of *Euripides, and in his three Shakespeare productions at the Savoy in 1912 and 1914 (as Hermione, Viola, and Helena in *A Midsummer Night's Dream*). They divorced in 1917, to her dismay; at first she continued acting but without Barker's direction her career was effectively over. DK

McClendon, Rose (1884–1936) *African-American actress. In 1916 McClendon studied acting in order to coach children's drama in Harlem. A series of major professional roles followed, including *Galsworthy's *Justice* in 1919, a revival of *Roseanne* in 1924, and *Greene's *In Abraham's Bosom* in 1926. Her graceful performance in *Deep River* that same year impressed Ethel *Barrymore. The next year she appeared in the *Heywards' play *Porgy*. Her last role was in Langston *Hughes's *Mulatto* (1935). With Dick Campbell, McClendon formed the Negro People's Theatre to give training and opportunity to black actors, which merged in 1935 with the Negro Theatre Unit of the *Federal Theatre Project. BBL

McClintic, Guthrie (1893–1961) American director and *producer. Though he began his career in 1914 as an actor, McClintic became one of the most admired directors of his era, directing 94 productions between 1921 and 1952. Twenty-eight of his productions featured his wife Katharine *Cornell. Their careers reached simultaneous zeniths in the 1930s and 1940s with a series of productions noted for their intelligent casting, elegant design, and literary quality, including *The Barretts of Wimpole Street* (1931), *Romeo and Juliet* (1933), *Ethan Frome* (1936), *Hamlet* (1936), *High Tor* (1937), *Candida* (1937), *The Doctor's Dilemma* (1941), and *Medea* (1949). MAF

McCowen, Alec (1925–) Restrained and intelligent English actor who worked with *regional repertory theatres in the 1940s. He joined the *Old Vic in 1959 and was quickly established as a versatile actor in both the classic and modern repertoire: *A Comedy of Errors* and *King Lear* (both 1964), *After the Rain* (1967), and *Hadrian VII* (1969). He was well cast in *Hampton's *The Philanthropist* (1970), as Alceste in *Dexter's production of *The Misanthrope* (1972), and as Higgins in the West End revival of *Pygmalion* (1974). He began performing his one-person shows *St Mark's Gospel* in 1978 and *Kipling* in 1984. At the *National Theatre he was a moving Crocker-Harris in *Rudman's revival of *The

Browning Version (1980) and a thoughtful Vladimir in his production of *Waiting for Godot* (1987). In 1991 he appeared as Jack in *Friel's *Dancing at Lughnasa* and the following year was the English hostage in Frank *McGuinness's *Someone Who'll Watch over Me*. AS

McDonagh, Martin (1971–) English playwright, born in London but writing in the idiom of his Irish heritage. Hailed as a cross between *Synge and film director Quentin Tarantino, McDonagh's carefully constructed *melodramas feature acute observations of the obsessions and innate violence of Irish country life in *farcical situations. His masterful manipulation of *audience emotions and expectations made his first play *The Beauty Queen of Leenane* (1996) a huge success in Ireland and abroad. Produced by the Druid Theatre, Galway, it won four Tony awards; it was the first of a trilogy including *A Skull in Connemara* and *The Lonesome West*. Subsequent plays, *The Cripple of Inishmaan* (1997) and *The Lieutenant of Inishmore* (2001), are also rural Irish melodramas, while *The Pillowman* (2003) is a black comedy set in a fictional totalitarian state. His directing of his screenplay *In Bruges* (2008) was internationally admired. BRS

McEwan, Geraldine (1932–) English actress. Early in her career McEwan was in the company of the *Shakespeare Memorial Theatre, appearing as Jean Rice in *Osborne's *The Entertainer* (1957), Olivia (1957, 1960), Beatrice and Ophelia (1961). She had a reputation for Restoration *comedy, where her roles included Lady Teazle (1962), Lady Brute (1980), Mrs Malaprop (1983), and Lady Wishfort (1995). She appeared opposite *vaudevillian Jimmy Jewel in *Bogdanov's revival of the *Kaufman and *Hart *musical *You Can't Take It with You* (1993), and in 1998 played the Old Woman in Simon *McBurney's production of *Ionesco's *The Chairs*. On television she appeared as the brittle and eccentric *heroine in *The Prime of Miss Jean Brodie* (1978), the monstrous mother in *Oranges Are Not the Only Fruit* (1990), and *Christie's Miss Marple in a 2004 series. AS

Macgowan, Kenneth (1888–1963) American *producer and critic. *The Theatre of Tomorrow* (1921) and *Continental Stagecraft* (with Robert Edmond *Jones, 1922) made him a leading proponent of the New Stagecraft and experimental techniques in playwriting. Macgowan was appointed head of the *Provincetown Players in 1923, managed with *O'Neill and Jones. In 1924 operations were reorganized as the Experimental Theatre, Inc., and staged *The Great God Brown and other works by O'Neill. In the early 1930s Macgowan became a major film producer in Hollywood.   MAF

MacGowran, Jack (1918–73) Irish actor. Notable early stage performances were in Irish-language *pantomimes at the *Abbey Theatre (1947–9). He was much praised as the Dauphin in *Shaw's *St Joan* (1953), Nicola in Shaw's *Arms and the Man* (1955), and Joxer in *O'Casey's *Juno and the Paycock* to Peter O'Toole's Boyle (1966), all in Dublin. He was in John Ford's film *The Quiet Man* (1952), Polanski's *Dance of the Vampires* (1967), and Lean's *Ryan's Daughter* (1970). He was acclaimed in the first English-language productions of four plays by *Beckett: Tommy in *All that Fall* (1957), Clov in *Endgame* (1958), Henry in *Embers* (1959), and Joe in *Eh Joe* (1956). Awards included British TV actor of the year for Vladimir in *Waiting for Godot* (1961) and New York Critics' for his Beckett compilation *Beginning to End* (1971). His brooding presence and lugubrious countenance produced an extraordinary effect, at once tragic and comic.   CFS

McGrath, John (1935–2002) British writer, director, *producer, a cultural presence working across theatre, television, and film. He came to attention as one of the writers for the *English Stage Company in the late 1950s, and as a principal creator of *Z Cars*, the legendary television police drama series, while a director at the BBC in the early 1960s. McGrath had further success in the theatre, with *Events While Guarding the Bofors Gun* (1965), and as a screenwriter with *Billion Dollar Brain* (1967). In the early 1970s with his wife Elizabeth McLennan he established 7:84 and 7:84 (Scotland), *touring companies committed to performing socialist popular theatre to working-class *audiences. *The Cheviot, the Stag and the Black, Black Oil* (1973) became one of the most influential post-war political plays and was televised by the BBC in 1974. McGrath reflected critically on his work, popular theatre generally, and cultural politics in *A Good Night Out* (1981), and *The Bone Won't Break* (1990). Thereafter he continued to produce theatre (mainly in Scotland) and films for television through his company, Freeway Films.   SWL

McGuinness, Frank (1953–) Irish playwright, renowned for sensitivity to the traditions, beliefs, and sensibilities of others. His representation of Protestants, most notably in *Observe the Sons of Ulster Marching towards the Somme* (1985), interrogates their loyalism to England and loyalties to each other in the First World War in an *expressionistic, moral stage battle.

Mutabilitie (*National Theatre, London, 1997), washes up William Shakespeare in an Ireland governed by Edmund Spenser and pits the brutalities of opposing ideologies with the loves of good men. *Dolly West's Kitchen* (*Abbey Theatre, 1999) questions Ireland's neutrality in the Second World War, and permits Irish nationalism to embrace homosexuality. His most commercially successful play, *Someone Who'll Watch over Me* (1992) features the plight of three Western hostages in an unnamed Middle Eastern country. All his work, including many celebrated translations of European classics, challenges the myths, traditions, and taboos that breed intolerance.   BRS

Machiavelli, Niccolò (1469–1527) Florentine political theorist and playwright. A devoted student of classical literature, Machiavelli was the author of two original prose *comedies in the new humanist style, and one translation from *Terence. *The Mandrake* (c.1518) is regarded by many as the masterpiece of *commedia erudita*: it deals in single-minded fashion with a plot to seduce a virtuous wife with the cooperation of her incredibly stupid husband and a corrupt friar. The wife herself is not a willing collaborator (unlike the *heroines of most traditional comic adultery tales), and modern *audiences might be uncomfortable with the way in which her role is treated, but the play contains some devastating moments of black comedy. *Clizia* (1525) shows the resourceful wife Sofronia foiling her husband's erotic designs on their young ward: the play thus has a socially acceptable *denouement.   RAA

MacIntyre, Tom (1935–) Irish playwright, poet, and fiction writer, a restless experimenter in different styles and media, including an early political play *Eye-Winker, Tom Tinker* (1972). His most significant contribution to Irish theatre has been a series of image- and movement-based plays of the 1980s, staged at the *Abbey in collaboration with the director Patrick *Mason and the actor Tom Hickey. These included *The Bearded Lady* (1984), centred on the writings of Swift, *Rise up Lovely Sweeney* (1985), based on Irish mythological material, and paticulary the adaptation of Patrick Kavanagh's long poem *The Great Hunger* (1983). Working from certain central images in Kavanagh's bleak evocation of the sexual and spiritual repressions of mid-century rural Ireland, MacIntyre choreographed a drama of *lighting, *mime, and movement. Later plays, *Sheep's Milk on the Boil* (1994), *Good Evening Mr Collins* (1995), and *What Happened Bridgie Cleary*

(2005), have been more conventionally language based. NG

MacKaye, Percy (1875–1956) American theorist and playwright. Son of Steele *MacKaye, Percy began writing on commission for the actor E. H. *Sothern. His *Jeanne d'Arc* was premièred by Sothern and Julia *Marlowe in 1906 and *The Scarecrow* was a New York success in 1911. Seeing theatrical activity as a pathway to meaning in an increasingly mechanized world, MacKaye wrote several influential books encouraging 'participatory drama', including *The Civic Theatre in Relation to the Redemption of Leisure* (1912) and *Community Drama* (1917). His mass spectacles put these principles to use, such as a 'masque' celebrating the 150th anniversary of the founding of St Louis, performed in the open air with a cast of 8,000. When the vogue for pageantry faded during the First World War, MacKaye turned to folk drama based on research in Kentucky and New England and wrote plays commemorating historical events. *See also* COMMUNITY THEATRE; LITTLE THEATRE MOVEMENT. MAF

MacKaye, Steele (1842–94) American actor, playwright, *manager, and inventor. After studying with *Delsarte in Paris in 1869, McKaye opened a Delsartian *acting school in New York in 1871. He made his professional debut as actor and writer the following year in *Monaldi*, but his first major writing successes did not come until an adaptation, *Rose Michel* (1875), and his original piece *Won at Last* (1877). His insistence upon *realistic acting and natural *dialogue are evident even in historical romances such as *Anarchy* (1887). McKaye's best play, *Hazel Kirke* (1880), ran for more than a year at his Madison Square Theatre. His interest in theatrical modernization was evident in this venue, which introduced elevator stages and folding chairs, both of McKaye's own design, and an electrical *lighting system designed by Thomas Edison. McKaye subsequently opened the Lyceum Theatre complex, which incorporated innovative fire-fighting equipment, rising orchestra pit, and rooms for an acting school. GAR

McKellen, Ian (1939–) English actor. McKellen worked widely before his performances as Richard II (1968) and a camp extrovert incarnation of *Marlowe's Edward II (1969) brought him prominence as a brilliant classical actor, sensitive to language and complex in characterization. He was a founder member of the Actors' Company in 1972, an attempt to diminish *directors' power. In 1974 he began working for the *Royal Shakespeare Company, moving from a romantic Romeo to a tortured Macbeth (both 1976). In Martin

Sherman's *Bent* (1979, 1989) he used the role as part of his campaign for *gay rights. He toured his one-person show *Acting Shakespeare* from 1980 to 1983. His seasons at the *National included *Chekhov's Platonov (1986), Coriolanus (1984), and a 1930s fascist Richard III (1989), the basis of a powerful film adaptation (1995) which he wrote and starred in. His search for *realism in Shakespeare generated a paranoid and punctilious Iago (RSC, 1989), while dislike of the major companies led him to a season at West Yorkshire Playhouse (*The Seagull*, Prospero, and *Coward's Garry Essendine, 1998–9). He played the wizard Gandalf in the film of *The Lord of the Rings* (2001) and Widow Twankey in *Aladdin* (*Old Vic *pantomime, 2004). His *King Lear* (RSC, 2007) was widely praised and filmed for television. PDH

McKenna, Siobhán (1922–86) Irish actress. Born in Belfast, her stage career began in the Irish language at An Taibhdhearc Theatre in Galway, where she played Lady Macbeth and St Joan (1941). She was at the *Abbey Theatre in Dublin (1943–6), and starting in 1947 established a career in London and New York. Her appearances in *Shaw's *St Joan* (this time in English) and as Pegeen in *Synge's *Playboy* (filmed in 1961) were highly acclaimed. A candid, earthy energy and poetic verve drove these performances; she also excelled in the painfully vulnerable title role in *Friel's *The Loves of Cass Maguire* (1967). She first played her one-person show *Here Are Ladies* (1970) in Oxford. Subsequently televised in Ireland, the work illustrated her extraordinary range from high *comedy to Molly Bloom's *soliloquy from Joyce's *Ulysses*. Tom *Murphy wrote the part of Mommo in *Bailegangaire* (1985) for her; she gave an unforgettable performance as an obsessive, bedridden storyteller, which was her last. CAL

McKern, Leo (1920–2002) Australian actor. Most famous for his creation of a very English *character, Rumpole of the Bailey in the television series written by John *Mortimer, McKern had a long and successful stage career. McKern left Australia for the UK in 1946, following, and then marrying, the actress Jane Holland. *Guthrie directed him in Molière's *The Miser* at the *Old Vic, where he stayed for a number of years, and he also took major roles (including Iago) for the *Shakespeare Memorial Theatre *tour of Australia in 1952–3. Despite his extensive British career, in Australia McKern played the iconic role of Ned Kelly, in Douglas Stewart's poetic drama of the same name (1956), and had great commercial success with the one-person show *Boswell for the Defence*, which toured extensively in 1988. He also played the lead in the 1987 Australian film of David *Williamson's *Travelling North*, and in many international films.   EJS

Mackintosh, Cameron (1946–) English *producer. His first real hit was the 1976 London production of *Side by Side by Sondheim*. He reached the top of the profession when he produced *Lloyd Webber's *Cats* (1981), followed by *Boublil and Schönberg's *Les Misérables* (1985) and *Miss Saigon* (1989), and Lloyd Webber's *The Phantom of the Opera* (1986). He has produced hundreds of *musicals—new and old, large and small—becoming the world's most successful theatre entrepreneur. 'It's called show *business*,' he has said, and he has revolutionized that business, largely by keeping tight supervisory control (or 'franchising') over all his productions, assuring a standard of quality in every venue internationally. He produced the musical *Mary Poppins* (London 2004, New York 2006), and a revival of *Bart's *Oliver!* at *Drury Lane (2009). He has contributed substantial sums to the *National Theatre to produce large-scale musicals, in each of which he retains co-producer interest, supervising subsequent commercial transfers. He owns seven West End theatres.   JD

Macklin, Charles (1699–1797) Irish actor and playwright, one of the most famous and longest lived of his day. He capitalized on the *Drury Lane actors' rebellion of 1733, making his London debut there during the absence of the regular company. He became an invaluable *stage manager for Charles Fleetwood and began to acquire more roles. His greatest triumph was as Shylock in 1741. Macklin revolutionized the play by restoring Shakespeare's text and treating the *character as fiercely malevolent in a *realistic manner, adapting the *costuming to a more historically correct style. His range was not great: he was at his best in cantankerous old man roles, such as Sir Gilber Wrangle in *Cibber's *The Refusal*. As a playwright Macklin tended to write similar roles for himself, like Sir Archy MacSarcasm in *Love à la Mode* (1759) and Sir Pertinax MacSycophant in *The Man of the World* (1781). Famously litigious, he made important legal strides for actors and authors, defending his plays from pirated editions and performances (*see* COPYRIGHT), successfully prosecuting *audience members for conspiring to have him fired from *Covent Garden in 1773, and then the *managers for firing him. He died famous, but not rich, just a few years shy of 100.   MJK

MacLíammóir, Micheál (1899–1978) Irish actor, designer, and writer. Born Alfred Willmore in London, he visited Ireland as a child actor in

Peter Pan, studied art and the Irish language in London, and following an Irish Shakespearian *tour with Anew *McMaster settled in Dublin in 1927. He was instrumental in founding the Irish-language theatre An Taibhdhearc in Galway in 1928, the year he co-founded Dublin Gate Theatre Productions with Hilton *Edwards; their production style derived largely from romantic German *expressionism. His most admired roles were Speaker/Emmet in Denis *Johnston's *The Old Lady Says, 'No!'*, Brack in *Ibsen's *Hedda Gabler*, and the title parts in *Pirandello's *Henry IV* and Shakespeare's *Richard II* and *Hamlet*—all produced several times, the latter also at Elsinore. His one-person show *The Importance of Being Oscar* was seen in nineteen countries from 1960 to 1975. The most enduring of his eight plays are *Diarmuid agus Gráinne* (1927), *Where Stars Walk* (1940), and *Ill Met by Moonlight* (1946).   CFS

McMahon, Gregan (1874–1941) Australian actor and director. From 1911 to 1917, McMahon established and ran the mostly amateur Melbourne Repertory Theatre Company, and remained centrally involved in the repertory theatre movement until his death. He introduced the drama of *Shaw, *Galsworthy, *Chekhov, and *Ibsen to Australian *audiences, and championed Australian playwrights, staging thirteen new Australian plays in six years. McMahon's professional directing career included working for J. C. *Williamson's company (1920–8 and 1935–41), running their repertory companies in Sydney and Melbourne.   KMN

McMaster, Anew (1891–1962) Irish *actor-manager. At 19 Anew (Andrew) forsook a banking career for the stage; his first major success came in 1920 as Jack O'Hara in *Paddy the Next Best Thing* at the Savoy. He *toured Australia in this and other plays, and in 1925 formed his own company to tour Shakespeare, chiefly in Ireland but also in Britain and Australia, continuing until the early 1960s. At the *Shakespeare Memorial Theatre in Stratford he appeared as Hamlet, Coriolanus, Macduff, Leonato, Escalus, and Petruchio (1933). His greatest roles were Othello and Shylock, adding Lear in 1952. He toured the United States as James Tyrone in *O'Neill's *Long Day's Journey into Night* in 1956. The possessor of 'a great organ voice', *Pinter, who acted in his company in Ireland, described him as 'evasive, proud, affectionate, shrewd, merry'. He married Marjorie Willmore, actress and designer, sister of *MacLíammóir.   CFS

McNally, Terrence (1939–) American playwright. *And Things That Go Bump in the Night*

(1964) was a quick flop on Broadway, and much later work was done *Off-Broadway. Starting in 1987 with *Frankie and Johnny in the Clair de Lune*, McNally found an artistic home at the Manhattan Theatre Club, with many transfers to commercial engagements (*Lips Together, Teeth Apart*, 1991; *A Perfect Ganesh*, 1993; *Love! Valour! Compassion!*, 1994). His *Master Class* (1995) achieved immense popularity, while his 1997 *Corpus Christi*, which featured a gay Jesus-like figure and his disciples in modern-day Texas, aroused storms of protest at each production. McNally was also a *musical comedy librettist: *The Rink* (1984), his first musical, was regarded as a weak vehicle for stars Chita Rivera and Liza Minelli. Rivera also starred in *Kiss of the Spider Woman* (1990). McNally's librettos for *Ragtime* (1997) and *The Full Monty* (2000) were better received. *Deuce* with Angela *Lansbury opened on Broadway in 2007.   AW

McPherson, Conor (1971–) Irish dramatist. McPherson's first plays were characterized by the monologue form, from *This Lime Tree Bower* (1995) to *Port Authority* (2001). His 1997 commission by the *Royal Court, *The Weir*, ran for over two years and transferred to Broadway, winning a host of awards. *The Seafarer* (2006), first produced at the *National Theatre, had a similar trajectory. As well as writing three screenplays, he also directs for theatre and film. His work centres on evocative fables of troubled men.   BRS

Macready, William Charles (1793–1873) English actor and *manager. In 1816 he made his London debut and soon established himself as a major actor. Before his first period of management Macready had played many leading Shakespearian roles and was indisputably at the head of his profession. His managements at *Covent Garden (1837–9) and *Drury Lane (1841–3) were financially unrewarding, but distinguished and influential. A dedicated, hard-working manager, Macready *rehearsed as thoroughly as he could, given the size of his repertory, searched endlessly for new plays of merit, worked extensively with inexperienced dramatists on their scripts, as with *Bulwer-Lytton on *Richelieu* (1837), introduced the pictorial illustration of Shakespeare's texts through scenery and spectacle, and used large numbers of crowd scenes with skill. He respected the text, and restored the Fool to Shakespeare's *King Lear*, not seen since *Tate's 1681 version. Stressing unity and coherence in production, he led the way to *Phelps, Charles *Kean, and *Irving. Macready's problems were largely those of personality and temperament. Regarding himself as a gentleman, he disliked actors, but felt he must carry on for the sake of his family, to which he was devoted. His friendships with the literary elite—*Dickens and Browning among them—made him overprotective of the worth of *legitimate drama. As an actor, he was a great Lear and Macbeth, and strong in any role, such as Virginius in *Knowles's play (1820). He retired in 1851.   MRB

Madách, Imre (1823–64) Hungarian playwright and poet. Madách graduated as a lawyer and was a Member of Parliament from 1861. In the same year he published his masterpiece *The Tragedy of Man*, a great success that gained him entrance to literary circles and the Hungarian Academy of Sciences. Although he wrote poems and fiction, and was an acknowledged journalist and orator, his main interest lay in drama. His work includes historical plays such as *Commodus* (1839) and *Andrew of Naples* (1841–2) and a *comedy, *The Civilizer* (1859) in the style of *Aristophanes. *The Tragedy of Man*, a sweeping philosophical play about destiny, was influenced by *Goethe's *Faust* and seems to look forward to *Ibsen's *Peer Gynt*. The work was not staged until 1883 and received international recognition in 1892. It has been translated into many languages and produced frequently in Central Europe. It remains central to the Hungarian repertoire; the new National Theatre in Budapest opened with it in 2002.   JHA

Madani, Izzedine (1938–) Short-story writer and playwright, the most popular Tunisian dramatist of the 1970s and 1980s. His dramatic career began when Ali *Ben Ayed produced *The Revolt of the Man on the Ass* (Tunis, 1970). Madani has written nine further plays, which have been produced widely: in Casablanca, Tayeb *Saddiki directed *Forgiveness* (1976); in Cairo, Samir Asfouri staged *To Round and to Square* (1985); in Tunis and Paris, Cherif Khaznadar directed *The Voyage* (1985). The most important period of Madani's career, however, was in tandem with Moncef Souissi, director of the regional Tunisian company El Kef. Taking *Brecht as a point of reference, Madani wrote plays about revolutions and *characters drawn from Arabic and Islamic history. MMe

Maddy, Yulisa Amadu (1936–) Sierra Leonean dramatist, actor, director, and dancer. After drama study in London (1962–4), his first play, *Yonkon*, was broadcast by the BBC. Other work followed in abundance, including *Life Everlasting*, *Alla Gba*, *Take Tem Draw Di Rope*, *Naw We Yone Dehn Sco*, *Big Berrin*, *A Journey into Christmas* and *Drums, Voices and Worlds*. Back in Freetown in 1968 as head of radio drama, he also directed national *dance troupes there and in Zambia and founded his long-lived theatre company Gba-kanda Afrikan Tiata. Maddy was imprisoned in Sierra Leone in 1977, possibly in connection with his play *Big Berrin*, and on his release moved to London where he directed Alem Mez-gebe's *Pulse* (1979). Maddy has since carried his high ideals for African theatre to Ibadan in 1980, where he directed *Pulse*, *Jero*, and *Big Breeze*, and, over a twenty-year period, to Britain and the USA.   JMG

Maeterlinck, Maurice (1862-1949) Belgian *symbolist playwright and poet. Paul *Fort direct-ed two of Maeterlinck's early one-acts at the Thé-âtre d'*Art, *The Intruder* (1891) and *The Blind* (1892), productions which gave rise to the term 'static theatre'. In these plays actors barely move, as the spirit world is evoked through atmosphere and the performers' reactions. *The Blind* features a split stage dividing the human race by sex, and a host of blind *characters, led into a forest by a priest; they cannot see that the priest is dead and they are abandoned. The verse is incantatory and liturgical, the fear is vague but palpable, presaging *Beckett's early plays and other *absurdist dra-mas. Death is a tangible presence, and perhaps even the play's greatest (though unseen) charac-ter. *Pelléas and Mélisande*, first directed by *Lugné-Poe in 1893, and set to music by Debussy in 1902, frees characters from stasis and permits spatial and temporal progression in a retelling of the story of Paolo and Francesca. Life, like the course of Maeterlinck's dramas, is determined by unknown forces; his characters are led to their deaths but fail to understand their predica-ment or fate, even at their final moments. Mae-terlinck believed his work was not best performed by human actors and in 1894 wrote three plays specifically for *puppets (*Alladine et Palomides*, *Intérieur*, *La Mort de Tintagiles*). Other notable works include *Monna Vanna* (directed by Lugné-Poe, 1902), and the much filmed *Blue Bird*, first produced by *Stanislavsky at the *Moscow Art The-atre in 1908. Most of Maeterlinck's later career was as an essayist and poet. He was awarded the Nobel Prize for Literature in 1911.   BRS

Maffei, Francesco Scipione (1675-1755) Italian scholar, playwright, and librettist. Attribut-ing the decadence of Italian theatre to a depen-dence on French writers such as *Corneille, the rationalist Maffei urged a return to the tradition of sixteenth-century Italian *tragedy. He enlisted Luigi and Elena *Riccoboni, who were in the ser-vice of the Duke of Modena, to present contem-porary tragedies specifically written for them, as well as sixteenth- and seventeenth-century works

such as *Trissino's *Sofonisba*, *Tasso's *Torris-mondo*, and his own extremely successful tragedy *Merope* (1713). Considered an ideal of *neoclassical simplicity and verisimilitude, this play inspired *Voltaire's of the same title.   JEH

Magaña, Sergio (1924-90) Mexican play-wright, novelist, and theatre critic. A member of the so-called Generation of 1950, his first success-ful piece, *The Signs of the Zodiac* (1951), is still considered among the best twentieth-century Mexican plays. Set in a tenement in the older part of Mexico City, the text explores the comings and goings of the lower middle class whose lives are determined by the physical and psychological restrictions of their cramped quarters; *The Small Case of Jorge Lívido* (1958) deals with similar sub-ject matter. While a critic of the social inequities of Mexican society, Magaña also struck a patriotic note in historical plays such as *Moctezuma II* (1954), an attempt at modern *tragedy which, like many of his plays, was a popular success. His *Frozen Rents* (1960) is one of a handful of modern Mexican *musicals.   KFN

Maggi, Carlos (1922-) Uruguayan play-wright, scriptwriter, and novelist. A lawyer with a highly visible public persona, Maggi began to write in the 1950s and became the most re-nowned Uruguayan playwright of his generation. His work scrutinizes the social, political, and in-tellectual conditions of the nation, drawing upon strategies related to *expressionism, the *absurd, and the grotesque. Major early plays include *The Library* (1959), *Waiting for Rodó* (1961), and *The Pianist and Love* (1965). During Uruguay's dicta-torial period (1973-85) Maggi was persecuted and stopped writing for the theatre, but he reappeared with *Don Frutos* (1985), a look at the life of Presi-dent Fructuoso Rivera, and a number of new works in the 1990s.   JCC

magic shows In the third century AD the Roman Alciphron recorded street performers of-fering the 'cup and ball' trick, making pebbles disappear and reappear under dishes and cups, and out of spectators' noses and ears. Street con-jurors were a common sight in the medieval fairs of Europe. By the eighteenth century more lavish conjuring *fairground booths, such as that of Isaac Fawkes, were found at Bartholomew Fair; Fawkes's great illusion was a tree that bore ripe apples in less than a minute. By the nineteenth century magic and spectacular effects were im-portant features of popular drama. The 'transfor-mation scene' became a standard element of *pantomime, and Pepper's *ghost (an apparition created by projecting an image onto a tilted mirror) enlivened otherwise unremarkable dramas. *Illusion was frequently dissected in popular magazines, with cutaways showing stage effects and techniques. The availability of simple conjuring apparatus in the second half of the nineteenth century, and the publication of magicians' manuals such as Professor Hoffman's *Modern Magic* (1876), prompted growth in amateur conjuring.

Robert-Houdin (1805–71), the 'father of modern magic', rose from watchmaker to *manager of the Théâtre des Soirées Fantastiques in the *Palais Royal in Paris (1845). His levitation trick called 'Ethereal Suspension'—in which his son was supposedly rendered weightless by the inhalation of ether—was typical of his fascination with mechanics and technology. Another watchmaker, John Nevil Maskelyne (1839–1917), and his friend George Alfred Cooke (cabinetmaker and cornetplayer), successfully debunked popular spiritualist acts (the Davenport Brothers in particular), whilst establishing themselves at the forefront of British magic in the Egyptian Hall in London's Piccadilly, 'Home of Mystery' for almost 30 years (1873–1904).

*Music-hall and *variety entertainment encouraged magicians such as David Devant (1868–1941) and P. T. Selbit, who specialized in short and sensational programmes. Selbit promoted the involvement of the female magician's assistant, variously chained, impaled, and dismembered in a series of torture effects. Infamous on the variety stage was Carl Hertz, an American conjuror specializing in disappearing canaries; in 1921 he was forced to play before a House of Commons Select Committee on Performing *Animals to prove that he did not kill a bird each time he made it disappear. Though the Committee was satisfied, there is little doubt that Hertz's skill in substituting a lookalike bird saved his reputation and his act. Harry *Kellar, who joined spiritualism with escape, was enormously popular in America at the turn of the twentieth century. But Harry *Houdini, as flamboyant and self-promoting as Hertz, was the great escapologist, 'The Handcuff King'. Most of his sensational escapes were performed in public: manacled, laced, and chained, he was confined within the embalmed body of a whale in Boston in 1911. William Robinson (1861–1918), known as Chung Ling Soo, also risked personal injury in his extraordinary bullet-catching illusion; he died when he was hit by one of the two bullets he purportedly caught.

In the latter part of the twentieth century, magic underwent a major television revival, with the extravagant performances of conjurors like David Copperfield, who memorably made the Concorde aircraft disappear. David Blane, in a determinedly streetwise approach, continues to appeal to the younger television *audience, offering variations on card tricks, levitation, and spectacularly sealing himself in a block of ice for three days in New York's Times Square.   AF

Mahelot, Laurent (fl. 1625–40) French *scenographer. Mahelot, whose non-professional life remains a mystery, probably succeeded Georges Buffequin in the late 1620s as resident scenic designer–stage director at the *Hôtel de Bourgogne in Paris. He is known to us exclusively through the manuscript commonly called the *Mémoire de Mahelot*, to which he was the first of three contributors. Mahelot's section—notes describing the production requirements of 71 plays in the company's repertory in the early 1630s, plus ink-and-wash sketches of his settings for 47 of them—illustrates the *medieval tradition of multiple staging, as it moved onto the enclosed end-stage of the seventeenth-century *playhouse. The various scenic elements representing the locations required by a play's *action—prisons, palaces, caves, temples, shops, and gardens, all chosen from stock—are arranged on three sides of a central, unoccupied acting space. While he rarely attempted to compose these elements into homogeneous stage pictures similar to *Serlio's, Mahelot's frequent use of *perspective reflects Italian practice. The *Mémoire* records the moment at which the medieval and the *early modern scenographies collide, moving towards scenic *illusion.   JG

Mahendravikramavarman (580–630) Sanskrit poet, playwright, and musician. His father Simhavishnuvarman, the founder of the Pallava dynasty, established an extensive kingdom in south India. Mahendravikramavarman's many accomplishments traditionally include *Mattavilasa*, his best-known play (*Drunken Reveller*), which belongs to the *prahasana* (*farce) category in Sanskrit drama. *Bhagavadajjukiyam* (*Hermit and Harlot*) is also sometimes attributed to him. *Mattavilasa* involves a Saivite mendicant, who goes through Kanchi visiting liquor shops along with Devasoma, his attractive female companion. In their drunken revelry Kapalin loses his begging bowl. Later he picks a quarrel with a Buddhist monk whose begging bowl he claims as his own. A devotee of Lord Siva tries in vain to arbitrate the dispute, and finally a madman retrieves the bowl from a dog's mouth, proving himself more sane than the others. The *characters in this farce, drawn from contemporary life, are all degenerate, regardless of their religious beliefs, and the royal author, an ardent Saivite himself, vehemently *satirizes them.   KNP

Maillet, Antonine (1929-   ) French-Canadian dramatist and novelist, born in Acadia. Her first major success was *The Slattern* (1971), the play for which she is best known. A series of sixteen poignant *monologues in the archaic Acadian dialect, spoken by an elderly cleaning woman, reflect with mordant but balanced humour on the injustices to which she, her social class, and indeed all Acadians have been subject. It was an instant success in Canada, on stage and television. Published in France in 1976, it has been staged there and in other European countries. Maillet's other plays (some fifteen), although often successful, have not received such acclaim. Typical is *Evangeline the Second* (1976), an impassioned rejection of Longfellow's passive, tearful *heroine. Also a major novelist, she received France's prestigious Prix Goncourt in 1979 for her novel *Pélagie-la-Charrette*, a semi-historic recounting of the Acadian nation's return from exile.   LED

Mairet, Jean (1604-86) French dramatist. A rival of *Corneille, Mairet is generally regarded as responsible for the introduction of the three *unities into serious French drama, first in a preface to *Silvanire*, a *pastoral *tragedy of 1630, then in practice in his masterpiece *Sophonisbe* (1634), the first play to illustrate the *bienséances* (decorum) as well as the unities, thereby achieving the fourth unity—that of tone—which was to be the hallmark of French tragedy throughout the *neoclassical period. Mairet, a protégé of *Richelieu and for a time a member, with Corneille, of the 'cinq auteurs' who composed plays under the Cardinal's direction, wrote one of the most hostile attacks on Corneille's *Le Cid* (acting, it is assumed, on Richelieu's orders); indeed, the 'Quarrel of the *Cid*' can fairly be regarded as a controversy originating in, and kept alive by, the vanity and touchiness of both Corneille and his principal adversary.   WDH

Maleczech, Ruth (1939-   ) American actor and director. After work with the San Francisco Mime Troupe, Maleczech travelled in Europe where she acted in *Beckett's *Play* (1965) and studied with *Grotowski. With *Akalaitis, *Breuer, David Warrilow, and *Glass, she formed *Mabou Mines in 1969. Maleczech acted in five productions at the *New York Shakespeare Festival, including *Dead End Kids* by Akalaitis (1980), a play about nuclear power, and Breuer's poetic performance piece *Hajj* (1983). She acted the role of a submissive butcher in *Kroetz's *Through the Leaves*; played the title role in a cross-gendered *Lear*, set by Breuer in the 1950s American south-

east (1987); and performed Winnie in Beckett's *Happy Days* (1997). Though she writes and directs, her focus remains on *acting, where her meticulous, straightforward approach and wide-ranging experimental techniques make her a major artist. She directed *A Song for New York* for Mabou Mines (2007).   FL

male impersonation Women cross-dressing to represent men or boys, within a context of public performance, does not appear to have the long history or the roots in *ritual practice that could be said to legitimize cross-dressing by men (*see* FEMALE IMPERSONATION). Nor does it have the same range of meanings, and such difference may account for its relative rarity. Historically, male cross-dressing is a commonplace of performance, accommodated relatively comfortably within both social hierarchies and the conventions of *gender ordering. Not so for women. Their gradual appearance on European professional stages during the sixteenth and seventeenth centuries led at once to their performing in male clothes (*see* BREECHES ROLE), but such appearances were usually defused of any possible threat by being sexualized in a mode which emphasized the femininity of the performer, if simply by the physical exposure of wearing the breeches. Only in the later nineteenth century in Britain and America did the 'impersonation' of men, in the sense of an *illusionistic and sometimes *satirical intent to replicate their dress and physical demeanour, become a popular performance speciality. It has not remained so; since the coming of a general awareness in the early twentieth century of possible challenges to white male definitions of masculinity and of *lesbian meanings in such performance, the psychological discomforts and social transgressiveness of being or of seeing a woman dressing up (as opposed to a man dressing down) in their performance of gender have stood in the way of widespread male impersonation for entertainment.

The flowering of male impersonation was on the nineteenth-century stage, in *vaudeville and *music hall. The habit of simple cross-playing, girls representing boys in dramatic sketches simply for convenience, survived unchecked, and there were also still *dancers who used elements of male dress simply to display their own bodies with a freedom denied by voluminous skirts; but singers, especially, had begun to use a more thoroughgoing gender transformation on stage. According to physical type, ability, and temperament, they might represent slender youths in fashionable dress and especially in attractive uniforms (Vesta *Tilley, Bessie Bonehill, Hetty King are examples of this mode) or heavyweight roistering swells or dudes (early examples were Annie Hindle and Ella Wesner in America, Fanny Robina in England, Louise Rott in Germany, and later the Australian Ella Shields, and the black vaudeville 'bull dagger' Gladys Bentley). There were many variations in *realism of representation: Robina wore corsets under her tail-coated *costume, while Tilley was so immaculately androgynous that she was supposed to have set male fashions. But she had a soprano voice. How far the gender play extended, that is, whether their representation of masculinity was mocking or idealized, and whether the personae projected and received were sexually ambiguous or romantically innocent, must have varied not only between individual performers but between venues, and been differently read even across parts of the house, by working men and middle-class loungers; and certainly the response must have differed between men and women in the *audience. Such an absence of common agreement about how to understand the act of full-dress male impersonation is arguably the reason for its fading, rather than becoming an established and acceptable form of gender play: it is too uncomfortable for a general audience.

Twentieth-century examples of its use endorse that conclusion in two distinct ways. In 1914 Kobayashi Ichizō organized an all-girl acting company in a small town in Japan, from which the *Takarazuka took its name. Still thriving, and with a huge following of Japanese women, this lavishly mounted song-and-dance entertainment is characterized by young women playing *otoko-yaku*, idealized young men, more perfect than any male self-representation. Their material typically draws on Western music and cultural icons, and their polished routines present a perfect simulacrum of glamorous romantic relationships whose remoteness from real life guarantees a safe subsexual thrill which is in no way challenging or unsettling. On the other hand, some Western *feminist performers have taken up male impersonation as an explicit challenge to patriarchal hegemony. Peggy Shaw's performances such as *A Menopausal Gentleman* openly explore gender boundaries and transgressive experience (*see* SPLIT BRITCHES); while some British television *satire, such as the representation of Prime Minister Margaret Thatcher in the *puppet show *Spitting Image*, or the disgusting sexism of the fat middle-aged working men in sketches presented by Dawn French and Jennifer Saunders, make male impersonation a route to explicit critique of masculine attitudes and supremacy. Since there is still no generally understood and easy way of integrating such performance into light entertainment

in the West, such acts remain a minority interest, and an aggressive statement.   JSB

Malina, Judith (1926–   ) American director, actor, playwright, and activist. Born in Germany, she trained with *Piscator in New York. In 1947 she founded the *Living Theatre with her husband Julian *Beck, and promoted an experimental approach with productions of playwrights such as *Stein, *Cocteau, *Brecht, and *Pirandello. Malina's anarcho-pacifist beliefs led the Living Theatre to explore new forms of theatre-making through *collective creation and *improvisation, while developing an aesthetic of physicality and confrontation. She performed throughout Europe and the Americas in such landmark productions as *Mysteries and Smaller Pieces* (1964), *Frankenstein* (1965), *Antigone* (1967), and *Paradise Now* (1968). She won eight Obie awards, including one for best actress in her translation and adaptation of Brecht's *Antigone* (1969). After Beck's death in 1985, Malina continued the work of the Living Theatre with her partner Hannon Resnikov, performing new works throughout the world. As an actress she has appeared in such films as *Dog Day Afternoon* (1975), *Radio Days* (1987), *The Addams Family* (1991), and *Looking for Richard* (1996).   MDC

Mamet, David (1947–   ) American writer and director. Born and raised in Chicago, Mamet joined its vibrant theatre scene as co-founder of the St Nicholas Theater Company and has since become a major dramatist. *American Buffalo* (1975) thrust Mamet into the national spotlight, partly for its earthy and liberal use of profanity. Its taut *naturalistic tale of three lowlifes who botch the theft of a coin collection introduced some of Mamet's enduring themes: trust and betrayal, vernacular speech, the intimacy of machismo, spiritual vacuity. These themes were advanced in two major works of the 1980s, the Pulitzer Prize-winning *Glengarry Glen Ross* (1984), about a group of unscrupulous Chicago real-estate agents, and *Speed-the-Plow* (1988), about two Hollywood insiders and the innocent woman who comes between them. *Oleanna* (1992) was Mamet's provocative take on political correctness and sexual harassment, while the quasi-autobiographical *The Cryptogram* (1994) and *Boston Marriage* (1999) effected a more serene demeanour. In the 1990s the prolific Mamet concentrated more on film. He began writing screenplays for hire in the 1980s (*The Postman Always Rings Twice*, 1981; *The Verdict*, 1982; *The Untouchables*, 1987) and directing his own scripts (*House of Games*, 1987; *Things Change*, 1988). Later films written and directed by Mamet include *The Spanish Prisoner* (1997), an adaptation of *Rattigan's *The Winslow Boy* (1999), *State and Main* (2000), and *Redbelt* (2008). All told, he has written more than two dozen screenplays and directed a dozen films. *Writing in Restaurants* (1986), his first collection of occasional pieces, was followed by other volumes of fiction and poetry.   STC

Mamoulian, Rouben (1898–1987) Georgian-born American director. When his studies at *Vakhtangov's Third Studio in Moscow were disrupted by the Russian Revolution, he co-founded a theatre in his native Tbilisi. He emigrated to London in 1921 where he directed Russian émigrés; his West End debut came in 1922. Mamoulian headed the *opera programme at the Eastman School of Music in Rochester, New York, from 1923 to 1925, and the *Theatre Guild's *acting school in 1926. He staged nine Guild productions, including *Porgy* (1927), *Marco Millions* (1928), *Wings over Europe* (1928), the American première of *A Month in the Country* (1930), and the *musicals *Porgy and Bess* (1935), *Oklahoma!* (1943), and *Carousel* (1945). His musicals were notable for advancing the seamless integration of elements. Among other significant shows directed by Mamoulian, who also directed a number of films, were *St Louis Woman* (1946) and *Lost in the Stars* (1949).   SLL

manager A person responsible for organizing the practical necessities of bringing a theatrical performance into being, including the choice of play, selection and hiring of personnel (and often casting of actors), procurement of a venue, and controlling the *finances. Functioning at the juncture of art and business, managers find their roots in both theatre and commerce. Managers drawn from the world of playwrights, *actors—and later, *directors—appeared in England and France at the end of the sixteenth century, usually as the leading members of acting troupes in which all shared the risk and the profits. A more markedly entrepreneurial model emerged when managers (like Shakespeare) were able to control the *playhouse as well as the acting company, a profitable combination that began in England in the 1590s and continued in England and then America through most of the nineteenth century. The 'sharer' system broke down completely in the seventeenth century, and was replaced by a system in which risk and profit were taken by managers (and external investors) and the actors were salaried.

The period from the mid-eighteenth century to the First World War in England and America was the era of the *actor manager, many of whom—

*Macready, *Vestris, *Tree—strongly influenced theatrical style. In France and the German-speaking lands, the entrepreneurial role of the manager was made largely redundant by the *early modern system of court theatres, and then by the introduction of state funding in the early nineteenth century, which released managers to concentrate on theatrical art, but which also brought state supervision. In Germany, the state-appointed manager (*Intendant*) was sometimes considered an impediment to art as late as the 1960s, though many major German directors in the later twentieth century succeeded in that role at high levels of creativity and originality. In the English-speaking theatre the manager's twofold function has devolved onto (*a*) the *artistic director, a theatrically trained manager who supervises the production, protected in varying degrees from the vicissitudes of the market-place by state or philanthropic funding, boards of directors, and legal contracts; and (*b*) the *producer, an entrepreneur who markets stars and theatrical productions within the context of 'show business'. RWV

Manaka, Matsemela (1956–98) South African director and playwright. While working as a teacher, the 1976 Soweto student uprising provoked his theatrical career. He founded the Soyikwa African Theatre group, which developed *satirical plays in response to current events. Between 1977 and 1991 Manaka wrote fourteen plays in the workshop context, as well as the important essays 'Theatre of the Dispossessed' and 'Theatre as a Physical Word'. Committed to the Pan-African and Black Consciousness movements, his work integrated European and African forms of *dance, *music, and *physical theatre to explore issues of apartheid and post-colonial Africa, including rural poverty, urbanization, detribalization, migrant labour, forced removals, social disintegration in the townships, and crime. His plays include *Egoli: city of gold* (1978), *Imbumba* (1979), *Vuka* (1980), *Pula* (1982), *Children of Asazi* (1984), and *Gorée* (1989).   YH

Manohar, R. S. (1925–2006) Actor and director from Tamil Nadu in the south of India who joined the Tamil film industry as an actor in 1950, strayed into the theatre, and became a major star and impresario. In 1954 he founded a company called the National Theatre, which specialized in plays on social themes that exploited the patriotic fervour of post-independence India. His major breakthrough was his shrewd retelling of the *Ramayana* in his own play *The God of Lanka* (1956), which replaced the role of Rama with Ravana, the alleged *villain of the epic who abducts Sita. Manohar *produced, directed, and acted the lead roles in at least 29 major productions. His company employed 60 actors and gave close to 8,000 performances all over India and in many other Asian countries. Most drew on legendary figures, sensationalized in a *mise-en-scène packed with tricks and special effects. Experimenting with the first stereo sound system in Tamil theatre, Manohar also drew heavily on the technology and conventions of the popular *Parsi theatre. PR/RB

Mansfield, Richard (1854–1907) English-American *actor-manager and playwright. Born in Berlin, raised in England, Mansfield began his career in New England (1876), chiefly with the works of *Gilbert and *Sullivan. He created a sensation as a dissolute roué in *A Parisian Romance* (New York, 1883). He first played Shakespeare in London (*Richard III*, 1889), then returned to America, where his major career was shaped with *Beau Brummell* (1890), *The Scarlet Letter* (1892), *Arms and the Man* (1894), *Cyrano de Bergerac* (1898), *Beaucaire* (1901), and the première of *Ibsen's *Peer Gynt* in the United States (1906). He wrote several plays, none of which remained long in his repertory. Mansfield often responded publicly to perceived critical malice and was widely regarded as eccentric, both in personality and in performance. His supporters found his performances intensely individual in their *realism, marking a sharp break with traditional *acting style; his detractors characterized his work as idiosyncratic and highly mannered, with artificial vocal choices. AW

Mantell, Robert B. (1854–1928) British-American actor. Born in Scotland, Mantell made his professional debut in 1876, followed by extensive *touring in the provinces. Throughout his career he was one of the few actors to adhere to an old-fashioned unrestrained style with plenty of bombast and exaggerated gesturing—which impressed some and dismayed others. But there was no denying his extraordinary personal magnetism. From 1882 on, he performed almost entirely in America, not just in New York but all over the country in large cities and small towns. His first important Broadway vehicle was *The Romany Rye* (1882), followed the next year by *Sardou's *Fedora*. He achieved stardom as a matinée idol in the *melodrama *Tangled Lives* (1886). Starting in 1904 he concentrated almost entirely on Shakespeare, performing Richard III and Othello, and adding Iago, King John, Brutus, and Hamlet. He was at his best as Shylock, Macbeth, and Lear—performing Lear more than 500 times. CT

Manzoni, Alessandro (1785–1873) Italian writer. Author of the famous novel *The Betrothed* (1825–7), Manzoni was a leader of the Italian *romantic movement that manifested itself about 1815 in a yearning for political independence from Austria, freedom from the French *neoclassical tradition, and a new national literature. Inspired by Shakespeare and the German romantics, Manzoni's verse *tragedies, *Il conte di Carmagnola* (1828) and *Adelchi* (1843), take local history as their tragic subject, defy the *unities, and employ a language that departs from the neoclassical rhetorical tradition. While these tragedies have not met with much success in the theatre (though *Adelchi* was directed in 1960 by *Gassman), excerpts from *Adelchi* served as *monologues for the great Italian actors like *Modena. Manzoni's *Preface* to *Carmagnola* and his *Lettre à M. C[hauvet]* (1823) are important theoretical documents of Italian romanticism. JEH

Marais, Théâtre du Paris's second public *playhouse, a converted *tennis court, was opened in 1634. Rebuilt after a fire in 1644, the Marais measured 34.4 m (113 feet) by 11.7 m (38 feet), its raked stage was 9.7 m (32 feet) deep, with a practicable upper stage at the rear. Around a standing pit, the *auditorium was fitted with two tiers of *boxes, parallel to the walls, a *paradis* above the seven side boxes, and a tiered *amphithéâtre* behind the four rear boxes. In the 1650s and 1660s the Marais's fortunes were maintained by the success of spectacular machine-plays, the accommodation of which required extensive remodelling: the stage was extended and equipped with machinery, the *auditorium boxes realigned into an Italianate horseshoe, and the *amphithéâtre* relocated to the rear of the pit. But the Marais had little future. Its leading actors were forced in 1673 to merge with those of the recently deceased *Molière at the Guénégaud, after which it briefly housed a *puppet troupe in 1677 and then disappeared from the records. JG

Marber, Patrick (1964–   ) English playwright, actor, and director. Marber emerged initially as a comic writer and actor, contributing to the unsettlingly brilliant news *parodies *On the Hour* and *The Day Today* for BBC radio and television respectively. His first play, *Dealer's Choice* (1995), uses the rituals of the all-male poker game to investigate the bluffs and gambles of masculinity in crisis. This piece was developed at the *National Theatre, which also staged *Closer* (1997), a searing portrait of contemporary male–female relationships and the caverns that open up between sex and understanding. Both plays transferred to the West End. *Howard Katz* (2001), directed like the first two by Marber himself, concerns a successful actor's agent falling from success to squalid loneliness; its anguished ethical concerns chimed with a turn towards moral investigation in British theatre. Marber has also directed well-received productions of *Potter's Blue Remembered Hills* (1996), *Mamet's The Old Neighbourhood* (1998), and *Pinter's The Caretaker* (2002).   DR

Marceau, Marcel (1923–2007) French *mime. Son of a kosher butcher killed at Auschwitz, Marcel Mangel became Marcel Marceau when he moved to Paris in 1944 from Limoges, where he and his brother worked for the Resistance. He first studied with *Decroux in *Dullin's school, and in 1946 joined *Barrault's company to perform in the *Baptiste* pantomime Barrault created following the success of his starring role in the film *Les Enfants du paradis*. In 1955, after years of European *touring, Marceau's six months of sold-out performances in New York, and his coincidental television appearances, made him a household word. He defined the art of mime for millions of people who never knew it existed. Finally more influenced by silent film actors and by the nineteenth-century whitefaced silent pantomime of *Deburau than by the radical and austere modernism of Decroux, Marceau's stage persona Bip became synonymous with mime and with himself. He toured internationally for half a century, and his school in Paris attracted students from everywhere in the world.   TL

March, Fredric (Frederick McIntyre Bickel) (1897–1975) American actor. He made his debut in a *Belasco production of *Guitry's De-burau* (1920) and played his first major role in I. E. Goodman's *melodrama *The Law Breaker* (1922). He then acquired his stage name and performed in several plays before meeting Florence Eldridge in summer *stock. They married in 1927, *toured with the *Theatre Guild Repertory Company, and continued to act together. After 1928 March worked in films before returning to Broadway with Eldridge to co-star in *Yr. Obedient Husband* (1938). Commuting between Hollywood and New York, he played Mr Antrobus in *Wilder's *The Skin of our Teeth* (1942), Major Joppolo in Paul *Osborn's *A Bell for Adano* (1944), Nicholas Denery in *Hellman's *The Autumn Garden* (1951), James Tyrone in *O'Neill's *A Long Day's Journey into Night* (1956), and the Angel in Paddy Chayefsky's *Gideon* (1961). His performance of Tyrone was the masterpiece of his stage career. He made 69 films.   TL

Marchessault, Jovette (1938–) Québec playwright, novelist, painter, sculptor. Largely self-taught, her radical *feminist perspectives are evident in all that she produces, most of it intended to provoke patriarchal reaction. Her first stage success was *The Saga of the Wet Hens* (1981), in which four female writers reject oppressive male authority. Similar themes are explored in plays such as *The Earth is Too Small, Violette Leduc* (1982), and *Anaïs [Nin] in the Comet's Tail* (1985), dealing with famous *lesbian writers of the past.   LED

Marcos, Plínio (1935–99) Brazilian playwright. The most *censored dramatist during the worst period of the dictatorship (1964–79), Marcos nonetheless attracted a wide range of production interest from student, alternative, amateur, and professional companies. Writing about São Paulo's most abjectly dispossessed, his plays focus on pivotal moments in the lives of criminals and outcasts: prostitutes, transvestites, homosexuals, pimps, small-time crooks, conmen, prisoners, and addicts. His hyper-*naturalistic and often brutal *dialogue nonetheless creates an imagistic language that stands in contrast to the grim themes, notably apparent in his searing AIDS play *Scarlet Mark* (1989), an allegory about the redemptive powers of community in a women's penitentiary. Its large cast is unusual for Marcos, whose works generally are duets or trios of desperate persons who shift back and forth from victims to victimizers, as in *Knife through Flesh* (1967).   LHD

Mardzhanov, Konstantin (1872–1933) Georgian/Soviet director. From 1910 to 1913 Mardzhanov worked as assistant director at the *Moscow Art Theatre, collaborating with *Stanislavsky and *Craig on *Hamlet* and with *Nemirovich Danchenko on *Peer Gynt* and *The Brothers Karamazov*. He left to found his own Free Theatre in Moscow in 1913, where he specialized in *operetta, *pantomime, and the work of *Offenbach. Mardzhanov was fascinated by the notion of the carnivalesque and staged a production of Lope de *Vega's *Fuente Ovejuna* in Kiev in 1919, followed by a number of mass performances of revolutionary spectacles, and planned a production of *Mayakovsky's *Mystery-Bouffe* on top of a mountain. In 1922, Mardzhanov became virtual founder of a Soviet Georgian theatre when he staged productions at the Rustaveli Theatre in Tbilisi of plays by Georgian writers. In 1928 he created a second Rustaveli Theatre in Kutaisi, where he staged *Toller's *Hoppla, We're Alive!* (1928), plays by Georgian and Soviet playwrights, and *Shelley's *The Cenci* (1930).   NW

Marinetti, Filippo Tommaso (1876–1944) Italian poet, playwright, and theoretician, best known as the founder of *futurism. As a late *symbolist in turn-of-the-century Paris he shocked *audiences with his anarchist poetry declamations and *Jarry-inspired productions of *Le Roi Bombance* and *Poupées électriques* (1909). Creating theatre scandals became a favoured method of the early futurist movement, which Marinetti set up in various Italian cities. He published several theatre manifestos and wrote a large number of playlets for the new genres he created in the 1910s and 1920s (Synthetic Theatre, Theatre of Surprise, Tactile Theatre). When futurism began to have an impact on conventional *playhouses, Marinetti wrote several full-length plays that were staged in Italy and abroad: *Bianca e Rosso* (1923), *Prigionieri* (1925), *Vulcano* (1926), *L'oceano del cuore* (1927), *Simultanina* (1931). As a champion of modern technology and scientific modernity he immediately seized upon the new invention of radio and wrote several dramas for this medium. Marinetti also tried his hand at architectural design and took Gropius' *total theatre as a starting point for his own project of a *Teatro totale per masse* (1933). GB

marionette The term arose in France in the seventeenth century as a generic word for *puppets, but was little used before the nineteenth. In English it refers uniquely to puppets operated from above by strings, rods, or wires. Most marionettes are jointed, usually at the neck, shoulder, elbows, hips, and knees. In China even the fingers may be jointed, but in Rajasthan unjointed figures are used. Jointed figures survive from classical antiquity. Europe favoured operation by a rod or wire to the head, and one or more ancillary strings. The success of the widely travelled Holden Company from England in the 1870s ensured the abandonment of the head rod in most of Europe. Strings may be held directly in the hand (Rajasthan) or attached to a control bar or bars, with additional ones held in the hand (Myanmar, China). In modern times carefully balanced and highly elaborate controls have developed. JMCC

Marivaux, Pierre Carlet de Chamblain de (1688–1763) French dramatist and man of letters. Marivaux wrote two *comedies for the *Comédie Italienne in 1720, as well as a *tragedy for the *Comédie-Française. Thereafter his dramatic output was shared between the two theatres. Reliance on tradition regarding *character, and preference for simplicity in terms of plot, helped Marivaux to produce the subtlety of *dialogue by which he is best known. In what has remained his most popular play, *The Game of

Love and Chance (1730), the plot has something in common with that of *She Stoops to Conquer*, but the misunderstandings are handled with a light-hearted subtlety that is quite foreign to *Goldsmith's play. At first used disparagingly by contemporaries, who criticized what they saw as preciosity, the term 'le marivaudage' has survived as an appreciative definition of the mixture of wordplay, psychological exploration, and revelation which marks the author's distinctive style, as in *The Double Inconstancy* (1723) or *Misleading Confessions* (1737). The tragedy *Annibal*, a failure in 1720, was again unsuccessful when revived at the Comédie-Française in 1747, after Marivaux's election to the Académie Française.

Meanwhile he had tried his hand with mixed success outside the formula he inherited from the Italians. *La Mère confidente* (1735) was popular with contemporary *audiences, and its theme of confidence and trust between mother and daughter anticipates that of *Diderot's *drame* *bourgeois. Island of Slaves* (1725), presenting an island community where social equality rules, enjoyed the longest opening run of any Marivaux play. Whereas the adoption by the Comédie-Française of plays that had been premièred by the Italians was not immediately successful, by the end of the century, especially under Mlle *Contat's influence, Marivaux had been well assimilated to the repertory of the national theatre. The process continued throughout the next century, and in the post-1950 period Marivaux was to become, after *Molière, the French classical dramatist most frequently performed on the French stage. Pride of place during this period should go to the company founded by *Barrault and *Renaud at the Marigny Theatre in 1946. Productions here, and foreign tours by the company, brought Marivaux to a new worldwide audience. His work is now frequently performed outside France. WDH

Marlowe, Christopher (1564–93) English dramatist. The eldest son of a debt-ridden Canterbury shoemaker, Marlowe was awarded a scholarship to the King's School in that city in 1578, and later earned a second scholarship to Corpus Christi College, Cambridge. By 1587 his *Tamburlaine the Great, Part I* had taken London by storm. The play was so successful that its author was immediately commissioned to write a sequel; and the actor who memorialized the lead role, the young Edward *Alleyn, went on to make his career in other Marlowe plays. Marlowe followed the *Tamburlaine* plays with four others: *Dr Faustus* (c.1588), *The Jew of Malta* (1589–90), *The Massacre at Paris* (c.1591–2), and *Edward II* (c.1591–2). The first three were performed at the *Rose playhouse by the Lord *Admiral's Men, and Marlowe's work became the mainstay of the company for generations. *Edward II* was performed by the Earl of Pembroke's Men at an indeterminable theatre.

Marlowe seems to have been a turbulent personality. On 30 May 1593 he journeyed to a tavern in Deptford with two acquaintances who, some think, were government spies working in association with the Elizabethan secret police. A fight broke out over the payment of the bill, and Marlowe was stabbed to death and buried with dispatch in Deptford. This odd meeting has fuelled many popular theories concerning Marlowe's involvement in espionage. Furthermore, it has—in combination with *Edward II* and selections from Marlowe's poems—prompted some scholars to conclude that Marlowe's sexuality was ambiguous; that he, in fact, lived many double lives. Yet his professional life had an enormous impact on the drama of his contemporaries. The main *characters in his plays can be distinguished by what their author referred to as 'high astounding terms' and what literary critics characterize as 'overreaching'. It is clear that the playgoers who first heard Marlowe's 'mighty line' were astonished by its resonance.

Productions of *Dr Faustus*, *Tamburlaine*, and *The Jew of Malta* were plentiful in the 1590s, and well into the next century. Thereafter they were virtually absent from the stage until the early twentieth century. *Faustus* was seen in England in 1904, 1925, and 1944, was at the *Shakespeare Memorial Theatre (1946-7), and the *Old Vic (1948). *Welles directed a production (and played Faustus) for the *Federal Theatre Project in the USA in 1937, and again took the part in Paris in 1950 in his own version, which featured Eartha Kitt as Helen and music by Duke Ellington. Productions of *Tamburlaine* have been fewer but *Hall inaugurated the Olivier stage at the new *National Theatre in London with a version of both parts in 1976, with *Finney in the title role. At the *Royal Shakespeare Company's *Swan Theatre (1992) *Hands returned to the savage spectacle of earlier productions.

Since 1940 *The Jew of Malta* on both sides of the Atlantic has been steadily on stage, with seven productions in the 1960s in England alone. The best known of these was Clifford *Williams's for the RSC (London, 1964). Most interesting has been the increasing popularity of *Edward II*, produced steadily in the twentieth century with special attention to its homosexual themes. Toby Robertson's production (1969) starred *McKellen, and *Beale played the role for the RSC in 1990. There have also been numerous radio versions. A film version by Derek Jarman (1993) has become a cult classic, and in 1995 the play became a ballet by David Bintley in Stuttgart.   SPC

Marlowe, Julia (1866–1950) Anglo-American actress. She was born Sarah Francis Frost in England, and at 4 emigrated to the state of Ohio, where she was known as Fanny Brough. In 1876 she first appeared on stage in a nine-month *tour of *HMS Pinafore*. In 1882 she went to New York for several years of arduous coaching, chose her new stage name, and starred as Parthenia in *Ingomar* (1887), which was enthusiastically received. This propelled her into Shakespeare, beginning with Juliet (which *Duse proclaimed the greatest in her experience) and Viola, and proceeding to Rosalind, Beatrice, Imogen, even Prince Hal, Ophelia, Portia, Katherine, Cleopatra, and Lady Macbeth (often opposite *Sothern, whom she married in 1911). Her moral standards led her to avoid *Ibsen and *Shaw, though she did act successfully in some historical dramas: the title roles in *The Countess Valeska* (1898), *Colinette* (1899), and *Barbara Frietchie* (1899), and Mary Tudor in *When Knighthood Was in Flower* (1901, a huge hit). She was lauded for her velvety contralto voice and magnetic charm.   CT

Marowitz, Charles (1934–   ) American director, dramatist, and critic who moved to Britain in the 1950s. He worked with *Brook on *King Lear* (1962) and on the Theatre of *Cruelty season in 1963, and was *artistic director of the small Open Space Theatre in London (1968–79). The company's many experimental productions included new plays by *Hare, *Brenton, *Griffiths, and *Shepard; Marowitz's own 'collage' variations on Shakespeare, including *Hamlet*, a *feminist *Shrew*, and a Black Power *Othello*; and *environmental productions such as *Fortune and Men's Eyes*, for which the theatre was transformed into a prison. His work, partly influenced by *Artaud, was notable for rapidly changing images and *lighting, and verbal and visual shocks. In 1980 he moved to California, where he has taught in universities and directed at the Los Angeles Theatre Center and at the Malibu Stage Company, which he founded in 1990. *Sherlock's Last Case* (1984), which he called a pot-boiler, was successfully produced on Broadway. He has published some two dozen books of plays, criticism, reflections on *acting, and autobiography.   EEC

Marqués, René (1919–79) Puerto Rico's most important twentieth-century dramatist. Marqués conquered the national stage in 1953 with *La carreta* (*The Oxcart*). Performed in Spanish in New York the same year, it encouraged Puerto

Rican theatrical activity in the USA, enlarged when the Puerto Rican Travelling Theatre presented it in English (1967). The play depicts the movement of Puerto Ricans from the countryside to deprived urban outskirts to the American metropolis, ending with a utopian return to the motherland to rescue national identity. In 1958 *Broken Suns* had huge success at the Puerto Rican Theatre Festival. Marqués followed with *The House without a Clock* (1961), *A Blue Boy for that Shadow* (1962), *El apartamiento* (1964), and *Marina; or, The Dawn* (1966). *Carnival Outside, Carnival Inside* was performed in Havana in 1962, but banned at home until 1979 because of its commitment to Puerto Rican independence. A constant experimenter, Marqués turned to parables in the 1970s with *Sacrifice on Mount Moriah, Titus y Bernice*, and *David y Jonathan*.   JLRE

Mars, Mlle (Anne-Françoise-Hippolyte Boutet) (1779–1847) French actress, admitted to the *Comédie-Française in 1799. She made her reputation in *Molière and *Marivaux, impressing *audiences by her perfectly modulated diction, as well as by the elegance and refinement of her manner, attributes she used to good effect outside the theatre, becoming a leader of fashion in her own salon, where she set an example of style and good taste. Adapting badly to the *romantic revolution, she played an important part in the events leading up to the 'bataille d'*Hernani' (*see* RIOTS). Cast as the young heroine Doña Sol (at the age of 51), she spearheaded the opposition to *Hugo in matters of staging, versification, and imagery. In the case of Hugo's *Angelo*, hostility towards the author was accompanied by a personal vendetta against Marie *Dorval, recently brought in from the *boulevard theatre.   WDH

Marshall, Norman (1901–80) English director and *manager. He emerged as a director with *Gray's Cambridge Festival Theatre in the 1920s. In 1932, under his own management, he directed *O'Neill's *Marco Millions*, and in 1934 took over the Gate Theatre (London), where he produced and directed a range of plays from *Aristophanes' *Lysistrata* to Steinbeck's *Of Mice and Men*. He also staged the annual Gate *revues. He served in the army in 1940–2, then returned to directing with *Sherwood's *The Petrified Forest* (1942). In 1950 he *toured in India with abridged versions of Shakespeare's plays. Throughout the 1950s and 1960s he continued to direct. He was chairman of the British Council's Drama Committee (1961–8) and served with *Olivier as joint chairman of the National Theatre Building Committee. His book *The Other Theatre* (1947) is an important treat-

ment of the British alternative theatre movement of the first half of the twentieth century.   TP

Marston, John (1576–1634) English playwright. After receiving his BA at Oxford in 1594, Marston moved to the Middle Temple in London, where he published fashionable satiric and erotic poetry. Around 1599, soon after the Children of Paul's resumed acting, he provided the troupe with self-consciously innovative plays. *Antonio and Mellida* (1602) and *Antonio's Revenge* (1602) are marked by flamboyant linguistic inventiveness and the use of *boy actors to burlesque the adult world and to *parody plays performed by adult companies. In *Jack Drum's Entertainment* (1601), he mocked other Paul's plays as 'the mustie fopperies of antiquity'. In *Satiromastix* (1602), co-authored with *Dekker, and *What You Will* (1607), he traded caricatures with *Jonson in 'the War of the Theatres'. After 1603 he wrote for the children's troupe at *Blackfriars: *The Malcontent* (1604), his revenge *comedy stolen by Shakespeare's troupe; *Eastward Hoe* (1605), the city comedy he wrote with Jonson and *Chapman and which landed the authors in jail; *The Dutch Courtesan* (1605), a warning to gallants about prostitutes; *The Fawn* (1606), an Italianate anticourt *satire; and *Sophonisba* (1606), the *tragedy of a virtuous Roman matron. Several of his satires offended the ecclesiastical authorities, and he was often in legal difficulties. In 1609 he became a country clergyman, abandoning a play about an aristocratic nymphomaniac later completed by William Barkstead under the title of *The Insatiate Countess* (1613).   MS

Martin, Karl Heinz (1888–1948) German director, one of the earliest proponents of *expressionism. He staged Carl *Sternheim in Frankfurt and *Kaiser's *From Morn to Midnight* in Hamburg (1918), which he also directed as a film. Martin was a founding member of the expressionist Die Tribüne in Berlin, where he directed *Toller's *Transfiguration* (1919). The bare stage, striking *acting from *Kortner, and innovative *lighting effects defined the aesthetics of the movement. Throughout the Weimar Republic, Martin worked at major theatres in Berlin, Munich, and Vienna. After 1933 he was mainly in the film industry, returning to the Berlin theatre during the war, chiefly at the *Volksbühne. From 1945 to 1948 he was *artistic director of the Hebbeltheater in Berlin.   CBB

Martin, Mary (1913–90) American *musical comedy actress-singer. Her Broadway debut was in *Leave It to Me* (1938), where her striptease-like number 'My Heart Belongs to Daddy' made her a star. This led to a series of mostly forgettable films in the early 1940s. She returned to Broadway for *One Touch of Venus* (1943), moved on to *Lute Song* (1946), appeared in London in *Pacific 1860*, and *toured the United States in *Annie Get your Gun* (1947). Her signature role came with *Rodgers and *Hammerstein's *South Pacific* (1949), when she played the spirited military nurse Nellie Forbush, washing her hair nightly onstage as she sang 'I'm Gonna Wash That Man Right Outa my Hair'. Martin played Nellie for two years in London (1951-3). She was on Broadway in *Kind Sir* (1953), toured in *The Skin of our Teeth* (1955), and starred in various television specials, most memorably in *Peter Pan* (1954) following its brief Broadway run. She was the novice nun in *The Sound of Music* (1959). Other major shows includ ed *Hello, Dolly!* (1965), *I Do, I Do* (1966), and *Do You Turn Somersaults?* (1978).   SLL

Martinelli family Mantuan *commedia dell'-arte* actors. **Drusiano** is known to have appeared with various companies: his brother **Tristano** (1557-1630) was far more famous, as interpreter of the role of Arlecchino or *Harlequin. It seems likely that a Martinelli invented this mask for the theatre, basing it on a demonic figure from French legend; and that Tristano adapted it as a lowlife role for Italian *comedies, one which later became assimilated to other 'servant' or *Zanni stereotypes. Like all improvising performers, Martinelli has left us few clues as to his material and manner, though roles in two comedies by Giovan Battista *Andreini may capture some of his aggressive style. Correspondence by and about Martinelli shows him as a selfish, obsessed performer who changed companies frequently, adapted badly to the new corporate discipline of the *arte* troupes, and was constantly seeking autonomous star status together with a star income.   RAA

Martínez Sierra, Gregorio (1881-1948) Spanish director, *manager, and playwright who collaborated with his wife María de la O Lejárraga on most titles that bear his name. *The Cradle Song* (1911) and *The Kingdom of God* (1915) were performed internationally. In England, Helen and Harley Granville *Barker were champions of their plays and *Le Gallienne's Civic Repertory Theatre staged *The Cradle Song* in New York in 1927. As a director, Martínez Sierra was instrumental in introducing new European and *avant-garde Spanish works through his Teatro Eslava in the 1920s, and staged *García Lorca's first play. In 1930 he went to Hollywood, where he wrote scripts in the Spanish divisions of several studios and oversaw the filming of several productions.

After the victory of Franco, he lived in Argentina, his long career virtually at an end.   MPH

Martin-Harvey, John (1863-1944) English *actor-manager. He began with *Irving's Lyceum company (1882-96), and in 1898 he appeared with Mrs Patrick *Campbell in *Maeterlinck's *Pelléas and Mélisande*. The following year he became a popular star in *melodrama when he appeared as Sydney Carton in *The Only Way*, a dramatization of *Dickens's *A Tale of Two Cities*. Work in several melodramas and Shakespeare culminated in a successful *Hamlet* in 1904. In 1912 he played Oedipus in *Reinhardt's London production, and during the 1920s he made a successful *tour of North America; back in London he performed in *Shaw, including *The Devil's Disciple*, for the rest of his career he was featured mainly in revivals of his famous roles.   TP

Marx Brothers American comic performers. The three eldest Marx brothers—**Chico** (Leonard) (1887-1961), **Harpo** (Adolph Arthur) (1888-1964), and **Groucho** (Julius Henry) (1890-1977)—formed the core and substance of the family *variety act that went on to Broadway musical *revues, Hollywood films, and iconic status in Western culture. **Gummo** (Milton) (1892-1977), and **Zeppo** (Herbert) (1901-79) each served as comic foil at different times during the performing brothers' incubation period in *vaudeville, and Zeppo appeared in films up to *Duck Soup* (1933). It was, however, the trio of Groucho, Chico, and Harpo which imprinted itself indelibly on the face of American comic performance with a *surreal, anarchic humour.

By the time of their early successes on Broadway in the 1920s, they had adopted their trademark guises: Groucho wore a greasepaint moustache and walked with a stoop; Chico spoke with an Italian accent; Harpo wore a red fright wig and became known as the silent one. The Marx Brothers' Broadway shows hung songs and routines on the bones of a romantic plot. The formula served just as well for the movies, and from the mid-1920s to the late 1930s the comics traced a legendary arc of success. Stage productions like *The Cocoanuts* (1925) and *Animal Crackers* (1928), were subsequently translated to the screen; *Monkey Business* (1931) was their first film written directly for Hollywood. In the 1940s, the brothers began turning to individual pursuits, though they did reunite for several more films. They each appeared variously on the rapidly growing medium of television, and Groucho made the most of his wisecracking persona as host of the quiz series *You Bet your Life*, which aired on radio and then television (1947–61). Martin Esslin observed that the Marx Brothers 'bridge the tradition between the *commedia dell'- arte* and vaudeville, on the one hand, and the theatre of the *absurd*, on the other'. *Artaud and *Beckett are among the figures who drew inspiration from their zany and often disturbing physical and verbal comedy.   EW

Masefield, John (1878–1967) English poet and playwright who laboured to revive poetic drama. His plays include the *melodramas *The Campden Wonder* (1907) and *The Witch* (1910), the Shavian historical drama *The Tragedy of Pompey the Great* (1910), the *kabuki-inspired *The Faithful* (1914), and a *Racine adaptation, *Esther* (1921). Masefield achieved critical success with *The Tragedy of Nan* (1908), directed by Granville *Barker and featuring Lillah *McCarthy. Masefield's plays have been little performed since their premières, suffering as they do from the tendency of verse drama towards untheatrical stasis. After the First World War, Masefield moved away from commercial theatre and formed the Hill Players, an amateur group devoted to verse drama. He became Poet Laureate in 1930.   MDG

mask and masking Masking carries with it a double notion of hiding and of transforming identity. A potent force in performance, its uses can also range from religious *ritual to architectural embellishment. The mask occurs in virtually every culture. Commonly perceived as an object that covers all or part of the face, the mask usually must be seen in the full context of an accompanying *costume.

Origins and sacred function. The earliest use of the mask was probably in the context of animist magic. By wearing a skin or other animal attribute a man might take on some of the qualities of that animal; large animal figures with concealed performers are still used in initiation ceremonies in Mali. Shamans employed masks so as to become vehicles for a spirit. In certain cultures in Africa and Asia today the donning of a mask allows the wearer to enter into a state of trance. Where cult made way for theatrical representation the mask began to lose its shamanic and seasonal or ritual functions, but could retain ambivalent status. *Nō masks in Japan are still idealized forms, intended as vehicles for the spiritual and not as *realistic portrayals of *characters, and are treated with reverence.

Wild man. The wild man, a hirsute counterpart of 'civilized' man clad in animal accoutrements, erupts in a context of carnival. Ancient *Greek *satyr-plays took over the wild man, and slave masks likewise reflected uncivilized man. The Christian Church perceived links between masks and pagan practices, and this may explain the proscription on masquerading in *medieval England. Hallow'en (the Celtic new year) was the festival of the dead, when those from the underworld were thought to roam, prompting bands of young men to go through the countryside, often disguised as wild men. A popular figure from Austria was *Harlequin (Hellequin). When he appeared as a stage servant in northern Italy in the sixteenth century, *audiences would have immediately recognized the diabolical and animalistic associations suggested by his black leather mask.

The sixteenth- and seventeenth-century court *masque in England, and the closely related French *ballet de cour*, originated in popular mummings and disguisings, but lifted them to the level of courtly allegory. The grotesque antimasque elements, often performed by professional entertainers, related in a contained way to carnival and the wild man tradition. The fantastic creations of the court masque, and later the *opera, required huge papier mâché masks. Later such masks were the stock in trade of the nineteenth-century theatrical extravaganza, and similar masks continue to be employed in street carnival, especially in Iberia. In the twentieth century the carnival use of the mask, because of its power and visibility, was adopted for political theatre by Russian *agitprop groups of the 1920s, and this idea was repeated in the 1960s and 1970s, most notably by the *Bread and Puppet Theatre in the USA.

The theatrical mask. The mask is often seen as an emblem of theatre, and theatrical performance in most cultures can involve masks. Performance masks can cover just the face, or a part of it, or the whole head (Greek satyr masks). In *kathakali the actor's face itself is built up with rice paste until it becomes virtually a mask. Various forms of traditional Indian theatre have shown how the actor, with supreme control over the facial muscles, can model his own face into a mask. *Mime artist *Marceau developed this skill, as did *Grotowski, and the Japanese *butoh theatre.

Reacting against the *naturalism of the nineteenth century, modernist European theatre returned to the masks of *commedia dell'arte and Asian theatre. *Copeau used the mask for actor training because of the emphasis on the whole body as a means of expression, while *Yeats tried to create a repertoire for the masked performer. *Artaud, drawing on the cultural and sacred origins of the mask, was among the practitioners to recommend giant masks. In the 1970s the Swiss company Mummenschanz devised a form of body mask that concealed actors totally within abstract amorphous shapes which they brought to life. *Interculturalism in contemporary theatre has drawn heavily on different masking traditions. Sometimes worn, sometimes carried, sometimes completely divorced from the live performer, sometimes superimposed on stages or performers by techniques of projection, the mask is now extensively used in visual and *physical theatre.   JMcC

Mason, Bruce (1921–82) New Zealand playwright. Mason's lifelong crusade against New Zealand philistinism was evident in his bleakly *realist 1950s one-act plays for Wellington's Unity Theatre, but his idealism was more evident in the romantic, almost operatic, *dramaturgy of his full-length plays, several on the then unusual topic of Maori and bicultural issues, especially *The Pohutukawa Tree* (1957; BBC television 1959), which became the first New Zealand play to be a set text for schools. With the collapse of the New Zealand Players in 1960, he turned to radio and solo performance as the only avenues for a professional playwright; and his nearly 2,000 performances of *The End of the Golden Weather*, many in small towns, displayed his gifts of rhetoric and mimicry (over 40 *characters) to the full.   DC

Mason, Patrick (1951–) Irish director, born in Britain. From 1992 to 1999 he was *artistic director of the Irish National Theatre (*Abbey Theatre), where he achieved a high degree of stability in a troubled institution, and gained international recognition for his productions of new plays. Earlier he directed many notable premières there including an adaptation of Patrick Kavanagh's poem *The Great Hunger* (1983), Frank *McGuinness's *Observe the Sons of Ulster Marching toward the Somme* (1985), and, to international acclaim, *Friel's *Dancing at Lughnasa* (1990), which won him a Tony award in New York. As artistic director he continued a strong repertoire of new work, directing the premières of *Kilroy's *The Secret Fall of Constance Wilde* (1997), Marina *Carr's *By the Bog of Cats* (1998), and McGuinness's *Dolly West's Kitchen* (1999). All his work manifests a strong sense of symbolism appropriate for his subsequent work as a director of *opera. Recent stage work includes the UK *tour of *McGuinness's adaptation of *Rebecca* (2005) and Seamus Heaney's *The Burial at Thebes* (Abbey, 2008).   BRS

masque A stylized form of drama performed in the sixteenth and seventeenth centuries at the English court and aristocratic country houses. According to the chronicler Edward Hall, the masque was 'a thing not seen afore in England'

when, on Twelfth Night 1513, King Henry VIII and eleven of his courtiers arrived at Greenwich in disguise and asked the ladies to *dance. Later Tudor masques incorporated narrative elements which 'explained' the characters' visit, and by Elizabeth's reign they were scripted as well as choreographed. The genre reached its full formal development in the early seventeenth century, combining elaborate pageantry with literary and musical virtuosity, usually written and designed by established professional figures such as the poet-dramatists Samuel Daniel and *Jonson, and the architect Inigo *Jones.

A typical masque would feature allegorical or mythological *characters, often all of the same gender, either enacting some simple fable or visiting the performance venue for some benevolent purpose. Everything would lead up to a sequence of stately figure dances, after which the masquers would 'take out' members of the *audience for livelier, more sexually charged dancing, and the dramatic fiction would dissolve into the social reality of a court revel; finally the masquers would make their departure. This recognized format was extended in 1609 when Queen Anne asked Jonson to provide *The Masque of Queens* with 'some dance or show that might precede hers', and he wrote an antimasque of witches, a threatening presence banished by the arrival of the masquing queens. Thereafter the antimasque became a standard feature, counterpointing the main masque's elegance with grotesque figures, and later grew increasingly prominent and disconnected from the central action: for example, the antimasque of Jonson's *News from the New World Discovered in the Moon* (1620), *satirizing newsmongers, reads like a *revue sketch.

Masques took place indoors in the evening, and dancing usually went on until the small hours; Jonson's *Oberon, the Fairy Prince* (1611) is designed to end as dawn breaks. Though antimasque roles were often played by professional actors, the main performers in a masque were always amateurs, usually courtiers (of either sex) or members of the Inns of Court; audiences regularly included foreign ambassadors. *Music was an important feature of the performance. The survival of masque music is haphazard, but we are better served for the visuals: the *costume and scenic designs by Inigo Jones, supplemented by the court's financial records, give us a good sense of the events' spectacular *scenography. Beginning with Jones's *Masque of Blackness* (1605; libretto by Jonson), the action took place on a stage set at one end of the hall; an open space between the stage and the audience's seating was reserved for the dancing. There was elaborate architectural scenery, sometimes solid and sometimes mechanically sophisticated. Costumes, too, were flamboyant, made of costly, luxurious materials like taffeta, silk, and cloth of gold. Female masquing costumes were often sexually provocative, exposing the performer's nipples or legs: one innocent, unmarried courtier remarked that he never knew women *had* legs before seeing the Queen's when she appeared in Daniel's *The Vision of the Twelve Goddesses* (1604).

A masque's ostensible purpose was to celebrate a special occasion such as an aristocratic wedding, a calendar festival like Shrovetide or Christmas, or a state event such as the investiture of Prince Henry as Prince of Wales in 1610. Its political significance was complex. Under the early Stuart monarchs masques were seen as latent expressions of the royal will, and were scrutinized by ambassadors and politicians seeking to decode the King's intentions; Jonson called them 'court hieroglyphics'. Most fundamentally, though, the genre was political in that it existed to praise and support the ruling elite. A typical masque narrative develops towards hierarchical order and harmony, which is not so much established as confirmed by the action, so effortlessly are the discordant forces expelled; this proclaimed a more than fictitious state of affairs because the courtier performers' actual identities were never entirely effaced by their roles. The performance, too, worked to honour the most exalted member of the audience: the King was sometimes expected to intervene in the *action as the agent of its concluding concord; even the *perspective scenery was designed to ensure that the image was least distorted when seen from his canopied throne of state. The expense of the occasion was an assertion and display of the power of the crown—in 1610, for instance, James I authorized unlimited expenditure on Daniel's *Tethys' Festival*; its actual cost was in excess of £2,000—and in the *early modern court culture of gifts and compliments, some masques were financed by prominent politicians seeking to declare their devotion and cement their status.

Masques were a recognized feature of court life in the early seventeenth century, and some commercial playwrights used miniature inset masques as an element of court settings: sometimes they merely represented a social practice, but in *tragedies they are often a powerful metaphor for duplicity and corruption, used as a cover for one or more murder plots. The last court masque was *Davenant's *Salmacida Spolia* (1640), there are some later masques written for private performance during the Interregnum, notably *Shirley's *Cupid and Death* (1653), but the genre did not

return with the Stuart monarchy in 1660. Some of its features are seen, however, in Restoration drama and early English *opera.

Sometimes masques were repeated, but fundamentally they were designed as single-occasion events. Accordingly, most individual masques have no subsequent stage history beyond antiquarian reconstruction attempts. However, Milton's *Comus* (1634) has a strong enough narrative to sustain occasional amateur revival.   MJW

Massey, Raymond (1896–1983) Canadian actor. Best known for portraying Abraham Lincoln in Robert *Anderson's *Abe Lincoln in Illinois* (1938, filmed 1941), Massey had a long career as an actor and occasional director. Appearing in numerous London productions between the wars, he was mainly associated with the London Everyman Theatre, where he also directed. Massey made his New York debut in *Hamlet* (1931), followed by *Ethan Frome* (1936) and *Idiot's Delight* (1938). He also appeared with Katharine *Cornell in *The Doctor's Dilemma* (1940) and *Candida* (1942). After the war, Massey spent most of the rest of his career in America, where his roles included Brutus and Prospero for the American Shakespeare Theatre (1955) and Mr Zuss in Macliesh's *JB*, directed by *Kazan (1957). Massey featured in the long-running television drama *Dr Kildare*. His numerous films include *Fire over England* (1936), *Arsenic and Old Lace* (1944), *Mourning Becomes Electra* (1947), and *East of Eden* (1955). Massey's children Anna and Daniel both became actors.   MDG

Massinger, Philip (1583–1640) English playwright. Attached to the King's Men (*see* CHAMBERLAIN's MEN, LORD) for most of his dramatic career, he collaborated with *Fletcher on a number of plays (most notably *The Tragedy of Sir John van Olden Barnavelt*, 1619) before succeeding him as resident dramatist in 1625. Massinger was a protégé of the Herbert family, who were active in supporting opposition artists throughout the 1620s, and most of his plays deal with controversial topical issues. The *tragicomedy *The Bondman* (1623), for instance, is an attack on Buckingham, Charles I's protégé and a favourite target of the opposition, while *The Maid of Honour* (c.1621) uses its Sicilian setting to deal with English foreign policy. Massinger's best-known *comedy, *A New Way to Pay Old Debts* (c.1621), is a combination of topical and general *satire against court greed and corruption, while his most famous *tragedy, *The Roman Actor* (1626), is an outspoken defence of the freedom of the stage, which he considered as an agent of social reformation.   PCR

Mathews, Charles (1776–1835) English actor and dramatist. In 1803 he appeared at the *Haymarket, later acting at *Drury Lane and *Covent Garden, distinguishing himself for eccentric *comedy in a decade when London was blessed with excellent comedians. Many of his parts were especially written for him, but he also played Falstaff and Sir Peter Teazle in *The School for Scandal*. Mathews was a superb, protean mimic, and he devised an entertainment in which he would play all, or most of the parts. The first was *The Mail Coach Adventure* (1808), and the idea evolved into a series entitled *Mr Mathews at Home*, which he performed in London during the season and the provinces in the summer, as well as in America. These energetic entertainments, to which comic writers contributed scripts tailored to Mathews's talents, featured him as a player of widely different eccentric *characters, quick-change artist, singer of comic songs, speaker of rapid patter, and storyteller. He is sometimes referred to as Charles Mathews the Elder in distinction to his son, Charles James *Mathews. MRB

Mathews, Charles James (1803–78) English actor and dramatist, the son of Charles *Mathews. He joined *Vestris's Olympic Theatre company in 1835, marrying his *manager in 1838. They then assumed the management of *Covent Garden (1839–42) and the Lyceum (1847–55). Both managements were financially disastrous, and Mathews was twice imprisoned for debt. Vestris died in 1856, and Mathews married the American actress Lizzie Davenport, spending much of the rest of his life *touring, abroad and at home. Mathews was the leading light comedian of his time, although he did not regard himself as belonging to a particular *line of business. On stage he was brisk and lively, with a rapid and distinctly enunciated delivery. Like his father he was an excellent and versatile mimic. These talents showed themselves in his own *farce, *Patter versus Clatter* (1838), which is a virtual *monologue in several impersonations, and his elegant man-about-town Dazzle in *Boucicault's *London Assurance* (1841). He wrote many farces and comediettas for his inimitable style of performance; when he died his repertory died with him.   MRB

Matsui Sumako (1886–1919) Japanese actress in *shingeki. Matsui entered the training programme of *Tsubouchi Shōyō's newly created Bungei Kyōkai (Literary Society) and soon appeared with particular success in 1911 as Ophelia in *Hamlet* and as Nora in *Ibsen's *A Doll's House*, a

production that made her famous. In *kabuki women's roles are played by men, so that Matsui can be said to be the first actress in the history of modern Japanese theatre. (She had a predecessor in Sada Yacco (1872–1946), a former geisha who performed in bowdlerized Japanese historical plays in Europe at the turn of the century.) Matsui had a powerful temperament, and her love affair with Shōyō's associate, the writer and director Shimamura Hōgetsu (1871–1918), was the scandal of the decade. The pair withdrew from the Literary Society and began their own company in 1915, when Matsui had her greatest triumph as Katsusha in Shimamura's adaption of *Tolstoy's novel *Resurrection*. Shimamura fell ill and died in 1918; Matsui, distraught, committed suicide a short time later, ending a brilliant if unstable career.   JTR

Matthison, Edith Wynne (1875–1955) English actress. Matthison began her professional career with *Greet's company, playing, among other roles, Portia in *The Merchant of Venice* and Queen Katherine in *Henry VIII*, which she later reprised opposite *Irving (1904) and *Tree (1916). Her first public acclaim came when at short notice she played Violet Oglander in *Jones's *The Lackey's Carnival* (1900), but her sustained reputation rested upon classical roles from *Greek *tragedy to Shakespeare. Her success in *Poel's production of the *morality play *Everyman* (1902) —she played the title role cross-dressed—led to an American performance the same year. Thereafter she spent almost equal time working on opposite sides of the Atlantic. She was married to Charles Rann Kennedy, in whose plays she occasionally appeared, and she worked frequently with Granville *Barker.   TK

Matura, Mustapha (1939–) Trinidadian playwright. Matura left at the age of 21 for London, where he has had a highly successful career as a dramatist at the *Royal Court, the *National Theatre, and elsewhere. He writes about Trinidad, as in *Play Mas* (1974), and about the tensions of West Indian exiles in Britain, as in *As Time Goes By* (1971). His output of over twenty plays includes *Rum and Coca Cola* (1976), about a calypsonian whose relationship with his assistant turns violent, *Welcome Home, Jacko* (1979), which deals with the alienation of West Indian adolescents in Britain, and *The Coup* (1991), a bitterly funny portrayal of a bungled revolution, partly based on the 1970 Black Power uprising in Trinidad. His work has been widely produced in English-speaking countries. He is also a director, and a founder of the Black Theatre Cooperative in London. In 1984 Matura adapted *Synge's *comedy as *The Playboy of the West Indies*, and *Chekhov's *The Three Sisters* as *Trinidad Sisters*. His scripts for British television include *Bakerloo Line* (1972), the series *No Problem* (1983), and *Black Silk* (1985).   AS

Maude, Cyril Francis (1862–1951) English *actor-manager, adept at light *comedy and in elderly roles. He first appeared in London in 1886, and in 1890 began his long association with eighteenth-century comedies, playing Joseph Surface in *Sheridan's *The School for Scandal*. He went on to play Benjamin Backbite in the same play in 1890 and 1896, and the ageing Peter Teazle in 1900 at the age of 38. He played opposite *Wyndham and *Alexander in the 1890s. Between 1896 and 1905, together with Frederick Harrison, he *managed the *Haymarket Theatre, reviving *Goldsmith's *She Stoops to Conquer*, Sheridan's *The Rivals* (both in 1900), and *Colman and *Garrick's *The Clandestine Marriage* (1903), as well as appearing in plays by *Barrie and *Jones. After 1913 he went on extended *tours of North America and Australia with occasional returns to England, and went into semi-retirement in 1932.   VEE

Maugham, Somerset (1874–1965) English writer. Most of Maugham's tightly constructed *comedies, like his novel *Of Human Bondage* (1915), depict enslavement to marriage and society. He had early success with lightweight comedies, with four running in the West End in 1908. *Penelope* (1909) and *The Unattainable* (1916) were directed by the younger Dion Boucicault. In *The Circle* (1921), his most revived play, a young woman on the verge of leaving her stodgy marriage comes into contact with her mother-in-law, who had deserted her own husband, with subversive romantic results; Rex *Harrison starred in a 1989 Broadway revival. *The Sacred Flame* (1928) deals with euthanasia, while *For Services Rendered* (1932) pessimistically examines England after the First World War by focusing on one family. In *Sheppey* (1933), adapted from his own short story 'A Bad Example', a lottery-winning barber models himself after Christ while his family plot to have him committed. The play's bitterness and its mixture of comedy, social commentary, and allegory confused *audiences and critics alike, and Maugham stopped writing plays.   GAO

May, Elaine (1932–   ) American actress, director, and playwright. May began performing as a child with her father, the Yiddish actor Jack Berlin. After studying *acting in New York, she moved to Chicago where she met Mike *Nichols. With others, they formed an *improvisational theatre group in 1954 at the Compass Theatre (a forerunner to Second City). The two refashioned themselves as the comedy duo Nichols and May, moved to New York in 1957, and achieved quick fame after television appearances. In 1960 they created a successful stage version, *An Evening with Mike Nichols and Elaine May*, which they revised and performed off and on until 1965. May also wrote three plays: *A Matter of Position* (1962), *Not Enough Rope* (1962), and *Adaptation* (1969), which she also directed. Primarily a screenwriter since then (including *Primary Colors*, 1998), she appeared with Nichols in a revival of *Who's Afraid of Virginia Woolf?* in 1980.   JAB

Mayakovsky, Vladimir (1893–1930) Russian/Soviet poet, dramatist, painter. He made his stage debut in St Petersburg in 1913 in his own *'tragedy', *Vladimir Mayakovsky*, in a double bill with Kruchonykh's futurist extravaganza *Victory over the Sun*. Rallying to the Revolution, Mayakovsky and *Meyerhold staged 'the first Soviet play', *Mystery-Bouffe* (1918), in which Mayakovsky played the role of 'Man, Pure and Simple'. Like Meyerhold, Mayakovsky was drawn to popular entertainment such as the *mystery play, *commedia dell'arte*, *pantomime, and *circus. Although his energies during the 1920s were devoted to poetry, he found time to write short propaganda plays for circus performance as well as film scripts. In 1928, Meyerhold persuaded Mayakovsky to return to dramatic writing. His *satire on the New Economic Policy period and the new Soviet bourgeoisie, *The Bedbug*, with music by Shostakovich for firemen's band (1929), got a mixed reception, while his dystopian satire on future prospects for the Soviet Union, *The Bathhouse* (1930), although written and staged in a genuinely comradely spirit, proved too much for his major antagonists. A combination of overwork, hostile criticism, a failed love affair, and disillusionment with the Revolution led him to shoot himself.   NW

Mayo, Frank (1839–96) American actor, *manager, and playwright. Mayo sought his fortune in California's gold fields of the early 1850s, but found his way onto the San Francisco stage. After supporting such *touring stars as Laura *Keene and Junius Brutus *Booth, he returned to his native Boston as a leading man in 1865. While he played Shakespearian roles opposite such stars as Edwin *Booth, his greatest initial success came as Badger in *Boucicault's *The Streets of New York*. In 1872 Mayo secured the rights to Frank Murdoch's *Davy Crockett*, the play that gave him his signature role for more than two decades. A chance 1894 meeting with old friend Mark Twain led to Mayo's enormously successful adaptation of *Pudd'nhead Wilson* (1895), which he was touring when he died.   GAR

Ma Zhiyuan (Ma Chih-yüan) (1260–1325) Chinese playwright. Ma was ranked among the finest dramatists of his age and fully half of his sixteen known *zaju* plays have survived in complete or partial versions. Suffused with an otherworldly outlook, his work tends to stress the futility of fame and fortune. Ma collaborated with actors affiliated with the court entertainment bureau on the *Yellow Millet Dream*, the sort of deliverance play that may have been performed on *ritual occasions at local temples or at court. For early Ming imperial drama enthusiasts, Ma's work resonated with their own interest in Taoist immortality, while in the late Ming the literati approved his handling of the conflict between private sentiments and public duty. The definitive literati *zaju* anthology, *The One Hundred Yuan Plays*, gave pride of place to Ma's tale of love lost to political exigency, *Autumn in the Han Palace*, and included six of his other plays, including *Yellow Millet Dream* and *Tears on the Blue Gown*.   PS

Mbowa, Rose (1943–99) Ugandan actress, director, and playwright. She began her career with the Makerere Travelling Theatre in the 1960s. After an MA from Leeds she worked for *Serumaga's Abafumi Theatre, Radio Uganda, and Jimmy Katumba before becoming director of the department of music, dance, and drama at Makerere University. Her most influential play is *Mother Uganda and her Children* (1987) about Uganda's devastation through ethnic politics and the rebuilding of the nation on the principles of cultural diversity. She produced *Mine by Right* for the investigations of human rights violations, and works with her students in a variety of theatre for *development projects. She was last seen on stage as Mother Courage in a Luganda adaptation of *Brecht's classic.   EB

Mda, Zakes (1948–) South African playwright, novelist, and artist. He has written many literary and theatre for *development plays which call for community social action, particularly with the Lesotho-based Maratholi Travelling Theatre Company, foregrounding the complexities of southern African issues. In 1978 *We Shall Sing for the Fatherland* won his first Amstel Playwright of the Year Award, which he won again in 1979 for *The Hill*. Other plays include *Dead End, Dark Voices Ring* (both 1979), *The Road* (1982), *And Girls in their Sunday Dresses* (*Edinburgh Festival,

1988), *Joys of War* (1989), *Broken Dreams* (1995), and *The Whale Caller* (2005). *The Nun's Romantic Story* (1995), about the relationship between Church and state in an unnamed post-colonial country, has been performed in South America as well.   YH

Meckler, Nancy (1941–) American director. Meckler pursued a freelance directing career in England from the late 1960s, founding Freehold Theatre Company, and moved on to be associate director for Hampstead Theatre and the Leicester Haymarket. In 1981 she became the first woman to direct a mainhouse production at the *National Theatre (*Albee's *Who's Afraid of Virginia Woolf?*). Since 1988 she has been the *artistic director of Shared Experience, making highly *physical and actor-based productions of classic drama and literary adaptations, including world *tours of *The Mill on the Floss* and *Anna Karenina*. Her production of *Comedy of Errors* (2005) marked her RSC debut. For film she directed *Sister my Sister* (1994) and *Alive and Kicking* (1997).   KN

medieval theatre in Europe The somewhat amorphous term 'medieval' commonly refers to the theatre in Europe between roughly 900 and 1550, a period relatively well documented. The evidence from the early middle ages (400–900) is scanty and inconclusive. Medieval theatre was characterized by a wide variety of forms, venues, purposes, and auspices, and much of this activity was non-literary and occasional, bequeathing little in the way of dramatic text or self-consciously prepared 'theatrical' records. Spectacle, pageantry and ceremony—though often *mimetic in nature—served political, social, military, diplomatic, religious, and recreational purposes, embodying values appropriate to the circumstance. Only in material from the late middle ages is it possible to detect a growing awareness of dramatic activity as a distinct kind of performance, based on a written script, confined to particular places and circumstances, and focused on a performance aesthetic rather than on worship or instruction. While there is evidence that the medieval theatre was as much secular as religious, the high survival rate of religious texts and records has skewed our perceptions.

*Folk drama undoubtedly existed from an early date, but surviving texts date from the eighteenth century and later. Secular *farces and *interludes are numerous in the fifteenth and sixteenth centuries; otherwise, the bulk of the evidence for text-centred dramatic performance is religious. The *liturgical drama of the medieval church is represented by approximately one thousand Latin texts. Scripture and related legends provided material for *Corpus Christi plays, *Passion plays, and cycle plays (*see* BIBLICAL PLAYS). *Saint plays and especially *morality plays were designed to inculcate Christian virtue and morality, although the morality could be and was adapted to a variety of didactic purposes. As various as the medieval theatre was, it shared certain performance practices: procession, spectacle, emblematic *costume and *scenography, place-and-scaffold staging. The medieval theatre is best conceived as a single theatre distinguished by a finite number of variations brought about by differences in motivation and circumstance.   RWV

Medwall, Henry (fl. 1495) English playwright. Medwall was chaplain to Cardinal John Morton, archbishop of Canterbury, and both of his *interludes are assumed to have been performed at the Great Hall at Lambeth. *Nature* (*c.*1495), a *morality play in two parts, retains the conventions of the form, including the fall and redemption pattern and *farcical vices. Of more interest is *Fulgens and Lucrece* (*c.*1497), the earliest extant secular play in English. In it a debate on birth versus worth between Lucrece's two suitors in ancient Rome is made relevant to Medwall's aristocratic *audience through the device of a framing plot featuring two pages who emerge from the audience, to comment on the *action and take part in a comic parallel wooing of Lucrece's maid. Both plays are indebted to the popular theatrical tradition and were probably performed by professionals. RWV

Mee, Charles L. (1938–) American playwright and historian. In the middle of a career in American political history, Mee resumed an interest in theatre in 1986 when he provided the texts for Martha *Clarke's *Vienna Lusthaus*. He went on to create a series of radical reconstructions of *Greek *tragedies or modern classics that led to collaborations with experimental directors including *Bogart. Inspired by the collage techniques of Max Ernst and Robert Rauschenberg, Mee often borrows excerpts from wide-ranging sources and includes them verbatim in the *dialogue of his plays. Productions in New York alternative venues led to relationships with a number of *regional theatres, including Steppenwolf and *American Repertory Theatre, each of which produced *Full Circle*, Mee's take on *Brecht's *Caucasian Chalk Circle*. *Actors Theatre of Louisville premièred two of his plays, *Big Love* (2000), which went on to the Next Wave Festival at the Brooklyn Academy of Music, and *bobrauschenbergamerica* (2001) written for Bogart's SITI Company. His output is prodigious. STC

Mei Lanfang (1894–1961) World-famous Chinese actor of *jingju* (Beijing opera). Beginning his career as a *qingyi* ('black robe' or singing female) at the age of 8, Mei had become one of the chief actors of the *dan* (female) category before he was 20. After 1915 he gradually formed his own style through reforms in singing, *costume, and make-up, and by creating his own repertoire. He also merged the once rigid division between *qingyi*, pantomime, and dance and acrobatic roles. The result was a new category he called *huashan* (colourful robe). In 1927 Mei was chosen the best *dan* actor in China by popular vote. He made three *tours to Japan between 1919 and 1924, and in 1930 he performed in the USA for about half a year, including two months on Broadway. His 1935 tour to the Soviet Union received high praise from *Stanislavsky, *Meyerhold, *Eisenstein, and *Brecht. During the Sino-Japanese War Mei remained in Hong Kong; when the Japanese occupied the city in 1942 he grew a moustache and abandoned the stage. He returned to China and resumed performance after the war.   SYL

Meilhac, Henri (1831–97) and **Ludovic Halévy** (1834–1908) A prolific partnership of Parisian playwrights under the Second Empire; during their long joint career they wrote journalism, novels, and more than 50 plays and librettos. They are now mainly remembered for the lively and witty librettos for *Offenbach's *operettas, including *Orpheus in the Underworld* (Halévy alone, 1861), *La Belle Hélène* (1864), *La Grande Duchesse de Gérolstein* (1867), and *La Vie parisienne* (1867). They also wrote a successful *tragicomedy, *Froufrou* (1869), in which *Bernhardt had great success; and Halévy wrote the libretto for Bizet's *Carmen*. *Gilbert adapted *Les Brigands* and *Le Réveillon* (as *On Bail*).   EEC

Meiningen Players German theatre company. Although the court theatre in Meiningen, a small town in Thuringia, was founded in 1831, the fame of the Meiningen players (known in Germany as 'Die Meininger') is linked with Duke Georg II of Saxe-Meiningen (1826–1914), who assumed direct responsibility for the company in 1870. Under his direction, a provincial court theatre developed into one of the most influential theatres in Europe. His first reform had been the abolition of *opera four years earlier to concentrate entirely on drama. Although the Duke did not assume the official position of *director—this task was carried out by Ludwig *Chronegk—his control of central aspects of production effectively made him one. His overriding artistic principle was historical authenticity in the manner of historicist painting (*see* ANTIQUARIANISM). To achieve this end, he conducted extensive research into the cultural, historical, and archaeological context of the plays to be staged. Innovations included *realistic sound effects and the creation of a three-dimensional stage with a system of steps and rostra to manage dynamic spatial arrangements for crowd scenes. Another innovation was the creation of a true ensemble, in which even famous actors had to take turns playing smaller parts. The Meiningen Players demonstrated their new style on extended *tours throughout Europe. Between 1874 and 1890 they visited 38 cities and gave a total of 2,591 performances. Their influence was considerable, particularly on the *naturalistic theatre of the 1890s. Their admirers included *Irving, *Brahm, *Antoine, and *Stanislavsky.   CBB

Melo, Jorge Silva (1948–   ) Portuguese actor, playwright, and director, co-founder with *Cintra of the Teatro da Cornucópia in 1973. He acted and directed there, but left in 1979 to take up film directing. He worked with *Stein and *Strehler in the early 1980s, and later joined Jean Jourdheuil in France. Back in Lisbon in the 1990s, he combined film, cultural criticism in newspapers, and theatre activity as director of Artistas Unidos, a company he founded in 1996 devoted to contemporary work. Committed to *Brecht's and *Müller's idea of theatre as a 'poetry of politics', he is the author of three provocative plays—*António, a Young Man from Lisbon* (1995), *The End; or, Have Mercy on Us*, and *Prometheus* (both 1997)—focusing, in a tragic atmosphere, on the problems and fears of young men in modern society (violence, drugs, unemployment) and the question of political revolution.   MHS

melodrama The term 'melodrama' originally meant a performance blending *music and *action, with or without speech, to tell a story (*see* MÉLODRAME). It has sometimes been used merely as a formal description, denoting a drama of simple moral imperatives in which embattled goodness eventually triumphs. Such a category may then be used alongside *comedy and *tragedy in describing representations from all periods: it has been suggested that the mixed genre to which *Corneille's *Le Cid* (1636) belongs, or the moral structure of *Macbeth*, ending unequivocally with the death of the *villain, qualify these plays as melodrama rather than tragedy. But the term is more useful when confined to a particular kind of staged fiction whose conventions and sensibilities began to develop in Europe in the late eighteenth century, marked by new formal characteristics which were the result of cultural shifts expressed through new emphasis upon technical interac-

tions between theatre arts. Rather than being chiefly realized in the actors' performance of a writer's work, melodrama calls on all theatre systems, weaving its complexity from music, *mime, comedy, and spectacle. New technical capabilities in the theatre—larger stages, ever increasing possibilities of *lighting and scenery, as well as large casts and orchestras—were used to explore radical ideas and often to democratize moral assumptions.

The melodramatic stage embodied the newly conceptualized inner world of *romantic psychology and the resulting changed perception of the outer world of natural wonder and exotic sensation. It was organized by the new, anthropocentric moral order of personal sensibility, nationalism, prescriptive *gender roles, and family values. The result is a genre that externalizes conflicts and personifies cultural meanings in iconic roles—*hero, heroine, villain—within an *action rendered through the entire repertoire of physical performance. Thus music is an essential part of high melodrama, as is athletic, expressive movement; stage setting will strive for visual and aural excitement to match the size and importance of the issues dramatized. The internal and external discoveries of the post-revolutionary years—exotic distant places, and inner psychological depths—are rendered visible and sensationally present; and to keep the *audience both engaged and protected, the extreme theatricality of the genre continually advertises and refers to itself, in heroic, comic, and ironic interplay.

Exactly how the emergence of melodrama correlated with late eighteenth-century upheavals in European society and revolutionary politics is a vexed question. The link was certainly felt to be very real at the time: *Schiller's *The Robbers* (1781) was banned; Europe-wide performances of *Masaniello*, about the rise and fall of a humble man, were suspected of contributing to the revolutions of 1830–1; strict *censorship was enforced on the London stage, where the only apparent consensus between many contending interests was that politics should never be allowed in drama. Modern scholars are divided, some arguing that melodrama was a creative expression of French revolutionary culture, asserting its democratic character, while others regard melodrama as emerging from the tradition of the *drame *bourgeois* and corroborating its values.

There is less debate about whose plays were the first melodramas proper: in Germany August von *Kotzebue built successful popular plays out of the revolutionary sentiments, extreme situations, and new morality first expressed on stage by Schiller. In France Guilbert de *Pixérécourt renounced the dominant *neoclassicism of the stage in favour of a form of writing avowedly aimed at offering to those who could not read sensational stories illustrating the new moral world of the post-revolutionary republic. Radical British writers, excited by the new continental modes, soon generated a frightened backlash when translations of 'sickly German tragedies' deluged the London stage, to the delight of audiences. In 1802, significantly during the brief truce of Amiens between Britain and France, the radical Thomas *Holcroft brought a Pixérécourt play, *Cœlina* (1800), to *Covent Garden as *A Tale of Mystery*, and the model for the first generation of British melodramas was established. The picturesque setting of this play and its imitations, in a remote Gothic time and place, should not distract us from the contemporaneity of its romantic structure of feeling, in which innocence makes itself triumphantly known in the language of the heart— silent gesture and expressive music—and self-sacrificing love is powerful enough to overcome and convert both aristocratic selfishness and bourgeois caution. It is significant, too, that in the English version honest simplicity and right feeling are also embodied in Paulina, a woman servant, who adds comedy to the mix of music, spectacle, and mime.

Gothic-romantic melodrama, with its evocation of the sublime and picturesque through massive sets, violent action, and expressive music, and its egalitarian sentiments, was for a time high fashion. In England, as political reaction set in during the post-Napoleonic period, Walter Scott's novels provided a conservative turn to plots and setting. In France a further generation of dramatists— *Hugo, *Dumas *père*—developed the genre poetically; the addition of a literary dimension was facilitated by the legal situation in French theatre, which paid writers well for their work (see ROYALTIES). In England writers of the next generation who had a natural bent towards melodrama, such as *Dickens, were called away from the stage by the much greater rewards of the novel. Nevertheless, by the time Victoria came to the throne in 1837, the melodramatic had become established as simply the perceived story of today, the universal way of reading modern life. High comedy and classic tragedy had ceased to speak to the general audience; melodrama was the modality of the Victorians. And as the basic pattern for theatre, melodrama rapidly developed differentiation according to national and class tastes.

In Britain after Scott and the turn to history, the most significant shift was to settings in modern England. Douglas *Jerrold and other middle-class reformist writers sought to dramatize more explicitly the sufferings of the poor and the injustices of pre-Reform governments. *Black-Ey'd Susan* (1829) was his most successful championing of the honest Briton against all oppressions, since the sailor was already a national hero; more hard-hitting in their class critique were his *Press Gang* (1830) and *The Rent Day* (1832), the latter shifting to the significant locale of an idealized rural England, but this time in the present, menaced by enclosure and industrialization. Class confrontation in such plays was always important, and was personalized: evil systems, whether of landlordism or factory production, tended to be personified in the wicked mill owner or absentee lordling, and solved by the individual virtue of the heroine, the pluck of the sailor, or the sufferings of a humble family. But the simple solutions offered by the claptraps of heroism and repentance were undercut in the mode of melodrama by the ever present irony of the comic characters and their cheerfully pragmatic view of life, often cowardly, normally stoic, and always undeceived.

In the 1850s and 1860s the sensational strand of the melodramatic resurfaced, expressed first in the work of women writers, and therefore as novels. Harriet Beecher Stowe's *Uncle Tom's Cabin* (1852; see TOM SHOWS), Mary Braddon's *Lady Audley's Secret* (1862), and Ellen Wood's *East Lynne* (1861) were rapidly dramatized. Their huge success on both sides of the Atlantic was followed up by writers for the stage who produced dramas of crime and madness, the nightmare underside of the now strongly established and potentially suffocating Victorian dispensation: crime melodramas like Charles *Reade's *It's Never Too Late to Mend* (1853), Tom *Taylor's *The Ticket-of-Leave Man* (1863), and eventually *Irving's star vehicle *The Bells* (by Leopold Lewis, 1871) explored panic, pressure, guilt, and punishment for a middle-class audience. *Boucicault was the master of sensational melodrama, and his Irish plays in particular, but also his exploitation of the human costs of the growth of the cities, British imperialism, and interracial strife, were successful across the English-speaking world. The strength of such pieces was their heightening deployment of all possible theatre systems, exploding the internalized tensions of modern life into actualization by highly expressive *acting, feats of physical performance— mime, disguise, fighting—in impressive settings. Sensation melodrama was modern life illuminated and expanded by new technologies of gaslight and hydraulics.

Such dramas, pursued seriously by middle-class audiences as theatregoing became a fashionable pastime again in the 1870s, led on to the sophistications of *Pinero and H. A. *Jones, and writer's theatre reasserted itself as *copyright laws in England were established; increasingly full-blooded histrionics were left to the large suburban and East End houses. The West End exception was *Drury Lane, where an annual spectacular melodrama with amazing stage effects—sinking ships, steaming trains, or racing horses—purveyed the cruder heroics of empire to a large and various audience. In America the same development occurred; and on both sides of the Atlantic, therefore, the spectacular stage drama was ready to take up the next technical development—the cinematograph. *Birth of a Nation* (1915) and *Ben-Hur* (1925) feed melodrama through to Indiana Jones and James Bond; naval battles staged in real water and horse races run on revolves are the forerunners of daredevil stunts and digitally enhanced imaging on film.

In the silent years of film, not only visual spectacle and music remind us of earlier melodrama: mute acting reached a new flowering, and in such films as *The Wind* (1928) we may glimpse the scope of bodily expression possible within such a performance genre. In film criticism, however, the term has been shifted to denote not the big action movie, which is arguably the nineteenth-century play's most direct descendant, but the 'woman's film', especially the self-conscious saturation with high colour and emotion found in such work as Douglas Sirk's in the 1950s. This manifestation shares with stage melodrama the externalization of intensity into music, colour, and extremity.

Modernism's disdain for the arts of mass appeal discounted any serious appreciation of melodrama, especially when it found new vitality in the early twentieth century by spreading from the popular stage to popular film. Critical commentary on the genre during most of the twentieth century was either derogatory or, at best, defensive. This has at last given way to a deeper interest, the result of a postmodern realization that melodrama is not 'the *realism of dreams' (Eric Bentley), but precisely a non-realist dramatic form, suited to a sophisticated interactive relationship between writer, performers, and audience. *See also* OPERA.   JSB

mélodrame French genre, current *c.*1800–40. The literal translation of *mélodrame* (music drama) is misleading, as is the English term *melodrama derived from it. The freeing of controls on Paris theatres in 1791 led to a proliferation of small houses, in which new dramatic forms flourished: the *musical accompaniment was a relatively unimportant feature of this movement, which has been variously defined as 'trag-

edy for popular audiences' (Geoffroy), 'a product of the development of *drame *bourgeois*' (Gaiffe), and even 'the logical end-term of the evolution of the whole eighteenth-century theatre' (Marsan). Other theatre historians have rightly emphasized the lack of any cultural background on the part of the new *audiences produced by the revolution; hence their appetite for sensational *action, simplistic *characterization based on the opposition of good and evil, and countless variations on the theme of innocence persecuted. It is not surprising that this new class of spectators should share so many characteristics with the audiences of the early silent film 100 years later. There is an undoubted continuity between *le mélodrame* and the *romantic drama of the 1830s, despite the literary pretensions of the latter.   WDH

Menander (*c.*342–*c.*291 BC) Athenian comic playwright, the only writer of *New Comedy whose work has survived. Until the twentieth century he was known mainly by reputation or through quotations. Substantial fragments of his plays then turned up in Egypt and elsewhere through a series of lucky accidents. In 1957 Martin Bodmer published *Dyskolus* (*The Bad-Tempered Man*, sometimes translated as *The Malcontent* or *The Grumbler*), which is all but complete, and in 1969 *The Woman from Samos*, 85 per cent of which survives. From these, and substantial sections of at least three other plays, *The Arbitration*, *The Shorn Girl* (*The Rape of the Locks*), and *The Shield*, it became possible to uncover some of the reasons for Menander's huge popularity in the ancient world. Aristophanes of Byzantium considered him the supreme realist: 'O Menander and Life! Which of you imitated the other?' Plutarch, comparing him with *Aristophanes, wondered why anyone would go to the theatre except to see a play by Menander. The two virtually complete plays demonstrate a radical departure from the political bite of Aristophanes. Menander's plays are social *comedies in which the *characters are recognizably human and ultimately humane. Cnemon, the central figure of *The Bad-Tempered Man*, tries to live as a recluse, and to shelter his daughter from the outside world. When the wealthy Sostratus falls in love with her he has to resort to all manner of subterfuge to try to gain her hand. Cnemon himself is far more than a cardboard caricature. Menander reveals himself as less the harbinger of *commedia dell'-arte* than the forebear of *Molière, *Chekhov, and *Ayckbourn. The careful mix of *farcical comedy and genuine feeling is explored more deeply in *The Woman from Samos*. Most twentieth-century productions of Menander have been imaginative, if improbable, reconstructions from earlier fragmented texts, but the balance of the comic and the heart-wrenching was finely brought out in a production in 1994 at the Getty Museum in Malibu. JMW

Mendes, Sam (1965–) English director. Precocious success in *Chichester led Mendes quickly to the West End with *Cherry Orchard* (1989) with Judi *Dench. In 1990 he directed *Troilus and Cressida* for the *Royal Shakespeare Company at the *Swan Theatre, a production brutal in tone, virtuosic in manner. His skill in creating exciting theatre in small spaces brought *Jonson's *The Alchemist* and *Richard III* (1992), though he was less successful in large theatres at the RSC and *National Theatre. In 1992 he became *artistic director of the Donmar Warehouse in London, combining a flair for attracting major stars with an interest in less familiar plays, for instance in reviving *Sondheim's previously unsuccessful *musical *Assassins* (1992) and directing Nicole Kidman in *The Blue Room* (1998). Mendes's has combined Oscar-winning success in film (*American Beauty*, 1999) with theatre work, including awards for *Uncle Vanya* and *Twelfth Night* in 2002 and productions of *Stoppard's translation of *The Cherry Orchard* and *The Winter's Tale* in 2009. His latest film is *Away We Go* (2009). PDH

Méndez Ballester, Manuel (1909–2002) Puerto Rican playwright. *Outcry of the Furrows* (1939) strongly objected to land monopolizing by sugar refineries and the resulting impoverishment of the farming class. The *tragedy *Dead Season* (1940) established Méndez Ballester as the leading playwright of his generation; the production was enhanced by a neo-*naturalistic set that established new standards. He next turned to *comedy with *A Decent Ghost* (1950), *The Miracle* (1961), *Bienvenido, don Goyito* (1965), *Hail to the Women* (1968), and *The Circus* (1979). His late work *Caribbean Drums* was staged in 1996. JLRE

Meng Jinghui (Meng Ching-hui) (1965–) Chinese director, playwright, and actor. Meng became a director at the Central Experimental Theatre in Beijing and rose to prominence with his 1993 production of *The World of the Mortals Beckons*—an adaptation of a little-known work by an anonymous writer of the Ming Dynasty (1368–1644) combined with Boccaccio's *The Decameron*. Naughty, playful, wicked, the production made experimental theatre fascinating and accessible to the *audience. Since then he has become a major figure in the *avant-garde movement in China. Particularly memorable are his productions of *I Love XXX* (1994) and his pop-music

experimental drama *Rhinoceros in Love* (1999). He uses adaptation as a creative tool, most successfully in *Faust: a pirated version* (1999) and *Twelfth Night* (2000). He has participated in festivals around the world with productions of *Waiting for Godot* (1993) and *King Lear* (2000), among others. His 1998 production of *Fo's *Accidental Death of an Anarchist* went on world *tour in 2000 and his first film, *The Chicken Poets*, opened in 2002. MPYC

Mercer, David (1928–80) English playwright. Born into working-class Yorkshire, Mercer became a successful writer of witty yet substantial stage and television plays in the 1960s, often dealing with social alienation and class loyalties. These themes appear in Mercer's first successful play, *Ride à Cock Horse* (1965), as well as in *After Haggerty* (1970), an ironic *comedy in which a theatre critic, lecturing about the British theatrical revolution of 1956 in the face of real, political revolutions, must also confront his offensive working-class father. Mercer specialized in creating vivid, eccentric (and sometimes insane) *characters such as the artist Morgan in *A Suitable Case for Treatment* (broadcast 1962; filmed 1965, with David *Warner) and the renegade vicar in *Flint* (1970) who burns down his church. Other plays include *Belcher's Luck* (1966), *Duck Song* (1974), and *Cousin Vladimir* (1978). MDG

Merchant, Vivien (Ada Thompson) (1929–82) English actress. Playing cool, sexually charged *characters, Merchant was best known as an interpreter of *Pinter, to whom she was married. She originated the role of Ruth, the trophy-wife-turned-prostitute, in *The Homecoming*, directed by Peter *Hall for the *Royal Shakespeare Company (1965), a role she reprised in the 1973 film. She appeared as Anna in Pinter's *Old Times* (1971), also directed by Hall for the RSC. Her non-Pinter work for the RSC includes *Macbeth* (1967), *Mercer's *Flint* (1970), and James Joyce's *Exiles* (1970). Her films include *Alfie* (1966), *The Accident* (1967, scripted by Pinter), Alfred Hitchcock's *Frenzy* (1970), and *Genet's *The Maids* (1974). Merchant's career suffered after the break-up of her marriage with Pinter in the mid-1970s. MDG

Mercier, Louis-Sébastien (1740–1814) French playwright. Mercier was a pre-*romantic iconoclast. A staunch opponent of elitism who sought to abolish the *neoclassical tradition, he was an Anglophile, who championed the *drame *bourgeois* with its scenic *realism as the appropriate forum for debating moral, social, and political issues. *The Deserter* (1770) pleads against the mandatory death penalty for army deserters, and *The Vinegar-Seller's Barrow* (1775), answering *Diderot's wish that the stage portray all professions, urges the tolerance of marriage across class lines. His adaptations of Shakespeare have a similar naive optimism, cloying sentiment, and rhetorical tone. In *The Tombs of Verona* (1782) he campaigns for freedom of choice in marriage and protests against female oppression. Accepted at small theatres, at fairgrounds, in the provinces, and abroad, Mercier was *persona non grata* at the *Comédie-Française and supported *Beaumarchais's campaign against the Comédie for authors' rights. In 1792, as a deputy to the revolutionary Convention, he voted against the execution of Louis XVI. Subsequently imprisoned, he was saved from the guillotine by the fall of Robespierre in 1794.   JG

Mercouri, Melina (1923–94) Greek actress and politician. Mercouri made her first appearance in 1944 in Alexis Solomos's *Path of Freedom*. In 1949 her interpretation of Blanche Dubois in the Art Theatre's production of *A Streetcar Named Desire* established her as a leading actress. She made her screen debut in 1955 in Michalis Kakogiannis's *Stella*. In 1960 she shared the award for best actress at the Cannes Film Festival (with Jeanne Moreau) and was nominated for an Academy award for *Never on Sunday*, directed by her husband, the American expatriate Jules Dassin. She also starred in Dassin's films *Phaedra* (1961) and *Topkapi* (1964), and in Norman Jewison's *Gaily, Gaily* (1969). During 1966–7 she made her New York debut in Dassin's *Ilya Darling*, a stage adaptation of *Never on Sunday*. She actively opposed the military dictatorship in Greece (1967–74) while in exile abroad. In 1976 she played Medea for the State Theatre of Northern Greece. She was elected to Parliament on the socialist ticket in 1977 and became Greece's Minister of Culture in 1981.   KGO

Merman, Ethel (1909–84) American singer and actress. Born Ethel Zimmerman, the former stenographer was vaulted to fame in the *Gershwins' *Girl Crazy* (1930), in which she introduced 'I Got Rhythm'. With her brassy personality, clarion voice, and immaculate enunciation, she remained a box-office star in *musical theatre for three decades. Star vehicles were created for her by Cole *Porter (*Anything Goes* and four others, all big hits) and Irving *Berlin (*Annie Get your Gun*, *Call Me Madam*). Her final original role was perhaps her greatest—Mama Rose in *Gypsy* (1959). The title role in *Hello, Dolly!* was written for her, but she chose not to create it, although she was Broadway's final Dolly in 1970. While her outsize

stage persona was generally too large for film, she still made several motion pictures, repeating her stage role in the film of *Call Me Madam*. A dedicated performer, she typically stayed with her shows for their entire runs, and nearly all of them made a profit. 'Broadway has been awfully good to me', she noted on her retirement, 'but then I've been awfully good to Broadway.'   JD

Meron, Hannah (1923–) Israeli actress, leading lady of the Cameri Theatre, of which she was a founding member in 1945. Born in Berlin, she was a child star, appearing on screen in Fritz Lang's *M* before moving to Palestine in 1933. On stage she projected a modern and sophisticated presence, always recognized by her uniquely rasping voice. She played nearly 60 roles, representing a wide spectrum of native Israeli, classical, and modern plays: Shamir's *He Walked in the Fields*, *Shaw's *Pygmalion*, Shakespeare's *As You Like It*, *Schiller's *Mary Stuart*, and *Ibsen's *Hedda Gabler*. Always eager for new challenges, she left the Cameri to work in experimental productions as well as commercial *musicals such as *Hello, Dolly!* and *My Fair Lady*. She appeared with various orchestras, in film and television, and taught and directed at Tel Aviv University. In 1970 she lost a leg in an Arab machine gun attack at Munich airport.   EN

Merrick, David (1912–2000) American producer. Merrick, originally a lawyer, began producing with *Fanny* (1954), and was responsible for 88 Broadway plays and *musicals, many imported from London, some of them challenging and provocative. His contributions included *The Matchmaker* (1955), *Look Back in Anger* (1957), *The Entertainer* (1958), *Gypsy* (1959), *A Taste of Honey* (1960), *Stop the World I Want to Get off* (1962), *Oliver!* (1963), *Oh! What a Lovely War* (1964), *Hello, Dolly!* (1964), *Marat/Sade* (1965), *I Do, I Do* (1966), *Rosencrantz and Guildenstern are Dead* (1967), *Promises, Promises* (1968), *Travesties* (1975), and *42nd Street* (1981). Merrick also produced four films. Dubbed the 'abominable showman', he employed outrageous publicity stunts, such as paying an *audience member to slap an actor onstage in *Look Back in Anger*, advertising rave quotes for *Subways Are for Sleeping* (1961) signed by men with the same names as the leading critics, and, on *42nd Street*'s opening day, keeping secret news of director Gower *Champion's death so that he could announce it during the curtain call. He often feuded with New York's critics.   SLL

Mesguich, Daniel (1952–) Algerian-French actor and director. Mesguich studied under *Vitez at the Conservatoire in Paris, where he has himself taught since 1983. After founding Théâtre du Miroir in 1974, he headed the Théâtre Gérard-Philipe (1986-9) and Théâtre National de Lille, renamed La Métaphore (1991-8). Like Vitez, Mesguish is interested in the role of verse in the classical repertoire and is known for his reinterpretations of Shakespeare and *Racine, often based on ideas gained from his reading of French literary and cultural theory. He has directed several productions at the *Comédie-Française, including a popular version of *Offenbach's *La Vie parisienne* (1997), Shakespeare's *The Tempest* (1997), and Racine's *Mithridate* and *Andromaque* (1999). His *opera stagings have been seen at the *Opéra, the *Opéra-Comique, and in Brussels. As an actor Mesguich has appeared on television and in many films by noted directors, including Costa-Gavras, Truffaut, *Mnouchkine, and James Ivory. DGM

Messel, Oliver (1904-78) English artist and designer. A student of the Slade School of Art, Messel's style tended towards a *romantic, imaginative, and sometimes sinister aesthetic. His work for C. B. *Cochran between 1926 and 1932 included macabre *masks for *Coward's *This Year of Grace* (1928) and a striking white-on-white setting for *Reinhardt's *Helen* (1932). Among his designs were a tulle and gauze Victorian pastiche for *Guthrie's *A Midsummer Night's Dream* (1937), and a delicate, innovatively constructed Winter Garden for *Brook's *Ring round the Moon* (1950). His designs for *ballet included the celebrated and lavish *Sleeping Beauty* at *Covent Garden (1946), and for *opera, a light and elegant *La Cenerentola* at Glyndebourne (1952). His rich, colourful, painterly style was appropriate to stagings which used backcloths and *flats. VRS

Metastasio (Pietro Trapassi) (1698-1782) Italian dramatist, uncontested master of *melodramma*, a form of *musical drama which employs poetic language and the heroic style. Unfortunately its pursuit of pathos or grandiloquence makes it appear merely overwrought to modern tastes. The composers who vied to write music for his works included Vivaldi, Pergolesi, Scarlatti, Salieri, and Albinoni. *Mozart used his *Clemenza di Tito*, albeit adapted by Carlo Mazzolà, for his *opera of the same name. Metastasio's *Didone abbandonata*, a classic tale of unrequited love and descent into madness, was produced in Naples in 1724 and five years and five *melodrammi* later he was summoned to Vienna as court poet in succession to Apostolo Zeno, the other great writer of *melodramma*. Metastasio was afflicted by the eighteenth-century urge to reform. His programme was aimed at eliminating

from *melodramma* baroque excess, giving less prominence to design and more to the lyrics and *music, reducing the role of the *chorus, attaining a sober simplicity of style, and ensuring that the resultant work was imbued with high moral standards. He considered his best work to be *Attilio Regolo* (composed 1740), though his most enduring script is *Olimpiade* (1733), a poetic reworking of ancient legends of a child found abandoned as a consequence of prophecies of patricide. JF

metatheatre Self-reflexive drama or performance that reveals its artistic status to the *audience. The reflexivity may be embedded in a script's structure by the playwright, when it can be called metadrama, or superimposed in production by the *director or designer. In either instance, aesthetic self-consciousness is often presented in both artistic and metaphysical terms, especially in works that speculate on alternative versions of reality, including the artifice of representation. The play-within-the-play in *Hamlet* (*c.*1600) set the standard for the elevation of theatricality to metaphysical proportions in Western drama. As Lionel Abel observed (*Metatheatre*, 1963), because the play-within-the-play seems to have been scripted by Hamlet himself, he is the 'first stage figure with an acute awareness of what it means to be staged'. While it can be argued that some ancient *Greek plays also lean in this direction, it is certain that Shakespeare's concern with performativity resurfaced often, most tellingly in *The Tempest* (1611), when Prospero comments on his devotion to theatrical magic. No wonder the work is a favourite of modern directors such as *Strehler, whose 1978 production infused text and *mise-en-scène with a concern with directorial and *scenographic artifice. Self-consciously dramatic *characters are also apparent in *early modern Spanish dramatists, some of whom extended a baroque preoccupation with artifice to themes not traditionally associated with aesthetics, most notably in *Calderón, whose *Life Is a Dream* (*c.*1629) is widely acknowledged as the precursor to the deployment of metatheatre in modernism.

In the age of psychology, preoccupation with the dynamics of personality would assume diverse forms, from *naturalism at one end to the exposure of the mechanisms of *illusionism on the other. Strindberg explored the theatre's potential to mirror subjective processes in *A Dream Play* (1907), where plot and scenography are material emanating from the unconscious mind of the dreamer/author (*see also* SYMBOLISM; EXPRESSIONISM). In the trilogy comprised of *Six Characters in Search of an Author* (1921), *Each in his Own Way* (1924), and *Tonight We Improvise*

(1930), *Pirandello builds tension among the constituents of theatrical events, pitting characters against playwrights, actors against characters, and performers against the audience.

What links the metatheatre of the sixteenth with that of the late nineteenth and early twentieth centuries is the presumption of a cohesive system of social values that may be compared (or reduced) to the theatrical realm. The metaphor of theatricality, in other words, implies that life itself is fixed on a stage of limited scope. It is the absence of such social givens that most typified versions of metatheatre after the Second World War. If the slipperiness of metaphor resides at the heart of *absurdist despair, the opening up of interpretative possibilities is one of its happier by-products, as can be seen from the metatheatrics of *Ionesco, *Genet, and *Beckett. The indeterminateness of meaning has been borne out in formal experimentation with metatheatre in some postmodern theatre, particularly in the work of Robert *Wilson, *Foreman, *LeCompte, *Bausch, and *Lepage. And the solo activity of *performance art, often taking the body of the playwright-performer as the entire site of theatricality, suggests that metatheatre has transcended its status as metaphor by becoming a major representational mode, and one no longer confined to the theatrical realm.   DRP

Method A term usually applied to the *acting techniques developed by Lee *Strasberg to enable the actor to create truthful behaviour. Strasberg's Method was based on the System of *Stanislavsky and additional ideas of Stanislavsky's student *Vakhtangov. Strasberg encountered the ideas while studying with *Moscow Art Theatre actors at the American Laboratory Theatre in New York in 1924 and over the course of his long teaching career, especially at the *Group Theatre in the 1930s and the *Actors Studio (1948–82), Strasberg developed his own exercises for accomplishing Stanislavsky's goals of relaxation, concentration, and creativity. Strasberg was sometimes criticized for his reliance on 'affective (or emotional) memory' and Vakhtangov's related technique of the 'adjustment'. Suggested by the Russians' reading of Pavlov, the techniques are designed to assist the actor in bringing to consciousness a set of feelings from a past event and then devising a physical or mental cue so that the recalled emotion can be brought forward during performance. During the 1950s the Method became a matter of public controversy, accused by some of promoting self-absorbed and inarticulate performances (from *Brando, James Dean, and others) while praised by many as a path into truth and away from theatrical clichés. The Method has worked well in the intimate and psychologically intense area of Hollywood film drama.   MAF

Meyerhold, Vsevolod (1874–1940) Russian/Soviet actor, director, and theorist who, as a protégé of *Nemirovich-Danchenko, was among the founding members of the *Moscow Art Theatre in 1898 and the original Konstantin there in *Chekhov's *Seagull*. At first an enthusiastic admirer of *Stanislavsky, Meyerhold became attracted by the non-*naturalistic possibilities of the *symbolist theatre movement and left the MAT in 1902 to lead his own troupe in the Russian provinces where between 1902 and 1905 he staged over 170 productions. After returning briefly to the MAT in 1905, in order to assist Stanislavsky's own experiments in symbolist staging, Meyerhold was invited by *Komissarzhevskaya to head her theatre in St Petersburg, a post which he held in 1906 and 1907, and where he staged groundbreaking productions of *Blok's symbolist *The Fairground Booth* (or *The Puppet Show*), as well as highly original, stylized versions of *Ibsen's *Hedda Gabler* and *Andreev's *Life of Man*. Meyerhold was then invited to become head of the imperial theatres in St Petersburg and between 1908 and 1917 staged major productions of drama and *opera.

But his unofficial work in private and fringe venues in St Petersburg was more significant. He and fellow enthusiasts staged experimental productions based on conventions of pre-Renaissance theatre, and with a special debt to popular forms such as the *pantomime, the *circus, *commedia dell'arte, and the harlequinade, experimenting with ideas drawn from Asian theatre and modernist sources (including *Craig, *Appia, *Fuchs, and *Wagner), foregrounding overt theatricality and the grotesque. The radicalism of Meyerhold's approach was reflected in his acceptance of the October Revolution and led to his appointment, by *Lunacharsky, as head of the theatre section of the Moscow Cultural Commissariat. Having staged what became known as 'the first Soviet play', *Mystery-Bouffe*, in collaboration with its author, *Mayakovsky, Meyerhold threw himself into the task of converting theatres to the communist cause with the kind of zeal that so alarmed his political superiors that he was rapidly relieved of his post. This had the effect of setting him free to pursue the revolutionizing of Soviet theatre on his own terms and in his own way.

At the various theatre workshops which he established in Moscow during and after the Civil War, Meyerhold surrounded himself with a remarkable group of actors and future directors, including *Okhlopkov and *Eisenstein, and prepared productions combining *constructivist staging with his own actor-training method of *biomechanics. Principal among these was Crommelynck's farce *The Magnanimous Cuckold* (1922), with constructivist *scenography by *Popova. Acquiring his own theatre in 1924, which became known as the Meyerhold Theatre, Meyerhold staged brilliantly original productions during the 1920s, notably *Ostrovsky's *The Forest* (1924) and *Gogol's *The Government Inspector* (1926). Never an easy person to work with, Meyerhold attracted violent antipathy and unqualified allegiance in equal measure, as did his wife Zinaida Raikh, who was given leading roles in many of his productions.

His association with Mayakovsky, *Tretyakov, and the flagrant modernism of the Left Front of the Arts, came under increasing scrutiny in the early 1930s, as Stalin tightened his grip on power and began to insist on conservative forms of art. Meyerhold's staging of Mayakovsky's *satirical plays *The Bedbug* and *The Bathhouse* (1929, 1930) challenged bureaucracy and the betrayal of revolutionary ideals, only to be criticized as anti-Soviet, as were other productions during the 1930s. Meyerhold sought to confirm his political allegiance with *Vishnevsky's *The Last Decisive* (1931) and Yury German's *The Prelude* (1933), both of which had anti-fascist or anti-bourgeois themes. By the mid-1930s, however, the writing was on the wall, and not even an attempt to stage *How the Steel Was Tempered* (1937), based on a novel by the conspicuously pro-Soviet writer Nikolai Ostrovsky, could save him. It was banned and his theatre closed in 1938. Notwithstanding painful efforts to justify himself and prove his pro-Soviet loyalties at a conference of directors in 1939, Meyerhold was arrested and imprisoned that June. Despite desperate appeals to high officials like Molotov, wherein he sought to refute the ludicrous charges of Trotskyism and espionage, Meyerhold was shot on 2 February 1940 and buried in a common grave. His name was erased from public records, just as his image was airbrushed from photographs, until his rehabilitation by a Military Court of the USSR in 1955.

Meyerhold's main legacy has been less his theory than his practice. Crucially, he was the first modernist to bring open theatricality back into play and to do so in a radically populist manner. His left-wing ideology and his foregrounding of 'the means of theatrical production' has enabled us the better to understand work of like-minded practitioners such as *Piscator and *Brecht, and to

weigh the merits of social and political theatre against the more personal and psychological forms of Stanislavsky, or the therapeutic and spiritually convulsive intensities of *Artaud and *Grotowski. In terms which *Brook has provided, Meyerhold may be said to have raised 'rough' theatre to 'holy' heights of achievement.   NW

Mhlanga, Cont (1958–) Zimbabwean playwright and director. In 1982 he founded Amakhosi Theatre in Makokoba Township, Bulawayo, which remains Zimbabwe's most famous theatre company. He remained playwright and *artistic director of the group until 1999, professionalizing its structures and expanding it into film, radio drama, and music. *Workshop Negative* (1986) was Mhlanga's most controversial play, causing a nationwide debate on race relations, reconciliation, and corruption. Other plays include *Nansi LeNdoda* (1985), *Stitsha* (1990), *Dabulap* (1992), and *Hoyayaho* (1994), the last a *musical on AIDS with predominantly *mimed *action. Mhlanga's plays, most of them written in what he calls 'ndenglish'—the typical township mixture of SiNdebele and English—and his direction have won several awards.   MRO

Mhlope, Gcina (1958–) South African writer, director, and actress. Her first play, *Have You Seen Zandile?* (1985), was collaboratively written, and she also collaborated with Barney *Simon on *Born in the RSA* the same year. In 1989 she became the in-house director of the Market Theatre in Johannesburg, where she wrote and directed *Somdaka* (*Proud to be Dark-Skinned*, 1989). She co-authored *The Good Person of Sharkeville* with Janet *Suzman (an adaptation of *Brecht, 1995) and her *Love Child* premièred in Grahamstown in 1998. She founded Zanendaba Storyteller in 1992, a group that performs traditional stories for children and adults. She won best actress awards in America for *Born in the RSA* (New York, 1987) and *Have You Seen Zandile?* (Chicago, 1988). Her role in reclaiming and teaching oral performance forms, particularly in the urban context, has been profound.   YH

Michell, Keith (1928–) Australian actor, designer, and director. Michell trained at the *Old Vic in London and achieved major successes in the UK. He had leading roles at Stratford in the 1950s, *toured Australia with the *Shakespeare Memorial Theatre (1952-3), and was *artistic director of the *Chichester Festival (1974-7). He also worked in *musicals—*Robert and Elizabeth* (1964) and *La Cage aux folles* (1985), for example—but is most famous for his King Henry in the BBC television series *The Six Wives of*

Henry VIII (1970). He worked extensively in Australia as well, and wrote and acted in an Australianized version of *Peer Gynt* (*Pete McGynty and the Dreamtime*, Melbourne, 1981). EJS

Mickiewicz, Adam (1798–1855) Poet and playwright, considered the greatest Polish writer. As a student in Vilnius, Mickiewicz joined the anti-Russian cause, was jailed, exiled, and eventually settled in Paris, where he was a professor at the Collège de France (1840–4). He died of cholera in Turkey, organizing a Polish military force. Among his masterworks is the *romantic Forefathers' Eve*, a dramatic poem published in five parts (1823–32). Long and anarchic, it is an explosive call for Poland's spiritual and political freedom, prohibited in Poland in the nineteenth century and on several occasions *censored by the communist regime after 1945. It was staged for the first time by *Wyspiański (Cracow, 1901) in an adapted text, and since then has remained central to Polish theatre, often seen in rich spectacles with *music, monumental *scenography, crowd scenes, and powerful *acting. Leon *Schiller's production (1932–4), designed by Andrzej Pornaszko, is remembered for its vast, open platform crowned with three crosses, equating the suffering of Poland with the suffering of Christ. *Forefathers' Eve* was frequently produced after the war, notably by *Grotowski (1961) and *Swinarski (1973). KB

Middle Comedy The transitional *comedy in the Greek world in the fourth century BC. The term covers the period from the last two plays of *Aristophanes, *Ecclesiazusae* (or *Women in the Assembly*, 392/1 BC) and *Plutus* (388 BC), to the first play of *Menander (*c.*323 BC). There are no other surviving plays from the period, only titles from a number of writers which suggest a mix of mythological theme and *character comedy, but without either the hard edge or the fantasy in which the previous century rejoiced. The two late Aristophanes comedies are noticeably different in tone and structure from his earlier work. The *choruses have far less influence on the plot, and what they actually say, or sing, is often omitted in the received text in favour of a choral interlude. *Ecclesiazusae*, in which the women of Athens disguise themselves as men in order to go to the Assembly and vote themselves into power, does have the feel of the authentic Aristophanes, complete with its directed *satire against Platonic social engineering. *Plutus* is social satire too in its story of the return to sight of the blind god of money. Neither, though, shows the exuberance or the personal attacks on living characters which made *Old Comedy seem both dangerous

and volatile. In a time of political change in Athens there was no place for the comedy of the Peloponnesian War that had so fiercely mocked institutions and politicians. *See also* NEW COMEDY. JMW

Middleton, Thomas (1580–1627) English dramatist. Educated at Oxford, Middleton had begun to work in the theatre by 1601. A period of intense activity in 1604–6 produced *satirical *comedies for the Paul's *boy company, including *A Mad World, my Masters, A Trick to Catch the Old One*, and *Michaelmas Term*. These plays adapt the characteristic preoccupations of sixteenth-century Italian comedy to a contemporary London setting, with unscrupulous, predatory young men tricking their elders in a quest for money and sex. For the King's Men (*see* CHAMBERLAIN'S MEN, LORD) he began as a writer of sardonic *tragedies of sexual and political intrigue in foreign courts, notably *The Revenger's Tragedy* (1606) and *The Maiden's Tragedy* (1611). Some late twentieth-century scholarship claimed that Middleton was Shakespeare's collaborator on *Timon of Athens* and the reviser, after Shakespeare's retirement, of *Macbeth* and *Measure for Measure*.

The mid-Jacobean fashion for romance tempered Middleton's satirical tendencies, beginning with his comedy, *No Wit, No Help Like a Woman's* (1611). The plays of this middle period are less harsh in tone, more *tragicomic in incident, and the presence of uncomplicatedly sympathetic figures, like the title *character of *A Chaste Maid in Cheapside* (1613), make the happy endings the more joyous. The year 1613 also saw the first of a series of eight city pageants, which he continued to write on and off for the rest of his life, and the beginning of an intermittent collaboration with *Rowley. Middleton's later work includes his great tragic studies of female psychology and sexuality, *Women Beware Women* (1621) and *The Changeling* (1622, with Rowley), which have proved his most enduring contributions to the repertory: both had notable revivals at the *Royal Shakespeare Company (1962 and 1979). Middleton's last extant play is the political satire *A Game at Chess* (1624), which uses its chessboard analogy to represent the worsening diplomatic relations between England and Spain, and played for nine consecutive days before it was closed by the authorities. MJW

Mielziner, Jo (**Joseph**) (1901–76) American *scenographer. Under the spell of R. E. *Jones's New Stagecraft, Mielziner made his mark with the *Theatre Guild production of *Molnár's *The Guardsman* (1924). Rising quickly to the top of his profession, for the next 50 years he matured into the finest set and *lighting designer of his time. The favourite of Katharine *Cornell's company, *Rodgers and *Hammerstein, and a number of Broadway playwrights and *producers, he gained a reputation as a problem solver. His notable successes were *Annie Get your Gun* by *Berlin (1946), *A Streetcar Named Desire* by *Williams (1947), *Death of a Salesman* by *Miller (1949), *Guys and Dolls* by *Loesser (1950), and *The King and I* by Rodgers and Hammerstein (1951). Chafing against the restrictions of Broadway, he sought to make changes in the design of *playhouses, and in the early 1960s he worked with Eero Saarinen on the design of the Vivian Beaumont Theatre in *Lincoln Center, and served as designer or consultant on a number of university theatres.   MCH

Mihura, Miguel (1905–77) Spanish playwright, director, and humorist. His first and most acclaimed play, *Three Top Hats*, was written in 1932 but not staged until 1952, initiating a career of almost two decades. At the end of the Spanish Civil War, he founded the popular satirical magazine *La Cordoniz*, which thrived in spite of *censorship restrictions. *Sublime Decision* (1955) and *The Fair Dorothea* (1963) rank with the best seriocomic plays of their time and illustrate his gift for brilliant, near *absurdist *dialogue. In *Carlota* (1954), one of his several crime plays, he anticipates postmodernism by inverting the conventions of the murder mystery genre and denying his *audience a definitive ending. He directed brisk and stylish productions of many of his own plays in Madrid's leading commercial venues.   MPH

Mikhoels, Solomon (1890–1948) Soviet-Jewish actor and director who led the Moscow State Yiddish Theatre from 1929. Mikhoels made a name for himself as an actor in plays by *Aleichem but most notably in *Radlov's 1935 production of *King Lear*. His approach to *acting derived from forms of Jewish folk theatre, allied with sophisticated forms of *expressionism based on stylized gesture and speech, together with *mask-like make-up redolent of the grotesque. This style lent itself well to forms of folk *comedy but could also be refined, in Mikhoels's hands, to produce more poignant and subtly tragic creations, such as his Jewish 'Don Quixote' in *The Voyage of Veniamin III* (1927) and his Teve in Aleichem's *Tevye the Milkman* (1937). Mikhoels had a prominent public profile and did much to encourage popular interest in a state-sponsored Jewish theatre. His death in a car accident in mysterious circumstances was rumoured to have

been contrived at Stalin's behest in the year in which Mikhoels had also suffered the closure of his theatre.   NW

Miller, Arthur (1915–2005) American playwright. Beginning with *All my Sons* in 1947, Miller acquired a worldwide reputation and joined the ranks of *O'Neill and *Williams as one of the most accomplished American dramatists. More than 25 Miller plays have been produced and several have entered the world repertory: *All my Sons* (1947), *Death of a Salesman* (1949), *The Crucible* (1953), *A View from the Bridge* (1955), *After the Fall* (1964), *Incident at Vichy* (1964), and *The Price* (1968). Of the later work, *The Ride down Mount Morgan* (1991), and *Broken Glass* (1994) have seen major productions in London and New York. Miller's work began and to a degree continued within the modern *realistic tradition developed by *Ibsen—psychologically complex and logically motivated *characters move through strong plots driven by external social pressures, the *protagonists finding resolutions which conclude the *action and deliver potent but satisfyingly ambiguous moral reflections. Nevertheless Miller stretched the realistic form by interweaving dream states and subjective imaginings into the fabric of his dramatic world. In *Death of a Salesman*, widely regarded as his masterpiece and one of the outstanding English-language plays of the modern period, the playwright provides the objectively viewed realistic scenes of the present-day salesman Willie Loman—ageing, confused, and on the verge of disaster. The play also moves freely about in Willie's memory and imagination, mingling the 'real' scenes of the present with Willie's replaying of scenes from his past as well as his present-time conversations with the imagined presence of a dead relative. The allure, necessity, and unreliability of memory in relation to one's own sense of moral responsibility is a persistent theme in Miller's work, as is the related issue of time and the ability of the human to 'bend' it through memory and art. Two Miller one-act plays bear the title *Danger! Memory!* (1987) and Miller's memoir of the same year is called *Timebends*.

Despite these interests, Miller was not a relativist. There is a truth to be found, and the struggle of human beings, with their limited capacities to find that truth, is the central drama of existence. The clearest model for Miller's lifelong project may be *After the Fall*, which takes place in the mind of its protagonist who seeks, if not exoneration, then at least insight, clarity, the kind of redemption that could come with understanding. *Death of a Salesman* and *The Cru-*

cible were criticized by some who felt that Miller over-articulated the message of the plays in their final scenes. Later works put greater trust in metaphor.

Miller was a major public figure and, at times, a celebrity. He was associated with a number of pro-communist activities during the 1940s and became a focus of the House Un-American Activities Committee during the 1950s. *The Crucible* (1953), his historically based play about witch trials in Salem, Massachusetts, was widely interpreted as offering a parallel to tactics of congressional investigators, by which witnesses were intimidated into naming communists as a means of saving themselves, just as seventeenth-century colonists were frightened into naming witches. Miller became the focus of intense media scrutiny when at about the same time that he was called to testify before HUAC (1956), he announced his impending marriage to Marilyn Monroe. (They divorced in 1961.) Having refused to 'name names', the playwright was indicted for contempt of Congress (1957), but the conviction was overturned on appeal in 1958. From 1965 to 1969, Miller was international president of PEN (the organization of Poets, Essayists, and Novelists) and used this position to advocate freedom of expression for writers in totalitarian states of the left or the right. His 1969 travel journal *In Russia*, and his public attacks on the oppression of dissident writers, led to the banning of his works by the Soviet regime. *The Theater Essays of Arthur Miller* (1978) include his influential 'Tragedy and the Common Man', first published in 1949. Miller argued that 'tragic stature' is achieved for modern audiences not in the *Greek sense of a 'person of high estate' whose fall affects the whole community, but rather through the commonality of the *hero, a shared status that allows the audience to identify with the protagonist. MAF

Miller, Jonathan (1934–) English director. Trained as a doctor, Miller became known as a comedian through *Beyond the Fringe* (with Alan *Bennett, Peter Cook, and Dudley Moore, 1961) but quickly moved to directing with *Osborne's *Under Plain Cover* (*Royal Court, 1962). Since then, in classic drama and in *opera, though very rarely with new work, Miller has been sensitive to the psychology of *character (Lear's ageing or Ophelia as a latent schizophrenic) and the social implications of the text. Often willing to direct the same play (he has done four productions of *King Lear*), his research interests and immense intellect have enabled him to theorize the practice of revivals, writing brilliantly about it in *Subsequent Performances* (1986). Miller's use of

alternative period settings, for instance setting *The Merchant of Venice* in the late nineteenth century for the *National Theatre (1970), *Rigoletto* in the New York mafia of the 1930s (English National Opera, 1984), or *The Mikado* in a Victorian hotel (ENO, 1986), is always the consequence of careful examination of the text's original social context. In *The Taming of the Shrew* (*Royal Shakespeare Company, 1987), he made the play a detailed study of the emerging belief in companionate marriage. But intellectual justification never becomes arid in Miller's work: his productions have a freshness and energy which many directors envy. PDH

Mills, John (1908–2005) English actor who began his career in *musical theatre but made his name playing plucky Brits in a succession of war films that included *In Which We Serve* (1942), *This Happy Breed* (1944), and *Ice Cold in Alex* (1958). He made his London debut in 1927 in the *chorus of *The Five O'Clock Review*, thereafter joining the repertory company the Quaints and *touring the Far East. In 1931 he appeared in *Coward's *Cavalcade*, and in 1938 joined *Guthrie's *Old Vic company. He made his Broadway debut in 1961 in *Rattigan's *Ross* and again appeared in a Rattigan play, *Separate Tables*, in London in 1977. Later stage roles include *Goodbye Mr Chips* (1982), *Little Lies* (1983), and *Pygmalion* (1987). His most successful film roles were Barrow in *Tunes of Glory* (1960) and Michael in *Ryan's Daughter* (1970). AS

mime Contemporary dictionaries define the verb 'to mime' as 'to play a part with gestures and actions, but usually without words'. A more inclusive definition comes from *Decroux: mime is not mute theatre, but actor centred theatre. In 1931 he proposed that theatre become silent for 30 years, but this was to allow the presence of the *actor to displace literature from its central position. Decroux's assertion set the stage for a host of diverse and sometimes contradictory contemporary performance activities. Decroux suggested that the play be *rehearsed before it is written, that is, the actors should determine the spoken text and physical text simultaneously, not begin with pre-existing script to interpret; decades later companies as different as Theatre de *Complicité and the Odin Teatret did just that.

Decroux's definition helps us to understand history better. Records of Greek mime and Roman pantomime (the terms are often used interchangeably) mention that the actors spoke, or were accompanied by narrators or *chorus, but differed from other actors in that they did not use a text established by a playwright. In *commedia dell'arte* (*c.*1550–*c.*1750) actors also *improvised and developed their own *scenarios. As they relied heavily on gesture, *acrobatics, *masks, and facial expression, *commedia* performers could *tour in many countries while speaking only Italian. In Paris they were prohibited from speaking on stage by Louis XIV in 1697, as they were competing with the two official French theatres (*see* Comédie Italienne). In order to survive they performed silent mime for the duration of the proscription, and their performances gave rise to the best-known pantomime performer of the nineteenth century, *Deburau, who also played mute because of restrictions on the fairground theatres where he performed. In the late 1940s *Marceau perfected his mute *character Bip, inspired by *Barrault's portrayal of Deburau in the film *Les Enfants du paradis* (1945); Marceau also admired the work of silent stars Charlie Chaplin and Buster Keaton. In these examples muteness was more an accident of history (or technology) than a prerequisite of mime.

Much *performance art and a host of activity generically entitled *physical theatre, despite dissimilarities, find certain common ground: none is mute, all are actor centred. Mime, instead of a light diversion for a child's birthday party or a simplistic street corner amusement, has become central to the work of contemporary performance, a powerful alternative to logocentric theatre.

At international mime festivals the work may include *puppetry, object animation, masks, acrobatics, *commedia*, *butoh, and myriad other forms and combinations. For the most part performers use text and voice, in addition to very strong physical and gestural components; mime differs from mainstream theatre in that those who create it also perform it. What is rarely seen at the festivals is the mute, whitefaced, illusionist pantomime which tells stories through gesture, which seems to have reached its logical conclusion with Marceau. Students of the three great mime teachers of the twentieth century—Decroux, Marceau, and *Lecoq—are to be found in many parts of the world. While a few of Marceau's students carry on his tradition, for the most part mime has come to mean a postmodern blend of varied elements that does not begin with written text, nor exclude it.   TL

mimesis The term mimesis first assumes a central function in the writings of Plato. The basis of reality, according to Plato, is the realm of pure 'Ideas', dimly reflected in the material world and in turn copied by art. This copying, imitation, or mimesis, is viewed negatively, especially in Pla-

to's *Republic*, since it creates a product twice removed from the reality sought by philosophy. *Aristotle, who viewed reality as a process in which the partially realized forms of the physical world were moving toward more complete realizations, saw mimesis in a much more positive light. His *Poetics* suggests that the poet's concern should not be imitating things 'as they are' but 'as they ought to be'. Through the influence of Aristotle, mimesis became a central, if often disputed, critical term in Western dramatic and literary theory. During the medieval period, the Latin term *imitatio* became associated with the imitation not of reality, but of existing and admired models, an emphasis that continued through the *early modern period, when classic authors were widely assumed to provide the ideal models for modern authors to imitate.

During the Enlightenment the term 'mimesis' generally gave way to 'imitation', and the focus shifted with the rise of modern *bourgeois society away from imitation of abstract reality or earlier models to models of social action and self-understanding. The late eighteenth-century drama offered social and psychological mimetic models, and gradually the idea of society itself as mimetic role playing, suggested by such theorists as *Rousseau and *Diderot, became part of social consciousness.

Mimesis regained popularity as a critical term in the twentieth century, though its historical association with *realism and models of social action led many critics, notably Eric Auerbach in *Mimesis* (1946), to apply it to discussions of the novel rather than of drama. Among theatre theorists, those same associations led socially engaged writers like *Brecht and *Boal to distrust mimesis, seeing it as a device for encouraging acceptance of and conformity with the existing social order, while some feminist critics asked if there could be a feminist use of the term.   MC

Minetti, Bernhard (1905–98) German actor. With a career spanning over 70 years, Minetti was a living legend. The stations of his life, from training under *Jessner in the 1920s, to major roles at the Berlin state theatre under *Gründgens and *Fehling in the 1930s and 1940s, to various theatres in the post-war period (Hamburg, Frankfurt, Düsseldorf), to a return to Berlin in 1965, provided Minetti with experience of most major aesthetic developments from *expressionism to postmodernism. He was equally at home in classical and contemporary roles and was particularly drawn to the plays of *Beckett and *Bernhard. The latter even wrote a play for him, called *Minetti* (1976).   CBB

Minks, Wilfried (1930–   ) German designer and director. In Ulm (1959–62) and then in Bremen (1962–9) Minks began a fruitful cooperation with Kurt Hübner and *Zadek. At Bremen, then one of the most innovative theatres in Germany, Minks's designs incorporated elements of *environmental staging as well as a new pictoralism, with citations from pop art and the media. His visual contributions were a crucial element of German director's theatre, particularly associated with Zadek (*Spring's Awakening* and *The Robbers*, both 1966), *Palitzsch (*Wars of the Roses*, 1967), and *Grüber (*The Tempest*, 1969). It was only logical that after 1971 Minks combined both functions. Productions he directed and designed, such as *Mary Stuart* (1972) and *The Maid of Orleans* (1973), were hailed as inaugurating a visual turn in German theatre, and since then Minks has seldom worked for other directors. His work has decisively influenced younger designers such as Karl-Ernst *Herrmann.   CBB

minstrel show Minstrelsy was the most popular form of American entertainment from the middle to the end of the nineteenth century. Minstrel performers, mostly white males, many of them of Irish and Jewish descent, applied burnt cork as make-up to change their racial appearance and sang, danced, played musical instruments, and told jokes as caricatures of the inept and inarticulate slave or free black. Also known as blackface, and performed on both national and international stages, minstrelsy developed the template for how the racial other was portrayed as a juvenile halfwit not to be taken seriously. More often than not, minstrelsy was racially demeaning, but it also provided the point of entry into mainstream entertainment for *African-American performers.

The genre evolved through three phases: early, solo, and group. Early minstrel performance originated in the eighteenth century, when blackface characters were included in *legitimate dramas such as *Othello* and *The Padlock*. The solo minstrel performer emerged at the beginning of the nineteenth century. While the form occasionally attracted major actors like Charles *Mathews and *Forrest, it was most associated with Thomas Dartmouth *Rice. In the 1830s he introduced a between-acts skit in which he mimicked the song and *dance of a disadvantaged black labourer. *Audiences went wild for his 'crippled step' routine, delighted by his depiction of black diminishment, and the name of Rice's borrowed song, 'Jim Crow', became an institution. Jim Dandy and Jim Crow, the urban image and the agricultural, became the bookends of black limitation in Ameri-

ca. Subsequently these two were transmuted into 'endmen', the comic duo essential to the semicircle formed by minstrel performers onstage.

In its group phase, minstrelsy was headquartered in New York, where minstrel houses eventually lined both sides of lower Broadway. The Christy Minstrels dominated, featuring the songs of Stephen Foster, *female impersonation, introducing the whitefaced mediator Mr Interlocutor to communicate with the endmen, and establishing the three-act minstrel form. The first act included songs and banter with the endmen, beginning with a cakewalk and the command, 'Gentlemen Be Seated'. The second act, called the olio, consisted of a *variety show and often concluded with a stump speech. The third act was a short drama set on the plantation or a *burlesque of a serious play, perhaps Shakespeare or a popular *melodrama.

Minstrelsy's immense popularity was due in part to its unifying function, bringing whites of different ethnic, socio-economic, and historical backgrounds together in differentiation from racial outsiders. After the Civil War, African-American performers began to enter the ranks of minstrelsy, gaining an arena to develop their own abilities and attain celebrity, although they were usually forced to wear the blackface mask, and so minstrelsy gradually became a repository and workshop for black humour and songs. W. C. Handy, Bert *Williams, Ma Rainey, and Jelly Roll Morton are among the many African-American performers who received early training on the minstrel stage.

Though live minstrel shows were in serious decline at the beginning of the twentieth century, their appeal continued in the recorded media, *variety shows, and early *musicals, including *Minstrel Misses* (1903), *A Snapshot of Dixie* (1904), and *Lulu Belle* (1926). In film, Al *Jolson blacked up in the first talkie, *The Jazz Singer* (1927), and so did Bing Crosby in *Dixie* (1943). While live minstrel productions continued at Radio City Music Hall in New York in the 1930s and 1940s, it was in radio (Jack Benny, Fred Allen, Tallulah Bankhead) and television (Ed Sullivan, Milton Berle, Dean Martin, and Jerry Lewis) that the tradition continued most forcefully. In Britain, the Black and White Minstrels enjoyed a two-decade tenure on television until 1978, when minstrelsy was finally perceived as unacceptable. Yet amateur productions flourished in American social, church, and school clubs, and in fraternal organizations as well, for much of the century. And at its end, the black film director Spike Lee signalled a renewed, revisionist interest in minstrelsy in *Bamboozled* (2000).   BBL

Mira de Amescua, Antonio (*c.*1574–1644) Spanish dramatist, active and highly regarded from *c.*1600 to 1632. An exuberant but somewhat erratic disciple of Lope de *Vega, he nevertheless foreshadowed *Calderón. His plays, though they include accomplished *comedies, are predominantly serious, on religious, biblical, and historical subjects. Several chart the rise and fall of favourites, like *The Wheel of Fortune*, but the most famous and influential was his complex *melodrama *The Devil's Slave*, in which a hermit turns bandit and sells his soul, but is ultimately redeemed. VFD

Mirii, Ngugi wa (1951–2008) Kenyan director, actor, playwright, and teacher. Trained as a social welfare officer, wa Mirii was a facilitator for the Kamariithu Community Cultural and Educational Centre (KCCEC) in his home village near Limuru. At the KCCEC's invitation wa Mirii and his cousin Ngugi wa *Thiong'o wrote a controversial play, *Ngaahika Ndeenda* (*I Will Marry When I Want*). The community built a theatre for the 1977 performances. After the play's banning and the detention of Thiong'o (*see* CENSORSHIP), wa Mirii tried to build Kamariithu into an egalitarian cultural centre. In 1981 the government ordered the destruction of the theatre and began a purge of intellectuals, whereupon wa Mirii, like several other Kenyan theatre activists, fled to Zimbabwe. He joined Foundation for Education with Production in 1983, and as director of the Zimbabwe Association of Community Theatres from 1986 was active in promoting Zimbabwean community theatre and running numerous training workshops and theatre for *development projects. DaK

Mirren, Helen (Ilyena Lydia Mironoff) (1946–) English actress. Performances with the National Youth Theatre while in her teens led to Cleopatra at the *Old Vic in 1965. From 1967 to 1970 she had leading roles with the *Royal Shakespeare Company, including Cressida and *Strindberg's Miss Julie. In 1972 she joined *Brook's International Centre for Theatre Research and *toured *The Conference of Birds* throughout North Africa. Back in England, she made a remarkable impression as the rock singer in *Hare's *Teeth and Smiles* (1975) as well as in frequent Shakespearian parts in the 1980s. In 1995 she received a Tony award for *Turgenev's *A Month in the Country*, and was noted for her Lady Torrance in *Williams's *Orpheus Descending* (2000). She has appeared in numerous films, including *Cal* (1984), Peter Greenaway's *The Cook, the Thief, His Wife and Her Lover* (1989), Queen Charlotte in *The Madness of King George* (1994), and Elizabeth II in *The Queen* (Academy award, 2006). On TV she played another queen in *Elizabeth I* (2005) and famously created the role of Detective Chief Inspector Tennison in the occasional series *Prime Suspect* (1991–2006). TK

mise-en-scène French for 'the placing [or setting] of the scene'. Strictly speaking, the term refers to painted scenery, scenic effects, stage pieces, and properties. But it has a more expansive meaning, signifying not only the stage setting but also *lighting, *costuming, and all other related aspects of the spatial and temporal order of a theatrical performance. In this more comprehensive meaning, mise-en-scène refers to what happens in the spatio-temporal continuum, including the actions and movements of all the performers (*actors, singers, or *dancers). In the modern period, the role of the *director is to organize these elements into a unified artwork. In this sense mise-en-scène and *Wagner's concept of the *Gesamtkunstwerk*, or total artwork, are related, both evoking all the features and principles of a theatrical presentation, from language, speaking, and *music, to gesture, movement, and design (*see* TOTAL THEATRE). Likewise, in film theory mise-en-scène refers to all the elements before the camera: settings, costumes, behaviour of actors, make-up, lighting, and properties. *See also* SCENOGRAPHY. TP

Mishima Yukio (1925–70) Japanese novelist and playwright. Mishima's fiction, flamboyant life, and spectacular suicide have obscured his stature as a dramatist. A brilliant and widely read author, his works demonstrate a penetrating intelligence, a love of paradox, and a taste for the aristocratic, the artificial, the exotic, and the decadent. *The Burning House* (1949) was followed by 40 plays in a wide variety of styles. His *Modern Noh Plays* (1950–6) were written for the *naturalistic *shingeki* stage. In contrast, his *kabuki plays, including one of his last works, *The Crescent Moon* (1969), were written in the classical language and baroque style of that theatre. Mishima's preoccupation with the tension between aesthetic contemplation and political action is reflected in dramas like *Rokumeikan* (1957) and *My Friend Hitler* (1968). In the same vein is his most famous play, *Madame de Sade* (1965); *Bergman's celebrated production for the *Dramaten in Stockholm (1989) subsequently toured Tokyo, London, and New York. Mishima also directed and acted in a number of stage and screen productions. CP

Mistinguett (Jeanne-Marie Bourgeois) (1873–1956) French actress, *dancer, and singer. Legendary queen of the Parisian *music hall, she was renowned more for her beautiful legs than for her talent as a singer. She began her career at the Casino de Paris under the name 'Miss Tinguett', then made her debut in comic roles at the Trianon-Concert in 1885, followed by a ten-year engagement at the Eldorado (1897–1907). In 1909 she danced with Max Dearly at the *Moulin-Rouge, which propelled her to stardom. In 1912 she appeared in 'la valse renversante' at the *Folies-Bergère with Maurice *Chevalier, who was to become her partner and lover for several years. From 1919 to 1923 she enjoyed great success in *tours of both Americas in such *revues as *Paris qui danse* and *Paris qui jazz*. She also appeared in several films, including *Les Misérables* in 1913 and *Rigolboche* in 1936. Mistinguett retired from the stage in 1951. CHB

Mitchell, Adrian (1932–2008) English playwright, translator, lyricist, and performance poet. Mitchell became an icon of the 1960s when he performed 'Tell Me Lies about Vietnam' at the 1965 Albert Hall Poetry Olympics. His plays, like the anti-racist *Man Friday* (1977), often reflect his committed left-wing views, or celebrate counter-cultural heroes such as Eric Satie (*Satie Day/Night*, 1986) and William Blake (*Tyger*, 1971, revised as *Tyger Two*, 1994). Mitchell's first theatre work was writing the lyrics for *Brook's production of *Weiss's *Marat/Sade* (1964). As a translator, he was instrumental in introducing English-speaking *audiences to the Spanish Golden Age with versions of *Calderón (*The Mayor of Zalamea*, 1981; *Life Is a Dream*, with *Barton, 1983) and Lope de *Vega (*Fuente Ovejuna*, 1989). An immensely prolific author, Mitchell also wrote many plays for *youth, adapting children's classics such as *The Pied Piper* (1986), *The Lion, the Witch and the Wardrobe* (1999), and *Alice in Wonderland* (2001). CDC

Mitchell, Julian (1935–) English writer. Already known as a novelist, Mitchell began his playwriting career adapting novels for performance, starting with several Ivy Compton-Burnett works, including *Heritage and History* (1965), *A Family and a Fortune* (1966), and *Half-Life* (1977). For television he adapted Austen's *Persuasion* (1971), Paul Scott's *Staying On* (1980), and Ford's *The Good Soldier* (1981). Of his original plays, his biggest success came with *Another Country* (1981; film 1984), concerning the sexual and political tensions in an English public school in the 1930s, with a thinly disguised Guy Burgess as the main *character. Mitchell's other stage plays include *The Enemy Within* (1980), *Francis* (1983), and *After Aida* (1986). In 1998 he wrote the screenplay for *Wilde*. MDG

Mitchell, Katie (1964–) English director. Productions for her company, Classics on a Shoestring, at the Gate Theatre, London, in the early 1990s—*Women of Troy*, *The House of Bernarda Alba*, and *Vassa Zheleznova*—bore the hallmarks of intimate, *acting-led ensemble work. *The Dybbuk* (1992), *Henry VI* (1994), and *The Phoenician Women* (1995) were influenced by Eastern European culture and reflected the atrocities of Bosnia. *Sowerby's *Rutherford and Son* (1994) and *Toller's *The Machine Wreckers* (1995) at the *National Theatre were painstakingly researched. From 1997 to 1999 Mitchell was *artistic director of the *Royal Shakespeare Company's Other Place, Stratford, where she directed *The Mysteries* and *Beckett pieces with a team of women designers. In the late 1990s she also began to work with living writers, directing Martin *Crimp's *Attempts on her Life* and his translation of *Genet's *The Maids*. Since 2001 she has been associate director at the NT where she has directed an acclaimed version of Euripides's *Iphigenia at Aulis* (2004) and *multimedia work (Virginia Woolf's *The Waves*, 2006). *The Director's Craft* was published in 2008. KN

Mitra, Dinabandhu (1830–73) Bengali dramatist. An employee of the colonial administration in India, he wrote his first play *Nil Darpan* (*Indigo Mirror*, published 1860) under a pseudonym, because it dealt with British indigo planters' oppression of Indian peasants. Its translation into English by Michael Madhusadan Dutt (1861) resulted in imprisonment and a fine for the Calcutta publisher. The original, a watershed work, inspired innumerable scripts suffixed *darpan* (mirror), but its provocative content prevented a complete staging until 1872, when the National Theatre's historic production inaugurated professional Bengali theatre. The script's *realism made it politically potent even after the British Raj, and many left-wing troupes exploited its anti-feudalism. Mitra's best *farce, *Sadhabar Ekadasi* (*The Wife's Ritual Fast*, 1868), gave the celebrated *actor-manager Girish *Ghosh one of his biggest hits. Its *satire of dissipated Anglophile Bengalis ensured revivals into the late twentieth century. AL

Mitra, Sombhu (1915–97) Bengali actor and director. Mitra joined the leftist Indian People's Theatre Association and co-directed the harbinger of the new drama movement, *Nabanna* (*New Harvest*, 1944) by *Bhattacharya. In 1945 he married Tripti Mitra, who also acted in IPTA productions, and both left to form their own group, Bohurupee, in 1948. He directed several *Tagore classics, beginning with an adaptation of the novel *Four Chapters* (1951), and continuing with the plays *Red Oleander* (1954), *Muktadhara* (1959), *Sacrifice* (1961), and *Raja* (1964). Mitra also directed *Ibsen (*An Enemy of the People*, 1952; *A Doll's House*, 1958), *Sophocles (*Oedipus the King*, 1964), *Sircar's *Remaining History* (1967) and *Pagla Ghora* (*Mad Horse*, 1971), and *Tendulkar (*Silence! The Court Is in Session*, 1971). He had tremendous presence as an actor, and played the *hero in most Bohurupee productions, exploiting his peculiar musical-recitative delivery and a finely tuned body. He worked under other directors as well, as Thakurda in Tagore's *The Post Office* (1957), Chanakya in Visakhadatta's *The Signet Ring of Rakshasa* (1970), and the king in *Karnad's *Tughlaq* (1972).   AL

Mlama, Penina (Penina Muhando) (1948–) Tanzanian director and playwright. Like Ebrahim *Hussein, Mlama writes her plays in Swahili about the project of *Ujamaa* (an African form of socialism or communalism) and liberation. *Recognize our Rights* (1973), *Liberation Struggles* (1982), and *An Antidote to Rot* (1984) reveal a shift from enthusiasm for *Ujamaa* socialism to its critical appreciation. Her study *Culture and Development: the popular theatre approach* (1991) summarized the experiences of the theatre for *development movement that flourished in Tanzania from the 1980s. She advocated the change from *vichekesho* (*farce) to *ngonjera*, a performance style combining traditional *dance, song, and *mime with modern political issues.   EB

Mnouchkine, Ariane (1939–) French director, one of the most celebrated in contemporary theatre. With a group of friends from the Sorbonne she formed the Théâtre du *Soleil in Paris in 1964 along the lines of a workers' cooperative. After brief encounters with psychological *realism and *commedia dell'arte*, training at the école Jacques *Lecoq proved the key influence. An opening *mime in her production of *Wesker's *The Kitchen* (1967) demonstrated her leftist desire for a people's theatre, while in subsequent productions she deliberately exposed the process of *acting and the machinery of theatre to make a political point about the conditions of labour. After the upheaval of May 1968 she abandoned play texts and developed a series of five *devised 'créations *collectives' in which she saw herself as a leader of *rehearsals. The most famous of these was *1789; or, The Revolution Must Stop at the Perfection of Happiness* (1970), a promenade, multi-focused spectacle of popular theatre forms applied to French history. Her interest in the theatre of Asia, however, was to have the most

enduring effect. From 1981 to 2005 she developed a highly declamatory style of *acting ('*jouer frontal*'), *mask work, and Asian-inspired *dance and movement. An oriental *interculturalism defined her practice with two major groups of classics (a Shakespeare sequence, 1981–4, and the *Greek *tragedies *Les Atrides*, 1990–3), and contemporary Asian-themed plays by *Cixous. Thereafter she returned to collective creation to tell the stories of individuals caught up in a maelstrom of transnational migration (*The Last Halting Site*, 2005) and the traces of marginalized lives in post-war France (*Ephemera*, 2007). Since 1971 she has worked at the Cartoucherie in Vincennes outside of Paris, inventing an environment for each production, creating work of great *physical and visual beauty which critiques colonialism and imperialism in all its manifestations as well as championing a politics of *gender.   BRS

Modena, Gustavo (1803–61) Italian *actor-manager and political activist. Modena's greatest roles were in *Saul* by *Alfieri and *Louis XI* by Delavigne. From 1843 to 1846 he headed an extremely influential company; his teaching directly influenced *Salvini and *Rossi, and led to important reforms in the Italian theatre. He demanded that the recitation of *tragic verse be based not on declamatory techniques that approached those of *operatic singing but on solid *character analysis and psychological truth. He taught that the art of *acting demanded political commitment, that theatre should have an educational and civic purpose, that it should open people's eyes, rid them of their prejudices and superstitions, and make them think. The company relied on recent French dramas—*Hugo, *Scribe, *Dumas *père*—for its repertory but introduced the new Italian historical drama that featured *melodramatic spectacle. His own political commitment to the Risorgimento, Mazzini, and the 'Young Italy' movement led him into confrontation with the Austrian rulers of the northern Italian states and to many years of exile.   JEH

Modjeska, Helena (1840–1909) Polish actress. Born Helena Opid, Modjeska was a successful actress in Poland from 1861 until 1876, when she and her politically radical second husband Karol Bozenta Chlapowski emigrated to America with friends to establish a cooperative Polish colony in California. Modjeska first performed in the USA in 1877 as Adrienne Lecouvreur in San Francisco and in New York later that year. She played in Poland in 1878, then returned to America. During subsequent successful *tours of England, Poland, and the USA she played Nora in adaptations of *Ibsen's *A Doll's House*, *Schiller's Maria Stuart, and hundreds of other roles. LQM

Moeller, Philip (1880–1958) American director. A founding member of New York's *Washington Square Players (1914–18), Moeller continued as frequent director with the reconstituted *Theatre Guild throughout the 1920s and early 1930s, directing 70 plays between 1915 and 1935. Admired for his stage composition, Moeller excelled in a wide variety of styles. Most notable were his concepts for *O'Neill—including first productions of *Strange Interlude* (1928), *Mourning Becomes Electra* (1931), and *Ah, Wilderness!* (1933)—as well as the first American productions of *Shaw's *St Joan* (1923) and *Major Barbara* (1928). MAF

Moisewitsch, Tanya (1914–2003) English designer who began her career working regularly for Hugh *Hunt's productions, particularly at the *Abbey Theatre, Dublin, after 1935. For many years from 1953 she was associated with the *Stratford Festival, Ontario, designing the thrust stage to *Guthrie's specifications, where the prime concern was to foster intimacy between actor and spectator. The stage comprised a series of wide, rising platforms backed by a raised balcony, where design was calculated to support the actor. This is the hallmark of the many productions on which Moisewitsch worked (they number in excess of 60, not including an early period (1941–4) working in repertory at Oxford Playhouse). A characteristic venture was the permanent setting for Shakespeare's history cycle at the *Shakespeare Memorial Theatre in 1951, where a *constructivist-style structure of wooden platforms and bridges could quickly be transformed by swags or arrangements of heraldic emblems, to avoid disrupting the rhythmic impetus of the action, creating evocative but unassuming environments. Moisewitsch designed *opera at *Covent Garden and the Metropolitan, for *Strehler's Piccolo Teatro, the *Guthrie Theatre, and the *National Theatre, London, during *Olivier's directorship. RAC

Moissi, Alexander (1880–1935) Austrian actor. The son of an Albanian merchant and an Italian mother, Moissi came to Vienna in 1897 to train as an *opera singer. While working as an extra at the *Burgtheater he was discovered by Josef *Kainz, and his first success was at the German theatre in Prague. In 1903 he joined *Reinhardt in Berlin where he became one of the most important actors in the ensemble. His notable roles before the war include Osvald in *Ibsen's *Ghosts* (1906), the title part in *Sophocles' *Oedipus* (1909), and, most famously, Fedja in Lev

*Tolstoy's *The Living Corpse* (1913). During the war Moissi was interned in Switzerland, though he was able to perform in that country until his release in 1917. After the war his fame waned. He performed principally in *touring productions and occasionally for Reinhardt in Vienna and at the *Salzburg Festival—he played the original Everyman in *Hofmannsthal's *Jedermann* (1922). Moissi's voice, with its strongly melodic, almost operatic range, was legendary. He specialized in troubled *characters whom he played with great introspection. CBB

Molander, Olof (1892–1966) Swedish director. Molander began his career as an actor at *Dramaten in Stockholm (1914–19), but thereafter concentrated on *directing and was responsible for some 120 productions at Dramaten until his retirement in 1963. From 1934 to 1938 he was artistic director of the theatre, directing epoch-making productions of *Strindberg's plays which gave *audiences a uniquely Swedish view of Strindberg's most complex work, including *A Dream Play* (1935) and *To Damascus* (1937). Previously, a Germanic, angst-ridden, and *expressionist view of Strindberg had prevailed in Swedish theatre, the legacy of *Reinhardt who had directed at Dramaten in the 1910s and 1920s. But Molander's *Dream Play* stressed the sense of compassion and humanity running through the text. He also made use of projected images from Strindberg's Stockholm to conjure up a dreamlike reality. In his later career Molander returned repeatedly to *Dream Play*, mounting productions in Denmark and Norway. DT

Molière (Jean-Baptiste Poquelin) (1622–73) French actor, playwright, and *manager. Molière changed the face of French theatre and raised *comedy to a status almost equal to that of *tragedy, and he did this in a career in Paris that lasted only fourteen years. He was born into the solid bourgeoisie in the heart of Paris; his father, an interior decorator like both grandfathers, had prospered greatly and secured an appointment at court. At the age of 21 he joined a young company, headed by Madeleine *Béjart and her siblings, that rashly attempted to compete with the *Hôtel de Bourgogne and the Théâtre du *Marais. Bankruptcy followed, and Molière and the Béjarts disappeared into the provinces. Thirteen years later, in 1658, the company, now headed by Molière, returned to Paris. The king's brother secured them an audition before the court; a tragedy by *Corneille was tepidly received, but Molière's *farce afterpiece, now lost, was so successful that Louis XIV allowed the company to share the *Petit-Bourbon theatre with the *commedia dell'arte troupe of Scaramouche.

At this point Molière had written two competent comedies in five acts and verse, the obligatory format for 'regular' literary drama (see NEOCLASSICISM), and several one-act farces, of which two survive. The troupe supplemented this material with old plays by other authors and with the personal repertory of *Jodelet, who soon joined from the Marais; it subsisted thus for over a year until Molière produced his first new play in Paris, the one-act afterpiece Les Précieuses ridicules (The Affected Damsels, 1659). This *satire on contemporary affectations was so unlike standard theatrical fare that it quadrupled receipts and made Molière a controversial celebrity; another successful new farce, Sganarelle; or, The Imaginary Cuckold (1660), solidified his position.

The demolition of the Petit-Bourbon forced the troupe to move to the derelict *Palais Royal, which, after repairs, opened in January 1661. Two weeks later Molière offered a project intended to establish him as an actor of serious roles: his 'heroic' play Dom Garcie de Navarre; or, The Jealous Prince. The failure was humiliating and complete, but it was followed in the same year by two great successes: The School for Husbands and Les Fâcheux (The Bores), the first of the *comédies-ballets. This hybrid venture, commissioned by Foucquet to entertain the king, alternated a series of caricatures of courtly eccentrics, of whom Molière played four, with *dances by Beauchamps in an outdoor setting by *Torelli, his last project in France. Like most of the comédies-ballets that followed, The Bores was later adapted for public performance at the Palais Royal.

Within three years of his arrival, Molière had learned that in tragic roles his vocal delivery was too choppy, his bearing too ungainly, his approach too conversational to gain favour with *audiences. In comedy he was a revelation: he was admired for the expressiveness of his face (reputedly learned from Scaramouche), the sharp observation of contemporary social behaviour, and what was described rather helplessly as the naturalness of his acting. Still, for an actor and an author, comedy was inferior in prestige to tragedy, and the afterpiece was a minor form. His next work, sixteen months later, was a 'regular' five-act verse play standing alone on the bill: The School for Wives (1662). It was a novel treatment of a traditional plot and a tour de force for himself, Mlle de *Brie, and *La Grange, the troupe's three best actors. Some moralists found the play indecent and impious; its popularity enraged the rival Hôtel de Bourgogne; and a flurry of pamphlets and polemical afterpieces ensued that lasted two years and raised attendance at both houses. Armande *Béjart, the 19-year-old sister (or daughter) of Madeleine, had married Molière earlier in the year; now she made her first appearances in the two plays that Molière contributed to the controversy, The Critique of the School for Wives and The Versailles Impromptu. *Montfleury, satirized in these plays, so far forgot himself as to accuse Molière of having married his own daughter; the king, to whom this complaint was addressed, responded by standing godfather to the couple's first child and by commissioning and dancing in Molière's second comédie-ballet, The Forced Marriage.

Molière was no longer a mere entertainer but a literary author to be taken seriously, a favourite of the king, and a man with enemies, who began working to suppress Tartuffe even before it was performed. The preliminary three-act version that was presented as part of a festival at Versailles was banned within days, after pressure from the Archbishop of Paris and perhaps also the queen mother. The ban was not lifted until 1669, after five years of revisions and appeals. Meanwhile, after producing the first play of *Racine, the troupe presented a spectacle-play on a popular subject, Don Juan (1665), in which La Grange played the charming, amoral aristocrat. Denunciations from the pulpit were thunderous, focusing on the performance of Molière in the role of the nattering, moralistic valet. Attendance was excellent, but for reasons we can only guess at, the play abruptly and permanently vanished from the repertory. The king's favour continued, however; in August 1665 he gave the company the title of the Comédiens du Roi and an annual subsidy, and in September commissioned another comédie-ballet. In June 1666, after a lengthy illness which forced the theatre to close, Molière presented the third of his great plays on hypocrisy, The Misanthrope, with himself as Alceste and his wife as Célimène; the play drew puzzled admiration and reasonably good receipts. The Misanthrope was a watershed in Molière's career: after it he wrote only one more 'regular' play, The Learned Ladies (1672), and prose, fantasy, and visual spectacle dominated the second half of his career as verse and *realism had the first. Most of Molière's later plays defy traditional classification: even The Doctor in Spite of Himself, the next play after The Misanthrope, is a play-within-a-play, a commedia plot framed by a native French farce, while The Tricks of Scapin (1671), ostensibly a throwback to commedia, seems to ironize that genre's conventions. Amphitryon (1668), his most poetic play, was written in free verse rather than traditional alexandrines; furthermore, it was a 'machine-play' like *Psyché* (1671), a 'tragedy-ballet' with settings by Carlo *Vigarani and text by Molière, *Quinault, and Corneille that was transferred at vast expense from the Tuileries to the Palais Royal, where it became the troupe's most reliable producer of income. Many of the *comédies-ballets* lose their meaning outside the matrix of court production: *George Dandin* (1668), shorn of its *pastoral interludes, is like an antimasque without the *masque. Two of Molière's most enduringly popular works, *The Would-Be Gentleman* (1670) and *The Hypochondriac* (1673), combine the characteristics of the *comédie-ballet* and character comedy; and each *denouement, instead of restoring the deluded central *character to reality, carries him off in a final *ballet sequence into the realms of permanent fantasy.

During that ballet in the fourth performance of *The Hypochondriac*, Molière was fatally stricken, finished the show, and died at home a few hours later. Implacable to the end, the church first refused burial, then permitted maimèd rites. At the end of the season, four actors defected to the Hôtel de Bourgogne and *Lully, composer for many of the *comédies-ballets*, seized the Palais Royal. The remaining members moved to the rue Guénégaud and absorbed the Marais troupe; in 1680 a merger with the Hôtel de Bourgogne created what soon became known as the *Comédie-Française.

Molière's role was always the comic lead, a list that includes heavy fathers, clever or befuddled valets, hapless husbands, rustics, and foolish courtiers. The constant is what contemporaries called the 'naturalness' of his acting style. This term implied a contrast with his predecessors, who had achieved success by creating and satisfying audience expectations of a familiar stage persona with a recurrent name, *costume, and bag of tricks; Molière regularly defied expectation, and he individualized the name and costume of each character he played. In *scenography also, the setting, though it might use stock elements, was specific to the play and frequently situated the characters in their private interior environment, a practice then rare.

The Comédie-Française is called the 'house of Molière' with some reason, but the boast of a continuous performance tradition is misleading. From the moment of its founding the Comédie jettisoned Molière's scenic reforms in favour of stock sets—it used the same decor for *Tartuffe* and *The Miser* as late as 1907—while Molière's own roles were parcelled out among several actors. Thus the personal repertory of Molière became fragmented into various *lines of business which in the following centuries developed their own performance traditions, coloured by the work of later authors.

Molière's modern status in the pantheon of French and world literature reflects a long critical tradition, symbiotic with the practices of the Comédie-Française, that concentrated on the 'serious' masterpieces, that saw him as the exponent of a benign, cautious moral philosophy, and that valued the dramatic over the theatrical and the verbal over the visual. The landmark productions of Molière in the twentieth century took place outside the Comédie: *Antoine's *Tartuffe* at the *Odéon (1907), *Jouvet's *School for Wives* at the Athénée (1936), *Planchon's *Tartuffe* at the *Théâtre National Populaire in Lyon (1962), *Vitez's 'tetralogy' at *Avignon (1978). Since the mid-1980s the Comédie has belatedly begun to embrace untraditional stagings. Some of these were merely repackaging of the standard reading of the plays as tragic autobiography, but some have achieved genuinely fresh interpretations. One of the Comédie's important actors, the Polish-trained Andrzej Seweryn, staged the relatively unfamiliar *Forced Marriage* as a mordant, surreal fable of modern despotism (1999), while Jean-Louis Benoit's production of the beloved *Would-Be Gentleman* (2000), with a stunning design by Alain Chambon, rediscovered a balance between comedy and ballet, farce and fantasy, that honoured the seventeenth century while delighting audiences of the twenty-first.   RWH

Molina, Tirso de See TIRSO DE MOLINA.

Molnár, Ferenc (1878–1952) Hungarian playwright. Molnár's first original play was *The Doctor* (1902) but international fame came with *The Devil* in 1907 and for many years thereafter a new work of his was performed almost annually in Budapest. His *dramaturgy often follows the pattern of nineteenth-century French *comedies and *well-made plays, but his *dialogue and use of dramatic situation are unique. He often directed his own work, and was also successful as a writer for *cabaret. His most famous plays, including *Liliom* (1909), *The Guardsman* (1910), and *The Play's the Thing* (1926), were translated and frequently performed in Vienna, Paris, London, and New York, often provided vehicles for star actors (like the American *Lunts), and continued to be revived in Hungary and abroad. He also wrote *The Boys of Pál Street*, one of the best-known Hungarian juvenile novels, which has been adapted for the stage. His international success helped him to escape Nazism; he lived in the USA from 1939 with his actress wife Lili Darvas. The story of *Rodgers and *Hammerstein's *musical *Carousel* (1945) is borrowed from *Liliom*. HJA

Moncrieff, Gladys (1892–1976) Australian singer known as 'Australia's Queen of song', and 'our Glad.' Moncrieff was contracted to J. C. *Williamson's company in 1911, and made her debut as Josephine in *HMS Pinafore* in 1914. She became a national star with *The Maid of the Mountains* in 1921. From 1926 Moncrieff starred in London *musicals, returning to Australia in 1928 for *The Chocolate Soldier* and a reprise of *The Maid of the Mountains*. Her status as national icon was confirmed by her work as entertainer in the Second World War and Korea. After the wars, she was a popular performer live, on radio, and later on television. KMN

Moncrieff, William Thomas (1794–1857) English playwright and *manager. The author of over 100 *melodramas, *comedies, *burlettas, *farces, and adaptations of novels, the manager of several theatres in London, Moncrieff churned out plays to suit the taste of his mostly working and lower-middle-class *audiences. On the whole, his most popular plays were melodramas, among them *The Shipwreck of the Medusa* (1820), one of the many nineteenth- century plays based on well-known paintings; *The Lear of Private Life* (1820), a version of a novel by Amelia Opie; *The Cataract of the Ganges* (1823), a *Drury Lane play with an exotic setting and a real waterfall on stage; and *The Scamps of London* (1843), a lowlife play from the French. *Tom and Jerry; or, Life in London* (1821), a farcical burletta based on Pierce Egan's sketches *Life in London*, was his greatest comic success. MRB

Monk, Meredith (1942–) American composer, singer, filmmaker, and director/choreographer. She was a trained musician and contributor to the new era of postmodern *dance coming out of New York's Judson Church performance *collective during the mid-1960s. Monk founded her own company, the House, in 1968 and began creating large interdisciplinary, site-specific pieces which layered storytelling, visual imagery, movement, and *music into the creation of a 'new world . . . where the elements are not separated'. Monk's career has been consistently multidisciplinary, routinely crossing genre boundaries as she explores the terrain of differing media. In the 1980s Monk's music-theatre pieces pioneered her 'extended vocal technique', a ritualistic singing style evocative of found sounds but also filled with emotionality and imagery. She formed Meredith Monk & Vocal Ensemble in 1978 and has produced a series of recordings. Her films and videos include *Quarry*, *Ellis Island*, and *Book of Days*. Major stage works include *The Games* (1983), created with Ping *Chong, and *Atlas*, a full-length *opera commissioned by the Houston Grand Opera in 1991. LTC

monologue Most simply, a dramatic utterance that is not *dialogue; a speech of extended length and internal coherence, delivered by a single speaker, that does not include another's response. Monologues of *exposition, reflection, or deliberation can be addressed to the *audience, to another *character, to the speaker herself (an 'interior monologue'), or even to an inanimate object. They can be dramatically motivated or simply a theatrical convention, delivered from outside the *action by a *chorus figure or from inside the action by a character. A 'protatic figure' like a *confidant, whose only function is to facilitate the monologue through brief interjections, is occasionally present. Monologue is sometimes used as a synonym for *soliloquy. RWV

monopoly, theatrical *See* PATENT THEATRES.

Montdory (Guillaume) (1594–1653/4) French *actor-manager. Montdory spent his early years as an itinerant actor before settling in Paris as leader of the company at the *Marais Theatre. Here he acted in Pierre *Corneille's earliest plays, including *L'Illusion comique*, where the role of Clindor, a young man of good family who has left home to become an actor, reflects the circumstances of Montdory's own life; and also playing Rodrigue in Corneille's masterpiece *Le Cid*. His prestigious career was soon cut short when he suffered an apoplectic fit on stage while playing Herod in Tristan's *La Mariane* (evidence, perhaps, of a highly physical acting style). He retired from the stage with a generous pension from *Richelieu. WDH

Montez, Lola (1818–61) Irish dancer and actress. Montez was a beauty who made her stage debut in London as a dancer in 1843 after the failure of her first marriage. She performed in Europe and was for a short time mistress of Franz Liszt and of King Ludwig I of Bavaria (1847–8) before making her debut in New York in *Betley the Tyrolean* (1851). In 1852 she played the title role in a play written to capitalize on her European experiences by C. P. T. Ware, *Lola Montez in Bavaria*. She subsequently went to California, then in the throes of the gold rush, scandalizing San Francisco *audiences with her spider *dance, performed on *tour in Australia in 1855. She also tutored the child actress Lotta

*Crabtree. From 1856 she appeared on the lecture circuit. After a religious conversion in 1859 she became a recluse, dying in poverty on Long Island, New York.   JTD

Montfleury (Zacharie Jacob) (*c.*1600–67) French actor. Montfleury has the misfortune of being remembered chiefly for his worst features: he was lampooned by Cyrano de Bergerac for his spectacular obesity and by *Molière for his roaring delivery and shameless begging for *applause, and in retaliation he disgraced himself by attempting without success to denounce Molière for incest. The fact remains that, between the sudden retirement of *Montdory and the gradual emergence of *Floridor, Montfleury was the leading tragedian of mid century. After making his early reputation in the provinces as a wildly emotional interpreter of the *tragicomedies and *pastorals of the 1630s, he joined the *Hôtel de Bourgogne in 1638, where he was a favourite of *Richelieu, the court, and the public, and where for three decades he was a fixture in roles of kings and emperors. However, his bellowing style seemed increasingly outlandish as playwriting and performance shifted towards greater restraint and *realism. *Racine tailored the role of Oreste in *Andromaque* to his talents, and he died of his exertions in the mad scene.   RWH

Montgomery, Elizabeth *See* MOTLEY.

Montherlant, Henry de (1896–1972) French writer. Already an established essayist and novelist, Montherlant came to the theatre in 1942 with the success of *The Dead Queen* at the *Comédie-Française. This was followed by a series of contemporary and historical dramas: *No Man's Son* (1943), *Those We Take in our Arms* (1950), *Malatesta* (1946), *The Master of Santiago* (1948), and *Port-Royal* (1954). In post-war France Montherlant's works were admired for their subtle poetic style and for their glorification of the soul, capable always of resisting the inherent fallibility of the material world. The last of his plays was *The Town Whose Prince Is a Child*, which depicts the intimate yet ambiguous relationships between boys and priests at a Catholic seminary. Written in 1951, Montherlant did not allow its production until 1967. Afraid that he was losing his sight, he committed suicide.   CHB

Monti, Ricardo (1944–) Argentinian playwright and screenwriter. Although he has written less than many of his contemporaries, he has been called Argentina's most important recent dramatist. In his theatre, classical *tragedy fuses with Christian *Passion plays; history, myth, and dreams converge; and the personal is both political and metaphysical. The mixture has created plays of dynamic, *metatheatrical tension. *An Evening with Mr Magnus and Sons* (1970) was one of the first Argentine plays to meld reflective realism with *avant-garde experimentation. *Tendentious History of the Argentine Middle Class* (1971) was openly political, and during the years of the dictatorship he produced *Visit* (1977), *Marathon* (1980), and *The Beaded Curtain* (1981), plays that poetically eluded the *censor to examine the possibility of revolution under repression and individual complicity within history. Monti's post-dictatorship works (*A South American Passion*, 1989; *Asunción*, 1992; *The Obscurity of Reason*, 1993) cross national borders, locating themselves in a mythic 'America'. *Hotel Columbus* (1998) and *Finland* (1999, condensed from *South American Passion*, continue in the vein of what he calls 'broader realism', also exploring *gender construction.   JGJ

Montigny, Adolphe (*c.*1812–1880) French actor, playwright, and *manager, also known under the name Lemoine-Montigny. He made his debut at the *Comédie-Française in 1829, although he never received much recognition on the national stage. He eventually moved to the *boulevard circuit, where he enjoyed some success in dramatic roles, and wrote several dramas and *vaudevilles, including the collaborative *The Finger of God* (1834), *Amazampo; or, The Discovery of Quinine* (1836), *Zarah* (1837), and *Samuel the Merchant* (1838), and his solo work, *A Son* (1839). In 1841 he was appointed co-director of the Gaîté, then in 1844 he took over the Théâtre du Gymnase, and with his wife, actress-dancer Rose Chéri, brought the Gymnase back into fashion with a repertoire that included works by Balzac, George Sand, *Dumas *fils*, and *Scribe. An extremely capable director, Montigny specialized in contemporary situational dramas and the *well-made play.   CHB

Moody, William Vaughn (1869–1910) American playwright. Born in Indiana and orphaned in his teens, Moody worked his way through Harvard College. While teaching at the University of Chicago (1895–1902) he published acclaimed lyric poetry and wrote verse dramas. His 1906 prose drama *The Great Divide*, in which the untamed west is contrasted with eastern gentility as a metaphor for the battle of the sexes, ranks as a masterpiece of its era. A second prose play, *The Faith Healer* (1909), reached New York in 1910, nine months before its author died of a brain tumour.   FHL

morality play A popular genre of *medieval theatre in Europe. Although there are examples from the tenth century onwards, moral plays do not become frequent until the early fourteenth century, when their marked increase was probably a result of the Christian Church stressing the need for regular confession and penance to ensure God's forgiveness, reinforced by the presence of the Black Death, which threatened to snatch people away at any moment with their sins upon their heads. The so-called Dance of Death, a literary/visual representation of the coming of death to an unheeding and worldly society, is the subject of the well-known *Everyman*. The earliest moral plays used the triumph of saints over temptation and persecution as an example for Christians to imitate. Such plays became a distinctive form of morality, called the miracle play, which could be applied to virtually any saint.

Miracle plays tended to use direct narrative, but the distinguishing mark of most morality plays was the use of allegorical *characters to represent the interplay of various positive and negative forces in human life. Characters representing the soul, sins, and virtues came to be treated as forces acting within the human mind, thus making possible a simple form of psychological analysis. The application of the allegorical method could be very flexible. It could be used to analyse institutions, political situations, people's impulses and objectives, or particular problems like preparing oneself for death. Most moralities, however, are centred around an 'Everyman' figure, who often undergoes a process of spiritual death and resurrection, a pattern with obvious parallels to the *folk plays involving the death and resurrection of St George. A second pattern, the *psychomachia* or battle for the soul, sometimes in combination with that of death and resurrection, involves the central 'Everyman' figure being dragged to and fro between sins, who tempt him towards damnation, and virtues, who try to save his soul. Some of these plays, such as *The Castle of Perseverance* (early fifteenth century), represent the whole life of man as a series of different ages, each governed by a particular vice, while others, such as *Lusty Iuventus* (c.1550), deal with the sins of a specific age like youth. In the case of *Everyman*, adapted from a Flemish original, *Elkerlijc* (late fifteenth century), rather than sins being the central focus, the subject is how best to prepare for death. The central character has to overcome his weaknesses in order to win a place in heaven, but no separate sins are specified.

During the fifteenth century, *Rederijkerskamers* (*Chambers of Rhetoric) in the Netherlands pro-

duced many moral pieces known as *Spelen van Sinne* ('meaningful' or serious plays). These could be varied, some relying on symbolic and allegorical argument, others presenting quite realistic motivations and actions. *Mariken of Nijmegen* has a *heroine who repents after seeing a play where the Virgin Mary appeals to God to save Mankind. Another group called *Abele Spelen* ('seemly' plays), sometimes described as romances because they deal with the world of chivalry, centre upon moral questions of knighthood. In *Lancelot of Denmark*, the discourteous hero loses his love to a more considerate lover and is left in bitter remorse.

Perhaps the most unusual of the serious moral plays are the *autos sacramentales* (sacred plays) of Spain, regularly presented on the feast of *Corpus Christi from the fifteenth century. These employed allegorical figures to illustrate the main dogmas of the Catholic Church, using characters like Faith, Thought, and Grace to clarify the dogma involved and trace a movement towards understanding in the central character's mind. The *autos* were brought to a very high level by *Calderón in the seventeenth century.

Most early moral pieces are rather serious, but many later examples are humorous and bawdy, and often contain a new central character called the Vice, a leader and organizer of sins who incorporates many of them in himself. He is a cynical commentator whose role could only be sustained by an accomplished comedian, and he probably appeared because the pieces were now being played by professional players who depended upon their *audience for their living. The best known of these late professional dramas is *Mankind* (1465). In the Netherlands such humorous moralities were called *Esbatementen* ('revels' or *'farces').

By the sixteenth century moralities were usually called *interludes and seem mainly to have been entertainments to accompany a banquet. The moral plays helped lay the basis for Elizabethan *tragedies and city comedies, the tragedies benefiting from the moral conflict of sins and virtues within the individual and the *comedies from the vivid and constantly varying catalogue of colourful types presented as the lesser actors changed quickly from role to role. Professional moral interludes disappeared when permanent companies like Shakespeare's began to perform in London so they clearly could not compete with the new drama. However, they continued to be written for amateurs to perform in schools and universities until about 1610.   JWH

Moratín, Leandro Fernández de (1760–1828) Spanish poet and playwright. The son of a celebrated writer, he was exiled to Paris following the Spanish War of Independence. Returning in 1820, he helped implement the reforms of Carlos III. A confirmed *neoclassicist, Moratín's strict respect for the *unities of time, place, and *action was coupled with a didactic conception of *comedy as the corrector of ignorant behaviour and outmoded or decadent customs. The marriage of convenience between an old man and an adolescent female was the target of *satire in *The Maidens' Consent* (1806), while in the earlier *The New Play; or, The Café* (1792), Moratín had mounted a swingeing attack on contemporary theatrical tastes.   KG

Moreno, Rita (1931–) American actress, *dancer, and singer, born Rosita Dolores Alverio in Puerto Rico. A Spanish dancer and entertainer by her early teens, Moreno made her Broadway debut in *Skydrift* (1945). At 17 she was signed to an MGM contract, appearing in many films, including *Singin' in the Rain* (1952), though often cast as an ethnic stereotype. Moreno's talent and range were given freer rein following her Oscar-winning performance as Anita in the film version of *West Side Story* (1961). She appeared in the London première in *She Loves Me* (1962), then returned to New York to star in *The Sign in Sidney Brustein's Window* (1964). She later originated the role of Googie Gomez in *The Ritz* (1975), played Olive Madison in Neil *Simon's *gender-reversed version of *The Odd Couple* (1985), and Amanda in *The Glass Menagerie* (Berkeley, 2006). She was featured on *The Electric Company* children's television show in the 1970s, and has since made many other appearances on TV and film.   EW

moresca Energetic and humorous *dance-drama, presumably Moorish in origin, that spread from post-Muslim Spain throughout Europe in the late fifteenth and early sixteenth centuries via companies of travelling performers. The dancers wore exuberant *costumes studded with bells, and after a brief spoken *prologue danced to fife and tabor, around bonfires, in villages, manors, and castles. Despite the complaints of the clergy, the *moresca* has persisted to this day, where it lives on as an ancient festival in parts of the Adriatic, as well as being a possible, if unproven, source of certain forms of *morris dance in England.   KG

Morley, Christopher (1937–) English designer. The structural simplicity of Morley's *scenographic approach came to prominence in 1966 in his brightly lit golden box within a larger box for

*Gaskill's controversial *Royal Court *Macbeth*. The same year his collaboration with Trevor *Nunn on *The Revenger's Tragedy* for the *Royal Shakespeare Company produced a grotesque *comedy played out in black and silver *costumes on a painted silver circle, luridly bathed in light. Appointed head of design for the RSC (1968–74), Morley continued to work with Nunn to create a company style stripped of extraneous detail. In 1969 Morley's great empty white box, illuminated from above with a huge cone of *lighting, provided the permanent frame for the whole season including a brilliant-white design for Nunn's *The Winter's Tale* and an atmospheric cage of latticed wicker for John *Barton's *Twelfth Night*. The new stage, operated on a system of hydraulics, which Morley designed for Nunn's season of the Roman plays in 1972, was less successful. In the 1970s and 1980s his other work in theatre and *opera included productions at *Birmingham Rep.   CEC

morris dance References to morris dance are found in Britain as early as the fifteenth century, but they do not enable us to characterize the performance clearly. A pattern *dance with the brandishing of swords is common in surviving accounts, however. As with other medieval *folk plays and performances, the morris dance carried social implications. The combative element, for example, would have altered its social meaning after the performances were banned from their traditional role at parish fundraising festivals and performed in defiance of the episcopacy. Morris dances continue into the twenty-first century in numerous locales within and without Great Britain, with great variety in their form and social setting. *See also* MORESCA; MUMMERS' PLAY.   JCD

Mortimer, John Clifford (1923–2009) English playwright and novelist. Mortimer was a barrister and novelist when he turned to radio and television writing in the 1950s. Somewhat like *Rattigan, Mortimer specialized in creating beleaguered middle-class *characters confronting their life-sustaining illusions. His first play for radio, *The Dock Brief* (1957), was his most successful, being reincarnated on television, stage, and film. *The Wrong Side of the Park* (1960) focuses on a woman coming to terms with false fantasies of her first marriage which are impinging on her second. The play's thin plot and final-act revelation, worthy of *Pinero, suggested that Mortimer was more comfortable with the one-act format fitting radio and television. Indeed, his best-known work comes from television and includes *Brideshead Revisited* (1981) and the series *Rumpole of the Bailey*, which originated in 1978. Other notable plays include an adaptation of *Feydeau's *A Flea in her Ear* (1966) for the *National Theatre, *A Voyage round my Father* (1972), *I, Claudius* (the stage version, 1972), and *Collaborators* (1973) with Glenda *Jackson.   MDG

Morton, Thomas (*c.*1764–1838) English dramatist. Morton's first play, the melodramatic *Columbus; or, A World Discovered*, was performed in 1792. He wrote two dozen plays altogether, almost all for *Covent Garden, mostly *comedies, of which the best known in their time are *The Way to Get Married* (1796), *A Cure for the Heart-Ache* (1797), *Speed the Plough* (1800, containing the *character of the unseen but fearsome Mrs Grundy), *The School of Reform* (1805), and the *farce *A Roland for an Oliver* (1819). Morton's plays are heavily sentimental, moralistic, anti-aristocratic, bustling with plot, intensely idealistic about virtue and rural domestic life. They are full of low comedy as well as *melodrama, and the pathetic and potentially tragic elements are in equal balance with the comic and farcical. This type of comedy represented the most popular *legitimate drama of its age and established a distinctive pattern inherited by the Victorian theatre.   MRB

Moscow Art Theatre Russian company, founded by *Stanislavsky and *Nemirovich-Danchenko in 1897. Like the free theatres of *Antoine and *Brahm, the Moscow Art Theatre set out to correct existing practice by a serious, contemporary repertoire, encouraging ensemble organization and playing, raising standards of design and production in the pursuit of authenticity (*see* NATURALISM), and educating a serious, more democratic *audience. MAT opened in 1898 with Aleksei *Tolstoy's previously banned historical play *Tsar Fyodor Ioannovich* and from 1898 to 1905 consolidated its reputation for *realist drama in plays by *Chekhov, *Gorky, *Ibsen, and *Hauptmann. Nemirovich-Danchenko operated as literary manager, administrator, and *director, while Stanislavsky—sometimes acting, sometimes co-directing—created a series of productions that are still admired. Nemirovich-Danchenko brought in his students *Knipper, Ivan Moskvin, and *Meyerhold and *scenography was by Viktor *Simov. After 1904 the MAT turned to the modernists, *Maeterlinck, Hamsun, and *Andreev, causing some criticism, not least from Stanislavsky. Relations between the two directors deteriorated so that by 1908 Stanislavsky had resigned from the board to develop his 'system', a theory of acting based on realist drama, its results first visible in *Turgenev's *A Month in the Country*

(1909). Nemirovich-Danchenko returned to classic realism with the work of *Griboedov and Lev *Tolstoy.

The first of the several studios was set up in 1913, for Stanislavsky to work on his theories with *Sulerzhitsky, which became known as MAT 2 in 1924 under the actor-director Michael *Chekhov (closed 1936). In 1920 the Third Studio was operated by *Vakhtangov, and a fourth was set up by actors from the mother company (1921). These studios enlarged the repertoire and bridged the gap between the founding members and the Soviet generation. In 1922–4 a second foreign *tour to Europe and America (the company visited Europe in 1906), led by Stanislavsky, secured the theatre's international reputation. Stanislavsky introduced new writers in the 1920s, notably *Bulgakov (*Days of the Turbins*, 1926) and *Ivanov (*Armoured Train 14–69*, 1927).

MAT's political standing with the Soviet regime was not helped by the pre-revolutionary productions still in the repertoire. Chekhov was readdressed (*Cherry Orchard*, 1927) and politically acceptable writers such as Afinogenov (*Fear*, 1931) and *Kirshon (*Bread*, 1931) were embraced. With Gorky's new work (*Egor Bulychov and the Others*, 1934) MAT demonstrated its conformity with *socialist realism. For much of the remaining Stalinist period, MAT became a museum of earlier successes, a national institution surviving by inertia rather then creativity, until revitalized by *Efremov with a programme of reform in 1970 with fresh productions of the classics, a more international repertoire, and new writers such as Aleksandr Gelman and *Shatrov. Yet allegiance to Stanislavsky's system is still strong. A crisis in the wake of perestroika in 1987 forced a split in the company. Efremov's group called itself the Chekhov Art Theatre, while a group led by Tatyana Doronina became the Gorky Art Theatre. Efremov's productions of once-controversial writers, Bulgakov, Solzhenitsyn, and *Petrushevskaya, have been followed by restagings of classics by Chekhov, Griboedov, and *Pushkin in tune with the 1990s. Since Efremov's death in 2000 the theatre has been led by Oleg Tabakov. A third performance space was added in 2001 and the theatre school has become an international institution, training students from a number of countries as well as Russia.   CM

Mostel, Zero (1915–77) American actor. With soulful eyes, baggy face, and portly elegance, Mostel was an 'inspired lunatic' regarded by *Beckett as a *clown of Chaplinesque stature. A career that began auspiciously on Broadway in 1942 stalled by the early 1950s when Mostel became branded along with other Hollywood artists as a communist sympathizer. He eventually regained momentum, notably with a portrayal of Leopold Bloom in *Ulysses in Nighttown* (1958), which earned an Obie award and first prize for acting at the Théâtre des Nations festival in Paris. Although he performed in works by *Molière, *Brecht, and *Ionesco, Mostel's singular stamp remains associated with his award-winning *musical roles: Pseudolus in *A Funny Thing Happened on the Way to the Forum* (1962) and Tevye in *Fiddler on the Roof* (1964). His films include *The Producers* (1968) and *The Front* (1976). Poised to redefine himself as a tragedian in the title role of *Wesker's *Shylock* (originally named *The Merchant*), Mostel died during its pre-Broadway tryout.   EW

Motley English design firm, comprised of Audrey ('Sophie') **Harris** (1901–66), **Margaret** ('Percy') **Harris** (1904–2000), and **Elizabeth Montgomery** (1902–93). Motley started in 1932 at Oxford designing scenery and *costumes for *Gielgud's *Romeo and Juliet*. In 1933 their first big London success, *Richard of Bordeaux* by Gordon Daviot, starring Gielgud in the title role, pioneered their characteristic use of simple *scenography from ordinary materials. After collaborating with Gielgud on some sixteen productions in the decade, including his revival of *Romeo* (1935), the threesome created designs for many important classical and commercial productions, *musicals, *operas, and *ballets, in the West End, on Broadway, and in Hollywood. Montgomery created most of their work in the United States, beginning with the 1941 *Romeo* of *Olivier and Vivien *Leigh, which she worked on with Sophie Harris. Among the musicals Motley designed were *South Pacific* (1949) and *Can-Can* (1953) in New York, and the film version of *Oklahoma!* (1955).

Motley was largely responsible for the ascetic visual style of the *Royal Court and the early *National Theatre. Among productions at the Royal Court were a charming *The Country Wife* (1956) and a chilling *Requiem for a Nun* (1957). With George *Devine, who married Sophie, Percy worked to establish a permanent stage surround at the Royal Court. For the National's first season (1963–4) Motley designed *Coward's *Hay Fever*. In 1966 Percy founded the Motley Theatre Design course, and its students have carried Motley design principles throughout the world.   TK

Moulin-Rouge, Bal du *Café-concert and *music hall in Montmartre in Paris, opened in 1889 to offer the controversial 'quadrille natur-

aliste', the *dance of the cancan, to more respectable *audiences. A huge theatrical windmill dominated the entrance, providing the name. Dancers like La Goulue, Nini Pattes-en-l'air, and Môme Fromage impressed the patrons with suggestive moves such as the 'porte-d'armes' and the 'grand écart'. The building burned in 1915, then reopened with a repertoire of cancans and dinner *revues. Some of the most famous international entertainers of the music-hall era have graced the stage, including *Mistinguett, Joséphine *Baker, and *Chevalier. After 1929 the space was converted to a cinema. It reopened for live entertainment in 1953, and continues to offer upscale *burlesques and lavish *cabaret.   CHB

Mounet-Sully (Jean Mounet) (1841–1916) French actor. Mounet worked for a minor Paris theatre where his vocal accomplishments attracted the notice of the director of the *Odéon. At the end of the Franco-Prussian War, having adopted Mounet-Sully as his professional name, he was accepted into the *Comédie-Française. Making his debut in *Racine's *Andromaque*, he was highly praised for his convincingly 'oriental' Oreste. From the early 1870s to the beginning of the twentieth century he was the outstanding interpreter of the tragic repertoire at the Comédie-Française, particularly in partnership with *Bernhardt up to her stormy departure in 1880. Their success in a revival of *Hugo's *Hernani* in 1878 was especially notable, as was Mounet-Sully's Hamlet; though his Oedipus received some criticism for its 'excessive' violence. His younger brother Paul Mounet made his debut at the Comédie-Française in the title role in *Corneille's *Horace*.   WDH

Mou Sen (Mou Sēn) (1963–) Chinese director. Mou established himself as a freelance director in Beijing with *Ionesco's *Rhinoceros* (1987). Since then he has attracted sponsorships—foreign and local—for his productions, including translated plays such as Ramuz's *Histoire du soldat* (1988) and *O'Neill's *The Great God Brown* (1989), and controversial successes such as '*The Other Side' and a Discussion about Grammar in 'The Other Side'* (1993), *Something to Do with AIDS* (1994), and *Yellow Flowers* (1995). In 1995, he took *File Zero*—an *avant-garde rendition of a long poem by his contemporary Yu Jian—on a highly successful international *tour, and became a symbol of alternative theatre in China. He concentrated on documentary films when his self-financed *Confession* (1997) was a box-office disaster.   MPYC

Mowatt, Anna Cora (1819-70) American playwright and actress. Anna Ogden seemed destined for a conventional middle-class life when at 15 she married James Mowatt, an attorney. Her husband's subsequent debilitating illness led to her writing career. In 1845 she wrote *Fashion*, a spritely *satire of American high society's pretension that has remained popular since its première. Needing more money than playwriting could provide, Mowatt became an actress, making her debut as Pauline in *Bulwer-Lytton's *The Lady of Lyons* in 1845. Although not professionally trained, Mowatt was attractive, had a good voice, possessed a ready intelligence, and abandoned herself to the emotions of her roles. It was a combination that engrossed *audiences, and she was highly successful until she abandoned the stage to marry William Ritchie in 1854.   GAR

Mozart, Wolfgang Amadeus (1756-91) Austrian composer. One of the most versatile composers in history, Mozart especially prized *opera. As a youth he showed himself adept in the conventional genres, *Idomeneo* (Munich, 1781) being the most accessible of all *opera seria*. Mozart's greatness is revealed in the operas he wrote to librettos by Lorenzo da Ponte. *The Marriage of Figaro* (*Burgtheater, 1786), still the most revived of all comic operas, has a vitality, pathos, and humanity that intensifies the revolutionary message of *Beaumarchais's original. Mozart's masterpiece *Don Giovanni* (Prague, 1787) is perhaps the only successful *tragicomedy in the operatic repertoire; music is used throughout to create an ironic perspective on *action and *character. *Così fan tutte* (Burgtheater, 1790) is a searching, ultimately painful *comedy on the instability of sexual desire. His two operas in the style of the *Singspiel, *The Abduction from the Seraglio* (Burgtheater, 1782) and the well-loved *The Magic Flute* (Vienna, 1791), demonstrated his capacity to write in the popular styles of his time. Although Mozart's operas are divided into separate musical numbers linked by recitative, the extended finales to the acts of his mature work did much to develop music as a continuous dramatic language.   SJCW

Mrożek, Sławomir (1930-) Polish playwright and humorist who from 1963 lived in the West before returning to Poland in the 1990s. In satirical *cabaret sketches—*Out at Sea* (1960), *Striptease*, and *Charlie* (both 1961) Mrożek developed a parable form of drama using model situations to explore the operations of power. *Tango* (1964), in the guise of a family drama,

charts the descent of liberal Europe into totalitarianism; its *absurd humour, grotesque *characterization, and *slapstick precision made it the most widely performed Polish play of the decade. Moving beyond political repression, *Vatzlav* (1970) and *Émigrés* (1974) examine the paradoxes of freedom and ironies of exile. *On Foot* (1981) offers a panorama of dislocated lives during the Second World War, including an apocalyptic artist patterned after *Witkiewicz; *Portrait* (1988) settles accounts with Stalin's poisoned heritage; *Widows* (1990) reinstates parable as an existential dance of death; and *Love in the Crimea* (1993) traces the collapse of Russia through a pastiche of *Chekhovian themes. Jerzy Jarocki's 1998 production *A History of People's Poland According to Mrożek*, based on a montage of the author's plays, reaffirmed Mrożek's pre-eminence as chronicler of life in communist Poland and master *parodist of theatrical styles.   DG

Mtshali, Thulani (*c*.1963–2002) South African writer, director, and *producer. Born in Kwa-Zulu Natal, he grew up in Soweto. He wrote or co-wrote nine plays, which include *Memories* (1981), *Prisons* (1985), *Burning Ambers* (*Edinburgh Festival, 1986), *Top Down* (1987), *Target* and *Devil's Den* (both 1994), *Golden Gloves* (1993), *Sekoto* (1995), and *WEEMEN* (1996). From 1984 to 1986 Mtshali trained in Johannesburg, and in 1987 co-founded Bachaki (Visitors) Theatre, through which he produced all his plays. It also creates *community theatre, involving *collective playmaking and praise poetry, a traditional southern African performance form of oral poetry, charged with emotion and a strong rhythm.   YH

mua roi nuoc A unique form of water *puppetry (literally 'puppets dancing on water') originating in the Red River Delta of Vietnam, records of which go back to 1121. It is traditionally performed by all-male guilds (who keep their manipulation techniques secret) in a village pond at festival time. A bamboo scene-house is erected in the centre of the pond, within which the puppeteers stand chest-deep in water and manipulate the puppets by controls beneath the pond's surface. The *audience sits on the pond bank. The puppets are either mounted on long rods or on wires stretched between posts hammered into the pond bed. All puppet heads and most bodies are carved from wood and may be hollow to contain apparatus to move them. The appearance of the puppets reflects the iconography of traditional wooden statuary and most are about 30 to 50 cm (12–20 inches) tall. Performances centre on a series of vignettes which are sometimes combined

to form extended narrative or thematic sequences. Subjects are distilled from aspects
of Vietnamese rural life, mythology, legend, or
history, usually connected with water. Over 200
different scenes have been recorded and an individual performance typically features about twenty scenes in a programme of some 40 minutes'
duration. Performances rely primarily on visual
impact, percussive and some melodic accompaniment, snatches of verse and song, occasional
pyrotechnics, and interaction with the audience.
There is little spoken *dialogue. By the late 1990s
Vietnam had two professional city-based water
puppetry troupes operating from specially built
theatres and *touring abroad with tank-stages. MJ

Müller, Heiner (1929–95) German playwright
and director. Müller's plays mix *Brechtian, *Artaudian, and postmodern techniques, and a vast
range of reference to European literature, in
blood-drenched collages of the catastrophes of
European Enlightenment in general and German
history in particular. Yet as his characteristically
grim aphorism 'I am an optimist: I believe in the
Fourth World War'—suggests, he extracted a utopian dialectic from these images of humanity's
interlocking drives to self-destruction and survival. In the 1950s and early 1960s, plays such as
Construction (1964) subverted the heroics of *socialist realism with critical images of the German
Democratic Republic's troubled transition from
capitalism to socialism. Production, when permitted at all, brought Müller repeated difficulties.

From the 1970s Müller radically rejected linear
progress and the self-determining subject. In
Germania Death in Berlin (1978), *The Battle*,
1975), or *Germania 3* (1995), brutal yet grotesque-
ly comic images of betrayal, dismemberment, or
cannibalism link the GDR with the disasters of
German history. Other plays such as *Desolate
Shore*, *Medea Material*, and *Landscape with Argo-
nauts* (all 1983) link patriarchy and colonialism in
a radical indictment of the European legacy.
Hamletmachine (1978) dismantles the Enlightenment individual, paralleling the artistic subject as
moulder of his material and the machine as symbol of dominance over nature. Meanwhile, in the
'ruins of Europe' Ophelia's resistance to *gender
determination generates revolutionary energy.
(Because of *censorship difficulties, the production dates listed often differ substantially from the
dates of composition.)

Müller's texts are often monologic and non-
verbal images are central; Müller admired Robert
*Wilson (who directed *Hamletmachine* in 1986)
and the *dance-theatre of *Bausch. For Müller,
aesthetic value emerged only from conflict, be-

tween text and production, or production and *audience. His plays challenge the production process
through unrealizable stage directions or blocks of
unattributed *dialogue.

His *directing work also sought to provoke, not
elucidate. He avoided psychological *realism, favouring montage, clownish exaggeration, fluid
intertextuality, and often grandiose visual symbolism (as with *Wagner's *Tristan and Isolde* at
*Bayreuth, 1993). His *Hamlet*, whose conception,
*rehearsal, and première in 1990 accompanied
the GDR's rapid disintegration, dismembered
and reassembled both Shakespeare's play and
Hamletmachine. The result was an eight-hour ne-
crology for the decayed and doomed East
German state but also for Müller's own work as
subversive art.   MMcG

multimedia performance Strategy combining varied media including juxtapositions of theatre, *dance, *music, projections of film, video,
and slides, computer technologies, virtual environments, plastic arts, and popular entertainments
in a single performance. The history of multimedia performance may be seen as running concurrently with the history of the Euro-American
*avant-garde. *Wagner's notion of *Gesamtkunst-
werk* is a prototype for the convergence of varied
art forms in one performance (*see* TOTAL THE-
ATRE). The *symbolists explored synaesthesia by
using aromas and abstract lighting to heighten the
performance. The *futurists, *dadaists, and *surrealists in their *cabarets combined a variety of
popular and high art forms into a single presentation. However, the work of *Piscator marks some
of the first experiments in combining media technologies and live performance. His 'living backdrop' created through film projections in a live
performance attempted to redefine theatrical
space and time through the addition of mechanical reproductions. *Happenings, developed during the 1950s and 1960s by painters and
sculptors, applied a form of multimedia performance through the addition of plastic art production, film, video, and daily activity in live art.

New media *performance artists such as the
*Wooster Group, *Lepage, and Japan's company
called dumbtype employ extensive use of video
and new technologies in live performances, extending the stage to combine both live and pre-
recorded performers. A technological and multimedia stage of analogue and digital recording
apparatus creates a performative space unrestricted by the 'here and now', toward a live
performance which can include a technological
space of 'not here and not now'. Once the province of experimental and avant-garde theatre and

performance, multimedia is now a tool of art performance and a popular entertainment as well. Currently multimedia performance can be seen in the popular entertainments of theme parks, rock concerts, and the spectacles of Las Vegas, utilized in art installations and interactive sculptures, and as a common element in both traditional and experimental theatre. MDC

mummers' play English *folk play. Traditionally divided into Hero Combats, Sword Dances, and Wooing plays, mummers' plays have in common performance by disguised local amateurs during the winter months in Britain, concluding with the demand for donations or drink. The earliest surviving texts date from the eighteenth century, but similar dramatic elements in *medieval *morality plays suggest a much longer heritage. The troupe has traditionally been composed only of men and boys who visit private homes and public houses during a holiday period and perform a traditional text using loud and relatively uninflected voices. Movement within the playing space is likewise formal and restricted. *Costuming varies from *realistic dress for the *character to adoption of 'ribbon costumes' for the troupe, with strips of bright cloth or paper in many colours worn over the performers' own clothing. Plays typically mix the comic with the serious. Repeated plot elements include combats between St George and a Turkish Knight, the competition to woo a wife, and the resurrection of a slain combatant from the dead; the theme of triumph over death, sterility, and destruction led early twentieth-century scholars to regard the plays as survivals of ancient seasonal *rituals. Later, interest shifted away from questions of *origin and turned to the function of the plays as community-affirming rituals, and, more recently, as a form of resistance by local lords to the centralizing agenda of the monarchy. JCD

Munday, Anthony (1560–1633) English playwright. Munday, who wrote ballads, pamphlets, and Lord Mayor's pageants and translated several French chivalric romances, was author or co-author of over a dozen plays, most of them commissioned by *Henslowe for the *Admiral's Men. Between 1590 and 1601 he collaborated with *Dekker and *Middleton, as well as Shakespeare and others, in writing *Sir Thomas More* (probably c.1593). In 1598 Francis Meres described him as one of 'the best for comedy' and 'our best plotter'. The artisan acting troupe in his *John a Kent and John a Cumber* (probably c.1594) invites comparison with Shakespeare's 'rude mechanicals' in *A Midsummer Night's Dream*. Munday also wrote

two *Robin Hood plays, *The Downfall of Robert Earl of Huntingdon* and *The Death of Robert Earl of Huntingdon* (both 1601). MS

Muni, Paul (1896–1967) American actor, born Muni Weisenfreund in Ukraine, to a family of itinerant actors who emigrated to the United States in 1901. Muni acted over 300 roles in Yiddish theatres, specializing in old men. His English-language debut (*We Americans*, 1926) was as an old man; he first played a young role in *Four Walls* (1927). He moved to films in the 1930s, starring in a series of major biographical films (*The Story of Louis Pasteur*, 1935, *The Life of Émile Zola*, 1937; *Juarez*, 1939), along with such successes as *Scarface* (1932), *The Good Earth* (1937), and his final film, *The Last Angry Man* (1958). He regularly appeared on Broadway (*Counsellor-at-Law*, 1931, 1942; *Key Largo*, 1939; *Inherit the Wind*, 1955). Muni was celebrated for his thorough and careful preparation, and his ability to vanish within the *character. AW

Munk, Kaj (1892–1944) Controversial Danish playwright. After his ordination as a priest in 1924, he wrote the miracle play *The Word* (performed 1932). Copenhagen's Kongelige Teater accepted his next play, *An Idealist* (1928). In pastiche Shakespearian style, it shows King Herod defying all his foes, even God, and was violently attacked by the critics. Munk went on to write a series of plays that echoed his fascination with superhuman figures, including King Henry VIII in *Cant* (1931) and King David in *The Chosen Ones* (1933). Admiration for strong leaders led him to write a Nazi adaptation of *Hamlet* in 1935, in which Fortinbras, dressed as a Danish Nazi, comes to liberate Denmark from democracy. As war threatened, Munk lost faith in strong dictator figures, reflected in *He Sits by the Melting Pot* (1938), and during the occupation of Denmark spoke out strongly against the Germans and their collaborators. He was murdered by Gestapo thugs. DT

Muñoz, Eunice (1928–) Portuguese actress. Born into a family of *variety artists, she made her professional debut in Lisbon at 13. She has worked with some of the most important Portuguese directors (*Lourenço, *Pais), in a diversity of productions and styles, proving equally creative in *comedy, drama, *tragedy, and more popular forms, including film. Over the years she has developed a technique that combines heightened intuition with a rare attention to detail and characterization. Amongst her most memorable roles are Maria in *Garrett's *Frei Luís de Souza* (1943), *Anouilh's Joan of Arc (*The Lark*, 1955),

Shakespeare's Viola (1957), *Racine's *Phèdre* (1967), Claire in *Genet's *The Maids* (1972), *García Lorca's *Bernarda Alba* (1983), and *Brecht's *Mother Courage* (1986), widely considered her most accomplished performance.   PEC

Murphy, Arthur (1727–1805) The Irish Murphy had a brief career as an actor and a long one as an essayist, playwright, and lawyer. He was introduced to the stage by *Foote and played Othello in 1754 at *Covent Garden. Over the next two years he performed there and at *Drury Lane, acting competently in some major roles, such as Jaffeir in *Otway's *Venice Preserv'd* and Young Bevil in *Steele's *The Conscious Lovers*. But his theatrical criticism in the *Gray's Inn Journal*, his biographies of *Fielding and *Garrick, and his plays constitute Murphy's important contributions. Of his plays, *The Grecian Daughter* (1772) and *Know your Own Mind* (1777) are among the best.   MJK

Murphy, Tom (1935–) Irish playwright. *A Whistle in the Dark* (1961), produced in London by the *Theatre Workshop, aroused controversy by showing the violence of an Irish emigrant family living in Coventry, but its theatrical energies carried it to a successful West End run. Its *naturalism was replaced by more experimental styles in *Famine* (1968), an *expressionist rendering of the Irish potato famine, the fable-like *Morning after Optimism* (1971), and *The Sanctuary Lamp* (1975), which brought protests over its outspoken anticlericalism. Three plays of the 1980s represent the finest examples of Murphy's innovative *dramaturgy. *The Gigli Concert* (1983) counterpoints its three-actor drama with operatic arias; *Bailegangaire* (1985), which gave a last starring role to Siobhán *McKenna, makes imaginative theatrical use of traditional Irish storytelling, *Conversations on a Homecoming* (1985) brilliantly choreographs an uninterrupted night's drinking in a country pub. Murphy's preferred themes, the nullities of small-town life and the rootlessness of the emigrant, reappear in *The Wake* (1998) and *The House* (2000). *The Last Days of a Reluctant Tyrant* (Abbey, 2009) is based on *Saltykov-Shchedrin's *The Golovlyovs*.   NG

Murray, Gilbert (1866–1957) Australian classicist, dramatist, and translator. Murray's play *Carlyon Sahib* (1889) had been championed by *Archer before London production by Mrs Patrick *Campbell, but it was his vivid translations, which used rhyme and decorative language to approximate the effect of the verse of *Greek *tragedy, that most affected British theatre. Granville *Barker staged three of Murray's works at the *Royal

Court (*Hippolytus*, 1904; *The Trojan Women*, 1905; *Electra*, 1906), using modernist stage effects, and *Reinhardt used Murray's *Oedipus Rex* at *Covent Garden (1912). Barker toured America with *The Trojan Women* and *Iphigenia in Tauris* (1915; Lillah *McCarthy as Hecuba). Particularly influential to America's *Little Theatre and university theatre movements, Murray was *Shaw's model for Cusins in *Major Barbara*. Associated with the Cambridge School of Anthropologists (*see* ORIGINS OF THEATRE), Murray's passion for civilization led to work with the League of Nations.   GAO

Murray, T. C. (Thomas Cornelius) (1873–1959) Irish schoolmaster who turned to playwriting as a hobby. Associating in Cork with Lennox *Robinson, who staged Murray's *comedy *The Wheel of Fortune* there (1909), doubtless helped Murray get a hearing at the *Abbey. *Birthright* (1910), *Maurice Harte* (1912), *Sovereign Love* (a revision of his comedy, 1913), *Spring* (1918), *The Serf* (1920), *Aftermath* (1922), *Autumn Fire* (1924), *The Pipe in the Fields* (1927), *The Blind Wolf* (1928), *Michaelmas Eve* (1932), all Abbey plays, many directed by Robinson, are remarkable for their patient *realism, which avoids any sensationalism in depicting rural lives knowing only desperation, penury, lovelessness, and greed. His best plays intimate situations resonant with mythical or biblical parallels, which bring tragic dignity to the *characters. When after 1930 Murray endeavoured to write of urban, middle-class life (*A Flutter of Wings*, *A Spot in the Sun*, *Illumination*) the results were disappointingly thin by comparison.   RAC

Murrell, John (1945–) Canadian playwright. Born in the USA, Murrell settled in Calgary and left teaching to work as an actor, writer, and director. *Waiting for the Parade* (1977) intertwines the lives of women on the home front during the Second World War; its use of *music and space have made it popular in Canada and abroad. In *Memoir* (1978), *Bernhardt demands that her secretary replay scenes from her life. Siobhán *McKenna performed in the première at the Guelph Spring Festival, a French version had a lengthy run in Paris, and the work has been translated into 35 languages and performed in fifteen countries. Robin *Phillips directed *Farther West* (1982), *New World* (1984), and *Democracy* (1991). Other plays include *October* (1988) and translations of *Chekhov, *Ibsen, *Machiavelli, and *Racine.   FL

musical play (Also called musical comedy, musical theatre, or musical.) A play in which *music, usually in the form of songs, is essential to the narrative. A musical typically relies on the alternation of *dialogue and song, as opposed to the continuous music, sung speech, and arias of *opera. Although the term 'musical comedy' generally connotes light humorous or romantic material, contemporary musical plays are diverse in both subject matter and style. As in related forms, such as *revues, *music hall, *vaudeville, opera, and *operetta, there is frequent use of *dance and a *chorus of singers or dancers, as well as featured performers and spectacular *scenography.

The modern musical began to separate itself from opera in the early eighteenth century with the development of *ballad opera, beginning in 1728 with the success in London of *Gay's *The Beggar's Opera*, a robust *parody of the mythological subjects and settings of serious opera. Until the early nineteenth century, light opera and operetta were the main musical theatre offerings in Europe and America. But despite a debt to extant forms, musical plays also developed by combining and differently emphasizing the elements of performance and blending the popular stage and musical traditions of Europe and the United States. Musicals are avid borrowers from different periods and forms, frequently crossing borders and stealing from *variety, music hall, *pantomime, as well as from opera and its descendants.

In the mid-nineteenth century these multiple strains came together and developed unique native forms in the United States. Slavery, its aftermath, and the tremendous influx of immigration in the country produced the *minstrel show, vaudeville, and a distinctive form of American popular song. Musical theatre also owed its evolving character to cross-pollination between Europe (particularly England and France) and the United States. Burlesque, music hall, light opera ballet, and spectacle converged in an 1866 production that changed the course of popular musical plays. *The Black Crook* was a *melodrama based on the Faust legend into which the producers inserted a French *ballet troupe. Its lavish sets, dancers in flesh-coloured tights, and interpolation of popular melodies made it a hit, spawning numerous imitations in New York and London in the 1870s and 1880s.

By 1900 operetta, revues, and variety performance dominated. It was then that American musical plays began to find their voice—musically and theatrically. George M. *Cohan, an Irish-American theatrical jack of all trades, began writing and starring in his own patriotically saturated shows such as *Little Johnny Jones* (1904). The development of ragtime piano by Scott Joplin and other American black musicians provided a driving rhythmic platform from which Irving *Berlin, George *Gershwin, and later songwriters fashioned

a new popular music. Berlin followed his first hit, 'Alexander's Ragtime Band' (1911), with more than half a century of memorable songs and shows. A few years later, Jerome *Kern blended the European penchant for melody, the emerging American pulse of ragtime, and his own desire for musical plays with more fully integrated elements. The result was a series of 'Princess Theatre musicals', written with *Wodehouse and *Bolton between 1915 and 1918, which set a new standard for the integration of song, dialogue, and *character.

In the 1920s jazz and musical-theatre songs became the mainstays of popular music, as major songwriters turned their talents to Broadway. George and Ira *Gershwin, *Porter, *Rodgers, and *Hart were among the major forces in the United States. In England the musical productions of *Coward and *Novello gained popularity. Lavish annual revues, such as *Ziegfeld's *Follies*, were sumptuously costumed and staged entertainments that have seldom been equalled. However, despite the innovations of Kern's Princess Theatre shows, 1920s musicals featured formulaic plots, thin characterization, and little real integration of their elements.

Kern's *Show Boat* (1927, lyrics and book by *Hammerstein) provided a new model for the unification of song and story. Based on the novel by Edna Ferber, it spanned three generations of a showboat family in the American south after the Civil War. The 1930s and 1940s saw the further development of more sophisticated musical plays. The satiric musicals of the Gershwin brothers (*Strike up the Band*, 1930; *Of Thee I Sing*, 1931; *Let 'Em Eat Cake*, 1933) were followed in 1935 by their most adventurous show, *Porgy and Bess*. This operatic work, set in a black community in Charleston, brought together the complex blend of jazz, blues, popular melodies, and classical influences. Porter brought urbane sophistication and playfulness to the music and lyrics for *Anything Goes* (1934) and *Kiss Me, Kate* (1948). The 1930s also saw experimentation with dance as a narrative element, as seen in choreographer *Balanchine's 'Slaughter on 10th Avenue' in *On your Toes* (1936), the first ballet conceived as an integral part of a musical comedy. Rodgers and Hart also blazed new trails with *Pal Joey* (1940), a dark, unsparing tale of a small-time nightclub host. By the late 1930s, musicals reached worldwide *audiences through the films of choreographer Busby Berkeley (a former Broadway dance director) and Fred *Astaire, who had starred in Broadway musicals.

The most significant production since *Show Boat* came in 1943 with *Oklahoma!*, the first collaboration between Rodgers and Hammerstein.

Set in the last days of the American frontier, *Oklahoma!* employed dance to further plot and character. Agnes *de Mille's choreography used folk idioms, ballet, tap, and modern dance in a manner new to musical theatre. The success of Rodgers and Hammerstein shows, such as *Carousel* (1945), *South Pacific* (1949), and *The King and I* (1951), became the touchstones for the development of subsequent musicals.

The late 1940s to the mid-1960s were a particularly rich and productive period. Among the practitioners who emerged after the Second World War was Frank *Loesser, whose range as a composer-lyricist was equalled only by Berlin. Loesser's *Guys and Dolls* (1950) achieves a rare balance between comic and romantic elements. Other notable post war composers include Jule *Styne, who (like Loesser) began writing film songs in Hollywood. Styne's shows include *Gentlemen Prefer Blondes* (1949), *Gypsy* (1959), and *Funny Girl* (1964). *Lerner and Loewe gave romantic material a special wit and sophistication with *Brigadoon* (1947), *My Fair Lady* (1956), and *Camelot* (1960), among others. They managed in *My Fair Lady* a deft musicalization of *Shaw's *Pygmalion*.

The post-war period also saw noteworthy contributions from composer *Bernstein, whose *West Side Story* (1957) was another advance in the integration of music, dialogue, dance, and staging. Working with choreographer-director *Robbins and librettist *Laurents, Bernstein's music served a novel retelling of *Romeo and Juliet* as a street-gang conflict on New York's Upper West Side. Robbins staged an opening number that established atmosphere, setting, and character dynamics before a word was uttered. The show also established Stephen *Sondheim, who wrote the lyrics, as a significant emerging talent. Mentored by Hammerstein, Sondheim went on to write lyrics for Styne's *Gypsy* (1959) and music and lyrics for the broadly *farcical *A Funny Thing Happened on the Way to the Forum* (1962). He firmly established himself as an innovator with *Company* (1970), *Follies* (1971), and *A Little Night Music* (1973), which featured his most popular song, 'Send in the Clowns'. In 1979 he blended operetta, spectacle, and *Grand Guignol in *Sweeney Todd*. Imaginatively staged by Hal *Prince, the show remains controversial for both its content and stark satire. Sondheim's later work includes *Sunday in the Park with George* (1984) and *Passion* (1994).

The 1960s and 1970s produced shows that stand in the first rank of modern musicals. *Fiddler on the Roof* (1964), by composer Jerry *Bock and lyricist Sheldon Harnick, brought the stories of *Aleichem vividly to life. That same year *Hello, Dolly!* began a run of 2,844 performances with stars like Carol *Channing, Pearl Bailey, and Ethel *Merman in the title role. *Kander and Ebb created the hits *Cabaret* (1966) and *Chicago* (1975) that looked at the darker side of the 1930s. In 1975 *A Chorus Line* started its fifteen-year run on Broadway. Director-choreographer Michael *Bennett developed the show from tape recordings of musical-theatre dancers talking about their lives.

The 1970s also saw the re-emergence of British influence through the work of *Lloyd Webber. While Sondheim placed a premium on innovation and seldom produced commercially successful shows, Lloyd Webber demonstrated a cagey awareness of both musical theatre and the business of popular music. With lyricist Tim *Rice, his first hit, *Jesus Christ Superstar* (1971), began life as a successful sung-through pop-rock album prior to its first live performance. In 1978 the collaborators created *Evita*, a study in power, stardom, and the ambition and charisma of those that achieve it. In 1981 Lloyd Webber, working with director *Nunn, adapted *Eliot's light poems *Old Possum's Book of Practical Cats* (1939). Essentially a revue with spectacular costumes, make-up, choreography, and no dialogue, *Cats* became the longest running musical in the stage history of both New York and London.

The 1980s found spectacle reasserting itself with productions of *Les Misérables* (1985) and *Miss Saigon* (1989) by the French team *Boublil and Schönberg, Lloyd Webber's *Phantom of the Opera* (1986), and the entry of the Walt Disney Company into live production. Starting with a stage version of their animated film *Beauty and the Beast* (1993), Disney then presented an innovative staging of another animated hit, *The Lion King* (1998), directed and designed by Julie *Taymor, followed by a pop version of *Aida* (1999) with a score by Elton John and words by Tim Rice.

Although new musicals were rarer each season, the decade produced *Rent* (1998), and *Ragtime* (1997), based on the novel by E. L. Doctorow. The comedy writer and director Mel Brooks took Broadway by storm in 2001 with a stage version of his film *The Producers*. The modern musical is unlikely to return to the prominence it enjoyed from the 1940s to the 1960s when its songs were heard everywhere and cast albums topped the record charts. Yet it remains popular worldwide and adds a few shows each year to the canon of one of history's most widely enjoyed theatrical forms.   SN

music hall The music hall in Britain came into existence as Queen Victoria was crowned, flowered with her reign, and entered the twentieth century ready to decline; its heyday was roughly from 1890 to 1910. The first purpose-built halls began to be erected in numbers in the early 1840s. Signs of the end were the 1907 performers' strike and the 1912 Royal Command performance, which signalled the arrival of the respectable *variety theatre. At first the growth of the halls provided a leisure service to growing urban populations, and enabled talented individuals to develop star careers and fortunes. Cultural change and aspiration, the broadening of the *audience, and concomitant moves to increase discipline and market control shifted power into the hands of business *managers and investors. They spent venture capital on large, sumptuous *auditoriums laid out as theatres rather than 'halls', transforming the audience–performer relationship; and they protected their investments by the *censorship of material and the contractual disciplining of performers. The transformation resulted not only in the shifting character of the large halls themselves, as they developed into 'variety theatres', but also the suppression of small independent halls.

Music hall was the primary, but not the only, Victorian home of professional entertainment. It shared the development of popular song and dance with *musical theatre and *operetta in upper-class venues. *Freaks and novelties, feats of strength and agility, and technical mastery continued to be exhibited in *circuses, fairs, and pleasure gardens as well as on the halls. Verbal and physical *clowning overlapped into *farce and *pantomime in popular theatres. The cultural politics of pleasure and leisure was a multi-layered and important discourse, then as now, touching upon many significant beliefs and practices; a concentration of financial, class, and *gender issues made the halls a prime focus of Victorian identity formation.

This is most obvious in the character songs and their singers, still recalled as the characteristic product of the halls and partially preserved in the published song sheets so popular in drawing rooms. The songs of the 'lions comiques' like Alfred Vance and George Leybourne (whose version of urban masculinity celebrated good companionship, promoted the cheap pleasures of mass-produced fashion, set modern drinking habits, and mocked aristocratic exclusivity) became a model to which large swathes of the young male population aspired. Character songs setting female fashion, behaviour, and self-image suggest a range of class types: Jenny *Hill depicted working women, chiefly for their own amusement, while Marie *Lloyd evoked the fun had by a series of Daisies and Millies, lower-middle-class girls who were the working counterparts of the young men of the City. Some performers specializing in working-class depictions, like Dan *Leno, were lionized by the West End, and translated, in Leno's case, to the famous Christmas pantomime at *Drury Lane, which was a ritual exposure to theatreland for the middle-class child. Fewer song sheets record one of the most significant turns of the music hall, the *male impersonators, presumably because there were fewer girls with pianos who would want to sing such songs themselves, however fascinated they were by Vesta *Tilley on the stage. The vivid imagery of the song sheets should not obscure the importance of other music-hall acts, like the ubiquitous clowning routines done in blackface (*see* MINSTREL SHOW), the surreal and uproarious playlets which could sometimes be of the most anti-establishment, counter-imperial character, or the feats of strength and agility and novelty acts that filled out every bill. The halls were an important and highly specific Victorian phenomenon which reverberated in the cultural imagination of Britain through most of the twentieth century.   JSB

music in the theatre Pure music is commonly regarded as an abstract language, but when it is used in the theatre it can take on highly specific meaning. Music can make more rather than less precise the *subtext of *dialogue and can give clarity to the shape of dramatic *action. Music was employed in the earliest phases of spoken theatre. The *chorus in ancient *Greek theatre was accompanied by a piper, playing the double pipes: he marked the rhythm of the verse for its delivery and for *dancing. Most spoken dialogue in later periods of the theatre has been delivered without such rhythmic support, though it can be heard occasionally in the modern theatre in the revival of classical drama or in spoken dramas whenever there is an attempt to create an atmosphere of *ritual or grandeur.

Historically, theatrical performance has made liberal use of music. In the theatres of England, Italy, and Spain during the *early modern period, breaks between the acts of spoken plays would usually provide the opportunity for *dances, songs, and other musical turns, a pattern of programming that lasted well into the eighteenth and, in some instances, the nineteenth century. Songs and dances were often incorporated into the action as well, as, for example, in Shakespeare's *comedies. In London and Paris, where the performance of spoken drama was the privilege of a few *patent theatres, plays were often staged in other theatres in conjunction with musical performances, under the pretence that the event was a concert with spoken interludes. Yet there were few systematic attempts to wed music and the spoken word until the latter half of the eighteenth century with the advent of *melodrama. Initially referring to the formal recitation of a spoken text to instrumental accompaniment (*see* MÉLODRAME), melodrama by the beginning of the nineteenth century was recognized as a distinct genre, of which music was an integral part. Much of the spoken dialogue in melodrama was delivered to orchestral accompaniment, particularly in passages designed to arouse an atmosphere of intense pathos or great tension and excitement. Usually, scripts would indicate where music should be played, so the dialogue was written with musical accompaniment in mind. This practice began to decline in the latter part of the nineteenth century and is rarely in use today. Frequently modern productions of spoken drama will employ recordings or live musicians to set the atmosphere, bridge scenes, or divert audiences during scene changes, but in film music is still constantly used to intensify the emotional impact of the scene and heighten dramatic tension.

Various genres of *musical theatre arose in the nineteenth century which still dominate the repertoire of commercial theatres around the globe. While the *operetta and its national sub-genres prevailed in the nineteenth century, in the twentieth century the musical has thrived. Both forms usually require orchestra and chorus, and usually both contain passages of dialogue that lead to musical numbers, solo songs, duets, larger concerted and choral pieces, and dance sequences. It is impossible to specify all occasions on which music is a more appropriate medium of expression than spoken words, but music is employed whenever the action reaches an emotional, sentimental, or dramatic highpoint, whenever festive occasions are represented on stage or set pieces are required to represent the social world of the drama. Music in the theatre tends to formalize and frequently idealize both social and personal experiences. In recent decades, some musicals have entirely dispensed with the spoken word, which brings them formally close to *opera, the one genre in which solo, concerted, and choral singing to orchestral accompaniment is the chief medium of expression. Although the practice of performing music, songs, dances, and *acrobatics between the acts of spoken plays died out at the

beginning of the twentieth century, compiling theatre programmes from a variety of acts continued, most notably in the *music halls of Great Britain and in *revues, which originated in Paris, but soon spread throughout Europe and the United States, where they continue still.   SJCW

Musset, Alfred de (1810–57) French poet and
dramatist. The youngest and most original of the *romantic playwrights, Musset was little performed in his lifetime. After the failure of *La Nuit vénitienne* (1830), many of his plays were published as *closet drama. One of them, *Lorenzaccio* (1834), marks a complete break from French *neoclassical tradition, with its construction (39 separate scenes), the wide social spread of its *characters, and how the *hero is presented. The clear-cut conflict or dilemma exhibited in *Corneille or *Racine is replaced by Lorenzo's gradual development from an unsympathetic, if enigmatic, character to one whose motivation is laid bare in a series of emotionally charged scenes: comparison with *Hamlet* has become commonplace. When first produced, at the Renaissance Theatre in 1896, Sarah *Bernhardt played Lorenzo, starting a *male impersonation tradition; the *Théâtre National Populaire at *Avignon saw the first major production with a male actor (Gérard *Philipe) in the role in 1952. Musset's *Un caprice* was performed at St Petersburg by a French actress, Mme Allan, in 1837; and it was she whose performance in the same play on her return to Paris in 1847 led to the belated recognition of Musset's comedies. Among the more substantial plays, *Les Caprices de Marianne* (1851) and *Don't Joke with Love* (1861) suggest the *tragicomic mood of Shakespeare's *Measure for Measure*.   WDH

Muthuswamy, Na (1936–) Indian writer
and director, based in Chennai (Madras). From his breakthrough in 1979 with *From Time Immemorial*, Muthuswamy has continued to explore the conflicting values of the metropolis in relation to pre-modern traditions. Working within a stylized and disjunctive narrative structure, Muthuswamy is known for experimental plays that are marked by an extremely inventive use of the Tamil language, including *Umbilical Cord*, *Wall Posters*, *A God*, and *A Scene from the Movie*. As the *artistic director of Koothuppattarai (1979), re-established as a *repertory company by 1986, he has brought together diverse talents from *terukkuttu* with contemporary painters, choreographers, *dancers, and critics. Muthuswamy's translation of a Sanskrit play by *Bhasa

(*Dhuthagatothkajam*) was matched by his reinterpretation of the 'Burning of the Khandava Forest' episode from the *Mahabharata*, where environmental issues were placed within the tradition of *terukkuttu*.   PR/RB

mystery plays The term *mystère* appears first in 1374 in the records of Rouen linked with 'miracle', where a *confrérie* is commanded to play 'aucun vrai mistere ou miracle'. The terms seem to be interchangeable in late medieval French usage. Later French use of the term refers to *Passion plays, *biblical plays, dumb shows, and even plays on profane subjects. Because one of the meanings of the French word *mystère* is 'craft', English scholars of the late nineteenth century applied the phrase 'mystery play' to works thought to have been performed by craft guilds—particularly those sequences that dramatize salvation history: the York, Chester, Towneley, N-Town plays, and the *Cornish Ordinalia*. *See also* CORPUS CHRISTI PLAYS.   AFJ

Nakamura Utaemon VI (1917–2001) Japanese *kabuki actor and *onnagata (woman's role specialist). The son of Nakamura Utaemon V, he began performing at 5 years of age under the name of Kotarō and went through successive name changes as Fukusuke (1933) and Shikan (1941) before assuming the name Utaemon VI in 1951. Equally strong at dance roles and at playing courtesans, maidens, and princesses, Utaemon's style is elegant and subtle. In the 1950s and 1960s he was the favourite actor of *Mishima Yukio, who wrote several new kabuki plays for him. At his death Utaemon was the senior *onnagata* and a leader of the art, exerting strong influence on play selection and actor promotion.   LRK

Namiki Sōsuke (Senryū) (1695–1751) Japanese dramatist, a Buddhist priest before becoming a playwright at the Toyotake-za *puppet theatre in Osaka. He produced about 47 *bunraku and ten *kabuki plays, most written in collaboration under his direction. He became the senior playwright in 1727, after only one year with the troupe. He briefly went to Edo (Tokyo) around the end of 1741, and then in 1742–5 wrote kabuki for Osaka theatres. In 1745 he moved to the Takemoto-za, and under the name Senryū collaborated with *Takeda Izumo II and Miyoshi Shōraku to produce ten works, including three famous plays, *Sugawara and the Secrets of Calligraphy* (1746), *Yoshitsune and the Thousand Cherry Trees* (1747), and *Chūshingura. the treasury of loyal retainers* (1748). In 1751 he returned to the Toyotake-za to write two works under the name Sōsuke; he died after completing Act III of *The Battles at Ichinotani* (1751). His works are known for their critical and tragic view of Tokugawa period society, and today he is considered the second greatest Japanese playwright after *Chikamatsu Monzaemon.   CAG

Napier, John (1944–) English designer who trained with Ralph *Koltai. Work for *Marowitz's Open Space and the *Royal Court led to appointment as associate designer for the *Royal Shakespeare Company (1974). He was part of the team that restructured the RSC main stage (1976) and achieved international recognition for *The Greeks* (1980) and a *constructivist *Nicholas Nickleby*

(1980). Napier is associated with bravura West End *musicals such as *Les Misérables* (1985) and *Sunset Boulevard* (1993). Stripping the stage of decor, he replaces it with an evocative object such as the 'American dream' Cadillac in *Miss Saigon* (1989). His sets include the *audience as part of the design, requiring transformation of *auditorium and stage space: seats were removed for skaters' tracks in *Starlight Express* (1984), and *Cats* (1981) extended its junkyard set into the auditorium. Recent work includes *Once in a Lifetime* (2005), the *pantomime *Aladdin*, with *McKellan as the Widow Twankey (2005), and a revival of *Equus* (2007).   RVL

Nation, Théâtre de la See COMÉDIE-FRANÇAISE.

National Theatre of Great Britain (Royal National Theatre) Honouring Shakespeare and showing that Britain deserved a 'state' theatre like those of its European neighbours were strong motives for the founding of a National Theatre in London. (The 'Royal' of its title was not approved until 1988, and in 2002 the company began to de-emphasize the regal designation in its publicity.) Bringing the theatre to life was a long and tortuous process. In 1848 a publisher, Effingham Wilson, wrote a short pamphlet with the grand title *A House for Shakespeare: a proposition for the consideration of the nation.* This he sent to eminent persons whose reactions were mixed, state interference and competition with commercial theatres being among the objections. Effingham gave up hope, but in the 1870s the cause was taken up by Matthew Arnold and *Irving, the man of letters making common cause with the *actor-manager. Their motives were different, however, and in succeeding years the theatre's history seldom ran smoothly, despite the existence of the *Shakespeare Memorial Theatre at Stratford-upon-Avon and the *Old Vic in London, and the efforts of Granville *Barker and *Archer in the early decades of the twentieth century.

Eventually, in 1948, both Houses of Parliament voted £1 million towards building a national theatre on the South Bank in London, but not until 1963 did a company, formed and led by *Olivier, open at the Old Vic with a production of *Hamlet*. Remaining there for over a decade, Olivier produced some highly acclaimed work on a small scale suitable for a temporary home. A board of trustees had been established and a committee of theatre professionals was appointed to advise Denys Lasdun as architect for an impressive new building. He designed two major *auditoriums, the Olivier, with 1,160 seats curved fan shaped around a thrust stage, and the Lyttelton, with 890 seats on two levels in almost straight rows facing a wide straight-fronted stage. The best of everything was prescribed, including the latest technical equipment that promised to reduce operating costs and make a frequently changing repertoire practicable. In a space originally left conveniently empty, a third auditorium, the Cottesloe, was created in which a stage and some 300 seats could be variously configured. The fittings of this theatre, intended for small-scale and experimental work, were much less luxurious.

Construction was slow and not until 1977 was the National in full occupation with Peter *Hall in charge, having replaced Olivier. A red, white, and blue poster, featuring a partially obscured Union Jack, proclaimed that 'The New National Theatre is yours', but it was to face harsh criticism, political manoeuvring, unofficial strikes, and shortage of funds. With the National mocked and envied as the 'establishment', a seemingly tireless Hall argued eloquently for sufficient finance to ensure the company's health. Attracting talented dramatists, directors, actors, designers, and technicians of all kinds, he was criticized for stripping other theatres of the personnel as well as the subsidy they needed. He also assembled a group of associates, including *Blakemore, *Bury, Jonathan *Miller, and *Pinter, together with the composer Harrison Birtwistle and the film director John Schlesinger, to meet regularly and advise on planning and repertoire. In 1988, Hall handed over to Richard *Eyre, director of the National's *Guys and Dolls* and previously *artistic director of the Nottingham Playhouse. In 1998 Trevor *Nunn succeeded Eyre, having previously run the *Royal Shakespeare Company and directed a string of successful West End *musicals. In 2001 Nicholas *Hytner took over on the retirement of Nunn; he had directed several long-running productions on the National's main stages but had no experience as artistic director of a theatre building or theatre company.

With changes in leadership and in British politics, mood, and prospects, the National developed from a theatre committed to maintaining a wide repertoire of new productions in its own theatres to a more diverse organization. During the first

three weeks of September 1977, by which time all three theatres were in operation, nine productions were in the repertoire, four of them of new plays. In the same three weeks of 2001, the repertoire was one visiting production, one revival from a previous season, three new plays, and a UK première of an American double-bill, but that was only part of the National's activity. Three productions from earlier seasons were playing in the West End. In the 1999–2000 financial year, an education department had mounted small-scale *touring productions, *youth theatre projects, in-service teacher training, workshops, school visits, and much else. The National's Studio, based in the former workshops of the Old Vic, was busy with master classes, training, play readings and exploratory workshops, and productions. A fundraising development department had raised £2,077,000, or more than an eighth of the theatre's total income.

The story has continued in much the same broad course but with ever-more emphasis on reaching out to new and diverse audiences and productions that could attract whole families. *WarHorse* was a prime example of a family show: based on a novel by Michael Morpurgo, produced in association with Handspring Puppet Company, and billed as suitable for audiences of 12+, the production sold out at the National over many months and then moved in March 2009 to a West End venue large enough to accommodate a show originally devised for the Olivier. *Warhorse* also exemplified the National's growing dependence on plays adapted from previously successful novels, films, and current events. 'New plays' in the National's repertoire for February 2009 told stories about immigrants in Britain, 'examined' post-colonial Nigerian corruption, 'adapted' a Russian screenplay, and took 'inspiration' from *Ibsen's *Little Eyolf* and William Feaver's account of the Pitmen Painters. The state-subsidized National Theatre looks set to continue to try every means of fighting for its acceptance and existence. JRB

naturalism Although the term has come to be applied to any drama which depicts recognizable *characters in everyday situations, naturalism properly refers to a nineteenth-century European movement influenced by positivist sociology, natural history, and empirical scientific method. It is marked by a realistic representation of contemporary life, in *acting, writing and *mise-en-scène, with an emphasis on revealing the darker corners of social experience not usually acknowledged in bourgeois society. Although theatrical *realism was hardly new, it took on particular importance in Paris in the 1880s. *Zola's advocacy of naturalism in his own novels prepared the way for his polemical *Naturalism in the Theatre* (1881), which demanded that the naturalist experiment be repeated on stage, which was mostly given over to harmless entertainments in the tradition of the *well-made play. *Becque's *Crows* (written 1876), about the sexual and financial corruption of a family, did not find a production for six years and then was coolly received. Meanwhile adaptations of Zola's novels, notably *Thérèse Raquin* (1867), *Nana* (1881), and *Germinal* (1888), compromised too readily with conventional dramatic forms, and the scientific scrutiny of the novels seemed cheapened as a result.

The first successful naturalist theatre was *Antoine's Théâtre *Libre (1887). The opening production included a short piece by Zola, *Jacques Damour*, and the company was soon celebrated for its intimate acting style and the detailed authenticity of its settings. Antoine removed the *footlights, dimmed the *auditorium, and experimented with stage *lighting. He championed foreign dramatists of a naturalist bent like *Tolstoy, *Ibsen, *Strindberg, and *Hauptmann. The Théâtre Libre sparked similar independent companies across Europe: *Brahm's *Freie Bühne in Berlin (1889), *Grein's *Independent Theatre in London (1891), Strindberg's Intima Teatern in Stockholm (1907). Italian realism, *verismo*, produced important naturalist plays, such as *Giacosa's *Sad Loves* (1887) and *Like the Leaves* (1900), and *Capuana's *The Rosary* (1912); the movement's most acclaimed writer, Giovanni Verga, successfully adapted some of his stories for the stage, including *Cavalleria rusticana* (1884) and *The She-Wolf* (1896).

Antoine often spoke of his indebtedness to Zola, whose own inspiration lay not just in novels of Balzac and Stendahl but also in Darwin, Taine, and Comte. In his *Course in Positive Philosophy* (1830–42) Auguste Comte argued that the history of the human mind shows a progression from theological to metaphysical and finally to scientific (or positive) understanding of the world. In the preface to the second edition of *Thérèse Raquin* Zola's scientism is visible in his assertion that he is dissecting the behaviour of his *characters as dispassionately as a surgeon in an operating theatre. Hippolyte Taine's highly deterministic view of human behaviour, most clearly expressed in *History of English Literature* (1864), assumed that the human being is 'a machine with well-arranged cogs; he is a system'. Taine argued that behaviour was determined by *race* (inherited factors), *milieu* (social and political environment), and *moment* (the historical forces that bear upon the present).

This displacement of morality and divinity from the field of human endeavour was still shocking to a society reeling from Charles Darwin's view of humanity created not by the invisible hand of God but by gradual adaptation to the environment. The application of Darwinian natural history to society (social Darwinism), fostered by writers like Herbert Spencer who saw society as a struggle between the weak and the strong, is a pervasive presence in naturalist writing.

Despite the broadly liberal or socialist views of many naturalists there is often a political ambiguity, notably in Ibsen's and Strindberg's work, between extreme individualism and its critique. There were considerable theatrical and philosophical anxieties in the naturalist enterprise as well, and the *audience's sense of the fictiveness of the theatrical event was in many ways heightened, rather than suppressed, by the highly theatrical innovations for which the naturalists were famous. Not only are most naturalist plays visibly shaped, albeit unconsciously, by the structures and styles of *melodrama or the well-made play, but the collaborative nature of theatre makes it hard for a single vision to dominate. Indeed writers found themselves displaced by the *director in the very form they had so vehemently called for, as the demands of increased realism necessitated a single eye that could place the script in a coherent visual structure (*see* SCENOGRAPHY). Naturalism's bequest to the theatre was not just a theatrical genre but the figure of the director as well.

In the most artistically successful plays of the naturalist period there is a tension between undiluted representation and *symbolism that suggests a struggle between materialism and idealism in late nineteenth-century European culture. Throughout Ibsen's work, for example, metaphors seem to transcend the purely rational, and *Chekhov wrote with a detached calmness that put *action into the background. Chekhov's plays are witty and ironic, sometimes bleak, sometimes broadly comic in tone; yet his collaborating director, *Stanislavsky, developed a detailed naturalist mise-en-scène for them at the *Moscow Art Theatre. Stanislavsky's influential theories of acting tended towards an internalization of the actor's craft, and suited the *bourgeois, individualist aspects of naturalism more than they did its political and critical role.

The symbolist theatres of Paris in the 1890s were indebted to naturalism as much as they turned away from its every principle. Despite its relatively short flowering, the theatre of the twentieth century was largely given to working out its contradictions. DR

Natyasastra Earliest known Sanskrit compendium on Indian theatre, attributed to the sage Bharata. Allegedly written almost two millennia ago, this encyclopedic text incorporated interpolations over the years which have been tacitly approved by generations of gurus and performers. In the opening chapters, the divine *origin of drama is established with a graphic description of how the first play was enacted—and interrupted—in the presence of gods and demons by Bharata and his sons. The open-air performance was later shifted to a *playhouse. Broadly dividing the art of acting into two different modes, *natyadharmi* (stylized) and *lokadharmi* (real), the *Nastyasastra* outlines numerous components of *dance, drama, *music, and spectacle. It attaches great importance to *rasas (aesthetic sentiments) in acting. In addition to physical and vocal acting, the *Natyasastra* also elaborates on *sattvikabhinaya* (acting of the innermost sentiments) and *aharyabhinaya*, which is concerned with the histrionic and visual possibilities of *costumes, make-up, ornaments, weapons, and carriages, as well as the practicalities of the acting area (entries and exits) and the positions and postures of the actors. The text also emphasizes the characteristics of an ideal *preksaka* (spectator) and the aesthetic preparation needed for the full appreciation of *rasa*. Reflecting a unity of purpose and integrated vision of *dramaturgy with related arts, the *Natyasastra* remains an invaluable reference for all classically trained artists in drama, music, and dance, as well as for contemporary Indian artists inspired by traditional resources. KNP

naumachia The most extensive form of dramatized punishment at Rome (*damnatio) was the *naumachia*, a staged naval battle based upon a real or imaginary episode from Greek history that demonstrated the emperor's control over human resources and simultaneously his power to re-create history. In 2 BC Augustus dug an enormous lake in Trastevere so as to stage the battle of Salamis (480 BC) during the inaugural celebrations for the temple of Mars Ultor, which commemorated the avenging of Caesar's death. Excluding marines, 3,500 men were involved. The result was faithful to the historical outcome: 'Athens' won. In AD 52 Claudius used a *naumachia* as an advertisement for an engineering project by staging a sea battle between Rhodes and Sicily on the Fucine Lake just before he drained it in a land-reclamation scheme; 19,000 prisoners participated; some survived. Some emperors effected a miracle by flooding a venue associated with terrestrial displays: in AD 80 at the 100 days of celebrations to inaugurate the Colosseum a small

naumachia was held in the Colosseum itself to re-enact a battle between Corfu and Corinth from the Peloponnesian War. An emperor might also rewrite the past. During the same inaugural celebrations Augustus' lake was the venue for a re-enactment of the Athenian expedition against Syracuse later in the war (414 BC), but this time history was reversed in that the 'Athenians' routed the 'Syracusans'. Domitian (AD 81–96) and Trajan (AD 98–117) constructed their own lakes for *naumachiae*. The last recorded *naumachia* in the city was staged by Philip the Arab in AD 248 to celebrate Rome's millennium. KMC

nautanki Hindi- and Urdu-language theatre popular in the villages and towns of northern India that combines sophisticated folk singing and drumming, *dancing by female artists and transvestites, and dramatic recitation of poetic tales. *Nautanki* belongs to the class of rural theatre forms originating in pre-modern contexts, like *jatra* of Bengal and *tamasha* of Maharashtra, that have become urbanized popular entertainments to varying degrees. *Nautanki* is performed at fairs, religious festivals, and weddings. Troupes may be sponsored by a patron (often a merchant or landlord) or booked for ticketed performances, and the personnel come from a mixture of castes with artisan groups dominating. *Audiences are drawn from the semi-urban working class and agriculturalists, and include women and children (though they are often discouraged from attending). Stories of romance are prevalent in the secular *nautanki*, with plots frequently derived from legends of Arabic, Persian, or Indo-Islamic origin. The genre is named for the Princess Nautanki, an alluring heroine famed for her delicacy and beauty. In these dramas pure love is pursued even unto death, though romance is also combined with ascetic virtue in cautionary tales that warn against the dangers of sensual attachment, and some plays laud saints who renounced sexuality. Martial prowess is another preoccupation. With the advent of the mass media the frequency of performances began to decline, yet several directors such as Habib *Tanvir have adopted its features. KH

Ndao, Cheik Aliou (1933–) Francophone Senegalese writer whose plays re-imagine African history in order to recover heroic figures of the past. *The Lodge of the Initiate* (1973) treats traditional customs, especially the initiation associated with circumcision *rituals. Three plays are devoted to the rehabilitation of heroes of anti-colonial resistance: *Albouri's Exile* (1967), *Almamy's Son* (1973), and *Blood for a Throne* (1983).

Two further works, *La Décision* (1967) and *L'Île de Bahila* (1975), treat American history. His work has been performed in many African countries and has earned him a reputation far beyond Senegal.   OD trans. JCM

Neher, Caspar (1897–1962) German *scenographer, whose career was inextricably linked with that of his school friend *Brecht. His first design was for *Kleist's *Heilbronn's Casket* (Berlin, 1923), and his collaborations with Brecht began with *The Life of Edward II* (Munich, 1923) and *Baal* (Berlin, 1926). Thereafter Neher worked closely with Brecht and his disciple *Engel, designing the premières of *In the Jungle of the Cities* (1923) and, most famously, *The Threepenny Opera* (1928). Neher also designed for *Jessner and *Reinhardt, and from 1927 to 1932 was head of design for the municipal theatre in Essen. In the 1930s he began to design for *opera in Vienna and Hamburg. From 1946 to 1949 Neher was at the Zurich Schauspielhaus, working again with Brecht (*Antigone*, 1948); in 1949 they reunited at the *Berliner Ensemble, where Neher designed some of the most famous productions. Characteristic of Neher's style was a spare, anti-*illusionistic stage which stressed use of space rather than pictorial elements. Design elements frequently highlighted theatricality, citing historical styles or genres, sometimes employing projections. The famous, bare, Brechtian stage was largely Neher's invention.   CBB

Nekrošius, Eimuntas (1952–) Lithuanian director. Nekrošius trained in Moscow; back in Vilnius he produced *Love and Death in Verona* (a rock *opera based on *Romeo and Juliet*, 1982) and Aitmatov's *A Day Longer than a Century* (1983). During the 1980s his productions focused on *characters close to death, experiencing a last burst of energy. In *Chekhov's *Uncle Vanya* (1986) and *Three Sisters* (1995) Nekrošius offered fresh readings of plays often crippled by the restraints of psychological *realism. He directed *Pushkin's *Mozart and Salieri* (1994) and *Hamlet* (1997) for the Lithuanian International Theatre Festival. Since 1998 he has headed his own theatre in Vilnius, Menofortas, where he directed *Macbeth* (1999) and *Othello* (2000). His productions impress by their clarity and their closed system of visual references.   BB

Nelson, Richard (1950–) His early plays, *The Killing of Yablonski* (1975), *Conjuring an Event* (1976), and *Jungle Coup* (1978), reflect both Nelson's criticism of American political reportage and his enthusiasm for Sam *Shepard. Later Nelson entered what he called a 'classical' phase

which emphasized elements of *Brecht and *Chekhov to create a more ironic political drama. The first work to appear was *Principia Scriptoriae* (1986), about two political activists who were tortured in a Central American country. It failed in the United States, but won acclaim in a *Royal Shakespeare Company production directed by David *Jones. Since then Nelson has written a series of plays exploring Anglo-American themes which have premièred in Britain, including *Some Americans Abroad* (1989), *Two Shakespearean Actors* (1990), *New England* (1994), *The General from America* (1996), and *Goodnight Children Everywhere* (1997). His adaptations include plays by *Molière, *Strindberg, Chekhov, and *Fo.   JAB

Nemirovich-Danchenko, Vladimir (1858–1943) Russian director, playwright, and *dramaturg. After a period as a critic, he trained actors at the Moscow Philharmonic Society's Institute of Music and Drama (1891–1902). His desire for a contemporary repertoire and better performance standards nurtured a union with *Stanislavsky, and together they founded the *Moscow Art Theatre in 1897. Nemirovich-Danchenko's literary and organizational skills complemented Stanislavsky's success in *acting and *directing. They co-directed many early productions, with Stanislavsky often acting a major role, including the four *Chekhov plays (1898–1904), and *Gorky's *Philistines* and *The Lower Depths* (both 1902). Nemirovich-Danchenko interested Moscow in *Ibsen and *Hauptmann and directed *Julius Caesar* (1903) in a new historical *realist style. His working relationship with Stanislavsky, under strain for several years, broke down as their differences built into opposition, causing Stanislavsky to resign from the MAT board in 1908. Nemirovich-Danchenko directed classic productions at this time, including *Griboedov's *Woe from Wit* (1906), *Pushkin's *Boris Godunov* (1907), and controversial new adaptations of Dostoevsky (*The Brothers Karamazov*, 1910; *Nikolai Stavrogin*, 1913). Nemirovich-Danchenko founded a musical studio at MAT in 1919, producing *operas and *operettas. In the 1930s he brought MAT back into political favour by staging *Gorky (*Egor Bulychov and the Others*, 1934, and the revised *Enemies*, 1935) as models for *socialist realism, but with MAT's exacting standards still in place.   CM

neoclassicism Historical/critical term, describing European drama, literature, and the fine arts that acknowledged the influence of the literary culture of Greece and Rome. A fairly recent coining, it is absent from general dictionaries and from specialist works of reference until about 1930. In its most straightforward use, neoclassicism is interchangeable with 'classicism'—though this term, whose primary meaning was 'suitable for use in the classroom', was adopted only in the mid-eighteenth century. Neoclassicism is largely, though not exclusively, a French phenomenon. Du Bellay (1549) argued that the way to eclipse Italian Renaissance achievement, and establish French literature as the equivalent of the ages of Pericles and Augustus, was through close familiarity with the classical texts and faithful imitation of the models handed down by the ancients.

The head start of Italian theorists and playwrights in both *tragedy and *comedy, was already yielding to French competition; by the end of the 1630s, after the success of *Mairet's *Sophonisbe*, *Corneille's *Médée*, and *Rotrou's *Hercule mourant*, 'regular' tragedy was victorious, based on *Aristotle and his *early modern commentators. Irregular *tragicomedy had had its day, despite the success of Corneille's *Le Cid* (1637); and in his Roman plays from *Horace* (1640), *Cinna* (1640), and *Polyeucte* (1642) onwards, as well as in his theoretical writings, Corneille became his generation's leading practitioner of neoclassical tragedy. Its principal features were a five-act structure closely adhering to the *unities: a single setting (unity of place), a single, closely related series of events (unity of *action), and a concentration of action into a single day (unity of time). The *Greek *chorus had by now been dispensed with; superfluous action took place offstage, and was narrated onstage by servants, messengers, or *confidants of the *protagonists. Lytton Strachey, writing about *Racine's *Bérénice* (1670), called this the aesthetic of 'concentration', by contrast to the Shakespearian aesthetic of 'comprehension' illustrated in *Antony and Cleopatra*. In his historical plays and his adaptations of Greek myth, of which *Phèdre* (1677) stands as the supreme example, Racine exploits the full possibilities of the neoclassical idiom. His contemporary *Molière was able to realize, in the no less testing medium of five-act verse *comedy, a dramatic form capable of expressing both a sophisticated portrait of the society of his own day and a provocative theatre of ideas, as in *The Misanthrope* (1666) or *Tartuffe* (1669).

The cultural imperialism of neoclassicism was the counterpart of the political imperialism of *Richelieu and Louis XIV, for courtier-poets were already flattering the King by comparing the Age of Louis to the Age of Augustus. While the regular tragedy did not go unchallenged in the theatre, the creation of a national theatre (the Théâtre Français, founded in 1680 under royal patronage; *see* COMÉDIE-FRANÇAISE) helped to maintain a hierarchy of genres, in which the popular machine-plays (*see* SALLE DES MACHINES) and other mixed-genre forms took second place to the revivals of seventeenth-century tragic masterpieces. In comedy, the hierarchy was just as rigid, with the 'grandes comédies' (five acts in verse) taking pride of place, even if the public came to prefer the freer compositions of the *Comédie Italienne and the fairground players.

Particularly in tragedy, when we come to the eighteenth century the guiding principles were no longer positive and creative but negative and restrictive, the 'rules' being overshadowed by the dead hand of the *bienséances* (decorum), those conventions which governed what could and could not be shown on stage or expressed in verse. *Voltaire, forward-looking and iconoclastic in his thinking, was nonetheless a fervent supporter of the status quo in drama; he thought the 'ignoble' phrase 'Not a mouse stirring' in *Hamlet* was quite incompatible with the dignity of tragedy.

The dead hand of this aesthetic, hardly challenged at the ultra-conservative Comédie-Française through most of the eighteenth century, was seen in a declamatory *acting style, producing static (even statuesque) delivery; in derivative forms of writing, which shunned any suggestion of local colour in favour of abstract rhetoric; in *costume, where attempts at historical *realism were regularly defeated by leading actors determined to show off their sumptuous wardrobe; and in *mise-en-scène, where any call for greater realism in setting was frustrated by the presence of scores of onstage spectators. However, the stage was freed from spectators in 1759, and the pioneering attitudes to costume of Mlle *Clairon and *Lekain did gradually achieve something of a breakthrough; but the language of tragedy remained an arcane idiom.

Elsewhere in Europe Shakespeare found a more ready acceptance and French cultural imperialism failed to sweep the board. Although the neoclassical formula was exported with some success to other European lands—in *Addison's *Cato*, *Johnson's *Irene*, *Gottsched's *Der sterbende Cato*, or some of the plays of *Maffei and *Alfieri—playwrights and their publics outside France on the whole remained much more eclectic in their choices. While *Goethe, for instance, produced in *Iphigenie* (1787), one of the most perfect neoclassical dramas of his time, his *Götz von Berlichingen* (1773) looked towards Shakespeare to express *Sturm und Drang fervour. *Schiller was likewise capable of writing a play of classical inspiration like *The Bride of Messina* (1803), alongside the sprawling history trilogy *Wallenstein* (1798–9). The cultural relativism of a new generation was to spell the end of the dominance of neoclassicism, even in France. Stendhal's *Racine et Shakespeare* (1823) led to *Hugo's *Préface de Cromwell* (1827), before the final showdown of *Hernani* in 1830. The 'bataille d'*Hernani*' was between two generations: the predominantly conservative establishment of the Comédie-Française and their diehard supporters, versus the young promoters of *romanticism who succeeded in carrying the day (*see* RIOTS). Henceforward, dramatists might choose to write on 'classical' subjects, from Ponsard in *Lucrèce* (1843) down to *Cocteau in *La Machine infernale* (1934) and *Anouilh in *Antigone* (1944), but the idiom of French neoclassical tragedy would never be resurrected.   WDH

Nesbitt, Cathleen (1888–1982) English actress who first distinguished herself in 1912 with the *Abbey Irish Players, appearing in New York and London in *Synge and *Yeats, and as Perdita in Granville *Barker's *The Winter's Tale*. During the First World War she acted in the USA, taking on roles in *Galsworthy and *Shaw, and returned to London in 1919 to play the lead in *Webster's *The Duchess of Malfi*. In the 1920s she performed mainly in modern works, and in 1935 played Katherine in *The Taming of the Shrew*. She *toured in Shakespeare with the *Old Vic in 1939, and in 1940 played Goneril in *Gielgud's *King Lear*. During the Second World War she performed in England, but in 1950 shifted to America for the next two decades, notably in plays by *Eliot and *Williams. On occasion she returned to London, appearing, for example, in Robin Maugham's *The Claimant* (1964). She continued to act into her nineties.   TP

Nestroy, Johann Nepomuk (1801–62) Austrian actor and dramatist, who made his debut in 1822 as Sarastro in *Mozart's *The Magic Flute* in Vienna. Following successful engagements abroad as a singer, he returned to Vienna in 1831, where he quickly established himself as a popular comedian in the suburban theatres. His coarse and aggressive *acting affronted *bourgeois *audiences, however, and political authorities repeatedly intervened against his poignant criticism of Church and state. To avoid *censorship, he became a master of the extempore, for which he was several times imprisoned. He began writing plays in order to provide himself and his associates with adequate roles, and following the success of *The Evil Spirit Lumpazivagabundus* (1832) he became the most popular playwright in Vienna. Displeasure with the censor's interven-

tions into his texts forced him into dangerous high-wire acts of *improvisation and *mime, which made him an idol of the opposition forces before the 1848 Revolution. Nestroy's plays are full of caustic caricatures and acerbic commentaries on social ills. He was an astute observer of class and the effects of industrialization, with skill in both Viennese dialect and literary language. Nestroy keenly observed the 1848 Revolution and exposed the political immaturity of the Viennese bourgeoisie in the *satirical *comedy *Freedom Comes to Krähwinkel*. Following the defeat of the revolution, he wrote some of his most melancholic works, including the bleak, dystopian *farce *Chief Zephyr; or, The Gruesome Banquet*. Of his more than 80 plays about a dozen are still regularly performed, including *The Talisman*, *The Girl from the Suburbs*, *Einen Jux will er sich machen* (adapted by *Wilder as *The Merchant of Yonkers* and *The Matchmaker*, and by *Stoppard as *On the Razzle*), and *The Old Man with the Young Wife*.   GB

Nethersole, Olga (1863/1870–1951) English actress and *manager. First appearing in London in 1887, she gravitated toward the roles of fallen or unconventional women, beginning with a revival of *Sardou's *Diplomacy* in 1893. During the 1890s and 1900s she managed several London theatres for short periods, often performing plays by *Dumas *fils*, *Sudermann, and *Pinero. Her success as an emotional actress in siren roles carried her to New York, where she was arrested in 1900 for the supposed moral indecency of Clyde *Fitch's *Sappho*. She won an acquittal and much fame, which made her a star in both New York and London. She retired in 1914.   TP

Neuber, Caroline (Weisenborn) (1697–1760) German actress and *manager. The daughter of a lawyer, she eloped with the student Johann Neuber in 1717 to join an itinerant theatre troupe, eventually establishing their own company in Leipzig. Between 1727 and 1737 she was closely associated with *Gottsched and together they initiated one of the most important reform projects in German theatre, directed initially against the debased dramatic forms of the time. Neuber devoted her energies to improving the status of actors as well as purifying the repertoire. In 1737 she symbolically banned Hanswurst from the stage by burning a *puppet dressed as the comic figure. The gesture had more symbolic than immediate consequences, however; after falling out with Gottsched her influence waned and her troupe fell into disfavour. She died impoverished and largely forgotten.   CBB

Neville, John (1925–) English actor and director. At the *Old Vic, he notably alternated as Iago and Othello with *Burton (1955), played Romeo to Claire *Bloom's Juliet (1956), and Hamlet with Judi *Dench as Ophelia (1958). In the 1960s he worked at Nottingham Playhouse as actor, associate producer (1961–3), and joint director (1963–7). After moving to Canada in 1972, he became director of the Citadel Theatre, Edmonton (1973), where he invited Peggy *Ashcroft to appear in *Beckett's *Happy Days* (1977). He became director of the Neptune Theatre, Halifax (1978), and *artistic director of the *Stratford Festival (1986–9), where his productions included *Hamlet* (1986), *Mother Courage* (1987), and *The Three Sisters* (1989). His long film career included the title role in Terry Gilliam's *The Adventures of Baron Munchausen* (1988).   VRS

New Comedy The *comedy of Greece and Rome from the late fourth to the second century BC. *Greek New Comedy emerged from the *Middle Comedy of the fourth century with the work of *Menander, but so vague is the nature of the transitional period that some commentators choose to refer only to *Old Comedy (fifth century BC Athens), and New Comedy (anything after the defeat of Athens in the Peloponnesian War in 404 BC). That the war had brought an effective end to political comedy is beyond dispute, for Menander's world is one where the central issues are those of family life. Plots revolve around love affairs and marriage; disputes over children and their legitimacy; misunderstandings over relationships. The location is usually Athens or the countryside of Attica, and the *characters are recognizable types distinguished in the main by age, class, and gender. Gods are reduced to the occasional *prologue and the *chorus to entr'actes which the manuscripts omit. Though still acted in *masks and, for the most part, in the Theatre of *Dionysus now rebuilt in stone, the range of situation and character is both complex and subtle, allowing for pathos and even tragic potential.

After the death of Menander's rival Philemon in about 263 BC, New Comedy in Greece went into stagnation. It re-emerged in Rome with the work of *Plautus (c.250–184 BC) and *Terence (193 or 183–159 BC), both writing in Latin. Twenty plays of Plautus have survived, more than from any other playwright in the ancient world, and all six of those written by Terence, who drowned when still quite young. Both playwrights confessedly adapted their work from Greek Middle and New Comedy originals anything up to 200 years old. This *Roman comedy was known as *fabula palliata*, 'comedy wearing the pallium', a short Greek cloak. The plays were set in Greece or a Greek city; the characters are Greek and live according to a Greek morality, in strong contrast to the staid and respectable world of the Roman Republic; even the metre and the ethos are Greek with 'citizens' meaning Athenians, anyone else being foreigners.

But there are many aspects of Plautus and Terence which are wholly un-Greek. The plays were presented on makeshift stages—no permanent theatre was allowed in Rome until the first century BC—during Roman public festivals. They vied for attention with the alternative attractions of the fairground. There is a strong colouring from Roman public life; there are *metatheatrical in-jokes; and especially a love of words and wordplay with puns, alliteration and, despite the metrical form, the argot of the street. In other ways Plautus and Terence are very different. Plautus was a writer of *farces with a strong enough *musical content for some to consider him the founder of comic *opera. Still performed in masks, they provide one strand of the Italian street tradition which would eventually turn into the improvised comedy of the *commedia dell'arte*. Terence wrote more Menandrian comedy, less broad and with hardly any *slapstick, but his characters are living and breathing. In the fourteenth century Petrarch revived the study of Terence, and an enthusiasm for both Terence and Plautus was confirmed by the rediscovery of a missing Plautine manuscript in 1428 and the commentary on Terence by Donatus five years later. Performances in translation were regularly presented at the court at Ferrara and, together with the *commedia dell'arte*, provided a platform for the whole European tradition of physical and character comedy.   JMW

Newton, Christopher (1936–) English-Canadian actor and director. After acting in *regional theatres, in New York, and for three seasons with the *Stratford Festival, in 1968 he was appointed founding *artistic director of Theatre Calgary. In 1973 he moved to the Vancouver Playhouse, where he revitalized the artistic fortunes of the company and established a prestigious training school. He was artistic director of the *Shaw Festival (1979–2002), where he developed a highly skilled acting ensemble dedicated to the plays of *Shaw and his contemporaries. There Newton became a leading interpreter of Shaw and *Coward, having directed at least twenty of their plays, including Shaw's *Misalliance* (1980, 1990), *St Joan* (1991), *Caesar and Cleopatra* (1993 and 2002), *Heartbreak House* (1985), *You Never Can Tell* (1988 and 1995), *Man and Superman* (1989), *Pygmalion* (1992), and *The Doctor's Dilemma* (2000). In 2002 he resumed a freelance career, but has returned to the Shaw Festival to direct *Hankin's *The Cassilis Engagement* (2008) and other works.   DWJ

New York Shakespeare Festival/Joseph Papp Public Theatre

American company, the brainchild and lifetime project of Joseph *Papp, who first brought a group of actors together as the Shakespeare Workshop in 1954. In 1956 the renamed New York Shakespeare Festival presented free outdoor performances in the East River Park, which expanded to productions of Shakespeare around all five boroughs of New York, transporting sets and actors in a flatbed truck. In 1962 the company opened its first *playhouse, the Delacorte Theatre, in Central Park. Wanting to expand repertoire, Papp discovered the Astor Library on Lafayette Street, which had fallen into disuse and was scheduled for demolition. He persuaded the city to declare it a landmark, and it opened as the Public Theatre in 1967. Its first production, the *musical *Hair*, was a huge success and transferred to Broadway.

Papp was interested in nurturing new talents from diverse backgrounds, and the Public became a haven for young playwrights, composers, directors, and actors. Papp championed the work of writers *Rabe, *Guare, *Shange, and Miguel Pinero; actors Meryl Streep, Kevin *Kline, and Mandy Patinkin; and directors A. J. Antoon, and Michael *Bennett. Bennett's musical about Broadway dancers, *A Chorus Line*, premièred at the Public in 1975 and ran on Broadway for fifteen years, providing *financial stability for the Public. Throughout the 1980s Papp continued his spirited if idiosyncratic programming, founding an annual celebration of Latin American writing talent, Festival Latino, and producing a number of groundbreaking and lucrative shows including Larry Kramer's seminal AIDS play *The Normal Heart* (1985), and *The Pirates of Penzance* (1980). In 1990, secretly suffering from prostate cancer, Papp reorganized the theatre, appointing JoAnne *Akalaitis his artistic associate. After Papp's death, Akalaitis took over the theatre, but her reign was troubled, and she was succeeded by George C. *Wolfe in 1993, who effected a high-profile and sometimes controversial programme. Oskar Eustis assumed the helm in 2005. Shakespeare in the Park continues as a New York summer institution.   KF

Ngema, Mbongeni

(1955–) South African actor, playwright, and director, born in Natal. He began his career as a guitarist in the theatre, and his first play, *The Last Generation* (1978), was produced at the Stable Theatre in Durban. While working for Gibson *Kente, he met Percy Mtwa

and created *Woza Albert!* (1981) with him and Barney *Simon. Moving to the Market Theatre in Johannesburg, he created *Asinamali!* (*We Have No Money*, 1985) a *musical exploration of township rent strikes. *Sarafina* (1986), which celebrated the spirit of South African youth, was produced internationally. He unsuccessfully attempted *community theatre with *Sarafina 2* (1987), an AIDS play. In *Maria, Maria* (1997) he created a musical mixing the Christ story with that of Steve Biko. His latest work is *The House of Shaka* (2006).   YH

Nichols, Mike

(1931–) American director, *producer, and actor with six Tony awards for best director between 1964 and 1984, for *Simon's *Barefoot in the Park*, *The Odd Couple*, *Plaza Suite*, and *The Prisoner of Second Avenue*, Murray Schisgal's *Luv*, *Stoppard's *The Real Thing*, and an Oscar for best director (*The Graduate*, 1967). Fleeing from Nazi Germany with his family at the age of 8, he studied with *Strasberg, and in 1955 formed an *improvisational comedy troupe called the Compass Players (later Second City), whose members included Elaine *May and Alan Arkin. *An Evening with Mike Nichols and Elaine May* (Broadway, 1960) brought socio political *satire and wry observations about the sexes to a mainstream *audience. Though he is chiefly known for his success with *comedy, Nichols also directed serious works like *Rabe's *Streamers* and *Griffiths's *Comedians* (both 1976). *Albee's *Who's Afraid of Virginia Woolf?* starring Elizabeth Taylor and Richard *Burton was his film debut; other work includes *Beckett's *Waiting for Godot* on Broadway (1988). Nichols occasionally returned to acting, as in *The Designated Mourner* by Wallace *Shawn (London, 1997).   GAO

Nichols, Peter

(1927–) English playwright. Nichols acted in *regional theatre before turning to television and film writing (including the script for *Georgy Girl*, 1966). His first play, *A Day in the Death of Joe Egg* (1967), was a hugely successful black *comedy on the unlikely topic of a couple with a brain-damaged child. His next, commissioned by *Tynan, was *The National Health* (1969), a *parody of television soap operas tinged with an underlying bitterness. *Forget-Me-Not Lane* (1971), a nostalgic family drama, has proven a continuing success with regional theatres. Nichols struggled with *Chez Nous* (1974) and *The Freeway* (1974), but returned to success with the *musical *Privates on Parade* (1977), based on his RAF experiences in Malaysia. *Passion Play* (1981), produced by the *Royal Shakespeare Company, was also a hit and his second musical, *Poppy* (1983), a parody Victorian *panto-mime, centred on the opium wars in China. Nichols gave up playwriting for novels in 1983, but returned to the stage in 1987 with *A Piece of my Mind*, about a novelist with writer's block.   MDG

Ninagawa Yukio (1935-) Japanese director. Ninagawa began as a painter but became an actor after seeing a production of *Abe Kōbō's *The Uniform*. He founded the Contemporary People's Theatre in Tokyo in 1968 and made his directorial debut the following year with *Shimizu Kunio's *Sincere Frivolity*. During the 1960s and early 1970s, Ninagawa's work (frequently with Shimizu) was experimental and politically engaged, but since 1974 he has won a reputation for his commercial productions, often for the Tōhō Group, of Shakespeare and *Greek *tragedy. His productions of *Medea* (1979), *Macbeth* (1980), and *The Tempest* (1987) have *toured abroad to great acclaim. At the same time, he has been active cultivating younger talent with his Ninagawa Company. He also continues to direct contemporary Japanese drama, by Shimizu, *Akimoto, *Mishima, *Kara, and *Terayama. His English-language production of Shimizu's *Tango at the End of Winter* premièred at the *Edinburgh Festival in 1991. Ninagawa regularly stages productions in London, including *Midsummer Night's Dream* (1994), *Hamlet* (1995), *King Lear* (in English for the *Royal Shakespeare Company, 1999), *Pericles* (2005), *Coriolanus* (2007) and *Twelfth Night* (2009). His productions are distinguished by their innovative and spectacular staging; designer *Asakura frequently works with him. He has also directed *opera, notably *The Flying Dutchman* (1992), and an English-language production of *Peer Gynt* in 1994. *See also* INTERCULTURALISM.   CP

nō (noh) Japanese theatrical tradition which combines poetic texts, *dance, and *music with elaborate *costumes and simple props. Developed from earlier performing arts by *Kan'ami and *Zeami in the fourteenth and fifteenth centuries, nō maintains an unbroken performance tradition. The nō stage, a small architectural gem with an austere beauty uncompromised by scenery, developed in the seventeenth century. It is a raised and roofed structure, about 6 m (20 feet) square, with ceramic jugs strategically placed underneath the highly polished floor to add resonance to foot stamps. The back wall is decorated with the painting of a large pine tree, in front of which is a small area used by instrumentalists. At stage left another small area holds the *chorus. A bridgeway, approximately 2 m by 10 m

(5 by 33 feet), leads obliquely from rear stage right to a curtained exit into the dressing rooms and serves as a secondary performing area. After any large props are carried in by stage attendants, the musicians and the chorus (eight to ten *shite* actors) enter the stage before the *waki*, the secondary actor who generally introduces himself and travels to the site of the play's *action.

Most plays are in two acts: the first introduces a narrative—the establishment of a shrine, the death of a warrior, the loss of a loved one—and the second presents some part or result of that story. A single player, normally the *shite*, performs most of the action and is the visual centre of interest. He is garbed in a large, brightly coloured costume and a carved, wooden *mask, both of which may be of museum quality. The *shite*, however, is always surrounded by supporting performers, a large number for such a small stage, and it is the interaction among the entire ensemble that creates the power and the beauty of the performance. Nō plays rarely focus on *character development or dramatic conflict; rather they explore an emotion (love, anguish, longing, regret, resentment); celebrate deities, poetry, longevity, fertility, or harmony; or exorcize external or internal ghosts and demons. Some plays feature a supernatural being or the *ghost of a human recalling its life on earth; others present real (but sometimes deranged) people living in the dramatic present. Nō plays are divided into five categories—deities, warriors, women, miscellaneous (including most living-people plays), and demons or strong characters—and one play from each group made up a traditional, formal programme with four *kyōgen plays performed between the nō. Since the Second World War, however, programmes have been shortened drastically, sometimes to a single nō play. The current nō repertory contains approximately 250 plays.

Nō texts are expressed in music and dance. A flute and two or three drums play in all nō performances. Drummers play two types of hand drums and one larger stick drum and issue calls (*yo*, *ho*, *yoi*), whose quality helps establish the mood of a piece and whose precise placement in the drum patterns is an important means of controlling the rhythm. A chorus chants large portions of the text, which may describe and comment on the settings and the characters' actions or feelings. *Dialogue plays a relatively minor role: the chorus sometimes speaks in the first person for a character; an actor is not restricted to remaining in character, and two actors or the *shite* and the chorus often share lines. All movement is choreographed, and the *shite* often dances during the chanting of the most intense sections of the text and usually performs a dance to instrumental music. Professional performers (approximately 1,500 actors and musicians currently) undergo intensive training from childhood to early adulthood, and the discipline and control they develop are widely admired by their Western counterparts. To augment their performance fees, most performers give lessons in nō chanting and dancing to amateurs, who in turn constitute a dedicated *audience.

Because the stage is sparsely decorated, costumes and masks provide most of the colour and visual beauty as well as indicating the age, gender, social status, and nature of the characters. Many hand props are used, including swords, branches, and letters, and the *shite* and *waki* carry spreadtip fans which may be used to pour sake, represent the wind, or point out the moon.

In the twentieth century nō became an international art, its players performing throughout the world and playwrights using nō in new compositions, from *Brecht's *Der Jasager* and *Yeats's *At the Hawk's Well* to *Mishima's modern nō plays. In Japan traditional nō attracts large crowds at outdoor, torchlight performances, and in the twenty-first century elements of nō have entered Japanese pop culture in comics, animations, and youthful fashions.   KWB

Noble, Adrian (1950–) English director. Noble began working at the *Royal Shakespeare Company in 1980, and was its *artistic director from 1991 to 2003. Almost all his work since 1982 was for the company, with large-scale projects including *The Plantagenets* (from Shakespeare's histories) and *Sophocles' Theban plays. He was responsible for *Branagh's first RSC season and for reviving the career of Robert *Stephens (Falstaff in 1991 and King Lear in 1993). Unafraid of the largest stages, Noble created emotionally powerful productions within the traditions of British classical theatre. His control of the RSC in difficult economic circumstances removed the last traces of its leftist political image. Noble sought to attract new family *audiences (*The Lion, the Witch and the Wardrobe*, 1998). His reorganization of the RSC in 2001 abandoned the tradition of ensemble *repertory in favour of project-based companies, new funding partnerships, and plans for new theatres for Stratford. He resigned as artistic director after successful reviews for his West End production of *Chitty Chitty Bang Bang* (2002).   PDH

Noda Hideki (1955–) Japanese playwright, director, and actor. In 1976 he established his own theatre company, Yume no Yuminsha (Dream Idlers), while still an undergraduate at Tokyo University. With their colourful sets, frenetic athleticism, and speedy delivery, Noda's fragmented and irreverent productions were a hallmark of the hedonistic spirit of the Japanese bubble economy of the 1980s. His plays are typically *surrealistic pastiches of elements derived from Japanese and Western popular culture, filled with gags, pratfalls, and puns. Watching one of his plays has been compared to channel surfing. His productions for Dream Idlers include *The Prisoner of Zenda* (1981) and *Descent of the Brutes* (1982); *Comet Messenger Siegfried* (1985) and *Half a God* (1986) have been performed in Europe and the USA. In 1992, Noda disbanded the Dream Idlers and took a sabbatical in England, returning the following year to found a new company called Noda Map. Recent productions include *Taboo* (1996). Noda is also famous for his riotous versions of Shakespeare and *kabuki. *The Bee*, written in English with playwright Colin Teevan, was staged in London in 2007.   CP

Noer, Arifin C. (1941–c.1996) Indonesian playwright, filmmaker, and director. Best known for his masterwork *Moths* (1970), Arifin was a major influence on late twentieth-century theatre, television, and film. In the 1960s he worked with *Rendra's Bengkel (Workshop) Teater and Teater Muslim in Yogyakarta. In 1968 he founded Teater Kecil (Little Theatre). He produced regularly at TIM, the art centre in Jakarta, doing both Western plays like *Caligula* and *Macbeth* and his own works like *Beloved Grandmother*, *Ozone* (set in a post-apocalyptic future), and *The Bottomless Well* (1964, 1989). His 25 scripts combined metaphysics, poetry, and deep self-questioning of society in the Suharto era. *Moths*, which has been performed internationally, is a *surreal play dealing with the light and darkness of human nature. Films include *Suci, the Prima Donna* (1977) and *The Dawn* (1982).   KFO

Nomura Manzō VI (1898–1978) *Kyōgen actor of the *Izumi school. The eldest son of Nomura Manzō V, Manzō VI succeeded to the Nomura family headship in 1922 (Nomura Manzō I was active in the early 1700s). In 1920 Manzō VI joined his father and younger brother in founding the kyōgen performance series Yoiya-kai which produced some 200 all-kyōgen shows to 1944. In the post-war period Manzō organized three performance series that showcased his talents and those of his three sons. Early in his career his *acting was known for its rigidity and strictness, but it later evolved into a witty, unconstrained style. He garnered fans and supporters from many quarters and was largely responsible for the pre-eminence of his family in Tokyo kyōgen. LRK

Norman, Marsha (1947-) American playwright. Jon *Jory directed *Getting Out* (*Actors Theatre of Louisville, 1977), about an ex-convict who makes peace with her violent younger self, and *Third and Oak* (1978) about loss. In *'night, Mother* (1982, Pulitzer Prize), a mother fails to prevent her middle-aged daughter's suicide; it has been produced in 36 countries and 23 languages. For the next eight years her new work, treating comedy, myth, and religious scepticism, was seen at American *regional theatres (*The Holdup*, 1983; *Traveler in the Dark*, 1984; *Sarah and Abraham*, 1988). Norman returned to Broadway with books for the *musicals *The Secret Garden* (1991), *The Red Shoes* (1993), and *The Color Purple* (2005). She complained that she could not get a straight play accepted unless Jory had commissioned it. Jory did present *Loving Daniel Boone* (1992) and *Trudy Blue* (1995), which succeeded in New York in 1999. FL

Norton, Thomas *See* SACKVILLE, THOMAS.

Novello, Ivor (David Ivor Davies) (1893-1951) Welsh composer, actor, dramatist, and impresario celebrated for his stylish performances and glamorous image as much as for his popular songs and romantic *musicals. In 1914 he wrote one of the First World War's most popular standards, 'Keep the Home Fires Burning', and 'We'll Gather Lilacs' (1945) was a similarly successful response to the next war. After serving in the Royal Naval Air Service he made his acting debut in *Duburau* (1921) in London, and subsequently became an *actor-manager, beginning with *The Rat* (1924). His many other plays include *Symphony in Two Flats* (1929) and *The Truth Game* (1930). Novello's musicals have simple, often *melodramatic plots, and lush and sentimental scores; they include *Glamorous Night* (1935), *Careless Rapture* (1936), *Crest of a Wave* (1937), *The Dancing Years* (1939), *Arc de Triomphe* (1943), *Perchance to Dream* (1945), and *King's Rhapsody* (1949). Novello also wrote original and adapted screenplays and acted in several films. AS

Novo, Salvador (1904-74) Mexican playwright, director, poet, and novelist. As a member of the experimental Teatro de Ulises (1928), he sought to modernize the Mexican stage. A translator of *O'Neill, *Beckett, and *Synge, Novo was appointed the first director of the theatre section of the National Institute of Fine Arts in 1947. His first significant play was *The Cultured Lady* (1951), a vitriolic *satire of Mexican high society. *At Eight Columns* (1956) is a critique of the press and *The Third Faust* (1956) is one of the first Mexican plays to deal openly with homosexuality. KFN

Nowra, Louis (1950-) Australian playwright. Nowra's earlier plays, such as *The Precious Woman* (1980), are historical fantasies set outside but still relevant to Australia. Later work focused on contemporary predicaments shaped by historical traumas, such as the effects of colonization—particularly for indigenous Australians—and class oppression, best exemplified in *The Golden Age* (1985). A prolific decade in the 1990s saw the production of semi-autobiographical *comedies such as *Cosi* (1992), Aboriginal-centred dramas such as *Radiance* (1993), and plays such as *The Temple* (1993) which offered *satires of contemporary situations. The 'Boyce Trilogy' (*The Woman with Dog's Eyes*, *The Marvellous Boy*, and *The Emperor of Sydney*) concluded in 2006. Nowra has also written for film, television, radio, and *opera. SBS

Ntshona, Winston (1941-) South African actor. Ntshona was working in the Ford plant when *Kani introduced him to *Fugard in 1967, and by 1972 was a full-time professional performer. Classified as Fugard's domestic workers, Ntshona and Kani workshopped *Sizwe Bansi Is Dead* (1972) and *The Island* (1973) with him, based on their personal experiences of apartheid South Africa. The two were imprisoned in the Transkei for remarks criticizing the government's 'Bantustan policy' of total separation of blacks in *Statements after an Arrest under the Immorality Act* (1972), but released under pressure from Europe. YH

Nuñez, José Gabriel (1937-) Venezuelan playwright, screenwriter, and economist. His most important works are *I Remain the Same* (1963), *The Bat Route* (1964), *Fish in the Aquarium* (1967), *Bang bang* (1968), *You Want the Tiger to Eat Me* (1975), *Madame pompinette* (1980) and *Maria Cristina Wants to Rule Me* (1989). His dramatic world abounds with alienated people fighting a battle of wits to maintain their dignity. He draws on *realism, the *absurd, *epic theatre, and the folkloric approach to manners and customs, always with a touch of black humour. LCL trans. AMCS

Nunn, Trevor (1940-) English director. Nunn joined *Hall's *Royal Shakespeare Company early in his career, making his mark with *The Revenger's Tragedy* (1966), succeeding Hall in 1968 as *artistic director, a role he shared with *Hands after 1978 and gave up in 1986. Under Nunn the company moved into the Barbican Theatre as its

London home and developed two new spaces in Stratford (the Other Place and the *Swan Theatre). His own work showed an ability to adapt to every kind of space: his small-scale *Macbeth* (1976) was an intense study of the working of evil, while he rescued the company from *financial disaster with an eight-hour, two-part, spectacular version of *Nicholas Nickleby* (1980) that explored the social conditions of Victorian England in a *Dickensian spirit. He was just as adept in establishing large-scale Shakespeare projects (such as the season of Roman plays in 1972) as in turning *The Comedy of Errors* into a *musical in 1976.

Hands's presence enabled him to work outside the RSC. His commercial productions of *Lloyd Webber's *Cats* (1981) and *Starlight Express* (1984), and of *Boublil and Schönberg's *Les Misérables* (1985), established a new model for theatre as a global product, with mountings all over the world obliged to reproduce his version exactly (*see also* MACKINTOSH, CAMERON). If his work in classical theatre was never marked by innovation, the invention, freshness, and commercial acuity of these productions redefined musical theatre

(and made Nunn by far the richest English director). It also provided a model for successful work in *opera (*Porgy and Bess*, Glyndebourne, 1986). Returning to Shakespeare for *Othello* (RSC, 1989), Nunn moved far from the broad strokes of his musical work by developing the style of minute social *realism he had used for *Porgy and Bess*, locating the play in a precise milieu and filling it with carefully observed social detail. Musicals apart, Nunn showed only limited interest in new work, though he directed the première of *Stoppard's *Arcadia* (1993). In 1997 he was a surprising choice to succeed *Eyre as artistic director of the *National Theatre, where he tried to recreate the RSC's ensemble company. His own success with small-scale Shakespeare (*The Merchant of Venice*, 1999) and large-scale musicals (*My Fair Lady*, 2001) continued the best of his previous work but his regime was marked by a narrow repertoire and a failure to encourage young directors or writers. He stepped down in 2003 and since then directed both Shakespeare (*King Lear* with Ian *McKellen in 2007) and new plays (Stoppard's *Rock 'n' Roll*, 2007).   PDH

O

Oakley, Annie (1860–1926) American sharp-shooter, who learned her skills providing game for restaurants near her Ohio home. As a young girl she defeated professional shooter Frank Butler. Eventually they married and he became her *manager. The diminutive performer joined Buffalo Bill *Cody's *Wild West show in 1885. Known as 'Little Sureshoot', a name given her by her friend and fellow Wild West star Sitting Bull, one of her tricks involved shooting holes in playing cards; by association, punched complimentary passes came to be known as 'Annie Oakleys'. With brief interruptions when she appeared in action-oriented *melodramas, Oakley *toured with the Wild West show for seventeen seasons until a disastrous 1901 railway accident, though she continued to perform occasionally over the next twenty years. Her career inspired the Irving *Berlin *musical *Annie Get your Gun* (1946). RAH

Oberammergau At the beginning of each decade between May and September the villagers of Oberammergau in Bavaria mount approximately 100 performances of a *Passion play that lasts all day, in fulfilment of a pledge made in 1633. The first texts have not survived. In 1750 Ferdinand Rosner produced a baroque drama in rhyming couplets which remained in use until the early nineteenth century. In 1811 a new prose version by Othmar Weiss created a form in which dramatized *dialogue alternated with *tableaux illustrating the central moments of the Passion. Weiss depicted the Jews in a harsh light, making them responsible for Christ's death. This interpretation survived the 1860 revision by Daisenberger, the version which remained current until 2000, when a new text purged of all anti-Jewish sentiments was produced. The first performances presumably took place in the parish church and after 1700 on a temporary open-air stage. After 1800 a *perspective stage was constructed which remained in use until the end of the century. The present theatre was built in 1920–9 and retains an outside stage, while the spectators sit in a covered *auditorium holding up to 4,700. By the end of the nineteenth century the play had already become a major tourist attraction, a function which has increasingly replaced its religious significance. CBB

Obey, André (1892–1975) French dramatist. In Paris from 1919, he wrote music and drama criticism. After writing two plays with Denys Amiel, he met *Copeau, whose skill at blending physicality and poetry influenced Obey's subsequent style. Obey's best plays resulted from his collaborative work with Copeau and disciples; *Noé*, *Le Viol de Lucrèce*, and *La Bataille de la Marne* were all produced at the Théâtre du Vieux-Colombier in 1931. His *Eight Hundred Metres* (1941) was performed in a *sports stadium. Obey wrote three plays about Don Juan and translated or adapted works of *Aeschylus, Shakespeare, and *Williams. As director of the *Comédie-Française (1945–7), he initiated reforms to allow production of contemporary works. Obey's skill at *mime-based storytelling is said to have influenced both *Barrault and *Wilder. FHL

Obolensky, Chloe (1942–) Greek *scenographer who studied in Paris. She designed *Aristophanes' *Frogs* (directed by *Koun, Athens, 1967) and *Verdi's *Aida* (*Zeffirelli, Milan), and productions at the *Comedie-Française and the Spoleto Festival with Gian Carlo Menotti. She is especially noted for her extensive work with *Brook in Paris, including *The Cherry Orchard*, *The Tragedy of Carmen* (both 1981), *The Mahabharata* (1985, film 1989), *The Tempest* (1990), *Impressions of Pelléas* (1992), *Don Giovanni*, and *Hamlet* (2000). Her simplicity of colour and objects has been particularly suited to Brook's work. She has also designed the *opera *La Dame de Picques* (directed by *Dodin, Paris, 1998) and *Chekhov's *The Seagull* (Dodin, St Petersburg, 2001). PH

O'Brien, Timothy (1929–) English designer. Born in India, he studied history at Cambridge and design at Yale with *Oenslager. Not interested in *realism, he created kinetic stage units that evolve as working symbols of thematic concerns. His collaborations with Tazeena Firth at the *Royal Shakespeare Company in the 1960s and 1970s include *Richard II* (1973): two giant escalators conveying the hapless king offered a visual metaphor for his loss of power. *Evita* (1978) combined projection and mobile units into a self described 'machine for presenting a play'. The tumult of *War and Peace* (St Petersburg, 1991) was suggested by hinged walls, which reconfigured the stage and contrasted with an enduring Russian oak. For the endless journey of *Outis* (La Scala, 1996), monolithic figures disappeared and appeared from the void of the revolve.   RVL

O'Casey, Sean (1880–1964) Irish playwright. The alliance of the socialist Irish Citizen Army with the nationalist Volunteers disillusioned him with the 1916 Easter Rising, political views reflected in the three Dublin plays that brought him international success. *The Shadow of a Gunman* (*Abbey, 1923) made an immediate impact with its comic vignettes of Dublin slum life and its tragic background of the just-ended Irish War of Independence. *Juno and the Paycock* (1924), set during the Irish Civil War (1922–3), provided major roles for Sara *Allgood and Barry *Fitzgerald with its mixture of *melodrama and *character *comedy. *The Plough and the Stars* (1926), O'Casey's version of the Easter Rising itself, was felt to be intolerably provocative in its anti-heroic perspective. Once again, as with *Synge's *Playboy*, *Yeats for the Abbey *management vehemently defended the play.

O'Casey's situation at the Abbey changed with the humiliating rejection of his next play, *The Silver Tassie*, in 1928: the irascible O'Casey quarrelled loudly and publicly with the management and cut his links with the Irish theatre. Though the experimental *Silver Tassie*, with its *expressionist dramatization of the Flanders trenches, had a *succès d'estime* in London in 1929 with *Laughton, and the more fully expressionist *Within the Gates* (1934) was well received in New York, for the rest of his long life O'Casey never regained an assured position as a working dramatist in any theatre. His later plays, including *Red Roses for Me* (1943), *Cock-a-Doodle Dandy* (1949), and *The Drums of Father Ned* (1959), were fantastic in idiom, promoting a fervently socialist and anticlerical utopianism.   NG

Odéon The Théâtre de l'Odéon, as it became in 1797, was originally built as the Théâtre-Français (*see* COMÉDIE-FRANÇAISE) by de Wailly and Peyre on the site of the former Hôtel de Condé. Opened in 1782, it was the first *playhouse in Paris to be conceived as a significant free-standing architectural entity and the central feature of a major urban redevelopment. The building was enclosed by an open arcade, and from each side of its

majestic Doric pillared façade bridges led to cafés incorporated into adjacent pavilions. Its circular *auditorium accommodated four tiers of *boxes, set in slight retreat, and—for the first time—a seated pit. Twice destroyed by fire, in 1799 and 1818, and twice rebuilt, by Chalgrin in 1808 and Baraguey and Provost in 1819, the Odéon, now the Odéon-Théâtre de l'Europe, still stands and, if bereft of its original setting, retains much of its original monumental austerity.   JG

Odeon Ancient *Greek 'music hall'. The best known was in Athens, next to the Theatre of *Dionysus, and was built by Pericles and used for recitations of all kinds but also for other public functions. The term is used generally for the smaller roofed theatres that developed in Hellenistic times from the *ecclesiasterion* or assembly room; these were suitable for more intimate musical, rhetorical, and dramatic functions. However, very large roofed or partially roofed music halls were then constructed in many cities under the *Roman empire, such as the Odeon of Herodes Atticus in Athens and the Odeon of Domitian in Rome.   WJS

Odets, Clifford (1906–63) American playwright and director. Odets burst onto the New York scene in 1935 with four plays on Broadway. *Waiting for Lefty* was an hour-long episodic play which used the flashback technique to dramatize reasons behind the New York cab drivers' strike of 1934. Its *Group Theatre production was rapturously received by its left-wing *audience and it transferred to Broadway, paired with *Till the Day I Die*, an anti-Nazi one-act hastily readied by Odets. But a month before *Lefty* got to Broadway, Odets's *Awake and Sing!*—a *realistic drama about a working-class Bronx family—opened there (in February), and in December *Paradise Lost*, a *character driven family drama, appeared in the theatre which had just housed *Lefty*. Success brought Hollywood offers, and Odets would remain a Hollywood-based writer for the rest of his life. The Group produced three more plays, including *Golden Boy* (1937), before their 1940 dissolution, but Odets's relationship with them was strained. *The Country Girl* (1950), about an alcoholic actor and his salvific wife, and *The Flowering Peach* (1954), a retelling of the Noah myth, were commercial successes in Broadway productions directed by Odets.   MAF

Odin Teatret *See* BARBA, EUGENIO.

Oenslager, Donald (1902–75) American *scenographer and teacher. Oenslager first came into notice as a protégé of *Baker, who later hired him as design teacher at the newly founded Yale School of Drama (1925). Oenslager balanced professional careers as Broadway set and *lighting designer and teacher throughout his life. A follower of Robert Edmond *Jones, he designed for early experimental groups and later for *regional theatre and the Metropolitan Opera. Known for his ability to design *box sets that reflected the personalities of their inhabitants in their psychological detail, he was sought after by *Kaufman, *Kanin, *Hart, *Connelly, and other contemporary playwrights. He also designed *musicals and *revues: *Anything Goes* (1934), *Red, Hot, and Blue!* (1936), and *Three to Make Ready* (1946). Among his most notable achievements were *Of Mice and Men* (1937), *The Man Who Came to Dinner* (1939), *Born Yesterday* (1946), and *JB* (1958). His book *Stage Design* (1975) has been influential.   MCH

Œuvre, Théâtre de l' *See* LUGNÉ-POE, AURÉLIEN.

Off-Broadway New York movement, intended as an alternative to the commercial methods of Broadway. Off-Broadway emerged after the Second World War, as a cosmopolitan group of theatres dedicated to introducing modern European classics and new American playwrights to more sophisticated *audiences in the 1950s. Since that decade the Off-Broadway theatre has gone through phases of commercialization that made it a smaller version of Broadway or a mirror of *regional repertory theatres.

The movement was formalized in 1949 when five theatre companies formed the Off-Broadway Theatre League and struck a deal with Actors' Equity that permitted union members to work on a reduced pay scale. Circle in the Square's revival of *Williams's *Summer and Smoke* (1952), directed by *Quintero, was Off-Broadway's first popular success and compelled the attention of major critics. In 1957 the *Village Voice* newspaper initiated the Obie awards to recognize the best new plays, performers, and productions Off-Broadway. Other important companies were the Phoenix Theatre, the *Living Theatre, and the *New York Shakespeare Festival. By the end of the 1950s Off-Broadway venues began to showcase a new generation of young American playwrights, with successes ranging from *Gelber's *The Connection* (1959) and *Albee's *The Zoo Story* (1960) to *Kopit's *Oh Dad, Poor Dad*... (1961). Albee's quick graduation to Broadway with his first full-length play, *Who's Afraid of Virginia Woolf?* (1962), suggested that Off-Broadway was less an alternative and more a proving ground. But as expectations and production

values increased, the cost to mount an Off-Broadway show soared. Corporate foundations and public agencies were enlisted to subsidize whole seasons.

The dramatic rise of *Off-Off-Broadway during the 1960s eventually distanced Off-Broadway from *avant-garde circles. The long-running *musical *The Fantastiks*, which opened in 1960, remained Off-Broadway for 42 years. *Papp's Public Theatre (1966) used transfers to Broadway like *A Chorus Line* (1975) to underwrite more daring productions, particularly by racially marginalized playwrights such as *Shange, and *Hwang. Identity politics continued to fuel much of the best Off-Broadway theatre of the 1980s. The redevelopment of Times Square in the 1990s brought record numbers of new tourist audiences, but escalating real-estate values and other costs meant that by the end of the century even a three-*character, one-set Off-Broadway play needed a capitalization of over $400,000. As a result New York companies increasingly co-produce shows with theatres outside the city, an arrangement that further blurs the distinction between Off-Broadway and the regional theatre movement.   JAB

Offenbach, Jacques (1819-80) French *operetta composer of German birth. A talented instrumentalist and conductor, in 1855 Offenbach founded the Bouffes-Parisiens, a company devoted to the performance of satirical light *opera, which he directed until 1862. He was a prolific composer, turning out almost 100 stage works from 1847. In his masterpieces—*Orpheus in the Underworld* (1858), *La Belle Hélène* (1864), *La Vie parisienne* (1866), and *La Périchole* (1868)—Offenbach's graceful, energetic, and tuneful music is a perfect foil to the witty text. The works not only effectively satirized the Second Empire, they achieved a level of comic ebullience that has since guaranteed their survival. Offenbach's fortunes declined after the fall of Napoleon III in 1871, public taste no longer favouring his brand of *satire, though a romantic opera, *The Tales of Hoffmann* (incomplete at his death), has assured his lasting fame.   SJCW

Off-Off-Broadway A critic for the *Village Voice* coined the term to describe a collection of bohemian performance spaces springing up in lower Manhattan in the early 1960s, marking them as distinct from the *Off-Broadway movement which was becoming commercialized. *Caffe Cino is credited with founding the new development in 1958. A coffee shop with a tiny stage, its owner, Joe Cino, offered a cheap venue for a wide range of performance that included poetry, *dance, music, and theatre. Ellen Stewart's *La Mama Experimental Theatre Club (1962) and Ralph Cook's Theatre Genesis (1964) focused more directly on the theatrical side of this emerging arts counter-culture. Among the playwrights featured in early Off-Off Broadway houses were *Terry, *Shepard, *Fornés, *Van Itallie, Lanford *Wilson, *Ludlam, *McNally, *Guare, *Bullins, *Kennedy, *Owens, and *Horovitz. The *Open Theatre, founded by *Chaikin in 1963, may have best realized Off-Off-Broadway's aesthetic tendency to incorporate dance, poetry, and the visual arts into theatrical performance. The most controversial production associated with the movement was the *ritualistic Paradise Now (1968), created by the *Living Theatre, formerly an Off-Broadway company. Other important Off Off Broadway theatres and artists to emerge from the tumultuous 1960s were the *Performance Group, *Mabou Mines, Andre *Gregory, *Şerban, *Monk, and *Foreman.

After the impact of the New Left, the Vietnam War, and the influence of *Grotowski, some artists, like *Schechner, sought to subordinate or eliminate dramatic texts in favour of a more comprehensive principle of performance. The result was often a war between playwrights and *directors during the 1970s that led many dramatists to write for mainstream and *regional theatres. The rise of identity politics in the 1980s gave Off-Off-Broadway writing a new lease on life. *Gay and *lesbian artists, for example, found dramatic performance an effective rhetorical strategy for resisting the new cultural conservatism of the Reagan era as well as coping with the AIDS crisis.

Off-Off-Broadway was increasingly vertically integrated into the commercial theatre system during the 1990s. 'Showcases'—limited-run performances primarily designed to place new actors in the eye of casting directors—became increasingly important. At the same time Off Off Broadway theatres assumed a greater role in the development of new plays with commercial aspirations. Resolutely *avant-garde companies like the *Wooster Group and Foreman's Ontological Hysteric Theatre have become the exception to a trend that is erasing the cultural-geographical distinctions that marked New York theatre from 1955 or so. By the start of the new millennium, *performance art emerged as the heir to the anti-establishment spirit of the 1960s and 1970s. The category 'Off-Off' no longer seemed distinct or meaningful.   JAB

Ogunde, Hubert (Chief) (1916–90) Playwright, musician, and *manager, the 'father of Nigerian theatre'. While employed as a policeman, Ogunde produced an innovative 'native air opera' in

Lagos, Garden of Eden and the Throne of God (1944), which started a 45-year career of more than 50 stage productions and several films. Concerned chiefly with the Yoruba experience, his plays include Africa and God (1944), which explored the *Yoruba oral tradition, Strike and Hunger (1946), The Tiger's Empire (1946), an attack on colonial rule in which women professionals appeared on the Nigerian stage for the first time, the nationalistic Herbert Macaulay (1946), and Bread and Bullet (1950), based on the Enugu miners' strike. In the cauldron of post-independence politics, Ogunde wrote Yoruba Ronu! (Yoruba Awake!, 1964), which, like Bread and Bullet, was banned (see CENSORSHIP). Yoruba mask theatre directly influenced Ogunde's method, combined with rehearsed songs, *stock characters, *music hall routines, and *slapstick in productions created through *improvisation. A compelling actor on screen as well as stage, as a manager Ogunde played a key role in the settlement of artistic disputes and the general development of Nigerian theatre.   JMG

Ogunyemi, Wale (1939–2001) Nigerian dramatist, director, and actor. Since the mid-1960s his life was, in his own words, 'write—produce—act, write—produce—act'. Deeply grounded in *Yoruba verbal arts and performance, Ogunmola has been involved in theatre in Ibadan at almost every point. His output includes scripts for the stage, radio, television, and film, and covers the mythological and historical, farcical and domestic, the adapted and the highly original. An actor with experience of the gamut of European forms, Ogunyemi has moved with assurance between English and Yoruba.   JMG

Oida Yoshi (1933–) Paris-based Japanese actor and director. Oida studied both modern (*shingeki) and classical theatre in Japan before being invited by *Barrault to work with *Brook at the Théâtre des Nations festival in Paris in 1968. He played Ariel in a production of The Tempest directed by Brook that year, and later returned to Paris to join Brook's International Centre for Theatre Research for such productions as The Conference of the Birds (1979), The Ik (1975), and The Mahabharata (1985). Oida has been active as an independent stage and film actor as well as director and teacher. His own productions include Japanese Liturgical Games and The Divine Comedy. He has also directed operas, notably Britten's Curlew River and Stravinsky's The Nightingale. CP

O'Keeffe, John (1747–1833) Irish playwright and actor. O'Keeffe performed for twelve years with Henry Mossop's *Smock Alley company, until blindness forced him to retire from acting. Turning to playwriting, he had his first London success with *Tony Lumpkin in Town* (1778), based on a *character by *Goldsmith. O'Keeffe's plays are often structured around innovative stage effects presenting exotic landscapes. For instance, *Omai* (*Covent Garden, 1785) was a showcase for designs by *Loutherbourg, whose South Pacific sets catered to public interest generated by the voyages of Captain Cook. Between 1766 and 1826, O'Keeffe wrote 64 *operas and *comedies, of which *Wild Oats* (1791) was revived successfully in 1976 by the *Royal Shakespeare Company. His most enduring legacies are his Irish plays, particularly *The Poor Soldier* (1782) and *The Wicklow Mountains* (1795). Exceptionally popular in Ireland, England, and America until the 1820s, O'Keeffe's Irish plays established many of the basic conventions that would be developed by *Boucicault and others into the Irish *melodrama, which in turn formed the basis for the earliest Irish films.   ChM

Okhlopkov, Nikolai (1900–67) Russian/Soviet actor and director. Okhlopkov joined *Meyerhold's Moscow troupe, acting in *Tarelkin's Death* (1922), *Bubus the Teacher* (1925), and *Roar, China!* (1926). Deeply committed to the communist cause, and to the cause of overt theatricality, Okhlopkov acquired the leadership of the Realistic Theatre in 1932 where he sought to implement his idea of a communal theatre. Reconfiguring actor-*audience relationships so as to encourage emotional involvement, Okhlopkov staged plays on revolutionary and Civil War themes. Ironically the establishment rewarded him by merging his theatre with *Tairov's—the theatrical equivalent of chalk with cheese. Following film appearances, which included *Eisenstein's *Aleksandr Nevsky*, Okhlopkov's career resumed its course when he took over the Mayakovsky Theatre, mounting a stage version of Fadeev's anti-fascist novel *The Young Guard* (1947) in a style of elevated romantic *realism, and a *Hamlet* (1954) in a famous cellular setting by Vadim Ryndin, reflecting Hamlet's sense of Denmark as a prison and constituting a surreptitious post-mortem examination of Stalin's Russia.   NW

Okuni (Izumo no Okuni) (fl.1590–1613) Japanese performer, prostitute, and legendary creator of *kabuki. Born *c.*1578, she began her career as a *miko* (shrine maiden), performing *music and *dances based on *nō, *kyōgen, and Shinto *rituals. In Kyoto she devised in 1603 a hybrid dance-drama called kabuki, in which she combined sacred temple dances with sensual skits about samurai procuring prostitutes. Okuni became famous for her performances of *rōnin*, the masterless samurai warriors. Suffusing her roles with flamboyant sensuality by dressing in Portuguese men's trousers, kimono, a dangling crucifix, and samurai swords, she toyed with the icons of male authority and forged links between the supernatural, the dramatic, and the erotic, an attribute of kabuki that has continued to the present. By stamping the form with a lush and socially transgressive character, she prepared the way for women to become celebrities in the world of prostitution and performance. The government found this development dangerous: in 1629 female prostitution fell under official licensing and professional women performers were banned from the stage until the beginning of the twentieth century. *See also* MALE IMPERSONATION.   KMM

Old Comedy The festival *comedy of Athens during the fifth century BC. By the time of *Aristophanes, the only writer of Old Comedy whose work has survived, comedy held almost as important a position in Athens as did *tragedy. Plays were presented in competition at the Great, or City, *Dionysia and at the *Lenaea, both held in honour of Dionysus, god of the theatre. Comedy was first presented in competition at the Great Dionysia of 486 BC. The Lenaea was more closely associated with the presentation of Old Comedies but did not offer prizes for playwrights or actors until after 440 BC. The Great Dionysia was held in spring when the sailing season had resumed and Athens could play host to visiting traders, guests, and diplomats. The Lenaea was in the dead of winter and exclusive to Athenians and resident aliens.

Old Comedy was played in *masks. It was topical and political, but it was also social and *satirical fantasy in which gods and heroes from the mythological past could consort with celebrated contemporary figures and fictional *characters. The plays contained a fair sprinkling of scatological and sexual references, as well as explicit comic business, and in later centuries much of Aristophanes was banned from both schoolroom and public stage. The plays often feature a confrontation between opposing parties and usually a *parabasis* in which the *chorus becomes a mouthpiece for the author, addressing the *audience directly on contemporary issues. Singing and *dancing choruses of 24 members might represent the animal kingdom or some original theatrical conceit. Writers from the earlier part of the fifth century, and Aristophanes' own rivals, have survived only in fragments or by title. *See also* MIDDLE COMEDY; NEW COMEDY.   JMW

Old Vic Theatre London *playhouse in Waterloo Bridge Road, which opened as the Coburg Theatre in 1818, a handsome building with a beautifully proportioned *auditorium. Renamed the Royal Victoria in 1833, it remained a local house with a popular repertoire until 1880, when it became the Royal Victoria Hall and Coffee Tavern, run by the temperance reformer Emma Cons. Her niece Lilian *Baylis joined her in 1898, and took over in 1912. In 1914 she started Shakespeare seasons which continued until 1941; from 1914 to 1923 she presented all the plays in the First Folio, at popular prices. Throughout the 1930s most leading English actors appeared at the theatre, and the directors included *Guthrie and *Saint-Denis. Baylis died in 1937, and the theatre was bombed in 1941. In 1963 the *National Theatre Company under *Olivier took over, staging numerous important productions until the National's move to the South Bank in 1976. Since then the Old Vic's status has been much debated, operated by a series of entrepreneurs and agencies and producing a variety of work. In 2003 its direction was assumed by the film actor Kevin Spacey.   EEC

Olimpico, Teatro An *early modern playhouse designed by *Palladio for the Olympian Academy in Vicenza, still in use. This circle of learned connoisseurs took an interest in the revival of classical drama and organized performances of ancient and modern plays. The temporary stages erected by Palladio for these occasions were fairly sophisticated structures, but costly and restrictive. In 1580 the Academy acquired the site of an old prison building, where they had a permanent theatre built to Palladio's design. The architect died a few months after work began in 1580. *Scamozzi finished the theatre in 1584 in accordance with Palladio's design, except for the stage, which he extended to the rear. The *auditorium had an elliptical plan to allow better sightlines. The stage was a long and narrow rectangular (29 by 8 m; 95 by 26 feet) in front of an ornamented architectural façade. In its centre a large arch opened up, flanked by two lesser doors with two further doors at the sides. Palladio's idea placed *perspective scenery behind the arches; Scamozzi opened them up into alleyways with wood-and-plaster houses constructed in diminishing perspective. This setting thus fixed the prototypical urban scene, which *Serlio had constructed in painterly fashion, in a three-dimensional manner. *See also* SCENOGRAPHY.   GB

Olivier, Laurence (1907–89) English actor and *manager. The greatest heroic actor of his age, Olivier always made sure his performances were

marked by extremes. His abilities were recognized early. He worked with Barry *Jackson at the *Birmingham Rep, where from 1926 he learned his craft in a variety of classic and *stock roles. A long run as Ralph in *Coward's *Private Lives* (1930) brought him a measure of success and proved his skills in *comedy. But it was his Romeo and Mercutio opposite *Ashcroft (exchanging the roles with *Gielgud during the run) that made him a star, helped by the production's move to New York. Lacking Gielgud's sensitivity to the verse, Olivier made his Romeo a dashing romantic *hero of great erotic charge.

With *Guthrie's *Old Vic company he played Hamlet, taking the performance to Elsinore in 1937, but also Macbeth, Henry V, Iago, Coriolanus, and Sir Toby Belch. His Hamlet and Iago were strongly influenced by a Freudian reading of *character, but Olivier's style was less psychological study than sheer theatrical power and panache. It led to a spell in Hollywood as a matinée idol (*Wuthering Heights*, 1939; *Rebecca*, 1940) and marriage to Vivien *Leigh. The glamorous couple left Hollywood for Olivier to take up war service, initially in the navy but soon by making films, especially *Henry V* (1944), supported by the Ministry of Information and released on the eve of the Normandy invasion. Patriotism and a commitment to Shakespeare on screen combined perfectly, and subsequently led to *Hamlet* (1947) and *Richard III* (1954).

With Ralph Richardson he ran the *Old Vic company at the New Theatre (1944–9), where he learned management, created an extraordinary ensemble, and extended his own range of work. As a brutally sardonic Richard III, tempestuous Hotspur, and tortured Oedipus, he confirmed his status as energetic hero, but was also brilliantly funny as Justice Shallow (*2 Henry IV*) and *Sheridan's Mr Puff in *The Critic* (on a double bill with *Oedipus*).

Olivier tried commercial management but it did not appeal and he returned to classical theatre. His Titus, directed by *Brook (1955), was the first ever production of *Titus Andronicus* in Stratford and was an astonishing success, its tragic power matched by his eccentric Malvolio (1955) and deeply patrician Coriolanus (1959). But Olivier was also prepared to engage with the new forms of drama then emerging, quickly sensing both their significance and their opportunities for actors. As *Osborne's *music-hall comic Archie Rice in *The Entertainer* (*Royal Court, 1957) Olivier appropriated the role for an extraordinary display of *acting skills. He also played in *Ionesco's *Rhinoceros* (1960) and *Anouilh's *Becket* (New York, 1960).

Olivier's marriage to Leigh collapsed as her mental health deteriorated and, after divorce in 1960, he married Joan *Plowright, whom he had met in the cast of *The Entertainer*. In 1962 he became director of the *Chichester Festival Theatre and planned the long-awaited *National Theatre, of which he became the first director in 1963 when it opened at the Old Vic. Olivier assembled a genuine company of actors, encouraging younger actors including *Jacobi, Robert *Stephens, and *Blakely. Helped and provoked by *Tynan, Olivier established a broadly based and often experimental *repertory of classical and new drama which won immediate and intense admiration. Though exhausted by illness, endless battles for subsidy, and the delays in constructing the National's home on the South Bank, Olivier also gave some of his finest performances. His Othello (1964) was a colossus, for which he added lower octaves to his vocal range, the last great Othello by a white actor blacked up. As *Congreve's Tattle in *Love for Love* (1965), Edgar in *Strindberg's *Dance of Death* (1967), Chebutikhin in *Chekhov's *Three Sisters* (1969), and Tyrone in *O'Neill's *Long Day's Journey into Night* (1971), he showed his continuing determination to experiment, to create memorable stage images, and to steal almost every scene.

Olivier had been knighted in 1947 but his life peerage in 1970 (making him Lord Olivier of Brighton) was the first ever given to an actor, apt state recognition of his status in the profession. Struggling with illness, Olivier stopped acting and left the National Theatre in 1973, distressed by the secrecy which kept Peter *Hall's appointment as his successor from him. The largest *auditorium of the National Theatre was named after him. But his film work had continued both in blockbusters and in recording his stage performances. He won a number of Academy awards, including a lifetime achievement award (1979). In 1984, though seriously ill, he played King Lear for a television production in which, while the heroic fire was a pale shadow, the final scenes were profoundly moving. He published an autobiography, *Confessions of an Actor* (1982), and further thoughts *On Acting* (1986).   PDH

Olivier Theatre See NATIONAL THEATRE OF GREAT BRITAIN.

O'Neill, Eugene (1888–1953) The only US playwright to win the Nobel Prize (1936), O'Neill brought a native *tragedy to the American stage. With his innovative major works—among them *The Emperor Jones* and *Anna Christie* (1920), *The Hairy Ape* (1921), *Desire under the Elms* (1924), *Strange Interlude* (1927), and *Mourning Becomes Electra* (1931)—he paved the way for an enlightened cadre of home-grown dramatists. O'Neill's father, James *O'Neill, born in Ireland,

was a matinée idol in America, and Eugene accompanied his father on *tour, absorbing the life of the theatre. Eugene's mother Ella Quinlan found it increasingly difficult to endure the touring life, the dirty trains, the lack of a permanent home; Eugene, her third child, was born in a hotel on Broadway. Her eventual morphine addiction, coupled with Eugene's knowledge that he had been unwanted, became the defining facts of his life, material he turned to use in *Long Day's Journey into Night* (written 1941). O'Neill's other masterworks, *The Iceman Cometh* (1939) and *A Moon for the Misbegotten* (1943), were also drawn from his life.

He entered Princeton at 18, but was dismissed in his freshman year. Pursuing what he liked to call 'life experience', by the time he began writing plays at 25, he had carelessly fathered a child, spent almost two years drifting as a sailor and dock worker, and nearly drunk himself to death in Buenos Aires and at a New York saloon called Jimmy the Priest's, the basis for the setting of *The Iceman Cometh*. He worked briefly as a reporter and satiric poet in Connecticut, and in 1912 suffered a bout of tuberculosis, after which he began to write one-act plays. His enrolment in *Baker's playwriting course (1913–14) was followed by a mostly drunken year in Greenwich Village, at the end of which he found recognition through the *Provincetown Players, who mounted his sea play *Bound East for Cardiff* in 1916.

By 1924 O'Neill had won two Pulitzer Prizes, for *Beyond the Horizon* and *Anna Christie*. By 1926 his marriage to Agnes Boulton had become problematic and he fell in love with the actress Carlotta Monterey, who had appeared in *The Hairy Ape*. They were married in France in 1929 as O'Neill was starting work on *Mourning Becomes Electra*. In the late 1930s he suffered from a nervous disorder that caused his hands and body to shake and eventually forced him to give up work on a cycle of eleven plays, *A Tale of Possessors Self-Dispossessed*, tracing the fortunes of an Irish-American family from 1754 to 1935. He died in a Boston hotel of pneumonia. His last words: 'Born in a hotel room and—Goddammit—died in a hotel room!'

In performance O'Neill has become one of the most durable of twentieth-century playwrights. After the initial Broadway successes, *Langner brought O'Neill into the *Theatre Guild in 1927 with *Strange Interlude*. It became a sensation, not least for its *Wagnerian length of six hours (including dinner break). The Guild also produced *Mourning Becomes Electra* and O'Neill's only *comedy, *Ah, Wilderness!* (1933), starring *Cohan. All three productions were directed by *Moeller. Although O'Neill is now praised for his later plays, they achieved success only after his death, chiefly through the efforts of *Quintero and Jason *Robards, who became associated through the revival of *Iceman* and the première of *Long Day's Journey into Night* (both 1956). Their subsequent productions greatly enhanced O'Neill's international reputation.									ANG/BSG/YS

O'Neill, James (1845–1920) Irish-American actor. Born in County Kilkenny during the famine, at age 6 his family emigrated to Buffalo, New York, where his father deserted them. At 20 James started acting and soon was supporting stars, including Charlotte *Cushman and Edwin *Booth. O'Neill achieved great fame as Edmond Dantès in the adaptation of *Dumas *père*'s novel *The Count of Monte Cristo*, in which he *toured the United States for more than 30 years. Despite huge promise, O'Neill found himself trapped in the role; *audiences flocked when he played it, and stayed away when he took other parts. In 1877 he married Ella Quinlan, who bore him three sons, among them the playwright Eugene *O'Neill. In his *tragedy *Long Day's Journey into Night*, Eugene dramatized his mother's addiction to morphine and depicted his father as the actor James Tyrone, a man psychologically crippled by his terror of poverty.									ANG/BSG

Ong Keng Sen (1963–) Singaporean director, *artistic director of Theatre Works Singapore. In 1994 he established the Flying Circus Project, a biennial workshop bringing performers from many Asian countries together for collaboration. His experimental productions often use English as the shared language of the different cultures, but depend more on visual and physical elements, including *music, *ritual, film, and *documentary, to create disjunctive perspectives on Asian identity. *Descendants of the Eunuch Admiral* (1995) focused on male sexuality and hierarchies, *Broken Birds* (1995) depicted Japanese prostitutes, and *Workhorse Afloat* (1997) juxtaposed foreign workers in nineteenth-century and contemporary Singapore. Ong's best-known works internationally are *Lear* (Tokyo, 1997, and *tour), *Desdemona* (Singapore, 2000), and *Search: Hamlet* (Elsinore, 2002), which combined different performance forms and languages in an Asian *intercultural response to Shakespeare. *The Continuum: Beyond the Killing Fields* (2001) showcased traditional Cambodian dancers speaking in Cambodian about their personal histories. Other recent productions that have travelled internationally include *The Buddha Project* (2003), *Geisha* (2006), *Diaspora* (2008), and *130* (2009).									YLI

onnagata Male *actors in *kabuki who specialize in female roles. The term first appeared in Japan after 1629, when women were banned from the public stage, and was used to designate boys playing female roles. *Yoshizawa Ayame, along with Segawa Kikunojo I (1693–1748), created the physical techniques and iconography, Ayame establishing *onnagata* as an art of female-likeness, as recorded in his treatise 'The Words of Ayame' in *The Actors' Analects*. The 'gender acts' that *onnagata* use to inhabit female roles were devised over time as elaborate methods of disguise and transformation, necessitated by government bans on eroticism and violence on stage. Major *onnagata* roles are classified by age and status: *yūjo* (courtesan), *himesama* (princess), *musume* (young girl), *jidainyōbō* (period wife), *sewanyōbō* (contemporary wife), *haha* (old woman or grandmother), and *akuba* (evil female). *Onnagata* have always held a lower status in kabuki troupes than the *tachiyaku*, the male-gender specialists. Contemporary *onnagata* include *Bandō Tamasaburō V. Nakamura Ganjirō III is exceptional in that he plays both male and female roles. *See also* FEMALE IMPERSONATION; GENDER AND PERFORMANCE.									KMM

Ōno Kazuo (1906–2010) Japanese *butoh dancer. Ōno was inspired to study modern *dance by seeing a performance of the flamenco dancer La Argentina (Antonia Mercé) in 1929. He studied under the leaders of German *Neue Tanz* in Japan, Ishii Baku and Eguchi Takuya. Converted to Christianity in 1930, for much of his career he worked as a gymnastics teacher (and, later, janitor) at a private mission school in Yokohama. His first public performance was not until 1949; thereafter he or his son Yoshito collaborated with *Hijikata Tatsumi on a number of seminal butoh pieces, starting with *The Old Man and the Sea* (1959) and *Forbidden Colours* (1959). From 1980 Ōno regularly gave performances and workshops in Japan and abroad, sometimes with his son; his last public performance was in 2007. In contrast to Hijikata's fascination for the darker side of life, Ōno's work was marked by its tenderness. His most famous pieces, *Admiring La Argentina* (1977) and *My Mother* (1981), featured him in women's dress.					CP

Ontological Hysteric Theatre *See* FOREMAN, RICHARD.

Open Theatre American experimental company, formed in 1963 by Joseph *Chaikin to explore new *acting and performance strategies through *improvisation, training, and *physically *devised *collective creation. The company included actors Raymond Barry, Tina Shephard, and Paul Zimet, writers *Van Itallie, and Susan Yankowitz, and *dramaturgs Gordon Rogoff and Richard Gilman. Productions included Megan *Terry's *Viet Rock* (1966), as well as *The Serpent* (1969), *Terminal* (1971), *The Mutation Show* (1973), and *Nightwalk* (1973). Like other collectives of the 1960s, the Open Theatre followed workshop process rather than standard *rehearsals, to develop techniques for freeing the body and voice. Chaikin had earlier worked as an actor for the *Living Theatre and many of the performers in the Open Theatre studied with Nola Chilton, who developed physicalized acting techniques in response to the demands of *absurdist drama; her exercises, and the improvisation work of Viola Spolin, became the starting point. Works of the Open Theatre were physically devised pieces developed with single authors around such themes as biblical myths in *The Serpent* (developed with Van Itallie), and death in *Terminal* (with Yankowitz). The performance aesthetic included a focus on the presence, physicality, and art of the actor, while the texts and performances exhibited narrative fragmentation, fluid subjectivities, and presentational theatrics. The Open Theatre had wide influence in the West and its techniques continue to be reworked in contemporary devised performance. The company disbanded in 1973. MDC

opera Dramatic work in which the *action is sung by solo singers and often a *chorus, to orchestral, instrumental, or keyboard accompaniment. Some operas include passages of spoken *dialogue over accompaniment. Opera by nature of its musical idiom is most suited to the representation of the extremes of human conduct. The actions of many operas, therefore, involve the spectacular *rituals, conflicts, and confrontations of political, social, and military life, but they also explore the most intimate human emotions. On the whole opera does not successfully represent the transactions of everyday life (*realism) or easily incorporate dramatic actions that generate discursive ideas. Originating in Europe, opera has spread to all parts of the world, though it remains primarily a Western form.

The first theatrical works that consistently explored *music as a dramatic medium arose in the courts of northern Italy. (*Opera* means 'work' in Italian.) The operas of Jacopo Peri in Florence (*Dafne*, 1598; *Euridice*, 1600), Claudio Monteverdi, and others were presented as revivals of the style of ancient *Greek *tragedy, though they were related to the *intermezzi* performed between acts of plays and other events at court. In Rome, an operatic tradition was founded on the patronage of rich families and princes of the Church, while from 1637 opera was performed in Venice on a commercial basis. Opera narratives were taken from a wide range of sources, including classical mythology, biblical stories, and history. By the end of the seventeenth century, opera had spread throughout Italy and to the major courts and larger cities of Europe. Although Italian opera was not popular at the French court when introduced in 1645, it laid the groundwork for the foundation of the Paris Opéra in 1669, where the *tragédies lyriques* of its director, *Lully, were staged. This eclectic form, which incorporated elements from *neoclassical tragedy, *ballet, and *pastoral, dominated French opera until well into the eighteenth century.

The splendour of opera's music and the opportunities it offered for extravagant spectacle made it the ideal vehicle by which European monarchs could manifest their power. In the eighteenth century, royal governments installed companies in specially constructed theatres to give opera performances, sometimes under the direct supervision of the monarch, on a regular rather than occasional basis, and municipal communities supported opera, sometimes under commercial auspices. All the larger cities of German-speaking Europe and Italy housed regular companies.

There was a constant demand for new material, so composers had to be extremely prolific. It was not unusual for a popular composer to write more than 80 operas in his career. By and large, Italian was the preferred language for most of the eighteenth century.

Opera seria (serious opera) was an action, usually based on ancient history and involving a small number of royal or aristocratic figures, in which such virtues as courage, fidelity, patriotism, and honesty were put to the test and invariably emerged triumphant in obligatory happy endings. Neo-*Aristotelian *unities were observed and *comedy rigorously eschewed. Many *opera seria* were based on the tightly constructed librettos of *Metastasio, which were also noted for the elegance of their poetry and were highly suitable for singing. Several of Metastasio's librettos were set many times; there were, for example, 90 settings of his most popular libretto, *Artaserse*, between 1730 and 1840. Gluck was especially important as a composer, notably *Orpheus and Eurydice* (Vienna, 1762), and *Alceste* (Vienna, 1767). *Mozart recalled the earlier *seria* in *Idomeneo* (Munich, 1781) and *La clemenza di Tito* (Prague, 1791). The heroic dimensions of *seria* action required splendour in setting and wealthier theatres devoted considerable resources to grandiose *scenography.

Opera buffa (comic opera)   originated in Naples but swiftly moved northward. Less subject to convention, *buffa* represented the everyday life of the bourgeoisie and peasantry. Its high point was reached in Mozart's ironic masterpieces *The Marriage of Figaro* (Vienna, 1786), *Don Giovanni* (Prague, 1787), and *Così fan tutte* (Vienna, 1790). *Buffa* gave rise to national comic opera genres, notably the *Singspiel, *opéra-comique, *zarzuela, and *operetta.

The Industrial Revolution and the increase of global trade led to the growth of immense cities in Europe and the United States in the nineteenth century, demanding mass entertainment. While opera did not expand as rapidly as other forms of theatre, it maintained its cultural centrality. As the bourgeoisie aspired to display its new wealth in the way the aristocracy had done, opera's prestige was enhanced. New opera houses were built and the stage equipped with increasingly complex machinery for scene shifting. By the middle of the century a canon had developed, centred initially around Gluck, Mozart, Cimarosa, and Rossini; Bellini, Donizetti, *Verdi, and *Wagner would be added.

The most characteristic operatic genre of the nineteenth century was **grand opera**, which originated at the Paris Opéra. A successor to *opera seria*, the action was most frequently set during the Middle Ages or the Renaissance: Rossini's *William Tell* (1829) is a well-known example. Although Italian composers contributed generously to this repertoire, their focus tended to individual experience. Early nineteenth-century Italian opera is commonly referred to as bel canto (fine singing), indicating beauty of voice is the prime interest. The great bel canto composers—Gioachino Rossini (1792–1868), Gaetano Donizetti (1797–1848), and Vincenzo Bellini (1801–35)—effectively dramatize the concerns of *romanticism, though display of the virtuoso voice, especially of the coloratura soprano, was a major appeal.

The modes of bel canto and grand opera were most effectively combined by Italy's greatest composer, Giuseppe Verdi. Verdi's reputation was built on work with extended choruses in grand operatic settings that seemed to articulate the aspirations of his countrymen for national unity. However, his capacity to use music to endow the heroic striving of the individual with theatrical credibility meant dramatic interest was focused on how *characters face social and political coercion.

The other towering figure of nineteenth-century opera is the German Richard Wagner. Although skilled at grand opera, Wagner was profoundly alienated from the theatre of his time by a disjunction between music, design, and staging. Wagner through-composed the action so that it was clearly articulated by the flow of the music. Although it is possible to identify formal musical numbers such as arias, duets, and ensembles in his great tetralogy *The Ring of the Nibelung* (*Bayreuth Festival, 1876), the continuous music is structured on the repetition of myriad themes (leitmotifs) rather than on discrete musical forms, and the drama unfolds without hiatus for musical embellishment. Wagner's festival theatre at Bayreuth provided a viable alternative to the horse-shoe-shaped auditorium, while the care with which his music dramas were produced contrasted with the slapdash practices of several European opera houses.

The large number of personnel required by opera, its lavish spectacle, and the large stipends commanded by singers have meant that for most of its history opera has been difficult to produce commercially. It has traditionally depended upon the patronage of politically powerful or wealthy individuals and, in the modern age, upon heavy government subsidy. Ticket prices have always been considerably higher than for spoken theatre. Consequently opera has found it difficult to shed its reputation as an elitist art in the egalitarian twentieth century. The heroic dimensions of much operatic action, its tendency to treat the past with nostalgia, and the formal display still found in the conduct of both singers and the well-heeled segments of the *audience have given opera an air of archaism and exclusiveness that potentially alienates newcomers. Nevertheless, after signs of decline in the middle decades of the twentieth century, opera at the start of the new millennium was undergoing a surprisingly vigorous revival, especially in the United States.

The canon was substantially expanded. The emotionally stirring operas of *Puccini are among the most frequently performed, while the post-Wagnerian compositions of Richard Strauss are firmly in the repertoire. The tersely intense operas on Moravian and Russian themes by the Czech Leoš Janáček (1854–1928) have undergone a spectacular international renaissance since 1970. As in previous centuries, some composers have made their mark with one opera: Dmitry Shostakovich's *Lady Macbeth of the Mtsensk District* (Leningrad, 1924), Alban Berg's *Wozzeck* (Berlin, 1925), and *Weill's *The Rise and Fall of the City of Mahagonny* (text by *Brecht, 1930) are regularly performed. These works have succeeded in part because they use music to articulate the experience of social alienation that was salient to serious theatre in the century. But it has not been easy for modern composers to find large audiences. The latest composer who regularly features is the Englishman Benjamin Britten (1913–76). Toward the end of the century, American composers were particularly productive: *Einstein on the Beach* (1976), *Satyagraha* (1980), and *The Voyage* (1992) by *Glass, *Nixon in China* (1987) and *The Death of Klinghoffer* (1991) by John Adams, and *Emmeline* (1996) by Tobias Picker have found enthusiastic audiences. But, however successful a new work may be at its première, the odds against it finding acceptance into the 60 or so works that form the core of the canon are overwhelming, whatever the quality of the musical drama.

Under these circumstances, it might be puzzling why opera appeals today. The answer may lie as much in the interpreters as in the music. From its beginnings, singers with opulent voices and flamboyant personalities have found opera their natural medium. At the start of the twenty-first century singers such as Cecilia Bartoli, Placido Domingo, Luciano Pavarotti, and Bryn Terfel sang via recordings to audiences far more numerous than those which attend live opera, and at the same time expand the audience for live performance.

Opera offers stage *directors and designers attractive challenges. Given the limitations of the repertoire, directors have to devise ways to give theatrical life to operas which have been performed so frequently that most of the audience are likely to be intimately familiar with them. From 1900 the scenic abstraction of *symbolism gradually eroded the literalness of operatic sets, but it was not until the productions of Wolfgang and Wieland *Wagner at Bayreuth in the 1950s, influenced by *Appia, that symbolist principles were completely embraced. From the 1970s on, aesthetic unity was no longer a prime consideration. Now it is rare to see a production designed and directed in a style resembling its first staging, or its imagined staging by the librettist and composer. Noted contemporary directors include Jonathan *Miller, *Chéreau, *Dorn, *Ronconi, *Sellars, and Robert *Wilson, all from spoken theatre. Opera audiences, being of a somewhat conservative bent, have not always taken kindly to what they regard as unwarranted liberties with pieces dear to their hearts, but the vitality of opera in the present is in part guaranteed by these directors' work.   SJCW

opéra-comique The name *opéra-comique* appears in 1715, applied to the distinctive productions of the fairground theatres. It became the generic term for various kinds of popular entertainment with musical accompaniment, produced under constant harassment from the official theatres, the *Comédie-Française and the Opéra. In 1721 a poor tax was levied on the fairground theatres, putting them on an equal footing with the monopoly companies. The future of the *opéra-comique* remained precarious and in 1745 the Opéra managed its complete closure until 1751. In 1762, after premises at the Saint-Germaine fairground had been destroyed by fire, the *opéra-comique* amalgamated with the *Comédie Italienne at the *Hôtel de Bourgogne, the joint company taking the official title in 1780 and moving into the present-day premises of the Théâtre de l'Opéra-Comique in 1783. In opera history the term *opéra-comique* has retained from its origins a more technical meaning: a work containing spoken *dialogue, whether 'comic' in tone or not (thus Bizet's *Carmen* ranks as an *opéra-comique*).   WDH

operetta A light *opera in which musical numbers, songs, and *dances are linked by spoken *dialogue. Although the term dates from mid-eighteenth-century Italy, operetta was first recognizable as an independent genre in 1850s Paris. One-act stage works by *Offenbach were designated 'operettes', or 'little operas', while his full-length works were labelled 'opéra-bouffes'. Nevertheless, his great *satires—*Orpheus in the Underworld* (1858), *La Belle Hélène* (1864), *La Vie parisienne* (1866), and *La Périchole* (1868)—are, along with the flamboyant historical *burlesques of his associate Hervé (1825–92), acknowledged as the first operettas. When Paris fell to the Prussians in 1870, the centre for operetta shifted to Vienna. Viennese operetta provided the perfect antidotal entertainment for a society experiencing anxiety over modernization. The fairy-tale atmosphere of its plots, usually set among the colourful peasantry and glamorous aristocracy of the Austro-Hungarian Empire, the seductive lilt of its waltzes, and the sentimental allure of melodies conjuring up dreams of Old Vienna had a potent appeal to Austrians and Europeans alike. Although Johann Strauss the Younger (1825–99) is regarded as the pre-eminent operetta composer, of his nineteen stage works, only *Die Fledermaus* (*The Bat*, 1874) has achieved lasting popularity, his later *Night in Venice* (1883) and *Gypsy Baron* (1885) surviving more for their music than dramatic qualities. Perhaps the true father of Viennese operetta was Franz von Suppé (1819–95), who wrote close to 200 theatre scores. Some of his works, in particular *The Beautiful Galathea*

(1865), *Fatinitza* (1876), and *Boccaccio* (1879), still have theatrical appeal.

Operetta in London was dominated by the partnership of *Gilbert and *Sullivan, whose 'Savoy Operas' represent some of the highest achievements in the genre. Gilbert and Sullivan's most popular collaborations, such as *The Pirates of Penzance* (1879), *Patience* (1881), *Iolanthe* (1881), *The Mikado* (1885), *The Yeomen of the Guard* (1888), and *The Gondoliers* (1889), often satirized contemporary London life and burlesqued serious theatrical and operatic forms. Consequently only *The Mikado*, a comic masterpiece, found an international *audience.

Viennese operetta survived the convulsions of the First World War to remain a vital part of the city's theatrical culture. The pre eminent com poser in the twentieth century was Franz Lehár (1870–1948), whose *Merry Widow* (1905) has proved to be the most successful of all operettas. His other hits included *The Count of Luxemburg* (1909), *Gypsy Love* (1910), *Paganini* (1925), and *The Land of Smiles* (1929). Viewed from the twenty-first century, operetta looks like a genre that was always in transition. Emerging from the disparate traditions of *opéra-comique, English burlesque, *Singspiel, and *opera buffa*, it achieved distinctive form only in the latter half of the nineteenth century, to be replaced in the early twentieth by the American *musical. It contributed greatly to the development of the musical; distinct vestiges of its music can be heard in the work of *Kern, *Rodgers, and *Sondheim. Yet it has survived as part of the repertoire only in Vienna, where one theatre, the Volksoper, is devoted largely to preserving it. Operetta seems destined to remain a delightful but dated curiosity, whose works give an intriguing, sometimes touching view of the playful fantasies and nostalgic yearnings of an earlier age.   SJCW

oppressed, theatre of the A system designed to encourage the public to be participants ('spect-actors') in identifying and dramatizing the connections between socio-cultural problems, economic and political repression, and internal or personal oppressions. Gradually elaborated by the Brazilian Augusto *Boal in collaboration with numerous theatre and community projects since the 1970s, theatre of the oppressed is now practised in some 70 countries worldwide, according to Boal's estimate. Inspired by Paulo Freire's participatory teaching system developed in the drought- and poverty-stricken Brazilian north-east (*Pedagogy of the Oppressed*, 1970), Boal's first theoretical book, *Theatre of the Oppressed and Other Political Poetics* (published in Spanish in 1974, with translations into about 25 languages), argues that an oppressed people can learn to change their circumstances by actively discovering the nature of their oppressions, rather than being told what they are. 'You can only teach if you learn' is Boal's advice to political theatre artists: do not show people what is wrong, use your skills to let them discover it themselves.

The techniques of the theatre of the oppressed have evolved since the early 1970s. The initial schemes were conceived in the climate of political dictatorship, to find avenues for protest and social mobilization. In 'forum theatre', actors dramatize a problem common to the community, then represent the scene again with a community member taking over the *protagonist's role, improvising solutions in *dialogue with other spect-actors. 'Invisible theatre' arose from the need for anonymity: already in exile in Argentina, which had just itself suffered a military coup (1976), Boal knew it was too dangerous to mount overt protest; instead actors staged scenes in public places, such as racial or class discrimination in a restaurant, designed to provoke polemic while planted observers instigated and directed commentary. In 1979, exiled in Europe, Boal developed further variations, such as 'the cop-in-the-head', which focused on internalized oppression and psychological stresses. After his return to Brazil in 1986 after re-democratization, he developed 'legislative theatre' to address the legal codification of citizen rights and responsibilities. Both are articulated in his book *The Rainbow of Desire* (1995). *See also* DEVELOPMENT, THEATRE FOR; COMMUNITY THEATRE.   LHD

origins of theatre The 'ritual theory of origin', itself of nineteenth-century origin and first proposed in scientific guise by the Cambridge School of Anthropology, swiftly became a commonplace even beyond the circles of theatre scholarship. Although repeatedly refuted, the influence of the CSA is still felt in subsequent theories. While alternative arguments have been suggested, the main thesis—that theatre originated in *ritual—remains firm.

Eventually this theory was also adopted by leading directors, such as *Brook, *Grotowski, *Schechner, *Mnouchkine, and *Barba, who attempted to restore the ritual qualities they assumed had been lost and that they considered vital for the rejuvenation of theatre. Their created elements were not genuinely ritual, however, but no more than inventions of stagecraft.

The grip of the ritual theory of origin is enigmatic, for it contradicts the rather obvious perception that ritual and theatre belong in different spheres of human activity. Whereas a ritual is a complex act, whose main purposes are to affect a divine sphere for the benefit of a community of believers and buttress their beliefs, theatre is a particular medium that may be employed for either reconfirming or refuting common beliefs. The latter function cannot be imagined in any ritual. If ritual and theatre are indeed independent of each other, it is sensible to assume that ancient rituals may have included theatrical components, just as they equally well may have not.

The advent of ancient theatre Despite changing arguments, three major contributions to the theory of ritual origin can be discerned; in chronological order these are: the CSA theory, the shamanist theory, and Schechner's performance theory.

(a) *Cambridge School of Anthropology.* In its scientific form, the theory that ancient *Greek *tragedy and *comedy originated in Dionysiac ritual was suggested by a group of English scholars known as the Cambridge School of Anthropology at the beginning of the twentieth century. Its leading proponents were Jane Harrison, Gilbert *Murray, and Francis McDonald Cornford. The CSA accepted *Aristotle's account (in the *Poetics*) regarding the development of tragedy from dithyrambic poetry. However, in contrast to Aristotle, who was closest to the process, they argued for continuity—mediated by *dithyramb—between Dionysiac ritual and tragedy. Murray suggested an apparently sophisticated method for detecting the traces of Dionysiac ritual in the pattern of recurrent narrative components featuring: *agon*, a struggle between the Spring Daimon and its enemy (winter); *pathos*, the ritual death of the Daimon; *messenger*, the report of death or display of corpse; *threnos* or *lamentation*, the expression of grief; *anagnorisis*, the recognition of the dead Daimon; and *epiphany* or *theophany*, his resurrection and apotheosis.

As early as 1927 Pickard-Cambridge (*Dithyramb, Tragedy and Comedy*) challenged the existence of these narrative components in their stipulated order, and demonstrated that they are not to be found either in any known form of Dionysiac ritual or in dithyramb, tragedy, or comedy. Even in *Euripides' The Bacchae*, the only extant tragedy that dramatizes an episode of Dionysus' life, there is no death and resurrection. If the intention of the CSA was to discover the origin of the theatre medium, their main fallacy was to look for it in the fictional worlds of dithyramb, tragedy, and comedy. Moreover, there is evidence for the existence of a theatre medium

prior to the creation of both tragedy and comedy in pictures on early sixth-century BC vases and names of theatrical burlesques. Aristotle suggests that Attic comedy developed from popular forms of comedy. Cornford accepts this account and quotes *Aristophanes' contemptuous remarks on earlier Megarean *farce. *Thespis, credited with the creation of tragedy, may have figured out the possibility of performing the Homeric narratives and sublime style typical of dithyramb in a medium that was already in existence. Tragedy could have developed the dialogic element found in dithyramb itself, as in other forms of storytelling too. The moment Thespis, as a member of the dithyrambic *chorus, enacted *dialogue in *character, the existent theatre medium was employed and tragedy was born.

(b) *Shamanistic theory.* In contrast to the CSA, Ernest T. Kirby (*Ur-Drama; the origins of theatre*, 1975) focuses on the shaman exhibiting another identity. Enacting a character, allegedly shared by both shaman in the state of trance and actor on stage, indeed regards a crucial property of theatre. The shaman is believed to enter a state of trance, travelling other worlds, taking control of spirits and compelling them to cure people. While in trance, the shaman behaves as if possessed by a spirit, speaking in his voice. Kirby thus establishes him as the prototype of the *actor, because of his embodying an entity other than himself. From the perspective of the shamanist culture, however, the shaman is definitely not enacting a spirit but constitutes a means for its revelation in the world. The efficacy of the ritual depends on the community's belief that the spirit is real and operates through the shaman. If the shaman is suspected of impersonation, he is seen as a fraud and efficacy is impaired. In contrast, an actor genuinely enacts a character, a fictional entity that reaches existence only in the spectator's imagination, which is not perceived as fraudulent but as essential to the art. Moreover, ecstasy cannot be a necessary condition of acting.

Although the community's participation is shared by ritual and theatre, its meaning is different. Whereas in ritual it means a community involved in a common effort to produce a change in the human world, in theatre it means an *audience sharing a form of thinking and experiencing the potentialities of human nature.

(c) *Performance theory.* While denying a generative link between ritual and theatre, Richard Schechner (*Performance Theory*, 1977) suggests an even stronger bond. they are different manifestations of the single comprehensive category of 'performance', a combination of two ubiquitous elements of 'entertainment' and 'efficacy'. In varying proportions these create the continuum of all kinds of performance: when entertainment overweighs efficacy, the result is 'aesthetic theatre'; and when efficacy overweighs entertainment, the result is 'ritual'.

Inclusion of such disparate activities as ritual, football (*see* SPORT), and theatre under 'performance' necessarily leads to an over-abstract definition: 'a performance is an activity done by an individual or group *in the presence* of and for the benefit of another individual or group.' Whereas this applies to almost any kind of human activity, including, for example, a fire brigade rescuing people from a fire in front of a gathering of curious observers, it excludes activities most akin to theatre, such as imaginative play, writing fiction, and making films.

Furthermore, instead of unravelling the relationship between ritual and theatre, questions about it multiply. For example, does the category of 'entertainment' apply to subversive kinds of theatre, whose main aim is to baffle and even shock audiences? In fact, by means of this category Schechner gives a reductive account of a medium which can serve any purpose. The notion of 'efficacy' raises similar difficulties.

Schechner claims that a performance is an 'actual', in the sense of not representing anything, but being identical with itself, here and now. The 'actual' thus contrasts with the *'mimetic'. He also maintains that 'aesthetic theatre' reflects both representation and actuality; that is, they do not exclude each other, and may complement each other. Indeed, focusing attention on the mechanism of producing the stage text, including actors, can highlight the 'actual' elements of theatre. In contrast, ritual is only an actual. Schechner thus provides the ideology for creating *performance art, which professedly aims at pure actuality. Whereas the category of 'performance' may correctly explain some shared characteristics of different domains, it cannot account for their specific differences.

The re-creation of theatre by the Church

Controversy also surrounds the theory of re-creation of theatre *ex nihilo* within Christian ritual, about the tenth century, after a prolonged discontinuity from early *medieval theatre. This theory is of *romantic origin. In 1809 *Schlegel declared that no theatre could be found in all of Europe throughout the Middle Ages. In 1839 Charles Magnin claimed, well prior to the CSA, that the new theatre was created from the festivals of the Christian Church during the tenth and eleventh centuries, exactly as it had been created from the religious festivals of ancient Greece. In contrast,

Benjamin Hunningher (*The Origin of the Theater*, 1961) claimed that the Church could not have re-created theatre because, *inter alia*, the re-creation thesis requires demonstration of total discontinuity. It would appear that absence of documentation about any form of theatre unquestionably supports discontinuity. Paradoxically, from the third to the tenth centuries, the only sources on possible theatrical activity are decisions of the Church, which consistently denounced the art of the *mimes (*mimi*) and their successors, and blamed even the clergy for indulging in this 'Satanic' activity. However, the frequency of decisions clearly decreases during the tenth century, when the supposed re-creation took place; the relative silence of the Church can be interpreted as evidence of final disappearance, or as mitigation of hostility towards theatre, and even awareness of its educational potential. The Church probably objected to stage artists reflecting a heretical attitude to sacred matters.

A. M. Nagler claims that in the *Quem Quaeritis* 'the birth of medieval drama from the spirit of liturgy lies clearly before us'. In contrast, for Hunningher it only bears witness to its adoption within a continuous dramatic tradition. Indeed, analysis of the text reveals a degree of acquaintance with theatre practice that definitely contradicts spontaneous re-creation. *See also* LITURGICAL DRAMA; BIBLICAL PLAYS.

Egyptian coronation ritual In 1950 Theodor H. Gaster (*Thespis*) published an interpretation, couched in theatrical terms, of the *Ramesseum Dramatic Papyrus*, usually called the *Egyptian Coronation Drama* which pre-dates the origins of Greek theatre by more than 2,000 years. Gaster meant to infuse new blood into the CSA thesis. The papyrus was written during the reign of Sesostris (Senusret) I, a king of the Twelfth Dynasty (*c.*1970 BC), and is probably a transcription of a papyrus written during the First Dynasty (*c.*3300 BC). The text is meant to be narrated by a reader and is interspersed with dialogue. It relates Horus' victory over Seth, who had previously vanquished and killed Osiris, and Horus' installation as the god/king of united Upper and Lower Egypt. Dialogue was performed by the king and his followers: the king represented Horus, and his followers the other characters of the myth. The ritual was performed for the king's installation or annual reconfirmation as a descendant of Horus, and for the opening of the Nile for navigation. Identification with the divine ancestors was probably meant to attach a divine aura to the new king, and thus legitimize his power.

However, the mere assumption that the king was believed to be only enacting Horus would have destroyed the ritual nature of the event. Nonetheless, there are episodes that indicate use of enacted dialogue which support the thesis that ritual can make use of the theatre as a medium.

An alternative theory The continued persistence and vitality of the main thesis of ritual origin, despite repeated criticism, is puzzling. Its charm may be due to its lending to theatre a numinous aura which it does not always possess. The theoretical stalemate probably stems from the methodologies employed in researching the elusive question of origins. While theatre historiography is limited by available documentation, theatrical phenomena probably hark back to prehistoric times which by and large have left scanty and deficient traces. Analogously, cultural anthropology is limited by its tendency to broad categories which, based on extreme abstraction of singularities, allow almost uninhibited application and hardly fit any given culture. In addition to ritual, almost every cultural domain has been suggested as an ancestor of theatre. For example, Karl Groos (*The Play of Man*, 1899) considers *imaginative play of children* as the source of theatrical drama. In enacting fictional characters, such as doctor and patient, children imprint images of human beings on their own bodies. Jane Harrison (*Ancient Art and Ritual*, 1913) suggests a *ritual dance* in honour of Dionysus as the origin of drama and traces the origins of mimetic dance back to the dawn of human culture: 'all rites *qua* rites are mimetic'. Kurt Sachs (*World History of Dance*, 1933) provides examples of primitive 'image dances' performed even today. J. Michael Walton (*Greek Theatre Practice*, 1980) suggests *oral storytelling* as the source of acting. This is a verbal art, which naturally includes the verbal components of dialogue. This element of acting in performed dialogue could have been the ground for transition from dithyrambic storytelling to tragic theatre. Indeed, the moment the oral storyteller performs dialogue 'in character' there is acting. Rock and cave paintings and engravings from the Stone Age are usually conceived as objects of ritual or depictions of ritual acts. Rock paintings and engravings at Tassili n'Ajjer (central Sahara, *c.*6000–3500 BC) display masked men, *masks, processions, dancing groups, and possibly jesters. Although physical distortion, long noses, and swollen bellies do call to mind comic actors in pictures of popular comedy in ancient Greece, masks and jesters are not necessary elements of theatre. However, jesting, although a possible element of ritual, does not necessarily indicate acting. In any case, lack of verbal description precludes definite interpretation. In its present state 'The Sorcerer' (*c.*14000 BC), discovered and possibly reconstructed by Breuil, reveals a man wearing a skin and head of a deer. Although different interpretations are possible, many scholars consider it as the earliest theatrical document. However, there is no indication of acting, unless an essential connection between disguise and theatre is presupposed. Nonetheless, these pictures, especially the amazing cave paintings at Altamira (*c.*14000 BC) and Lascaux (*c.*18000 BC), reflect the use of imprinted images (although not on bodies) for signification and communication. Even if used for magic purposes, their descriptive function must be presupposed.

The common denominator of all these alternative approaches to the origin of theatre is not the often invoked instinct for impersonation, but rather the crucial role of imagination: the propensity of the human brain to produce mental images and use them for thinking. Since theatre is a medium that operates by the use of imprinted images, it is sensible to search for its *roots* in this elementary ability of the human brain. Whereas a history of theatre could determine the origins of particular theatrical genres in ancient Greece or medieval Europe, the quest for roots assumes that proto-theatrical activities may have emerged any time and anywhere. The roots of theatre must lie in the very structure of the human psyche.

Sigmund Freud (*The Interpretation of Dreams*, 1900) was probably the first in claiming that dreams think in images and that this mode of thinking is of preverbal origin. Following the thesis that childhood replicates early stages in the development of humankind, Jean Piaget (*Play, Dreams and Imitation in Childhood*, 1945) provides empirical evidence for viewing the imagistic play and drawings of children as a mode of thinking. Susanne Langer (*Philosophy in a New Key*, 1942) perceives images as basic units of thought. This is amply corroborated by recent findings through digital neurobiology.

Mental images cannot be communicated unless they are imprinted on matter, as illustrated by rock and cave engraving and painting, image, dance, and theatre. Theatre extends the principle of the similarity underlying images to the imprinting matter: that is, images of human beings are imprinted on human actors. This also applies to some kinds of play and dance. Despite similarities, however, none of these domains should be conceived as originating theatre; but all of them attest to common roots in the mental imagery spontaneously produced by the human psyche.

The imagistic method of representation, which was superseded by natural language and probably residually left as the 'language' of the unconscious, is socially permitted to re-enter verbal culture only within predetermined domains, mainly in the form of art. If that is so, we must assume both a primeval phase of spontaneous creation of imagistic media, and a subsequent phase of formalization, in which natural language fulfilled a crucial role, in order to conform with a mind conditioned by language. It is in this transitional phase in the development of culture, which assumedly conjoined imagistic thinking and incipient language, probably replicated in children's imaginative play and drawing, that the roots of the medium of theatre may be found.

Primeval ritual was probably a conglomerate of forms of representation, which eventually developed into independent media and/or arts and outlived the cults in which they were initially employed. Yet despite the use of these rudimentary arts in primitive rituals, only theatre has been accorded the groundless privilege of originating in ritual. ER

Orlik, Emil (1870–1932) German-Czech artist and designer. Best known as a painter and graphic artist, Orlik was associated with the art nouveau movement in Munich in the 1890s. In Berlin Orlik worked with *Reinhardt at the *Deutsches Theater, and his design for *The Winter's Tale* (1906) may have been the first major application of art nouveau aesthetics to *scenography. After seeing the production *Craig accused Reinhardt of plagiarism, which Orlik took as a compliment. His next design was for *Schiller's *The Robbers* (1908), after which he became more directly involved in staging and the entire visual effect. In 1900–1 Orlik had spent a year in Japan studying artistic techniques. This experience was decisive in the construction of a *kabuki-style stage with a *hanamichi (ramp) for the *pantomime *Sumurun* (1910), a massive and wordless Reinhardt show performed in Berlin, Paris, London, and New York. Other set designs for Reinhardt included *Oedipus the King* (1910). CBB

Orton, Joe (1933–67) English playwright. Before his violent murder at the hands of his lover, Orton was one of the most promising young playwrights of the 1960s, specializing in slightly *absurdist black *comedies in which his *characters' observation of social form and primness of speech clash spectacularly with their situations. His first play, *Entertaining Mr Sloane* (1964) transferred to the West End. The situation of its plot—a brother and sister blackmail their father's killer into becoming a sexual toy for both of them—inspired just enough controversy to ensure notoriety. His next, *Loot*, won both the *Evening Standard* and *Plays and Players* awards for best play of 1966. *What the Butler Saw*, more in line with traditional *farce than his earlier works, was still being revised at the time of his death. It received a posthumous West End production starring Ralph *Richardson in 1969, although it was not a great success. Orton's other dramatic works include the short plays *The Ruffian on the Stair* (1967), *The Erpingham Camp* (1967), and *Funeral Games* (produced 1970). MDG

Osanai Kaoru (1881–1928) Japanese playwright and director. Along with *Tsubouchi Shōyō, Osanai took a strong interest in introducing concepts of modern Western theatre and performance into Japan (*see* SHINGEKI). Inspired by *Chekhov and *Ibsen, Osanai formed a theatre company to present such plays in Tokyo, which he named Jiyū Gekijō (the Free Theatre), based on the model of *Antoine's Théâtre *Libre. Their first production was a translation of Ibsen's *John Gabriel Borkman* prepared by the great contemporary novelist Mori Ōgai. Osanai had available only *kabuki actors so that the women's roles were performed by men. A trip to Europe in 1912 helped him see what reforms were needed and his growing knowledge and enthusiasm resulted in the establishment of Tokyo's Tsukiji Little Theatre in 1924. It chiefly produced European plays in translation until his death, at which point the company split into literary and political factions. Osanai was a charismatic figure who inspired a generation of artists and intellectuals. JTR

Osborn, Paul (1901–88) American playwright and screenwriter. Osborn studied playwriting with *Baker at Yale (1927). His play *Hotbed* was produced on Broadway in 1928 and *Mornings at Seven*, a gentle *comedy about four eccentric sisters in a small town, in 1939. Osborn's other plays, some of them adaptations from novels by others, included *A Ledge* (1929), *The Vinegar Tree* (1930), *Oliver, Oliver* (1934), *Tomorrow's Monday* (1936), *On Borrowed Time* (1938), *The Innocent Voyage* (1943), *A Bell for Adano* (1944), and *Point of No Return* (1951). Osborn was well known as a screenwriter for, among others, *The Yearling* (1946), *East of Eden* (1955), and *South Pacific* (1958). MAF

Osborne, John (1929–94) English playwright. Osborne was a jobbing actor when his fourth play, *Look Back in Anger* (1956), was accepted by *Devine at the *English Stage Company. It marked a revolution in British theatre. Its anti-*hero, Jimmy

Porter, became the archetype of the 'angry young man', marking the arrival of a new generation of disenchanted, socially conscious, undeferential artists. There are *Brechtian influences (always denied) in *The Entertainer* (1957), an extraordinary state-of-the-nation play about the decline of the empire which gave *Olivier one of his greatest parts, and *Luther* (1961), which equally suited *Finney. In *Inadmissible Evidence* (1964), Osborne takes us into the mind of his *protagonist Bill Maitland (played by Nicol *Williamson), yet allows a complex structure of ironies to trouble the vicious hatreds and suspicions that rend Bill's mind. Even more daring is the *metatheatrical *A Sense of Detachment* (1972), seemingly designed to provoke *audiences into leaving. In his last play, *Déjàvu* (1992), a sequel to *Look Back in Anger*, Jimmy is a curiously *Pirandellian *character, aware of his fictional status and burdened by his notorious eloquence.

Osborne's anger was initially thought to be left wing, and his eventual move to the right seemed to some like a betrayal. But in *Time Present, A Hotel in Amsterdam* (1968), and *West of Suez* (1971) his ambivalence towards the left was as evident as his hostility to the new radicals of the late 1960s.   DR

Osofisan, Femi (1946-) Nigerian writer and director. Osofisan's plays, written in English, are complex and multi-layered. Influenced by Marx, Fanon, and Cabral, the politically confrontational dimension of his work has been combined with an appreciation of Yoruba mythology and of Nigeria's colonial and neocolonial experience. Osofisan deploys a range of devices to make spectators self-aware, so that his theatre is a place of constant reinterpretation, interrogation, and subversion. He extended *Brecht's model for a reconsideration of history in works such as *The Chattering and the Song* (1976) and *Morountodun* (1979), and in those that embody challenges on social issues, such as *Once upon Four Robbers* (1979), and has also adapted *Gogol's *The Government Inspector* (*Who's Afraid of Tai Solarin?*) and *Feydeau's *Paradise Hotel* (*Midnight Hotel*). Osofisan has worked with *Soyinka but has adopted a radically different position. He critiqued Soyinka's *The Strong Breed* with his own *No Longer the Wasted Breed* (1981), insisting on the value of concerted action. He treated *Clark-Bekederemo's *The Raft* with a similar reply in *Another Raft* (1989). An experienced director who has worked in the United States and Ghana as well as Nigeria, Osofisan was general *manager of the National Theatre in Lagos (2000-8). JMG

Ostermeier, Thomas (1968-) German director. Ostermeier quickly established himself as one of the most important directors in Germany. He was invited in 1996 to run a small experimental stage attached to the *Deutsches Theater in Berlin. Known as the Baracke, its repertoire of contemporary plays, especially by English authors such as Mark *Ravenhill and Sarah *Kane, soon attained cult status. He regards his commitment to contemporary drama as indicative of a 'new *realism' and a departure from the usual focus on the classics in German theatre. In 1999 he became co-director of the *Schaubühne, where his productions of *Ibsen have received especial praise: *Nora* (2002), *Hedda Gabler* (2005), *The Master Builder* (2006), and *John Gabriel Borkman* (2009).   CBB

Ostrovsky, Aleksandr (1823-86) Widely acknowledged as Russia's greatest playwright, he was also the most prolific, producing 47 original dramas and 22 translations of foreign plays. Comparatively unknown in the West, his main subject is the manners and mores of the Russian merchant class. Most of Ostrovsky's work premièred at the Imperial Maly Theatre in Moscow. He sought to bring about substantial changes in the internal organization of the Russian theatre, campaigning for the removal of the imperial monopoly and seeking to develop *acting through a training school. Ostrovsky's first play of note, *It's a Family Affair—We'll Settle It Ourselves* (1849), was banned for its unflattering depiction of the merchant class. His cause was taken up by the Slavophiles, who encouraged him to write what would be his first play to be staged (1853), *Don't Sit in Another's Sleigh*. His next three plays found critical success when published in the *Muscovite*, particularly *The Poor Bride* (1851).

In 1856 Ostrovsky volunteered for an ethnological excursion to the Upper Volga. This led to *The Thunderstorm* (published 1860), now generally considered to be his masterpiece. The central character, Katerina, is a compound of provincial backwardness and obscurantism, engendered by mystical religious beliefs, domestic tyranny, and sexual repression, which leads to rebellion, guilt, and suicide. During the 1860s Ostrovsky turned to historical dramas as well as articles on the state of Russian theatre. In 1870 he organized the Association of Russian Playwrights and later the Actors' Circle. In the wake of *Enough Stupidity in Every Wise Man* in 1868, he wrote *The Forest* (1870) and *Talents and Admirers* (1881) which, alongside *The Thunderstorm*, are the plays best known abroad. His final days were spent working on a translation of *Antony and Cleopatra*.   NW

O T'ae-sŏk (1940–) Korean director and playwright. The author of over 30 plays, he has directed nearly all of them for the Mokhwa Theatre Company in Seoul. O T'ae-sŏk emerged in modern Korean theatre (*shingŭk*) in the late 1960s. *Glass Tomb* (1973) characteristically dealt with the conflict between civilization and the primitiveness of Korean life; it was performed under the title *The Order* at *La Mama in New York in 1974. In his directing, O T'ae-sŏk has applied the *Gestus* of *Brecht's *epic theatre, and *Artaud's theatre of *cruelty to indigenous themes. His representative plays, published in English in *The Metacultural Theatre of Oh T'ae-Sŏk* (1999), are *Lifecord* (1974), *Ch'un-p'ung's Wife* (1976), *Bicycle* (1983), and *Intimacy between Father and Son* (1987). JOC

Ōta Shōgo (1939–2007) Japanese playwright and director. Born in China and evacuated to Japan after the Second World War, Ōta began writing plays in high school and was active in both theatre and politics for most of the 1960s. In 1968 he helped found Tenkei Gekijō (the Transformation Theatre) in Tokyo for which he served as house playwright and *artistic director until the group was disbanded in 1988. His first major critical success was the *nō-inspired *Legend of Komachi* (1977). In contrast to the speed, noise, and garrulousness of much contemporary Japanese theatre, Ota's plays are distinguished by their austerity, silence, stillness, and glacial pace. The nature of being, rather than doing, informed his *dramaturgy. Ota's works reflect his 'desire to stage living silence' in order to capture the most basic elements of human experience. His best-known piece, *Water Station* (1981), performed widely abroad, has no *dialogue whatsoever. Other works include *Sarachi* (1992). CP

O'Toole, Peter (1932–) Irish-born actor who spent his childhood in Leeds. His London debut was in *Shaw's *Major Barbara* (*Old Vic, 1956), followed by *The Long and the Short and the Tall* (*Royal Court, 1958), and a season with the *Royal Shakespeare Company playing Shylock, Thersites, and Petruchio (1960). Thereafter his career became ever more international: productions included *Brecht's *Baal* (1963), *Hamlet* (1964), *O'Casey's *Juno and the Paycock* (1966), Shaw's *Man and Superman* (1967), and *Beckett's *Waiting for Godot* (1967). In 1984 he appeared as Higgins in *Pygmalion* in the West End, a role he revived on Broadway in 1987. In 1989 he appeared as the eponymous journalist in *Jeffrey Bernard Is Unwell*, a role he recreated in 1999 at the Old Vic. On screen, his gripping performance in

David Lean's *Lawrence of Arabia* (1962) brought O'Toole huge international recognition; other films included *Becket* (1964), *The Lion in Winter* (1968), the remake of *Goodbye Mr Chips* (1969), *The Ruling Class* (1971), *The Stunt Man* (1979), *My Favourite Year* (1982), and *Venus* (2006). AS

Otto, Teo (1904–68) German designer. After study at the *Bauhaus, Otto began designing *opera in Kassel. In 1931 he became chief designer at the Berlin State Theatre. In 1933 he was forced to emigrate to Switzerland, where he was associated with the Zurich Schauspielhaus. During this time Otto began a lasting collaboration with *Brecht, designing the first productions of *Mother Courage* (1941), *Galileo* (1943), and *The Good Person of Setzuan* (1943). After the war he became an internationally known *scenographer with productions in major European cities and at New York's Metropolitan Opera. Besides Brecht, he worked with the leading directors of the early post-war period, including *Gründgens (*Faust*, 1957) and *Kortner. He designed the premières of the plays of *Frisch and *Dürrenmatt's *The Visit* (New York, 1958). Otto's designs, exceptionally varied stylistically, range from *realism to abstract stylization. CBB

Otway, Thomas (1652–85) English playwright. Clergyman's son, Oxford drop-out, and failed actor, Otway turned to playwriting with *Alcibiades* (1675), a moderately successful *heroic tragedy, and followed it with *Don Carlos* (1676), which adds individual psychology to the heroics, and *The History and Fall of Caius Marius* (1679), which grafts the pathos of *Romeo and Juliet* onto Roman political history. Otway's penchant for tragic pathos found expression in the two blank verse *tragedies for which he is best known. *The Orphan* (1680) is a domestic *melodrama in which the inadequacies of human nature replace villainy in bringing about tragic suffering. *Venice Preserv'd* (1682), Otway's masterpiece, explores love, honour, and the pathos of undeserved suffering in the context of a political conspiracy. On the other hand, there is little pathos in Otway's *comedies. *Friendship in Fashion* (1678) is a bitter and violent social *satire. *The Soldier's Fortune* (1680) is an equally sardonic sex comedy that recognizes the real social problems underlying adulterous behaviour. *The Atheist* (1683) includes a dark view of the ugly reality that follows the romantic union with which conventional comedies end. RWV

Ouyang Yuqian (Ou-yang Yü-chien) (1889–1962) Chinese actor, director, and playwright of both *jingju (Beijing opera) and the Western-style *huajü* (spoken drama). As a student in Japan, he performed in the *Chunliu She production of *Uncle Tom's Cabin*, the first Western-style play in Chinese. After returning to Shanghai in 1910 he became active in the new drama movement, performing and writing *wenming xi* (civilized drama). Meanwhile he also studied Beijing opera as a *dan* (female) actor, becoming professional in 1916; for over ten years he was the leading *dan* actor in Shanghai, where he enjoyed equal fame with *Mei Lanfang in Beijing. Ouyang also wrote some of the Beijing operas he performed, including *Pan Jinlian* (1927) in which he transformed a traditional loose woman into an individualist who lived and died for the sake of love. Some of his plays include: *Liang Hongyu* (1937), *Li Xiucheng, the Duke of Loyalty* (1941), and *The Peach Blossom Fan*, a *chuanqi* play he adapted first into *jingju* (1937) and then *huajü* (1946). After 1949 he was president of the Central Academy of Drama in Beijing.   SYL

Owen, Alun (1925–94) English playwright. A prolific writer for stage, screen, and radio, Owen was appreciated for his precise ear for speech and his depiction of life in Liverpool. He began his career as an actor but turned in 1958 to writing with the television play *The Rough and Ready Lot*. His reputation as a Liverpool playwright began with *Progress to the Park* (1958; *Theatre Workshop, 1959) which depicts two star-crossed lovers whose relationship is ruined by the religious bigotry of their elders. Other television and stage plays about Liverpool include *No Trams to Lime Street* (1959), *Lena, Oh my Lena* (1960), *After the Funeral* (1960), and the book for Lionel *Bart's *musical *Maggie May* (1964). Owen is probably most popularly remembered as the screenwriter of the Beatles' *A Hard Day's Night* (1964).   MDG

Owens, Rochelle (1936–) American playwright and poet, a leading exponent of *avant-garde drama. Her most famous work is *Futz* (published 1961, New York production 1967). A farmer enjoys sodomizing his pet pig, whom he regards as his wife; and the reactions of outraged villagers result in several deaths. *Homo* (1966) deals with greed, xenophobia, and racial purity. The savage excesses of *Beclch* (pronounced 'bek-lek', 1966) lead to elephantiasis and self-strangulation. Owens occasionally turned to historical *characters—George and Martha Washington, Karl Marx, Emma Goldman. Her works have been staged widely in Europe and translated into half a dozen languages. She also published more than a dozen volumes of poetry.   CT

Page, Geraldine (1924–87) American actress. After years of summer and winter *stock, she joined *Off-Broadway's Circle in the Square, making her breakthrough as the spinster in a revival of *Summer and Smoke* (1952) that demonstrated her affinity for *Williams *heroines. In 1954, a year after her first appearance on Broadway, she had a hit as Lizzie in *The Rainmaker* (1954), which she also played in London. She appeared in sixteen other Broadway plays, including *Sweet Bird of Youth* (1959), *Strange Interlude* (1963), *Three Sisters* (1964), and *Agnes of God* (1982). Page acted in *regional theatres, on television, and in 27 films. She and her husband, actor Rip Torn, founded Off-Broadway's Sanctuary Theatre in 1976. SLL

Page, Louise (1955–) English playwright. Page first received notice in 1978 with *Tissue*, a play about breast cancer. She was resident playwright at the *Royal Court (1982–3). Her best-known play, *Salonika* (1982), received the George Devine award. Other major plays include *Real Estate* (1984), *Golden Girls* (1984), *Beauty and the Beast* (1985), and *Diplomatic Wives* (1989). Page's work, which has been widely produced, focuses on *gender and issues of ambition and choice in contemporary life. AHK

Pais, Ricardo (1945–) Portuguese director. Pais trained at the Drama Centre, London. Back in Lisbon in 1974, he began to create seductive stage metaphors and powerful visual and aural landscapes, dominated by experiments with space, body, movement, and voice. He directed classical and contemporary plays (*Vicente, *Machiavelli, Shakespeare, *Otway, *Garrett, *Wedekind, *Ionesco, *Bernhard) as well as creating productions, mostly written or conceived by him, in which *music or *dance played a leading role. His *Fausto. Fernando. Fragmentos* (1988, after Fernando Pessoa's poem on the Faust myth) remains one of the most imaginative Portuguese productions of the time. He was in charge of major cultural initiatives in Oporto, where he brought a radically new approach to the Teatro Nacional de S. João (1995–2000). PEC

Pak Sŭng-hŭi (1901–64) Korean actor, director, and playwright of modern commercial theatre (*shinp'agŭk*). He was a founding member of the Towolhoe (Earth and Moon) group in 1922 while a student in Tokyo. After returning to Korea, he led the group for over twenty years, exhausting his inheritance to maintain its activities. He sought to revolutionize dramatic form by writing complete play scripts and abandoning the improvised *dialogue common in Korean theatre. His most successful play, *Arirang Pass* (1929), which was lost and reconstructed through the director's recollection, dealt with lovers forced to part because of family bankruptcy caused by Japanese exploitation. This play, which sentimentalized life under Japanese suppression, is still loved by *audiences. He wrote over 200 plays, including translations and adaptations; all but four were lost in a fire during the Korean War. Of those which survive, *Offspring* (1929) and *Hometown* (1933) also portray the repression of Korean life under the Japanese. JOC

Palais Royal, Théâtre du Seventeenth- and eighteenth-century Paris *playhouse, or one of later theatres with the same name. The larger of two private *proscenium theatres constructed for Cardinal *Richelieu within his Parisian palace, it was originally supplied with an *auditorium of gently sloping steps and equipped with the latest Italianate stage machinery. Opening with Jean Desmarets's *Mirame* in 1641, it typically housed spectacular productions that explicitly glorified France. After Richelieu's death it passed into the control of the French royal family, who often used it for court performances. In 1660 Louis XIV granted the use of the theatre to *Molière's company, which shared the space with the King's Italian players throughout the height of the writer's career (*see* COMÉDIE ITALIENNE). After Molière's death in 1673, the theatre passed into the hands of his rival *Lully, and afterwards remained the site of the Opéra until it was destroyed by fire in 1763. CJW

Palitzsch, Peter (1918–2004) German director who began his career at the end of the 1940s at the Volksbühne in Dresden. In 1949 he joined *Brecht as assistant and *dramaturg at the *Berliner Ensemble. Between 1956 and 1959 he directed (with *Wekwerth) *Synge's *Playboy of the Western World*, *Vishnevsky's *Optimistic Tragedy*, and (with Ekkehard Schall) Brecht's *Arturo Ui*. In 1961 he left for West Germany, and became *artistic director at Stuttgart's State Theatre (1966–72), then co-director of the municipal theatre in Frankfurt (1972–80). From 1980 Palitzsch worked freelance in Germany and abroad, and in 1992 joined the board of the Berliner Ensemble. As a Brechtian he had a major impact on West German theatre in the 1960s and 1970s, directing classics and contemporary work (*Frisch, *Pinter, *Beckett) with precise dramaturgy and clarity, theatrical wit balancing a dialectical approach.   CBB

Palladio, Andrea (1508–80) Italian architect, whose attempts to resurrect the principles of antiquity had a decisive influence on *neoclassical architecture. Through his patron *Trissino he became involved with the Olympian Academy in Vicenza, which took an active interest in the revival of classical drama. In 1556 he illustrated the Vitruvius edition of Daniele Barbaro, which allowed him to develop a clearer picture of classical playhouse architecture. In 1558 he constructed for the Academy a small stage for the performances of 'Olympic Games' (semi-scenic poetry recitations and play readings), and a few years later a temporary stage in the Palazzo della Ragione, complete with *scaenae frons* and *perspective scenery, which was used for productions of Piccolomini's *Unceasing Love* (1561) and Trissino's *Sophonisba* (1562). In 1564 he constructed another temporary theatre for the Compagnia della Calza in Venice for a performance of Conte di Monte's *Antigono*, which *Vasari described as 'a wooden half-theatre in the style of the Colosseum'. These preparatory studies allowed Palladio to design his masterpiece, the Teatro *Olimpico in Vicenza, begun in February 1580, shortly before his death the same year, and completed by his pupil *Scamozzi in 1584.   GB

Pallenberg, Max (1877–1934) Austrian actor. *Reinhardt engaged Pallenberg in 1914 for the *Deutsches Theater, Berlin, where he remained for the rest of his career. His important roles included the leads in *Molnár's *Liliom* (1922) and *Hofmannsthal's *Der Unbestechliche* (Vienna, 1923), and the father in *Pirandello's *Six Characters in Search of an Author* (1924). He created the part of Schwejk in *Piscator's *The Adventures of the Good Soldier Schwejk* (1928), which remained one of his most important performances. Pallenberg's special gift for gesture, facial mimicry, and

*improvisation enabled him to add political insight and critique to the petty bourgeois *characters he so often played. He is acknowledged as one of the greatest German-speaking actors of the Weimar period. His exceptional range spanned low comic roles to Mephisto in Reinhardt's production of *Faust* (*Salzburg Festival, 1933).   CBB

Panikkar, Kavalam Narayana (1928–   ) Indian playwright, director, poet, composer, and critic. In 1968 he formed Kuthambalam, an experimental theatre in Kerala, and wrote and produced *The Witness* (1964), *The Revered God* (1973), and *Tiruvazhithan* (1974). Moving to Thiruvananthapuram, he renamed his troupe Tiruvarang, and it functioned under the umbrella of Sopanam, a centre for performing arts and research. His major productions in the Malayalam language were *One's Own Impediment* (1975) and *The Black Guy* (1983), noted for their use of regional folk idioms and *acting methods. Panikkar was also known for inventive productions of Sanskrit dramas which draw on the tenets of the *Natyasastra*. They have included *Bhasa's *The Middle One* (1979), *Karna's Task* (1984), *The Broken Thighs* (1988), and *The Vision of Vasavadatta* (1990); and *Kalidasa's *Shakuntala* (1982) and *Vikramorvasiya* (1981). Panikkar's ethnographic research on the *sopanam* music style has been widely recognized.   JOG

p'ansori Korean folk opera. *P'ansori* (literally, 'story singing') utilizes a single singer-actor and a drummer. It needs no props except a hand fan for the singer, a double-headed barrel drum for the drummer, and a straw mat. The fan can represent anything and the mat any location. Traditionally, *p'ansori* was performed almost anywhere: a market-place, town square, a courtyard, a king's palace. The singer-actor performs all the parts and produces all sound effects. The performance contains three elements: singing in verse, *dialogue and narration in prose, and *acting and movement expressing emotion. The singer-actor, who can be male or female, undergoes years of vocal training. Although the origin of the form is unclear, in the early eighteenth century twelve *p'ansori* works existed. The number fell to six in the late nineteenth century when Sin Jae-hyo (1817–84), a *p'ansori* master, set down the texts of the oral tradition. Of these only five are popularly performed today: *Song of Ch'un-hyang*, on a wife's sincere feelings for her husband; *Song of Shim Ch'ong* on filial piety; *Song of Hung-bu* on virtue and vice; *Song of the Water Palace*, based on an animal fable; and *Song of the Red Cliff*, from Chinese folklore.   JOC

pantomime, British For above three centuries pantomime has been a continually mutating genre. During much of this span it has been characterized by rhyming doggerel verse, orchestral *music, song, *dance, allegorical or mythic *characters sharing the stage with comic roles, and spectacular scenic *illusions or 'transformations'. Despite the implications of its name, pantomime is not silent and is, in its later manifestations, highly verbal. It is an entertainment whose core remains largely persistent despite constant demands for novelty, yet, in response to taste and cultural pressures, pantomime's structure, purpose, frequency, and *audience have all changed dramatically. Today pantomime is a Christmas family entertainment, whereas it was a *satirical drama intended for adults meant to be offered year round.

The immediate ancestor of pantomime was created in 1702 when Paris suppressed illegal theatres performing *commedia dell'arte style in fairgrounds. A mixed handful of French and English actor-dancers sought work in London. The French-speaking performers could be understood only when they danced and *mimed their roles, so the entertainments offered were *commedia* episodes transposed to the English environment and set to music. These were billed as 'night scenes' or 'Italian night scenes' and featured comic episodes in which London tradesmen mingled with the *commedia* characters. In 1716 John Weaver, the dancing master at *Drury Lane, devised *The Loves of Mars and Venus*, which was advertised as a 'new Entertainment in Dancing after the manner of the Antient Pantomimes' (i.e. pantomimes of the late Roman Empire). The rival *Lincoln's Inn Fields offered its own 'pantomime' with characters from Roman mythology suddenly transformed into or replaced by characters from the night scenes, and the mythic setting transformed to modern London. Thus a pantomime was a drama in two halves: a mythic, musical opening, and a briefer comic modern knockabout segment, somewhat like the Jacobean *masque.

The *manager at Lincoln's Inn Fields was John *Rich, whose talents lay in dancing and devising spectacles. Under the stage name of Lun, Rich developed the role of *Harlequin and made him the *hero of the English harlequinade. Armed with a magic sword or bat (actually a *slapstick), Rich's Harlequin treated his weapon as a wand, striking the scenery to sustain the illusion of changing the setting from one locale to another. Objects, too, were transformed.

Under Rich's influence pantomimes acquired their form for the next 50 years. Rich began with a plot from Greek or Roman mythology. Later in the century the search for plots for the openings widened to include British folk tales, popular literature, and, in the 1780s and 1790s, nursery tales. As the opening concluded, an enchantress with remarkable powers intervened to conduct the 'transformation scene'. Here the characters were transformed as if by magic to the identities of the harlequinade. The performers' outer *costumes, often papier-maché *masks or 'big-heads', were removed by wires tugged from the wings. In the harlequinade were Harlequin, his female companion Columbine, Columbine's parent or guardian Pantaloon, and a miscellany of topical English characters. Harlequin and Columbine tried to elude the pursuing Pantaloon using Harlequin's magic to stave off capture, their flight meanwhile taking them in successive scenes to places currently in the news, offering wry comment on persons and events. Harlequinades featured topical satire, and, because visual rather than spoken, were less provocative to *censors. 'Panto' was available to all classes at theatres royal and fit-up *fairground booth theatres, even at *puppet booths and primitive *circuses.

In the next 60 years its growth was due largely to the talents of Joseph *Grimaldi, and to the astute showmanship of the actor and pantomime 'arranger' Charles Farley (1771–1859). By 1815 Grimaldi had deflected its centre from Harlequin to *Clown. The overall structure of pantomime again changed to what was to be its most elaborate form, and pantomime was recognized by its champions as an effective mirror of British life as the nation adjusted to the Industrial Revolution, trade, empire, and coped with foreign conflicts and domestic crises.

With Grimaldi's success the opening became little more than a pretext for introducing the characters to be transformed into the harlequinade. Harlequin always received his magic bat from a benevolent agent or good fairy, thus signalling the start of a harlequinade which could extend for as many as ten or fifteen scenes. Finally, in a scene set in a gloomy forest, cavern, or ruined castle—the 'dark scene'—Harlequin's attention wandered long enough for Clown or Pantaloon to seize the magic bat and render the lovers helpless. Again the benevolent agent appeared, restored Harlequin's power at the return of the bat, and effected a reconciliation in a final splendid scene. Grimaldi's individual approach had ossified into a national style and determined the form of pantomimes for the four decades to follow: clowns thereafter called 'Joey'.

Pantomime has long featured *female and *male impersonation: the dame is a man, and the principal boy is a girl. Both roles reveal efforts to control, if only in fantasy, female power and to limit the areas in which women may hold power. Pantomimes from the Regency and Victorian periods offered biased stereotypes of ageing females: ugliness allied to misplaced vanity, sexual voracity paired with squeamishness, assertiveness, slovenly housekeeping, appalling taste in clothes, excessive curiosity, and chronic and indiscriminate gossiping.

Although attempted as early as 1819, the principal boy was not accepted into pantomime until the 1830s and even then was performed by adolescent or pre-pubescent girls, not by mature actresses. The principal boy appeared in the opening, as she does today—as the male lover courting the girl who will become Columbine. However, in the Victorian transformation scene, the principal boy was replaced by a male Harlequin. Only a real male was allowed Harlequin's potent weapon, the bat, and permitted to win Columbine. Further, the principal boy did not appear until women began to compete with men for jobs in industries where the first 'factory girls' were children and adolescents. As the median age of female employment in factories rose through the 1860s, so the age and appearance of the principal boy changed, from immature adolescent to sexually mature woman with full hips and padded thighs.

As early as the 1830s arrangers looked for means of enhancing a Grimaldi-less pantomime, and the following seven decades leisurely altered the flavour and structure of pantomime with infusions from *burlesque and *music hall. By the 1850s burlesque had largely replaced pantomime at all seasons but Christmas. By the 1870s music-hall artistes were cast in pantomime opening roles and were contracted to perform their variety turns, regardless of the relevance of the material, and strongly satiric topical jokes disappeared, replaced by dazzling scenic effects.

Pantomime continues to change. The structure that now survives is a confused residue of the Edwardian form: the 'dark' penultimate scene is now the 'dark opening' in which a Demon King arrives to spread blight on the happiness of a nursery tale character; the opening itself is swollen to great length; the final scene is wholly absorbed into the transformation scene; the harlequinade has vanished altogether. The once wide range of subjects has shrunk as well. The overwhelming preference is for *Cinderella*, followed by *Aladdin, Dick Whittington, Jack and the Beanstalk, Babes in the Wood, Mother Goose*, and *Robinson Crusoe*. Rarely do we see any one of the hundreds of subjects from fairy tales and English folklore which formerly found their way into pantomimes. Changes came from other directions as

well. Rock 'n' roll stars Tommy Steele and Cliff Richard were among the first male principal boys since the early 1830s; today the female principal boy is more likely to be found in regional and northern pantomimes than in the south of England.

In the twentieth century it became commonplace for leading pantomime roles to be cast from film, radio, and television. It is not uncommon now to find actors known to British audiences through Australian television serials, American situation comedy, and international professional athletics. Although such performers add a certain topicality, and although jokes identify the performer with her or his usual vehicle, pantomime has become more generalized in addressing comic subjects and much less specific in selecting targets for even mild satire. Sanctioned by economies of cost, some pantomimes are now planned for ten years of hard stage life: the new script, with fresh costumes, scenery, and music, is first performed in a major urban centre, then, with different casts, annually recycled to progressively smaller cities and lesser theatres until sets and costumes are threadbare.

Shakespeare may be the national dramatist, but pantomime is still the British national entertainment. It accounts for approximately 20 per cent of all live performance, and approximately the same percentage of work for actors in live entertainments occurring between December and March. *See also* FÉERIE. DM

Papp, Joseph (1921–91) American *producer and director. Born Joseph Papirofsky in Brooklyn, he trained as an actor in Hollywood, and worked behind the scenes in theatre and television through the mid-1950s. In 1954 he formed the Shakespeare Workshop—the organization that became the *New York Shakespeare Festival in 1956—and directed its first productions. Papp was a brilliant organizer and fundraiser, and a tireless and inventive promoter of his theatre. He was known to appear uninvited in newsrooms to harangue reporters and critics; and in 1957 claimed the festival's flatbed truck broke down in the middle of Central Park so that the group could perform there. In 1962, after Papp's aggressive lobbying with funders and city officials, the festival opened the Delacorte Theatre in Central Park, and in 1967 opened its downtown home, the Public Theatre. Papp controlled all aspects of his theatre along with a tight group of deputies including his fourth wife Gail Merrifield, the company's literary manager. The Public was renamed the Joseph Papp Public Theater in 1992. KF

parades and processions Events in which people move in groups through public spaces for purposes of display or *ritual celebration. Though in practice they often overlap, parades and processions differ essentially in their styles and functions. Parades are designed primarily for presentation before an *audience, the energy directed outward to the spectators. Parades have many different functions, ranging from civic festivals to state displays and shows of power. In contrast, processions direct their energy into the processional group, which may be commemorating a religious or civil rite, or engaging in a festival occasion, or both. Whereas parades are ordinarily out of doors, in the street or on a designated parade ground, processions take place indoors as well as out. They are frequently characterized by a mood of solemnity lacking in parades.

Parades and processions manifest the human need to congregate for purposes of communal expression. They may celebrate the triumphs of military victories (Roman triumphal entries, tickertape parades following the world wars), or of *sporting events (championships, the parades of the nations in Olympic games). Processional audiences may mourn collectively at times of local, regional, or national loss. They may mark annual holidays, whether seasonal festivals (new year celebrations, carnival parades), religious feasts (Shiite Muharram processions, Catholic festivals honouring the Virgin Mary), celebrations of ethnic solidarity (St Patrick's Day or Columbus Day parades), or patriotic occasions (Independence Day in the USA, 1 October celebrations in communist China).

Parades and processions do not in themselves serve a single political or sociological function. They may be utilized as instruments of power or protest. They may allow an ethnic or religious population to celebrate its identity within a complex culture. They offer opportunities for subversion. They may be more simply occasions for celebration, or rituals of worship. But whatever the rationale, the impulse to parade or process through the streets or in other public places or areas of private worship seems basic to the human herding instinct. *See also* ENTRIES, ROYAL.   MR

Parker, Stewart (1941–88) Irish playwright whose first success was *Spokesong* at the Dublin Theatre Festival in 1975. His seriously playful dramas, usually involving music, explore the politics, history, and life of Northern Ireland with full-blooded theatricality. He stretched theatrical form to accommodate black *comedy, irony and paradox, and to undermine the clichés of Irish sectarianism. He described his trilogy—*Northern*

Star (1984), *Heavenly Bodies* (1986), and *Pentecost* (1987)—as a 'continuing comedy of terrors'. *Northern Star* contains brilliant pastiches of Irish theatrical styles from *Boucicault to *Behan, as well as dramatizing the tragedy of the 1798 Protestant rebel Henry Joy McCracken. Other plays include *Catchpenny Twist* (1977), *Nightshade* (1985), and works for radio and television.   CAL

Parks, Suzan-Lori (1963–   ) *African-American playwright who first attracted notice in 1990 with *Imperceptible Mutabilities in the Third Kingdom*. Fascinated by the play of history in the contemporary landscape, her *The Death of the Last Black Man in the Whole Entire World* (1990) and *Devotees in the Garden of Love* (1992) work postmodern twists on American myths and icons. This characteristic came to the fore the next year with *The America Play*, which includes Abraham Lincoln (played by a black actor in the original production) musing on the 'great hole of history'. *Venus* (1996), about a large African woman exhibited as an anatomical oddity in the nineteenth century, was directed by Robert *Wilson in New York. *In the Blood* (1999) updated Hawthorne's Hester Prynne from *The Scarlet Letter* into a homeless woman living under a bridge with a ragtag brood of cross-racial children. *Topdog/Underdog* (2001) is about sibling rivalry experienced by two black brothers named Lincoln and *Booth. *365 Days/365 Plays*, a series of mini-dramas written over a single year, played around the US in 2005-6.   BBL

parody Parody mimics human behaviour, and can be the funniest and at the same time the most unscrupulous and wounding form of *satire, a slightly skewed version of its prey. Even when a *puppet and its handler carry out the impersonation, as in the British television series *Spitting Image*, the moving likeness and distortions of bodily and facial features accentuate, rather than temper, the insults. Meanwhile, the *audience may not be able to repress its tears of joy. In the American *Saturday Night Live* TV series, some actors, under false hair and exaggerated cosmetics, lampoon celebrities, garble political speeches, and smirk shamelessly at their fans. Most parodies are performances about the arts of performing. For example, *Fielding's *Tragedy of Tragedies; or, The Life and Death of Tom Thumb the Great* (1731) parodied the *heroic drama of the seventeenth century, and most tenaciously its hysterical seriousness. *Sheridan composed *The Critic; or, A Tragedy Rehearsed* (1779) to parody the *rehearsal process, as *Buckingham and Fielding had done.

A parody can present a community, real or imaginary, in a new and scornful light. *Gay's *The Beggar's Opera* (1728) turns London's police force into crooks, and Macheath, a gang leader, into the *hero, as *Brecht would do two centuries later with his adaptation, *The Threepenny Opera* (1928). In the modern era, despite the plethora of parodies, their topics have mostly proved commonplace or their treatments erratic. But *Barnes's tragifarce *Laughter!* (1968) takes place in a concentration camp and ends with a Jewish *vaudeville duo putting on a brief turn, after which 'they die in darkness'. Barnes, prolific writer of comedies and *farces, knows that, in assuaging our grief over fiendishness, parody and laughter take us only so far. ACB

Parsi theatre The dominant form of entertainment in urban India from the 1860s to the 1930s. Influenced by British travelling companies and amateur theatricals, Parsi theatre blended European and South Asian practices. Professional *touring companies performed on *proscenium stages decorated with richly painted curtains. Orchestral *music, declamatory *acting, and mechanical devices created spectacular effects. Parsi theatre ushered in modern theatre throughout South and South-East Asia, and lent its genres, aesthetics, and economic base to popular Indian film. Parsi theatre's appeal extended far beyond the Parsi community, and its content had little to do with Parsi religion or culture. Followers of the prophet Zarathustra, the Parsis emigrated from Iran to Gujarat over 1,000 years ago. Settling in Bombay in the eighteenth century, prominent families made fortunes as bankers and traders. Social interaction with colonial elites, exposure to English-language theatre, and entrepreneurial skill inclined Parsis to organize the first modern theatrical companies. Although companies remained under Parsi management into the twentieth century, actors and writers increasingly were drawn from other Indian communities.

Initially companies performed in Gujarati or English and spectators were urban Parsis and Europeans. In 1871 Urdu-language dramas were introduced and the *audience rapidly expanded to all classes and communities. Parsi theatre appealed through its performative vocabulary rather than linguistic medium, much like the present-day Hindi cinema. The early repertoire comprised heroic legends from the Persian *Shahnamah*, Indo-Islamic fairy romances (*Indar Sabha*), and adapted Shakespearian *comedies and *tragedies. Later the focus turned to historical tales, mythological material, and contemporary social dramas. Women's parts were commonly played by *female

impersonators who attracted large followings. Actresses began to appear in the 1870s. Hundreds of Parsi theatre companies existed, including spin-off troupes outside Bombay, but sound film in 1931 led to a rapid decline. Most of its personnel found employment in cinema, and audiences too switched loyalties. The Moonlight Theatre of Calcutta, however, continued under the direction of Fida *Hussain up to the 1950s. KH

Pasqual, Lluís (1951–) Spanish-Catalan director. After an apprenticeship with *Strehler in Milan, he was the co-founder (with Fabià *Puigserver) in 1976 of the Teatre Lliure, Barcelona's leading independent company dedicated to innovative stagings of classical and modern world drama. In 1983 he became director of Spain's national theatre and in his first season startled *audiences by replacing the orchestra seats of the historic Teatro Nacional María Guerrero with a vast sandpit for the *Marlowe/*Brecht *Edward II*. Landmark productions were *Valle-Inclán's *Bohemian Lights* (1984), Brecht's *Mother Courage* (1985), and *García Lorca's *The Public* (1986). After leaving the national theatre in 1989, he directed *opera in Spain, Italy, France, and Belgium and became director of the Théâtre de l'Europe in Paris. He returned to the Teatre Lliure in 1998 and was involved in the company's move to a larger space in Barcelona's new Ciutat de Teatre. In 2000, as a farewell to the Lliure's original home, he directed an unconventional staging of *Chekhov's *The Cherry Orchard*, which extended into the lobby and encompassed the audience. MPH

Passion play In the strict sense, a play depicting the sufferings of Christ on the cross. In fact, the need to explain the meaning of the Passion often led to the depiction of other events in human and divine history. The origins of the Passion play are obscure, but it is probable that the impetus was the new emphasis during the eleventh and twelfth centuries on the humanity of Christ, so that the Passion play arose in the context of Christocentric mysticism and piety.

A Latin Passion play from the Benedictine monastery in Monte Cassino dates from the twelfth century, and references to other Passion plays throughout the thirteenth century suggest an early tradition of Latin Passions in Italy. In Germany, two Passion plays from the monastery of Benediktbeuern in Bavaria have survived in a thirteenth-century manuscript, but they might actually be older. In the longer of the German plays, both Mary Magdalene and the Virgin make extensive use of the vernacular.

By the end of the fourteenth century, the vernacular Passion play was firmly established. Those performed in Germany and France during the fifteenth and sixteenth centuries were remarkable achievements. Based on the Vulgate Bible, on *The Golden Legend* (a collection of saints lives and short treatises on Christian festivals), and on other works of piety, they furnished dramatic material for some of the most spectacular productions in the history of the theatre. In Germany it has been possible to distinguish at least five regional textual traditions, but expansions, redactions, and alterations were constant, and extant manuscripts represent freeze-frame versions of ever changing texts. The situation in France is similar, although we know the names of several playwrights. These were large, sprawling plays, over 25,000 lines long and requiring anywhere from two to several days to perform. Passion plays for the most part did not long survive the sixteenth century. The Parlement de Paris banned their performance in 1548; the last recorded performance at Lucerne was in 1616. The tradition carries on, however, at *Oberammergau. *See also* BIBLICAL PLAYS.   RWV

Pastor, Tony (1837–1908) American blackface *minstrel and entrepreneur. Pastor transformed the lower-class entertainment of minstrelsy and *vaudeville into respectable family fare. He began at *Barnum's American Museum in New York in 1846. At 10 he became a blackface minstrel with the Raymond and Waring Menagerie. He also performed in *circus and *variety shows. In 1861 he sang the 'Star Spangled Banner' on the eve of the Civil War, and from then on interspersed all his work with patriotic songs. Pastor is said to have formulated the idea of a vaudeville show, essentially a variety show with a diversity of acts from other forms of American popular entertainment such as minstrelsy, the circus, Shakespeare *burlesques, comedy sketches, and popular *music and *dances. By 1881 Tony Pastor's New Fourteenth Street Theatre opened with the specific purpose of presenting vaudeville 'for the amusement of the cultivated and aesthetic'.   AB

pastoral drama A form of drama evolved from poetry—particularly the idyll, eclogue, or bucolic—which idealizes nature and the rural life. Ostensibly the pastoral tells stories of shepherds but at root the form problematizes social relationships and ideas of modernization: the purity and simplicity of shepherd life is contrasted with the corruption and artificiality of the court, the town, or the city. The pastoral sometimes uses the device of 'singing matches' between two or

more shepherds, and it often presents the poet and his friends in the personae of shepherds and shepherdesses. Classical models are drawn from Theocritus and Virgil and from the idea of a lost golden age, imagined by Hesiod and Ovid, in which humans lived close to and at one with nature. In Theocritus' idylls the convention and dramatis personae were established: his verse celebrates the beauty and simplicity of rustic life in Sicily, his *characters including Daphnis, Lycidas, Corydon, and Amaryllis.

The form won renewed significance in the *early modern period. In Italy Poliziano and Beccari set a tone for *Tasso's *Aminta* (1573), generally regarded as the first pastoral play. *Il pastor fido* by *Guarini (c.1597) influenced *Fletcher's *The Faithful Shepherdess* (1608) and *Lyly's *Love's Metamorphosis* (c.1600). The best known pastoral play, Shakespeare's *As You Like It* (c.1599), found a source in the earlier pastoral romance of *Rosalynde* by Thomas Lodge (1590). Shakespeare's play *parodied the vogue for pastoral verse while also reimagining the form as a counter-pastoral: despite being a drama of transformation in the woods, it is also full of scepticism about the perceived delights of the rural. The eighteenth century began to adapt the convention to more *realistic depictions of rural life and the genre all but disappeared thereafter, though the dialectic of the rural and the urban, of nature and civilization, remained common dramatic themes.   AS

patent theatres In anticipation of Charles II's return from exile, the remnants of the old London acting companies began to perform plays in the spring of 1660. That summer, however, Charles gave a joint theatrical monopoly to the courtiers *Davenant and *Killigrew, who suppressed other companies and forced actors to join their theatres, the King's Company (Killigrew) and Duke's Company (Davenant). Formal patents were granted to them in 1662 and they had eliminated all competition by 1667. The patents were exclusive and granted in perpetuity, creating a dispensation that, although frequently challenged and altered, was to exist for nearly 200 years. After *Betterton led an actors' revolt against Christopher *Rich in 1695, the rebels operated a rival theatre in *Lincoln's Inn Fields under a licence. Unlike a patent, a licence could be withdrawn at the pleasure of the Lord Chamberlain. By the 1720s the rules about who could legally offer plays had become fuzzy and their enforcement lax. Thomas Odell, Henry Giffard, and *Fielding all established theatres without patent or licence, but the Stage *Licensing Act of 1737 reasserted that only theatres holding royal patents could operate, though their productions were now subject to pre-*censorship. Thereafter the patentees of *Drury Lane and *Covent Garden frequently acted to enforce their monopolies, but in the early nineteenth century the proliferation of small venues and transpontine theatres put the system under great stress. While spoken drama was technically limited to the patent houses, other venues began to stretch the boundaries of *melodrama, bringing it closer to the patent house fare. The patent system came to an end with the Theatre Regulation Act of 1843, which lifted the prohibition on spoken drama at non-patent houses (but maintained censorship). MJK

Pavlovsky, Eduardo (1933-) Argentinian playwright, actor, and psychoanalyst. After *absurdist plays such as *We Are* and *The Tragic Wait* (1962), politics revolutionized his work, resulting in the hugely successful *Mr Galíndez* (1972), which violently portrayed an omnipresent repressive system. *Spiderwebs* (1977) was banned for distorting traditional values. Several months later, after Pavlovsky's office was invaded by men disguised as gas meter-readers (as *Spiderwebs'* two paramilitaries had been), Pavlovsky escaped to Spain, returning in 1980. In the 1980s his *characters, already typified by their split condition as the shared subconscious of repressor and victim, began to discard psychological unity, so that *Potestad* (1986) and *Pablo* (1987) display an 'aesthetic of multiplicity'. Two actresses shared the role of 'She' in Laura *Yusem's controversial 1990 staging of *Pas de deux*: one played the naked, raped body, the other the character's ethos which survives to defy her assassin. An 'anti-postmodern' resistance in the face of national and personal physical decay informs such plays as *Red Balloons Red* (1994) and the *monologue *The Death of Marguerite Duras* (2000).   JGJ

Payne, B. Iden (1881–1976) English actor, *manager, and director. After a brief term at the *Abbey Theatre, he worked with Miss *Horniman in 1907 to develop a *regional repertory theatre in Manchester, acting regularly and serving as general manager until 1911. In 1913 he moved to the USA where he worked in the alternative theatre movement in New York (*Theatre Guild), Chicago, and Philadelphia. He served as head of the school of drama, Carnegie Institute of Technology (1914–34), then succeeded *Bridges-Adams as director of the *Shakespeare Memorial Theatre, staging ten productions. He moved to the University of Texas in 1946 and founded the Shakespeare festival in San Diego in 1949.   TP

Payne, John Howard (1791–1852) American actor and playwright. Payne began a weekly theatrical journal at the age of 14 and composed his first full-length play at 15. He made his acting debut in 1809 and became the first native-born star on the American stage. He was a prolific playwright and adapter. His *Brutus* (1818) was a vehicle for both Edmund *Kean and Edwin *Forrest, while *Thérèse* (1821), *Clari* (1823), *Charles II* (1824), and *Richelieu* (1826) proved that an American could write successfully for English *audiences. He is best remembered as the lyricist of 'Home, Sweet Home' from *Clari*.   GAR

Peele, George (1558–96) English playwright. A graduate of Oxford, Peele turned his hand to a variety of composition. *The Arraignment of Paris* (c.1581–4) was performed at court by the Children of the *Chapel; *Anglorum Feriae* (1595) describes a court tilt. *Woolstone Dixie* (1585) and *Descensus Astreae* (1591) were London civic pageants. Peele's plays for the professional stage are similarly various. *The Battle of Alcazar* (1588–9) is based on contemporary history, *Edward I* (1590–3) on chronicle history, and *David and Bathsabe* (c.1594?) on biblical narrative. All three plays are elaborated by apocryphal and imaginative adventure. Peele's best play, *The Old Wives' Tale* (c.1588–94), is a delightful combination of folk story and *romance that good-humouredly mocks the conventions of both. Other plays, now lost, may have contributed to his contemporary reputation.   RWV

Peking opera See JINGJU.

Penhall, Joe (1967-) English playwright. With *Some Voices* (*Royal Court, 1994), Penhall established himself as a leading figure in a new wave of British dramatists. Filmed in 2000, the play concerns the misadventures of a young schizophrenic man released into the care of his brother. *Pale Horse* (1995) deepened the melancholy in an investigation of contemporary moral emptiness. *Love and Understanding* (1997) and *The Bullet* (1998) repeated the male double act of *Some Voices*, in their pairs of lawless and conventional male leads. Penhall's breakthrough came with *Blue/Orange* (2000), which centres on the deliberation of two psychiatrists over the diagnosis of a young black man's mental illness. Though he shares with his contemporaries largely urban locations and a sense of underlying violence, there is a delicate compassion in his plays and a sense of impassioned social debate.   DR

Pennington, Michael (1943-) English actor. Pennington learned fine verse speaking and concern with complex texts at Cambridge, adding his rich and cutting voice and lithe stage presence. He soon began working with the *Royal Shakespeare Company, with especial successes as Berowne in *Love's Labour's Lost* (1978), Angelo (1974) and the Duke (1978) in *Measure for Measure*, and Hamlet (1980). Though established as one of the leading classical actors of his generation, he became disillusioned with both the RSC and the *National Theatre and, with *Bogdanov, established the *English Shakespeare Company in 1986 to create a new brash style of Shakespeare production for a popular *audience. In their successful cycles of Shakespeare's history plays he played Richard II and Prince Henry (later Henry V) as well as a brutal Jack Cade. With the collapse of the ESC's funding in 1994, he joined Peter *Hall at the *Old Vic in 1997 to play Trigorin in *The Seagull* and returned to the RSC in 1999 in the title role of *Timon of Athens*.   PDH

penny theatres Also called 'gaffs', penny theatres were common in the poorer districts of many Victorian cities. Gaffs were a permanent feature for the nineteenth-century inhabitants of London's New Cut, Shoreditch, and Whitechapel Road. They were housed in converted factories and warehouses and accommodated thousands, or in dwelling houses or shops with room for only a few spectators. Though children and teenagers probably made up a large portion of the *audience, adults, male and female, were also regularly found in the gaffs. In the larger venues performances were announced on handbills. Shakespeare, *melodramas, and *music-hall programmes were the usual fare, in performances lasting no more than an hour and repeated many times during the evening. Dramas were sometimes performed in dumb show (in a vain attempt to evade *licensing regulations), but usually caution was thrown to the wind, and *dialogue, often of a very coarse and lurid nature, was used. Companies varied from the extremely small to a substantial ten or twelve, with individuals doubling parts, acting as ticket takers, and running a lottery in the interval.   AF

Pepys, Samuel (1633-1703) English diarist and government official. Pepys's *Diary*, written 1660-9, is a storehouse of information concerning the Restoration theatre. As a regular theatregoer Pepys commented on plays, actors, *costumes, scenes, and *audiences. He inspected stage machinery and visited the tiring room. He interviewed *Killigrew, the *manager of the Theatre Royal. Some of his comments on Shakespearian revivals and adaptations are legendary: *Romeo and Juliet* was 'the worst that ever I heard in my

life'; *Twelfth Night* was 'a silly play'; *Macbeth* was 'one of the best plays for a stage, and variety of *dancing and *music, that ever I saw'.   RWV

performance art/art performance These two terms, and the more general term 'Performance', emerged in the early 1970s to describe international contemporary work which straddled the boundaries of the performing and visual arts. (In this entry the word 'Performance', when capitalized, is intended to convey the category of work covered by 'performance art' and 'art performance'.) That activity derived from a long *avant-garde tradition, issuing from experiments in theatre, visual art, *music, poetry, and *dance, and from the various artistic movements in which the separate forms coalesced and cross-fertilized. Performance in this sense seems to defy definition 'beyond the simple declaration that it is live art by artists' (RoseLee Goldberg).

What differentiates Performance from other arts? Clearly it is not a matter of medium. Music, for instance, might be identified as the art form whose medium is sound, while literature can be identified as the art whose medium is language. But Performance makes use of every available medium, material, or even art form, including film, music, painting, sculpture, theatre, dance, architecture, photography, and so on. Many Performance pieces employ more than one medium, for instance Laurie *Anderson's use of music with technologically altered instruments and voices, choreographed actions, slide and film projections, video, and holograms. But that does not imply that Performance is necessarily *multimedia. For example, performances by action artists and body artists like Vito Acconci, Chris Burden, Otto Muehl, Joseph Beuys, and Ulay/Abramović in the mid-1970s involved the stark confrontation of bodies and objects in social situations, without extraneous media.

One might think that Performance requires the presence of a performer. But even that broad generalization is thwarted when we consider that a Performance piece may be comprised of the action of *puppets or automata, the movement of objects or machinery (like those of Survival Research Laboratories), or a succession of slide images. Nor does Performance require the presence of an *audience, as *Kaprow's participatory performances, evolving out of *happenings, and Anna Halprin's movement *rituals show. Contemporary Performance seems to emerge from two dominant sources. On the one hand, it was a reaction by certain painters and sculptors to what they believed to be the fundamental theoretical limitations of gallery aesthetics in the

1960s: *art performance*. On the other hand, at roughly the same time, practitioners of theatre initiated a revolt against the dominant and prevailing forms of drama: *performance art*.

Art performance Many of the European avant-garde art movements of the first half of the twentieth century included para-theatrical auxiliaries (e.g. *futurism, *dada), as did both American and Japanese avant-garde painting and sculpture following the Second World War. Harold Rosenberg dubbed Jackson Pollock's work 'Action Paintings' and treated his canvases as the tracery of the artist's performative act of painting. Although static, paintings were reconceived in action terms, rather than object terms, under the category of performance. Another interpretation, championed by Clement Greenberg, glossed abstract expressionism as reflexive reductionism which strove to reveal the essential conditions of painting. Art performance grew out of the repudiation of this essentialist approach to art, the belief that each art form has its own delimited nature, fixed by its medium.

The most vividly remembered strategy of 1960s art performances is the happening. One important precedent for happenings was a multimedia event staged by John Cage at Black Mountain College in 1952, in which a film was shown while choreographer Merce *Cunningham danced, Charles Olson and M. C. Richards recited poetry, David Tudor played the piano, and painter Robert Rauschenberg displayed his work and played music of his choosing on an old record player. The anti-essentialist message was that anything could become art. Inspired by Cage, fine artists displaced their concerns from the canvas and embodied them in performative genres like happenings and Fluxus. In a parallel development, the Japanese groups Gutai Art Association and Hi Red Centre made art out of actions with objects.

A reaction against another aspect of mainstream gallery aesthetics—its formalism—led, in another way, to 'body art' in the 1970s. Eschewing the flamboyant theatricality of happenings, body artists like Vito Acconi, Chris Burden, Stuart Brisley, and Gina Pane explored issues of risk, death, decision-making, and the psychosexual, often through an existentialist focus on the self through the insistent presence of the body. Also in the 1970s, the closely related movement of conceptual art arose, criticizing the commercial nature of the art world and the commodity status of the art object. For example, in *Catalysis III* (1970), Adrian Piper walked through the streets with 'Wet Paint' printed on her shirt, suggesting the idea 'don't touch' in a way that conflated her rights to sexual autonomy with a gibe aimed at the art world's elevation of the materiality of paint.

By the 1980s, postmodernism in gallery art, with its programme of exploring and interrogating representations, especially in the mass media and popular iconography, had a performance component. Laurie Anderson's rock star image had the postmodern quality of both criticizing and participating in contemporary pop culture. And this connected to postmodernism in the theatre, which involved recycling plays, images, and genres, as in the work of director Peter *Sellars. If art performance originally emerged in a cultural moment that valued authenticity and spontaneity, by the 1980s it participated in a cultural moment of anxiety about life as a hollow product of signs and signifying systems.

In the 1970s and 1980s Performance proved a fertile ground for advancing and embodying feminist politics, allowing an open space for the expression of feelings, fantasies, and political action. In Los Angeles, Womanhouse, organized by visual artists including Judy Chicago, and the Woman's Building were the site of many installations and performances; during the 1970s, also in California, several women's performance *collectives were founded. In the 1980s and 1990s the French artist Orlan's impossible project of using plastic surgery to mimic images of female beauty in various canonical works by male artists combined feminist social criticism and conceptual art with a new spin on the body art of the 1970s. Janine Antoni's *Loving Care* (1992-6), in which she used her hair as a mop to cover a gallery floor with hair dye, parodically criticized the legacy of male artists like Yves Klein and asserted the female artist's agency. Beginning in 1985, the Guerrilla Girls, a group of anonymous performers wearing gorilla masks, picketed American museums for discriminating against women artists.

By the 1990s American art performance was dominated by identity politics, as not only women but artists of colour asserted their presence in museum exhibitions and in other venues. Coco Fusco and Guillermo *Gómez-Peña underlined the marginalization of Americans of colour and the politics of exhibition when they displayed themselves in art museums and natural history museums as caged exotic specimens of a primitive culture in *Two Undiscovered Amerindians* (1992-4). Toward the end of the twentieth century, new works in art museums were as likely to use new media, such as video and computers, as paint and canvas. A number of visual artists have explored the intersection of the possibilities and drawbacks of intensifying technology through live performance, such as Mona Hatoum and Stelarc.

Performance art was initially a reaction to the polemics and practices of the theatre world in the 1950s and 1960s. Avant-gardists criticized the representationalism of Shakespeare and the modern classics, as well as of popular shows on Broadway and the West End, the spectatorial aspects of mainstream theatre, and its text-oriented or verbal emphasis. Instead they proposed a theatre that would be presentational, participatory (or at least challenging to the division between spectator and performer), and image oriented as well as kinesthetic. Theatrical performance art brought the performative aspects back to the theatre. One strategy was to install real events (rather than fictive ones) on stage. So, for different reasons, the art world and the theatre world moved in similar directions.

The first stage of performance art stemmed from an Artaudian vision of an anti-literary theatre. According to *Artaud and those inspired by his vision, theatre should be *'cruel': emotional and visceral, rather than intellectual. The *Living Theatre, for example, staged *Mysteries and Smaller Pieces* (1964) as a series of ritual games without plot or *characters, as in happenings. However, there was a difference between the art performance and the performance art of the 1950s and 1960s. While happenings and Fluxus were anti-essentialist, ironically the Living Theatre, the *Open Theatre, and the 'poor theatre' of *Grotowski were essentialist, searching for the core elements of theatre and theatricality and trying to purify theatre, to strip theatre down to its essence. The actor became a performer rather than a character.

Not only did the happenings makers and postmodern dancers evince a special interest in articulating space, but so did *Foreman and *Brook. Foreman's preoccupation with perspective, perception, and indexical devices, physicalized in production, connected his work in the theatre with the concerns of gallery artists/art performance makers like Michael Snow and Robert Morris. Moreover, the emphasis on the visual moved performance art toward the visual arts, strikingly in Robert *Wilson, Meredith *Monk, Ping *Chong, and Jan *Fabre in the 1970s and 1980s.

As in art performance, feminism had an impact on avant-garde theatre internationally, for instance in the many performances at WOW Café in New York. In Britain, Rose English and Sally Potter's feminist performances tended toward cinematic imagery, before Potter moved into independent filmmaking. Bobby Baker makes visible and ironic the daily activities of ordinary housewives. Annie Sprinkle, a former *pornographic actress, frankly celebrates women's sexuality with tales and demonstrations of eroticism as well as vulnerability, while Karen *Finley speaks in a Cassandra-like voice of prophecy and possession about women's oppression and abuse.

Feminism was by the 1990s only one branch of multiculturalism, which also included the politics of ethnic identities, sexuality, and ability. Multicultural performance art often took the form of autobiographical confessionals, as in Tim Miller's narratives of gay life in America and Robbie McCauley's stories of her African-American family. This genre was born partly of the widespread use of performance art by feminists (especially in California) in the 1970s, partly of the use of the solo form, which lends itself to autobiography, and partly of the changing, increasingly multicultural demographics of the avant-garde art and theatre worlds. With the expansion of ethnically diverse populations both in the United States and Europe, as well as the intensification of economic and cultural globalization, by the 1990s artists raised questions about who we are, what made us this way, and what is to be done about it.

Video and computer technologies have increasingly attracted performance artists in the 1990s and after, just as they have attracted art performers like Mona Hatoum and Stelarc. New technologies can extend the possibilities of bodies, space, imagery, and point of view in live performance, as well as contrast live and mediated events.

In the United States, performance art became notorious and was often censured in the popular press during the 'culture wars', especially when in 1990 the National Endowment for the Arts, contravening the recommendations of peer panels, denied funding to four performance artists (Finley, John Fleck, Holly *Hughes, and Tim Miller). In the 1990s US funding shrank for both individual artists and producing organizations, and American performance art was also decimated by the proliferation of cable television and the Internet, which multiplied venues for the subversive acts of social and political criticism that previously had been live performance's domain. In Europe at the turn of the twenty-first century, however, art performance and performance art flourished, often underwritten by state arts funding.   SB/NC

Performance Group New York company, founded in 1967 by *Schechner to challenge the distinction between *audience and performer and between performance and 'real life'. The goal was an experience of transcendence for all present at the theatre event; Schechner believed in the potential of theatre as *ritual. The Group's pieces were created in collage style and used existing texts and found material as well as the members' personal contributions. As such the company formed part of a continuum of American *collectives that stretches back to the *Group Theatre of the 1930s. The Performance Group's most famous production was *Dionysus in 69*, based on *Euripides' *The Bacchae*, which they created in 1968-9. The Dionysus actors were encouraged to interact with the audience, and some performances dissolved when the orgiastic experience overtook the theatrical one. After one other production, *Makbeth* (1970), the original group disbanded. Schechner reformed the Group and continued to create collage-like productions including *Commune* (begun in 1970). Many important experimental theatre artists worked with the Performance Group, including the founding members of the *Wooster Group, who took over the Performing Garage when Schechner's troupe disbanded in 1980.   KF

peripeteia An unexpected reversal or a sudden turn of events in the plot of a drama that leads to an opposite state of affairs. *Aristotle identified *peripeteia* as an element in a complex plot and linked it with *anagnorisis* (recognition), a new perception or discovery on the part of the *protagonist. Since there can be several instances of *peripeteia* in a play (for instance *Sophocles' *Oedipus the King*) it ought not to be confused with *metabasis*, a general change over the course of a play from prosperity to adversity or vice versa. Aristotle's examples of *peripeteia* underscore the irony of blasted expectation that characterizes this acute form of *metabasis*.   RWV

Perlini, Amelio ('Memé') (1947-) Italian actor, director, and cinematographer. In 1973, with the *lighting artist and designer Antonello Aglioti and the musician Alain Curran, Perlini formed Teatro La Maschera, Rome, and established himself as an important voice in the Italian *avant-garde with the productions of *Pirandello chi?* (1973), *Tarzan* (1975), *Yellow Whiteness, with Sounds of the Sea* (1974), *Othello perche?* (1975), *Landscape No. 5* (1975), and *Locus Solus* (1976). Perlini aimed not to please but to provoke his *audience, to jangle their expectations of theatre as a spectacle of scenery and *costumes designed to support a literary text involving specific *characters. Thus he shrank text to segmented phrases and sounds and, from a position in front of the stage, manipulated lighting in such a way as to reduce actors, objects, and scenery to fragments, the *surreal, dreamlike atmosphere was heightened by contemporary *music, such as that of Philip *Glass.   JEH

Perry, João (1940-) Portuguese actor and director. He began his career in 1953 at the Teatro Nacional D. Maria II and became a permanent actor there in 1978, but during the 1960s and 1970s he worked with alternative companies. He played in a wide variety of productions: drama, *comedy, *variety, television, and film. Productions such as *Tango, Equus, Baal*, and *Emigrants* were valued for his meticulous and creative characterization and *Stanislavskian exploration of the psychological. He worked with *La Mama in New York, where he made his debut as a director in *Stolen Words* (1971). He has since directed Herman Broch, *Marivaux, Shakespeare, and an *opera by Cimarosa.   MJB

perspective Shortly after the rediscovery of Vitruvius in the *early modern period, and in accord with the rapid development of perspective in the graphic arts, experiments began in Italy with painted scenes in perspective in the early sixteenth century. *Serlio's 1545 treatise transmitted the idea to the rest of Europe, where it caught on over the next 100 years, especially in aristocratic theatres under the influence of *neoclassicism. Perspective's ability to create apparent *reality, provided that the visual angle subtended is kept small, made an important difference: the *audience now seemed to look through a window into the *illusion of another world. Unlike *medieval theatre traditions, which depicted the actor against a simple or unencumbered ground, in the perspective stage the fictive world is actualized primarily by *trompe l'œil*. Serlio designed with single-point perspective, a natural choice for the streets or squares of an Italian town. But single-point perspective poses severe problems, since it creates an extremely forced perspective that looks cavernous and renders upstage scenery comically small next to actors, requires distortions in the painting of *flats and wings, and is fully effective for only one seat in the house: the 'king's seat', elevated and at the centre of the *auditorium, some distance from the stage. For everyone else the picture appears distorted. Around 1700, *scena per angolo* (two-point perspective) revolutionized scene painting, its gentler perspective obtained by placing the two vanishing points far offstage. Perspective scenery, once Ferdinando *Bibiena disseminated its techniques in 1732, remained part of the visual theatre until well into the twentieth century. Since the Second World War, perspective scenery has tended to be three dimensional and designers have preferred to use it only for deliberately forced perspective.   JB

Petherbridge, Edward (1936–) Lean and poised English actor and director. He began a long association with the *National Theatre in 1964, appearing in *Trelawny of the 'Wells'* (1965), *Rosencrantz and Guildenstern Are Dead* (1967), *Volpone* (1968), *The Way of the World*, and *The White Devil* (both 1969). He was a founder member of the Actors' Company, appearing in *'Tis Pity She's a Whore*, *The Way of the World*, *Tartuffe*, and *King Lear* (all 1972). For the *Royal Shakespeare Company he was a touching Newman Noggs in *Nicholas Nickleby* (1980). He was co-director of the *McKellen and Petherbridge group at the National (1984–6), acting in *The Duchess of Malfi*, *The Cherry Orchard*, *The Real Inspector Hound*, and *The Critic* (all 1985). He was seen as Cyrano at Greenwich (1990), in *The Seagull* opposite Judi *Dench at the National (1994), and *Cymbeline* at the RSC (1997). On television he was Dorothy L. Sayers's eponymous detective *hero in *Lord Peter Wimsey* (1987). AS

Petit-Bourbon, Théâtre du A long vaulted hall, at 54.6 m (179 feet) the longest in Paris, used intermittently for court entertainments and, from 1577, when the *Gelosi played there, by travelling professional troupes. It had a high, vaulted apse at one end. Its stage was raised above a flat pit, which also served for performance, and it extended, probably forward of the apse, by some 15.6 m (53 feet). Two superimposed galleries of open *boxes ran along the walls of the *auditorium. In 1645, for Strozzi's machine-play *The Counterfeit Madwoman*, *Torelli built a new stage on which he installed, for the first time in France, his revolutionary counterweight scene-shifting machinery. In 1658 the Petit-Bourbon became *Molière's first Paris home, to be shared with Tiberio Fiorilli's *commedia dell'arte company. Two years later, however, it was demolished, to make way for the colonnade of the Louvre, and Molière was transferred to the *Palais Royal. JG

Petrushevskaya, Lyudmila (1938–) Soviet/Russian playwright whose work reached the stage only after glasnost. *Music Lessons* (1972) had been written for the *Moscow Art Theatre but was never staged there; an amateur production at Moscow State University (1987) was closed after it caused too much publicity. Her second play, *Cinzano* (1973, staged 1987), was one of the first swallows of glasnost, portraying the squalor of everyday life and addressing openly the issue of alcoholism. By the late 1980s, *Three Girls in Blue* (1983) and *Columbine's Apartment* (1988) were seen in Moscow, and *Cin-*

zano was *touring European festivals. Petrushevskaya strikes a balance between everyday life scenes and their absurd, grotesque, and ironic theatricalization. Her plays provide glimpses of mundane existence, void of any development, and beyond the wit and irony lies the bleakness of Soviet life. BB

Peymann, Claus (1937–) German director. Peymann attracted national attention with *Handke's *Offending the Audience* (Frankfurt, 1966). After a short period as a co-director at the *Schaubühne in Berlin (1971), he worked freelance at major theatres. From 1974 to 1979 he was *artistic director at Stuttgart's State Theatre but was forced to resign in 1979 after a scandal surrounding his alleged sympathies with the terrorist movement the Red Army Faction. He moved with his troupe to Bochum where he remained until 1986, when he assumed control of Vienna's *Burgtheater. In 1999 he was appointed *artistic director of the *Berliner Ensemble, where he has recently directed Brecht (*Mother Courage*, 2005) and Shakespeare (*Richard III*, 2008). Peymann is representative of a group of German directors in the late 1960s who tried to reform the established theatre through collective management and politically inflected productions. His career has always been accompanied by carefully orchestrated controversy, both artistic and political. His productions are characterized by careful *dramaturgical preparation and topical interpretations of the classics. He has developed special relationships with Austrian dramatists such as Handke and *Bernhard. CBB

phallus A false penis worn by actors in certain forms of classical and classically derived *comedy. Carried also as a serious symbol of regeneration in religious processions, an exaggerated phallus made of leather was sported by some *characters in *Old Comedy and in a variety of local *farces in ancient *Greece and Italy. JMW

Phelps, Samuel (1804–78) English actor and *manager. Phelps first appeared in London in 1837 in a series of Shakespearian roles and played supporting roles with *Macready at *Covent Garden (1837–9). In 1844, taking advantage of changes in the *licensing act permitting any theatre to perform *legitimate drama, Phelps leased *Sadler's Wells, an entirely unfashionable theatre in north-east London, remote from the West End. Here Phelps presented 31 of Shakespeare's plays in eighteen seasons (fourteen in 1856–7 alone), new plays, and other revivals. He attracted a loyal local *audience and some support from West End theatregoers. Lacking Macready's jealousy of potential rivals, Phelps stressed thorough *rehearsals, ensemble, unified productions, and pleasingly illustrative but not lavish scenery and spectacle. In this last respect his *Pericles* (1854) and *Midsummer Night's Dream* (1853) were outstanding. After he left Sadler's Wells in 1862, Phelps spent his time fishing, returning to the stage in the provinces and in London. His last role was Cardinal Wolsey in *Henry VIII* in 1878. In his large repertory, Phelps was especially admired as Lear and Othello, and although he was not a natural comedian his Bottom and Falstaff were the best of their time.   MRB

Philipe, Gérard (1922–59) French actor. Often considered one of the finest of his generation, and elevated to cult status after his untimely death from cancer, Philipe starred in many acclaimed films after the Second World War, working with some of the finest directors of French cinema. His iconic status in French culture is also due to *Vilar's vision for the *Théâtre National Populaire, where Philipe attracted large popular *audiences, performing in classical roles for which he became celebrated as a romantic *hero for the modern age: *Corneille's *Le Cid*, *Hugo's *Ruy Blas*, and *Kleist's *Prince of Homburg*.   DGM

Phillips, Robin (1942–) Anglo-Canadian director. Born in Surrey, Phillips acted and directed with the *Chichester Festival and *Royal Shakespeare Company, and served as *artistic director of the Greenwich Company Theatre in London. In 1975 he was appointed artistic director of Canada's *Stratford Festival, which he revitalized with several productions that combined audacious staging with brilliant illumination of text. Enormously energetic, in six seasons there Phillips directed 29 productions and six revivals, including celebrated versions of *Measure for Measure*, *As You Like It*, and *Richard III*. But his tenure at Stratford began in controversy—a foreigner appointed in nationalistic times—and his departure in 1980 sparked a lengthy struggle over succession. Since then Phillips has served as artistic director of the Grand Theatre in London, Ontario (1983–4), and the Citadel Theatre in Edmonton (1990–5), but has worked mainly as a freelance. Acclaimed productions have included *Lloyd Webber's *Aspects of Love* (Edmonton, 1991), *Schiller's *Don Carlos* (Toronto, 1998), and several productions for the Stratford Festival and the Canadian Opera Company.   DWJ

Phillips, Stephen (1864–1915) English playwright. For a brief period Phillips, a cousin of *Benson, was celebrated as a new poetic dramatist. Beerbohm *Tree produced *Herod* (1900) and *Ulysses* (1902); *Alexander produced *Paolo and Francesca* (1902). The praise was excessive, setting up expectations that Phillips was unable to meet. *Nero* (1906) and *Faust* (1908), both produced by Tree, failed, and with that Phillips's career collapsed. His last two plays, *Iole* (1913) and *The Sin of David* (1914), found little support, and he died destitute.   TP

physical theatre A relatively new term open to debate. Theatre based on physicality has always existed, ranging from the *circus (using skills like *juggling, *acrobatics, trapeze, and *clowning) and *commedia dell'arte* to *mime, *pantomime, and *dance-theatre. 'Physical theatre', however, attempts to describe a type of hybridized non-traditional theatre which places emphasis on physical virtuosity but is not exclusively dance, and which, although it often uses words, usually does not begin with a written text (*see* DEVISING). Its creators often use an image, an object, a movement, or a gesture as a point of departure.

Many early twentieth-century theatre visionaries (*Craig, *Appia, *Jaques-Dalcroze, *Artaud) prepared the way for physical theatre, but perhaps none more than *Copeau, who sought an open playing space which demanded actors who could occupy it with authority. To achieve this, he instituted training in many forms of movement: *ballet, gymnastics, *masked *improvisation, corporeal mime, *nō, and clowning, paving the way for a synthesis of physical forms. Exercises from Copeau's École du Vieux-Colombier gave rise to the careers of *Decroux and *Lecoq, and through them to *Barrault, *Marceau, *Mnouchkine, Robert *Wilson, *Lepage, *McBurney, and many who, rather than 'saying the text and making appropriate gestures' (*Grotowski's words), relegated the script to a secondary role, created it or adapted it themselves, or treated it unconventionally. Copeau, who was not alone in opening this Pandora's box, would be shocked by what he provoked, since he believed the theatre's task was to serve the playwright faithfully.

The development of physical theatre also coincided with a growing awareness of Asian forms and the rediscovery of the body through *sport. Western innovators of the early twentieth century were in many cases inspired by glimpses of non-Western forms in which actors were also dancers, singers, and acrobats, and where scenery, when it existed, was sparse and symbolic, allowing space for movement of the actors' bodies and the spectator's imagination (*see* SCENOGRAPHY). In 1931 Artaud saw Balinese dancers at the Colonial Exposition in Paris, and wrote enthusiastically about them. *Brecht, who saw *Mei Lanfang's Beijing opera (*jingju*) performance in 1936, greatly admired the actors' acrobatic quality.

At the beginning of the twenty first century physical theatre was a hybridized and hyphenated art, relying on the physical skills from the Western tradition and the rigorous physical training of Asian forms, and combining them in an exemplary fashion to create something that is simultaneously new and old.   TL

Piaf, Édith (1915-63) Famed French singer who supported herself as a child by singing in the Paris streets. As a *cabaret and *music-hall artist, her intensity, nostalgic lyrics, and strident yet controlled voice greatly moved her *audiences, especially coming from such a tiny, waifish figure. Piaf *toured widely as a singer, and acted in films as well as stagings of *Cocteau's *The Indifferent Beau* (1941) and Marcel Achard's *Little Lili* (1951). Among her famous songs are 'Je ne regrette rien', 'La Vie en rose', and 'Pour deux sous d'amour'.   SBB

Picard, Louis-Benoît (1769-1828) French actor and *manager. Picard's early career as a manager in Paris was peripatetic: the *Odéon burned down in 1799, and his company played in six different theatres before settling at the Louvois in 1801, which he was to manage with considerable success. Meanwhile, he had begun to write *comedies, which range from light-hearted *satires (*The Little City*, 1801) to *Duhautcours* (1801), whose *realism foreshadows *Scribe, and *Capitulations of Conscience* (1809), a character comedy in the tradition of *Molière. Favoured by Napoleon, Picard was awarded the Légion d'Honneur. Renouncing his acting career, he was elected to the Académie Française in 1807, also becoming manager of the Opéra.   WDH

Picasso, Pablo (1881-1973) Spanish artist. Throughout his long career Picasso made numerous incursions into the theatre. As early as 1917, in the midst of his cubist phase and at the behest of *Cocteau, he designed the *Ballets Russes production of *Parade*. His collaboration with *Diaghilev's company continued in productions of Manuel de Falla's *El sombrero de tres picos*, Stravinsky's *Pulcinella*, and Milhaud's *The Blue Train*, for the curtain of which Picasso reproduced an enormous version of his own painting *Two Women Running on the Beach* (1922). Following his last trip to Spain in 1934, he started to write poems and other pieces, the best known of which was the play *Desire Caught by the Tail*, which was performed privately in Paris in 1944 with an improvised cast which included *Camus and *Sartre, but which would have to wait until 1988 for its professional première in New York.   KG

Piccolo Teatro di Milano *See* STREHLER, GIORGIO.

Pierrot French equivalent of the Italian Pedrolino, a *stock character in *commedia dell'arte*, he was an intriguing servant, familiarly *costumed in slack white trousers and blouse with a large ruff. Guiseppe Giaratone popularized Pierrot in the Italian version of *Molière's *Don Juan* (1665). Pierrot was lazy, outspoken, deliberately stupid, often misinterpreting orders, but later became a more sensitive, lonely, almost mystical figure. The agile Jean-Gaspard *Deburau turned him into a *mime at the Théâtre des Funambules in early nineteenth-century Paris, wearing the white costume, collar, make-up, and black skull cap that now define the role. In the twentieth century *Meyerhold was fascinated by Pierrot.   JTD

Pillai G., Shankara (1930-89) Indian playwright, critic, and director who explored *total theatre in a wide range of forms. In plays in the Malayalam language like *Messenger of Love* (1956), *Mirage* (1965), *The Bond* (1977), *In Search of the Black God* (1980), and *Prayer Room* (1966) he focused on conflicts of the inner self and a psychological enquiry into the unknown. His *comedies, closely related to social *satire, include *Marriage Happens in Heaven* (1958), *Crazy World* (1969), *The Saviour* (1969), and *The Younger Brother Returns* (1965). He pioneered the theatre workshop movement in Kerala, wrote a number of one-act and radio plays for pedagogical purposes, and a major history of Malayalam drama (1980).   JoG

Piñera, Virgilio (1912-79) Cuban writer whose plays rely on a variety of formal experiments while engaging directly with Cuban culture and society. *Electra Garrigó* (written 1941, premièred 1948) anticipated existentialism and the theatre of the *absurd on the Latin American stage. Piñera's lower-middle-class family background is revealed in an autobiographical and *realist play, *Cold Air* (1962). The fervent dogmatism of Cuban life from the late 1960s marginalized Piñera from public life, but though over a dozen of his plays remained unproduced, by the 1990s he had became the most frequently staged Cuban playwright. Other work includes *Jesus* (1950), *Falsa alarma* (1957), *The Wedding* (1958), *The Philanthropist* (1959), *The Thin and the Fat* (1960), *Two Old Panics* (1968), and *Dear Little Girl* (1993).   MMu

Pinero, Arthur Wing (1855-1934) English playwright. Pinero's acting career (1874-84) gave him grounding in dramatic construction, and he conducted careful *rehearsals of his own plays throughout his life, during which he wrote 54 plays. Pinero's first real successes in London were *farces for the *Royal Court, notably *The Magistrate* (1885), *The Schoolmistress* (1886), and *Dandy Dick* (1887), which are still regularly revived. The 'problem plays', which brought him fame, began with *The Profligate* (1889). His greatest contemporary success, *The Second Mrs Tanqueray* (1893), was generally thought to have improved the status of the English theatre by giving a *realistic and complex picture of the 'woman with a past'. (*Shaw thought it thoroughly unrealistic, and wrote *Mrs Warren's Profession* as a corrective.) The part of Paula Tanqueray brought Mrs Patrick *Campbell fame at the age of 28; she played it until she was 55.

Pinero's other plays turning on current social attitudes to women and the double standard of morality, *The Notorious Mrs Ebbsmith* (1895), *Iris* (1901), and *Mid-Channel* (1909), have not survived the problems they dealt with. *Trelawny of the 'Wells'* (1898) is an affectionate, sentimental tribute to the mid-Victorian theatre of *Robertson. Pinero's social *comedies, such as *The Benefit of the Doubt* (1895) and *His House in Order* (1906), combine an astringent and cynical view of human nature with able plotting. The later plays were not well received. He supported the struggle against *censorship and the campaign for a *national theatre.   EEC

Pinnock, Winsome (1961–) English playwright. Most associated with the *Royal Court, she is one of a very small group of black women playwrights to achieve sustained success in Britain. Her work is rooted in the experience of the black communities of England, particularly those of Caribbean extraction. Her plays are often political, focusing on issues of civil rights, the tensions between traditional cultures and modern society, interracial relationships, and recent black history: all themes that shape or underscore *A Hero's Welcome* (1989), *A Rock in Water* (1989, about the founder of the Notting Hill Carnival), *Leave Taking* (1988), *Talking in Tongues* (1991), and *Mules* (1996).   AS

Pinter, Harold (1930–2008) English playwright, actor, and director. After training in London, Pinter acted until 1960 under the stage name of David Baron (with *McMaster, among others). His second full-length play, *The Caretaker* (1960), brought him a West End reputation, while *Hall's staging of *The Collection* in 1962 began a long association between dramatist and director, first with the *Royal Shakespeare Company and subsequently with the *National

Theatre. Pinter's plays were at first variously described as *absurdist, 'comedies of menace', and *Beckettian; but no label aptly fits his unique and constantly changing style. It next became fashionable to define distinct periods in Pinter: plays of menace gave place to a lyrical phase of dramatizing memory, while his later work was categorized as political. Social and sexual politics are now seen to operate as strongly in early plays such as *The Birthday Party* (1958), *The Lover* (1963), or *The Homecoming* (1965) as in *One for the Road* (1984) with its analysis of the evils of absolutism, victimization, and torture. Certainly politics became an explicit concern since his involvement with Amnesty International and PEN, but it is the energizing dynamic of all his plays, even those most preoccupied with intimate relations: *Landscape* (1969), *Old Times* (1971), *Moonlight* (1993), *Ashes to Ashes* (1996), and *Celebration* (2000).

Pinter's style was often caricatured as overly deploying the pregnant pause. This is a crude reduction, but silence does contribute as powerfully to the rhythm and meaning of his plays as it does to music, allowing *characters momentarily to disguise their motives or hide their intentions, stave off attack, shield their vulnerability, or sustain an advantage. Simultaneously the pauses allow spectators space in which to reassess characters and situation by exploring the *subtext to the dramatic *action, especially what is intimated through the subtle tonal placing of speech and the spatial relations of the actors. Pinter's female characters have been dismissed as chauvinistic by feminist critics, but women in his plays often emerge as the more powerful (Ruth in *The Homecoming*, Kate in *Old Times*) by exploiting the very dependency implicit within the male characters' gaze and their questionable assertions of superiority. Men are frequently the victims or losers for their want of sensitivity. The shortcomings of what passes for masculinity are relentlessly exposed, particularly in the dramas with all-male casts (*The Caretaker*, and *No Man's Land* of 1975). Betrayal is perhaps Pinter's most enduring theme: subtle betrayals that reap devastating personal consequences (Davies in *The Caretaker*, Spooner in *No Man's Land*), and the casual betrayals of the self that bring spiritual and emotional desiccation (the fate of all three characters in *Betrayal* of 1978, and of Deeley and Anna in *Old Times*).

The most notable British actors were attracted to Pinter's work. Invariably this has resulted in their extending their known techniques, the role challenging the performer's conventional stage persona, in turn challenging *audience expectation. Judi *Dench's assumption of a vital, girlish innocence, for example, was tragic in *A

Kind of Alaska when it voiced the inner isolation of a middle-aged woman waking from the nightmarish void that is sleeping sickness, which she had entered as a teenager; and Alan *Bates's customary geniality became a terrifying mask for Nicolas's intricate games of sadism in *One for the Road*. Pinter acted in several of his plays and directed his own work and over twenty plays by such dramatists as Simon *Gray, James Joyce, *Coward, *Williams, *Giraudoux, and *Mamet. Many of Pinter's plays were originally conceived for radio or television before being staged; and over ten of his film scripts have been realized by directors including Elia *Kazan. Joseph Losey's project to film Pinter's 1972 adaptation of Proust's *Remembrance of Things Past* was not produced, but the script was staged by Pinter and Di Trevis at the National Theatre in 2000. Diagnosed with cancer in 2002, Pinter continued actively in the theatre, playing (for example) Beckett's *Krapp's Last Tape* in a motorized wheelchair (*Royal Court, 2006). His many honours were crowned by the Nobel Prize for Literature in 2005.   RAC

Pintilie, Lucian (1933–) Romanian director. His stage, television, and film productions in Romania were known for their varying styles, from the grotesque to refined lyricism. But his 1972 staging of *Gogol's *The Government Inspector* so inflamed the *censors (who saw in it a *parody of Leonid Brezhnev) that Pintilie was banned from theatre in Romania. In artistic exile, he directed *opera and theatre extensively in France. He also worked at the *Guthrie Theatre in Minneapolis at the invitation of Liviu *Ciulei. His 1979 film of I. L. Caragiale's *Carnival Doings* was suppressed by Romanian censors and not released until 1991. After the overthrow of communism in 1989, Pintilie returned to Bucharest to run the government-funded Cinema Creation Studio. His films, notably *The Oak* (1992), *An Unforgettable Summer* (1994), and *Terminus paradis* (1998) have been invited to major festivals, including Cannes and Venice.   EEP

Pirandello, Luigi (1867–1936) Italian writer, born in Sicily. Most of his early writing stems from *verismo*, the Italian form of *realism established by Giovanni Verga and *Capuana. Success came in 1904 with the novel *The Late Mattia Pascal*. Profoundly influenced by Freud and Alfred Binet, the complexity of the human psyche and the split nature of personality are at the core of all of Pirandello's mature fiction, most notably his novel *One, None, and a Hundred Thousand* (1926). The playwright-director Nino Martoglio drew him into the Sicilian dialect movement and

produced his first plays: *Think It over, Giacomino* (1916), *Liolà* (1916), and *Cap and Bells* (1917). Pirandello wrote many roles for Angelo Musco, who became a major interpreter of his work, along with the director Virgilio Talli who staged *It's So, If You Think So* (1916) with *Ruggeri in the lead, and *The Pleasure of Honesty* (1917). In 1920 Ruggeri was acclaimed for his interpretation in *All for the Best*.

Pirandello's best-known play, *Sei personaggi in cerca d'autore* (*Six Characters in Search of an Author*), was a flop in Rome in 1921, where *audiences were scandalized by its supposed immorality. A classic work of *metatheatre, calling into question the truth of performance and the performance of truth, *Six Characters* became one of the most influential plays of the first half of the twentieth century, a complex example of theatre-within-theatre which dramatizes the discrepancy between *illusion and reality. Its reputation began with a highly successful production in Milan in 1922. His play of that year, *Enrico IV* (*Henry IV*), a subtle investigation of sanity and madness, is also based on concepts of the performance of the self, *acting and honesty, pretence and sincerity. Like much of his work, both plays reveal a strong *melodramatic undercurrent to the narrative and a pessimistic outlook on life, veiled by a formal theatricality.

In 1924 Pirandello publically joined the Italian Fascist Party. His decision provoked disdain among fellow intellectuals, and his relationship with the party was strained, but Pirandello remained a member throughout his life. In 1925 he formed the modernist Teatro d'Arte in Rome, with his son Stefano and several other writers. Though *financially supported by the Fascist Party, its purpose was to promote and experiment with new dramatic techniques, which it did with vigour until 1928. In addition to Ruggeri, the company hired Marta Abba, who became Pirandello's principal actress and muse, prompting him to write a number of works with female leads, including *Diana e la Tuda* (1926), *The Wives' Friend* (1927), *The New Colony* (1928), *Tonight We Improvise* (1930), *When Somebody Is Somebody* (1933), *No One Knows How* (1935), and the unfinished *The Mountain Giants* (1937).

In 1934 Pirandello was awarded the Nobel Prize for Literature, by which time his plays were broadly known and admired. Starting in the 1960s directors such as *Strehler and *Squarzina produced new interpretations which revitalized critical opinion, and the works continue to enjoy a prominent place in the repertoire of Italian theatres. Though their innovation now seems dated and the writing overly philosophical, they are still produced abroad and remain central to the theatre. DMcM/DK

Pirchan, Emil (1884–1957) Austrian designer. Pirchan began his career at Munich's State Theatre. In 1919 he joined *Jessner at the Staatstheater in Berlin and collaborated with him until 1932. There followed positions in Prague and Vienna where he was head of design at the *Burgtheater (1936–48). In 1936 he was also appointed professor of stage design at the Vienna Academy and subsequently wrote books on theatre biography and design. Pirchan had a symbiotic relationship with Jessner. Their work included landmark productions such as *Schiller's *William Tell* (1919), *Wedekind's *Der Marquis von Keith* (1920), Shakespeare's *Richard III* (1920); for the last Pirchan created the famous *Jessnertreppen* (Jessner steps), using a giant staircase as the chief scenic element. Pirchan's designs can be characterized as *expressionist with a preference for bold *lighting and symbolic architectural forms. CBB

Pisarev, Aleksandr (1803–28) Russian dramatist and critic. Considered among the best writers of *comedies and Russian *vaudevilles of his day, Pisarev wrote more than twenty plays, many of which were either translations or adaptations of foreign models. One of his most popular was *The Tutor and the Pupil* (1824) in which *Shchepkin played the pedantic tutor who proves more stupid than his pupil. Shchepkin was also excellent as the landowner with a passion for the sea in Pisarev's *A Trip to Kronstadt*. A typical Pisarev play is *Lukavin*, in which a young man flirts with another man's wife but with his eyes on the daughter's dowry (anticipating *Gogol's *The Government Inspector*). Pisarev was hostile to the poetic style of *Griboedov's *Woe from Wit* and attacked Nikolai Polevoy for believing that the theatre was something more than entertainment. NW

Piscator, Erwin (1893–1966) German director who, together with *Brecht, developed *epic theatre. Piscator is credited with inventing *documentary drama, the political *revue, and many scenic devices. Drafted into the German Front Theatre in 1915, like many others Piscator was disillusioned and radicalized by the destruction and propaganda of the war, as well as by the complicity of capitalist industry, the art establishment, and the Church. In 1918 he joined the Berlin *dadaists in several leftist events, then founded the Proletarian Theatre (1920–1), producing plays by *Gorky and *satirical 'agitprop works such as *Russia's Day* (1920), which combined projections and posters of documentary material, narration, songs, and actors playing car-

toon-like stereotypes, devices he would later identify as epic.

In 1924 Piscator was invited by the Berlin *Volksbühne to direct *Fahnen* (*Flags*) and the *Rowdy Red Revue*. *In Spite of Everything* (1925) regularly filled the 3,500 seats at the Grosses Schauspielhaus, re-enacting historical events from 1914 to the 1919 crushing of the Spartakus Revolution, using film footage from the national archives and other epic devices. Piscator's international reputation was made with four productions in 1927–8 at the new Piscatorbühne: *Hoppla, Wir Leben!* (*Hoppla, We're Alive!*), *Rasputin, Boom*, and *Adventures of the Good Soldier Schweik*. The last was adapted from Jaroslav Hašek's Czech novel: Brecht helped write the script and George Grosz's animated cartoons, life-size *puppets, and cut-out set pieces appeared with live actors on the conveyor-belt stage. Piscator's *The Political Theatre* (1929) outlines his theory of epic theatre and the discoveries made in practice.

He fled Germany in 1931, first to Russia, then Paris, and in 1938 to New York, where he founded the Dramatic Workshop in the New School for Social Research, and taught, most notably, Tennessee *Williams and Judith *Malina. Although Brecht offered him a position at the *Berliner Ensemble in East Berlin after the war, Piscator instead moved to West Germany in 1951, where he first worked freelance and then became *artistic director of the West Berlin Freie Volksbühne in 1962. He mounted a courageous version of *The Merchant of Venice* the next year that looked forthrightly at Germany's responsibility for the Jewish Holocaust, and highly influential productions in the documentary epic style, including the premières of *Hochhuth's *The Representative* (1963), Heinar *Kipphardt's *In the Matter of J. Robert Oppenheimer* (1964), and *Weiss's *The Investigation* (1965). Piscator's work also inspired a new generation of political directors, including *Stein, *Littlewood, *Mnouchkine, *Strehler, and *Boal. SBB

Pisemsky, Aleksei (1821–81) Russian writer. After a successful start with his *comedy *The Hypochondriac* (1855), Pisemsky wrote his best-known play, *A Bitter Fate*, two years before the Emancipation of the Serfs in 1861. The play pits a peasant, Anany, against his owner who, while Anany is away earning money in the city, fathers a child by Anany's wife. On his return, maddened with jealousy, Anany kills the baby, runs away, but ultimately returns to beg forgiveness and accept imprisonment. The play's shocking *naturalistic approach in theme and language troubled spectators by its coarse *realism. Among Pisemsky's other plays are *Vaal* (1873) and *The Financial

Genius (1876), targeting the materialism of the expanding middle classes.　　　　　　　　CM

Pitoëff, Georges (1884–1939) and **Ludmilla** (1895–1951) Russian-French actor, director, designer; and Russian-French actress. Georges Pitoëff's early efforts were influenced by *Meyerhold, *Tairov, and *Komissarzhevskaya, whose troupe he joined in 1908. Later he and his wife Ludmilla founded a company in Geneva, *touring regularly to Paris before settling there. Throughout the 1920s and 1930s they produced many modern playwrights, including *Wilde, *Shaw, *Strindberg, *Gorky, *Ibsen, *Molnár, *O'Neill, *Cocteau, and *Anouilh. Their mounting of *Pirandello's *Six Characters in Search of an Author* (1923) was particularly important. While sharing the philosophy of the *Cartel des Quatre, including an emphasis on *mise-en-scène in service of the text, Pitoëff differed by offering an extremely large repertoire of foreign plays for an insular French public. Responsible for his own *scenography, his geometric visual rhetoric owed much to cubism and *expressionism, and often exploited simple means in concert with experiments in *lighting. Unlike *Copeau and *Jouvet, Pitoëff confined his scenographic innovation to the 'empty space' of a given stage, allowing the actor to reign supreme. None more so than Ludmilla, whose virtuosic *acting sustained the ambitions of the company, even after her husband's death.　　　　　　　　　　　　　　　DGM

Pix, Mary (1666–1709) English playwright, who had at least thirteen plays on the London stage between 1696 and 1706. Eight of these were written for Elizabeth *Barry and Anne *Bracegirdle at *Lincoln's Inn Fields (1695–1705). Pix's plays anticipated the sentimental reform *comedies of the eighteenth century but present a female perspective on society, particularly on love and marriage. Her complex plotting and witty *dialogue are apparent in her more successful works *The Innocent Mistress* (1697) and *The Beau Defeated* (1700).　GBB

Pixérécourt, René-Charles Guilbert de (1773–1844) French playwright; along with the German *Kotzebue, the originator of the *romantic *melodrama which dominated Western theatre in the nineteenth century. Having written an anti-Jacobin play, and narrowly escaped with his life, Pixérécourt continued to write without success until *Victor; or, The Child of the Forest* (1797). Becoming the principal exponent of *mélodrame* with more than 100 plays, Pixérécourt catered for popular taste for over 30 years. A simplified form of *drame *bourgeois* for an uneducated public—Pixérécourt claimed he wrote for 'those who cannot read'—melodrama offered moral instruction as well as spectacular entertainment; and, profiting from the ending of the ban on independent houses, its authors were to provide the staple fare of the *boulevard theatres.

The standard plot concerned the persecution of innocence by the unscrupulous wielders of power—political, or domestic. Pixérécourt's *Coelina; or, The Child of Mystery* (1800) is exemplary (translated by *Holcroft for *Covent Garden, 1802). Coelina's plight as persecuted *heroine is shared with Francisque, her father, whose tongue has been cut out years earlier by the villain Truguelin, to prevent disclosing the secret of Coelina's birth. The *villain is brought to book after a spectacular chase up a stream and across a waterfall. The sentimental appeal of the mutilated or handicapped is further illustrated in *The Woman with Two Husbands* (1802) and in *Valentine; ou, Le Séducteur* (1821). The appeal of *animals is illustrated in *The Dog of Montargis* (1814), in which the eponymous dog prevents a miscarriage of justice.

Though his *dialogue is turgid and sententious, Pixérécourt took close interest in *directing his plays, and claimed responsibility for special effects, such as the finale of *Death's Head* (1827) with an eruption of Vesuvius, whose lava engulfs the stage. Pixérécourt *managed the Gaîté Theatre with success from 1825, but lost a fortune when it burned in 1835. He suffered a severe stroke, and retired to Nancy, half-blind, to prepare the edition of his selected plays.　WDH

Planché, J. R. (James Robertson) (1796–1880) English playwright and designer. A successful *burlesque, a speaking harlequinade, the translation of a French *melodrama with a novelty trap (*The Vampire*, 1820), and research for *Kemble in 'authentic' *costuming and heraldry for Shakespeare's *King John* (*Drury Lane, 1823) brought him friends in the business, and in 1831 he became a valued member of *Vestris's team. He wrote the spectacular quasi-classical extravaganzas in which she so brilliantly starred (*Olympic Revels*, 1831). He failed as *manager of the Olympic in her absence in 1838 but was retained as designer and occasional writer at *Covent Garden and the Lyceum. Meanwhile he pursued interests in history and pageantry via the Society of Antiquaries and a gentlemanly appointment to the Herald's Office. He continued to write for the stage, as well as producing a source-book for Victorian historical painting and theatre in *The History of British Costumes* (1834). His autobiography, *Recollections and Reflections* (1872), shows how his respectable *antiquarianism and skill in creating amusing fantasies contributed to the genteel rehabilitation of stage entertainment.   JSB

Planchon, Roger (1931–2009) French actor, director, and playwright, the successor to *Vilar in espousing decentralized, popular theatre. Planchon founded the Théâtre de la Comédie in Lyon in 1953, presenting *Marlowe, *Brecht, and *Ionesco, and began long-standing collaborations with playwrights *Vinaver and *Adamov and *scenographer René *Allio. Allio was crucial in defining the Planchon aesthetic: a spectacular, often cinematic, Brechtian style that attempted to reach a wide *audience. In 1957 Planchon became director of the Théâtre de la Cité at Villeurbanne, a working-class suburb of Lyon, where he and Allio collaborated on many important productions, of which Shakespeare's *Henry IV* (1957), *Marivaux's *The Second Surprise of Love* (1959), Brecht's *Schweik in the Second World War* (1960), and *Molière's *George Dandin* (1958) and *Tartuffe* (1962) were most celebrated. At this time Planchon formulated 'scenic writing', a concept he ascribed to Brecht, in which scenic and *directorial choices were given equal responsibility to the text in creating meaning, which had the force of political action, ideological engagement, and *epic scope; it became a central concept in French theatre during the 1960s and 1970s.

In 1972 Planchon, offered the directorship of the *Théâtre National Populaire in Paris, declined the move; instead his Théâtre de la Cité was accorded the title of TNP, to be co-*managed with *Chéreau. Planchon continued to direct Shakespeare, *Racine, Molière, and Marivaux, as well as groundbreaking productions of contemporary plays such as Vinaver and *Pinter, and began a series of collaborations with scenographer Ezio *Frigerio.

Planchon became a successful playwright himself, producing many of his own works, which ranged from *musical comedies like *The Three Musketeers* (1958), to modern *comedies like *White Paw* (1965) and *Trendies* (1968), to 'provincial plays' such as *The Return* (1962), *The Villain* (1969), *The Black Pig* (1973), and *Gilles de Rais* (1976). In the late 1980s he began directing films and creating productions for other companies including the *Comédie-Française, while continuing his association with the TNP. Never retiring, Planchon continued to act and direct until his death.   DGM

Plautus, Titus Maccius (c.254–184 BC) Roman dramatist. The earliest Latin author whose works are preserved, Plautus was the father of *farce and the most successful *Roman

dramatist. His influence upon later playwrights has been immense. His 21 surviving plays were most likely based on *Greek *New Comedy. But instead of translating them directly, Plautus, as he freely admitted, 'transformed' them into 'barbarian' versions which reflected Roman taste, injecting the urbane and decorous Greek *comedies with vitality and vulgarity. The *dialogue is cruder, more ribald and playful, but also more complex in imagery. For his holiday *audience Plautus greatly increased the amount of song and *dance, adding many references to Roman customs, and often breaking the dramatic illusion with direct address.

Plautus' plots abound in deception and comic conspiracy, and serving as their mischievous agents (and foils) he made extensive use of slave characters, as in *Miles Gloriosus* or *Pseudolus*. These slaves are regularly threatened with extreme violence as a consequence of their cleverness and trickery. But the pain, beatings, and threats of torture are not merely a source of fun; they serve as important motivations of plot and *action. Plautus' plays are also inclined towards coarse or indecent humour, a fondness for disguise and crude deception, a preference for fooling over emotional interest, and a festive conclusion. Less frequently (in for example, the *Rudens* or *Captivi*) the play is informed by more ethical and philosophical concerns while still reaching a happy conclusion.

One of the recurrent elements of Plautine drama is that characters appear to make up the plot as they go along. Probably this reflects the legacy of a more tentative dramatic fare: improvised, non-literary entertainments long favoured by his audience, which the actors are thought to have assembled on the basis of *stock characters and situations, some well-worn but ever popular bits of comic business, and the barest outline of a *scenario. The chief agent of this *dramaturgical self-consciousness is again the clever slave who fashions the play around himself by wit and intelligence, triumphing over adversity and social fact in a way no actual Roman slave could have done. Masters are tricked, freedom is won, and the slave enjoys impunity. In fact, Plautus' *protagonists make a point of disdaining and mocking the fates which, but for their success in fashioning unlikely plots, would tumble down upon them. This is one key to his enduring popularity. The audience enjoys the pretence of the *actors'* theatrical improvisation, while in the process admiring and experiencing a mildly subversive and liberating pleasure in the *characters'* ability to salvage something redemptive. For his audience the pleasure and release of tension was compounded by setting plots and characters unthreateningly in Greece: for Romans a Plautine play was one extended Greek joke.

Although the changes Plautus made to Greek models helped ensure success in performance, they did little to endear him to generations of classicists, who often considered him a hack translator and adaptor of what were believed to be sublime comedies of the Greek playwrights. This is both mistaken (as the discovery of *Menander's texts has shown), and ironic in the light of the immense influence Plautus had upon dramatic composition since the *early modern period. Plautus and *Terence were the first ancient dramatists whose works were revived. The first translation of a Roman comedy, Plautus' *Menaechmi*, was performed at Ferrara in 1486 before an audience of over 10,000. Whereas previously the study and presentation of Roman drama had been the preserve of scholars, the way was now open for its exploitation as vernacular entertainment. Further productions followed, and the earliest Italian comedies, notably *Ariosto's *La Cassaria* of 1513, were closely modelled upon Plautine models. Countless works (including Shakespeare's *Comedy of Errors*, based on *Menaechmi*) have recycled his plots, characters, theatrical playfulness, and jokes.

In recent decades have been presented in schools, universities, and festivals of ancient drama. Although relatively few commercial productions occur, Plautus continues to influence farce and comedy, from *Sondheim's *musical *A Funny Thing Happened on the Way to the Forum* (1962) to the latest Hollywood romantic comedy.　RCB

Playfair, Nigel (1874–1934) English actor, *manager, and director. Beginning as an actor with *Benson, Playfair appeared in *Shaw's *John Bull's Other Island* (1904) and *Fanny's First Play* (1911), Granville *Barker cast him as Bottom in *A Midsummer Night's Dream* (1914), and with Barker as a model he took up *directing in 1918 when he renovated the Lyric Theatre Hammersmith. The theatre was launched with Barry *Jackson's production of John Drinkwater's *Abraham Lincoln* (1919). For the next decade the Lyric's stylish productions, especially of Restoration and eighteenth-century drama, delighted London *audiences. Playfair's major successes included *Gay's *The Beggar's Opera* (1920; 1,463 performances), *Congreve's *The Way of the World* (1924) with Edith *Evans, *Farquhar's *The Beaux' Stratagem* (1927) with Evans again, and *Wilde's *The Importance of Being Earnest* (1930) with *Gielgud. Playfair also acted in several of the productions.　TP

playhouse A building constructed for the purpose of presenting drama to an *audience. A term equally common in English is *theatre (derived from the Greek *theatron*, 'place for seeing'), which was the name given to the first such building erected for the purpose in *early modern England, the *Theatre, in 1576.

Ancient Europe Although theatre performances have in different times and in different cultures taken place in a wide variety of locations, indoors and out—in churches, private homes, palaces, factories, market-places, town squares, parks— most cultures have developed particular structures devoted to this activity. In classical times (*Greek, *Roman, and Hellenistic) the theatres were large, open-air places of assembly for entire communities, and the remains of many of these still surround the Mediterranean. The Theatre of *Epidaurus has been considered since classic times the outstanding example of the Greek theatre. It is an outdoor structure, with a circular orchestra in the centre for the movements of the *chorus. Sweeping around this, in slightly more than a half-circle, are rows of steps for seating, and facing them was a building for the actors, the *skene*. Separating the *skene* from the audience were two passageways through which the chorus entered and exited (the *parodoi*). The Hellenistic theatre retained many of these features, but notably shifted focus from the orchestra to a raised platform, the *logeion*, in front of the *skene*. The *skene* was also moved forward, taking over part of the circle of the old orchestra. The most fully elaborated Roman theatres carried this process further, reducing the orchestra to a half-circle (still surrounded by a half-circle of seats), and developing a highly elaborate permanent façade several storeys high for the stage house, the *scaenae frons*. The *parodoi* were also roofed over and became part of an architectural element connecting the stage and *auditorium into a single structure.

After the classical period the great public playhouses of Greece and Rome fell into ruins, and although these ruins were occasionally used in the late Middle Ages, when theatre appeared again it appeared in a variety of performance spaces, but not in buildings created for this purpose. Churches, monasteries, town squares, open fields, even cemeteries saw dramatic performances. Even the elaborate *biblical plays of *medieval England were not offered in playhouses, but in a variety of locations in the open air.

Early modern Permanent theatres were not built again in Europe until the *early modern period, when the term playhouse becomes more suitable, since these were often more like houses than the great outdoor places of assembly of classical times, smaller, more intimate, and normally made up of interior spaces. The first such theatres were built in Renaissance Italy during the sixteenth century. The oldest surviving of them is the Teatro *Olimpico, built in Vicenza by *Palladio on the model of a Roman theatre. After Palladio's death, *Scamozzi, who completed the theatre for its 1585 opening, added street scenes, built in *perspective, behind each of the doors in the Roman-style stage façade. Palladio's Roman stage was soon abandoned for a stage with a single large *proscenium arch, the first surviving example of which is the Teatro *Farnese in Parma.

These theatres were built for academic societies, like the Olimpico, or ruling families, like the Farnese, but alongside them a tradition of public theatres was being established in Venice which reached its full development after the introduction of *opera in the early seventeenth century. The Venetian opera houses utilized what would become the standard pattern for European auditoriums for the next 300 years: an open area on the ground floor (the pit or parterre) provided the least expensive admission, and surrounding it were several tiers of boxes for more affluent spectators, descending in value as one ascended. An area of open seating, the gallery, later commonly replaced the upper rank of balconies, and the *box, pit, gallery arrangement became standard throughout Europe.

While the inspiration for these public playhouses of the Renaissance was from classical sources, inspiration in other countries was often recent and local. At least nine *public theatres were built in areas neighbouring the city of London between 1576 and 1642, when all playhouses were officially closed. Public inn yards, used for dramatic performances before the first theatres, have generally been considered the primary models, which surrounded a pit (without seats) with rows of boxes. The first permanent playhouses in Spain, the Corral de la *Cruz (1579) and the Corral del *Príncipe (1583), both located in Madrid, also took their design, as well as their name, from the courtyards (*corrales) inside of which they were built. Again, the pit and box arrangement of seating was utilized. In England and Spain the public playhouses had auditoriums open to the sky to maximize interior *light. In Paris and elsewhere in Europe, most early public theatres were converted from indoor *tennis courts, which already possessed the requisite pit, boxes, and gallery, and often needed only a raised platform for a stage to complete the ensemble. The first French public playhouse was the *Hôtel de Bourgogne, opened in 1548; a royal monopoly protected it

until 1625 when a second permanent theatre, the *Marais, opened, also converted from a tennis court.

London's first indoor playhouse, the *Blackfriars, was rebuilt from a great hall in 1576, the same year as the Theatre, but the outdoor houses dominated the scene until 1596, when James *Burbage built the second Blackfriars, which shared the services of Shakespeare's company with the open-air *Globe. During the early seventeenth century indoor *private theatres, generally catering to a more aristocratic public, gradually replaced the outdoor theatres. Their interior arrangements are not certain, but they did have galleries, some boxes, and a seated pit.

Asia Asian theatrical performances, while often quite elaborate, were offered in temporary and improvised performance spaces until about the time that permanent playhouses began to appear in Europe. In China, as in Europe, the first permanent theatres were inspired by earlier non-theatrical spaces which had been previously used for theatrical offerings, in this case the popular tea houses. Here the area corresponding to the European pit was filled with tables and chairs where spectators were served tea while watching the play. The poorer spectators were placed not in the pit, but on benches on raised platforms at the sides and back of the auditorium. In larger theatres a balcony might be added for women or wealthier spectators. This style of playhouse remained essentially unchanged in China until the arrival of Western models in the early twentieth century.

Japan's *nō theatre was developed in the late fourteenth and early fifteenth centuries and its arrangements have changed little since that time. Whether located indoors or out, it consists of a square main stage area extending out into the audience with a long walkway, the bridge, at the rear, leading off to the dressing room. Both stage and bridge are covered with their traditional roofs, even when they are erected within an encompassing auditorium. The more popular *kabuki theatre first used the established nō stage. By the 1730s a forestage had appeared, upon which most of the action occurred, and the nō bridge was replaced in importance by the distinctive 'flower path', the *hanamichi, which extended directly out through the audience to the rear of the auditorium. By 1830 the traditional nō roof had been abandoned, and the kabuki stage, like its Western counterpart, occupied the full width of the auditorium, without a proscenium arch, which was introduced under European influence in 1908. The pit was divided into individual boxes and others ran in rows along the sides and back of the auditorium.

Neoclassic Europe When the first new playhouses were created in London in the 1660s after the Restoration, they reflected the style of France rather than the public theatres. The new playhouses, the most important of which were *Lincoln's Inn Fields, *Drury Lane, and Dorset Garden, were all indoor theatres whose auditoriums were divided into pit (now provided with benches), two or three rows of boxes, and one or two galleries. The stage differed from continental stages by including in front of the proscenium a substantial forestage, called the apron, a remnant of the thrust stages of Elizabethan *amphitheatres. This forestage was the main acting area, and was normally entered by doors on either side of the proscenium arch, with small balconies above them. The area behind the proscenium arch was in England used primarily for scenery, which in this period became an important part of the theatre experience (*see* FLATS AND WINGS; SCENOGRAPHY).

Both in England and the Continent, the new playhouses were fairly modest structures, not highly visible in the urban landscape. They were often converted from other modest structures, such as tennis courts, and the most economical space for a large structure in the city was generally within the open space in the centre of an urban block, with other buildings on all sides facing the surrounding streets. The façade of the theatre was at best a decorated portico the size of which gave little indication of the theatre behind it, as was the Amsterdam *Schouwburg (1637), and often the theatre had no street façade at all, but was reached through a series of narrow passageways, as were the leading theatres in London in the early eighteenth century, Drury Lane and *Covent Garden.

The general structure of European playhouses did not change a great deal in the course of the eighteenth century, although their size gradually increased, especially late in the century, as the population of the major cities rapidly increased. Drury Lane, extensively remodelled several times, began with a seating capacity of about 650 and after the renovations of 1775 could accommodate around 1,800. Covent Garden, when it was built in 1732, had roughly the same capacity as the older Lincoln's Inn Fields Theatre which it replaced, about 1,400, but subsequent alterations provided seating for over 2,000 by the 1780s and for 3,000 in 1793, at which time Drury Lane was enlarged to accommodate 3,600. The stage also grew wider and deeper, and the traditional forestage gradual-

ly diminished, though it remained the primary acting area.

The first permanent playhouse built in America was the Southwark, opening in 1766 in Philadelphia. The following year the John Street Theatre opened in New York. These, and the more elegant and ambitious playhouses that followed in the 1790s, the Chestnut Street in Philadelphia, the Park in New York, and the Federal Street in Boston, were all designed and *managed by actors with British backgrounds, and they differed in no substantial way from British playhouses of the same period.

Paris theatres also increased in size. Although France dominated the dramatic repertoire, Italy, thanks to the great families of designers—*Bibiena, Quaglio, Galliari—dominated the field of architecture and scenic design. Late eighteenth-century French works dealing with playhouse architecture invariably considered Italian design superior, due to the capacious stages and ovoid auditoriums, which provided better sightlines than the French rectangular boxes, still reminiscent of tennis courts. Among the French architects who imported Italian features, the most influential were Marie-Joseph Peyre and Charles de Wailly, who designed a handsome new home for the *Comédie-Française in 1782 (renamed the *Odéon, still one of the major playhouses).

Even more important than the internal changes at the new Comédie was the fact that it was a free-standing building with a monumental façade overlooking a public square, in every sense a civic monument. The change to such highly visible public structures was also a product of eighteenth-century thought. As early as the 1740s *Voltaire called for the cities of Europe to return to the practice of Greece and Rome and create magnificent public edifices for theatre. The first monumental theatre of modern times was erected by Voltaire's friend and disciple Friedrich the Great. In 1745 he created a huge free-standing opera house in an open square in he centre of Berlin, which Friedrich hoped to make a modern Athens.

The playhouse as public monument gradually spread across Europe. The new Berlin Royal Theatre, designed by the leading German architect *Schinkel, opened in 1820 and served in turn as a model for theatres all over Germany and Central Europe, where the state theatre building is still in many cities one of the most visible public structures. England's first monumental public playhouse was the rebuilt Covent Garden of 1809 designed by Robert Smirke. On the Continent an important encouragement for the development of the idea of the playhouse as public monument was the close relationship between theatre and the spreading idea of nationalism. In many countries, especially in Central and Eastern Europe, the theatre served as a focus for the display of national myths, legends, and history, presented in the national language. The urban and architectural visibility of the new 'national' theatres of the early nineteenth century reflected their symbolic importance in the building of a national consciousness and memory.

Opera houses Although the inspiration for monumental playhouses did not disappear, it was overtaken in importance by the appropriation of opera by the new moneyed classes as their central example of high art. Except in Italy, opera had largely been the concern of royalty, and its production very often took place in spaces within princely residences. But as the moneyed middle class assumed the dominant position in society that had been that of the aristocracy, they became the new patrons of opera. Perhaps no single architectural feature of the late nineteenth century became so emblematic of high bourgeois culture as the monumental opera house. In the early 1860s, as plans were developed for Charles Garnier's Paris Opéra, César Daly, the editor of France's leading architectural journal, wrote a series of articles claiming that the morals and values of every society were echoed in its most prominent public buildings, and that for the late nineteenth century that meant the church, the railway station, and the opera house.

For the next century, from the opening of the Garnier Opéra in 1875 to that of the Opera House in Sydney in 1976, the monumental opera house remained an obligatory emblem for any city in the world attracted to European high culture, in the Far East, in Cairo, even in the city of Manaus deep in the Amazonian jungle. Nor were such structures confined to urban centres. *Wagner's 1876 Festspielhaus in *Bayreuth popularized another version of the monumental playhouse, erected, like the great pilgrimage churches of the Middle Ages, as an attraction for a public drawn from great distances. During the twentieth century the most important development of the festival playhouse outside urban centres was not in opera but in the spoken drama, of which the first *Shakespeare Memorial Theatre at Stratford, opened just three years after the Bayreuth Festspielhaus, was the first great example. Especially after the Second World War, festival theatres sprang up across Europe and America, where the major sources of inspiration were the *Stratford Shakespeare Festival Theatre in Ontario and the *Guthrie Theatre in Minneapolis.

A common development in the playhouse as public monument in the late twentieth century was the arts complex, where several playhouses, and perhaps other cultural structures as well, were grouped into an artistic enclave within the city. The most familiar example in New York is *Lincoln Center, which includes performing spaces for dance, opera, and theatre, as well as auxiliary spaces for films, musical events, and a performing arts library. In London, the South Bank complex similarly combines a wide range of cultural structures, most notably the *National Theatre, a building which houses three different performance spaces.

Wagner's Festival Theatre at Bayreuth was revolutionary and influential in its internal arrangements. His design radically altered the normal interior arrangements of the standard European playhouse for both drama and opera. Instead of the traditional pit, boxes, and galleries, Bayreuth offered a large fan-shaped auditorium with a single ramp of seats (and a few vestigial boxes at the rear). The sides were lateral walls that suggested repeated proscenium arches extending into the auditorium, between which were multiple entrances to that space. This more democratic plan was widely adopted in European theatres built during the next century, and its general arrangement came to be known as 'continental seating'.

Modernism to the present In the late nineteenth and early twentieth century playhouses felt the effects of the technological revolution, as electricity, steam, and hydraulic power were utilized to make ever more elaborate technical effects. In New York Steele *Mackaye dazzled audiences at his Madison Square Theatre and Lyceum Theatre during the 1880s with hydraulic lifts for the entire stage, an elevator orchestra pit, the latest in electric *lighting, and similar marvels. German scenic practice was revolutionized by pioneers like Karl Lautenschläger, who created the first permanent revolving stage in a Western theatre in Munich in 1896 (it had long been a feature of the kabuki stage), and Adolf Linnebach, who developed the modern *cyclorama and the first successful device for projecting images of scenery.

Technological advances, increasing urbanization, and improved public transport all combined at the end of the nineteenth century to make public playhouses ever larger and more elaborate. Improved machinery for lifting or sliding scenery forced the fly-tower over the stage higher and the side wings wider. In the auditorium, steel cantilevering, which became general by the 1890s, allowed balconies to become larger and deeper, and reduced the once dominant boxes, in the theatres that still had them, to a few remnants hugging the proscenium arch. The coming of electricity in the 1880s improved illumination both in the auditoriums and onstage, and moreover provided a far safer lighting source than gas, which had been the standard means of illumination during the nineteenth century.

Although gas lighting provided playhouses with more flexible illumination than they had ever previously enjoyed, it was a very dangerous technology, and this, combined with the ever increasing size of theatres in Europe and America, resulted in more and more catastrophic fires in theatres as the century progressed, culminating in the Ring Theatre fire in Vienna in 1881, which claimed 450 lives. The result was the enactment of strong fire codes in many countries, which remained in effect even though the coming of electricity reduced the danger, and which had distinct effects on playhouse design. Stages and auditoriums were now required to be separated by a fireproof safety curtain, construction material had to be more fire resistant, and multiple exits had to be provided for quick evacuation.

The coming of the First World War and the rise of the cinema brought to an end the steady increase in the size, number, and complexity of theatre buildings around the world, particularly in Europe and America. Nevertheless the years after the Second World War saw a boom in theatre construction and innovation headed by the widespread rebuilding of city centres destroyed by bombing, especially in Germany, and in the 1960s there was a boom in festival, university, and *regional theatre buildings in the United States. The majority of these new playhouses were in the general tradition of the nineteenth-century theatre as civic monument but both exteriors and interiors were distinctly of another era. On the exterior, the columns and pediments of traditional *neoclassical and baroque playhouses were replaced by features more characteristic of high modernist architecture: open glass façade-walls as in the 1955 State Opera in Hamburg, or sweeping, curved opaque walls in the manner of Le Corbusier in the 1969 Düsseldorf Schauspielhaus.

Equally radical adjustments were seen within these buildings. The rise of experimental theatres and an interest in breaking out of the proscenium arch, both significant turn-of-the-century developments throughout Europe, began to be widely reflected in the design of post-war European and American playhouses. From the early twentieth-century work in experimental theatre came the idea of each national or state theatre having a

large theatre for the traditional repertoire and a smaller, more flexible auditorium for new and unconventional work. The first major playhouse of the post-war renaissance was the Stadtstheater of Malmö, Sweden, which featured one of the first glass façades as well as a large and small auditorium under a single roof. In many such theatres the large auditorium was a conventional proscenium theatre, but Malmö's large space was flexible as well, altering its shape by means of false walls and movable stage sections. Its basic pattern reflected the growing interest in breaking out of the proscenium arch. Provision was made for a large thrust stage to extend out into the audience, seated in sweeping rows on three sides rather like a classical theatre.

The thrust stage enjoyed enormous popularity in the late 1950s and 1960s, a time of major theatre construction in Europe and America. The playhouse built by *Guthrie for the Stratford Festival in Ontario in 1957 offered a thrust stage based on a modified Shakespearian public theatre, with surrounding ranks of seats in the style of Malmö. This design in turn influenced that of the Guthrie Theatre in Minneapolis (1962) and the *Chichester Festival Theatre (1963), both of them in turn inspiring subsequent playhouses in the USA and the UK. Many playhouse designers of the 1960s regarded the thrust stage as the auditorium of the future, a prophecy which has not proven correct; but clear testimony to the power of this belief remains in London's National Theatre, which incorporates under one modernist roof a large theatre of a somewhat modified thrust design, a medium-sized conventional proscenium-arch theatre, and a small experimental theatre which can be arranged variously.

The most innovative playhouse design of the century occurred in these large civic and festival theatres, but two other basic types of playhouses also contributed significantly. Commercial playhouses and those experimental playhouses not attached to larger theatres. Commercial playhouses were normally found during most of the century clustered near one another in entertainment districts in large cities, and were often generically designated by the name of the district: Broadway in New York, West End in London, *boulevard theatres in Paris. They followed a fairly standard pattern. Their entrance was through a rather narrow decorated façade on a commercial street, with the auditorium fitted in behind small adjacent commercial structures, and they were almost invariably proscenium-arch theatres with vestigial boxes and one or more wall-to-wall balconies. Due to the space constraints in their expensive and crowded commercial locations, they could also not offer the spacious lobbies, grand staircases, and other impressive public areas that were typical of the free-standing monumental theatres.

The smaller experimental playhouses shared a few common features. Economically, experimental playhouses normally lacked the means available to other venues, thus adjusting physical arrangements to a wide variety of pre-existing spaces. Artistically, many were founded by groups with little interest in replicating the configurations of the past. At mid-century, arena theatre, or theatre in-the-round, with audiences completely surrounding the action, enjoyed a strong vogue in the United States, and a number of playhouses were built in this pattern. Almost every possible type of audience–actor relationship was attempted in one experimental theatre or another; probably the most common and most challenging of all was the 'black box', which simply provided an open and neutral space for the placement of seating, raised platforms, and lighting, and could accommodate an almost infinite variety of such relationships. In the latter part of the twentieth century, when theatre was often produced in spaces not designed for that purpose—as it had been in the Middle Ages and Renaissance—the interest in a large, open, neutral performance space attracted a number of directors and designers to abandoned industrial buildings for site-specific or *environmental theatre. At the end of the century a number of European cities, among them London, Paris, Berlin, and Zurich, converted such spaces into important new theatrical venues.   MC

Pleasence, Donald (1919–95) English actor whose career was interrupted by national service and time as a prisoner of war. Thereafter work included *The Brothers Karamazov* at the Lyric Hammersmith (1946) and productions with the *Birmingham Rep (1948–50), Bristol Old Vic (1950–1), and *Shakespeare Memorial Theatre (1953). His unusual looks—at once soft and vulnerable and then sinister and vaguely psychotic—as well as his distinctive voice cast him as a British character actor on screen and stage. Although he worked regularly in London through the 1950s, it was as the tramp Davies in *Pinter's *The Caretaker* (1960) that his reputation was secured. Two other major roles were in *Anouilh's *Poor Bitos* (1963) and as Eichmann in Pinter's production of Robert Shaw's *The Man in the Glass Booth* (1967). All three productions transferred to Broadway. Although most of his subsequent career was on film, he did return to the stage in Pinter's 1991 revival of *The Caretaker*.   AS

Plowright, Joan (1929–) English actress. Plowright joined the *English Stage Company, run by her former teacher George *Devine, in *Miller's *The Crucible* in 1956. At the *Royal Court she met *Olivier while in *The Country Wife*; she married him in 1961. Her reputation increased through her virtuosity in *Ionesco (*The Chairs* in 1957, *The Lesson* in 1958, *Rhinoceros* in 1960 under the direction of *Welles). Through her performance as Beatie Bryant in *Wesker's *Roots* (1959), Plowright established herself as a leading actress of her generation. She joined the *National Theatre with Olivier for its first season in 1963, and continued to work there in the following decade. Thereafter Plowright focused more on film, appearing in such successes as *Revolution* (1985), *Enchanted April* (1991), and *Tea with Mussolini* (1999, directed by *Zeffirelli, who had directed Plowright and Olivier in *de Filippo's *Saturday, Sunday, Monday* at the National in 1973). Her latest film is a thriller, *Knife Edge* (2008).   TK

Plummer, Christopher (1929–) Canadian actor. After work in Canada (from 1945) and Broadway (1954–5), Plummer's appearance at the American Shakespeare Festival in Connecticut (1955) was eclipsed by *Henry V* at the 1956 *Stratford Festival in Ontario. Acclaimed for his regal bearing, charismatic stage presence, and lyrical sense of language, Plummer developed an international reputation for his classical work in Canada, with the *Royal Shakespeare Company (1961), the *National Theatre (London, 1981), and in New York (Iago opposite James Earl *Jones, 1981). His Tony-winning *Barrymore* (1996–8) invited comparisons with John *Barrymore as a classical actor. But Plummer's prolific, versatile canon also includes complex contemporary roles (*Pinter's *No Man's Land* with Jason *Robards, Jr., 1995), *musicals (Anthony Burgess's *Cyrano*, adapted from *Rostand, 1973), extensive television work, and over 60 films including *The Sound of Music* (1965).   MJD

Podestá, José Juan (1858–1936) Uruguayan-Argentinian *circus performer, actor, director, and *producer. Podestá was the fourth of nine children, with whom he went on to found a performance dynasty. He is best known for portraying two *characters: the *clown Pepino the 88 and the outlaw gaucho Juan Moreira. After *touring Uruguay as clowns and *acrobats, the Podestá brothers established their own circus company in Buenos Aires in 1880. Because of his physical skill, 'Pepe' was asked to play Juan Moreira in a pantomime based on Eduardo Gutiérrez's *melodrama. The circus company's production was a great success, the action taking place on a movable stage as well as in the ring itself. In 1886 a spoken version of *Juan Moreira* premièred in Chivilcoy, later playing to record *audiences in Montevideo and Buenos Aires. In the 1890s Podestá staged *Martín Fierro* and Leguizamón's *Calandria*, trading the circus ring for the stage, where he continued to perform, direct, and produce, sponsoring Argentina's first three-act play competition in 1903. JGJ

Poel, William (1852-1934) English actor, director, and playwright, pioneer of restoring Elizabethan stage conditions for Shakespeare. He was *stage manager of two Shakespearian institutions in their infancies—Emma Cons's Victoria Coffee Palace (the *Old Vic, 1881-3), and *Benson's *touring company (1884). Poel's approach attracted attention in 1881, when he presented the First Quarto text of *Hamlet* on a minimally furnished stage with red curtains. In 1892 he staged *Webster's *The Duchess of Malfi* for the *Independent Theatre: the production showed both Poel's interest in reviving neglected English plays (notably, *Marlowe's *Dr Faustus*, 1896, *Arden of Faversham*, 1897, Milton's *Samson Agonistes*, 1900, *Everyman*, 1901, *Jonson's *Poetaster*, 1916) and his tendency to take greater liberties with such texts than he did with Shakespeare, which he often cut but rarely rearranged or interpolated. For *Measure for Measure* (1893) he devised a portable stage modelled upon the contract for the *Fortune Theatre. From 1894 he campaigned for the full reconstruction of an Elizabethan *playhouse in London, and formed the *Elizabethan Stage Society in 1895 to further this goal. Unorthodox in his time, Poel's doctrine was popularized by individuals who worked with him early in their careers—notably, *Atkins, Granville *Barker, *Casson, Edith *Evans, Lillah *McCarthy, Nugent Monck, and *Payne. MOC

Poisson, Raymond (*c.*1633-90) French actor and playwright. Known as Belleroche in *tragedy, his greatest fame came in *comedy as Crispin, a likeable, mumbling, wide-mouthed, scheming valet *costumed in a Spanish-style black jacket, cape, and knee-length boots. This *character, invented by *Scarron in 1654, was taken over by Poisson in 1660 when he arrived in Paris, and over the next 25 years at the *Hôtel de Bourgogne and the *Comédie-Française he played Crispin in comedies by himself and other authors. After his retirement his son Paul and grandson Philippe, known as Crispin II and III, starred in vehicles by *Dancourt, *Lesage, and *Regnard; a second

grandson and a great-grandson, Crispin IV and V, exhausted the line. RWH

Poliakoff, Stephen (1952-) English dramatist and film director. Poliakoff had work produced at the *Royal Court (*Lay-By*, 1971) and Bush Theatre (*The Carnation Gang*, 1973; *Hitting Town* and *City Sugar*, 1975). These early plays about post-industrial urban living feature *characters who are lonely, isolated, and under intense pressure. After time as writer-in-residence at the *National Theatre (1976-7), Poliakoff saw his work at the *Royal Shakespeare Company; plays from this time include *Shout across the River* (1978), *Breaking the Silence* (1984), and *Playing with Trains* (1989). *Coming into Land* (1987) and *Sienna Red* (1992) were less successful and were easily topped by his film and television screenplays, which include *Caught on a Train* (1980), *She's Been Away* (1989), *Close my Eyes* (1991), and *Shooting the Past* (1999), which he also directed. The last is archetypal Poliakoff in its intelligence and attention to detail, distinctively televisual in its narrative, characterization, and its central metaphor of the still photographic image. AS

Polish Laboratory Theatre *See* GROTOWSKI, JERZY

Pollock, Sharon (1936-) Canadian playwright and actress. Pollock examines events in Canada's past that bring out unresolved issues in the present, for example, racism in *Walsh* (1974) and *The Komagata Maru Incident* (1976), and the legacy of colonialism in *Fair Liberty's Call* (1993). Past and present interweave in plays of private life: in her best-known play, *Blood Relations* (1980), Lizzie Borden, acquitted of the murders of her stepmother and father, challenges her actress friend to come to her own verdict by playing Lizzie as she was, or could have been, at the time of the murders. Past and present overlap also in *Doc* (1984), in which a woman and her father struggle over their conflicting memories of the suicide of her mother. Her latest play, *Man out of Joint* (2007), concerns restrictions on liberty since the attacks of 11 September. RCN

Ponnelle, Jean-Pierre (1932-88) French director and designer. Ponnelle began an extraordinary career in *opera and *ballet by designing for composer Hans Werner Henze (*Boulevard Solitude*, 1952; *König Hirsch*, 1965). He became one of the most important opera directors of his generation, often designing his own productions. He was sought after by major companies throughout the world, including the *Salzburg Festival, where he created renowned productions of Monteverdi and *Mozart. Reintroducing a taste for the baroque in staging, and with a painstaking attention to visual detail, Ponnelle was one of the first directors to oversee the filming of his opera productions.   DGM

Popov, Oleg (1930-   ) Russian/Soviet *circus artist and *clown whose career began in 1950 as a high-wire trick cyclist, sporting a trademark tow-haired peasant wig and outsize chequered peaked cap. With his mobile features, characterized by minimal make-up, he developed the persona of the good-natured simpleton who wants to get involved in other circus acts, such as bareback riding or the trapeze, then succeeding in a *parody of the skills of the experts. Popov was inclined to include political comment on home and foreign affairs as part of his act. Among the most popular clowns of his generation, his work was seen widely abroad.   NW

Popova, Lyubov (1889-1924) Russian/Soviet painter and *scenographer who became a prominent member of the *constructivist movement in the early 1920s. She contributed designs to the *Tairov-*Ekster production of *Romeo and Juliet* (1921), but her most influential construction was for *Meyerhold's 1922 production of Crommelynck's *The Magnanimous Cuckold*. Set in a flour mill, the scene consisted of an open, skeletal structure of plain latticed wood, comprising levels, inclined planes, ladders, revolving doors, vestigial mill sails, and three painted wheels, one large and enclosed, the other two spoked, all of which revolved in accompaniment to intense emotional moments of action. The whole was mounted on a bare stage against a background of the theatre's plain brick walls. The *biomechanical style of *acting was enhanced by *costumes which established the actors as a workers' collective. To this end, Popova designed 'acting overalls' to which individual items of *characterization could be added. Popova later designed properties and propaganda slogans for Meyerhold's 1923 production of *Tretyakov and Martinet's *Earth Rampant*.   NW

pornography and performance Pornography—from the Greek *pornei* and *graphos*, meaning, literally, 'whore writing'—refers to representations that are perceived to have sexual arousal as their primary objective. Its definition involves both content and effect and is subject to culturally specific, historically shifting standards of sexual normalcy and deviance. While almost all forms of representation might theoretically be pornographic because it is impossible to limit what every person may find sexually arousing,

the most widely recognized forms of pornography intend to incite sexual performance, and in the process create models by which consumers judge themselves and others in the sexual arena. Pornography is thus by common definition highly performative.

The interpenetrations of pornography and performance are documentable from ancient times, at least since Xenophon's *Symposium* recorded nude erotic *dancers who enacted the marriage of Dionysus and Ariadne at a banquet for the patriarchal intelligentsia in classical Greece. Pornographic performance has often reproduced the dynamics of imperial regimes, eroticizing those colonized as Other in terms of sexuality, *gender, race, ethnicity, and/or class. For many feminists, the Marquis de Sade (1740-1814) epitomizes the phallocentric ethos of sex as power over and violence against women. But others, emphasizing the performative aspects of his enterprise, find subversion of that paradigm in the ways his purposefully staged and exaggerated actions—elaborated to still greater excess in his major writings—ultimately *satirized and thus critiqued the excesses of the tyrannous regimes under which he operated.

In Asia, as in Europe, the development of pornography as a distinctive genre was linked to the spread of printing technology and flowering of literature. If *kunqu drama espoused Confucian orthodoxy in China, its performance by prostitute troupes titillated aristocratic audiences in the Ming and Qing dynasties. By contrast, native Polynesian culture, while figuring in Western imperialist erotica, did not develop a comparable pornography of its own; sexual mores permitted a wider range of behaviour, including public sexual intercourse during some religious festivals, which mitigated against pornographic production and consumption.

In Europe and America, official *censorship of pornography intensified in the nineteenth century as the bourgeoisie solidified its political and cultural power. However, far from eliminating the genre, legal repression fostered its subterranean efflorescence in cities such as London and New York, creating a bifurcated culture with a forbidden but frequented underworld. Tracy C. Davis has demonstrated that pervasive consumption of printed pornography (mostly by males) fuelled the continuing association of actresses with prostitutes through the nineteenth and into the twentieth centuries. As spectacular public women, actresses were readily available objects for the projection of male sexual fantasies. Theatrical producers and performers became expert at playing to pornographically literate audiences, manipulating sexual codes more boldly in leg shows and *burlesque, and more subtly but no less consciously in performances of *legitimate drama. Sexual desires aroused could be satisfied by prostitutes who remained available outside the theatres and concert saloons.

Graphic portrayal of sexual acts generally remained suppressed in public venues until late in the twentieth century, although there is evidence of secret black market erotic theatres, such as those that sprang up in Germany after the First World War. In official culture, widening knowledge of the so-called sexual perversions made imputations of eroticism permissible in a heterosexual context but censorable in a homosexual one, as in the New York productions of *Asch's *The God of Vengeance* (1922) and Mae *West's *The Drag* (1927) and *The Pleasure Ma* (1928), all shut down under the auspices of the Society for the Suppression of Vice. While Anglo-American censorial standards subsequently shifted (from increased legal crackdowns in the 1930s and their more paranoid enforcement following World War II to the greater liberation of the 1970s), overt performances of *lesbian and *gay desire remain more feared for their arousing impact on susceptible audiences and thus more subject to obscene and pornographic classification than heterosexual depictions.

With the so-called sexual revolution that began in the 1960s, more explicit sexual acts became a feature of performances across a wider range of venues. On the legitimate stage at the end of the decade, *Arrabal incorporated graphic scenes of sadism and bestiality; *Tynan celebrated orgasm in *Oh! Calcutta!*; *Hair* glorified free love; and orgies were mounted in Peter *Hall's *opera production of *Moses and Aaron* and *Schechner's *Performance Group's *Dionysus in 69*. Meanwhile, performance elements enlivened the expansion of sexual emporia. Film pornography peaked in the 1970s, working along with more mainstream print media like *Hustler* and *Playboy* to shape the fantasies audiences projected onto performers in all sorts of venues. More cheaply produceable and privately consumable, video supplanted film pornography in the 1980s and enlarged the possibilities of vicarious sexual performance just as the AIDS epidemic called the ethos of lived promiscuity into question.

In alternative theatre spaces, performers engaged in more self-conscious, critical explorations of pornography. For example, in New York, *Le-Compte and the *Wooster Group imitated the 'depthless' performance style of porn films in *Route 1 & 9* (1981). *Foreman's *The Birth of a Poet* (1985) pushed the seminal stereotype of the

lust-ridden whore to deconstructive extremes. Karen *Finley, in *performance art works such as *The Constant State of Desire* (1986), thwarted the objectifying gaze with spectacularly obscene defilements of her own body, while 'sex-positive' Annie Sprinkle, appearing in Schechner's *Prometheus Project* (1985) and her own *Post-Post Porn Modernist* (1990), both revelled in and subverted the pornographic economy with elaborate displays of self-commodification on- and offstage.

At the beginning of the new century, the interpenetrations of pornography and performance proliferated with the mass marketing of computers and the growth of Internet and Web-based technologies. Redrawing the boundaries of liveness, interactive media allow consumers new voyeuristic and participatory pleasures, including unprecedented ability to access and customize images and sounds and play any role for real-time sexual intercourse in cyberspace, which in turn shape the production and reception of the performing arts. By some estimations, the United States is engaged in a cynical pastiche of Victorian bifurcation as official culture, pushing the rhetoric of church and family, cleaned up Times Square and fulminated over the sexual indiscretions of a president while pornography ballooned to an industry with an annual turnover in the billions of dollars. By some estimates Americans, though few will admit it, spend more money per year on porn than they do on other kinds of movies and all the performing arts combined.   KM

Porres (Porras), **Gaspar de** (1550–*c*.1615) Spanish *actor-manager. Performing between 1585 (when he bought two plays from *Cervantes) and 1608, Porres was probably the most important and prosperous impresario of his day. His company played throughout the country, and employed several actors famous later. A close associate and friend of Lope de *Vega, he bought and first performed dozens of that author's plays, twelve of which he published, with Lope's help, in Madrid in 1614.   VFD

Porter, Cole (1891–1964) American composer and lyricist. Porter made his name at Yale (1909–13) by writing music and lyrics for college shows, and co-wrote *See America First* (Broadway, 1916), a patriotic *musical in the manner of *Gilbert and *Sullivan. After volunteering with an ambulance corps in the First World War, Porter—wealthy by birth and married to the even wealthier Linda Lee Thomas—spent much of the 1920s with high society in Paris and Venice. He grew more disciplined about his composing in the 1930s and created a series of successful scores. *Gay Divorce*

(1932), in which Fred *Astaire introduced the song 'Night and Day'; *Anything Goes* (1934), a long-running show starring Ethel *Merman and featuring 'I Get a Kick Out of You' and 'You're the Top'; *Leave It to Me!* (1938), in which Mary *Martin sang 'My Heart Belongs to Daddy'; and *Du Barry Was a Lady* (1939), which concluded with Merman and Bert *Lahr singing 'Friendship'. Severely injured and in chronic pain after a 1937 riding accident, Porter grew dependent on medication and alcohol and became less productive. *Kiss Me, Kate* (1948) supplied many hit songs in the context of a soundly constructed plot (adapted from *The Taming of the Shrew*), while *Can-Can* (1953) and *Silk Stockings* (1955) also saw long commercial runs. Many of Porter's witty songs became popular standards and the shows *Anything Goes* and *Kiss Me, Kate* have seen frequent revivals.   MAF

Porter, Eric (1928–95) English actor whose long stage career was overshadowed by his television role of Soames Forsyte in the landmark series *The Forsyte Saga* (1967). Porter made his first professional appearance at the *Shakespeare Memorial Theatre in 1945, and was a member of the *Birmingham Rep (1948–50). In the 1950s he worked for H. M. Tennent, the Bristol Old Vic, and the *Old Vic in London, playing roles that included Lear, Vanya, Volpone, Henry IV, and Bolingbroke. In 1957–8 he *toured with the *Lunts, appearing on Broadway in *Dürrenmatt's *The Visit*. Following a celebrated Rosmersholm (*Royal Court, 1959), he joined the *Royal Shakespeare Company, where roles included Malvolio, Leontes (1960), Pope Pius XII in *Hochhuth's *The Representative* (1963), Bolingbroke, Henry IV, Shylock (all 1965), Faustus, and Lear (1968). Later stage appearances included an unlikely (but successful) Big Daddy at the *National Theatre in *Cat on a Hot Tin Roof* (1988), Lear for the Old Vic (1989), and Serebriakov in *Uncle Vanya* at the National (1992).   AS

Potter, Dennis (1935–94) English television dramatist, one of the 'angry' generation of anti-establishment writers of the 1950s. Unlike most of them, Potter made an early commitment to the new and untried medium of television, producing 43 original plays, series, and adaptations, mostly for the BBC. Widely regarded as the most significant television dramatist, his work was characterized by a concern with the forms and possibilities of television drama, often drawing on, and reworking, genres of popular culture: *Pennies from Heaven* (BBC, 1978), for example, introduced the device of 'lip-synch' miming to popular music which was to become a Potter trademark. Potter also drew, often controversially, on his own life and obsessions, as in his final plays, *Karaoke* (BBC, 1996) and *Cold Lazarus* (Channel 4, 1996). Potter suffered from psoriatic arthropathy, a condition which affects the skin and joints, and which necessitated long periods of hospitalization, an experience dramatized in *The Singing Detective* (BBC, 1986), perhaps his most accomplished work. He also wrote screenplays, and directed for television and the cinema.   SWL

Power family Irish-American acting dynasty. The line begins with (William Grattan) **Tyrone** (1797–1841), born in Ireland, who from 1826 was London's most popular enacter of comic Irish *characters. Between 1833 (when he made his New York debut in *The Irish Ambassador*) and 1841 he *toured America three times, repeating his acclaim. He also wrote six original plays. Two of his four sons—**Maurice** (d.1849) and **Harold**— became minor actors. Harold's marriage to actress Ethel Lavenu produced a prominent player, (Frederick) **Tyrone** (1869–1931), born in London. From 1888 his career was mainly centred in New York, where he acted in many important productions, including the *musical *Chu Chin Chow* (1917). His later years emphasized Shakespeare—Brutus in *Julius Caesar*, reprised many times, being his signature role. He wed the actress **Helen Reaume** and sired **Tyrone** (Edmund) (1914–58), born in Cincinnati. The sometimes inaccurately billed Tyrone Power, Jr., acted with his mother at 7 and in 1931 did a Shakespearian season in Chicago. On Broadway he appeared with Katharine *Cornell in *Romeo and Juliet* (1935) and *St Joan* (1936). After many years as a film star, he returned to the stage in the 1950s in *Mister Roberts*, *John Brown's Body*, and *Back to Methuselah*. His son **Tyrone** (William) (1959–   ), born in Los Angeles, began his career in 1978 as Malcolm in *Macbeth*.   CT

Praga, Marco (1862–1929) Italian playwright and critic. Praga dominated the Italian stage at the turn of the century. Companies interested in the new *realistic (*verismo*) style premièred his plays: Virginia Marini performed *The Virgins* (1889), *Duse *The Ideal Wife* (1890), Ermete Novelli *Alleluja* (1892), Cesare Rossi *The Spell* (1892), Andò-Leigheb *Il bell'Apollo* (1894), and C. Reiter *La crisi* (1904). At the Manzoni Theatre company (1912–15) in Milan, Praga headed an experimental playwriting and *directing project. This company premièred his *The Closed Door* (1913) which became a vehicle for Duse, and *Il divorzio* (1915). Like *Becque, *Strindberg, *Ibsen, and *Chekhov,

Praga centred most of his twenty plays on women—*ingénues, wives, and mothers—and while he portrayed seducers in all their rascality, he usually condemned the 'fallen' or sinful woman and her confused, irrational emotions for destroying the social order.   JEH

Prampolini, Enrico (1894-1956) Italian painter, *scenographer, and theoretician, a key figure in the *futurist movement. His early manifestos, *Futurist Scenography and Choreography* and *Dynamic Stage Architecture* (1915), abolished the traditional divide between *playhouse design and architecture, between stage and *auditorium, between *actor and scenery, and introduced the idea of an 'electro-dynamic luminous stage architecture', which would unfold as a total work of art. He was a prominent exponent of the Futurist Mechanical Theatre through his production of the *puppet plays *Matoum et Tévibar* (1919) and *Night Divers* (1923), the 'mechanical *ballets' *Renaissance of the Spirit, Metallic Night* (both 1922), *Dance of the Propeller* (1923), and *Psychology of the Machines* (1924), and the manifestos *The Aesthetics of the Machine* (1922), *Futurist Mechanical Art* (1923), and *Futurist Scenic Atmosphere* (1924). In 1925 he exhibited a model for a Magnetic Theatre at the Exposition Internationale des Arts Décoratifs in Paris, which won him the grand prize for theatre. He consolidated his international success by directing and designing a season of futurist pantomimes in Paris (1927). In the following years he designed over 80 (mainly non-futurist) plays and *operas.   GB

Presnyakov, Vladimir (1974–) and **Oleg** (1969–) Playwrights from Ekaterinburg in central Russia, part of the Russian 'New Drama', whose work includes *Terrorism* (2002) and *Playing the Victim* (2004), both staged at the *Moscow Art Theatre and later at London's *Royal Court. The Presnyakovs explore a world where the performance of violence is the only means of emotional expression.   BB

Préville (Pierre-Louis Dubus) (1721-99) French actor. Arguably the finest comic actor of the eighteenth century, Préville played in the provinces and at the Saint-Laurent Fair before joining the *Comédie-Française in 1753, to assume the Crispin and Sganarelle valet roles. Admired by *Garrick, amongst others, for a naturalness and versatility which enabled him to play both the classic comic repertory and contemporary *bourgeois drama, in 1775 he created Figaro in *Beaumarchais's *The Barber of Seville*.   JG

Price, Stephen (1783-1840) American *manager and producer whose business acumen and commercial sense propelled him to the pinnacle of American theatre in the early nineteenth century. Son of a loyalist New York farmer, Price was licensed to practise law in 1804 and served in the city's criminal courts until 1808 when he bought a management share in the Park Theatre under the direction of his friend, the actor Thomas A. Cooper. Price turned the Park into New York's leading *playhouse by bringing in English stars and signing them to profitable *touring contracts; his successes included G. F. *Cooke, Edmund *Kean, and Charles *Mathews, and he soon had a virtual monopoly on such English imports. From 1826 to 1830 Price was the manager of *Drury Lane in London.   PAD

Priestley, J. B. (John Boynton) (1894-1975) English writer. Priestley broke into theatre with a successful adaptation of his comic novel about a theatre company, *The Good Companions* (1932). Most of his work was informed by his humanistic socialism, as in *Cornelius* (1935), *They Came to a City* (1943), and *An Inspector Calls* (1946), or his occult, cyclical theories of time, as in *Dangerous Corner* (1932), *Time and the Conways*, and *I Have Been Here Before* (both 1937). Priestley was also important in bringing European modernism to West End theatre. *Johnson over Jordan* (1939) reviews the life of an everyman *character, and in production encouraged the use of *expressionist imagery and modernist choreography, *masks, *lighting, and *music. Those elements have continued to fascinate *audiences, most notably in *Daldry's acclaimed mounting of *An Inspector Calls* at the *National Theatre in 1992, with a design by Ian McNeil which perched the elegant house of the central *characters on stilts lifted above a post-war wasteland.   DR

Prince, Hal (Harold) (1928–) American director and *producer, one of the most influential forces in *musical theatre. Prince apprenticed to George *Abbott, and in 1953 began producing musicals himself. Among his many producing successes in the 1950s were *New Girl in Town*, *West Side Story*, and *Fiorello*. He began *directing in the 1960s, and scored successes with *She Loves Me*, *Zorba*, and *Cabaret*. In the 1970s Prince began collaborating with composer *Sondheim; their productions, including *Company* (1970), *Follies* (1971), *Pacific Overtures* (1976), and *Sweeney Todd* (1979), dealt with topical and sometimes controversial subject matter and often functioned as a layering of ideas and songs rather than through a strong plot. Prince also directed *Lloyd Webber's blockbuster *Evita* (1978) and *The Phantom of the Opera* (1986), and in the 1990s a major revival of the classic *Show Boat*. He has also directed *opera at major houses including New York City Opera and the Metropolitan Opera. In the 1990s Prince became increasingly involved in promoting the work of young composers. He directed *Love-Musik*, based on the music of *Weill, on Broadway in 2007.   KF

Príncipe, Corral del The second of Madrid's two permanent *playhouses or *corrales de comedias*, the other being the Corral de la *Cruz. The Príncipe opened in 1583 (on a site now occupied by the Teatro Español) and lasted, albeit much modified, until replaced by a *coliseo* (*proscenium theatre) in 1744. Like the Cruz, it was built by two charitable brotherhoods (*cofradías*), the Pasión and the Soledad, in an enclosed yard (19 m or 62 feet square) behind a converted house, through which the *audience entered; its rear façade contained a women's gallery, some *boxes above, and a further gallery in the attic. At the far end (east) was a tiring house with a lower and upper gallery and a machine loft; projecting from this was a roofed stage the same size as in the Cruz. There were benches and *gradas* (raked seating) on roofed platforms at the sides of the yard, adjoining the stage. Lateral boxes gradually appeared after 1600 in neighbouring buildings. The yard was roofed in 1713.   CD

Pritchard, Hannah (1709-68) English actress. Her first recorded performance was in 1733 at *Drury Lane, where she played mostly comic roles and *pantomimes. Greatly admired for her Rosalind in *As You Like It* (1741), by the end of that decade she scored hits in a number of Shakespearian roles, especially Lady Macbeth. Mrs Pritchard was the original Clarinda in Benjamin Hoadly's *The Suspicious Husband* and the title *character in *Johnson's *Irene*. In 1760 she was appointed dresser to Queen Charlotte for her wedding to George III, and she retired from the stage in the year of her death.   MJK

private theatres The indoor *playhouses in London were called 'private' when first built in 'liberties' in 1575 and 1576. The term differentiated them from the *public theatres used by the adult professional companies. Although they charged money at the door for public admission, they pretended to give private shows, of the kind that noblemen and the court gave for their friends in private houses. This freed impresarios from the attentions of the Master of the Revels, appointed in 1578 to oversee public performances by *censoring playbooks and requiring playing

companies to be licensed. It also affirmed the superior social status of the boys' companies. Even when the King's Men (*see* CHAMBERLAIN'S MEN, LORD) took over the *Blackfriars the title pages of their plays in print proclaimed they had been acted 'publicly' at the *Globe and 'privately' at the Blackfriars. After 1606, when the Master of the Revels secured the right to censor all playbooks, the real advantage of mounting private performances was lost and the claim of 'private' became a complete fiction.   AJG

producer Since the early nineteenth century in English, 'production' has meant the mounted performance on stage, yet the person who produces has been called the *manager, the *director, and the financial controller. The confusion probably arose at the beginning of the twentieth century in England and America, when traditional managers were first displaced by businessmen with commercial profit in mind rather than the long-term development of a company. The new breed hired venues and put together casts for specific productions only, and thus were 'producers of product' more obviously than *actor-managers with stable theatres under them. At the same time, the first anglophone artists who thought of themselves as directors were appearing, such as Granville *Barker and *Belasco. Barker called his directing work producing; his credit on playbills often read 'the play produced by H. Granville Barker'. The result was that in Britain 'producer' tended to mean director in the first half of the century, and was occasionally used in that sense much longer. In America, perhaps by analogy with Hollywood film practice, 'director' caught on earlier. But by the last quarter of the century, on both sides of the Atlantic 'producer' had come to be applied to a person responsible for *finance, organization, publicity, hiring, and the other complex aspects of contemporary production, especially in the commercial sector. Producers can wield extraordinary power over the production like *Beaumont or *Mackintosh, involve themselves heavily in promotion like *Merrick, or allow their creative employees scope like Emanuel Azenberg.   DK

prologue The opening section of a dramatic performance, presented either as an integral part of the play or as a dissociated address on a topic unrelated to the *action. The integrated prologue in *Greek theatre, the part of a *tragedy that precedes the entry of the *chorus, eventually devolved into an introductory *monologue, delivered in *Euripides by a *character, in *Seneca often by a non-dramatic supernatural figure, and on the Elizabethan stage by a *chorus figure. These prologues functioned as *exposition or commentary on the ensuing action. The semi-independent or dissociated prologue served a variety of extra-dramatic functions: to defend a particular dramatic theory or practice, to establish a theatrical 'frame', to comment on current political or social issues; and, of course, to curry *audience favour. Prologues connect the stage world with that of the audience, but they also establish the fictitious nature of the performance. They are therefore shunned in *realistic theatre, although they are occasionally resurrected in modern anti-illusionist theatre. *See* EPILOGUE.   RWV

promenade performance *See* ENVIRON-MENTAL THEATRE

prompter The person, often culturally assumed to be invisible, who reminds actors of lines and movements; now rare in Western theatre, though surviving in some *opera houses. Until well after 1900, *rehearsal pay was the exception rather than the rule in professional theatre, and since most theatrical traditions have been popular traditions in which the actors were either unpaid or part time, most plays historically have been given by casts who did not fully know their lines and blocking. Images of *medieval theatre occasionally show a man with a book and a long pointer standing in front of the performers, apparently *directing the actors; in *kabuki, the *koken* (the visible props and *costume assistant assigned to an individual actor) prompts; in *Ram lila* in north India, prompting is done by the *vyas*, who also comments on the action and talks to the *audience.

The eighteenth- and nineteenth-century European prompter had duties similar to those of the modern *stage manager's 'run' duties. Standing concealed in the prompter's box—partially sunk below the stage down centre—he cued the *lighting operator after the introduction of gas, and the crews at the pinrail and machines, made small sound effects himself, blew a whistle to cue the act drop, and often read nearly the entire script aloud to the actors on stage. The job was a highly skilled one, and the prompter greatly respected, yet his presence goes virtually unmentioned in documents from the period. In Britain the prompter stood at a desk in the wings stage left ('prompt side'; stage right is OP or 'opposite prompt'). More rehearsal time eventually put an end to continuous need for prompters, though they can still be heard occasionally on opening nights and in some theatres with *repertory playing systems. The prompter's show running duties

were reassigned in the early part of the twentieth century.

Prompting is still essential while actors are learning a script, and so it continues as part of the rehearsal process. Some film prompting is now done via wireless earpieces.   JB

proscenium An opening, framed by an arch, through which an *audience views a play, or the arch itself. In ancient *Greek theatre *proskenion* was 'that in front of the *skene*', that is, the low platform between the *skene* on which modern scholars believe most of the *acting took place. *Early modern *perspective scenery made the arched opening essential to restrict the angle of the spectator's view. A form of proscenium arch was first erected for the Teatro *Farnese in 1618. In early baroque theatre the platform of the Renaissance thrust stages became the apron or forestage on which the action took place, while behind the proscenium perspective scenery depicted the location (the 'Italian stage'). Actors entered through doors in the arch. From about 1680 to 1850, as the *action moved upstage, the forestage and the proscenium shrank while the doors disappeared.

The proscenium arch intensely privileges figure over ground, and suited *romantic theatre well, as *Schlegel pointed out. The *box sets of *realism further benefited from the proscenium, because realism is also dependent on *illusion more than convention. After 1910, as modernist taste returned toward convention, the proscenium appeared conservative and restrictive, encouraging a private response in each spectator rather than a shared audience experience. To socialist critics the proscenium spoke of a capitalist *bourgeois approach, a feeling still widely current among both practitioners and theoreticians. *See also* SCENOGRAPHY.   JD

protagonist From *protos* (first) and *agon* (struggle), meaning 'first contestant'. The term used to designate the leading *actor in a *Greek *tragedy—a performer purported to have been introduced as the *hypocrites* (answerer) by *Thespis in the sixth century BC—after *Aeschylus introduced a second actor (the *deuteragonist*, 'second contestant') and *Sophocles a third (the *tritagonist*, 'third contestant') in the fifth century. By extension, *protagonist* came to refer to the main *character in a tragedy as well as to the main actor. A character in opposition to or in conflict with the protagonist as character was thus the *antagonist.* Three protagonists were customarily selected by the archon and each assigned to one of the three competing tragic poets. The protagonists in turn selected the subordinate deuteragonists and tritagonists and assigned them their roles. (As the number of characters increased the doubling of parts became necessary.) In the fifth century BC each group of three actors played in all the plays of a single poet; but in the fourth century the system was altered in the interests of fairness so that each actor played in one drama from each of the three poets. In modern usage, 'protagonist' is used to refer to the central character in a play, the one at the centre of the conflicts, and frequently the *hero.   RWV

Provincetown Players American company operating 1915–29. Some of the founders of the *Washington Square Players in 1915 spent that summer and the next in Provincetown, Massachusetts. They staged twelve short plays over two summers, including *O'Neill's *Bound East for Cardiff* and *Glaspell's *Trifles*, then created a small theatre on Macdougal Street in Greenwich Village in New York. Productions of O'Neill's *The Emperor Jones* (1920) and *The Hairy Ape* (1922) brought them much attention, and transferred to Broadway. Between 1915 and 1922 they produced 93 new American plays by 47 playwrights. With the departure of the group's president Jig Cook and Glaspell for Greece in 1923, a remnant reorganized under O'Neill, Robert Edmond *Jones, and *Macgowan, but the success of their production of O'Neill's *Desire under the Elms* (1924) helped to bring about the venture's end, now that O'Neill was established with Broadway *producers.   MAF

Prowse, Philip (1937–) English director and designer. Prowse worked at *Covent Garden and Watford during the 1960s, where his highly expressive sets functioned as a dramatic *character. In 1969 he moved to the *Citizens' Theatre in Glasgow with Watford's director Giles *Havergal, and with writer Robert David MacDonald established a highly successful enterprise, stepping down in 2004. Since directing *Coward's *Semi-Monde* in 1971 he increasingly worked as a director-designer; at Glasgow his work has included *Genet, *Wilde, *Anna Karenina* (1978), *Phèdre* (1984), *The Duchess of Malfi* (1985), and *Brecht's *Mother Courage* with Glenda *Jackson (1990). Prowse directed *Webster at the *National Theatre with mixed success (*Duchess of Malfi*, 1985; *The White Devil*, 1991). In the 1980s he designed widely for *opera (Jonathan *Miller's production of *Don Giovanni*, and his own *The Pearl Fishers*) In the 1990s his authoritarian, *Zeffirelli-inspired productions with rich *costumes and lavish sets proved successful in the West End: *Lady Wind-

ermere's Fan, The Vortex, A Woman of No Importance.   KN

Pryce, Jonathan (1947–) Welsh actor. His breakthrough role was Gethin Price in *Comedians* (1975) for which he won his first Tony award. Through the 1970s he appeared in a succession of *Royal Shakespeare Company productions, including *Measure for Measure, Antony and Cleopatra*, and *The Taming of the Shrew*, while in 1979 he was Hamlet and the Ghost in *Eyre's *Royal Court production. In 1986 he played Macbeth for *Noble. He created the role of the Engineer in the West End and Broadway productions of *Miss Saigon* (1989, 1991), winning a second Tony for the role, and appeared as Fagin in the West End revival of *Oliver!* (1994). In 2001 he was Higgins in the National Theatre's *My Fair Lady*, and played Levene in *Mamet's *Glengarry Glen Ross* (London, 2007). For television he has appeared in *Selling Hitler* (1991) and *Mr Wroe's Virgins* (1993), while his extensive film roles include Sam in *Brazil* (1985), Perón in *Evita* (1996), the *villain in the James Bond film *Tomorrow Never Dies* (1997), and Governor Swann in the *Pirates of the Caribbean* sequence (2003–7).   AS

Prynne, William (1600–69) English *anti-theatrical writer. His *Histriomastix; or, The Actor's Tragedy* (1632), derisively organized like a play into acts and scenes, is a torrent of elaborately documented invective against the immorality of the stage. Unfortunately for him, its publication coincided too closely with a high-profile court show starring the Queen, *The Shepherd's Paradise*: his condemnation of female performers as 'notorious whores' was taken as a libel, and his attacks on drama-friendly rulers were construed as referring to King Charles I. He was sentenced to life imprisonment and his ears were cropped, but the Long Parliament released him in 1640. MJW

Przybyszewska, Stanisława (1901–35) Polish playwright. Illegitimate daughter of novelist and dramatist Stanisław Przybyszewski, in 1925–9 she wrote a trilogy (first published in 1975)— *Ninety-Three, The Danton Case*, and *Thermidor*— about the French Revolution based on revisionist historiography sympathetic to Robespierre. His *character, challenging *Büchner's *Danton's Death* and influenced by *Shaw's *Caesar and Cleopatra*, is portrayed as brilliant and far-sighted. Although only her masterpiece, *The Danton Case*, was staged in her lifetime, since her rediscovery in the 1960s Przybyszewska's plays have been widely staged in Poland and abroad, the most notable being *Wajda's *Danton Case* (1975) and his film version, *Danton*, with Gérard

Depardieu (1983). Przybyszewska's extensive correspondence reveals her incisive analysis of revolution and her harrowing life of self-chosen isolation, leading to death from malnutrition and morphine addiction at 34; these letters have served as the basis for several stage and television dramatizations of her life.   DG

Ptushkina, Nadezhda (1949–) Soviet/Russian playwright. Ptushkina gained huge popularity in the post-Soviet era, writing chiefly about domestic problems, such as *By the Light of Others' Candles* (1995) about two women trapped in unfulfilled lives. Her plays have been staged in commercial projects and repertory theatres. *As a Lamb* (1996), starring Inna Churikova, created furore for its outspoken eroticism. The play draws on the tale of Jacob's love for Rachel and his enticement by her sister Leah for an exploration of lust and love.   BB

public theatres The name given to the *playhouses built in London from 1576 for professional adult companies. It referred to open-air *amphitheatres such as the *Theatre, the *Curtain, the *Rose, the *Globe, and the *Fortune. They were populist venues, some of them capable of accommodating as many as 3,000 people. Their open structure with only the galleries and the stage roofed, and performances each afternoon, gave the best possible light for viewing the plays, while the two doors for *audience access gave the players a reliable income. While the more costly places included seating and a roof overhead, the main crowd stood in the yard around the stage itself. This was the cheapest place from which to see a play, and also the most powerful, in full view of the players. The people whom Hamlet called 'groundlings' had to stand throughout the play and got wet if it rained, but they had the closest access to the show. The roofed *private theatres set the cheapest places at the back of the *auditorium, furthest from the stage. The term 'public' was used dismissively, and such entertainment was thought by many writers to be common and therefore degrading to the gentry, the social rank from which most writers came.   AJG

Puccini, Giacomo (1858–1924) Italian *opera composer. Widely acknowledged as the heir to *Verdi, Puccini's reputation rests primarily on *La Bohème* (Turin, 1896), *Tosca* (Rome, 1900), *Madama Butterfly* (Milan, 1904), and *Turandot* (Milan, 1926). Puccini combined a melodic gift and the capacity to write a *quasi-Wagnerian through-composed score with unerring theatrical sense. While his operas characterize Italian *realism (*verismo*) in tone and milieu, his librettists

borrowed widely from plays by *Sardou, *Belasco, and *Gozzi. Puccini raised his underprivileged *characters to a genuinely tragic status: Butterfly's death speaks powerfully against the indifference of modern society, and Mimi's death at the end of *La Bohème* achieves a pathos unequalled in operatic theatre. *Tosca*, the most unified of his works, has exceptional momentum and sweeping emotional range. Puccini's versatility is apparent from his final work, *Turandot*, which is the last of the major grand operas. No opera house with an extended season omits Puccini from its repertoire.   SJCW

Puigserver, Fabià (1938–91) Catalan designer and director who revolutionized the Spanish stage with his conceptual *scenography. By the time he co-founded the Teatre Lliure in Barcelona in 1976 Puigserver was an internationally recognized designer, having produced the trampoline like canvas scenery for Víctor *García's production of *Yerma* (1971). He also worked with major Spanish directors: Albert Boadella, Ricard Salvat, Adolfo Marsillach, and José Luis Gómez. His minimalist eye stripped the stage of superficial decor and provided a visual analogy for dramatic tension. He maintained a fifteen-year collaboration with Lluís *Pasqual which provided radical, audacious reimaginings of the Teatro Nacional María Guerrero's stage for the Spanish premières of *García Lorca's unknown plays *The Public* (1987) and *Play without a Title* (1989). While known primarily as a designer, Puigserver's lean, measured directing of works like Per Olov Enquist's *The Night of the Tribades* (Teatre Lliure, 1978) created alternative actor–*audience relationships. The new Teatre Lliure building now bears Puigserver's name.   MMD

Punch and Judy English *puppet theatre which acquired its present form early in the nineteenth century. The show is a glove-puppet performance of an episodic nature with little plot, built around a lord of misrule, whose antisocial behaviour would be intolerable in any other context. Punch's violent fights with his wife Judy are the material of the oldest of *farces, whilst his confrontations with death and the Devil express a fundamental aspect of the human condition. Punch's name originated with the sixteenth-century Neapolitan *commedia dell'arte* figure of Pulcinella, who wore a pointed hat and a loose-fitting *costume of cheap white fabric, and his performers travelled widely abroad. The *character became Polichinelle in France and Punchinello in England, where he had arrived as a *marionette by the 1660s, probably with Pietro Gimondi.

Pulcinella rapidly lost his Italian accent and melded with local characters of *folk farce. In Andalusia he became Don Cristobal, and in the German lands Hanswurst and, later, *Kasper, whilst in nineteenth-century Russia Petrushka took over his characteristics.

In England street performances of Punch were popular with the young, but not considered exclusively children's shows: at night the showmen sometimes turned their stages into a shadow or 'galanty' show, and Punch and Judy could be seen at race courses. Once the railways and new concepts of leisure made seaside holidays possible, Punch could be found on beaches and piers and in the parks of seaside towns. Private engagements brought him more and more into middle-class children's parties, with a consequent effect on the content of the show. Nonetheless Punch was generally perceived as subversive and, like many European puppet figures, used for satiric comment on the follies of the day. The magazine *Punch* was named after him.   JMcC

puppet theatre Puppet theatre can range from an approximation of *actors' theatre to an adjunct of storytelling to a form of *performance art. In East and South-East Asia there are strong parallels between repertoires of actors' theatre and puppet theatre, especially in Chinese opera and Indonesian *wayang*. The *wayang kulit* is thought to have preceded theatre with actors, and in eighteenth-century Japan *kabuki actors borrowed the repertoire of the *ningyo-joruri* (puppet theatre, or *bunraku). Even their gestures and acting styles, like those of live performers in Indonesia, were partly based on the puppet theatre. In the West, on the other hand, puppet theatre has often been perceived as an imitation of actors' theatre. Nineteenth-century puppeteers tried to persuade themselves and their *audiences of the *realistic nature of their shows, informing the public that figures 80 cm (2.6 feet) high were 'life-size' (as well as lifelike).

Unlike the human performer the puppet must be animated externally. A puppet in a museum is a material object, in performance it is a channel of communication, but however 'realistic' it may seem to be, its value is purely metonymic. This is one reason why the European *symbolists were attracted to the puppet, and why *Maeterlinck designated some of his dreamlike plays as being for puppets. The move towards stylization and simplification in *avant-garde theatre was supported in part by the use of puppets, and as a result the older folk puppeteer was replaced by a new generation of puppet artists.

Definition A puppet is an object which a performer is able to invest with a suggestion of life, and into which an audience is prepared to project life. Puppets are mostly anthropomorphic or zoomorphic figures and are usually classified by their mode of operation. The major forms are the *marionette, a fully or partially jointed figure operated from above; the glove puppet, or hand puppet, worn on the hand and operated from below; and the rod puppet, operated, usually from below, and sometimes from the back (as in China), by rods which both support and permit specific movement. The *shadow-puppet theatre is an extension of the rod puppet, using flat figures against a screen. Japanese bunraku, involving three manipulators standing behind the puppet, which is operated by various rods and levers, is an extension of the rod puppet. Much imitated outside Japan after 1960, this form opened the way for the table-top puppet, where the visible or semi-visible manipulator stands behind the figure whose only control is usually a short rod protruding from the back of the head.

Water puppets, which survive in Vietnam as a national form (*mua roi nuoc*), were also known in China. They are operated from the back by means of long rods under the water. Africa has some unique puppet forms, amongst which are 2- or 3-m (6.5- or 9.8-foot) high figures of Mali, surmounted by a tiny head and operated by a puppeteer inside the body. There are also *masks with articulated mobile figures attached, or else large *animals, such as buffalo, that perform dances and then become puppet stages themselves. In this situation the distinction between the puppet and the mask is minimal. Like the mask the puppet has a performer behind it and is a way of presenting a *character or entity. In modern puppetry masks are widely used; in some cases the figure is operated by a puppeteer concealed within it, and in others a full or partial figure, often called a 'body puppet', is attached to the performer.

Automata were long confused with puppets, sometimes deliberately by showmen, who presented and described their theatres as 'mechanical'. Even allowing for modern technology, the distinction remains. A puppet requires a human impulse for each movement, an automaton merely requires the mechanism to be set in motion.

Origins The origins of puppets are uncertain, but much evidence points to shamanistic use. In many cultures dolls or puppets have been used as substitute human beings for magic purposes, and vestiges of this survive today in fetish and *voodoo dolls. Nearly everywhere, puppetry was first practised in a religious or cultic context, then going through a process of secularization. In Japan the *ningyo-joruri* evolved out of religious performances given by itinerant monks, partly to raise funds for their shrine. The *medieval Christian Church adopted animated figures to assist in the teaching of the scriptures. The first specific reference to a Christian puppet was the artificial serpent that climbs the Tree of Knowledge in the twelfth-century Anglo-Norman *Play of Adam*, but animated statues were already known earlier (*see* LITURGICAL DRAMA). By the end of the sixteenth century, England had a tradition of puppet plays ('motions') drawn from biblical material, whilst much of Europe also had puppet plays based on the birth and *Passion of Christ and on the lives of saints.

In India and Indonesia puppetry was firmly associated with the religious epics of the *Mahabharata* and *Ramayana*. In Karnataka the shadow performer still recites part of the text of the *Ramayana* and also provides his own glosses and commentaries on it. In sub-Saharan Africa puppets were often used during initiation and circumcision rituals. Performances were given in conjunction with the seasons of the agricultural year, encouraging fertility. A popular subject involved a male and female figure, the male provided with an erectile penis. The male sex organ is common to many puppet traditions, even if its religious overtones have made way for comedy. Turkish *Karagöz, Iranian Mobarrak, Japanese Noroma, and Italian Pulcinella all have penises, and often use them to urinate on the audience. Ironically, puppets are now often used in a number of developing nations as a teaching aid in order to promote birth control rather than fertility (*see* DEVELOPMENT, THEATRE FOR).

Repertoires From the medieval *joculatores* of Europe to the Skomorokhi of Russia, popular and secular entertainers combined puppetry with *juggling, *acrobatics, *magic shows, and storytelling. Narrative and storytelling are the starting points for much puppet performance. The *joruri* singer, seated at the side of the stage, provides all the voices for the bunraku theatre. The Indonesian *dalang* works through a gamut of linguistic levels, alternating old court Javanese and vernacular dialect and mixing singing, recitation, narrative, and *dialogue. In Europe the presenter of the show initially provided the voices, a practice depicted by *Jonson in *Bartholomew Fair* (1614), and still employed by a Mr Stretch, whose theatre ran for some 40 years in eighteenth-century Dublin.

Short dialogues, *farces, and knockabout scenes are common to all puppet theatre. Some-times they are mere interludes, sometimes, in the simple one-man street glove-puppet performance, they are the show itself. A central *hero (e.g. *Punch, *Kasper) goes through a series of encounters, each concluding with a fight. In most traditional puppet theatre the verbal element is at least as important as the physical batterings and the puppet can become the mouthpiece for the improvisation of the puppeteer. In much of the world, an extra comic effect is provided by a squeaker or 'swazzle' which distorts the voice.

The puppet can give an uncanny imitation of a human being and do things which are inconceivable for the human. Many are designed in terms of the tricks they can perform—expanding and contracting puppets, dismembering skeletons, transforming figures on the one hand, and imitators of acrobats and popular entertainers on the other. Before 1800 many European performers were both actors and puppeteers, passing from one medium to the other according to the political, social, religious, or economic climate. Masks of the *commedia dell'arte* spread to the puppet stage and generally outlived their stage models. Traces of *commedia* characters, often transformed, re-dressed, and absorbed into local types, can be found in much of Europe. The eighteenth-century European marionette stage presented both folk and hagiographic plays, and in the nineteenth century *melodrama provided an endless stream of dramatic fodder which was supplemented by adaptations of the popular novels.

Puppets can be perceived as diminutive humans, and as such lend themselves to *parody and *satire. *Bartholomew Fair* introduces a puppet parody of classical mythology, and the fairground theatres of eighteenth-century Paris frequently resorted to puppets to parody the live theatres that were trying to have them closed down. In the nineteenth century anti-government satire often depicted puppets, whilst Punch, *Guignol, and other puppet figures gave their names to satirical magazines. Satirical *cabarets of the turn of the twentieth century, such as the Green Balloon in Cracow, introduced puppet versions of well-known literary and political figures. In the late twentieth century British television's *Spitting Image* brought wickedly accurate puppet caricatures of political figures and the royal family into the living room.

Stages Puppet stages range from the non-existent to accurately scaled miniature versions of European *opera houses. In India for performances of the *kundhei-nacha* of Orissa and the *pava-kuthu* of Kerala (where the puppets are miniature versions of *kathakali actors), the puppeteers simply squat on the ground in full view of the audience. In eighteenth- and nineteenth-century Iberia a street performer might play an instrument and use his own cloak as a stage (with his puppeteer-assistant inside). Early puppeteers in Japan hung a miniature stage in front of them like a vendor's tray. In parts of Russia, Mongolia, and China the puppeteer would sometimes mount his booth on his head, with a curtain hanging to conceal the body. The simple glove puppet and rod puppets used by the poor itinerant puppeteers in China and Japan require the most minimal screen as a stage, while the traditional glove-puppet stage of south China was an elaborately carved two-storey wooden structure, the upper level being reserved for the 'gods'.

Many puppeteers in Europe and Africa have simply suspended a cloth on a line between two trees (or across a doorway) and popped the figures up over it. In Africa, some puppeteers travel with a light frame construction about a metre (3.3 feet) high, under which they climb and over which they throw cloths to conceal themselves. The traditional Rajasthan stage has a distinctive background of a coloured cloth with a series of arcades cut in it.

In Europe a simple screen, sometimes surmounted by a miniature stage, was a common sight in the streets. A fourteenth-century manuscript of the *Roman d'Alexandre* depicts a stage in the form of a small castle (hence the French term *castelet* for a puppet stage). The court marionette stages of Burma in the late nineteenth century were very wide and the show involved numerous puppets, performers, and an orchestra. The purpose-built bunraku stage can measure over 10 m (33 feet) in width, with a separate side stage for the musician(s) and reciter/singer. Marionette opera in the aristocratic palaces of eighteenth-century Europe allowed for miniaturized versions of baroque performances and employed the greatest scene painters (for instance *Juvarra). Nineteenth-century European showmen had elaborate stages that could be set up in available halls or *fairground booths. They created complete theatres in miniature, with scenery, *lighting, and even an orchestra. Some travelled with their own portable theatres, measuring about 20 by 10 m (65 by 33 feet) and able to accommodate several hundred spectators. Much smaller theatres existed in cellars and living rooms of the poorer areas of industrial towns in Belgium and northern France and in the back streets of Naples and Palermo.

Today the *scenography of the puppet theatre has often abandoned the conventions of wings and backcloths for a fuller exploration of the space in which the puppet operates. For example, Drak's designer, Petr Matasek, has taken his cue from the Russian *constructivists: all his sets are carefully devised mechanisms with which the puppet can interact. They are placed on the stage and in no sense are mere scenic backgrounds. Philippe Genty likewise eschews the purely scenic and his productions seem to grow organically out of objects and fabrics placed in the centre of the stage.

Film and television Puppet sequences were incorporated into a number of films of the 1940s, but with the spread of television in the 1950s and 1960s puppets came to the fore in children's programmes such as the English *Muffin the Mule* and *Thunderbirds*, whose extremely realistic puppets aimed to imitate humans to perfection. The real breakaway from the filmed puppet show came with Jim Henson in the USA, who treated the televised puppet as if 'real'. Where viewers had been used to the presenter or newsreader, Henson filled the screen with the speaking head of a puppet looking directly into the camera. His most celebrated creation was *The Muppet Show*, and his most endearing characters Kermit the Frog and Miss Piggy.   JMcC

Purcărete, Silviu (1950–) Romanian director. Purcărete was director of Teatrul Mic in Bucharest before going to the National Theatre in Craiova in the late 1980s. His 1989 season, which included *Ubu roi with Scenes from Macbeth*, *Phèdre*, *Titus Andronicus*, and D. R. Popescu's *The Dwarf in a Summer Garden* earned him great praise within Romania and work abroad, from France and Britain to Norway and Portugal. He assumed the directorship of the Centre Dramatique National du Limousin in 1996. His large-cast, international projects have included the French-Romanian production of *Les Danaïdes* (1995) and the Italian-French production of *De Sade* (1999). *Les Danaïdes*, adapted from *Aeschylus' *The Suppliants*, employed an extravagant but low-tech theatricality. The cast of 107 used cloth, fire, water, movement, and voice to evoke images and moods. The 50 suitcases carried by the daughters of Danaos became tombstones, temples, beds, city walls, and dominos. He directed *Twelfth Night* for the *National Theatre in London (2006) and *Ionesco's *Macbett* for the *Royal Shakespeare Company (2007).   EEP

Purim play Traditional playlet or *monologue performed on the carnival holiday of Purim, on which Jews celebrate the events described in the Book of Esther. Purim plays were already popular in Europe in the sixteenth century and were maintained until the Second World War; some Hasidic communities preserve the genre to this day. The plays began as rhymed *monologues and in the sixteenth century were enlarged to include several performers, with the subject matter drawn from contemporary Jewish life and folk tales, with biblical themes such as the sacrifice of Isaac introduced in the late seventeenth century. The performances were usually presented in private homes during the holiday meal by male students clad in *masks and simple *costumes. Later on, craftsmen, apprentices, and quasi-professional entertainers formed their own holiday troupes. Performances were sometimes characterized by vulgar language and bawdy innuendoes, leading to their occasional banning. The Purim play was the primary theatrical event in traditional European Jewish life and is considered one of the main contributors toward the creation of modern Yiddish theatre. *See* DIASPORA.   EN

Pushkin, Aleksandr (1799–1837) Russia's greatest poet, one of its greatest prose writers; on the basis of a single play, its greatest tragedian. After an early attempt at a *tragedy, Pushkin turned to the 'time of troubles' at the turn of the seventeenth century. The play which resulted, *Boris Godunov* (1825), written in Shakespearian blank verse, as opposed to alexandrines, is episodic rather than *neoclassical in form, ignores the *unities, and moves freely between Russia and Poland, from a palace to an inn, from moonlit garden to palace square. Making use of Karamzin's *History of the Russian State*, the play charts the rise and fall of Boris. After a struggle with the *censor, Pushkin managed to have sections published and, in 1830, the play received imperial sanction, though it waited until 1870 for its première, at the Mariinsky Theatre, St Petersburg.

Pushkin also wrote some 'Little Tragedies' in verse, *The Miserly Knight, The Stone Guest, Mozart and Salieri,* and *Feast in Time of Plague,* set in Elizabethan London. Only *Mozart and Salieri* was staged during Pushkin's lifetime. The poet was also instrumental in furthering *Gogol's career and is popularly believed to have lent him the plot of *The Government Inspector,* based on incidents in Pushkin's own life. *Boris Godunov* is more famous abroad in Mussorgsky's *operatic version of 1873, although Pushkin's play proved popular during the Soviet period and was given a memorable revival during the 1980s by *Lyubimov, seen at the *Edinburgh Festival in 1989. Declan *Donellan staged a modern-dress version in Moscow in 2001 with a Russian cast, which had a successful *tour in Britain.   NW

Py, Olivier (1965–   ) French playwright, director, and actor. A prolific theatrical and cinematic talent, Py founded his own company in 1988, producing close to twenty of his own plays, many of them at the *Avignon Festival, including the *cabaret performance *Miss Knife* (1996) in which he performed the title role. Beginning in 1998 he was director of the Centre Dramatique National at Orléans-Loiret, where he created *Requiem for Srebrenica* (1999), an indictment of the massacre in Bosnia, which later *toured Europe and the United States. His other major plays include *The Exaltation of the Labyrinth* (2001) and *The Conquerors* (2005). In 2007 he became director of the newly refurbished *Odéon/Théâtre de l'Europe.   DGM

Quayle, Anthony (1913–89) English actor and director. Six years of war service interrupted a promising career, and afterwards he turned down a Hollywood offer to run the *Shakespeare Memorial Theatre in Stratford (1948–56). Without the help of subsidy, he oversaw the theatre's change from a provincial festival *playhouse to a national institution that could recruit leading directors and actors, including *Gielgud, *Olivier, *Ashcroft, and the young *Brook. He directed a version of the Shakespeare history plays and undertook international *tours. As an actor he was well received in secondary parts such as Aaron, Iago, Pandarus, and Enobarbus, but less well as Othello and Macbeth. He left Stratford to pursue a more varied acting career, and took part in several films, but was never asked back to the *Royal Shakespeare Company when it assumed control of the SMT. He joined the Prospect Theatre Company in 1978, and founded his last touring company, Compass Productions, in 1984.   EEC

Queen's Men (Queen Elizabeth's Men) Formed in 1583, the Queen's Men was a large acting company for London, founded by Secretary of State Walsingham and the Master of the Revels with the twelve best players from leading companies. It was the chief performer at court and the only company licensed to play at *public theatres. When on *tour, towns usually gave twice what other travelling companies received because the actors wore the royal livery; perhaps the company was founded to parade the Queen's colours round England and her political and religious ideas. The exceptional size of the Queen's Men prompted the composition of ambitious plays with large casts, like Shakespeare's *King John* and *Richard III*. After the first few years, though, they divided into two groups, one entertaining with tumbling and *juggling as well as plays. Quality declined once the original players such as the *clown Richard *Tarlton died or left, and by 1590 they were outstripped at court by other groups. They still travelled the country as late as 1623.   AJG

Quem Quaeritis trope A literary-musical elaboration of the *medieval Easter liturgy consisting of a short *dialogue between the Angel guarding Christ's empty tomb and the three Marys. It begins with the Angel's question, 'Whom do you seek?' (*Quem quaeritis*). The *Quem Quaeritis* trope preserved in the *Regularis Concordia*, a collection of rules for Benedictine monasteries compiled by Ethelwold, Bishop of Winchester (*c.*970), has traditionally been interpreted as an extra-liturgical ceremony. Moreover, Ethelwold's instructions for its performance suggest a dramatic enactment, and the trope has thus been seen as the seed from which the later, clearly dramatic examples of the *Visitatio Sepulchri* developed. It has been argued with equal force that these tenth-century tropes were liturgical, not dramatic, and that some other catalyst was needed to bring the true *liturgical drama of the eleventh and twelfth centuries into being. The *Quem Quaeritis* trope, considered in isolation, does appear to be drama; considered in its liturgical context, it appears to be *ritual. The distinction lies less in formal qualities or techniques of presentation than in differences in purpose and perception.   RWV

Quin, James (1693–1766) English actor, singer, and *manager, the last great actor of the old school before the rise of *Garrick and *Macklin in 1741. Quin began in Dublin and was performing in London by 1715, from the start playing parts big and small, comic and tragic. He was a popular Falstaff and Sir John Brute in *Vanbrugh's *The Provok'd Wife*, but he also excelled as Macbeth and as *Addison's Cato. The 'natural' *acting of Garrick and Macklin provided a strong contrast to Quin's more formal, declamatory style, most evident when he played Horatio to Garrick's Lothario in *Rowe's *The Fair Penitent* in 1746. Quin was admired for the force and dignity he lent to tragic roles and the exuberance of his comic ones, but he was criticized for his inability to express the softer passions of pity and delicacy that *audiences increasingly desired.   MJK

Quinault, Philippe (1635–88) French dramatist and librettist. Educated and introduced to the theatre by Tristan l'Hermite, he wrote his first *comedy at 18 and produced several successful plays for both the *Hôtel de Bourgogne and

*Marais. Oustanding among his successes were *Astrate, roi de Tyr* (1664, a target for Boileau's satire in *L'Art poétique*) and a *comedy, *La Mère coquette* (1665). Having collaborated with *Molière and *Corneille in the *tragédie-ballet Psyché* (1671), Quinault began a fruitful career as librettist for *Lully's *operas, including *Cadmus et Hermione* (1673), *Alceste* (1674), *Atys* (1676), helping to assure the success of this new genre with King and court.   WDH

Quintero, José (1924–99) Panamanian-born American director. In 1951 Quintero and Theodore Mann turned a Greenwich Village nightclub into the Circle in the Square, producing in an intimate semi-arena format. The company moved to a new space in 1960. Quintero had to use a minimalist style, focusing on psychological depth. Among his many fine productions were *Dark of the Moon* (1951); *Summer and Smoke* (1952); a landmark revival of *O'Neill's *The Iceman Cometh* (1956), which boosted Jason *Robards's career; *Children of Darkness* (1958), which brought George C. *Scott and Colleen *Dewhurst to prominence; *Our Town* (1959); and *Desire under the Elms* (1963). New foreign plays included *The Quare Fellow* (1958) and *The Balcony* (1960). Meanwhile he worked in film and television, and freelanced on Broadway, his chief contribution being *Long Day's Journey into Night* (1956). After he left the Circle in the Square in 1963, Quintero confirmed his status as O'Neill's foremost interpreter with numerous productions, including the American première of *Hughie* (1964) and the world première of *More Stately Mansions* (1967).   DLL

Rabe, David (1940–) American playwright. Rabe was drafted into the army in 1966 and sent to Vietnam. Upon his return he wrote a series of plays exploring the connections between American masculinity and militarism, all produced by *Papp at the *New York Shakespeare Festival. *The Basic Training of Pavlo Hummel* (1971) described the traumatic effects of the war on a disillusioned draftee, *Sticks and Bones* (1972) is an *absurdist depiction of a blind veteran's homecoming, and *The Orphan* (1973) is about a rural family who lost a son in Vietnam. Rabe returned to the war in *Streamers* (1976), which uses an army barracks as a metaphor for American life in the 1960s. His broader concern with the construction of American masculinity is also evident in *In the Boom Boom Room* (1973), about the misogyny of the strip-club scene, and *Hurlyburly* (1984), a *satire on male rivalry and violence in Hollywood. Recent work includes *A Question of Mercy* (1997), which sympathetically portrays a gay couple living with AIDS, and *The Dog Problem* (2001). JAB

Rabinal Achi The only extant script from the indigenous Maya prior to the conquest. A story of two enemy warriors, one of whom is captured and sacrificed at the end, the play proceeds by a long series of formal challenges interspersed with *dance and *music. AV

Rachel (Élisa Félix) (1821–58) French actress. Born into an impoverished Jewish family, Rachel eventually attracted the attention of the *Comédie-Française actor Samson, who taught his protégée elocution and *acting technique, as well as rudiments of the education and culture she lacked, turning her into the actress who quickly enchanted Paris *audiences by her grace and poise. Making her debut at the Comédie-Française in 1838 as Camille in *Corneille's *Horace*, by the early 1840s she had performed all the leading roles in *Racine's tragedies, and in the plays of Corneille still in the repertoire; contemporary tributes agree that her Phèdre in 1843 was the high point of her career. Although she captivated audiences, critics, and society hostesses by her charm and talent, the rapacious attitude of her family, and Rachel's own greed, led to diffi-

culties. She was soon earning an unheard-of 60,000 francs a year, but in addition to her work in Paris she arranged *tours in the provinces and abroad; by the late 1840s there were quarrels with the Comédie over contracts and conditions, causing the resentment of her colleagues. In 1849 she negotiated a reduction of salary to 42,000 francs but also six months' leave a year, during which she was free to arrange lucrative tours: it is reported that her tour to Russia in 1853–4 brought in 300,000 francs for Rachel herself as well as 100,000 for her brother Raphael as her *manager. By 1855, suffering the strain of combining foreign tours with her schedule in Paris—and aware that she was in danger of being eclipsed by the popularity of the new star *Ristori—she resigned from the Comédie-Française altogether, and formed her own company. The onset of tuberculosis forced her to dissolve the company in 1856, and she died at the age of 37. WDH

Rachilde (Marguerite Eymery) (1860–1953) French writer. Rachilde won notoriety for fiction whose inversion of *gender roles caused her to be called 'Mademoiselle Baudelaire'. The risqué image attracted *symbolist writers to her salon, and she wrote her first plays for the Théâtre d'*Art, helping to define its anti-*realist aesthetic with *Madame la Mort* (1891). Rachilde advised *Lugné-Poe in his *directing of the Théâtre de l'Œuvre, persuaded him to produce *Jarry's *Ubu roi*, and concocted misinformation about the opening night in 1897. Her *The Crystal Spider* (1894) was the first French play Lugné-Poe produced, but none of her twenty other pieces were performed at the theatre she championed, and she repudiated Lugné-Poe when he attacked the symbolists. An anti-feminist pamphlet (1928) deepened her isolation from women writers. Other plays include *Pleasure* (1896), *The Transparent Doll* (1919), and *The Prowler* (1928). Rachilde's sardonic humour and preoccupation with sexuality make her plays more performable in the twenty-first century than the work of some of her symbolist contemporaries. FL

Racine, Jean (1639–99) French playwright. Racine's early religious education by the Jansenists at Port-Royal instilled a mastery of Greek and Latin authors, including *Euripides, *Seneca, and Virgil, that provided the foundation for his *tragedies, regarded as the pinnacle of *neoclassicism. *Molière encouraged Racine's ambition and first performed his *The Story of Thebes; or, The Enemy Brothers* (1664), which was followed by a more successful production of his *Alexandre le Grand* (1665). Unbeknown to Molière, Racine ventured the same play to the rival troupe at the *Hôtel de Bourgogne. This unscrupulous move, coupled with the defection from Molière's company of Racine's presumed mistress, Mlle Du Parc, and her subsequent triumph in his *Andromaque* (1667), launched Racine's theatrical career but created a permanent rift between the authors. Such rivalries, a staple of Parisian theatrical life, punctuated Racine's career, which continued with major plays: *The Litigants* (his only produced comedy, based on *Aristophanes' *Wasps*, 1668), *Britannicus* (1669), *Bérénice* (1670), *Bajazet* (1672), *Mithridate* (1673), *Iphigénie* (1674), and *Phèdre et Hippolyte* (later published as *Phèdre*, 1677). All were performed at the Hôtel de Bourgogne. During the first performances of *Phèdre*, a cabal ensued when the late Molière's company performed Jacques Pradon's more successful play on the same subject. Racine retired from the theatre, married, and assumed the duties of his new appointment, with Nicolas Boileau, as historiographer to Louis XIV. Racine wrote two additional tragedies on biblical subjects, *Esther* (1689) and *Athalie* (1691), performed privately by the pupils at the school for girls at Saint-Cyr.

In 1680, the creation of the *Comédie-Française began a continuous tradition of Racine's plays that ensured their classic status. Between 1680 and 1990 the Comédie-Française offered more than 9,000 performances of Racine. Over the course of three centuries many of France's finest actors have been celebrated for their portrayal of Racinian roles, including *Lecouvreur, *Clairon, *Talma, *Rachel, *Mounet-Sully, and *Bernhardt. The study of Racine has been a fundamental component of actor training in France.

Racine's plays have been staged by some of the most important French directors of the past century. *Antoine's production of *Andromaque* at the *Odéon (1904) was the first to historicize the action of the tragedy by setting the play in an anteroom at Versailles and *costuming the actors in seventeenth-century dress rather than that of ancient Greece. This interpretative shift would be repeated often. *Baty's 'Jansenist' *Phèdre* (1940) attempted to evoke Knossos, Athens, Versailles, and Port-Royal simultaneously, with a complex interpretation that emphasized the title

*character's fear of damnation rather than her incestuous desire. The production marked a trend toward *scenographic abstraction that continued with *Barrault's *Phèdre* at the Comédie-Française (1946), a production that coincided with the publication of his detailed *mise-en-scène, a testament to the painstaking attention that can be lavished on the intricacies of Racinian verse. With the arrival of *Brecht's ideas came several noteworthy productions, many of which carried scenographic minimalism to extremes. These included *Vilar's austere *Phèdre* for the *Théâtre National Populaire at Chaillot (1957), *Planchon's *Bérénice* for the TNP at Villeurbanne (1963), and *Vitez's *Andromaque* for the Théâtre des Quartiers d'Ivry (1971), in which the actors, in jeans and T-shirts, self consciously recounted the story of the play instead of embodying its characters. In the 1990s, directors like *Kokkos and *Mesguich turned their attention to Racine, some producing multiple plays in 'cycles' involving overarching interpretations.

Outside of France, the most notable production of Racine in the twentieth century was the Kamerny Theatre's *Phèdre* (1923). Directed by *Tairov with cubist design, the production demonstrated a synthesis of *Stanislavsky's psychological *realism, the *symbolism of *Craig, and the *biomechanics of *Meyerhold. In the Anglo-American theatre, where Racine's plays have suffered from a notorious difficulty in translation, the *Stratford Festival in Ontario and the Almeida Theatre in London presented noteworthy productions in the 1990s.   DGM

Radlov, Sergei (1892–1958) Russian/Soviet playwright and director. At his own Theatre of Popular Comedy he collaborated with the designer Valentina Khodasevich on a number of his plays (1920–1), while directing mass performances like *Towards the World Commune* (1920). Between 1925 and 1934 he staged *operas in Leningrad, and ran his own Studio Theatre between 1928 and 1942, where he staged *Othello* (a play he returned to several times), *Hamlet*, *Romeo and Juliet*, and *Ibsen's *Ghosts*, among twenty or so other productions. He directed at the Leningrad *circus in 1927, and at the Moscow State Yiddish Theatre between 1930 and 1935, including a magnificent *King Lear* starring *Mikhoels. During the 1950s he worked in Latvia. He staged over 100 productions at more than 30 different venues during his lifetime, including the work of *Aristophanes, *Sophocles, *Plautus, *Calderón, Shakespeare, *Molière, *Goldoni, *Goldsmith, *Lessing, *Hugo, *Pushkin, *Ostrovsky, *Wilde, *Toller, and *Zamyatin.   NW

Radok, Alfréd (1914–76) Czech director and playwright. After the war he staged *operas and *operettas, usually with *Svoboda's *scenography. In 1948 he entered the Czech National Theatre but was dismissed, for political reasons, the next year; he was readmitted in 1954, and again forced to leave in 1959. The highlights of that period were productions of *Leonov's *Golden Coach*, *Hellman's *The Autumn Garden*, and *Osborne's *The Entertainer*, all in 1957. In the Chamber Theatre (Prague, 1964), he enlarged *Rolland's intimate *Play on Love and Death* into a social epic with strong contemporary connotations. With Svoboda, he conceived *Laterna Magika for Expo 58 in Brussels; its second programme was banned, however, and Radok cut off from its future development. He emigrated to Sweden in 1968. Radok had a unique spatial imagination, used music lavishly to create atmosphere, and did not hesitate to adapt the script to his own vision. A perfectionist, he was very demanding with actors, but he enjoyed working with promising young talents like Miloš Forman and *Havel.　　　　ML

Radrigán, Juan (1937–　) Chilean playwright. Since *Testimony of Sabina's Death* (1979), Radrigán was recognized for works about marginality. He deals with the underworld and underclass, with drug addicts and prostitutes, and uses black *comedy and colloquial language rich in image and metaphor. Because his stagecraft is simple his work is easily produced by groups with scant resources. Although his plays tend to be specific about the social and political situation of Chile, his *characters struggle for self-respect and search for meaning in their lives in a manner recognizable elsewhere. His most accomplished plays are *Bull by the Horns* (1982), *The Guest, When All Is Said and Done* (1981), and *Destined to Live without Love* (1986).　　　　MAR

Radzinsky, Edvard (1936–　) Soviet/Russian playwright. Radzinsky displayed a concern for history in plays and novels about Stalin and Nicholas II (*The Last Tsar* was adapted for the stage as *The Last Night of the Last Tsar*, 1995). His play *Lunin; or, The Death of Jacques* (1974) deals with the last hour of the Decembrist Mikhail Lunin, while *The Seducer Kolobashkin* explores the legend of Don Quixote. Radzinsky has also written non-historical plays, in which he demonstrates a critical attitude to Soviet reality: *A Film Is Being Shot* (1964) addresses film "censorship, and *104 Pages about Love* (1974) involves a stewardess in a romantic plot though she ultimately dies in a plane crash. Radzinsky never flattered the regime

and remained a critical voice in post-Soviet Russia.　　　　BB

Raimund, Ferdinand (1790–1836) Austrian actor and playwright, the major representative of old Viennese popular theatre. His first plays belonged to the 'fairy play' tradition and described in rather sentimental terms aspects of ordinary Viennese life influenced by a benign metaphysical world. Fantastic adventures in the realm of spirits offered scope for magical stage spectacle and fascinating transformations. The main characters' attempts to escape their humble stations are always regretted in the end and they are reconciled to the limits of a modest existence. Raimund's aspiration to write serious drama conflicted with the commercial framework of the Theater in der Leopoldstadt, where he was engaged from 1817 to 1830. Nonetheless he introduced tragic and melancholic aspects in his allegorical *comedies, as well as good-humoured *satire on popular life in Vienna. The depth and complexity of his masterpieces, *The Peasant as Millionaire* (1826), *The Alpine King and the Misanthrope* (1828), and *The Prodigal* (1834), ensure that they occupy a secure position in the German-language repertoire.　　GB

Rakesh, Mohan (1929–72) Indian writer in Hindi whose stories and plays on urban relationships deal with identity, the limits of communication, and the impossibility of self-definition and self-fulfilment. The first of his full-length plays, *A Day in the Month of Asadh* (1958), which concerns the romantic relationship of *Kalidasa with his village beloved Mallika, debunked the sacrosanct image of the Sanskrit poet. Directed by *Alkazi in 1962 in Delhi, it established Rakesh as the most promising playwright of the new generation. His final full-length play, *Neither Half nor Whole* (1969), continues to engage urban *audiences through its central character, Savitri, damned to an impossible situation with a hopeless husband. After this Rakesh regarded *dialogue as a dated convention and experimented with wordless plays before his early death.　　　　VDa

Rakotoson, Michèle (1948–　) Francophone playwright and novelist from Madagascar. She has worked as cultural programme director for the French International Radio service, researched the traditional dramatic form *hira gasy*, and wrote her first plays in Malagasy. Political upheavals sent her into exile in Paris in the early 1980s and provided the inspiration for her major plays on dictatorship: *One Day, my Memory* (1988), *The Dead House* (1991), and *She Danced on the Waves* (1999). Her sister Christiane

Ramanatsoa staged her bilingual drama in Madagascar (*Iboniamasiboniamanoro*, 2001). CJM

Rama VI (1880–1925) King of Thailand from 1911 to his death, the most significant force in Thai theatre history. Involved in court performances from his childhood, he wrote, produced, and directed plays while studying military history and law in England, and started his own **khon* (*masked play) troupe soon after he returned to Thailand in 1902. He wrote 151 plays of various types: for traditional, folk, and modern theatre, adaptations of Western plays, translations of Shakespeare, and dramas in English and French. He also produced, directed, and acted for the court *audience. Many actors, dancers, and comedians were granted noble status during his reign. He established the Royal Department of Performing Arts to assist traditional theatre, then in decline, and founded the Royal School for Performing Arts to nurture young artists. He used theatre to promote nationalism and to counter colonialism and wrote many scholarly works. EV

Rame, Franca (1929–) Italian actress and playwright, who came from a family of travelling players. While performing in Milan with a *variety company she met Dario *Fo, and married him in 1954. Her subsequent career is inseparable from his. She introduced him to popular theatre, to the Italian tradition centred on the actor-author and on *improvisational skills, and she employed her deep, almost instinctive knowledge of theatrical techniques and rhythms to provide him with trenchant criticism of his writing. The two established the Fo–Rame company in 1958 and, at the height of the 1968 movement, they set up a *touring cooperative, similar to the Rame family company, to perform political theatre. Her contribution to Fo's plays has been undervalued, and with the rise of feminism she herself wrote several one-person shows, such as *All Bed Board and Church*, on the condition of women. JF

Ram lila Dramatization of the epic story about the Hindu deity Ram, which takes place every autumn across northern India. The story of Ram's birth, marriage, exile, and epic battle to regain his abducted wife Sita has been a foundational narrative of South and South-East Asia for over two millennia. It encapsulates central tenets of kingship, statehood, moral behaviour, and family and *gender relations, and is represented in a variety of styles including *puppetry, singing, *dancing, and *acting. *Ram lila* is based upon *Ramcharitmanas* by Tulsidas, a long poem in the Awadhi dialect of Hindi. Infused with the fervour of devotional poetry, *Ram lila* inspires reverence for the gods and inculcates an understanding of *dharma* or righteous action. It is also notable for its inclusive public character. Open-air performances of episodes from Ram's life are played before large crowds for at least ten days leading up to the festival of Dussehra, when the effigy of Ravana, the demon king, is destroyed by burning. Spectators come from all classes and castes, and historically include Muslims and Christians as well as Hindus. In episodes such as the march against Ravana, the crowd falls in behind the monkey-warriors and becomes part of the army. In Varanasi, episodes are associated with and enacted at specific localities identified by their mythic place names. As in the *ras lila, the actors are all male; Sita, Ram, and his brothers are played by prepubescent boys. Other *characters usually wear *masks, notably Hanuman, Ravana, and Kumbhakarna. But unlike the *ras lila* the performers are amateurs, and sponsorship through subscriptions is the most common form of patronage. The present form of the *Ram lila* began soon after Tulsidas's death in 1624. In the nineteenth century the royal house of Banaras established hereditary sponsorship of the Ramnagar *Ram lila*. In this presentation, passages from Tulsidas's text are recited by a *vyas* or Brahman specialist, in alternation with chanted passages by a *chorus accompanied by musical instruments. *Dialogue is interspersed between these sung and chanted lines. The style is *ritualistic, highly verbal, and somewhat static, and little emphasis is placed upon mimetic representation. KH

Ramly, Lenin El- (1945–) Egyptian playwright, screenwriter, and *manager. Ramly's *expressionism interlocks with his flair for popular *comedy, and serves to pose topical social and political questions. His best-known play internationally is *In Plain Arabic* (1991), a devastating *satire of the time-honoured ideal of pan-Arabism. The play also marked the end of Ramly's collaboration with actor-director Mohamed Sobhi, originally a classmate at the Egyptian Theater Institute; the two had founded in 1980 Estudio Tamaneen, a private troupe with justifiable claims to artistic experimentation. As film writer Ramly received media attention, both at home and abroad, for his attack on Islamist militants in *The Terrorist* (1994), a reworking of his 1967 short television drama. HMA

Ramos-Perea, Roberto (1959–) Puerto Rican playwright and director, winner of the Tirso de Molina award in Spain for *Lie to Me More* (1993). Author of more than 30 plays, his work alternates between neo-*realism, as in

Module 104 (1983), and the postmodern, as in *Mistiblú* (1991) and *To Die at Night* (1995). He often directs his own work, which has been translated into English and French and performed internationally. JLRE

Rana, Juan (Cosme Pérez) (fl. 1622–72) The most famous Spanish comedian of his day. Having acted in leading companies, by the mid-1630s Pérez was identified with his *clownish persona Juan Rana. This *character, originally a rustic magistrate, appeared in many other guises in over 40 playlets. Advancing years brought infirmity, but he emerged from retirement for major festivals, and rode on a chariot in *Juan Rana's Triumph*, an *interlude performed at court in 1672. VFD

Rand, Sally (1904–79) American fan and bubble dancer. As Billy Beck, she made her debut at 13 and after a few years in *vaudeville, she acted in silent films. Cecil B. DeMille reportedly chose her stage name from his Rand-McNally atlas. Rand catapulted to fame in 1933 when she rented a horse and crashed the Chicago World's Fair midway as Lady Godiva. This led to her engagement as a dancer at the fair, where she developed her celebrated fan *dance: swirling huge ostrich feather fans to conceal ('the Rand is quicker than the eye') her naked body. Her signature melodies were Debussy's '*Clair de lune*' and, for her finale, Chopin's 'Valse in C-sharp minor'. Nude dancing with fans or semi-transparent balloons remained central to her career in nightclubs and *burlesque, even as late as 1978. FHL

randai Folk *dance-drama of the Minangkabau ethnic group in west Sumatra (Indonesia) which evolved at the turn of the twentieth century as a composite of martial arts, dance, instrumental music, song, and *acting. Originally an all-male tradition with *female impersonators, most *randai* groups today are mixed. The indigenous martial arts (*silek*) continue to be featured prominently, including circular dances called *galombang*, based on martial arts movements, which are accompanied by songs and flute music. A unique feature of *galombang* is the *tapuak* percussion, performed by dancers slapping their trousers. The *galombang* alternate with acted scenes in performances that typically last three to four hours. The narratives are derived from traditional Minangkabau tales (*kaba*). Though the form uses electric *lighting and amplified sound, more *realistic acting techniques, and an array of modern *costuming, it remains firmly rooted in *silek* and strives to educate its *audiences about Minangkabau customs and tradition. KP

rasa Literally 'flavour', *rasa* is one of the most important concepts in Indian aesthetics. In theatre it refers to the pleasure involved in 'tasting' a performance through a heightened experience that transcends temporal, spatial, and personal conditions and constraints. Grounded in a spectrum of at least nine distinct emotional registers—erotic, comic, pathetic, furious, heroic, terrifying, odious, marvellous, and peaceful—the *rasa* is produced through the exploration of dominant states of emotion, supported by determinant, consequent, and transitory states of emotion. The Kashimiri Saivite seer Abhinavagupta (tenth century) offered the most complex theory of *rasa* in which it prefigures the entire aesthetic experience, rather like the essence underlying the transformation of a seed into a tree. Approximating the *ananda* (bliss) experienced by yogis in touch with the Absolute, the experience of *rasa* falls short of spiritual self-realization. Nonetheless, its pleasure is made possible to connoisseurs of the arts, who are called *rasika* or *sahridaya*, whose 'consent of the heart' makes the experience of *rasa* at once immediate and indivisible. RB

Rascón Banda, Víctor Hugo (1948–2008) Mexican playwright and novelist. A prominent member of the 'New Dramaturgy', his plays are hard-hitting, dark, and violent explorations of political corruption (*Blue Beach*, 1990), drug trafficking (*Contraband*, 1991), and a social system that has forgotten its poor (*The Fierce Woman of Ajusco*, 1985). Born in the state of Chihuahua, he also wrote powerful texts about that region (*Voices on the Threshold*, 1983) and USA–Mexico border issues (*The Illegals*, 1979; *Murder with Malice*, 1994). As a banker, Rascón had his pulse on the law of money in Mexico and the courage to expose its inner machinations in plays such as *The Bank* and *The Executives* (1997). His playwriting evolved from a crude *realism to a more poetical one and, later, to a form of hyper-realism. With *La Malinche* (1998), Rascón ventured into the excesses of the postmodern with a production that both intrigued and outraged Mexican *audiences and critics. KFN

ras lila Devotional Hindi-language theatre found in the Braj region of Uttar Pradesh in India. It is a specific form of *Krishna lila*, the dramatic telling of miraculous episodes from the life of the Hindu deity Krishna. The circle *dance (*ras*) symbolic of the mystic union between the human Radha and the divine Krishna is the principal medium for the arousal of religious emotion (*bhakti*).

In its present form *ras lila* dates to the sixteenth century when saint-poets disseminated an accessible form of religious faith in Krishna, one of the incarnations of Vishnu, through the common languages of north India. It is performed in temple courtyards by professionals, typically during the monsoon season, before pilgrims and local followers of Vaishnavism. Temple priests are the usual patrons, although affluent devotees may also fill this function. The roles of Krishna, Radha, and the *gopis* (Krishna's girlfriends, who, like Krishna, tend cattle) are played by pre-pubescent boys chosen from local Brahman families. They are worshipped as divine manifestations during the performance and offstage as well. *Costumes date from the Mughal period, and facial stencils, long black artificial braids, and glittering headgear complete the distinctive look. The stage consists of a demarcated circular area where the dancing and acting take place. Viewers respond through clapping, swaying, and dancing in response to the devotional atmosphere. At significant moments the Radha-Krishna pair assume iconic stances, freezing in a tableau (*jhanki*). Framed by an ornamental border like enshrined deities, the actors become gods and the spectators worshippers as they advance to prostrate themselves and make offerings.

The repertoire of *lila* numbers over 100 episodes. The dominant emotion of erotic love pervades the *ras lila*, but comic *improvisations are also intermixed, particularly through the character Mansukha, who serves as a jester. The dancing in *ras lila* includes virtuoso elements such as rapid spins, twirling on the knees, and acrobatic manoeuvres. *See also* RAM LILA.   KH

Rattigan, Terence (1911–77) English playwright. Rattigan made his name with the long-running *comedy, *French without Tears* (1936), followed by the darker *After the Dance* (1939). *The Winslow Boy* (1946), the tale of a boy expelled from naval college for allegedly stealing a postal order, gained him critical respect, while *The Browning Version* (1948), a one-act about a failed schoolmaster and his wretched marriage, is a miniature masterpiece. *The Deep Blue Sea* (1952), probably his greatest work, concerns a woman who abandons her rich husband only to find herself trapped in a hopeless relationship with a young airman. Despite taking greater risks in subject matter and form, few of Rattigan's plays were successes after the revolutions in British theatre led by *Osborne's *Look Back in Anger* in 1956. *Ross* (1960) and *Cause Célèbre* (1977) used filmic, almost epic, structures, while *Variations on a Theme* (1957), *Man and Boy* (1963), and *In Praise of Love* (1973) continued to explore the nature of sexual desire and repression. The final scene of

Separate Tables (1954) shows a tempestuous battle between judgemental sexual conservatism and liberal decency, conducted entirely through glances and small talk in the dining room of a seaside hotel.   DR

Raucourt, Mlle (Françoise-Marie-Antoinette-Josèphe Saucerotte) (1756–1815) French actress. The sensational debut of this tall, handsome 16-year-old at the *Comédie-Française in 1772 earned her the protection of Louis XV and the mercenary attentions of aristocrats eager for her virginity. Her sexual proclivities, however, were lesbian and, after a series of highly publicized scandals and arrest for debt, she was exiled for three years. Reinstated in 1779 by order of Marie Antoinette, she rebuilt her reputation during the 1780s, starring in tragic-queen roles such as *Racine's Athalie and *Voltaire's Sémiramis. In 1782 she appeared cross-dressed as a young soldier in *Henriette*, a play of her own composition. With other counter-revolutionaries, she was imprisoned in 1793 and narrowly escaped the guillotine. In 1796, dreaming of re-establishing the Comédie-Française in a new home, she formed a 'Second Théâtre-Français' at the Théâtre Louvois. In 1799 she joined the reconstituted Comédie. In 1806 she was entrusted by Napoleon to organize a company to *tour Italy. She returned seven years later and in 1814 gave her last performance, as Catherine de Médicis in François Raynouard's *The Blois Parliament*.   JG

Raupach, Ernst (1784–1852) German dramatist. After studying theology and philosophy in Halle, Raupach taught literature and history at St Petersburg University. In 1824 he settled in Berlin where he wrote 117 plays, mainly historical and mythological *tragedies in the tradition of *Schiller, as well as *melodramas and sentimental *comedies. Raupach was one of the most performed German dramatists of the late *romantic period. Best known are his play *The Miller and his Child* (1830), for its prevalent death symbolism and fatalistic tone, as well as his skilfully constructed eight-play cycle *The Hohenstaufens* (1837).   CBB

Ravenhill, Mark (1967–) English playwright. *Shopping and Fucking* (1996) angrily satirizes the vacuity of his generation's lives and aspirations, a theme which became clearer in *Faust Is Dead* (1997), which pitilessly identified the worst excesses of postmodern thought in a tale of a philosophical guru's journey with a young boy into the American desert. *Some Explicit Polaroids* (1999) places the *satire in a broader context, juxtaposing the empty-headed narcissism of its characters with the unforgiving forces of globalization.

Mother Clap's Molly House (2001) is a *Brechtian piece, interweaving scenes set in the early eighteenth century with a contemporary gay sex party, subtly questioning the relationship between sexual liberation and market economics. Greater formal experimentation is apparent in the elliptical political parable *The Cut* (2006), the self-performed satirical monologue *Product* (2006), the text for *dance theatre *pool (no water)* (2006), and the seventeen short texts of the global-political epic, *Shoot/Get Treasure/Repeat* (2008). He has also written a number of successful plays for young people, including *Totally Over You* (2003), and *Scenes from Family Life* (2008).   DR

Ravenscroft, Edward (fl. 1671–97) English playwright. Ravenscroft wrote a dozen plays, many of them imitations or adaptations of European *comedies, some successful, none of them particularly distinguished. A master of the bedroom *farce, in his first play, *The Citizen Turned Gentleman* (1672), he was relatively restrained, but in his later comedies—*The Careless Lovers* (1673), *The Wrangling Lovers* (1676), *The Canterbury Guests* (1694)—he catered shamelessly to Restoration taste. His masterpiece, *The London Cuckold* (1681), spices adulterous *action with smutty *dialogue, and was so popular that it was annually revived on the Lord Mayor's Day until 1751. *The Anatomist* (1697), reduced to an afterpiece, held the stage for over a century. Ravenscroft also adapted Shakespeare's *Titus Andronicus* (1686), and experimented with *commedia dell'arte* with *Scaramouche a Philosopher* (1677). *The Italian Husband* (1697), a domestic horror play, is an unsentimental examination of a brutal murder. RWV

Razumovskaya, Lyudmila (1946–) Soviet/Russian playwright. Razumovskaya began writing plays in the mid-1970s. *Dear Elena Sergeevna* (1980, staged 1988, film 1988) is about a group of pupils who visit their teacher in order to steal exam questions; she does not surrender, but is driven to the brink of suicide by the realization that she has brought up monsters. *Garden without Soil* (1982) explores loveless marriage. The theme of moral corruption caused by the Soviet system runs through Razumovskaya's work. BB

Reade, Charles (1814–84) English writer. Reade was better known for his novels, such as *The Cloister and the Hearth* (1861), but wrote some 35 plays, almost all *melodramas. Among them is the popular *comedy *Masks and Faces* (1852), which he wrote with Tom Taylor, whose liveliest *character is *Garrick's actress Peg *Woffington. *The Courier of Lyons* (1854), a crime drama about mistaken identity, was played with

great effect by *Irving as *The Lyons Mail* (1877). *It's Never Too Late to Mend* (1864) contained a grim and controversial scene showing punishment on a prison treadmill, which illustrated Reade's social reformist tendencies. He was responsible for persuading Ellen *Terry to return to the theatre in 1874 to act in one of his own plays. The theatre was not good to Reade: he estimated his total income from the drama at £35 a year.   MRB

realism and reality Realism is the generic name for various philosophical arguments through the ages which counter the philosophy of idealism. Although the terms did not emerge until the eighteenth century, the concepts were central to classical Greek philosophy. *Aristotle was the promoter of common-sense realism (the world is as it appears, material objects are what they seem). Aristotle wrote in reaction to Plato, who held that ideal forms lay under appearance (the world and its objects are degraded copies of the idea of things). Western philosophy has struggled ever since to describe the relation between the Real and the Ideal (or the world and idea). These philosophical debates chart major difficulties in human understanding, including the problem of how the mind, apart from the material world yet still in it, is able to perceive, know, and represent the world accurately and fully. Various dialectical terms (reality and appearance, truth and falsehood, essence and existence, materialism and formalism) have been used to articulate this problem.

When the concepts of *reality*, the *real*, and the *realistic* are taken up by theatre artists, dramatic theorists, and theatre scholars, they are usually anchored in Aristotelian philosophy. The relation between art and reality has been negotiated by the general (and often vague) principle of *mimesis, defined variously as representation, likeness, imitation, resemblance, and verisimilitude. Yet despite the recurring appeal to some kind of principle of reality through theatre history, the concept of realism acquired new meanings in modern times, especially between the 1870s and the 1920s. Three interrelated developments are noteworthy.

1. Both theatre artists and theorists put forward a new concept of realism—not just the familiar idea of realistic or representative theatre—to refer to an artistic movement identified with the drama of *Zola, *Ibsen, early *Strindberg, *Hauptmann, *Chekhov, and *Gorky. In basic accord with the novelists who were already articulating a new realism (such as Balzac, Flaubert, *Tolstoy, and Zola himself), the dramatists sought to produce plays that presented a candid, concrete, and exact picture of contemporary life and society. In this

sense realism was an early stage of modernism, one of the revolts against not only *romanticism and *melodramatic conventions but also *bourgeois culture. Modern realism is also closely related to *naturalism—a term that Zola used in his essay 'Naturalism in the Theatre' (1881). He called for 'the return to nature and to man, direct observation, correct anatomy, the acceptance and depiction of that which *is*'. Likewise, in the preface to *Miss Julie* (1888) Strindberg spelled out his own version of the naturalistic programme. Ibsen did not write manifestos, but like Chekhov was determined to represent ordinary details in order to capture both the texture of material life and the *subtextual pulse of the *characters' lives—their psychological, social, economic, and moral beings. By representing the illusion of actual experience, realistic drama aimed to reveal not only the social registers of contemporary life but also the sordid, empty, and even tragic nature of modern society.

The aesthetic philosophies of realism and naturalism, influenced by positivism in the sciences, urged writers to be objective in order to dissect society and human character. Both programmes also revealed the influence of Darwinism and the idea of the struggle for survival. Naturalist drama, such as Hauptmann's *The Weavers* (1892) and Gorky's *The Lower Depths* (1902), tended to represent the economic and environmental forces that controlled, even determined, the characters' behaviour. By contrast, realistic drama, such as Ibsen's *Hedda Gabler* (1890) and Chekhov's *The Cherry Orchard* (1904), located the suffering of the characters in their social values and psychological self-deceptions, though a strain of economic, social, and hereditary determinism may operate in these plays as well.

2. The new realistic drama served as a catalyst for *actors and *directors who attempted to develop new realistic methods of acting and staging. Indeed, the figure of the director (e.g. *Saxe-Meiningen, *Reinhardt, Granville *Barker) emerges in this era as a solution, at least in part, to the problem of how to unify the many detailed elements of performance and production in the new realism. New acting companies also emerged at the end of the nineteenth century to perform realist and naturalist drama: *Antoine's Théâtre *Libre in Paris, *Brahm's *Freie Bühne in Berlin, the *Independent Theatre Society and the partnership of *Archer and Elizabeth *Robins in London, and, most tellingly, the *Moscow Art Theatre, founded by *Stanislavsky and *Nemirovich-Danchenko. In addition, some actors and directors, notably Stanislavsky, attempted to develop a new system of actor training and performance.

3. In conjunction with the new acting and directing methods, a new realistic *scenography developed. Although the nineteenth-century stage had already taken up historical *antiquarianism in the production of historical drama and Shakespeare, thus achieving one kind of realism, the new realistic drama called for a natural or realistic environment, so detailed and accurate that it looked exactly like a Norwegian parlour in *A Doll's House* or a basement lodging in *The Lower Depths*. *Costumes as well had to be accurate for the time and place of the play, right down to the buttons on Hedda Gabler's dress. And the new stage *lighting, enhanced at the turn of the century by the development of instruments for controlling electric lights, contributed to the aura of a natural environment.

For a few decades the theatre seemed to achieve a new realism that answered the demands of representing reality. And yet no sooner did realism proclaim itself as the instrument of modernism than a *symbolist—or idealistic—alternative asserted itself. Even the careers of Ibsen and Strindberg show that the dialectic between the Real and the Ideal is abiding in the theatre. In the early decades of the twentieth century, modernism promoted various non-realistic agendas, from *futurism, *dada, and *surrealism to *expressionism, *constructivism, and *epic theatre. But realism did not disappear from the modern theatre; it continued to be the preferred mode of representation for many playwrights, actors, designers, and directors. And in film realism has served as a defining principle of *mise-en-scène and acting.

Advocates for modern realism often claim that it is truer to life than all previous modes of representation. If so, did it achieve a solution to the debate initiated by Plato and Aristotle? Apparently not, for theatre in every age and locale has developed its particular method for representation. This is why the natural acting of one age, locale, or medium often looks stylized and unnatural to observers from any other age, locale, or medium. Realism is yet one more theatrical style, not a mode of representation without theatrical features. In consequence, it is impossible to define the terms realism and reality in any acceptable manner, especially if we expect them to carry and maintain a shared set of meanings that apply throughout human history, operate across diverse cultures and societies, and fit all art forms. All workable definitions must be local definitions, specific to time and place, particular to a group of people who have agreed upon a set of meanings for the concepts. Change any of these conditions and the meanings also change, sometimes radically. TP

Reaney, James (1926–2008) Canadian poet and playwright. His most famous work is the 'Donnelly trilogy' about an Irish family destroyed by sectarian violence in nineteenth-century Ontario. Employing a fluid improvisational style and richly poetic language, these plays—*Sticks and Stones, The St Nicholas Hotel,* and *Handcuffs*—attracted enormous attention at Toronto's Tarragon Theatre (1973–5) and *toured nationally. Reaney's other plays include *One Man Masque* (1960), *The Killdeer* (1960), *The Sun and the Moon* (1962), *The Easter Egg* (1962), *Listen to the Wind* (1966), and *Colours in the Dark* (1967). He wrote several plays for *youth, notably *Names and Nicknames* (1963), and his adaptation of *Alice through the Looking Glass* premièred at the *Stratford Festival in 1994. Most of Reaney's plays reflect his upbringing in rural Ontario.   DWJ

recognition *See* ANAGNORISIS.

Redgrave, Michael (1908–85) English actor. At the *Old Vic he played Orlando to Edith *Evans's Rosalind in *As You Like It* (1936) and Laertes to *Olivier's Hamlet (1937). In contemporary plays his roles included Harry in *Eliot's *The Family Reunion* (1939). Redgrave's imposing height but gentle personal magnetism lent him a striking stage presence. At the *Shakespeare Memorial Theatre he was Richard II (1951), Prospero (1952), King Lear, and Shylock (1953); he also played opposite *Ashcroft in *Antony and Cleopatra* (1953) and in 1958 was Hamlet at the age of 50. He appeared as Uncle Vanya at *Chichester in 1962. He had a lengthy film career, ranging from Hitchcock's *The Lady Vanishes* (1939) to Losey's *The Go-Between* (1971). Influenced by *Stanislavsky, Redgrave wrote on the craft of *acting in *The Actor's Ways and Means* (1953) and *Mask or Face* (1958), and the autobiographical *In my Mind's Eye* (1983). From a theatrical family, he married actress Rachel Kempson in 1935; their children Corin (1939–2010), Lynn (1943–2010), and Vanessa *Redgrave all pursued theatrical careers.   VRS

Redgrave, Vanessa (1937–) English actress, eldest daughter of Michael *Redgrave. Her London debut was opposite her father in N. C. *Hunter's *A Touch of the Sun* (1958). She joined the *Shakespeare Memorial Theatre in 1959, as Helena in *A Midsummer Night's Dream* and Valeria in *Coriolanus.* Later roles included Jean Brodie in *The Prime of Miss Jean Brodie* (1966), Gilda in *Design for Living* (1973), Boletta in *The Lady from the Sea* (1976), Arkadina in *Three Sisters*

(1985), Katherine in *The Taming of the Shrew,* Mrs Alving in *Ghosts* (both 1986–7), and Hesione in *Heartbreak House* (1992). In 1994 she played Vita Sackville-West to Eileen *Atkins's Virginia Woolf in *Vita and Virginia* in New York, and in 1999 she was Carlotta in *A Song at Twilight* in London. In 2000 she was Prospero in *The Tempest* at the new *Globe, and Madame Ranevskaya in *Nunn's *Cherry Orchard.* Her film appearances have been hugely varied and include Antonioni's *Blow-Up* (1966), Frears's *Prick up your Ears* (1987), *Mission Impossible* (1996), and *Atonement* (2007).   AS

Rees, Roger (1944–) Welsh actor and director, who worked as a *stage manager for a variety of theatres including Wimbledon, where he made his acting debut in *Murder at the Vicarage* (1965). The following year he joined the *Royal Shakespeare Company. Through the 1960s and 1970s he appeared in numerous RSC productions, gradually gaining larger roles. In 1980 he was the eponymous *hero in the company's *Nicholas Nickleby*; the Broadway transfer won him a Tony award as best actor. Subsequent appearances include Terry Johnson's *Cries from the Mammal House* (*Royal Court), and Hamlet and Berowne for the RSC (all 1984). Much of his career has been in the USA and has included Broadway productions of *Cocteau's *Indiscretions* (1995), *Anouilh's *The Rehearsal* (1996), and *Chekhov's *Uncle Vanya* (2000), playing Astrov opposite *Jacobi. Rees was a regular in the television sitcom *Cheers* (1989–90).   AS

regional repertory theatres, UK The term repertory theatre (or 'rep') refers to the network of publicly subsidized regional theatres throughout the UK that operate regular seasons of plays produced by a resident *management. Such theatres differ from the major city repertory theatres in continental Europe in that they rarely maintain a permanent acting company (the *National Theatre and *Royal Shakespeare Company are exceptions); and the pattern of production is seldom true *repertory playing. More usually each production will run for three to four weeks, to be replaced by a new production with a new cast. What has animated the repertory movement throughout its history is the ideal of offering a varied and balanced fare of plays—new and classic, serious and comic—and related events that command the interest and feed the imagination of the community. Theatre in this sense is seen as a cultural service rather than a commercial enterprise.

The history of the repertory movement in Britain aligns itself almost exactly with the course of the twentieth century. Its seeds lay in the campaigns mounted at the end of the nineteenth century to establish a national theatre, forcefully articulated by Granville *Barker and *Archer in their 1904 manifesto, but it effectively began in the regions, which were less constrained by London's major commercial ventures and costly rents. The first repertory theatre in mainland Britain was founded in 1907 in Manchester by the wealthy theatre enthusiast Annie *Horniman. Having helped found the *Abbey Theatre in Dublin three years earlier, she was keen to establish a permanent company dedicated to high standards of production and opposed to the long run and star system. She presented a range of high quality drama and fostered the development of new, home-grown writing. Following Manchester came reps in Liverpool (1911) and *Birmingham (1913), and, after the war, smaller but often just as innovative ventures in Northampton, Sheffield, Oxford, Cambridge, and elsewhere. By 1938 there were over 30 reps in the UK—subsidized not by the state but by wealthy entrepreneurs, charitable trusts, and subscription.

The rebuilding of cities following the Second World War and the arrival of public subsidy produced a rapid expansion. Arts Council subsidy enabled the rep companies to move out of the straitjacket of weekly repertory (involving a new production every week, usually with one week's *rehearsal), raise production standards, and build new *audiences, aided by subsidized ticket prices. From the Belgrade, Coventry (1958), to the West Yorkshire Playhouse, Leeds (1990), there was a surge of new or radically renovated *playhouses which reflected a fresh vision of the repertory theatre and its relationship to its community. Theatres were seen now as arts centres—they incorporated cafés and studio theatres, ran *youth, *educational, and community outreach teams, and hosted *touring companies as well as staging their own productions. By 1980 the number of new theatres (including major conversions) totalled 40, of which 34 were outside London. The scale of renewal was all the more remarkable at a time of declining fortunes in the commercial touring sector and the increasing dominance of television. Although the early designs were mostly conventional *proscenium-arch affairs, many of the later theatres are impressive for their exploration of theatre space and actor-audience relationships, notably the thrust stages of the *Chichester Festival Theatre (1962) and Sheffield's Crucible Theatre (1971), and the in-the-round *auditoriums at Manchester's Royal Exchange (1976), Scarbor-

ough's Stephen Joseph Theatre (1976), and Stoke-on-Trent's New Victoria Theatre (1986).

A few enterprising reps in this period stand out. The Nottingham Playhouse, especially under *Eyre (1973–8), premièred some of the most penetrating English plays of the 1970s including *Brenton's *Churchill Play* and *Griffiths's *Comedians*. The small but lively Victoria Theatre, Stoke-on-Trent, is best known for its *documentary dramas, such as *The Knotty* and *Fight for Shelton Bar*, fashioned out of the region's own history and topical concerns to celebrate a community's own stories. The *Citizens' Theatre in Glasgow, under the artistic triumvirate of *Havergal, *Prowse, and Robert David Macdonald, created a visually stunning style and a radical reinterpretation of the classics. The Everyman in Liverpool (1964) signalled the emergence of an alternative to the mainstream; playwrights John *McGrath, Chris Bond, Adrian *Mitchell, Willy *Russell, and Alan Bleasdale all cut their teeth at the Everyman.

Public arts subsidy came under pressure in the 1970s following sudden hikes in oil prices and soaring inflation, accelerated by the arrival in 1979 of the Thatcher administration with its market-forces philosophy. Some of the smaller reps closed; larger theatres economized by closing down community outreach and drastically reducing studio production. The voices clamouring for a fairer distribution of resources between London and the regions became louder, and in response the Arts Council began to decentralize funding, leading to a wholesale devolution, beginning in 1990, to newly constituted regional arts boards. Only the National, Royal Shakespeare Company, and national touring companies remained funded from the centre.

But decentralization did not counter under funding. In 1990 the Arts Council drama panel reported that 31 regional theatres were on the verge of bankruptcy. Some adventurous work continued, but by the end of the twentieth century the British repertory theatre was unsustainable in a great many of the towns and communities it had served for most of the century. Funding was a major factor, but so too were the rapidly changing tastes and leisure habits of the communities themselves. If theatres were to respond positively to the needs of a multicultural society and make programmes accessible to all sections of society, not least to disaffected urban youth, then the rep, geared primarily to generating its own productions, could no longer be seen as the dominant model for regional theatre. Theatres were needed that could host a variety of work targeted at different facets of the community, respond rapidly to changing interests, and offer far greater opportunity for community involvement. Following the publication of the influential 'Boyden Report' (2000), Arts Council England committed substantial new funding from 2002, to help stabilize the many building-based theatres and encourage innovative and socially inclusive programming. The additional funds restored a degree of health to an ailing system. Scotland attacked the problem differently, by creating the National Theatre of Scotland in 2006 without a base in a building, and with a brief to tour the Scottish regions.   ARJ

regional theatres, USA Theatre in the United States has been centred in New York for much of the past 300 years. There have always been theatres elsewhere, of course, rising and falling with the larger history of dramatic entertainment in the country, but in the second half of the twentieth century the establishment of a network of permanent professional theatres represented a development of lasting significance. Known variously as regional, resident, non-profit, and institutional theatres, they have decentralized American theatre in important ways, though without displacing New York from its primary position.

The movement was pioneered by three dynamic and determined women. In 1947 Margo *Jones established a resident repertory theatre in Dallas and inspired others with a manifesto, *Theatre-in-the-Round* (1951). That same year Nina Vance marshalled efforts to launch the Alley Theatre in Houston, which she ran for more than 30 years. In 1950 Zelda *Fichandler co-founded *Arena Stage in Washington, DC, which she led with distinction for 40 years. Other early regional theatres include *Blau and Jules Irving's Actors Workshop in San Francisco (1952–66), and the Milwaukee Repertory Theatre (1954). These represented a typical pattern: led by a dominant personality, a small, dedicated group of aspiring professionals with limited resources and roots in the community or local university produced in inadequate, rented facilities. Another pattern featured a team of professionals, sometimes alienated by Broadway, who moved to a city and joined with civic and business leaders to establish an institution parallel to the local symphony and art museum. This pattern was epitomized by the *Guthrie Theatre (1963), founded in Minneapolis after several cities were considered. Its emphasis on a repertory of American and European classics highlighted the shared mission of regional theatres to preserve and refresh past traditions, styles, and playwrights, most obviously Shakespeare. The Guthrie heralded a mid-1960s explosion of regional theatres in cities around the country, including Seattle,

Hartford, Baltimore, Louisville, Providence, San Francisco, New Haven, and Los Angeles.

The first-generation shared characteristics that set standards for future institutions. Artistic freedom was sought by organizing as tax-exempt, 'not-for-profit' corporations, often led by an *artistic director and *managing director in tandem. Fundraising and subsidy became keys to survival. *Financial crises were chronic as theatres struggled to find or build adequate facilities. On the model of symphony orchestras, stability was sought by programming a season of plays sold in advance to a core subscription *audience of mostly upper-middle-class citizens. The pull between establishing a permanent institution and pursuing artistic goals led to a dynamic and sometimes fiery tension between artists, administrators, and boards of directors. Through it all, a missionary zeal about saving the art of theatre prevailed. That same mission motivated the concurrent *Off-Broadway movement in New York, equally concerned to establish an alternative to Broadway.

By 1966 regional theatres in aggregate employed more actors than New York, and this growth continued into the 1970s. The subscription season became a fixture and led to a flexible but standard repertoire that combined classics, modern dramas, American plays, theatrical chestnuts, and new works. A Shakespeare play is often the cornerstone for a season, with *Molière, *Shaw, and *Chekhov making more frequent appearances than *Ibsen, *Pirandello, or *Brecht. The perpetual search for a *comedy to balance the season has prompted frequent revivals of *Coward and *Kaufman and *Hart. Many theatres will mount an American *musical, while others have embraced the holiday tradition of adaptations of *Dickens's *A Christmas Carol*. These cash cows help to offset production of more obscure or challenging work.

At more daring theatres, that work included the development of new plays and playwrights, which led to the occasional practice of transferring a regional production to Broadway. For the non-profits, success in New York had huge benefits back home for individual artists and the institution. For Broadway *producers, the provinces became a new source of commercially viable plays. The *Actors Theatre of Louisville launched the Humana Festival of New American Plays in 1977, which evolved into a celebrated national showcase. The regional theatres' role in nurturing new American plays seemed to climax in the late 1980s and early 1990s, when no fewer than five of August *Wilson's plays originated at the Yale Repertory Theatre before moving to Broadway. In 1993, after years of development at the Eureka

Theatre and the Mark Taper Forum, *Kushner's *Angels in America* premièred on Broadway to great acclaim.

By this time a community of institutional theatres was well established, some with permanent endowments but many more with nagging deficits. Economic pressures contributed to the formation of in-house conservatories, internship programmes, or alliances with local universities. Some theatres early recognized a need or obligation to reach beyond their middle-class, middle-aged constituency to find ways to serve the larger community. At larger institutions this led to extensive outreach and *educational programmes which attract non-traditional audiences or take special projects into neighbourhoods and institutions where the arts are missing. Less complimentary aspects have been a general failure to maintain permanent companies of actors or to promote experiment and innovation, the second stemming in part from the innate conservatism of institutions and the difficulty of establishing a permanent second stage for riskier productions.

A 2000 survey of 262 theatres revealed that they mounted 3,200 productions for an audience of 21.7 million. On average, they financed two-thirds of total expenses from earned income, relying on contributions and subsidy for the other third. Though the quality of work varies widely, the regional movement has brought theatre to the nation. It established a network of institutions that produced and promoted theatre as a vital art form on the local level, enhancing the cultural landscape and decentralizing the American theatre in the process.   STC

Regnard, Jean-François (1655–1709) French writer. During his travels Regnard was captured by corsairs in 1678, and held prisoner at Algiers until ransomed, an experience he was able to exploit in his own fiction. As playwright he had a personal style, perhaps because his first plays were composed for the *Comédie Italienne, which helped to give him a distinctive approach to the master–servant relationship. From 1695 he wrote for the *Comédie-Française. In *Le Joueur* (1696), the best known of his *comedies, he treats the addiction to gambling in a light-hearted rather than a moralistic manner; *Le Distrait* (1697) is an amusing treatment of absent-mindedness; while *Le Légataire universel* (1708) uses a gaily amoral story of the 'correction' of an uncle's will in favour of his nephew—and also in favour of the valet Crispin who has impersonated the dying uncle.   WDH

Rehan, Ada (1857–1916) Irish-American actress. Born Ada Crehan in Limerick, her family emigrated to New York in 1862. In 1873 she followed several siblings into the theatre, serving a long apprenticeship in regional theatres. In 1879 she joined Augustin *Daly's company in an alliance that would last twenty years. Under Daly's tutelage, Rehan became the company's leading comedienne, playing over 200 roles as varied as Nelly in *Love's Young Dreams* (1879), Lu Ten Eyck in a revival of *Divorce* (1879), Sylvia in *The Recruiting Officer* (1885), and Lady Teazle in *The School for Scandal* (1894). Daly produced numerous Shakespearian *comedies as vehicles for her and she responded with widely praised performances, most notably as Katherine, Viola, and Rosalind. After Daly's death she rarely performed, the last time being on *tour with Otis *Skinner in *The Taming of the Shrew* (1904–5).   GAR

rehearsal The activity of actors and technicians preparing a play or other performance for presentation before an *audience. Rehearsal of some type has probably been central since the beginning of theatre as an institution, though what it has meant has varied greatly. We know that the playwright rehearsed *actors in ancient *Greek theatre (though apparently not the *chorus), and in the *early modern period the author was probably in charge of preparing actors for new plays. But we know little about how those rehearsals proceeded or how much authority the leader exercised. In succeeding centuries in most countries actors were organized according to *lines of business, playing similar or type roles across a range of plays, reducing or eliminating the need for detailed *character investigation. They depended on the *prompter for onstage help with words and movements, and had little incentive for practice runs since they were not paid for them. Star actors, whether or not they *managed their own companies, would set the standard for rehearsal, and because most plays were kept in some form of rotating *repertory prior to the rise of the long run, actors were expected to step into roles they already knew with little or no warning.

As the technology of theatre became more complex in the late nineteenth century, and more concerned with innovative styles like *realism and *naturalism, rehearsal became more important. The advent of modernism solidified the change through the introduction of the *director, who emerged as a functionary separate from actor, playwright, or manager specifically to lead rehearsals, with the goals of textual explication and stylistic unity foremost in mind. *Stanislavsky was the most influential theorist of rehearsal in the twentieth century, establishing a practice in which actors used solitary and group preparation to delve deeply into the psychology of their characters, often relying on the concept of *subtext. This combination of circumstances—coupled with the contracted payment to actors for rehearsal instituted by trade unions in many countries—led to greatly expanded periods of preparation.

Professionals and amateurs alike now take rehearsal most seriously, knowing that each new production of a play is considered by Western culture as a new work of art, and aware as well that the audience expects a sophisticated interpretation of even minor characters. What goes on during rehearsal will nonetheless vary enormously, and could range from the complete *devising of a new piece through *improvisation to seemingly endless reiteration of difficult scenes. How long a period is devoted to rehearsal is determined by the material and *financial conditions of the organization. In modes dependent on improvisation such as *commedia dell'arte, *agitprop, and *street theatre, preparation before a specific performance may involve only a quick consultation among actors to adapt a stock *scenario to local circumstance.   DK

Reid, Christina (1942–   ) Irish playwright. Several of her plays offer female perspectives on Belfast working-class lives, including *Tea in a China Cup* (1983), *Joyriders* (1986), *The Belle of the Belfast City* (1986), *Did You Hear the One about the Irishman?* (1987), and *Clowns* (1996), a sequel to *Joyriders*. Reid was writer-in-residence at the Lyric Theatre, Belfast (1983–4), moved to London in 1987, and was playwright-in-residence at the Young Vic (1988–9). She has written for theatre for *youth and schools, and for radio and television.   AEM

Reid, Kate (1930–93) Canadian actor, born in London. Reid built her classical repertoire at the *Stratford Festival between 1959 and 1965, while her Broadway performances as Martha in *Albee's *Who's Afraid of Virginia Woolf?* (1962) and Caitlin Thomas opposite *Guinness in Sidney Michael's *Dylan* (1964) demonstrated her versatility in contemporary roles. *Williams (*Slapstick Tragedy*, 1966), *Miller (*The Price*, 1968), and Albee (*A Delicate Balance*, film version, 1973) all wrote roles for her. An exceptional interpreter of tough, complex survivors, whether bawds (Mistress Overdone in *Measure for Measure*, 1992) or queens (Clytemnestra in *Aeschylus' *Oresteia*, 1983), Reid's vulnerable, earthy, compassionate portrayal of Linda in Dustin Hoffman's 1985 revival of *Death of a Salesman* remains a highlight of a prolific career in North American theatre, film, radio, and television.   MJD

Reinhardt, Max (1873–1943) Austrian director, probably the most prolific and influential director of the first half of the twentieth century. Born Max Goldmann near Vienna of Jewish parentage, Reinhardt began his career as an actor in Austria, but in 1894 moved to Berlin, where he specialized in playing old men. In 1901 he opened his cabaret 'Schall und Rauch' (later the Kleines Theater), the initial step leading to his domination of Berlin theatre for almost two decades. In his earliest major production, *A Midsummer Night's Dream* at the Neues Theater in 1905, a revolving stage with a realistic forest was used for the first time in Europe. In 1906 he acquired the *Deutsches Theater, where he controversially staged *Ibsen's *Ghosts*, with designs by Edvard Munch, and *Wedekind's *Spring's Awakening*, which had been banned by the *censor since publication in 1891. In 1910, finding the conventional *proscenium theatre too restricting, he staged the first of his massive productions in a *circus arena, *Sophocles' *Oedipus the King*, using hundreds of extras as the populace of Thebes. In 1911 there followed similar large-scale productions, *The Oresteia* and *Hofmannsthal's version of *Everyman*, which was revived many times, most notably as the centrepiece of the *Salzburg Festival from 1920. At the end of 1911 Reinhardt undertook his most ambitious project when he produced a *mime piece based on a medieval legend, Karl Vollmoeller's *The Miracle*, at the Olympia Exhibition Hall in London, converted by his favourite designer, Ernst *Stern, to resemble a cathedral. *The Miracle* was later (1924) also performed in New York and *toured America until 1930. Reinhardt's love of huge performance spaces finally found expression in his plans for the 'Theatre of Five Thousand', the Grosses Schauspielhaus in Berlin. This building, with its large, horseshoe-shaped *auditorium and arena stage, was opened in 1919 with a revival of *The Oresteia*, but within a few years had run into *financial difficulties and was given over to commercial *revues.

During the First World War, Reinhardt was controversially appointed director of the Berlin *Volksbühne (1915–18), a nominally left-wing foundation, which he saved from closure. In 1917 he also launched the 'Young Germany' season at the Deutsches Theater, devoted to work by young writers, himself directing the first piece, *Sorge's *The Beggar*, though he had little sympathy with the strident images of *expressionism. From 1920 he felt ever more out of tune with the new theatre of the Weimar Republic and was drawn back to his more conservative homeland: with Richard Strauss, Hofmannsthal, and the conductor Bruno Walter he founded the Salzburg Festival; in 1924 became director of the refurbished Theater in der Josefstadt, Vienna; and opened the new Salzburg Festival Theatre in 1925. After further successes in Vienna and Berlin, including the German premières of *Shaw's St Joan and *Pirandello's Six Characters in Search of an Author in 1924, and having given performances in London, Manchester, and Oxford, he was dispossessed of his theatres when the Nazis came to power in 1933. He responded by courageously writing an open letter to Goering and Goebbels. In 1934 he went to Hollywood to direct a sugary film version of A Midsummer Night's Dream. Offered by Goebbels the status of 'honorary Aryan' if he agreed to return to Germany to direct, he preferred to emigrate permanently to the United States in 1937 with his wife, the actress Helene Thimig. He died of a stroke in New York, where he directed for the stage for the last time.

Reinhardt's achievements were many: he staged classics in spectacularly theatrical ways, he discovered elegance and beauty—his so-called 'stylized *realism' or 'impressionism'—in a wide variety of scripts, he paid considerable attention to crowd scenes, he made serious theatre accessible to everyone, and he nurtured the talents of young playwrights and leading actors. Above all, he played a major part in transforming theatre practice from a nineteenth-century craft to a twentieth-century art form.   MWP

Réjane (Gabrielle Réju) (1856–1920) French actress and *manager. Réjane excelled as a student at the Conservatoire, but chose to make her career chiefly in *boulevard theatres, especially the Théâtre de Vaudeville, appearing there first in 1875. As a result, while the list of her performances includes the leading roles in *naturalist plays like Germinie Lacerteux (1888) and *Becque's La Parisienne (1893), as well as in *Ibsen's A Doll's House (1894) and *Claudel's Break of Noon (1898), her more typical vehicle remained drawing-room *comedy and second-rate *well-made plays. She maintained the same tradition as a manager when she took over the Théâtre Nouveau in 1906 and renamed it Théâtre Réjane. Like *Bernhardt, Réjane's career took her abroad, performing for the first time in London in 1894 and New York the following year. Of her films, the most notable was Madame Sans-gêne (1911), based on the *Sardou play she had premièred in 1893.   WDH

Renaissance See EARLY MODERN PERIOD IN EUROPE.

Renaud, Madeleine (1900–94) French actress. At the *Comédie-Française from 1921 to 1946, she became distinguished for her charm, incisive intelligence, beautiful voice and person, and finely tuned wit and timing, especially in roles in *Molière and *Marivaux. In 1940 she married Jean-Louis *Barrault, who had just joined the company as an actor and director. When the Comédie-Française was reorganized in 1946, the couple left to form their own Compagnie Renaud-Barrault, housed mainly at the Théâtre Marigny from 1946 to 1956. During her long association with Barrault there and at other venues, Renaud continued to expand her repertory to include *Claudel, *Genet, Lope de *Vega, *Chekhov, *Fry, *Anouilh, *Kopit, and *Duras, and became world famous as Winnie in Oh! Les Beaux Jours! (Happy Days, 1963), and in other *Beckett plays, many directed by *Blin. Uneasy with her performance in Pas moi (Not I, 1975), Beckett did not cast her in Rockaby, causing Barrault to break off relationships with the playwright. Barrault noted that Renaud achieved eminence by the direct route of a classically trained artist, while he himself succeeded by trial and error.   SBB

Rendra, W. S. (1935–2009) Indonesian playwright, director, and actor, a charismatic Javanese who fought *censorship and set the stage for political activism. He founded Bengkel (Workshop) Teater in 1967. His minikata (minimal word pieces), which used stylized chanting of slogans, were a response to the devaluation of language by Suharto's government. Though he produced Western work like Caligula and The Bald Soprano, he is best known for his own plays. Mastodon and Condor (1973) contrasts government aims with the individual spirit and The Struggle of the Naga Tribe (1975) shows the resistance of villagers to rapacious foreign development, relying on traditional gamelan music and a dulang (traditional *puppet master) as narrator. Regional Administrator (1977) and Prince Reso in the 1980s attacked government corruption. Rendra's plays were frequently banned in the Suharto era and he was held under house arrest in the late 1970s. Among those he inspired are playwrights Arifin C. *Noer and Putu *Wijaya.   KFO

Renée (1929–) New Zealand playwright (formerly known as Renée Taylor). Renée came to prominence with Wednesday to Come (1984), in which four generations of working women respond to the death of the male breadwinner in a relief camp of the 1930s, with clear political implications for a contemporary *audience. Her spare *realism derives from long experience directing rural amateur drama. A sequel, *Pass It On* (1986), adopts *Brechtian *dramaturgy to anatomize New Zealand's savagely divisive 1951 waterfront dispute. *Jeannie Once* (1990) completes the trilogy. Set in Dunedin in 1879 on the eve of a twenty-year depression, it benefits from Renée's feminist *revue experience to incorporate *music hall with audience participation as counterpoint to the serious political themes. Other plays, stories, and novels similarly affirm working-class and lesbian women, and draw on Renée's Maori heritage.   DC

Rengifo, César (1915–80) Venezuelan painter and playwright. His first work, *Why the People Sing*, dates from 1938, though he was not much performed until the 1950s, when the company Máscaras began to stage his work. Historical themes dominate, as apparent in *Obscéneba* (1958), which deals with the Spanish Conquest, *Snow Rope* (1954), about colonization, and *What the Storm Left Behind* (1957), about the nineteenth-century civil war. Oil forms the backdrop for *The Towers and the Wind* (1956), which takes issue with social injustice.   LCL trans. AMCS

repertory playing A theatre system, dependent on a stable company of actors, in which various plays are rotated on the bill over a season. While the repertory ensemble in the aristocratic theatres of eighteenth- and nineteenth-century Europe (such as the *Comédie-Française) could lead to productions of the first order, in Britain it had a chequered history. Its seeds lay first in the establishment during the Restoration of semi-permanent acting companies at the *patent theatres and in the growth during the eighteenth century of the 'circuit' companies which *toured well-defined geographical areas of the country. These *stock companies were led by *actor-managers who staged stock (or recycled) productions using stock sets and relying on actors playing *lines of business. At their best, they provided a valuable training ground and a lively, varied fare for their small audiences, while at their worst production standards were shoddy, *rehearsals were almost non-existent, and stereotyped acting was encouraged. They could not compete in the middle of the nineteenth century with the rising commercial companies, now able, with the aid of the rapidly expanding railway system, to tour major productions of single plays across the country with dedicated casts and scenery, meeting the increasingly sophisticated demands of their growing, industrialized audiences. The attendant use of the long run and the star system soon became common practice and put an end to the repertory

company. It was this box-office-driven theatre that in its turn was challenged by the *regional repertory movement in the UK at the start of the twentieth century.

The virtues of the repertory ensemble, once freed from the straitjacket of 'weekly rep' with the aid of public subsidy, were particularly manifest during the 1960s, 1970s, and 1980s in the UK: the *devised productions of *Littlewood's *Theatre Workshop, the *Royal Shakespeare Company's cycles of Shakespeare's history plays and *Nicholas Nickleby* (1980), the *National Theatre's *The Mysteries* (1985). All were dependent upon a company of actors working together over many months (sometimes years) and in a variety of plays, each actor able to take an assortment of roles, with stars sometimes playing supporting parts. In the final decades of the century many repertory theatres found themselves increasingly hard pressed to compete with other sectors of the leisure industry, particularly the multiplex cinemas. In the UK, 'true rep' is kept alive now only by the large national companies and the summer resort theatres. In the 1990s even the National Theatre began to abandon the ensemble in its endeavour to create productions that would transfer to the West End. And in mainland Europe, where the permanent company has been more firmly embedded, the willingness of actors to commit to career-long contracts has severely diminished as lucrative film and television opportunities beckon.   ARJ

République, Théâtre de la *See* COMÉDIE-FRANÇAISE.

revenge tragedy With roots in classical antiquity, revenge *tragedy pits an individual's urge for justice against collective social and religious laws. *Greek tragedy—*Aeschylus' *Eumenides* or *Euripides' *Medea*—employed bloody retribution to fulfil a social purgative function, at least in *Aristotle's view of *catharsis. *Senecan drama became highly influential on the *early modern stage, and was adapted in *Kyd's *The Spanish Tragedy* (*c.*1586), which inaugurated the 'tragedy of blood' that reached its height in the revenge drama of *Marlowe, Shakespeare, *Webster, *Marston, *Corneille, and *Racine, to name a few.

The most notorious revenge play is *Hamlet*, which exploits the revenge motif while simultaneously undermining it with a *protagonist who spends the play trying to talk himself into avenging his father's murder. Jacobean revenge tragedy offered a disturbing view of the many class and *gender tensions riddling Jacobean society, and expressed a considerable degree of cynicism about the possibility of attaining justice through

Judaeo-Christian laws. The thirst for violent individual retribution, often going against the powers of legitimate justice, remains. We are heirs to the imagination of the bloody Jacobean stage, evident in the phenomenal popularity of revenge films such as *Dirty Harry*, *Lethal Weapon*, *Blade Runner*, and *The Terminator*   LC

reversal *See* PERIPETEIA.

revolutionary modern drama (revolutionary model drama) *See* GEMING XIANDAI XI.

revue A programme of light entertainments, largely *musical but including often *satiric sketches, may be called a revue if it focuses on a topical theme or if it is presented in a periodic series. In some instances, the frivolity is intended to throw *censors off the scent of the political gibes. Or the display of beautiful women in gorgeous yet scanty *costumes could be the basic appeal. The visual and thematic unity of a revue lends greater sophistication than one expects of *burlesque or *vaudeville, to which the revue is related. *Fielding's *The Historical Register for the Year 1736* (1737) might be an early prototype, but the term is French, where it was long used interchangeably with *le* *music-hall. From the mid-nineteenth century, Paris enjoyed periodic editions at the *Folies-Bergère and the *Moulin-Rouge, as well as one-time creations like *La Revue nègre* (1925) featuring Joséphine *Baker. The golden age of the revue was on Broadway from the 1890s to the 1920s. Notable series were the lavish *Ziegfeld Follies* (1907–31), the *Shuberts' *Passing Show* (1912–24), *Greenwich Village Follies* (1919–28), *George* *White's Scandals* (1919–39), Irving *Berlin's *Music Box Revues* (1921–4), and Earl Carroll's *Vanities* (1923–32). In London, C. B. *Cochran produced successful revues from the 1910s, followed by André Charlot and, at mid-century, *Coward and Herbert Farjeon. Greece, Portugal, and Brazil have strong traditions of political revues.   FHI

Revuelta, Vicente (1929–) Cuban actor and director. Revuelta trained several generations of theatre artists while maintaining an experimental outlook. A founder of Teatro Estudio in 1958 with his staging of *O'Neill's *Long Day's Journey into Night*, he has also been one of the most versatile and creative actors in Cuba. He has played, among others, *Brecht's Galileo, Jerry in *Albee's *Zoo Story* (1965), Lalo in *Triana's *Night of the Assassins* (1966), and Feste in *Twelfth Night* (1982), all directed by him. He has also directed *Joan of Lorraine* (1956), *The Good Person of Setzuan* (1959), *Mother Courage* (1961), Lope de

*Vega's *Fuente Ovejuna* (1963), *Chekhov's *Three Sisters* (1972), *Miller's *The Price* (1979), *The Story of a Horse* (1986), and *The Shoemaker's Prodigious Wife* (1998).   MMu

Reza, Yasmina (1959–) French playwright. Having completed studies at the University of Paris and at the *Lecoq drama school, she began a career as an actress and in 1987 wrote her first play, *Conversations after a Burial*, which won the Molière award for best author. Her next two plays, *Winter Crossing* (1990) and *Art* (1994), also won Molière awards, the latter taking the 1998 Tony award in New York as well. Other plays include *The Unexpected Man* (1995), *Life X 3* (2000), and *The God of Carnage* (2006, Tony 2009). Her work, equally well received by *audiences in Paris, London, and New York, generally consists of witty *dialogues between 'bobos', the French bohemian bourgeois, and touches on the tensions between the *characters' true natures and their often artificial social identities.   CHB

Rhone, Trevor (1940–2009) Jamaican dramatist who founded Theatre 77 (later the Barn Theatre) in Kingston in 1965. Rhone's early play *The Gadget* (1969) eventually became the highly successful *Old Story Time* (1979). His concerns are social: *satire of the tourist industry in *Smile Orange* (1970), witty treatment of education in *School's Out* (1975) and of skin shade in *Old Story Time*. *Two Can Play* (1982) is a humorous and disturbing portrait of Jamaicans forced to become infinitely resourceful to save their families amid the political violence of the late 1970s. His film scripts include *The Harder They Come* (1972) and *Milk and Honey* (1989).   ES

Riantiarno, Nano (1949–) Indonesian playwright and director, founder of Teater Koma. His productions, replete with colour and comedy, present social issues, including those dealing with income disparity, with a *Brechtian spirit. He has adapted Western work, including *The Threepenny Opera* (1983) and *Animal Farm* (1987), while his own *Cockroach Opera* (1987) satirized the persecutions of Jakarta transsexual prostitutes. *Sam Pek Eng Tay* (1988), a humorous adaptation of a Chinese *melodrama, was banned in Sumatra and barred from *touring abroad because officials thought the Chinese theme would fan racial tensions. *Primadonna Opera* (1988, 2000), an entertaining story of an ageing star who refuses to yield the stage to a successor, reflected President Suharto's unwillingness to yield power. Teater Koma attracts a young and diverse *audience and is one of the few troupes in

Indonesia that has survived the loss of government subsidy.   KFo

Riccoboni family Italian actors. **Luigi** (1686–1753) followed his father **Antonio**, a celebrated Pantalone, into *commedia dell'arte*, playing the part of Lelio, the Innamorato. Lelio, as he became known, worked in Venice (1702–15), and there married **Elena Balletti**, a writer and actress who took the role of Flaminia, the Innamorata. Like *Goldoni, Lelio aspired to reform contemporary theatre. In *comedy, his aim was to achieve reform of a moral and literary character but his deeper goal was to elevate Italian theatre by reintroducing *tragedy. He translated *Racine, performed tragedies by *Maffei and *early modern playwrights, but had only moderate success with an *audience which demanded lighter fare. Lelio and Flaminia moved their company to Paris in 1716. Often performing Lelio's own scripts, the new *Comédie Italienne enjoyed such success at court and in the city as to arouse the resentment of French companies, but Lelio's ability to imbue the traditional 'masks' with individual *character had a profound influence on French eighteenth-century drama. The young *Marivaux had his early work staged, anonymously, by the Riccoboni company. Lelio's *Histoire du théâtre italien* (1726) and *Dell'arte rappresentativa* (1728), helped spread knowledge of Italian culture and stage techniques across Europe. He abandoned the theatre in 1729, but his work was carried on by his son **Francesco** (1707–72), actor-author of around 30 plays and of writings on the art of *acting.   JF

Rice, Elmer (Elmer Reizenstein) (1892–1967) American dramatist. The author of more than 50 plays in multiple styles, Rice *produced and *directed most of his work after 1929 and directed plays by others, most notably *Sherwood's *Abe Lincoln in Illinois* (1938). Rice gave up the law when his courtroom drama *On Trial* (1914) earned him $100,000. His next play was the anti-war *The Iron Cross* (1917). *The Adding Machine* (1923) was not the first *expressionist play on Broadway, but Rice's story of Mr Zero's journey from earthly to eternal monotony was given an unforgettable production in the *Theatre Guild, featuring *Simonson's expressionistic *scenography: walls covered with projected numbers, a slanting courtroom, a gigantic adding machine with movable keys. *Street Scene* (1929), a *naturalistic picture of tenement life, ran for over 600 performances (Pulitzer Prize). During the 1930s his entertainment vehicles, such as *Counsellor-at-Law* (1931), were outnumbered by brooding, discursive social dramas praising democracy and attacking *fascism. Rice was New York director for the *Federal Theatre Project (1935–6), resigning in a public fight over *censorship. He wrote two successful *comedies, *Two on an Island* (1940) and *Dream Girl* (1945).   MAF

Rice, Thomas D. (1808–60) American actor and playwright. By the late 1820s Rice played minor roles in Louisville. According to legend, Rice copied a crippled black stablehand's singing and dancing for a blackface act. Performed at New York's Bowery Theatre in *The Kentucky Rifle* (1832), his 'Jim Crow' persona and song and dance were instantly successful, leading to national *tours and circuits of England. Although Rice is often credited with popularizing blackface performances and laying the groundwork for *minstrel shows, his Jim Crow routine remained a solo act. He adapted the persona for several plays and occasionally acted other roles, notably the title *character in the Bowery production of *Uncle Tom's Cabin* (1858).   GAR

Rice, Tim (1944–) English lyricist and librettist who found fame with the lyrics and books for three *musicals composed by *Lloyd Webber—*Joseph and the Amazing Technicolor Dreamcoat* (1968), *Jesus Christ Superstar* (1970), and *Evita* (1978). After this collaboration ended, he worked with a number of composers—Stephen Oliver on *Blondel* (1983), Benny Andersson and Bjorn Ulvaeus of ABBA on *Chess* (1985)—before finding a new career scoring Walt Disney animated features. He wrote the score for *Aladdin* (1992) with Alan Menken, with whom he also wrote six new songs for the stage version of Disney's *Beauty and the Beast* (1994). Teaming with Elton John, he wrote lyrics for both film (1994) and stage (1997) versions of *The Lion King*, and for *Aida* (2000). Rice's typical subject has been the results of sudden fame on the individual.   JD

Rich, Christopher (c.1657–1714) English *manager. Taking control of the ailing *patent company at *Drury Lane around 1693, Rich is cast as the tyrannical villain of theatre history largely because he made the commercial success of the company his first priority. His attempt to cut salaries caused a revolt by the leading players, who formed a rival company at *Lincoln's Inn Fields in 1695. This competition prompted Rich to import foreign and domestic attractions, a device that proved profitable and established the popularity of the mixed bill. Dogged by disagreements, Rich was eventually ousted from Drury Lane. He died before the completion of a new theatre in Lincoln's Inn Fields, which passed into the hands of his son John *Rich.   GBB

Rich, John (Lun) (1692–1761) English dancer and *actor-manager. The son of Christopher *Rich, John took over *Lincoln's Inn Fields on his father's death. The elegant house with mirrored interior became the home of popular adaptations of Italian-style *pantomime in which Rich excelled as *Harlequin. *The Necromancer; or, Harlequin Doctor Faustus* (1723) was his most successful and he spared no expense in providing spectacular *costumes and scenery. In 1728 Rich premièred *Gay's *Beggar's Opera*, which ran for an unprecedented 32 nights. By 1730 Rich had built a larger theatre in *Covent Garden in which he mounted a mix of popular plays and pantomime.   GBB

Richards, Lloyd (1922–2006) *African-American director. Richards was teaching *acting when one of his students, Sidney Poitier, recommended him as the director of *Hansberry's *Raisin in the Sun* in 1959. Richards thus became the first African-American to direct on Broadway, just as he was the first African-American to head the Playwrights Conference at the Eugene O'Neill Theatre Center (1969–99) and to be dean of the Yale School of Drama (1979–91). One novice dramatist under his wing at the O'Neill Center was August *Wilson, who brought him *Ma Rainey's Black Bottom* in 1984, followed by his next plays; in 1987 Richards won a Tony award for his direction of Wilson's *Fences* (and received many other awards). He made the Yale Repertory Theatre into a major force in the *regional theatre movement, and steered the early careers of a number of new playwrights. Richards also directed work from Africa: *A Lesson from Aloes* and other plays by *Fugard, and *The Lion and the Jewel* by *Soyinka.   BBL

Richardson, Ian (1934–2007) Scottish actor who joined the *Birmingham Rep in 1958 with a range of roles including Hamlet. At the *Shakespeare Memorial Theatre he was Sir Andrew Aguecheek (1960) and Oberon (1961), and for the newly formed *Royal Shakespeare Company he performed leading roles in *The Representative* (1963), *King Lear* (1964), *Marat/Sade* (1964), *Coriolanus* (1966), *Julius Caesar* (1968), *Pericles* (1969), *Measure for Measure* (1970), and *Love's Labour's Lost* (1973). In *Barton's *Richard II* he alternated the roles of Richard and Bolingbroke with Richard Pasco (1973). On Broadway he was Higgins in *My Fair Lady* (1976) and played opposite Donald Sutherland in a short-lived production of *Lolita*, adapted by *Albee (1981). For television he was Bill Hayden, the mole, in the spy thriller *Tinker, Tailor, Soldier, Spy* (1979) and

Francis Urquhart, the machiavellian politician, in *House of Cards* (1990), *To Play the King* (1993), and *Final Cut* (1995). He appeared at *Chichester in *The Miser* (1995) and *The Magistrate* (1997). AS

Richardson, Ralph (1902–83) English actor. With neither the characteristic nobility of *Gielgud nor the heroism of *Olivier, Richardson excelled at *character roles in classical plays, though his pre-war reputation rested on contemporary plays, including Phillpotts's *Yellow Sands* (1926), *Maugham's *Sheppey* (1933), and *Priestley's *Eden End* (1934) and *Johnson over Jordan* (1939). In 1944 Richardson joined Olivier in *managing the *Old Vic Company, giving performances which were to become legendary in British theatre: Peer Gynt, Falstaff, Bluntschli, and the original Inspector in Priestley's *An Inspector Calls* (1946). Throughout the 1950s his roles included Ruth and Augustus Goetz's *The Heiress* (1949), N. C. *Hunter's *A Day by the Sea* (1953), and Robert *Bolt's *Flowering Cherry* (1957). Initially finding himself out of step with the new drama of the 1960s, Richardson rebounded in the 1970s, appearing with Gielgud in *Storey's *Home* (1970) at the *Royal Court and *Pinter's *No Man's Land* (1975) at the *National, where he was also acclaimed in *John Gabriel Borkman* (1975), *The Cherry Orchard* (1978), and *The Wild Duck* (1979). He appeared in two *Home plays in the West End: *Lloyd George Knew my Father* (1972) and *The Kingfisher* (1977). Significant film appearances include *The Fallen Idol* (1948), *The Heiress* (1950), *Richard III* (1955), and *A Long Day's Journey into Night* (1960).   MDG

Richardson, Tony (1928–91) English director. Richardson began as an assistant to *Devine at the *Royal Court, later directing *Osborne's landmark *Look Back in Anger* (1956) and *The Entertainer* (starring *Olivier, 1957). Both productions transferred to New York. At Stratford, Richardson directed a notorious *Othello* with Paul *Robeson (1959). Richardson's direction of new writing for the screen was remarkable: *Look Back in Anger* (1959), *The Entertainer* (1960), *Delaney's *A Taste of Honey* (1961), *The Loneliness of the Long Distance Runner* (1962). In 1963 he won an Oscar for best direction and best film for *Tom Jones*. From the early 1970s Richardson directed only film and television drama, though his critics claim that he never equalled the successes of the 1960s. His short marriage to Vanessa *Redgrave produced actor-daughters Natasha and Joely.   KN

Richelieu, Cardinal Armand-Jean du Plessis (1585–1642) French statesman, chief minister under Louis XIII. In addition to leading military campaigns and solidifying the power of the French monarchy, he was a prominent patron of the arts, employing notable architects, painters, and sculptors to design and decorate his numerous houses. In the Palais Cardinal (later the *Palais Royal), he built the first two permanent *proscenium *playhouses in France. In these spaces he commanded performances of *tragedies and elaborate spectacular productions. He also established and funded a company of five writers (including *Corneille and *Rotrou) to produce new works. One of his most lasting legacies was the creation of the Académie Française in 1634. Controversially, he personally influenced the outcome of the Académie's first official action, which was to condemn Corneille's *Le Cid* for violating *neoclassical standards for tragedy. CJW

Ridiculous Theatrical Company *See* LUD-LAM, CHARLES.

Rigby, Terence (1937–2008) English actor. Rigby was Joey in the revival of *The Homecoming* in 1969, when *Pinter played Lenny, and in 1975 he was Briggs in the première of Pinter's *No Man's Land* at the *National Theatre. He was directed by Peter *Hall in *Macbeth* and *The Cherry Orchard* at the NT (1978), where he also appeared in *Eyre's *Richard III* (1992). He was in Hall's revival of *Amadeus* (1999) in London and New York, where he also played Agamemnon in *Troilus and Cressida* (2001). In 1994–5 he was the *ghost, Player King, and Gravedigger in Jonathan Kent's *Hamlet* in London and New York, where in 2001 he was Harry in *Bond's *Saved*. His Davies in *The Caretaker* (Bristol, 2003) prompted Michael Billington of *The Guardian* to call him 'the Pinter actor par excellence'. On screen he appeared in British art cinema (*Accident*, 1967), as a definitive British gangster (*Get Carter*, 1971), in a James Bond film (*Tomorrow Never Dies*, 1997), and in *Elizabeth* (1998). AS

Rigg, Diana (1938–) English actress. Early roles at Stratford included Helena in *Hall's *A Midsummer Night's Dream*, Bianca in *The Taming of the Shrew*, and Cordelia in *Brook's *King Lear* (all 1962). In the 1960s she was the unforgettably sexy Mrs Peel in the cult television series *The Avengers* (1965–7). At the *National Theatre her roles (1972–3) included Dolly in *Stoppard's *Jumpers*, Lady Macbeth, and Célimène in *The Misanthrope*. She starred in *Little Eyolf* at the Lyric Hammersmith (1985), *All for Love* at the Almeida (1991), *Mother Courage* at the National (1995), *Who's Afraid of Virginia Woolf?* at the Almeida (1996), and *Phèdre* and *Britannicus* at the Albery (1998). Having been nominated for a Tony award

on two previous occasions—for *Abelard and Heloise* (1971) and for *The Misanthrope*—Rigg won for Jonathan Kent's *Medea* (London, 1992, New York, 1994). At *Chichester she starred in *Cherry Orchard* (2008) and *Hay Fever* (2009). Later television roles include the eponymous sleuth in *The Mrs Bradley Mysteries* (1998, 2000). AS

Rihany, Naguib el- (1892–1949) Egyptian actor, *manager, and director. He collaborated with Badie Khairy and others in reworking French *vaudevilles into purely Egyptian versions, creating memorable interpretations on stage and screen of the Egyptian petite bourgeoisie. After the First World War Rihany moved from comic folk performance (he won fame as the *commedia-like *character of Kish-Kish Bey, a gullible country mayor) to Western psychological *acting in Egyptian colloquial Arabic (Ammeya). The literary Standard Arabic (Fus'ha) of the Levantine troupes had long been considered essential on the Egyptian stage, but Rihany's status legitimized performing in the colloquial language. HMA

Ringwood, Gwen Pharis (1910–84) Canadian playwright and *community theatre activist who wrote her best-known play, the one-act *tragedy *Still Stands the House* (1938), while a graduate student. Like her subsequent plays *Dark Harvest* (1939), *Jack and the Joker* (1944), and *The Rainmaker* (1946), it reflected Ringwood's upbringing on the prairie frontier. After moving to central British Columbia in 1953, she continued to write and to produce community theatre. Several later plays, from *Lament for Harmonica* (1959) to *The Furies* (1981), are set among the native people there. DWJ

riots In England disorder and riots were frequent during the eighteenth and nineteenth centuries. Some riots, as in the 1730s, were politically motivated, but *Covent Garden witnessed a violent response to its attempts to raise prices in 1736, while footmen rampaged in 1737 after their privilege of free gallery seats was withdrawn. In 1755 anti-French sentiment led to rioting over several evenings during the *ballet *The Chinese Festival* at *Drury Lane. In 1763 Thaddeus Fitzpatrick organized riots protesting abolition of half-price admission for late arrivals. The rioters rushed onto the stage at Drury Lane, broke woodwork and shattered chandeliers, while at Covent Garden they destroyed the entire fabric of the theatre.

The last major riot in an English theatre was the Old Price riots at Covent Garden in 1809. The *management had rebuilt the theatre after a fire in 1808, raised the prices of seats in the pit, removed inexpensive seats to accommodate more *boxes, and employed the Italian singer Madame Catalani at great expense. The opening-night performance was disrupted by demands for old prices, which were finally restored (along with the dismissal of Catalani and a reduction in private boxes) after 67 nights of organized rioting. Throughout the intervening period not a word was heard on stage. Horns, bugles, bells, and rattles, the clatter of sticks, and the display of banners, as well as an 'OP dance', contributed to the disorder. Actors were pelted, fights occurred in the *auditorium. The OP riots became an expression of political and social dissent and of national identity, focusing on issues far beyond the immediate circumstances.

One year later 31 were killed and 150 wounded by soldiers during the Astor Place riot in New York, caused by an actors' rivalry. Supporters of *Forrest, who was convinced *Macready had been responsible for his poor reception in England, stormed the theatre, but were quelled by the military. As with the William Farren riot in the USA in 1834, social and racial tensions lay behind the disruption.

France's most famous riot was motivated by an assault on tradition. In 1830 riots occurred at the Thèâtre-Français (*Comédie-Française) after the performance of *Hugo's *Hernani*, which deliberately broke with *neoclassical rules. During the first three performances the theatre was stacked with Hugo's friends and supporters, but the play's opponents were equally vociferous. In 1896 another assault on convention provoked strong reaction, *Jarry's *Ubu roi*. Since Jarry may have orchestrated the cabal protesting against the play, this hardly constitutes an authentic riot. Modernism's assault on convention also triggered violent responses to *The Rite of Spring* (Paris, 1913) when the noise of the audience prevented the *dancers from hearing Stravinsky's music, and to *Pirandello's *Six Characters in Search of an Author* (Rome, 1921).

Among the most notorious riots of the twentieth century were those at the *Abbey Theatre in Dublin after the première of *Synge's *The Playboy of the Western World* in 1907. Synge's depiction of peasant *characters as flawed and immoral inflamed audiences, whose nationalist sensibilities were upset. When the Abbey *toured the USA in 1911, *Playboy* again provoked riots at a number of theatres. *Yeats sprang to Synge's defence in 1907, as he did on behalf of *O'Casey, whose irreverent representation of the myths of Easter 1916 in *The Plough and the Stars* (1926) also enraged Abbey spectators. The declining importance of the theatre in the latter half of the twentieth century has meant that it has not been considered as significant a

venue as formerly for public protest. Nevertheless, from 15 May to 14 June 1968, student protesters occupied the *Odéon in Paris, which led to the resignation of its director, *Barrault.   JTD

Ristori, Adelaide (1822–1906) The first Italian actor since the *early modern period to establish an international reputation. Ristori's career paralleled the struggle for freedom from foreign domination and for unification of the Italian states, which was accomplished by 1871; she brought international attention to this cause and served as honorary ambassador abroad. After a major success playing the title role in Pellico's *Francesca da Rimini* at the age of 14, she joined Turin's prestigious Reale Sarda Company as *ingénue (1837–41). Over the next ten years she became a leading actress in the Mascherpa company and, opposite a young *Salvini, in the Domeniconi–Coltellini company. Her repertory consisted of popular sentimental drama, *Goldonian comedy, *tragedy, and translations of the French *well-made play. Through marriage to a nobleman she became Marchesa Capranica del Grillo (1847). In 1853 she rejoined the Reale Sarda and during the company's 1855 Paris tour, which starred Ristori and *Rossi in *Francesca da Rimini*, *Alfieri's *Mirra*, and *Schiller's *Mary Stuart*, she found herself the toast of Parisian critics and literati.

Returning home, state authorities considered Ristori's repertory inflammatory and subjected her material to *censorship. She turned to international *touring and, from the late 1850s to 1885, travelled the world to great acclaim, performing sometimes in English and French. Her standard international repertory consisted of exceptional women whom she interpreted as victims of hostile forces. Ristori dismissed the fixed vocal and gestural conventions of the past and searched for a new *realism of expression. She was noted for her careful study of a *character's moods, inner conflicts, and transitions from one state of mind to the other.   JEH

ritual and theatre Since the 1980s cooperation between the disciplines of anthropology, with its focus on ethnographic recording of rituals, and theatre studies, with its theoretical attention to performance, has demonstrated the difficulty of separating the modes of ritual from theatrical performance. The field of performance studies in particular has attempted to establish a theoretical frame for the effectiveness of ritual in a cross-cultural perspective, at the same time considering the larger resonance of theatrical and para-theatrical productions. This development is largely due to the interdisciplinary work of two thinkers. The first is the anthropologist Victor Turner, who applied concepts of drama to ritual processes which remember, refashion, or remedy structures and conflicts of social reality. The second is the critic and director Richard *Schechner, who has explored and incorporated non-European rituals and theatrical practices into his practical and theoretical work. Their collaboration replays theorizing on the *origins of theatre by the Cambridge School of Anthropology, chiefly Jane Harrison, Gilbert *Murray, and Francis Cornford, who postulated the derivation of *tragedy from early Greek sacrificial practices and of *comedy from the Dionysian revels and mystery cults. Their genealogical or 'genetic' method, asserting that theatre derived from the sacred domain in the manner of an evolutionary event, was extremely influential in the twentieth century. It was eventually opposed by a more 'generic' comparison between theatre and ritual, one that saw social action as modelled on the formal element of the performative, a view evident in *Brecht's notion of 'everyday theatre', and enlarged into a social theory by Erving Goffman.

But the similarity between ritual and theatre does not lie only in formal aspects. More recent anthropological theories have suggested that ritual carries the quality of 'efficacy' (or effectivity) in symbolic communication. In this view the performative possesses not only the traits of conventionality, stereotype, and repetition, but also the power of constituting and reconstituting reality. Borrowing from the 'speech act' theories of J. L. Austin and John Searle, some commentators have claimed that the performative can be an 'illocutionary force' to constitute and change reality, an idea equally applicable to ritual and theatre. Traditionally, theatrical performances are assumed to function within the conceptual frame of pretence, of an 'as if' reality, while ritual operates in a mode that has actual effects on lived reality. Since both are staged and *rehearsed practices, the distinction between theatrical performances and ritual actions is somewhat arbitrary, yet some differences remain important. The change of perception of both actor and *audience, for example, depends on the expectations and intentions with which they approach the performance: if, as in ordinary *bourgeois theatre, actors and audience expect to create and derive only entertainment from the event, then the mental and spiritual result is not likely to be the same as that of a ritual ceremony where priest and congregation might well expect immanence and transformation. But even this has been contested. Some theoretical discussions of *acting insist that theatre, just as ritual, can transform experience and therefore

transform reality. This assumption has been present from the very beginning of theories of drama, since *Aristotle claimed that *catharsis was central to the experience of tragedy. Another example lies in German classical writings after *Schiller, which asserted the innovative power of *mimesis.

Recent theories on ritual, such as the approach by Humphrey and Laidlaw in *The Archetypal Actions of Ritual* (1994), imply or insist that ritual action is 'meaningless', since the intentions of both actor and spectator are unknowable: all that is known is their ritual commitment to perform the act and subscribe to a traditional 'stipulation'. Nonetheless a common denominator can be found in many debates on theatre and ritual—that the efficacy of any performative action depends upon its impact on perception. This calls into question the idea of framing concepts that distinguish the two practices. Schechner, a leading light of performance theory, has proposed the metaphor of 'porous nets' for expectations, leaving scope for shifting the boundaries of reality and experience, and also allowing for the possibility that both ritual and theatre can change lived reality. Notions about 'ritual play' meshed well with earlier *avant-garde approaches to acting, most famously proposed in *Artaud's *The Theatre and its Double* (1938) with a call for the revitalization of theatre practice through the 'magic of ritual', which significantly influenced practitioners like *Grotowski.

Performative action—and through it the transformation of performers, contexts, and social functions—connects and merges the domains of theatre and ritual as much as it separates and distinguishes them. Whether transformations will occur as the result of an actual performance is unpredictable. Both ritual and theatre performances, therefore, involve risk for the performer, whose ability to evoke divinities, fictional *characters, the dead or their ghosts, will be judged by criteria known to the culturally conditioned audience. The result of a healing ritual may be the recuperation of the sick person, but failing to achieve this may not diminish the 'success' of the ritual. People like the Kaluli of New Guinea consider performative failure or success according to theatrical elements of stagecraft and acting ability, whether or not the shaman evoked resonance about the divine presence in his audience.

According to Bruce Kapferer in *The Feast of the Sorcerer* (1997), one of the specific identifiers for ritual action is that it constitutes a sphere of virtuality, a non-contingent reality, which is opposed to that of actuality. If this is so, then theatrical and ritual performances both represent and constitute realities in their own right, worlds of the imagination which evolve according to their own logic. These virtual or imaginary realities become real and transformative for actual life through being bodily performed—even if the body practice is meticulously trained in accordance with (diverse) cosmological ideas. Through performance both theatre and ritual create and constitute a world which is neither a representation of lived reality nor an ideal model for it, but rather a separate reality.

The creation of what Turner calls 'liminal' space and time enables both theatre and ritual to effect a desired or expected transformation of reality. The virtuality of the performative event relies on the ambiguous nature of its liminal or on-the-threshold reality, which enables it to become creative or constitutive of new forms of perception and cognition. The ambiguity of the performative also makes it dangerous for established powers, secular or sacred, and can make 'play' a matter of life and death. But we should not forget that virtuality can only occur in the liminal and limited space and time of ritual and theatre, for the virtual world they create must feed on the larger, contingent reality of the actual world. We underplay the actual world as source for virtual performances at the risk of stultifying the performative itself.   KPK

Rix, Brian (1924–) English actor and *manager, who began his career in 1942 and was for a while a member of *Wolfit's company during its London wartime seasons. He made his reputation as a farceur, performing in and *producing the series of *farces associated with the Whitehall Theatre (1950–69), notably *Reluctant Heroes* (1950), *Dry Rot* (1954), *Simple Spymen* (1958), *Chase Me Comrade* (1964), and *Uproar in the House* (1967). Himself expert in farcical timing, Rix's productions set a style of knowing, sexually based humour entirely different from the earlier Aldwych farces by Ben *Travers of the 1920s. After 1980 he devoted his energies to the charity for the mentally handicapped, for which work he was ennobled in 1992.   VEE

RNT *See* NATIONAL THEATRE OF GREAT BRITAIN.

Robards, Jason (1922–2000) American actor. Robards was universally acclaimed the greatest interpreter of *O'Neill's tortured *characters. After ten years as an actor and *stage manager (and a stint as a sailor), he won acclaim as Hickey in the historic Circle in the Square production of *The Iceman Cometh* (1956), revived on Broadway in 1985. He created the roles of Jamie in *Long Day's Journey into Night* (1956)—also playing in the film (1962)—and Erie Smith in *Hughie* (1964).

Other O'Neill roles included Jim Tyrone in *A Moon for the Misbegotten* (1973), Con Melody in *A Touch of the Poet* (1977), James Tyrone in *Long Day's Journey* (1976, 1988), and Nat Miller in *Ah, Wilderness!* (1988). Robards also distinguished himself in *Toys in the Attic* (1960) and *After the Fall* (1964). Equally adept at *comedy, he triumphed in *A Thousand Clowns* (1962) and a revival of *You Can't Take It with You* (1983). His career of over 50 films included *Tender Is the Night* (1961), *The Hour of the Gun* (1967), *All the President's Men* (Academy award, 1976), and *Philadelphia* (1993).   TFC

Robbins, Jerome (1918–98) Born Jerome Rabinowitz, Robbins was the foremost American choreographer of the mid twentieth century. While he infused classical *ballet with a modern American spirit, his theatre choreography integrated *dance as a fully expressive element. Already dancing on Broadway by 1940, Robbins made his mark as a choreographer with *Bernstein's *Fancy Free* (1944), a jazz-inflected ballet which grew the next year into *On the Town*. In 1948 Robbins was invited by *Balanchine to join the fledgling New York City Ballet, where he choreographed in earnest, producing *L'Après-midi d'un faune* (1953), among many others. He kept pace on Broadway, staging dances for several shows before directing and choreographing a string of musical classics. *West Side Story* (1957; he co-directed the film, 1962) used the discipline of classical dance as a scaffold for the expression of ethnicity, street-gang conflict, and forbidden love, using split-stage counterpoint to unprecedented effect. Following *Gypsy* (1959) and *Fiddler on the Roof* (1964), Robbins concentrated on ballet, save for a triumphant reprise of his most popular dance numbers, titled *Jerome Robbins' Broadway* (1989).   EW

Robertson, T. W. (Thomas William) (1829–71) English dramatist. The eldest of 22 children, Robertson's father was *manager of the Lincoln circuit and one of his sisters was Madge *Kendal. Robertson was an actor, scene painter, *prompter, *stage manager, songwriter, and unsuccessful author of sixteen plays before his first success, *David Garrick* (1864), at the *Haymarket. In 1865 his *comedy *Society* was staged by Marie *Wilton at the Prince of Wales's Theatre; it was followed there by *Ours* (1866), *Caste* (1867), *Play* (1868), *School* (1869), and *MP* (1870). During these years Robertson also wrote *melodramas and comedies for other theatres. The Prince of Wales's made a fortune from the enormous success of the Robertson comedies and gave a little of it back to him. Robertson's themes were familiar: social ambition, class antagonism, wealth, the idealizing of young womanhood, and the faith in romantic love. Yet he wrote with a distinctly un-Victorian delicacy and restraint: a quiet twilight scene of courtship in *Society*, the making of roly-poly pudding in the middle of the Crimean War in *Ours*, a tea party in *Caste* with comic business involving bread and butter and teacups (thus the term 'cup-and-saucer drama' for the plays)—all this contributed to a gentle middle-class domestic verisimilitude that *audiences found greatly appealing. Robertson ensured the *realism of his domestic interiors and restrained playing, even of intensely emotional moments (*see* DIRECTING/DIRECTOR). The vogue for his plays abated by 1890, and after about 1910 they were rarely performed, though still occasionally revived today.   MRB

Robeson, Paul (1898–1976) *African-American actor and singer. *O'Neill cast Robeson in the title role of the *Provincetown Players' revival of *The Emperor Jones*, as well as Jim Harris in *All God's Chillun Got Wings* (1924–5). Twice an All-American athlete at Rutgers, he played professional football (1920–2) while studying law at Columbia. He chose performing instead, first appearing on Broadway in *Taboo* (1922), and scored a concert triumph as bass-baritone at Carnegie Hall (1925), with a groundbreaking programme of spirituals and folk songs. He made more than 300 recordings, frequent concert *tours, and radio broadcasts. He was particularly associated with *Kern's 'Ol' Man River', which he sang in revivals of *Show Boat* in London (1928), New York (1932), and Los Angeles (1940).

Robeson first played Othello opposite *Ashcroft in London (1930). He was the first African American to play the role in the United States (opposite *Hagen in 1943), and repeated it opposite Mary Ure at Stratford (1959). His career on stage and film (*The Emperor Jones*, 1933; *Show Boat*, 1936; *Song of Freedom*, 1936; *King Solomon's Mines*, 1937; *The Proud Valley*, 1940) was interrupted by anti-communist pressure. Having performed widely in the Soviet Union and supported republican troops in Spain, Robeson denied membership in the Communist Party but refused to retract statements praising the USSR as a model of racial justice. He was intensely investigated and the State Department withdrew his passport in 1950. Blacklisted, he completed a short autobiography in 1958 (*Here I Stand*) and, passport restored, toured the Soviet Union. He returned to the USA in 1961 in poor physical and mental health.   MAF

Robey, George (George Wade) (1869–1954) Almost the last of the great English *music-hall comedians. Known as the 'Prime Minister of Mirth', Robey threw up a career in civil engineering to begin performing as an amateur, making his professional debut in 1891. Risqué rather than vulgar, he *toured extensively throughout the British Isles and abroad, conspicuous on stage through his bowler hat, large bushy eyebrows, and short, solid figure. A great *pantomime dame, he was also renowned for his songs, delivered in a machine-gun staccato. Songs written for him included 'If You Were the Only Girl in the World'. In the 1930s he appeared in C. B. *Cochran's *Helen* (based on *Offenbach's *La Belle Hélène*) and film versions of *Chu Chin Chow* and *Don Quixote*. In 1935 he played Falstaff in *Henry IV* at Her Majesty's Theatre, later playing the dying Falstaff in *Olivier's film of *Henry V*.   JTD

Robin Hood play *Medieval English *folk play. References to Robin Hood plays date back to the thirteenth century, and in 1473 Sir John Paston noted the loss of a servant who had performed in one. Surviving texts are difficult to date but show the *hero flouting traditional authority, such as the Sheriff of Nottingham, and stealing from the rich to preserve a greater justice and to provide for the poor. Records indicate parish fundraising fêtes as common performance sites, and criticism has speculated about the power of the plays to express resistance against the growth of a market economy, centralized authority, and economic individualism.   JCD

Robins, Elizabeth (1862–1952) Anglo-American actress and writer. Robins made her debut in 1881 with Junius Brutus *Booth in New York, then *toured with James *O'Neill, and in 1883 joined the Boston Museum Company. Marriage in 1885 to a fellow actor cost Robins her contract and she returned to touring with O'Neill, playing Mercedes in *The Count of Monte Cristo*. In 1887 her husband drowned himself. Taking up residence in England, Robins figured prominently in London's belated reception of *Ibsen. In 1889, a few weeks after Janet *Achurch presented *A Doll's House*, Robins played Martha in a single matinée of *The Pillars of Society*. Over the next decade she appeared in another twelve London Ibsen productions, most notably the UK premières of *Hedda Gabler* (1891) and *The Master Builder* (1893). With Florence Bell, she was anonymously responsible for *Alan's Wife*, which sympathetically represented maternal infanticide as natural selection (*Independent Theatre, 1893). After 1902 she concentrated upon writing. Women's issues and feminist objectives became explicit in her work, especially in *Votes for Women*. Granville *Barker directed it at the *Royal Court (1907), and Robins recast it as a novel, *The Convert*, the same year.   MOC

Robinson, Bill ('Bojangles') (1878–1949) *African-American song-and-dance man. An orphan, Bojangles danced on street corners and at the age of 12 joined the *vaudeville troupe headed by the Whitman sisters. He expanded his repertory and became a big draw in nightclubs. When he was 50 he made his debut with white *audiences in Lew Leslie's *Blackbirds of 1928*, followed by a series of similar Broadway *musicals. He is best remembered for the roles he performed with Shirley Temple in a series of films from the 1930s. An inveterate hoofer, Bojangles revolutionized tap *dancing with fast, syncopated footwork.   BBL

Robinson, Lennox (1886–1958) Irish playwright and director who became *manager of the *Abbey Theatre at *Yeats's invitation in 1910, on the strength of his first play *The Clancy Name* (1908). Except for a few short periods, he remained at the Abbey in a number of capacities until 1956. He directed over 100 productions, among them the premières of *O'Casey's *The Shadow of a Gunman* and *The Plough and the Stars*. He earned immense public affection through his gently ironic and deftly constructed *comedies of provincial life; *The Whiteheaded Boy* (1916), *The Far-Off Hills* (1928), and *Drama at Inish* (1933) stayed in the repertory until the end of the century. Among his other plays are *The Dreamers* (1915), *The Lost Leader* (1918), *The White Blackbird* (1925), *The Big House* (1926), and *Killycreggs in Twilight* (1937). *Ibsen and *Chekhov were his masters, though *Church Street* (1934) is consciously *Pirandellan.   CFS

Robson, Flora (1902–84) English actress. Robson's early opportunities were scarce, but by the early 1930s she had appeared in London in plays by *O'Neill, *Pirandello, *Wilde, *Maugham, and Shakespeare, establishing herself as a powerful actress who could both suggest and tap great depths of feeling. In 1933 she joined the *Old Vic-*Sadler's Wells company, taking on Shakespeare as well as *Chekhov and *Congreve. She played in both London and New York during the 1940s. By the 1950s her career was well established, with major successes in *Gielgud's *The Winter's Tale* and *Redgrave's adaptation of *James's *The Aspern Papers*. She also appeared in *Ibsen's *Ghosts* and *John Gabriel Borkman*. Toward the end of her career she did some *tour-

ing, from Edinburgh to South Africa. From the mid-1930s she acted regularly in film.   TP

Robson, Frederick (1821–64) English actor and *manager. Robson began singing comic songs in London's East End, then moved in 1850 to act in extravaganza and *burlesque at the Olympic, where he became co-manager. Robson was very short and possessed the capacity to blend the ridiculousness of burlesque with *tragedy. *Planché, who wrote the *character of the Dwarf for him in *The Yellow Dwarf* (1854), said that his impersonation of the cunning, malignity, passion, and despair of the monster was so powerful that it elevated extravaganza into tragedy. Another *tour de force* was Medea in Robert Brough's burlesque *Medea* (1856). Again Robson's portrayal of grief, rage, and despair in the supposedly light-hearted doggerel of burlesque was extraordinary. He played Shylock and Macbeth in burlesques with similar strength, carried over to parts written for him in *comedy and drama which elicited his great powers of pathos and anguish. All he lacked to be a great tragic actor, his contemporaries believed, was height.   MRB

Rodgers, Richard (1902–79) American composer. With the librettists Lorenz *Hart and Oscar *Hammerstein II, Rodgers wrote some of the most beloved *musicals in the canon – more than 900 songs and 40 Broadway shows. After several amateur shows with Hart, the pair had their first professional success with *The Garrick Gaieties* in 1925, which featured the groundbreaking jazz *ballet 'Slaughter on 10th Avenue', choreographed by *Balanchine. Rodgers and Hart worked in Hollywood (1931–5) and wrote scores for a number of films. From 1936 to Hart's death in 1943, the duo created a number of musical comedies including *Babes in Arms* (1937), *The Boys from Syracuse* (1938), and *Pal Joey* (1940). Rodgers and Hammerstein's first collaboration was to change the face of American theatre. *Oklahoma!* (1943), based on Lynn Riggs's play *Green Grow the Lilacs*, ran on Broadway for a record 2,248 performances. The musical revolutionized the form through its emphasis on plot and *character; before that time musicals tended to string songs together and emphasize entertainment over content. The production was also praised for the seamless integration of Agnes *de Mille's *dances. Other successes in Rodgers and Hammerstein's seventeen-year collaboration were *Carousel* (1945), *South Pacific* (1949), *The King and I* (1951), and *The Sound of Music* (1959). Collectively their musicals earned 34 Tony awards, fifteen Academy awards, two

Pulitzer Prizes, two Grammy awards, and two Emmy awards. After Hammerstein's death in 1960, Rodgers wrote for Broadway, television, and film. In 1990 the 46th Street Theatre was renamed in his honour. KF

Rodrigues, Nelson (1912–80) Brazilian playwright, internationally known for lacerating studies of lower-middle-class suburban life in Rio. Rodrigues's plays intended to 'transform a simple kiss into an act of eternal degradation', and 'cause typhus and malaria in the public'. Also author of a newspaper column, chronicles of everyday life, and of pornographic novels under a pseudonym, among his favourite themes were incest, poverty and corruption, soccer and suburban politics, violence, and social and sexual prejudice. Rodrigues's complicated work, often written with strangely chaste and economic *dialogue, has inspired innovative and varied interpretations on stage, such as Zbigniew Ziembinski's *expressionist production of *The Wedding Dress* (1943), José Antunes Filho's mythopoetic cycle *Nelson Rodrigues: the eternal return* (1981), and Martinez *Corrêa's sexually explicit and scatological treatment of *Teeth Made of Gold* (1999). LHD

Rodríguez, Jesusa (1955–   ) Mexican director, actor, and *producer. Rodríguez gained international attention with her iconoclastic production of *Donna Giovanna* (1983), a liberal adaptation of *Mozart's *opera in which roles were played by women whose nudity was meant to deconstruct the traditional discourse of the Don Juan figure. Among her full-length productions are an adaptation of Panizza's *Council of Love* (1988), her original *Yourcenar; or, Marguerite* (1989), *Ambrosio the Monk; or, The Fable of Love* (1990), a three-act opera adapted from Matthew G. Lewis's Gothic novel *The Monk*, and *The Sky of Below* (1993), a postmodern take on the sacred book of the Maya, the *Popol Vuh*. She is best known for political sketches that have attracted *audiences from around the world to her *cabaret El Hábito and small chapel/theatre, La Capilla. In these she casts her *satirical net wide to include corrupt politicians, the church hierarchy, machismo, globalization, NAFTA, abortion, and any other current topic that is ripe for debunking. KFN

Rogers, Will (1879–1935) American humorist and actor. A cowboy from Oklahoma, Rogers entered show business in 1904 as 'lasso-artist' in a *Wild West show. In a 1905 performance at New York's Madison Square Garden, Rogers introduced his special trick of simultaneously roping a horse and its rider with two ropes. His honesty

and charm were immediately apparent when he said in his Oklahoma drawl, 'A rope ain't bad to get tangled up in, if it ain't around your neck.' *Audiences warmed to him at once and he became a *vaudeville headliner for whom the rope tricks were incidental to the real show—his homespun, self-mocking, and hilarious philosophic *monologues. By 1921 he was *touring in a *Shubert *revue at $3,000 per week. Rogers starred in five issues of the *Ziegfeld Follies* between 1915 and 1924, but reached larger audiences with his humour column (1922–35) and films (24 between 1919 and 1935). He played the father in *O'Neill's *Ah, Wilderness!* in 1934. He was lost in a plane over Alaska. MAF

Rojas, Fernando de (c.1465–c.1541) Spanish dramatist. Born into a family of *conversos* and possibly under perpetual suspicion for his 'contaminated' Jewish origins, he is credited with the authorship of the vastly influential *La Celestina*, which remains his only literary testament. This 21-act *tragicomedy on the doomed amour of Calixto and Melibea and their go-between (or *celestina*) builds on the classical *comic tradition but goes beyond it in both its unforgiving moral resolution and its pithy *dialogue, ranging from the urbane, sophisticated language of court to the downright bawdy. Though probably not intended for the stage, *La Celestina* has been translated and staged in a variety of languages into the present. The superabundance of dialogue and the absence of explicit *action does not detract from the play's often frenetic pace and cinematic ending, with the accidental fall of Calixto and the suicidal leap of Melibea. KG

Rojas Zorrilla, Francisco de (1607–48) Spanish dramatist. Active mainly in the 1630s, he sought to astonish his *audience by presenting unconventional *characters in extraordinary situations. His plays divide, unusually clearly, into *tragedies and *comedies. The former, centred on *revenge and often on classical subjects, were traditionally regarded as the more characteristic, and *No One Lower than the King*, whose *hero believes himself dishonoured by his monarch, enjoyed lasting popularity. He is more admired today for his lighter, *satirical works, like *It's a Fool's Game*, an excellent early example of the *comedia de figurón*. VFD

Rolland, Romain (1866–1944) French writer. In an age of fervent nationalism, Rolland placed his faith in pacifism and communism, and railed against the elitism of the artistic establishment. With his 1903 essay *Theatre of the People*, he emerged as one of the first vocal proponents of the 'théâtre populaire'. His major work for the stage was the monumental *Théâtre de la Révolution*, comprising eight plays written between 1898 and 1938. They include *The Wolves* (1898), inspired by the Dreyfus case; *Danton* (1900); and *The Fourteenth of July* (1902). His other plays include *The Time Will Come* (1902), a condemnation of imperialism and colonial genocide; and *Liluli* (1919), a biting critique of capitalism. Rolland received the Nobel Prize for Literature in 1915.   CHB

Roller, Alfred (1864–1935) Austrian painter and *scenographer. A founding member of the Vienna Secession, as a set designer he developed the ideas of *Appia and *Craig. In 1903 Gustav Mahler engaged him for the Vienna Court Opera. From 1909 onward he worked with *Reinhardt, designing *Goethe's *Faust I and II* (1909, 1911), the première of Strauss's *Der Rosenkavalier* (1911), *Sophocles' *Oedipus the King* (1910), *Aeschylus' *Oresteia* (1911), and the première of *Hofmannsthal's *Everyman* (1911). In 1920 Roller became a board member of the *Salzburg Festival where he created the famous platform before the cathedral for *Everyman* (1920) and constructed a medieval stage in a church for Hofmannsthal's *The Great Theatre of the World* (1922). Roller was noted for his ability to create simultaneous playing spaces. Best known are the 'Roller Türme', three mobile corner towers which replaced the fixed *proscenium in order to change the look of the scenic space.   CBB

Romains, Jules (1885–1972) French writer whose plays were popular triumphs in the 1920s. His most enduring success was *Knock; or, The Triumph of Medicine*, produced by *Jouvet (1923), which was much revived and *toured. Jouvet himself played the lead in this *satirical *comedy of trickery and gullibility. Other notable plays feature an eponymous pompous professor in *Monsieur Le Trouhadec saisi par la débauche* (1923) and *Le Mariage de Monsieur Le Trouhadec* (1925), both directed by Jouvet. Earlier his play *Old Crommrdeyre* was directed by *Copeau in his relaunched Théâtre du Vieux-Colombier, and Romains reworked *Zweig's adaptation of *Jonson's *Volpone*, creating one of *Dullin's greatest successes in 1929. He was elected to the Académie Française in 1946 after self-imposed exile in the USA during the war, after which his energies were directed to politics.   BRS

Roman theatre Theatrical activity flourished at Rome from at least the fourth century BC to the end of the sixth century AD. The occasion, content, and manner of presentation varied enormously, and it is not easy to summarize its evolution and nature, requiring a good deal of guess work and generalization.

Republican period (to mid-first century BC) Most public theatrical entertainments during this period were centred on the formal religious festivals and the public games (*ludi*) that marked them. By the mid-fourth century stage shows (*ludi scaenici*) had been introduced, multiplying to 60 or 70 days of performances each year by the end of the republic. In addition, victorious Roman generals dedicated games and noble families staged funeral games (*munera*) to honour deceased relatives.

The provision and management of the official state games was the responsibility of the elected magistrates, most commonly the aediles. At first the Senate voted a fixed sum for particular holidays, but by the second century BC the individual magistrate supplemented state funds to promote a successful political career.

Admission to the games was probably open to all: citizens and slaves, men, women, and foreigners. The diversity of the *audience was reflected by the variety of theatrical entertainments offered it. Both the evolution and nature of these is difficult to trace in detail, though Etruscan and native Roman entertainments likely were influenced by performances in areas settled by *Greeks, who built numerous theatres in southern Italy and Sicily. The first scripted drama at Rome was attributed to a former Greek slave, Livius Andronicus, who in 240 BC staged his translation of a Greek play at the Ludi Romani.

Judging from titles, Andronicus created Latin versions of Greek *tragedies and *comedies refashioned for a relatively unsophisticated audience. Others followed his successful lead, and Roman authorities recognized the importance of maintaining civic morale during the dark days of the second Punic War (218–201BC), establishing additional games to satisfy popular demand. These games enjoyed a particular status by virtue of their religious basis, but at the same time their content and performance were severely circumscribed and tightly control by the Roman aristocracy. This tended more towards the restriction of potentially subversive political or social content, while considerable latitude was allowed for ribaldry and sexual jesting (*see* CENSORSHIP).

In the case of comedy, because the Roman playwrights based their plots on Greek *New Comedy, and these were notionally set in Greece, the Roman audience could enjoy watching the 'foreign' *characters' scandalous or ridiculous behaviour without any directly implied criticism of

Roman customs or values. Nevertheless the early comic authors, *Plautus, *Terence, and Naevius, faced the challenge of having to entertain a demanding popular audience whose prior experience of theatre was conditioned by *satire and ribald abuse and who would have been quick to pick up (or misconstrue) political references, while simultaneously avoiding giving offence to religious or political interests. Writers of tragedy, including Ennius, Pacuvius, and Accius, also based their works upon Greek models, but no complete example of republican tragedy survives. The titles and a few scraps of text suggest reliance on flamboyant emotion, spectacle, violence, and rhetorical display.

The composition of both comedy and tragedy appears to have died out by the mid-first century BC, although revivals of earlier works continued and other genres appeared. Spectators could freely move from one attraction to another at holiday entertainments, and short *farces may have had better success in holding attention than longer complex plots. By the mid-first century BC, Atellan farces had acquired literary form, and were widely performed in Latin, although at least occasionally still presented in the original Oscan language as well.

Long before the introduction of scripted comedy, Romans were probably familiar with *mime, which had originated in Greece and been imported into southern Italy by colonists: *acrobatics, song and *dance, jokes, and conjuring were grafted onto the flimsiest of impromptu *scenarios to create a variety show.

Until 55 BC all theatres were temporary wooden structures built for particular occasions. Based on evidence from the surviving plays of Plautus and Terence, the scene building, called the *scaena*, backed a raised wooden stage. The front façade of this building had three openings that could be fitted with serviceable doors. In addition, entrance onto the stage was afforded from either side, used by characters coming from or going to the harbour or the forum. The area in front of the three doors was considered an open street, thus the doorways functioned conventionally as entrances to houses along the street. From literary sources we know that from the beginning of the second century BC these temporary stages were increasingly lavish—sometimes astonishingly so. The officials sponsoring the games commissioned elaborate, multi-storeyed and multicoloured structures, decorated with *perspective painting and architectural embellishment, hoping that their future electoral success might benefit from ostentatious munificence. Elaborate public entertainments simultaneously validated personal power, while contributing to the public's sense

of being paid the honour and enjoying the splendour that was its due.

The imperial period The construction of the first permanent theatre by the victorious general Pompey the Great in 55 BC represented an extension of this concept. Its attraction was the provision of a site where he and later politicians and rulers could appear before a huge crowd to display and validate the popular basis for their authority. Pompey's theatre (prototype for many throughout the Empire) may have held as many as 20,000 spectators. With a stage almost 90 m (300 feet) in width, it was probably the largest of all Roman theatres, and also one of the most sumptuous. The three-storey façade of its scene building was adorned with stone and stucco and embellished with fine decorative detail, and numerous statues. The *auditorium (*cavea*) was covered with a huge coloured linen awning (the *vela*), attached to masts located around the perimeter wall, to shade the spectators from the sun. The most striking element in Pompey's edifice was a temple to Venus Victrix at the top and rear of the auditorium, directly opposite the stage. It was said that when Pompey's political rivals objected to a permanent theatre, he claimed that he was merely building a temple beneath which steps (the semicircular rows of seating) would be provided for watching the games honouring the gods. For six centuries this splendid theatre was one of Rome's foremost cultural and political monuments.

Under the emperors, presentations in the theatre (with those in the Circus Maximus and Colosseum; see CIRCUS, ROMAN) were of major political significance, since they provided one of the few occasions in which the rulers and the people could see and communicate directly, through proclamations by the former, and acclamations, chanted expressions of discontent, and petitions from the latter. The population throughout the empire was presented with dazzling spectacles calculated to impress and to cast glory upon the rulers or their local representatives. The games increased in frequency and splendour; at Rome the emperor and his people might spend as much as a third of the year together at shows.

By the end of the first century BC, the composition of new plays for the theatre had virtually ceased, as alternative entertainments displaced comedy and tragedy. In addition to revivals of old plays, and the perennially popular mime, in the early imperial period the new art of pantomime rapidly spread throughout the empire, attracting huge, partisan, and enthusiastic audiences. Pantomime was presented by a single non-speaking actor (accompanied by a *chorus and musicians) who enacted an entire plot, drawn from mythology or earlier dramatic compositions, performing all the roles himself and seeking to represent characterization, emotion, and narrative entirely through the movements and gestures of his body. Despite the skill and sophistication demanded of such performers (many of whom acquired star status) they were, like all Roman actors, officially considered disreputable, subject to severe legal restrictions, denied Roman citizenship, and from time to time banned altogether because of the scandals and frequent public disorders associated with their behaviour.

The fact that a number of emperors, notably Caligula and Nero, were generous supporters of scenic presentations (which increasingly encompassed *gladiatorial contests, *animal fights, *damnatio, and *naumachia) did not enable the theatre to overcome the antipathy of Roman moralists, whose traditional hostility was continued by the emergent Christian Church. For Christian leaders the games themselves were an affront and an annoyance, and morally repugnant; the pagan religion, however (of which, from earliest times, the theatre was an expression), was a present danger to the very survival of the Church. Christians were urged to avoid the games, and during the last centuries of the Roman Empire in the West, as Christian influence and political power grew, theatrical performance was subjected to regulation, restriction, and outright prohibition. Yet despite the ascendancy of the new religion and social, economic, and political disruption, at the end of antiquity in the sixth century we can discern the same mixture of sophistication and vulgarity, the same conjunction of diverse entertainments, that were first evident in Roman theatrical practice seven centuries before.

The last recorded scenic entertainments at Rome were in 549, and the formal theatre ceased within a few decades. In the Byzantine Empire some vestige of the traditional games continued, but official theatrical activity was officially banned by the Trullan Council in 692. Yet the legacy of the Roman theatre is immense. Theatre since the *early modern period owes far more in virtually all its manifestations to Roman custom and achievement than to Greek.   RCB

romanticism A complex artistic and intellectual movement, romanticism articulated the ideals and aspirations of radical forces that had been unleashed by the French Revolution. In its early phases, romantic culture was optimistic, reflecting confidence that the utopia sought for by revolution was achievable; in its latter phases, especially after the fall of Napoleon in 1815, romanticism was marked by deep pessimism as reactionary governments were installed throughout Europe. Romantic art has many characteristics, among them the prizing of subjective vision above objectively verifiable truths; the elevation of feeling above reason; the worship of nature; and the understanding of the individual human soul as the site of universal conflicts.

Although ultimately the theatre was as altered by romanticism as the other arts, the process of change took much longer. Technically, in performance and production the theatre of the late eighteenth century was not capable of representing adequately the romantic vision. It was also ill-prepared as an institution. Until the latter part of the nineteenth century, both commercial and state-sponsored theatre in Europe and America largely sustained the ideology of the Enlightenment that promoted and preserved social harmony. Nevertheless, theatre did respond to different aspects of the movement, so that in the course of the nineteenth century the romantic transformation took place piecemeal.

In playwriting, the romantic impetus was first apparent in the work of the German *Sturm und Drang (1770–84). Inspired by *Rousseau's natural philosophy, Gothic literature, and Enlightenment humanism, the drama of Sturm und Drang set forth themes of social and familial alienation and was often centred around *characters who experience severe mental conflict. The episodic structure of these plays owed much to Shakespeare and decisively rejected *neoclassicism. Both *Goethe and *Schiller began in Sturm und Drang, with Götz von Berlichingen (Berlin, 1771) and The Robbers (Mannheim, 1782) respectively, but much of their mature drama, performed at the *Weimar Court Theatre, represents a culmination of Enlightenment theatre rather than an embodiment of romanticism. At best, Schiller's William Tell (1804), with its romantic setting in the Swiss Alps, can be regarded as a play about a romantic personality and different modes of romantic experience; it does not use the stage to materialize the subjective romantic experience. The one play of Goethe's that does, Faust I (completed 1808), was considered by its author unsuitable for representation, and, when it was first staged in 1829, its most romantic aspects were cut.

Romantic poets throughout Europe aspired to write drama that would incorporate subjectivism on stage. Some achieved minor success (*Byron, *Tieck), but most wrote *closet drama. In the German-speaking theatre, only *Raimund achieved a sustained romantic ambience in his fairy plays, *The Alpine King and the Misanthrope* (Vienna, 1828) and *The Spendthrift* (1834). There was, however, one extended period of romantic playwriting in Paris, in the liberal environment following the Revolution of 1830. Under the leadership of *Hugo and *Dumas *père*, a series of plays flouted the *unities by setting their frequently violent and irregular *actions in the colourful ambience of the Middle Ages and Renaissance. Hugo's *Hernani* was a *succès de scandale* when it was staged at that bastion of neoclassicism the *Comédie-Française in 1830 (*see* RIOTS); his later successes, in particular *Lucrèce Borgia* (1833) and *Ruy Blas* (1838), were staged in commercial theatres devoted mainly to *melodrama. Indeed the ubiquitous genre of melodrama was the abiding response of the popular theatre to romanticism. While melodrama retained the ethos of eighteenth-century sentimentalism, its Gothic landscapes and the tendency to focus the conflict of the action within the souls of either the *hero or the *villain show the distinct influence of romantic culture.

At the turn of the century, the most admired style of acting was that practised in England by John Philip *Kemble and Sarah *Siddons or in Germany by *Iffland, which presented elevated or idealized characters, reminiscent of the Enlightenment theatre. However, in the first decades of the nineteenth century, some actors powerfully represented the agony of the romantic hero, most frequently in Shakespeare. Notable was the German *Devrient, who uncannily brought to life the unconscious of his characters, the English Edmund *Kean, who raised melodramatic acting to a sensational tragic level, and the American *Forrest, who strove to corporealize the idea of America as a land of untrammelled nature. The impact was ephemeral, however, as romantic acting is inimitable and can never be developed into a tangible discipline, the principles of which can be handed down from generation to generation.

*Scenography and *costuming responded more immediately to romanticism. They readily accommodated demands for historically accurate environments with an abundance of local and period colour (*see* ANTIQUARIANISM), and had no difficulty in providing the wild and rugged landscapes so characteristic of melodrama in the first half of the nineteenth century. By the middle of the century, romantic *realism, which was consummated in the productions of Charles *Kean, *Dingelstedt, and Richard *Wagner, had become the dominant scenic style of the European theatre.

In some ways *opera was more compatible with romanticism. *Music could convey with immediacy the volatile emotions of characters. The bel

canto operas of Bellini, Donizetti, and Rossini memorably explore extreme states of mind and the intricacies of sexual desire, usually in exotic or historical settings. Wagner most fully recognized the essence of Romantic theatre. From his Byronic music drama *The Flying Dutchman* (1843) on, he was acutely aware of the potential the setting possessed to serve as a metaphor for the inner life of characters. His great hymn to romantic love, *Tristan and Isolde* (1865), cannot be coherently staged without embracing the principle of romantic scenography. Unfortunately, when it came to *directing his own works Wagner did not put his ideas into practice.

It remained to later generations to fulfil the potential of the romantic stage. The introduction of electric *lighting allowed infinitely more subtle gradations in mood and atmosphere. It enabled *Appia, in *symbolist designs for Wagner, to demonstrate how abstract form and pure space could be used to embody characters' inner worlds, though his ideas would not be successfully applied until the mid-twentieth century. While *Ibsen was rigorously anti-romantic in his view of the world, the manner in which he closely tied scenic elements to his characters' volitional being and to the symbolic structure of the play represents a fulfilment of both romantic scenography and *dramaturgy. This also applies to *Chekhov's work, while *Strindberg, a more overtly experimental dramatist, realized the potential of romanticism in theme and form in his symbolist *A Dream Play* (1901). The German *expressionists were strongly influenced by Strindberg, and their 'ego-centred' dramas are seen as the consummation of the romantic ideal in the German theatre. Thus while romanticism arose from the revolutionary consciousness of the late eighteenth century, it was only in the twentieth that the theatre could rise fully to the challenges it offered. sJcw

Romberg, Sigmund (1887–1951) American composer. Born in Hungary and educated in Vienna, where he learned *operetta, he emigrated to New York in 1909 and tried his hand at writing American music. In 1913 he was hired by the *Shuberts as a staff composer, for whom he cranked out serviceable, undistinguished scores for more than 30 *revues and *musical comedies. Frustrated and threatening to quit, he was given a chance to write a few original operettas, several of which—*Maytime* (1917), *Blossom Time* (1921) —established him as a leading composer of the form. In 1924 he wrote perhaps the most enduring American operetta, *The Student Prince*, which was the longest-running Broadway show of the 1920s, followed by *The Desert Song* (1926) and

The New Moon (1928). Romberg's work was enhanced by his introduction of a contemporary popular idiom amid the conventions of traditional *romantic operetta. When the age of the 1920s operetta passed, Romberg continued to evolve his style, leading a popular dance band and finding late-career success in 1945 with *Up in Central Park*. JD

Romeril, John (1945–) Australian playwright. A founding member of the Australian Performing Group, Romeril has remained committed to its ideals of collaboration, socialism, and focus on Australian subject matter. He is best known for *The Floating World* (1974), which confronts Australia's post-war relationship with Japan, and *Marvellous Melbourne* (1970, written with Jack Hibberd), a *revue inspired by the nineteenth-century Australian play of the same name. Romeril has also worked extensively in *community theatre and has a sustained interest in Japanese theatre techniques. EJS

Romero, Mariela (1949–) Venezuelan playwright, actress, and television writer. Her debut play was *Something around the Mirror* (1967), though recognition only came with *The Game* (1976), concerned with young beggar girls. *The Inevitable Destiny of Rosa of the Night* (1980) deals with child prostitution, *The Seller* (1984) is about the sale of women, and *Waiting for the Italian* (1988) about mature women who prostitute themselves. Her recurrent themes are the disadvantaged position of women, solitude, and the impossibility of human relationships, which she expresses through colloquial and direct *dialogue layered with meaning. LCL trans. AMCS

Ronconi, Luca (1933–) Italian director. In subversive productions of *Measure for Measure* and *Richard III* (1967), Ronconi's use of space and movement, amplified by complicated *scenography, created a strong visual impression. Influenced by *Artaud's Theatre of *Cruelty, Ronconi's early productions included *Middleton and *Rowley's *The Changeling*, Middleton's *A Game at Chess* and *The Revenger's Tragedy* (all roles were played by women), and Bruno's *Il candelaio* (1968). International acclaim greeted his *environmental version of *Ariosto's epic *Orlando furioso* (1968), written with Eduardo Sanguineti. The design by Uberto Bertacca allowed for simultaneous staging of multiple scenes: performers and *audience interacted on an equal basis and spectators were asked to shift scenery and move platforms with actors riding on them. During the 1970s, Ronconi's productions included an *environmental production called *XX*

in Paris (1971), *Kleist's *Das Kätchen von Heillbron* on barges on the lake in Zurich, and *Aeschylus' *Oresteia* at the 1972 Belgrade Festival. Disappointed by the response, he turned to *opera and worked for television as well. In 1975 he was named director of the Venice Biennale festival, mounting seven *comedies by *Aristophanes updated to the present in a single show. In his own experimental studio in Prato he staged *Euripides' *The Bacchae* and *Calderón's *Life Is a Dream*. In 1989 he was named director of the Teatro Stabile in Turin. Despite frequent hostility to his work, Ronconi persisted with productions of Botho *Strauss, *Pirandello, Ariosto, and *Ibsen. Notable were Karl Kraus's *The Last Days of Mankind* (1990), *O'Neill's *Strange Interlude* (1991), and radical remakes of *Measure for Measure* (1991) and *Tasso's *Aminta* (1994). He continues to direct opera, including *Puccini's *Il Trittico* at La Scala (2008). DMCM/DK

Ronfard, Jean-Pierre (1929–2003) Québec playwright and director. Born in France, he came to Canada in 1960 as director of the National Theatre School in Montréal. After some time with the Théâtre du Nouveau Monde he opted for less traditional dramatic values and forms, helping to found in 1975 what has become the Nouveau Théâtre Expérimental de Montréal. Typical of Ronfard's outrageous, abundant *dramaturgy is the seven-play cycle *Life and Death of the Lame King* (1981–2), a vaguely Shakespearian *parody of Western myths and values. *Hitler*, another controversial, cartoon-like portrayal, played to packed houses in 2001. LED

Roscius Gallus, Quintus (*c*.120–62 BC) *Roman comic actor. Roscius was born a slave, but his success caused him to be freed by Sulla, who in 82 BC admitted him to the equestrian order, an unprecedented honour for an actor at Rome. He subsequently acquired great wealth and prestige, and his name became proverbial for excellence and popularity. He instructed his close friend Cicero in elocution, and was defended by him in a lawsuit; the oration survives. Roscius was admired for his grace and style. He was meticulous in his roles, noted for his observation and careful *rehearsal of gestures and vocal delivery, as well as his skill at *improvisation. Although he occasionally played *tragic roles, he excelled in *comic parts and was noted for his impersonation of parasites, famously for Ballio, the maniacal pimp in *Plautus' *Pseudolus*. RCB

Rose, Billy (1899–1966) American *producer. Born William Rosenberg, he began in Tin Pan Alley writing the words for popular songs, among them 'It's Only a Paper Moon'. In 1925 he opened the first of his Manhattan nightclubs. He was brought into the theatre when Fanny *Brice, who had performed several of his songs, asked to meet him. They were married in 1927, and in 1930 he produced his first Broadway *revue, featuring Brice. His productions were typically lavish, vulgar, and spectacular—none more spectacular than *Jumbo* (1935), a *circus-cum-*musical in New York's Hippodrome with aerialists and a menagerie of *animals, including the titular elephant. After producing expositions and aquacades in the late 1930s, he returned to musicals and plays in the 1940s and 1950s. He also owned two Broadway theatres—the Ziegfeld and the Billy Rose. The foundation which he established in the late 1950s generously funded the New York Public Library's theatre collection.   JD

Rosencof, Mauricio (1933–) Uruguayan playwright and journalist. The son of Jewish immigrants, Rosencof was a political activist and a journalist early in life. Before he was imprisoned by the military dictatorship in 1972, he wrote a number of plays for El Galpón, including *The Great Tuleque* (1960), *The Frogs* (1961), and *The Horses* (1967). From 1973 until 1984 he was in isolation, but guards paid him with cigarettes and extra food for writing poems and letters for them; he used the cigarette papers to write *dialogue, which was eventually smuggled out. Although he composed about eight plays during his imprisonment, he was able to remember and reassemble only four of them. The best known is *Fight in the Stable* (Montevideo, 1985), in which two men are jailed in a stable until they become cows. The younger resists complete transformation by crafting a crude flute, resisting oppression by holding on to humanity.   EJW

Rosenthal, Jean (1912–69) American pioneer *lighting designer who studied with *Baker at Yale. In 1935 she worked with the *Federal Theatre Project in New York with *Houseman and *Welles, and became principal lighting designer after the two founded the Mercury Theatre in 1937. By the early 1950s Rosenthal was in high demand. Some of her most original designs were achieved in collaboration with the Martha *Graham Dance Company, and she also designed for big Broadway *musicals, including *West Side Story* (1957), *The Sound of Music* (1959), *A Funny Thing Happened on the Way to the Forum* (1962), *Fiddler on the Roof* (1964), and *Cabaret* (1966). Her work was seen at the American Ballet Theatre, the New York City Opera, and the American Shakespeare Theatre. Her book on theatrical lighting, *The

Magic of Light, was published posthumously in 1972.   JAB

Rose Theatre The third amphitheatre *playhouse built in London after the *Theatre and the *Curtain in Shoreditch, the only one to be extensively excavated. The Rose was paid for by *Henslowe in collaboration with a local grocer who was to sell food and drink there. Built on Bankside in 1587 near the bear- and bull-*baiting houses, the Rose became, along with the Theatre, one of the two playhouses licensed in 1594 by the Master of the Revels for use by a resident playing company. Its residents were the *Admiral's Men; their leading player, *Alleyn, married Henslowe's stepdaughter in 1592. Depicted in engravings as a six-sided polygon, when its remains were excavated in 1989 the Rose turned out to be a fourteen-sided structure, 22.5 m (74 feet) in diameter, with a stage on the northern flank. The excavation showed that it was enlarged in 1592, when Henslowe spent £108 on it, by extending two sides of the previously symmetrical polygon towards the north, making a tulip shape, with the stage in the newly built section. In 1600 Henslowe replaced the Rose with the *Fortune Theatre, and put in another company which used it till 1604.   AJG

Rossi, Ernesto (1829–1906) Italian *actor-manager. After acting with *Modena, in 1852 Rossi joined Turin's prestigious Reale Sarda Company, displaying his versatility in Italian and French *comedies, *tragedies, and sentimental works and playing opposite *Ristori in *Francesca da Rimini* in an 1855 Paris *tour. With new verse translations of Shakespeare by Giulio Carcano, Rossi successfully performed *Othello* and *Hamlet* at Teatro Re, Milan (1856). Short of stature and burly, Rossi had a flexible face, a body capable of supple movement and expressive gesture, and a voice that shifted volume and tone with facility. The tempestuous and unpredictable nature of his passions earned him the title of a '*romantic' actor as compared to *Salvini, who was described as 'classical'.

From 1864 until his death, he managed the Ernesto Rossi Company in a repertory of Italian (*Alfieri, *Giacometti, *Ferrari) and foreign playwrights (*Corneille, *Hugo, *Scribe, *Goethe, *Iffland, *Laube, *Byron, *Calderón) as well as Shakespeare. After 1868, in an age of the international star, Rossi toured throughout the world like Ristori and Salvini. All three experimented with bilingual productions, but Rossi relied on a Shakespearian repertory more than they. Although lauded elsewhere, particularly in Spain, Portugal, South America, and Romania, his

Shakespearian performances in London met with a cold reception.   JEH

Rostand, Edmond (1868–1918) French playwright. Rostand's historical drama *Cyrano de Bergerac* (1897) filled a national need, felt far outside the theatre. His earliest plays suggested a lightweight talent, but *Cyrano*, written at the invitation of *Coquelin, who had been impressed by *The Far Princess* (1895), at once took the public by storm, at a time when national spirit had still not recovered from the humiliation of defeat in the Franco-Prussian War. The bizarre *character with whom the public identified for an unprecedented 600 performances was the Poet as *Hero: but a swashbuckling poet able to disarm a bully while composing a ballad, before entertaining us with a fantasy about travel to the moon; and whose courage inspires the French troops at the siege of Arras before his pathetic death moves us to tears in the final act. Often scorned by the critical intelligentsia, *Cyrano de Bergerac* is a striking example of pure theatre, captivating *audiences by brilliant stagecraft and verbal virtuosity, and illustrating that juxtaposition of the sublime (the poet with the exalted imagination) and the grotesque (the ugly lover handicapped by his long nose) in which *Hugo had seen the essence of *romantic drama. Rostand was elected to the Académie Française in 1901 on the strength of *Cyrano* and of *L'Aiglon* (1900), in which *Bernhardt played Napoleon's ill-fated son.   WDH

Roswitha *See* Hrotsvitha of Gandersheim.

Rotimi, Ola (1938–2000) Nigerian playwright and director. His first play, a robust indictment of political charlatans, was *Our Husband Has Gone Mad Again* (1966). Three years later *The Gods Are Not to Blame* established him more widely, a bold adaptation of *Oedipus the King*, which he directed with panache and *toured extensively. For the next 35 years, Rotimi was a major figure in Nigerian theatre, writing a series of strong, sometimes *melodramatic, occasionally broadly comic plays that contributed to the reappraisal of Nigerian history and politics, often combining *dialogue, *music, song, and *dance. *Kurunmi* (1969) and *Ovonramwen Nogbaisi* (1971) began as examinations of episodes from Nigerian history. *Holding Talks* (1977) took a *satirical approach to contemporary events. Rotimi responded to the shift to the left on Nigerian campuses in *If* (1983), which he described as 'a full-length socio-political *tragedy', and the historical *Hopes of the Living Dead* (1988). He worked abroad for several years from 1991, and

died in Ife while on a mission to establish a new theatre company.   JMG

Rotrou, Jean (1609–50) After *Corneille, Rotrou was the most significant French dramatist of the 1630s and 1640s. His first effort was at the *Hôtel de Bourgogne (1628), where by 1632 he had succeeded *Hardy as salaried playwright. Fourteen of his plays were in the repertory in the early 1630s. Rotrou was enlisted as one of the five who wrote under *Richelieu's direction. By the mid-1630s he claimed authorship of 30 plays. Largely *tragicomedies and *comedies drawn from Spanish, Italian, and Latin sources, composed in an exuberantly *melodramatic manner without regard for *neoclassical rules, these were mostly intended for an elaborate multiple *scenography. In 1639 Rotrou purchased a legal post in his native Dreux and retired there to produce his most durable work, in particular three plays illustrating the new aesthetic: *Venceslas* (1647), a tragicomedy adapted from *Rojas Zorrilla, played at the *Comédie-Française until 1857; *Cosroès* (1648), a regular *tragedy that remained in the repertory until the eighteenth century; and *Le Véritable Saint Genest* (1645), a quasi-regular baroque tragedy inspired by Lope de *Vega and influenced by Corneille.   JG

Rousseau, Jean-Jacques (1712–78) French philosopher. Although author of the *anti-theatrical polemic known as the *Lettre à M. d'Alembert*, in the 1740s and 1750s Rousseau sought success as a playwright and composer. He began seven plays, one of which, *Narcisse*, failed at the *Comédie-Française. His 'heroic *ballet' *Les Muses galantes* was *rehearsed by the Opéra, but withdrawn before performance. Only his *operetta *Le Devin du village* was successful when produced in 1753. Rousseau considered himself a musician and supported himself as a musical copyist. He was a gleeful participant in the war of the *buffons*, when he and other *philosophes* defended the Italian *opera buffa* against Rameau and his French *tragédie lyrique*. Five years after the success of *Le Devin*, however, Rousseau broke with Paris, the *philosophes*, and the theatre, which he then attacked as a symbol of the corruption of a hypocritical urban society.   VS

Roux, Jean-Louis (1923–) Québécois actor, director and playwright. Trained as an actor in France, he returned to Montréal in 1950 and founded, with *Gascon, the Théâtre du Nouveau Monde, which became the foremost company in French Canada. For the next 30 years Roux was associated with it, directing and acting in plays from the classical French canon while introducing modern works by French and Québécois authors. Equally at home in French and English, he was recognized as one of the finest actors of his generation. Roux also had a distinguished career as actor and writer for radio, television, and film.   LED

Rovina, Hanna (1889–1980) Russian-Israeli actress admired for her regal appearance and impressive voice. In 1917 she became a founding member of the Moscow Habima company. Her role as Leah in *The Dybbuk* (1922) made her into a visual icon and earned her a reputation as the Hebrew theatre's leading actress. She settled in Palestine with the rest of the company in 1928. Her repertoire was wide, but she was especially admired for her mother roles, notably in Pinsky's *The Eternal Jew* (1923), *Gordin's *Mirele Efros* (1939), *Čapek's *Mother* (1939), *Sophocles' *Oedipus the King* (1947), *Brecht's *Mother Courage* (1950), *Euripides' *Medea* (1955), Meged's *Hannah Szenesh* (1958), and *O'Neill's *Desire under the Elms* (1958). See DIASPORA.   EN

Rovner, Eduardo (1942–) Argentinian playwright and critic. His more than twenty plays—including *Anniversary Concert* (1983), *Castaway Dreams* (1985), and *She Returned One Night* (1993)—combine *realist theses with concentrated, *absurdist stagings, often built upon *sainete models. Rovner was *artistic director of the Teatro Municipal San Martín (1991–4).   JGJ

Rowe, Nicholas (1674–1718) English writer. Although Rowe was Poet Laureate (from 1715), he is now remembered for his six-volume edition of Shakespeare (1709), which contained the first biography of Shakespeare, introduced act and scene divisions still in use, and began an industry of Shakespeare editing. In Rowe's own day, he was best known for extremely popular 'she-*tragedies' like *The Fair Penitent* (1703), *Jane Shore* (1713), and *Lady Jane Grey* (1715). The plays feature a strong enunciation of female subjectivity, but ultimately focus on the pity, distress, and death of the female *protagonists. The rebellious *heroines either become admirably penitent or are excluded from their social worlds, so that the plays tend to side with *bourgeois patriarchal values, often revealing a Whig bias, but provided excellent roles for actresses from Anne Oldfield to Sarah *Siddons.   MJK

Rowley, Samuel (c.1575–c.1624) English actor and dramatist, possibly brother to William *Rowley. *Henslowe's accounts show he was an important member of the *Admiral's Men by 1597, and he was still with them in 1613. Although Henslowe paid Rowley for writing scripts—including

additions to *Marlowe's *Dr Faustus* in 1602—the company's terms may have precluded their publication: only one Rowley play certainly survives, *When You See Me, You Know Me* (printed 1605). This engaging (if inaccurate) portrait of Henry VIII—which influenced Shakespeare's *Henry VIII* (1613)—includes lively episodes in which the incognito King meets a London gangster, and in which his son Edward chooses Protestantism after comparing letters from his half-sisters Mary and Elizabeth.   MD

Rowley, William (c.1585–1626) English actor and dramatist. In 1607 he collaborated with John Day and George Wilkins to write the topical play *The Travels of the Three English Brothers* for Queen Anne's Men, but it is likely that he was already working as an actor, always the principal strand of his career. He specialized in comic roles, especially rotund *clowns, raising *laughter by exploiting his ungainly physique. By 1609 he was with the Duke of York's Men, and in the 1620s transferred to the King's Men (*see* CHAMBERLAIN'S MEN, LORD); for them he played, among others, the Fat Bishop in *Middleton's *A Game at Chess* (1624). As a dramatist Rowley mainly worked in collaboration, notably on *A Fair Quarrel* (1616) and *The Changeling* (1622) with Middleton, *The Witch of Edmonton* (1621) with *Dekker and *Ford, *The Birth of Merlin* (1622) with an unknown collaborator, and *A Cure for a Cuckold* (1624) with *Webster; his role seems to have been to script the comic subplots.   MJW

Royal Court Theatre Small *playhouse, opened in 1888 in Sloane Square in London, home to two of the most influential ventures in British theatre. The first occurred from 1904 to 1907, when Granville *Barker and his business *manager J. E. Vedrenne presented a series of matinée and evening performances, the Vedrenne-Barker seasons. *Maeterlinck, *Yeats, *Schnitzler, and *Hauptmann were seen alongside *Galsworthy, *Hankin, *Robins, and, most prominently, *Shaw, whose plays were recognized for the first time as stageworthy and commercially viable. Barker also established the role of the *director as a creative force in British theatre. The Court struggled between the wars, eventually suffering the twin misfortunes of conversion into a cinema in 1934 and bombing in 1940. Four years after its renovation, the *English Stage Company began residency in a season that included *Osborne's *Look Back in Anger* (1956). George *Devine, the company's first *artistic director, remodelled the venue in imitation of the *Berliner Ensemble's home in Berlin: he ripped out the gilt *proscenium arch and added a forestage, converting two of the lower *boxes into downstage entrances. In 1971 a *rehearsal room at the top of the building was con verted to a small experimental space, the Theatre Upstairs. The building was extensively renovated between 1997 and 2000.   DR

Royal National Theatre See NATIONAL THEATRE OF GREAT BRITAIN.

Royal Shakespeare Company From the opening of the *Shakespeare Memorial Theatre in 1879 until 1960, performances in Stratford were a summer festival season. In 1958 Fordham Flower, chairman of the board, and Peter *Hall, as the new *artistic director, planned a strikingly different future. Hall proposed a permanent company on the European model with actors on long contracts, a wider repertory, and with the Stratford shows transferring to a second home in London, where they would join productions of new plays. Hall conceived the model as a national company with substantial state support. In 1961 the enterprise was renamed the Royal Shakespeare Company with the Aldwych Theatre as the London base. Hall involved young directors like *Brook and *Barton but also *Saint-Denis, whose non-British perspective was crucial to the company's development.

Hall's company became known for its innovative Shakespeare productions, like Brook's *King Lear* (1962) and Hall and Barton's *The Wars of the Roses* (1963), but also for its exploration of the European repertory in *Brecht's *The Caucasian Chalk Circle* (directed by *Gaskill, 1962) and *Weiss's *Marat/Sade* (Brook, 1964). The RSC commissioned new plays (such as *Whiting's *The Devils*, 1961) and brought controversial plays like *Hochhuth's *The Representative* (1963) to Britain. Its willingness to experiment was typified by the Theatre of *Cruelty season in London in 1964 exploring *Artaud. In 1966 the RSC became more visibly radical in its politics with Brook's *US*, attacking American involvement in Vietnam. Where *Olivier's *National Theatre was emphatically an *actors' theatre, Hall's RSC was a *directors' theatre—but also a playwrights' theatre, with new work encouraged and with Shakespeare's plays treated as if newly written.

In Stratford the RSC made underrated Shakespeare plays popular (*Troilus and Cressida*, 1960), popular plays contemporary (Hall's *Hamlet* with *Warner, 1965), and placed Shakespeare among his contemporaries by playing *Marlowe's *The Jew of Malta* beside *The Merchant of Venice* (1965). Theatregoround was created for small-scale *touring, primarily of Shakespeare, in 1965,

eventually closing in the 1970s, though the emphasis on touring continues.

In 1968 Hall handed the company over to *Nunn who, like Hall, was 28 when given the responsibility. Nunn made Barton, *Hands, and David *Jones his associates and continued Hall's model, creating two companies to alternate between Stratford and London. The Shakespeare repertory continued to gather praise, especially Brook's *A Midsummer Night's Dream* (1970), with the influence of the London repertory (including *Pinter, *Ibsen, and *Barnes) on the Shakespeare productions increasingly marked. In Stratford Buzz *Goodbody established a studio theatre in a tin shack that opened as the Other Place in 1974 with her *King Lear*, followed by her modern dress *Hamlet* in 1975. The exploration of small-scale Shakespeare continued with Nunn's *Macbeth* (1976), which underscored the increasing difficulty for designers, directors, and actors of finding a contemporary style for Shakespeare in the Royal Shakespeare Theatre (as the main house has been called since 1961). The Other Place was also used for new drama by *Edgar, *Rudkin, *Gems, and others. Nunn also began in 1977 the practice of taking the entire Stratford season to Newcastle-upon-Tyne, ensuring the company's work was accessible to *audiences in the north of England.

In 1978 Nunn made Hands associate director. The RSC had grown into a massive enterprise, by far the largest theatre institution in the world. In 1979 the company mounted 33 productions with 175 actors, playing in Stratford and London and touring in the UK and to Broadway. Best known for its large-scale shows—for example, in 1980 both Barton's ten-play Greek cycle and Edgar's eight-hour adaptation of *Nicholas Nickleby*—the RSC also developed other modes: *The Dillen* (1983), for instance, used local amateur actors and the audience journeyed through Stratford to follow the *action.

In 1982 the company finally opened its London home at the Barbican. The poor design of the Barbican complex and the struggles to secure funding from the City of London made the venture a continual burden. Yet in 1986 Frederick Koch's benefaction enabled the RSC to build the *Swan Theatre in the shell of the old Victorian house in Stratford as a 450-seat space, to explore *early modern drama in a brilliant design that echoes Renaissance *playhouses without any attempt at authenticity. The Swan's exhilarating dynamics encouraged some of the RSC's finest work. Nunn's production of *Les Misérables* (1985) showed that the RSC could make a commercial as well as artistic success of a *musical, providing a much needed source of revenue for many years.

Nunn left the RSC in 1986 and under Hands it flourished along similar, if increasingly predictable, lines. The Other Place was closed in 1989 and rebuilt to include much-needed *rehearsal space in 1991. *Financial constraints led to the closing of the Barbican for four months in 1990. In the same year Hands resigned and *Noble became artistic director. The range of work continued, though in an even less politicized mode. The company began looking to the USA as a major source of income with regular visits to New York. In 2001 Noble announced radical plans to restructure the enterprise, abandoning the Barbican and the tradition of a large-scale ensemble in favour of small ad hoc companies to tour increasingly in the USA, and planning two new theatres in Stratford. Michael Boyd replaced Noble in 2003, returning the RSC to an ensemble company, especially in his productions of Shakespeare's English history plays, and supervising a complete reconstruction of the Royal Shakespeare Theatre to turn it from a proscenium-arch space into a larger-scale version of the Swan's thrust stage. As the RSC continues to adapt to changing economic, political, and cultural climates, it maintains its position as the world's largest theatre company and the major site for contemporary Shakespeare production.   PDH

Royal Shakespeare Theatre *See* SHAKE-SPEARE MEMORIAL THEATRE.

royalties A percentage of box-office receipts paid to the author of a play. From 1791 playwrights in France received royalties on the night's receipts, the percentages varying according to the importance of the theatre and the number of acts in the play. Popular dramatists lived handsomely on this system. In England dramatists had done reasonably well early in the nineteenth century from substantial fees for the *copyright of a published play and fixed payments of £33 6s. 8d. for each performance (replacing the old *benefit system on the third, sixth, ninth, and twentieth nights of a new play). However, by the 1830s and 1840s, with the slump in attendance and economic depression, dramatists were paid derisory sums: usually—with some generous exceptions—£50 an act at West End theatres, far less at minor theatres, and almost nothing for the copyright. Indeed, there was no copyright whatever in a performed play until the Dramatic Authors Act of 1833. Royalty and sharing agreements were not common until the 1880s. International and American copyright agreements in 1886 and 1891 re-spectively further strengthened the royalty position of the published dramatist.   MRB

Różewicz, Tadeusz (1920–   ) Polish writer. Blurring distinctions of genre and using stage directions to challenge artistic convention, Różewicz's poetic *realism questions *mimesis and produces an 'open *dramaturgy' that regards the text as a work in progress to be completed by actors and director. His first performed play, *The Card Index* (1959), introduced a new theatrical language of fragmented structure and imagistic collage made from the scrap heap of modern civilization. In the wake of Auschwitz, his anti-*hero's experiences of alienation and loss cannot be communicated through ideologies, moral judgements, or intellectual speculations, but only through the bare facts of human existence and ultimately silence. Różewicz has been a restless experimenter with form. Following a path leading from *Chekhov through Kafka to *Beckett, he has moved toward an interior drama played out in the empty spaces between events. *The Old Woman Broods* (1968) contemplates the persistence of life amidst post-apocalyptic rubble. *White Marriage* (1974) is a pastiche of *fin de siècle* sexual obsession seen through the eyes of two pubescent girls; and *The Trap* (1982) reveals Kafka's sexual and familial entanglements. Różewicz the playwright has been silent since then.   DG

Rozov, Viktor (1913–2004) Soviet/Russian playwright. Rozov's plays focus on children on the way to adulthood, and became the main source for the repertoire of *Efros and *Efremov. In his *In Search of Joy* (1957) the *hero demolishes a piece of furniture, symbol of the petty bourgeoisie, with his father's sabre; the gesture accompanying this act became symbolic for the break with tradition. *Alive Forever* (1943, 1956) deals with the compromising moral values of the immediate post-war years, and formed the basis for Mikhail Kalatozov's film *The Cranes Are Flying*.   BB

Rozovsky, Mark (1937–   ) Russian/Soviet playwright and director. His credo, 'Theatrical Circles Arranged in a Spiral', appeared in 1972. Rozovsky is best known outside Russia for a stage adaptation of *Tolstoy's *Kholstomer* as *The Story of a Horse*, which was given a memorable production by *Tovstonogov in Leningrad. It was seen at the *Edinburgh Festival in 1987 and also in English-language productions in New York and London (1984, the latter directed by *Bogdanov). In 1989 Rozovsky was responsible for staging *Tretyakov's controversial play on sexual mores, *I Want a Baby*, banned since *Meyerhold first attempted to produce it in 1930.   NW

Rudkin, David (1936–) English playwright, who achieved success with *Afore Night Come* (*Royal Shakespeare Company, 1963). It is characteristic in its examination of violence and *ritual, its sympathy for an outsider casually welcomed into a closed community and as casually killed, and its deployment of imagery linking *dialogue and *action. *Ashes* (1978) elides a Belfast couple's infertility with the political impasse in Northern Ireland. *The Sons of Light* (1981), *The Triumph of Death* (1981), and *The Saxon Shore* (1986) show Rudkin increasingly working with mythopoeic material to illuminate history, place, and contemporary life and to show how ritual is often the means to access the seemingly incommunicable and the darkest of human tendencies. Rudkin has created a *scenario for *dance (Darrell's *Sun into Darkness*), and proved a fine translator of classical drama (*Hippolytus*), *Ibsen's plays (*Peer Gynt, When We Dead Awaken, Rosmersholm*), and *opera librettos (*Moses and Aaron* for Solti/*Hall at *Covent Garden, 1965), a form of music theatre for which he also created original work (*Broken Strings, Inquest of Love*). RAC

Rudman, Michael (1939–) American director in Britain. From the mid-1960s to the 1970s, he worked in *regional repertory theatres, and was *artistic director of the Hampstead Theatre Club until 1979. Subsequently he became director of the Lyttelton Theatre at the *National Theatre, where he mounted *Death of a Salesman* (1979) (revisited with Dustin Hoffman in New York in 1984), *For Services Rendered* (1979), *Measure for Measure* (1980), *The Browning Version/Harlequinade* (1980), and *The Magistrate* (1986). His work at the National made him seem a natural choice as the new artistic director of the *Chichester Festival in 1990, but he was dismissed after a year following the commercial failures of an adaptation of *Greene's *The Power and the Glory* and a *musical version of *Ionesco's *Rhinoceros*. In 1993 he directed *Frayn's *Donkey's Years* at the Sheffield Crucible and in 2000 he directed his ex-wife, Felicity Kendal, in a revival of *Coward's *Fallen Angels*. MDG

Rueda, Lope de (*c.*1512–1565) Spanish playwright and *actor-manager who, as leader of a troupe of travelling players, performed a variety of religious and secular plays at religious festivals, in private houses and courtly halls before aristocratic *audiences, and in city squares, courtyards, fairs, etc., on simple board-and-trestle stages. The repertory consisted of *autos sacramentales, religious plays in honour of the feast of *Corpus Christi, *comedias, full-length secular plays; and

Rueda's own contribution—*pasos*, short, comic pieces usually played in conjunction with *comedias*. His four *comedias* and two "pastoral colloquies' were published in 1576, his two collections of *pasos* in 1567 and 1570. RWV

Ruganda, John (1941–2007) Ugandan director and playwright. A founding member of the Makerere Travelling Theatre, Ruganda left Idi Amin's Uganda in 1973 for Kenya, where he founded the Nairobi University Free Travelling Theatre. His early plays, *The Burdens* (1972), *Black Mamba* (1973), and *The Floods* (1980), deal with the social and political upheavals in Uganda since independence. His dramatic style was influenced by *Brecht's *epic theatre. While *The Burdens* and *The Floods* figure on school and university curricula, the later plays like *Echoes of Silence* (1986) and *The Glutton* (1989) gained little critical attention although they are more sophisticated, merging elements of the theatre of the *absurd with *Serumaga's allegorical style. ED

Ruggeri, Ruggero (1871–1953) Italian actor who gained international notoriety during a career of 65 years. He performed an extensive repertoire of Italian and European plays and led various theatrical companies. In 1925 he was invited by *Pirandello to join his company, Teatro d'Arte. Ruggeri *toured with Teatro d'Arte in London and Paris, where he performed in *Henry IV* and *Six Characters in Search of an Author*. He became one of the best interpreters of Pirandello's work, noted in particular for his portrayal of Henry IV. In his later years he performed under the direction of both *Strehler and *Visconti, including Jaques in the latter's *As You Like It*. ATS

Ruiz de Alarcón y Mendoza, Juan (*c.*1581–1639) Dramatist who wrote in Spain though born in Mexico. A 'colonial', a much-mocked hunchback, and a lawyer, in 1626 he abandoned playwriting after only a single decade, having written fewer than 30 works, which rarely foreground conventional themes like romantic love or honour. *The Antichrist* mixes spectacle and theology, three others centre on magic, and a few are heroic dramas, but most characteristic are his moralistic *comedies. His moralizing, however, is less otherworldly than ethical and *satirical; the virtues he celebrates are integrity, truthfulness, loyalty, and friendship. His plots are precisely constructed, his *characters sharply etched, and his language direct, almost devoid of lyricism or rhetoric. In his masterpiece, *The Truth is Suspect*, a compulsive liar is defeated in love by a truthful rival, though his fabrications are so inventive that one feels tempted to forgive him; in *Corneille's adaptation,

Le Menteur, he is indeed allowed to get the girl. In *Walls Have Ears* a rich and handsome slanderer similarly loses out to a poor but honourable hunchback. But Alarcón's most original creation is the *hero of *Don Domingo de don Blas*, who defends with engaging logic his comfort-seeking lifestyle; when duty calls, however, both he and a thieving ne'er-do-well prove nobly patriotic. VFD

Rush, Geoffrey (1951–) Australian actor and director. Despite his mesmerizing, Oscar-winning performance in *Shine* (1996), Rush trained with *Lecoq and is a highly theatrical actor. His strengths are in broad *comedy and in working an *audience, but he is equally powerful in mannered roles. Of his many Australian performances his Proposhkin in *Armfield's production of *Diary of a Madman* was particularly acclaimed, and *toured Russia and Georgia. Rush's fondness for irreverence and clowning were in evidence in his direction of *The Popular Mechanicals* and its sequel *Pop Mex 2*, plays inspired by the workmen in *A Midsummer Night's Dream*, which became cult hits throughout Australia. Although now a major film star (*The Life and Death of Peter Sellers*, 2004; *Pirates of the Caribbean*, 2003–7), Rush continues in theatre, particularly in collaboration with Armfield (e.g. *Ionesco's *Exit the King*, 2007, on Broadway 2009). EJS

Russell, Lillian (1861–1922) American singer and actress. Born Helen Leonard, Russell made her debut in Chicago at 16 in *Time Tries All*. Moving to New York, she toyed with the idea of *opera, but opted for a career in *operetta. In 1879 she was a *chorus girl in *HMS Pinafore*, and had her first major role in *The Grand Mogul* (1881). From then until 1899 she starred in nearly 30 works—many written for her—including *Polly* (1884), *La Cigale* (1891), and *An American Beauty* (1896). From 1899 to 1904 she appeared in the *revues of *Weber and Fields, notably *Twirly-Whirly* (1902), in which she introduced John Stromberg's sentimental song 'Come Down, ma Evenin' Star', thereafter her trademark number. Although her offstage behaviour was far from exemplary, her unsurpassed beauty and onstage charm rendered her the reigning queen of light opera. CT

Russell, Willy (1947–) English playwright. Russell's commercially popular plays and *musicals frequently focus on *characters struggling to escape the confines of class or *gender roles in his native Liverpool. His first success, the musical *John, Paul, George, Ringo. . .and Bert* (Liverpool Everyman, 1974), transferred to the West End. After several other plays for the Everyman, Russell's next hit was *Educating Rita* (1980), commissioned by the *Royal Shakespeare Company. It transferred to the West End and ran for over two years and was filmed. *Blood Brothers*, another musical, again examined emergent class-consciousness, through the providential theme of twins separated at birth. It began life at the Liverpool Playhouse in 1983 and became a West End hit in 1988, running for several years. *Shirley Valentine*, a one-woman play (Liverpool, 1986) moved to the West End and Broadway, and was filmed in 1989. MDG

Ruzante (*c*.1495–1542) Stage name of the Paduan actor and playwright Angelo Beolco. In his earlier surviving sketches he explored and impersonated the world of Paduan peasants, rather than the urban scene which *commedia erudita* took from *Plautus. His farcical but persuasive evocations of the underdog and the loser draw a fine line between mocking derision and subversive sympathy—his *Conversation of Ruzante Returned from the Wars* (*c*.1529) is the only Italian text of the century to present war in a *realistic manner. He eventually accepted the five-act format of *commedia erudita*, and even openly imitated Plautus, but always retained his own inimitable voice. In his use of a mixture of different Italian dialects, in his performance-oriented *dramaturgy, and in his semi-professional merging of his own identity in his stage role, he is seen as a precursor of *commedia dell'-arte*. RAA

Rylance, Mark (1960–) English actor and director. Rylance first worked with the *Royal Shakespeare Company in 1982 but made a substantial mark with his Hamlet (for Ron *Daniels) at Stratford and on a lengthy *tour. His Benedick in Matthew *Warchus's production of *Much ado about Nothing* (London, 1993) won an Olivier award. In 1995 he was named the first *artistic director of Shakespeare's *Globe in London and saw the new theatre through opening and a further ten years, acting and directing every season. Notable roles included Proteus in *Two Gentlemen of Verona* (1996), Henry V (1997), Bassanio in *Merchant of Venice* (1998), Cleopatra (1999), Hamlet (2000), Olivia in *Twelfth Night* (2003), and Richard II (2004). After the Globe he played *Ibsen's Peer Gynt (*Guthrie Theatre, 2008) and Hamm in *Beckett's *Endgame* (*Complicité, London, 2009), among other parts. He has worked frequently on television, often in classical or period roles. DK

Sacco, Antonio (1708–88) Italian *actor-manager (surname sometimes recorded as Sacchi). He perfected the *Harlequin-type role of Truffaldino, importing material from recognizable literary sources which were pleasingly attributed to this improvised mask. He began his career in Florence, and *toured widely, but is associated with occupancies of theatres in Venice. *Goldoni's early *commedia dell'arte *scenarios, including The Servant of Two Masters which was later written out in full, were composed around his favoured mask. Later his company realized the very different 'Fables' of *Gozzi, starting with The Love for Three Oranges (Pomegranates in the original) in 1761.   RAA

Sackville, Thomas (1536–1608) and **Thomas Norton** (1532–84) English politicians and dramatists. As young barristers, they wrote Gorboduc (1562) for the Inner Temple's Twelfth Night revels. The *tragedy of a legendary British monarch who divides his kingdom, it made a covert political statement in favour of Elizabeth I's establishing the succession by marriage. It is notable for its formal and stylistic innovations in the use of blank verse and allegorical dumb shows, and inaugurated a fashion for *Senecan tragedy at the Inns of Court. Much admired in the sixteenth century as a literary work, it was revived theatrically in Dublin in 1601.   MJW

sacra rappresentazione A form of Italian popular drama, without division into acts or change of scenery, based on religious themes and stories from the scriptures. It differed from religious theatre in Spain and France in that it did not originate with the clergy. It is presumed to have evolved from the lauda drammatica and it was the foundation of the dramma sacro. Begun in Umbria in the thirteenth century as part of a movement of religious renewal, it spread to the rest of Italy, and is still practised in some rural communities.   GGE

Saddiki, Tayeb (1930–) The most important force in modern Moroccan theatre. He *managed a number of companies, from his own People's Theatre to the Casablanca Municipal Theatre (1964–76). At first he directed plays from the world repertory, such as *Gogol's Revizor (1958), *Aristophanes's Ecclesiazusae (1959), *Jonson's Volpone (1960), *Beckett's Waiting for Godot (1960), and *Ionesco's Amédée (1964). He then devoted himself to Moroccan and Arabic work, including Saghrouchni's Last Act (1962), Chakroun's Hammad and Hamid (1964), Kenfaoui's Sultan Attoulba (1965), al-*Eulj's The Rams Involve Themselves (1969), and *Madani's Forgiveness (1976). Searching for forms that would resonate in his country, he staged experimental adaptations from the Arab classics (Meetings of Humudhuni, 1971) and others from the Moroccan popular tradition (Al Harraz of Chra'bi, 1970; The Caftan of Love Crimped by Passion, 1999).   MMe

Sadler's Wells Theatre Sadler's Wells grew out of a late seventeenth-century London pleasure garden in Finsbury and opened as a theatre in 1765. Unable to perform the *legitimate drama, it concentrated on dancing, performing *animals, *pantomime—*Grimaldi was the theatre's great *clown—and spectacle entertainments like the sea battles in a stage water tank (fed by the New River) from 1804 to 1815. The best years were during the tenure of *Phelps (1844–62), which saw the production of 31 of Shakespeare's plays—carefully *rehearsed, stressing unity and ensemble, pictorially pleasing but not spectacular. Sadler's Wells then went through a lean period. After presenting *melodrama, boxing, skating, and *music hall, it closed in 1906 and became derelict. In 1931 *Baylis erected a new theatre on the site, intended as a northern counterpart to the *Old Vic. It was later used for *opera, *ballet, and performances by visiting companies, becoming the home of Sadler's Wells Royal Ballet in 1977. It has been extensively renovated for *dance, opera, and experimental theatre.   MRB

Sadovsky, Prov (1818–72) Russian actor, senior member of a famous acting family. Sadovsky made his Moscow debut at the Maly Theatre in 1839, where he developed into a first-rate character actor especially in the plays of *Ostrovsky. Graduating from the role of simpleton in Russian *vaudevilles, he made his mark as the Fool in King

Lear (1843) and as Podkolyosin in *Gogol's *Marriage* the same year. He next triumphed in *Molière as M. Jourdain in *The Would-Be Gentleman* (1844) and Argan in *The Imaginary Invalid* (1846). He also acted the role of the servant Osip in Gogol's *The Government Inspector* (1845) but offended some with the *realistic coarseness of his interpretation, which was also true of his Gravedigger in *Hamlet*. During the 1850s and 1860s he appeared in 26 different roles in plays by Ostrovsky, as well as in *Turgenev, *Pisemsky, and *Sukhovo-Kobylin.   NW

sainete Short, generally one-act, mode of Spanish *comedy, originally performed in the interval or at the end of a more serious piece or as the finale to a series of entertainments. An eighteenth-century derivation of the traditional *early modern forms of the *paso* and the *entremés*, popularized among Madrid *audiences and given generous amounts of local colour by established authors such as Ramón de la Cruz, the *sainete* continued to evolve in the nineteenth century and reached its pinnacle in the early twentieth, especially at the hands of Carlos Arniches and the *Álvarez Quintero brothers, where it was used as a lively evocation of popular culture in the lowlife quarters of Madrid and Andalusia. Many *sainetes* were intended as *parodies of, and were often produced at the same theatres as, plays of a more serious kind by both Spanish and foreign playwrights. An Argentinian variant of the genre is the *sainete criollo*.   KG

Saint-Denis, Michel (1897–1971) French actor, director, and teacher. Nephew and student of *Copeau, Saint-Denis later headed the Compagnie des Quinze, for which he directed several noteworthy productions at the Théâtre du Vieux-Colombier, including four major plays by *Obey. He took the troupe to London where it made a huge impression before disbanding. He established the London Theatre Studio (1935–9), coming into contact with *Guthrie, *Gielgud, and *Olivier. From 1946 to 1952 he founded and ran the *Old Vic Centre, which included a training school and a *touring company of young professionals, the Young Vic, where his idea of an organic theatre institution with a programme to connect training to the profession was fully articulated. Returning to France in 1953, he headed the Centre Dramatique de l'Est in Strasbourg, where he continued to develop this organic model, later continued in the curriculum for the National Theatre School of Canada and the Juilliard School in New York. His two books, *Theatre:*

the rediscovery of style (1960) and *Training for the Theatre* (1982), solidified his reputation.   DGM

St Denis, Ruth (1879–1968) The first American dancer to incorporate the traditions of *vaudeville and *legitimate stages into the emerging indigenous concert *dance movement. Beginning with *Radha*, her 1905 self-described 'dance translation', St Denis combined popular and ethnic dance steps with a visually entertaining, fully theatricalized *mise-en-scène, winning her acceptance in the United States and Europe as a 'classic' dancer in the same category as *Duncan. In 1916 she and husband Ted Shawn founded Denishawn, a Los Angeles-based dance school and *touring company. A watershed experiment in dance pedagogy and performance, Denishawn was responsible for several generations of influential dance and theatre artists, among them Martha *Graham and Doris Humphrey.   LTC

saint play *Medieval drama based on the lives of saints, either biblical or extra-biblical, featuring conversion, miracle, and martyrdom. The treatment of biblical saints in the *liturgical drama was confined largely to single scenes. The only Latin saint plays that anticipate the later vernacular versions are several on the extra-biblical St Nicholas. Saint plays were produced in England, Spain, and Italy, but the bulk of those extant are French. The saints featured were, like St Nicholas, extra-biblical figures around whom legends had accumulated. While conversion, either of or by the saint, continued as a theme, the emphasis of saint plays gradually shifted to miracle and martyrdom. Martyrdom in particular afforded opportunity for grisly special effects, as saints were mutilated, grilled, boiled in lead, beheaded, or drowned. Later writers occasionally essayed the form: *Dekker and *Massinger in *The Virgin Martyr* (1620) and *Rotrou in *Saint Genest* (1646).   RWV

Sakata Tōjūrō (1647–1709) *Kabuki actor, *manager, and playwright. Born in north-west Japan, Tōjūrō became the most famous exponent of *wagoto*, or the 'gentle style', associated with Kyoto and Osaka. He was famous for his lover roles, particularly those of wealthy, effeminate men who lose their positions due to profligacy or the machinations of others and must go into disguise. *Chikamatsu wrote kabuki plays for Tōjūrō: *Letter from the Pleasure Quarter* is a magnificent example that reveals something of Tōjūrō's manner. He emphasized *realism in *acting and was known for his witty declamatory style, and his legacy of realism and depiction of fallen figures lives on in Chikamatsu's domestic plays. His ideas on acting are preserved in *The Actors' Analects*, a fascinating collection of writings by actors from Tōjūrō's era.   CAG

Salazar Bondy, Sebastián (1924–65) Peruvian playwright, teacher, poet, and critic. He studied in the University of San Marcos and at the Paris Conservatoire, obtaining the Peruvian National Theatre award for *Love, the Great Labyrinth* (1947), a satirical middle-class *farce. Inspired by European models, he also wrote historical plays such as *Rodil* (1952) and *Flora Tristán* (1958). Using *Brechtian techniques of *satire, humour, and social commentary, Salazar explored the contradictions of Lima's traditional bourgeois class in *The Debt Arranger* (1962), *The Diviner* (1965), and several one-act plays.   LRG

Salcedo, Hugo (1964–) Mexican playwright. He won national and international recognition with *The Singers' Trip* (1990), based on the real-life tragic fate of Mexicans who suffocated in a train car as they tried to enter the United States illegally. Border themes and types are recurrent in Salcedo's plays, with depiction of gratuitous violence in *The Desert Burns with Winds from the South* (1990) and *Boulevard* (1995), both of which use myth and *tragedy in journeys through the labyrinthine and often dangerous world of Tijuana, where Salcedo resides.   KFN

Salem, Ali (1936–) Egyptian playwright. A *puppeteer by training, Salem creates *characters resembling those of popular *comedy in spirit and form (hence his ability to cross over to commercial theatre), but also living in a pseudo-*realistic world that, as the play unfolds, takes on fantastical and Kafkaesque dimensions. The three targets of Salem's attacks are bureaucracy, corruption, and despotism. *You Killed the Beast* (1970), subtitled 'the comedy of Oedipus', was a daring criticism of Nasser, represented by Oedipus.   HMA

Salle des Machines Paris *playhouse, built in 1662 for Louis XIV to replace the demolished *Petit-Bourbon as a private court theatre for spectacular entertainments. The theatre, a long rectangle some 78 m (256 feet) in depth, took up the entire north wing of the Tuileries Palace. Its stage, designed and equipped with machinery by the *Vigarani family, was the deepest in Europe to accommodate *perspective effects. Because of its appalling acoustics, the theatre was little used, though in 1671 it did see performances of *Psyché*, by *Corneille and *Molière, with a finale in which one of Vigarani's cloud machines carried 300 divinities. It was the ideal venue for the annual mute spectacles devised by *Servandoni in the eighteenth century. From 1764 the Opéra was

temporarily relocated in the Salle des Machines and from 1770 the *Comédie-Française spent twelve damp, draughty years there. It ceased theatrical function at the Revolution, was redesigned as the Théâtre des Tuileries under Napoleon, and was destroyed under the Commune in 1871, when the entire north wing of the Tuileries was burned down.   JG

Salmawy, Mohammed (1945–) Egyptian journalist, playwright, and novelist. In 1984, only three years after the assassination of President Sadat, Al-Talia Theatre presented two one-act plays: *Come Back Tomorrow* and *Who's Next*. Their indictment of *Infitah*, Sadat's notoriously corrupt version of capitalism, marked the return of the long-repressed voice of his predecessor Nasser. Salmawy's style has ranged from *expressionism (with an *absurdist slant) to *realism, yet all his plays attempt to depict the Egyptian socio-political condition. Thanks, perhaps, to their topical nature, Salmawy's plays are widely endorsed by the media and frequently performed and translated.   HMA

Saltykov-Shchedrin, Mikhail (1826–89) Russian writer. His first play, *Dramatic Scenes and Monologues*, an adaptation of his *Provincial Sketches* (1856) and a *satire on bureaucratic rule, was prohibited by the *censor. *Mrs Muzovkin's Story*, also adapted from *Provincial Sketches*, was staged in 1857. In the same year his *comedy *The Death of Pazukhin*, about a family of repulsive legacy hunters, appeared in print but was not staged until 1893 and next revived at the *Moscow Art Theatre in 1914 by *Nemirovich-Danchenko. Saltykov's major claim to fame is his saga of provincial family life, *The Golovlyovs*, which chronicles the decline of a family as a consequence of alcoholism and material greed. It was dramatized as *Little Judas* (1880), revived in more complete versions in 1910 and 1931.   NW

Salvini, Tommaso (1829–1915) Italian *actor-manager. Salvini was tall of stature and had a powerful physical presence and expressive features; his melodious voice could reflect many shades of meaning. Critics described him as a classical actor because he shaped his roles very carefully, exerting great control over his *character's emotional life and gestures, and usually repeating a part exactly each performance. Like his contemporary *Rossi, Salvini learned his approach from *Modena (1843–5), showing signs of his exceptional abilities as David in *Alfieri's *Saul*. He acted opposite *Ristori in several plays, including *Francesca da Rimini*, and then opposite Clementina Cazzola, his companion until her death in 1868, in *Voltaire's *Zaïre*, Alfieri's *Saul*, and *Othello* and *Hamlet*. His Othello also triumphed in Paris in 1857, Salvini's first venture abroad. From 1864 to 1867, during the political upheavals of unification, Salvini directed the Fiorentini company in Naples, bringing in 40 new plays and adding several roles to his repertory—King Lear, the suffering husband in *Giacometti's *La Morte civile*, and the title role in D'Aste's *Samson*. Thereafter he would add to his permanent repertory only *Macbeth*, *Coriolanus*, and A. Soumet's *Gladiator*. Having discovered the profitability of performing abroad, and finding little state support for theatre in unified Italy, from 1871 to 1889 Salvini alternated long *tours to South America, the USA, Russia, Europe, and Egypt with short stays at home. His interpretations, especially of Othello, served as compelling models for many, including *Poel, *Stanislavsky, *Zola and Edwin *Booth, who appeared with him in *Hamlet* and *Othello*.   JEH

Salzburg Festival Austrian festival of the performing arts, founded by *Hofmannsthal, *Reinhardt, and Richard Strauss in 1920. Intended to vitalize the cultural vacuum of the modern world by reviving the glories of Central European high and folk art, from the start it failed to attract popular *audiences because of high prices. Subsequently it has become the most exclusive of European festivals, a feature that one long-standing director (1964–87), the conductor Herbert von Karajan, did little to discourage. Artistic standards are of the highest, and all major *opera stars, leading actors and directors of the Austrian and German theatres, and international symphony orchestras have performed there. Under Gerard Mortier (*artistic director, 1991–2001), the conservative image of the festival was, controversially, challenged by innovative productions of classic opera and drama and by the successful presentation of experimental works.   SJCW

Sánchez, Florencio (1875–1910) Uruguayan writer, the River Plate region's first great playwright, producing at least sixteen plays during the golden age of theatre in the area. Before his untimely death in Italy, Sánchez saw his plays sell out in Montevideo and Buenos Aires. He also worked as a journalist for both literary and anarchist weekly papers. Although most of his plays take place in the city, he is best known today for his rural gaucho *tragedies: *My Son the Doctor* (1903), *The Immigrant's Daughter* (1904), and *Down the Ravine* (1905). He wrote *naturalistic thesis plays about conflicts between the old creole populace and new immigrants. Designed for an urban, *bourgeois *audience, his plays reinforced official policy about the benefits of foreign immigration to the region. Despite his anarchist, bohemian, and socially critical tendencies, Sánchez ironically served to consolidate the theatre of *realism as the region's dominant model.   JGJ

Sánchez, Luis Rafael (1936–) Puerto Rico's most renowned contemporary writer. *The Farce of Commercial Love* and *13 Sol, Interior* (1961) were well received, but *The Passion According to Antigone Pérez* (1968) gained him universal acclaim. Its staging (by Pablo Cabrera) was noteworthy for the use of *Brechtian techniques to convey *tragedy in a tale about a Latin American dictator. *Quíntuples* (1984) was a success in Brazil, Venezuela, Colombia, Mexico, Dominican Republic, Spain, and several North American cities.   JLRE

Sanchez-Scott, Milcha (1953–) American playwright of Indonesian, Chinese, Dutch, and Colombian heritage who spent her early years in Colombia, Mexico, and London. In Los Angeles to pursue an acting career, she was discouraged by the paucity of roles for Hispanics and turned to playwriting. *Latina* (1980) was based on her experiences as a receptionist in a maid's agency in Beverly Hills. Sanchez-Scott's most produced play is *Roosters* (1987), which explores relationships in a rural Chicano household through a style of magical *realism infused with heightened language, a poetic interpretation of the way working-class Chicanos speak. *See also* DIASPORA. JAH

Sanchis Sinisterra, José (1940–) Spanish playwright, director, and *dramaturg. Founder of Barcelona's independent Teatro Fronterizo, he became a guiding force in the resurgence of Catalan-language drama in the post-Franco period. His early plays, written in Spanish, were often postmodern adaptations of novels or stories. *The Night of Molly Bloom* (1979) was based on the final chapter of *Ulysses* and *The Great Natural Theatre of Oklahoma* (1982) on Kafka texts. *Ay, Carmela!* (1986), an original play about an acting couple caught behind the lines during the Spanish Civil War, was his first major success. In 1999, Catalonia's new National Theatre staged his *The Hired Reader*, a brilliant, enigmatic play in which excerpts from Conrad, Faulkner, and Durrell are integrated into the text.   MPH

sandiwara Popular Malay theatre in the 1950s and 1960s in Malaysia and Indonesia. The emergence of *sandiwara* after the decline of the *bangsawan* (Malay opera) marked the beginning of a modern Malay theatre in which written scripts and *directing became essential, encouraging many literary figures to write plays for the first time. *Acting techniques shifted from the vocalist-actor-dancer routine of the *bangsawan* to a *naturalistic mode, and scenes were changed behind curtains rather than by a retinue of *dancers and singers in full view. In place of mystical and legendary scenes on painted backdrops, properties and scenery were now designed to provide a *realistic ambience. *Sandiwara* stories were linear and centred around issues of social class and social conflicts, both romantic and melodramatic. Plays by well-known writers became classics of the *sandiwara* era, such as Kala Dewata's *Tile and Thatched Roofs*, Awang Had Salleh's *To Wipe away Tears*, Kalam Hamidy's *Child Pledged to the Seven Saints*, and Osman Awang's *Guest at Kenny Hill*. Before *sandiwara* gave way to modern Malay theatre and television dramas in the 1970s, it also had a large impact through radio broadcasts.   MA

Sandow, Eugen (Ernst Friedrich Möller) (1876–1925) German strongman and actor. Known as the 'Mighty Monarch of Muscle', Sandow appeared in 1889 in London, wrestling and lifting weights (including a carthorse). In 1893 he was brought to America but received little attention until he came to the notice of *Ziegfeld, who engaged Sandow for the 1898 Chicago Columbian Exposition. Ziegfeld's promotion launched an international career for both. After they fell out Sandow continued to perform in *vaudeville until his vogue waned. His performances combined feats of strength with an aestheticization and eroticization of the male body. Wealthy women reputedly paid up to $300 to feel his biceps backstage. As an advertiser of cosmetic aids such as corsets and health oils, he was one of the first promoters and popularizers of physical culture, developing a system of body building based on classical statuary.   CDD

Sanger, 'Lord' George (1827–1911) English *circus proprietor. His father owned a travelling peep-show, and George established his own show of trained mice and canaries, after which he opened a tent circus with his brother John in 1853. He bought *Astley's Amphitheatre in 1871, giving command performances before Queen Victoria in 1885 and 1898. His circus *toured Europe as well as America. Sanger claimed the title 'Lord' in response to Buffalo Bill's advertising hype as the 'Honourable' William *Cody. In 1911, Sanger was murdered by a man who had worked as a labourer on his farm—and who was bequeathed £50 in Sanger's will. His reminiscences in *Seventy Years a Showman* (1910) pro-

vide a fascinating insight into the travelling shows of the nineteenth century.   AF

sanghyang Various types of Balinese exorcistic trance *dances involving spirit possession. The best-known form is *sanghyang dedari*, in which two pre-pubescent girl dancers enter a trance in which they are believed to become possessed by spirits of heavenly nymphs. Other forms of *sanghyang* possession trance are associated with animal spirits, in which male dancers are possessed by the spirits of horses, pigs, monkeys, or snakes. These trance *rituals are intended for purification, healing, or protection of the village community from epidemics, bad harvests, or evil spirits; generally to prevent misfortune. Trance induction begins in the innermost temple ground and is facilitated by incense smoke, chanting by female and male *choruses, and prayers by the head priest. Once in a trance state, the dancers take on the character of the invoked celestial or animal spirits, often performing feats such as dancing on burning coconut husks. In *sanghyang dedari*, the young girls are sometimes lifted onto the shoulders of attendants, where they perform delicate dance movements while their eyes are closed. They are often paraded through the village to purify and bless the area. The trance state is sustained by continued chanting or gamelan music. While in trance, the *sanghyang dedari* dancers often prescribe ritual remedies required for purification or healing. At the conclusion of the ritual, holy water is sprinkled on the dancers by the priest to guide them out of trance. Several aspects of these trance rituals have influenced the development of more recent secular performances; for instance, the dance of the *sanghyang dedari* is re-created and refined in *legong, and the male chorus is a central feature of *kecak. KP

Sannu, Yacub (1839–1912) Egyptian playwright, actor, *manager, and director. In 1870 Sannu founded the first Egyptian theatrical troupe, in response to the visiting European companies that performed under the auspices of Khedive Ismail, Egypt's westernizing Ottoman viceroy. Sannu drew upon the *comedies of *Molière, *Goldoni, and *Sheridan, as well as on indigenous spectacles such as *Karagöz. Sannu's overriding interest was to communicate with Egyptians, aesthetically and politically, and eventually he sacrificed European models in favour of audience participation, allowing spectators to change the plot of the play while in progress, even determining its ending. *Improvisations sanctioned by the audience became part of the performance on subsequent nights. When the government closed Sannu's theatre in 1872 for political reasons, the preference for populist performance died away. Levantine troupes, travelling to Egypt from 1876 onwards, consolidated a text-oriented tradition that established literary Arabic (Fus'ha) as the standard language on stage. HMA

Sanskrit theatre and drama See ABHINAYA; BHASA; BHAVABHUTI; HASTA; KALIDASA; MAHEN-DRAVIKRAMAVARMAN; NATYASASTRA; RASA; SUDRAKA.

Santana, Rodolfo (1944–) Venezuelan playwright who received recognition with *The Death of Alfredo Gris* (1964). He was appointed director of Casa de la Cultura in Petare, which led to *Some on the Island* (1965) and experimental works. *The Place* (1967) is about social revolution. Other plays include *Our Father Dracula* (1968), *Red Beard* (1970), *The Company Forgives a Moment of Madness* (1976), which was highly acclaimed internationally, and *Thank You for the Favours Received* (1977). LCL trans. AMCS

Santander, Felipe (1934–2001) Mexican playwright. Drawing on his training as an agricultural engineer, Santander had a resounding success with *The Extension Agent* (1978), a critique of ill-conceived agrarian reform and social injustice in rural Mexico. Using *Brechtian techniques adapted to Mexican culture with *corridos* or sung ballads, Santander has his singing narrator (the *cancionero*) ask theatregoers to provide the play's *denouement. *The Extension Agent* *toured Mexico and Latin American countries, as well as the United States; it played for over six years in Mexico City. Its companion piece, *The Two Brothers* (1984), had some success at home and in the US. KFN

Santareno, Bernardo (1957–81) Portuguese playwright, pseudonym of António Martinho do Rosário, a doctor and psychiatrist, whose work registers the upheavals of the Revolution of 1974. Led by the search for a national subject matter that is not devoid of universal appeal, his *tragedies deal with love (lyrical, violent, wasted) regulated by social constrictions, jealousy, sex, the flesh, and the instincts. They include *The Promise* (1957), *Murder in the Old Village* (1959), and *Portuguese. Writer. 45 Years Old* (1974). In these and other works religion is represented in its most reactionary form, as an obsessive mystical experience; his *characters alternate between the entremes of symbolic good and satanic evil. Santareno reveals a Portuguese society that left citizens in ignorance in order to continue an obscurantist form of power. He developed dramatic

structures in line with European tendencies, such as *Brecht's and *Piscator's didacticism and *García Lorca's folk lyricism. JOB

Sardou, Victorien (1831–1908) French dramatist. Sardou carried on from *Scribe, exploiting the *well-made play with success from 1860 until after the turn of the century—sometimes at the *Comédie-Française, more often in independent *boulevard theatres, and also in London and the United States. His subject matter ranged from *farce and light *comedy, such as *A Scrap of Paper*, his first success (1860), and *Let's Get a Divorce* (1880); through comedy of manners (*La Famille Benoîton*, 1865), political comedy (*Rabagas*, 1872), and comedy in a historical setting (*Madame Sans-gêne*, 1893) to historical drama with serious pretensions (*Thermidor*, 1891). In London the works were the butt of *Shaw's criticism, in the essay 'Sardoodledom', or in his devastating analysis of *Fedora*; but Sardou's well-developed sense of theatre and meticulous craftsmanship made him the most successful dramatist of his day.

In a fruitful collaboration with *Bernhardt, he wrote *Fedora* (1882), *Théodora* (1884), *La Tosca* (1887), and *Gismonda* (1894) for her theatre; while *Robespierre* was premièred by *Irving in English translation (1899). *Thermidor* sought to re-evaluate the Revolution and caused a *riot by left-wing students outraged by its condemnation of the Terror. *Robespierre* offered a sentimental rehabilitation of its subject as historical *melodrama (with 69 speaking parts and 250 supernumeraries). The end of Sardou's career was marked by protracted litigation, when he sued the librettists of *Puccini's *Tosca* for plagiarism; the case was resolved (in his favour) only in the year of his death. WDH

Saro-Wiwa, Ken (1941–95) Nigerian dramatist, also involved in publishing, television production, politics, and the environment. During the early 1970s he reworked an undergraduate *revue sketch, *The Transistor Radio*, as a radio play, and subsequently as the pilot for what became a television sitcom with attitude, *Basi and Company*. He wrote dozens of scripts for this phenomenally successful series, which he produced during the mid-1980s. The *farce and *satire of *Transistor Radio* can also be found in (unpublished) later plays; an adaptation of *Gogol's *The Government Inspector, The Supreme Commander*, was staged shortly after the Nigerian Civil War; *Enoka* was so provocative that the group that staged it in Port Harcourt (*c.*1971) was disbanded. In commenting on events at the tribunal that sentenced him to death, Saro-Wiwa, a thorn in the side of a ruthless regime, quoted Shakespeare, creating an extraordinary fusion between the actual and the theatrical.   JMG

Saroyan, William (1908–81) American writer. The author of some 45 plays, 22 volumes of short stories, eleven novels, and six volumes of memoirs, Saroyan professed indifference to commercial or critical acceptance. When *The Time of your Life* (1939) was awarded the Pulitzer Prize, Saroyan returned the $1,000 cheque, explaining that art and business do not mix. Born to Armenian-American parents in California, Saroyan left school at 15 and reached national attention in 1934 with the short story 'The Daring Young Man on the Flying Trapeze'. The long one-act play *My Heart's in the Highlands* (1939) was produced by the *Group Theatre and the *Theatre Guild. Saroyan offered the Group *The Time of your Life*, but *Clurman declined it, a move he soon regretted. The play is a loosely structured fable about likeable eccentrics who find refuge in a San Francisco saloon. When threatened by a brutish police detective, a comic eccentric restores the sanctuary for misfits, at least temporarily. Saroyan's other plays tend toward a similar mood, philosophy, and outcome. *Love's Old Sweet Song* (1940), *The Beautiful People* (1941), *Across the Board on Tomorrow Morning* and *Talking with You* (1942), and *The Cave Dwellers* (1957) all saw brief Broadway runs. Saroyan's one-act *Hello, Out There* (1942) has been admired as a small masterpiece, the playwright's most disciplined work.   MAF

Sartre, Jean-Paul (1905–80) French philosopher, novelist, and playwright, who in 1964 rejected the Nobel Prize. Sartre spent a formative year as a prisoner of war, which helped him link existentialism with political struggle. His plays, termed the 'theatre of situations', feature *characters locked in combat with one another, struggling for supremacy. *The Flies* (directed by *Dullin, 1943) is an updated version of the Electra myth, read at the time as a call to resist the Nazi occupation. *Huis clos* (*No Exit*, or *In Camera*, 1944), his most famous play, is a post-death *ménage à trois* featuring a woman and her male and lesbian lovers who vie for her affection while vilifying each other. One of the most famous lines of modern French theatre, 'hell is other people', sums up Sartre's philosophy and *dramaturgy.

Dirty Hands (1948) features a young intellectual who fails as a revolutionary through self-doubt. The *hero in his sequel, *The Devil and the Good Lord* (directed by *Jouvet, 1951), manages to break out of inaction, but this action is limited because accomplished in a quest to define his own existence. Other notable plays include an adaptation of *Kean* by *Dumas *père* (1954) and *The Condemned of Altona* (1959). Sartre's final theatrical work was an adaptation of *Euripides' *The Trojan Women* at the *Théâtre National Populaire in 1965. He wrote a study of *Genet (*Saint-Genet, Actor and Martyr*, 1952), but unlike its subject and unlike the *absurdists, Sartre's own theatre was limited by a nineteenth-century concept of drawing-room dramaturgy.   BRS

Sastre, Alfonso (1926–) Spanish writer. Largely outlawed by the Francoist regime, his work developed as a response to the *bourgeois dramas of *Benavente, defending the theatre as an instrument for social change. After a frustrated attempt in 1950 to found the Teatro de Agitación Social, Sastre embarked on a wide-ranging investigation of theatrical *realism, theoretically and practically (through the foundation of the Grupo de Teatro Realista). In Sastre's view, the 'definitive' start of his theatrical career occurred in 1953 with the première of *The Death Squad*, a series of six bleak tableaux linked by blackouts, a 'cry of protest against the threatening prospect of a new world war', and *The Gag* (1954). His work developed with the 'complex *tragedies' of the late 1960s and 1970s, slices of Spanish social reality collected in his *Teatro penúltimo* (1972). To this 'penultimate' phase should be added an 'ultimate' one in which Sastre produced powerful revisions of *Rojas's *La Celestina* and *Plautus' *Amphitruo*.   KG

satire One of the two most common forms of mockery, the other being *parody. Satire is literary, parody an enactment, but the line of separation wavers and at times disappears. Both boast a range of weapons: irony or saying more or less the opposite of what is meant, sarcasm or saying something in an uncomplimentary or hurtful way, understatement, and hyperbole. Satire and parody send cross-currents of morality, acerbity, and topical additions through three of the formal genres—*comedy, *tragicomedy, *farce.

Since *Aristophanes, satire has defended its occasional savagery as a cleansing function. Aristophanes assailed his targets with what might be called smiling distaste. He expressed disappointment with the bluster of Athenian statesmen, compared with a principled (but fictitious) community founded above Earth by the *Birds*; contempt for the self-righteous teaching and philosophy attributed to Socrates in *Clouds*; men addicted to legal cases and law courts in *Wasps*. He disparaged other poets' plays (*Frogs*) and advised women to defeat war by denying sex to their partners (*Lysistrata*).

The scope of his mockery and the gallery of laughing stocks was nearly matched by *Molière, more than two-thirds of whose 33 plays rely on satire. Molière depicted extreme examples of what *Jonson called humours, roles dominated by one characteristic. Molière's list takes in Harpagon in *The Miser* (1668); his opposite, Monsieur Jourdain, the extravagant spender in *The Would-Be Gentleman* (1670); the hypocritical priest-cum-cadger, and his mark, Orgon, in *Tartuffe* (1668–9); Argan in *The Imaginary Invalid* (1673); the less-than-effective seducer who is the *protagonist of *Don Juan* (1665); the snobbish girls in *The Affected Damsels* (1659). Alceste, the social critic of *The Misanthrope* (1666), along with other male characters, bring misery into their lives by marrying or coveting much younger women—the Sganarelles in *The Imaginary Cuckold* (1660), *The School for Husbands* (1661), and *The Forced Marriage* (1664), or Arnolphe in *The School for Wives* (1662).

Scores of playwrights all over Europe tried their hands at satirical theatre. Restoration authors from *Dryden and *Wycherley to *Congreve and *Farquhar, purloined Molière's plots. In Denmark *Holberg wrote more than twenty comedies streaked with satire; in Italy *Goldoni sustained Molière's satirizing of *petits commerçants*; and in Russia the outstanding theatre satirist of the nineteenth century, *Gogol, wrote *The Government Inspector* (1836), a sceptical look at tax chicanery in a remote Russian community. The twentieth century was crammed with satirical scenes by *Brecht (*Mahagonny*, 1930; *Arturo Ui*, 1941), *Dürrenmatt (*The Visit*, 1956), *Genet (*The Balcony*, 1956), Vian (*The Knacker's ABC*, 1950), and many worthy others. Among them is the most striking American drama since *O'Neill, *Kushner's two-part *Angels in America* (1993), with its devastating picture of Roy Cohn's anti-Semitism, homophobia, anti-communism, and influence in Washington, as well as the loathing of everyone who passed through his tawdry life.   ACB

Satoh Makoto (1943–) Japanese director and playwright. A veteran of the 1960s underground (*angura*) theatre movement, Satoh was instrumental in forming what is now called the Black Tent Theatre in Tokyo. His *Brechtian, political theatre is apparent in such plays as *Ismene* (1966), *My Beatles* (1967), *Nezumi Kozō: The Rat* (1969), and *The Dance of Angels Who Burn their Own Wings* (1970, a radical revision of *Weiss's *Marat/Sade*). His trilogy *The Comic World of Shōwa* (1975–9) cast a sharply critical gaze on the ultra-nationalist ideology of pre-war Japan.

Satoh's company have toured Japan with their trademark black tent since the 1970s, and have linked with other leftist theatre groups like the Philippine Educational Theatre Association on projects such as *Journey to the West* (1980). Since then, Satoh has been increasingly active as a director, notably of *Brecht, but also of *avant-garde Japanese playwrights like *Kara Jūrō and *Terayama Shūji. He has also distinguished himself as a director of *opera, including a production of *Wozzeck* at *Avignon in 1995.   CP

satyr-play An ancient *Greek drama with *chorus of satyrs engaged in lively *dances. Satyrs, or more properly *silens*, were half-horse, half-human mythical companions of Dionysus. Satyr costume consisted of a *mask with equine ears, a snub nose, unkempt hair and beard, and a girdle fitted with horse tail and *phallus. Wide use of satyr *costume in Dionysiac *ritual, sometimes in processions and mummeries with mythological themes, led *Aristotle to suppose that *tragedy *originated in 'satyr-play-like performances'. The satyr-play was integral to the original programme of the City *Dionysia. *Aeschylus regularly added a satyr-play (often thematically connected) to each tragic trilogy. It soon declined in popularity, however; omitted from the dramatic contests, it was added to the *Lenaea and to various Rural Dionysia in and after 440 BC. *Euripides is the first dramatist known to have substituted a fourth tragedy for a satyr-play, with *Alcestis* in 438. By 341 BC tragic poets competed at the City Dionysia with three tragedies only, while a single 'old' satyr-play was performed outside the competition. The plots of the earliest satyr-plays employ myths, and typically evoke moments when humanity progressed from savagery to civilization. Euripides' *Cyclops* is the only complete satyr-play, but substantial fragments of others survive.   EGC

Savary, Jérôme (1942–) French director. Born in Buenos Aires, Savary emigrated to Paris and co-founded the anarchic 'anti-movement' called Panique, which *toured fringe festivals with popular theatre that ridiculed the cultural establishment. In 1966 his production of *Arrabal's *The Labyrinth* as a *happening toured to Frankfurt, London, and New York. His company, now called the Grand Magic Circus, created a sensation with *Zartan* in 1970. In 1988 he succeeded *Vitez as director of the Théâtre National du Chaillot, where he was successful in creating a large popular theatre that alternated classics (Shakespeare, *Molière, *Rostand) with new works, especially *musical spectacles that forged popular culture with myth, such as *Zazou* (1990), based on popular *chansons* of the 1940s and 1950s. From 2000 to 2006 he was director of the beleaguered *Opéra-Comique, where his intention was to create a thoroughly popular musical theatre.   DGM

Savits, Jocza (1847–1915) Hungarian actor, director, and scholar, co-founder of the German stage employees' union. From 1885 to 1906 he was director at the Munich Court Theatre, where he worked with Karl Lautenschläger to construct a 'Shakespeare stage'. First used in 1889 for *King Lear*, this 'reform' stage devoid of decor enabled performances of the complete texts of Shakespeare's plays without the usual lengthy pauses for scene changes. The stage consisted of three parts: a curtain which divided the main stage from a forestage; a raised upstage area behind a closed backdrop; and wing curtains on both sides of the stage for entrances and exits. For over two decades Savits presented Shakespeare to a Munich *audience which he demanded 'accept the dramatist-poet's call for imaginary settings' rather than elaborate scenery.   CBB

Saxe-Meiningen *See* MEININGEN PLAYERS.

Scamozzi, Vincenzo (1552–1616) Italian architect and *scenographer. In 1582 he won a competition for the completion of Sansovino's Biblioteca Marciana in Venice. Frequent travels in Italy and abroad rounded off his learning, which he demonstrated in his *Discourses on the Antiquities of Rome* (1583) and *The Idea of a Universal Architecture* (1616). He designed festive decor for the royal *entry of Maria of Austria in Vicenza (1581) and the coronation of Morosina Grimani in Venice (1597). He is best known for the completion of the Teatro *Olimpico in Vicenza and the construction of the Teatro Olimpico in Sabbioneta.   GB

Scaparro, Maurizio (1932–   ) Italian director. Scaparro began as a critic but he switched to practice, becoming *artistic director of the Teatro Stabile in Bologna and making his directing debut in 1964 with *Festa grande di aprile*. In 1965 in Spoleto he presented *La Venexiana* (an anonymous play of the sixteenth century), which established him as a major director. Scaparro mounted more than 60 productions in his career, among them *Our Lord of the Ship* by *Pirandello (1967), *Chicchignola* by Ettore Petrolini (1969), *Hamlet* (1972), *Rostand's *Cyrano de Bergerac* (1977, 1985, 1995), and *Brecht's *Galileo*. He has also managed the theatre festival at the Venice Biennale. At the Teatro di Roma he directed *Camus's *Caligula*, an adaptation of *Cervantes's *Don Quixote* (both 1983), and Pirandello's *The Late Mattia

Pascal (1986), often incorporating *multimedia devices.   DMcM

Scarpetta, Eduardo (1853–1925) Italian *actor-manager and playwright. In 1880 Scarpetta began presenting adaptations of such French *boulevard authors as Hennequin, *Feydeau, and Halévy (*see* MEILHAC) at Naples' San Carlino Theatre in an attempt to bring recognizable contemporary *characters to the dialect theatre. He became identified with the new 'mask' of Felice Sciosciammocca, the *protagonist for many of his Neapolitan *farces. The finest of these are *Misery and Nobility* (1888) and *Doctor for the Mad* (1908). He was the father of Vincenzo Scarpetta, who acted in his plays and succeeded him as actor-manager, and of Eduardo, Titina, and Peppino *de Filippo.   JEH

Scarron, Paul (1610–60) French writer. Seriously disabled by rheumatism, Scarron was the husband of Françoise d'Aubigné, the future Mme de Maintenon. He achieved considerable success with his *comedies *Jodelet; ou, Le Maître valet* (1645) and *Dom Japhet d'Arménie* (1652), which were still in the repertory of *Molière's company in the 1660s. His novel *Le Roman comique* (1651–7), based on the travels of an itinerant company of actors, contains considerable historical interest about *touring companies in the seventeenth century.   WDH

scenario One of the terms used by Italian *commedia dell'arte actors for the plot summary which they used instead of a written script: other words were *soggetto* and *canovaccio*. The great majority of documents which have survived are in unpublished manuscripts, since a company wished to retain control of its material. Just one practitioner, Flaminio Scala, chose to publish a collection of 50 scenari (1611). A scenario was a scene by scene account of the essential events or business which needed to take place between *characters to advance the plot. Each entrance of a new character was signalled by a name in the left-hand margin, so actors could quickly spot the moment at which they would next be needed. At the beginning were listed the characters and their relationships (grouped in family units), and the essential properties needed. What tends to be missing from scenarios is information about jokes or comic effects (when *lazzi are mentioned, no details are given), or about the balance between ridiculous and sentimental tones in scenes involving more 'serious' characters. Concrete facts about methodology and comic content have to be deduced from other sources.   RAA

scenography The accumulation of spatial and visual elements that creates a stage setting. Scenography (literally, painting of the **skene*) thus includes stage architecture, scenery, machines, *costumes, and *lighting, but does not include speech, non-verbal sounds, *actors' actions, actors' personal properties, or the non-ludic areas of the *playhouse such as lobbies and bars. Scenography, often referred to as design, has a history too lengthy and complicated to detail here; this entry deals with only some of the most important issues and developments.

Elements The first major element in scenography is the architectural form of the stage itself and its relationship to the *audience. Stage forms can vary in terms of size, shape, elevation, acting surface, and distance from the audience. In contemporary Western societies, for example, a 'blackbox' stage (small, square, zero elevation, very close to the spectators) generally prepares audiences to receive a more experimental production than would a large, elevated stage.

A second major element is scenery or stage decoration. Scenery can range from the highly stylized and emblematic (a single branch to represent 'forest') to the utterly *illusionistic (a woodland scene re-created to the last bramble). It may be a three-dimensional imitation of a two-dimensional painting, as in much *early modern and *neoclassical scenery, or it may choose to emphasize the three-dimensionality of the stage space, as in the designs of *Appia. Some stage decorations remain uniform throughout, while others change repeatedly.

Stage machinery is a third element. Stage machines have often been used to change sets quickly, allowing a more or less uninterrupted performance. Stage machines may also be used to transgress limitations imposed by architecture and decoration. In one of the earliest instances, a crane with a rope and pulley called a *mechane* was used to 'fly' gods, animals, and *heroes above the *skene*, thus adding a vertical axis to the otherwise horizontal field of ancient *Greek stagecraft. In some instances, such as English court *masques and nineteenth-century disaster spectacles, the illusions produced by stage machines have been central to performance.

Lighting is the element that owes the most to modern innovation. Stage lighting may be artificially or naturally produced, and may have both a practical function (making the space visible) and a scenographic one. Throughout most of theatre history, the use of natural light predominated. Artificial lighting became essential during the Italian Renaissance with the construction of the first

indoor theatres. Though artificial lighting prior to the nineteenth century was largely a practical affair of mere illumination, London's Lyceum Theatre installed the first gaslit stage in 1817, and gas lighting became standard in theatres by 1850. Though dangerous, gas allowed far greater control and greatly enhanced the scenographic possibilities of light. This control was increased, and the dangers reduced, with the introduction of electric lighting around 1880. By the twentieth century, lighting was widely considered a major aspect of scenography. Some modern designers, following Appia, have made it the central element of stage design, while others, following the *Berliner Ensemble, have de-emphasized its dramatic role.

Non-Western traditions Most traditional performance styles East and West place relatively little emphasis on scenography. Stage decoration is rarely used in the traditional performance genres of Asia, Africa, and the Middle East. While certain genres of Indian, Chinese, and Japanese theatre have relatively complex scenic styles, scenery has not received the emphasis in these traditions that it has in the mainstream European theatre since the early modern period, with the major exception of *kabuki.

For example, the *nō theatre of Japan is visually striking but uses a sparsely decorated stage. The stage itself is a platform of polished cypress wood, about 6 m square (about 19 feet) which rises less than a metre (2 feet 7 inches, to be exact) off the ground. It is open on three sides and covered by a wooden roof supported by four pillars. An aged pine tree is painted on the back wall. A long railed bridgeway (*hashigakari*) extends to the left of the stage, leading to a curtained doorway. The bridgeway leads to the actors' dressing room and is the entrance and exit route for all the principal characters. It is decorated by three small trees, which stand at intervals alongside it. At the beginning of a play, four musicians enter along the *hashigakari* and seat themselves at the back of the stage, where they are visible to the audience throughout. Simple stage properties such as bamboo poles and coloured cloth may be used to represent wagons, boats, houses, and other scenic elements. Otherwise, props and scenery are almost entirely absent.

The spectacle of kabuki stands in stark contrast. Kabuki was originally performed on the same stage as the nō, but by the end of the seventeenth century the bridgeway had been widened, a curtain added to conceal the performing area, and a dance floor occasionally used. The *hanamichi was introduced between 1724 and 1735. A walkway approximately

1.5 m (5 feet) wide, the *hanamichi* begins at stage right and extends through the audience to the back of the *auditorium. It is used for entrances, exits, and as an extension of the stage space. Coloured floor cloths may represent distinct settings: blue for water, grey for earth, white for snow. At other times, settings are far more illusionistic. One-half of the stage might contain an entire interior of a house, complete with furnishings and working doors, while the other half holds a garden or wilderness scene complete with trees, bushes, rocks, and a backdrop depicting a vista. Since roughly the 1760s, in response to the influence of Western illustration, kabuki scenographers began to design such houses and paint accompanying backdrops by using *perspective. Of all the techniques of transforming the stage space quickly, none is simpler or more effective than the sudden curtain drop. Night can suddenly fall by the drop of a black curtain, or, as in *The Forest of Suzu*, dawn can arrive when a black curtain hung at the back of the stage drops to reveal a painted morning vista.

Europe to 1600 *Aristotle dates the origin of scenography with the plays of *Sophocles, but writing in the first century BC, Vitruvius calls Agatharchus of Samos the first scenographer, and claims that he painted scenes for *Aeschylus. While most *tragedies are set in a single location, some (such as Aeschylus' *Eumenides*) change locations, as do many *comedies. If the Greeks had developed illusionistic scenography, then they may have developed a means to change scenes within plays as well. Two basic devices have been suggested for this purpose: *pinakes* (painted panels much like modern *flats) and *periaktoi* (triangular prisms that could be rotated to change scenes).

By the beginning of the fourth century BC, two stage machines were in use. The *mechane* (a stage crane) was chiefly used to show a character in flight, either in a chariot, on the back of a beast, or suspended alone in a harness, and was likely placed to the side and behind the *skene* to lift the character over the top of the playing space. The *ekkyklema* (a wheeled platform) was used for revealing tableaux, and was probably wheeled out from the inside of the *skene*. In tragedies it most often displayed the bodies of characters killed offstage.

Though strongly influenced by Greek theatrical practices, *Roman scenography developed its distinctive style by the beginning of the first century BC, when the plain wooden platform of the Roman stage gave way to a performing space before an elaborate architectural façade. This façade, or *scaenae frons*, was often three storeys high, with between three and five doors and numerous niches,

frescos, statues, and pediments. In tragedy, the *scaenae frons* represented a temple or royal palace; in comedy it stood for a city street. According to Vitruvius, setting was also provided by means of *periaktoi*.

After the collapse of the Roman theatre in the early sixth century AD, European performing arts largely survived through popular entertainments, state spectacles, and church liturgy. In Western Europe in the twelfth century, *liturgical drama took place in churches, where scenic requirements included benches or low platforms (*sedes*) and simple 'houses' (referred to by the Latin *domus* or the French *mansion*), as well as a stage area (*locus*) that might be raised from the floor and furnished.

Mansion staging consisted of two basic elements: mansions and an open playing area (*platea*). Mansions served to locate the scene (Daniel's house, the lion's den) and store any required properties, and were generally equipped with curtains and open on four sides. The number of mansions varied according to the production, but heaven and hell were almost always included, and usually placed at opposite ends of the performing space. As impressive as heaven was, hell was the spectacular highlight of the *medieval stage. A gaping, bestial mouth of teeth, fire, smoke, screaming sinners, and flying demons, *hell mouth made use of the full range of effects.

Most European performances occurred on fixed stages, but pageant wagons were used for Spanish *autos sacramentales* and English *biblical plays. Most scholars now agree that each play was mounted on a separate wagon, that the wagons were wheeled to a series of predetermined points around town, and that the play was performed anew at each point. Over the course of the festival, an audience member standing at one of the points could therefore witness the full cycle of plays.

By the sixteenth century, permanent companies with distinctive regional traditions had established themselves in Germany, the Netherlands, and England. But the most important innovations in scenography would come from Italy, where stage design would attract some of the greatest artists. Vitruvius' treatise on Roman architecture, *De Architectura* (rediscovered 1414, printed 1486), had become by 1500 a central authority on theatre architecture and scenography.

Perspective illustration evolved slowly but by the 1530s Italian stage settings regularly featured geometrical perspective with a single central vanishing point. *Serlio systematized the innovations of the previous decades in his *Second Book of Architecture* (1545), the first early modern work to include a chapter on the theatre. Inspired by

Vitruvius, Serlio used perspective techniques to create an influential series of illustrations of tragic, comic, and satyric (*pastoral) settings, consisting of a painted backdrop and three pairs of angled side wings receding symmetrically at right angles to the front of the stage. The stage was level in the front, where the actors performed, but steeply raked toward the back, where the scenery was placed. Finally, the vantage point of the ruler was made the organizing principle of the stage as a whole, with the height of the platform raised to the ruler's eye level and the ruler's chair placed directly in line with the vanishing point of the scenery.

Designers lost little time finding ways to create a more flexible stage. Of all the innovations, it was the *flat wing that proved most effective and outlived the Renaissance. In the first decade of the seventeenth century, scenes made up entirely of flat wings appeared in drawings by *Aleotti. Fifty years later, flat wings would become the dominant element on the Italian stage. A further innovation was the *proscenium arch (around 1560), which hid offstage space and significantly deepened the separation between stage and auditorium, spectacle and spectator. Particularly when combined with the elaborate stage machinery developed at the same time—flying devices, traps, rotating platforms, wave simulators, and collapsible walls—the proscenium arch reinforced the emerging conception of performance as a moving painting.

Neoclassicism Most of the changes in the next two centuries were extensions and refinements of Italian discoveries. Flat wings made possible systems for quick scene shifting that were often executed for no reason beyond the pleasure of the metamorphosis. Of the many scenographers of the seventeenth-century, none contributed more than *Torelli, who designed the Teatro Novissimo in Venice, where his experiments with stage design earned him the nickname 'the great sorcerer'. Between 1641 and 1645, he introduced the carriage-and-frame (or 'chariot-and-pole') method. The system worked by mounting flat wings on rectangular frames, which passed through long slits in the stage floor to wheeled platforms (or 'chariots') running on rails in the cellar. The carriage-and-frame contraption was duplicated on either side of the stage, with all of the carriages connected by a complex system of ropes and pulleys to a single winch. When the winch was turned, one set of flats would be moved into the proscenium while its double was simultaneously drawn off. The offstage frame could then be fitted with a new wing, and the entire process could be repeated for the next scene change. A very effective method of changing scenes, it was soon adopted by theatres throughout Europe, with the exception of England and the Netherlands.

Torelli went to Paris in 1645 to design productions for the *Petit-Bourbon and the *Palais Royal, both remodelled with his techniques. His staging of *Corneille's *Andromède* (1650) started a lengthy vogue for 'machine-plays', performances that featured little outside the mechanical spectacle which became the stock-in-trade of the *Marais Theatre and the *Salle des Machines.

England emerged as an important centre for design when James I and Charles I opened their purse strings to a variety of spectacles, especially for the court *masque, closely identified with the architect and designer Inigo *Jones. Jones visited Italy at least twice and Paris once, and the influence of the Italian style is clearly apparent in his work. He introduced perspective scenery to England for *The Masque of Blackness* (written by *Jonson, 1605), featuring an array of machines far surpassing anything yet seen in England. A groove system was developed for the last masque of all, *Davenant's *Salmacida Spolia* (c.1640). Jones used grooves for the side wings as well as the back shutters, thus allowing the entire stage space to change scene without great interruption. Though never quite so lavish as their continental counterparts, English theatres such as Jones's *Whitehall Banqueting House (1622) were well equipped with machinery, including multiple cloud devices and large traps through which whole scenes could rise. Complaining of 'the Machines and the showes' that had banished 'prose, or verse, or sense', Jonson broke off his collaboration with Jones and began the battle between text and spectacle that has consumed theatre theory ever since.

Around 1703 Ferdinando Galli-*Bibiena introduced angled perspective (*scena per angolo*) to a theatre in Bologna. Previous designers had organized their perspective illustrations around a single vanishing point at the centre of the picture, with architectural features marching along either side toward a central vista. Bibiena established two or more vanishing points, often placing the architectural features in the middle of the painting with the vistas out to the sides. The result was a looser, less static image, one that strives for harmony through asymmetry. *Scena per angolo* extends the eye beyond the visible stage, forcing the spectator to complete the stage picture in his or her imagination. Moreover, the avoidance of strict symmetry disperses the spectatorial gaze, allowing for greater visual autonomy and a diminution of the symbolic power of the prince, who had previously occupied the position of the ideal spectator.

Bibiena's aesthetics were spread through the wide-ranging accomplishments of his family, along with *Juvarra, *Servandoni, and the Quaglio and Galliari families, who gave baroque scenography its characteristics of opulence, grandiosity, asymmetry, and attention to mood though chiaroscuro effects.

The nineteenth century Stage design in Europe and the Americas moved in a variety of directions. In much *melodrama, dramatic action featured less prominently than did natural disaster, with volcano eruptions, floods, and fires drawing large crowds. Exotic locales, antique historical periods, and supernatural happenings proved equally popular. The increasing demand for spectacle, particularly after about 1820, put great pressure on *managers to develop elaborate stage machines, and continued the alliance between science and stagecraft that had first emerged in the Renaissance. By the second decade of the century, *box sets an arrangement of flats forming three walls and a ceiling—were being used to stage interiors, representing intimate domestic spaces with attention to illusion, the first step toward *naturalism. In France, *Antoine continued the development with his Théâtre *Libre (1887), insisting interiors give the impression that the fourth wall had disappeared, filling them with quotidian bric-a-brac; for a scene in a butcher's shop, Antoine hung sides of real meat. In England, the movement toward realistic visuals and *antiquarianism had gained momentum with *Planché's costumes, reaching its apex with the Shakespeare productions (1850–9) of Charles *Kean, whose enthusiasm for historical accuracy extended even to the plants on stage.

As actor-manager of the Lyceum in 1881, *Irving ceased using the groove system in favour of 'free plantation', meaning scenery could be placed anywhere on the stage, which in turn encouraged three-dimensional set pieces. Commanding an army of over 100 set changers, Irving moved toward a plastic, three-dimensional stage space and decreased reliance on the flat surfaces of perspective painting.

Irving's scenographic work was surpassed by the experiments of the *Meiningen company at the court of Georg II. Duke Georg, who founded the company in 1874, directed the productions (alongside his *stage manager *Chronegk) and designed scenery, properties, and costumes himself. He brought to these productions a thoroughgoing antiquarianism, insisting upon historical accuracy in speech, gesture, and bearing as well.

The movement of actors, famously in the form of enormous crowds, was inseparable from the conception of the setting. As a result of several successful European *tours, the impact of the Meiningen company far exceeded its brief lifespan, counting Antoine and *Stanislavsky among its many admirers.

The towering figures of scenographic modernism were *Appia and *Craig. Appia was a passionate *Wagnerite who argued that music was the apex of the arts and wrote a study of scene designs for imaginary productions, *The Staging of Wagner's Music Dramas* (1895), followed by *Music and Stage Design* (1899). Appia argued that, since the actor was three dimensional, instead of attempting to simulate depth through perspective, designers ought to exploit the three-dimensionality inherent in the stage space itself.

Appia felt that Wagner's music called for stark, sculptural abstractions on a minimally decorated stage. 'We need not try to represent a forest,' he wrote of his designs for *Siegfried*, 'what we must give the spectator is man in the atmosphere of a forest.' And what this atmosphere called for, especially, were landscapes formed of light and shadow. Light in Appia's designs was used not merely to illuminate or give atmosphere, but to construct and define stage space. Such an aesthetic idea could not have been conceived without nineteenth-century developments in stage lighting, and would not be realized fully until the arrival of electricity.

Craig, an able self-promoter, insisted production be guided by a single artistic will, who would forge staging and design into a unified work of art, a kinetic abstraction of architectural masses, darkness, shadows, and light. He called for a stage filled with great moving cubes, rising and falling like the tones of an organ, while folding screens furled and unfurled and coloured lights continuously played. One aspect of this dream, the folding screens, he experimented with his entire life, though never with much success.

After Appia and Craig, scenographers and *directors increasingly abandoned illusionistic techniques for a sense of three-dimensionality, so that the period from 1880 to 1920 marked the most significant break in Western scenography since the Renaissance.

After 1900 In Russia a call to arms was sounded by the periodical *World of Art*, begun in 1898 by *Diaghilev, whose vision reached a wide audience after the Paris performance of the *Ballets Russes in 1909. Working with designers including *Bakst, *Goncharova, and *Benois, Diaghilev developed a widely imitated scenographic style. Though traditional in many ways (the sets generally consisted of a large painted backdrop), the scenography tended toward abstraction. Unlike Appia and Craig, the Ballets Russes embraced an exotic opulence, bold colour, and rich ornamentation, a vision of the orient with Bakst, of Byzantium and folk painting with Goncharova and others, a mood at once modern and primal, decadent and holy, an evocative setting for Stravinsky's music and Nijinsky's *dancing.

Some of the greatest innovations would be made in post-revolutionary Russia, where *constructivism emerged around 1920. A 1921 *Romeo and Juliet*, directed by *Tairov in Moscow, featured a cubist-influenced design of swirling, abstract forms by *Ekster that anticipated the daring innovations the same year in *Meyerhold's production of *Mayakovsky's *Mystery-Bouffe*, designed by Anton Lavinsky and Vladimir Khrakovsky. Here the painterly gave way entirely to the architectural: platforms of differing levels criss-crossed by ladders, catwalks, and a ramp stretching deep into the auditorium. The following year constructivism came of age with *Popova's design for Meyerhold's production of *The Magnanimous Cuckold*. Popova's creation was an autonomous stage machine that could be placed anywhere or used for almost any production. Multifunctional and non-representative, it resembled a cross between a jungle gym and the interior of some gigantic clock, a combination perfectly suited to the *biomechanical practices of Meyerhold's troupe. The stage was realized as a 'machine for acting', celebrating the power of mechanics.

More consistent with the heritage of Appia was *expressionist scenography, which emphasized formal abstraction, simplification of colour, exaggeration of central images, and heavy chiaroscuro effects. Instead of an objective picture, expressionism aimed to re-create the mood of a setting or envision how it might appear mediated through an extreme mental state. Innovations in light proved ideal for the stream-of-consciousness typical of expressionist writing. In Germany and northern Europe, expressionist techniques were adopted broadly, associated with the directors *Fehling and *Jessner and designer *Pirchan.

By the mid-1920s in Germany, the *epic theatre of *Piscator presented sharply critical visions of mass mechanization that made use of functional and mechanistic stage designs. His scenography aimed to engage the critical functions of the audience through collage: revolving stages, elevators, conveyor belts, transparent screens, projections, dramatic lighting changes. While arguing that the practices of such *avant-gardists as Piscator and Meyerhold were 'passive and reproductive' and therefore 'anti-revolutionary', *Brecht developed a theory of scenography that owed much to them. According to Brecht, disparate stage effects should be combined not to create a unified space, but to show the constructed nature of stagecraft and the independent function of each theatrical element, encouraging the audience to pay critical attention to the ideas behind the performance. Of the three scenographers with whom Brecht worked (*Neher, *Otto, and Karl von Appen), Neher had the closest relationship with Brecht, from 1923 to 1953. Neher might use any device if it suited the dramatic purpose: screen projections, placards, painted scenery, platforms, curtains, folding screens, rolling carts, lit with a bright, uniform light that eschewed atmospheric effect and refused to direct the attention of the spectator to any particular part of the stage. The effect of such designs has been enormous on numerous contemporary director-designers and companies.

In the early part of the century, American scenography was largely defined by *Belasco, whose style of 'Belasco realism' was highly naturalistic. The first major challenge was issued by Robert Edmond *Jones, who designed Granville *Barker's production of *The Man Who Married a Dumb Wife* (New York, 1915), influenced by Jones's recent European visit. This was the birth of American 'New Stagecraft', an abstract, minimal, and modern style associated with Jones, *Simonson, and *Bel Geddes, and further developed by *Oenslager, *Aronson, and *Mielziner. Mielziner became a central figure with 'poetic realism', a style well suited to *Williams's *The Glass Menagerie* and *A Streetcar Named Desire* and *Miller's *Death of a Salesman* (all Mielziner designed, 1945–9). His scenography emphasized the dreamy, half-remembered quality of reality, creating subjective moods through the employment of scrims, hazy lighting, and partially deconstructed set pieces. Mielziner's former assistant Ming Cho *Lee was responsible for many American scenographic developments since the 1960s. Influenced by the Berliner Ensemble, Lee's designs largely discarded the pictorial style of New Stagecraft for a sculptural stage space.

The most influential scenographer of the late twentieth century was the Czech *Svoboda. Affected by Meyerhold, Piscator, the Czech avant-garde, and the *multimedia experiments of *Burian, Svoboda is best known for his innovative technology, particularly in the realm of film and slide projection. Taking advantage of the thawing of Soviet *socialist realism in the late 1950s, Svoboda and the director *Radok developed *Laterna

Magika, which fused projection spectacle with live actors, dancers, singers, and musicians. Svoboda used that and other forms either as *total theatres in themselves or in conventional theatre design, breaking down barriers between the arts and challenging distinctions between high art and television.

The styles of contemporary scenography are too varied to permit generalization. Particularly in the 1960s and 1970s, many directors and designers were influenced by *environmental theatre, with its integration of spectacle and spectator, a radicalization of the avant-garde attack on the proscenium stage. Most innovation, however, continues to occur in conventional theatres. Designers such as *Frigerio, *Conklin, and *Herrmann, and companies such as *Societas Raffaello Sanzio and the *Wooster Group, among countless others, have continued to expand the possibilities of indoor stage space. Most intriguingly, the director-designer *Taymor has proved that the artistic potential of scenographic experimentation has mass appeal, in staging Disney's *The Lion King* (1997).   MWS

Schaubühne Berlin theatre. Founded in 1962 by the students Jürgen Schitthelm and Klaus Weiffenbach, the history of the Schaubühne has four phases. The first saw a number of innovative productions at the Schaubühne am Halleschen Ufer in West Berlin which did not attract significant critical attention. The second and most important phase began in 1970 when Schitthelm and Weiffenbach invited the director Peter *Stein and a group of actors, directors, designers, and *dramaturgs to form a new company based on democratic principles. The constitution provided (and still provides) for participation of all members of the theatre in the production process. The production process was characterized by long *rehearsal periods, intensive research into the social and historical background of the plays, and substantial dramaturgical intervention. Major productions included *Ibsen's *Peer Gynt* (1972), *Gorky's *Summerfolk* (1974), *Shakespeare's Memory* (1976), and *Aeschylus' *Oresteia* (1980). Together they established the Schaubühne as the leading German-speaking theatre, assuming the position once held by the *Berliner Ensemble.

The second phase culminated in 1981 with the opening of a new building at Lehninger Platz (on Kurfürstendamm), a three-stage complex with variable seating facilities, and ended in 1985 with Stein's departure. The third phase (1985–99) was marked by a succession of *artistic directors (*Bondy, *Breth, among others) and a gradual decline in the status of the theatre. The fourth phase began with a new artistic board with *Ostermeier as director. Although its pre-eminent position is now contested, the Schaubühne has a secure place in history.   CBB

Schechner, Richard (1934–) American director and scholar. Schechner was among the first to appreciate and discuss the dimension of performance beyond the strict confines of theatre. He was instrumental in developing the discipline of performance studies during the 1960s and 1970s with his groundbreaking investigations of the links among performative behaviour, daily life, play theory, and anthropology, which led to a series of *intercultural studies of performance as well as his influential definition of it as 'restored' (that is, 'twice behaved') behaviour. Among his books, *Performance Theory* (1988), *Between Theater and Anthropology* (1985), and *The Future of Ritual* (1993) continue to be influential, as does his editorship of *The Drama Review* (*TDR*). He founded the Department of Performance Studies at New York University, where he holds a professorship.

The founder-director of the New York-based *Performance Group (1967–80), he mounted numerous innovative productions, including *Dionysus in 69*, *Makbeth*, and a notable *environmental production of *Shepard's *The Tooth of Crime*. Schechner also championed experiments in performer training, *collective creation, and various forms of *audience participation. He continues to direct and conduct workshops around the world.   IDW

Schiaretti, Christian (1955–) French director. A student of philosophy as well as theatre, Schiaretti was named director of the Comédie de Reims in 1991, the youngest director ever to administer a national theatre in France. There he established a permanent resident troupe, the first since the decentralization of the French theatre. He has staged a great variety of works, ranging from *Greek classics to twentieth-century European *avant-garde. He has also collaborated with contemporary writers on new creations, such as the *Ahmed* suite (1994–6) with Alain Badiou and *Stabat Mater Furiosa* (1999) with Jean-Pierre Siméon. He has also staged several *operas, including *Puccini's *Madame Butterfly* (1997), and Strauss's *Ariadne on Naxos* (2001). In 2001 he succeeded *Planchon as director of the *Théâtre National Populaire.   CHB

Schikaneder, Emanuel (1751–1812) Austrian actor, director, *manager, dramatist, and singer. A central figure in Viennese popular theatre, Schikaneder was director of an itinerant theatre group until 1789 when he became director of the Wiener Vorstadttheater auf der Wieden. In 1801 he founded the Theater an der Wien and remained director until 1806. As an actor Schikaneder was a successor to Felix Kurz, firmly rooted in the tradition of Viennese broad comedy. He wrote numerous light *comedies, *burlesques, and *musical plays. Having met *Mozart in Salzburg in 1780, Schikaneder became famous as librettist for *The Magic Flute* (1791) and performed Papageno on opening night. CBB

Schiller, Friedrich (1759–1805) German dramatist, director, and poet, author of the finest verse *tragedies in the German language. Born in Marbach, he began writing plays while still at military academy in Württemberg, from which he was expelled in 1780. In 1782 he fled from the repressive regime in Stuttgart and eventually was appointed poet at the Mannheim Court Theatre, where his revolutionary *Sturm und Drang* prose drama *The Robbers* (1782) caused a sensation. Despite its *melodramatic language and incidents, *The Robbers* has remained popular in the German repertoire, most famously in *Piscator's controversial staging at the *Volksbühne in 1926. Schiller's next plays, *The Conspiracy of Fiesco in Genoa* (1783) and *Intrigue and Love* (1784), have been called the first political plays in German. *Don Carlos* (1787), a long and complex verse tragedy, on which *Verdi's opera is loosely based, portrays two young idealists, Don Carlos and the Marquis of Posa, whose attempt to end Spanish tyranny in the Netherlands is crushed by reactionary forces in sixteenth-century Spain.

In 1789 Schiller became professor of history at Jena University, not far from the cultural centre of Weimar, and in 1794 he began a deep friendship with *Goethe. Having for ten years devoted himself to historical and philosophical studies, he began to write once more for the stage. In 1799 he moved permanently and directed for the *Weimar Court Theatre, the work including Goethe's *Iphigenia* in 1802 and the première of his own epic trilogy about the Thirty Years War, *Wallenstein* (1798–9). In 1800 the theatre premièred *Mary Stuart*, Schiller's finest play, depicting the final days and execution of Mary on the orders of Elizabeth I. While ostensibly the tragic *heroine, Mary attains sublimity in her death, and Elizabeth has to live on, isolated and unable to escape from the contamination of political life.

There followed *The Maid of Orleans* (1801), in which Joan of Arc dies heroically on the battlefield, *The Bride of Messina* (1803), a classical piece employing a *chorus about the enmity of two brothers, and *William Tell* (1804), which sets the legendary hero against the background of the Swiss War of Independence against the Austrians. It became a great favourite in revolutionary situations, most memorably by *Jessner after the First World War. Schiller also published important theoretical essays, including *The Stage Regarded as a Moral Institution* (1784), a document that helped to raise the theatre to become an important element in German culture; *On Pathos* (1793); and *On the Sublime* (1793). *See* ROMANTICISM MWP

Schiller, Leon (1887–1954) Polish director, composer, and *manager. Schiller studied with *Craig in Paris before his debut as director in 1917. He headed theatres in Warsaw, Łódź, and elsewhere. A committed socialist, he joined the Communist Party after the Second World War and was a member of the Polish parliament, but in 1950 he was disgraced by the regime. Schiller was a man of sharp contradictions: he first promoted the *avant-garde but in old age accepted Soviet *socialist realism, and he oscillated between Catholicism and Marxism. He directed about 150 productions, the core being in the tradition of Polish *romanticism, including *Słowacki's *Kordian* (1930, 1935, 1939), *Mickiewicz's *Forefathers' Eve* (1932, 1933, 1934, 1938), and *Wyspiański's *Achilles* (1925). He also directed Shakespeare and other classics. He sought a 'monumental theatre' or a 'theatre greater than life', often collaborating with modernist *scenographers on work based in anti-*illusionism, *symbolism, or *expressionism, creating grand and complex spectacles with an abundance of crowds and *music, elaborate *lighting, and expressive *acting. KB

Schinkel, Karl Friedrich (1781–1841) Painter, designer, and one of the most famous architects of the nineteenth century. He developed a style which combined the utopian potential of French revolutionary *neoclassicism with a convincing functionality. He studied in Italy and Paris, and after 1805 he worked under *Iffland at the Berlin Royal Theatre where he designed scenery for about 40 productions (most notably *The Magic Flute*, 1816; *Schiller's *Maid of Orleans*, 1817; *Goethe's *Faust II*, 1832). Between 1818 and 1824 Schinkel rebuilt the Royal Theatre at the Gendarmenmarkt, a famous example of neoclassical *playhouse architecture. He broke with the baroque conventions by trying to bridge the gap between stage and 'audience. Unlike the traditional *illusionist stage of the time, his strongly symbolic sets emphasized three-dimensional space. CBB

Schlegel, August Wilhelm (1767–1845) German literary historian. A congenial poet-translator, Schlegel remains best known for his part in the translation of Shakespeare with *Tieck (1797–1820). Schlegel translated seventeen of the plays for the series completed by Dorothea Tieck and Wolf von Baudissin in 1833. Although now sounding dated, this translation is still the most widely performed in Germany and regarded by some as highly faithful to the original. Schlegel did much to publicize *romanticism, especially in his *Lectures on Dramatic Art and Literature*, which insist that drama is a text for performance, not to be valued for its literary merit alone. CBB

Schlemmer, Oskar (1888–1943) German artist, director, and theorist. Schlemmer directed the theatre department of the *Bauhaus (1923–9), where he created his *Triadic Ballet* (1922) based on ideas expressed in his essay 'Man and Art Figure' (1925). For theatre to become a true art form, Schlemmer argued, the human performer must be transformed into an abstract figuration. In the *Triadic Ballet* actors disappeared beneath all-encompassing *masks and *costumes, the performance made of *dance movement along geometrical lines. He also worked as a designer in the conventional theatre for *Piscator, among others. Schlemmer's work was highly influential on postwar dance and *performance art. CBB

Schmidhuber de la Mora, Guillermo (1943–   ) Mexican playwright and scholar. An early success was the award-winning *The Heirs of Segismundo* (1980), about imaginary beings descended from *Calderón's *hero in *Life Is a Dream*. In 1987 Schmidhuber won the Golden Prize of the University of Miami for the best Spanish-language play written by someone in the United States, for *In the Lands of Columbus*. With productions in the USA (1989), Mexico City (1989), and Spain (1994), it is the first part of a trilogy about Columbus in America. *Columbus's Fifth Voyage* (1992) concerns a trip that Columbus should have taken, while *Good-bye to Columbus* (1992) deals with the loss of culture and language among Latinos in the United States. KFN

Schneider, Alan (1917–84) American director. Born Abram Leopoldovich Schneider in Kharkhov, he went to the USA as a child. He had a peripatetic career in regional and commercial theatre, achieving early success on Broadway with *The Remarkable Mr Pennypacker* (1953) and *Anastasia* (1954). He directed many productions for *Arena Stage, where he was *artistic director for one season (1952–3). He staged the American première of *Waiting for Godot* in

Miami in 1956, which led to a long-standing friendship with *Beckett. Schneider directed the American premières of most Beckett plays, as well as *Film* (1964) with Buster Keaton. In the 1960s he also became associated with *Albee and *Pinter, directing world or American premières of many works, including *Who's Afraid of Virginia Woolf?* (1963), for which he won a Tony award. Known as a playwright's director, he was scrupulous in placing the demands of the script ahead of his own interpretative impulses. STC

Schnitzler, Arthur (1862–1931) Austrian dramatist and novelist. His first play, *Anatol* (written 1889–92), describes a bourgeois youth like himself who drifts through endless, superficial pleasures. In 1891 he established his career with *The Adventure of his Life*, but attempts to stage *Anatol* in Vienna led to *censorship problems, and *The Fairy Tale* (1893) caused such a scandal that performances were cancelled after two nights. *Liebelei* (*Love Games*, *Burgtheater, 1895) was an enormous success, produced in ten German theatres. The trouble did not stop, however: *The Eccentric* (published 1896, acted 1932), *Fair Game* (Berlin, 1896), and most of all *Der Reigen* (*La Ronde*, 1900, produced 1920) brought notoriety and charges of immorality. Nonetheless in the years preceding the First World War he wrote a string of highly successful works and became one of the most widely performed dramatists in the German-speaking countries.

Schnitzler was an acute observer of the disintegration of the Habsburg Empire. His plays are characterized by elegant, charming *dialogue and a *dramaturgy of apparent formlessness that hides a precise and musical structure. Following a court case against *La Ronde* in 1921, Schnitzler withdrew the performing rights as he feared that the play was not properly understood. When the ban was lifted in 1982 it was performed in a large number of major playhouses. Other plays still regularly performed are *The Green Cockatoo*, *The Lonely Way*, *Life's Calling*, *Countess Mizzi*, *Undiscovered Country*, and *Professor Bernhardi*. GB

Schoenaerts, Julien (1925–2006) Greatest Flemish actor of the post-war period. After his studies at the Studio Herman Teirlinck in Antwerp, Schoenaerts joined the Royal Dutch theatre (National Theatre) in Antwerp, acted in The Netherlands, and set up several impressive solo productions. His most creative work was in collaboration with *Tillemans, who directed some of his greatest performances: Kaspar in *Handke's eponymous play, Davies in *Pinter's *The Caretaker*, Hamm in *Beckett's *Endgame*, and Vladimir in

Waiting for Godot. Schoenaerts possessed a uniquely energetic theatrical presence. His *acting was characterized by utmost control of expression and by an impressive talent for exploring the emotional value of sound and rhythm in the text.   JDV

Schönberg, Claude-Michel *See* BOUBLIL, ALAIN.

Schouwburg The first municipal theatre of Amsterdam, inaugurated January 1638. Jacob van Campen used stone for the building after the merger in 1632 of the two Amsterdam *Chambers of Rhetoric and the demise of the first Dutch Academy, on whose site the theatre was erected. The Schouwburg opened with Joost van den *Vondel's *Gijsbrecht van Aemstel*, written especially for the occasion; until the late twentieth century this play, combining local history with abundant praise of marriage, was performed almost annually during the Christmas season. The original *playhouse was soon redesigned in the Italian style with *proscenium arch and stage machinery. Destroyed by fire in 1772, a wooden structure was built two years later, which lasted until a fire of 1890 when it was replaced by the present edifice (1894). The Schouwburg has maintained a vital role in the capital's theatre scene. It has three in-house companies and hosts four theatre festivals as well as numerous premières each year.   TH

Schröder, Friedrich Ludwig (1744–1816) German actor and director. The son of Sophie Charlotte *Schröder and stepson of *Ackermann, Friedrich joined his stepfather's group in Switzerland in 1759 and followed him to Hamburg in 1764. Under the tutelage of *Ekhof he performed in comic parts and in larger character roles including King Lear, Othello, Richard II, and Shylock. With his mother he *managed the Hamburg Comödienhaus am Gänsemarkt after Ackermann's death in 1771, which they directed until 1780. He was a member of the *Burgtheater in Vienna (1781–5), and again became director of the Hamburg theatre (1785–98). Schröder encouraged contemporary drama, especially authors of the *Sturm und Drang movement: *Lessing's *Emilia Galotti* (1772), *Goethe's *Clavigo* and *Götz von Berlichingen* (1774), *Schiller's *The Robbers* and *Love and Intrigue*, and Klinger's *The Twins* (1776) were among those he mounted. He also contributed to the breakthrough of Shakespeare on the German stage, first in adaptations, later in versions closer to the original.   CBB

Schröder, Sophie Charlotte (Ackermann) (1714–93) German actress and *manager. After a short-lived marriage to the Berlin organist J. D. Schröder, she joined the Schönemann troupe in 1740. In 1741 she founded her own acting company in Hamburg, which was dissolved in 1744. In 1747 she joined the Theater Danzig and followed *Ackermann on his *tour through Russia, and married him in Moscow in 1749. The couple founded the renowned Ackermannsche Gesellschaft, which travelled throughout the German-speaking countries. As the company's teacher and leading actress she was noted for her intellect and energy as well as for a refined *acting style. CBB

Schumann, Peter *See* BREAD AND PUPPET THEATRE.

Schwab, Werner (1958–94) Austrian dramatist and prose writer. Educated in fine arts, Schwab was among the most provocative and successful young dramatists of the mid-1990s. His plays are primarily interested in language, dialect-inflected speech presented as verbal attacks, playing freely with word associations, paradoxes, and misspellings. His *characters find themselves in extreme situations: murder, rape, incest, and cannibalism are among the atrocities that often end in grotesque and comic travesty. Schwab died of an alcohol overdose. Notable plays include *The Lady Presidents* (1990) and *Genocide; or, My Life Is Blameless: a radical comedy* (1992).   CBB

Scofield, Paul (1922–2008) English actor who established his reputation at the *Birmingham Repertory Company before moving to Stratford in 1946, where he played a wide variety of roles over the next three seasons, from the Clown in *The Winter's Tale* to Henry V. He demonstrated that his intelligence and his extraordinary voice could turn parts thought almost unactable, like Don Armado in *Love's Labour's Lost*, into deeply humane studies of individuals. In 1948 he was, for *Tynan, simply 'the best Hamlet I have seen'. As Thomas More in *Bolt's *A Man for All Seasons* (1960), Scofield created a study of conscience that gained him a wider international reputation. But it was his King Lear (1962), directed by *Brook for the *Royal Shakespeare Company, which marked his greatness; its searching of Lear's rigidity at the opening made the transition to mad outsider painful and colossal in a nihilistic universe which drew Shakespeare close to *Beckett. Scofield returned to the role for Brook's film (1971) and in a new radio production in 2002.

As Timon of Athens in 1965 he charted a similar collapse. After the comparative failure of his Macbeth in 1967, he left Stratford and became carefully selective, never playing a role unless fully committed to it and the production. As *Chekhov's Vanya (1970), Salieri (*Shaffer's *Amadeus*, 1979), or *Ibsen's John Gabriel Borkman (1996), he showed his fascination with failures. But he was also gifted in *comedy: as the delicately drunk Khlestakov in *Gogol's *The Government Inspector* (1965), *Zuckmayer's Captain of Köpenick (1971), or *Jonson's Volpone (1977). Scrupulously private and deeply committed to his art and the actor's responsibility to the dramatist, Scofield was never a conventional star but was admired as one of the most provocative actors of his age.   PDH

Scott, Dennis (1939–91) Jamaican writer, director, and actor. He joined the National Dance Theatre Company of Jamaica in 1965, and won prizes in 1966 and 1969 for his early plays *Chariots of Wrath* and *The Passionate Cabbage*. *The Crime of Anabel Campbell* (1970) transposed the *character of Clytemnestra to contemporary Jamaica. The remarkable *Echo in the Bone* (1974) relates the story of the murder of a white plantation owner, and the man who may have killed him, in a non-linear and highly theatrical form, using elements from Caribbean spirit possession. *Dog* (1978) is a disturbing Orwellian fable about rich and poor. In 1977 Scott became director of the Jamaica School of Drama, and from 1983 taught playwriting and *directing at the Yale School of Drama. In the USA he also worked with the National Theatre of the Deaf, which commissioned his adaptation of *Sir Gawain and the Green Knight*. He acted regularly on the US television series *The Cosby Show*, before his early death. AS

Scott, George C. (1927–99) American actor who made his New York debut as Richard III with the *New York Shakespeare Festival (1957). He subsequently appeared in *The Andersonville Trial* (1959), *Desire under the Elms* (1963), *The Little Foxes* (1967), *Uncle Vanya* (1973), as Willy Loman in his own production of *Death of a Salesman* (1975), and in *Sly Fox* (1976). At the Circle in the Square, he directed and acted in *Present Laughter* (1982) and *On Borrowed Time* (1991). Best known as a film actor, he had major roles in *Anatomy of a Murder* (1959), *Dr Strangelove* (1964), *The Flim-Flam Man* (1967), and the powerful title role in *Patton* (1970).   JDM

Scribe, Augustin-Eugène (1791–1861) French dramatist. Scribe's first play was performed in 1815, and at his death he had written nearly 500 plays, mostly in collaboration with less well-known authors. Many were produced for the Gymnase Theatre, where he was appointed house

dramatist in 1821. Scribe specialized at first in *vaudeville*, or light *comedy, with a reputation for effective dramatic construction. His name soon became synonymous with the term *well-made play which was to be so important in nineteenth-century theatre history, even though later ridiculed by *Shaw. The tight logic of plot, the subordination of *character to situation, the contrived or mechanical creation of suspense, and the inevitable resolution in a *scène à faire* were appropriate to the *comédie-vaudeville*, and the *farces of *Labiche or *Feydeau. But the formula of the well-made play had the effect in more serious drama of turning characters into puppets controlled by chance. For instance, in *The Glass of Water* (*Comédie-Française, 1840), designed to show that important events can have trivial causes, the *denouement depends on the request for a glass of water at a court reception. A tragic outcome is seen in the historical drama *Adrienne Lecouvreur* (1849), when the young actress's misinterpretation of the behaviour of her lover leads to her death after inhaling poison from a bouquet sent by her rival. Both plays retained their popularity up to the end of the nineteenth century. *Adrienne Lecouvreur*, written in collaboration with Legouvé as a vehicle for *Rachel, was frequently revived by *Bernhardt. Scribe enjoyed a parallel career as the librettist for successful *operas and *opéras-comiques*, from Rossini's *Le Comte Ory* (1828) and Boieldieu's *La Dame blanche* (1825) to several works by Meyerbeer, including *Robert the Devil* (1831) and *L'Africaine* (1865). He was also the librettist for *Verdi's *Sicilian Vespers* in 1855.   WDH

Scudéry, Georges de (1601–67) Prolific French playwright of *tragedies, *tragicomedies, and *comedies. The most interesting is *La Comédie des comédiens*, one of two plays with this name staged during the 1632–3 Paris season showing a theatre company at *rehearsal and in performance: Scudéry's work features *Montdory's company at the *Marais Theatre, while the alternative by Gougenot presents their rivals at the *Hôtel de Bourgogne. Scudéry played a prominent role in the 'Querelle du *Cid', his hostile *Observations* (1637) containing a pedantic commentary on *Corneille's play. *See also* NEOCLASSICISM.   WDH

Segal, Zohra (1912–) Indian dancer and actress. Of aristocratic Muslim Pathan parentage, Segal broke *gender norms and pioneered a career in performing arts. After study in Lahore, she travelled to Germany to pursue *dance. In 1935 she joined Uday Shankar's *ballet company and as a principal dancer performed throughout the world. From 1945 to 1959 she was a member of Prithvi Theatres, serving as dance director and acting alongside *Kapoor. The company gave some 2,000 performances by *touring over 100 towns in India. In the 1960s she moved to London, working for the BBC, the *Old Vic, and the British Drama League. She achieved acclaim in two Merchant-Ivory films, *The Guru* and *Courtesans of Bombay*, in the television serial *Jewel in the Crown*, and in two films about the Indian diaspora, *Bhaji on the Beach* and *Masala*. Segal continued to perform in her nineties, notably in the *Ajoka production of *Ek Thi Nani* in Lahore.   KH

Sellars, Peter (1957–) American director. Using eclectic staging techniques derived from European and American *avant-garde theatre and non-Western performance, Sellars's modern-dress productions of the classics always address the culture and politics of contemporary America. At Andover and Harvard he directed scores of productions, culminating in his first professional assignment, *Gogol's *Inspector General* at the *American Repertory Theatre in 1980. As *artistic director of the Boston Shakespeare Company (1983–4) and later of the American National Theatre at Washington's Kennedy Center (1985–6), Sellars developed a performance style that juxtaposes psychological *realism with precisely choreographed physicality. Strongly influenced by *Meyerhold and *Lyubimov, *music always plays a central role in Sellars's theatre. In the late 1980s he focused exclusively on *opera, most notably the *Mozart–da Ponte trilogy which he set in New York. In collaboration with composer John Adams, Sellars developed a repertoire of new opera that combines national politics with intense spiritual yearning, evident in works like *Nixon in China* (1987), *The Death of Klinghoffer* (1991), and *El Niño* (2000). In the 1990s this spiritual theme dominated his productions of Messiaen's *St François d'Assise* (1992), Handel's *Theodora* (1996), *Tang Xianzu's *Peony Pavilion* (1998), and Stravinsky's *Biblical Pieces* (1999). He was the director of the Los Angeles Festivals of 1990 and 1993, and of the New Crowned Hope Festival (part of the Vienna Mozart Year 2006), where he directed Adams's new opera *A Flowering Tree*. That year he also directed Mozart's unfinished *Zaide* at *Lincoln Center.   MPB

Semyonova, Ekaterina (1786–1849) Russian actress. Semyonova rose from rags to riches to become one of the finest tragic actresses of her day. Blessed with a powerful temperament, she starred in plays by *Racine, *Voltaire, and *Schiller before abandoning the professional stage and marrying a prince. She became one of the highest-paid actresses of her day and very popular with aristocratic men of letters as well as with *audiences. She made a point of observing and then imitating *touring performers, such as Mlle *George. The 'Russian George', as she became known, competed with her rival in 1811 when they found themselves playing the same role in Moscow. Her status as classical tragedienne was affected by the advent of *romantic drama but Pushkin declared that 'When one speaks of Russian *tragedy, one mentions Semyonova—and, perhaps, her alone.'   NW

Senda Koreya (1904–94) Japanese director and actor, born Itō Kunio. His brother Itō Michio (1893–1961) was a famous dancer who began his career performing in *At the Hawk's Well* by *Yeats in 1916. A second brother, Itō Kisaku (1899–1967), was the foremost stage designer of his generation for the modern theatre (*shingeki). Senda joined the Tsukiji Little Theatre as an actor in 1924, then left to pursue his interests in political theatre in Germany from 1927 to 1931. On his return to Tokyo he staged the first Japanese production of *Brecht's *Threepenny Opera* and performed often as an actor, most notably as Hamlet. Imprisoned during the war for his political views, Senda founded a new company, Haiyûza (the Actors' Theatre), in 1945, dedicated to improving the standards of Japanese performance. During his long tenure he mounted memorable productions of Shakespeare, Brecht, *Chekhov, and such Japanese playwrights as *Abe Kōbō. A major figure in post-war Japanese theatre, Senda's high artistic standards and progressive political stance helped define the accomplishments of the entire period.   JTR

Seneca, Lucius Annaeus (5/4 BC–AD 65) Roman philosopher and tragic playwright, who served as a senator under Caligula and Claudius and tutored the future Emperor Nero. During the first years of Nero's reign, Seneca was virtual ruler of Rome, but later, perhaps jealous of Seneca's wealth and prestige, Nero ordered him to commit suicide for allegedly conspiring against his life.

Seneca's nine Latin *tragedies are based loosely on *Greek originals: *Hercules Furens, Hercules Oetaeus, Troades, Phoenissae, Medea, Phaedra, Oedipus, Agamemnon*, and *Thyestes*. A tenth, *Octavia*, based on events in the reign of Nero, is sometimes attributed to Seneca (almost certainly erroneously). It is a matter of debate whether they were written primarily for recitation, or intended to be staged (*see* CLOSET DRAMA). Seneca does not aim at subtle or consistent *character delineation and still less at effective stage *actions, concerned instead with rhetorical impact and the excitement of raw emotion through lurid descriptive passages. The works contain highly effective set speeches, and some stirring *choral odes, as well as numerous examples of precepts and 'lessons' based on Seneca's stoic philosophy. Whatever his effect in ancient Rome, the plays greatly appealed to *early modern playwrights and audiences through their sensational violence and *melodramatic horror, prevalence of *ghosts and black magic, evocation of direst woe and *catastrophe, and recourse to rant and bombast, which excited widespread imitation. His Latin was accessible, and his five-act format easy to emulate.

The first English translation of Seneca appeared in 1559, and the Elizabethan stage was soon strewn with his demons, tyrants, fustian, and corpses. If Senecan *revenge tragedy spawned such offspring as Shakespeare's *Titus Andronicus*, it also deeply influenced *Richard III* and left more than its mark on *Hamlet*, as well as on *Kyd and *Marlowe. In recent years prominent revivals of Seneca have included Ted Hughes's translation of *Oedipus*, staged by *Brook for the *National Theatre at the *Old Vic (1968), with *Gielgud and Irene *Worth in a *total theatre production conceived as a primitive rite. In 1994 *Churchill's translation of *Thyestes* was *toured by the *English Stage Company.   RCB

Şerban, Andrei (1943–   ) Romanian-born director working in the USA. *Fragments of a Trilogy: Medea, Electra*, and *The Trojan Women* (*La Mama, 1974) established him as a leader of the *avant-garde. Controversial classics followed: *Good Woman of Setzuan* (1975); *The Cherry Orchard* (1977); *Ghost Sonata* (1977), and *Happy Days* (1979). In *Sganarelle*, based on *Molière, the director explored a new theatrical language anchored in the musicality of words (1978) by reinventing the tradition of *commedia dell'arte. This led to *Gozzi's fables: *King Stag* (1984) and *The Serpent Woman* (1988), at the *American Repertory Theatre. With *Puccini's *Turandot*, also based on Gozzi (Los Angeles and *Covent Garden, 1984), Şerban scored another international success. These spectacular productions should not overshadow Şerban's chamber theatre: his *Three Sisters* (ART, 1982) stripped *Chekhov's *realism to a haunting memory play.

From 1990 to 1993 he headed the Romanian National Theatre in Bucharest, and he has increasingly turned his attention to *opera: *Glass's *The Juniper Tree* (ART, 1985), *Lucia di Lammermoor* (Chicago, 1990), Strauss's *Elektra* (1991), *Offenbach's *Tales of Hoffmann* (Vienna, 1993), *Khovanshchina* (Paris, 2001). Starting in the late 1980s, a series of radical stagings put Şerban in the forefront of Shakespeare interpreters: *Twelfth Night* (1989), *Cymbeline* (1998), *Hamlet* (1999), *The Merchant of Venice* (*Comédie-Française, 2001), *Richard III* (2001), *Pericles* (2003). He heads the Hammerstein Center for Theatre Studies at Columbia University.   ACH

Serlio, Sebastiano (1475–1554) Italian architect, painter, and theorist. His only known theatrical commission was to build a temporary theatre in Vicenza, probably in 1539. On the theoretical side, however, he became a fundamental source for later historians, on the basis of six chapters of his *Second Book of Architecture* (French translation, 1545; Italian, 1560). His printed designs for three standard stage settings, for *comedy, *pastoral, and *tragedy, are constantly reproduced in modern studies. There was probably little that was innovative in what he proposed: he summarized, at a crucial moment, everything which had been done in classical-style static *scenography, just before the vogue for elaborate machinery and scene changes took over.

Serlio's recommended design for a theatre was based as much as he could manage on interpretations of classical theatre ruins, and on the Roman author Vitruvius. This revival was not fully authentic, because it was adapted to the kinds of indoor space which court and academic theatres used in the early sixteenth century. Raked seats, in semicircle or horseshoe plan, faced a platform stage; seating areas were divided and assigned to different sexes and social classes. The stage itself did not yet involve a genuine *proscenium arch, but nevertheless assumed that scenery should provide *illusionistic *perspective, with a receding panorama painted on a *flat backcloth and practicable buildings at each side. For tragedy, the setting evoked would be palatial and aristocratic; for comedy, urban and domestic; for the new genre of pastoral, rustic and Arcadian.   RAA

Serumaga, Robert (1939–81) Ugandan director, playwright, and novelist. Serumaga read economics at Trinity College, Dublin, and trained with the BBC radio drama department. Informed by *Beckett's theatre of the *absurd and *Stanislavsky's concept of training actors, he returned to Uganda in 1966 and founded the semi-professional Abafumi Players. His published plays, *A Play* (1967), *The Elephants* (1970), and *Majangwa* (1971), follow the absurdist mode but address the political and social disintegration in Uganda under Obote and Amin. With *Renga Moi* (1972) and *Amerykitti* (1974) he created a new style of abstract *dance-drama representing the political atrocities in visual images and movements. Serumaga joined the liberation army that ousted Amin, but died mysteriously in Nairobi.　　EB

Servandoni, Jean-Nicolas (1695–1766) Italian designer. Servandoni worked principally in Paris, where he designed settings for the Opéra from 1726 to 1735, and for his own mute spectaculars at the *Salle des Machines between 1738 and 1758. Reacting against the more painterly style, he introduced into France the full baroque *scenography of Ferdinando *Bibiena's *scena per angolo*: replacing central one-point *perspective settings with oblique and diagonal arrangements of wing-*flats, he sought to create a more three-dimensional stage picture, into which the dramatic *action might be fully integrated.　　JG

set/setting *See* SCENOGRAPHY.

Settle, Elkanah (1648–1724) English playwright. Settle was active in the London theatre for nearly 50 years, producing a score of plays at both *patent theatres, drolls at the fairs, and civic pageants as City Poet. His first success, *The Emperor of Morocco* (1673), provoked a quarrel with *Dryden, a pattern that continued with John Crowne, *Shadwell, and *Otway. Settle's plays were characterized by stage violence, extravagant machine effects, and, in the case of *The Fairy Queen* (1692, with Henry Purcell), spectacular scenes of *music and *dancing. He died a pauper.　　RWV

Sewell, Stephen (1953–) Australian playwright. Sewell's plays are uncompromising Marxist critiques with a broad interest in political, economic, and social life. Grand in style, often requiring large casts, his plays have won much critical acclaim. Nineteen fifties working-class conservatism is examined in *The Father We Loved on a Beach by the Sea* (1977), and *Traitors* (1979) explores human relationships to socio-political processes. While his most ambitious play, *Dreams in an Empty City* (1986), further engages with the relationship of morality to capitalism, later smaller-scale works, such as *The Garden of Granddaughters* (1993), focus on the politics of family relationships. Recent work includes *Three Furies: Scenes From the Life of Francis Bacon* (2005, directed by *Sharman) and *The United States of Nothing* (2005).　　SBS

sex shows and dances *See* PORNOGRAPHY AND PERFORMANCE.

Seyler, Athene (1889–1990) English actress. Seyler's career was primarily in *comedy, at which she excelled—from Shakespeare, *Congreve, and *Wycherley to *Sheridan, *Shaw, and *Wilde. She first demonstrated her skills in Restoration comedy when she played Cynthia in Congreve's *The Double Dealer* (1916). Her Shakespearian roles began in 1920 with Rosalind in *As You Like It*, and over the next four decades she was a beloved comic actress, appearing in Restoration plays and Shakespeare on a regular basis. She also played a few more serious roles, including Emilia in *Othello*, the Nurse in *Romeo and Juliet*, and Madame Ranevskaya in *The Cherry Orchard*. Her last role in 1966 was in *Arsenic and Old Lace*.　　TP

shadow-puppet theatre Performance with light projections of *puppets that ranks in importance with live *acting in parts of Asia. The Indonesian tradition reached Mameluke Egypt by the twelfth century, brought by traders, and shadow theatre subsequently spread through the Ottoman Empire and North Africa. Shadows are often classified separately from puppets because the *audience sees a shadow, not an object. This distinction made performances possible during Lent in nineteenth-century Catalonia, when no other theatre was allowed. If the shadow has no substance, the object that casts it does, and is operated in a manner similar to many rod puppets. Some are highly articulated, some not at all. In Indonesian *wayang kulit, part of the audience is on the same side of the screen as the flat figures employed to project the shadows. In Thailand the large leather *nang talung* figures show complete scenes and are held in front of a screen by dancers. Sometimes a single performer handles a huge number of figures (Indonesia), but the main puppeteer, who generally provides all the speech, may have a number of assistants (Kerala). Musicians vary from a single instrument to an orchestra, and singing may be provided by one of the musicians (*Karagöz) or by the puppeteer himself (as the Indonesian *dalang* does). The screen varies in size and is usually lit from the back by a lamp hung above and behind the performer; the size of the image can be modified according to the proximity of the figure to the light source, a tactic that can give a sense of depth and perspective.

Shadow performance using the hands existed in Europe long before 'Italian' or 'Chinese' shadows with animated silhouette figures became popular through Dominque Séraphim in Paris in 1784. Henri Rivière at the Chat Noir *Cabaret in the same city (1885–97) developed an art shadow theatre involving projected and coloured scenery from two magic lanterns. In the 1970s Gioco Vita (Piacenza) freed shadow theatre from a single fixed screen, introducing a large variety of light sources in *Gilgamesh* (1982).   JMcC

Shadwell, Thomas (*c.*1642–1692) English playwright. Shadwell turned to playwriting in 1668 with *The Sullen Lovers*. Most of the twenty plays that he wrote over the next 23 years were *comedies, and at his best he was able to exploit the titillation of sex and *satirize its participants simultaneously. *The Virtuoso* (1676) is equally mocking of libertinism, romantic love, and science. *The Squire of Alsatia* (1688), which held the stage for 80 years, presents an unsettling reversal of *Terence's *The Brothers* by contrasting the praise of a liberal education with its ambiguous results. Shadwell's *tragedies, a rewriting of *Timon of Athens* (1678) and a Don Juan play, *The Libertine* (1675), are both satirical attacks on the libertine moral code of contemporary comedy. He also tried his hand at *opera with adaptations of *Davenant's *Tempest* (1674) and *Lully's *Psyche* (1675). Shadwell was himself satirized in *Dryden's *MacFlecknoe* (1678), but undoubtedly took some satisfaction in his succession to Dryden as Poet Laureate ten years later.   RWV

Shaffer, Peter (1926–) English dramatist. Shaffer achieved success with *Five Finger Exercise* (1958) and the one-acts *The Private Ear* and *The Public Eye* (1962), but *The Royal Hunt of the Sun* (*National Theatre, 1964) revealed epic qualities. Through its opposition of Atahualpa, Sun King of the Incas, and Pizarro, the Spanish conquistador, it explored the relationship of man and God, a recurrent theme in Shaffer's work. *Black Comedy* (NT, 1965) depended on the simple trick of reversing light and dark, so that a play taking place in pitch blackness is clearly seen by the *audience. *Equus* (NT, 1973) effectively explored issues of faith, belief, and sexuality through the story of a psychiatrist treating a stable boy who has blinded six horses. The theme of man and God resurfaces in *Amadeus* (NT, 1979), which depicts *Mozart through the eyes of his jealous rival Salieri, whose fight with Mozart becomes a fight against God and divine inspiration. Such concerns are echoed in *Yonadab* (1985). *Lettice and Lovage* was staged in 1987. Shaffer has also written for radio and television, and completed several thrillers with his twin brother Anthony (1926–2001).   JTD

Shakespeare, William (1564–1616) English actor, playwright, *manager, poet, and landowner.

Career The most popular and influential dramatist in world history was baptized in provincial Stratford-upon-Avon on 26 April 1564, and it is a mark of his canonization as Britain's national writer that his birthday (which may have been any time over the preceding few days) has been celebrated since the eighteenth century on the feast day of England's patron saint George, 23 April. As the eldest son of a local glover who rose to be alderman and town bailiff, Shakespeare was entitled to be educated at the local grammar school (traces of its standard syllabus in Latin literature and rhetoric are visible throughout his works). Immediately after leaving school he was married at 18 to Anne Hathaway, who was 26 and already pregnant with their daughter Susanna, but at some point after the birth of their twins Judith and Hamnet in 1585 Shakespeare left Stratford to enter the London-based theatrical profession.

Shakespeare probably began his stage career as an actor, but, to judge by the style of his first play, the *Lyly-influenced *The Two Gentlemen of Verona*, he was already writing by the late 1580s. Within a short time the scope and power of Shakespeare's plays about the Wars of the Roses (three parts of *Henry VI*, 1591–2) were unnerving established university-educated playwrights such as *Greene. This first sequence of English chronicle plays (a genre Shakespeare practically invented) culminated in *Richard III* (*c.*1592–3), and by then Shakespeare was not only writing under the influence of his contemporary *Marlowe but was influencing him in turn. Furthermore, the young Shakespeare's ambition extended across history and *tragedy and into one genre Marlowe never touched, *comedy: the assured pursuit of a single theme across the interwoven plots of *The Taming of the Shrew* (*c.*1590–1) marks an immense technical advance on all its English forebears in this mode. This thirst for new artistic territory combined happily with Shakespeare's social aspirations when, during the closure of the theatres by plague in 1593–4, he dedicated two narrative poems to the Earl of Southampton, *Venus and Adonis* and *The Rape of Lucrece*.

After the theatres reopened the dramatist became a member of the *Chamberlain's Men, initially formed to play at Elizabeth's court during the Christmas season of 1594–5 and destined to become the official royal company, the King's Men, on the accession of James I in 1603. Shakespeare would remain with them—as actor, writer, and a managing shareholder—for the rest of his working life, the only contemporary playwright to enjoy so settled a working relationship with a single company (and with particular actors, among them Richard *Burbage, who created many of his leading roles). It was a lucrative arrangement: in 1596 Shakespeare obtained a grant of arms for his father, and in 1597 bought the second-largest house in Stratford.

Shakespeare's *dramaturgy entered a more lyrical phase after the narrative poems, with *The Comedy of Errors* and *Love's Labour's Lost* (*c.*1594–5), and this lyricism found bravura expression in three plays of 1595–6: *Romeo and Juliet*, *Richard II*, and *A Midsummer Night's Dream*. He produced four more chronicles, first *King John* (1596) and then the three plays which extend the story of *Richard II* to make up a second tetralogy depicting the dynastic events which preceded the first, the two parts of *Henry IV* (*c.*1596–8) and their sequel *Henry V* (1599). They are contemporary with four mature romantic comedies, *The Merchant of Venice* (1596–7), *The Merry Wives of Windsor* (1597–8), *Much Ado About Nothing* (1598), and *As You Like It* (1599). By now printers were placing Shakespeare's name on title pages to advertise quarto editions of his plays, and his literary achievements, including his sonnets, were being hymned.

His remaining comedies grow ever more bitter, from the exquisite *Twelfth Night* (1601) to the intellectual 'problem plays' *Measure for Measure* (1603) and *All's Well That Ends Well* (1604–5), which seem deliberately to test how much suffering and moral conflict a comedy can dramatize without renouncing the conventions of the happy ending altogether. But for the best part of a decade most of Shakespeare's energies were devoted to writing tragedy proper. *Julius Caesar* (1599) may have been the first play staged at the *Globe on Bankside, and it would in time be followed by two further dramatizations from Plutarch of the lives of doomed Romans, the expansive *Antony and Cleopatra* (1607) and the concertedly political *Coriolanus* (1608). In between came *Hamlet* (*c.*1600), *Troilus and Cressida* (1602), *Othello* (1603–4), *Timon of Athens* (written with *Middleton around 1605), *King Lear* (1605–6), and *Macbeth* (1606).

By now Shakespeare had apparently given up acting, and investments in land and tithes suggest that he was spending more time in Stratford. His remaining plays look at once to the fashionable present and to the archaic past. *Pericles* (1607–8), probably written with George Wilkins, dramatizes a medieval romance in an affectingly simple mock-medieval style, and its successors, though belonging to the courtly vogue for sophisticated *tragicomedy initiated by Shakespeare's juniors *Beaumont and *Fletcher (and written with the company's new indoor theatre, the *Blackfriars, in mind), also echo much earlier and more naive works in their pursuit of wonderful reconciliations between fathers and daughters, politics, and

magic. *The Winter's Tale* (1609) adapts a twenty-year-old prose romance by Shakespeare's first critic, Greene; *Cymbeline* (1610), a tour de force of multiple narrative, offers an astonishing mix and match of motifs drawn from nearly all of Shakespeare's earlier plays at once; and his last unassisted play, *The Tempest* (1611), achieves a visionary, lyrical fusion of elements drawn from accounts of a contemporary shipwreck in the Bermudas, from Montaigne, from Ovid, and from his own earlier explorations of usurpation and paternity. After these came three collaborations with Fletcher, rapidly replacing him as the King's Men's chief dramatist: an adaptation of a subplot from *Cervantes' newly translated *Don Quixote*, *Cardenio* (1612–13, now lost); the sceptical pageant history *Henry VIII* (1613); and a tragicomedy based on Chaucer's *Knight's Tale*, *The Two Noble Kinsmen* (1613–14).

Shakespeare was in Stratford involved in disputes over land enclosures during the next two years, and on 25 March 1616 he was there altering his will to make it more difficult for his daughter Judith's new husband (convicted of fornication with another woman during their engagement) to gain access to her share of his estate. The signature looks shaky, and only a month intervened before the will was put into effect: the playwright died on 23 April, probably his 52nd birthday.

Theatrical afterlives Shakespeare's unclassical sense of *character, and the increasingly outdated linguistic density of the plays, encouraged later seventeenth-century dramatists such as *Davenant, *Dryden, *Tate, and *Cibber to rewrite Shakespeare's works to make them approximate more closely to *neoclassical notions of the self, of verbal decorum, and of poetic justice—though such adaptations were also shaped by a desire to rewrite female roles written for performance by *boy actors in order to provide greater opportunities for the display of the Restoration theatre's most exciting innovation, the professional actress. Shakespeare's plays remained staples of the London theatre into the 1620s (and would continue to do so to the closing of the playhouses in the 1640s), but after the Restoration, though a handful were revived in their pre-war forms (notably *Hamlet*, *Othello*, and *1 Henry IV*), some of what are now Shakespeare's most valued plays—*The Tempest*, *Macbeth*, *King Lear*—reappeared only in heavily modified versions; *Lear* was supplied by Tate with a happy ending.

Even so, the great Shakespearian tragic roles stayed the touchstones of serious *acting—as with Burbage, so with *Betterton—and their rewritten variants were gradually replaced, as the patriotic celebration of Shakespeare (promulgated in particular by *Garrick) increasingly made adapting the national poet's works seem like a treasonous surrender to French critical dogmas. This British canonization of Shakespeare as solid middle-class antitype to all things French paved the way for his pan-European adoption as the archetypal *romantic artist during the early nineteenth century, when the French translations of *Ducis gave place to those produced by enthusiastically anti-classical Germans such as *Schlegel and *Tieck. In Germany, indeed, Shakespeare was adopted as honorary father of the national theatre, in France, his plays inspired the romantic drama of *Dumas *père*, and in Italy gave rise to the three great Shakespearian *operas of *Verdi (*Macbeth, Otello, Falstaff*).

But in Britain, although a line of heroic actors continued to shine on increasingly elaborate pictorial sets (from *Siddons and the *Kembles to the *Keano, *Macready, *Irving, and *Terry), Shakespeare's influence was often more successfully incorporated in literature than on the stage. The novels of Sir Walter Scott, for example, mediated the social, generic, and linguistic scope of Shakespearian history for the nineteenth century far more effectively than did the sub-Shakespearian verse dramas of *Byron and Tennyson. Byron, indeed, recognized that Shakespeare was 'the worst of models—though the most extraordinary of writers', and it may be that Shakespeare substantially exhausted the particular forms he developed: his influence on subsequent playwrights has been more often (and more safely) registered in pervasive allusion (as in the works of *Chekhov or *Stoppard) than in direct imitation.

A backlash against pictorial *realism in Shakespearian staging at the end of the nineteenth century, led in part by the zealous antiquarian *Poel and his more pragmatic disciple Granville *Barker, coincided with the rise of the individual *director, and opened up Shakespearian performance the world over to the aesthetics of modernism. This movement was comparatively slow to take hold in Britain: through the 1930s and 1940s figures such as *Olivier, *Gielgud, and *Wolfit were still working in modes inherited from the *actor-managers of the Victorian age, and anglophone directors have in any case been held back from some of their continental colleagues' wilder flights by the necessity to work with Shakespeare's now partly archaic language rather than fresh modern translations. In stage design, the Royal Shakespeare Theatre in Stratford (which replaced the original 1879 *Shakespeare Memorial Theatre, and has been the headquarters of the *Royal Shakespeare

Company since 1960) was built with a Victorian-style proscenium arch as recently as 1932 (even though some of the first productions mounted there featured what were then *avant-garde sets by *Komisarjevsky). But elsewhere new theatres were increasingly given open, thrust stages with the non-*illusionistic, *flat-free production of Shakespeare in mind (*Guthrie's experiments at the *Stratford Festival in Ontario in the early 1950s were much imitated), and it would be fair to say that theatregoers arriving to see a new production of a Shakespeare play anywhere have since about 1950 been substantially unable to predict what it will look like. Performances in modern dress, in attempted re-creations of Elizabethan dress, in *costumes chosen from some period in between, in costumes borrowed from other cultures, and in costumes drawn from some eclectic blend of all these are only a few among the many options with which post-war designers have experimented (*see* SCENOGRAPHY).

Just as they have been the obligatory test-cases for every new school of literary criticism since the eighteenth century, so Shakespeare's plays have provided occasions for the development of each successive movement in the modern and postmodern theatre (and, increasingly, film): *Artaud, *Stanislavsky, *Brecht, *Welles, *Brook, *Zeffirelli, *Mnouchkine, *Zadek, *Lepage, *Ninagawa, *Ong, all have had careers shaped to a large extent by their encounters with Shakespeare. To look a little way downmarket, even big-time, large-cast contemporary *musicals owe much of their style at least indirectly to Shakespeare: their baleful progenitor *Les Misérables* (itself based on *Hugo's Shakespeare-influenced novel) was originally produced by the Royal Shakespeare Company (using techniques pioneered in the RSC's stage adaptation of *Dickens's Shakespeare-influenced novel *Nicholas Nickleby*, a show which had itself adapted them from productions of Shakespeare's histories), and the most long-running of them all—*Cats*—was directed by the former RSC *artistic director *Nunn. Highbrow and low, the post-Renaissance theatre has as much evolved around the playing of Shakespeare as life on earth has evolved around the breathing of oxygen. Giving up the former would be almost as difficult—and just as undesirable—as giving up the latter.   MD

Shakespeare Memorial Theatre

Shakespeare Memorial Theatre The first Shakespeare Memorial Theatre, designed by Dodgshun and Unsworth, was completed in 1879, a Victorian extravaganza of mixed Gothic and Tudor styles. It was the first *playhouse in history dedicated to a single dramatist. It burned down in 1926; *Shaw announced that 'Stratford-on-Avon is to be congratulated . . . It is very cheerful news.' The competition for the new theatre was won by Elisabeth Scott, aged only 29; she was the first woman architect to design a major public building in the country. It opened in 1932, to mockery of its exterior (described as 'a jam-factory' and as a crematorium), admiration for its elegant foyer, and anxiety about the relationship of stage to *auditorium. The distance between actors and *audience was difficult: Baliol Holloway commented that 'it is like acting to Calais from the cliffs of Dover', while *Bridges-Adams complained that 'what we eventually got . . . was the theatre . . . in which it is hardest to make an audience laugh or cry'. The original capacity of 1,000 seats was progressively increased by expanding the back of the gallery and adding cantilevered side slips for the gallery and side *boxes in the circle to connect the audience to the stage until, by the 1990s, there were 1,500 places (including standing room). The theatre was renamed the Royal Shakespeare Theatre in 1961 upon the formation of the *Royal Shakespeare Company. There were repeated attempts to remodel the stage to solve the problems and reduce the divisive effect of the *proscenium. With backstage space increasingly cramped, and the need to create more room for the *Swan Theatre (opened in the shell of the Victorian theatre in 1986), the RSC is building a completely new auditorium (seating 1000) with a thrust stage inside the 1932 building, scheduled to open in 2010.   PDH

Shakhovskoy, Prince Aleksandr (1777–1846) Russian dramatist and director. A member of the imperial theatre committee, Shakhovskoy was sent to France in 1802 to study European methods. On his return he became head of a St Petersburg theatre and wrote about 100 plays. His *The New Sterne* (1805), a polemical *comedy aimed at the vogue for sentimentalism, brought him to public notice, as did plays on Russian historical subjects and *vaudevilles with a patriotic slant, such as *Lomonosov; or, The Poet Recruit* (1814) and *The Cossack Poet* (1812). His comedy *A Lesson for Coquettes; or, The Lipetsk Spa* (1815) *satirized Gallomania and romantic poetry. In the 1820s and 1830s he adapted Walter Scott and Shakespeare and wrote plays incorporating songs and *dances, sieges, and conflagrations, suggesting compromise with the popular taste for *romantic subject matter; his *The Bigamous Wife* (1830) is typical. He was a successful teacher, numbering *Semyonova and *Karatygin among his pupils, and wrote articles on the history of Russian theatre.   nw

Shange, Ntozake (Paulette Williams) (1948–) *African-American playwright and novelist. Shange created enormous excitement with her first play, *for colored girls who have considered suicide / when the rainbow is enuf* (1974), a 'choreopoem' which moved from small venues in California to the *New York Shakespeare Festival and Broadway. It greatly moved *audiences with its unconventional language and self-celebratory female postures, and caused a storm cloud of commentary, some of it charging that the play castigated African-American males. *From Okra to Greens* followed in 1978, along with *A Photograph: Lovers in Motion* (the title was revised at least twice) and with *Spell # 7*, another cross-genre choreopoem, this one relying on *dance, *masks, and song. *Boogie Woogie Landscapes* was produced in 1979. She won an Obie in 1982 for her adaptation of *Brecht's *Mother Courage*, and Crossroads Theatre staged *The Love Space Demands* in 1992. To commemorate the twentieth anniversary of *for colored girls*, it was revived in 1994 at a number of theatres across the USA, introducing the work to a new generation of women.   BBL

Sharman, Jim (1945–) Australian director. Sharman's first shows were non-*naturalistic productions at in Sydney. In 1969 his Sydney production of the *musical *Hair* was seen by 1.3 million people, and after the success of his 1972 version of *Jesus Christ Superstar* he went on to direct the première in London (1973), later also mounting David *Williamson's *The Removalists* and *The Rocky Horror Show*. He also directed the cult film of that piece, *The Rocky Horror Picture Show* (1975), for which he is best known. Sharman's *directorial style is big, bold, and very visual. Apart from a dazzling international box-office success in musicals, he was responsible for encouraging Patrick *White back to the theatre. While he ran the Lighthouse Company in Adelaide, Sharman also encouraged the work of director *Armfield and playwrights *Nowra and *Sewell. Sharman wrote and directed *The Burning Piano* (1993), a television tribute to Patrick White. He directed Sewell's *Three Furies: Scenes from the Life of Francis Bacon* (2005).   SBS

Shatrov, Mikhail (Mikhail Marshak) (1932–2010) Soviet/Russian playwright. Shatrov's plays are ideologically challenging and highly theatricalized, using narrators, documents, posters, and a *chorus. Frequently *characters from the present comment about the past in a *Brechtian manner. *The Peace of Brest-Litovsk* (1963, staged 1987) tackled too openly the figures of Bukharin, Trotsky, and Zinoviev and was banned. *Day of Silence, Sixth of July*, and *The Bolsheviks* form Shatrov's Lenin trilogy, staged by *Efremov (1965–6). *Blue Horses on Red Grass* (1979), a play about the Third Youth League Congress, was directed by *Zakharov. During the period of glasnost Shatrov gained major attention with *Thus We Shall Conquer* (1984) and *The Dictatorship of Conscience* (1988). *Dictatorship* draws on non-contemporaries and fictional characters to support Lenin's case, and Zakharov's bold staging brought the director to the forefront of theatre politics. *Onward, Onward, Onward* (1987) was the last of Shatrov's glasnost plays before he turned his attention to the construction of a cultural centre.   BB

Shaw, Fiona (1958–) Irish actress who trained at Royal Academy of Dramatic Art, London. She joined the *National Theatre to play Julia in *Sheridan's *The Rivals*, followed by a four-year stint with the *Royal Shakespeare Company, playing such roles as Celia in *As You Like It* and Kate in *The Taming of the Shrew*. Work with director Deborah *Warner raised much international attention, including lead roles in *Brecht's *Good Person of Setzuan* (1988), *Sophocles' *Electra* (1988), a highly agitated Hedda Gabler (*Abbey Theatre, 1991), a cross-dressed Richard II (1995), a raw and moving Medea (2000), and a hugely entertaining Winnie in *Beckett's *Happy Days* (2007). Her style combines *Method acting with a personal, highly charged emotionalism, which deconstructs and challenges preconceived notions of *character and text. Her extensive film career includes, most famously, Aunt Petunia in the Harry Potter films.   BRS

Shaw, George Bernard (1856–1950) Irish writer and public personality. Born in Dublin into the class he called 'downstarts', downwardly mobile Anglo-Irish Protestants, he never attended university but started work as a clerk at the age of 15. Escaping to London in 1876, he never returned to live in Ireland. A prolonged period of unemployment, self-education, and unsuccessful novel-writing, was ended by work as a journalist, reviewing successively art, books, music, and theatre for London journals and newspapers. A zealous convert to socialism in the 1880s, he became a leading member of the left-wing, middle-class Fabian Society and a well-known lecturer and political publicist.

Shaw came to playwriting in the 1890s as a convinced socialist and a crusader for *avant-garde theatre, both evident in his doctrinaire *Quintessence of Ibsenism* (1891). His first play, *Widowers' Houses* (1892), written for *Grein's *Independent Theatre, was a polemic *Ibsenian problem play, designed to accuse its middle-

class *audience of capitalist complicity in slum-landlordism. Even more scandalous was *Mrs Warren's Profession* (written 1893), exposing the cash–sex nexus of prostitution as the unspeakable counterpart of respectable marriage. *Mrs Warren* was denied a public licence in Britain for over 30 years, and provoked a prosecution for immorality in New York in 1905 (*see* CENSORSHIP). Shaw's technique was to borrow plots, *characters, and situations from the conventional nineteenth-century theatre, which he knew intimately from his experience as a reviewer, and to overturn and subvert all of the audience's expectations. So his *Arms and the Man* (1894) mocked military romance; *Candida* (1897) was a counterpart to *A Doll's House* to show that in the Victorian family it was the male who was the petted doll. *The Devil's Disciple* (1807) was intended as an Adelphi *melo-drama, *You Never Can Tell* (1899) a *farce for the *Haymarket, *Caesar and Cleopatra* (1901) a historical epic for leading actors *Forbes-Robertson and Mrs Patrick *Campbell. But in nearly every case they proved too difficult for contemporary *managements and Shaw was forced to publish two volumes of *Plays Pleasant and Unpleasant* (1898) and *Three Plays for Puritans* (1901) in default of satisfactory productions. His one major success in the nineteenth century was the American staging of *The Devil's Disciple* by the British *actor-manager *Mansfield.

The money made from this production and his marriage in 1898 to the wealthy Irishwoman Charlotte Payne-Townshend enabled Shaw to retire as theatre critic for the *Saturday Review*, a position he held since 1895. (His collected criticism was published as *Our Theatres in the Nineties*, 1930.) Ironically, it was not long after he had completed *Man and Superman* (1903), a 'comedy and a philosophy' intended to be beyond staging, that Shaw found a theatre able to do justice to his work.

The Vedrenne–Barker management at the *Royal Court Theatre (1904–7), and collaboration with Harley Granville *Barker, brought the production of eleven Shaw plays, both new and earlier works, including *John Bull's Other Island* (1904), a *satiric treatment of the 'Irish question'. The Court productions showed that Shaw could grip audiences, especially with *Man and Superman* and *Major Barbara* (1905). Though his discussion plays *Getting Married* (1908) and *Misalliance* (1910) were less well received, Shaw was to achieve great success with *Pygmalion* (1914), written for Mrs Patrick Campbell. The sugar-coated *musical comedy adaptation, *Lerner and Loewe's *My Fair Lady* (1956), went on to make more money for the Shaw estate than all his plays put together.

The First World War brought Shaw intense unpopularity in Britain for his unseasonably cool *Common Sense about the War* (1914) and the disillusionment in *Heartbreak House* (written 1916–17), which indicted the irresponsibility of the intelligentsia that had led to the war. Both *Heartbreak House* (1920) and the immense *Back to Methuselah* (1922), dramatizing Shaw's religion of Creative Evolution, were produced abroad, by the *Theatre Guild in New York. Shaw's theatrical fortunes were again revived by *St Joan* (1923), an enormous success particularly for Sybil *Thorndike, and helped to win Shaw the Nobel Prize for Literature for 1925. In the 25 remaining years of his long life Shaw continued to be immensely productive, with *The Apple Cart* (1929), *Too True to Be Good* (1932), and a dozen further plays, often on political themes with fantastic or futuristic settings. Few of these had commercial success, but the Malvern Festival, founded by Barry *Jackson, provided a dedicated space for Shaw productions in the 1930s.

Shaw, arguably the most important English-language playwright after Shakespeare, produced an immense oeuvre, of which at least half a dozen plays remain part of the world repertoire. In the English-speaking world they are often staged as part of a classic middlebrow repertoire, generally in conservative, period-style productions, and works such as *Heartbreak House* and *St Joan* are periodically revived as star vehicles. The specialist *Shaw Festival in Niagara-on-the-Lake, Ontario, mounts much more imaginative and innovative productions, notably *Misalliance* (1990) and *The Doctor's Dilemma* (2000), both directed by Christopher *Newton. Academically unfashionable, of limited influence even in areas such as Irish drama and British political theatre where influence might be expected, Shaw's unique plays keep escaping from the safely dated category of period piece to which they have often been consigned.   NG

Shaw, Glen Byam (1904–86) English actor and director. His substantial *acting experience, which included Horatio to *Gielgud's Hamlet (1939), rendered him sympathetic but authoritative in his later *directing work. His productions, often designed by *Motley, were clear and unobtrusive, allowing actors space for *characterization. He was co-director of the *Shakespeare Memorial Theatre with *Quayle (1953–6), and then sole director (1956–9) during a phase of glamorous casts and celebrated productions. In 1953 Shaw controversially but successfully cast *Ashcroft against type as the Egyptian Queen in *Antony and Cleopatra*, with Michael *Redgrave as Antony; *Olivier

and *Leigh featured in Shaw's *Macbeth* and also in *Brook's *Titus Andronicus* in 1955. Peter *Hall emerged as Shaw's protégé, succeeding to the directorship in 1960. Shaw's later work in *opera included *The Rake's Progress* (1962) and *The Ring* (1973).   VRS

Shaw Festival Canadian company, founded 1962 in Niagara-on-the-Lake, Ontario, in tribute to George Bernard *Shaw. From small beginnings the Festival evolved into an internationally renowned enterprise featuring an ensemble of 80 actors in three theatres. Offering a season of almost 800 performances to *audiences of over 300,000, the Shaw became adept at interpreting its original classical mandate. Under Andrew Allan (1963–5) and Barry Morse (1966–7) only one of the fourteen plays was outside the Shaw canon. Under Christopher *Newton (1980–2002) the festival took Shaw's lifetime (1856–1950) as the period of its concern, developed a strong ensemble company, and expanded to produce American classic plays, series devoted to *Priestley and Granville *Barker, and the works of Shaw's European contemporaries (*Andreev, *Erdman, *Wedekind, *Witkiewicz). Period *musicals, *farces, and thrillers became a feature of the repertoire, and educational programmes for students and others have been remarkably successful. Jackie Maxwell succeeded Newton as *artistic director in 2002. The 2009 season included *Coward's cycle of ten one-acts, played in *repertory.   MJD

Shawn, Wallace (1943–) American playwright and actor. Shawn won an Obie award for his first play, *Our Late Night* (1975), which was produced by Andre *Gregory's The Manhattan Project. His next play, *A Thought in Three Parts* (1977), created a scandal in London for its graphic sexual depictions. Shawn collaborated with Gregory to create the film *My Dinner with Andre* (1981). The centre of the piece, assembled from actual conversations, is Shawn's sceptical interrogation of Gregory's rationale for leaving the theatre to explore para-theatrical experiments with *Grotowski. Returning to England to work with the *Royal Court, Shawn's writing took a strong political turn in *Aunt Dan and Lemon* (1985), about the legacy of Nazism. The *National Theatre subsequently produced *The Fever* (1991), a single-character play affirming a Marxist critique of Third World poverty, and *The Designated Mourner* (1996), a *monologue-driven play for three actors that explores the failure of democracy in an unspecified South American country. His translation of the *Brecht-*Weill *Threepenny*

Opera played in New York in 2006, and his *Grasses of a Thousand Colours*, directed by Gregory and starring Shawn and Miranda Richardson, was at the Royal Court in 2009. Shawn has also appeared in a number of films. JAB

Shchepkin, Mikhail (1788–1863) Russian actor who introduced *realistic *acting. Rising from the serf theatres, Shchepkin made his debut on the Moscow imperial stage in 1822, proving himself an outstanding and popular actor, becoming close friends with *Pushkin, *Lermontov, *Griboedov, *Gogol, and *Turgenev. Shchepkin's importance lay also in his attitude to the theatre as a serious art form. The examples he set by strict professionalism, attention to detail, *rehearsal procedures, and questions of ensemble and *mise-en-scène were crucial for both playwriting and production. Those who were immediately affected included Turgenev and Gogol; others who inherited his tradition were *Ostrovsky, *Stanislavsky, and *Nemirovich-Danchenko. Belinsky admired his performances, especially as the mayor in Gogol's *The Government Inspector*. His playing in Turgenev's *The Bachelor* (1850) and *The Parasite* (1862) served to establish that writer's reputation as a dramatist, while his own observations on the Russian theatre were, in Stanislavsky's words, those of Russian theatre's 'great legislator'. NW

Sheldon, Edward (1886–1946) American playwright. Sheldon's *Salvation Nell* (1908) was produced soon after Harvard, where he studied playwriting with *Baker. The production, starring Minnie Maddern *Fiske, was admired for its eventful script, convincing *acting, and *naturalistic scenery. Sheldon saw himself as a craftsman more than an artist and sought out subjects likely to become hits. *The Nigger* (1909, about a southern governor who discovers his own black ancestry) and *The Boss* (1911, a labour play) surged with *melodramatic power and controversial *dialogue and *action. *The High Road* (1912) and *Romance* (1913) turned toward more whimsical topics. Stricken by severe arthritis in 1917 and bedridden for the rest of his life, Sheldon was visited regularly by writers and actors as a benevolent sage on *dramaturgical questions. He was credited as co-author with *Howard for *Bewitched* (1924) and with *MacArthur for *Lulu Belle* (1926). MAF

Shelley, Percy Bysshe (1792–1822) English poet, author of four weighty verse dramas, the best known being *The Cenci* (1819). Since this excessively poetic (rather than dramatic) Elizabethan-style *tragedy dealt with a real case of incest and parricide in sixteenth-century Italy, it could not be licensed for performance and was first done privately by the Shelley Society in 1886 (*see* CENSORSHIP). In the twentieth century it was seen with Sybil *Thorndike (1922, 1926) and Barbara *Jefford (1959) as Beatrice. A 1935 version by *Artaud in Paris represented one of his few actual productions. MRB

Shelving, Paul (1888–1968) English designer. After study in fine art and service in the war, he became resident designer and scene painter at the *Birmingham Repertory Theatre under *Jackson, and designed *Shaw's *Back to Methuselah* (1923) and the famous modern-dress Shakespeare productions (1925–8). For a decade from 1929 he was resident designer at the new Malvern Festival with Shaw and Jackson, and after the Second World War he returned to Birmingham for *Man and Superman*, *King John*, and *Ibsen's *Lady from the Sea* with *Brook as director. Shelving's personal signature was simplicity of colour and line, with bold colourful patterns and great attention to ornamental detail. PH

Shen Jing (Shen Ching) (1553–1610) Chinese playwright for *kunqu. Ranked with *Tang Xianzu as a genius of the late Ming dynasty, Shen's reputation subsequently declined because of his formalism. Six of seventeen plays are extant, the most popular of them being *The Altruistic Knight-Errant*, based on the exploits of Wu Song in the novel *Water Margin*. Six of its 36 scenes were performed as highlights throughout the Qing Dynasty. Shen's *Manual of Nine Modes and Thirteen Keys for Southern Drama* codifies 652 tunes for the *kunqu* musical style, responding to and further enabling its emergence as the pre-eminent form, until Beijing opera (*jingju) replaced it in the eighteenth century. Shen's concern with performability distinguished him from contemporary *chuanqi playwrights. He was among the first to write Wu dialect for the *jing* (painted-face actor who depicts *villainous or comical *characters) and *chou* (comic actor who performs using dialect), and featured those roles in playlets that depict inept magistrates, thugs, monks and priests, and merchants. CS

Shepard, Sam (1943–) American playwright, actor, and director. A prominent figure *Off-Off-Broadway in the 1960s, his work is regarded as unmistakably American in its energies, jargons, and pop-culture trappings, yet harbours the existential undertow of *Beckett. Shepard's avalanche of early works exposed the raw patchwork of inner experience at the expense of conventional *character and plot. During this period he met *Chaikin, with whom he would establish a lifelong creative relationship. *The Tooth of Crime* reflects his passion for rock and roll—he wrote the music for its songs—though he disagreed openly with famous productions by *Marowitz (London, 1972) and *Schechner (New York, 1973).

Shepard found an artistic home at San Francisco's Magic Theatre with director Robert Woodruff, where his 'family' plays were produced, beginning with *Curse of the Starving Class* (1977) and *Buried Child* (1978), for which he received the Pulitzer Prize. The honour, along with his debut as a film actor in *Days of Heaven,* swept the fiercely individualistic playwright into the mainstream of American theatre. *True West* (1980) renewed his ascendancy, followed by *Fool for Love* (1983), which earned one of many Obie awards for Shepard as playwright and his first as director. These pieces lay bare dysfunctioning family bonds and the betrayed promises of American myths, drawing on a roughly hewn *realism amid scruffy Western landscapes, hinging on reversible images of the mundane and the apocalyptic. His plays have come sporadically since the mid-1980s. His latter-day cowboy persona has won popularity as a film actor and drawn him closer to the screen as writer and director.   EW

Sher, Antony (1949-) South African actor. After leaving apartheid South Africa, Sher went to drama school in London and worked in *regional repertory companies and on the fringe. His *absurdist *music-hall *clown Fool in *King Lear* (*Royal Shakespeare Company, 1982) and spider-like Richard III (1984) established him as a viscerally exciting and dangerous classical actor, physicalizing *characters in new ways that dominated the stage (often at the expense of other actors). A novelist and painter as well, he documented the experience of playing Richard III in *The Year of the King* (1985). He returned to South Africa to play Titus Andronicus (1995) as a grizzled Boer. Refusing a narrow definition of range, his roles have been deliberately spread wide: Tartuffe and Shylock, *Marlowe's Tamburlaine and *Rostand's Cyrano, the painter Stanley Spencer and the composer Mahler, *Brecht's Arturo Ui and *Stoppard's Henry Carr, and his film career has further expanded his scope. His thorough research work before *rehearsal includes psychological analysis, for example interviewing murderers before playing Macbeth (1999). He was knighted in 2000.   PDH

Sheridan, Richard Brinsley (1751-1816) Irish playwright and *manager, the son of the actor Thomas Sheridan and the novelist and playwright Frances Sheridan. Born in Dublin and educated at Harrow, Sheridan married the singer Elizabeth Linley while they were both minors and fought two duels with a rival suitor on her behalf; throughout his career, Sheridan retained a lively talent for transforming the incidents of his life into the raw material of theatre. His first play was *The Rivals* (1775), a light-hearted *burlesque of sentimental *comedy, set in Bath and featuring the inimitable Mrs Malaprop. *St Patrick's Day* (a *farce) and *The Duenna* (a comic *opera) were performed the same year. In 1776 Sheridan bought *Garrick's half-share in *Drury Lane. The theatre's *finances were already in disarray; Sheridan's reckless extravagance further exacerbated the situation.

Sheridan created sparkling dramas which combined the *stock characters and conventions of Restoration comedy with topical humour and moral *satire. In 1777 he produced *A Trip to Scarborough,* a moralized adaptation of *Vanbrugh's *The Relapse,* and later that year *The School for Scandal.* Witty repartee and a colourful cast of scandalmongers created one of the most enduring and cherished plays in the history of British comedy. This success was followed by a topical entertainment entitled *The Camp* (1778), and *The Critic* (1779), an afterpiece satirizing contemporary drama.

In 1780 Sheridan became a Member of Parliament and combined his theatrical career with the drama of politics. He was appointed Secretary to the Treasury in 1783 and played an important role in the impeachment of Warren Hastings for his maladministration as governor-general of India. Sheridan's intense opposition to colonial tyranny also provided the inspiration for *Pizarro,* his controversial adaptation of *Kotzebue's play about the Spanish conqueror of Peru, starring John Philip *Kemble as Rolla. Between 1791 and 1794 Sheridan presided over the demolition of Wren's Drury Lane, and its replacement by a huge and luxurious new theatre designed by Henry Holland. But after Drury Lane was destroyed by fire in 1809 Samuel Whitbread barred Sheridan from the management; the playwright lost his parliamentary seat in 1811 and was arrested for debt two years later. He was buried close to Garrick in Westminster Abbey.   JM

Sherriff, R. C. (Robert Cedric) (1896-1975) English playwright and screenwriter. Sherriff began writing for an amateur company but his seventh play, *Journey's End* (1928), propelled him into professional theatre. The script had been turned down by every *management in London, who believed that its subject matter, the behaviour of a group of soldiers in a dugout trench towards the end of the First World War, was inherently uncommercial. Produced by the *Stage Society for two nights, with *Olivier in lead, a hit production soon followed, inspiring a revival of serious dramatic writing about the war. Sherriff never repeated this success, though his well-crafted thrillers *Miss Mabel* (1948), *Home at Seven* (1950), and *The White Carnation* (1953) chimed with the mood of post-war *audiences. After the rise of *Osborne and the *Royal Court, Sherriff's last play, *A Shred of Evidence* (1960), was denounced by the critics as from a time gone by.   DR

Sherwood, Robert E. (1896–1955) American playwright. *Reunion in Vienna* (1931), a *comedy about the lost world of pre-war Europe written for the *Lunts, was a major success and established Sherwood as a mainstay of the *Theatre Guild. *The Petrified Forest* (1935), starring Humphrey Bogart as a desperate killer and Leslie Howard as a spiritually exhausted poet, is a parable about civilization's self hatred and desire for destruction by brutes (filmed the next year with the same actors). *Idiot's Delight* (1936) is a complex mixture of *comedy, *musical, and drama and ends with an imagined beginning of the Second World War. *Abe Lincoln in Illinois* (1938) chronicles Lincoln's transition from innocent idealist to practical man of action. *There Shall Be No Night* (1940) uses the Soviet invasion of Finland as the setting for a didactic drama on the necessity of fighting against totalitarian expansion. Sherwood served as speech writer for Franklin Roosevelt during the war and later won his fourth Pulitzer Prize for his book *Roosevelt and Hopkins* (1948). He won an Academy award for his script of *The Best Years of our Lives* (1946).   MAF

Shiels, George (1886–1949) Irish dramatist. Paralysed in a railway accident in Canada, Shiels returned to Ireland in 1913, and settled into life in a wheelchair. He became a mainstay of the *Abbey Theatre between 1921 and 1948, writing two dozen popular *comedies. Despite his personal difficulties, his plays are mostly light-hearted, teasing the Irish with a constrained *satire. His popular work includes *Paul Twyning* (1922), *Professor Tim* (1925), *The New Gossoon* (1930), *The Passing Day* (1936), and *Tenants at Will* (1945). In a more serious mode, *The Rugged Path* (1940) and *The Summit* (1941) reveal a darker critique of Irish self-deceptions.   TP

Shimizu Kunio (1936–   ) Japanese playwright. Shimizu began as a student radical during the 1960s, working closely with the young director *Ninagawa. After graduation Shimizu wrote for the small *avant garde companies that prolifer-

ated in Tokyo, his greatest early success being *The Dressing Room* (1977), a *metatheatrical piece mixing *Chekhov with contemporary Japanese politics. Among his later works are *Older Sister Burning Like a Flame* (1978), in which a Shakespearian actor from Tokyo falls prey to dark forces in his past, and a second play about memory and the theatre, *Tango at the End of Winter* (1984), successfully produced in London in 1991 with a British cast, directed by Ninagawa. Unlike some of his contemporaries, Shimizu continues to place the text at the centre of theatre. His plays are among the most eloquent and unsettling written in contemporary Japan.   JTR

shimpa The first Japanese modern theatre. *Shimpa* (new school) set itself as distinct from the 'old school', *kabuki. The fathers of *shimpa*, Sudō Sadanori (1867–1907) and Kawakami Otojirō (1864–1911), began as political activists for democratic rights in the 1880s using theatre as *agitprop, but as *shimpa* became more professional its political message waned. By the 1890s Kawakami had created a popular repertory based largely on sensational treatments of news items like the Sino-Japanese War or adaptations of melodramatic novels by writers like *Izumi. Kawakami and his wife, Sadayakko (1872–1946) were the most colourful and enterprising figures in early twentieth-century Japanese theatre. On their American and European *tours, Sadayakko (Japan's first modern professional actress) was compared favourably to *Duse and *Bernhardt. With their pastiches of kabuki, the troupe pandered to Western *audiences hungry for *Japonisme*, but introduced Western scenic and *lighting effects to Japan, as well as plays by Shakespeare, *Maeterlinck, and *Sardou. By 1910 *shimpa*'s melodramatic repertory and reliance on kabuki-esque conventions made it fall increasingly out of favour with reformers like *Osanai, though it remained popular thanks to the work of *onnagata like Kitamura Rokurō (1871–1961) and Hanayagi Shōtarō (1894–1965), and actresses like Mizutani Yaeko (1905–79). *Shimpa* celebrated its 100th anniversary in 1988 to sold-out houses, indicating that there was still a place for good *melodrama. Newer plays by *shingeki (new theatre) writers like *Inoue, and guest appearances by kabuki stars like *Bandō Tamasaburō V, have helped keep *shimpa* alive, but it suffers from a lack of fresh material and good acting.   CP

shingeki 'New theatre', the leading movement in modern Japanese theatre until the 1960s. For much of the twentieth century the modernization of theatre in Japan meant westernization, a project that created its own contradictions. In its attempt to emulate European stagecraft, *acting, repertory, and *dramaturgy, *shingeki* rejected traditional Japanese theatre, especially *kabuki. Where traditional theatre focused on the sensual qualities of a performance (including *music and the physical appeal of the actor), *shingeki* appealed to the *audience's intellect; spoken drama thus came to replace music and *dance. Kabuki's presentational style of acting was abandoned in favour of greater *realism; at the same time, innovations in theatre architecture, such as the *proscenium arch, helped create the *illusion of a fourth wall between actors and audience. Japanese theatre was slow to modernize, in large part because of the popularity and technical brilliance of kabuki, which as late as the 1890s still boasted excellent actors and playwrights. By the beginning of the twentieth century it was clear that kabuki had become impervious to change. 'New' became the buzzword, but *shimpa* (new school), *shin-kabuki* (new kabuki), and *shinkokugeki* (new national theatre) retained many kabuki conventions like the *hanamichi* runway and the female impersonator (*onnagata*).

In Japan the *director was promoted before a dramatic literature could develop fully. Both *Tsubouchi and *Osanai attempted to introduce Western plays, staging, and acting techniques, and to raise literary standards, but these were not easy tasks. Tsubouchi founded the Literary Society (Bungei Kyōkai) in Tokyo in 1906 to train amateur actors and stage European works; Osanai established the Free Theatre (Jiyū Gekijō), modelled after *Antoine's Théâtre *Libre, in 1909. Their productions of European drama had enormous impact. The repertoire was eclectic, reflecting changes in contemporary European theatre: Shakespeare, *Ibsen, *Chekhov, and *Gorky were favourites, but productions of *Hauptmann, *Maeterlinck, *Strindberg, and *Wedekind also excited debate. Though the Free Theatre staged original Japanese drama, translated plays continued to dominate *shingeki* until well into the 1930s. The Literary Society disbanded in 1913, and after the closing of Osanai's Free Theatre in 1919, there were practically no attempts at collaboration between the traditional and modern theatres again until the 1960s.

In 1924 Osanai joined with *Hijikata to open the state-of-the-art Tsukiji Little Theatre. Osanai idolized *Stanislavsky, but Hijikata's models were *Piscator, *Reinhardt, and *Meyerhold; their tastes indicated the polarization between apolitical *naturalism and leftist *expressionism that was to last in *shingeki* until the 1960s. The TLT became

a fertile training ground for actors and directors like *Senda, but Osanai's reluctance to stage Japanese plays was a blow to native playwrights. After his untimely death in 1928, the TLT split into two camps. The leftists, led by Hijikata, spawned one of the major works of *socialist realism in Japan, *Kubo's *Land of Volcanic Ash* (1937). The Literary Theatre (Bungakuza), organized around playwrights like *Kishida, concerned itself with purely aesthetic criteria and with the development of a Japanese repertory. Proletarian theatre flourished before the war until it was crushed by the militarists. The Literary Theatre fared better, in part due to Kishida's collaboration with the authorities; it was one of the few theatres allowed to perform throughout the Second World War.

Two leftist *shingeki* troupes emerged soon after the war, the Mingei (People's Theatre) founded by Kubo, and the Haiyūza (Actors' Theatre) led by Senda. The Rōen (Workers' Council on Theatre), founded in the 1950s by progressive labour unions, ensured large audiences for *shingeki* troupes through its sales of subscription tickets. American and European drama dominated the post-war Japanese stage, with Senda responsible for the interest in *Brecht. Several excellent Japanese playwrights appeared, however, including Tanaka and *Kinoshita. Two prominent novelists, *Abe and *Mishima, also distinguished themselves in the 1950s as *shingeki* playwrights; their works were among the first to be translated from post-war Japanese drama. By the 1960s, however, the rise of *absurdism, the discrediting of the Stalinist Old Left, and the quest for more native sources of theatrical inspiration led to the demise of *shingeki*'s artistic and political dominance over modern Japanese theatre. *See also* ANGURA.   CP

Shipenko, Aleksei (1961–) Soviet/Russian playwright, almost a classic among contemporary Russian dramatists, though he moved to Berlin in 1992. *The Observer* (1984) was an anthology of rock music in the Soviet Union, and *Van Halen's Death* (1987), also dealing with rock culture, was still in several theatre repertoires in 2000. *Natural Housekeeping in Shambale* (1989) explores a journey into the other world, reflecting Shipenko's preoccupation with archaic and Eastern culture, staged by both the Formal Theatre (St Petersburg) and Omsk Drama Theatre. Other plays include two from 1988, *Archeology* and *La Funf in der Luft* (a macaronic nonsense phrase muttered by the *protagonist, more or less meaning 'la five in the sky'.   BB

Shirley, James (1596–1666) English playwright, headmaster of St Albans grammar school before turning to the theatre in 1623. He was resident dramatist for the Queen's Men (1625–36), then moved to Dublin, where he helped established the first Irish *playhouse, the Werburgh Street Theatre. Upon return to London in 1640 he became attached to the King's Men (*see* CHAMBERLAIN'S MEN, LORD). After the Civil War (he took the royalist side) he went back to teaching, setting up a school and publishing a Latin grammar. Among Shirley's best-known works are *Hyde Park* (1632) and *The Lady of Pleasure* (1635), witty *comedies of London life which foreshadow the drama of the Restoration, albeit displaying a much stricter moral strain. *The Cardinal* (1641) is a *revenge tragedy on religious dissention. He also wrote *tragicomedies and romantic comedies, and *The Triumph of Peace*, a *masque presented to Charles I in 1634. Of the handful of plays he wrote for Dublin, *St Patrick for Ireland* (1639) deserves special mention as an example of English colonialist propaganda thinly disguised as a tribute to Irish folklore.   PCR

shite See NŌ; KYŌGEN.

Shubert brothers American *managers, *producers, and theatre owners. **Lee** (1873–1953), **Sam S.** (1876–1905), and **J. J.** ('Jake') (1878–1963), born in Lithuania, were raised in Syracuse, New York. After gaining control over the Syracuse theatre, the trio moved to Broadway. Between the time of their finest regular production, *The Brixton Burglary* (1901), at the Herald Square Theatre, and their final production before Lee's death, *The Starcross Story* (1954), they produced over 520 shows, mostly ephemera aimed at escape-hungry *audiences. At one point, they controlled the booking in more than 1,000 national theatres, and owned 31 Broadway theatres, 63 elsewhere in America, and held part ownership in five London theatres. They possessed a huge stock of *costumes and scenery, and had numerous designers, writers, and performers under contract.

After Sam's early death in a train crash his brothers divided the firm's many responsibilities and in 1916 successfully defeated the *Theatrical Syndicate for control of the American theatre. They fought often with the press, even barring certain critics from productions. Notoriously secretive, penny-pinching, and humourless, the Shuberts engaged in ruthless, even devious business methods, which helped them to overcome bankruptcy during the Depression. Eventually they were responsible for almost one-quarter of all Broadway productions and two-thirds of all ticket sales. In 1956 the Supreme Court found the firm guilty of monopolistic practices and

forced divestiture of various holdings and the abandonment of its booking business.   SLL

Sichuan opera See DIFANGXI.

Siddons, Sarah (1755–1831) English actress. The eldest daughter of Roger *Kemble, she made an early marriage while working in her family troupe. A first London debut failed, but a second, in 1782, was a triumph. For the next 30 years Siddons was regarded as the leading tragic performer of her time. She specialized in roles which required tenderness, sorrow, indignation, remorse, resolution, and heroic dignity. When young she was acclaimed for her beauty and in later years her impressiveness was not diminished. Her famous roles included Isabella in *Southerne's *The Fatal Marriage*, Belvidera in *Otway's *Venice Preserv'd*, Euphrasia in *Murphy's *The Grecian Daughter*, Zara in *Congreve's *The Mourning Bride*, Calista in *Rowe's *The Fair Penitent*, and the title role in his *Jane Shore*. Her greatest Shakespearian *characters were Constance, Lady Macbeth, Volumnia, and Queen Katherine. In many of these roles she was partnered by her brother John Philip *Kemble. Her private life was at times unhappy but her public life was conducted with intelligence and propriety. She loved her profession and retired from it with reluctance, causing a good deal of mirth by the number of her farewells.   FD

Sierra, Gregorio Martínez See MARTÍNEZ SIERRA, GREGORIO.

Sieveking, Alejandro (1935–) Chilean playwright, actor, and director. His first plays were psychological in nature, such as *My Brother Christian* (1957) and *The Stepbrothers* (1960). Thereafter he turned to Chilean tradition, myths, and folklore, and avoided the conventions of *naturalism. In this category are *Spirits by Daylight* (1962) and the well-received *melodrama *The Rave* (1965). *Everything Will Go, Has Gone, Is Going to the Dogs* (1968), an incisive *satire of the upper middle class, was hailed by the critics for its original stage setting. He and the Teatro del Ángel, a group he created with his wife Bélgica Castro, remained in political exile in Costa Rica from 1974 to 1984.   MAR

Silva, António José da (1705–39) Portuguese playwright. Born in Rio de Janeiro, he grew up and studied in Lisbon during the heyday of the Portuguese baroque. Known as the Jew (he was a 'New Christian' through enforced conversion), his was a short literary career: imprisoned in 1726, he suffered with his family from the Inquisition and was burned at the stake (*see* EXECUTIONS,

PUBLIC). Between 1733 and 1738 he wrote eight *tragicomic *operas: *Don Quixote*, *The Life of Aesop*, *The Wars between Rosemary and Marjoram*, *Medea's Charms*, *Metamorphoses of Proteus*, *Phaeton's Fall*, *Amphitryon*, and *Crete's Labyrinth*. A high point in the history of Portuguese playwriting, his work is the national model of *neoclassical drama, resulting from a cross-fertilization of Spanish and Italian influences, appropriating themes with wide European currency. He combined borrowed motifs with topical references to Portuguese culture and society that could easily be grasped by the popular *audiences at the theatre in Bairro Alto, where his plays were performed by *puppets (*bonifrates*). His work was rediscovered in the early twentieth century, though infrequently performed until the 1960s.   JOB

Sim, Alastair (1900–76) Scottish actor and director. His eccentric and sometimes lugubrious style, mixing pathos and irony with subtlety and assurance, was particularly suited to *Bridie's morally ambiguous *characters such as the eponymous *Dr Angelus* (1947). Beginning his career as late as 1930, he progressed swiftly to Banquo in 1932 and two seasons with the *Old Vic in London. In parallel with his film career he was a West End regular, making frequent appearances as Hook in *Peter Pan*, where his ability to convey irascible foolishness, bemused humiliation, and wheedling and malicious *villainy was particularly appropriate. Later in life he appeared in critically acclaimed seasons at *Chichester. His film roles include Inspector Cockerill in *Green for Danger* (1946), the headmaster pitched against Margaret Rutherford in *The Happiest Days of your Life* (1950), Scrooge in *A Christmas Carol* (1951), and Miss Fritton in *The Belles of St Trinian's* (1954).   AS

Simon, Barney (1933–95) South African director and playwright. In the 1970s Simon worked in Zululand and the Transkei running workshops. With Mannie Manim he formed the Company and the Market Theatre, which opened in 1976 with Simon as *artistic director. Shaped by the workshop process, his collaborative plays include *Hey Listen!* (1974, adapted from his *Jo'burg, Sis!* stories), *Cincinnati* (1979), *Woza Albert!* (1981, with Percy Mtwa and *Ngema), *Black Dog/Inj'emnyama* (1984), *Outers* (1985), *Born in the RSA* (1985), *Score Me the Ages* (1989), and *Silent Movie* (1992). Influenced by *Littlewood, *Fugard, and his own experiences in America in the 1960s, Simon's plays focus on the experience of the individual and the restoration of dignity for those on the social margins.   YH

Simon, Neil (1927–) American playwright and screenwriter, one of the most successful playwrights of all time. Until his autobiographical trilogy (*Brighton Beach Memoirs*, 1983; *Biloxi Blues*, 1985, film, 1988; *Broadway Bound*, 1986) critics often dismissed his plays as glib domestic *comedies that substituted one-liners for *character development. *Lost in Yonkers* (1991), dealing with abandonment as well as love, proved Simon could use his comic sensibility to serve a painful story as well as smooth it out.

Simon began his career as part of a comedy-writing team with his brother Danny for several television *variety shows, experiences that encouraged quick gags and stock situations. His first Broadway play, with brother Danny, was *Catch a Star!* (1955), and *Come Blow your Horn* (1961) was his first original Broadway play. *Barefoot in the Park* (1964; film, 1967), about a newly-wed free spirit and her conservative husband, typifies Simon's motifs of attraction and compromise, as well as quirky characters and New York settings. *The Odd Couple* (1965), about two divorced men attempting to room together, was later filmed (1968) and became a long-running television series. Other hits include *Plaza Suite* (1968; film, 1971), *The Prisoner of Second Avenue* (1972; film, 1974), and *The Sunshine Boys* (1972; film, 1975). Simon also wrote the books for *Sweet Charity* (1966) and *Promises, Promises* (1967).

The death of his first wife in 1973 led to attention to serious issues. *The Gingerbread Lady* (1970) had portrayed an alcoholic actress, but it was *Chapter Two* (1977; film, 1978), about a widower's sudden remarriage, based on his own remarriage to actress Marsha Mason, that impressed critics as an honest exploration of pain. Mason starred in that and many other of his works, including the film *The Goodbye Girl* (1977). Simon increasingly experimented with darker themes: *Jake's Women* (1992) attempts *surreal stream-of-consciousness; *Laughter on the 23rd Floor* (1993), recalling his days writing for Sid Caesar, is a comedy addressing McCarthyism. *Proposals* (1997) is a nostalgic romance narrated by a black maid, while *The Dinner Party* (2000) is an attempt at a *farce that turns serious. Winner of numerous awards, in 1983 he became the only living playwright with a New York theatre named after him.   GAO

Simonson, Lee (1888–1967) American designer. After studying with *Baker at Harvard, Simonson's first professional set designs were for the *Washington Square Players. After service in the First World War, he helped found and direct the *Theatre Guild, for which he created many of the most important designs of the 1920s, including *RUR* (1922), *Peer Gynt* (1923), *The Adding Machine* (1923), *Marco Millions* (1928), *Roar China* (1930), and *Dynamo* (1930). He also designed for *opera, including *Wagner's *Ring* and Stravinsky's *Le Pas d'acier* at the Metropolitan Opera in the 1940s. Simonson garnered early praise for his range of styles from *realism and *naturalism to *expressionism and *constructivism. Often compared with Robert Edmond *Jones, Simonson clarified his own vision for *scenography in a number of books. *The Stage Is Set* (1932) distanced him from *Craig while championing many practical applications of modernist design. He also wrote an influential primer entitled *The Art of Scene Design* (1950).   JAB

Simov, Viktor (1858–1935) Russian designer. Simov worked as an artist and architect and designed sets for the Society for Art and Literature before joining the *Moscow Art Theatre at its inception in 1898. He remained chief designer until 1912, when he joined the Svobodny (Free) Theatre set up by *Mardzhanov, but returned to MAT in 1925 and remained until his death. Simov was responsible for the designs of many key MAT productions such as *Tolstoy's *Tsar Fyodor Ioannovich* (1898) and the four groundbreaking *Chekhov productions (1898–1904). Working closely with *Stanislavsky, he initiated the practice of field research, visiting a Moscow doss-house for *Gorky's *The Lower Depths* (1902) and Rome for *Julius Caesar* (1903). Simov brought three-dimensional *realism and historical and location accuracy to Russian stage design, contributing much to the MAT reputation for authenticity.   CM

sinakulo A theatrical rendition of the life, death, and resurrection of Jesus Christ performed annually during Holy Week in lowland Philippines, especially in provinces around Manila, and (under alternative names) in the region of Bicol, the town of Iloilo, and the island of Leyte. Traditional *sinakulo* is staged over eight nights (Palm Sunday to Easter Sunday). Abridged versions, which start in the Garden of Gethsemane and culminate with the Crucifixion, take place on Good Friday, often in a church plaza. Stylized forms of chanting, marching, and *acting distinguish holy *characters (*banal*), notably Jesus and the Virgin Mary, from the evil *hudyo* (soldiers) and *hari* (Herod, Pilate). Participation in the *sinakulo* is a form of religious devotion and sacrifice, involving a vow (*panata*), pledged as supplication or thanksgiving. The first *sinakulo* followed publication in 1704 of the *pasyon*, a vernacular narrative in verse of the life of Christ by Gaspar Aquino

de Belen, although a revised version, the *Pasyong Genesis* (1814), proved more influential. The traditional *Passion play declined after independence in 1946, but successfully evolved in the last two decades of the twentieth century. The inclusion of corporeal self-mortification (*ritual self-flagellation and crucifixion) both attracted and distracted *audiences, while in Manila political *sinakulos* emerged as a form of social activism.   NHB

Sinden, Donald (1923–) English actor, celebrated and *parodied in equal measure for his distinctive plummy vocal quality. He joined the *Shakespeare Memorial Theatre company in 1946, was later with the Bristol Old Vic and from 1963 the *Royal Shakespeare Company. An assured and sophisticated actor, Sinden has been particularly successful in high *comedy: he was a definitive Lord Foppington in *The Relapse* (1967) and Sir Peter Teazle in *The School for Scandal* (1983). His darker roles include Romeo (1947), and for the RSC, Richard Plantagenet in *The Wars of the Roses* (1963), Malvolio in *Twelfth Night* (1969), Lear (1977), and Othello (1979). In the modern repertoire he appeared at *Chichester in *Rattigan's *In Praise of Love* (1973), Stockman in *Ibsen's *An Enemy of the People* (1975), and the Duke of Altair in *Fry's *Venus Observed* (1992). More recently he was with Peter *Hall's company in *She Stoops to Conquer* (1993) and *Hamlet* (1998) and in the première of *Harwood's elegy on ageing, *Quartet* (1999).   AS

Singspiel 'Song play', a popular form of *musical drama in the second half of the eighteenth century in Germany, is distinguished from *opera, mainly because the *dialogue is spoken not sung. *Singspiele* have a light touch, tuneful songs, often about love, in a bucolic or magic setting. *Goethe wrote a number of them, staged by the amateur theatre at the *Weimar court, sometimes in the open air. The highest achievements of the genre were *Mozart's *Abduction from the Seraglio* (1782) and *The Magic Flute* (1791). The nineteenth-century *operetta and *mélodrame* reveal the influence of the *Singspiel*.   MWP

Sircar, Badal (1925–) Bengali director, dramatist, and actor. Trained as a civil engineer, in 1962 he composed the *absurdist *Evam Indrajit*, about identity and conformity in the metropolitan jungle; published and staged in 1965, it created a sensation across India and was translated into many Indian languages. Meanwhile Sircar had gone on official work to Nigeria (1964–7), where he wrote a string of plays, including *Remaining*

History, Thirtieth Century, and *Mad Horse*, which highlight existential meaninglessness. On returning to Calcutta he started the group Satabdi, and soon was experimenting with a form of theatre-in-the-round which he called 'Third Theatre'—as opposed to the urban and rural varieties. In 1973 he finally rejected the *proscenium, dramatizing Howard Fast's novel *Spartacus* in a bare room with the *audience seated in clusters on the floor. His original scripts for this flexible theatre included *Procession* (1974), *Bhoma* (1976), and *Stale News* (1979). His plays are characterized by socially conscious themes, a wry sense of humour, pithy *dialogue, and simple, direct language which attains an aphoristic, even poetic quality. In 1977 Sircar devoted himself entirely to theatre and to writing *The Third Theatre* (1978), which created many disciples all over India. AL

Sissle, Noble *See* BLAKE, EUBIE.

site-specific performance *See* ENVIRON-MENTAL THEATRE.

Sjöberg, Alf (1903–80) Swedish actor and director. Despite numerous international offers, Sjöberg rarely worked outside the Royal Dramatic Theatre in Stockholm. In his more than 50-year tenure at *Dramaten, he was lauded for visually evocative productions of *Ibsen, *Strindberg, and contemporary writers, and his innovative modern Shakespeare productions created a new tradition for playing the classics. His *directing was always vital, often poetic, and frequently committed to social issues. Sjöberg strove to balance a keen inner *realism with a richer outer visual image. He introduced the contemporary international repertory to Sweden, foremost the work of *Brecht and *Sartre, but extending to new writers from South Africa, Latin America, and Eastern Europe. His film version of Strindberg's *Miss Julie* won a Palme d'Or at Cannes in 1951. DLF

Skelton, John (*c*.1464–1529) English poet and dramatist. Skelton's only drama, *Magnificence* (1515–16), is a *morality play in which the allegorized Magnificence is brought to ruin and despair through the advice of evil counsellors, but is ultimately restored to a wiser though less opulent happiness by good counsellors. The language is commendable; the characterization, structure, and thematic focus less so. *Magnificence* seems to reflect the necessity of doubling (the eighteen *characters could be played by five actors), and there are over 50 stage directions in English and Latin; but we know nothing of an original performance. RWV

skene Originally Greek 'hut', meaning the simple building before which ancient *Greek drama was performed. The early addition of a *proskenion*, the low construction supporting the stage 'before the hut', and accessible by a short wooden stair from the orchestra, created a true stage building. The classical theatre of 400 BC (Theatre of *Dionysus) could use the roof as well as the stage and orchestra levels simultaneously with machinery (especially the *ekkyklema and *mechane* or crane), and had the capacity to simulate effects such as fire and thunder. Though one door was perhaps usual, it could be converted quickly to a cave and other doors or windows could be created if required. Projecting wings enclosing the stage, found after 330 BC, are thus *paraskenia* ('things beside the *skene*') even though they may be only access doorways. About 300 BC the classical stage proper was raised to *c*. 2.5 m (8 feet), with access from below only from the sides, and a *proskenion* was thereby created with a pillared façade into which flats (*pinakes*) were fitted. This required that the entire building then be raised to two storeys, with the upper façade also consisting of pillared openings with *paraskenia*. The term *skene* (Latin *scaena*) never applied to the seating area. *See* PLAYHOUSE. WJS

Skinner, Cornelia Otis (1901–79) American actress and playwright. The daughter of actors Maud and Otis *Skinner, she was best known for the one-person evenings of *character sketches and *monologues which she created and performed in New York, London, and on *tour between 1925 and 1961. Of her plays, *The Pleasure of his Company* (with Samuel Taylor, 1958) was most successful, and her memoir, *Our Hearts Were Young and Gay* (1942), became a popular 1944 film. Among her one-woman creations were *The Wives of Henry VIII* (1931), *The Loves of Charles II* (1933), *Mansion on the Hudson* (1935), and *Paris '90* (1952). Also a respected character actress, Skinner appeared in Broadway productions which included *Hellman's *The Searching Wind* (1944), *Wilde's *Lady Windermere's Fan* (1946), and as Lady Britomart in *Shaw's *Major Barbara* (1956). MAF

Skinner, Otis (1858–1942) American actor. He gained his early experience with a Philadelphia troupe in which he played 92 roles in his first season (1877–8). Following his New York debut in 1879, he had important supporting roles with major companies, eventually heading his own *touring troupe from 1894. A rather flamboyant actor, he scored a success with the blustering ex-soldier in *The Honor of the Family* (1908), and his greatest triumph as the beggar Hajj in *Kismet* (1911), which he played for four years. After some 325 roles, his Broadway valedictory came in *A Hundred Years Old* (1929). His daughter was Cornelia Otis *Skinner.   CT

Slabolepszy, Paul (1948–   ) South African actor and playwright, who founded the Space Theatre in 1972 with *Fugard, *Bryceland, and her husband Brian Astbury. Later he joined the Company at the Market Theatre in Johannesburg. His plays include *Saturday Night at the Palace* (1982), *Over the Hill* (1985), *Boo to the Moon* (1987), *Fordsburg's Finest* (1988), *Smallholding* (1989), *Mooi Street Moves* (1992), *The Return of Elvis du Pisanie* (1992, which won more awards than any other production in the history of South African theatre), *Victoria Almost Falls* (1994), and *Life's a Pitch* (2001). His work focuses on the dreams, unease, and insularity of the lower-middle-class white male in South Africa.   YH

slapstick Literally a prop paddle used for meting out punishment in *music hall or *vaudeville, but more generally a term embracing exaggerated or knockabout comedy and its stylistic features. The slapstick derives from Arlecchino's *batocchio* and *Harlequin's *batte* in *commedia dell'arte*. Its two slats of wood hinged together at one end make a sharp crack upon contact with, for example, a victim's posterior. The brand of physical, comic extravagance conjured by the slapstick label can be traced to ancient western *comedy and seen in other cultures—for example, a comparable comic weapon is described in accounts of thirteenth-century Chinese variety plays (*zaju).   EW

Slavkin, Viktor (1935–   ) Soviet/Russian playwright. Slavkin's plays offered genuinely new themes (the subculture of stagnation) in a collage of various sources new to the theatre. *A Young Man's Grown-up Daughter* (1979) deals with the meeting of old university friends, who were once jazz fans and 'teddy boys'. *Cerceau* (1985) uses a collage of texts to treat the midlife crisis of a group of 40-year-olds, who lead lives of tragic isolation and cannot share feelings. At the end they see a glimpse of hope in the possibility of living together, yet at this point they all leave.   BB

Słowacki, Juliusz (1809–49) Polish poet and playwright. Like *Mickiewicz, Słowacki eventually settled in Paris. He wrote some fifteen plays indebted to Shakespeare and the *romantic movement, with subjects that range from legendary Poland (*Balladyna, Lilla Weneda, Mindowe*) to Polish and European history (*Samuel Zborowski,* *The Golden Skull, Mazepa, Beatrix Cenci, Mary Stuart*) to the 1830s and 1840s (*Kordian, Fantazy*). They offer rich, complex, and imaginative material for spectacular stagings and excellent roles for actors. Prohibited by the *censor in the early nineteenth century, Słowacki's dramas were gradually mounted in Poland after 1851, though *Kordian*, a biography of a romantic *hero who plots the assassination of the Russian Tsar, had to wait until the end of the century (1899). Thereafter Słowacki's works became part of the Polish repertoire, regularly encountered by major directors (including *Schiller) and actors. *The Constant Prince*, based on *Calderón, was notably directed and acted by Juliusz Osterwa, who treated it as a *morality play in an open-air spectacle with dozens of extras on horseback (1926). *Grotowski's condensed study, with *Cieślak, which forced the *audience to peer on events as at a *ritual or operating theatre, was one of the finest achievements of the Polish Laboratory Theatre (1965). KB

Sly, William (fl.1590–1608) English actor. Sly played two roles (Porrex, and a lord) in *Tarlton's *The Seven Deadly Sins, Part II*. From around 1598 until his death he performed with the *Chamberlain's Men. He is listed among the cast for three of *Jonson's plays (*Sejanus, Every Man in his Humour,* and *Every Man out of his Humour*), although the roles he took are unknown, and his name also appears in the list of 'principall actors' in the First Folio of Shakespeare's plays (1623). Sly was on the King's Livery list in 1604, and bequeathed to actor Robert Browne his share in the *Globe.   SPC

Smith, Albert (1816–60) English performer and writer who began his career as a journalist and author of theatrical extravaganzas. His 1850 performance *The Overland Mail* initiated a series of humorous travelogues that included panoramas, songs, and special effects. Smith's second production, *The Ascent of Mt Blanc* (1852), was one of the most successful theatrical events of its time, running for over 2,000 performances at the Egyptian Hall in London. It provided a fast-paced, ironic account of Alpine travel that exploited contemporary interest in that region, further developed in *Mt Blanc to China* (1858).   SF

Smith, Anna Deavere (1950–   ) *African-American actor and playwright. In the late 1970s she developed a *documentary theatre that combines mimicry, journalism, and oral history. She created solo performance pieces that portrayed a real-life community or conflict by interviewing dozens of people, editing the results, and performing them verbatim as a series of *character sketches, retaining the subject's speech patterns and vocal intonations. Two pieces made Smith a major cultural figure. *Fires in the Mirror: Crown Heights, Brooklyn and Other Identities* (1992) depicted 26 people connected to racial disturbances that erupted between blacks and Jews in a New York neighbourhood in 1991. In a similar vein, *Twilight: Los Angeles, 1992* (1993) investigated the explosive aftermath of the Rodney King verdict. The juxtaposition of numerous voices and the virtuosity of Smith's performance yielded a powerful portrait of racial identity in the USA. In *House Arrest* (1997), first staged with a cast of fifteen before reverting to a solo piece, Smith broadened her focus to examine the US presidency and the media. *Let Me Down Easy* (*American Repertory Theatre, 2008) contiuned the documentary style. Smith has appeared in political films and television series. STC

Smith, Maggie (1934–) English actress. She made her New York debut in the *New Faces of 56 Revue* (1956), and her London debut the next year with *Share my Lettuce* with Kenneth Williams. She was a member of the *Old Vic company in 1959–60, appearing as Lady Pliant in *Congreve's *The Double-Dealer*, Celia, the Queen in *Richard II*, and Maggie Wylie in *Barrie's *What Every Woman Knows*. In 1963 she joined the *National Theatre to play Desdemona to *Olivier's Othello. Subsequent roles included Hilde Wangel, Myra in *Hay Fever*, Beatrice, and Miss Julie. She was already recognized as a talented comedienne and dramatic actress specializing in eccentric English women of a certain age when she won her first Oscar for the film *The Prime of Miss Jean Brodie* (1968). In the 1970s she was a regular at the *Stratford Festival in Canada, appearing as Cleopatra, Millamant, and Lady Macbeth (1976), Titania, Hippolyta, Judith Bliss, and Rosalind (1977). Later stage work includes *Virginia* (1980), *Lettice and Lovage* (1987), Lady Bracknell in *The Importance of Being Earnest* (1993), and a revival of *Albee's *The Lady from Dubuque* (2007). She received a further Oscar for her role in *California Suite* (1977), and as Minerva McGonagall remains central to the series of Harry Potter films (2001–). Among her numerous television roles, her appearance in *Bennett's *Talking Heads* (1989) was exceptional. AS

Smithson, Harriet Constance (1800–54) Irish actress and muse. She made her Dublin debut at 14 and her *Drury Lane debut at 17, after which she stayed in London playing roles which required grace and beauty. She was a useful performer but not a contender for the most demanding tragic *characters. She went with an English company to Paris in 1827 and was required to play Ophelia: she had an immense success and thereafter played leading roles including Juliet, Desdemona, and *Rowe's Jane Shore. For the first time French *audiences, accustomed to the rules of *neoclassical *tragedy, were deeply moved by Shakespeare. Miss Smithson's image was incorporated into every young poet's *romantic fantasies. An unlucky accident in 1833 lamed her and more or less ended her career. Hector Berlioz married her and paid her debts, and for a time they were happy. FD

Smock Alley Theatre The first Irish Restoration theatre was built in 1662 by John Ogilby. Its stage was smaller than the main London theatres, but it shared their basic configuration of a large apron, *proscenium arch, *boxes, pit, and two rows of galleries. Initially, the theatre had strong links with nearby Dublin Castle, the administrative centre for British rule in Ireland, and many early actors held commissions in Castle regiments, though these ties weakened over time. Rebuilt in 1735, its *management was assumed by Thomas Sheridan in 1745. Sheridan (father of Richard Brinsley *Sheridan) introduced a number of reforms, including banning spectators from the stage. In spite of a *riot that almost destroyed the building in 1754, Smock Alley remained among the most important theatres in the British Isles, launching the careers of *Barry and *Woffington, among others. Competition forced its closure in 1788. ChM

Sobol, Joshua (1939–) One of Israel's foremost playwrights, known for politically provocative work. Sobol's first play was produced in 1971 by the Haifa Municipal Theatre, where he served as playwright in residence and *artistic director from 1984 to 1988. He is the author of nearly 40 plays, including *The Night of the Twenty* (1976), *The Soul of a Jew* (1982), *Ghetto* (1984), *The Palestinian* (1985), *The Jerusalem Syndrome* (1987), and *Village* (1996). His work has been produced internationally and has received prestigious awards in Israel, Britain, and Germany. EN

socialist realism A prescriptive term for socialist artistic practice, which emerged from the First Soviet Writers' Conference in 1934, used in opposition to 'formalism'. Socialist realism required adherence to four basic principles. The first was *narodnost*, and implied that whatever an artist wrote, painted, or composed must be recognizable by or intelligible to the people (*narod*). This excluded anything elitist, abstract, modernist, or aesthetically remote from ordinary experience (normally including the *avant-garde).

The second principle was *ideinost*, which meant that a work of art should be ideologically sound and reflect a progressive, socialist view of history and social development. The third principle, *partiinost*, required that literature serve the interests of the Communist Party; this demand was based on a probable misunderstanding of Lenin's essay 'On Party Organization and Party Literature', which was interpreted as if his edicts applied to creative literature as well. The fourth principle was *tipichnost* (typicality), and meant not what is typical of the present (which is necessarily susceptible to criticism) but what will be typical of the socialist future. Therefore every artwork needed to contain some promise of that likely future, usually an idealized version of the man or woman who will constitute it—the 'positive' *hero or heroine—who may be shown as opposed or even destroyed by negative forces, but only if coupled with the assurance that his or her virtues will eventually triumph. This last scenario can be seen, typically, in *Vishnevsky's classic socialist realist play *An Optimistic Tragedy* (1932), where the self-sacrifice and eventual death of a female commissar represents triumph over the forces of anarchy and the welding together of collective forces that will construct the future in her name, and in the name of the Party. Socialist realism effectively became the mandated artistic style of the Stalinist period in the USSR and other states ruled by a Communist Party. *See also* REALISM.   NW

Societas Raffaello Sanzio Contemporary Italian *collective, located in Cesena, named after the painter Raphael. Under the direction of Romeo Castellucci (1960–), the company has presented a series of *touring performances whose *mise-en-scène includes complex imagery, dense audio scores, technological apparatus, performing objects, *animals, and children in linguistically minimal works devised from deconstructed classic texts. The company has gained notoriety for its use of special performers with various conditions of advanced anorexia, morbid obesity, and post-operative conditions of tracheotomy and mastectomy. *Giulio Cesare* (1997) based in part on Shakespeare, was a performative meditation on the power of rhetoric, and *Genesi: from the Museum of Sleep* (1999), which explored the relations of creation and destruction in myth and science, included young children of company members as performers. Earlier productions of the company include *The Fall of Inanna* (1989), *Gilgamesh* (1990), and *Masoch* (1993). The company is also active in developing children's theatre, such as *Buchettino* (2001), directed by Chiara

Guidi, which attempts to mine the dangerous creativity of the child. *Tragedia Endogonidia*, a major project that opened in ten European cities from 2001 to 2004, consisted of eleven separate pieces investigating the meaning of tragedy in the contemporary world. The imagistic *Hey Girl* premiered in 2007. Castellucci has theorized his work as an aesthetic of the 'dis-human' and the 'dis-real', that resists *acting, metaphor, and narrative in favour of embodiment, metonymy, and image.   MDC

Sofola, Zulu (1938–95) Nigerian playwright, director, and teacher. Educated in Nigeria and the USA, Sofola was a pioneering woman who made provocative interventions in politics, religion, and theatre. Some of her plays, such as the farcical *Wizard at Law* and the sombre *Ivory Tower* (1991), draw very obviously on European originals. Others, like *Queen Omu Ako of Oligbo* (1988), for which she carried out extensive research into local conventions, were deliberately Afrocentric in approach. Always relevant, sometimes reactionary, her plays often comment on *gender issues and topical concerns. *Ivory Tower* was significantly subtitled 'a new spirit of African womanhood' and confronted the secret cults that were disrupting life on Nigerian campuses.   JMG

Soleil, Théâtre du French theatre company founded in Paris by *Mnouchkine (and ten former Sorbonne students) in 1964, modelled on their student theatre *collective, formed with equality of responsibilities. A version of *Wesker's *The Kitchen* (1967) and *A Midsummer Night's Dream* (1968) were performed in the Cirque Médrano, a suitable space for a people's theatre. The events of May 1968 saw the company members turn political activists, developing an association with trade unions, a rejection of the classical repertoire, and the beginnings of a *devised form called 'collective creation'. Four works were created in this style: *The Clowns* (1969), two on the French Revolution, *1789* and *1793* (1970 and 1972), and a play of contemporary life, *L'Âge d'or* (1975). *1789; or, The Revolution Must Stop at the Perfection of Happiness*, the first production in what was to become their permanent home, a disused munitions factory (Cartoucherie) in the Vincennes forest, was created by the actors playing fairground workers who told their personal histories of the revolution. *L'Âge d'or* was a *commedia dell'arte-inspired story of a North African immigrant worker falling victim to corruption and social inequalities.

In 1979 Mnouchkine's adaptation of Klaus Mann's novel *Méphisto* was marked by a more conciliatory politics which outraged the left, and the unions withdrew their support. Experimentation with Eastern theatre forms followed, applied to the canonical texts (three plays by Shakespeare, 1981–4; a tetralogy of plays by *Euripides and *Aeschlyus, *Les Atrides*, 1990–3; and *Molière's *Tartuffe*, 1995). These lavish, highly physicalized, and *intercultural spectacles were enormously successful. The same approach to commissioned plays set in Asia by *Cixous (*The Terrible but Unfinished History of Norodom Sihanouk, King of Cambodia* in 1985, and *The Indiade* in 1987) retained the pictorialism of the Orient but the hybridized *acting style was absent. This was rectified in 1999 in *Drums on the Dyke*, an imagined Chinese fable in which live actors were manipulated as *bunraku puppets. From the beginning of this orientalist period the Soleil came to resemble a global village of ethnicities, and the stage a mêlée of accents and bodies, a characteristic that took on thematic force in *The Last Halting Site* (2005) and *Ephemera* (2007), about contemporary migration and marginalized lives.   BRS

soliloquy Literally 'single speech', the Latin-derived eqivalent of the Greek-derived *monologue, soliloquy is most often used of a form of monologue in which a speaker, alone on the stage, or believing himself to be alone, delivers an extended speech within the context of the dramatic fiction. A soliloquy cannot go beyond the competence and knowledge of the *character, and, as the speaker is alone, cannot be intended to deceive. A soliloquy is either 'conventional', a function of the theatrical code (the Elizabethan practice), or 'motivated', a function of dramatic characterization (the *realistic practice). It tends to be (a) an introspective revelation of character, (b) a reflective commentary on the dramatic *action, or (c) a deliberation of future action. A soliloquy can be addressed to the *audience (*Richard III*) but it is more often an interior monologue (*Hamlet*).   RWV

Sologub, Fyodor (1863–1927) Russian writer, whose well-known novel *The Little Demon* was dramatized in 1910. The conflict between the material and the spiritual is a persistent feature of his work and finds expression in plays such as *The Triumph of Death*, staged by *Meyerhold in 1907, and *The Gift of the Wise Bees*, his treatment of the Laodameia legend. A theorist of *symbolist theatre, his influential essay 'The Theatre of a Single Will' (1908) advocated stylized modes of writing and performance. In the spirit of *Craig, Sologub was hostile to the actor's living presence and wished to return the theatre to the poet. His *Nocturnal Dances* (1908) is a version of a fairy tale presenting the triumph of the aesthetic over the commonplace. Sologub's ideas were unpopular during the Soviet period and his work neglected.   NW

Solórzano, Carlos (1922–   ) Guatemala-born Mexican playwright, director, and scholar. A self-described *expressionist, Solórzano's plays blend Mesoamerican culture with French existentialism, as in *The Doll Puppets* (1958). The oppression of the poor is the main theme of *The Hands of God* (1958), a kind of modern *mystery play which inverts notions of good and evil. In *The Crucified One* (1958), a Pontius Pilate-like priest symbolically washes his hands when the young actor playing Christ in a local *Passion play is killed by drunken celebrants. Solórzano was fundamental in establishing the professional University Theatre of the National Autonomous University of Mexico in 1952; in 1973 he was named head of the department of dramatic literature and theatre of that university. He is the author of important studies of Mexican and Latin American theatre.   KFN

Somigliana, Carlos (1932–87) Argentinian playwright and director who figured prominently in the development of a critical neorealism (*see* REALISM AND REALITY). From *Yellow* (written 1959, produced 1965) to *Lavalle, the Story of a Statue* (1983) his works stand out for their crisp *dialogue and focus on historical conflict. *Official Number One* (1982) buried the stage in corpses in one of the first explicit representations of the disappeared.   JGJ

Sondheim, Stephen (1930–   ) American composer-lyricist, the pre-eminent *musical theatre composer of his generation. Often labelled misanthropic, his sharp, unsparing wit and carefully crafted lyrics grace shows with strong narrative power and musically delineated *characters. Encouraged by Oscar *Hammerstein II, Sondheim made his Broadway debut as lyricist for *Bernstein's *West Side Story* (1957), followed in 1959 with the words for *Styne's *Gypsy*.

Sondheim began writing both words and music with *A Funny Thing Happened on the Way to the Forum* (1962), a broad *farce based on *Plautus that featured *Mostel. After an unsuccessful collaboration with Richard *Rodgers on *Do I Hear a Waltz?* (1965), Sondheim came into his own with the innovative *Company* (1970), directed by *Prince and choreographed by *Bennett. *Follies* (1971) used a reunion of former showgirls to explore the myths of show business. *A Little Night Music* (1973) featured Sondheim's most popular song, 'Send in the Clowns'. In 1976 he offered

Pacific Overtures, based on the opening of Japan to the West in 1853; though designed by *Aronson, the work was too unusual for *audiences.

Sweeney Todd (1979) was Sondheim's most theatrically effective production. Based on the gruesome 1847 play by George Dibdin Pitt (adapted by Christopher Bond in 1973), it blended *operetta, *melodrama, and horror with Prince's fluid staging. The tale of a vengeful barber in mid-nineteenth-century London was performed with great verve by *Cariou and *Lansbury as Mrs Lovett, who bakes Sweeney's victims into meat pies, and is frequently revived (film, 2007, directed Tim Burton). After the failure of *Merrily We Roll Along* (1981), Sondheim won the Pulitzer Prize in 1984 for *Sunday in the Park with George*, a visually striking musical about the painter Georges Seurat. *Into the Woods* (1988) was a novel examination of fairy tales and their archetypal motifs. *Assassins* (1991) presented the killers of American presidents in a *revue.

Passion (1994), based on Ettore Scola's film *Passione d'amore*, had a solid critical reaction but struggled to find an audience. *Road Show* (originally called *Bounce*) played briefly at the *New York Shakespeare Festival's Public Theatre in 2008.　　　　　　　　　　　　　　　　　SN

Sophocles (*c*.495–406 BC) Athenian *tragic dramatist. During his long and supremely successful career Sophocles was said to have introduced the third actor (*see* PROTAGONIST) and scene painting to the *Greek theatre. Of more than 120 plays (with which he won at least twenty victories, eighteen of them at the City *Dionysia), only seven survive. *Philoctetes* was performed in 409 and *Oedipus at Colonus* in 401 (posthumously), but there is no evidence for the dates of *Ajax*, *Electra*, *Oedipus the King*, or *Women of Trachis*, and little for *Antigone*, though it is often thought an early play.

It is clear from *Aristophanes' *Frogs*, *Aristotle's high regard for *Oedipus the King*, and Sophocles' highly respectable political career, that he and his work were greatly admired in his time, though his surviving plays are often uncomfortable. His *heroes can suffer terribly despite being fundamentally good, and he challenged some of the most cherished assumptions of his society.

As a dramatist Sophocles was hugely theatrical. His use of significant properties, for example, focus the audience's attention and articulate the progress of the plot. The sword with which Ajax kills himself is an instance; and after Ajax's suicide, his dead body becomes the visual and thematic focus of the last part of the play. In *Electra* the focus similarly shifts from an object to a corpse, but in a way which emphasizes this

play's multiple bitter ironies: the disguised Orestes presents his sister, who believes him dead, with an urn he says contains Orestes' ashes. She laments wildly over it, and refuses to be parted from it even as Orestes tries to make himself known to her. At the play's shocking climax, the corpse of Clytemnestra (only in Sophocles is she murdered before her lover Aegisthus) is brought out on the *ekkyklema and is misidentified as that of Orestes by the deluded Aegisthus before he is killed. So Orestes is falsely presumed dead twice, and twice a visual symbol is used to convince those on stage that false is true, and simultaneously to illustrate the irony for the audience. Related to this is Sophocles' interweaving of metaphorical and actual blindness in the Oedipus plays. In *Oedipus the King*, when Oedipus has sight he is blind, unlike the blind Teiresias; only when he re-enters in his bloodied and blinded *mask can he see clearly.

The power of Sophocles' plays, and their beauty of language, ensured their continued performance after his death: a number of famous actors in the fourth century BC were known for their interpretations of his roles. After the *early modern period, Sophocles remained the most popular of ancient dramatists. *Oedipus the King* and *Antigone* in particular have been constantly performed, translated, and adapted, and it was Sophocles' Oedipus and Electra after whom Freud named his complexes. In 1585 at the Teatro *Olimpico in Vicenza, *Oedipus the King* was the first Greek tragedy to be performed in modern times, though it was not until the nineteenth century that regular performances of Greek tragedy took place. In 1841 a production of *Antigone* with music by Mendelssohn was produced at Potsdam under the aegis of Friedrich Wilhelm IV, and proved to be the first of many across Europe. Later an extremely influential *Oedipus the King* with *Mounet-Sully was performed at the *Comédie-Française in 1881.

In the nineteenth and early twentieth centuries the play was banned from the public stage in Britain (*see* CENSORSHIP). Eventually it was performed in 1912 to acclaim, with *Martin-Harvey as Oedipus and Lillah *McCarthy as Jocasta, directed by *Reinhardt. *Olivier probably remains the most famous of many post-war Oedipuses, playing opposite *Thorndike at the *Old Vic in 1945, in the version by *Yeats first performed at the *Abbey Theatre in 1926. The play has been adapted by such diverse talents as *Corneille (1659), *Voltaire (1718), *Gide (1930), and *Cocteau (*La Machine infernale*, 1932), among many others. There are also numerous versions of *Antigone*, notably that of *Anouilh (1944), performed under the Nazi occupation of

France and using the Sophoclean story to negotiate the moral tensions between idealism and pragmatism in the face of *force majeure*. More recent important adaptations include Seamus Heaney's version of *Philoctetes*, called *The Cure at Troy* (1990); and his version of *Antigone*, called *The Burial at Thebes* (2004). JMM

Sorescu, Marin (1936–96) Romanian poet and dramatist. Sorescu's *Jonah* was first produced by *Şerban in Bucharest in 1969 to great praise. Although the *censors' distrust of Sorescu's poetic ambiguity limited production of his works in Romania prior to 1989, *Jonah* received numerous stagings in Europe, India, and the United States, as did a companion piece, *The Matrix* (1974). Since 1989 many of his works, including the history plays *A Cold* (1977) and *A Third Stake* (1979, also translated as *Vlad Dracula the Impaler*), have become key elements in the national repertory. EEP

Sorge, Reinhard Johannes (1892–1916) German dramatist. A victim of the First World War, Sorge is remembered chiefly for his play *The Beggar* (1912), which was staged posthumously by *Reinhardt at the *Deutsches Theater in 1917. Both play and production epitomized *expressionism: the episodic structure, focus on a single *protagonist, father–son conflict, and theme of spiritual renewal. Reinhardt's production, with a star-studded cast including Ernst *Deutsch and Jannings, marked a departure to new staging techniques through symbolic *lighting and the use of a bare stage. CBB

Sorma, Agnes (1865–1927) German actress. After work in various provincial theatres, Sorma came to the *Deutsches Theater in 1883, where she performed under *L'Arronge. From 1894 to 1898 she was a member of *Brahm's ensemble at the Deutsches Theater. She worked freelance at various Berlin theatres and went on many international *tours, often performing next to *Kainz. Important parts included Nora in *Ibsen's *A Doll's House* (1892) and Portia in *The Merchant of Venice* (1905) directed by *Reinhardt. She was a principal actress of *naturalism in the plays of *Hauptmann, Ibsen, and *Shaw, as well as a passionate and intense interpreter of the classical roles. Her finely nuanced, psychological *acting style became increasingly superficial after she left Brahm's ensemble to become a star performer. CBB

Sothern, E. A. (Edward Askew) (1820–81) and **E. H. (Edward Hugh)** (1859–1933) Anglo-American actors, father and son. E. A. moved to the USA in 1852, joining Wallack's company in New York in 1854. His signature role came in 1858 when he reluctantly agreed to play Lord Dundreary in Laura *Keene's production of *Taylor's *Our American Cousin*, a performance celebrated as one the funniest on the American stage, and he furthered his reputation playing a relative of Dundreary's in *Brother Sam* (1862). He also attempted more serious roles with varying degrees of success. Unlike his lanky father, E. H. was small and handsome. For ten years he *toured, becoming a popular leading man. In 1887 he joined *Frohman's company at the Lyceum in New York where he took his most famous roles, including *The Prisoner of Zenda* (1895), adapted from Anthony Hope's novel, playing both Prince Rudolf and his lookalike nemesis. But it was his work with his second wife, Julia *Marlowe, that defined his reputation. Together they acted in a series of hallmark Shakespeare productions beginning in 1904 and continuing until Marlowe's retirement in 1924. PAD

Southerne, Thomas (1660–1746) Irish playwright. Southerne's first play, *The Loyal Brother* (1682), was performed at *Drury Lane with a *prologue and *epilogue by his friend *Dryden. The successful mingling of *heroic and sentimental *tragedy was repeated in his dramatic adaptations of Aphra *Behn's novels *The Fatal Marriage* (1694) and *Oroonoko* (1695). Southerne's unusually sympathetic treatment of a female perspective is most obvious in his three *comedies of manners. The most popular of these, *Sir Anthony Love* (1690), directly *satirizes male behaviour through the witty and skilful intrigues of the heroine Lucia, who dominates the *action disguised as the titular Sir Anthony: a *breeches role written for Susannah Mountfort. *Congreve contributed a song to Southerne's comedy *The Maid's Last Prayer* (1693) and Southerne was instrumental in revising Congreve's first play, *The Old Bachelor* (1693), performed a few weeks later. Southerne was a commercial playwright, seeking to please an *audience in transition between Restoration libertinism and eighteenth-century sentiment, but his writing also attracted critical praise. GBB

Sowande, Bode (1948–) Nigerian playwright, director, and *manager. Best known in Nigeria for his television scripts, Sowande's plays include *The Night Before* (Ibadan, 1972), *A Sanctus for Women* (produced as *The Angry Bridegroom*, Sheffield, 1976), and *Farewell to Babylon* (Ibadan, 1979). His international reputation is partly based on *Circus of Freedom Square* (1985) and *Ajantala-Pinocchio* (1992), both produced in Italy. A graduate in French, he received a commission for the bicentenary of the French Revolution (*Tornadoes Full of Dreams*, Lagos, 1989), and the next year wrote a localized version of *Molière's The Miser* called *Arelu*. Sowande's work has often confronted social and political issues. He frequently mixes fact with fiction, explores the relationship between anarchy and revolution, and draws attention to the process that changes idealists into cynics. The richness of his mixture of Yoruba and European elements, together with his religious preoccupations—mostly clearly seen in *Barabas and the Master Jesus* (1980)—mean that he is out of step with the more radical of the second generation of Nigerian dramatists.   JMG

Sowerby, Githa (1876–1970) English playwright whose best-known work is the powerful *Rutherford and Son* (1912). Set in the north Yorkshire home of the oppressive patriarch, the portrayal of a father's obsession with his glass manufacturing business and his tyranny over the wrecked lives of his family was influenced by *Ibsen and Granville *Barker (revived at the *National Theatre by Katie *Mitchell, 1994). Sowerby's other work includes *Ruth* and *Before Breakfast* (both 1912), *A Man and Some Women* (1914), *Sheila* (1917), *The Stepmother* (1924), and *The Policeman's Whistle* (1935).   AS

Soyinka, Wole (1934–   ) Nigerian actor, writer, and political activist. Winner of the Nobel Prize for Literature in 1986, Soyinka is commonly regarded as Africa's greatest playwright. An anticolonial stance persisted from *The Lion and the Jewel* (1959) to *Death and the King's Horseman* (1976), but he is also a post-colonial writer, forging in the 1960s a distinctive local theatre that, while written in English, drew basic structural elements from Yoruba *rituals and festivals, as in *A Dance of the Forests* (1960), *The Strong Breed* (film, 1963; staged, Ibadan, 1966), *The Road* (London, 1965), and *Kongi's Harvest* (Lagos, 1965). In the 1970s Soyinka turned to European models, particularly in *The Bacchae of Euripides* (*National Theatre, London, 1973), and *Opera Wonyosi* (Ile-Ife, 1977), based on *Brecht's *The Threepenny Opera*.

After study at Leeds University (1954–7), he was a play reader at the *Royal Court Theatre before his return to Nigeria in 1960, where he established the 1960 Masks, and the Orisun Theatre. From *Swamp Dwellers* (London, 1958), which was triggered by the announcement that oil had been found in the Niger Delta, Soyinka demonstrated passionate responses to Nigerian events, notable especially in his writing for radio, television, and

satirical *revues, including *The New Republican* (1964), *Before the Blackout* (1965), and *Before the Deluge* (1991). The popular *Jero Plays* (1960, 1974), together with *Requiem for a Futurologist* (1983), came from a similar compulsion, as did *From Zia, with Love* (Siena, 1992). *Beatification of Area Boy* (Leeds, 1995) included songs from Soyinka's own record, *Unlimited Liability Company* (1983).

As his international reputation grew, Soyinka's situation at home worsened. He was detained in 1967 during the Biafran War, released two years later, going into exile in Ghana and Britain, and not returning until 1976. Despite the Nobel Prize—Africa's first for literature—and his high public profile, his opposition to the repressive military dictatorship forced him into exile again in 1994. He was charged with treason in 1997, eventually returning after the charges were lifted in 1998, though he chose to remain based outside Nigeria.

His 1990 *satire on American political correctness, *1994*, was presented at Emory University in Atlanta when Soyinka took up a chair there in 1996. He responded to a request for a play for young British actors with *Travel Club and the Boy Soldier* (1997), which confronted 'First World' youths with 'Third World' issues. Much of Soyinka's writing during the 1990s was polemical; almost all was in prose, some of it bilious. Lacking direct contact with his primary *audience and in touch with only a few trusted companions, his recent plays have lacked the resonance of the earlier ones. The best works, however, *From Zia* and *Area Boy*, exhibit a continuing interest in mixing the music and conventions found in popular Nigerian theatre. This was also apparent in the international production of *King Baabu* (Lagos, 2001), a radical reworking of *Jarry's *Ubu roi*. Directed by Soyinka, with a cast from Nigeria and Britain, it subsequently *toured nationally and abroad.   JMG

Specht, Kerstin (1956–   ) German dramatist and film director. At the Munich Film and Television School she produced three short films: *The Silent Woman, Africa*, and *Wilgefort*. As a stage writer she came into prominence in 1990 with *The Radiant Mannikin* (Bonn, 1990) and *Yankee Fields* (1990). Further plays include *Carceri* (1996), *The Frog Princess* (1998), and *Solitude* (2003). Her earlier plays are written in the tradition of critical folk theatre, relying on dialect and containing references to fairy tales and folk songs; in *Carceri* she deals with the French philosopher Althusser, who killed his wife in 1980.   CBB

spectator *See* AUDIENCE.

Sperr, Martin (1944–2002) German dramatist. Sperr came to prominence in the late 1960s with his *Bavarian Trilogy*. *Hunting Scenes from Lower Bavaria* (1966) deals with social behaviour in a Bavarian village, exposing the stupidity of villagers hounding a young homosexual in 1949. *Tales from Landshut* (1967) shows two rural entrepreneurs fighting for control of a local monopoly and reveals brutal scheming, mendacity, and anti-Semitic behaviour. The last and least accomplished of the three, *Münchener Freiheit* (1971), deals with unscrupulous profit making in Munich real estate. Sperr wrote a version of *Bond's *Saved* for Munich Kammerspiele (directed by *Stein, 1966), as well as a translation and adaptation of Shakespeare's *Measure for Measure* for *Zadek (1967, Bremen). Sperr also worked as an actor and translator. CBB

Split Britches American *lesbian-*feminist performance group. Peggy Shaw, Lois Weaver, and Deborah Margolin formed the company after their successful collaboration on a play by the same name for the WOW Café in New York in 1980. The group draws on *cabaret, *satirical *revue, and the drag show to create often campy performances about lesbian sexuality and, particularly, butch–femme role playing. By the late 1980s the *collective began to create longer dramatic performances like *Belle Reprieve* (1991), a queer deconstruction of *Williams's *A Streetcar Named Desire*. Academic feminists have described the group as a model of *gender-subversive performance. JAB

spoken Chinese theatre *See* HUAJÜ.

sport The spectacular nature of athletic contests has been apparent at least since the eight century BC. The Greek Olympiads, which offered competitions of physical speed, strength, and accuracy, were directly parallel to the dramatic contests presented annually in the *Dionysia festivals in Athens. Like the arts of war, sporting events can be pleasing in themselves to watch and exciting in terms of outcome. In one sense sport is *ritualized, sublimated, or regulated fighting—performed fighting—allied to the tactics of classical warfare. Both require physical stamina and aggression; the events of the Olympiad (running, jumping, wrestling, throwing the javelin, discus, and hammer) were directly modelled on the techniques of land battle common in the Greek experience. Both war and sport are inherently teleological or end-directed (like the plot of a *tragedy). Both can be adapted into entertainment events, and can also blend easily, as they did in *Roman *gladiatorial contests, *animal fights, *naumachia, and *circus races, in the tour-

naments of the *medieval period. The presence of spectators not only theatricalizes, it also transforms the purpose of an athletic contest, moving sport from the realm of pure play to the realm of display.

In the modern period, the rise of professional sports in the latter half of the nineteenth century commodified the bodies of competitors for entertainment and laid the groundwork for the adulation of athletes in the twentieth century and beyond. English Association Football ('soccer' is a nickname derived from 'association'), which began as a gentleman's sport in upper-class schools, soon was vigorously appropriated by the working classes, partly because it required so little specialized equipment. A series of parliamentary Acts after 1847 gradually released British industrial workers on Saturday afternoons, which were often used to play or watch football. By the end of the century local clubs were common, matches and leagues became regulated, and some payments were made to players. The stage was set for the huge commercial development of professional sport that spread globally and incorporated many other amateur games.

The aesthetic and dramatic implications of sport are magnified by the relationship that usually develops between fans ('fanatics') and a home team. Despite the fact that many sports are now big businesses operated for profit, *audiences regularly take a passionate interest in the fortunes of their side, assuming a pride of ownership in the civic or national team. The absorption of a sporting match, amplified by rivalry, gambling, or alcohol, sparks a febrile excitement among spectators that no theatrical or filmed show can hope to equal. The spectacle of men or women engaging all their cunning and strength to achieve a clear victory is an appealing release from the ambiguities of contemporary life. But since a clear victory for one side always means a clear defeat for the other, the emotion of fans, especially male fans, whether in celebration or despair, can easily spill over into violent expression, as it did so often in British football in the latter twentieth century. The soccer riot, parallel in some ways to theatre *riots, which also fed upon the proximity of numerous spectators in an agitated state, is one example of how sport creates opportunities for audience participation.

By the end of the twentieth century spectator sports had become intensely commodified and international in scope, especially in Grand Slam tennis championships, the World Cup, or the Super Bowl. The modern Olympics, started in 1896 as a celebration of amateurism and international understanding, have been most notably altered as cultural attitudes to sport changed through the Cold War and after. As the pretence of the amateur standing of athletes was gradually abandoned, and the number and nature of events greatly expanded, the quadrennial meeting became more and more a product manufactured by a multinational firm called the International Olympic Committee. In such a marketable environment, it is not surprising that the spectacularization of sport has reached a high point with the Olympic opening ceremonies in the 1990s and beyond. Often designed by leading stage *scenographers, these gigantic demonstrations of *dance, music, *fireworks, and other live events, globally televised, have contextualized Olympic sport as a form of theatre.   DK

Sprinq Willow Society *See* CHUNLIU SHE.

Squarzina, Luigi (1922–2010) Italian playwright and director. Squarzina was one of the generation of people, like *Strehler and *Visconti, who introduced the new *director-led theatre to Italy. He worked with *Gassman in the Teatro d'Arte Italiano, producing the first complete Italian *Hamlet* (1952) and taking works by *Pirandello to South America. He is most closely associated with the Genoa Teatro Stabile, but later worked in Rome. His own plays, which include *Three Quarters of the Moon* (1955) and *The Five Senses* (1987), show Squarzina as an acute, disenchanted observer of his own time.   JF

Sriranga (Adya Rangacharya) (1904–86) Indian dramatist, director, and scholar who worked in Kannada theatre. Sriranga wrote extensively on Sanskrit drama and translated the *Natyasastra, the classical Indian treatise on *dramaturgy, into English and Kannada. Starting in 1930 he wrote more than 40 plays in Kannada. *Harijanvara*, one of his earliest, depicts the social tensions created during Gandhi's anti-untouchability movement. Later his social critique turned ironic, as in *The Wheel of Grief* (1952), where a Gandhian politician anguishes over the loss of traditional values. After the 1950s Sriranga often employed the device of a play-within-a-play, as in *Darkness and Light* (1959) and *Rangabharata* (1965). An active practitioner, he directed many of his own plays and spearheaded the amateur theatre movement in Karnataka. His plays have been widely translated into other Indian languages.   KVA

Stafford-Clark, Max (1943–) English director, particularly associated with new writing. He was *artistic director of Edinburgh's Traverse Theatre (1968–71), then founded Joint Stock (with *Hare and David Aukin, 1974), a company which involved actors in the writing process and developed many

of *Churchill's works. He has directed six Churchill premières, including *Cloud Nine* (1979), *Serious Money* (1987), and *Blue Heart* (1999). As artistic director of London's *Royal Court (1979–93), his premières included Michael Hastings's *Tom and Viv* (1985) and *Wertenbaker's *Our Country's Good* (1987), which ran in *repertory with *Farquhar's *The Recruiting Officer*. He co-founded the *touring company Out of Joint in 1993, developing and directing Sebastian *Barry's *The Steward of Christendom* (1995), *Ravenhill's *Shopping and Fucking* (1996), Alistair Beaton's political *farce *Feelgod* (2001), and Stella Feehily's *Dreams of Violence*, among other works.   GAO

stage design *See* SCENOGRAPHY.

stage lighting *See* LIGHTING.

stage manager A complicated term that changes meaning according to historical and traditional circumstances. In England and America it was sometimes used to refer to *actor-managers of the nineteenth or early twentieth centuries, or to a functionary delegated by them to organize actor movement on stage, a prototype of the modernist *director. In translating certain Asian theatre roles into English, the stage manager could be an onstage performer separate from the *action of the play, who may variously serve as narrator, master of ceremonies, coordinator of the stage crew, *prompter, onstage *acting coach, cheerleader, or effects person, who may be conventionally visible or invisible and may or may not interact with the *characters, *audience, or actors-as-actors. Functionaries as different as the *kyogen kata* of *kabuki in Japan, or the *Adhikari of *jatra and the *Vyas* of *Ram lila in India, have become the 'stage manager' in some English translations.

In the modern Western theatre, the stage manager is the chief operations officer for a production, and the liaison between the artistic, technical, and production management teams. In the Anglo-American tradition, the stage manager is the director's assistant, secretary, and executive officer; she or he schedules *rehearsals and conducts the business side of them; records movements, stage business, and cues in the promptbook; heads the production crew; maintains the director's version once the show is running; and calls the cues during the run, in addition to numerous other duties. Normally the stage manager will have a number of assistants. Because of the complexities of technology and production, stage management is almost indispensable in modern theatre and among its most highly honoured crafts.   JD

Stage Society London play-producing society, founded 1899, incorporated 1904, closed 1948. The largest of the British independent theatres, its membership was initially held to 300 but eventually rose to 1,500. Performers were professionals acting for little or nothing, and its venues were commercial theatre buildings on dark nights. Productions were given only one or two performances in the interstices in West End schedules, usually Sunday evenings and Monday matinées. A notable handful of Stage Society productions were of plays which had been refused a licence (*see* CENSOR-SHIP) and were nominally private performances, including *Shaw's *Mrs Warren's Profession* (1902), Granville *Barker's *Waste* (1907), and *Pirandello's *Six Characters in Search of an Author* (1925). Performances could also prove to be try-outs for the commercial theatre: *Houghton's *Hindle Wakes* (1912) and *Sherriff's *Journey's End* (1928) moved on to West End *managements. *See also* INDEPEN-DENT THEATRE. MOC

Stanfield, Clarkson (1793–1867) English designer, influential at the Royal Coburg (*Old Vic) and *Drury Lane theatres. From the early 1820s he also enjoyed considerable success as an easel artist and after 1840 this became his principal occupation. Benefiting from the development of gas *lighting on stage, he was most admired for the clarity of his painting in scenes of landscape and Eastern exoticism. He also painted *dioramas of great splendour and accuracy for Drury Lane *pantomimes during the 1830s. His panoramic scene of the Agincourt battlefield for *Macready's *Henry V* at *Covent Garden (1839), and his designs for *Acis and Galatea* at Drury Lane (1842), were his last significant theatre works. CLB

Stanislavsky, Konstantin (1863–1938) Russian actor and director, the most influential theorist of modern *acting. Stanislavsky changed his name from Alekseev in 1885 when he performed in the amateur theatre movement in Moscow. Along with others, he founded an amateur group, the Society of Art and Literature, in 1888, where his acting and *directing reached professional standards. Ten years later he founded a professional company with *Nemirovich-Danchenko, the Moscow Art Theatre. Their joint agenda focused on ensemble, modern standards of *scenography, authenticity in sets and *costumes, discipline and dedication, in-depth *rehearsal, and creating a contemporary repertoire of high quality. Stanislavsky's task was to act and direct. In the early years he created a number of major roles, including in the four major *Chekhov plays: Trigorin (*Seagull*, 1898), Astrov (*Uncle Vanya*,

1899), Vershinin (*Three Sisters*, 1901), and Gaev (*Cherry Orchard*, 1904). Other notable parts were Stockmann in *Ibsen's *An Enemy of the People* (1900), the title role in *Hauptmann's *Michael Kramer* (1901), and Satin in *Gorky's *Lower Depths* (1902). Stanislavsky directed some of these with Nemirovich-Danchenko (the Chekhov plays), and directed others alone (*Ivan the Terrible*, 1899; *Power of Darkness*, 1902) or with another colleague (*Tsar Fyodor Ioannovich*, with A. Sanin, 1898). Tall, attractively built, imaginative, disciplined, and self-critical, Stanislavsky excelled as an actor. His natural introspection led him to dissect his roles in minute detail and relate every aspect to the overall production, a practice he encouraged among the members of the young company and which led him to the notion that acting could be systematically taught.

After an experimental studio headed by *Meyerhold failed (in Stanislavsky's view) in 1905, he reached a crisis in his own technique and began subsequently to record his observations towards the creation of what eventually became known as the 'system'. This period of development coincided with a difficult time at MAT, particularly in his relationship with Nemirovich-Danchenko. Resigning from the board in 1908, Stanislavsky embarked on an experimental journey, rehearsing *Turgenev's *Month in the Country* (1909). An intimate psychological drama, the play gave opportunity for Stanislavsky to work on his theories about imagination, memory, and the emotions. The key was an idea garnered from the French psychologist Ribot that it is possible to retrieve the emotional impact of memories given an appropriate external stimulus. This led to the central principle of the system, that by using 'affective memory' or 'emotional memory' an actor can create fusion between his or her own self and the *character by stimulating emotions the actor has experienced. A strong imagination is paramount, as well as a willingness to create, as if true, the external circumstances for the character (the 'magic if'). Such use of the imagination and emotions would prevent the mechanistic repetition of roles which Stanislavsky had experienced, and would ensure vitality on stage. The fusion of the actor's self with the role also implied immense self-control, concentration, and discipline, and a willingness to believe in the truth of what is being created at the expense of a conscious awareness of its theatricality. Physical training and exercises to sustain concentration became requisites.

Stanislavsky allied this psychological approach to close study of the text to establish a 'throughline of *action' to which all the analyses of the individual roles would cohere. Crucial to this development was his work on Chekhov's plays, which led Stanislavsky to assert that a latent drama or *subtext operated under the spoken *dialogue, revealing hidden desires and 'objectives' of the characters, who were treated as psychological mechanisms. Such an agenda was particularly appropriate to the *realistic plays in *naturalistic productions he favoured, which also called for the establishment of a 'fourth wall', the pretence that the audience is not present, in order to preserve the semblance of reality. In 1912 Stanislavsky set up a studio at MAT with *Sulerzhitsky as a training centre for young actors to develop his system.

After the 1917 Revolution, Stanislavsky introduced his demanding standards of acting into *opera at the Bolshoi Opera Studio in 1918 (subsequently the Stanislavsky Opera Theatre). He was in demand as a teacher and managed MAT's European and American *tour (1922–4). He staged two plays reflecting the mixed politics of the period: *Bulgakov's *Days of the Turbins* (1926) and *Ivanov's *Armoured Train 14-69* (1927). A heart attack in 1928 left him debilitated and housebound but with time to write. He had already published a hasty autobiography (*My Life in Art*, 1924). Now he assembled *An Actor Prepares* (1936) and *Building a Character* (published posthumously, 1950). *Creating a Role* (1961) is an edited collection of remaining pieces.

Stanislavsky's collected works were published in Russian (1954–61) and form the core of the system, which became enshrined in training in Soviet Russia and highly influential elsewhere. *Boleslavsky imported the ideas to America in the 1920s, where they were notably taken up by *Strasberg and developed as the *Method at the *Actors Studio, though the Method ignores Stanislavsky's changes to the system in later years. CM

Stapleton, Maureen (1925–2006) American actress. Stapleton studied at the *Actors Studio and made her debut in the 1946 Broadway revival of *Synge's *The Playboy of the Western World*. Her breakthrough performance came as the earthy Serafina delle Rose in *Williams's *The Rose Tattoo* (1951). Stapleton, who over the course of her career demonstrated a formidable emotional range as well as a knack for *comedy, played in Broadway premières of *The Crucible* (1953), *Orpheus Descending* (1957), *Toys in the Attic* (1960), and *The Gingerbread Lady* (1970). Her last notable stage performance was Birdie in the 1981 revival of *Hellman's *The Little Foxes*. Stapleton also worked in television and film, including *Airport* (1970), *Interiors* (1978), and *Reds* (1981).   EW

Steele, Richard (1672-1729) Irish writer, editor, and *manager. Best known for his collaborations with *Addison on the *Tatler* and the *Spectator*, Steele was deeply involved with the theatre for much of his life. His first play, *The Funeral* (1701), remained in the repertory throughout the eighteenth century. His next plays, *The Lying Lover* (1703) and *The Tender Husband* (1705), show him attempting to accommodate *Collier's strictures against immorality into comic drama. Steele was genuinely interested in the moral reformation of the stage. Upon the accession of George I, Steele became governor of *Drury Lane, and in 1715 its *patentee. While Steele left the business affairs of his *playhouse to the *actor-managers, he considered himself its moral arbiter. He even experimented with a semi-private theatrical venture called 'The Censorium', which was part theatre, part concert hall, part self-improvement seminar. His dramatic masterpiece *The Conscious Lovers* (1721) was an instant hit and an enduring success.   MJK

Stein, Gertrude (1874-1946) American writer. A central presence in modernism, Stein applied principles of fragmentation and simultaneity gathered from *Picasso and Braque to theatre. Her 77 'plays' and *'operas' (bearing no *character names or distinctions between stage direction, *dialogue, or texts for singing) were composed between 1913 and 1946, though staged rarely. Stein wrote that theatre was the appropriate literary form for the modern era in that, unlike a novel, theatre happens in a continuous physical present. Her theatre attempted to render the 'actual present' without plot or *action. Stark *Young captured Stein's objective when he wrote of *Houseman's production of *Four Saints in Three Acts: an opera to be sung* (1934, music by Virgil Thomson), 'the opera turns itself in one's hand, like a melon or a flower'. Stein's *Dr Faustus Lights the Lights* (1938) saw New York stagings by the *Living Theatre (1951), Maxine Klein at *La Mama (1972), *Foreman (1982), and Robert *Wilson (1992).   MAF

Stein, Peter (1937–) German director, arguably the most important of his generation. His work is characterized by great intellectual rigour and attention to detail, but without dryness. In 1964 he joined the Munich Kammerspiele under *Kortner, who, together with *Brecht, was a major influence. His direction of a Bavarian dialect version of *Bond's *Saved* in 1967 was a remarkable professional debut, named production of the year by *Theater heute*. It was distinguished by the *realism of its performances, its shocking contemporary content, and its imaginative staging. His career in Munich came to an abrupt end in 1968, when the Kammerspiele banned his production of *Weiss's *Vietnam-Discourse*, a virulent attack on US policy in South-East Asia. Stein worked in Bremen until he once again resigned in protest at the infringement of artistic freedom, debating this problem in his production of *Goethe's *Torquato Tasso* (1969).

In 1970 Stein relocated to Berlin and was a driving force in founding a theatre *collective at the *Schaubühne am Halleschen Ufer. Provocatively, it opened with Stein's production of Brecht's *The Mother*, in which a simple woman is converted to communism, and became one of the many sources of conflict between Stein and the West Berlin Senate, concerned about subsidizing left-wing attacks on the so-called Free World. Yet so strong did Stein's international reputation become that he needed only to threaten to leave Berlin for the Senate to concede ever greater subsidies. His next major production was *Ibsen's *Peer Gynt*, staged over two nights in 1971, which challenged the bourgeois concept of the individual, revealing Peer as an infinitely reproducible nonentity. There followed *Kleist's *Prince of Homburg* (1972), *Gorky's *Summerfolk* (1974), and *As You Like It* (1977). For Shakespeare's *comedy, which was staged in a film studio with the Forest of Arden created with real trees and a pond, Stein worked with his ensemble for six years, presenting the results of their research in a spectacular living exhibition, *Shakespeare's Memory* (1976). After *Aeschylus' *Oresteia* (1980), and *Chekhov's *Three Sisters* (1984), Stein left the Schaubühne to work internationally as freelance director of *opera, *O'Neill's *The Hairy Ape* (1987), Chekhov's *Cherry Orchard* (1989), and on a 21-hour staging of Goethe's *Faust* (2000). He also revisited Shakespeare with a grandiose *Julius Caesar* (1992) and a lacklustre *Troilus and Cressida* (2006), both seen at the *Edinburgh Festival, and returned to *Greek drama in *Euripides' *Medea* (2005) and *Sophocles' *Electra* (2007).   MWP

Stepanova, Varvara (1894–1958) Russian/ Soviet painter, designer, and founder member of the Working Group of Constructivists. Her designs for *Meyerhold's 1922 production of *Sukhovo-Kobylin's *Tarelkin's Death* consisted of *constructivist items made out of wooden slats in the shape of crates large enough to contain individual actors (when functioning as prison cells, for example), plus exploding and collapsing stools. The central crate was designed to resemble a giant mincing machine and stood as a metaphor for tsarist Russia. Her *costume designs, like

working overalls, were intended to tone in with the decor.   NW

Stephens, Robert (1931–95) English actor. At the *Royal Court his dashing good looks saw him veer between heroic leads and languid ne'er-do-wells in *Miller's *The Crucible* (1956), and *Osborne's *The Entertainer* (1957) and *Epitaph for George Dillon* (1958). Joining *Olivier's *National Theatre at the *Old Vic in 1963, his reputation as a weighty and significant actor was won in *Hamlet* (as Horatio in the inaugural production), *Farquhar's *The Recruiting Officer* (1963), *Shaffer's *The Royal Hunt of the Sun* (1964), *Arden's *Armstrong's Last Goodnight*, and *Pinero's *Trelawny of the 'Wells'* (both 1965). Although his star waned somewhat, he returned to the NT in *The Cherry Orchard* and *Brand* (both 1978). A high-profile film and television career never quite translated into commercial stardom. Towards the end of his life his reputation as an actor of power and pathos was secured when he appeared at the *Royal Shakespeare Company as Falstaff (1992) and as Lear, his last stage role (1993).   AS

Stephens, Simon (1971–) English writer of unsentimental plays about lives lived in extremis. *Herons* (2001), *Port* (2002), *One Minute* (2003), *Country Music* (2004), and *Harper Regan* (2008) are domestic, somewhat *naturalistic dramas depicting the effect on ordinary people of violence, scandal, and loss. *Motortown* (2006) and *Pornography* (2007) capture, through increasingly complex theatrical forms, the mindset of a society blighted by lovelessness and terrorism.   DR

Stephenson, Elie (1944–) Guianese writer who became French Guiana's first playwright with *O Mayouri* (1974). All his plays, whether *tragedies, *satires, or historical dramas, interrogate Guianese society, weaving French and creole scenes as a representation of French Guiana's socio-linguistic condition and to communicate more readily with the creole-speaking *audience. They include *A Speck of a Country*, (1976), *Les Voyageurs* (1977), *The Earth* (1979), *Les Delinters* (1979), and *A New Legend of d'Chimbo* (1984). Stephenson's plays have been performed in French Guiana and in numerous festivals throughout the francophone Caribbean.   LEM

Stern, Ernst (1876–1954) German *scenographer, *Reinhardt's main collaborator in Berlin from 1906. An eclectic designer, his work was normally characterized by stylized *realism. He designed several of Reinhardt's Shakespeare productions, notably *Twelfth Night* (1907), *Hamlet* (1909), and *A Midsummer Night's Dream* (1913).

He helped Reinhardt's *The Miracle* (1911) to be an international success, first at the Olympia in London, which he transformed into a massive cathedral, and later in New York. His most successful *expressionist collaboration with Reinhardt was *Sorge's *The Beggar* (1917), though he was never fully suited to the style and was less successful with *Goering's *Naval Encounter* (1918) and Felix Hollaender's production of *Kaiser's *From Morning to Midnight* (1919). Stern was more comfortable with the classics, as in *Büchner's *Danton's Death* (1916) and *Ibsen's *John Gabriel Borkman* (1917). When he began to work in London from the late 1920s, he designed *Coward's *Bitter Sweet* (1929) and other popular *musicals. In 1937 he was in charge of Selfridge's designs for the coronation of George VI. During the Second World War, by which time he had changed his first name to Ernest, he returned to Shakespeare, working on *Wolfit's productions (1943–5). MWP

Sternheim, Carl (1878–1942) German dramatist. Sternheim is best known for his dramatic cycle *From a Bourgeois Hero's Life*, satiric *comedies portraying Wilhelmenian Germany on the eve of the First World War. Plays such as *The Cash Box* (1911), *The Underpants* (1911), and *Der Snob* (1914) created scandals because of their 'immorality' and were banned during the war. Other works include *Bürger Schippel* (1913) and *Die Marquise von Arcis* (1919, translated as *The Mask of Virtue*, 1919). Sternheim was initially deemed *expressionist for stylistic reasons but his plays are formally quite traditional, owing more to *Molière than to *Toller. His career declined during the Weimar Republic and he was banned by the Nazis. CBB

Stevenson, Juliet (1956–) English actress. With the *Royal Shakespeare Company her repertoire included Titania and Hippolyta in *A Midsummer's Night's Dream* (1981), Isabella in *Measure for Measure* (1983), Rosalind in *As You Like It*, Cressida in *Troilus and Cressida* (both 1985), and Mme de Tourvel in *Les Liaisons dangereuses* (1985). At the *Royal Court she was Paulina in Ariel Dorfman's *Death and the Maiden* (1992), while at the *National Theatre she played Hedda Gabler in 1989 and Amanda in *Private Lives* in 1999. Her screen appearances include a touching Nina in the delightful *Truly, Madly, Deeply* (1990) and a satisfyingly pompous Mrs Elton in *Emma* (1996). Her *métier* is intelligent, rather introspective *characters edged with steel or mild eccentricity. AS

Stewart, Ellen *See* La Mama Experimental Theatre Club.

Stewart, Nellie (1858–1931) Australian actor and singer. She made her debut aged 5 with Charles *Kean in *The Stranger* in Melbourne in 1864, and as an adult was a versatile actor and singer, appearing for J. C. *Williamson's company in a variety of comic and dramatic operatic starring roles. She left Williamson's in 1887, establishing a permanent professional and personal partnership with George Musgrove. In 1902 she played the first non-singing role of her career, as Nell *Gwynn in *Sweet Nell of Old Drury*, which established her as Australia's leading comedy actress, known as 'Australia's idol'. KMN

Stewart, Patrick (1940–) English actor. Stewart was associated with the *Royal Shakespeare Company from 1966 for almost three decades, appearing in numberous productions, including *The Revenger's Tragedy*, *Henry V*, *Titus Andronicus*, and *A Midsummer Night's Dream*. His distinctive voice and commanding presence made him equally attractive for BBC television, where he played Sejanus in *I, Claudius* (1976) and Karla, John le Carré's master spy, in the serializations of *Tinker, Tailor, Soldier, Spy* (1978) and *Smiley's People* (1982). But international celebrity came with the role of Captain Jean-Luc Picard in *Star Trek: The Next Generation* (television 1987–94, films 1994–2006). Other film appearances include *Dune* (1984) and the *X-Men* series (2000–9), which pitted his Professor Xavier against fellow RSC alumnus *McKellen's Magneto. Stewart's later stage work includes Prospero, a one-person dramatization of *Dickens's *A Christmas Carol* (1991), *Othello* (Washington, 1997), *Miller's *The Ride down Mount Morgan* (2000), *Priestley's *Johnson over Jordan* (2001), and *Waiting for Godot* with McKellen (2009). AS

stock character A *character of the same general type appearing in a number of different plays. The Italian *commedia dell'arte* offered traditional general types—the young lovers, the comic servants, the foolish old men—but also more specific stock characters that were also endlessly repeated: the flamboyant but cowardly Spanish captain, the foolish pedant, the elderly lover of the young wife. The comic tradition has continued through the centuries to make much use of this device, but stock characters have also been important in serious drama, every historical period developing certain type characters that were often repeated, such as the dashing heroes of the Spanish *early modern 'cape and sword' plays or the darker and more introspective machiavels or *revengers of England. During the English Restoration the stock comic characters of the fops, the witty couples, and the country bumpkins had their stock parallels in the noble leading figures of the *heroic dramas, influenced by *Corneille.

Nineteenth-century *melodrama excelled in stock characters, noble *heroes, persecuted maidens, aristocratic *villains, stalwart British sailors, but before melodrama actors throughout the European tradition had specialized in noble fathers, male romantic leads, tyrants, soubrettes, and *ingénues, since most *stock companies hired, trained, and cast actors according to certain general stock types that were called *emplois* in France and *lines of business in England. In India, the classic Sanskrit theatre manual, the *Natyasastra*, contains lengthy descriptions of a great array of traditional stock character types. Japanese *kabuki contains similar carefully delineated traditional role categories, as does Beijing Opera (*jingju*).

The rise of modern *realism with its emphasis upon the originality and uniqueness of each new drama, has muted (though by no means terminated) theatrical reliance upon stock types. Radio, film, and television continue to rely on stock characters, as in television series like soap operas or sitcoms. MC

stock company A means of organizing a resident acting company into specialist *lines of business, dating from the Elizabethan period. Each actor, such as the *clown in the Elizabethan company, would play many parts, but all within his own range as clown. By the nineteenth century this system had been codified, and actors were hired as a Light Comedian, a First Old Man, or a Female Juvenile Lead. Such a company could handle anything in the *repertory: *tragedy, *comedy, *farce, or *melodrama. The stock company had an extensive repertory, which changed frequently, and therefore very little time or necessity for *rehearsals, since each actor in the company was already in the possession of a large number of parts, which he or she could play at a moment's notice with minimal rehearsal (and with the aid of the *prompter). With the advent of the long run, and with the *touring company taking a single hit out of London or New York, the stock company disappeared rapidly in the 1870s and 1880s. A nostalgic picture of a stock company appears in *Pinero's *Trelawny of the 'Wells'* (1898). MRB

Stoklos, Denise (1950–) Working as playwright, director, and performer in solo performance pieces since 1979, Brazilian artist Stoklos has won a large international *audience. Her pieces, such as *Mary Stuart* (1987), *500 Years: a fax to Christopher Columbus* (1992), and *Civil Disobedience* (1997), are generally grounded in historical reference. Though often produced in languages other than Portuguese, her work remains rooted in Brazilian life. A consummate *mime, dependent on Brazilian gestural codes, her *actor-based theory of 'essential theatre' opts for a utopian humanism in response to cultural, political, and sexual repression. Many of her pieces have been created while visiting artist with New York's *La Mama, including *Louise Bourgeois: I do, I undo, I redo* (2000), a *monologue taken from Bourgeois's autobiography, and *Deconstructing and Reconstructing the Father*, which was visually enriched by a sculpture set designed by Bourgeois herself. LHD

Stoppard, Tom (1937–) Playwright. Born in Czechoslovakia, Stoppard grew up in Singapore before moving to England in 1946. His first major play, *Rosencrantz and Guildenstern Are Dead* (1966-7), retold *Hamlet* through the eyes of its two unfortunate courtiers, reconceived as a *Beckettian double act. It established several characteristics of Stoppard's *dramaturgy: his word-playing intellectuality, audacious, paradoxical, and self-conscious theatricality, and preference for reworking pre-existing narratives. In *Jumpers* (1972) a professor of moral philosophy is placed alongside radical gymnasts in a murder-mystery thriller. *Travesties* (1974), based on the fact that Lenin, Joyce, and Tristan Tzara were all in Zurich during the First World War, exploits the dazzling possibilities of their incongruous encounter in a *Wildean context.

Stoppard's plays have been sometimes dismissed as pieces of clever showmanship, lacking in substance, social commitment, or emotional weight. His theatrical surfaces serve to conceal rather than reveal their author's views, and his fondness for towers of paradox spirals away from social comment. This is seen most clearly in his *comedies *The Real Inspector Hound* (1968) and *After Magritte* (1970), which create their humour through highly formal devices of reframing and juxtaposition. Stoppard has eloquently defended his refusal of commitment with increasing sophistication in his epic trilogy about nineteenth-century Russian revolutionaries and radicals, *The Coast of Utopia* (2002), and in *Rock 'n' Roll* (2006), but his plays about *censorship, human rights, and state repression—notably *Every Good Boy Deserves Favour*, 'a play for actors and orchestra' (1977), and two television works, *Professional Foul* (1977) and *Squaring the Circle* (1984)—are unmistakably engaged politically.

Many of Stoppard's later works bring a profound emotional depth to his characteristic intellectual sparkle. *The Real Thing* (1982) uses a *metatheatrical structure to consider the pain of an adulterous relationship, and in *Arcadia* (1993) a dual time scheme produces a real and surprising pathos lurking within its investigation of chaos theory, historiography, and landscape gardening. *The Invention of Love* (1997) has a similar effect with an exploration of love and passion. Other works include *Night and Day* (1978), *Undiscovered Country* (1979, adapted from *Schnitzler), *On the Razzle* (1981, from *Nestroy), and *Hapgood* (1988). Radio plays, some subsequently adapted for the stage, include *If You're Glad I'll Be Frank* (1966), *Albert's Bridge* (1967), and *Artist Descending a Staircase* (1972). Stoppard has been a mainstay of the *National Theatre and is one of the most internationally performed dramatists of his generation.   DR

Storey, David (1933-) English writer. Although he considers himself a novelist first (he won the Booker Prize for *Saville* in 1976), Storey earned great critical acclaim for a number of plays that appeared in quick succession between 1967 and 1975. Like fellow Yorkshire dramatist *Mercer, several of Storey's works refract elements of his 'split' life as the rugby-playing son of a miner and a Slade School of Art graduate and writer. His first play, *The Restoration of Arnold Middleton* (1967), about the mental breakdown of a schoolteacher, was produced at the *Royal Court and transferred to the West End. With his second play for the Royal Court, *In Celebration* (1969), Storey teamed up with Lindsay Anderson, who had previously directed the film version of Storey's novel, *This Sporting Life* (1963). Anderson directed Storey's subsequent major plays, all of them marked by a *Chekhovian quality: *The Contractor* (1969), *Home* (1970), *The Changing Room* (1971), *Life Class* (1974), and *Early Days* (1980).   MDG

storm and stress *See* STURM UND DRANG.

Stranitzky, Joseph Anton (1676-1726) Austrian comic actor. Stranitzky began as an itinerant comedian in southern Germany in 1699 and moved to Vienna in 1705, where he set up as a dentist and fair *booth actor. He developed the *stock character of the Salzburg peasant Hanswurst, which was to become his leading role. In 1711-12 he assumed control of the new Kärntnertor Theatre, the first permanent German language theatre. Plays came from a variety of sources but all were laced with Stranitzky's earthy Hanswurst *improvisations. Stranitzky established the tradition of Viennese folk theatre which continued into the mid-nineteenth century.   CRB

Strasberg, Lee (1901-82) With the *Group Theatre (1931-7) and the *Actors Studio (1948-82), Strasberg was identified as the pre-eminent *acting teacher of his day and—through his work with film actors such as *Brando and James Dean—helped to shape the notion of *realistic acting around the world. The productions he directed for the Group Theatre, especially *The House of Connelly* (1931) and *Men in White* (1933), were admired by critics for their ensemble acting and graceful staging. Born in Galicia, Strasberg emigrated at the age of 7. From 1924 in New York he studied with *Boleslavsky and Maria Ouspenskaya, alumni of the *Moscow Art Theatre and the studios of *Stanislavsky and *Vakhtangov. Strasberg later described his own system—known as the *Method—as a blending of Stanislavsky and Vakhtangov techniques. Strasberg joined *Clurman and Cheryl Crawford in forming the Group Theatre in 1930, but resigned in 1937 and directed freelance until he began at the Actors Studio. He was named its *artistic director in 1951. Late in his life, Strasberg emerged as a film actor himself, notably as a mobster in *The Godfather, Part II* (1974).   MAF

Stratford Festival Canadian company in Ontario, the largest repertory theatre in North America. While centred on classics, it also produces twentieth-century works, *musicals, and new plays. In 1952 Tom Patterson persuaded *Guthrie to give advice, and he eventually became the first *artistic director. Guthrie directed both productions in the first season, *Richard III* and *All's Well That Ends Well*, which ran in repertory for six weeks in the summer of 1953. Guthrie and his designer Tanya *Moisewitsch created a revolutionary thrust stage which influenced *playhouse architecture for decades, housed initially in a *circus tent and then in a new building that opened in 1957.

At first the acting company consisted of international stars supported by a predominantly Canadian ensemble. Famous names at Stratford have included *Guinness and *Worth (1953), *McKenna (1957), *Robards (1958, 1969), Julie Harris (1960), *Scofield (1961), *Bates (1967), Maggie *Smith (1976-8, 1980), and *Ustinov (1979-80). But the company also developed its own Canadian stars, such as *Hutt, *Plummer, Martha *Henry, and more recently has brought in television celebrities.

Guthrie's hand-picked successor was *Langham (1956-67), who brought international fame to the company with his devotion to the classics and his mastery of the thrust stage, and took productions abroad. Subsequent artistic directors have been Canadians, either native born or naturalized: *Gascon (1968-74), *Phillips (1975-80), *Hirsch (1981-5), *Neville (1986-9), David William

(1990-3), Richard Monette (1994-2007), and Des McAnuff (2008-). Further *tours have included Europe (1973), Australia (1974), and New York (frequently).

Stratford's Festival Theatre is one of the most recognizable playhouses in the world. Major renovations in 1996-7 reduced both its seating capacity (from 2,276 to 1,824) and the span of its fan-shaped *auditorium. The company also has three further playhouses. Since its first season, the Festival's *audience has grown from 68,000 to over 500,000 annually.   DWJ

Strauss, Botho (1944-) German dramatist. In 1970 Strauss joined *Stein at the *Schaubühne as a *dramaturg, became freelance in 1975, and is now acknowledged as a significant German dramatist. His first plays, *Die Hypochonder* (1972) and *Well-known Faces, Mixed Feelings* (1975), were moderately successful, but his breakthrough was *Three Acts of Recognition* (1977) with its fluid, interlocking conversation exposing the vapidity of a provincial arts society. *Great and Small* (1980) is a kind of *expressionist *Stationendrama* featuring a woman *protagonist on a journey through the indifference of West German society; *Kalldewey Farce* (1982) is a rare example of German intellectual *farce. Other plays include *Der Park* (loosely based on *Midsummer Night's Dream*, 1984), *The Tour Guide* (1986), *Visitors* (1988), *Seven Doors* (1988), and *The Time and the Room*, (1989). *Final Chorus* (1991) refers to German reunification. Strauss's work is grounded on a fine ear for speech and a satirical eye for posturing. Despite often hilarious *dialogue the plays are philosophically inflected; the mythical themes and figures are married with the trivia of quotidian middle-class existence. *Ithaka* (1996) was attacked for its apparent desire for restoration of conservative metaphysics.   CBB

street theatre Many street entertainments probably had their genesis in the skills of *juggling, *magic acts, or *acrobatics that took *audiences out of the everyday with minimal means, and street theatre is as old as the most ancient crossroads. Street theatre also connects with carnival, festival, revels and riotous assemblies, popular gatherings that disrupt routine with rudeness, insert the miraculous into the mundane, challenge authority with the cheapest of jokes, and give power a poke in the eye. The *mimes, minstrels, and strolling players that peopled every fair and market-place in *medieval Europe were simply one aspect of a vast and enduring transcultural web of often illicit pleasures enjoyed by millions at street level. Given such traditions, and the raw, high-risk nature of its territory, street theatre can be both sublime and ridiculous, sophisticated and crude, seductive and provocative —sometimes all at once. It is therefore extremely difficult to do well.

The accelerating urbanization of Western societies in the final two centuries of the last millennium ensured that street theatre was a regular and widespread trade. It had its gruesome dimensions in public *executions and tortures everywhere, in the nineteenth-century reflected in Britain in the comic grotesque *puppet shows of *Punch and Judy, and in America in the sidewalk shenanigans of blackface *minstrelsy. In the mid-twentieth-century it served a widening range of purposes, from entertainment that pretended a pristine innocence—in the between-wars *pierrot shows of English seaside towns—through intense participation in political struggle and upheaval—in the *agitprop of the 1930s, or the unbuttoned provocations in 1960s American civil rights and Vietnam War protests (*Bread and Puppet Theatre leading the way). Later it engaged with more or less ambivalence in the international festivals, in the competition between 'cultural capitals', and in the merry-go-round of special events (including the Olympic Games) mounted for transcultural tourists, all tending to place it in service to capitalist globalization as the millennium drew to a close (*see* INTER-CULTURALISM). Yet its original rebellious spirit survived, and even sometimes thrived, in the uncontainable invention of thousands of street theatre groups around the world, especially in India. BRK

Strehler, Giorgio (1921-97) The preeminent Italian director of his time. With *Visconti and *Squarzina, Strehler ensured that the vision of the *director was primary, replacing the traditional dominance of the actor in Italy. Born near Trieste into a family of musicians and artists, he studied drama in Milan, worked as an actor, was enlisted in the Fascist army, but fled to Switzerland where, in a refugee camp, he gained his first experience directing. In liberated Milan he and Paolo Grassi established a theatre of a new type called the Piccolo Teatro, which opened in 1947 with Strehler's production of *Gorky's *The Lower Depths*. In the early years the Piccolo produced a total of 80 plays, the vast majority directed by Strehler. *Pirandello and *Goldoni, authors who were to figure prominently in his output, appeared in the first season. In 1947 Strehler also produced *Verdi and Prokofiev at La Scala, and would all his life move between drama and *opera. Strehler and Grassi divided responsibilties, but in the 1960s the Piccolo itself, once in the vanguard, was viewed as stale and conservative. Strehler was criticized so heavily by the militant student movement that he resigned to set up a new company, Gruppo Teatro e Azione, whose aim was to present political work by authors such as *Brecht, *Gorky, and *Weiss. Strehler returned to the Piccolo in 1972, assuming sole charge. In 1982 Jack Lang, French Minister for Culture, offered Strehler the *artistic directorship of both the *Comédie-Francaise and the *Odéon in Paris. Instead he accepted a newly created post at the Odéon alone as director of Théâtre de l'Europe. He held the position in conjunction with his post with the Piccolo, and in 1991, the Piccolo, together with theatres in Madrid and Paris, became part of one overarching Theatre of Europe. His last years were spent defending himself, successfully, from a charge of having embezzled European Union funds.

Strehler published an influential book, *Per un teatro umano* (*Towards a Human Theatre*, 1974), and the adjective 'humanist' or the equally unhelpful 'eclectic' has been attached to his directing. He was not an experimentalist, he did little to encourage new writing, and preferred to work and rework a few scripts from the classical canon. He refused to be associated with one school or tradition, and any quest for a constant aesthetic standard in his long career is futile. His genius was an ability to release an energy in an individual script by meticulous critical analysis and by attention to the individual scene, but it is worth underlining that, having reduced the power of the actor, he held to the collaborative notion of production, first outlined in the manifesto of the Piccolo: 'The word in the first place, the gesture in the second in a process which reaches completion only in front of an *audience.' He had a privilege granted to few directors, of returning time and again to a few plays. The first production of Goldoni's *Arlecchino, Servant of Two Masters* was in 1947, and it remained in his repertoire over 40 years through six separate productions. In it he harnessed the acrobatic talents of Marcello Moretti, his first Arlecchino, to produce a unique synthesis of the words of Goldoni the theatrical reformer and the styles of *commedia dell'arte* Goldoni had tamed. Pirandello, Shakespeare (most notably *The Tempest*, 1978), and Brecht were the other authors who dominated his portfolio. His first Brecht production was *The Three-penny Opera* in 1956, but although the meeting between the two came relatively late, the contact with Brecht's methods was a watershed, even if, idiosyncratically, he blended Brecht with *Stanislavsky. In his last decade, he directed only the Promethean spirits of European theatre, mounting his sixth production of Pirandello's enigmatic *The Mountain Giants* in 1993, and between 1987

and 1992, he produced a version of *Goethe called *Fragments of Faust I and II*, returning to the stage himself in the title role.   JF

Strindberg, August (1849–1912) Swedish playwright. Strindberg's father was a shipping administrator who married his former domestic servant. Strindberg never completely came to terms with his mother's lowly station; he called his autobiography *The Son of a Serving Woman* (1886). He became an assistant at the Royal Library in Stockholm (1874–81). During this period he wrote his first major historical drama, *Master Olof* (1876); a much acclaimed novel on artistic life in Stockholm, *The Red Room* (1879); and works of cultural history, *Old Stockholm* (1882) and *The Swedish People* (1882). In 1877 he married the divorced actress Siri von Essen, a tempestuous union that lasted twelve years. In self-imposed exile from 1883 to 1897, he returned briefly in 1884 to face a trial for blasphemy for his collection of stories *Married Life* (he was acquitted).

During the 1880s Strindberg wrote a series of plays inspired by the *naturalist movement: *The Father* (1887), *Miss Julie* (1888), and *Creditors* (1888), depicting the warfare between the sexes he experienced in his marriage. Following an acrimonious divorce, Strindberg moved to Berlin and married a young Austrian journalist, Frida Uhl in 1893; after a year of misery, they too divorced. Strindberg moved to Paris to pursue experiments in alchemy, where a production of *The Father* in 1894 brought him public recognition. But the repeated failures of his personal life precipitated a severe mental crisis (1895–6), a time he called the 'Inferno period'. Remarkably, even at the height of his anguish, he was able to make precise notes that permitted him to write a novel about his suffering called *Inferno* (1897) and an *expressionist dream play, *To Damascus* (1898), in which he attempted to come to terms with his failed marriages.

In 1897 he returned to Sweden, moved back to Stockholm in 1899, and remained there until his death. The production of *To Damascus* at *Dramaten in 1900 led to his meeting Harriet Bosse, a young actress who became his third wife in 1901. Their marriage was even more tempestuous than his previous two and resulted in a pattern of separation and reconciliation until 1904 when they divorced. Despite the upheavals in his emotional life, these were enormously productive years. He wrote a cycle of historical dramas to bring alive Swedish history, from *Gustav Vasa* (1899) to *Gustaf III* (1902). He wrote an *absurdist black *comedy, *The Dance of Death* (1900), two further parts of *To Damascus*, and completed *A*

Dream Play (1901). He wrote the major novels *Gothic Rooms* (1904) and *Black Banners* (1904). He founded Intima Teatern (Intimate Theatre) with the actor August Falck in 1907 and wrote his chamber plays for that company: *The Storm, The Ghost Sonata,* and *The Pelikan.* Intima presented 24 of his plays until it closed in 1910. In *Open Letters to the Intimate Theatre* (1909) Strindberg set down his advice on *acting and staging. In the final years of his life he wrote *The Great Highway* (1909) and a series of works of cultural history. This brief listing gives only a taste of the range and scope of his creative genius.

Miss Julie is the most frequently performed of Strindberg's plays but in its time evoked shocked horror. It was refused by Strindberg's publisher and frequently banned by *censors across Europe. It offered a brutally frank insight into the naturalist world that *Zola had depicted in his novels, while the preface stressed the complex motivation for the *characters' behaviour suggested by Hippolyte Taine. Jean and Miss Julie are shown to be amoral predators, using sex as a weapon in their struggle for mutual domination. Further to the naturalist cause, the stage directions insist on a real kitchen, with real utensils and furniture, in place of the painted scenery of the *illusionist stage.

Equally revolutionary were Strindberg's dream plays written after his Inferno crisis: *To Damascus* and *A Dream Play.* In these works Strindberg conjures up a spiritual landscape in which his own sufferings are the starting point for a meditation upon life and relationships, hope and despair. Settings blend and merge, as the figures strike out on a quest for the meaning of existence. The inevitable failures that confront the characters are shown with the certainty of one who has looked into the abyss and is no longer terrified of the emptiness. The works represent the aesthetic transcendence of absurdity, the sensitive creation of dreamlike beauty out of the chaos of darkness and despair.

Strindberg wrote in advance of his age, as the contemporary theatre lacked the technological resources to stage the dream images he suggested. After his death, directors in Sweden such as *Molander in the 1930s and *Bergman in the 1970s were able to create the dreamlike atmosphere Strindberg had envisaged. Throughout the twentieth century Strindberg's dramas and ideas on practice proved highly influential.   DT

striptease *See* BURLESQUE; PORNOGRAPHY AND PERFORMANCE.

Strouse, Charles (1928–) American composer. Strouse began writing theatre *music for

*stock productions at an upstate New York resort, where he first met lyricist Lee Adams. In 1960 they made their joint Broadway debut with the successful *Bye Bye Birdie,* integrating traditional Broadway sound with satirical rock and roll rhythms. He and Adams wrote four more Broadway *musicals together, ending their exclusive collaboration in 1970 after *Applause,* a powerful vehicle for Lauren Bacall. They reunited only twice, both times with disastrous results. Strouse continued to write for the musical theatre in New York and London with new lyricists, finding his greatest success with *Annie* (1977), written with Martin Charnin. He also wrote scores for several films and the theme song for the popular television series *All in the Family.*   JD

Sturm und Drang 'Storm and stress', an influential literary movement in late eighteenth-century Germany, took its name from the title of a play of 1776 by Friedrich Maximilian Klinger. The period began with *Goethe's youthful drama set in medieval Germany *Götz von Berlichingen* in 1773, and ended with *Schiller's contemporary domestic *tragedy *Intrigue and Love* in 1784. *Sturm und Drang* plays were strongly influenced by Shakespeare, who had been upheld by *Lessing as a model to replace the stultifying effect of French *neoclassicism. The resulting works were characterized by a focus on a powerful central figure, usually in revolt against a corrupt and flaccid society. Emulating Shakespeare, the portrayal of vibrant *heroes was achieved by tracing their progress through many locations and across several years. Such extravagant technical demands for multiple settings, together with the provocative subject material and charged, occasionally obscene, language, made staging of most of the plays impossible at the time. Thus the major pieces of the period, *Lenz's *The Tutor* (1774) and Schiller's *The Robbers* (1781), could be performed only in bowdlerized versions, while Lenz's *The Soldiers* (1776) had to wait a century. Only Heinrich Leopold Wagner (1747–79), who was less demanding of stage resources, had modest contemporary success with *Remorse after the Deed* in 1775 and with his most famous play, *The Child Murderess* (1777). Nevertheless *Sturm und Drang* had a powerful influence on *romanticism, and the episodic character of their plays re-emerged in *expressionist drama and in *Brecht, who wrote an adaptation of Lenz's *Tutor.*   MWP

Sturua, Robert (1938–) Georgian director, head of the Rustaveli Theatre in Tbilisi since 1978. Sturua came to international attention in the late 1970s, when his productions of *Brecht's *The Caucasian Chalk Circle* and Shakespeare's *Richard III* were seen abroad to acclaim. Sturua drew inspiration from Georgian folk theatre, popular music, cinematic montage, and the formalist theories of Bakhtin. He has staged drama and *opera abroad, including productions in the 1990s of *Hamlet* with Alan Rickman, *Three Sisters* with Vanessa, Lynn, and Jemma Redgrave, and *The Seagull*. None was especially well received. If Sturua tends not to travel well, work with his own company has been outstanding and his leading actor, Ramaz Chkhikvadse (known as the Georgian *Olivier), played an important part in his success. Sturua's Vakhtangov Theatre production of *Shatrov's *The Treaty of Brest* was also seen in London in the late 1980s during the period of glasnost, when excerpts from his production of *King Lear* were staged in Leicester. His revelatory *Merchant of Venice* was in Moscow in 2000. In Tbilisi he staged *Waiting for Godot* (2002) and two separate versions of *Hamlet* (2001, 2006). NW

Styne, Jule (1905–94) Prolific American composer of *musicals. He was playing for dance bands, conducting, and coaching vocalists in 1930s New York when he was brought to Hollywood to work with singers like Shirley Temple and Mary *Martin. In the 1940s he struck up a partnership with lyricist Sammy Cahn, scoring the film *Anchors Aweigh* (1945) and writing the Oscar-winning title song for *Three Coins in the Fountain* (1954). But Styne longed for Broadway, and he and Cahn had their first hit in 1947 with *High Button Shoes*. Styne went on to compose scores for more than 25 shows, among them *Bells Are Ringing* (1956), with lyrics by his frequent collaborators *Comden and Green. Styne endowed several singers with their signature tunes, including *Channing's 'Diamonds Are a Girl's Best Friend' from *Gentlemen Prefer Blondes* (1949), and Barbra Streisand's 'People' from *Funny Girl* (1964). Still composing in relative anonymity at the time, Styne gained overdue recognition with *Merman's powerhouse performance in *Gypsy* (1959).   EW

Suassuna, Ariano (1927–) One of Brazil's best-loved playwrights. His comic parables about society and religion mix the forms of Iberian religious plays with Portuguese-Brazilian folk legends. *Auto da compadecida* (*The Rogue's Trial*, 1956) uses the *auto sacramental* to present the trials of two tricksters who appeal to the Virgin Mary and a black Jesus for help against social injustice. The co-founder of important regional theatre groups in Recife in the 1940s, in 1970

Suassuna organized the Armorial movement, encouraging north-eastern artists and writers to study and preserve the living traditions of popular culture.   LHD

subsidy *See* FINANCE.

subtext A *Stanislavskian concept, subtext suggests, on the most basic level, that the written words of a play are incomplete, that a meaning is to be found beneath them. Underlying what a *character says is the subtext, the inner life which motivates and informs speech, *action, and even silence. The notion that an *actor must locate or create the subtext of a script, then convey it onstage, is central to the practices of both Stanislavsky's system and its descendant, the American *Method. On a larger level, subtext can also refer to the ineffable contribution actors make to the performance of scripted material, offering *audiences readings of plays which may be deeper and psychologically more complex than the plays themselves; the meaning of a script is therefore dependent upon actors' performance of both text and subtext.

The idea of subtext is linked historically to psychological *realism, and specifically to Stanislavsky's work on *Chekhov's plays at the *Moscow Art Theatre at the turn of the twentieth century. In *My Life in Art* (1924), Stanislavsky hints at the essence of subtext when he says of Chekhov's plays: 'Their charm does not lie in the *dialogue; it lies in the meaning behind this dialogue, in the pauses, in the looks of the actors, in the way they display emotions.' These observations opened up a world of experimentation for Stanislavsky, as he discovered how much could be revealed by actors through 'rays' of communication. He sought ways for actors to take characters from the written page and make them appear to audiences as 'real' human beings, who listen, think, reflect, react, and speak from an ongoing inner life (*see* REHEARSAL).

The idea of subtext assumes there can be a marked difference between what characters say and what they mean; the meaning is dependent upon the given circumstances. Thus subtext invites close reading and careful interpretation of the text, often in collaboration with a *director. Stanislavsky-inspired New York teachers such as *Adler, *Strasberg, and Sanford Meisner have placed different values on the relationship of the playwright's text to actor-derived subtext, but all subtext practices shift the status of both actor and text. Through the use of subtext, the actor is no less important than the playwright; the actor becomes co-creator, filling in what is not written.   RM

Sudermann, Hermann (1857–1928) German playwright. Sudermann's debut came in 1889 with *Honour*. He attained prominence along with *Hauptmann and was the most performed German playwright at the turn of the century, thought to be as powerful as *Ibsen. His *naturalistic plays deal with social problems and the threat of an increasingly oppressive environment. *Honour* projects the classical seduction motif into a Berlin working-class milieu, while *Sodom's End* (1890) deals with the conflict between emancipated artists and conservative bourgeoisie, a theme that he further developed in *Heimat* (*Homeland* or *Magda*, 1893). His *comedy *The Tempestuous Fellow Socrates* (1903), about the 1848 democrats, provoked both aesthetic and political attack. Sudermann was strongly influenced by Nietzsche, Flaubert, *Zola, and Fontane. Despite his skill (he wrote about 35 plays) his work is now dated and very seldom revived.   CBB

Sudraka Ancient Indian playwright of *Mricchakatika* (*The Little Clay Cart*). The *prologue identifies Sudraka as a Kshatriya king with wide expertise, though his dates are highly uncertain (ranging from second century BC to fifth century AD). Allegedly derived from *Bhasa's *Charudatta*, *Mricchakatika* deals with the love of a noble Brahman, Charudatta, for the courtesan Vasantsena, in a broad canvas of epic action involving intrigue, murder, reconciliation, and a subplot about the overthrow of a despotic ruler by a shepherd. Cast in the *prakarana* category of Sanskrit drama, this ten-act blockbuster draws on real life rather than on a classical tale or legend, incorporating a large number of low-class characters, who speak a wide range of Prakrit dialects. One of the earliest Sanskrit plays to attract European attention, two celebrated productions were staged in Paris in the nineteenth century—Gérard de Nerval and Méry's highly *romanticized rendering (1850), and Victor Barrucand's more 'anarchist' interpretation (1895).   LSR/RB

Sukhovo-Kobylin, Aleksandr (1817–1903) Russian playwright and philosopher. Having studied in Moscow, Heidelberg, and Berlin (1834–42), his career was cut short when he was accused in 1850 of the murder of his French mistress. After two spells in prison, he was acquitted in 1857. His trilogy of plays reflects these experiences. *Krechinsky's Wedding* (1855) is a *comedy modelled on the *well-made play which attacks the pretensions and moral bankruptcy of the bureaucracy. Several *characters are carried over into *The Case* (1861, but *censored until 1882), which spells out the fate of the duped *heroine of

the first play, whose father now attempts to bribe her out of the clutches of two corrupt officials. *Tarelkin's Death* (1869, banned until an amateur performance in St Petersburg, 1900) follows one of the corrupt officials as he adopts the identity of a dead neighbour and attempts to blackmail his colleague. He is caught and tortured by the police until he confesses. The trilogy was directed by *Meyerhold (1917–22), who turned *Tarelkin's Death* (1922) into a political work.   CM

Sulerzhitsky, Leopold (1872–1916) Russian director. Sulerzhitsky was introduced to the *Moscow Art Theatre by *Gorky and *Chekhov before commencing work in 1905, assisting *Stanislavsky with productions of Hamsun's *The Drama of Life* (1907), *Andreev's *The Life of Man* (1907), *Maeterlinck's *The Blue Bird* (1908), and the *Craig-Stanislavsky *Hamlet* (1911). Before his premature death in a boating accident, 'Suler' spent the last period of his life nurturing the spiritual atmosphere of the Art Theatre's First Studio where, in close collaboration with *Vakhtangov, he attempted to put Stanislavsky's *acting theories into practice. Prolonged and often agonizing *rehearsal periods culminated in productions of *Heijermans's *The Wreck of 'The Hope'* (1913), a dramatized version of *Dickens's *The Cricket on the Hearth* (1914), and Johann Henning Berger's *The Flood*.   NW

Sullivan, Arthur (1842–1900) English composer of comic *operas or *operettas. As a young man Sullivan made a considerable mark as a composer and conductor. But by the time he embarked on his first collaboration with *Gilbert, *Thespis* (1875), it was clear that his talents were best suited to light music. Over the following 25 years Gilbert and Sullivan collaborated on thirteen stage-works, the 'Savoy Operas' (produced at the Savoy Theatre by Richard D'Oyly Carte), which stand at the apex of English operetta and light opera. Sullivan's skill at imitating the idiom of Italian lyric and French grand opera complemented Gilbert's *parodies of *melodrama and *satires of London life. His music is noted for its good humour and its capacity to set atmosphere. It is distinguished by a sweetness of melody and tone, which expresses perfectly the winsome innocence that the British at this time considered to be expressive of the national character. Sullivan wrote one grand opera, *Ivanhoe* (*Covent Garden, 1891), but although this achieved a remarkable run of over 160 performances, it has disappeared from the repertoire. The Savoy operas, however, have maintained their popularity throughout the English-speaking world.   SJCW

Sullivan, Barry (1821–91) Irish actor. Sullivan played in Ireland, Scotland, and the English provinces before appearing in London in 1852 at the *Haymarket as Hamlet. He was a tragedian of the old school, never especially popular in London, and spent a great deal of time *touring in provinces, America, and Australia. His Benedick opposite *Faucit's Beatrice opened the *Shakespeare Memorial Theatre in Stratford-upon-Avon in 1879. Sullivan was not strong in *comedy and made his reputation in Shakespearian *tragedy and *romantic drama. His Hamlet was much praised for its grace, restraint, clarity, elocutionary power, and careful study. The young *Shaw greatly admired it, and considered Sullivan, 'a splendidly monstrous performer', to be the last exponent of the tradition of superhuman *acting. Sullivan also played Iago, Lear, Cassius, Richard III, Shylock, Hotspur, and Falstaff in a 50-year career.   MRB

Sumarokov, Aleksandr (1717–77) Russian writer. The first to break with the tradition of church Slavonic, Sumarokov laid the foundations of a European Russian culture founded on French *neoclassicism. The first writer of Russian *tragedy and *comedy, Sumarokov was also the first Russian theatre theorist. Of his nine tragedies and twelve comedies, the latter tend to imitate *Molière and the former are pale versions of *Racine. His first tragedy, *Khorev* (1747), was followed by *Hamlet* (1748) and a range of worthy but forgettable work whose themes were taken from Russian history. With *The False Dmitry* (1771) Sumarokov discovered an original voice, in a play which suggested that even an illegitimate successor could be legitimized by good rule. It provided an example for Russian historical drama later developed along Shakespearian lines by *Pushkin in *Boris Godunov* (1825). Sumarokov considered tragedy a means of social education and was among the first to champion women's right to an independent emotional life.   NW

Sunarya, Asep Sunander (1953–   ) Sundanese *dalang* (puppet master) of Indonesia. Descended from a noted line of *dalang*, Sunarya is the foremost performer in a family renowned for *wayang golek purwa*, the rod-*puppet theatre of West Java. He began his career in the 1970s, won the Binojakrama (biennial contest of Sundanese puppetry) in the early 1980s, and developed into the most innovative performer of the genre. Ogres with heads that split or who vomit spaghetti were among the new breed of figures he introduced. Musical innovations include a gamelan which can play in different scales.   KPD

Sundari, Jaishanker (1889–1975) Indian actor of Gujarati theatre, who enthralled his *audiences as a *female impersonator from 1901 to 1932. Later he made his mark as a director of plays like *Ibsen's *A Doll's House* and *The Lady from the Sea* in Gujarati adaptation. At 11 he achieved instant stardom as Sundari (Desdemona) in *Saubhagya Sundari*, a loose adaptation of *Othello*. His performance achieved such fame that he became known as Sundari. Like his contemporary *Balgandharva of the Marathi stage, Sundari played female roles with so much grace and style that women were inspired to imitate his mannerisms and *costumes in real life. With his good looks, *acting talent, and extremely melodious voice, he became the prototype of the ideal Indian woman. He retired from playing female roles in 1932, but continued to direct.   KJ

Supple, Tim (1962–   ) British director. Under his *artistic directorship (1993–9) the Young Vic Theatre flourished. His Christmas production, a visual retelling of *The Grimm Tales* (1994), subsequently transferred to Broadway (1998). Productions such as *OMMA: Oedipus and the Luck of Thebes* (1994), *The Jungle Book*, *Blood Wedding* (1996), and *Twelfth Night* demonstrated a range of interests. His innovative staging methods integrate organic, *physical *acting with strongly atmospheric staging and *music. Since leaving the Young Vic, Supple has taken his visual staging to the *Royal Shakespeare Company (*The Comedy of Errors*, 1996; *Tales from Ovid*, *A Servant of Two Masters*, both 1999) and the *National Theatre (*Haroun and the Sea of Stories*, *The Epic of Gilgamesh*). He directed a West End and Broadway adaptation of Salman Rushdie's *Midnight's Children* and, under the aegis of Dash Arts, a company he co-founded, an epic multi-lingual *A Midsummer's Night's Dream* (2006).   KN

surrealism European *avant-garde movement which emphasized chance and automatism, along with irrational modes of cognition and creativity, in order to activate or represent a liberation of the self and culture from the restrictions of rationality. Surrealism began in Paris with a group of artists, poets, and theatre practitioners such as *Artaud, Philippe Soupault, and Paul Éluard, led by André Breton (1896–1966) and Tristan Tzara (1896–1963). Tzara arrived in Paris in 1920 from Zurich where he had led the *dada movement. Surrealism drew from a similar rejection of bourgeois norms, through Breton's interest in Freud, in particular *The Interpretation of Dreams* (1900), turned more towards liberatory change through the irrational. The first *Manifesto of Surrealism* was written by Breton in 1924, though Guillaume Apollinaire (1880–1918) had coined the term 'surrealism' in the preface to *The Breasts of Teiresias* (written 1903, produced 1917). Apollinaire's text is deeply indebted to *Jarry's *Ubu roi* (1896), following a comparable self-reflexive, *satiric, and imagistic style. A verse drama, the play's *characters and *action are liquid with sudden transformations of subjects and illogical shifts in plot. Typical surrealist *dramaturgy is exemplified in *Cocteau's *The Wedding on the Eiffel Tower* (1921), a *dialogue of clichés between two phonographs, and Artaud's *The Jet of Blood* (1925), a nightmarish scenario of lust and apocalypse.

Surrealist staging practice was a convergence of *symbolist, *futurist, dadaist, and cubist aesthetics and theory. Major productions included Cocteau's *Parade* (1917, *music by Satie, *costumes by *Picasso), performed by *Diaghilev's *Ballets Russes; *The Breasts of Teiresias* at the Conservatoire Renée Maubel; and Cocteau's *The Wedding on the Eiffel Tower* at the Théâtre des Champs-Élysées. *Masks and costumes were used to alter the performer's body through cubistic fragments with caricatured and cartoonish emblems. The stage was likewise distorted in fantastic imagery, bold colours, and a general sense of play. Surrealism continued to exert a wide influence in twentieth-century theatre and performance. The postwar theatre of the *absurd, the chance strategies of John Cage, and the theatre of images of Robert *Wilson and *Foreman borrow heavily from the early surrealist experiments.   MDC

Sutherland, Efua (1927–96) Leading Ghanaian playwright and director whose ideas continue to be influential. Educated at Cambridge and London, Sutherland was acutely aware that she was cut off from Ghanaian village communities and the artistic conventions they fostered. A great collaborator, she used her national and international position to develop a performance tradition that, while open to influences from the world, drew its strength from the local. She secured funds for a drama studio in Accra whose construction was inspired by the architecture of local compounds, and at Atwia Ekumfi she had a 'Story House' built in which the community kept alive performance traditions. She also established a professional theatre company, Kusum Agoromba, that produced the home-grown and adaptations of the foreign (such as *Everyman*). The company performed throughout the country in both English and Akan. Although Sutherland was responsible for several important initiatives and wrote or *devised a number of important texts, it was *The Marriage of Anansewa* (1975), which draws on Ananse storytelling tradi-

tions, that has made an enduring mark on Ghanaian playwriting.   JMG

Sütő, András (1927–2006) Transylvanian playwright. His first work, *The Barefooted Bride*, written with Zoltán Hajdú, was one of the most frequently performed plays in Kolozsvár in the late 1940s. *Gorgeous Gideon* (1968), a *tragicomedy more elaborate dramatically and stylistically, consolidated his position as a leading Hungarian-speaking writer in Romania, and his fame was further ensured by a tetralogy of plays staged in Kolozsvár from 1975 to 1981. Sütő strongly opposed the nationalistic communist regime of Romania in the 1980s; much of his work concerns the violent destruction of Transylvanian villages and the plight of their residents.   HJA

sutradhara Literally the 'holder of strings', the *sutradhara* is the *stage manager and *director of Sanskrit drama, though he has been conventionalized in other traditions in India. In classical Sanskrit plays, he first orchestrates the *rituals and prayers of the opening. Assisted by an attendant and the jester-like *character of the *vidush-aka*, he performs dance steps and gestures during the *purvaranga*, the ritualistic preliminaries of the play. Later he enters in the *prologue. More than a character, the *sutradhara* should be, according to the *Natyasastra*, knowledgeable in music, song, and *dance, and also in geography, astrology, medicine, and the other *shastras* (disciplines). LSR/RB

Suzman, Janet (1939–) South African actress, the niece of anti-apartheid campaigner Helen Suzman and herself a prominent human rights campaigner. Trained in London, Suzman joined the *Royal Shakespeare Company in 1962. Over the next decade she appeared in major Shakespearian roles, including Viola (1962), Lady Anne (1963), Rosaline, Portia, Ophelia (all 1965), Katherine and Celia (1967), Beatrice and Rosalind (1968), and Lavinia and Cleopatra (1972). In the 1970s and 1980s Suzman acted in London productions, including *Hedda Gabler* (1977) and *Andromache* (1987). In 1991 she appeared in *The Cruel Grasp* at the *Edinburgh Festival. Her film appearances include *A Day in the Death of Joe Egg* (1970), *Nijinski* (1978), and *Leon the Pig Farmer* (1992). She returned to South Africa to make her debut as a director at the Market Theatre in Johannesburg, of which she was a founding member, with a production of *Othello* with *Kani in the title role. She also directed a television version of *Othello* in 1988, and appeared in many TV productions, including *Robin Hood* (CBS, 1983) and *The Singing Detective* (BBC, 1986).   AS

Suzuki Tadashi (1939–   ) Japanese director. Co-founder with *Betsuyaku of the Waseda Little Theatre in 1966, Suzuki's innovative stagings of works by Betsuyaku, *Satō, and *Kara were crucial to the breakaway from orthodox *shingeki* (new theatre) *realism. Suzuki's experience of seeing the *nō actor *Kanze perform in Paris in 1972 made him reappraise classical Japanese theatre. His direction of Kanze and actress Shiraishi Kazuko in productions of *The Trojan Women* (1974) and *The Bacchae* (1978) defined the Suzuki style: an intense synthesis of traditional Japanese theatre and the *avant-garde. He is also famous for the 'Suzuki method' of *actors' training, a series of physical exercises aimed to reinvest performance with an 'animal energy' he feels has been lost in modern civilization. Inspired by *Grotowski's Poor Theatre, Suzuki moved the WLT in 1976 to Toga, a remote mountain village in Toyama prefecture, where he held the first of his annual international festivals in 1982. He officially changed the name of his company to SCOT (Suzuki Company of Toga) in 1985. He regularly *tours abroad, directing *Greek *tragedies, Shakespeare, and *Chekhov. He frequently collaborates with *Bogart and others in workshops on his Suzuki exercises, and his book, *The Way of Acting*, was translated into English in 1985. Since 2000 he has been the director of the Japan Performing Arts Foundation.   CP

Svoboda, Josef (1920–2002) Czech *scenographer and architect. By 1946 Svoboda was in charge of stage design in Prague's biggest *opera house, a flexible partner of the provocative directors *Radok and Václav Kašlík (1917–89). In the Czech National Theatre, which he entered in 1948, his talent flourished in Radok's productions of the late 1950s. Fascinated by the possibilities of modern technology, Svoboda developed *Laterna Magika and a system of simultaneous projection, which he used on a regular stage in 1959 in *Krejča's production of Topol's *Their Day*. Radok's dismissal restricted the development of Laterna Magika. Svoboda was Krejča's partner at the National Theatre and the Theatre Beyond the Gate from 1958, where his famous designs for *Chekhov were seen for the first time (*The Seagull*, 1960 and 1972; *Three Sisters*, 1966; *Ivanov*, 1970). He also worked abroad frequently, where he enjoyed more artistic freedom, better technical resources, and perhaps less control from directors. The principles of his scenography sometimes showed better in an *opera by *Wagner in *Bayreuth, or for Luigi Nono's opera *Intoleranza* in Boston (1965), where he used live telecast long before doing so more extensively for Laterna

Magika (1981). Svoboda strived for a scenography able to express movement, rhythm, and even *action. He believed theatre must allow modern technology to invade it, including holography and new synthetic fabrics, which can appear transparent or solid under light. Thus *characters on the stage may appear and disappear almost unnoticed, as if they moved from being to nonbeing, as in his production of his own piece *The Trap* (1999). Svoboda was the great beneficiary of *Craig's legacy, but also an ardent follower of the magic baroque designs of the *Bibienas. Widely recognized as one of the world's greatest scenographers, his work was the model for generations of designers and directors.   ML

Swann, Donald *See* FLANDERS, MICHAEL.

Swan Theatre Built in 1595 as the second *amphitheatre on London's Bankside, the original Swan was used in 1597 by a group who broke away from the nearby *Rose company. The Privy Council ordered it demolished, and although it survived it seems never to have been used regularly for playing. The only play known to have been performed there is *Middleton's *A Chaste Maid in Cheapside* (1611). Otherwise it was used for fencing matches and other shows.

Built on a polygonal frame, its square stage had two large pillars supporting its cover. The Swan's main claim to fame is the drawing of it discovered in 1888 at Utrecht. Made by Johannes de Witt, a Dutch visitor in 1596, it survives in a copy made by a friend, along with a Latin text describing the four theatres of London. De Witt's drawing is the only surviving picture of the interior of an open air London playhouse. Its accuracy, or the accuracy of the copy, has been extensively disputed.

The name 'Swan' was reused at Stratford-upon-Avon in 1986 for a third theatre to supplement the *Royal Shakespeare Company's two other spaces. It was built behind the main house on the site of the Victorian *Shakespeare Memorial Theatre, burned down in 1926. Conceived chiefly to stage neglected Elizabethan, Jacobean, and Restoration plays, its wooden *auditorium seats 460 people on three sides, using a thrust stage.   AJG

Swinarski, Konrad (1929–75) Polish director and designer. Bilingual in Polish and German, Swinarski was at the *Berliner Ensemble (1955–7), for a while one of *Brecht's assistants. He then worked in Warsaw and Cracow and developed a reputation in Europe, Israel, the USA, and the Soviet Union. His range was eclectic, taking in modern drama, classics, and *opera. He directed more than a dozen of Brecht's plays and work by *Dürrenmatt, *Genet, *Kopit, and *Weiss. He returned frequently to the Elizabethans, mounting *Twelfth Night, Hamlet, All's Well That Ends Well, A Midsummer Night's Dream, Richard III,* *Marlowe's *Edward II,* and the anonymous *Arden of Faversham.* He directed a number of Polish classics at the Stary Theatre in Cracow, including *Słowacki's *Fantasy* (1967), *Wyspiański's *The Judges* and *The Spell* (1968), *Mickiewicz's *Forefathers' Eve* (1973), and Wyspiański's *Deliverance* (1974). In general Swinarski sought to blend the *romantic, spiritual, and anarchic Polish heritage with German structured and practical culture, often relying on *Verfremdung* and other *epic theatre methods yet creating a distinctive and spectacular theatricality. He died in a plane crash.   KB

symbolism European movement which promoted the use of art, music, theatre, and writing to uncover the 'hidden realities' of metaphysics. The basic strategy of symbolism—the use of signs to deliver meanings otherwise unavailable—has been present in most aspects of theatre, but the specific movement began in Paris in the late nineteenth century. Symbolist artists, such as the playwright *Maeterlinck and directors *Fort and *Lugné-Poe, sought to create new theatre forms based on representations of metaphysical realms depicted through occult and spiritual material. Precursors of symbolist theatre included the French poets Baudelaire, Verlaine, Rimbaud, and Mallarmé, whose use of symbolism to express the inexpressible, and theory of the correspondences and synaesthesia, became critical elements in later symbolist *dramaturgy and practice. *Wagner's notions of a total artwork and the spiritual content of his *operas, along with Nietzsche's philosophy of a Dionysian unity attainable through the Apollonian art, were likewise influential.

Symbolist theatre developed, in part, through a reaction to the objective and scientific representations of *naturalism as exemplified in the theories and dramaturgy of *Zola and the practice of *Antoine at the Théâtre *Libre. As an antithetical response to and rejection of naturalism, symbolism can be understood as beginning the structure of thesis and antithesis of the historical *avant-garde. However, the repertory at the Théâtre Libre, Théâtre d'*Art, and Théâtre de l'Œuvre contained a mix of plays that can be considered as exemplary of both movements. Symbolist productions of quasi-*realist plays such as the Théâtre de l'Œuvre's *Rosmersholm* and *The Master Builder* by *Ibsen further upset any neat portioning.

Symbolist performance theory developed before actual productions through the writings of Mallarmé, Maeterlinck, and Gustave Kahn, all concerned with how the material stage can present the metaphysical realm. Maeterlinck suggested the use of *puppets in place of actors, whose bodily materiality would always confine the theatre to naturalist representations. The problem of the body of the actor on a stage of abstraction would later be developed by *Craig, the *futurists, and *Schlemmer.

Symbolist drama, such as Maeterlinck's *The Intruder* and *The Blind* (1891), developed *characters and plots of a generalized or eternal nature, representations of imagined psychic states between life and death. The symbolist plays, some of which used verse and *mime, were often static, with long pauses added in an attempt to evoke a reverie in the spectator necessary for the contemplation of the higher realms of existence.

Similarly, symbolist *scenography attempted to depict a space of mystery and the metaphysical, the stage often dark, the *action sometimes seen through gauze scrims. The theatre also employed synesthesia, attempting to engage all of the senses; during some performances scents were delivered across the *auditorium from atomizers controlled by actors in the aisles.

Fort's Théâtre d'Art closed in 1892, but Lugné-Poe established the Théâtre de l'Œuvre that same year and continued producing symbolist drama, including Maeterlinck's *Pelléas and Mélisande* (1893) and symbolist stagings of works by Ibsen, *Strindberg, and *Bjørnson. In 1896, the theatre presented *Jarry's *Ubu roi,* a landmark production in the history of the avant-garde. It also marked a closure of sorts to French symbolism, with a move away from the *romantic exploration of metaphysics toward the *satiric and confrontational modes of the later futurism and *dada. Although symbolist theatre in France did not survive after the 1890s, with the exception of *Claudel's early plays, the movement continued as a force in Poland, Russia, Spain, Portugal, and Ireland, often operating as a tool for the representation of national identity, as in *Yeats's *Cathleen Ni Houlihan* (1903).

Symbolist aesthetics continued to exert an influence on European and American theatre practice throughout the twentieth century. The designs of *Appia and Craig extended the use of a symbolic and ahistorical *mise-en-scène, creating stages that represented a timeless space of interiority and mysticism. In contemporary practice symbolist strategies are often quoted by such artists as Robert *Wilson and Socìetas Raffaello *Sanzio.   MDC

Synge, John Millington (1871–1909) Irish writer. An 1898 visit to the Aran Islands off the west coast of Ireland provided him with a subject and style. Having met *Yeats in Paris in 1896, he was encouraged to participate in the Irish literary revival, and over his five visits to Aran (1898–1902) he gathered folk tales, observed customs, and heard a dialect of English heavily influenced by the Irish language, which contributed to his plays, as in his one-act *tragedy *Riders to the Sea* (1904).

Synge's plays corresponded to the aspirations of the Irish national theatre movement, and when the *Abbey Theatre was founded in 1904, he joined Yeats and Augusta *Gregory as a director. However, his dramatic vision clashed with the expectations of the nationalist *audiences. His first produced play, the one-act *tragicomedy *The Shadow of the Glen* (1903), provoked protests for its representation of an unhappily married countrywoman going off with a tramp. *The Well of the Saints* (1905), a fable-like drama of blind beggars who prefer blindness to sight, was almost equally unpopular, and *The Playboy of the Western World* (1907) was received with *riots. Synge's ironic vision of the Irish country community puzzled and outraged Dublin audiences who looked for more idealizing and traditional representations of Ireland in the Irish national theatre. His two-act *comedy *The Tinker's Wedding,* which showed a priest attacked by tinkers, was judged to be too dangerous to stage, and he did not live to complete his last play, *Deirdre of the Sorrows,* a dramatisation of old Irish saga material (produced 1910).

Despite these troubles, Synge's unusual poetic speech helped to win him an early and lasting international reputation. Translated into Czech and German within his lifetime, Synge became a classic figure, influencing *O'Neill, *Brecht, and *Walcott. *The Playboy of the Western World* has ironically become one of the most frequently revived plays in Ireland, and holds its place in the repertoire of world theatre. NG

Szajna, Józef (1922–2008) Polish designer and director who was a prisoner in Auschwitz in his youth. After establishing himself as a designer, he became head of Teatr Ludowy in Nowa Huta (1963–6), where he started directing, followed by a decade as director of the Studio Theater in Warsaw (1972–82). In the 1970s he *toured Europe and the USA with his productions and from the 1980s directed, designed, exhibited paintings, and lectured all over the world. His best productions, some of which he wrote, include *Replika* (1972, 1995), *Gulgutiera* (1973), *Dante* (1974, 1992), and *Cervantes* (1976). As a *director, Szajna exercised control over every aspect of production, using space in an innovative way and incorporating found objects into the *scenography. KB

Szyfman, Arnold (1882–1967) Polish *manager and director. Szyfman supervised the construction of Teatr Polski in Warsaw (1913), one of the most beautiful *playhouses in Europe. Equipped with a revolving stage and up-to-date *lighting, it was under Szyfman's management from 1913 until 1939, except for his two-year internment in Russia in the First World War. In hiding during the next war, Szyfman resumed management of the Polski in 1945, was fired by the communist authorities in 1949, and returned a final time from 1955 to 1957. He also was manager of other Warsaw theatres and companies. At the Polski he employed the best artists and directed numerous memorable productions himself, including *Mickiewicz's *Forefathers' Eve* (1934, 1955) and other national masterpieces, 22 Shakespeare plays, eighteen by *Shaw (including the world première of *The Apple Cart,* 1929), and many contemporary plays, domestic and foreign. KB

tableau vivant The 'living picture' was usually created by arranging a person or group of persons to represent a scene from a painting or sculpture. The form may have originated as an allegorical or narrative representation of episodes of the Gospels or classical mythology, and was common at feasts and religious festivals in Europe from the *medieval to the *early modern periods. In eighteenth-century polite society, *tableaux vivants* became popular entertainments, genteel 'charades' with detailed imitation of well-known paintings and sculpture groups in private theatres and salons. By the mid-nineteenth century, the subject matter had been extended to embrace literary and historical episodes. In London, the notorious 'Judge and Jury' clubs and the Coal Hole in the Strand had female performers in 'fleshings' (flesh-coloured tights) posing as classical statuary. Ever sensitive to popular demand, the *music hall also imported the *tableau vivant*. The Canterbury Hall, with a change of subjects every Monday, produced *tableaux* after popular or epic paintings in 1873, such as Titian's *Venus Rising from the Sea*. Opposition became fierce as proprietors dared more, and stage 'realization' of pictures became a barely disguised excuse for the exhibition of female nudity. In the early twentieth century the *variety theatre saw the rise of 'adagio' acts such as the Ganjou Brothers and Juanita and Gaston and Andree. In the 1930s the Windmill Theatre offered copies of Victorian *tableaux vivants*, protected from prosecution because they were classical pictures in frozen poses (*see* CENSORSHIP; PORNOGRAPHY AND PERFORMANCE).

Living pictures also appeared in the regular theatres. From the early nineteenth century, representations of the passions and of moral positions or dilemmas were realized in frozen attitudes, with accompanying *music. In 1832 painting combined with drama in *Jerrold's play *The Rent Day* and David Wilkie's painting of the same name. Dramatic tableaux became a feature of act endings in *melodrama, freezing a frame of emotions and attitudes, giving added weight to the *crisis or climax rather than animating a narrative or allegorical image. AF

Tabori, George (1914–2007) Hungarian-English dramatist and director. Born in Budapest into a Jewish family, Tabori studied in Berlin before emigrating to England in 1936. He moved to the USA in 1947, where he wrote for the screen (for Hitchcock, Litvak, and Losey) and the stage (with *Brecht, *Kazan, and *Strasberg). After moderate success in New York Tabori began working in Germany in the late 1960s where he established a major reputation as a dramatist and experimental director, mainly of his own work. Influences include Brecht, the *Living Theatre, *Beckett, Kafka, psychoanalysis, and gestalt therapy. The dominant theme in Tabori's writing is the Jewish experience seen from a variety of perspectives: familial (*My Mother's Courage*, 1979; *Cannibals*, 1968); historical (*Jubilee*, 1983; *Mein Kampf*, 1987; *Masada*, 1988); theological (*Goldberg Variations*, 1991); literary (*Shylock*, 1978; *Nathan's Death*, 1991). Although the Holocaust is explicit or implicit in almost all his work, Tabori's plays are shaped by Jewish humour and witty *dialogue. Written in English, most have been premièred and published in German translation. CBB

Tagore, Rabindranath (1861–1941) Bengali writer and director, artistic icon of modern India. The first non-European to win the Nobel Prize for Literature (1913), Tagore's fame focused on his poetry, but his path-breaking dramas (over 60 plays) became central to Indian theatre. In the 1880s and 1890s he wrote musicals on Indian subjects, verse dramas, and several *comedies and *farces. In 1902 his outlook changed. His essay 'The Stage' rejected Western *illusionism, exhorting Indian artists to return to classical Sanskrit theatre and folk forms. Meanwhile he made the village of Santiniketan his base for an experimental school, and in 1908 created a new kind of drama: 'season plays' which celebrated the natural cycle, performed by the children under his direction.

Tagore moved to more thematically elaborate plays, which he premièred at Santiniketan and were often seen in Calcutta. Three masterpieces followed. The allegorical *Raja* (1911) is about spiritual quest, the moving story of a boy's death, *Dakghar*, had its première as *The Post Office* by his admirer *Yeats at the *Abbey Theatre (1913); and *Immovable Institution* (1914) is a scathing attack on religious orthodoxy. Tagore did not direct his finest works of the early 1920s: *Muktadhara*, opposing the damming of rivers, and the exposé of materialistic totalitarianism in *Red Oleander*. He did direct the all-women *The Dancer's Puja* (1926), about egalitarian reforms of Buddhism, and *Tapati* (1929), about female independence. Toward the end of his life he created a hybrid *dance-drama inspired by visits to South-East Asia, as in *Chitrangada* (1936), *Chandalika* (1938), and *Shyama* (1939), which *toured Indian cities and Sri Lanka. *Music remained central to his work—the final version of *Raja* (*Formless Jewel*, 1935) contains 25 songs—with melodies based on classical ragas or folk tunes.   AL

Tairov, Aleksandr (1885–1950) Russian/Soviet director. After a period as an actor, Tairov's first important post was at Mardzhanov's Free Theatre in 1913, where he directed his future wife *Koonen in *Schnitzler's *The Veil of Pierrette*. In 1914 Tairov and Koonen established the Kamerny (Chamber) Theatre in Moscow. Here Tairov staged outstanding productions in accordance with his manifesto, *Notes of a Director* (1921). Tairov insisted on a unified aesthetic, involving actor's movement, designer's concept, and *music, under the control of a *director. Hostile to *Stanislavskian 'psychologism' and *Meyerholdian *biomechanics, Tairov sought the 'universal' actor who had expertise as singer, dancer, *acrobat, and theatrical performer. The ideal exponent proved to be Koonen who, for 36 years, performed leading roles in most of Tairov's productions, commencing with *Kalidasa's Shakuntala and *Wilde's Salome, and concluding with *Chekhov's Nina in *Seagull*.

During the 1920s Tairov worked with some of leading *avant-garde *scenographers, including *Ekster, *Goncharova, and Vadim Ryndin. Among Tairov's most memorable productions were *Romeo and Juliet* (1921), *Racine's *Phèdre* (1922), and three plays by *O'Neill, *The Hairy Ape* and *Desire under the Elms* (1926), and *All God's Chillun Got Wings* (1929). He made significant contributions to *constructivist production with Annensky's *Famira Kifared* (1916), and a version of Chesterton's *The Man Who Was Thursday* (1923). Tairov also staged *operetta, extravaganzas such as E. T. A. Hoffmann's *Princess Brambilla* (1920), *Shaw's *St Joan* (1924), and the first foreign production of *Brecht's *The Threepenny Opera* (1930). Tairov's apolitical theatre inevitably fell foul of authority (his production of *Bulgakov's *The Crimson Island* was banned after opening). Such pressure did produce one outstanding production, in 1933, of *Vishnevsky's

Soviet Civil War classic, *An Optimistic Tragedy*, but this success was not enough to appease the authorities, who closed the Kamerny in 1938 and merged it with *Okhlopkov's Realistic Theatre. The situation was rescued by the outbreak of war and the evacuation of the Kamerny company to the east, where they resumed their work before returning to Moscow after the war. With Stalinist paranoia at its height, however, and anti-Semitism once more on the agenda (Tairov's real name was Aleksandr Yakovlevich Kornblit), he and Koonen were removed from control of their theatre in 1950.   NW

Takarazuka Revue Japanese company of all-female performers, founded in 1913 in the hot-spring resort of Takarazuka, about 25 km (15 miles) from Osaka, by the railroad magnate Kobayashi Ichizō (1873–1957) to attract patrons to the area. The company now maintains an additional theatre in Tokyo, and both venues continue to provide spectacle entertainment to an enormous circle of fans. *Kabuki, the most popular form of Japanese theatre until the early twentieth century, used only male actors. The few actresses who performed in the modern forms of *shimpu and *shingeki in the early 1900s were looked down upon socially, whatever their talents. Kobayashi's troupe was thus a daring attempt to place female performers on the stage. Dedicated to 'wholesome family entertainment', the romantic stories performed, with women in both male and female parts, range in subject matter from adaptations of classical Japanese tales to European stories of royalty, versions of Shakespeare, and occasional Broadway *musicals. Potential performers are chosen by examination and train for two years at the troupe's academy, where they perfect singing and *dancing skills. Performers are divided into five troupes; once they begin their professional careers, they may perform for a limited number of years only. *See also* MALE IMPERSONATION. JTR

Takeda Izumo II (1691–1756) Japanese playwright and *manager. Son of the manager-playwright Takeda Izumo I, he used the name Takeda Koizumo until his father's death in 1747. He contributed to the writing of 28 works produced at the Osaka Takemoto-za *bunraku *puppet theatre, the most famous of which are in collaboration with *Namiki. These include three outstanding plays: *Sugawara and the Secrets of Calligraphy* (1746), *Yoshitsune and the Thousand Cherry Trees* (1747), and *Chūshingura: the treasury of loyal retainers* (1748). Works such as *The Rise and Fall of the Heike* (1739), *Summer Festival and the Mirrors of Osaka* (1745), and *Two Sumo*

Wrestlers and their Pleasure Quarter Diaries (1749) are also still regularly performed on the bunraku and *kabuki stages.   CAG

Takemoto Gidayū (1651–1714) *Bunraku chanter. Born the son of a farmer, he was the most famous chanter of his age, his name *gidayū* becoming the term for bunraku singing. He was granted the honorary court title of Chikugonojō in 1701. Initially an apprentice to Kaganojō in Kyoto, he founded his own theatre, Takemoto-za, in Osaka in 1684, and invited *Chikamatsu Monzaemon to write plays for him the next year. After the success of *Love Suicides at Sonezaki* in 1703, Chikamatsu gave up writing for *kabuki and became the Takemotoza staff playwright in 1705. Gidayū was known for his powerful voice. He wrote several short treatises on the art of bunraku chanting which were important for Chikamatsu and show a master actor's sense of how to capture and keep attention. In his view, entertaining the *audience meant leading them into the depths of *tragedy and suffering to show the nobility of ordinary men and women, and then out again into a brighter world of hope.   CAG

Talma, François-Joseph (1763–1826) French actor. Reared in London on English theatre, he trained in Paris before making his debut at the *Comédie-Française in *Voltaire's *Mahomet* in 1787. He made his name in 1789 in the title role in Chénier's inflammatory anti-monarchical play about the St Bartholomew's Day massacre, *Charles IX*. The scandal aroused by Chénier's play eventually split the Comédie ideologically and physically, and in 1791, after the liberation of the theatres made their classical repertoire freely available, the radical faction, led by Talma, defected to the newly built Variétés-Amusantes (later Théâtre de la République). There, alongside plays by *Corneille and *Racine, he staged work by authors with whom he collaborated closely—five more plays by Chénier, three of *Ducis's Shakespearian *tragedies, and new plays which also challenged the conservatism of his former colleagues. Talma was clearly republican in his sympathies, and in 1795 became friends with Napoleon.
In 1799 Talma rejoined the reintegrated Comédie-Française, though for most of the next two decades he was only part-time in Paris. Not only was he required, for the prestige of France and its Emperor, to supply entertainment at court and abroad, but also the debts incurred through his generosity and extravagance forced him to undertake lucrative provincial and foreign *tours. Talma helped effect a radical transition from a *neoclassical to a *romantic aesthetic in both *acting and

*costume. His playing was described as 'a combination of *Racine and Shakespeare' (Mme de Staël). To the declamatory formality of traditional verse speaking he brought a new English conversational naturalism, plus a liberal use of expressive gesture and business when he was not speaking. No *hero, knight, or lover, his talent was for the portrayal of intense, manic, doom-laden passion: of the 247 roles he played at the Comédie-Française, Oreste and Néron (Racine's *Andromaque* and *Britannicus*), and Hamlet (Ducis's version) were among his most celebrated. From the outset of his career he followed *Lekain in the pursuit of historical authenticity of dress. Talma was the undisputed leader of his profession for almost 40 years and such was the extent of his celebrity, that his death, of intestinal cancer, was reported as far away as Sydney, Australia. JG

tamasha Folk theatre performed in Maharashtra, India. The Urdu word *tamasha* (spectacle) entered Marathi during Aurangzeb's occupation of Maharashtra from 1680 to 1707. It referred to the songs and *dances performed by the low-caste Mahar and Mang communities for the entertainment of soldiers in the Mughal army. By the mid-eighteenth century, *tamasha* evolved into a more structured form under the patronage of the Peshwas, administrators to the Maratha kings. The *gan* (invocation to Ganapati, the deity of the Peshwas) and the *gaulan*, the milkmaid's song to Lord Krishna, were followed by erotic songs, known as *lavanis*, danced by *nachas* (*female impersonators). With the collapse of Maratha rule in 1818, *tamasha* lost its urban upper-caste patronage and turned for support to rural *audiences, who were primarily attracted to *lavanis*, and women's troupes developed to meet this demand. The practice of *daulatjada*, in which a patron showed appreciation of a dancer's skill by offering a coin that she had to fetch from him, became even more explicit when women dancers from the Mahar and Kolhati communities replaced the *nachas*.
By the 1920s *tamasha* had settled into its present five-part structure, in which the *gan* is followed by the *gaulan*, in which a dancer performs tantalizingly with her back to the audience. She then assumes the role of Lord Krishna's beloved Radha and calls out to her aunt Maushibai, played by the *songadya*, or *clown. Their repartee with Krishna is followed by the third part, the *lavani* dances. Next, the *shahir* (composer-singer) introduces the theme of the *vag* (narrative), assisted by the *songadya* who comments satirically on current affairs. The *vag* itself is a full-fledged play drawn from historical or legendary sources

with *satire and *slapstick. At the end comes the *mujra* or dance asking for blessing. Strong *musical accompaniment is provided by drum, one-stringed drone, tambourine, and at times, harmonium.

During the independence struggle, political parties used the *tamasha* to raise consciousness against British rule. From the 1960s onwards, the *tamasha* was staged in a sanitized form for urban audiences. After 1955 a *lavani* dance sequence became almost obligatory for every Marathi film, with live *tamashas* imitating them in their performances. Despite its adaptability, however, the full-fledged *tamasha* has been dying a slow death, while glamourized *sangeet baris* are doing lively business in urban centres.   SGG

Tandy, Jessica (1909–94) Anglo-American actress. Tandy joined the *Birmingham Repertory Theatre in 1928, and the next year made her London debut at the *Royal Court in *The Rumour*. Her reputation was established when she appeared as Manuela in *Children in Uniform* in 1934. Thereafter she played in the major venues in London, receiving greatest recognition for her Shakespearean roles, which included Ophelia to *Gielgud's 1934 Hamlet; Viola and Sebastian in *Twelfth Night* and Katherine in *Henry V* at the *Old Vic under *Guthrie (1937); Cordelia to Gielgud's *Lear* (a production supervised by Granville *Barker), and Miranda to Gielgud's first Prospero in 1940. During the war she went to the United States and a Broadway career, which culminated as Blanche in *A Streetcar Named Desire*, for which she won her first Tony award. She won a second Tony as Fonsia Dorsey in *The Gin Game* (1978) and a third as Annie Nations in *Foxfire* (1983). In 1989 she became the oldest actress to win an Academy award for best actress as Daisy Werthen in the film of *Driving Miss Daisy*. She married *Cronyn in 1942, and they appeared together often.   TK

Tang Xianzu (T'ang Hsien-tsu) (1550–1617) China's greatest pre-modern playwright. Tang left five plays, of which the most famous is *The Peony Pavilion*, also known as *The Return of the Soul* (1598), about a young girl from a respectable family who sees a scholar in a dream, pines for him, and dies. She visits him as a ghost and makes love to him, then conquers death and marries him. The play caused a sensation in its time, its *heroine seen as icon of passionate self-determination, and continues to be one of the most popular in the Chinese opera repertoire. *The Purple Flute* and *The Purple Hairpin* were written earlier; both tell the story of the ill-fated

romance between the Tang Dynasty courtesan Huo Xiaoyu and Li Yi. Two later plays, *The Story of Handan* and *The Story of Southern Branch*, also based on Tang classical tales, concern the vanity of earthly rewards, good fortune, and honour. Tang Xianzu had been a loyal civil servant who criticized corruption in his youth and was exiled to present-day Canton. He retired from office in 1598 to write plays.   SYV

Tanvir, Habib (1929–2009) Indian playwright, poet, and director, pioneer of a movement that sought to close the urban-rural divide in the arts. Tanvir worked in Urdu, Hindi, and, most inventively, in Chhattisgarhi, the language of the tribal actors with whom he was associated from 1958.

Earlier Tanvir wrote and produced *Agra Bazar* (1954). Earthy and replete with robust *characters and the songs and cries of vendors in a bazaar, it became a classic of its kind, focusing on the Urdu poet Nazir Akbarabadi. Another of Tanvir's famous productions, *Mitti ki Gadi*, a fluid adaptation of *Sudraka's Sanskrit play *The Little Clay Cart*, was conceptualized while he was *touring Europe in 1956–7. Tanvir is most remembered for *Charanadas Chor* (1974). A *Brechtian adaptation of a Rajasthani folk story, this play narrates the trials of a charismatic thief (*chor*), representative of a common man, who makes good in spite of himself, and who ultimately gets entrapped within his own vows. Since its acclaimed exposure at the *Edinburgh Festival in 1982, *Charanadas Chor* has played all over the world. Tanvir produced many other plays that question the complacency and corruption of post-independence India.   VDa/RB

Tarkington, Booth (1869–1946) American playwright and novelist, part of the 'Indiana school' of writers whose work saw wide popularity between 1900 and 1925. He wrote more than 21 plays, most adapted by him from his own novels. Though he first came to theatrical attention in 1901 by adapting his historical romance *Monsieur Beaucaire* for *Mansfield, Tarkington was at his best in coming-of-age stories about charming and precocious Midwestern teenagers, such as *Seventeen* (1917), which featured Ruth *Gordon, and *Clarence* (1919), written for the comic abilities of Alfred *Lunt. *Welles adapted the Pulitzer Prize-winning novel *The Magnificent Ambersons* (1918) into a highly regarded film in 1942.   MAF

Tarlton, Richard (d.1588) English actor. From 1583 to his death, Tarlton acted with the *Queen's Men, playing at the *Curtain, at London inns, and on company *tours. Whatever the play, Tarlton inhabited his *stock character of stage rustic, such as Derick in *The Famous Victories of Henry

V. Dressed in peasant attire and playing on the tabor and pipe, Tarlton was the company's *clown, its chief comic actor and a country bumpkin, often transposed to urban settings as a displaced farmworker forced to find employment. Despite this rustic simplicity, his *character usually bested others in verbal combat. He was celebrated for his skill at *improvisation, not only within plays, where he was famous for retaliating to spectators' rhymed taunts with clever verses of his own, but also in *jigs, the short afterpieces of song and *dance improvised in response to suggestions from spectators. He wrote a play entitled *The Seven Deadly Sins,* which survives only in abbreviated form. He was often hired to attend banquets at court or aristocratic homes as a kind of professional jester. Some of his exploits on and off the stage are described in *Tarlton's Jests* (1600).   MS

Tasso, Torquato (1544–95) Italian poet and dramatist. Born in Sorrento, he found his most continuous patronage from the Este dukes of Ferrara, in whose court he composed his major epic poem *Gerusalemme liberata.* It was here also that (it is believed) the *Gelosi company performed in 1573 Tasso's five-act *pastoral drama *Aminta,* which was read and translated all over Europe for many generations. The plot is simple: will the nymph Silvia surrender herself to the love of the shepherd Aminta, before he commits suicide out of desperation? In the end she makes the passage from celibacy to love. Some highly emotional events precede the happy ending, but they are narrated rather than enacted, and the two lovers never appear on stage together, even for a final *tableau of union. The work is thus close to *closet drama, and its influence on pastoral theatre was minimal, though its highly charged but oblique eroticism created a poetic tone for later pastoral works, literary or dramatic. Tasso also wrote a *tragedy, *Torrismondo* (published 1587). Although set in a romanticized Scandinavia, this story of incest is clearly based on *Sophocles' *Oedipus the King.* The *comedy *Intrigues of Love* was begun in the 1570s and completed after his death by academic colleagues.   RAA

Tate, Nahum (1652–1715) Irish playwright. Tate moved to London in 1672 and began his career with two *tragedies, *Brutus of Alba* (1678) and *The Loyal General* (1679). His adaptation of *Richard II* (1680) was banned for political reasons (*see* CENSORSHIP), and his attempt to title the play *The Sicilian Usurper* was similarly unsuccessful. The following year, Tate produced *The Ingratitude of a Commonwealth,* based on *Coriolanus,* and a now-infamous version of *King Lear* that

eliminated the Fool, made Edgar and Cordelia lovers, and restored Lear to his throne. His *Lear* replaced Shakespeare's text on the English stage for the next 157 years. Tate scored a success with *A Duke and No Duke* (1684), a *farce based on Aston Cokain's *Trappolin Supposed a Prince* (1633), but fared less well with *Cuckold's Haven* (1685), derived from *Eastward Hoe* (1605). He wrote *The Island Princess* (1687) and the libretto for Henry Purcell's *Dido and Aeneas* (1689), but thereafter ceased playwriting.   RWV

Tavira, Luis de (1948–   ) Mexican director. As a young Jesuit priest, he was sent to study at the National Autonomous University of Mexico in 1968. Coming into contact with radical figures in theatre, de Tavira left the order and quickly became Mexico's most celebrated and controversial director. A champion of the *director as *auteur,* de Tavira has thrilled and outraged critics and *audiences with his highly idiosyncratic, free adaptations of Shakespeare, Lope de *Vega, *Calderón, *Büchner, *Brecht, among many others. He has worked closely with the Mexican playwright *Leñero, as in *The Martyrdom of Morelos* (1982), *No One Knows Anything* (1988), and *The Night of Hernán Cortés* (1992). With echoes of his Jesuit past, he considers the theatre to be a mystical space where actors should overcome their inherent narcissism to dominate their intellect. The much debated results can be surprising and make stunning, if sometimes excessive, use of stage effects. He has held important administrative positions, where controversy has followed him.   KFN

Taylor, C. P. (Cecil Philip) (1928–81) Scottish dramatist. His first professional production was *Aa Went to Blaydon Races* in 1962 at Newcastle Playhouse, and in 1965 Taylor began a productive relationship with the Edinburgh Traverse Theatre with *Happy Days Are Here Again.* Subsequent plays include *Of Hope and Glory* (1965), *Allergy* (1966), *Lies about Vietnam/Truth about Sarajevo* (1969), *Bread and Butter* (1969), *Passion Play* (1971), *The Black and White Minstrels* (1972), *Schippel* (1974), *Me* (1976), and *Walter* (1977). Taylor worked extensively with *community theatre groups, the mentally handicapped, and theatre for *youth. He died shortly after the opening of *Good,* which was premièred by the *Royal Shakespeare Company in 1981. Set in Germany, the play shows the fall of a liberal professor whose moral and physical cowardice leads him to join the Nazi Party and work in Auschwitz. A major retrospective occurred at the *Edinburgh Festival in 1992.   AS

Taylor, Laurette (Cooney) (1884–1946) Distinctive American actress who began acting in 1903. The critic John Corbin wrote that Taylor had 'the greatest talent, the greatest spirit of our times', but that her ability was wasted in poor dramatic material. In 1911 she married the English playwright J. Hartley Manners and starred in a series of immensely popular plays by him, most notably *Peg o' my Heart*. Taylor performed more than 1,000 times the role of the plucky young Irishwoman who inherits a fortune and wins the heart of London society. After Manners's death in 1928, Taylor became an alcoholic and was frequently out of work. She emerged to acclaim in 1938 in a revival of Sutton Vane's *Outward Bound* and again in 1944 as Amanda in *Williams's The Glass Menagerie*.   MAF

Taylor, Tom (1817–80) English playwright. Taylor was a civil servant for 21 years, art critic of *The Times*, editor of *Punch* (1874–80), and professor of English in London. He wrote or adapted around 80 plays. His adaptations show an acute understanding of dramatic narrative, a good example being *A Tale of Two Cities* (1860), which he wrote in consultation with *Dickens. The *comedy *Our American Cousin* is famous for establishing *Sothern's reputation in 1858; it is infamous for being performed at Ford's Theatre in Washington when Abraham Lincoln was assassinated by John Wilkes *Booth in 1865.

The Ticket-of-Leave Man (1863) was long popular, and was even recast in *fairground booth theatres as *The Ticket-of-Leave Woman*. The play conveys the atmosphere of place through the precise detail of its 'cup-and-saucer' scenes in a drawing room, a kitchen, a city office, and the Bellevue Tea Gardens. Taylor collaborated with *Reade on *Masks and Faces* (1852) and with Augustus Dubourg on *New Men and Old Acres* (1869), both sentimental comedies, but he also turned his hand to *pantomimes and a *hippodrama, *Garibaldi*, at *Astley's Amphitheatre (1859). His more serious dramas were often derived from French sources. They include *Still Waters Run Deep* (1855) and *The Fool's Revenge* (1859, from *Rigoletto*). Taylor's ability to imbue foreign plots with English familiarity and sentiment were important factors in his continuing popularity. His last play was *Love and Life* (1878).   AF

Taymor, Julie (1952–) American director and designer. At Oberlin College, she joined *Blau's ensemble KRAKEN. In the mid-1970s, she spent four years in Java and Bali, studying and experimenting with traditional forms of *mask and *puppet theatre. Back in the USA, she

designed *costumes, masks, and puppets for directors such as *Şerban until she began directing. Productions included an original piece titled *Juan Darien: A Carnival Mass* (1988), which was later *toured extensively. In the 1990s her innovative fusion of movement, music, and design led to invitations to direct *opera internationally and to her transformation of Disney's film *The Lion King* into a Broadway *musical (1997). Catapulted to fame, she pursued film adaptations of Shakespeare in *Titus* (1999, with Anthony *Hopkins) and *The Tempest* (2010, with Helen *Mirren). She directed *Mozart's *The Magic Flute* (Metropolitan Opera, 2005), and the accident-prone *Spider-Man: Turn Off the Dark* (2011), the most expensive musical in Broadway history.   STC

Ta'zieh The Ta'zieh (consolation) plays of Persia (present-day Iran) are similar in structure and function to the *Passion plays of *medieval Europe. Most scholars assume that the form developed from a variety of religious observances. Its historical basis was the heroic martyrdom of Husayn, grandson of the prophet Muhammad and the redemptive figure of the Shiite branch of Islam. His death on the plains of Karbala in 680 is the central episode of any Ta'zieh cycle, but like the European Passion plays, each Ta'zieh cycle contains a wide variety of material. As early as the tenth century, elaborate processions mourning the death of the martyr were a standard feature of festivals in the month of Muharram, when his death occurred. These festivals received royal encouragement in the sixteenth century under the Shiite Safavid dynasty, with *costumed processions, tableaux, and mock battles. During this period another Muharram tradition developed, the recitation of the life and deeds of Shiite martyrs by professional storytellers. These two traditions, one largely visual, the other largely auditory, are thought to have provided the basis for the elaborate Ta'zieh cycles, which first appeared in the eighteenth century and flourished under the Kajar kings (1786–1926). Performances are still presented by amateur and professional companies both in small improvised theatres and in elaborate, permanent structures. The most famous of the latter was the State Tekya, built in Tehran in the late nineteenth century and seating up to 20,000 spectators.   MC

Teirlinck, Herman (1879–1967) Flemish writer, born in Brussels, where his *expressionist plays were performed in the Royal Flemish Theatre. *Film in Slow Motion* (1922) is located in a modern city with a middle act underwater, showing what passes through the heads of a young couple who commit suicide by drowning. *I Serve* (1924) is a secularized version of the medieval *Beatrijs* legend, while *The Man without Body* (1925) gives concrete shape to a split personality. Teirlinck promoted a new theatrical style marked by varying rhythms and the inclusion of *masks and *acrobatics. After the war he became the founder of the National Theatre, based in Antwerp. Strongly influenced by *Craig, he initially emphasized the role of the *director, but in his major theoretical work *Wijding voor een derde geboorte* (1956) he saw the *actor as the autonomous creator of theatre art.   JDV

Téllez, Fray Gabriel *See* TIRSO DE MOLINA.

Tempest, Marie (1862–1942) English actress. A popular performer and vocalist at the turn of the century, she appeared in London in *musical comedies such as *The Geisha* (1896) and *San Toy* (1899), and *comedies such as *Robertson's *Caste* (1902) and *The Marriage of Kitty* (1903) by her husband Cosmo Gordon Lennox. Her association with the *manager George *Edwardes during *San Toy* was terminated when, playing a Chinese boy, she insisted on wearing the more flattering shorts instead of trousers. Her considerable talent was rarely exploited, and she was often cast as a charming, beautiful, but essentially decorative addition to the cup-and-saucer *comedies with which she was generally associated. At the end of her career, Dodie Smith's *Dear Octopus* (1938) provided a vehicle for her considerable talent. AF

Tendulkar, Vijay (1928–2008) Marathi writer, one of the leaders of the new theatre movement of the 1950s. His *Shrimant* (*The Wealthy*, 1955) questions the middle-class values of marriage, family, and human relationships. *An Island Called Man* (1958) subverts the cosy drawing-room setting of mainstream plays by portraying the reality of unemployed middle-class youth facing homelessness. In *Silence! The Court Is in Session* (1968) Tendulkar used a play-within-the-play to reveal the psychological violence the middle class can wreak on those who contravene its hypocritical social conventions. Other plays in this vein include *Vultures* (1971) and *Sakharam Binder* (1972). Tendulkar's most notable play, *Police Chief Ghashiram* (1973), was condemned in orthodox circles for its anti-Brahmanism. Drawing on folk theatre traditions of song, *dance, and actor deployment, he turned a historical event into an allegory of the prevailing political situation, depicting ordinary men growing into monsters under the patronage of self-serving politicians. Tendulkar wrote 29 plays, many of them produced in other Indian languages.   SGG

tennis-court theatres As the medieval French sport of 'real tennis' declined during the seventeenth century, its indoor courts became available as *playhouses. A tennis court was a long, rectangular structure with a flat stone floor, a covered, ground-level spectator gallery running around three walls, and a tiled roof. The installation of a raised stage at one end, the division of the side galleries into *boxes, and the addition of a second tier above them, were sufficient to convert it into a theatre—one easily dismantled when the tenant actors moved on. Although its sight lines were unsatisfactory, the geometry of the tennis court was enormously influential on French theatre architecture until the mid-eighteenth century.

The nation's first permanent public theatres were both so constructed in Paris. While the *Hôtel de Bourgogne had not been a tennis court when it was built in 1548, it had broadly similar internal dimensions. The *Marais, on the other hand, had been a tennis court until *Montdory undertook its permanent conversion in 1634. Moreover, the first home of *Molière's company, the Illustre Théâtre, in 1643 was the Mestayers tennis court. The first Paris *opera house was a former tennis court; renamed the Guénégaud theatre in 1673, this was also the initial home of the *Comédie-Française from 1680 to 1689.

While tennis was imitated outside France, only in England did tennis-court theatres play any significant role. The first London tennis court converted to a permanent theatre was Gibbons's tennis court, opened in 1660 by *Killigrew. The following year Lisle's tennis court in *Lincoln's Inn Fields was leased by *Davenant for his *The Siege of Rhodes*, the first play to employ changeable scenery in a permanent *public playhouse in England.   JG

Terayama Shūji (1935–83) Japanese director and writer. A seminal figure in *avant-garde culture during the 1960s and 1970s, Terayama's life was plagued by ill-health. A published poet at 16, he went on to a distinguished and diverse career as a writer and director for stage, television, radio, and film. His first play, *Blood Sleeps Standing Up*, was staged in 1960. In 1967 he founded his own theatre company, Tenjō Sajiki (Les Enfants du Paradis), which, inspired by *Artaud, carried out radical experiments with dramatic text, performance, venue, and *audience relationships. A poet with visual images as well as words, the look of a Terayama production defined Japanese counter-culture: grotesque, *surrealistic, sexy, violent, rebellious yet strangely nostalgic. He was famous for *street performances like *Man-Pow-ered Airplane Solomon* (1970) and *Knock* (1975). Other plays include *Mink Marie* (1967), *Lessons for Servants* (1978), and *Lemmings* (1980). Terayama and his company frequently *toured Europe and the USA.   CP

Terence (Publius Terentius Afer) (195/185–159 BC) Roman comic playwright. Terence came to Rome as a slave, probably brought from North Africa by a Roman senator who educated and eventually freed him. Little is known about his life, though a leading actor, Lucius Ambivius Turpio, promoted his career. Terence wrote six plays: *Andria*, *Hecyra*, *Heauton Timoroumenos*, *Eunuchus*, *Phormio*, and *Adelphi*. He based them upon *Greek originals, primarily by *Menander (*see* NEW COMEDY).

Terence was born either some ten years before or at the time of *Plautus' death, but the surviving works of Rome's great comic playwrights display radically different approaches. Unlike Plautus, Terence appears to have been relatively faithful to the plots, characterization, and atmosphere of his models while rendering them more acceptable to the conditions of performance at Rome. He created more realistically drawn *characters, with greater emphasis on individual psychology, and rarely resorted to the *stock figures used by Plautus. Terentian characters are not single-minded types but are motivated in more complex and ambiguous ways, which enhances the ethical relevance of the plays.

This loosening of dramatic stereotype and conventional comic morality is accompanied by greater sobriety in language. There is none of the wordplay, indecencies, irrelevant jokes, extravagant fantasies, or sudden outbursts of song characteristic of Plautine drama. Terence sought to write pure and elegant Latin, which was simple, flexible, and concise, but also capable of irony and wit; the language spoken perhaps by the cosmopolitan circle with which he is thought to have associated. Staging conventions are more *realistically employed. The plot is rarely interrupted for comic asides, or for audience address, topical allusion, or *slapstick.

Like other Roman dramatists, Terence presented his works to holiday audiences who were looking to be entertained. It is not surprising that these spectators were at times distracted by the attractions of rival entertainments. The first performance of Terence's *Hecyra*, for example, was abandoned by the audience in favour of a tight-rope walker and boxers; the second attempt suffered a similar fate caused by a competing *gladiatorial display. Evidently at least a portion

of the audience had little regard for the relatively sophisticated, complex, and restrained *comedies Terence offered them, or for the *prologues he employed to lecture on dramatic technique, argue with his critics, defend his craft, and plead for a fair hearing. Terence also suffered the taunts of a rival dramatist, Luscius Lanuvinus, who claimed that he had taken liberties in translating his Greek originals.

Terence seems to have been less concerned with accurate translation than with creating careful reconceptions of the originals. His *Eunuchus* evidently marked a turning point. Terence added extra characters and scenes from another play and the result was extremely successful, winning the largest fee ever paid for a comedy. In his subsequent plays, the *Phormio* and *Adelphi*, he continued to employ a judicious mixture of traditional farcical elements and familiar characters while retaining the naturalism, ethical complexity, and intelligence of the original works.

Terence's influence upon European drama has been immense. His works were widely admired and discussed in antiquity, extensively copied, annotated, and analysed in the *medieval period, and published in numerous editions during the *early modern period. Many of these were illustrated, and examples produced in the last decade of the fifteenth century contain important visual evidence of the earliest attempts by scholars to understand and to stage ancient drama. In turn, such experiments led to new plays composed in direct imitation of Terence and of Plautus. Thus the *dramaturgy, representation of character, and wit and elegance of Terence's *dialogue left an indelible mark upon subsequent practice, providing the models for modern comedy.

Masked performances of *Heauton Timoroumenos*, *Andria*, and *Adelphi* were presented at the *Weimar Court Theatre in the first decade of the nineteenth century. Revivals of Terence's plays have been infrequent in the modern era, despite his virtues as a skilled playwright. Translators and directors have found it difficult to determine an appropriate style for his language and its enactment.   RCB

Terriss, William (1847–97) English actor. His early career as a tea planter and sheep farmer added to his reputation for athletic and vigorous roles, which he assumed with ease, and he was universally known as 'Breezy Bill' for his devil-may-care demeanour and association with the *heroes of nautical *melodrama, notably William in *Jerrold's *Black-Ey'd Susan*. He played athletic heroes at *Drury Lane (Captain Molyneux in *Boucicault's *The Shaughraun* in 1875) and with

*Irving at the Lyceum. Though he played Shakespeare—Edgar in *King Lear*, Laertes in *Hamlet*, Mercutio in *Romeo and Juliet*—he had difficulty with the verse, complaining of *King Lear* that it was 'a damned dull play you know. Damned dull. Heavy as anything.' At the Adelphi from 1885 he was more comfortable, playing the popular soldier-sailor heroes in melodramas like *Harbour Lights* (1885) and *The Swordsman's Daughter* (1895). Attacked in a fit of madness and stabbed to death outside the Adelphi by Richard Prince, an ambitious young actor, Terriss's funeral procession was lined by an estimated 50,000 mourners. AF

Terry, Ellen (1847–1928) English actress. Part of a great theatrical dynasty (*Terry family), Ellen began acting professionally as a child for Charles *Kean. Yet she took some time before achieving serious success. First she left the stage to marry the much older painter G. F. Watts in 1864; the marriage soon collapsed and Terry returned to the stage. In 1868 she suddenly eloped with the architect Edwin Godwin, by whom she had two theatrical reformist children: Edith *Craig and Edward Gordon *Craig. Terry's career began in earnest in 1874 when *Reade persuaded her to act in *The Wandering Heir*, and in 1875 she played her first Portia in a *Merchant of Venice* sumptuously mounted by *Wilton and *Bancroft. In 1878 she joined forces with *Irving for a twenty-year partnership at the Lyceum Theatre. Here Terry starred as Beatrice, Portia, Queen Katherine in *Henry VIII*, and Imogen. Terry's forte was in charming the public with her Pre-Raphaelite good looks, merry laugh, and appearance of spontaneity, but she never played the part that seemed made for her, Rosalind in *As You Like It*, presumably because there was not a significant role for Irving. She also had success with less classical plays, such as *Bulwer-Lytton's *The Lady of Lyons*, and was popular as Marguerite in *Faust*.

Irving and Terry *toured America several times and their partnership flourished. In 1892 she began an extended correspondence with *Shaw (published 1931). Shaw encouraged Terry to branch out and wrote the role of Lady Cicely Waynflete in *Captain Brassbound's Conversion* for her. In 1902 she played in Shakespeare away from the Lyceum, as Mistress Page in *Tree's *Merry Wives of Windsor*, and in 1903 moved into *management with *Much Ado About Nothing* and *Ibsen's *The Vikings*, starring herself in productions directed by her son and designed by him and her daughter, though the project was a *financial failure. In 1906 the Golden Jubilee of her first appearance was celebrated in an all-star mat-

inée at *Drury Lane. From 1910 to 1921 Terry toured England, Australia, and the USA, lecturing on Shakespeare, a format that also allowed her to recite favourite speeches without relying on her failing memory for lines; *Four Lectures on Shakespeare* (1931) reveal her as a lively and important critic. Late in life Terry appeared in five silent films. Although she had made several fortunes during her career, her habit of giving money away left her financially insecure. Terry's autobiography is *The Story of my Life* (1908, 1933). EJS

Terry, Megan (1932–) American playwright. Terry began to write during the late 1950s, then moved to New York and co-founded the *Open Theatre in 1963 with *Chaikin. As director of the company's playwriting workshop, she rejected psychological *realism and created scripts that would allow actors to undergo 'transformation' in performance. Transformation-plays, like *Calm down Mother* (1965) and *Comings and Goings* (1966), require actors to undergo rapid shifts in time, place, and persona. *Viet Rock* (1967), a protest piece about the Vietnam War, also achieved recognition as the first rock *opera. After leaving the Open Theatre, she wrote *Approaching Simone* (1970), a play about the French religious philosopher Simone Weil, produced at the *La Mama. In 1971 she became playwright-in-residence at the Omaha Magic Theatre. Her concern with *feminism and American politics is reflected in such plays as *Babes in the Bighouse* (1974) and *Mollie Bailey's Traveling Family Circus, Featuring Scenes from the Life of Mother Jones* (1983). JAB

Terry family English theatre dynasty, embracing the descendants of the English provincial actors **Benjamin Terry** (1818–96) and **Sarah Ballard** (1817–92). Usually the successes of this family are measured by the careers of their daughter Ellen *Terry, her son Edward Gordon *Craig and her daughter Edy *Craig, and of Ellen's great-nephew *Gielgud. But also significant were the other children of the family founders, **Fred** (1866–1933), **Marion** (1852–1930), and **Kate** (1844–1924). Fred Terry, for example, pursued a successful acting career and together with his wife Julia Neilson (1868–1957) embarked from 1900 on a 30-year association in romantic *melodramas such as *The Scarlet Pimpernel* and *Sweet Nell of Old Drury* which endeared them to English provincial *audiences in particular. Their daughter **Phyllis Neilson-Terry** (1892–1977) followed in her parent's footsteps and had extensive experience with Shakespeare, taking Viola and Juliet under *Tree (1910–12), and *toured the American *vaudeville circuit. Her brother **Dennis**

Neilson-Terry (1895–1932) began his career as a Shakespearian actor with the *Benson company before the First World War. Thereafter he toured the English provinces and South Africa in mainly commercial vehicles.

Kate Terry retired in 1867 after a relatively short acting career. She was equally adept at Shakespeare and the Victorian repertoire like *Bulwer-Lytton's *Money* and *The Lady of Lyons* or *Knowles's *The Hunchback*. Marion Terry was in the *Bancrofts' first season at the *Haymarket (1880–1), replaced her sister Ellen as Viola in *Irving's *Twelfth Night* (1884), toured extensively with him as Marguerite in *Faust* (1884) and as Portia (1894). Her greatest successes occurred during her two years with *Alexander at the St James's Theatre (1891–3). She was the original Mrs Erlynne in *Wilde's *Lady Windermere's Fan*, a role she revived as late as 1911.

Others who pursued successful acting careers include **Beatrice** (1890–?) and **Minnie** (1882–?); **Hazel Terry** (1918–74), the daughter of Dennis; **Olive** (1884–1957); and **Mabel Terry-Lewis** (1872–1957), the daughter of Kate. The entire dynasty, especially the female line, appeared to share many of the same qualities: charm, creative energy, and individual distinctiveness.   VEE

teyyam A colloquial expression meaning god, *teyyam* refers to the spirits, deified heroes, lineage ancestors, and pan-Indian deities propitiated in *ritual performances in northern Kerala, India. *Teyyam* is unique to this region, and is the primary form of popular Hinduism. It may date from as early as the first century AD when heroes killed in battle were deified by erecting stones to be worshipped in their honour. Today over 300 different *teyyams* are propitiated at special festivals in community or lineage shrines on schedules that range from annual to once every twelve years. Each *teyyam* is unique, has its own story of origin, and can serve quite different functions. Some are worshipped exclusively by a joint family, or an individual household, while others are worshipped by a specific caste. Worship may benefit an individual, an extended family, or entire community.

Performances in community shrines are on fixed dates, some set by astrological calculations. Some propitiate a single *teyyam* and are modest affairs involving the central performer accompanied by drummers and assistants. Others may propitiate as many as 32 gods in a festival lasting up to seven days and nights, and include feeding the entire community. Occasionally an individual may commission a new *teyyam* as a 'vow to god'—as did one householder who, cured of lep-

rosy, built a shrine to the *teyyam* Visnumurti for annual propitiation.

Teyyam performances are organized in a series of stages through which a low-caste dancer (*kolakarran*) is eventually transformed into the deity, becoming a vehicle for visitation by the god who interacts with his devotees. The performance sequence begins with preliminary rituals, progresses through the chanting of songs about the origin and history of the deity invoked, may include a special *dance representing the deity in its youthful stage, and culminates in the full visitation of the performer *costumed as the deity. The event concludes when the deity, led by assistants, interacts with the devotees present by answering questions, offering prophecies, giving blessings, and receiving offerings, which often include palmwine or the sacrifice of cocks. Make-up helps transform the performer as the deity is 'painted' into his face. As the make-up is prepared, the ingredients are charged with the god's 'power' (*sakti*) by breathing into the mixture, and through repetition of sacred phrases (*mantra*). The performer receives the deity's full power at the moment when he looks in a mirror, witnessing and manifesting his transformation.

Society in Kerala was transformed in the twentieth century. Where caste rules once regulated a hierarchically ordered society, today democratically elected governments in the area often include communists. Not surprisingly *teyyam*'s role and function has changed radically for many performers, patrons, and devotees of the gods.   PZ

Thacker, David (1950–) English director. Since the mid-1980s Thacker has been a proponent of *Miller's work in Britain, directing the world premières of *Two-Way Mirror* (1989) and *The Last Yankee* (1993). Thacker's emotional and psychological explorations of texts place an emphasis on clarity of *acting, a style suitable for Miller's work, which also found success with *Ibsen (*Ghosts*, 1986, with Vanessa *Redgrave; a BBC television version of *A Doll's House*, 1994). Thacker's clear readings have led to numerous successful productions of Shakespeare; as *artistic director of the Young Vic from 1984 to 1993 he directed *Othello*, *Macbeth*, *Hamlet*, *Measure for Measure*, *Julius Caesar*, and *Romeo and Juliet*. Since 1993 he has been with the *Royal Shakespeare Company, where he directed an award-winning *Pericles* (1989), and innovative productions of *Two Gentlemen of Verona* (1991), *The Merchant of Venice*, *Julius Caesar* (both 1993), *Coriolanus*, and *Measure for Measure* (both 1994). More recently he has directed for television, including *The Mayor of Casterbridge* (2003).   KN

Thalbach, Katharina (1954–   ) German actress and director. The daughter of Benno *Besson, her debut at the *Berliner Ensemble in 1968 immediately established Thalbach as a major acting talent. In 1977 she began working in West Germany, and has performed in a large variety of classical and contemporary roles ranging from Shakespeare to *Kleist to *Brecht. She is also a versatile film actor, best known in *The Tin Drum* (1979). Her performances are noted for their original and often unorthodox readings of roles. Her interest in discovery and experiment led her into *directing, in which she showed the same talent for unconventional readings of classical plays. Most noteworthy were her *Macbeth* (Berlin, 1987) and Brecht's *A Man's a Man* (Hamburg, 1989).   CBB

Theatertreffen German theatre festival. Founded in 1964, this showcase of the German theatre takes place annually in May in Berlin, assembling ten notable productions from Germany, Austria, and Switzerland (East German theatres were excluded before reunification). The productions are selected by a jury of seven theatre critics, the selected plays showing an 'extraordinary collaboration between dramatic text, *dramaturgy, *direction, *actors' performance, and design'. The jury's work and judgement have been controversial throughout the festival's existence for a tendency to focus on the director's theatre of *Stein, *Zadek, *Peymann, and others. Neglected smaller theatres and troupes frequently complained that the jury was biased and the meeting a showcase for the highly subsidized public theatres. The Theatertreffen is accompanied by a programme of international productions and a seminar for younger theatre practitioners.   CBB

theatre For most topics beginning with some form of the word 'theatre', see the next significant word of the item's title or name. For example, for 'theatre of the absurd' *see* ABSURD, THEATRE OF THE; for 'Théâtre du Soleil' *see* SOLEIL, THÉÂTRE DU.

theatre Derived from *theatron*, the ancient Greek word for 'seeing place', the word 'theatre' has over the centuries lost much of its original optic meaning, and through a series of inflations and associations is now commonly used to refer to (*a*) a building designed for the performance or exhibition of plays, *operas, or film; (*b*) the art of producing plays; (*c*) the institution of theatre generally. (Other, more obviously metaphoric usages do not concern us here.) More recently, theoreticians have urged that for a performance to be 'theatre' requires two sets of participants—*audience and *actors—and an organized spatial relationship between them. A theatrical event, a

collaboration between spectators and performers, is a construct of its participants.

The tentative nature of any definition of theatre, however abstract or general, is made necessary by the great variety of theatrical traditions and forms that have flourished throughout the world and continue to expand in their diversity. Moreover, definitions of theatre, like its formal characteristics, are culturally and historically determined. *Schechner places theatre in a continuum 'that reaches from the *ritualizations of animals (including humans) through performances in everyday life—greetings, displays of emotion, family scenes, professional roles, and so on—through to play, *sports, theatre, *dance, ceremonies, rites, and performances of great magnitude' (*Performance Theory*, 1988). The performances in Schechner's continuum that qualify as 'theatre', however, can shift with time and place.

In spite of widespread recognition that theatre defies definition, Western theory in general clings to the intersection of drama and performance as the locus of theatre. That is, together with spectators, performers, and organized space, *action or the representation of an action (*Aristotelian *mimesis) is deemed indispensable to theatre. The mimesis test nevertheless excludes many forms that both practitioners and scholars regard as theatre. The notion of mimetic theatre is undoubtedly useful, but it cannot be allowed more than tentative and temporary status. 'Theatre' is no more limited by its function as a medium for drama than 'drama' is limited to the single medium of theatre.   RWV

Theatre, the Built by James *Burbage in 1576 in Shoreditch, on the main road north out of the city, the Theatre was the first successful custom-built *playhouse in London. It was the second attempt by Burbage, once a player with Leicester's Men, after the Red Lion of 1567. A large twenty-sided polygon, its design and its name were meant to be reminders of the D-shaped classical *Roman theatres. Its stage thrust out halfway into the open yard. In 1594 it became the home to a new playing company, the Lord *Chamberlain's Men, whose leader was Richard *Burbage, James's son, and whose chief writer was Shakespeare. When the lease of the land it was built on expired in 1597, the landlord closed it down. Two years later it was dismantled and its timbers were taken for reuse as the frame for the *Globe on the other side of the river.   AJG

theatre design *See* PLAYHOUSE; SCENOGRAPHY.

Théâtre-Français *See* COMÉDIE-FRANÇAISE.

Theatre Guild American art theatre that emerged from the *Washington Square Players in 1918, reconstituted as fully professional through the efforts of Lawrence Langner (who maintained his job as a patent attorney). The Guild choose to produce only important full-evening plays, to lease or build a theatre accommodating 500–600 persons and thus 'larger than the usual *Little Theatre', to organize on a subscription basis, and to produce no plays written by its board members. These principles propelled the Guild during the years 1919–1939 to succeed as an art theatre in the Broadway environment. By 1930 the original subscription list of 135 had grown to 35,000 in New York and 45,000 in 132 cities and towns around the country. The introducer of numerous plays by *Shaw to the United States, meticulous productions of key works by *O'Neill, *Rice, *Sherwood, Philip *Barry, and *Behrman added to its enormous prestige, attracting the talents of the *Lunts, among others. After the loss of some younger members (and some cultural currency) to the *Group Theatre in 1931, of major playwrights to the Playwrights Company in 1938, and their *playhouse in 1943, the Guild existed largely as a commercial enterprise. MAF

theatre-in-education *See* EDUCATIONAL THEATRE.

Théâtre National Populaire Theatre company founded by *Gémier in 1920 in Paris to fulfil his dream for a popular state-subsidized theatre. He received only limited support from the French government, but a modern performance space in the Palais du Chaillot, opened in 1937, extended the possibilities, though they were not fully exploited until *Vilar became director in 1951. Vilar transformed the Chaillot into the focal point of a vision to popularize and decentralize the arts in France, which he thought enslaved to class hierarchy and elitism. He abolished *footlights, front curtains, and superfluous scenery, and preferred stylized, colourful *costumes. For the audience he abandoned evening dress and tipping, instituted a new system of subscriptions, theatre weekends and galas, as well as discussions with authors, actors, and directors. Vilar's repertoire was a mix of French classics, German *romantics, and European moderns, many of which were unfamiliar to Parisian *audiences at the time, and his company attracted some of the most talented actors of the era, notably Gérard *Philipe and María *Casares. Vilar associated the TNP with the *Avignon Festival, which he inaugurated in 1947, and for nearly twenty summers the Paris productions were recreated under the

stars by the Rhône River. Georges Wilson took over the direction of the TNP in 1963 and attempted to continue Vilar's legacy, but in a politicized decade Wilson was unable to attract younger audiences and by the late 1960s the *financial situation was dire.

Consequently, in 1972 the title of the TNP was transferred to the company run by *Planchon in Villeurbanne, near Lyon. Over the next 30 years the company was a vehicle for Planchon's distinctive *directorial style, where a creative *mise-en-scène stands on equal footing to the author's text. Inspired by *Brecht and the new wave cinematographers of the 1950s and 1960s, Planchon staged a series of spectacular productions depicting the personal torment of individual *characters as metaphors for greater ideological conflicts, featuring works by *Ionesco, *Vinaver, Dubillard, and *Pinter, as well as a number of his own plays. Planchon left the TNP in 2001, and was succeeded by *Schiaretti.   CHB

Theatre Workshop Highly influential English company, based (1953–78) at the Theatre Royal, Stratford East, London. Established in 1945, Theatre Workshop was the last in a long line of troupes set up by Joan *Littlewood (director) and Ewan MacColl (folk musician), committed to *touring to working-class *audiences in non-theatrical spaces. The Workshop specialized in new, company-*devised plays and the classics (including the first British production of *Brecht's *Mother Courage*, 1955). By the late 1950s Theatre Workshop (minus MacColl) had become an important part of the new wave of British theatre, largely through a series of remarkable productions of new plays, notably *Behan's *The Quare Fellow* (1956) and *The Hostage* (1958), *Delaney's *A Taste of Honey* (1958), and the *collectively written *Oh! What a Lovely War* (1963). All the Workshop's productions were shaped by Littlewood's distinctive personality and *directorial methods (which included the extensive use of *improvisation and the rewriting of plays in *rehearsal). The company's radical ethos was eventually compromised by systematic underfunding, which caused Littlewood to leave the professional theatre altogether. Although the title Theatre Workshop was dropped in 1978, a company continues to thrive at the Theatre Royal.   SWL

Theatrical Syndicate An association or 'trust' comprised of six booking agencies and theatre owners that joined together in 1896 to control most American production. The period of Syndicate dominance was the most centralized in the history of American theatre and offers a case study in monopolistic practices. The Syndicate consisted of the Klaw and Erlanger Exchange; Samuel Nixon and J. Fred Zimmerman; Al Hayman; and *Frohman. The trust owned or controlled booking for nearly all 'first-class' theatres in the United States and so was in a position to dictate script choices, production styles, salaries, *royalty agreements, ticket prices, and even advertising rates. The expansion of the railways and the absence of government regulation made it possible for entrepreneurs to buy theatre buildings along a transportation route, dissolve the local *stock company, and substitute a series of 'combination' productions that were cast, built, and *rehearsed in New York. Competitors were eliminated through outright purchase or by temporarily low ticket prices which drove them out of business. With an unchecked ability to drive down costs and set prices, the Syndicate flourished, fighting off challenges from independent theatre owners, booking agents, playwrights such as *Belasco, or recalcitrant actors such as Minnie Maddern *Fiske, who *toured the country performing in gymnasiums, tents, and skating rinks to avoid Syndicate control.

The Syndicate had no interest in theatre as an art: plays, actors, and designs were valued strictly in economic terms. Playwrights and composers, if they wished to sell their work, were required to produce standardized *comedies, *melodramas, and *operettas that conformed to proven formulas. Actors were regarded as interchangeable commodities and expected to play the same type or even the same role for years on end. Though the *Shuberts finally overwhelmed the Syndicate between 1910 and 1920, they substituted a new monopoly for the old. Soon after film and radio overwhelmed theatre as popular entertainment and 'the road' was largely converted to movie theatres. Theatre as a locally produced professional enterprise did not recover across the United States until a partial revival in the *regional theatre movement of the 1960s and 1970s. MAF

theatron Greek 'viewing place'. The architecture of the *Greek ancient theatre distinguished *skene (the stage building) from *theatron* (the seating), but since the stage building was in origin often temporary the word came to imply our *'theatre', which is the usual meaning of Latin *theatrum*. Seating was at first on a hillside, then by about 500 BC on wooden scaffolding, increasingly with stone seating fronting the orchestra for distinguished priests or magistrates (*prohedria*). But it is also possible, as in *Roman festivals, that occasionally the steps of temples were designed as seating with temporary stages erected before

them. After *c.*330 BC the Athenian model (Theatre of *Dionysus) of semicircular stone seating became standard, but with many variants based on different geometric models, such as those described by the architect Vitruvius. The different 'wedges' (Greek *kerkides*, Latin *cunei*) separated by gangways could vertically demarcate social or political groupings; under Roman influence a very complex hierarchy from front to back developed, with horizontal divisions enforced by walkways (Greek *diazoma*, Latin *praecinctio*), barriers (Latin *balteus*), and special ticketed entrances (Latin *vomitorium*), the orchestra now being reserved for the elite. Seats were always narrow (*c.*41 cm; 16 inches). *See* PLAYHOUSE. WJS

Theobald, Lewis (1688–1744) English author, immortalized as the king of the dunces in the first versions of Pope's *The Dunciad* (1728), a reward for attacking Pope's edition of Shakespeare (1725) in Theobald's *Shakespeare Restor'd* (1726). At *Lincoln's Inn Fields Theatre, Theobald wrote and produced *pantomimes with John *Rich. While these works—such as *Harlequin a Sorcerer* (1725), *Apollo and Daphne* (1726), and *The Rape of Proserpine* (1727)—were performed hundreds of times, his serious plays, such as his adaptation of *Richard II* (1719) and his more popular *Double Falsehood* (1727), were produced much less frequently. MJK

Thespis (fl.534 BC) Semi-mythical inventor of Athenian *tragedy. *Aristotle, later sources say, believed that Thespis added the *prologue and speech to *choral performance, creating a new genre. This may accurately represent the development of drama from choral lyric (*dithyramb), but attributing that development to one man probably owes more to the Greek love of finding causes than to fact. *See* GREEK THEATRE, ANCIENT. JMM

Thiong'o, Ngugi, wa (1938–   ) Kenyan writer. Although better known as a novelist, Thiong'o had an influential drama career. In the early 1960s at Makerere University he wrote, produced, and published a *melodrama, *Black Hermit*, and several short *realistic plays. In 1975 he co-authored with Micere Mugo an epic, nationalist play, *The Trial of Dedan Kimathi*. One of the first Kenyan productions at the National Theatre in Nairobi, it reached a wider *audience through travelling performances in Kiswahili. In 1976 Thiong'o, invited along with his cousin Ngugi wa *Mirii to write a play for the Kamariithu Community Educational and Cultural Centre (KCECC), created *I Will Marry When I Want*, a popular, class-conscious attack on neocolonialism. The play's licence for performance was withdrawn and Thiong'o jailed without trial (*see* CENSORSHIP). The experience made him realize the need to work closely with subaltern classes and through indigenous languages and cultures. After his release in 1978 he returned to KCECC but the resultant play, *Mother Weep for Me*, was refused a licence. Controversial *rehearsals in 1982 provoked the Kenyan government into destroying Kamariithu Theatre and Thiong'o fled into exile. He continued to advocate anti-imperialist literature and theatre in African languages through such polemical essay collections as *Decolonising the Mind* (1986) and *Moving the Centre* (1993). DaK

Thiyam, Ratan (1948–) Artistic director of Chorus Repertory Theatre in Imphal, Manipur. As India's most internationally recognized director, Thiyam is known for his visually spectacular productions that reflect the state of global and national violence through a modernist reading of the epics. At least three of his major productions—*Urubhangu* (1981), *Chakravyuha* (1984), and *Karnabhara* (1991)—deal with critical events from the *Mahabharata*, tracing affinities to contemporary Manipur, a military state ridden with insurgency and intertribal conflicts. The search for peace has taken Thiyam beyond polemical productions on corruption and civic decay like *Imphal Imphal* and *Imphal Karusi*, towards more meditative reflections on violence, like Agneya's Hindi poem *Uttarapriyadarshi*. Elaborating on this poem in a highly layered and *surreal *mise-en-scène, Thiyam's production depicted the aftermath of the Kalinga war in which the Emperor Ashoka (Priyadarshi) survives a nightmarish vision of hell to embrace the eightfold path of the Buddha. The hell was contemporary, made up of modern instruments of torture and human limbs cooked in the kitchen of a five star hotel, a metaphoric evocation of Manipur today. While some critics regard Thiyam's productions as export-quality spectacles, others claim he is reinventing tradition meaningfully. RB

Thomas, Augustus (1857–1934) American playwright. His insistent focus on American themes was evident from *Alabama* (1891), his first success, which deals with the reconciliation of an old Confederate and his nationalistic son. Subsequently, *In Mizzoura* (1893), *Arizona* (1900), and *Copperhead* (1918) revealed Thomas's talent for constructing compelling American *characters and drawing distinctly American locales. Thomas was also interested in topical themes, evident in *The Witching Hour* (1907), a study of the occult, and *As a Man Thinks* (1911), an examination of hypnotism. He also wrote

*comedies, the best being *The Earl of Pawtucket* (1903). Thomas served for many years as president of the Society of American Dramatists. GAR

Thomas, Brandon (1856–1914) English actor, playwright, and songwriter. Thomas composed songs for the *music halls, acted in *farces, *comedies, *melodramas, and an occasional Shakespeare, and wrote a dozen or so popular plays, but he is best known for writing and starring in the amazingly successful farce *Charley's Aunt* (1892), which ran for four years in London. Thomas revived it successfully in the following decade. The play was frequently performed by professional and amateur companies in the twentieth century. Translated into several dozen languages, it has few to rival it in popularity. TP

Thomas, Gerald (1954–) Brazilian director. A polemical figure in Brazilian theatre since his 1985 staging of *Four Times Beckett*, epitomizing the *director as *auteur*, he has been both criticized and admired for his striking imagery and *metatheatrical productions. His work consistently refers to *operas and literary classics, *Beckett and Kafka being constants. He offers pastiches of quotations, psychoanalytical dream images woven together by musical references, and autobiographical commentary. In the 1990s Thomas produced a series of *happenings and musical rave parties in Rio and São Paulo, and has since turned his attention to media critique. He returned to his favourite subject in *Waiting for Beckett* (2000), in which the television interviewer Maria Gabriela conducted a '*monologic' interview with Beckett, played by the immobile back of an 'actor-ghost'. LHD

Thompson, Judith (1954–) Canadian playwright. While at the National Theatre School, she realized that the *monologues she composed as *acting exercises indicated her true vocation. The materiality of the voice is the defining characteristic of her *dramaturgy. Her *characters are driven to speak by unconscious impulses; the border between conscious and unconscious is (in her words) a 'screen door'. Her plays have a surface *naturalism through which erupts language that is violently poetic, disorienting, and darkly comic. Likewise the past erupts into the present with hallucinatory intensity. Religious imagery pervades: the presence of evil in the world is set against redemptive impulses. She has also written for radio, television, and film. Her stage plays include *The Crackwalker* (1980), *White Biting Dog* (1984), *I Am Yours* (1987), *Lion in the Streets* (1990), *Sled* (1997), *Perfect Pie* (2000), and *Palace of the End* (2007). RCN

Thompson, Mervyn (1935-92) New Zealand director and playwright. Thompson championed cultural nationalism of the left, both as an *artistic director (of Christchurch's Court Theatre and Wellingon's Downstage) and as a charismatic university teacher and director. He was also a significant writer, notably of *documentary plays with music, including *O! Temperance!* (1972) on the temperance and women's suffrage movement, *Songs to Uncle Scrim* (1976) about the Depression, and *Songs to the Judges* (1980) championing Maori rights against a century of New Zealand colonial injustice. A passionate and controversial advocate of New Zealand plays, he was an outstanding developmental director for Greg McGee, *Renée, and emerging women playwrights at national workshops in the 1980s. His vulnerably autobiographical plays, the *expressionist and *Brechtian *First Return* (1974) and his one-person show *Passing Through* (1991), are moving retrospectives of three decades in New Zealand theatre.   DC

Thorndike, Sybil (1882-1976) English actress who worked first with *Greet's company, and then at the Gaiety Theatre, Manchester. There she married *Casson in 1908, and acted, often under his direction, for the next 60 years. She played leading Shakespearian parts at the *Old Vic (1914-18), including Beatrice, Portia, and Imogen, Prince Hal, and the Fool in *King Lear*. As an actress she was intense, intelligent, quick to take direction, somewhat androgynous in youth, with a deeply musical voice, and was capable of playing an amazing variety of strong parts, from Hecuba, Medea, and Candida to Mistress Quickly and the working-class *heroines of the Gaiety. She triumphed in *St Joan*, which *Shaw wrote for her (1922). She was a high Anglican and lifelong socialist, with a belief in the civilizing mission of theatre. In later life she took some character parts in films and television, and her distinctive voice was often heard in radio plays.   EEC

Throckmorton, Cleon (1897-1965) American scene and *lighting designer. A founding member of the *Provincetown Players in 1915, Throckmorton used simple materials and backlit silhouettes to create the haunting *expressionist environments for *O'Neill's *The Emperor Jones* (1920) and collaborated with Robert Edmond *Jones in designing O'Neill's *The Hairy Ape* (1922). Throckmorton provided scenery for the *Group Theatre's first production—*The House of Connelly* (1931)— and became a major commercial designer. He designed 66 productions during the decade of the 1930s, ranging from the stifling Midwestern interiors for *Howard's *Alien Corn* (1933) to the

elegantly simple unit set for the *Federal Theatre Project production of *Auden's *The Dance of Death* (1936).   MAF

Tian Han (T'ien Han) (1898-1968) Chinese playwright. After six years in Japan, Tian returned to China in 1922 as an avid proponent of Western-style drama, giving it the name *huajü in 1927. Apart from writing, translating, and critiquing new plays, he produced work with his Nanguo She (South China Society) in Shanghai, Nanjing, and Guangzhou, including new one-acts (his *Death of a Famous Actor*, 1929) and translations ranging from the Japanese *shimpa to *Wilde's *Salome*. He became a member of the Communist Party in 1931 and was actively involved in the left-wing dramatic movement. Some of his better-known *huajü plays of this period are *The Rainy Season* (1931), *The Moonlight Sonata* (1932), and *The Charming Ladies* (1947). He was a prominent figure in reforming traditional theatre, partly by writing new scripts for *jingju (Beijing opera) and regional forms. In 1949 he became president of the All-China Dramatists Association but continued to write influential work, including the Beijing operas *The White Snake* (1952) and *Xie Yaohuan* (1961), and the *huajü play *Guan Hanqing* (1958).   SYL

Tieck, Ludwig (1773-1853) German playwright, critic, and translator. In 1799 Tieck joined the early *romantics in Jena, including *Schlegel. During a visit to England in 1817 he gathered materials on the Elizabethan stage, an important event in a lifelong preoccupation with Shakespeare. In 1825 Tieck became *dramaturg at the Dresden Court Theatre and had a significant impact on its repertoire during the 1820s and 1830s, with productions of Shakespeare, *Calderón, Lope de *Vega, *Kleist, and *Grillparzer. In 1843 he produced his legendary *A Midsummer Night's Dream* in Berlin, utilizing many features of the Elizabethan stage, accompanied by Mendelssohn's *music.

As a dramatist Tieck is representative of romantic *comedy: his *Puss in Boots* (1797) and *The World Upside Down* (1799) are distinguished by their *parody of prevailing dramatic genres and styles, but the plays were ignored by the larger theatres in Germany, and have rarely been performed. Tieck was a tireless reformer, promulgating ensemble *acting and an abstract stage. Equally important are his critical writings and translations of *Cervantes. He (and his daughter Dorothea) helped to finish Schlegel's monumental translation of Shakespeare, which became the standard version in German-speaking lands.   CBB

Tillemans, Walter (1932–) Flemish director. Soon after his studies Tillemans was employed by the Royal Dutch Theatre (KNS) in Antwerp. His work was marked by a rough, popular style, social commitment, and a sense of pure theatricality. Convinced of the community value of theatre, he was the first director to introduce an authentic Brechtian style in Flanders; notable *Brecht productions in the 1960s were *The Good Person of Setzuan*, *The Life of Galileo*, and *A Man's a Man*, which he daringly transposed to Vietnam. He was also an important Shakespeare director, and in 1979 founded the Raamtheater in Antwerp which introduced writers such as *Mamet and Pavel Kohout.   JDV

Tilley, Vesta (Matilda Powles) (1864–1952) *Male impersonator and *music-hall artiste. She made her stage debut aged 3 or 4. Moving to Nottingham, the precocious 'Great Little Tilley' performed at miners' galas and pub music halls, wearing male *costume to sing songs written by her father. She was always immaculately tailored, whether as a 'masher', soldier, or curate, playing on the pretensions of the rising middle classes in carefully chosen songs such as 'The Seaside Sultan' and 'The Afternoon Parade'. Best known for 'Burlington Bertie—the Boy with the Hyde Park Drawl' and 'Algy—the Piccadilly Johnnie with the Little Glass Eye', she married her own 'young swell', theatrical entrepreneur Walter de Frece, in 1890. He became her *manager, furthering her career on the music-hall and *variety stages, in film, and in America.   AF

Tipton, Jennifer (1937–) One of the USA's busiest and most respected lighting designers for *dance, theatre, and *opera. Tipton collaborated with many innovative choreographers and directors, including Twyla Tharp, *Robbins, Mikhail Baryshnikov, *Sellars, *Akalaitis, *LeCompte, and Robert *Wilson. Her designs were noted for a subtle, cerebral, and sculptural quality that served the needs of the production without attracting undue attention. At the Yale School of Drama from 1981, she was mentor to a new generation of lighting designers, and the recipient of numerous awards.   STC

Tirso de Molina (Gabriel Téllez) (1579–1648) Spanish dramatist. In 1600 he entered the Order of Mercy as a novice, whose history he would complete in 1639. But by 1610 he was also known as a playwright, and in the early 1620s was Lope de *Vega's outstanding rival. In 1625, however, a Committee for Reform required him to leave Madrid and write no more plays, and thereafter his output was small. He nevertheless claimed in 1634 to have written over 400 *comedias, of which some 80 survive. Like Lope, whose innovations he staunchly defended, he had a rather more comic than tragic sense of life, but though he lacked Lope's spontaneity and genius as a poet, his mindset was more intellectual and satirical and his outlook more broadly humane. Like Lope's, his plays are uneven, but their range is extremely wide. He portrayed some strikingly strong and intelligent women, like the eponymous *Antona García* (*c*.1623) and Queen María de Molina, in *Prudence in Woman* (*c*.1623). His his works are full of unusual *characters carefully portrayed, like David's son Amnon in *La venganza de Tamar* (*c*.1621-4), one of several *biblical plays, performed by the *Royal Shakespeare Company as *Tamar's Revenge* (*Swan, 2004).

Some of his finest works are urban *comedies, like *Martha the Pious* (*c*.1615) or *Don Gil of the Green Breeches* (1615); the latter exploits ingeniously the popular plot motif of the woman who regains her faithless lover by dint of deceit and disguise. *The Shy Man at Court* (1609-13), remarkable for its multiplicity of interwoven plots, its exploitation of role play, and the characterization of one of its *heroines, the narcissistic Serafina, is by contrast a model of that other comic genre, the *comedia palatina*.

His religious plays include some notable *autos sacramentales*, but above all two *comedias* (though his authorship of both has been questioned) whose *protagonists merit the unusual fate of damnation. *Damned for Despair* (*c*.1624), a powerfully visual drama, tells, in counterpoint with the tale of a double-dyed *villain who is ultimately saved, that of a doubt-driven hermit, whose paranoia is harrowingly portrayed. By contrast, Don Juan Tenorio's fundamental error, in *The Trickster of Seville* (*c*.1622), is that he can indulge an obsessive delight in deceit, but indefinitely postpone the reckoning the Stone Guest eventually brings. Reworkings from *Molière to *Mozart to *Shaw have made his character and story a universal myth, variously interpreted, but Tirso's seminal drama is in essence a dynamic, colourful sermon.   VFD

Toller, Ernst (1893-1939) German playwright. One of the most influential exponents of *expressionism, Toller came to attention with his 1919 play *Die Wandlung* (translated as *Transfiguration*), a personal and general treatment of the transformation of German society from patriotism to pacifism during the First World War. His involvement with the abortive Munich Soviet Republic in 1919 led to five years in prison (1919 24). After his release Toller moved to Berlin and, while avoiding direct political activism, channelled his radical socialist convictions into writing. His exile to the USA in 1933 led to depression and suicide. The experiences of the war form the background of *Die Wandlung* and *Hinkemann* (1923). Political activism is explored in a variety of styles and settings, ranging from *choral works performed by amateur working-class actors to *scenarios for mass performances and expressionist works featuring dream sequences. Important plays include *Masses and Men* (1920), in which *realistic scenes alternate with dream interludes in a debate on violence and left-wing politics. *The Machine Wreckers* (1922) deals with the Luddite revolt. *Hoppla, wir leben!* (*Hoppla, We're Alive!*, 1927) shows a cross-section of Berlin society; *Piscator's production featured a famous set with simultaneous playing areas.   CBB

Tolstoy, Aleksei (Konstantinovich) (1817–75) Russian writer. Well known for his short stories, poetry, and a novel, he retired from the civil service in 1861 to concentrate on literary work. Several 'dramatic ballads' were followed by a trilogy of historical dramas set in the late sixteenth century: *The Death of Ivan the Terrible* (1866), *Tsar Fyodor Ioannovich* (1868), and *Tsar Boris* (1870). Good contacts at court facilitated lavish funding for the première of *Ivan the Terrible* in St Petersburg (1867): historical *realism arrived on the Russian stage in design, *costume, and *acting style. The other two plays were severely *censored for performance because of their implicit discussion of Russian autocracy. *Tsar Fyodor* premièred in 1898 (Petersburg), and was also the opening production of the *Moscow Art Theatre that year. A censored version of *Tsar Boris* (Moscow, 1881) was followed by full versions (1898, 1899). Tolstoy's final play, *The General*, set in thirteenth-century Novgorod, written in 1870, was performed posthumously in 1877.   CM

Tolstoy, Lev (Leo) (1828–1910) Russian writer. Count Tolstoy's best plays are generally in a *naturalistic vein and have a didactic slant. His views on the theatre are in his essay *What Is Art?* (1897-8), which claims art should be accessible to all, not just an elite. He famously said of *Chekhov's plays that they were bad, but not as bad as those of Shakespeare. Nevertheless he considered drama 'probably the most influential province of art' and wrote sixteen plays, none as memorable as his novels *War and Peace* or *Anna Karenina* but at least two will probably survive, *The Power of Darkness* (1886) and *The Fruits of Enlightenment* (1889). The former was based on an actual case of murder of a newborn child by its peasant

father who, racked by a guilty conscience, eventually made a public confession of his crime. It was banned from performance until 1895 (*see* CENSORSHIP). The latter was a *satire directed at the inability of the landowning class to understand the peasantry. His first plays, *A Contaminated Family* and *The Nihilist*, date from the 1860s, and he only resumed playwriting after a twenty-year gap, with *The First Distiller* (1886), a comic fantasy on temperance themes based on his short story, 'The Imp and the Crust'. Most of his other plays were published posthumously, including *The Living Corpse* (1900) and *The Light Shines in Darkness* (1900), an autobiographical work about an aristocrat at odds with his family. *The Cause of It All* (1910), a temperance play featuring a worker, proved popular in Soviet times. A four-act play set in third-century Syria, *Peter the Baker*, was staged by *Meyerhold (1918). Other noteworthy productions include the première of *The Fruits of Enlightenment*, with *Komissarzhevskaya, directed by *Stanislavsky (1891), and the latter's revival of *The Power of Darkness*, in grimly naturalistic mode, at the *Moscow Art Theatre (1902).   NW

Tomashefsky, Boris (*c.*1866–1939) Ukrainian-American Yiddish actor. Tomashefsky arrived in New York in 1881, in possession of a melodious voice and good looks, and in 1882 participated in the first Yiddish performance in America, *The Witch* by *Goldfaden. Increasing competition forced him to play on the road beginning in 1893, where he became popular and began to write and compose for the stage. In Baltimore he met his actress wife Bessie (1873–1962), and in 1891 the Tomashefskys returned to New York, where he cultivated a career as the ultimate matinée idol of the Yiddish stage. Though he excelled in *musical comedy and *melodrama, he was also committed to a more serious repertoire in adaptations of classics and in literary Yiddish drama. *See* DIASPORA.   EN

Tom show George L. Aiken's adaptation of Harriet Beecher Stowe's 1851 novel *Uncle Tom's Cabin* appeared in 1852, and quickly became as sensationally popular as the novel. In various forms *Uncle Tom's Cabin* held the stage for the next 90 years, spawning a distinct genre, the Tom show. *Touring groups, often playing in tents and accompanied by a parade and brass band, crossed North America, performing in tiny rural communities as well as in urban centres. Forty-nine Tom shows were on the road in 1879; by the end of the century, the number had reached nearly 450. Connections to the Stowe novel were often tenuous, but the spectacle (Eliza crossing the ice; the bloodhounds) and sentimentality (Little Eva's death and apotheosis) remained intact. Although Tom shows lingered on until the 1940s, most had disbanded a decade early, under pressure from radio, sound films, and the Depression.   AW

topeng Various forms of *masked *dance in Java and Bali in Indonesia, and in Malaysia. Roving companies of masked players appear in records by 850 in Java and 882 in Bali, though little is known of these traditions. In Java and Malaysia, the term *wayang topeng* is now most frequently used to describe masked dance-dramas based on the romantic tales of Prince Panji, which, though set in earlier times, seem to have emanated from the Majapahit courts in eastern Java from the fourteenth to sixteenth centuries. In the several regional variants of this tradition, *characters present a continuum of human behaviour, from the extremely refined Panji to the lustful and crude Klana.

As Islam became the dominant religion of Java during the sixteenth century, performance genres often became more abstract and contemplative. The central Javanese courts of Surakarta and Yogyakarta maintained an active masked dance rivalry, while the regions of Sunda, Cirebon, Malang, and Madura all developed distinctive variations of *wayang topeng*, with a narrator (*dalang*) providing the *dialogue. With the dissolution of the Majapahit kingdom, many members of its Hindu elite migrated to Bali, where masked dance continued to develop. The present tradition of *topeng* in Bali seems to have originated in the late seventeenth century and uses stories drawn from the *Chronicles of the Kings*.

In the oldest form of Balinese *topeng* (*topeng pajegan*), one man portrays all the characters—alternating full-faced masks used for dancing with half-masks that allow greater scope for improvised storytelling and commentary. *Topeng pajegan* is commonly presented at temple anniversaries and at life-cycle events (tooth filings, marriages, cremations) celebrated by Balinese families; its performances end with a public offering. Near the end of the nineteenth century, it became more common to present *topeng* with troupes of players. The less sacred *topeng panca* (five-person *topeng*) encouraged more extensive comic byplay among the performers, as well as a more theatrical depiction of dramatic confrontations.   JE

Torelli, Giacomo (1608–78) Italian architect and *scenographer. He began in the early 1640s in Venice, where he left behind detailed illustra-

tions of his work. Invited by Cardinal Mazarin to France in 1645, he designed a number of spectacles, *dances, weddings, and plays. He repeated his design for Strozzi's *The Counterfeit Madwoman*, first mounted in Venice in 1641: to conform to French taste it was performed with comic *ballet interludes. He was involved in mounting the first *opera in Paris, Luigi Rossi's *Orfeo* at the Palais Cardinal (1647). Possibly influenced by Sabbatini, he was known for his dramatic special effects—flights through the air, sudden spectacular appearances, all the *illusionistic surprises of baroque theatre, which led to his being known as 'the miracle-worker' or the 'Great Sorcerer'. He staged *Molière's *The Bores* in 1661; but by this time the *Vigarani family were working to supplant him. Gaspare Vigarani burned all Torelli's sets from the *Petit-Bourbon in 1660, though the drawings survived and reappeared in *Diderot's *Encyclopédie* (1772), indicating a substantial influence in French theatre. Sent away from Paris, Torelli returned to his home town of Fano, where he enjoyed renewed success with the Italian public.   RAA

Torres Molina, Susana (1946–) Argentinian writer and director. Her most frequently staged plays emphasize role playing, from her first, *Strange Plaything* (1977), to the cross-gendered *That's Enough of That* (1981), which she directed after returning from political exile. Later works, inspired by Japanese *butoh, *dance-theatre, and image-theatre, are more lyrical and improvisational. *Amantissima* (1988) explores mother–daughter relationships, and *Unio mystica* (1991) pioneered Argentine theatrical exploration of the effects of the AIDS epidemic.   JGJ

total theatre Term used in the twentieth century to describe performance that uses, or aspires to use, numerous artistic elements to create a powerful or overwhelming experience for the *audience. The urge to draw upon and exploit the totality of performative devices—*music, *dance, *acting, *scenography and the plastic arts, *costume, *masks, *lighting, *playhouse architecture, the configuration of the stage and *auditorium, and spectator environment—is particularly modernist, rising from *Wagner's intention to produce a *Gesamtkunstwerk* or 'total work of art' in his music dramas (*see* OPERA) and *Craig's attempt to elevate the *director-designer into the prime artist of the theatre. The major theoretical proponent of total theatre was *Artaud, who in the 1930s demanded that the stage abandon its logocentric history in favour of a theatre of *cruelty: a sensory, kinetic, and visceral strategy that would invoke the darker or Dionysiac side of human life. Artaud's influence, combined with the theatre of the *absurd, led to major experiments in total theatre in the West in the 1960s. Notable examples included the season of theatre of cruelty by *Brook with the *Royal Shakespeare Company in London, especially *Weiss's *Marat/Sade* (1964); the *ritualistic work of *Schechner's *Dionysus in 69* with the *Performance Group in New York, and the *Living Theatre's *Paradise Now* (both 1968); and in Paris, the carnivalesque approach of *Barrault's *Rabelais* (1969) and of *Mnouchkine's *1789* with Théâtre du *Soleil (1970). Despite the radical politics of many of these groups, and the reliance by some of them on *collective creation, in important ways the movement has been chiefly aestheticist, standing in opposition to the clarity and simplicity demanded by earlier political theatre movements of the century, exemplified in the *epic theatre of *Piscator and *Brecht. Postmodern examples of total theatre include the large-scale operas of Robert *Wilson, such as *Einstein on the Beach* (music by *Glass, 1976), the marathon *intercultural work of Brook (*The Mahabharata*, 1985) and Mnouchkine (*Les Atrides*, 1990–3), and the globalized festival productions of *Lepage (*The Seven Streams of the River Ota*, 1994).   DK

touring Moving a show from one venue to another, generally over a planned route. Despite its tendency to move into permanent *playhouses, the *acting profession is essentially mobile, requiring only 'two boards and a passion' for performance. We know that ancient *Greek actors journeyed widely throughout the Mediterranean under the protection of the *Artists of Dionysus, and professional players of all types in *medieval Europe lived a life of continuous travel. In a modern commercial setting, when the long run is the economic norm (as opposed to *repertory playing), once the local *audience is exhausted the company must mount a new play or tour, taking the production to fresh audiences. Nineteenth-century *managers calculated to the day when to pack up a show from a major city and tour the provinces.

When the decision to tour is not economic, it is often political: it might be wise to get away from the politically volatile capital, as French royalist actors (1791–5) and Jacobin actors did (1795–8), and theatre companies sometimes left London for months to avoid association with endemic *rioting. Or touring might be a career move, as *Molière's company allowed the memory of its first disastrous Paris performance to die, or as some Chinese companies would tour extensively while

another company's actor was the Emperor's favourite. Technologies of transport are clearly relevant. The extension of the railways to most parts of Britain in the second half of the nineteenth century vastly increased the economic viability of theatrical touring, and rock shows at the start of the twenty-first century can tour extensively by relying on large motorized trucks that are effectively houses on wheels, which carry all the equipment needed and are comfortable for the performers.

Whatever the cause, touring has had profound effects upon the theatre. First and foremost, by broadening the scope of competition, it forces improvements in quality and the rapid transfer of artistic techniques and of technology. If the provinces receive tours, they become more capable, as provincial technicians and actors measure themselves by higher standards. *Irving's first tours of the United States (1883–4), for example, had to travel with nearly every piece of equipment, but by his last (1903–4) he could count on finding most of what he needed, and the technicians to operate it, in almost any large city. Even today, many young theatre technicians get their first look at new innovations by working as casual labour for touring *musicals or for rock concerts. Secondly, in many parts of the world, touring encouraged the emergence of professional theatre; the economic advantages of touring were enough to allow full-time performers to make a living and the professional theatres of many European and Asian nations have their origins in touring. Finally, touring has fostered a tradition of portability, reusability, and flexibility in theatrical equipment; much of the way that things are done backstage is predicated on the assumption that everything must be packed up and moved soon, whether this is true or not.   JB

Tourneur, Cyril (c.1575–1626) English dramatist. His traditional reputation rests on a play he did not write, *Middleton's *The Revenger's Tragedy*, erroneously attributed to him in 1656. His only extant play is *The Atheist's Tragedy* (1609), an overtly Christian treatment of common Jacobean *tragic themes: here, in contrast to Shakespeare's *Hamlet*, a murdered father's *ghost recommends that his son 'leave revenge unto the King of kings', and providence intervenes to destroy the Machiavellian *villain at the climax of his schemes.   MJW

Tovstonogov, Georgy (1915–89) Soviet/Russian director. Appointed artistic director of the Bolshoi Drama Theatre in Leningrad in 1957, Tovstonogov merged the approaches of *Stanislavsky and *Meyerhold, mixing figurative stylization with psychological analysis. Relying on cinematic devices to maintain narrative, his repertoire included contemporary and classical Russian plays as well as prose adaptations. A remarkable example was the version of *Tolstoy's *The Story of a Horse* (1975, directed with *Rozovsky), which achieved wide international success. Set on a stage veiled in sackcloth, with *costumes of the same material, Tovstonogov interpreted the condition of the horse as a tragic metaphor for human life, creating at the same time an allegory about how we deform nature by claiming it as property. His work tended to stay general rather than make explicit social criticism, echoing his neutral position in the politics of Soviet theatre.   BB

township musicals South African *musical theatre characterized by multilingual *dialogue, dynamic vocal and *physical theatre. In the 1920s and 1930s urban African communities in South Africa expanded rapidly. Slum yards became the focus of black recreational life and the 'shebeen society' of informal (and illegal) pubs became the centre for entertainment. Miners and contract workers brought African, Afro-Western, and Afrikaans folk music together in a syncretic urban musical style called *marabi*, widely adopted by the working class. By the 1950s African-American performance culture had been identified with urban cultural autonomy, and Sophiatown was the black cultural centre. Other influential forms were *tsaba-tsaba*, a local adaptation of American jive; *kwela*, or penny-whistle players, which in turn fused into *mbaqanga*, the people's own jazz. Ian Bernhardt promoted the Township Jazz Concerts, which culminated in *King Kong* (1959). Influenced by that piece, *Fugard's collaboration with the Serpent Players, and Alan Paton's musical *Mkumbane*, *Kente revolutionized urban African popular theatre during the 1960s by incorporating gospel, jazz, and local music to create a syncretic spectacle of township life in song and *dance. Sam Mhangwane and the Sea Pearls Drama Society produced these township musicals in Sowetan Tsotsitaal (a street slang), including *Crime Does Not Pay* (1963), *Unfaithful Woman* (1964, which *toured for twelve years), *Blame Yourself* (1966), and *Thembi* (1978). Though the form is no longer vital, older examples are occasionally revived and new pieces written in a nostalgic mode.   YH

toy theatre In London in 1811 William West issued sheets of engraved *characters from popular plays. By 1812 multiple sheets were on sale, together with *proscenium stage fronts and wooden stages. Sheets were plain or coloured

and, once mounted on cardboard, the characters were cut out and fitted on slides. The pieces were performed, usually by children, in front of painted scenes. West published 140 plays between 1811 and 1843, employing carpenters to make the little stages. In the first half of the nineteenth century many firms were active and about 300 plays were published. After 1835 cheaper sheets were produced by Skelt, Green, and Pollock, the latter surviving in a small shop in Hoxton until the Second World War. A perennial favourite was the *melodrama *The Miller and his Men*. *Dickens refers to his fascination with toy theatres in *A Christmas Tree*, while Robert Louis Stevenson popularized the toy theatre in his essay 'A Penny Plain and Twopence Coloured', although some of his assertions are inaccurate. An interest in toy theatres developed on the Continent a little later than in England. Germany was especially prolific, its first major publisher of toy theatres being Winkelmann in Berlin around 1830, and its last Schreiber, in business until 1939. Heavier in style than the English equivalents, the sheets were later lithographed in colour. In Austria, Trentsensky, established about 1840, was the outstanding publisher, producing some of the most imposing toy sets ever seen. Denmark developed toy theatre publications later in the nineteenth century, while toy theatres were also produced in Czechoslovakia, France, and Spain.   JTD

tragedy Few plays called tragedies have been written for theatre performance since the two world wars and yet the word 'tragedy' is heard almost daily as real events are presented on television and in newspapers. Individual lives, the future of the globe, politics, *sports, and humanitarian issues bring before us many of the constituents of stage tragedies: violence, suffering, endurance, a sense of inevitability. In the actions of exceptional persons and numbers of anonymous witnesses commenting on events, the tragic *heroes and *choruses are reborn in actuality for us to see on screens and in newsprint. What are missing are dramatists to manipulate the action, create the *characters, and with eloquent, sensitive, arresting speeches record how these events have come to pass and how men and women confront them.

Nevertheless tragedies written for earlier theatres are still honoured in criticism and performed alongside plays of our own time. Nostalgia for theatre of the past may be partly responsible, as ruins of theatres built to stage these plays are witness to the large *audiences they once attracted, and the texts remain an enduring and irresistible challenge to theatre companies. The old tragedies have not died in European culture and are increasingly finding new life in theatres around the world.

From its earliest times, in Athens of the fifth century BC, when tragedy was the dominant dramatic form of *Greek theatre, its attractions and significance have been much discussed. Among tragedy's *origins were the public assemblies and debates which were the foundation of Athenian democracy and, in keeping with tradition, the plays were written to provoke questions and demand judgement. Tragedy also derived from choral singing (*dithyramb), enacted narratives, and civic and religious ceremonies. *Aristotle wrote the first sustained analysis of the form in his *Poetics* and has influenced scholars and practitioners ever since.

That tragedy is 'an imitation of an *action' is Aristotle's central idea, which he illustrated with reference to *Sophocles' *Oedipus* and other plays known to him. This action must be 'serious, complete, and of a certain magnitude' and the handling of it in the 'plot' is the dramatist's primary task. Second and third in importance are the creation of 'characters' and provision of the tragedy's 'thought' or argument. The action should present a change of fortune (*peripeteia) from prosperity to adversity in a way that both satisfies moral sensibility and 'arouses pity and fear' in its audience. In consequence, the *protagonist cannot be entirely evil or entirely good: if the hero were evil, Aristotle argued, the misfortune would call for no pity; if good, there would be no fear. By arousing both these feelings, a tragedy purged them from spectators. (This concept of purgation, or *catharsis, has far-reaching implications for aesthetic theory and has been much debated.) The misfortune must derive, Aristotle concluded, not from vice or depravity, but from 'some error or frailty' within a good man, later to be called the hero's 'tragic flaw' (*hamartia). From his basic concept of art as imitation (*mimesis), Aristotle also required characters to be true to life and consistent in thought and feeling, however conflicting they might be. In plot, the dramatist should always aim 'either at the necessary or the probable' and, in imitating what he found in life, should seek to make it more noble.

Not all the tragedies known to Aristotle followed his formulation in all respects and after his time, as theatre practice and writing changed, other theories about what constitutes a tragedy were offered. Most of these required the action to end with the death of the principal character or characters. In *Roman times, when *comedy had become the dominant dramatic form, *Seneca's tragedies emphasized the influence of passion and fate and showed how injustice motivates violent and cruel actions; perhaps never intended for performance, their claim for attention lies in the fear and horror provoked, rather than in the arousal of pity. In *medieval theatre, the central tenets of Christianity were represented in religious dramas that replaced wayward fortune with a provident God and demonstrated how the death of Jesus brought blessing and not misfortune. Tragedy did not thrive in this culture except in moral narratives.

Only with a rebirth of classical learning in the *early modern period were tragedies again written for the stage, regaining much of the prestige they had originally enjoyed. Shakespeare and his London contemporaries, having read Seneca attentively, developed their own 'tragedy of blood'. One variant is *revenge tragedy, the hero of which seeks justice or restitution of honour by violent means; *Kyd's *Spanish Tragedy* (1590) and Shakespeare's *Hamlet* (1600–3) are famous examples. Other variants were the tragedies of ambition, such as *Marlowe's *Tamburlaine* (c.1587) and Shakespeare's *Macbeth* (1606), and of passion, such as *Othello* (c.1602) and *Webster's *White Devil* (1612). Like the medieval narratives, they customarily showed the rise and fall of great men and the punishment of evil.

These tragedies differ from classical example in being peopled by many distinctive characters, some of them simple folk or *fools. These interact with the protagonists and help to define their natures by demonstrating contrasting motives, abilities, and feelings, in the analogical manner of earlier *morality plays. An audience gains a deepening knowledge of the hero or heroine as their inner thoughts and feelings are progressively exposed by what they say and do, and by what happens to them. With its attention held by increasing terror and fear of consequences, an audience can find that empathy with the protagonists increases, despite any crimes they have committed.

After a few decades tragedy lost popular favour in England while in another form it grew to prominence in France, playing to smaller audiences. The nine tragedies that *Racine wrote between 1664 and 1676 were carefully modelled on classical example, excluding the minor characters and comic interludes of Elizabethan and Jacobean practice (*see* UNITIES). The mental and emotional dilemmas of their leading characters, especially the women, are expressed in lengthy speeches of great sensitivity. Action turns on violent feelings and intractable conflicts that reflect the politically troubled and unsettled times, with civil war threatening and intellectual controversy and scepticism increasing. In *Andromaque* (1667), for example, Racine's first triumph, the passionate clarity of language and remorseless interlocking of action helped establish a new and *neoclassical form of tragedy. Pierre *Corneille had written his first tragedy, *Médée* (1635), almost 30 years before Racine's; in contrast to Racine's doomed protagonists, Corneille's are noble and virtuous, his audiences roused to amazement and admiration rather than pity.

After this triumph in Paris, tragedies never regained dominance. In their place during the eighteenth century, *melodramas and *romantic dramas became popular successes. In England, *Lillo's *London Merchant* (1731) was an unusual throwback to Elizabethan domestic tragedies that had considerable influence in France as a model for a brief vogue of *bourgeois tragedy. *Voltaire wrote numerous neoclassical tragedies which were respectfully received but of little lasting value. In Germany, where leading poets wrote for the theatre, tragedy found most favour, *Schiller's *Mary Stuart* (1800) having a long and varied stage history. Tragedy's prestige was to be reaffirmed by Nietzsche in *The Birth of Tragedy* (1872), which asserted that the earliest tragedies were informed by a Dionysian freedom of spirit and enquiry that had later been stifled, in art as in life, by an Apollonian order and sobriety: *Aeschylus and Sophocles are seen in opposition to *Euripides and Socrates, *music as a direct expression of tragedy's affirmation of life. Nietzsche's enthusiastic endorsement of *Wagner's music dramas as the true inheritors of tragedy has the facts of history on its side in that *operas composed by *Verdi, *Puccini, Berg, Britten, and many others have presented tragic actions and expressed them through music and roles requiring amazing vocal technique in performance. When considering the birth of tragedy, Nietzsche was also announcing that it had died as text-based drama.

In the twentieth century, tragedies have occasionally been written, though seldom in classical, Elizabethan, or any other consistent tradition. One discernible tendency has been to set tragic action in rural communities; for example, *Synge's *Riders to the Sea* (1904), *O'Neill's *Desire under the Elms* (1924), and *García Lorca's *Blood Wedding* (1933). In these plays, an inherited morality and way of life bring intolerable burdens on the principal characters, leading to death. Some of *Ibsen's nineteenth-century dramas set in close-knit families with inherited ideals that the characters cannot or will not sustain have some of the features of tragedies—misfortune, necessity, error, commanding characters—for example,

Ghosts (1881) and *John Gabriel Borkman* (1896) —and later dramatists have, more or less consciously, followed his lead. In the USA, O'Neill wrote a trilogy in imitation of Greek predecessors, *Mourning Becomes Electra* (1929–31), and slowly developed his own, more Ibsen-like, tragic form, notably in *Long Day's Journey into Night* (written 1939–41; produced 1956). *Miller also brought social drama and tragedy together in *A View from the Bridge* (1955).

In twentieth-century tragic dramas, an audience is led to follow a group of persons in a recognizable and familiar contemporary setting, rather than witness the misfortune of one exceptionally gifted protagonist at one time of crisis. Its perception of an entire society is called in question, as well as its judgement of individual persons. If the term tragedy is widened to include all such plays (and some films), then this form of drama has not died but found new life. *See also* TRAGICOMEDY; FARCE.   JRB

tragicomedy In a preface to his *Faithful Shepherdess* (1608–9), *Fletcher reports that it had failed on stage because its *audience failed to recognize a tragicomedy. Such a play, he explains, lacks deaths, 'which is enough to make it no *tragedy, yet brings some near it, which is enough to make it no *comedy' Fletcher's title alludes to *Guarini's *Il pastor fido* (written 1580s) and his defence of it seems indebted to *Il compendio della poesia tragicomica* in which Guarini explained that this form of drama should take 'great persons' from tragedy 'but not great *action; a plot which is life-like but not true…the danger, not the death'; and from comedy should come 'a feigned complication, a happy reversal, and above all, comic order'.

Leaving the *pastoral setting and collaborating with *Beaumont, Fletcher went on to write a number of tragicomedies, notably *Philaster* (1608–10) and *A King and No King* (1611). A vogue had been started that lasted in England until *Dryden's *The Secret Love; or, The Maiden Queen* of 1667. While *characters are natural in manners, they are remote from ordinary experience and involved in an intricate plot that often rests on improbable circumstances. Strong passions, horror, unmitigated evil, improbable disguise, and moral transformation are all present and expressed in lively and often florid language. To latter-day readers, such as *Eliot, the style can seem superficial. But in performance in their own day, *audiences wept openly. An enjoyment of these tragicomedies depends on an ability to admire virtuosity of expression and dramatic construction and, at the same time, to be moved by the sentiments of the characters.

Tragic and comedic elements have often been found within a single play, but without that sustained and equal attention to both that justifies calling it a tragicomedy. Clowns in tragedies had long been sanctioned by ancient and popular tradition in many countries. In the English *biblical plays, torturers occupied in crucifixion or soldiers slaughtering innocent babies make jokes as they engage in their familiar business. In practice there was no fixed line between tragedy and comedy. The two appear side by side in separate plots in Greene's *Friar Bacon and Friar Bungay* (c.1589). A tragic action is presented with comic irony and its *hero possesses a keen comic awareness in *Marlowe's *Jew of Malta* (c.1589) and Shakespeare's *Richard III* (1593) and *Titus Andronicus* (1594). The Porter's appearance in *Macbeth* (c.1606) to make jokes about damnation and drunkenness is a famous example of a comic incident in a tragedy. Shakespeare had earlier taken comedy close to tragedy in *The Merchant of Venice* (1597) when Shylock voices his passion for revenge and Antonio faces death. At about the same time as Fletcher wrote his first tragicomedy, Shakespeare was moving towards a closer fusion of comedy and tragedy in *Cymbeline* and *The Winter's Tale*, both with two offstage deaths and an apparent death onstage.

The mingling of modes was found throughout *early modern Europe, especially in the *comedias* of sixteenth-century Spain, where comedy and disaster are often close together, their complicated plots giving rise to intense emotions and ending with unexpectedly happy reversals of fortune (*peripeteia*). Italian and Spanish example was followed in France during the early decades of the seventeenth century, among others by the prolific *Hardy and, in his earlier years, Pierre *Corneille. But as tragedy ceased to be a dominant form, its boundary with comedy became much less marked and tragicomedy dropped out of favour. As stage characters and speech became closer to those of real life, tragicomedy's obviously artificial style became increasingly unacceptable.

Many plays that contain a mixture of moods might be called tragicomedies but they do not approach the artificial and sophisticated manner that the term traditionally implies. The deaths, ironies, and jesting present in *Chekhov's *Seagull* (1896), *Gorky's *Lower Depths* (1902), *O'Casey's *Juno and the Paycock* (1924), and *Beckett's *Endgame* (1957) would entitle them tragicomedies if the term were used loosely; what they lack are the great persons, feigned complications, and, above all, the comic ordering that takes pleasure in danger while avoiding death. The playwrights of the

*absurd might lay the best claim to the term: *Ionesco entitled *The Chairs* (1952) a 'Tragic Farce'. Only when a play provokes *laughter, tears, and amazement does it come close to the original tragicomedies.   JRB

Travers, Ben (1886–1980) English playwright and novelist who enjoyed two periods of great popular success, the second 50 years after the first. From 1925 to 1933 he wrote nine 'Aldwych farces' tailored to a team of talented actors. The plays rely heavily on carefully constructed *characters; they play better than they read, but need careful timing and conviction. *A Cuckoo in the Nest* (1925), *Rookery Nook* (1926), *Thark* (1927), and *Plunder* (1928) are those most often revived by both professionals and amateurs. They rely on the usual British fear of scandal and sexuality, though *Plunder* does take burglary and murder in its stride. *Plunder* did well at the *National Theatre in 1976, as did Travers's late success *The Bed before Yesterday* (1975); the last shows a post-*censorship explicitness about the heroine's late-flowering sexual satisfaction.   EEC

Treadwell, Sophie (1885–1970) American writer. While working as a journalist, Treadwell wrote more than 30 plays, most of which were never produced. The *naturalistic *Gringo* (1922) was staged by *McClintic, and the romantic *comedy *Oh Nightingale* (1925) had a brief run. Treadwell's 1927 investigation of the Ruth Snyder-Judd Gray murder case (Snyder was the first woman executed in the electric chair) provided material for *Machinal* (1928), an economically crafted play depicting in nine hypnotic scenes the Young Woman's journey from office girl to boss's wife to victim of the chair. Apart from the play's topicality (it was staged only eight months after Snyder was put to death), it endures as a prototypical *expressionistic story of the human being's destruction by the machine of modern life (business systems, social systems, legal systems, the absence of love and compassion).   MAF

Tree, Ellen (1806–80) English actress. She was a strikingly beautiful young woman who first appeared on stage at *Covent Garden in 1823, acting Olivia for the *benefit of her sister, the singer Maria Tree; all four sisters went on the stage. After a spell at Edinburgh and Bath she was engaged at *Drury Lane, and at Covent Garden in 1829. For her benefit in 1832 she played Romeo to Fanny *Kemble's Juliet, and in 1836 created the male title part in Thomas Talfourd's *tragedy *Ion*. After *touring America between 1836 and 1839 she played Rosalind and Viola in London. Following her marriage to Charles *Kean (1842), she was his leading lady, playing more matronly parts as her figure filled out. The Fool in *King Lear* was a peculiar piece of casting; she played Hermione in *The Winter's Tale*, the Chorus in *Henry V* as the Muse of History, Katherine in *Henry VIII*, Constance in *King John*, Ophelia, and Lady Macbeth, but she was not outstanding in the great tragic parts.   MRB

Tree, Herbert Beerbohm (1853–1917) English actor and *manager. Tree had a notable success in *Hawtrey's *farce *The Private Secretary* (1884), and after 1887 as manager of the *Haymarket began to distinguish himself in both *melodrama and Shakespeare, following the model of *Irving, staging grand spectacles, *comedies, and social dramas that displayed his flamboyant *acting skills. In the 1890s Tree was a leading *actor-manager, his repertoire including *The Merry Wives of Windsor* (1891), *Wilde's *A Woman of No Importance* (1893), and Paul Potter's *Trilby* (1895), based on George du Maurier's novel. The profits of *Trilby* allowed him to build Her Majesty's Theatre, which opened in 1897. For the next two decades he produced major successes, including Stephen *Phillips's *Herod* (1900) and *Ulysses* (1902), *Belasco and Long's *The Darling of the Gods* (1903), and Phillips and Comyns Carr's *Faust* (1908). In 1914 he appeared with Mrs Patrick *Campbell in *Shaw's *Pygmalion*. During his career he staged eighteen of Shakespeare's plays, reviving some of them often. Though he did not excel in the major tragic roles, he was successful as Falstaff, Caliban, Bottom, Malvolio, and Cardinal Wolsey. Most tellingly, he was a threatening *villain: the Devil in H. A. *Jones's *The Tempter*, Svengali in *Trilby*, Fagin in *Oliver Twist*, and Shylock. In 1904 Tree developed an actor-training programme that became the Royal Academy of Dramatic Art. His annual Shakespeare festival, begun in 1905, proved to be the training ground for many promising actors. He was the half-brother of Max Beerbohm, the dramatic critic and caricaturist.   TP

Tremblay, Michel (1942–) Québec dramatist and novelist. His *Les Belles-Sœurs* (*Sisters-in-Law*, 1968) was a watershed for francophone *dramaturgy. The furore aroused by its use of *joual*, Montréal's working-class French, hitherto considered too vulgar for public display, diverted attention from the play's formal innovations, its stylized *monologues and *choruses, pervaded by an intense, sometimes startling poetry. Now a modern classic, it has been performed in more than twenty languages and dialects as diverse as Japanese, Yiddish, and Yorkshire English. Some

30 plays have followed, notably *Forever Yours, Marie-Lou* (1971), a *tragedy transcending scenic time/space; *Hosanna* (1973), where homosexual identity is examined; *Albertine, in Five Times* (1984), where one female character, portrayed by five actresses, relives critical stages of her long, troubled life; and *Marcel Pursued by Hounds* (1992), exploring the world beyond sanity. Tremblay was deeply influenced by *Greek authors (*Aeschylus in particular) and by *opera (his *Nelligan*, with music by André Gagnon, was performed by the Montréal Opera in 1990). His translations of authors as diverse as *Aristophanes, *Chekhov, and *Williams have also been staged with considerable success. Since the mid-1990s he has turned his attention to the novel, but the stage *monologue *Le Paradis à la fin de vos jours* (2008) gained attention.   LED

Trenyov, Konstantin (1876–1945) Russian/Soviet writer, putative founder of the *socialist realist school. His main plays are *Pugachev Times*, about the Pugachev peasant revolt (*Moscow Art Theatre, 1925), and *Lyubov Yarovaya* (1926), a Civil War drama depicting family members on opposed sides of the conflict—in this case, a Bolshevik wife, Lyubov Yarovaya, at war with her White husband. In a poignant finale, he is led away to be shot while she turns her attention, with minimal remorse, to the task of defeating the enemy. The play received a Stalin Prize in 1936. Of his later plays, *On the Banks of the Neva* (1937) is set during the revolution and offers a theatrical portrait of Lenin.   NW

Tretyakov, Sergei (1892–1939) Russian/Soviet writer associated with the *avant-garde LEF (Left Front of the Arts). He adapted *Ostrovsky's *Enough Stupidity in Every Wise Man* as an *agitprop political 'montage of attractions' for *Eisenstein's production (1923). His own propaganda plays, *Are You Listening, Moscow?!* and *Gas Masks* (1923), were staged by Eisenstein, the latter in a Moscow gas plant. Tretyakov's adaptation of Marcel Martinet's First World War novel *La Nuit* as a revolutionary drama, *Earth Rampant*, was staged by *Meyerhold in 1923, deploying Tretyakov's notion of 'speech montage' (propagandist, *choric declamation) in a production lit by military headlights, with a real army lorry onstage and a dispatch rider on a motorbike hurtling through the *auditorium. His schematic, anti-imperialist play *Roar, China!* was staged in 1926, and by agitprop groups in the West. *I Want a Baby*, provoking discussion on socially controlled reproduction, was banned before the première (directed by Meyerhold). Tretyakov met *Brecht during a Berlin tour and had become his Russian translator before being arrested in 1937. Following torture, he avoided implicating others by committing suicide in prison.   NW

Triana, José (1931–) Cuban writer, author of *Night of the Assassins* (1965), the most widely produced Cuban play internationally. Concerned with three adolescent brothers about to murder their parents, it was directed by *Revuelta, who also played the role of Lalo. In 1967 the production was seen at *Avignon Festival during an extensive European *tour. In 1960 Triana premièred *The Major General Will Speak on Teogony* and *Medea in the Mirror*; in 1963, *Fraternity Park*, *The House on Fire*, *The Visit of the Angel* and *Death of Ñeque*. Since 1980 he has lived in Paris, where his output has included *A Mess in the Champ de Mars* (1985); *Common Words* (1986), a free adaptation of Miguel de Carrión's novel *Las honradas*, produced by the *Royal Shakespeare Company; *Crossing the Bridge* (Valencia, 1992); and *La fiesta* (1995).   MMu

Trissino, Gian Giorgio (1478–1550) Italian humanist and playwright, born in Vicenza. His *Sofonisba* (1515) was the first original attempt to write a classical-style *tragedy in the *early modern period. It deals with a defeated Numidian queen who chooses death rather than slavery; and its structure was more based on *Greek tragedy than on the *Roman models which eventually found more favour. It remained unperformed until 1556: the first tragedies actually staged were by *Giraldi.   RAA

Trotter, Catherine (**Cockburn**) (1679–1749) English playwright. Trotter's first play was an adaptation of Aphra *Behn's novel *Agnes de Castro* and was performed at *Drury Lane (1696). A friend and contemporary of Delarivière Manley and Mary *Pix, Trotter largely escaped the personal attacks that other female playwrights endured. Her four plays (*tragedy and *tragicomedy) avoid topical references and contemporary settings although, like Behn, her female *characters challenge the social mores that promote marriage as a financial contract and preclude female sexual expression. *Love at a Loss* was first performed at Drury Lane in 1700.   GBB

Tsubouchi Shōyō (1859–1935) Japanese playwright, director, and translator. Born in Gifu prefecture, he discovered Western literature after the opening of Japan in 1868 and developed a strong interest in Shakespeare, eventually translating all the plays into Japanese for the first time. Wishing to stage Shakespeare as well, Shōyō (as he was known), by then a professor at Waseda University in Tokyo, formed Bungei Kyôkai (the Literary Society) in 1905, using student performers, both male and female. In 1911 the group performed *Hamlet* in his translation and *A Doll's House*, which made *Ibsen, as well as the leading lady *Matsui, famous. Matsui ran off with her lover, Shōyō's colleague Shimamura Hōgetsu, and the company was dissolved in 1913. Deeply discouraged, Shōyō retired from active involvement in the stage. His play *The Hermit*, chosen by *Osanai as the first Japanese drama to be performed at the Tsukiji Little Theatre in 1926, is the story of a master betrayed by his disciple.   JTR

Tsukiji Little Theatre *See* OSANAI KAORU.

Tsuruya Nanboku IV (1755–1829) *Kabuki playwright. Born in the centre of Edo (Tokyo) in a merchant house, he began his apprenticeship in 1776 and became senior playwright in 1803. He wrote under several names for various actors and theatres, finally as Nanboku IV from 1812. As senior playwright he wrote 120 plays; he also published 25 books of illustrated fiction. He is known for theatrical innovation, using frequent stage tricks and effects such as stage blood. He is also famous for his ghost plays, in particular *Yotsuya Ghost Stories* (1825), which revel in depictions of the grotesque. One recurring theme is the fall of high-born figures into Edo low life; *Princess Sakura and Letters from the East* (1817) is a fine example, often revived for the contemporary stage. His first great success was *The Foreign Adventures of 'India' Tokubei* (1804), in which the theme of a rebel who tries to overthrow the government proved be fascinating for his *audience.   CAG

Tsypin, George (1954–) American *scenographer, born in Kazakhstan. Layers of visual references, *multimedia technology, and an architectural approach to space characterize his work. Tsypin won a French set design competition while still a student in Moscow. He moved to the USA in 1979 as an architect, but was drawn back to theatre and studied with *Conklin. Influenced by *constructivism, Tsypin realized his desire to 'explode the box' in a series of poductions with *Sellars in the mid-1980s (*Dumas *père's Count of Monte Cristo*, *Sophocles' *Ajax*, *Mozart's *Don Giovanni*, *Wagner's *Tannhaüser*) which juxtaposed *realistic architectural fragments with abstract conceptual structures. In the 1990s his work assumed a minimalist character, his designs often resembling gallery installations (Messiaen's *St. François d'Assise*, Handel's *Theodora*, Wagner's *Ring*, Prokofiev's *War and Peace*). He has also worked regularly with *Taymor, Robert Falls, and *Akalaitis, and designed Disney's *The Little Mermaid* on Broadway (2008).   MPB

Tucker, Sophie (1884–1966) American *vaudeville singer and dancer. Born (probably) in Poland, Tucker began life on the road and eventually worked her way to New York and the Yiddish theatre (*see* DIASPORA). She spent much of her early life in small houses. Guided by the agent William Morris, Tucker eventually became a headline act on the vaudeville circuit with songs such as 'Who Paid the Rent for Mrs. Rip Van Winkle (When Rip Van Winkle Went Away)?' (1914). In her autobiography (*Some of These Days*, 1945), Tucker credits herself with developing the shimmy *dance and perfecting 'coon shouting' (blackface comic ballads) in vaudeville. She left vaudeville in 1918 to perform blues music in the *cabarets in New York and London. She also performed in six films and two Broadway shows.   AB

Tuileries, Théâtre des *See* SALLE DES MACHINES.

Tune, Tommy (1939–) American dancer, singer, director, and choreographer. His first featured role was in *Seesaw* (1973), then he branched into directing and choreography, beginning *Off-Broadway and moving to Broadway with *The Best Little Whorehouse in Texas* (1978). Other directing included *Churchill's *Cloud 9* (1981) before he entered the high ranks of director/choreographers with *Nine* (1982), *Grand Hotel* (1989), and *The Will Rogers Follies* (1991), and played in *My One and Only* (1983), tap *dancing with his gangly 2-m (6-foot 6-inch) frame. In the 1990s he returned to performing, both on *tour and in a Las Vegas extravaganza, *EFX*, and in 2009 he was touring in his own *Steps in Time: A Broadway Biography in Song and Dance*. With nine Tonys, he is the only person to have won the award in four different categories.   JD

Turgenev, Ivan (1818–83) Russian writer. Though he wrote ten plays of varying quality, *A Month in the Country* (1850) is responsible for his international status as a dramatist. Influenced by *Gogol, the early *satires suffered heavily from *censorship: *Indiscretion* (1843), *Penury* (1845, produced 1852), *The Parasite* (1849, produced 1862), and *An Evening in Sorrento* (1852, produced 1885). Only *The Bachelor* (1850), *Lunch with a Marshal of the Nobility* (1849), and *The Provincial Lady* (1851) reached the stage near the date of their composition. Turgenev fell foul of the authorities in the early 1850s for his views on serfdom, contacts with radicals, and publication of a forbidden obituary for Gogol; as a result *A Month in the Country* languished for 22 years (written 1850, produced 1872). It marks a move away from Gogol towards the *realism of *Ostrovsky, the subtlety of Turgenev's novels, and of *Chekhov half a century later. A psychological drama with little overt *action, it demanded a new style of *acting and staging only fully achieved in *Stanislavsky's production (*Moscow Art Theatre, 1909). This interpretation dominated the twentieth century until *Efros disturbed it with his 1977 version of passionately and physically expressed despair. There have been many notable productions outside Russia.   CM

Turlupin (Henri Legrand) (1587–1637) French actor, called Belleville when acting in *tragedy. The youngest member of the famous *farce trio at the *Hôtel de Bourgogne, Turlupin is first mentioned there in 1615. In contrast to the rotund *Gros-Guillaume and the spidery Gaultier-Garguille, he was well built and handsome; he played the knavish member of the trio, with a *mask that resembled the Italian *character Brighella's (*see* COMMEDIA DELL'ARTE). His stage name, which dates back to the fifteenth century, became a generic synonym for buffoon, and his comic speciality of low puns, or *turlupinades*, was still in vogue 40 years after his death among the idle younger courtiers of Louis XIV.   RWH

Turrini, Peter (1944–) Austrian dramatist. His first play, *Rat Hunt* (1971), established Turrini as one of a group of dramatists writing dialect plays, along with *Bauer, *Kroetz, and *Sperr. Six other plays immediately followed. With *Low Achievers* (1988), on unemployment in the steel industry, Turrini blended social *realism with *surrealistic sequences and heightened language to achieve a modern-day *Passion play. His innovative combination of folk theatre and experimental forms makes him one of the most interesting contemporary Austrian dramatists. Since the mid-1970s Turrini has also written for the television series *Alpensaga*, dealing with life in a small village community from the beginning of industrialization in 1900 to the end of the Second World War. His later plays include *Jedem das Seine* (written with Silke Hassler, 2007).   CBB

Tutin, Dorothy (1931–2001) English actress. Considered a leading young actress in the 1950s, her reputation was confirmed by her vivacious Cecily in Anthony Asquith's film of *Wilde's *The Importance of Being Earnest* (1952). After working with the *Old Vic in Bristol and London, she joined the *Shakespeare Memorial Company at Stratford, where her major roles included

Ophelia, Viola, and Juliet. In the West End she was a great success in *Greene's *The Living Room* (1953), and the next year she was equally celebrated as Sally Bowles in *I Am a Camera*. In 1971 and 1972 she starred as Peter Pan at the London Coliseum. Her screen appearances included *A Tale of Two Cities* (1958), Anne Boleyn in the BBC series *The Six Wives of Henry VIII* (1970), Goneril in *King Lear* (1984), and *Jake's Progress* (1995). She was also a regular at the *Chichester Festival.   AS

Tyl, Josef Kajetán (1808–56) Czech writer, actor, and *manager. He began as an actor with a German *touring company in 1829, but his efforts to perform plays in Czech increased after his return to Prague (1831), where he soon became the leading figure of Czech theatre and ardent organizer of Czech cultural life. His amateur company produced plays in Czech, and between 1846 and 1851 Tyl was the *dramaturg responsible for the Czech repertory in the Theatre of Estates. He wrote his most important plays in those years, both 'dramatic folk tales' and 'scenes from life', moving from late *romanticism to early *realism, but always with strong patriotic and sentimental touches. As a result of his political activities he was forced to leave Prague and tour the Czech regions, where he died in poverty. Some of Tyl's plays still appear on the repertory of Czech theatres, including *The Bagpiper of Strakonice* (1847), *The Bloody Trial* and *Jan Hus* (both 1848), and *A Stubborn Woman* (1849).   ML

Tyler, Royall (1757–1826) American jurist and playwright. Tyler served briefly during the Revo-lutionary War but returned to Harvard to finish his legal studies (1779). During a 1787 trip to New York, he saw a production of *Sheridan's *School for Scandal* and within weeks had written *The Contrast*. Mounted by *Wignell in 1787 at the John Street Theatre in New York, *The Contrast* became the first professionally produced American *comedy. The play introduced the *character of the Yankee, laying the groundwork for a comic line that lasted generations.   GAR

Tynan, Kenneth (1927–80) For a decade Tynan was the most influential theatre critic in Britain, working at the *Observer* from 1954 to 1963. His elegant prose made him standard-bearer for the new theatres of the 1950s and 1960s, an early champion of *Brecht, *Beckett, *Brook, *Littlewood, and the *Royal Court dramatists. Of *Osborne, he wrote famously that he doubted he 'could love anyone who did not wish to see *Look Back in Anger*'. Tynan always retained his youthful love of what he called 'high-definition performance' and charismatic stars like *Coward, *Welles, and *Olivier, for whom he worked between 1963 and 1969 as literary manager (or *dramaturg) of the new *National Theatre. There he persuaded Olivier to play Othello and Shylock, brought in directors like *Zeffirelli, and commissioned major plays, including *Shaffer's *Black Comedy* (1965) and *Nichols's *The National Health* (1969). A long-standing opponent of *censorship, he celebrated its abolition by producing the erotic *revue *Oh! Calcutta!* (1968). After his early death he was described by *Stoppard, one of his discoveries, as 'part of the luck we had'.   CDC

Udall, Nicholas (c.1505–1556) English playwright. One-time headmaster of Eton College and later master of Westminster School, Udall wrote *Ralph Roister Doister* (c.1550), the only play that can be attributed to him with certainty, probably for a school performance. Modelled on *Roman *comedy, the play balances comic inventiveness with pedagogical design. The parasite Merrygreek's mispronunciation of Roister Doister's love letter to Christian Custance leads to Roister Doister's rejection and a terrific mock battle in which the braggart soldier is routed. The play deliberately avoids scurrility and seeks to teach decency and modesty.   RWV

Ukala, Sam (1948–) Nigerian playwright, director, and teacher. A resolute supporter of decolonization, Ukala set out to explore African traditional aesthetics and progressively subvert Western *dramaturgy. His plays, including *Akpaland* and *The Placenta of Death*, explore the contemporary possibilities of folk styles. Building on a shared concern with popular theatre, Ukala worked with Bob Firth's UK-based Horse and Bamboo Theatre Company to create *Harvest of Ghosts*, a wordless piece of festival theatre that took the 'judicial murder' of Ken *Saro-Wiwa and eight Ogoni activists as a starting point. It made use of *masked figures in a carefully choreographed production that was successfully performed in Britain in 1999.   JMG

unities Theoretical position for *neoclassical *tragedy. The three unities—of time, place, and *action—were often traced back to *Aristotle, though the *Poetics* recommends only that of *action* as a binding condition; the unity of *time* is noted as a description: 'tragedy endeavours, as far as possible, to confine itself to a single revolution of the sun...' From this statement a dogmatic assertion of the rules for dramatic composition developed in the *early modern period, which were to retain their importance, especially in France, for over 200 years. The unity of *place* (or setting) was deemed (by J.-C. Scaliger, writing on Aristotle in 1561) to follow, as a logical consequence, from that of time; and the theory of the three unities, once established in Italy by Castelvetro's edition of the *Poetics* (1570), followed in France by Jean de La Taille in *De l'art de la tragédie* (1572), assumed the character of an immutable doctrine.

In practice, the new doctrine was largely ignored in the Spanish Golden Age and in the Elizabethan age, especially by Shakespeare. In France, however, there was little dissension about the basic doctrine of the unities: even during the aftermath of *Corneille's success with *Le Cid* in 1637 his adversaries criticized him for crowding too many events into the single day of the play's action. By the time of the publication of his *Discours des trois unités* in 1660 Corneille was almost as orthodox in his commentary on the 'rules' as his critic Aubignac. *Racine was masterful in handling the unities. Theorists paid less attention to *comedy than to tragedy in this respect; but few plays observe the unities more completely than *Molière's *The Misanthrope* (1666).

The formal technicalities of the three unities were often subsumed in the 'fourth unity': the unity of tone, or overall aesthetic coherence, together with that other pillar of neoclassical doctrine, the *bienséances* (decorum). The conservatism of the *Comédie-Française succeeded in encouraging new playwrights to adhere to the neoclassical formula; and it was left to *Hugo, by argument in his *Préface de Cromwell* (1827) and by demonstration in his play *Hernani* (1830), to prove the viability on the French stage of a radically different *dramaturgy.   WDH

Unity Theatre Influential left-wing company in London. Its first success was *Odets's *Waiting for Lefty* (1936), and though much of its material was written by members and its actors were usually amateur, it had an important international output, including *Señora Carrar's Rifles*, which was the first *Brecht play in Britain (1937), *O'Casey's *The Star Turns Red* (1940), *Sartre's *Nekrassov* (1956), and *Adamov's *Spring 71* (1962). Its actors and directors included *Robeson, Lionel *Bart, Alfie Bass, and Bob Hoskins, who presented and *toured *living newspapers, *documentary dramas, *satire, and political *pantomimes. Its rented base in Goldington Street was burnt out in 1975, and the theatre did not recover.   EEC

Unruh, Fritz von (1885-1970) German writer. Unruh came to the fore with his poetic *expressionist dramas *Before the Decision* (1914), a discussion of *Kleist, and *Officers* (1911), which treats the conflict between military discipline and self-determined action. Recipient of the prestigious Kleist award in 1915 and celebrated as the 'new Kleist', von Unruh's significance was partly dependent on his position as a representative of the Prussian military class who turned to pacifism around the time of the First World War. The poetic *tragedy *A Race* (1918) is an expressionist work in which the horror of war is transcended by a utopian vision of a new race of mankind. His later plays treat mainly historical themes in a variety of styles, though his work after the war never attained the same eminence. After a short political career in the 1920s, von Unruh moved to Italy and France in the 1930s. After internment in France, he escaped to New York, and returned to Germany in 1962.   CBB

Urban, Joseph (1872-1933) Austrian-American designer. At first an architect, Urban began to work with the Vienna *Burgtheater in 1905 and was quickly in demand as an *opera designer all over Europe. In 1912 he moved to the USA, collaborating with modernists R. E. *Jones, *Simonson, and *Bel Geddes, as well as designing for major opera houses, the *Ziegfeld Follies*, and *musicals. An important influence in American theatre, Urban belonged to the first generation who put the theories of *Appia and *Craig into practice. Innovative both technically and aesthetically, Urban applied pointillist techniques to scene painting, thus allowing for parts of the image to appear or disappear under different coloured lights; also he was one of the first to use platforms and portals which generated a frame and focus on the stage while providing continuous elements for unit sets.   CBB

Usigli, Rodolfo (1905-79) Mexican writer, author of some 40 plays. Self-proclaimed father of the modern stage, he championed a theatre that would hold up a mirror to Mexico's social and political realities. Usigli gained notoriety with *The Impostor*, an exploration of the psychology of political demagoguery. Written in 1938, its première ten years later elicited strong protests from the left and right, who both objected to the central delusional *character, César Rubio, a failed history professor who comes to believe that he is the military hero of the same name murdered during the revolution. In the historical trilogy *Crown of Shadows* (1947), *Crown of Fire* (1961), and *Crown of Light* (1964), he looked to Mexico's past to understand its painful entry into modernity. Other work focused on private lives, revealing the psychological effects of sexual repressions and social hypocrisies; *Jano Is a Woman* remains one of the best.   KFN

Ustinov, Peter (1921-2004) English actor, director, and writer. Ustinov made his debut in 1938 in *Chekhov's *The Wood Demon* and his London debut in his own *Late Joys* (1939). Although he performed a variety of plays, Ustinov was more closely associated with productions of his own work. He appeared in or directed *Fishing for Shadows* (1940), *The Love of Four Colonels* (1951), and *Romanoff and Juliet* (1957), and acted in, directed, and produced the latter's film version in 1961. Lear at the *Stratford Festival, Ontario (1979), was his first Shakespearian role. Later plays include *Photofinish* (1962), *The Unknown Soldier and his Wife* (1967), *Who's Who in Hell* (1974), *Overboard* (1981), and *Beethoven's Tenth* (1983). Film appearances of note include *Spartacus* (1960), *Topkapi* (1964)—both of which brought him Academy awards—*Logan's Run* (1976), and *Death on the Nile* (1978).   AS

U'Tamsi, Tchicaya (Gérard Félix) (1931-88) Born in Mpili, U'Tamsi went to France in 1946. Encouraged by *Césaire, he published several volumes of poetry in the 1950s. As a journalist with the overseas broadcasting station La France d'Outre-Mer, he dramatized African folk tales and wrote radio serials. In 1960 he went to Kinshasa to cover the independence celebrations centring around Patrice Lumumba, and subsequently worked for UNESCO in Paris until his retirement. His two-play sequence *Le Zulu* and *Vwène le fondateur* (1977), about a *clownish president who commits grotesque horrors, is similar to *Macbeth* in the destructive and tragic passion that grips the *hero. After *The Glorious Destiny of Marshal Nnikon Nniku, the Presentable Prince Consort* (1979), he returned to the events of the Congo in *Ndinga's Dance* (Paris, 1987).   PNN trans. JCM

Vaca, Jusepa (fl. 1602–34) The most famous actress of early seventeenth-century Spain. In 1602 she married the *actor-manager Juan de Morales Medrano, and the company they led was one of the most important until 1632, when their daughter Mariana married Antonio de Prado and they joined his. Jusepa's dynamic talent, especially in mannish and transvestite roles, was displayed in dramas written for her by playwrights like Lope de *Vega and *Vélez de Guevara.   VFD

Vakhtangov, Evgeny (1883–1922) Russian/ Soviet director who played minor roles at the *Moscow Art Theatre before *Stanislavsky established the First Studio in 1912 as a breeding ground for younger members of the company under the tutelage of Vakhtangov, *Sulerzhitsky, and Boris Sushkevich. Vakhtangov came into his own in the Third Studio of the MAT (after 1926, the Vakhtangov Theatre). Tired of the overcharged atmosphere of the First Studio, he had been excited by *Meyerhold's pre-revolutionary experiments in St Petersburg, the theatrical grotesque, and more overt forms of expressiveness. He established his own concept of 'fantastic *realism' in the early 1920s, before his untimely death from stomach cancer, with productions of *Maeterlinck's *The Miracle of St Anthony*, *Chekhov's *The Wedding*, *Gozzi's *Princess Turandot*, and Solomon Anski's *The Dybbuk* (Habima Theatre, rehearsed in Russian, acted in Hebrew). Vakhtangov's views changed in response to the Revolution. His post-revolutionary productions tended to be either ironic commentaries on a superannuated social and religious past (Chekhov, Maeterlinck) or, as with Gozzi, celebrated a new-found expressive freedom. The première of *Turandot* was a festive occasion, the exoticism of an Eastern fairy tale, supported by the ornately cubist design by Ignaty Nivinsky, merging with styles of popular Western acting and staging traditions which harked back to the medieval *mummers' play, the harlequinade, the *puppet show, and *commedia dell'arte. The production is considered one of the most memorable and influential in Russian theatre.   NW

Valdez, Luis (1940–) American playwright, director, actor, and filmmaker. Born in California to

Mexican farmworker parents, Valdez wrote his first play, *The Shrunken Head of Pancho Villa*, in 1964 while an undergraduate. In 1965 he founded the *touring Teatro *Campesino (Farmworkers' Theatre). Valdez's play with *music *Zoot Suit* (1978) exposes the racial discrimination suffered by Chicanos in Los Angeles in the 1940s. It was seen at the Mark Taper Forum in Los Angeles and was the first play by and about a Chicano to be produced on Broadway (1979). Valdez directed his film version in 1981; he also wrote and directed the film *La Bamba* (1987), about the 1950s rock singer Richie Valens. He directed his play *I Don't Have to Show You No Stinking Badges!* (1986), a *satire about Hollywood stereotyping, at the Taper. *The Mummified Deer* (2000) tells the story of a dying 80-year-old Mexican woman whose family becomes a metaphor for the Chicanos' history in the south-west. Valdez's career has been an eclectic and highly visible mixture of *actos* (sketches), plays, videos, films, and essays. *See also* DIASPORA.   JAH

Valentin, Karl (1882–1948) German comedian, author, and filmmaker. A product of the local *vaudeville and *cabaret tradition, together with his partner Liesl Karlstadt, he raised Bavarian folk *comedy to a high level by creating a comic world comprised of the recalcitrance of inanimate objects, cross-purpose language, and the malignity of human nature, prefiguring in many respects the theatre of the *absurd. He was admired by *Brecht, who compared him to Chaplin as an artist able to bridge the gap between the popular and the *avant-garde.   CBB

Valle-Inclán, Ramón del (1866–1936) Spanish writer. Although his first play was staged in 1899, his fame as a dramatist is largely based on plays written in the 1920s. *Bohemian Lights* (1921–5) is his masterpiece and the first of his *esperpentos*. As described in the play's *dialogue, the term represents an aesthetic of grotesque deformation such as occurs in the concave mirrors of a funhouse. *Divine Words* (1922), a grotesque exploration of superstition and debauchery in rural Galicia, was staged by *Xirgu in 1933, under the playwright's close supervision, and was not seen again until José Tamayo circumvented *censorship in Madrid in 1961. *Barbaric Plays*, an epic trilogy comprising two plays of 1907–8 and the later *Silver Face* (1922), was finally staged in its entirety in 1974 at Frankfurt's Stadt Schauspielhaus. In 1991 it received productions by *Lavelli in Paris and at Spain's National Theatre. The *Abbey Theatre staged the first production in English in 2000, directed by *Bieito, in a translation by *McGuinness called *Barbaric Comedies*. Seen as a precursor of *Artaud, *Brecht, and *Ionesco, Valle-Inclán is now ranked with *García Lorca in the hierarchy of modern Spanish theatre.   MPH

Vampilov, Aleksandr (1937–72) Soviet/Russian playwright. Vampilov's plays challenged a social type of his time, the egoist and materialist who lacks moral values. *Farewell in June* (1966) investigates corruption, *The Elder Son* (1970) explores self-betrayal of a materialistic nature, while *Duck-Hunting* (1970) and *Last Summer in Chulimsk* (1973) continue the concern with egoism. Vampilov's *dramaturgy was informed by a critical view of Soviet society: he attacked the corruption allowed by the system, bureaucracy that takes no account of individuals, and the suspiciousness that infects those who are themselves subjected to suspicion.   BB

van Bridge, Tony (1917–2004) Canadian actor and director. Born in England, he acted in weekly *repertory, and, after the war, spent seven years with the Young Vic and *Old Vic companies. In 1954 he emigrated to Canada where he became a leading classical actor, appearing with the *Stratford Festival (fifteen seasons), the *Shaw Festival (22 seasons), and many *regional theatres in Canada and the USA. At Stratford he excelled in comic parts such as Bottom (1960) and Falstaff (1965–7), and at the Shaw Festival directed three *Priestley plays in successive years (1988–90). He was an award-winning television actor (*Judge*, 1981–4) and for several years *toured as G. K. Chesterton in a one-person play he wrote.   DWJ

Vanbrugh, John (1664–1726) English playwright and architect. Vanbrugh established his credentials with two successful *comedies, *The Relapse* (1696), a sequel to and rebuttal of Colley *Cibber's *Love's Last Shift* (1696), featuring Cibber himself as Lord Foppington, and *The Provok'd Wife* (1697), an uncompromising look at the discord and bliss that defines marriage, later providing one of *Garrick's favourite roles. Vanbrugh replied to *Collier's *anti theatrical polemic in *A Vindication of the Relapse and the Provok'd Wife* (1698). The bulk of Vanbrugh's remaining plays were adaptations and translations of French

work, while *The Pilgrim* (1700) is an adaptation from *Fletcher. As an architect, Vanbrugh designed Castle Howard (1701), Blenheim Palace (1705), and the Haymarket Opera (1703), which he co-managed with *Congreve in 1705–6. His last play, *The Provok'd Husband*, left unfinished at his death, was completed by Cibber in 1728.   RWV

Van Druten, John (1901–57) Anglo-American playwright and director. Born in London, Van Druten moved to California in 1926 and in 1944 became a US citizen. His total output for the stage—sometimes adapted from other sources, and often directed by him—comes to 29 works. The cast of his first play, *The Return Half* (1924), was headed by the then unknown *Gielgud. After a few problem plays, he devoted himself largely to escapist middle-class *comedies, starting with *There's Always Juliet* (1931). His two greatest successes were the sophisticated three-character *The Voice of the Turtle* (1943, 1,557 performances in New York), and the folksy 23-person *I Remember Mama* (1944, 714 performances). His *I Am a Camera* (1951) was the basis of the *musical *Cabaret* (1966).   CT

Van Itallie, Jean-Claude (1936–) Belgian-born American dramatist, and playwright-in-residence for the *Open Theatre (1963–8). His plays for the company were characterized by a break with psychological *realism and an exploration of 'transformations', depictions of *characters undergoing rapid shifts of persona. *America Hurrah* (1966), a trilogy of one-acts, was written as an *absurdist *satire of American culture. His next major work, *The Serpent* (1968), broke new aesthetic ground and established Van Itallie as one of the premier playwrights of his generation. Written for an ensemble, the play interweaves the story of Genesis with disturbing re-enactments of the Zabruder film of President Kennedy's assassination. During the 1970s he became an important adaptor of *Chekhov. Frequently working with directors *Chaikin and *Şerban, his adaptations of *The Seagull* (1973), *The Cherry Orchard* (1977), *Three Sisters* (1979), and *Uncle Vanya* (1983) received numerous productions. He revisited the style of the Open Theatre with his ambitious adaptation of *The Tibetan Book of the Dead* for *La Mama in 1983. Van Itallie remained prolific during the 1980s and 1990s while holding a number of influential teaching positions.   JAB

variety Entertainment that consists of a collection of individual acts—such as song, *dance, comic *monologue, *acrobatics, *clowning, trained *animals, *magic shows—performed in succession on a bill. Long a staple of the English *music halls and American concert saloons (also known as 'free-and-easies' or 'honky-tonks'), variety was associated with a heavy-drinking male clientele. Beginning in the 1880s in New York, Tony *Pastor's success in presenting variety programmes without vulgarity in facilities more like *legitimate theatres than saloons transformed it into *vaudeville, which appealed to a broader *audience that included women and children. Meanwhile, variety continued in various venues, including dime museums.

In England the term 'variety' continued to be used, often disparagingly, while music-hall entertainment gained some respectability as it began to be formalized into twice-nightly programmes instead of the earlier continuous cycles of acts. Whatever the nomenclature, forms of variety entertainment can be found in most cultures: in Paris on the nineteenth-century boulevard du Temple and the twentieth-century *Folies-Bergère, in the 1920s Russian *Chauve-Souris* that *toured internationally, in the *carpas* of Mexico, and at the *concert parties of Ghana. Variety is quintessentially popular entertainment, because its rationale is to provide something for everyone. By the mid-twentieth century American variety shows had blended into related forms like *cabaret and *revues, as popular audiences turned to radio, film, and television (the long-popular *Ed Sullivan Show* epitomized media variety). In England the BBC kept radio variety alive into the 1950s with *Variety Bandbox* and *Take It from Here*. FHL

Varlamov, Konstantin (1848–1915) Russian actor who excelled in comic *character roles. Extremely popular throughout his career and familiarly known as Dyadya Kostya (Uncle Kostya), Varlamov joined the Aleksandrinsky Theatre in St Petersburg in 1875. Here he proved a superb comic improviser in Russian *vaudevilles, *farces, and *operettas, but his principal successes were in work by *Gogol and in 29 *Ostrovsky roles. From the 1880s onwards he suffered increasingly from elephantiasis, to the point of immobility. He still continued to appear on stage and was remarkably successful as a totally static Sganarelle in *Molière's *Don Juan*, directed by *Meyerhold in 1910. NW

Vasari, Giorgio (1511–74) Italian artist, *scenographer, and biographer, attached to the court of the Medici grand dukes of Tuscany. He organized and designed spectacles and pageants of all kinds for his princely patrons between 1536 and 1566. He also created some stage designs elsewhere—as in the set for *Aretino's *Talanta* in Venice in 1542. This offered a panoramic view of the monuments of Renaissance Rome, and may have involved some elements of moving scenery. His *Lives of the Artists* is also a source of information for other artists and episodes of stage history and design. RAA

Vasiliev, Anatoly (1942–) Soviet/Russian director. Vasiliev worked at the *Moscow Art Theatre during the 1970s. His production of *Slavkin's *A Young Man's Grown-up Daughter* (1979) at the Stanislavsky Theatre was spectacular for its use of jazz *music, condemned as decadent in the Soviet Union. For several years Vasiliev *rehearsed Slavkin's *Cerceau* (1985), a landmark in Russian theatrical history, a combination of lived experience and collated literary material about the mid-life crisis of a group of 40-year-olds. In 1987 Vasiliev founded his own theatre, the School of Dramatic Art, and worked with *improvisation based on rigid textual structures. Since *Amphitryon* (1995) and *The Stone Guest* (1998) he has been experimenting with text by depriving it of narrative function and reducing it to a pure sign system to enhance the meaning of the word, a technique best demonstrated in *Mozart and Salieri: Requiem* (2000). BB

vaudeville American *variety entertainment that sought to be dissociated from the male-oriented fare in the concert saloons, 'honky-tonks', and 'free-and-easies'. The adoption of a classy-sounding French term (used in France to mean light *comedies incorporating snatches of popular tunes) along with the move into venues free of drink and smoke allowed variety entertainment to expand its *audience by attracting respectable women to matinée and evening performances. Tony *Pastor led the way, first using the word 'vaudeville' in 1875 for his variety shows at the Metropolitan Theatre on Broadway. After the 1881 opening of his New 14th Street Theatre 'catering to the ladies', vaudeville soared in popularity. B. F. *Keith created the vaudeville circuit and introduced continuous performances, so that a spectator could enter at any time and stay until that act came around again. In partnership with E. F. Albee from 1883, by 1920 the Keith–Albee circuit controlled over 400 *playhouses. So rigorous were the partners about clean language and wholesome material that theirs was dubbed the 'Sunday school circuit'. Albee was a ruthless businessman whose exploitation of performers was epitomized in the monopolistic practices of his United Booking Office, which he created in 1906 and which maintained control of publicity, bookings, and facilities until vaudeville lost its audiences to talking films and motorcars.

*Hammerstein's Victoria Theatre dominated New York vaudeville from 1904 to 1914. Martin Beck (1867–1940) covered the Midwest and west with over 250 theatres on his Orpheum circuit, and opened the Palace Theatre in New York in 1913. To play the Palace was regarded as the apogee of any career in vaudeville.

*African-American vaudevillians had a southern circuit, but the vaudeville stage was better integrated than other aspects of American society between 1890 and the 1920s, with numerous black musical groups, monologists, singer-comedians like Bert *Williams, *opera singers, ventriloquists, and song-and-dance teams on the bill at top theatres. The legendary tap-dancing Nicholas brothers enlivened vaudeville's last two decades.

As the dominant American entertainment form, vaudeville generated a wealth of talent: regurgitators, singing *animals, contortionists, quick-change and sleight-of-hand artists, clog *dancers, and midget *acrobats. Specialists in ethnic or national humour included the Scottish Harry *Lauder, *Weber and Fields with their 'Dutch' act, Jewish comedienne Fanny *Brice, blackface duo Montgomery and Stone (*see* MINSTREL SHOWS), and Irish pairs like Gallagher and Shean. Other major stars included the comic monologists Will *Rogers and Ed *Wynn, and the comic team George *Burns and Gracie Allen. Comedy, song, and dance teams were particularly memorable, such as the *Marx Brothers, the Three Keatons, Eddie *Foy and the Seven Little Foys, as were the singers Lillian *Russell and Fay Templeton. The list goes on, with singer-comedians Eddie *Cantor, Marie *Dressler, and Mae *West; dancers Ray 'Rubberlegs' *Bolger and Bill 'Bojangles' *Robinson. *Magicians included *Houdini and *Kellar; a 'tramp act' brought W. C. *Fields to fame; body cultist *Sandow had an international reputation; and *female impersonator Julian Eltinge had a New York playhouse named after him.

The greatest star in vaudeville was Al *Jolson, though he devoted most of his career to *musical comedy, movies, and radio, and never played the Palace. Jolson's electrifying voice and engaging comic banter could hold an audience for hours while other performers waited their turn that might not come. Entertainers who acknowledged the influence of Jolson included Eddie Cantor, Bing Crosby, and Judy Garland, who carried vaudeville traditions into the early television variety shows. *See also* MUSIC HALL.   FHL

Vauthier, Jean (1910–92) Belgian playwright. An *absurdist contemporary of *Beckett, *Genet, and *Ionesco, Vauthier distrusted rational discourse and relied on fantasy and dream, which in his plays clash with trite reality. But he created a distinct poetic diction in which the French language expresses emotion by its physical quality. The eponymous *hero of *Capitaine Bada* (Paris, 1952) is a pathetic, *clown-like poet and emblematic of Vauthier's work. *Barrault acted Bada in a sequel, *The Fighting Character* (1956), and Marcel Maréchal revived the original play in 1966 and commissioned *Blood* (1970). Vauthier also wrote French adaptations of some of Shakespeare's plays and of *Marlowe's *The Massacre at Paris*.   JDV

Vedrenne–Barker seasons *See* BARKER, HARLEY GRANVILLE.

Vega (Carpio), Lope de (1562–1635) Spanish dramatist. Born in Madrid, the son of an embroiderer, he attended a Jesuit school and probably the University of Alcalá. He served a long series of noble masters, but though idolized by the public he never gained due recognition at court, and his last decade was overshadowed by disappointment and distress. Though sincerely devout, Lope de Vega was notoriously active sexually; he fathered eleven offspring by two wives and some of his (at least) six lovers. His ordination as a priest in 1614 did not appear to end his liaisons.

His literary activity was extraordinary. In addition to innumerable works in every verse and prose genre of his day, Lope (as he is known) was said to have written 1,800 *comedias (as well as over 400 *autos sacramentales). Since fewer than 400 survive, 600 or 700 is a likelier but still prodigious total; over half a century, roughly one a month. This productivity, his closeness to his public, and his genius as both a playwright and poet gave him the dominant role in the evolution of Golden Age drama. He gave the 'New Comedy' its fixed but flexible form, as well as unrestricted content. Rejecting the rigidity of the *neoclassical rules, he insisted on modifications, which were very far-reaching. The works of so fluent a dramatist are inevitably uneven, but even his weakest have flashes of startling originality, and most reveal more calculation than he is often credited with. His sources were of necessity very diverse. Some plays draw for instance on classical mythology, the Bible, or the lives of saints.

Very many quasi-historical plays are set in a huge range of countries and periods, but especially in late medieval Spain. *Fuente Ovejuna* (1612–14), the most frequently performed, dramatizes the murder of a nobleman by villagers he had tyrannized, and the solidarity under torture that won them a royal pardon. Like the eponymous *heroes of his *Peribáñez* (c. 1605) and *The Peasant in his Corner* (c. 1611), they clearly have Lope's sympathy, but he insists that they are loyal to the crown, and he is often seen in general as a political conformist, or even an establishment propagandist. Though many of his plays were commissioned as publicity by noblemen, the Church, or the court, and though he never questioned monarchy as a system, he must often have fuelled debate about its functioning in practice, since many of his rulers are badly flawed. One such is the paranoid King of Portugal who slays exemplary nobles in *The Duke of Viseu* (1608–9). Another is the lecherous Duke of Ferrara in Lope's masterpiece *Punishment without Revenge* (1632). A more characteristically lyrical tragedy is *The Knight of Olmedo* (1620–5), based in part on the *Celestina*, but mainly on a well-known semi-historical tale. Until well into the final act, life seems to be smiling on two young lovers, but their idyll is undermined by reminders of the fate we know awaits them.

Far more frequently, however, Lope's optimistic nature gives love a happy outcome. His best *comedies are in the 'cloak and sword' mould, like *The Shrewd Girl in Love* (1606), *Belisa's Extravagances* (1634), or the metatheatrical *La noche de San Juan* (*Midsummer's Eve*, 1631). *La dama boba* (*The Dumb Belle*) contrasts a blue-stocking with her initially stupid sister, who nevertheless proves the cleverer when educated by love, though ironically the gallant who effects the transformation is more intent on getting her larger dowry. Another comic but mildly subversive masterpiece is *El perro del hortelano*. Its 'Dog in the Manger' is a Countess who vacillates throughout between love for her secretary and regard for her noble rank. Eventually a triple *anagnorisis* enables them to marry; he too is revealed to be nobly born, but when he reveals to her that this is a fabrication she reveals that for her, as for society, appearances are enough, and the audience is invited to keep their secret.

Many of Lope's plays were performed worldwide in the twentieth century. In particular, *Fuente Ovejuna*, often heavily adapted, was frequently mounted as political propaganda. A balanced production by the *National Theatre (directed by *Donellan, 1989) was well received in Britain, and *The Dog in the Manger* was the hit of the *Royal Shakespeare Company's season of Golden Age plays (*Swan, 2004). VFD

Vélez de Guevara, Luis (1579–1644) Spanish dramatist. Popular and prolific, he claimed to have written 400 plays. Some 100 survive, largely on heroic themes, and notable both for their lyri-

cism and exploitation of visual effect. His *melodramatic *The Mountain Maid of La Vera* depicts the life and death by execution of a bloodthirsty female outlaw. *Queen after Death* is by contrast a moving *tragedy on the Inés de Castro legend. VFD

Veranna, Gubbi (1890–1972) *Actor-manager in Karnataka, south India. Rising from stagehand to its owner (1917), under his direction the Gubbi Theatre Company flourished. Veranna brought in important actors and playwrights, and introduced innovations in stagecraft, glittering *costumes, electric *lighting, and projectors. The company mounted spectacular productions on mythological subjects like *Kurukshetra* (1934), *Krishnalila* (1944), and *Dashavatara* (1958), which made a deep popular impression. With three branches and more than 300 employees, the Gubbi *toured extensively in Karnataka, Andhra Pradesh, and Tamil Nadu. Veranna himself is remembered especially as a comedian. Through elaborate improvisations he transformed minor roles into memorable comic *characters, like the thief in his popular hit *Sadarame*. KVA

Verdi, Giuseppe (1813–1901) Composer who dominates Italian *opera; well over half of his 28 operas remain in the repertoire. Verdi combines lyricism and spectacle in dramas that centre on conflicts between individuals of often heroic proportions. He used his formidable melodic gift to craft *characters of great power and psychological complexity and to give the *action a momentum unequalled in opera. His early works, of which *Nabucco* (1842), *Ernani* (1844), and *Macbeth* (1847) are the most revived, became popular for their rousing drama and stirring *choruses; in the 1850s they became briefly associated with growing Italian nationalism. *Rigoletto* (1851), *Il trovatore* (1853), and *La traviata* (1853) are the most popular, terse but moving dramas. In the latter part of his career he wrote more in the style of French grand opera, in which the action is not as economical as in Italian opera. Not all these works were instantly successful, but in recent years *Simon Boccanegra* (1857), *A Masked Ball* (1859), *The Force of Destiny* (1862), *Don Carlos* (1867), and *Aida* (Cairo, 1871) have achieved widespread popularity. After a silence of almost sixteen years, Verdi completed his career with *Otello* (1887) and *Falstaff* (1893), works widely considered to be equal to the Shakespearian plays upon which they are based. SJCW

Verdon, Gwen (1925–2000) American dancer and actress. Some years after her childhood debut as 'Baby Alice, the Fastest Little Tapper in the World' in Los Angeles in the late 1920s, Verdon began dancing with the Jack Cole Dancers at Columbia Pictures and in nightclub *revues around the country. Her astonishing *dance technique and vibrant, sexually charged stage presence helped her to win the first of her four Tony awards for *Can-Can* in 1953. Verdon began her long personal and professional partnership with choreographer-director *Fosse in the 1955 production of *Damn Yankees*, where her *acting, singing, and dancing crystallized her reputation as the most formidable 'triple threat' in *musical comedy. In later years she pursued straight film and television roles, including parts in the film *Cocoon* and in the television series *Magnum PI*.   LTC

Verfremdung Since *Brecht's first use of the term in 1936, the German word has been translated variously as 'disillusion', 'alienation', 'de-alienation', 'distanciation', 'estrangement', and 'defamiliarization', each of which alludes to a relevant feature of this concept. In his 1948 'Short Organum for the Theatre' Brecht described *Verfremdung* as aiming 'to free socially conditioned phenomena from that stamp of familiarity which protects them against our grasp today' through a defamiliarizing representation 'which allows us to recognize its subject, but at the same time makes it seem unfamiliar'. On occasion Brecht applied the term to the strategies of diverse artists down the ages who have sought to arouse new or revitalize old perceptions through a process of 'making strange'. However, Brecht remained critical of those *Verfremdungseffekten* ('defamiliarization effects', or 'V-effects'), which he felt made the objects represented seem incomprehensible, given, or unchangeable. Brecht wished to expose habitualized behaviour as the product of a socio-economic condition that is alterable.

A major component of Brecht's political aesthetic, *Verfremdung* is underpinned by his engagement with the Marxist tradition. Close to the practice of *Verfremdung* is Marx's idea that social reality is not timeless and universal but an ever-changing, man-made construct. Brecht defamiliarized those conventions of *illusionist theatre which he believed inhibited the appreciation of that idea: hence his overt display of human productivity and technology—making *lighting apparatus and musicians visible, or scene shifting behind a half-curtain—and his interruption of the flow of *action by inserting narration, song, and direct address. In addition Brecht introduced historicizing devices such as scene titles, projections, and summary reports which present the action played out as a critical recreation of past events. For performers, he devised a method of distancing actor from character through the *rehearsal technique of 'quoting' text and turning it into the past tense. Most importantly, Brecht asserted that the realization of a socialist *Verfremdung* was dependent upon a historicizing method of interpretation. For instance, in the case of Shakespeare's *Othello* he advocated that the fatalist tendency to interpret Othello's jealousy as eternal should be estranged by showing instead how the character's behaviour is a product of the battles for property and position specific to the *early modern context.

While Brecht initially argued that *Verfremdung* required the minimizing of familiarizing processes such as empathy, he later modified this position and placed greater emphasis on the dialectical interplay of empathy and detachment. In the Western world many of the playful and visually striking techniques employed by Brecht to create V-effects, such as non-illusionist stylization and overt displays of technology, have been adapted by the commercial theatre and mass media industry, where they are often disconnected from Brecht's socialist project and used to promote the consumption of pleasurable wit and spectacle. However, interventionist theatre critics and practitioners worldwide continue to find the interruptive, historicizing, and denaturalizing potential of *Verfremdung* an important source of inspiration. *See also* EPIC THEATRE. MM

Vestris, Madame (Lucia Elizabeth Bartolozzi) (1797–1856) English actress, singer, *manager. In 1813 she married Armand Vestris, and made her debut in 1815 at the King's Theatre where he was *ballet master. In 1816 they went to Paris; she returned in 1819, alone. The *succès de scandale* of her *breeches performance in *Giovanni in London* at *Drury Lane in 1820 made her a star. Vestris's appearances in breeches always emphasized feisty femininity, showing off her fabulously perfect legs. In 1830 she took a *burletta licence for the little Olympic, near the struggling *patent houses, remodelling her theatre as a modern, feminine alternative to their discomforts. In an intimate 'drawing-room' space, she offered pretty musical pieces and undemanding *farces, finishing by eleven. The standard was reliable and the class-segregated *auditorium, with no free admissions and no tipping, offered no unpleasant surprises. These simple changes made her theatre fashionable. Behind the scenes Vestris copied the best French *boulevard theatres, with fresh scenery, good working conditions and contracts, and adequate *rehearsal. She attracted loyal workers, including *Planché, *Liston, and Benjamin *Webster, and regularly appeared herself in Planché's *metatheatrical extravaganzas.

In 1835 she hired Charles *Mathews, Jr., and they developed a light *comedy partnership; in 1838 they married and unsuccessfully *toured America. In 1839 they took over *Covent Garden. Despite the disapproval of *Macready, Vestris's artistic practices transferred well to the *legitimate stage. For three seasons she staged classic comedy and new writing, such as *Boucicault's *London Assurance* (1841), and notable Shakespearian productions. But the expenses of the old theatre meant little profit, and Mathews declared bankruptcy in 1842. In 1847, after a period of unremitting work at the *Haymarket under Webster and in provincial touring, they took on the Lyceum. There the John Morton *farce *Cox and Box* prefaced eleven Planché extravaganzas. From 1849 modern French plays translated by *Lewes were used to develop their cool modern comedy style. Vestris took her farewell *benefit in 1854, as one of the most important practitioners of her generation. JSB

Viana Filho, Oduvaldo (Vianinha) (1936–74) Brazilian playwright and actor. Viana Filho's history as a playwright and leftist activist is tied to the political theatres of the 1950s and 1960s. Although he wrote *Brechtian *musical sketches and rural political *satire, his major theme was the alienation of the lower middle class in Rio. His varied theatrical styles sought to renew the Brazilian popular traditions of *street theatre, *revue, and *boulevard theatre. *Heart Torn Asunder* (1974), his major play, is a collage of historical fact and interpretation, created by using a *realist basis intercut with flashbacks, *Verfremdung techniques, and the conventions of musical *revues. LHD

Vicente, Gil (*c.*1465–*c.*1536) Portuguese poet and playwright. The history of his life is elusive, but his career began in 1502, when, as part of the court's celebration of the birth of the royal prince, he staged a short secular piece in the mode of a Christmas *pastoral. Vicente worked almost exclusively for the royal courts of Manuel I and João III until 1536, either commissioned by the sovereign or putting on plays 'of his own invention'. The most significant personality in early sixteenth-century Iberian drama, Vicente wrote in Portuguese and Castilian rhymed verse, often using both languages in the same play. His work has been regarded as a forerunner of the *auto sacramental* and the *comedia*, two of the main genres of the Spanish Golden Age. He was involved in all the aspects of production, but his entertainments were not produced for the *playhouse. Yuletide plays were usually performed in chapels, churches, and monasteries, while those

written to honour the birth of royal children were presented in palace chambers, great halls, and gardens. Taking advantage of the venues, the *audience, and the occasion, Vicente at first exploited the coincidence between the performance location and the fictional locale of the play, though later he moved toward the *early modern division between performers and audience.

The Vicente canon consists of 50 plays that have survived chiefly in a collection published in 1562 by his son and daughter, and organized in four books. Works of devotion include *Visitation, Castilian Pastoral, The Magi, The Sibyl Cassandra, Portuguese Pastoral, Ship of Hell, Purgatory, Ship of Heaven, History of God*, and *Resurrection*. *Comedies include *The Widower, The Crest of Coimbra*, and *Forest of Deceits*. *Tragicomedies consist of *Amadis of Gaul, Ship of Love, Forge of Love, Exhortation to War, Temple of Apollo*, and *Pilgrimage of the Aggrieved*. *Farces include *The Old Man of the Orchard, Fairies, The Judge of Beira, Gypsies, Lusitania*, and *The Physicians*. The *Minor Works*, the final book, is composed of assorted poems, a paraphrase of Psalm 50, and his own epitaph. JCa

vidushaka Comic *stock character in classical Sanskrit drama. A privileged *clown or jester who has licence to ridicule social norms, the *vidushaka* is the sounding board and alter ego of the *hero, who could be a god, a king, a minister, or a Brahman. Functioning as a surrogate for humour and love affairs, he intervenes in the plot only to complicate matters. The *Natyasastra* specifies the physical deformities of the *character—protruding teeth, a bald pate, red eyes, a limp, a dwarf-like stature, supplemented by his crooked stick and even more twisted face. This grotesquerie is matched by his gluttony and vulgar language in Prakrit dialect, which exposes his degraded Brahman status. The role of the *vidushaka* can also be conventionalized, as in his appearance in the *ritualistic preliminaries to Sanskrit plays. In performances of *kuttyattam in Kerala, the *vidushaka* continues to play a significant role through his critical commentary in colloquial Malayalam on the learned Sanskrit *dialogues used by the main characters. LSR/RB

Viganò, Salvatore (1769–1821) Italian dancer, choreographer, and composer. The nephew of Boccherini, Viganò learned from Jean Duberval a practice of choreography demanding mimic talent. After working principally in Vienna, Venice, and Milan, he became *ballet master in 1811 at La Scala. He invented the *coreodramma*, a highly theatrical work based on mythology, history, or a

Shakespeare play that synthesized *dance patterns with *mime. He created over 40 dances; among the greatest were *The Creatures of Prometheus* (1801), with music especially composed for him by Beethoven; *Othello* (1818); the mock heroic *The Guards* (1809); and *The Titans* (1819). JEH

Vigarani family Italian family of architects and *scenographers. **Gaspare** (1588–1663) built a long, successful career designing large-scale scenery and apparatuses in his native duchy of Modena, for public spectacles organized both by the court and by the religious authorities: in 1654 he constructed a theatre holding 3,000 spectators. Invited to Paris, he created the *Salle des Machines at the Tuileries in 1662; in the process he opposed and supplanted the influence of *Torelli, to the extent of confiscating and burning his sets from the *Petit-Bourbon. His son **Carlo** (1623–93) returned to Paris after his father's death and created major royal pageants and spectacles for Louis XIV between 1664 and 1675, in collaboration with his younger brother **Ludovico**. Carlo received French nationality and patents of nobility, after he associated with the composer *Lully (also Italian by birth), launching the foundation of the Opéra. RAA

Vigny, Alfred de (1797–1863) French playwright. In the early 1830s, when *romantic drama was becoming established in Paris, Vigny stood out as the intellectual among the leading dramatists. His theatrical debuts were marked by translations from Shakespeare (*Le More de Venise*, *Comédie-Française, 1829); while his masterpiece *Chatterton* (1835), which treats the last hours of the Bristol boy-poet's life with real pathos (notably contributed by Vigny's mistress Marie *Dorval in the role of Kitty Bell), was conceived as a philosophical plea on behalf of the sufferings of genius in a hostile, materialist society. WDH

Vilalta, Maruxa (1932–) Mexican playwright and director. The winner of ten awards for best play of the year, many of her pieces are concerned with social issues. *Number 9* (1965) is an *expressionist piece about the dehumanization of factory workers, while *Together Tonight, Loving Each Other So Much* (1970) is a dark, *absurdist *comedy about middle-class self-centredness. In *A Woman, Two Men and a Gun Shot* (1981) and *A Small Tale of Horror and Unbridled Love* (1985) Vilalta *parodies *melodrama and *gender identity. Subsequent plays, such as *A Voice in the Desert: the life of St Jerome* (1990), are religious in theme. KFN

Vilar, Jean (1912–71) French director and *actor-manager. Vilar acted his first major role in Paris in 1942 in *Synge's *The Well of the Saints*. As founding director of the Compagnie des Sept, he won acclaim for productions of *Strindberg, *Molière, and *Eliot. Expanding *Copeau's philosophy of popular theatre, Vilar founded and directed the *Avignon Theatre Festival from 1947 until his death, with the aim of bringing together troupes and spectators, especially young people, from all over Europe in a July holiday atmosphere to heal the bitterness of the war and rediscover the shared heritage of European classics. Vilar believed that theatre could bring social enlightenment to all classes, strengthen democracy, and make wars and tyranny less likely. He was the first in post-war France to direct German works, including *Büchner's *Danton's Death* (1948), *Brecht's *Mother Courage* (1951), and *Kleist's *Prince of Homburg* (1951), while his anchors remained Molière, *Corneille, and Shakespeare. In Avignon Vilar built an open-air stage in the courtyard of the ancient Palais des Papes, which accommodated thousands of spectators.

A fine actor himself, as a director Vilar emphasized *character and textual clarity over spectacle, and demanded that *actors make strong, intimate contact with the audience. At the *Théâtre National Populaire, which he managed from 1951 to 1963, Vilar remodelled the Palais de Chaillot in Paris, removing the orchestra pit, galleries, curtain, *proscenium, and *footlights, which greatly enlarged the *auditorium. He lowered prices, eliminated tips to ushers, provided inexpensive food, free programmes and buses, performances for schools and workers, public symposia, and a journal for patrons. Although not a radical, Vilar often produced plays that provoked critical reflection on political events. In the era of the Algerian War and Gaullist nationalism, he staged an antimilitarist *Ubu roi*, and produced Brecht's *Galileo* to protest French tests of the atom bomb. His vision of theatre as community was challenged at the 1968 Avignon Festival when the *Living Theatre led protests condemning Vilar as reactionary and the festival as 'a marketplace of culture'. Nonetheless, Vilar's innovations were emulated worldwide, and opened the way for decentralization of theatre in France. SBB

villain A *character who energizes dramatic *action by desiring or performing what the play represents as culturally evil. Directly opposed to the *hero or *protagonist, a villain is distinguished from a morally acceptable antagonist only by his or her wickedness, and the term might be applied equally to Clytemnestra in *Aeschylus'

Agamemnon (458 BC), Iago in Shakespeare's *Othello* (1603-4 in the cast of characters of the First Folio he is called 'a villain'), and Hannibal Lecter in the film *The Silence of the Lambs* (1990)—even though each of them could also be considered in part noble, attractive, or even heroic. Ravana in the Indian epic the *Ramayana* (upon which much South Asian and South-East Asian performance depends) is parallel: on one level he is a villain, but he is also heroic and artistic. The word, deriving from medieval French and English *villein*, originally meant a tenant feudal peasant, and thus a base or low-born person, suggesting a class-based definition of the villain that has been prevalent since *early modern drama.

The nineteenth century was heyday of the villain in the West. Once *romanticism had insisted that the hero of *tragedy need not be high-born, or that he might be alienated from society, an opposing figure was needed to clarify the protagonist's virtue. The dramatic usefulness of this strategy was abundantly clear in popular *melodrama, where the opposition between abstract good and evil was normally enacted over the body of a young, beautiful, and defenceless female character, the villain attempting to take advantage of his superior financial position to work his evil ways. Since his power had been gained improperly or illegally, often depriving the hero or the heroine of a rightful inheritance, the action of most melodramas consisted in exposing not so much the villain's iniquity as his imposture.

The presence of a villain in drama raises complicated issues about the nature of evil, which are often left unresolved. Coleridge famously gave up on explaining Iago, calling his actions 'motiveless malignity', though since Freud playwrights and critics have been more likely to posit a root cause in (fictional) childhood development that twisted the character into malevolence. Modernist theatre in general, consciously moving away from the incredible bad boys of melodrama, has tended to lessen the out-and-out evil of antagonists, but the villain has remained a powerful type figure in popular cinema, from the black hats of westerns to the *femmes fatales* of film noir. Villains are especially notable in Hollywood action films, where a master criminal, perverted politician, unscrupulous businessman, or megalomaniacal terrorist threatens worldwide horror and devastation that only the physically attractive hero can prevent or undo.   DK

Villegas, Oscar (1943-) Mexican playwright and director, whose work is testimony to the social and political unrest of the 1970s. *Renaissance*

(1971) is about Beatlemania, sexual liberation, and political repression; *Marlon Brando Is Someone Else* (1977) tells of gratuitous crime among alienated youth. The explicit treatment of sexual promiscuity in *The Pyre* (1983) caused something of a commotion with local authorities. Villegas is best known for *Santa Catarina* (1980), about same-sex encounters in a school for young boys, and for *Atlantida* (1977), which takes place among the lumpenproletariat.   KFN

Vinaver, Michel (1927-) French playwright. A successful international businessman, Vinaver became one the most important French dramatists of the post-1968 generation. *The Koreans* (1956), *Hotel Iphigenia* (1959), and *Planchon's production of the monumental *Overboard* (1973) solidified Vinaver's reputation. His plays experiment freely with dramatic structure and time, providing a mine for directorial interpretation. Like *Overboard*, the later works, including *Situation Vacant* (1971), *A Smile on the End of the Line* (1977), and *The Television Programme* (1988), often deal with the intrusion of larger economic and socio-political forces on the construction of personal life, language, and thought. His *dramaturgical technique is often considered 'juxtapositional' or deconstructive, resisting traditional narrative closure and seeking fragmentation and possibility in a *Brechtian vein. A champion of younger playwrights, Vinaver was instrumental in the resurgence of support for emerging talent, composing an influential government report in 1987 on the concerns of French dramatists. His play *11 September 2001* (2002) was a very early and challenging meditation on the terrorist attacks.   DGM

Vincent, Jean-Pierre (1942-) One of the leading French directors of the post-1968 generation, from 1975 to 1983 Vincent headed the Théâtre National de Strasbourg, where he championed the work of younger authors. Greatly influenced by *Brecht, whose minor works he championed early in his career, Vincent's deconstructive approach to the classical repertoire, akin to that of *Stein, foregrounds a text's ideological underpinnings as well as its contemporary relevance. Briefly (and turbulently) heading the *Comédie-Française (1983-6), he succeeded *Chéreau as director of the Théâtre des Amandiers at Nanterre in 1990. Since then he has directed widely throughout France, notably an acclaimed production of *Les Prétendants* by Jean-Luc Lagarce.   DGM

Visconti, Luchino (1906-76) Italian director. There were two souls in Visconti, one which laid bare harsh social reality (he was a communist)

and one which relished the opulence of style and splendour (he belonged to the nobility). He made his theatrical debut with *Cocteau's *Les Parents terribles* (1945), but his strong directorial stance was a novelty which made him unpopular with actors, who complained of his dictatorial ways. In 1954 he moved to opera, directing Spontini's *La Vestale*, and thereafter working with Maria Callas on Gluck, Bellini, and Donizetti. In cinema he served an apprenticeship with Jean Renoir, and made his debut in 1943 with *Ossessione*. The term neorealism was first used for this film, and in the post-war period he was one of the principal exponents of this approach. Later his cinema vision widened to such literary masterpieces as *Death in Venice* (1971) and *The Leopard* (1963).   JF

Vishnevsky, Vsevolod (1900–51) Russian/Soviet dramatist who served with the cavalry during the Civil War and wrote a play (*The First Cavalry Army*, 1929) based on his experiences. In 1921 he had organized an eight-hour outdoor epic about the Kronstadt sailors' revolt, but his revolutionary zeal is seen to best effect in *Optimistic Tragedy* (1932), staged memorably by *Tairov in 1933 on a spiralling tiered setting by Vadim Ryndin, and with Alisa *Koonen as the commissar sent by the Party to discipline a group of anarchist sailors. His *Unforgettable 1919* (1949) is a shameless, and factually dubious, celebration of Stalin.   NW

Vitez, Antoine (1930–90) French actor and director. Vitez, able to work in Russian, German, and Greek, was inspired by contemporary critical theory and the work of *Brecht and *Meyerhold. He began acting at 18 and taught *acting at the *Lecoq School and the Conservatoire National. He began as a director in 1966 with his adaptation of *Sophocles' *Electra* at Caen, and gained recognition *directing in the communist suburbs ringing Paris, including the Théâtre des Quartiers d'Ivry, which he led from 1971 to 1980. With his productions of *Electra* (1971), Brecht's *Mother Courage* (1973), and *Catherine* (1976), he attained an international reputation. Believing that 'theatre can be made from anything', Vitez adapted *Catherine* from a Louis Aragon novel, staging it with a group of actors who passed a book around and read passages as they ate a complete dinner. In 1978-9 he produced four *Molière plays in repertory, using only props and furniture listed by Molière's *stage manager.

His signature approach was to help actors render the intrinsic rhythm and music of the text, and the *scenography of his long-time collaborator *Kokkos lent an epic dimension to actors' move-

ment. As *artistic director of the Théâtre National du Chaillot (1981-8), and of the *Comédie-Française from 1988 until his unexpected death, he tried, like *Vilar, to democratize the theatre, offering a wide range of classical and modern works. Vitez's important productions of later years included *Hugo's *Hernani* (1985), *Claudel's *The Satin Slipper* (1987), and *Rojas's *La Célestine*, starring Jeanne Moreau (1989).   SBB

Vitrac, Roger (1899-1952) French dramatist. The bourgeois provincialism of Vitrac's childhood infused his writing, which often apprehended the adult world through the sensibility of a child, as in his best-known play *Victor; or, Children Take Over* (1928). After founding the literary journal *Aventure* in 1922 and publishing *dada poetry, Vitrac joined the *surrealists and signed the 1924 manifesto, but was dismissed, apparently for his obsession with theatre over poetry. He and *Artaud started their own theatre, the Alfred Jarry (1926-9), which produced two of Vitrac's plays: *Les Mystères de l'amour* (1927) and *Victor*. Attacking middle-class institutions and hypocrisy in a mix of *farce, dream elements, risqué humour, Artaudian *cruelty, and often *tragedy, Vitrac honed his *dramaturgical skills through sixteen plays that were largely unappreciated during his lifetime. *Le Sabre de mon père* (1951) scandalized critics by its military *satire, but won posthumous acclaim.   FHL

Viviani, Raffaele (1888-1950) Italian actor, composer, and playwright. Viviani taught himself to read and write and became a nationally known *variety performer by the age of 24. In 1917 he formed his own company and, building on his variety character sketches and songs, he wrote the *dialogue and composed the lyrics and music for over 40 *musical plays—many of them panoramic dramas that take place in specific areas of Naples. Among these are *Via Toledo by Night* (1918), *Street Urchin* (1918), *Sgueglia's Equestrian Circus* (1922), and *Have-Nots* (1929). He painted genuinely compassionate and often humorous portraits of the Neapolitan working class, the poor, and the disenfranchised. His *realistic depictions and his use of Neapolitan led to fascist *censorship from the late 1920s until the end of the Second World War.   JEH

Viviescas, Victor (1958-) Colombian playwright, director, and essayist. He won first prize in the National Playwriting Contest for *Crisanta Alone, Loneliness Crisanta* (1986) and for *Russian Roulette* (1993). One of the most important playwrights of his generation, his other works include *Anibal Is a Ghost Who Repeats Himself in the*

Mirrors (1986), *Promise Me I Will Not Scream* (1988), *The Obscene* (1997), and a version of *Chekhov's *Platonov* (1999). He is one of the co-authors of *The Crusade of the Street Children* staged in Madrid by *Sanchis Sinisterra (2000). He explores solitude, memory, intimacy, and betrayal in a language rich in connotation and metaphor, and his lyrical pessimism has been compared to *Müller and *Koltès.   BJR

Vodanovic, Sergio (1926-2001) Chilean playwright and lawyer. A master of *parody and *satire, Vodanovic usually targeted the Chilean upper middle class but also focused on the inner conflicts of individuals. His most accomplished play is *Viña: Three Comedies in Bathing Suits* (1964). During the 1970s his plays dealt with social and political unrest during the Allende regime and the Pinochet dictatorship. Representative of this period are *We Occupied the University* (1971) and *The Sea Was Calm* (1978), a metaphorical reference to the dictatorship.   MAR

Vogel, Paula (1951-) American playwright. Like *Churchill and *Fornés, Vogel's plays focus on women and *feminist issues. Through a mix of scatological humour, fantasy, and rage Vogel addresses such issues as incest and domestic violence. *How I Learned to Drive* (1998), about a young girl's sexually charged driving lessons with her uncle, evokes erotic confusion and healing rather than victimhood. *The Baltimore Waltz* (1992), inspired by her brother's death, likewise stands apart from other AIDS plays through its allegory about 'Acquired Toilet Disease'. Other plays include *Desdemona* (1979), a revisioning of *Othello*; *The Oldest Profession* (1981), about ageing prostitutes; *And Baby Makes Seven* (1984), about lesbian mothers of imaginary children; *Hot n' Throbbing* (1992), about *pornography; and *The Mineola Twins* (1997), about extremism. Recent work includes *The Long Christmas Ride Home* (2003) and *The Civil War Christmas* (2008).   GAO

Volkov, Fyodor (1729-63) Russian actor, called the father of the Russian Theatre. Keen to found a national theatre, Peter the Great's daughter, the Empress Elizaveta Petrovna, summoned Volkov's amateur troupe in Yaroslavl to St Petersburg in 1750, and in 1756 established them as a company under the directorship of *Sumarokov, laying the foundation for the imperial theatres. Volkov became the leading actor and, after 1761, took over the *management. Volkov was a highly intelligent performer, blessed with a powerful temperament, which found expression in a number of roles in Russian classical *tragedies such as Sumarokov's

Hamlet and *Khorev*. Volkov took part in the *coup d'état* against Peter III which brought the Empress Catherine to the throne, for which she offered him the post of cabinet minister and the Order of St Andrew, both of which he refused. He also officiated at her coronation, staging a street masquerade in her honour, *Minerva Triumphant*.   NW

Volksbühne (people's theatre) German term to describe a theatre movement and the buildings that emerged from it. The cultural movement was founded in 1890 by Franz Wille in Berlin as a subscription organization, the Freie Volksbühne. Disputes over programming led to a split in 1892. The social democratic journalist Franz Mehring took over the organization and Wille founded the Neue Freie Volksbühne. The two organizations merged in 1927 with a nationwide membership of half a million. Meanwhile a *playhouse had been built in 1914 as the 2,000-seat Volksbühne am Bülowplatz. The movement became a crucial forum for politically committed theatre during the Weimar Republic and is most closely associated with *Piscator's directorship (1924-7) and that of K. H. *Martin (1929-32). In 1933 the Nazi regime took over the Volksbühne, renaming it Theater am Horst-Wessel-Platz. After the war the movement was reconstituted in a divided Germany. The original playhouse reopened in 1954 as the Volksbühne am Rosa-Luxemburg-Platz. After 1969 it achieved renown under *Besson and again after 1992 under the controversial directorship of *Castorf. The West Berlin Freie Volksbühne, in a new building from 1963, had a series of *artistic directors, starting with Piscator, who staged important *documentary and historical drama, including the work of *Hochhuth. It lost its public subsidy in 1992 after reunification and was closed.   CBB

Volonakis, Minos (1925-99) Greek director. He directed for private companies starting in 1960, as well as for the State Theatre of Northern Greece in Thessaloniki (*artistic director, 1975-8), including the first Greek production of *Beckett's *Waiting for Godot*. His memorable productions included *Brecht's *Mr Puntila and his Man Matti* and *Euripides' *Medea* with Melina *Mercouri. In 1982 he directed *Sophocles' *Oedipus the King* for the Greek National Theatre and that same year, in an attempt to bring theatre closer to the working classes, inaugurated the Festival of the Rocks in Athens, an annual event that featured performances in open-air spaces. Volonakis is remembered for the visual aspects of his productions and for his numerous translations of ancient *Greek and American plays.   KGO

Voltaire (François-Marie Arouet) (1694–1778) French philosopher, historian, and poet. Voltaire was placed by contemporaries on a level with his predecessors *Corneille and *Racine as a writer of *tragedy. Many of his best-known plays were based on subjects from classical antiquity: *Oedipe* (1718), *Mariamne* (1725), *Mérope* (1743), *Sémiramis* (1748) among others; but *Zaïre* (1732), his tragedy with most lasting appeal, is set in Jerusalem during the Crusades, and *Alzire* (1736) in South America at the Spanish Conquest. In exile in London from 1726 to 1729, Voltaire acquired a good working knowledge of English, partly by attending theatres. His serious acquaintance with Shakespeare dates from this period; *Zaïre* and *La Mort de César* (1731) show the influence of *Othello* and *Julius Caesar*; the appearance of a *ghost in *Ériphile* (1732) and *Sémiramis* is an explicit borrowing from *Hamlet*. An important innovation in the field of tragedy was Voltaire's creation of philosophical tragedy, in which the harmful effects of religious fanaticism are shown, as in *Zaïre*, *Alzire*, *Mahomet* (1741), and *L'Orphelin de la Chine* (1755). Another was the choice of subjects from national history (*Zaïre*; *Adélaïde du Guesclin*, 1734; *Tancrède*, 1760) as an alternative to the legacy of classical antiquity.

But Voltaire was very much a *neoclassic traditionalist, and later became hostile to English influence, denouncing Shakespeare in intemperate terms on grounds of taste. In *comedy, Voltaire was equally hostile to the new 'tearful comedy' (*comédie larmoyante*), frequently castigating *La Chaussée for his pernicious influence. Voltaire played a prominent part in campaigns concerning the religious and civil status of the *acting profession. He had a close relationship with *Lekain, who acted (as Voltaire himself did) in his private theatricals at Ferney. He was paid a remarkable tribute shortly before his death, when he was crowned with a laurel wreath during a performance of his tragedy *Irène* at the *Comédie-Française.   WDH

Vondel, Joost van den (1587–1679) Dutch playwright and poet. Influenced by the *Chambers of Rhetoric, Vondel began with mock poems and patriotic poetry. He wrote *Gijsbrecht van Aemstel* for the opening of Amsterdam's new municipal theatre, the *Schouwburg (1638), a religious play that was performed there annually on New Year's Day until 1968. A founder of the Netherlands' national drama and its main representative of humanist drama, Vondel combined the classical with *characters that belonged to the *medieval tradition. His *biblical plays, such as *Lucifer* (1654) and *Adam in Exile* (1664), were

still performed occasionally at the end of the twentieth century.   CBB

Von Sydow, Max (1929–) Swedish actor. Soon after he started his career in the 1950s he joined *Bergman's company in Malmö, and subsequently performed in many of Bergman's films. His portrayal of a knight returning from the Crusades in *The Seventh Seal* (1957) brought him international acclaim. Further probing performances in *The Virgin Spring* (1959), *Through a Glass Darkly* (1962), and *Shame* (1968) confirmed his ability to portray emotionally tormented *characters. On stage he worked with Bergman on a gallery of equally complex roles, starting with *The Misanthrope* (Malmö, 1957), in which he played Alceste as a defiant and confused idealist. He gave emblematic performances of the embittered Lawyer in Bergman's production of *Strindberg's *A Dream Play* (1970) and an emotionally stunted Gregers in *Ibsen's *The Wild Duck* (1972). He has had a substantial Hollywood career, but was especially noted in Bille August's *Pelle the Conqueror* (1988) and as the Norwegian writer in Jan Troell's *Hamsun* (1996).   DT

voodoo Haitian *ritual practice with large performative elements. A voodoo ceremony takes place at the request of a devotee of a *loa* (spirit), and culminates with the trance of the possessed through whose mouth the spirit speaks. The possessed (medium) is assisted by the *oungan*, who is both *actor and *stage manager. By drawing *vêvês*, the symbolic designs of the *loas*, he prepares the decor, and by leading the participants in a round *dance he marks the performance space—a circle in the middle of which the *poto-mitan*, a column that supports the roof, symbolizes communication between earth and sky. The *oungan* performs prescribed gestures for ablutions, libations, or sacrificial offerings, using accessories like the *ason* (a ritual rattle), and a scarf to wipe the faces of the participants. The colours of the scarf and the sacrificial animal are also prescribed, and the *ounsis* (the temple servants) must be dressed in white. The ceremony involves intensely visual and auditory dimensions, as songs and dances are accompanied by insistent drumbeats that punctuate various stages of the action. Voodoo is a game of doubles, suggesting a performative universe of doubles: the *loa* spirits double as God, the devotee doubles as the *oungan* and the possessed, the possessed is doubled by the possession trance crisis.   MLa trans. JCM

Voss, Gert (1941–) German actor. Particularly linked with *Peymann since 1974, Voss performed a range of classical and contemporary roles.

In 1986 he moved with Peymann to Vienna's *Burgtheater and starred in the opening production of *Richard III*. Under *Zadek, Voss played Shylock, *Chekhov's Ivanov, and Antony in *Antony and Cleopatra* (*Berliner Ensemble, 1994). He also acted Othello for *Tabori (1990). Recently he starred in *Ibsen's *The Master Builder* (directed by *Ostermeier, 2004), *Williams's *Cat on a Hot Tin Roof* (*Breth, 2004), *Strindberg's *The Dance of Death* (Zadek, 2005), and *King Lear* (*Bondy, 2007). One of the most celebrated performers in German theatre, Voss's *acting is distinguished by keen intelligence and ironic wit. *Theater heute* named him actor of the year four times, and he has received many prestigious awards.   CBB

Vychodil, Ladislav (1920–2005) Slovak *scenographer. Vychodil became a designer of the Slovak National Theatre in 1945, and in 1951 head of its scenographic studios. In 1952 he established the department of scenography at the Academy of Performing Arts in Bratislava, and in 1968 was one of founders of International Organization of Scenographers, Theatre Architects, and Technicians. A student of the Czech inter-war *avant-garde, he worked for the unity of space, light, colour, and actors' presence. Vychodil was

sometimes restrained by resources, often using an open and minimally furnished stage. In the early 1960s, while working in Prague with *Radok, he acquired a more complex and playful style, using in an ironic way the *surrealist methods of montage and collage. He developed this further in 1990s in Josef Bednárik's lavish productions of *opera and *musicals, in both Prague and Bratislava.   ML

Vysotsky, Vladimir (1938–80) Russian actor and bard. Vysotsky trained at the *Moscow Art Theatre Studio and in 1964 joined the Taganka Theatre, where he soon emerged as a leading actor. He played the parts of *Brecht's Galileo, Dostoevsky's Svidrigailov, and Esenin's Khlopusha in *Lyubimov's productions. Most important was his performance as Hamlet: he turned the Danish prince into a man from the street, allowing ordinary people to understand Hamlet's ethical dilemma, and recited to guitar accompaniment Pasternak's poem 'Hamlet' (then unpublished). Vysotsky's fame as an actor was complemented by his reputation as a bard. His songs and poems dealt with themes incompatible with *socialist realism: alcoholism, the real street life, prostitution. They were very popular and circulated illegally on tape.   BB

Wagner, Richard (1813–83) German composer, librettist, theorist, conductor, and *director. Wagner made his name with *Rienzi* (1842), a grand *opera in the French style, which led to his appointment as musical director of the Dresden Court Opera. His first mature opera, *The Flying Dutchman* (1843), was not initially successful, but *Tannhäuser* (1845) and *Lohengrin* (1850), based on German material, established him as the leading opera composer of his generation.

Wagner's career was interrupted by his involvement in an abortive uprising against the Saxon monarchy in 1849, which led to an eleven-year exile in Switzerland. Here he wrote three major theoretical essays, *Art and Revolution* (1849), *The Artwork of the Future* (1850), and *Opera and Drama* (1852), in which he argued that each art can only fulfil itself in cooperation with all the others. Following the model of the *Dionysia in ancient Athens, Wagner intended to unite the arts once again, in works that would allow the people—the 'Volk'—to discover their own identity. He also explored how music can become a dramatic language. All this was preparatory to his central work, *The Ring of the Nibelung*, a tetralogy based upon medieval German romances and Norse sagas, which took him 25 years to complete. The music dramas of *The Rhinegold* (1869), *The Valkyrie* (1870), *Siegfried*, and *Twilight of the Gods* (1876), which take over fourteen hours to perform, are unified by Wagner's resourceful use of the leitmotif, a musical fragment, phrase, or melody that is given specific and frequently multiple dramatic meanings. The score for each act is continuous, so that musical and dramatic form are identical.

In 1857 he broke off composition for twelve years to complete *Tristan and Isolde* (1865), a hymn to romantic love, and *The Mastersingers of Nuremberg* (1868), his only *comedy. Wagner was notoriously improvident and his life was bedevilled by debt, until in 1864 when he came under the patronage of Ludwig II of Bavaria, who relieved his financial burdens. Ludwig also helped finance the building of the *Bayreuth Festival Theatre, where the first complete performance of the *Ring* was staged in 1876. Wagner intended an annual festival, though in his lifetime only his final music drama was seen there, *Parsifal* (1882), a quasi-religious work.

Wagner aroused rancorous dispute in his life and after. Few question that his music dramas, and his theories of the *Gesamtkunstwerk* or *'total work of art', have been immensely influential. But Wagner's works have been reviled successively for their decadence, militant nationalism, and anti-Semitism. Nevertheless, they are informed by a powerful tragic sense that addressed the political, economic, and social problems of his day and reintroduced European theatre to the themes of ancient drama. Today they play to packed houses whenever they are performed.   SJCW

Wagner, Robin (1933–) American *scenographer who entered the first rank of New York scene designers with *Hair* (1968). Often associated with large spectacular sets for *musicals (*Jesus Christ Superstar, On the Twentieth Century, 42nd Street*), many of his best designs featured a choreographic resculpting of space (*Dreamgirls, Chess*). One of his most famous sets, for *A Chorus Line* (1975), was one of his most minimal. His designs also displayed a sense of humour, as in *The Producers* (2001). He designed *opera and rock concerts as well.   JD

Wagner, Wieland (1917–66) German designer and director. The grandson of Richard *Wagner, Wieland became director of the *Bayreuth Festival and reopened it in 1951 with a production of *Parsifal*, rejecting the *realism which he had used as a director before the war. Instead, in a *symbolist manner that owed much to *Appia, scenery was abstract and staging sparse. Over the next fifteen years, when he co-directed the festival with his brother Wolfgang (1919–2010), Wieland restaged the entire canon of his grandfather's work, highlighting both mystical dimensions and, paradoxically, the less-than-heroic aspects of the *action. His greatest achievement was a *Tristan and Isolde* (1962) in which symbols combining erotic and Celtic themes were bathed in subtly changing *lighting that evoked the dreamlike action of the work. Wieland Wagner also directed elsewhere in Germany, applying his symbolist style to the *operas of Richard Strauss, Beethoven, *Verdi, and others.   SJCW

Wahba, Saad Eddin (1923–97) Egyptian writer. Motivated by a socialist suspicion of larger-than-life *heroes, Wahba built his plays around a large gallery of *characters, each with a story and voice interesting in its own right. His early plays, set in the countryside, were clever apologies for the 1952 Revolution satirizing the feudal society under the *ancien régime*. The second phase in his career showed a determination to expose the corruption and opportunism which then boded ill for the new socialist utopia. After 1970 he devoted more attention to film, and was for a time the president of the Cairo International Film Festival. But he also wrote a handful of plays *satirizing the consumerism and anti intellectualism of contemporary Egypt.   HMA

Wajda, Andrzej (1926–) Polish director, designer, and major filmmaker. From 1955 Wajda directed many films and television plays and dozens of theatre productions, the majority in Cracow. In 1980 he allied himself with the Solidarity movement, and during the martial-law period of the 1980s he directed illegal productions in churches. In his films he was keenly interested in national history and the national ethos (the remarkable *Ashes and Diamonds*, 1958), as well as contemporary struggles with communism (*Man of Marble*, 1978; *Man of Iron*, 1981). In the theatre Wajda created productions as if painting vast, colourful, and visionary moving canvases. His best works, often restaged at home and abroad, include his own adaptations of Dostoevsky novels: *The Possessed* (1963), *Nastasya Filipowna*, based on *The Idiot* (1977), and *Crime and Punishment* (1984). Among Polish classics he focused on *Wyspiański, directing *The Wedding* (1963, filmed 1962) and *November Night* (1974, filmed 1977), and staged *Przybyszewska's *The Danton Case* (1975, filmed 1982). Wajda also directed *Hamlet* (1960), *Antigone* (1984), *Romeo and Juliet* (1990), *Mrożek's *The Emigrants* (1976), and Kazimierz Moczarski's *Dialogues with the Executioner* (1977), and often developed the *scenography for his productions.   KB

Walcott, Derek (1930–) St Lucian playwright and poet, the towering figure of Caribbean theatre. In 1950 he directed his *Henri Christophe* for the St Lucia Arts Guild, which he had co-founded. His first important play, *The Sea at Dauphin* (1954), a revision of *Synge's *Riders to the Sea*, was produced by the same company. He studied in the USA (1958–9), and upon returning founded the Trinidad Theatre Workshop, the focus for his work for a number of years. Walcott has written

more than 40 plays, *musicals, and screenplays, which bring together different cultural influences to create a new language of Caribbean performance. Most notable are *Malcochon* (1959), *Ti-Jean and his Brothers* (1958), *Dream on Monkey Mountain* (1967), *The Joker of Seville* (*Royal Shakespeare Company, 1974), and *Pantomime* (1978), a brilliant variation on the Robinson Crusoe story. Also important are the more *realist *Remembrance* (1977), the adroit *farce *Beef, No Chicken* (1981), and a moving exploration of the difficulties of being an artist in the Caribbean, *A Branch of the Blue Nile* (1983). His work has been widely performed internationally. He received the Nobel Prize for Literature in 1992.   ES

Walker, George F. (1947–) Canadian playwright. Walker's plays, whose first productions he often directs, have the pace and absurdity of tragic *farce; his *characters live on the edge of disaster, against which they struggle desperately, inventively, and (almost) hopelessly. The plays of the 1970s, such as *Beyond Mozambique* (1974) and *Gossip* (1977), are ironic fantasias on themes from popular culture. *Criminals in Love* (1984) began a series set on his home turf, the working-class East End of Toronto, inhabited by characters whose lives are constricted by the power of wealthy elites and impersonal bureaucracies. Other notable plays include *Nothing Sacred* (1988), based on *Turgenev's *Fathers and Sons*, *Love and Anger* (1989), the six-play cycle *Suburban Motel* (1999), and *Heaven* (2000). His works are widely produced internationally.   RCN

Wall, Max (1908–90) English comedian and actor. Wall began his career in the 1920s as 'Max Wall and his Independent Legs', establishing a distinctive style of grotesque and sometimes menacing *clowning. He achieved success in *variety and *revue, appearing in the 1930 Royal Variety Performance, and was popular on radio and television in the 1940s and 1950s. After a period of obscurity, Wall pursued a second career in theatre, appearing at the *Royal Court in London in *Jarry's *Ubu roi* (1966), *Osborne's *The Entertainer* (1974), and in *Beckett's plays. His one-person show *Aspects of Max Wall* (1974) revived his earlier variety acts.   SF

Wallace, Nellie (1870–1948) Scottish vocalist and comedienne. Wallace appeared as a child actress in plays (Little Willie in *East Lynne*), graduating to clog *dancing with the Three Sisters Wallace, and finally to a solo act in *music halls. With her lanky frame, buck teeth, and generally unprepossessing appearance, suggestive and bizarre asides became her trademark—'If you're fond of anything tasty, what price me?'—along with similarly outrageous songs such as 'Let's Have a Tiddley at the Milk Bar' and 'The Blasted Oak'. AF

Waller, Lewis (1860–1915) English actor and *manager. Waller made his debut in 1883 in London. Exuding virility, with a splendid physique and a powerful voice, he was the prototypical romantic *hero, especially as D'Artagnan in *The Three Musketeers* (1898) and Monsieur Beaucaire (1902) in the play of that name. The heroic patriotism of his Henry V was never exceeded. Waller also played Hotspur, Brutus, Othello, and the Bastard in *King John*, and a wide variety of parts in modern *comedies and dramas, including *Ibsen. He acted in New York in Robert Hichens's *The Garden of Allah* (1911). His good looks and nobility of bearing caused a great flutter among his female *audience, and his more fervent admirers wore badges at the theatre proclaiming that they were KOW, keen on Waller. Much to his embarrassment, he had become a matinée idol. MRB

Wälterlin, Oskar (1895–1961) Swiss actor and director. Wälterlin directed *opera and drama in Basel in the 1920s (including *Wagner's *Ring* with *Appia, 1924–5). From 1938 until his death he was the director of the Zurich Schauspielhaus, which between 1933 and 1945 became a meeting place for exiled German theatre practitioners, including *Brecht, *Giehse, and Leopold Lindtberg. In the 1950s Wälterlin systematically promoted German-Swiss drama and directed the premières of many plays by *Frisch and *Dürrenmatt. Altogether he directed 125 plays for the Zurich Schauspielhaus, of which approximately 100 were designed by Teo *Otto. CBB

Walters, Sam (1939–   ) English director and actor. Walters performed in *regional repertory theatre before turning to directing in 1967. In 1971 he began producing unusual revivals and new writing in a room above a pub in Richmond in Surrey. The high standards of production turned his Orange Tree Theatre into an award-winning small venue, and in 1991 a significant sum was raised to build a permanent theatre-in-the-round. The Orange Tree has commissioned new writing by *Crimp, David Cregan, James Saunders, Fay Weldon, and Olwen Wymark. It has also produced revivals of D. H. *Lawrence plays, French *farce, obscure *musicals, *Glaspell, and Granville *Barker. The theatre has premièred work by *Havel since the 1970s, staging in 2008 *Leaving*, Havel's first play in 19 years. KN

Wanamaker, Sam (1919–93) American actor and director. Wanamaker visited London in 1952,

playing alongside *Redgrave in his own production of *Odets's *The Country Girl* (renamed *Winter Journey*), and stayed, preferring post-war England to the McCarthyism of America. Wanamaker's experience with the *Group Theatre in New York placed him to introduce *Method *acting to Britain, which he explored in Odets's *The Big Knife* (1954) and Richard Nash's *The Rainmaker* (1956). In 1957 he became director of the New Shakespeare Theatre in Liverpool, which he ran as a prototype arts centre with numerous outreach activities. His lifelong fascination with Shakespeare was kindled by his (poorly received) Iago to *Robeson's Othello (Stratford, 1959) and his appearance as Macbeth on a return visit to Chicago in 1964. In 1970 he founded the Playhouse Trust and World Centre for Shakespeare, where his vision and tireless fundraising overcame huge obstacles to reconstruct the *Globe Theatre near its Elizabethan site. He died a few months after the unveiling of the first building works. His production of Prokofiev's *War and Peace* opened the Sydney Opera House in 1973. His film acting included *The Spy Who Came in from the Cold* (1966) and *Private Benjamin* (1980), his directing included *Custer* (1967), and he appeared in TV programmes such as *Columbo* and *Hawaii Five-O*. British actress Zoe Wanamaker (1949–) is his daughter. KN

Wang Shifu (Wang Shih-fu) (probably mid- to late-thirteenth century) Chinese dramatist. The author of China's best-loved romantic drama *The Romance of the Western Chamber*, Wang is credited with a total of fourteen *zaju, of which only two others are extant: *The Hall of Beautiful Spring* and *The Tale of the Dilapidated Kiln*. As a cycle of five linked pieces, *The Romance of the Western Chamber* is almost unique in the Yuan Dynasty *zaju repertoire, nearly all of which consists of single four-act plays. Wang was dramatizing a love story already popular in a twelfth-century version, and five more of his plays are known to have shared plots with other *zaju. This apparent angling after popular success suggests Wang may have been an educated professional in the first great age of Chinese theatre. KC

Wannous, Sadallah (1941–97) Syrian playwright. Drama study in Paris exposed him to the theatre of the *absurd and the student uprisings of the late 1960s. Shattered by the 1967 Arab defeat by Israel, on his return to Syria he wrote a politically daring play, *An Entertainment on the Occasion of the 5th of June* (1969), which was published and produced in Beirut before it was licensed in Damascus in 1971. His other works include *The Elephant, Oh Lord of Ages* (1969) and *The

Adventure of Slave Jaber's Head (1972), both deeply influenced by *Brecht. He collaborated with Fawaz al-Sajer in launching the government-subsidized Experimental Theatre, and wrote adaptations from *Gogol, *Weiss, and *Buero-Vallejo. Diagnosed with cancer in 1992, Wannous feverishly wrote plays which had successful productions in Cairo, Damascus, and Beirut: *Historical Miniatures, Rituals of Signs and Transformations, The Drunken Days*, and *The Epic of Mirage*.   RI

Warchus, Matthew (1966–) English director. Since his West End debut with *Much Ado About Nothing* (1992), he has directed for the *Royal Shakespeare Company, the *National Theatre, the West End, and Broadway, associated at first with the plays of Ben *Jonson. Noted for his ability with classical and commercial theatre, *musicals, plays, and *opera, Warchus's characteristic skill is handling finely nuanced texts as well as large-scale spectacle. *Reza's three-hander, *Art* (London 1996, New York 1997), brought his first Tony nomination, while his version of *Lord of the Rings* (2007), for which he wrote book and lyrics, became the largest production ever on the West End stage. He won the 2009 Tony for Best Director (Reza's *God of Carnage*) and was also nominated that year for *Ayckbourn's *The Norman Conquests*.   MW

Ward, Douglas Turner (1930–) *African-American actor, director, and playwright. Ward acted *Off-Broadway and had a small part in the original cast of *Hansberry's *Raisin in the Sun* (1959), but his contributions in 1965–6 set his career. He wrote and acted in two one-act *comedies, *Day of Absence* and *Happy Ending*, which *satirized white supremacy and had an extended run Off-Broadway. Then he published an article in the *New York Times*, 'American Theatre: for whites only?', a call for a permanent African-American theatre, fashioned along lines set out by W. E. B. DuBois in the 1920s. Ward's timing was good; US cities were racially explosive and social countermeasures were urgently needed. With a large grant from the Ford Foundation, Ward established the Negro Ensemble Company in 1967, and became its *artistic director. He acted in or directed many of the company's major productions, including *Elder's *Ceremonies in Dark Old Men* (1969), Joseph Walker's *The River Niger* (1972), Samm-Art Williams's *Home* (1979), and *Fuller's *A Soldier's Story* (1981).   BBL

Ward, Nick (1962–) Anglo-Australian playwright and director. After winning *Edinburgh Festival Fringe First awards for student adaptations of Kafka and *Lawrence, Ward established

an intense, elliptical style with the Fenland *tragedy *Apart from George* (1987). The East Anglian landscape reappeared in *Trouble Sleeping* (1995). This reworks two *characters, a mother and son, from *The Strangeness of Others* (1988), in which an atypically large cast of disparate Londoners hides a very domestic story about two estranged brothers. After a period writing for the screen, Ward returned with *The Present* (1995), about a British-based Australian going home to a world of sexual tension and uncertain reality. Ward also co-wrote the libretto for *The Cenci* (1998), a *music drama based on *Artaud.   CDC

Warner, David (1939–) English actor. Warner joined the *Royal Shakespeare Company where he began fruitful collaborations with *Hall and *Richardson. He was Lysander in Hall's *A Midsummer Night's Dream* (1962), Henry VI in *The Wars of the Roses* (1963), the King in *Richard II* (1964), and Valentine Brose in Henry Livings's *Eh?* (1964). In 1965 he was one of the decade's definitive Hamlets in Hall's production, which failed with critics but captured the imagination of its young *audience. Subsequently he appeared in *Gogol's *The Government Inspector* (1970) and in *Hare's *The Great Exhibition* (1971). An eclectic catalogue of film roles veers from the extraordinary to the journeyman: among the most interesting are the title part in *Morgan: A Suitable Case for Treatment* (1966), Lance Bombardier Evans in *The Bofors Gun* (1968), and the father in *The Company of Wolves* (1984). A revival of his stage career brought King Lear at *Chichester (2005) and Falstaff in *Henry IV* at the RSC (2007).   AS

Warner, Deborah (1959–) English director who founded Kick Theatre in 1980. Warner was resident director at the *Royal Shakespeare Company 1987–9, where her *Titus Andronicus* and *King John* were praised for their clarity and energy. Her long collaboration with Fiona *Shaw began when she directed her in *Electra* (1988) and *Good Person of Setzuan* (*National Theatre, 1989). Warner's 1990 appointment as associate director for the NT established her as one of a new generation of innovators. That year she directed Brian Cox and *McKellen in *King Lear*, and in 1991 directed Shaw in *Hedda Gabler* (*Abbey Theatre) and in *Electra* (London), and in 1995 as Richard II (NT). Her direction has extended beyond classical texts to site-specific work in the St Pancras Chamber Project (1995) and Euston Tower Project (1999), *The Waste Land* (with Shaw, 1995), Britten's *The Turn of the Screw* (1995), the *St John Passion* (2000), and a film, *The Last September* (2000), based on Elizabeth

Bowen's novel. Her recent work with Shaw includes *Medea* (Dublin-London 2000-1), *Beckett's Happy Days* (NT, 2007), both of which went to New York, and Brecht's *Mother Courage* in *Kushner's translation (NT, 2009). RVL

Warren, Mercy Otis (1728-1814) American playwright and historian. Warren was intimately involved in American revolutionary pamphleteering before and during the War of Independence. Plays attributed to her, printed anonymously in periodicals and as pamphlets, include *The Adulateur* (1772), *The Defeat* (1773), and *The Group* (1775), all of which criticized Massachusetts Governor Thomas Hutchinson and British colonial policies, and encouraged revolutionary activity. After the war she wrote (among others) *The Sack of Rome* and *The Ladies of Castile* (1790). She also completed a three-volume history of the United States in 1805. SEW

Warren, William (the Elder) (1762-1832) English-born actor and *manager. He began his career in 1784, and joined Tate *Wilkinson's company in 1788 where he supported Sarah *Siddons. Emigrating to America in 1796, Warren was hired by *Wignell for Philadelphia's Chestnut Street Theatre, where his first role was Friar Laurence in *Romeo and Juliet*, followed by Bundle in *The Watermen*. An instant success, he devoted the remainder of his career to Philadelphia and Baltimore. With William Wood he took over the Chestnut Street and ran it successfully until his retirement in 1829, along the way discovering *Forrest. Primarily a comic actor, Warren was noted for his Anthony Absolute, Toby Belch, Falstaff, and Peter Teazle. With his third wife Esther Fortune (Joseph *Jefferson's sister-in-law) he had six children, all of whom worked in the theatre, the most famous being William Warren the Younger (1812-88). TFC

Washington Square Players American theatre group operating 1914-18, reorganized in 1919 to form the *Theatre Guild. Like the *Provincetown Players, the Washington Square Players emerged from a group of intellectuals, artists, and political radicals who frequented the Liberal Club, near Washington Square in Greenwich Village. They produced 62 one-act plays and six longer plays over the course of three and a half years and pushed the *Little Theatre movement toward a semi-professional state while mounting acclaimed productions of modern plays. Operating on a subscription basis and *managed by a five-member committee, the group offered a season in 1915, mixing short plays by *Maeterlinck, *Chekhov, and *Wedekind

with new American drama. The WSP expanded operations in 1916 to include *tours and moved to a larger theatre. The loss of personnel to the draft and overwhelming debt forced them to close in 1918. MAF

Wasserstein, Wendy (1950-2006) American playwright whose commercially successful *comedies show women trapped between modernity and convention. *Uncommon Women and Others* (New York, 1977) uses her undergraduate experience at Mt Holyoke College to critique the possibilities for women. In *Isn't It Romantic* (1981) two young women grapple with the pressure to marry. *The Heidi Chronicles* (1988) follows the feminist movement and its disillusions through one woman's life; it won both the Pulitzer Prize and the Tony award. In *The Sisters Rosensweig* (1992) three middle-aged sisters support and struggle with one another and come to terms with their Jewish heritage, while *An American Daughter* (1997) suggests pitfalls for women in public office. The last three plays were developed at the Seattle Repertory Theatre and directed by Daniel Sullivan. Wasserstein's other plays include *When Dinah Shore Ruled the Earth* (1975, with Yale classmate *Durang), *Tender Offer* (1983, film 1998), and *Miami* (1986). Her last produced play was *Third* (2005). FL

Waterhouse, Keith (1929-2009) English writer. Much of his theatre, film, and television writing was in collaboration with Willis Hall (1929-2005). Their early successes include the adaptation of Waterhouse's novel *Billy Liar* (1960), *Celebration* (1961), and *All Things Bright and Beautiful* (1962), which established their reputation as wry and astute observers of British provincial, and in particular Yorkshire, mores. In contrast their saucy hit play *Say Who You Are* (1965) tells of a *ménage à trois* in Knightsbridge. Independently and in partnership with Hall, Waterhouse adapted several foreign plays, including *de Filippo's *Saturday, Sunday, Monday* (1973) and *Filumena* (1977); adaptations of novels include *Mr and Mrs Nobody* (1986, from *The Diary of a Nobody*), *Bookends* (1990, from *The Marsh Marlowe Letters*), and *Our Song* (1992, from his own work). One of Waterhouse's most popular pieces is *Jeffrey Bernard Is Unwell* (1989), based on the louche writing of the *Spectator* columnist. AS

Waters, Ethel (1896-1977) *African-American singer and actress who began her career in Philadelphia, literally stopping the show with her rendition of 'St Louis Blues'. Eight years later she was billed as 'Sweet Mama Stringbean' in New York.

She soon appeared in *revues such as *Africana, Paris Bound, Blackbirds of 1928*, and in Irving *Berlin's *As Thousands Cheer* (1933), where she sang 'Suppertime'. She launched her acting career in 1939 with *Mamba's Daughters*, and appeared in *Member of the Wedding* (1950), which was made into a film. In her later years she toured with the evangelist Billy Graham.   BBL

Waterston, Sam (1940–) American actor. Waterston first appeared on Broadway as Jonathan in *Kopit's *absurdist Oedipal tale *Oh Dad, Poor Dad . . .*(1963), and then worked almost exclusively *Off-Broadway. He originated the roles of Kent in *Shepard's *La Turista* (1967) and Thomas Lewis in *The Trial of the Catonsville Nine* (1968). The turning point of his career occurred when *Papp cast him as Benedick in the *New York Shakespeare Festival's *Much Ado About Nothing* (1971). Waterston received Obie, Drama Desk, and New York Critics Circle awards for his performance, and played major roles for the festival throughout the 1970s, appearing in *The Tempest* (1974), *A Doll's House* (1975), *Hamlet* (1975), *Henry V* (1976), and *Measure for Measure* (1976). His Tom in a teleplay of *A Glass Menagerie* (1973) was well received, and thereafter he worked increasingly on screen, most notably as the journalist Sydney Schanberg in *The Killing Fields* (1984) and as prosecutor McCoy in the long-running TV series *Law & Order* (from 1990).   JAB

wayang kulit *Shadow-puppet theatre of Indonesia. *Wayang* ('puppet') is the traditional theatre of Java and Bali in which a *dalang* (puppet master) uses *puppets, *masks, or people to narrate a story to the percussive music of a gamelan orchestra. *Wayang kulit* (literally, 'hide puppet') uses figures made of water buffalo skin. The single puppeteer-narrator sits behind a white screen, using a lamp to create the shadows. The puppets are displayed on a horizontal banana tree board which sits atop wooden legs, where they lie ready for use. A set includes about 100 puppets on Bali and over 300 puppets on Java, and as many as 50 figures can be used in a single performance. Delicate manipulation, complex formulas in archaic language, virtuoso singing, dexterous vocal technique, intricate plot patterns, and bawdy humour are combined in a remarkable performance by the *dalang*, who improvises inside a pattern of formulaic songs and narratives. His presentations, which are hired by a family or village for a rite of passage celebration, may last up to eight hours. *Wayang kulit* relies on stories from the *Mahabharata* and *Ramayana*, while *wayang gedog* dramatizes the escapades of the amorous east

Javanese Prince Panji. Local histories and contemporary tales may also be performed.

Played on Java since at least the ninth century, *wayang kulit* was probably first introduced in the Hindu-Buddhist period which began in AD 78. Early Javanese models influenced shadow-puppet genres throughout all of South-East Asia. When the court of Majapahit, the last Javanese Hindu-Buddhist dynasty, moved to Bali at the end of the fifteenth century, some *dalang* followed, laying the framework for *wayang parwa*, the popular shadow-puppet theatre of that island. At the same time Islam brought innovations to Java, including an elaboration of music and a greater stylization of the figures. Philosophical developments were made in the Dutch colonial period also, as Javanese aristocrats, disenfranchised from political pursuits, invested enormous energy in court performance. Despite its traditional nature, Javanese *wayang kulit* has undergone numerous alterations. In the second half of the twentieth century the *dalang* Nartosabdho was a major innovator, while radio and television have tended to make performance less ritualistic and more entertaining.   KFO

Webb, John (1611–72) English architect and designer. Educated at the Merchant Taylors' School, London, Webb became Inigo *Jones's assistant in 1628 and later married into his family; some architectural plans for Jones's court *masques are in his hand, but may be later copies. In 1656 he designed the production of *Davenant's *The Siege of Rhodes* at Rutland House, which saw the English public stage's first use of the *proscenium arch and painted scenery, strategies that had been pioneered by Jones in the court theatre of the 1630s and before. In 1665 Webb designed the Hall Theatre, Whitehall, as a replacement for the *Cockpit-in-Court.   MJW

Webber, Andrew Lloyd See LLOYD WEBBER, ANDREW.

Weber, Joseph (1867–1942) and **Lew Fields** (1867–1941) American comedians and *producers. The two became childhood friends and began appearing at the age of 10 in *variety halls and beer gardens with their own song, *dance, and *slapstick acts—sometimes in Irish or German dialects. In 1881 they created their signature characters of Mike (the short, padded Weber) and Meyer (the lanky Fields), which they *toured across the country. By the 1890s they headed three touring companies. In 1896 they leased the Imperial Theatre and renamed it the Weber & Fields Music Hall, where they played and presented such talent as Lillian

*Russell. Following a disagreement, the pair separated in 1904, but reconciled in 1912 with shows titled *Hokey Pokey* and *Roly Poly*. From 1914 to 1927 they appeared in a series of silent films, including *Mike and Meyer*, and in the sound films *Blossoms on Broadway* (1937) and *Lillian Russell* (1940). CT

Webster, Benjamin (1797–1882) English actor, *manager, and playwright. Webster played *Harlequin and Pantaloon in *pantomime before joining *Vestris's company at the Olympic Theatre in 1830. He was *actor-manager at the *Haymarket (1837–53) and the Adelphi (1844–76), supported for some years by his partner, Madame *Celeste. At the Haymarket he introduced stall seats in 1843 and put backs on the pit benches. He secured the services of leading playwrights and engaged first-rank actors in good productions: the *Keans in *As You Like It*, *Bulwer-Lytton's *The Lady of Lyons*, and in *Knowles' new play *The Rose of Aragon* (1842); *Macready in the first performances of Bulwer-Lytton's *Money* (1840); *Taylor and *Reade's *Masks and Faces* (1852), with himself as the penurious poet Triplet. He also staged a revolutionary *Taming of the Shrew* in 1844 on an approximation of an Elizabethan stage. As a dramatist Webster wrote some 50 plays, mostly *melodramas and adaptations of novels. A versatile performer, he played *comedy and pathos with equal effect; in his later years he became an excellent character actor. Webster's Petruchio and Malvolio were much praised, and he was a sinister and malignant Tartuffe. MRB

Webster, John (*c.*1580–*c.*1633) English dramatist. The son of a coach-maker, he was born in London and educated at the Merchant Taylors' School. He first worked in the theatre in 1602 as a contributor to three syndicate-written plays for the *Henslowe companies. In 1604 the King's Men (*see* CHAMBERLAIN'S MEN, LORD) hired him to adapt *Marston's *The Malcontent* for adult actors, and in 1604–5 he collaborated with *Dekker on *Westward Hoe* and *Northward Hoe*. Webster offered his first solo play, *The White Devil* (1612), to the Red Bull, the most downmarket of the London *amphitheatres. It proved unsuccessful with the house's plebeian *audience, possibly because of the *tragedy's allusive language and dense storytelling. Webster's next play, *The Duchess of Malfi* (1613), has a similar style but a simpler narrative, and is more ambitious in its use of spectacle. A dark tragedy about the conflict between sexual desire and social honour, it was produced by the King's Men with John *Lowin and Richard *Burbage in the leading roles; it remained in their repertory until the 1630s.

These two tragedies are widely known for their gruesome qualities, a preconception that influenced productions in the twentieth century, which were frequent. They also display attention to latent psychological states, to disempowered figures like women and servants, the *characters' almost indestructible vitality in defiance of law and convention, and show deep political sophistication. Webster's later *tragicomedy *The Devil's Law-Case* (1619) is less often seen, but offers one of Jacobean drama's best roles for an older woman. During the 1620s he returned to collaboration, working with *Middleton (*Anything for a Quiet Life*, 1621), *Rowley (*A Cure for a Cuckold*, 1624), and *Heywood (*Appius and Virginia*, *c.*1627); he was also employed by the King's Men, along with *Massinger and *Ford, to finish *Fletcher's last play, *The Fair Maid of the Inn* (1626). MJW

Webster, Margaret (1905–72) English director. She began as a performer for *Greet's company and at the *Old Vic. Her first directorial triumph was *Richard II* in New York, starring Maurice *Evans (1937). Another notable success with Shakespeare was *Othello* in 1942; controversially, she cast the *African-American Paul *Robeson in the lead. Webster also directed many classical productions for Marweb, her bus and truck company which toured America in the late 1940s, and she was the first woman to direct at the Metropolitan Opera House. Webster liked bustle, crowds, energy, and visual detail. She did significant research for her productions, and wrote about her work in *The Same Only Different* (1969) and *Don't Put your Daughter on the Stage* (1972). Webster's career in America was disrupted after she was investigated by Senator Joseph McCarthy and subsequently she found it easier to find work within the university system and in the UK (for example, at Stratford in 1956 and the Old Vic in 1957). EJS

Wedekind, Frank (1864–1918) German playwright and actor. After visiting Paris in 1892 he appeared as an physically intense and accomplished performer in satirical *cabaret in Munich. Influenced by *naturalism, he began writing social dramas, but without the same level of *realism. His best-known play, *Spring's Awakening* (written 1891), was first performed in 1906, directed by *Reinhardt. Containing scenes of homosexual love, masturbation, and flagellation, the piece is a disturbing condemnation of how an oppressive society deals with puberty. Its provocative content, episodic structure, abrupt language, and two-dimensional and symbolic *characters, like the Man-in-the-Mask played at its première by the author, all anticipate *expressionism. His 'Lulu plays', *Earth Spirit* (1898) and *Pandora's Box* (1904), have as their central figure Lulu, memorably played by Louise Brooks in Pabst's silent film version (1929), a purely sexual creature who drives men to ruin. Finally she meets her nemesis by being murdered by Jack the Ripper, one creature of instinct destroyed by another. At the Leipzig première of *Earth Spirit* Wedekind played the male lead, Dr Schön. In both these plays, which deliberately sought to outrage bourgeois society, Wedekind reflects the concern of the time with sexuality and with the perceived threat of powerful women. His other major plays, while still satirical, are gentler in tone. *The Marquis of Keith* (1901), one of *Jessner's outstanding productions in 1920, deals with an amoral confidence trickster. Wedekind was repeatedly in trouble with the *censor and in 1899 was imprisoned for political *satire, a theme he addressed in his one-act play *Censorship* (1900).   MWP

Weigel, Helene (1900–71) Austrian actress and *manager. Weigel moved to Berlin in 1922, working with *Jessner and *Engel. She met *Brecht in 1923, and they married in 1929. Weigel was developing a reputation for performing working-class characters, enhanced by her performance in Brecht's *The Mother* (1932). Weigel, Brecht, and their two children fled Nazi Germany in 1933. Weigel performed the title role in the première of Brecht's *Señora Carrar's Rifles* (Paris, 1937), repeated in Denmark (1938), along with an early version of *Fear and Misery of the Third Reich*. She did not appear on stage again until 1948, when she played the title role in Brecht's adaptation of *Antigone* in Switzerland. The following year she played the title role in Brecht's *Mother Courage* in East Berlin, where its success helped win state support for the *Berliner Ensemble, which Brecht founded in 1949 with Weigel as *artistic director. The Ensemble *toured a 1951 restaging of *Courage* to Paris (1954) and London (1956). Weigel's performance, informed by simplicity and an understated emotional intensity, won recognition as one of the greatest in twentieth-century European theatre. Weigel led the Ensemble through a critical transition after Brecht's death in 1956, turning it into a company defined by Brecht's ideas rather than his ongoing work. She also continued to organize tours exhibiting old and new successes. These included Brecht's 1954 production of *The Caucasian Chalk Circle* with Weigel as Natella Abashvili and a 1964 production of *Coriolan* in which she played Volumnia. These tours secured the company an international reputation and helped provoke widespread interest in the principles and practices of *epic theatre.   JR

Wei Liangfu (fl.1522–73) Chinese music master, entertainer, and sometime physician; revered as the 'Sage of Song' by lovers of *kunqu. By 1600 he was a semi-legendary figure, reputed to have remained in a room for ten years while he forged a refined style of Kunshan music from folk forms. More likely he was one of several musicians who refined Kunshan music in a period from 1506 to 1566, establishing it as the pre-eminent style of southern drama (*kunqu*). His *Rules for Song* instructs composers to distinguish each song's mode and key and master each word's tone and articulation, so that tune and text will harmonize. Aesthetically, Wei sought to place southern opera on a par with that from the north. He believed that the slow and expressive southern songs, accompanied by woodwinds, complemented the taut and urgent northern songs, which were sung to stringed accompaniment.   CS

Weill, Kurt (1900–50) German composer. The son of a cantor, Weill established himself as a composer of instrumental music before devoting himself to theatre. He worked with *Kaiser on his first *opera, *The Protagonist* (1926), then collaborated with *Brecht in 1927 on the 'Songspiel' *Mahagonny* around Brecht's poems. Weill complemented the dark, socially critical texts with *music that powerfully combined the modernist idiom with popular traditions and contemporary 'low-art' music, especially jazz and ragtime. They developed the piece into a full-scale opera, *Rise and Fall of the City of Mahagonny* (1930). Meanwhile, they capitalized on their distinctive style with a work for singing actors, the wildly successful *The Threepenny Opera* (1928). A hurriedly completed follow-up project, *Happy End* (1929), was much less successful. Weill also helped Brecht develop the overtly political, didactic *Lehrstücke* (learning plays) he began writing in the late 1920s. Weill provided music for the 'school opera' *He Said Yes/He Said No* (1930) and, with Paul Hindemith, for the cantata *Lindbergh's Flight* (1928).

Weill married the actress and singer Lotte *Lenya in 1926; they divorced in 1933 when Weill left Nazi Germany but remarried in 1937. Emigrating to the USA after two years in Paris, he began a successful second career composing *musicals. Of his eight Broadway shows, the two biggest successes were *Lady in the Dark* (1941, book by Moss *Hart, lyrics by Ira *Gershwin) and *One Touch of Venus* (1943, Ogden Nash and

S. J. Perelman). Perhaps his most influential American work was his 'Broadway Opera' *Street Scene* (1947, Elmer *Rice and Langston *Hughes).   JR

Weimar Court Theatre Under the direction of *Goethe from 1791 to 1817, the court theatre at Weimar became the model for German repertory theatres during the nineteenth century. Its repertoire balanced classics, modern dramas, and light entertainment, its *acting company developed an ensemble approach to performance, and, during the years Goethe and *Schiller worked together (1799–1805), some basic principles of *directing were explored. In the performance of *tragedy the company was guided by Goethe's 'Rules for Actors', which encouraged a noble demeanour on stage, reminiscent of classical statuary, a style emulated by German actors throughout the nineteenth century. Only one Weimar actor, Pius Alexander Wolff, achieved national fame, when he left the company in 1816 to become leading tragic actor at the Berlin Royal Theatre. Goethe, who never greatly appreciated the position of director, resigned in 1817 when the Duke of Weimar insisted a dog be introduced on stage.   SJCW

Wei Minglun (1941–) Chinese playwright of *chuanju*, the regional music drama of Sichuan (*see* DIFANGXI). The son of a *chuanju* drummer and scriptwriter, Wei's career as an actor started at the age of 9 and he gradually learned directing and playwriting. He received nationwide recognition in the early 1980s when his *chuanju* scripts *Bold Yi*, *The Fourth Daughter*, and *The Scholar of Sichuan* won awards. His 1986 play *Pan Jinlian: the history of a fallen woman* sparked national controversy because of its modernist style and revisionist views of sex and women. Wei's '*chuanju* of the *absurd' was thought by some critics to herald the future of Chinese drama. *Pan Jinlian's* revisionist approach to the archetypal 'bad woman' of traditional Chinese literature and theatre made it appear to advocate sexual liberation. In the 1990s his plays (*Evening Glow on Mount Qi*, *Changing Faces*, and *Du Landuo, the Chinese Princess*) continued to attract critical attention.   SYL

Weiss, Peter (1916–82) German writer. Weiss left Nazi Germany with his parents in 1934. He initially pursued a career in painting, began publishing in 1946, and moved to *avant-garde film during the 1950s. After 1960 he became known in Germany for his fiction and his *puppet play *Night with Guests* (1963), then achieved international recognition with *The Persecution and Assassination of Jean-Paul Marat as Performed by the Inmates of the Asylum of Charenton under the Direction of the Marquis de Sade* (1964). Reflecting Weiss's own political concerns, *Marat/Sade* sets Marat's arguments for political revolution, however bloody, against Sade's endorsement of extreme individual liberation. Inspired by *Artaud's theatre of *cruelty and using songs drawn from *Brecht's *epic theatre, the work was immediately recognized for its power, thanks in part to the international success of *Brook's Artaudian production (*Royal Shakespeare Company, 1964). Weiss himself preferred the more soberly epic East German première, which favoured Marat over Sade.

The Investigation (1965) used transcripts from the 1964 West German investigation into war crimes at Auschwitz to show how the death camp's organization embodied values central to post-war capitalism. An important contribution to *documentary theatre, it premièred in West Berlin, directed by *Piscator, and simultaneously at thirteen other East and West German theatres. *Song of the Lusitanian Bogey* (1967) and the documentary *Vietnam Discourse* (1968) were informed by Weiss's increasing commitment to Marxism. Weiss explored the role of the revolutionary writer in *Trotsky in Exile* (1970) and political liberation and artistic vision in *Hölderlin* (1971). During the 1970s he devoted his energies to a massive three-part novel, *Ästhetik des Widerstands* (1975–81). He finished one more play before his death, *The New Investigation* (1981).   JR

Wekwerth, Manfred (1929–) German director. Wekwerth joined *Brecht as assistant director at the *Berliner Ensemble in 1951. After Brecht's death in 1956 and *Weigel's assumption of command, Wekwerth became the company's chief director from 1960 to 1969. His most famous production was Brecht's adaptation of *Coriolanus*, which *toured to London in 1965 and which he restaged at the *National Theatre in 1973. After a falling out with Weigel, he left the Ensemble in 1969 and wrote *Theatre and Science* (1975), insisting that the spectator was the most important part of the theatrical equation. In 1977 he was reappointed to the board of the Berliner Ensemble and fought to maintain Brecht's heritage and performance tradition. A staunch supporter of the German Democratic Republic, Wekwerth fell into disfavour after reunification and lost his official positions.   CBB

Welfare State International British company, founded in 1968 by John Fox and Sue Gill, that has worked across many hybrid forms of public art, incorporating *clowning, *puppetry, fire sculpture, lantern-making, and diverse *performance art practices. Along with performances, processions, and installations, they devise *rituals for a post-religious society for such moments as birth, naming, partnerships, and death, working with figures and myths from around the world which they see as archetypal. Their eclecticism often harkens back to premodern forms and notions of community. After a nomadic decade in caravans, in 1979 Fox and Gill settled in Ulverston, Cumbria, which has become the base for a loose association of artistic collaborators and for annual summer schools which have influenced many community arts workers and theatre-makers. The company also undertakes large-scale commissions, such as *Raising the Titanic* (1983), a performance in London's Docklands involving 150 people, in which the *Titanic* figured as a Ship of Fools and an image of capitalism, and *Glasgow All Lit Up!* (1990), in which 10,000 people carried lantern sculptures through the streets of Glasgow.   GJG

Weller, Michael (1942-) American playwright. Weller's 1970 London success *Cancer*, a drama of leave-taking about a group of college seniors, established his career at home when it received its American première at Washington's *Arena Stage under the title *Moonchildren* (1972). Directed by Alan *Schneider, the production transferred to New York where critics hailed Weller as a spokesman for the 1960s generation. Many of his later plays chronicle the progress of the counter-culture through the personal and political disillusionments of the 1970s and 1980s. Notable are *Fishing* (1975), *Loose Ends* (1979), and *Split*, a drama about divorce in two parts (1978–80). He also wrote the screenplays for the *musical *Hair* (1979) and *Ragtime* (1980), and has continued to write prolifically for *Off-Broadway and *regional theatres.   JAB

Welles, Orson (1915–85) American director and actor. A polymathic original, Welles often starred in his own productions and sometimes designed them. He made an immediate mark as director in 1936 with his Haitian-inflected (or *'voodoo') *Macbeth*, staged in Harlem in New York, inaugurating Welles's partnership with *producer *Houseman and the 'Negro People's Theatre' unit of the *Federal Theatre Project. The pair founded a classically based unit for the FTP, with Welles staging and starring in visually striking productions of *Horse Eats Hat* (from *Labiche, 1936) and *Marlowe's *Dr Faustus* (1937). When in 1937 *Blitzstein's leftist *opera *The Cradle Will Rock* was banned by the FTP due to political pressures, the pair founded the Mercury

Theatre and continued a remarkable string of productions. Welles set his heavily cut and rearranged *Julius Caesar* (1937) in a fascist state often eerily lit from below and against a blood-red up-stage wall. In 1938 the Mercury staged *The Shoemaker's Holiday, Heartbreak House*, and *Danton's Death*, after which the company dissolved as Welles was lured to Hollywood to begin his film *Citizen Kane* (1940). Welles's stage direction decreased, but his New York productions of *Native Son* (1941), *Around the World* (with music by Cole *Porter, 1946), and *King Lear* (1956), and his London productions of *Moby Dick* (1955) and *Rhinoceros* (1960), showed his abiding, if undisciplined, talent as director and (except for *Native Son* and *Rhinoceros*) centrifugal leading actor.   MAF

well-made play (*la pièce bien faite*) A dramatic structure pioneered by French playwright *Scribe and perfected by his successor *Sardou. The aim was to provide a constantly entertaining, exciting narrative which satisfyingly resolved the many complications and intrigues that drove the story. A well-made play is characteristically based on a secret known only to some of the *characters and usually shared with the *audience, one character trying to keep it hidden or another trying to uncover it. Initial *exposition is normally followed by ups and downs in the characters' fortunes, and will lead to the *scène à faire* (or 'obligatory scene') in which the characters confront each other with this information. The chains of events and the *denouement must all be logical and plausible. The overall structure should also be repeated in each act.

The term has always been a controversial one, *Shaw famously describing it as 'Sardoodledum'. Those for whom writing is a matter of inspiration and sensibility denounce the suggestion of soulless mechanics in the notion of making a play. The tight internal logic of the structure, sharply framed by exposition and denouement, is also anathema to dramatists who look to social and political realities. Further, the idea that there is a universal way of structuring a play 'well' is deeply problematic given the mercurial nature of audience tastes, expectations, and desires. Indeed, Scribe's and Sardou's ruthlessly plausible endings can seem ludicrous to contemporary spectators less concerned with neatness and more attuned to irresolution and moral ambiguity. Nonetheless the form has influenced many playwrights, including *Labiche, *Feydeau, and *Augier, *Robertson, H. A. *Jones, *Pinero, and even *Ibsen, *Rattigan, and *Priestley. Traces of the form continue to be found in writers like *Hare, and it also survives in the rigid rules for screenwriting promoted by Robert McKee in *Story* (1997).   DR

wenming xi *See* HUAJÜ.

Werfel, Franz (1890–1945) Austrian writer. Although primarily known as a novelist, Werfel wrote consistently for the stage. His first phase was *expressionist, with an adaptation of *Euripides' *The Trojan Women* (1916) as an anti-war statement. *The Mirror Man* (1921) is a Faustian story of man's temptation to self-deify, his fall, and his salvation, while *The Goat Song* (1922) deals with the unredeemed animal in man. In the 1920s Werfel turned to historical themes with *Juarez and Maximilian* (1925), followed by *God's Kingdom in Bohemia* (1930). *The Goat Song* and his '*comedy of a *tragedy', *Jacobowsky and the Colonel*, were both produced by the *Theatre Guild in New York in 1926, the latter taken to Broadway in 1944. *The Eternal Road*, a play about the persecution of the Jewish people, with music by *Weill, was directed by *Reinhardt in New York (1937). CBB

Werkteater Amsterdam company which began as a laboratory for theatre research in 1970. The objective of the *collective, founded by twelve actors including Peter Faber and Shireen Strooker, was to produce personal and politically committed work. Inspired by the *Living Theatre and *Grotowski, Werkteater ('work theatre') performances were created through *improvisation and *devising and were intended to initiate discussion with the *audience about current affairs. The company worked in alternative locations like a former factory building, as well as psychiatric and penal institutions, and nursing homes. Sets were bare and *costumes simple. The collective began to disintegrate in the late 1970s, leading to loss of state subsidy in 1988. Thereafter the Werkteater prepared tailor-made productions for trade, industry, government institutions, and other social organizations. TH

Wertenbaker, Timberlake (1951–) Anglo-French playwright, American born, associated with the *Royal Court Theatre in London and *Stafford-Clark. Much of her work, beginning with *New Anatomies* (1981) and *Abel's Sister* (1984), has focused upon history, mythic and documented, and analysed the relationship of language, *gender, and authority. *The Grace of Mary Traverse* (1985) is the picaresque journey of an eighteenth-century woman from innocence to experience; *The Love of a Nightingale* (1988) retells the Greek myth of Philomel and Procne; and *Our Country's Good*, based on Thomas Keneally's novel *The Playmaker*, traces the experience of mounting a theatrical production by the first convicts in Australia. The transformational ex-

perience of theatre is a theme she returns to in *After Darwin* (1998), while *The Break of Day* (1995) is a response to *Chekhov's *Three Sisters*. *Three Birds Alighting on a Field* (1991) explores the art world as a metaphor for contemporary Britain, while *Credible Witness* (2001) returns to loss and cultural identity. Recent plays include *Galileo's Daughter* (2004) and *Divine Intervention* (2006). She has translated works by *Sophocles, *Euripides, and *Marivaux, as well as *Mnouchkine's *Mephisto* (1986). LT

Wesker, Arnold (1932–) English dramatist, the son of Jewish émigrés, who achieved success with his first play, *Chicken Soup with Barley* (1958). His early works combined autobiography and *naturalist form with a strong cultural radicalism. Championed by *Devine and the *English Stage Company, Wesker found a home at the *Royal Court, forming a strong alliance with the director *Dexter. *The Kitchen* (1958) dramatized Wesker's experiences as a chef in a London restaurant. The *Trilogy* (comprising *Chicken Soup*, *Roots*, and *I'm Talking about Jerusalem*) was performed in 1960 to critical and popular acclaim. Wesker was prominent in the activities of Centre 42, an organization that attempted to involve the labour movement in supporting the arts. In the 1970s Wesker disowned his earlier radicalism and began experimenting with non-naturalist forms, seen, for example in *The Merchant* (1977, an adaptation of *The Merchant of Venice*), *Caritas* (1981), *Mothers* (1982), and *Annie Wobbler* (1983)—the last two plays being *monologues. Despite a successful revival of *The Kitchen* in 1994, Wesker was not a significant presence in Britain after 1980 and, like *Bond, has been more popular abroad. He was knighted in 2006. SWL

West, Mae (1893–1980) American actress, singer, and playwright. Born to a corset model and prizefighter, West would one day remark, 'I used to be Snow White, but I drifted.' Winning amateur contests and *stock roles from the age of 8, she performed in *vaudeville and Broadway *revues from 1911 to 1921. West shocked New York in 1926 by writing, *producing, and starring in *Sex*, a story of a prostitute that was closed by the police and landed her in jail. Undeterred, *The Drag* (1927) explored male homosexuality and transvestism. The wit and daring of *Diamond Lil* (1928) provided a perfect showcase for her stage personality, while *Pleasure Man* (1928) was also closed by police. After entering film in 1932, she appeared on stage less frequently: in her 1944 play *Catherine Was Great*, in a revival tour of *Diamond Lil* (1947–51), and in a nightclub act

(1954–9) in which she was worshipped by male bodybuilders.   MAF

West, Timothy (1934–) Versatile English actor whose classical stage work contrasts with his screen comedy. He made his first London appearance in *Caught Napping* in 1959. He was a member of the *Royal Shakespeare Company (1964–6) and of the Prospect Theatre (1966–72), where roles included Prospero, Bolingbroke, and Lear. He was Shpigelsky in *A Month in the Country* for the RSC (1975), Iago at Nottingham (1976), and Shylock at the *Old Vic (1980). For Bristol Old Vic he appeared in the title roles of *The Master Builder* (1989) and *Uncle Vanya* (1990) and as James Tyrone in *A Long Day's Journey into Night* (1991). He was Willie Loman for Theatre Clwyd in 1993, Gloucester opposite Ian *Holm in the *National Theatre's *King Lear* in 1997, and Falstaff, with his son Sam West as Hal, in the English Touring Theatre's *1 and 2 Henry IV* (1996).   AS

White, George (1890–1960) American *dancer, actor, and *producer. Born George Weitz in New York, he danced in *music halls for pennies as a child, and started as a song-and-dance man in *burlesque at 14, appearing prominently in the *Ziegfeld Follies* of 1915. He is best known for producing *George White's Scandals*, a series of *revues that ran through thirteen editions from 1919 to 1939. He had a gift for discovering talented showgirls and promising comedians, many of whom went on to stardom. He often contributed his own words and music, staged and performed numbers himself, and popularized such dances as the Charleston, Black Bottom, and Turkey Trot. CT

White, Patrick (1912–90) Australian writer, Nobel laureate, 1973. While best known as a novelist, White's first play, *The Ham Funeral*, was written in 1947. First seen at the Adelaide Festival in 1962, it was followed by *The Season at Sarsaparilla* (1962), *A Cheery Soul* (1963), and *Night on Bald Mountain* (1964). His non-*naturalistic style separated his work from the surge of nationalist playwriting that began in the late 1960s. However, from the late 1970s White forged important creative relationships with a new generation of Australian directors and actors. Jim *Sharman directed revivals of *Season at Sarsaparilla* (1976) and *A Cheery Soul* (1979), the premières of *Big Toys* (1982) and *Netherwood* (1983), and the film *The Night, the Prowler*. Neil *Armfield directed first productions of *Signal Driver* (1982) and *Shepherd on the Rocks* (1987), and revivals of *Season at Sarsaparilla* (1983) and *The Ham Funeral* (1989).   KMN

Whitehall Banqueting House The principal site for staging court plays in London in the Christmas season from Elizabeth's time. The Elizabethan structure was built in three weeks in 1582, as a wooden frame covered by canvas, shaped like a Tudor great hall, with a wooden dancing floor for staging *masques. A new brick and stone structure was constructed 1606–9, with a wooden interior with columns carved and painted in the Doric and Ionic modes, and elaborate decorative plasterwork. Again it was made to look like a theatre, although its chief role was to stage the elaborate masques of the Jacobean court. The third Banqueting House in Whitehall still survives. Designed by Inigo *Jones, it was completed in 1622. Its interior a perfect double cube, it is a brilliant example of the Palladian courtly style of the time. When the Rubens ceiling was installed in 1635, King Charles feared damage from candle smoke and banned the production of plays and masques.   AJG

Whitelaw, Billie (1932   ) English actress celebrated for *Beckett's plays, often his actress of first choice. Her work in this repertoire began in 1964 with *Play* for the *National Theatre, and continued with *Not I* (*Royal Court, 1973), *Footfalls* (1976), *Happy Days* (1979), and *Rockaby* and *Enough* (1982). She made her London debut in 1954 in *Feydeau's *Hotel Paradiso*. She then appeared in the *Theatre Workshop's *Progress to the Park* (1960), the *revue *England, our England* (1962), and *O'Neill's *A Touch of the Poet* (1962). From 1965 she appeared at the *Chichester Festival and the *Old Vic as well as at the *Royal Shakespeare Company where she played Clare in *Mercer's *After Haggerty* (1971). Other successes included Martha in *Who's Afraid of Virginia Woolf?* at the RSC in 1987. Her screen career was extensive, if never of the first order, including roles in *Lena, Oh my Lena* (1960), *Charlie Bubbles* (1968), *The Dressmaker* (1988), *Jane Eyre* (1996), and *Hot Fuzz* (2007).   AS

Whiting, John (1917–63) English playwright. Whiting was a rarity in pre-1956 British theatre: his plays were cerebral, experimental in form, and challenging in subject matter. Only *A Penny for a Song* (1951, revised 1962) was unreservedly successful. When *Saint's Day* (1951) won a playwriting competition at the Arts Theatre, London, the critics were scandalized by its symbolic textures, allegorical resonances, and strange clashes of register. *Marching Song* (1954), a meditation on the Nuremberg trials, achieves richness through layering classical allusions. *Guthrie, *Devine, *Brook, and *Ashcroft wrote in defence of *Saint's

Day and Peter *Hall commissioned *The Devils* for the *Royal Shakespeare Company's first Aldwych Theatre season in 1961. Loosely based on Aldous Huxley's *The Devils of Loudon* (1952), the play is a thrillingly ragged blending of history and desire that prefigures Howard *Barker. DR

Wignell, Thomas (1753–1803) Anglo-American actor and *manager. A member of *Garrick's company in England, Wignell joined his cousin Lewis *Hallam's American Company in 1774, though the Revolutionary War delayed his American debut until 1785. A small, stooped man with twinkling blue eyes, he became highly successful as a comic actor. After he played the role of Jonathan in *Tyler's *The Contrast* and financed publication of the play, Wignell became associated with the *stock 'Yankee' character. Breaking with Hallam in 1792, he joined the Philadelphia musician Alexander Reinagle to build the elegant Chestnut Street Theatre and assembled a brilliant acting company. Particularly known for comic *opera, they opened Washington's first *playhouse, then expanded to Baltimore, and Alexandria, Virginia. AHK

Wijaya, Putu (1944–) Indonesian playwright, director, and actor. A prolific writer and leader of post-1968 theatre, Wijaya is known for mixing Western and traditional Indonesian performance aesthetics and spirituality. Balinese-born, he performed with both *Rendra and *Noer before heading his own company, Teater Mandiri, in Jakarta in 1972, where he was exclusive playwright and director. Irreverently mixing fantasy and reality, he strove to invoke 'mental terror' in *audiences as an attack against the monotonous rhythms of daily life. His work includes *Ought* (1973), *Gerr* (1980), *Roar* 1982), and *Zetan* (2006). CRG

Wilbrandt, Adolf von (1837–1911) German playwright and director who worked at the *Burgtheater in Vienna in the 1870s and 1880s (*artistic director 1881–8). He maintained the Burgtheater's tradition of performing the classics but added *Raimund, *Gogol, and *Bjørnson to the repertoire. A playwright of considerable renown, he wrote in the tradition of *Schiller for *tragedy and Gustav Freytag for *comedy. *The Master of Palmyra* (1889), written after he had retired, is often thought his best work. CBB

Wilde, Oscar (1854–1900) Irish writer. Influenced by Walter Pater and the aesthetic movement, throughout the 1880s Wilde was prominent in London literary circles as a wit, essayist, and prolific journalist. His controversial novel *The*

Picture of Dorian Gray (1891) was enormously popular. Wilde had written two unsuccessful plays early in his career, but it was not until he turned to society *comedy with *Lady Windermere's Fan* (1892) that he found his mode. Produced by *Alexander in the fashionable St James's Theatre, it was hugely successful. *Lady Windermere* drew upon the French nineteenth-century tradition of the 'woman with a past' play going back to *Dumas *fils*, playing subversively with its implied ethics.

Wilde had established a formula for his next two successes, *A Woman of No Importance* (1893) and *An Ideal Husband* (1895). In each the sentimental architectonics of the *well-made play were retained, while a Wildean dandy voiced the epigrams that punctured and inverted traditional Victorian morality. In his last comedy *The Importance of Being Earnest* (1895), Wilde gave the play over to the dandies and turned the plot into *farce. This 'trivial play for serious people', with its deadpan concentration on muffins, cucumber sandwiches, and the name Ernest, joyously *satirized the surfaces of a society without depth or meaning. Much loved and continually revived throughout the English-speaking world, *Earnest* has sometimes been seen as a forerunner of the modern theatre of the *absurd. Wilde was always prepared to court controversy: his *symbolist drama *Salome*, written in French and translated by his lover Lord Alfred Douglas, was refused a licence by the British *censor. Produced by *Lugné-Poe (Paris, 1896), it was to prove influential in a European symbolist theatre. A series of trials in 1895 led to Wilde's imprisonment for homosexual offences. While in prison, he wrote his most important poem, 'The Ballad of Reading Gaol', and his passionate apologia *De Profundis*, but he was never able to re-establish his career, dying in Paris three years after his release. NG

Wilder, Thornton (1897–1975) American playwright. Sometimes ranked with *O'Neill, *Miller, and *Williams, Wilder was praised by Harold Bloom as 'the grand exception' to America's obsession with domestic *realism and dismissed by *Clurman as a sentimentalist. *The Trumpet Shall Sound* (written 1917) was performed by the American Laboratory Theatre in New York. *The Bridge of San Luis Rey* (1927) became a best-selling novel and won the Pulitzer Prize. A collection of experimental short plays, *The Angel That Troubled the Waters*, was published in 1928 and a group of theatrically challenging short works, *The Long Christmas Dinner and Other Plays*, in 1931. Wilder's reputation was secured when *Our Town* (1938) ran for more than a year and won the Pulitzer Prize. Now a classic, the play employs virtually no scenery and uses the *Stage Manager as a narrator who introduces and controls the *action in a simple telling of daily life, love, marriage, and death in a small New England town. *The Merchant of Yonkers* (1938) was Wilder's first treatment of a *Nestroy *comedy that was better received in *The Matchmaker* (1954) and wildly successful when adapted by Michael Stewart and Jerry *Herman as the *musical *Hello, Dolly!* (1964). Wilder's *The Skin of our Teeth* (1942) has entered the American repertory, beginning with a long-running Broadway production directed by *Kazan and starring Fredric *March and Florence Eldridge as a long-suffering couple who represent the human race's perseverance across millennia. *The Alcestiad* (1955) and *Plays from Bleecker Street* (1962) received respectful reviews but have been rarely revived. MAF

Wild West shows Late nineteenth-century phenomenon that attempted to re-create the American west with displays of riding and shooting and the dramatization of famous frontier incidents. Although *Barnum and others had staged demonstrations of frontier life, Buffalo Bill *Cody assembled a huge company in an outdoor arena in 1883, and his show gained enormous popularity. It featured prominent frontier personages, including Sioux Chief Sitting Bull, dramatizations of frontier incidents, such as Custer's Last Stand, and exhibitions of shooting and riding by performers like Annie *Oakley. Cody's Wild West became such a success in the United States and Europe that it spawned over a 100 imitators. His one-time partner William F. Carver launched his own Wild America company. Gordon W. 'Pawnee Bill' Lillie proved an able Wild West *manager, and his show eventually merged with Cody's. Other influential Wild West companies included the Miller Brothers' 101 Ranch Real Wild West, and Col. Zach Mulhall's Wild West, which starred Will *Rogers, who began as an expert roper before moving on to political commentary. The Wild West shows were a short-lived phenomenon, brought an end by the First World War and the Great Depression. RAH

Wilkinson, Norman (1882–1934) English designer and artist. Wilkinson began as a *costume designer for the *Frohman *repertory season in 1910 at the Duke of York's Theatre in London. Granville *Barker tapped him as scene designer for *The Winter's Tale* (1912) and for scenery and costumes for *Twelfth Night* (1912) and *A Midsummer Night's Dream* (1914). These beautiful, symbolic designs have become classics of modernist Shakespeare, especially the decorated curtains and the colourful, eclectic costumes. Of special note were the gilded fairies in *Dream* and the geometric set and costumes for *Twelfth Night*. In the 1920s Wilkinson worked for *Playfair at the Lyric Theatre Hammersmith, where he continued to work in a non-*realist, impressionist mode. In 1932 he redesigned *Dream* for the *Shakespeare Memorial Theatre at Stratford-upon-Avon. TP

Wilkinson, Tate (1739–1803) English actor and *manager. A highly skilled mimic, Wilkinson was sacked from John *Rich's company because of his indiscreet imitations on stage of Peg *Woffington. Lacking sensitivity—and possessing an overblown ego—he further irritated *Garrick by a similar performance. Fleeing north, he took joint ownership in 1763 of the York theatre, and seven years later became sole manager of the York circuit. Wilkinson used a full company, and gave many successful actors and actresses their first roles, including J. P. *Kemble and Sarah *Siddons. His blustering account, *The Wandering Patentee* (1795), gives valuable insight into provincial management in the eighteenth century. AF

Wilks, Robert (c.1665–1732) Irish actor and *manager, one of the most important actors of the early eighteenth century and a member of famous triumvirate (with Colley *Cibber and Barton *Booth) that ruled *Drury Lane from 1718 to 1732. He began acting in Dublin in 1691. He had an amazing memory and soon mastered a vast array of parts, many of them principal ones, such as Plume in *Farquhar's *The Recruiting Officer*, Sir Harry Wildair in Farquhar's *The Constant Couple*, and Sir Charles Easy in Cibber's *The Careless Husband*. In *comedy he excelled in genteel roles, in *tragedy pathetic ones. MJK

Williams, Bert (1876–1922) *African-American performer. In the 1890s Williams formed a partnership with George Walker and for over ten years produced and starred in popular shows including *In Dahomey, Abyssinia, Sons of Ham,* and *Bandana Land*. Williams and Walker productions were a training ground for many early African-American performers, such as Charles *Gilpin, Florence Mills, and Ada Overton Walker. Williams connected black *musical comedy with the mainstream stage when he joined the *Ziegfeld Follies* in 1910, singing his signature tune 'Nobody', and submerging his eloquence under the veneer of the *clown, the man who was and had nothing. BBL

Williams, Clifford (1926–2005) Welsh director, associate director of the *Royal Shakespeare Company, 1963–91. As director at the Arts Theatre in London his work included *García Lorca's

Yerma (1957) and *O'Neill's Moon for the Misbe-gotten* (1960). In 1963 he mounted *Hochhuth's *The Representative* for the RSC, opening one day after the première in Basel. His most influential Shakespeare production was a voguish all-male version of *As You Like It* (1967) for the *National Theatre, where he also directed *Shaw's *Back to Methuselah* (1969). Hits from this time include Anthony Shaffer's *Sleuth* (1970) and *Tynan's *Oh! Calcutta!* in London and Paris (1970). In 1975 he directed Shaw's *Too True to Be Good* at the Aldwych with *McKellen and *Dench. Following the Broadway revival of *Lonsdale's *Aren't We All?*, in 1986 he directed *Jacobi in *Breaking the Code* for the West End and Broadway. His musical work included *The Flying Dutchman* (London, 1966), *Dido and Aeneas* (1969), *The Rise and Fall of the City of Mahagonny* (Aalborg, 1984), and *Bellman's Opera* (Stockholm, 1990; London, 1992). In 1996 he mounted *Strindberg's *The Father* in New York.   AS

Williams, Emlyn (1905–87) The Welsh Williams ran parallel careers as playwright and actor, scoring an early success opposite *Laughton in Edgar Wallace's *On the Spot* (1930). His plays are characterized by his lyrical Welsh-speaker's English, *well-made construction, and a lifelong preoccupation with criminal psychology, most successfully expressed in *Night Must Fall* (1935). Centring on a young murderer who carries his victim's head in a hat-box and exerts a sexual attraction on the young woman who discovers his secret, the play has been frequently revived, usually as a star vehicle for handsome Welshmen like Richard *Burton and the author himself. Williams also played the lead in his *The Corn Is Green* (1938), a sentimentalized retelling of his own story as the working-class boy led to an Oxford scholarship by a formidable schoolmistress. *The Druid's Rest* (1944) is a witty self-*parody, and *The Wind of Heaven* (1945) locates the Second Coming in the Victorian Welsh valleys. He wrote only two original plays after 1950, concentrating on prose. He toured one-person shows based on the writings of *Dickens (1951), Dylan Thomas (1955), and H. H. Munro or 'Saki' (1977).   CDC

Williams, Harcourt (1880–1957) English actor and director. Williams joined *Benson's company in 1898, in 1903 *toured with Ellen *Terry, and in 1906–7 toured America with H. B. Irving (Henry *Irving's son). Returning to London, he played Valentine in a revival of *Shaw's *You Never Can Tell*, and from 1908 to 1916, when he joined the war effort, appeared in Shaw, Shakespeare, *Ibsen, and Granville *Barker. Influenced by

Barker, he directed innovative productions of Shakespeare at the *Old Vic, where he served as director (1929–33), and also staged Shaw. Much of the rest of his career was dedicated to acting in Shakespeare; he also performed in Barker, *Chekhov and *Pinero.   TP

Williams, Tennessee (Thomas Lanier Williams) (1911–83) American playwright. Born in Mississippi, Williams would mine his southern upbringing, the sufferings of his fragile sister, and experiences of travel and sexual exploration to write some 60 plays, two novels, eight volumes of short stories, three volumes of poetry, and a memoir sensational in its degree of self-revelation. Their depth and quality secured him a supreme stature in American theatre, rivalled only by *O'Neill and *Miller. Williams's childhood in an Episcopalian rectory (the home of his maternal grandparents) coupled with his growing awareness of his homosexual inclinations seems to have instilled in him an Augustinian fascination with the split between spirit and body. Prevented by social strictures from writing openly about homosexual *characters throughout most of his career, Williams transfigured his experiences into those of female characters who, in some of the outstanding plays of the twentieth century—*A Streetcar Named Desire* (1947), *Summer and Smoke* (1948), *The Night of the Iguana* (1961)—suffer the conflicting urges for spiritual transcendence and sexual desire for absolute masculinity, represented through a series of sleek, muscular, self-assured male figures. In some plays, like *Battle of Angels* (1940, revised as *Orpheus Descending*, 1957) and *Sweet Bird of Youth* (1959), an older female is the sexual aggressor and the younger man a stud-for-hire who by story's end is horribly punished by the community for the danger he represents. In others, the desirable man is unavailable to the woman due to probable homosexuality (*Cat on a Hot Tin Roof*, 1955; *Suddenly Last Summer*, 1958; *Period of Adjustment*, 1960), or a surpassing spirituality that has moved him toward chastity (*The Milk Train Doesn't Stop Here Anymore*, 1962). In rare works, such as *The Rose Tattoo* (1951), the frustrated woman and lusty male accommodate one another and the play ends happily.

Another category centres on the struggle of a sensitive artist to cope with life and create art from experience. Such a play began Williams's fame in *The Glass Menagerie* (1945) and he returned to the theme obsessively in works such as *The Two-Character Play* (1967, later as *Out Cry*, 1973) or *Vieux Carré* (1977). A few plays describe the artist's struggle through biography, such as *I*

Rise in Flame Cried the Phoenix: a play about D. H. Lawrence (1959) or *Clothes for a Summer Hotel* (1980) about Scott and Zelda Fitzgerald. Beginning around 1960, Williams entered what he called his 'Stoned Age', a period of fifteen years of alcohol, amphetamines, and barbiturates. He maintained a strict working schedule, but the results were denigrated by critics and did not attract large *audiences. Following the death of his long-time companion Frank Merlo in 1963, Williams suffered a series of psychological and physical breakdowns and hospitalizations. By the time of his *Memoirs* (1975), he claimed to have his addictions under control; but his 1983 death from choking on the cap of a pill bottle cast doubt upon this.

Williams' work often received outstanding productions. His emergence in post-war New York coincided with the careers of designers such as *Mielziner, directors such as *Kazan and *Quintero, and the flourishing of the *Method among a generation of American *actors expertly equipped to enact the poetic *realism of his psychologically complex creations. Kazan's 1947 direction of *A Streetcar Named Desire*, the multi-layered Mielziner set, and the Method performances of *Brando as Stanley Kowalski and Kim Hunter as Stella defined a new American style. Much of that magic was captured in Kazan's screen version (1951), which added the fascination of Vivien *Leigh as the tormented Blanche. Kazan's productions of *Cat on a Hot Tin Roof* and *Sweet Bird of Youth*, and Paul Newman's performances as the sexually charged young men who animated them, were archetypal creations of the realistic theatre of the 1950s. Though *Summer and Smoke* was unsuccessful in its original Broadway staging, Quintero's arena-style revival in 1952 was a landmark of intimate staging in the burgeoning *Off-Broadway movement.   MAF

Williamson, David (1942   ) Australia's most popular and successful playwright, Williamson has an international profile and many of his plays have become films. He established his reputation as a witty satirist dissecting the dilemmas and pretensions of the middle classes in a distinctive Australian vernacular, with plays such as *The Removalists* and *Don's Party* (both 1971). Primarily a *realist writer, Williamson's observations of Australian manners and mores, coupled with incisive social criticism delivered in a comic but confrontational style, saw him rapidly graduate from alternative to mainstream theatre, writing full time from 1972. In *A Handful of Friends* (1976), *Travelling North* (1979), *The Perfectionist* (1982), *Emerald City* (1987), *Money and Friends*

(1991), *Dead White Males* (1995), and *The Great Man and Sanctuary* (2000), Williamson charted the evolution of Australia's baby-boomer sensitivities to great commercial and critical acclaim. He regularly engaged in high-profile disputes with his critics in the newspapers. Recent work includes *Amigos* (2004) and *Influence* (2005).   SBS

Williamson, J. C. (James Cassius) (1844–1913) American *actor-manager who joined Lester Wallack's New York company in 1863, remaining until 1871. Williamson then moved to San Francisco, where he produced *Struck Oil* as a vehicle for himself and his first wife Maggie Moore (1851–1926). The Williamsons were engaged by George Coppin for a highly successful Australian *tour of *Struck Oil* in 1874, and the next year toured India, Britain, and the USA. They returned to Australia in 1879 after which Williamson became a major theatrical *manager. His policy was based on importing lavish British and American productions to Australia, with little reference to local conditions. He also acquired the Australasian performing rights to all *Gilbert and *Sullivan works. J. C. Williamson Ltd., established in 1911 and known as 'the Firm', dominated Australian commercial theatre, particularly in the presentation of *musicals, until its demise in 1976.   KMN

Williamson, Nicol (1938–) Scottish actor who joined the *Royal Court for *That's Us* and *Arden of Faversham* (both 1961). At the *Royal Shakespeare Company he appeared in Henry Livings's *Nil Carborundum* and *Gorky's *The Lower Depths* (both 1962). In 1964 the role of Maitland in *Osborne's *Inadmissible Evidence* won him the *Evening Standard* best actor award, and the New York Drama Critics award for the Broadway version. Through the 1960s he appeared as Vladimir in *Waiting for Godot* (1964), Sweeney in *Sweeney Agonistes* (1965), and Poprichtchine in *Diary of a Madman* (1967). In 1969 his performance as *Hamlet* as a rasping anti-*hero divided *audiences and critics. At the same time his reputation as self-destructive, self-critical, mad, bad, and dangerous to know saw his stage career falter. An eclectic catalogue of film roles includes Gunner O'Rourke in *The Bofors Gun* (1968), based on John *McGrath's play *Events While Guarding the Bofors Gun* (1966), Merlin in *Excalibur* (1981), and Badger in *The Wind in the Willows* (1996).   AS

Wills, W. G. (1828–91) Irish playwright and painter. Wills was a man of eccentric habits and bohemian lifestyle. He wrote 40 plays, mostly *romantic dramas. His first successful piece, *Olivia* (1878), at the *Royal Court in London, a version of

*Goldsmith's novel *The Vicar of Wakefield*, gave Ellen *Terry a great hit. A religious drama, *Claudian* (1884), had a good run for Wilson *Barrett at the Princess's. Wills wrote several poetic dramas for *Irving, notably *Charles the First* (1872) and *Faust* (1885), which Irving performed 792 times at the Lyceum, in the provinces, and in America— his greatest managerial success.   MRB

Wilson, August (1945–2005) American playwright. Born in Pittsburgh of mixed parentage, he took his mother's surname to confirm his *African-American heritage. He discovered the history and power of black culture through the blues: 'I got Bessie Smith one day and Malcolm X the next, and I was ready.' The first play in his authentic voice was *Jitney* (1979), using a gypsy cab office as the setting for a torrent of aspiration, conflict, and often comic storytelling. His breakthrough came in 1982 when the Eugene O' Neill Theatre Center accepted *Ma Rainey's Black Bottom* for development. That began his collaboration with black director Lloyd *Richards, who helped shape his first six plays. *Ma Rainey* went quickly to Broadway (1984), where it won the first of Wilson's unprecedented number of awards for best new American play.

From the start Wilson planned to set a play about black life in each decade of the twentieth century; he completed the ten just before his early death. After *Ma Rainey*, the 'Pittsburgh Cycle' continued with *Fences* (1985), *Joe Turner's Come and Gone* (1986), *The Piano Lesson* (1989), *Two Trains Running* (1990), *Seven Guitars* (1995), *Jitney* (revised, 1996), *King Hedley II* (1999), *Gem of the Ocean* (2003), and *Radio Golf* (2005). After changes at several *regional theatres, each achieved its final version on Broadway. Though not all were profitable, all went on to be widely staged in the US and abroad. He provided a showcase for an unexpected wealth of black *acting talent, and in controversial public pronouncements, such as his 1997 debate with *Brustein, he became a vigorous spokesman for a black theatre characteristically either marginalized or co-opted by the establishment.

Wilson is no structural innovator, but his fluent, allusive, and poetic vernacular rises to incantatory lyricism, as in the messianic vision in *Joe Turner* of the carnage of the Atlantic slavers. A frequent theme is the search for the individual 'song', the true self that reweaves a culture ravaged by *diaspora and oppression. He finds spiritual resource in historic imagination, such as the ghost at the climax of *Piano Lesson* or the 366-year-old prophet Aunt Esther, born the year African slaves were first forced to Virginia. Sometimes ribald, he can

rise to bleak *tragedy. His rank is with *O'Neill and *Williams as a quintessential American voice.   CR

Wilson, Lanford (1937–2011) American dramatist. Wilson's first work was seen *Off-Off-Broadway: *The Madness of Lady Bright* (1964), *Balm in Gilead* and *Ludlow Fair* (1965), and *The Rimers of Eldritch* (1966). He co-founded the Circle Repertory Theatre in 1969 and served as resident playwright; most of his plays were directed there by Marshall Mason and designed by *Beatty. *The Hot l Baltimore* (1973) was highly successful and became a television series. *The Fifth of July* (1978) presented a caustic picture of post-Vietnam disillusion. *Talley's Folly* (1979), starring Judd *Hirsch, and *A Tale Told* (1981), revised as *Talley and Son* (1985), completed the Talley family trilogy. Later work includes *Burn This* (1987), *Redwood Curtain* (1993), and *Sympathetic Magic* (1997). One of the first openly *gay playwrights to depict gay relationships as part of ordinary life, Wilson shows sympathy to a variety of outcasts. He also wrote for television and film, and translated *Chekhov's *Three Sisters*.   FL

Wilson, Robert (fl.1572–1600) English actor and playwright. Noted for his 'extemporal wit' with Leicester's company and the *Queen's Men from 1572 through 1588, Wilson probably ceased acting in the early 1590s and concentrated on playwriting. Between 1598 and 1600 he collaborated in the writing of fourteen plays for the *Admiral's Men. His extant plays—*The Three Ladies of London* (c.1581), *The Three Lords and the Three Ladies of London* (c.1589), and *The Cobbler's Prophecy* (c.1594)—owe a debt to the older moral *interlude in their emphasis on public ethics and the health of the body politic.   RWV

Wilson, Robert (1941–) American director, designer, playwright, performer, and visual artist, one of the most influential contemporary theatre artists. Born in Waco, Texas, in New York he became interested in choreographers *Cunningham, *Balanchine, and *Graham, and in 1968 set up an experimental theatre, the Byrd Hoffman School of Byrds. His first major productions were *The King of Spain* and *The Life and Times of Sigmund Freud* (1969). His works were praised and decried for their novel approach to the notion of the theatre event: dream-like and indebted to *symbolism, they often took many hours to unfold, seemingly in slow motion, and seldom featured conventionally defined plot, *characters, or *dialogue.

In the early 1970s Wilson worked closely with a deaf-mute boy, Raymond Andrews, whom he had adopted, and in 1971 the 'silent opera' he created with Andrews, *Deafman Glance*, became an international sensation. Some of Wilson's major pieces in the 1970s included *KA MOUNTain and GUARDenia Terrace*, in Shiraz, Iran (1972), and *A Letter to Queen Victoria* in Europe and America (1974–5). This period exhibited a new interest in the deconstruction of language, prompted by a writing and performing collaboration with an autistic young man, Christopher Knowles. Wilson's now legendary collaboration with composer *Glass, *Einstein on the Beach*, premièred in France in 1976 and was at the Metropolitan Opera that year. Wilson's career flourished in Europe in the next decades, when he created original works such as *Death, Destruction, and Detroit* at Berlin's *Schaubühne (1979) and *The Black Rider* (with Tom Waits) in Hamburg (1991). Wilson's most ambitious project remains unrealized: *the CIVIL warS: a tree is best measured when it is down*. This *opera was planned as a collaboration with many international artists and was to première in its entirety at the Olympic Arts Festival in Los Angeles in 1984, but organizational concerns, *finance, and internal politics prevented its completion. Several sections of the production, including its 'Knee Plays' (vignettes which fit between the major sections of action, with music by David Byrne), were produced in international locations.

Wilson has directed for many international opera companies. He has also collaborated with a number of acclaimed rock composers and *avant-garde artists, including playwright *Müller (*Hamletmachine*, 1986), *dancer Lucinda Childs (*Einstein on the Beach* and others), *performance artist Laurie *Anderson (*Alcestis*, 1986), writer Susan Sontag (*Alice in Bed*, 1993), and musician Lou Reed (*Time Rocker*, 1996; *POE-try*, 2000). In 1995 he took to the stage himself in a solo adaptation of *Hamlet*, which *toured around the world. His second collaboration with Waits, an adaptation of *Büchner's *Woyzeck*, premièred in Copenhagen in 2001. His highly active career has continued with productions of Strauss's *Die Frau ohne Schatten* (Paris, 2002), *Ibsen's *Peer Gynt* (Bergen, 2005), *Brecht-*Weill's *Threepenny Opera* (*Berliner Ensemble, 2007), and an adaptation of Shakespeare's sonnets with music by Rufus Wainwright at the same venue (2009). Wilson is the recipient of numerous international honours, and his designs and drawings are often exhibited.   KF

Wilton, Marie (1839–1919) English actress and *manager. She became a star in *burlesque in the 1850s in London. Lively and petite, she was also cast in saucy boys' parts, being much admired by *Dickens in H. J. *Byron's *The Maid and the Magpie* (1858). Tiring of typecasting, she borrowed £1,000 in 1865 and leased the run-down Queen's Theatre in Tottenham Street, renaming it the Prince of Wales's. Deliberately excluding the ginger-beer drinking, orange-eating *melodrama *audience, she renovated the theatre, put white lace antimacassars on the stall seats, flowers in the *auditorium, carpets in the aisles, raised prices, and successfully attracted the carriage trade. Seating only 814, the now-elegant Prince of Wales's resembled a well-appointed drawing room, and drawing-room plays replaced the burlesques of Byron, who withdrew from co-management in 1867. This largely meant the *comedies of Tom *Robertson, in which Wilton played his sunnier and more spirited *heroines, like Mary Netley in *Ours* (1866), Polly Eccles in *Caste* (1867), and Naomi Tighe in *School* (1869). After her marriage to Squire *Bancroft in 1867, she took a back seat in the management. So lucrative were the Robertson comedies that the Bancrofts were able to retire in 1885, after five years at the *Haymarket.   MRB

Winge, Stein (1940–) Norwegian director. Winge's father was a well-known *expressionist artist who designed the scenery for his son's experimental *Antigone* in 1970. Shortly after Winge became a director at the National Theatre in Oslo, where he astonished *audiences with unconventional stagings of *Ibsen, *Strindberg, *Brecht, *Verdi, and *Mozart. His reputation for controversial work grew after 1979, when he became director of the National Theatre's experimental space, especially with his 'poor theatre' *Shakespeare Project* (1983–4). His international career began with an irreverent *Three Sisters* at the Los Angeles Theatre Center in 1985, where he returned annually during the rest of the decade. In 1990 he was named director of the Norwegian National Theatre and inaugurated an annual international Ibsen Festival. In the 1990s he was acknowledged as one of Europe's leading experimental directors of both drama and *opera, outraging some spectators but dazzling others by his unconventional casting, his visual and narrative originality, and his imaginative use of crowds.   MC

Witkiewicz, Stanisław Ignacy (1885–1939) Polish playwright, novelist, painter, and philosopher, known as Witkacy. After service in the Tsarist army, he worked as a formist painter while earning his living as a portraitist. Between 1918 and 1926 he wrote over 30 plays—mostly unpublished and unperformed—that illustrate his theory 'Pure Form in the Theatre' (1920), an anti-*realist doctrine that sought to liberate drama from storytelling and psychology and make it an autonomous formal construction akin to modern painting and music. Characterized by grotesque humour, drug-induced dream logic, hyper-vivid colours, and spectacular stage effects, his plays are both social and existential. They include *They* (1920), *Water Hen* (1921), *Crazy Locomotive* (1923), *Madman and the Nun, Mother* (both 1924), *Beelzebub Sonata* (1925), and *Shoemakers* (1934).

Witkacy's flamboyant life and desperate suicide made him a hero to post-war intelligentsia, who used his works to battle Soviet-imposed *socialist realism. Following *Kantor's revival of *The Cuttlefish* in 1956, premières of Witkacy's plays became major events, his works gradually assimilated into popular culture, *cabaret performance, and rock *musicals. He is now recognized as Poland's leading playwright-theorist of the twentieth century. DG

Wodehouse, P. G. (Pelham Grenville) (1881–1975) English writer. Although chiefly remembered for his Bertie Wooster stories, Wodehouse was a prolific lyricist for *musicals between the wars. He collaborated with *Bolton and *Kern on the Princess Theatre shows in New York, notable for reorienting musical theatre towards an American idiom. Their work together includes *Have a Heart* (1917), *Oh, Boy!* (1917), *Leave It to Jane* (1917), and *Oh, Lady! Lady!* (1918). Wodehouse also contributed the words to the song 'Bill' in Kern's *Show Boat* (1927). His other musical collaborations with Bolton include *Oh, Kay!* (1926) with the *Gershwins and *Anything Goes* (1934) with Cole *Porter. Wodehouse also contributed lyrics to musicals by Irving *Berlin and Ivor *Novello. Comparatively less successful were his straight plays, including *A Damsel in Distress* (1928), *The Play's the Thing* (1926), an adaptation from *Molnár, and *Leave It to Psmith* (1930). MDG

Woffington, Peg (*c.*1720–60) Irish actress, performing in Dublin before 1731. London first saw her in the *breeches role of Silvia in *Farquhar's *The Recruiting Officer* in 1740 at *Covent Garden, but she moved to *Drury Lane the next year and remained for seven seasons, notably playing Cordelia to *Garrick's *Lear* (1742). Their relationship flourished during a *tour to Dublin that summer. She returned to Covent Garden in 1748 after breaking with Garrick (now *managing Drury Lane), but was enticed by Thomas Sheridan to join him at the *Smock Alley Theatre in Dublin (1751–4). When she rejoined Covent Garden in 1754, it was at a salary of £900 a year, making Woffington one of the highest-paid actresses of her day. Three years later she collapsed with a stroke while performing the *epilogue to *As You Like It*, retired to her home in Teddington, and died in London. During her short career Woffington excelled more in comic than tragic roles. RAC

Wolfe, George C. (1954–) *African-American playwright and director. Wolfe received widespread attention for his 1986 play *The Colored Museum*, a series of eleven vignettes satirizing stereotypical depictions of African Americans, seen at the *New York Shakespeare Festival, where *Papp became Wolfe's early champion. Other successes included the 1992 *musical *Jelly's Last Jam*, about jazz legend Jelly Roll Morton, which Wolfe wrote and directed; and *Kushner's *Angels in America*, which earned Wolfe the Tony award for direction in 1993. In that year, Wolfe succeeded *Akalaitis as *producer of the NYSF Joseph Papp Public Theatre and pursued a policy of cultural inclusiveness. He co-created the musical *Bring in 'da Noise, Bring in 'da Funk*, a history of African-Americans told through tap *dancing and rap music, for which he won his second Tony for direction in 1996. Under Wolfe the Public produced a number of new plays and musicals by emerging and established writers, including Anna Deavere *Smith and Suzan-Lori *Parks, and continued the tradition of free outdoor Shakespeare. At the same time Wolfe criticized for promoting his own work, particularly for opening the musical *The Wild Party* on Broadway in 2000, at a considerable loss. He had success again on Broadway with Parks's *Top Dog/Underdog* (2001) and Kushner's *Caroline, or Change* (2004). He left NYSF in 2004 but returned to direct *Brecht's *Mother Courage*, translated by Kushner, with NYSF alumni Meryl Streep and Kevin *Kline (Central Park, 2006). KF

Wolff, Egon (1926–) Chilean playwright. Wolff's first plays were psychological, and while he maintained interest in insecure, obsessive, or victimized *characters, he also treated the social forces that prevented them from living normal lives. In the 1960s he abandoned *naturalist conventions for a *surrealist style, depicting an ambiguous and dream-like world where reality and fiction mingled. *The Invaders* (1963), dealing with middle-class fears of losing social and economic power, anticipated the social conflicts of the Allende regime. *Paper Flowers* (1970), his most accomplished play, is also centred around the clash of social classes and mirrors the violence then escalating in most of Latin America. Although *The Raft of the Medusa* (1980) reiterates the subjects of earlier plays, its impact was heightened by a dictatorship that had deepened the gap between rich and poor. Wolff's other plays include *Kindergarten* (1977), *José* (1980), and *Laura, Talk to Me* (1988).   MAR

Wolfit, Donald (1902–68) Quintessential English *actor-manager. Wolfit was solidly built and somewhat moon-faced, but had undeniable power and stage presence, and a rich and versatile vocal technique (preserved in a number of films including *Room at the Top*, 1959, and *Decline and Fall*, 1968). He acted from 1920 with Matheson Lang's company, at the *Old Vic, and also at the *Shakespeare Memorial Theatre; in 1937 he founded his own company, and toured Britain and the USA for 30 years, giving regular London seasons, and putting on lunchtime Shakespeare performances during the Blitz. He was happy in strong 'heavy' parts, including Tamburlaine, Lear, Oedipus, and the Wandering Jew, but he also played in *Ibsen, *Galsworthy, *Barrie, *Sheridan, and *Shaw, and excelled as Long John Silver. He was sometimes criticized for using less than adequate supporting players, *costumes, and scenery, but his dedication to performing Shakespeare and the classics throughout the country was admirable. *Harwood's *The Dresser* (1980) gives an affectionate though apocryphal picture of Wolfit at work.   EEC

Wood, Charles (1932–) English playwright. Having served in the military, Wood made the absurdity and brutality of warfare a recurring theme in his drama. *Dingo* (1967), a bitter play attacking romantic notions of the Second World War, was written for the *National Theatre but withdrawn because of *censorship problems. He succeeded with his next play for the National, the spectacularly theatrical *H: being monologues at the front of burning cities* (1969), about the Lucknow campaign. During the 1960s Wood wrote the screenplays *The Knack . . . and How to Get It* (1965), *Help!* (1965), *How I Won the War* (1967), and, with *Osborne, *The Charge of the Light Brigade* (1968). The filming of the last of these was the subject of Wood's *comedy *Veterans* (1972), which starred *Gielgud at the *Royal Court. His other plays include *Cockade* (1963), *Meals on Wheels* (1965), *Fill the Stage with Happy Hours* (1966), *Jingo* (1975), *Has Washington Legs?* (1978), *Across from the Garden of Allah* (1986), and an adaptation of Shakespeare's first tetralogy, *The Plantagenets* (1988), for the *Royal Shakespeare Company.   MDG

Wood, John (1930–) Lean and elegant English actor. At the *Old Vic from 1954 and the *Royal Shakespeare Company from 1971, he developed a series of Shakespearian roles. He was

also closely associated with the work of *Stoppard: in 1974 he won awards in London and New York for his performance as Carr, the minor diplomat in *Travesties*. He played in Stoppard's version of *Schnitzler's *Undiscovered Country* at the *National Theatre (1979), where he also appeared in *The Provok'd Wife* (1980) and *Richard III* (1992). Later appearances at the RSC included Prospero in *The Tempest*, Solness in *The Master Builder*, Sheridan Whiteside in *The Man Who Came to Dinner* (all 1989), and the title role in *Hytner's production of *King Lear* in 1990, for which he won the *Evening Standard* award. Film and television appearances include *Nicholas and Alexandra* (1971), *The Purple Rose of Cairo* (1985), *Shadowlands* (1993), and *Chocolat* (2000).   AS

Wooster Group New York performance ensemble which creates dense and challenging works that have sparked praise and controversy around the world. Director Elizabeth *LeCompte and performer Spalding *Gray, among others, founded the company in 1980, out of the remnants of the *Performance Group. They are now resident at the Performing Garage on Wooster Street in SoHo. Their first piece, *The Rhode Island Trilogy*, was inspired by events in Gray's life; gradually the group established a practice of layering text, performance, sound effects, *music, and technical elements including live and recorded video. The company create their performances on a long-term basis, *improvising around ideas and research material. Often the base is an existing text, but one distorted or reshaped; *Miller tried to block the Wooster Group's 1983 production *LSD (Just the High Points . . .)*, because it included a cut-down and sped-up version of his play *The Crucible* alongside depictions and discussions of drug use; the production was forced to close early. The Group's later works, which have gained major international attention through *tours, include *Brace Up!* (based on *Chekhov's *Three Sisters*, 1991, 2003), *O'Neill's *The Emperor Jones* (1993, 2005) and *The Hairy Ape* (at a closed Broadway theatre, 1997), *To You, the Birdie!* (based on *Racine's *Phèdre*, 2002), and *Hamlet* (2007). The other members of the Wooster Group have included Jim Clayburgh, Willem Dafoe, Libby Howes, Peyton Smith, Kate Valk, and Ron Vawter (1948–94).   KF

Worth, Irene (1916–2002) American actress. Worth made her professional debut in 1942 in *Escape Me Never*. In 1944 she left New York for London, where she spent the next 30 years, in order to act and to study *acting. Her portrayal of Celia Coplestone in *Eliot's *The Cocktail Party*

at the *Edinburgh Festival in 1949 established her as one of the most commanding and sensitive actresses of her generation. In the early 1950s she joined the *Old Vic company, where she played Desdemona (1951), Helena in *A Midsummer Night's Dream* (1951), and Lady Macbeth (1952). She opened the *Stratford Festival in Ontario with *Guinness, playing Helena in *Guthrie's production of *All's Well That Ends Well* (1953), and was with the *Royal Shakespeare Company in 1962. She won three Tony awards—for Alice in *Albee's *Tiny Alice* (1965), for Princess Kosmonopolis in *Williams's *Sweet Bird of Youth* (1975), and for Grandma Kurnitz in *Simon's *Lost in Yonkers* (1991)—and an Obie for sustained achievement in 1989. TK

Wright, Garland (1946–98) American director. Wright moved east from Texas in 1969 to act at the American Shakespeare Festival in Stratford, Connecticut, where he made his directing debut in 1973 with *Julius Caesar*. In 1974 he founded the Lion Theatre Company in Manhattan where he defined his artistic style: collaborative script development, precise ensemble *acting, and minimalist staging. In 1976 Wright gained national attention with his production of Jack Heifner's *Vanities*, setting a record for longest-running non-musical *Off-Broadway. Wright won an Obie award in 1977 for his adaptation and production of *K*, based on Kafka's *The Trial*. He was associate *artistic director of the *Guthrie Theatre in Minneapolis from 1980 to 1983, and directed at *regional theatres around the United States. His production of Eric Overmeyer's *On the Verge* won Wright a second Obie (1987). MAF

Wu Hsing-kuo (*pinyin*, **Wu Xingguo**) (1953–) Taiwanese actor and director, whose own productions have toured the globe. Wu trained for the male warrior role type in Beijing opera (*jingju*) and as a modern dancer. After training and a short stint at the Cloud Gate Dance Theatre, Wu founded (with his wife Lin Hsiu-wei, a modern dancer) the Contemporary Legend Theatre in Taipei in 1986, an experimental company known for its adaptation of both traditional *jingju* methods and *Greek and Shakespearian tragedies, including *The Kingdom of Desire* (*Macbeth*, 1986), *Hamlet* (1990), *Medea* (1993), *The Oresteia* (1995), and *The Tempest* (2004). In *Lear Is Here* (2001), a solo performance, Wu played himself and nine characters from the play in various *jingju* role types, male and female. He played the title role in the world premiere of *Snow in August*, written and directed by *Gao Xingjian (Taipei, 2002), and Yin-Yang Master in

Tan Dun's *The First Emperor* at the Metropolitan Opera (New York, 2006). He has also appeared in a number of television series and Hong Kong films. AH

wujü (*wu chü*) Modern Chinese 'dance-drama', inspired by Western *ballet. After the Second World War Dai Ailian, who had studied at Dartington Hall, introduced English ballet to China. Dai became the head of the Beijing School of Dance in 1949 and engaged Russian choreographers to introduce the Russian method. Works such as *Le Corsaire*, *Swan Lake*, and *Giselle* helped produce a new generation of Chinese dancers. Attempts to mix ballet with traditional Chinese *dance resulted in the creation of the first *wujü* in 1959, *The Maid from the Sea*, a story about the love of a mermaid for a young hunter. In the 1960s political themes combined with *wujü* to create revolutionary modern dance-drama; two of these were included in the original eight revolutionary model plays (*geming xiandai xi*). *Red Detachment of Women* (Beijing) was about the struggle between a communist company of women soldiers and a local tyrant on a southern island in the 1920s. *The White-Haired Girl* (Shanghai) told of a girl's rescue by the communist army after living for years in the mountains to avoid a brutal landlord. Although they relied on ballet for their basic form, both *wujü* made considerable efforts to stress the theme of class struggle and the Chinese traditions of choreography, *costume, and *music. In the mid-1970s two more revolutionary *wujü* were created according to this model: *Ode to Yimeng* and *Children of the Grassland*. After the Cultural Revolution *wujü* based on Chinese folk dance were developed, a prominent example being *Legend of the Silk Road* (1985). SYL

Wycherley, William (1641–1715) English playwright. Wycherley's theatrical career was short and eventful. *Love in a Wood* (1671) earned him the friendship of *Buckingham and the favours of the Duchess of Cleveland. *The Gentleman Dancing-Master* (1672), also based on *Calderón, brought him the patronage of the King. Wycherley's two masterpieces, *The Country Wife* (1675) and *The Plain Dealer* (1676), were his last efforts in drama, and his subsequent life was the stuff of his own *comedy. He fell ill, recovered in France, married against the King's will and lost royal favour, engaged in lengthy litigation, was jailed for debt, and had his royal pension rescinded. Seldom debt free and encumbered by a bankrupt estate, Wycherley was tricked into marriage eleven days before his death. *The

Country Wife was controversial in its own time and remains open to a variety of interpretations, but contains lots of ridicule, lots of sex, lots of fun. *The Plain Dealer*, a dark and disturbing comedy, combines sex, sword-play, and intrigue in a bleak version of *Molière's *Misanthrope*.   RWV

Wyndham, Charles (1837–1919) English *actor-manager. Wyndham trained as a doctor and served as a surgeon with the Federal Army in the American Civil War. After acting and *touring in America he went into *management at the new Criterion Theatre in London in 1876. He succeeded with *The Pink Dominos* (1877), *Albery's adaptation of a risqué French *farce. *Robertson's *David Garrick*, which he revived in 1886 and 1888, portraying *Garrick himself, was his biggest hit. Wyndham played the leading characters of the older *comedy, such as Charles Surface in *Sheridan's *The School for Scandal*, and Dazzle in *Boucicault's *London Assurance*, with dash and polish. In the 1890s he took serious roles in the society dramas of Henry Arthur *Jones, especially *The Case of Rebellious Susan* (1894), *The Liars* (1897), and *Mrs Dane's Defence* (1900). With the profits of the Criterion he built the Wyndham Theatre (1899) and the New Theatre (1903). Handsome and distinguished, Wyndham was an actor of great charm and impeccable timing. MRB

Wynn, Ed (Isaiah Edwin Leopold) (1886–1966) American actor and comedian. Wynn entered *vaudeville as a child, taking his stage name in 1904 while *touring. By 1910, he was appearing in *musical comedy and in 1914 became a regular in the *Ziegfeld Follies. With a lisping, lilting voice, wispy hair, and bulbous nose, Wynn developed a devastating knack for absurd statements and the incongruous use of props. Wynn was blacklisted by *producers for his support of the Actors' Equity strike, and henceforward became his own producer for such vehicles as *Wynn's Carnival* (1920), *The Perfect Fool* (1921), and *The Grab Bag* (1924). Wynn's career gradually moved to radio during the 1930s, an exception being the long-running Broadway musical *Hooray for What?* (1937). In the 1950s, Wynn became a television regular and appeared in serious roles in the television production of *Requiem for a Heavyweight* (1956) and the film *The Diary of Anne*

Frank (1959). His last major appearance was as the lovable Uncle Albert in Disney's *Mary Poppins* (1964).   MAF

Wynyard, Diana (Dorothy Isobel Cox) (1906–64) English actress of great beauty and delicacy. Wynyard spent much of the 1920s on *tour or with the Liverpool Playhouse. During the early 1930s she established herself as a commercial star in West End theatre, but moved on to the *Shakespeare Memorial Theatre in Stratford, where she played a wide range of roles including Gertrude in *Hamlet* (1948), Portia in *The Merchant of Venice* (1948), Katherine in *The Taming of the Shrew* (1949), and Lady Macbeth (1949). Her Hermione in *The Winter's Tale* (1948) and Beatrice in *Much Ado* (1949) were considered by critics to be particularly engaging and were reprised opposite *Gielgud in 1951 and 1952. Her last performance was as Gertrude in *Hamlet* for the *National Theatre's opening season in 1963.   TK

Wyspiański, Stanisław (1869–1907) Polish playwright, director, theorist, painter, and poet, who paralleled *Appia and *Craig in creating a modernist *scenography. After his production of *Mickiewicz's *Forefathers' Eve* (1901) Wyspiański was viewed as the *romantic poet's successor. His own plays, including *The Wedding* (1901), *Deliverance* (1903), *Akropolis*, and *November Night* (both written in 1904, produced posthumously), combine *naturalism with *symbolism and historical truth with imaginative poetry. Wyspiański influenced and inspired Polish theatre throughout the twentieth century, his texts providing complex material for directors, designers, and actors. His early major follower was Juliusz Osterwa, who directed and performed in *Deliverance* several times after 1918. *Grotowski mounted *Akropolis* as a shocking and moving metaphor of Auschwitz (1962), while Mieczysław Kotlarczyk treated it as a glorification of culture and freedom and a hymn of hope (Cracow, 1966). *Wajda's production of *November Night* (Cracow, 1974) was the most faithful and most imaginative interpretation of Wyspiański in the latter twentieth century. Wajda, a painter and filmmaker, presented the play as a vast multi-layered canvas with astonishing images, expressive crowd scenes, and sung soliloquies.   KB

Xenopoulos, Gregorios (1867–1951) Greek playwright, born in Constantinople (Istanbul). His first play, *The Soul Father*, was produced by Nikolaos Lekatsas in 1895, followed by *The Third*, which shows *Ibsen's influence in its structure and *characters. In 1904 Constantine Christomanos directed *The Secret of Contessa Valeraina* for the New Stage, and thereafter Xenopoulos wrote over 40 dramas and *comedies, several novels and short stories, as well as essays on *realism and *naturalism. His plays, written in demotic, deal with the psychology and relationships of middle-class *characters in the changing Greek society of the early twentieth century. They include *Stella Violanti* (1909), *The Temptation* (1910), *The Students* (1919), and *Popolaros* (1933).   KGO

Xirgu, Margarita (1888–1969) Catalan actress and director. Beginning her career in the Catalan language in Barcelona, Xirgu moved into Castilian-language theatre after 1912. She dominated Madrid's stage with performances that merged the styles of *melodrama with more *realistic practice. Nurturing and promoting the work of living dramatists, including *García Lorca and *Casona, and staging radical foreign plays, Xirgu helped cultivate the rich theatrical climate of pre-Civil War Spain. *Touring in Latin America when the Civil War broke out, she chose to remain there until her death. She presented world premières in Buenos Aires of seminal works like Alberti's *The Absurdity* (1944) and García Lorca's *The House of Bernarda Alba* (1945), which could not be officially staged in the *censorious climate of Francoist Spain. She initiated various teaching methods in Chile and Uruguay which had a large impact on actor training in both countries.   MMD

Yacine, Kateb (1929-89) Algerian writer. He established his reputation with the experimental novel *Nedjma* in 1957, but the following year produced his first play, *Le Cadavre encerclé* (*The Surrounded Corpse*), and devoted himself primarily to theatre. Partly under the influence of *Brecht, whom he met in Paris in 1955, he turned from a *surrealistic to a more *epic theatre style with strong political engagement. After the independence of Algeria in 1962 he lived primarily in that country, though he wrote in French, and his plays were presented in Paris. In 1971 he turned to creating plays in colloquial Arabic, performed in Algeria by his own troupe, Action Culturelle des Travailleurs d'Alger. The Troupe also performed in Paris in 1975, and *toured the Arabic play *Mohammed, Take your Suitcase* and others to communities of Algerian workers in France. His best-known French play, the *farce *Intelligence Powder*, has also been presented in New York.   MC

yakshagana Traditional theatre form in coastal Karnataka in south India, with variants in other parts of the region. The name literally means 'the song (*gana*) of demi-gods (*yakshas*)' and its origin is obscure, though the *ritual genres in Karnataka, especially *bhutaradhane* (devil worship traditions), contributed to its conventions. Traditionally, *yakshagana* troupes are attached to temples but are not strictly religious. Financed by the village community, performances are held in any open space and last the whole night. The stage is normally a square of 6 m (20 feet) demarcated on the ground, with the *audience on three sides, musicians at a table at the far end. There are no props except a makeshift stool, which might represent a chariot or a throne. A small hand-held curtain often signals the entrance of *characters and there are stock *dances for typical actions, like the 'war-dance pattern' and the 'journey-dance pattern'. After opening procedures, a script based on epic stories is presented in a fast-paced, episodic narrative, mingling songs with improvised *dialogue. It usually climaxes with combat and concludes with a marriage. In the twentieth century *yakshagana* included plots from history and its performances became commercial. Since the 1950s new *yakshagana* troupes have popularized the form with travelling shows which incorporate modern equipment such as tents, chairs, and power generators. In a counter-movement, there have been attempts to salvage *yakshagana* from commercialization by impresarios like Shivarama Karanth, who created his own repertory and training institute to reinvigorate the tradition.   KVA

Yassin, Mustapha Kamil (1925–) Malaysian playwright, also known as Kala Dewata. Emergent in the post-independent Malaysia of the 1960s, he was a leading proponent of modern drama based on Western *naturalistic theatre. He criticized the popular Malaysian theatre of *bangsawan* and *sandiwara* as old-fashioned because of their poetic language, painted backdrops, and intricate or fantastical plots, advocating instead *realism in *dialogue and story. Often set in a living room, his plays tackle social issues such as intergenerational conflict, urban versus rural values, and interethnic disparities. His signature work is *Tile Roof, Thatched Roof* (1963).   CRG

Yates, Mary Ann (1728-87) English actress, the greatest tragedienne between Susannah *Cibber and Sarah *Siddons. Yates quickly came to *Garrick's attention and was employed at *Drury Lane starting in 1754. Her forte was haughty, imperious roles, but her repertory was varied. In *tragedy she played *Rowe's Jane Shore, Monimia in *Otway's *The Orphan*, and Cleopatra; in *comedy she ranged from Indiana in *Steele's *The Conscious Lovers* to Silvia in *Farquhar's *The Recruiting Officer*. Apart from a failed attempt to establish a third winter company at the King's Theatre (*Haymarket) in the 1770s, she acted mainly at Drury Lane and *Covent Garden.   MJK

Yeats, William Butler (1865–1939) Irish poet, who grew by experiment, self-criticism, and observation to a complete man of the theatre. Awarded the Nobel Prize for Literature in 1923, he devoted his speech of acceptance to his work not as poet but as playwright and founding director (1904), with Augusta *Gregory and *Synge, of Dublin's *Abbey Theatre, home of the National

Theatre Society. Yeats found kindred spirits in Lady Gregory and Edward Martyn in 1898, when they established the Irish Literary Theatre to promote a nationalist stage, achieved at the Abbey with the *financial assistance of Annie *Horniman with Yeats as *manager. Yeats became the apologist for the Abbey's aesthetic principles, gradually articulating a theatre distinctively Irish and devoid of English cultural influence.

In his dramas, mostly in verse, Yeats sought to break away from the Shakespearian model, taking variously *Maeterlinck, *Sophocles, *Racine, the *morality tradition, and ultimately Japanese *nō as his models. He required a play to demonstrate clarity, simplicity, and refinement; and meticulously revised his works after observing them staged until he achieved such qualities. For subject matter he turned to Irish sagas about Cuchulain, Deirdre, or Congal, to the Gospels and the life of Jonathan Swift, to Greek myth and Jungian archetypes. But always Yeats's focus was on a heroic life caught at an instant in time when its particular individuality most clearly defines itself through a momentous choice. He devised uniquely personal stage conventions, deploying *masks, *choric utterance, *ritual, or *dance, as ways of conveying his *audiences through the deeply psychological experience his *characters undergo. His plays include the nationalist *The Countess Cathleen* (1899) and *Cathleen ni Houlihan* (1903), *Deirdre* (1906), the nō-inspired *At the Hawk's Well* (1916), *The Dreaming of the Bones* (1931), and the almost-*Beckettian *Purgatory* (1938).

Staging revolutionary drama required a revolution in theatre practice, a new kind of concentration and focus. Disliking what he considered the *melodramatic, egocentric, or fussy mannerisms of English *acting, as a *director Yeats confined movement to the current speaker. This focused audience attention on the verse of the drama. He sought a similar concentration in *scenography, evolving a system of curtained hangings to offset the *costumes. After 1911 he deployed a set of *Craig's screens to achieve architectural settings, aided by sharply angled *lighting. For the dance-plays this system was reduced to a single screen and carpet, with the body of the actor as important as the voice, particularly when a mask limited facial movement.   RAC

Yiddish theatre See DIASPORA.

Ying Ruocheng (Ying Jo-ch'eng) (1929–2003) Chinese performer and director of *huaju (spoken drama). In 1949 he became a founding member of the Beijing People's Art Theatre, recognized as an ensemble devoted to a *realist *acting style. His

performances in *Lao She's *Teahouse* and *Cao Yu's *Thunderstorm* made him a national star. Widely read in Western literature, he played Hamlet, and translated *Stanislavsky into Chinese and twentieth-century Chinese drama into English. The Cultural Revolution interrupted Ying's career, but by 1979 he was able to travel with Cao Yu to the United States where the two avidly caught up on developments in Western theatre. During this visit Ying himself acted in American films and television (including Khubilai Khan in the American TV production of *Marco Polo*). In 1983 Ying brought *Miller to China to direct the People's Art Theatre in *Death of a Salesman*, which Ying had translated, and in which he starred as Willie Loman. In 1986 he was appointed Vice-Minister of Culture.   KC

yokthe pwe *Puppet theatre in Burma (Myanmar). Skilful manipulation of *marionettes is accompanied by spoken *dialogue, song, and orchestral *music. A traditional puppet set consists of 28 jointed, carved wooden figures (about 30 cm/12 inches high), dressed in elaborate silk *costumes, manipulated by twelve to sixteen strings. The puppeteers stand behind a screen or painted backdrop and hold the puppets over the top and in front of the screen on the stage floor. Shows, which might last an hour or all night, begin with an invocation. Routines with wild animals, ogres, and alchemists follow, referred to as the 'Himalayan scenes' and symbolize the chaos of creation. Then one or two puppet dramas will be performed. Their stories are often based on ancient tales of the Buddha's incarnations and include humorous improvised scenes with *clown puppets, and love scenes with a prince and princess. *Yokthe pwe* is thought to have been the inspiration for classical Burmese *dance and drama and was most popular in the eighteenth and nineteenth centuries. Since the late 1980s there has been renewed interest in the form and performances can be seen at pagoda festivals, art academies, and tourist sites.   MSH

Yoruba popular theatre Three Nigerian *actor-managers, Hubert *Ogunde, Duro *Ladipo, and Kola Ogunmola (1925–72) drew on tradition to create popular modern performance with groups willing to face the rigours of the road, presenting work normally developed from narratives they selected themselves. The plots were worked up through *improvisation by performers who tended to specialize in role types (*see* STOCK CHARACTER), relying on Western influenced methods and Yoruba traditions. Ladipo was concerned with authenticity and initially played in cultural centres and on university campuses rather than for the large-scale public attracted by Ogunde's showman tactics, while Ogunmola cultivated an extraordinary rapport with his *audiences through his talents as an *actor. Other popular groups have followed: at one point nearly 100 companies were members of the Union of Nigerian Dramatists and Playwrights.   JMG

Yoshizawa Ayame I (1673–1729) Japanese *kabuki actor. Famous as the founder of the *onnagata (*female impersonator) role in kabuki, he performed in Kyoto and Osaka. He was renowned for his realistic portrayal of women and perfected the role of the high-class courtesan (*keisei*). We know about his style from published 'actor critiques' and from his own ideas recorded in the treatise 'Ayamegusa' ('The Words of Ayame') in *The Actors' Analects*, where he provides considerable detail on his philosophy of *acting. He maintained the pose and mannerisms of a woman even offstage, and refused to let others see him eating. This concern for *realism (*jitsu*) was common to Kyoto-Osaka kabuki of the early era (*see* SAKATA TŌJŪRŌ). Two of Yoshizawa's sons became *onnagata* actors and took his name. Another son performed as a male lead, establishing the name Nakamura Tomijuro I, which still exists today.   CAG

Young, Stark (1886–1963) American critic, playwright, and director. A native of Mississippi, Young taught at the universities of Mississippi and Texas and at Amherst College. At the age of 40, he moved to New York and became an editor at *Theatre Arts Magazine* (1921–40) as well as theatre critic for the *New Republic* (1922–42). A friend and adviser to the *Provincetown Players, his play *The Saint* was staged by them in 1925; in the same season he directed *O'Neill's *Welded*. Young was a respected translator of *Chekhov and his six books on theatre emphasize the power of art to provide meaning by giving form to truth and beauty.   MAF

youth, theatre for An umbrella term that encompasses two age-related categories of performance work. *Theatre for children* means professionally produced plays aimed at children up to about the age of 12; *theatre for young people* refers to professional work designed for older age groups. Another term, *youth theatre*, generally refers to non-professional work performed by young people, rather than for them.

Theatre for children has for long been accorded a much higher status in continental Europe than in the UK. Most of the larger European cities, and several cities in North America, possess specialist children's and/or young people's theatre companies operating in their own well-equipped buildings. Many have long and impressive histories: the Moscow Theatre for Children was established as early as 1918. The work varies enormously, from the usual adaptations of fairy tales and classic novels to stylistically inventive plays dealing with contemporary social issues. Grips Theater in Berlin, Green Thumb in Vancouver, and Theatre Centre in London have been notable pioneers in this field. In the UK in general, however, *touring predominates.

Theatre for and with young people. Various examples have existed in British history, from the Elizabethan *boy actors to university and school drama to teach rhetoric, enliven the classics, and develop confidence and articulacy. But the real beginnings of professional theatre for youth were during the early years of the twentieth century. *Barrie's *Peter Pan* proved an extraordinary West End success with family *audiences in 1904, while matinée productions of Shakespeare for school audiences were given at *Baylis's *Old Vic during and immediately after the First World War. Bertha Waddell formed the pioneering Scottish Children's Theatre in 1927, giving performances of plays written and compiled especially for younger children; and Peter Slade founded the Parable Players in 1935 to perform in schools and other venues. Meanwhile, in the USA there was a parallel growth, led by pioneers such as Alice M. Herts and Winifred Ward; the establishment of the short-lived Federal Theatre for Children (1936–9), part of the *Federal Theatre Project, stimulated a longer-lasting interest in the field among writers and directors.

The end of the Second World War triggered renewed activity. In the USA, several dedicated professional companies were formed and children's theatre programmes were established in a number of universities, providing training, expanding the range of productions, and raising the status of the genre. In the UK, several specialist companies were founded, notably the London Children's Theatre (which became Theatre Centre), the Young Vic, and Caryl Jenner's Mobile Theatre Company, Amersham, later to transfer to London as Unicorn Theatre. Poorly funded, most companies struggled to survive, but a boost came with the Arts Council's injection of new money into both children's theatre of the more traditional kind after 1966, and the burgeoning theatre-in-education (TIE) movement (*see* EDUCATIONAL THEATRE). Many companies have their roots in participatory TIE, while others have always been more performance oriented. The boundary lines between TIE and young people's theatre became increasingly blurred through the 1980s and 1990s, due to funding pressures and a greater emphasis on production values and experimentation with *physical theatre and *mime. Occasional commercial productions of popular children's plays and adaptations of the classics continue to tour the larger theatres, and the *regional reps often cater for young people on a seasonal basis, but the general provision remains well below that of continental European countries.

Youth theatre flourishes in most large cities across Europe and in the USA and Canada, variously fostered by *regional theatres as part of their 'outreach' programmes, by local education authorities, and by community arts centres. In the UK, the National Youth Theatre, founded in 1956, has been a focal point in the development and raising of standards of performance by young people, while the National Association of Youth Theatres promotes training, festivals, and networking. *See also* COMMUNITY THEATRE. ARJ

Yu Ch'i-jin (1905-74) Director, *manager, and playwright of modern Korean theatre (*shingŭk*). With Hong Hae-sŏng (1893-1957), who acted in various productions of the Tsukiji Little Theatre in Japan, he founded the Drama-Cinema Club in 1931 and organized an exhibition of over 4,000 modern theatrical objects, including the Tsukiji's photographs, scripts, programmes, and ground plans. The same year he became a founding member of the Theatre Arts Research Society, a group that popularized Western *realistic theatre. His 30 plays, ranging from *tragedy to *comedy, made him the most influential playwright of the 1930s and 1940s, and he dealt courageously with the social and political implications of Japanese colonialism. His first play (*The Earthen Hut*, 1931) allusively exposed the Korean farmer's suffering under harsh military rule. He was appointed the first director of the National Theatre in 1950 and the first director of the Drama Centre in 1962. His representative plays are *The Cow* (1935), *Prince Maŭi* (1936), *The Fatherland* (1946), and *Wonsulrang* (1950). JOC

Yung, Danny (1943-) Hong Kong playwright, director, *producer. After completing his studies in America, Yung returned to Hong Kong and in 1979 presented his first theatre work, *Broken Record #1*. In 1982, he founded Zuni Icosahedron, a performing and visual arts *collective, and he has been *artistic director since 1985. His productions—provocative in their interrogation of different aspects of Chinese culture and uncompromising in their defiance of traditional theatre conventions—have become synonymous with *avant-garde theatre in Hong Kong. Controversial successes include the *One Hundred Years of Solitude* series, the *Chronicle of Women* series, the *Opium Wars* series, and the *Deep Structure of Chinese Culture* series. Since the mid-1990s, he became increasingly interested in cross-cultural, cross-region collaboration and, in productions such as the *Journey to the East* series and *King Lear—Experimental Shakespeare* (2000), experimented with cross-media and new art forms and concepts. He has directed and produced over 70 stage productions and his works have *toured widely. He also curates *multimedia exhibitions and organizes forums on cultural policy issues. MPYC

Yusem, Laura (1939-) Argentinian director. Ten years after staging her first play, Yusem achieved recognition in 1980 in Buenos Aires for *Różewicz's *White Wedding*. Noted for her collaborations with *Gambaro (*Antígona furiosa*, 1986) and *Pavlovsky (*Pas de deux*, 1990), Yusem has also staged the plays of other Argentinians like Oscar Viale, *Cossa and *Monti, as well as European classics. Yusem's *dance training is evident in choreographed high-concept productions set in unconventional spaces, or in unconventionally used traditional spaces, as when she closed off the house of the Teatro Cervantes, forcing the *audience to join *Antígona furiosa*'s actors onstage. JGJ

Yu Zhenfei (Yü Chen-fei) (1902-93) Chinese *kunqu and *jingju (Beijing opera) actor of the *xiaosheng* (young man) category. As the son of a distinguished authority on *kunqu*, the dominant lyrical form prior to Beijing opera, Yu received intensive training from the age of 6. Though he had over 200 *kunqu* scenes in his repertory he remained an amateur until an invitation from the Beijing opera actor *Cheng Yanqiu prompted him to resign his teaching post at Jinan University in 1931. His background helped him create many exquisite *xiaosheng *characters opposite Cheng's *heroines, including Li Jing in *The Story of Hongfu*, Emperor Xuanzong in *Princess Mei*, and Wang Hui in *Dream of a Maiden*. He also performed opposite such well-known Beijing opera actors as *Mei Lanfang, and was considered one of the most distinguished interpreters of the genre. He lived in Hong Kong in the 1940s but returned to Beijing in 1955. Two years later he became president of the Shanghai City School of *Jingju* and *Kunqu* Drama and *artistic director of Shanghai Youth *Jingju* Troupe in 1960. SYL

Zacconi, Ermete (1857–1948) Italian *actor-manager. An exponent of *realism, Zacconi had a natural and elegant delivery and slowly revealed his *character's psychological depth. Taking *Antoine's Théâtre *Libre as a model, he formed his own company and presented the new realistic canon at Milan's Manzoni Theatre (1894–5), including works by *Ibsen, *Maeterlinck, *Tolstoy, *Turgenev, *Hauptmann, *Giacometti, *Giacosa, and *Praga. Foreign *tours made him an international star by 1897; *Duse and he toured her *D'Annunzio repertory (1900, 1901, 1906) as well as Ibsen and Praga (1921). Among his major successes were Oswald in Ibsen's *Ghosts*, the title role in *Musset's *Lorenzaccio*, and, in his mature years, the title role in Testoni's *Cardinal Lambertini*. Critics accused him of misinterpreting some authors, particularly Shakespeare, and of placing too much emphasis on a character's neuroses.   JEH

Zadek, Peter (1926–2009) German director. Born in Berlin, he came to Britain with his Jewish parents in 1933. In 1943 he went to Oxford, left without a degree, studied *directing at the *Old Vic Theatre School, and had his first professional engagement in 1949. In 1957 he staged the world première of *Genet's *The Balcony* at the Arts Theatre Club, prompting Genet to threaten Zadek with a revolver—the first of many Zadek scandals. After 1960 he worked almost exclusively in Germany, producing Shakespeare's *Measure for Measure* in Ulm, where he began his long-term collaboration with the designer *Minks. Zadek's British background reveals itself in the inventive wit and spontaneity of his productions, a contrast to the precise work of a more typical German director like *Stein, who has described Zadek's productions as 'Shakespeare in underpants'.

Zadek had no political philosophy or defined aesthetic and frequently directed the same text in entirely different ways. In 1962 he went to Bremen, where he became *artistic director in 1964. Here he directed *Wedekind's *Spring's Awakening* and *Behan's *The Quare Fellow*, but went freelance again in 1967. In his spectacular 1967 production of *O'Casey's *The Silver Tassie* in Wuppertal he introduced a *chorus of dancing football players set against the horrors of the Great War. As director of the Schauspielhaus Bochum (1972–5) he staged novels by Hans Fallada, notably *Little Man,—What Now?* (1972, adapted with *Dorst). His production of *The Merchant of Venice* (1972) provocatively challenged German guilt about the Holocaust by presenting Shylock as a repulsive Yid. *King Lear* (1974) was presented in *vaudeville style, and in 1976 his Othello (Ulrich Wildgruber) wore a *minstrel blackface, and a naked Desdemona was violently murdered, her corpse slung over a curtain. *The Winter's Tale* in Hamburg (1978) was performed on two tons of green slime, a powerful visual image of the morass into which Leontes' jealousy drags the *action. In 1985 he became director of the Schauspielhaus Hamburg, where he made a particular effort to attract a wider *audience with productions of *As You Like It* (1986) and a popular *musical, *Andi* (1907). In his third staging of *The Merchant of Venice*, in Vienna in 1988, Shylock was played as a Wall Street broker. In 1989 he left Hamburg and after further entertaining productions as a freelance director, he joined the *Berliner Ensemble (1992–5), presenting *Antony and Cleopatra* in Vienna (1994) and *Pinter's *Moonlight* in Hamburg (1995). An acclaimed production of *The Cherry Orchard* (1996) was followed in 1999 by a *Hamlet* with Angela Winkler in the title role. He subsequently directed *Brecht's *Mother Courage* (2003), *Ibsen's *Peer Gynt* (2004), and *Shaw's *Major Barbara* (2009), and also directed for *opera, film, and television.   MWP

zaju (tsa-chü) Chinese variety play which arose in the Song (960–1279) and Yuan (1279–1360) periods, the first major musically based theatrical form. Combining tunes derived from a variety of sources—court music, lyrical poetry, folk song—zaju had a tight four-act structure and typically featured a *protagonist who sang arias from a subjective point of view. Role types, which would mark all subsequent operatic forms, were based on gender, prominence in the play, age, and moral tone.

Temple and court performances of *zaju* were often tied to *ritual or seasonal occasions, whereas the urban theatres, accommodating as many as 1,000 spectators, operated year-round as commercial undertakings. Musical accompaniment included string, wind, and percussion instruments, though no scores have survived.

The *zaju* repertoire featured stories about exalted as well as humble personages. Based on the 30 printed texts that have survived from the Yuan period, playwrights such as *Guan Hanqing and *Gao Wenxiu were irreverent toward the rich and powerful and often sympathetic to the lower orders.

The Ming court was fond of *zaju* but not of unflattering portrayals. In the early fifteenth-century the repertoire was revised at court and most extant plays (such as *Ma Zhiyuan's) made to celebrate Confucian virtues and Taoist notions of immortality.

Zaju ceased to be a vital performance tradition by the middle of the sixteenth century but became a significant textual influence on subsequent Chinese musical drama such as *kunqu and *jingju. Having attained to the status of 'ancient plays', the Yuan *zaju* encouraged writers to adopt a looser form, and the original Yuan texts were published in both popular and literary versions. One such collection, *The One Hundred Yuan Plays*, extensively redacted by the scholar-official Zang Maoxun (1615/16), projected the image of an orderly world governed by poetic rhyme and Confucian reason, and made *zaju* available in a compact and aesthetically appealing form.   PS

Zakharov, Mark (1933–) Soviet/Russian director. Zakharov came to the Theatre of the Lenin Komsomol in 1973 and developed a wide-ranging repertoire, including *musicals (*Troubadour and his Friends* and Grigorii Gorin's *Till*, both 1974), political plays by *Shatrov, contemporary plays by *Arbuzov and *Petrushevskaya, and classics in modern interpretation. His troupe was politically engaged in the early perestroika era when Zakharov was one of the first to support reform. He tackled historical issues with a hitherto unknown openness, as in Shatrov's *Dictatorship of Conscience* (1986), which for the first time mentioned figures such as Bukharin and Trotsky who had been blotted out of Soviet history. Zakharov caught the spirit of the time, attracting young *audiences with productions such as the rock *opera *Perchance* by Voznesensky and Rybnikov (1981). In subsequent years he continued to add visually stunning and psychologically convincing productions, always in collaboration with his set designer Oleg Sheintsis.   BB

Zaks, Jerry (1946–) German-born American director, known for *comedies and *musicals.

After appearing on Broadway as an actor in musicals, Zaks began directing *Off-Off-Broadway in the 1970s. He moved to *Off-Broadway in 1981 with *Durang's *Beyond Therapy, Sister Mary Ignatius Explains It All for You*, and *The Actor's Nightmare*. His later Off-Broadway credits include *Baby with the Bathwater* (1984), *The Foreigner* (1984), *The Marriage of Bette and Boo* (1985), *Wenceslas Square* (1988), and *Sondheim's *Assassins* (1991), while among his Broadway credits are *The House of Blue Leaves* (1986), *The Front Page* (1986), *Anything Goes* (1987), *Six Degrees of Separation* (1990), *Guys and Dolls* (1992), *Laughter on the 23rd Floor* (1993), *A Funny Thing Happened on the Way to the Forum* (1996), *The Civil War* (1999), and revivals of *The Man Who Came to Dinner* (2000) and *The Caine Mutiny Court Martial* (2006).   SLL

Zamyatin, Evgeny (1884–1937) Russian/Soviet writer who studied naval engineering in Newcastle. His first play, *The Society of Honorary Bell Ringers* (1925), was based on his novella *The Islanders* and *satirizes the English middle class. He is best known for his dystopian novel *We* (1920–1); a dramatized version was prepared for *Foregger's Mastfor Theatre, with designs by *Eisenstein, but was never staged. His other work includes a play in defence of heresy, *The Fires of St Dominic* (1922), and *The Flea* (1925), written in the style of a *clown show, poking fun at the backwardness of tsarist Russia and philistine bourgeois England. It was staged at the *Moscow Art Theatre and proved very popular, unlike his *tragedy *Attila*, which casts a favourable light on the marauder and was banned in *rehearsal (1928). Increasingly persecuted after 1929, Zamyatin applied to Stalin for permission to emigrate and, amazingly, this was granted. He settled in Paris in 1932 and spent the remaining five years of his life working on a novel, *The Scourge of God*.   NW

Zanni Stereotype mask—i.e. *character—in Italian *commedia dell'arte*. When the professionals took over the *Plautine plot formulas of *commedia erudita*, they needed a standard identity for the role of the ignorant *clownish servant. This was found in the figure of the peasant from the Bergamo area who had migrated to the city to find work, a phenomenon based in the social reality of the sixteenth century. The name Zani, or Zanni, is a Lombard version of Giovanni; and the Bergamo dialect is still seen within Italy as particularly impenetrable and comic. The master–servant confrontation between the Venetian merchant Pantalone and the Bergamask servant Zani became one of the core elements of Italian *comedy.

Individual actors multiplied their versions of the role, adding extra names to identify themselves, such as Zan *Ganassa, Zan Fritella, etc.; and the 'zany' contribution of these masks became so important that the whole genre was sometimes called simply 'commedia degli zanni'. Zannis were usually dressed in the roughest undyed material, with broad-brimmed hats and a dark, wolfish half-*mask. The notion that stage servants had to speak Bergamask lasted for two centuries on the Italian stage, and the initially intrusive alien mask of *Harlequin, dressed very differently, was quickly assimilated to this convention.   RAA

Zapolska, Gabriela (1857–1921) Polish actor, *manager, and writer. Appearing as Nora in *A Doll's House*, she introduced *Ibsen in Russia while on *tour in 1883. From 1889 to 1895 Zapolska studied *acting in Paris, appearing in minor roles at the Théâtre *Libre. Returning to Poland as a proponent of *naturalism with socialist sympathies, she wrote plays and novels about alcoholism, prostitution, class and ethnic conflicts, and oppression of women, embroiling her in scandal and controversy. She established a theatre school and ran a company bearing her name. Her satirical dramas and *comedies containing outstanding roles for women have constantly held the stage in Poland. *Malka Szwarcenkopf* (1895) depicts Warsaw Jewish life; *Miss Maliczewska* (1910) portrays a poor young actress battling against sexual exploitation. Zapolska's masterpiece, *The Morality of Mrs Dulska* (1906), exposes the hypocrisy of bourgeois family life (film scenario by the author, 1912). Many productions since the fall of communism have revealed Zapolska's *satire of the nouveaux riches to be more timely than ever.   DG

zarzuela Spanish musical genre, similar to the *operetta, which emerged in the seventeenth century as part of the entertainment for the court at the Palacio de la Zarzuela. The first known *zarzuelas* were by *Calderón, with *music by Juan de Hidalgo, combining witty librettos with melodies of high quality and great diversity. With the coming of Italian *opera in the eighteenth century, the popularity of the *zarzuela* began to wane. But the hybrid nature of the genre, with its brew of so-phisticated musical ensembles and arias, verse and prose *dialogue, popular songs, and lowlife comic *characters, appealed to nineteenth-century tastes and prompted the construction of a specialized venue, the Teatro de la Zarzuela, which opened in Madrid in 1856. In its related forms as *género grande*, long and operatic in scope, and *género chico*, short and often gently

titillating one-act *farces, mostly set in the poorer quarters of Madrid, the *zarzuela* has survived to the present.   KG

zat pwe Classical theatre of Burma (Myanmar) combining traditional and modern plays, song and *dance, and comic skits in all-night performances. Burmese court theatre emerged during the end of the Nyaugyan Dynasty (1599–1751), and refined literary court drama peaked during the reign of King Mindon in the works of dramatists U Kyin U (1819–53) and U Pon Nya (1807–66). With the annexation of Burma by the British in 1886, court patronage vanished and was replaced by popular support. The focus shifted from refined dramatic scripts back to song, dance, and comic scenes in a performer-centred style reminiscent of an older folk form. Since independence in 1948, modern plays (*pya zat*) have increasingly replaced or augmented classical stories. Popular during local pagoda festivals, these *variety shows feature comic skits, pop songs, and dance numbers in the all-night entertainment. Despite modernization, a performance always begins with a solo dance by the female *natkadaw* (spirit medium). Traditional *zat pwe* is accompanied by the *saing waing* orchestra which consists of the leading *pat waing*, a unique circular set of 21 tuned drums, the *kyi waing*, a circular set of bronze kettles, several other drums, gongs, clappers, cymbals, and wind instruments. A Western orchestra is often added in contemporary performances.   KP

Zeami (Kanze Motokiyo) (1363–1443) Japanese *nō actor, *manager, playwright, and theorist. In 1374 Zeami and his father *Kan'ami performed before the young shogun Ashikaga Yoshimitsu (1358–1408), winning military and aristocratic patronage. Zeami transformed the popular *sarugaku* of his talented father into an elegant art form known today as nō. In addition to performing before varied *audiences, Zeami wrote over 50 innovative, poetic plays, many of which are considered masterpieces today, and twenty extraordinary treatises about theatre. At the death of Kan'ami in 1384, Zeami took over the management of the Yūzaki (later Kanze) troupe, relinquishing leadership in 1422 to his son Motomasa, who died in 1432. Headship went to his nephew Onnami, but his son-in-law *Komparu Zenchiku was Zeami's artistic heir.

Zeami's treatises, written between 1400 and 1433, remained the protected property of acting troupes until 1909 when a manuscript was discovered in a second-hand bookshop. The earliest treatise, *Fushikaden* (*Teachings in Style and the*

Flower, 1400–18), includes descriptions of age-appropriate training, types of *miming (mono-mane)*, the interactions between actor and audience and between movement and text, and his aesthetic concept of *hana* (flowering). *Kyuui (Nine Levels, c.*1427) describes levels of *acting ability and relates them to the training and development of actors; *Kakyoo* (1424) analyses six principles of acting, including mind–body interaction, auditory and visual effects, and effective stage presence, as well as ideas about *yūgen* (mysterious beauty), *myō* (the wondrous), and *shoshin* (beginner's heart). Other treatises deal with music, voice production, composing plays, the two basic arts (song and *dance) and three modes (aged, martial, feminine), and strategies for managing a troupe.

Exactly which plays Zeami wrote and the order of their composition is a matter of debate as playwrights' names were not attached to texts and rewriting older works and joint composition were common. Many of the plays attributed to Zeami are *mugen* nō, plays which feature deities (*Unoha, Takasago, Oimatsu*), spirits of plants (*Saigyōzakura*), or ghosts (*Tadanori, Izutsu*), who appear as commoners in Act I and reveal their true natures in Act II. Themes of salvation, love, war, art, obsession, and celebration are expressed in densely beautiful poetry which is sung and danced on stage.   KWB

Zeffirelli, Franco (1923–) Italian designer and director. An architect by training, Zeffirelli designed films in the 1940s and 1950s with Vittorio de Sica, Roberto Rossellini, Michelangelo Antonioni, and *Visconti. For Visconti's stage productions in 1949 he designed scenery or *costumes for *A Streetcar Named Desire, As You Like It*, and *Troilus and Cressida*. He began directing and designing his own productions of *opera in 1951, working over the next five decades on more than 50 productions around the world. His *directing was marked by emotional and sexual energy and a comic sense almost manic in intensity, while his designs relied on sumptuous materials and visual luxury.

His work in the theatre began in earnest in 1960 when he was invited to design and direct *Romeo and Juliet* at the *Old Vic in London, a production of overheated mood that established the style for the play for the next generation. His other work included *Othello* for the *Royal Shakespeare Company (1961), *Hamlet* (1964), *Much Ado About Nothing* and *The Taming of the Shrew* (both 1965), and seminal productions of *de Filippo's *Saturday, Sunday, Monday* (1973) and *Filumena* (1977), most for the *National Theatre. Even when

he approached more modern texts, Zeffirelli never abandoned his taste for the spectacular: painstaking attention to the scene was evident in *Albee's *Who's Afraid of Virginia Woolf?* (Paris, 1964), *Miller's *After the Fall* (Rome, 1964), and *Musset's *Lorenzaccio* (*Comédie-Française, 1978).

He worked with major performers from Maria Callas and Placido Domingo to *Olivier, *Burton, Elizabeth Taylor, and Mel Gibson. His films of Verdi and Shakespeare were widely received, if sometimes criticized for excess. They include *The Taming of the Shrew* (1966), *Romeo and Juliet* (1968), *La traviata* (1982), *Otello* (1986), and *Hamlet* (1990). His film *Tea with Mussolini* (1999) was much admired. A supporter of the political right wing, Zeffirelli entered politics as a candidate for Forza Italia in 1994.   DMCM/DK

Zemach, Nahum (1887–1939) Russian pioneer of Hebrew theatre. His efforts began in his native Bialystock in 1912, where he organized Habima Ha'Ivrit (Hebrew Stage), which produced a Hebrew version of Ossip Dymow's *The Eternal Wanderer*, presented in 1913 at the Eleventh Zionist Congress in Vienna. Although the company disbanded, it was a precursor to the Habima Theatre founded by him in Moscow in 1917. Zemach interested *Stanislavsky in the fledgling troupe, which became incorporated into the *Moscow Art Theatre as an independent studio. Zemach stood at the helm of the Habima until 1927, when, during its American *tour, the company split. Zemach stayed in New York, his theatrical efforts faltering, and his later efforts to rejoin the Habima rejected. *See* DIASPORA.   EN

Ziegfeld, Florenz (1869–1932) American *producer and theatre owner. Emerging from a career as agent and *manager for *vaudeville performers, Ziegfeld left a lasting mark on American show business with the creation of his *Ziegfeld Follies* in 1907, a *revue of comedy, song, *dance, and female *choruses that enlivened Broadway in successive annual editions until 1931. The *Follies* were built upon four principles: glamour, pace, decency, and spectacle. The first-act ending of the 1927 edition featured a vast, semicircular staircase on which fourteen grand pianos and two complete orchestras slowly revolved as the entire enormous cast, attired in evening clothes and satin gowns, fringe, and plumed headdresses, entered singing and arranged themselves as elegant scenery. An artistically ambitious and perfectionist impresario, Ziegfeld spent ever larger sums to achieve novelty and surprise and to surpass his previous editions. Punctuating the spectacle were vaudeville performers such as Will *Rogers, *Brice, *Fields, *Cantor, and Ed *Wynn. Ziegfeld was a major customer for American songwriters, commissioning more than 500 songs from a stable of composers including *Berlin, *Kern, and *Herbert. He also produced book *musicals and was a force behind the landmark production of *Show Boat* (1927).   MAF

Zipprodt, Patricia (1925–98) American designer who launched her career by designing *costumes for Gore Vidal's *A Visit to a Small Planet* (1957). She worked constantly for established Broadway and *Off-Broadway companies, a favourite of some of the leading directors and *producers of her time, designing costumes for *Fiddler on the Roof, Cabaret, 1776, Chicago, The Crucible* by *Miller, *Brighton Beach Memoirs* and *Plaza Suite* by *Simon, *Period of Adjustment* by *Williams, and *The Gang's All Here* by *Lawrence and Lee, among many others. She added *opera, *ballet, television, and film credits to her résumé.   MCH

Zola, Émile (1840–1902) French writer whose theories of *naturalism altered French theatre production. His first major novel was *Thérèse Raquin* (1867), which he later adapted as a four-act play (1873) which became the template for the naturalist play. Zola's magnum opus was a twenty-volume series of novels entitled *Les Rougon-Macquart* (1871–93), a magnificent social history of Second Empire France fictionalized in the lives of two branches of one family, the petit bourgeois Rougons and the poacher-smuggler-alcoholic Macquarts. One novel made him the most talked-about writer of his generation. *L'Assommoir*, a hard-hitting indictment of the social conditions of working-class Parisians. It had a lucrative run on stage in 1879 in a version by the *melodramatist William Busnach, who was also responsible for adaptations of *Nana* and *Pot Bouille*. Zola's connection to the theatre extended to *Antoine's Théâtre *Libre, which staged a version of his story *Jacques Damour* in its first season (1887).

Zola's second major drive was as a literary and theatrical critic. In his reviews, he sought to rid French theatre of the *well-made play, calling for representation of all sections of society in scientific experiments of naturalism (published subsequently in *Naturalism in the Theatre* and *Our Playwrights* in 1881). In his early career Zola had been an avid reader of modern scientific theories: his mantra for literature and theatre ran, 'Determinism dominates everything'.

All his work had social and political implications, as it spanned the gamut of French society

and exposed weaknesses and vices at all levels, incurring the wrath of extreme right-wing politicians. Fame turned to notoriety with his intervention in the Dreyfus Affair. He was convicted of libel for his open letter to the President, *J'accuse*, in which he exposed institutional anti-Semitism. He was stripped of his national honours and forced into exile to London in 1898 to escape prison. When Dreyfus was pardoned in 1899, Zola was free to return. Three years later in Paris he died in bed of carbon monoxide poisoning from a faulty stove. The death was recorded as accidental, though there were suspicions he had been murdered.   BRS

Zorin, Leonid (1924–) Russian/Soviet dramatist, born in Azerbaijan. He came to international notice with *Guests* (1954), which deals with a new upper class spoiled by power and which places the blame on Soviet society. *Friends and Years* (1962) was among the first attempts to deal frankly with the facts of Stalinist oppression, while a satirical *comedy, *Dion* (1965), set during the time of the Roman Emperor Domitian, was removed from the stage in Leningrad when critics noted contemporary political allegories. His most popular play is *Warsaw Melody* (1967), 'a lyrical drama in two parts', which reflects the swing during the 1960s from the social to the personal in the wake of revelations about the legacy of Stalinism. It concerns a Russian boy and Polish girl (both students) whose relationship is frustrated, by laws which forbid Soviet citizens to marry foreigners. It was performed 4,000 times in its first year alone at various venues and on 150 separate occasions between 1967 and 1977.   NW

Zorrilla, José (1817–93) Spanish writer. His most celebrated play, *Don Juan Tenorio* (1844), was an adaptation of Tirso de *Molina's *The Trickster of Seville* with a *romantic overlay and a final redemption scene that appealed to conservative *audiences. Although less than a success at its première, it became immensely popular and was staged yearly in Spanish-speaking countries to coincide with All Saints' Day. A new production in Madrid in 2000 updated the *action with effective *mise-en-scène to attract younger audiences. Zorrilla's own favourite among his more than 30 works for the stage was *Traitor, Unconfessed, and Martyr* (1849), the last major work of Spanish romantic theatre.   MPH

Zuckmayer, Carl (1896–1977) German dramatist and novelist. Zuckmayer's first play, *Kreuzweg* (1920), was an exercise in *expressionism. His breakthrough came in 1925 with his folk *comedy *The Merry Vineyard*, a new form of critical *realism in the tradition of *Hauptmann. The play was an immediate success and a scandal for its satirical portrayal of conservatives. *The Captain of Köpenick* (1931), a *satire of the Prussian hierarchy and its cult of the uniform, became a German classic, made into several films. In 1938 Zuckmayer emigrated to the USA where he settled as a farmer and writer in Vermont. He returned to Germany in 1946 and achieved a major success with *The Devil's General*, written in exile in 1943. His post-war plays were less successful.   CBB

Zweig, Stefan (1881–1942) Austrian writer. Zweig's early work includes a *tragedy in blank verse, *Tersites* (1907), a *comedy in the style of *Marivaux, *The Actor Transformed* (1912), and the *naturalist *The House by the Sea* (1912). Zweig himself regarded his early plays as a stepping stone for his more mature essays and novels. In 1917 he emigrated to Switzerland, where his *tragedy *Jeremiah* (1917) premièred, an anti-war play pleading for reconciliation among the warring nations (produced in New York, 1939). Between the wars he became one of the most widely read and translated German authors. As a dramatist he was noted for his version of *Jonson's *Volpone* (1925) and he also wrote the libretto for Richard Strauss's *opera *Die Schweigsame Frau* (*The Silent Woman*, also based on Jonson). In 1941 Zweig and his second wife Lotte Altmann emigrated to Brazil where they committed suicide.   CBB

Timeline 🌿

Prepared by Diane DeVore

HISTORICAL/CULTURAL EVENTS	THEATRE AND PERFORMANCE EVENTS
BC	**BC**
c.3000–1500 Indus Valley Civilization	c.2600 First evidence of Egyptian ritual performances
c.1600–1028 Shang Dynasty in China	
c.1500 Aryans invade India; Brahmanism develops	c.1500 Evidence of importance of dance, ritual, and music in China
776 Traditional date for first Olympic Games in Greece	
630 Greek colony of Naukratis in Egypt	
508 New democratic constitution in ancient Greece	after 508 Greek tragedies at City Dionysia in Athens (traditional date is 534)
c.500 Buddhism and Jainism develop in India	c.500 Theatre of Dionysus built in Athens
490 Invasion of Greece repulsed by Athenians at Marathon	
	486 Prize for comedy introduced at City Dionysia
478 Beginnings of Athenian empire	
461 Era of Pericles begins in Athens	472 Aeschylus' *The Persians*
	458 Aeschylus' *Oresteia*
	456 Death of Aeschylus
431–429 Peloponnesian War between Athens and Sparta; death of Pericles (429)	431 Euripides' *Medea*
	424 Aristophanes' *Knights*
	411 Aristophanes' *Lysistrata*
	409 Sophocles' *Philoctetes*
	406 Deaths of Sophocles and Euripides
404 Athens loses war against Sparta	401 Sophocles' *Oedipus at Colonus* (produced posthumously)
	c.380 Death of Aristophanes
	363 Traditional date for first Etruscan performances in Rome
338 King Philip of Macedon defeats Thebes and Athens and takes over mainland Greece	
336–323 Alexander the Great rules Macedon; invades Asia 334	336–210 Hellenistic period: rise of New Comedy
	326 Theatre of Dionysus rebuilt in stone
311 Division of Alexander's territories into the Hellenistic kingdoms	

HISTORICAL/CULTURAL EVENTS	THEATRE AND PERFORMANCE EVENTS
BC	**BC**
	*c.*300 Artists of Dionysus in existence
	292 Death of Menander
279 Celts invade Greece	
218 Hannibal invades Italy	
*c.*206–AD 220 Han Dynasty in China	
	191 Plautus' *Pseudolus*
168 Rome conquers Macedon	184 Death of Plautus
	159 Death of Terence
	*c.*200–100 Sanskrit dramas in India
	*c.*200–AD *Natyasastra* composed in India, a
	200 compendium on drama and acting
	for Sanskrit theatre
	55 First permanent Roman theatre
30 Roman republic ends when Octavian (Augustus) assumes monarchical power	
AD	**AD**
64 First persecutions of Christians in Rome	
	65 Death of Seneca
79 Vesuvius erupts, buries Pompeii and Herculaneum	
*c.*300–500 Northern India united under Gupta dynasty, reign of Guptas ends with defeat by White Huns and India plunges into anarchy	*c.*300–400 Possible dates for Indian Sanskrit playwrights Bhasa, Sudraka, and Kalidasa
330 Constantine, first Christian Roman emperor, renames Byzantium as Constantinople and makes it his capital	
407 Germanic tribes invade Western Europe	
410 Sack of Rome by Visigoths	
476 The last Roman emperor in the West is deposed	
	*c.*500 Opposition to Roman entertainments begins by Christians in western and eastern empires
	526 Theatre and worship of Dionysus banned in Byzantium
	549 Last recorded scenic entertainments in Rome
618–907 Tang Dynasty in China	
	679 Council of Rome orders English Church to ban plays
711 Muslims seize Spain	
	714 Emperor Xuan Zong establishes school to train singers, dancers, and other court entertainers in China

HISTORICAL/CULTURAL EVENTS		**THEATRE AND PERFORMANCE EVENTS**	
772–814	Charlemagne's reign over European empire		
		c.900s	*Quem Quaeritis* tropes introduced in Easter services in Europe
960–1279	Rule of Song Dynasties in China	c.960–70	Hrotsvitha of Gandersheim composes six Christian plays modelled on Terence
c.1000	Leif Eriksson lands on North American continent	c.1000	End of classical Sanskrit drama and reformation of *kutiyattam*
		c.960–1270	Oldest extant Chinese drama, *The Doctor of Letters*
1066	Norman conquest of England		
1085	Christian reconquest of Spain begins (completed 1492)	c.1150	Hildegard of Bingen's *Ordo virtutum* (*The Way of the Virtues*)
		c.1160	Allegorical play *Antichristus* in Austria
1204	Western Crusaders seize Constantinople from Byzantines		
1226	Death of St Francis of Assisi		
1236–40	Mongols conquer Russia		
1264	Feast of Corpus Christi instituted		
1279–1368	Rule of Yuan Dynasty in China		
1287	Mongols invade Burma		
1291	Muslims take Acre, last Crusader state in Palestine		
1305–77	'Babylonian Captivity' of popes at Avignon		
1338–1453	The Hundred Years War		
1348	The Black Death begins in Europe	c.1350–1400	Biblical cycles first performed in England
1368	Rule of Ming Dynasty in China	1374	Kan'ami's troupe performs at shogun's court in Japan, leading to development of nō
		c.1400–25	*The Castle of Perseverance*, English morality play
1431	Fall of Angkor to the Thais	1431	Cambodian tradition imported to Ayutthaya (Thailand)
1453	Ottoman Turks take Constantinople		
1462–92	Lorenzo the Magnificent rules Florence		
		1476	First evidence of Corpus Christi play on pageant wagons in Spain
1492	Columbus lands in the New World	1495	*Everyman* printed in England
1497	Leonardo da Vinci completes *Last Supper* in Milan		
1498	Vasco da Gama reaches India		
1501	First African slaves to Caribbean		
1508–12	Michelangelo paints the Sistine Chapel in Rome	1508	Perspective used in painted scenery for Ariosto's *La Cassaria*
		1515	First recorded performance of *khon*, masked drama in Thai court

HISTORICAL/CULTURAL EVENTS	THEATRE AND PERFORMANCE EVENTS
1517 Protestant Reformation begins with the posting of Luther's 95 theses	
	c.1518 Machiavelli's *The Mandrake*
1519 Cortés takes Mexico City for Spain	
1520–2 Magellan circumnavigates the globe	
1527 Troops of the Holy Roman Emperor Charles V sack Rome	
1533 Ivan IV the Terrible reigns as the first Russian tsar	
1534 Henry VIII made supreme head of Church in England, Society of Jesus (Jesuits) formed in Counter Reformation	
	1539 Last carnival at Nuremberg
1543 Copernicus refutes prevalent theory of universe	
	1545 First document of Italian *commedia dell'arte* company
	1547 Valenciennes Passion play
	1548 Mystery plays banned in Paris; Confrérie de la Passion acquires Hotel de Bourgogne for secular plays, first permanent theatre in Paris
1559 Publication of Spain's first *Index of Prohibited Books*	
1561 Capital of Castile established at Madrid	
	1564 Birth of William Shakespeare
	1567 First London playhouse, the Red Lion, built in Stepney by John Brayne; two *comedias* performed at a Spanish mission in Florida
	1570s *Commedia dell'arte* troupes touring in England, France, and Spain
	1573 Tasso's pastoral drama *Aminta* in Ferrara
	1574 Queen Elizabeth of England issues patent to Leicester's Men
	1576 James Burbage builds the Theatre in Shoreditch, London
	1579 Corral de la Cruz in Madrid
	1583 Queen's Men founded in London; Corral del Príncipe in Madrid
	1585 Teatro Olimpico at Vicenza
	1587 Marlowe's *Tamburlaine the Great* in London
	1594 Shakespeare becomes shareholder in the Chamberlain's Men (known after 1603 as the King's Men)
	1599 Chamberlain's Men build the Globe
	1600 Shakespeare's *Hamlet*
	1600–1800 Continued development of rural forms of Indian drama

HISTORICAL/CULTURAL EVENTS	THEATRE AND PERFORMANCE EVENTS
1603 Takugawa shogunate established in Japan	1603 In Japan, the female dancer Okuni gives public performances in Kyoto, early form of kabuki.
1605 Cervantes' *Don Quixote*, part I (part II in 1615)	1605 *The Masque of Blackness* by Ben Jonson and Inigo Jones at the English court.
1607 Jamestown, first permanent Virginia settlement	1607 Monteverdi's opera *Orfeo* in Mantua
1609 Galileo invents telescope	
	1613 The Globe burns
	1616 Death of Shakespeare; last performance of the Lucerne Passion play
1618–48 Thirty Years War	
	1619 Teatro Farnese constructed in Parma with proscenium arch
	1622 First certain date of plays at the Alcázar
	1629 Women banned from the stage in Japan; first permanent company at Hôtel de Bourgogne in Paris
1637 Descartes's Discourse of Method	1637 Corneille's *Le Cid* in Paris
	1641 Richelieu's Paris theatre, the Palais Cardinal (later the Palais Royal)
1642 Rembrandt paints *Night Watch* in Amsterdam; Civil War in England; death of Cardinal Richelieu	1642 Parliament closes theatres in England
1643–1715 Rule of Louis XIV in France	
1644 Descartes's Principles of Philosophy	1644–51 Various restrictions on public performances of *comedias* in Spain
1644–1911 Rule of Qing Dynasty in China (last of dynastic rulers)	
1649 Charles I of England beheaded	
1652 Dutch settlement in South Africa	
1653 Taj Mahal built in Agra, India	
	1658 Molière's company performs in Paris
1660 Restoration of English monarchy with Charles II	1660 Charles II grants two theatre patents for London; professional actresses first appear on the English stage
	1661 Louis XIV establishes Académie Royale de Danse
	1665 William Darby's *Ye Bear and ye Cub* in Virginia, first English play recorded in the American colonies
1666 Great Fire of London	
1672 Royal African Company for slave trade founded	
	1673 Death of Molière
	1674 King's Company opens Drury Lane Theatre in London
	1677 Dryden's *All for Love* in London; Racine's *Phèdre* in Paris
	1680 Comédie-Française founded in Paris
	1684 Takemoto Gidayu founds bunraku company in Osaka

HISTORICAL/CULTURAL EVENTS		THEATRE AND PERFORMANCE EVENTS	
		1685	Alessandro Scarlatti founds the Neapolitan school of opera
1687	Newton's law of gravity		
1694	La Fontaine's *Fables* completed		
1701–4	War of Spanish Succession		
		1703–21	Chikamatsu's best-known bunraku plays
1710	St Paul's Cathedral completed in London		
		1716	Playhouse opens in Williamsburg, Virginia
1719	Daniel Defoe's *Robinson Crusoe*		
		1722	Ludvig Holberg's *The Pewterer Who Wanted to be a Politician* in Copenhagen
		1724	First acting company in Philadelphia
1726	Jonathan Swift's *Gulliver's Travels*		
		1728	John Gay's *The Beggar's Opera* in London
1729	Bach's *St Matthew Passion*		
		1731	George Lillo's *The London Merchant* in London; Voltaire's *Zaire* in Paris
		1737	Stage Licensing Act in England
1742	Handel's *Messiah*		
		1745	Goldoni's *The Servant of Two Masters* in Venice
		1746	David Garrick assumes management of Drury Lane
		1748	Takeda Izimo's bunraku play *Chushingura*
1750	Death of Bach		
1751–65	Diderot and d'Alembert's *Encyclopedie*		
		1752	First theatre company formed in Russia
1756–63	Seven Years War between England and France		
1759	Cook claims New Zealand for England		
c.1760	Beginning of Industrial Revolution in England		
1765	James Watts invents the steam engine		
1767	Fall of Thai capital, Ayutthaya, to Burmese	1767	Lessing's *Minna von Barnhelm* in Hamburg; first permanent playhouse in New York, John Street Theatre, opens with Farquhar's *The Beaux' Stratagem*
1773	Boston Tea Party		
		1774	In North America, Continental Congress discourages theatre performance
1775–83	American Revolution		
1776	US Declaration of Independence		

HISTORICAL/CULTURAL EVENTS	THEATRE AND PERFORMANCE EVENTS
	1777 Sheridan's *School for Scandal* in London; Klinger's *Sturm und Drang* published
	1779 Death of Garrick
	1782 Schiller's *The Robbers* in Mannheim
	1785 Mozart's *The Marriage of Figaro* in Vienna
1787 US Constitution drafted; Russia begins second war with Ottoman Empire	1787 Mozart's *Don Giovanni* in Prague
1788 First British settlers in Australia	1788 Dramaten (Royal Dramatic Theatre) founded in Stockholm
1789 Storming of Bastille marks beginning of French Revolution	1789 William Dunlap's *The Father; or, American Shandyism* in New York
	1790 Anhwei Troupes arrive in Beijing, starting movement towards *jingju* (Beijing opera)
1791 Death of Mozart	1791– Goethe director of court theatre at 1817 Weimar
1792 Mary Wollstonecraft's *Vindication of the Rights of Women*	
1793 Louis XVI of France beheaded	
1793–4 Reign of Terror in France, ending with Robespierre's fall	
1796 Buddhist revolt against Manchu rule in China	
	1800– Development of modern urban theatre 1900 in India
1801 Alexander I becomes emperor of Russia	
1803–15 Napoleonic Wars	
1808 Goethe's *Faust*, part I	
	1809 In London, Drury Lane Theatre burns, enlarged Covent Garden Theatre opens
1811 Jane Austen's *Sense and Sensibility*	
1815 Napoleon defeated at Waterloo; French monarchy restored	
1816 Samuel Taylor Coleridge's 'Kubla Khan'	1816 Gas used in stage lighting for first time, at Chestnut Street Theatre, Philadelphia
1818 Mary Shelley's *Frankenstein*	
1819 John Keats's 'Ode to a Grecian Urn'	
1820 Austria subdues revolt in Italy	
1821 Greeks rise against Turkish rule	
1824 Beethoven's Ninth Symphony in Vienna	
1827 Death of Beethoven	
	1828 Start of development of minstrelsy in USA
	1830 Hugo's *Hernani* causes riots at the Comédie-Française
1831 Pushkin's *Eugene Onegin*	1831 First American showboat
	1833 Dramatic Copyright Act in England; foundation of Dramatic Authors' Society

HISTORICAL/CULTURAL EVENTS	THEATRE AND PERFORMANCE EVENTS
1836 Dickens's *Oliver Twist*	
1837–1901 Reign of Queen Victoria	
1840 Start of Opium War in China	1840 Karl Immerman's open-stage production of *Twelfth Night* in Düsseldorf
	1843 In England Theatre Regulation Act abolishes stage monopoly and extends censorship powers
1845–51 Famine in Ireland	
1847 Charlotte Brontë's *Jane Eyre*; Emily Brontë's *Wuthering-Heights*	
1848 Marx and Engels's *The Communist Manifesto*; revolutions in Europe; California gold rush	
	1849 Debut of Edwin Booth, in Boston
1851 Napoleon III founds Second Empire in France	
1854–6 Crimean War	
1859 Darwin's *Origin of Species*	
1861–5 Civil War in USA	
1862 Bismarck Chancellor of Prussia	
1863 Manet's *Déjeuner sur l'herbe* exhibited in Paris	
	1864 Abolition of the monopoly of Comédie-Française on classic French drama
1865 Assassination of Abraham Lincoln; Tolstoy's *War and Peace*	1865 Tony Pastor opens the first variety theatre in New York
1867 Canada becomes a dominion; end of shogun rule in Japan and beginning of modernization	
1870–1 Franco-Prussian War	
1871 German unification complete; the Paris Commune	1871 Verdi's *Aida* premières in Cairo
	1872 Japanese government places actors under the control of the Ministry of Religious Instruction in attempt to improve public morals
1874 First Impressionist exhibition in Paris	
1876 Victoria proclaimed Empress of India; battle of Little Bighorn in the USA; Bell patents the telephone	1876 Wagner opens Bayreuth Festival with *The Rhinegold*
1876–8 Famine in India	1878 Irving becomes manager of Lyceum Theatre, London
	1879 Ibsen's *A Doll's House* premières in Copenhagen
1880 Edison develops light bulb	1880s Establishment of *bangsawan* performance style in Malaysia and Indonesia
	1881 First modern cabaret, Le Chat Noir, in Paris; Savoy Theatre in London reopens with all-electric lighting
	1882 Monopoly of imperial theatres abolished in Russia

HISTORICAL/CULTURAL EVENTS	THEATRE AND PERFORMANCE EVENTS
	1883 Metropolitan Opera House opens in New York
	1884 Buffalo Bill's first open-air Wild West show, in Nebraska
1885 Indian National Congress founded as focus for nationalism	
	1887 Antoine's Théâtre Libre in Paris
	1888 New Burgtheater opens on the Ring in Vienna; Strindberg's *Miss Julie*
1889 Eiffel Tower built in Paris; Rodin's *The Thinker*	1889 Braham's Freie Bühne in Berlin opens with Ibsen's *Ghosts*
	1891 Fort's Théâtre d'Art in Paris; Grein's Independent Theatre in London opens with *Ghosts*
	1893 Lugné-Poe's Théâtre de l'Œuvre opens in Paris
1895 Tchaikovsky's *Swan Lake* in St Petersburg	1895 Irving becomes first actor to be knighted
	1896 Jarry's *Ubu roi* at Théâtre de l'Œuvre
1898 Spanish-American War	1898 Stanislavsky and Nemirovich-Danchenko's Moscow Art Theatre founded
1900 Freud's *The Interpretation of Dreams*	
1900–1 Boxer Rebellion in China	
1901 Australia becomes a dominion	
1902 Conrad's 'Heart of Darkness', Mélies's film *A Voyage to the Moon*	
1903 Wright brothers' first flight	
	1904 Gregory and Yeats found Abbey Theatre in Dublin
	1904–7 Vedrenne–Barker seasons in London
1905 First Russian revolution	1905 Reinhardt takes over the Deutsches Theater, Berlin; Isadora Duncan's first school of modern dance, Berlin
	1906 Final full-scale court performance of *gambuh* dance-drama in Bali; death of Ibsen
1907 Picasso's *Les Demoiselles d'Avignon*	1907 First Chinese spoken drama (*The Black Slave's Cry to Heaven* in Chinese in Tokyo); *Playboy* riots in Dublin
1908–12 Cubism in Paris	1909 Ballets Russes in Paris
1912 Chinese Republic proclaimed; *Titanic* sinks	1912 Craig-Stanislavsky production of *Hamlet* at Moscow Art Theatre
1913 Stravinsky's *Rite of Spring* in Paris	1913 Jacques Copeau's Théâtre du Vieux-Colombier opens in Paris; *Darktown Follies* opens in Harlem in New York
1914–18 First World War	
1915 Einstein's general theory of relativity; Kafka's 'The Metamorphosis'	
1916 Easter Rising in Dublin	
1917 Bolshevik Revolution	

HISTORICAL/CULTURAL EVENTS	THEATRE AND PERFORMANCE EVENTS
1919 Ezra Pound begins the *Cantos*	
1920 Gandhi begins non-cooperation movement against British rule in India; Irish Civil War; League of Nations founded	1920 Salzburg Festival founded; O'Neill's *The Emperor Jones* in New York
1921 Irish Free State established	1921 Pirandello's *Six Characters in Search of an Author* opens in Rome
1922 Joyce's *Ulysses*; Elliot's *The Waste Land*; Mussolini in power in Italy	
	1923 Meyerhold Theatre founded in Moscow; The Cotton Club opens in Harlem
	1924 Stanislavsky's *My Life in Art*; Tsukuji (Little) Theatre in Tokyo
1925 Hitler's *Mein Kampf*; Fitzgerald's *The Great Gatsby*	1925 Pirandello's Teatro d'Arte founded in Rome; Shaw wins Nobel Prize for Literature
	1926 Martha Graham's dance troupe appears in New York
1927 First talking film, *The Jazz Singer*, Monet's *Water Lilies* in Paris	1927 Piscator takes over Volksbühne in Berlin
1928 First television in USA; Alexander Fleming discovers penicillin	1928 Brecht-Weill *The Threepenny Opera* in Berlin
1929 Wall Street crash starts Great Depression	
	1931 Group Theatre founded in New York
	1932 Artaud's 'First Manifesto of the Theatre of Cruelty'
1933 Hitler becomes Chancellor of Germany	1933 Brecht, Reinhardt, Piscator, and many other artists escape Nazi Germany
	1934 Pirandello wins Nobel Prize for Literature
1935 Italy invades Ethiopia; German rearmament	1935 Federal Theatre Project in USA; Gershwin's *Porgy and Bess*
1936 Spanish Civil War; Margaret Mitchell's *Gone with the Wind*	1936 O'Neill wins Nobel Prize for Literature
1937 Picasso paints *Guernica*	
1939–45 Second World War	
1940 Fall of France; Battle of Britain	1940 Meyerhold executed
1941 Germany invades USSR; Orson Welles's film *Citizen Kane*; Japan bombs Pearl Harbor	
	1942 Mao Zedong's 'Talks at the Yan'an Forum on Literature and Art'
	1943 Rodgers and Hammerstein's *Oklahoma!* in New York
1945 Newsreels of Nazi death camps as war in Europe ends; atomic bombs dropped on Hiroshima and Nagasaki; Japanese surrender	
	1946 New York City Ballet established
1947 Indian Independence and Partition	1947 Strehler and Grassi's Piccolo Theatre in Milan; Actors Studio founded in New York
1947–90 The Cold War	
1948 First Arab–Israeli War; Gandhi assassinated	

HISTORICAL/CULTURAL EVENTS	THEATRE AND PERFORMANCE EVENTS
1949 People's Republic of China established under Mao	
1950–1 Korean War	1950 Korean National Theatre founded
1952 Ralph Ellison's *Invisible Man*	1952 First All China Festival of traditional operas in Beijing
1953 Death of Stalin	1953 Beckett's *Waiting for Godot* in Paris
1954 Viet Minh victory at Dien Bien Phu	1954 Joseph Papp's New York Shakespeare
1954–62 Algerian War	Festival founded; National School of
c.1954–68 Civil Rights movement in America	Drama in New Delhi
c.1955–62 Beatnik movement	
1956 De-Stalinization in USSR; Allen Ginsberg's poem *Howl*	1956 Osborne's *Look Back in Anger* produced in London
1957 USSR launches Sputnik I and II	1957 O'Neill posthumously awarded Pulitzer Prize for *A Long Day's Journey into Night*; Efua Sutherland's open-air theatre, the Drama Studio, in Ghana
1958–69 De Gaulle president of France	1958 Off-Off-Broadway movement begins at Caffe Cino, New York
1959 Alan Resnais's film *Hiroshima mon amour*	
1960 Independence of African nations begins; Hitchcock's *Psycho*; Fellini's *La dolce vita*	
1961 Foucault's *Madness and Civilization*	1961 Death of Mei Lanfang; Royal Shakespeare Company founded in Stratford-upon-Avon
1962 Cuban Missile Crisis	1962 Ngugi wa Thiong'o's *The Black Hermit* in Kenya
1963 John Kennedy assassinated	1963 Tawfiq el-Hakim's *The Tree Climber*, in Cairo
	1964 Mnouchkine's Théâtre du Soleil founded in Paris; Imamu Baraka's *Dutchman* in New York
1965 Vietnam War begins	
c.1965–73 Hippie counter-culture movement	
1967 Six Day War in Middle East; the 'summer of love'	
1967–70 Nigerian Civil War	
1968 Worldwide student unrest and protest; Warsaw Pact invades Czechoslovakia; Martin Luther King and Robert Kennedy assassinated	1968 End of British stage censorship; Dario Fo and Franca Rama found Nuova Scena in Milan; *Hair!* on Broadway; Living Theatre's *Paradise Now* on tour in Europe and USA
1969 Neil Armstrong is first man on moon; Woodstock Music Festival	1969 Beckett wins Nobel Prize for Literature
	1970 Peter Brook founds International Centre for Theatre Research in Paris; Brook's *A Midsummer Night's Dream* for Royal Shakespeare Company; Laurence Olivier becomes first actor raised to peerage

HISTORICAL/CULTURAL EVENTS	THEATRE AND PERFORMANCE EVENTS
	1971 Yury Lyubimov's *Hamlet* in Moscow (for ten years); Lloyd Webber's *Jesus Christ Superstar*
1973 Watergate; Yom Kippur War	
1974 Nixon resigns as US president; start of the punk movement	
1975 Khmer Rouge takeover in Cambodia	1975 Khmer Rouge regime destroys performance traditions and executes performers in Cambodia; the Wooster Group founded in New York; National Theatre of Great Britain moves to new South Bank building in London; *A Chorus Line* in New York
	1976 Robert Wilson–Philip Glass *Einstein on the Beach* in New York; Market Theatre founded in Johannesburg; centennial production of Wagner's *The Ring* by Pierre Boulez and Patrice Chéreau opens at Bayreuth
	1980 Ninagawa Yukio's *Ninagawa Macbeth* in Tokyo
1981 IBM launches the personal computer	
1982 Falklands War	1982 Suzuki Tadashi's Toga International Arts Festival founded in Japan; Lloyd Webber's *Cats* in New York; Fugard's *Master Harold and the Boys* at Yale Repertory Theatre
	1983 Laurie Anderson's performance art piece *United States*
1984–5 Ethiopian famine	1985 Peter Brook's production of *The Mahabharata* at Avignon Festival
	1986 Wole Soyinka wins Nobel Prize for Literature; Karen Finley's performance art piece *The Constant State of Desire*
1989 Berlin Wall comes down; protests in Tiananmen Square; death of Japanese Emperor Hirohito; Václav Havel elected president of Czechoslovakia	1989 Death of Samuel Beckett
1990 Collapse of Soviet Union and satellite states in East Europe; Cold War ends; Nelson Mandela freed in South Africa	
1990s The rise of the Internet	1990s Drastic reductions of state subsidy for theatres in former socialist countries in Europe
1991 The Gulf War	
	1992 Derek Walcott wins Nobel Prize for Literature
	1993 Tony Kushner's *Angels in America* on Broadway

HISTORICAL/CULTURAL EVENTS	THEATRE AND PERFORMANCE EVENTS
	1997 The Globe Theatre opens in London; Dario Fo wins Nobel Prize for Literature
	2000 Gao Xingjian wins Nobel Prize for Literature
2001 Terrorist attacks on the World Trade Center in New York and Pentagon in Washington; USA invades Afghanistan and starts War on Terror	
2003 Completion of Human Genome Project; US-led coalition invades Iraq (Second Gulf War); deadly heat wave in Europe; increasing awareness of global warming	
2004 European Union expands from 15 to 25 nations; Madrid terrorist bombings; Indian Ocean tsunami kills at least 230,000 people in South and South-East Asia	
2005 London terrorist bombings; Hurricane Katrina submerges much of New Orleans	2005 Harold Pinter wins Nobel Prize for Literature; death of Arthur Miller
2007 European Union expands to 27 nations	2007 *Radio Golf* on Broadway, the last of August Wilson's ten-play Pittsburgh Cycle
2008 Mumbai terrorist attacks; 'subprime' mortgage crisis sparks worldwide economic recession	2008 Death of Harold Pinter
2009 Barack Hussein Obama inaugurated President of US	
2010 Earthquake in Haiti destroys capital and kills over 230,000 people	2010 Rebuilt Royal Shakespeare Theatre opened in Stratford
2011 UN estimates world population at almost 7 billion	

Further reading

A selection of important and useful books in English on general aspects of theatre and performance. Works on individual artists (playwrights, directors, etc.) have not been included unless they deal with larger issues.

1. Reference Works and Theatre Histories

Banham, Martin (ed.), *The Cambridge Guide to Theatre* (Cambridge, 1995)

Banham, Martin, Hill, Errol, and Woodyard, George (eds.), *The Cambridge Guide to African and Caribbean Theatre* (Cambridge, 1994)

Benson, Eugene, and Conolly, L. W. (eds.), *The Oxford Companion to Canadian Theatre* (Oxford, 1989)

Brandon, James R., *The Cambridge Guide to Asian Theatre* (Cambridge, 1993)

Bratton, Jacky, *New Readings in Theatre History* (Cambridge, 2003)

Brockett, Oscar G., and Hildy, Franklin, *History of Theatre*, 10th edn. (Boston, 2009)

Brown, John Russell (ed.), *The Oxford Illustrated History of Theatre* (Oxford, 1995)

Chambers, Colin (ed.), *The Continuum Companion to Twentieth Century Theatre* (London, 2002)

Farrell, Joseph, and Puppa, Paolo (eds.), *A History of Italian Theatre* (Cambridge, 2006)

Hamburger, Maik, and Williams, Simon (eds.), *A History of German Theatre* (Cambridge, 2009)

Hartnoll, Phyllis (ed.), *The Oxford Companion to the Theatre*, 4th edn. (Oxford, 1983)

Hawkins-Dady, Mark, and Pickering, David (eds.), *International Dictionary of Theatre*, 3 vols. (London, 1992–6)

Jurkowski, Henryk, *A History of European Puppetry*, 2 vols. (Lewiston, 1996–8)

Kennedy, Dennis (ed.), *The Oxford Encyclopedia of Theatre and Performance* (Oxford, 2003)

Lal, Ananda (ed.), *The Oxford Companion to Indian Theatre* (Oxford, 2004)

Leech, Christopher, et al. (eds.), *The Revels History of Drama in English*, 8 vols. (1976–83; reprinted London, 1996)

Londré, Felicia Hardison, *The History of World Theatre: from the Restoration to the present*, 2 vols. (New York, 1991)

Nagler, A. M. (ed.), *A Source Book in Theatrical History* (New York, 1952)

Nicoll, Allardyce, *World Drama*, revised edn. (London, 1976)

Oenslager, Donald, *Stage Design: four centuries of scenic invention* (New York, 1975)

Parsons, Philip, and Chance, Victoria (eds.), *Companion to Theatre in Australia* (Sydney, 1995)

Pavis, Patrice, *Dictionary of the Theatre: terms, concepts, and analysis*, trans. Christine Shantz (Toronto, 1998)

Rubin, Don, et al., *The World Encyclopedia of Contemporary Theatre*, 5 vols. (London, 1994–8)

Sadie, Stanley (ed.), *History of Opera* (London, 1989)

Southern, Richard, *Seven Ages of the Theatre* (London, 1964)

Thomson, Peter, and Salgado, Gamini, *The Everyman Companion to the Theatre* (London, 1987)

Thomson, Peter (gen. ed.), *The Cambridge History of British Theatre*, 3 vols. (Cambridge, 2004)

Trussler, Simon, *The Cambridge Illustrated History of British Theatre* (Cambridge, 1994)

Wiles, David, *A Short History of Western Performance Space* (Cambridge, 2003)

Wilmer, S. E. (ed.), *Writing and Rewriting National Theatre Histories* (Iowa City, 2004)

Wilmeth, Don B. (ed.), *The Cambridge Guide to American Theatre*, 2nd edn. (Cambridge, 2007)

Worthen, W. B., and Holland, Peter (eds.), *Theorizing Practice: redefining theatre history* (Basingstoke, 2003)

Wyckham, Glynne, *A History of the Theatre*, 3rd end. (Oxford, 1985)

Zarrilli, Phillip B., et al., *Theatre Histories: an introduction*, 2nd edn. (New York, 2009)

2. Theoretical and General Works

Abercrombie, Nicholas, and Longhurst, Brian, *Audiences: a sociological theory of performance and imagination* (London, 1998)

Aronson, Arnold, *Looking into the Abyss: essays on scenography* (Ann Arbor, 2005)

Aston, Elaine, *An Introduction to Feminism and Theatre* (London, 1995)

—— and Case, Sue-Ellen (eds.), *Staging International Feminisms* (Basingstoke, 2007)

Auslander, Philip, *Liveness: performance in a mediatized culture*, 2nd edn. (London, 2008)

Balme, Christopher, *Pacific Performances: theatricality and cross-cultural encounter in the South Seas* (Basingstoke, 2007)

Balme, Christopher, *The Cambridge Introduction to Theatre Studies* (Cambridge, 2008)

Barba, Eugenio, and Savarese, Nicola, *The Dictionary of Theatre Anthropology: the secret art of the performer*, trans. Richard Fowler (London, 1991)

Barish, Jonas, *The Antitheatrical Prejudice* (Berkeley, 1981)

Bennett, Susan, *Theatre Audiences: a theory of production and reception*, 2nd edn. (New York, 1997)

Bentley, Eric, *The Playwright as Thinker: a study of drama in modern times* (New York, 1946)

Berghaus, Günter, *Avant-Garde Performance: live events and electronic technologies* (Basingstoke, 2005)

Bharucha, Rustom, *The Politics of Cultural Practice: thinking through theatre in an age of globalization* (London, 2000)

—— *Theatre and the World: performance and the politics of culture* (London, 1993)

Blau, Herbert, *The Audience* (Baltimore, 1990)

Boal, Augusto, *Legislative Theatre* (London, 1999)

Boal, Augusto, *Theatre of the Oppressed*, trans. Charles A. and Maria-Odilia Leal McBride and Emily Fryer, new edn. (London, 2000)

Campbell, Patrick, and Kear, Adrian (eds.), *Psychoanalysis and Performance* (London, 2001)

Carlson, Marvin, *Performance: a critical introduction*, 2nd edn. (New York, 2004)

—— *Places of Performance: the semiotics of theatre* (Ithaca, NY, 1989)

—— *Theories of the Theatre: a historical and critical survey, from the Greeks to the present*, 2nd edn. (Ithaca, NY, 1993)

Case, Sue-Ellen, *The Domain-Matrix: performing lesbian at the end of print culture* (Bloomington, 1996)

—— *Feminism and the Theatre* (New York, 1987)

Causey, Matthew, *Theatre and Performance in Digital Culture: from simulation to embeddedness* (London, 2006)

Chaudhuri, Una, *Staging Place: the geography of modern drama* (Ann Arbor, 1995)

Clark, Barrett H., *European Theories of the Drama* (New York, 1965)

Cole, Toby, and Chinoy, Helen K. (eds.), *Actors on Acting*, rev. edn. (New York, 1980)

Davis, Tracy C., *The Cambridge Companion to Performance Studies* (Cambridge, 2008)

Delgado, Maria M., and Heritage, Paul (eds.), *In Contact with the Gods? directors talk theatre* (Manchester, 1996)

Diamond, Elin (ed.), *Performance and Cultural Politics* (London, 1996)

Dolan, Jill, *The Feminist Spectator as Critic* (Ann Arbor, 1991)

—— *Utopia in Performance: finding hope at the theatre* (Ann Arbor, 2005)

Dukore, Bernard, *Dramatic Theory and Criticism from the Greeks to Grotowski* (New York, 1974)

Elam, Keir, *The Semiotics of Theatre and Drama*, 2nd edn. (London, 2002)

Gerould, Daniel, *Theatre/Theory/Theatre: the major critical texts from Aristotle and Zeami to Soyinka and Havel* (New York, 2000)

Goffman, Erving, *The Presentation of Self in Everyday Life* (Garden City, NY, 1959)

Holland, Peter (ed.), *Shakespeare, Memory and Performance* (Cambridge, 2006)

Howard, Pamela, *What Is Scenography?* 2nd edn. (London, 2009)

Huxley, Mike, and Witts, Noel (eds.), *Twentieth Century Performance Reader* (New York, 1996)

Kennedy, Dennis, *The Spectator and the Spectacle: audiences in modernity and postmodernity* (Cambridge, 2009)

—— and Yong Li Lan (eds.), *Shakespeare in Asia: contemporary performance* (Cambridge, 2010)

Kershaw, Baz, *The Politics of Performance: radical theatre as cultural intervention* (London, 1992)

Kirshenblatt-Gimblett, Barbara, *Destination Culture: tourism, museums, and heritage* (Berkeley, 1998)

Leacroft, Richard, and Leacroft, Helen, *Theatre and Playhouse: an illustrated survey of theatre building from ancient Greece to the present day* (New York, 1984)

Lehmann, Hans-Thies, *Postdramatic Theatre*, trans. Karen Jürs-Munby (London, 2006)

Nuttall, A. D., *Why Does Tragedy Give Pleasure?* (Oxford, 1996)

Postlewait, Thomas, *The Cambridge Introduction to Theatre Historiography* (Cambridge, 2009)

—— and McConachie, Bruce (eds.), *Interpreting the Theatrical Past: essays in the historiography of performance* (Iowa City, 1989)

Pavis, Patrice (ed.), *The Intercultural Performance Reader* (New York, 1996)

Pavis, Patrice, *Languages of the Stage: essays on the semiology of the theatre* (New York, 1982)

—— *Theatre at the Crossroads of Culture* (London, 1992)

Phelan, Peggy, *Unmarked: the politics of performance* (London, 1993)

Reinelt, Janelle G., and Roach, Joseph R. (eds.), *Critical Theory and Performance*, rev. edn. (Ann Arbor, 2007)

Roach, Joseph R., *Cities of the Dead: circum-Atlantic performance* (New York, 1996)

—— *It* (Ann Arbor, 2007)

—— *The Player's Passion: studies in the science of acting* (Ann Arbor, 1993)

Rokem, Freddie, *Performing History: theatrical representations of the past in contemporary theatre* (Iowa City, 2000)

Rozik, Eli, *The Roots of Theatre: rethinking ritual and other theories of origin* (Iowa City, 2002)

Schechner, Richard, *Between Theatre and Anthropology* (Philadelphia, 1985)

—— *Essays on Performance Theory* (New York, 1977)

—— *Performance Studies: an introduction* (London, 2002)

Senelick, Laurence, *The Changing Room: sex, drag and theatre* (London, 2000)

Sidnell, Michael J. (ed.), *Sources of Dramatic Theory*, 2 vols. (Cambridge, 1991–4)

Steiner, George, *The Death of Tragedy* (London, 1961)

Turner, Victor, *From Ritual to Theatre* (New York, 1982)

Wallace, Jennifer, *The Cambridge Introduction to Tragedy* (Cambridge, 2007)

Weitz, Eric, *The Cambridge Introduction to Comedy* (Cambridge, 2009)

Zarrilli, Phillip B. (ed.), *Acting Reconsidered*, 2nd edn. (London, 2002)

3. Ancient Europe

Beacham, Richard C., *The Roman Theatre and Its Audience* (Cambridge, Mass., 1992)

—— *Spectacle Entertainments of Early Imperial Rome* (New Haven, 1999)

Beare, W., *The Roman Stage*, 3rd edn. (London, 1968)

Csapo, E. G., and Slater, W. J., *The Context of Ancient Drama* (Ann Arbor, 1995)

Easterling, P. E. (ed.), *The Cambridge Companion to Greek Tragedy* (Cambridge, 1997)

—— and Hall, Edith (eds.), *Greek and Roman Actors: aspects of an ancient profession* (Cambridge, 2002)

Goldhill, Simon, *Reading Greek Tragedy* (Cambridge, 1986)

Green, J. R., *Theatre in Ancient Greek Society* (London, 1994)

Hunter, Richard L., *The New Comedy of Greece and Rome* (Cambridge, 1985)

McDonald, Marianne, and Walton, J. Michael (eds.), *The Cambridge Companion to Greek and Roman Theatre* (Cambridge, 2007)

Moore, Timothy J., *The Theater of Plautus: playing to the audience* (Austin, Texas, 1998)

Pickard-Cambridge, A. W., *The Dramatic Festivals of Athens*, 2nd edn., rev. J. Gould and D. Lewis (Oxford, 1968, addenda 1988)

Segal, Erich (ed.), *Roman Laughter: the comedy of Plautus*, 2nd edn. (New York, 1987)

Simon, Erika, *The Ancient Theatre* (London, 1982)

Taplin, Oliver, *Greek Tragedy in Action*, rev. edn. (London, 1985)

—— *Pots and Plays: interactions between tragedy and Greek vase-painting of the fourth century BC* (Los Angeles, 2007)

Vernant, Jean-Pierre, and Vidal-Naquet, Pierre, *Myth and Tragedy in Ancient Greece* (New York, 1988)

Webb, Ruth, *Demons and Dancers: performance in late antiquity* (Cambridge, Mass., 2008)

Wiles, David, *The Masks of Menander: sign and meaning in Greek and Roman performance* (London, 1991)

—— *Greek Theatre Performance: an introduction* (Cambridge, 2000)

—— *Mask and Performance in Greek Tragedy: from ancient festival to modern experimentation* (Cambridge, 2007)

4. Medieval Europe

Axton, R., *European Drama of the Early Middle Ages*, (London, 1974)

Beadle, Richard, and Fletcher, Alan J. (eds.), *The Cambridge Companion to Medieval English Theatre*, 2nd edn. (Cambridge, 2008)

Bevington, David (ed.), *Medieval Drama* (Boston, 1975)

Burke, Peter, *Popular Culture in Early Modern Europe* (London, 1979)

Elliott, John R., *Playing God: medieval mysteries on the modern stage* (Toronto, 1989)

Harris, John Wesley, *Medieval Theatre in Context* (London, 1992)

Nicoll, Allardyce, *Masks, Mimes, and Miracles* (London, 1935)

Potter, Robert, *The English Morality Play* (London, 1975)

Records of Early English Drama (REED), records volumes (Toronto, 1979–)

Rossiter, A. P., *English Drama: from early times to the Elizabethans* (Folcroft, 1978)

Simon, Eckehard (ed.), *The Theatre of Medieval Europe: new research into early drama* (Cambridge, 1991)

Stevens, Martin, *Four Middle English Mystery Cycles* (Princeton, 1987)

Tydeman, William, *The Medieval European Stage, 500–1550* (Cambridge, 2001)

—— *The Theatre in the Middle Ages* (Cambridge, 1978)

Wickham, Glynne, *Early English Stages, 1300–1660*, 5 vols. (London, 1959–2002)

Wickham, Glynne, *Medieval Theatre*, 3rd edn. (Cambridge, 1987)

5. Europe 1500–1700

Allen, John J., *The Reconstruction of a Spanish Golden Age Playhouse: El Corral del Principe 1583–1744* (Gainesville, Florida, 1983)

Andrews, Richard, *Scripts and Scenarios: the performance of comedy of Renaissance Italy* (Cambridge, 1993)

Bate, Jonathan, and Jackson, Russell (eds.), *Shakespeare: an illustrated stage history* (Oxford, 1996)

Bentley, G. E., *The Jacobean and Caroline Stage*, 7 vols. (Oxford, 1941–68)

—— *The Profession of Player in Shakespeare's Time* (Princeton, 1984)

Brandt, George W., and W. Hogendoorn (eds.), *German and Dutch Theatre 1600–1848* (Cambridge, 1992)

Cairns, Christopher (ed.), *The Commedia dell'Arte from the Renaissance to Dario Fo* (Lewiston, NY, 1989)

Chambers, E. K., *The Elizabethan Stage*, 4 vols. (London, 1923)

Clubb, Louise George, *Italian Drama in Shakespeare's Time* (New Haven, 1989)

Cohen, Walter, *Drama of a Nation: public theater in Renaissance England and Spain* (Ithaca, NY, 1985)

Cox, John D., and Kastan, David (eds.), *A New History of Early English Drama* (New York, 1997)

Dawson, Antony, and Yachnin, Paul, *The Culture of Playgoing in Shakespeare's England* (Cambridge, 2001)

De Grazia, Margreta, and Wells, Stanley (eds.), *The Cambridge Companion to Shakespeare* (Cambridge, 2001)

Dillon, Janette, *The Cambridge Introduction to Early English Theatre* (Cambridge, 2009)

Dobson, Michael, with Wells, Stanley (eds.), *The Oxford Companion to Shakespeare* (Oxford, 2001)

Greenblatt, Stephen, *Renaissance Self-Fashioning* (Chicago, 1980)

Gurr, Andrew, *Playgoing in Shakespeare's London*, 3rd edn. (Cambridge, 2004)

—— *The Shakespearean Stage 1574–1642*, 4th edn. (Cambridge, 2009)

Herrick, Marvin T., *Italian Comedy in the Renaissance* (Urbana, Ill., 1965)

Hodgdon, Barbara, and Worthen, W. B. (eds.), *A Companion to Shakespeare and Performance* (Oxford, 2005)

Holland, Peter, *The Ornament of Action: text and performance in Restoration comedy* (Cambridge, 1979)

Howard, Jean, *The Stage and Social Struggle in Early Modern England* (London, 1994)

Howarth, William D. (ed.), *French Theatre in the Neoclassical Era, 1550–1789* (Cambridge, 1997)

Howarth, W. D., *Molière: a playwright and his audience* (Cambridge, 1982)

Howe, Elizabeth, *The First English Actresses* (Cambridge, 1992)

Hunter, G. K., *English Drama 1586–1642* (Oxford, 1997)

Jeffery, Brian, *French Renaissance Comedy, 1552–1630* (Oxford, 1969)

Johnson, Nora, *The Actor as Playwright in Early Modern Drama* (Cambridge, 2003)

Lough, John, *Seventeenth-Century French Drama: the background* (Oxford, 1979)

McKendrick, Melveena, *Theatre in Spain 1490–1700* (Cambridge, 1989)

—— *Women and Society in the Spanish Drama of the Golden Age* (Cambridge, 1974)

Munro, Lucy, *Children of the Queen's Revels: a Jacobean theatre repertory* (Cambridge, 2005)

Orgel, Stephen, *The Authentic Shakespeare and Other Problems of the Early Modern Stage* (New York, 2002)

Orgel, Stephen, *The Illusion of Power: political theatre in the English Renaissance* (Berkeley, 1975)

—— and Strong, Roy, *Inigo Jones: the theatre of the Stuart Court*, 2 vols. (Berkeley, 1973)

Powell, Jocelyn, *Restoration Theatre Production* (London, 1984)

Richards, Kenneth, and Richards, Laura, *The Commedia dell'Arte: a documentary history* (Oxford, 1990)

Scott, Virginia, *The Commedia Dell'Arte in Paris, 1644–1697* (Charlottesville, Virginia, 1990)

Stern, Tiffany, *Rehearsal from Shakespeare to Sheridan* (Oxford, 2000)

Thomson, Peter, *Shakespeare's Professional Career* (Cambridge, 1992)

—— *Shakespeare's Theatre*, 2nd edn. (London, 1992)

Vince, Ronald W., *Renaissance Theatre: a historiographical handbook* (Westport, Conn., 1984)

Wikander, Matthew H., *Princes to Act: royal audience and royal performance, 1578–1792* (Baltimore, 1993)

Wickham, Glynne, *Early English Stages, 1300–1660*, 5 vols (London, 1959–2002)

Weimann, Robert, *Shakespeare and the Popular Tradition in the Theater: studies in the social dimension of dramatic form and function*, ed. Robert Schwartz (Baltimore, 1978)

Weimann, Robert, and Bruster, Douglas, *Shakespeare and the Power of Performance: stage and page in the Elizabethan theatre* (Cambridge, 2008)

Wells, Stanley, and Stanton, Sarah (eds.), *The Cambridge Companion to Shakespeare on Stage* (Cambridge, 2002)

6. Europe 1700–1900

Bailey, Peter (ed.), *Music Hall: the business of pleasure* (Milton Keynes, 1986)

Baker, Michael, *The Rise of the Victorian Actor* (London, 1978)

Bevis, Richard W., *English Drama: Restoration and eighteenth century, 1660–1789* (London, 1988)

Bjurstrom, Per, *Giacomo Torelli and Baroque Stage Design* (Stockholm, 1961)

Booth, Michael R., *Theatre in the Victorian Age* (Cambridge, 1991)

—— *Victorian Spectacular Theatre 1850–1910* (London, 1981)

Bratton, J. S., et al. (eds.), *Melodrama: stage, picture, screen* (London, 1994)

Bratton, J. S. (ed.), *Music Hall: performance and style* (Milton Keynes, 1986)

Bratton, Jacky, *New Readings in Theatre History* (Cambridge, 2003)

Brown, Frederick, *Theatre and Revolution: the culture of the French stage* (New York, 1980)

Carlson, Marvin, *The French Stage in Nineteenth Century* (Metuchen, NJ, 1972)

—— *The German Stage in Nineteenth Century* (Metuchen, NJ, 1972)

—— *Goethe and the Weimar Theatre* (Ithaca, NY, 1978)

—— *The Italian Stage from Goldoni to D'Annunzio* (London, 1981)

Charnow, Sally Debra, *Theatre, Politics, and Markets in Fin-de-Siècle Paris: staging modernity* (New York, 2005)

Davis, Jim, and Emeljanow, Victor, *Reflecting the Audience: London theatregoing, 1840–1880* (Iowa City, 2001)

Davis, Tracy, *Actresses as Working Women: their social identity in Victorian culture* (New York, 1991)

—— *The Economics of the British Stage, 1800–1914* (Cambridge, 2000)

—— and Donkin, Ellen (eds.), *Women and Playwriting in Nineteenth-Century Britain* (Cambridge, 1999)

Donkin, Ellen, *Getting into the Act: women playwrights in London, 1776–1829* (London, 1994)

Donohue, Joseph, *Theatre in the Age of Kean* (Oxford, 1975)

Hays, Michael, and Nikolopoulou, Anastasia (eds.), *Melodrama: the cultural emergence of a genre* (New York, 1996)

Hemmings, F. W. J., *The Theatre Industry in Nineteenth-Century France* (Cambridge, 1993)

—— *Theatre and State in France, 1790–1905* (Cambridge, 1994)

Hume, Robert D. (ed.), *The London Theatre World, 1660–1800* (Carbondale, Ill., 1980)

Innes, Christopher (ed.), *A Sourcebook on Naturalist Theatre* (London, 2000)

Jackson, Russell (ed.), *Victorian Theatre* (London, 1989)

Kruger, Loren, *The National Stage: theatre and cultural legitimation in England, France, and America* (Chicago, 1992)

McCormick, John, and Pratasik, Bennie, *Popular Puppet Theatre in Europe, 1800–1914* (Cambridge, 1998)

Marker, Frederick J., and Marker, Lise-Lone, *A History of Scandinavian Theatre* (Cambridge, 1996)

Meisel, Martin, *Realizations: narrative, pictorial, and theatrical arts in nineteenth-century England* (Princeton, 1983)

Moody, Jane, and O'Quinn, Daniel (eds.), *The Cambridge Companion to British Theatre, 1730–1830* (Cambridge, 2007)

Morash, Christopher, *A History of Irish Theatre, 1601–2000* (Cambridge, 2002)

Nichol, Allardyce, *The Garrick Stage* (Manchester, 1980)

Odell, G. C. D., *Shakespeare from Betterton to Irving*, 2 vols. (New York, 1920)

Osbourne, John, *The Meiningen Court Theatre, 1866–1890* (Cambridge, 1988)

Patterson, Michael, *The First German Theatre: Schiller, Goethe, Kleist, and Büchner in performance* (London, 1990)

Powell, Kerry, *Women and Victorian Theatre* (Cambridge, 1997)

—— (ed.), *The Cambridge Companion to Victorian and Edwardian Theatre* (Cambridge, 2004)

Puchner, Martin, *Poetry of the Revolution: Marx, manifestos, and the avant-gardes* (Princeton, 2005)

Rees, Terence, *Theatre Lighting in the Age of Gas* (London, 1978)

Rowell, George, *The Victorian Theatre, 1792–1914*, 2nd edn. (London, 1979)

Schoch, Richard, *Shakespeare's Victorian Stage* (Cambridge, 1998)

Schumacher, Claude (ed.), *Naturalism and Symbolism in European Theatre, 1850–1918* (Cambridge, 1996)

Senelick, Laurence (ed.), *National Theatre in Northern and Eastern Europe, 1746–1900* (Cambridge, 1991)

Shaw, George Bernard, *Our Theatre in the Nineties*, 3 vols. (London, 1932)

Southern, Richard, *Changeable Scenery: its origin and development in the English theatre* (London, 1952)

Thomson, Peter, *The Cambridge Introduction to English Theatre, 1660–1900* (Cambridge, 2006)

Wikander, Matthew H., *Princes to Act: royal audience and royal performance, 1578–1792* (Baltimore, 1993)

Williams, Simon, *German Actors of the Eighteenth and Nineteenth Centuries: idealism, romanticism, realism* (Westport, Conn., 1985)

Ziter, Edward, *The Orient on the Victorian Stage* (Cambridge, 2008)

7. Europe since 1900

Appia, Adolphe, *Texts on Theatre*, ed. Richard C. Beacham (London, 1993)

Artaud, Antonin, *Theatre and its Double*, trans. Mary Caroline Richards (New York, 1958)

Aston, Elaine, and Reinelt, Janelle (eds.), *The Cambridge Companion to Modern British Women Playwrights* (Cambridge, 2000)

Bablet, Denis, *The Revolution in Stage Design in the Twentieth Century* (Paris, 1977)

Barker, Clive, and Gale, Maggie B. (eds.), *British Theatre Between the Wars, 1918–1939* (Cambridge, 2000)

Booth, Michael R., and Kaplan, Joel H. (eds.), *The Edwardian Theatre: essays on performance and the stage* (Cambridge, 1996)

Bradby, David, *Modern French Drama 1940–1990*, 2nd edn. (Cambridge, 1991)

—— and Williams, David, *Director's Theatre* (New York, 1988)

Braun, Edward, *The Director and the Stage: from naturalism to Grotowski* (New York, 1982)

Brecht, Bertolt, *Brecht on Theatre*, ed. John Willett (New York, 1964)

Brook, Peter, *The Empty Space* (New York, 1968)

——*The Shifting Point, 1946–1987* (New York, 1987)

Burian, Jarka M., *Leading Creators of Twentieth-Century Czech Theatre* (London, 2002)

Carlson, Marvin, *Theatre Is More Beautiful Than War: German stage directing in the late twentieth century* (Iowa City, 2009)

Craig, Edward Gordon, *On the Art of Theatre* (London, 1911)

Deak, Frantisek, *Symbolist Theater: the formation of an avant-garde* (New York, 1993)

Elsom, John, *Post War British Theatre* (London, 1979)

Esslin, Martin, *The Theatre of the Absurd*, new edn. (London, 2001)

Goldberg, RoseLee, *Performance Art: from futurism to the present*, rev. edn. (New York, 2001)

Goodman, Lizbeth, *Contemporary Feminist Theatres: to each her own* (London, 1993)

Grene, Nicholas, *The Politics of Irish Drama: plays in context from Boucicault to Friel* (Cambridge, 1999)

Grotowski, Jerzy, *Towards a Poor Theatre* (New York, 1968)

Hainaux, René (ed.), *Stage Design throughout the World*, 4 vols. (New York, 1956–76)

Holroyd, Michael, *Bernard Shaw*, 4 vols. (London, 1988–92)

Hortmann, Wilhelm, *Shakespeare on the German Stage: the twentieth century* (Cambridge, 1998)

Innes, Christopher, *Avant-Garde Theatre: 1892–1992* (London, 1993)

Jackson, Anthony, *The Repertory Movement: a history of regional theatre in Britain* (Cambridge, 1983)

Jelavich, Peter, *Munich and Theatrical Modernism, 1890–1914* (Cambridge, Mass., 1985)

Kaplan, Joel H., and Stowell, Sheila, *Theatre and Fashion: Oscar Wilde to the suffragettes* (Cambridge, 1994)

Kennedy, Dennis, *Granville Barker and the Dream of Theatre* (Cambridge, 1985)

——*Looking at Shakespeare: a visual history of twentieth-century performance*, 2nd edn. (Cambridge, 2001)

Kott, Jan, *Shakespeare Our Contemporary*, trans. Boleslaw Taborski (New York, 1966)

MacGowan, Kenneth, and Jones, R. E., *Continental Stagecraft* (New York, 1922).

McGrath, John, *A Good Night Out: popular theatre, audience, class and form* (London, 1981)

Meisel, Martin, *Shaw and the Nineteenth-Century Theater* (Princeton, 1963)

Morash, Christopher, *A History of Irish Theatre, 1601–2000* (Cambridge, 2002)

Patterson, Michael, *The Revolution in German Theatre, 1900–1933* (London, 1981)

Rebellato, Dan, *1956 and All That: the making of modern British drama* (London, 1999)

Roberts, Philip, *The Royal Court Theatre and the Modern Stage* (Cambridge, 1999)

Rouse, John, *Brecht and the West German Theatre: the practice and politics of interpretation* (Ann Arbor, 1989)

Saunderson, Michael, *From Irving to Olivier: a social history of the acting profession, 1880–1983* (New York, 1985)

Senelick, Laurence (ed.), *Cabaret Performance: Europe, 1890–1940* (Cambridge, 1993)

Shank, Theodore (ed.), *Contemporary British Theatre* (London, 1994)

Schechner, Richard, and Wolford, Lisa (eds.), *The Grotowski Sourcebook* (London, 1997)

Tynan, Kenneth, *A View of the English Stage, 1944–1965* (London, 1984)

Willett, John, *Theatre of the Weimar Republic* (New York, 1988)

Wilmer, S. E. (ed.), *National Theatres in a Changing Europe* (Basingstoke, 2008)

Worthen, W. B., *Shakespeare and the Force of Modern Performance* (Cambridge, 2003)

8. Russia and Soviet Union

Braun, Edward, *Meyerhold: a revolution in theatre* (London, 1995))

Carter, Huntly, *The New Spirit in the Russian Theatre* (London, 1929)

Gregor, Joseph, and Fülop-Miller, René, *The Russian Theatre* (London, 1930)

Karlinsky, Simon, *Russian Drama from its Beginnings to the Age of Pushkin* (Berkeley, 1985)

Kleberg, Lars, *Theatre as Action: Soviet Russian avant-garde aesthetics*, trans. Charles Rougle (London, 1993)

Leach, Robert, *Revolutionary Theatre* (London, 1994)

—— and Borovsky, Victor (eds.), *A History of Russian Theatre* (Cambridge, 1999)

Magarshack, David, *Stanislavsky: a life* (London, 1950)

Margarshack, David, *Chekhov, the Dramatist* (London, 1980)

Rudnitsky, Konstantin, *Russian and Soviet Theatre – Tradition and the Avant-Garde*, (London, 1988)

Russell, Robert, and Barratt, Andrew (eds.), *Russian Theatre in the Age of Modernism* (London, 1990)

Sayler, Oliver, *The Russian Theatre* (New York, 1922)

Segel, Harold, *Twentieth Century Russian Drama* (Baltimore, 1993)

Senelick, Laurence, *The Chekhov Theatre: a century of the plays in performance* (Cambridge, 1997)

Slonim, Marc, *Russian Theatre from the Empire to the Soviets* (Cleveland, 1961)

Smeliansky, Anatoly, *The Russian Theatre after Stalin* (Cambridge, 1999)

Van Norman Baer, Nancy (ed.), *Theatre in Revolution: Russian avant-garde stage design, 1913–1935* (London, 1992)

Worrall, Nick, *Modernism to Realism on the Soviet Stage* (Cambridge, 1989)

9. Africa

Arndt, Susan, et al. (eds.), *Theatre, Performance and New Media in Africa* (Bayreuth, 2007)

Banham, Martin (ed.), *A History of Theatre in Africa* (Cambridge, 2004)

Banham, Martin, Gibbs, James, and Osofisan, Femi (gen. eds.), *African Theatre*, series 1–8 (Oxford, 1999–2009)

Banham, Martin, and Plastow, Jane (eds.), *Contemporary African Plays* (London, 1999)

Banham, Martin, Hill, Errol, and Woodyard, George (eds.), *The Cambridge Guide to African and Caribbean Theatre* (Cambridge, 1994)

Barber, Karin, Collins, John, and Ricard, Alain, *West African Popular Theatre* (Bloomington, 1997)

Blair, Dorothy, *African Literature in French* (London, 1976)

Breitinger, Eckhard (ed.), *Theatre and Performance in Africa: intercultural perspectives* (Bayreuth, 1994)

—— *Theatre and Performance in Africa* (Bayreuth, 1993)

Conteh-Morgan, John, *Theatre and Drama in Francophone Africa* (Cambridge, 1994)

Dunton, Chris, *Make Man Talk True: Nigerian drama in English since 1970* (London, 1992)

Etherton, Michael, *The Development of African Drama* (London, 1982)

Graham-White, Anthony, *The Drama of Black Africa* (New York, 1974)

Gunner, Liz (ed.) *Politics and Performance: theatre, performance and song in southern Africa* (Johannesburg, 1994)

Jeyifo, Biodun, *The Yoruba Popular Travelling Theatre of Nigeria* (Lagos, 1984)

Kacke, Götrick, *Apidan Theatre and Modern Drama* (Stockholm, 1984)

Kamlongera, Christopher, *Theatre for Development in Africa: with case studies from Malawi and Zambia* (Bonn, 1989)

Kerr, David, *African Popular Theatre from Pre-colonial Times to the Present Day* (London, 1995)

Kruger, Loren, *The Drama of South Africa: plays, pageants and publics since 1910* (London, 1999)

Mda, Zakes, *When People Play People: development communication through theatre* (Johannesburg, 1993)

Ogunba, Oyin, and Irele, Abiola (eds.), *Theatre in Africa* (Ibadan, 1978)

Ogunbiyi, Yemi, *Drama and Theatre in Nigeria: a critical sourcebook* (Lagos, 1981)

Okagbue, Osita, *African Theatres and Performance* (London, 2007)

—— *Culture and Identity in African and Caribbean Theatre* (London, 2009)

Okpewho, Isodore, *African Oral Literature: backgrounds, character and continuity* (Bloomington, 1992)

Orkin, Martin, *Drama and the South African State* (Manchester, 1991)

Owomoyela, Oyekan, *African Literatures: an introduction* (Waltham, Mass., 1979)

—— *Visions and Revisions: essays on African literature and criticism* (Washington, 1991)

—— (ed.), *A History of Twentieth-Century African Literatures* (Lincoln, Neb., 1993)

Petersen, Bhekizizwe, *Monarchs, Missionaries and African Intellectuals: African theatre and the unmaking of colonial marginality* (Johannesburg, 2000)

Plastow, Jane, *African Theatre and Politics: the evolution of theatre in Ethiopia, Tanzania and Zimbabwe, a comparative study* (Amsterdam, 1996)

Prentki, Tim, and Preston, Sheila (eds.), *The Applied Theatre Reader* (London, 2009)

Schipper, Mineke, *Theatre and Society in Africa* (Johannesburg, 1982)

Soyinka, Wole, *Art, Dialogue and Outrage: essays on literature and culture* (Ibadan, 1988)

Soyinka, Wole, *Myth, Literature, and the African World* (Cambridge, 1976)

Thiong'o, Ngugi wa, *Penpoints, Gunpoints, and Dreams: the performance of literature and power in post-colonial Africa* (New York, 1998)

—— *Decolonising the Mind: the politics of language in African literature* (Oxford, 1986)

Walter, Harold, *Black Theatre in French: a guide* (Quebec, 1978)

10. South Asia

Ahmed, Syed Jamil, *Acin Pakhi Infinity: indigenous theatre of Bangladesh* (Dhaka, 2000)

Baumer, R., and Brandon, James (eds.), *Sanskrit Drama in Performance* (Honolulu, 1981)

Byrski, M. Christopher, *Concept of Ancient Indian Theatre* (New Delhi, 1974)

Bharucha, Rustom, *Theatre and the World: performance and the politics of culture* (London, 1993)

Bharucha, Rustom, *The Politics of Cultural Practice: thinking through theatre in an age of globalization* (London, 2000)

Dharwadker, Aparna Bhargava, *Theatres of Independence: drama, theory, and urban performance in India since 1947* (Iowa City, 2005)

Dutt, Utpal, *Towards a Revolutionary Theatre* (Calcutta, 1982)

Frasca, Richard Armand, *The Theatre of the Mahabharata: Terukuttu Performance in South India* (Honolulu, 1990)

Ghosh, Manmohan (ed. and trans.), *The Natyashastra Ascribed to Bharat Muni* (Calcutta, 1967)

Gokhale, Shanta, *Playwright at the Centre: Marathi drama from 1843 to the present* (Calcutta, 2000)

Hansen, Kathryn, *Grounds for Play: the Nautanki theatre of North India* (Berkeley, 1992)

Hashmi, Safdar, *The Right to Perform* (Delhi, 1989)

Kapur, Anuradha, *Actors, Pilgrims, Kings and Gods: the Ramlila at Ramnagar* (Calcutta, 1990)

Lal, Ananda (ed.), *The Oxford Companion to Indian Theatre* (Oxford, 2004)

Mukherjee, Sushil Kumar, *The Story of the Calcutta Theatres: 1753–1980* (Calcutta, 1982)

Obeyesekere, Ranjini, *Theater in a Time of Terror: satire in a permitted space* (New Delhi, 1999)

Panchal, Goverdhan, *Kuttampalam and Kutiyattam* (New Delhi, 1984)

Ranade, Ashok D., *Stage Music of Maharashtra* (New Delhi, 1986)

Richmond, Farley P., Swann, Darius L., and Zarrilli, Phillip (eds.), *Indian Theatre: traditions of performance* (Honolulu, 1990)

Schechner, Richard, *Performative Circumstances from the Avant Garde to Ramlila* (Calcutta, 1983)

Sircar, Badal, *The Third Theatre* (Calcutta, 1978)

Vatsyayan, Kapila, *Traditional Indian Theatre: multiple streams* (New Delhi, 1980)

Zarrilli, Phillip B., *When the Body Becomes All Eyes: paradigms, practices and discourses of power in Kalarippayattu* (New Delhi, 1998)

Zarrilli, Phillip B., *When Gods and Demons Come to Play: Kathakali dance-drama in performance and context* (London, 2000)

11. South-East Asia

General

Brandon, James R., *Theatre in Southeast Asia* (Cambridge, Mass., 1967)

Mietinnen, Yukka, *Classical Dance and Theatre in Southeast Asia* (Oxford, 1992).

Pong, Cuoa Soo, (ed.), *Traditional Theatre in Southeast Asia* (Singapore, 1995)

Yousof, Ghulam-Sarwar, *Dictionary of Traditional Southeast Asian Theatre* (Oxford, 1994)

Burma

Singer, Noel, *Burmese Theatre and Dance* (Oxford, 1995)

Cambodia

Cravath, Paul, *Earth in Flower: the divine mystery of the Cambodian dance drama* (Holmes Beach, Florida, 2007)

Kravel, Pech T. *Yike and Bassac: theatre of Cambodia* (Phnom Penh, 1997)

Indonesia

Bandem, I Madé, and Deboer, Frederik E., *Kaja and Kelod: Balinese dance in transition* (Oxford, 1982)

Brandon, James R. (ed.), *On Thrones of Gold: three Javanese shadow plays* (Honolulu, 1993)

Emigh, John, *Masked Performance: the play of self and other in ritual and theatre* (Philadelphia, 1996)

Malaysia

Yousof, Ghulam-Sarwar, *Panggung Inu: aspects of traditional Malay theatre* (Singapore, 2004)

Sweeney, Amin, *Malay Shadow Puppets: the Wayang Siam of Kelantan* (London, 1980)

Philippines

Tiongson, Nicanor G., *Komedya* (Quezon City, 1999)

—— *Sinakulo* (Quezon City, 1999)

Thailand

Rutnin, Mattani Mojdara, *Dance, Drama, and Theatre in Thailand: the process of development and modernization* (Toyo Bunko, 1993)

12. East Asia

China

Birch, Cyril, *Scenes for Mandarins: the elite theatre of the Ming* (New York, 1995)

Cheung, Martha P. Y., and Lai, Jane C. C. (eds.), *An Oxford Anthology of Contemporary Chinese Drama* (New York, 1997)

Crump, James Irving, *Chinese Theatre in the Days of Kublai Khan* (Tucson, 1980)

Dolby, William, *A History of Chinese Drama* (London, 1976)

Huang, Alexander C. Y., *Chinese Shakespeares: two centuries of cultural exchange* (New York, 2009)

Lei, Daphe Pi-Wei, *Operatic China: staging Chinese identity across the Pacific* (New York, 2006)

Lopez, Manuel D., *Chinese Drama: an annotated bibliography of commentary, criticism, and plays in English translation* (Metuchen, 1991)

Mackerras, Colin, and Tung, Constantine (eds.), *Drama in the People's Republic of China* (Albany, 1987)

Mackerras, Colin, *Chinese Drama from its Origins to the Present Day* (Honolulu, 1988)

—— *The Performing Arts in Contemporary China* (London, 1981)

Riley, Jo, *Chinese Theatre and the Actor in Performance* (Cambridge, 1997)

Scott, Adolphe C., *The Classical Theatre of China* (London, 1957)

Shih Chung-wen, *The Golden Age of Chinese Drama* (Princeton, 1976)

Yan Haiping (ed.), *Theatre and Society: an anthology of contemporary Chinese drama* (Armonk, 1998)

Yu Shio-ling (ed.), *Chinese Drama after the Cultural Revolution 1979–1989* (Lewiston, 1997)

Yung, Bell, *Cantonese Opera: performance as a creative process* (Cambridge, 1989)

Korea

Cho Oh-kon, *Korean Puppet Theatre: Kkoktu Kaksi* (East Lansing, 1979)

—— *Traditional Korean Theatre* (Berkeley, 1988)

Kardoss, John, *An Outline History of Korean Drama* (New York, 1966)

Korean ITI (ed.), *The Korean Theatre, Past and Present* (Seoul, 1981)

Lee Duhyun, *Korean Performing Arts: drama, dance, and music theater* (Seoul, 1997)

Yi Mi-wŏn (ed.), *Contemporary Korean Theatre: playwrights, directors, stage-designers* (Seoul, 2000)

Japan

Brandon, James R., and Leiter, Samuel L. (eds.), *Kabuki Plays on Stage*, 4 vols. (Honolulu, 2002–3)

Brandon, James R., *Nō and Kyōgen in the Contemporary World: brilliance and bravado, 1697–1766* (Honolulu, 1997)

—— *Kabuki's Foreign War: 1931–1945* (Honolulu, 2009)

Fraleigh, Sondra Horton, *Dancing into Darkness: Butoh, Zen, and Japan* (Pittsburgh, 1999)

Goodman, David, *Japanese Drama and Culture in the 1960s: the return of the gods* (London, 1988)

Jortner, David, McDonald, Keiko, and Wetmore, Kevin (eds.), *Modern Japanese Theatre and Performance* (New York, 2006)

Klein, Susan Blakeley, *Ankoku Butoh: the pre-modern and postmodern influences on the dance of utter darkness* (Ithaca, 1989)

Kominz, Lawrence R., *The Stars Who Created Kabuki: their lives, loves, and legacy* (New York, 1997)

Komparu Kunio, *The Noh Theatre: principles and perspectives* (New York, 1983)

Leiter, Samuel L., *New Kabuki Encyclopedia* (Westport, Conn., 1997)

—— *The Art of Kabuki: famous plays in performance* (Berkeley, 1979)

Ortolani, Benito, *The Japanese Theatre: from shamanistic ritual to contemporary pluralism* (Princeton, 1995)

Powell, Brian, *Japan's Modern Theatre, a Century of Change and Continuity* (London, 2002)

Rimer, J. Thomas, and Masakazu, Yamazaki (trans.), *On the Art of the No Drama: the major treatises of Zeami* (Princeton, 1984)

Rimer, J. Thomas, *Towards a Modern Japanese Theatre: Kishida Kunio* (Princeton, 1974)

Robertson, Jennifer, *Takarazuka: sexual politics and popular culture in modern Japan* (Berkeley, 1998)

Senda Akihiko, *The Voyage of Contemporary Japanese Theatre*, trans. J. Thomas Rimer (Honolulu, 1997)

Shaver, Ruth, *Kabuki Costumes* (Rutland, Vt., 1966)

Suzuki Tadashi, *The Way of Acting: the theatre writings of Suzuki Tadashi*, trans. J. Thomas Rimer (New York, 1986)

Thornbury, Barbara E., *Sukeroku's Double Identity: the dramatic structure of Edo Kabuki* (Ann Arbor, 1982)

Tsubioke, Eiko (ed.), *Theatre Japan*, 2nd edn. (Tokyo, 1993)

13. North America

Allen, Robert C., *Horrible Prettiness: burlesque and American culture* (Chapel Hill, 1991)

Aronson, Arnold, *American Avant-Garde Theatre: a history* (London, 2000)

Auslander, Philip, *Presence and Resistance: postmodernism and cultural politics in contemporary American performance* (Ann Arbor, 1994)

Banes, Sally, *Terpsichore in Sneakers: post-modern dance* (1980; Middletown, Conn., 1987)

—— *Subversive Expectations: performance art and paratheater in New York, 1976–85* (Ann Arbor, 1998)

Benson, Eugene, and Conolly, L. W. (eds.), *The Oxford Companion to Canadian Theatre* (Oxford, 1989)

Berkowitz, Gerald M., *New Broadways: theatre across America, approaching a new millennium* (New York, 1997)

Bigsby, C. W. E., *A Critical Introduction to Twentieth-Century American Drama*, 3 vols. (Cambridge, 1982–5)

Canning, Charlotte, *Feminist Theaters in the USA: staging women's experience* (London, 1996)

Clurman, Harold, *The Fervent Years: the story of the Group Theatre and the thirties* (New York, 1957).

Dudden, Faye E., *Women in the American Theatre: actresses and audiences, 1790–1870* (New Haven, 1994)

Durham, Weldon (ed.), *American Theatre Companies, 1888–1930* (Westport, Conn., 1987)

—— *American Theatre Companies, 1931–1986* (Westport, Conn., 1989)

Engle, Ron, and Miller, Tice L. (eds.), *The American Stage: social and economic forces from the colonial period to the present* (Cambridge, 1993)

Fuchs, Elinor, *The Death of Character: perspectives on theater after modernism* (Bloomington, 1996)

Fearnow, Mark, *The American Stage and the Great Depression: a cultural history of the grotesque* (New York, 1997)

Gelb, Arthur, and Gelb, Barbara, *O'Neill: life with Monte Cristo* (New York, 2000)

Gilbert, Douglas, *American Vaudeville* (New York, 1940)

Goldberg, RoseLee, *Performance Art: from futurism to the present*, rev. edn. (New York, 2001)

Goldstein, Malcolm, *The Political Stage: American drama and theater of the Great Depression* (New York, 1974)

Grimsted, David, *Melodrama Unveiled: American theater and culture 1800-1850* (Chicago, 1968)

Harris, Andrew B., *Broadway Theatre* (London, 1993)

Hart, Linda, and Phelan, Peggy (eds.), *Acting Out: feminist performances* (Ann Arbor, 1993)

Hay, Samuel A., *African American Theatre: a historical and critical analysis* (Cambridge, 1994)

Henderson, Mary, *Theater in America: 200 years of plays, players, and productions* (New York, 1986)

Hill, Errol G. (ed.), *The Theatre of Black Americans*, 2 vols. (Englewood Cliffs, NJ, 1980)

Hill, Errol G., and Hatch, James V., *A History of African American Theatre* (Cambridge, 2005)

Hirsch, Foster, *A Method to their Madness: the history of the Actor's Studio* (New York, 1984)

Kislan, Richard, *The Musical* (New York, 1999)

Larson, Orville K., *Scene Design in the American Theatre from 1915 to 1960* (Fayetteville, Arkansas, 1989)

Leiter, Samuel L., *The Encyclopedia of the New York Stage*, 3 vols. (Westport, Conn., 1985-92)

Levine, Lawrence W., *Highbrow/Lowbrow: the emergence of cultural hierarchy in America* (Cambridge, 1988)

Londré, Felicia Hardison, and Watermeier, Daniel J., *The History of North American Theater: the United States, Canada, and Mexico from pre-Columbian times to the present* (New York, 1998)

Marra, Kim, *Strange Duets: impresarios and actresses in the American theatre, 1865-1914* (Iowa City, 2006)

Marra, Kim, and Schanke, Robert A. (eds.), *Staging Desire: queer readings of American theater history* (Ann Arbor, 2002)

Marranca, Bonnie (ed.), *The Theatre of Images* (New York, 1977)

Mason, Jeffrey D., *Melodrama and the Myth of America* (Bloomington, 1993)

McArthur, Benjamin, *Actors and American Culture, 1880-1920* (Philadelphia, 1984)

McConachie, Bruce A., *American Theater in the Culture of the Cold War: producing and contesting containment, 1947-1962* (Iowa City, 2003)

—— *Melodramatic Formations: American Theatre and Society, 1820-1870* (Iowa City, 1992)

Meserve, Walter J., *An Emerging Entertainment: the drama of the American people to 1828* (Bloomington, 1977)

——*An Outline History of American Drama* (New York, 1994)

Murphy, Brenda, *Congressional Theatre: dramatizing McCarthyism on stage, film, and television* (Cambridge, 1999)

Norton, Richard C., *A Chronology of American Musical Theatre*, 3 vols. (Oxford, 2002)

O'Connor, John, and Brown, Lorraine, *Free, Adult, Uncensored: the living history of the Federal Theatre Project* (London, 1980).

Odell, G. C. D., *Annals of the New York Stage*, 15 vols. (New York, 1927-49)

Richardson, Gary A., *American Drama: from the colonial period through World War I* (Boston, 1993)

Shafer, Yvonne, *American Women Playwrights, 1900-1950* (New York, 1995)

Smith, Wendy, *Real-Life Drama: the Group Theatre and America, 1931-40* (New York, 1990)

Toll, Robert C., *Blacking Up: the minstrel show in nineteenth century America* (Oxford, 1974)

Wainscott, Ronald H., *The Emergence of the Modern American Theater, 1914-1929* (New Haven, 1997)

Wilmeth, Don B. (ed.), *The Cambridge Guide to American Theatre* 2nd edn. (Cambridge, 2007)

Wilmeth, Don B., and Bigsby, Christopher (eds.), *The Cambridge History of American Theatre*, 3 vols. (New York, 1998-2000)

Zeigler, Joseph Wesley, *Regional Theatre: the revolutionary stage* (New York, 1977)

14. Latin America and Caribbean

Albuquerque, Severino, *Violent Acts: a study of contemporary Latin American theatre* (Detroit, 1991)

Banham, Martin, Hill, Errol, and Woodyard, George (eds.), *The Cambridge Guide to African and Caribbean Theatre* (Cambridge, 1994)

Boyle, Catherine, *Thematic Development in Chilean Theatre since 1973: in search of the dramatic conflict* (Madison, 1992)

Dauster, Frank (ed.), *Perspectives on Contemporary Spanish American Theater* (Cranbury, NJ, 1997)

De Costa, Elena, *Collaborative Latin American Popular Theatre: from theory to form, from text to stage* (New York, 1992)

Ellis, Lorena, *Brecht's Reception In Brazil* (New York, 1995)

George, David, *Flash and Crash Days: Brazilian theater in the post-dictatorship period* (New York, 1999)

George, David, *The Modern Brazilian Stage* (Austin, Tex., 1992)

Glissant, Edouard, *Caribbean Discourses: selected essays* (Charlottesville, Va., 1003)

Graham-Jones, Jean, *Exorcising History: Argentine theater under dictatorship* (Cranbury, NJ, 2000)

Jones, Bridget Dickson, and Littlewood, Sita E., *Paradoxes of French Caribbean Theatre: an annotated checklist of dramatic works: Guadeloupe, Guyane, Martinique from 1900* (London, 1997)

Larson, Catherine, and Vargas, Margarita, *Latin American Women Dramatists: theater, texts, and theories* (Bloomington, Ind., 1998)

Leon-Portilla, Miguel, *Pre-Columbian Literature of Mexico* (Norman, Okla., 1969)

Luziaraga, Gerardo (ed.), *Popular Theater for Social Change in Latin America: essays in Spanish and English* (Los Angeles, 1978)

Martin, Randy, *Socialist Ensembles: theater and state in Cuba and Nicaragua* (Minneapolis, 1994)

Taylor, Diana, and Villegas, Juan (eds.), *Negotiating Performance: gender, sexuality, and theatricalism in Latin/o America* (Durham, 1994)

Taylor, Diana, *Disappearing Acts: spectacles of gender and nationalism in Argentina's Dirty War* (Raleigh, 1997)

Taylor, Diana, *Theatre of Crisis: drama and politics in Latin America* (Lexington, 1991)

Versényi, Adam, *Theatre in Latin America: religion, politics, and culture from Cortes to the 1980s* (Cambridge, 1993)

—— (ed.), *Latin American Dramatists*, first series (Detroit, 2005)

Weiss, Judith, et al., *Latin American Popular Theatre* (Albuquerque, 1993)

15. Principal journals

American Theatre
Asian Theatre Journal
Comparative Drama
Contemporary Theatre Review
Journal of Dramatic Theory and Criticism
Latin American Theatre Review
Modern Drama
New Theatre Quarterly
Nineteenth Century Theatre
Performance Research
Performing Arts Journal
Shakespeare Quarterly
Shakespeare Survey
Slavic and East European Performance
TDR (The Drama Review)
Theater (formerly Yale/Theater)
Theatre Arts (1939–64)
Theatre Arts Magazine (1916–39)
Theatre Design and Technology
Theatre History Studies
Theatre Journal
Theatre Notebook
Theatre Quarterly (1970–81)
Theatre Research International
Theatre Survey
Theatre Topics
Western European Stages
Women and Performance

Web resources

( ) SEE WEB LINKS

This is a web-linked dictionary. To access the websites, go to the dictionary's web page at www.oup.com/
uk/reference/resources/theatreandperformance, click on Web links in the Resources section and click
straight through to the relevant websites.

1. General

- Artslynx International Arts Resources: theatre
- Open Directory Project: resources for performing arts
- *The Oxford Encyclopedia of Theatre and Performance* (subscription)
- Virtual Library: theatre resources in libraries, conferences, training institutions, plays
- Yahoo!: links to numerous theatre categories

2. Theatre history

- The Costume Page: historical and practical resources
- Didaskalia: ancient Greek and Roman drama in performance
- Digital Bibliography: Brockett's *History of the Theatre*
- Internet Broadway Database: records from the beginnings of New York theatre until today
- Lortel Archives (Internet Off-Broadway Database): catalogue of shows produced
  Off-Broadway in New York
- The New Deal Stage: Federal Theatre Project (Library of Congress, USA)
- New York Public Library: Performing Arts in America, 1875–1923
- Records of Early English Drama (REED): medieval theatre history
- Theatre History on the Web: links to theatre history, research collections, archives of companies
- University of Bristol Theatre Collection: catalogue and links

3. Shakespeare

- Folger Shakespeare Library resources
- MIT Shakespeare Ensemble: complete texts and information
- Royal Shakespeare Company: resources, archives, library, online materials
- Shakespeare Birthplace Trust resources
- Shakespeare's Globe Theatre, education
- Shakespeare in Asia, Stanford University

4. Education and training

- Google Directory: international theatre education and training
- Virtual Library: training institutions

5. Major theatre companies

- Berliner Ensemble
- Comédie-Française, history and archive
- Deutsches Theater Berlin
- National Theatre of Great Britain (Royal National Theatre) archive
- New York Public Theatre
- Stratford Festival Canada, education and training

6. Organizations

- American Society for Theatre Research
- International Federation for Theatre Research
- International Organisation of Scenographers, Theatre Architects and Technicians
- International Theatre Institute: theatre organizations and events
- Performance Studies International
- Society for Theatre Research (British theatre)
- Society of British Theatre Designers